BUSINESS RESUMPTION PLANNING

1998 EDITION

EDWARD S. DEVLIN

COLE H. EMERSON

LEO A. WROBEL, JR.

AUERBACH

Boca Raton Boston London New York Washington, D.C.

ISBN 0-8493-9945-9

Printed in the United States of America

Auerbach
CRC Press LLC
2000 Corporate Blvd., N.W.
Boca Raton, FL 33431

About the Authors

EDWARD S. DEVLIN is often called "The Father of Disaster Recovery Planning." A leading consultant for over 20 years, Mr. Devlin has assisted hundreds of companies in formulating their emergency plans. He is a senior vice-president with Strohl Systems. He can be reached at (610) 768-4120.

COLE H. EMERSON is president of Cole Emerson & Associates. A recognized leader in the field of business resumption planning, he has assisted companies throughout the world in recovery planning. Emerson has written and spoken at numerous domestic and international conferences. He is a founder of the Information Systems Security Association and a charter member of the Disaster Recovery Institute Certification Board. He can be reached at (916) 729-6055.

LEO A. WROBEL, JR., president of Premiere Network Services, Inc., has more than two decades of experience in emerging network technology, disaster recovery planning, and technical training. An active author and lecturer, he as published nine books and dozens of trade articles on a wide variety of technical subjects. He can be reached at Premiere's web site (http://www.dallas.net/~premiere) or by calling (972) 515-5000.

Contents

Part III

Voice and Data Communications Recovery

WORKPAPERS

Introduction

Traditionally, resumption planning has focused on the recovery of computer systems. But experience has shown that the ability to recover computer systems does not necessarily guarantee the survival of an organization following a disaster. Quick recovery of a data center is useful only if the business units themselves are able to function–to communicate with customers and vendors, to receive and enter orders, to produce goods and services, and to collect revenue. The only way to ensure that is to plan for the resumption of all of the critical components of the business enterprise–its business operations, including personal computers and LANs, the data center, and voice and data communications services.

Business Resumption Planning is designed to provide a practical, hands-on guide for developing a comprehensive business recovery plan. The book consists of three modules:

- *Part I.* Business operations recovery.
- *Part II.* Data center recovery.
- *Part III.* Voice and data communications recovery.

Each module provides a step-by-step approach for developing the recovery plan; supporting checklists, questionnaires, procedures, and forms used in developing the recovery plan are provided on paper and on the accompanying CD-ROM.

Each of the three modules can be read and used independently of the other two. For example, if your company has already established a data center recovery plan, you may want to establish a plan for communications recovery. In that case, you can turn directly to Part III of this book and begin the process of developing the communications plan; all of the procedures, checklists, and forms you will need are provided in Part III. Of course, if your company has no recovery plan in place, you can begin with any of the three modules. (In practice, however, it makes most sense to proceed in sequential order, beginning with Part I. This is because information gathered in planning for business operations recovery can be useful when planning for data center and communications recovery.)

Business Resumption Planning is not only useful for developing recovery plans; it is also an invaluable source for evaluating the completeness of existing plans. For example, if your organization has already established a data center recovery plan, you might use Part II to ensure that the existing recovery plan is complete and follows the proven techniques described here. Given the step-by-step approach used in this book, its is easy to adapt specific procedures and forms to an existing plan and to the needs of specific organizations.

Now that you have an idea of what this book can do for you, let's look at why you need to plan for disasters.

DEFINING DISASTER

It is impossible to describe all of the events that might be considered disasters, but in the context of this book a disaster is any incident that causes an extended disruption of business functions. The first thought that comes to most minds are such common disasters as fire, hurricane, flood, and earthquake–that is, catastrophic acts of nature. This isn't surprising, given the unprecedented number of disasters the world has suffered in the past decade. The US, for example, has experienced three major earthquakes, several major hurricanes, and a massive flood that covered a large section of the Midwest. Hundreds of people were injured or killed in these natural disasters, tens of thousands lost their homes, and thousands of businesses were disrupted. Business and property losses were in the billions of dollars.

Despite the widespread association of disasters with natural disasters, most recovery specialists have expanded the definition of disaster to include any event that disrupts business operations. Given the variability in causes of disasters, recovery planners should not attempt to focus on specific types of disasters; rather, they should broaden their view to include any type of event that might disrupt business activity.

WHY PLAN?

Business survival is the primary rationale for planning. Avoidance of financial loss and embarrassment as well as ethical and legal obligations to employees, customers, and shareholders all support the need for planning. Without effective planning, the organization is forced to react to a disaster without an understanding of its recovery priorities, the time and resources needed to reestablish business functions, and sources of products and services needed during recovery. The delays caused by such lack of planning may be financially fatal. (For example, such technical resources as hot sites and communications services require long lead times to acquire and configure.) Indeed, history shows that most companies that suffer a disaster causing an extended disruption to information processing do not survive more than two years after the disaster.

The Need for Focus

Even with the most comprehensive plans for all major disruptions, the company can still be surprised. Therefore, it is recommended that organizations plan for the worst-case event rather than for specific types of disasters. The theory, proven many times, is that the company that is ready to respond to the worst disaster will also be able to handle lesser disruptions. If the planning team anticipates, plans for, and documents the recovery requirements and the company is prepared to meet most of those requirements at the time of a disaster, the recovery will succeed.

In addition, the recovery planner must plan within the scope of his or her control. It is always better to have an effective plan for one site than to be in the midst of planning for the world and not survive a single-site disaster. Ensuring that the highest-risk location is ready to respond and recover from an incident is always the more effective approach.

Hidden Benefits

As noted, the primary benefit of a recovery plan is ensuring the organization's survival in the event of a disaster. Yet other, less-obvious benefits are frequently overlooked. For example, in some cases a recovery plan may be a prerequisite for obtaining a business contract; conversely, lack of a plan may disqualify a company from consideration.

An effective recovery plan can also provide a competitive edge. Companies that have been able to quickly recover from regional disasters are often able to increase their share of the market because competitors are unable to conduct business. For example, one company reported that it was able to book $30 million in sales following the Hinsdale central office fire during a period when its competitors were unable to recover.

In developing a comprehensive plan, the recovery planner must learn how the business functions and how information, goods, and services move within and outside the organization. This may create opportunities for identifying potential cost reductions and improved operating efficiencies. The planner may also find opportunities for cost savings in business interruption insurance coverage and in company directors' and officers' insurance. Insurance professionals indicate that companies with resumption plans should save at least 10% on the cost of insurance premiums.

The planning process also forces a review of vital records management. One company was able to eliminate more than 110 tons of paper records, which in turn reduced the potential costs of restoring these records following a disaster.

HOW TO USE THE BOOK AND CD-ROM

Each part of this book is designed to provide a complete step-by-step approach to developing a recovery plan for its respective area; therefore, the chapters within each part should be read in sequential order. Although there are differences in methodology among the three parts, they do share a basic developmental framework:

- Obtaining senior management commitment and sponsorship of the planning project.
- Organizing the project and assembling the teams responsible for planning and recovery.
- Identifying recovery priorities, assumptions, and strategies.
- Gathering information to be included in the recovery plan.
- Developing detailed recovery procedures to be followed by the recovery teams in the event of a disaster.
- Establishing a program for testing and maintaining the recovery plan and for training recovery team members.

Differences among the three planning areas reflect the unique requirements of these areas as well as the practical experience of the authors in developing plans for clients.

In addition to providing step-by-step instructions on how to create the business resumption plan for each area, supporting checklists, questionnaires, procedures, and forms used in developing the recovery plan (collectively referred to as workpapers in this book) are provided on paper and on the accompanying CD-ROM.

On the CD-ROM, each workpaper is provided as a separate Microsoft Word 6.0 file. The file name matches the number of the workpaper referenced in the book.

The electronic files are designed so that users can easily customize the workpapers to meet the recovery planning requirements of his or her organization. Wherever possible, the files are formatted using Microsoft Word default settings; the base font is Courier, 10 characters per inch. Every attempt has been made to ensure that the page layout of the screen version of each workpaper matches the corresponding printed version contained in the book. The owner of this publication is permitted to make either paper or electronic copies of the workpapers without having to obtain permission from the publisher.

I BUSINESS OPERATIONS RECOVERY

I BUSINESS OPERATIONS RECOVERY

BUSINESS OPERATIONS RECOVERY

PART

I

Business operations recovery planning can be an overwhelming task if it is not properly structured and managed. Part I of this book presents a practical, straightforward approach to recovery planning for business operations.

The process of developing a business operations recovery plan can be broken into phases, each of which has its own objectives to achieve, actions to perform, and deliverables to produce. Breaking the project into phases makes it easier to establish and monitor progress against objectives. Although there are several alternatives, the following seven-phase approach is suggested. These seven phases of the planning project are covered in the following chapters of Part I:

- *Chapter I-1.* Obtaining senior management commitment and sponsorship of the planning project.
- *Chapter I-2.* Organizing the planning project. This includes assembling the team responsible for planning activities and establishing an action plan.
- *Chapter I-3.* Identifying the critical business functions by conducting a business impact analysis. These functions are identified first at the level of business units and their major supporting systems and applications. The objective is to identify the impact on the organization of the loss of these vital business functions and systems.
- *Chapter I-4.* Identifying and documenting critical business processes and tasks performed by each of the business units identified by the business impact analysis. This helps identify priorities for recovery of specific business operations and support systems.
- *Chapter I-5.* Identifying and documenting the resources needed to implement the plan.
- *Chapter I-6.* Organizing the teams responsible for carrying out the recovery plan in the event of a disaster.
- *Chapter I-8.* Establishing procedures for testing and maintaining the plan and training recovery team members.

The business operations recovery plan must address not only the recovery of critical business functions but also the recovery of the microcomputer and LAN resources on which they depend. Chapter I-7 discusses the issues that must be addressed in planning for microcomputer and LAN recovery.

The following paragraphs describe each of the components of successful business operations recovery planning.

OBTAINING SENIOR MANAGEMENT SPONSORSHIP

This requirement is a key to successful business resumption planning. The resumption plan affects the entire organization; therefore, senior management's involvement is critical. The person responsible for the project must be able to command management respect and be able to obtain a consensus from them. The planner must also have a good understanding of the current strategic direction of the business.

The first step is to perform a preliminary risk analysis to identify the potential level of interruption and financial loss if business operations and supporting information systems were interrupted by a disaster. To help ensure top management commitment, the planner should perform a high-level analysis identifying the most probable threats, their impact, and the financial consequences of the interruption. Legal and regulatory requirements for recovery planning should be identified at this stage. Potential threats and legal requirements identified during this initial analysis add weight to arguments for recovery planning and identify the initial priorities for recovery and risk mitigation.

Armed with this information, the recovery planner can then set out to build the business case for recovery planning. The results of the high-level analysis are then presented to management along with an overview of how the resumption plan meets the critical recovery needs identified by the analysis.

ORGANIZING THE RESUMPTION PLANNING PROJECT

This phase of the project involves assembling the project team, developing an action plan for carrying out the project, and allocating tasks and responsibilities for meeting plan objectives.

The recovery planner identifies the appropriate individuals to be involved in the planning effort. (These persons may also be selected as members of the recovery team itself.) The breadth of skills needed on the planning project team requires expertise in business operations, finance, information systems, communications, risk management, law, and auditing.

The recovery team should be composed of both senior managers and functional and technical experts. Participation by senior management is critical, because it establishes the appropriate level of authority necessary to obtain resources and cooperation throughout the enterprise. Functional and technical experts are needed because they possess the detailed knowledge of business operations and related systems, which is essential for gathering accurate information to create an effective recovery program.

The recovery planner, acting as planning project manager, must also develop an action plan that specifies the scope of the plan and its objectives. The objectives should be action-oriented; that is, they describe the steps that should be taken to complete discrete tasks. After these tasks have been defined, the project manager can then determine who is best suited to perform each task. He or she assigns one or more team members to each task and also identifies any other resources that may be needed to successfully execute the step. Completion dates for assigned tasks should be established in consultation with project team members to ensure that recovery planning tasks do not conflict with their other commitments.

CONDUCTING THE BUSINESS IMPACT ANALYSIS

The business impact analysis is designed to ensure a thorough understanding of the vital business functions and systems within the organization. The impact of loss on each of these functions is identified, evaluated, and categorized according to the required time frames for recovery of the function. The recovery priorities are set on the basis of this analysis.

The purpose of the impact analysis is to identify the consequences of the interruption in terms of financial loss, additional expense, embarrassment to the organization, and the maximum period of interruption that the organization can tolerate.

After the analysis is complete, it should be reviewed and verified by management and all participants. Management is then ready to establish recovery priorities. System and application recovery time frames are driven by the recovery priorities.

IDENTIFYING AND DOCUMENTING CRITICAL BUSINESS PROCESSES

The business impact analysis identified the critical business functions at the level of business units and their major supporting systems and applications. This next stage of developing the business operations resumption plan builds on that analysis. For each of the identified critical business units, the planner must now identify the critical processes performed by the business unit. An inventory of these processes is developed, and each process is broken down into its component tasks. (For example, order entry is a process; each activity performed to enter an order is a task.) The individual applications that support each of these processes must also be identified. Having established an inventory of processes and related tasks, the processes can be evaluated to identify those that are most critical and that should therefore receive a high priority for recovery.

Two structured methods can be used to obtain the necessary inventories of critical processes and tasks. The first method involves use of a questionnaire to collect data; the second involves interviews of key employees. These data collection methods are independent of each other, and either may be used.

IDENTIFYING AND DOCUMENTING RESOURCE REQUIREMENTS

For each process performed by the business unit, a set of resources or tools is necessary to complete the process. Resource planning identifies the resources that business units need to reestablish their operations at an alternate location.

First, the number and type of personnel needed for the recovery is determined. This information allows the planner to determine such other resource requirements as recovery facilities and equipment, because these depend, at least in part, on the number of people that need to be supported during the recovery effort. For example, the number of employees involved in the recovery helps determine the size of the recovery facility and the number of desks, phones, computers, and supplies that are needed. Planning for recovery of facilities and such basic resources as voice and data communications requires determining the expected volume and use of these resources.

Other types of dependences must also be taken into consideration. For example, the power requirements of specific items of equipment must be assessed to determine overall power requirements for the recovery facility.

Resource planning also identifies who is responsible for installing and configuring equipment. The results of this analysis must be shared with all participants in the planning process so that the parties responsible for providing the necessary resources understand what is expected of them. Depending on the availability of internal resources, the planner and service providers may have to go outside the organization for assistance.

ORGANIZING THE BUSINESS OPERATIONS RECOVERY TEAMS

The business operations recovery teams are responsible for responding to and managing any serious interruption of business operations. Some organizations choose to create separate programs and teams for handling specific types of threat events. A disaster recovery team might handle any immediately apparent disaster (e.g., an explosion, fire, or earthquake) that interrupts business operations. A crisis management team might be organized to handle such threats as criminal activity, workplace violence, product contamination, and accidents involving hazardous materials that pose a danger to the organization but do not interrupt operations. An emergency-preparedness team might be assigned responsibility for the safety of employees, customers, or the public in a crisis or disaster.

Other organizations choose to manage all types of crises and disasters using primarily two types of teams, one that is chiefly responsible for coordinating the companywide recovery effort and the other for managing recovery of specific business units at the alternate sites designated in the recovery plan. This is the approach presented in this book.

The purpose of recovery management is to minimize damage to the organization and its employees. The first priority is to protect human life, whether of employees or consumers of a company's products or services, while terminating and recovering from the incident as quickly as possible. The recovery teams must act prudently to ensure that a relatively minor incident does not become a major disaster.

The recovery teams must also attempt to protect the organization's assets. These include financial and commercial assets as well as such intangible assets as the company's goodwill and reputation.

In responding to a disaster, the organization must seek to maintain the confidence of its customers and shareholders. It must also maintain good relations with law enforcement, regulatory, and other governmental agencies and comply with all applicable laws and regulations. A key objective is to minimize the risk of legal liabilities to the organization.

Chapter I-6 offers guidelines on how to set up an emergency operations center and manage the disaster. It describes the chain of command, areas of responsibility for managing the recovery, and certain basic operational procedures. However, it is not possible to document how specific recovery decisions should be made. Such decisions will differ depending on the type of disaster and expected length of the outage, the nature of the affected organization, its organizational structure, and the mix of experts available at the emergency operations center.

It is possible to outline a basic framework for response and recovery activities. The emergency operations team must know under what circumstances it is to respond to a disaster or crisis. The organization might choose to designate response or escalation levels, each level assigned according to the expected length of the interruption and the appropriate response for that level. For ease of communication and use, one set of response procedures should be used by all parties involved in managing the incident. These procedures include notification of the disaster, damage assessment, activation of the emergency operations center and of the recovery teams, and restoration of facilities.

RECOVERY PLANNING FOR MICROCOMPUTERS AND LANS

Many applications that previously resided on mainframe systems are being moved to microcomputers and local area networks (LANs); this includes an increasingly large number of mission-critical applications. The local area networks may in turn be connected to other internal and external networks as well as to mainframes. Even if a system appears to serve a single business application, its applications and data may reside on multiple computers, although the connections may never be apparent to users. In addition to networked systems, standalone microcomputers are now sufficiently powerful to support important, mission-critical applications.

Whereas most companies have comprehensive programs in place for data center recovery, far fewer address recovery of microcomputers and LANs. A recent study found that LANs are extremely vulnerable to a disaster. This vulnerability results from failure to include LANs in business resumption planning.

Chapter I-7 presents an approach for recovery of microcomputers and LANs. Some of these procedures are adapted from procedures already used commonly in data center recovery programs; others have been created to address the specific requirements for recovery of small systems.

BUSINESS OPERATIONS RECOVERY PLAN TESTING, MAINTENANCE, AND TRAINING

The business operations resumption plan must change in response to changes in the organization. The plan must be maintained in a timely manner so that it reflects the most recent changes in operations, systems, and management structure. It must be periodically tested to ensure it is workable.

Recovery team members must be trained so that they understand how to perform their duties in a recovery operation. They must also be tested in the documented recovery procedures to ensure they are capable of carrying out the plan in a crisis.

The primary goal of testing is to ensure that the procedures for recovering business operations are feasible in practice. This involves testing the readiness of the organization to recover business operations as well as testing recovery of specific systems and applications.

The primary cause of failure for many plans is lack of proper maintenance. An inaccurate plan can be misleading and cause management to make incorrect decisions or delay the recovery. For example, if key vendor contact information is not valid, the delays in contacting and obtaining a response may extend the interruption. The users of the plan should provide the information and have primary responsibility to ensure that their specific part of the plan is kept current. To encourage active participation in maintaining the recovery plans, ease of plan use and maintenance are key.

Training provides an opportunity for team members to address problems that would almost never occur under normal business conditions and to do so in a more relaxed atmosphere. Tests and training exercises provide the best form of training for the recovery teams. They offer an opportunity for team members to use systems in an unfamiliar environment, accomplish critical tasks with minimal resources, and develop the team attitude and processes required for successful recovery.

CHAPTER I-1

Obtaining Senior Management Sponsorship

No business resumption project can succeed without both the initial and ongoing sponsorship of senior management. Starting the program is difficult; keeping it alive and growing is even more difficult. The object of the planner is to obtain and maintain senior management sponsorship. Without senior management sponsorship, neither the money nor the time will be made available to successfully complete the project.

How then does the planner obtain and keep this commitment? The most effective way to gain and maintain senior management commitment is to first make management aware of the risk of not having a recovery capability and then get it involved in the planning and recovery process. If senior managers do not understand the potential for interruption of business operations and the financial consequences if critical operations are interrupted, they cannot fully support the process.

The steps involved in obtaining senior management support include:

- Performing a preliminary risk analysis.
- Identifying any relevant laws or regulations.
- Building the business case for the business operations recovery plan.
- Obtaining management approval.

The following sections of this chapter describe these steps.

PERFORM A PRELIMINARY RISK ANALYSIS

STEP 1

The preliminary risk analysis identifies risks, their probability of occurrence, and their potential impact on the organization. The risk analysis differs from a business impact analysis in two important respects:

- A risk analysis only identifies overall impacts of a disaster to the organization. It does not attempt to identify financial and logistical impacts on specific organizational departments and functions; that is the purpose of the business impact analysis.
- The business impact analysis does not consider what types of incidents cause a disruption to business operations; it is concerned only with identifying consequences in terms of financial loss, additional expense, embarrassment, and the expected length of the interruption.

A full business impact analysis is conducted only after approval for the recovery planning project has been obtained from senior management. (Chapter I-3 describes how to perform the business impact analysis.)

In preparing to perform a risk analysis, the planner must accept that all possible risks cannot, and should not, be identified. The planner has neither the time nor money to invest in identifying every possible event that can interrupt business operations. It is a fact that meteors could do serious damage to business operations. But the potential is so remote and occurrence so infrequent that it would be a waste to include such

EXHIBIT I-1-A THREATS LIST

- Accidental explosion—off-site
- Accidental explosion—on-site
- Aircraft crash
- Ancillary equipment failure
- Arson
- Bomb threat
- Bombing
- Central computer equipment failure
- Data theft: physical assets ($2,500+)
- Earthquake (magnitude 5+)
- Epidemic
- Fire: external
- Fire: internal—catastrophic
- Fire: internal—major
- Fire: internal—minor
- Fraud/embezzlement
- High winds (70+ mph)
- Hostage taking
- Human error: maintenance
- Human error: operation
- Human error: programmers
- Human error: users
- Hurricane/typhoon
- HVAC failure/temperature inadequacy
- Ice storm
- Labor dispute
- Loss of key staff
- Major landslide/mudslide
- Media failure
- Medical emergency
- Misuse of resources
- Power flux
- Power outage—external
- Power outage—internal
- Purchased software failure
- Radioactive contamination
- Riot/civil disorder
- Sabotage: external—data and software
- Sabotage: external—physical
- Sabotage: internal—data and software
- Sabotage: internal—physical
- Sandstorm
- Seasonal/local flooding
- Snowstorm/blizzard
- Strike
- Subsidence faulting
- Telecommunications failure—data
- Telecommunications failure—voice
- Theft
- Thunder/electrical storm
- Tidal flooding
- Tornado
- Toxic contamination
- Tropical storm
- Tsunami
- Upstream dam/reservoir failure
- Vandalism
- Volcanic activity
- Water leak/plumbing failure

an event in any risk analysis. What the planner should focus on is the identification of the most probable set of risks that have the greatest impact on the company's business operations.

The objective of the risk analysis at this preliminary stage is to:

- Identify various risks to an organization.
- Identify the requirements of an organization to resume or continue business functions.
- Identify the general impact on the organization, both functionally and financially, of an occurrence of the risks.
- Identify a preliminary estimate of the costs to the organization to establish effective controls to reduce the risks.
- Establish priorities to address identified risks.

Before proceeding, it may be useful to clarify some terminology commonly used in risk analysis—the terms *threat, risk, controls,* and *vulnerabilities.* Threats are the triggers that cause a risk to become a loss. For example, the risk of fire is always present. If a threat called lightning or equipment failure occurs, a fire may happen and property may be damaged. Threats can also be risks. For example, sabotage is both a risk and a threat. A major objective of the planner is to identify the loss exposure due to threats. A comprehensive list of threats that the planner should be concerned with is illustrated in Exhibit I-1-A.

A primary objective of the risk analysis is to identify effective and appropriate controls. Controls are designed to either deter the threat or reduce the loss. Controls cannot do both. Controls may:

- Reduce the occurrence rate of a given threat.

- Reduce the magnitude of the loss.
- Reduce the intensity or severity of the threat, thereby reducing either the occurrence rate or the loss.

Fire sprinkler systems are an example of a control that can reduce the loss. Access controls can help deter the threat of intrusion.

Cost and effectiveness must be considered for controls. Cost is the initial investment in the control plus the annual maintenance. Because controls have a life expectancy and a return on investment, their benefits can be measured financially. The planner should always spend the most time identifying effective controls for those risks that are most likely to occur.

Some controls are specific in nature; others address more than one threat. A backup site acts as a control applicable to multiple threats, including earthquake, tornado, fire, and extended utility failure. An uninterruptible power source (UPS) addresses one threat, power failure.

Vulnerabilities are a weakness in the system of controls. If the control is absent, weak, or inadequate and cannot reduce the threat, the object of the threat is considered to be vulnerable.

Risk Assessment Tools

Explaining how to perform a risk analysis is beyond the scope of this book. Fortunately, there are a number of automated risk assessment tools that can be used to assist the business resumption planner at this stage. These include the Bayesian Decision Support System (Ozier, Peterse & Assoc) or RISKWATCH (Expert Systems Software Inc). These tools can help decrease the amount of time required to complete the risk analysis. However, risk assessment tools are not intuitive and require experienced risk analysis professionals to ensure a valid and useful result. The analyst will need to be trained to use the products; in addition, most users require ongoing assistance from the vendor in resolving problems using the software or interpreting the results.

Risk assessment tools address a wide array of threats, both natural and human-made, ranging from small fire to nuclear holocaust. The applicability of each threat and its impact on business operations are assessed. In addition, the tools identify the probability of the threat occurring and, by using a mathematical formula, determine the relationship between the threat, the impact on the operations, and the probability of occurrence. A risk priority is established along with the financial loss potential.

The classic school of risk analysis uses this information to establish how much should be invested to eliminate the threat or reduce its impact on operations and to set priorities for risk mitigation. Although historical data on such threats as earthquakes is not sufficiently detailed to provide a precise probability weighting, the authors of the tools claim to have a comprehensive set of historical occurrences that establish a credible probability of an occurrence. Nonetheless, there are often major debates within the organization about the validity of the probability algorithms used by these products.

Many risks that planners should concern themselves with are fairly evident and can be assessed without automated tools. For example, in southern California, earthquakes are the most significant risk that could cause catastrophic damage to business operations. Fires, both internal and external, pose major threats to business operations. Even if a fire does not directly affect a facility, it may require that it be evacuated. If the fire destroys employees' homes, the employees may not be available for several days. Power and communications failures also provide frequent challenges to businesses in both southern and northern California. Floods and landslides occur less frequently and with lesser impact. Without too much analysis, most California planners can identify and plan against the threats that are most probable and have the most catastrophic effect on business operations.

For the US Southeast and Gulf Coast, hurricanes and tornadoes are the major threats. In the Midwest, floods and tornadoes are major threats, with earthquakes being less likely but having a potentially catastrophic impact on the area. The Northeast faces both hurricanes and blizzards, sometimes simultaneously.

Risk assessments should address the threat of disruption of telephone, power, and water utilities. There are also subtler threats that might escape a novice planner—for example, contamination by a toxic spill near a company facility or a minor fire that causes a fluorescent light ballast containing PCBs to burn, thereby discharging carcinogenic agents into the surrounding area. Proximity to industries that use hazardous materials in their manufacturing process or actually manufacture the hazardous materials may pose a threat. So too may labor action that shuts down the manufacturing lines of a critical sole-source supplier. Major crimes against employees in the work place seem to be an increasing threat.

In the effort to present a solid business case for senior management, the planner should be ready to present the most likely risks. This preliminary risk analysis should be conducted at a high level; a more comprehensive risk assessment can be conducted after basic recovery capabilities have been established for the organization. The result of this high-level risk analysis may be expressed as a quantified risk value, but not to the degree that would be provided by a comprehensive risk assessment.

Sample Risk Assessment Report

Workpaper I1.01 provides a sample of an actual risk assessment extracted from a final report. This particular risk assessment focused on a data center and was conducted primarily as a qualitative analysis rather than quantitative, although numerical weighting was assigned to risk factors. Instead of a complicated formula, a simplified analysis was used with the objective of establishing priorities to address risks rather than determining the appropriate amount of money to spend to reduce or eliminate the risk.

STEP 2

IDENTIFY LEGAL AND REGULATORY MANDATES

It is only in the past ten years that federal and state regulators have recognized that resumption planning should include business operations and not just data processing. A legal or regulatory requirement to establish a plan does not necessarily mean that the company will comply with the requirement. All regulations are subject to interpretation; often a company can comply with the regulations without having actually implemented an effective business resumption plan. Nonetheless, management needs to be aware of how the recovery plan will be evaluated in the context of law and regulations.

The key regulations are summarized in the following paragraphs. Much of the regulatory focus is on financial institutions; therefore, the majority of the available regulations apply to a small but important set of business operations. The key legal and regulatory requirements include:

- Executive Order 11490.
- The Foreign Corrupt Practices Act of 1977.
- Comptroller of the Currency banking circulars.
- Federal Home Loan Bank Board regulations and memorandums.

In addition, common law related to negligence may also bear on the corporation's responsibility for recovery planning. Other regulations that may apply include: Office of Management and Budget Circular A-71; IRS Procedure 64-12; IRS Ruling 71-20; Occupational Safety and Health Administration regulations; and Environmental Protection Agency regulations.

Executive Order 11490

Since October 30, 1969, financial institutions have been mandated by Executive Order 11490 to prepare emergency plans that address the following issues:

- Assigning responsibility for emergency operations preparedness to a specific individual.
- Developing and distributing written emergency preparedness procedures.
- Training personnel periodically in emergency response procedures.
- Developing an effective program for safeguarding and duplicating records.
- Defining plans for succession of senior officers.

The Foreign Corrupt Practices Act

The Foreign Corrupt Practices Act is probably the most misused though frequently mentioned regulation in both the security and disaster recovery fields. In 1977, the Securities and Exchange Act of 1934 was amended by the Foreign Corrupt Practices Act to require all publicly held companies to keep accurate records and maintain internal control systems to safeguard assets. The courts have defined assets as including the computer system and all the data it contains. Critical records and original documents are also assets and should be protected. The company that fails to generate a record is as liable as the company that fails to preserve it. A company without adequate business resumption plans may not be able to create records for an extended period of time.

Commentators discussing computer disaster recovery generally agree that Section 13(b)(2) of the Securities and Exchange Act (as added by the Foreign Corrupt Practices Act of 1977) may be read to require executives of public companies to take reasonable precautions to preserve computer records from destruction. The act's internal audit and control requirement could conceivably extend into every aspect of corporate operations.

Courts have already indicated that its requirements apply not only to written documents, but to the preservation of accurate computer records as well (SEC vs. World-Wide Coin Investments Ltd.). The court defined *reasonable* on the basis of economic cost/benefit analysis: implementation of the required procedures was not to create a fail-safe system at all costs; rather, the cost should not exceed expected benefits.

Corporate executives who fail to determine the proper measure of disaster recovery preparation could become subject to certain criminal penalties. The Securities Exchange Commission, in enforcing this statute, may seek an injunction against noncompliance, institute administrative proceedings, or even institute criminal proceedings.

Originally corporate officers were personally responsible even if they were not aware of the deficiency. In 1992, Congress modified the law and significantly changed the responsibility of senior management. With the new amendment, senior management is not responsible unless it "knowingly" fails to put in place appropriate controls.

Comptroller of the Currency

The administrator of national banks is the Comptroller of the Currency. Over the past decade the Comptroller has issued several requirements related to disaster recovery planning. The following summarizes each publication.

Banking Circular 177. The Comptroller of the Currency originally issued Banking Circular 177 on June 29, 1983. Initially BC 177 emphasized contingency planning for computer systems processing but was revised on April 16, 1987 to include business operations. It states that contingency planning for bank's information systems should extend beyond the data center to the key operational areas of the bank. This is increasingly critical as information expands beyond traditional central operations. A principal objective of any contingency plan should be to ensure the ability of user departments to function effectively in an adverse environment.

Banking Circular 187. The Comptroller of the Currency issued Banking Circular 187 on January 18, 1985 to address the importance of reviewing the financial status of organizations that provide information processing services. Financial institutions using service bureaus should assure themselves of continued, uninterrupted data processing support. BC 187 states that to satisfy its fiduciary responsibilities regarding information processing services, a board of directors or its appointed committee should obtain and analyze the financial information of the data processing servicers on an annual basis. If a servicer's financial condition is deteriorating or unsound, alternative servicing arrangements should be considered to ensure continued information processing support. Prudent banking practices would usually include the documentation of contingency plans.

Banking Circular 226. One of the growing problems within the office environment is the protection of information resident on small distributed systems. The Comptroller of the Currency issued Banking Circular 226 on January 25, 1988. This circular was issued jointly by the Federal Financial Institutions Examination Council. This council includes the following organizations:

- Board of Governors of the Federal Reserve System.
- Federal Deposit Insurance Corporation.
- Federal Home Loan Bank Board.
- National Credit Union Administration.
- Office of the Comptroller of the Currency.

The circular addresses the risks associated with end-user computing activities. End-user computing includes information processing activities using microcomputers, minicomputers, small mainframes, or other computers to control and process data at the user level. BC 226 encourages bank management to evaluate the associated risks with its end-user computing networks and other forms of distributed computer operations. Control practices and responsibilities to manage these activities should be incorporated into an overall corporate information security policy. Such a policy should address areas such as:

- Management controls.
- Data security.
- Documentation.
- Data and file storage and backup.
- Systems and data integrity.
- Contingency plans.
- Audit responsibility.
- Training.

For each operational system, plans should be made to ensure that users can adequately recover from damage to hardware, software, and data. For some systems, an inability to process during recovery may mean that work can be held for later processing. For other systems, a manual backup may be appropriate. For some time-critical, highly automated systems, arrangements may have to be made for data reconstruction or for processing on other hardware. At a minimum, for all systems, there should be secure and remote backup storage of data files and programs. Beyond this, the backup and contingency requirements for individual systems may differ and need to be addressed separately.

Banking Circular 87-3. Banking Circular 87-3 was issued by the Comptroller of the Currency on February 12, 1987. It addresses risks associated with contracting long-term IS services. The comptroller recommends several considerations for contracts of information processing services, including establishing a method to develop and test contingency plans.

Federal Home Loan Bank Board

The Federal Home Loan Bank Board has issued several requirements related to disaster recovery planning. Regulation PA-7-1a states that a written contingency plan should be maintained for response to a wide variety of disasters, including potential disruption of the computer room, loss of computer hardware, and loss of data files. Contingency and use of backup hardware should be reviewed periodically and tested where appropriate.

Memorandum R67. The Federal Home Loan Bank Board issued Memorandum R67 on September 4, 1986. This regulation describes guidelines on contingency disaster recovery plans required for insured institutions and service corporations. Memorandum R67 addresses several important concerns, including reciprocal agreements and use of service bureaus. With respect to reciprocal agreements, the memorandum states that institutions often obtain a written letter of agreement from another institution, which provides for backup capability to each other, to serve as a contingency disaster plan. However, such agreements are often insufficient because:

- Agreements are not always current.
- The system owned by the institution providing the backup may not be capable of supporting the agreement.
- Backup capacity is not tested periodically to ensure compatibility of the systems.
- There is no guarantee that backup equipment will be available when needed.

With respect to service bureau users, the memorandum states that if an institution is using an IS service bureau, the institution must establish policies and responsibilities to ensure that the appropriate contingency disaster plans are developed and maintained. The institution must document a review of the service bureau's contingency plan to ensure that it is compatible with the institution's plan. If an institution uses both its own system and a service bureau, a combined plan must be developed and maintained.

Memorandum R67-1. The Office of Regulatory Policy, Oversight, and Supervision of the Federal Home Loan Bank System issued Memorandum R67-1 on March 22, 1988. This regulation is the same as Banking Circular 226, which addresses the risks associated with end-user computing activities.

Common Law Negligence

If a corporation owes a third party a duty and the corporate agent fails to perform that duty, the injured party may recover for the omission. However, recovery has been traditionally awarded only for physical damages; awards for monetary losses are usually granted only in cases in which the corporation is acting as a fiduciary or trustee.

Under common law, the legal responsibilities of a corporation's directors and officers include a fiduciary duty to the corporation. These executives must therefore exercise due care to safeguard corporate assets.

STEP 3

BUILD THE BUSINESS CASE

Although some organizations are mandated by regulations to establish a recovery plan, most organizations are not. The decision to put in place a resumption plan is a business decision. The investment of time and money must bring some benefits to the company.

As with any business plan, the objective is to identify the financial benefits of having a plan. In most cases, the planner is faced with having a non-profit-generating project that only offsets potential losses. The return on investment is loss avoidance contrasted with the cost of the program. In presenting the case, the planner must identify both the potential financial loss without the plan as well as the potential loss with the plan. The difference between the two provides the basis for justifying the investment.

At this preliminary project phase, the planner must create an informal business case providing a high-level analysis for management. Workpaper I1.02 provides a sample format for presenting the business case.

Financial estimates are developed using an iterative process, beginning with loss estimates determined in the preliminary risk analysis. The final estimates of potential loss for specific business functions and of the cost of equipment, personnel, and services are determined by conducting a business impact analysis (see Chapter I-3).

The planner should establish a minimum baseline of investment needed to initially recover the most critical business functions. As part of a more comprehensive business plan, the expansion of the program can be addressed. Each expansion of the program should be able to demonstrate a reduction in the loss potential of the organization.

STEP 4

OBTAIN MANAGEMENT APPROVAL

The most effective way for a planner to present a case for the planning project to senior management (as well as project participants) is to use a case study of a type of disaster that would most likely affect the organization. The planner should always use organizations that have been successful in responding to and recovering from major incidents. Describing those actions that were most effective—as well as those that were not—can help senior management better understand how the plan should be implemented. Although what worked for one organization will not necessarily guarantee success for another, it is more convincing to use actual incidents.

Conducting the Initial Presentation

The objective of the initial management presentation is to first gain management's interest and second present the intended message. The presentation must always address management's concerns before those of the planners. The level of presentation must remain at a high level; detail should be provided in handouts that can be read before the presentation.

The presentation materials should be provided to senior management a few days before the meeting for its review. The planner should anticipate that most managers will not read the materials. Therefore, the most important information should be presented in a crisp, concise format during the presentation.

The time provided by senior management will be short and the message must be precise and targeted for the audience. An initial meeting of one hour should be planned, though the planner may be given additional time for questions and answers. Any follow-up and status meetings should be about 30 minutes long.

The following sections describe the key components of an effective presentation.

Introduction and Meeting Objectives. The presentation starts with a statement of objectives for the meeting. If the planner has a senior management sponsor, the sponsor should state the purpose of the presentation and introduce the planner.

Case Studies. During the initial meeting, the planner should present a brief synopsis of disasters that have occurred at peer companies in the industry. The objective of this summary is to obtain management attention.

Qualities of an Effective Plan. The planner next describes what the plan should do. This can be accomplished by presenting the qualities of an effective business resumption plan. An effective plan should:

- Identify the most likely potential threats.
- Identify critical business and support functions.
- Estimate impacts because of a disruption of operations; these may include revenue loss, additional expenses, and embarrassment to the organization.
- Document how key assets move within and outside the business. Such assets include information and transactions, goods, and funds.
- Determine relationships and interdependences within the organization (e.g., between order entry and sales) and external to the organization (e.g., between telephone power and utilities and corporate emergency services).
- Determine space and supporting facility requirements, such as percentage of normal requirements for space, and proximity of related business units.
- Develop the prevention, planning, response, recovery, restoration, and resumption teams.

The purpose and objectives of the teams should also be introduced. In general, the objectives are to:

- Establish preventive engineering to eliminate threats or mitigate the consequences of the incident.
- Plan and prepare by identifying critical components, team members, impact of loss, time frame for recovery, proposed course of action, and roles of the participants.
- Respond through effective command and control to maintain the safety of personnel and transition to business and processing recovery.
- Initiate the recovery involving the movement of people, data, equipment, and operations to alternative locations.
- Initiate cleanup of facilities, paper, magnetic media, and equipment and rebuilding of the facilities.
- Transition from the temporary facilities and services to a precrisis operational status.

Current Planning Status. The planner presents where the company is in the planning process, focusing on the highest-priority items first.

Mission Statement. The planner presents the mission statement of the business resumption planning organization. For example, the mission might be to "provide a cost-effective approach to mitigating the financial impact of a significant business interruption."

Planning Project Objectives. The planner then presents the objectives of the planning project, which should flow from the mission statement. These objectives might include:

- Establishing a business resumption plan for critical headquarters functions.
- Establishing a command structure for effectively managing the response and recovery efforts.
- Training recovery team members in procedures required to recover critical business operations.
- Testing and exercising the recovery plan to ensure it can effectively respond to an actual disaster.

Defining Corporate Policies

After management's approval is obtained, a policy statement should be issued that clearly states the organization's commitment to ensuring continued business operations. In addition, policies for each business unit within the organization should establish responsibility for plan development, activation, and maintenance at the business unit level. The policy lays the initial foundation for establishing plan ownership at the appropriate and most effective level within the organization. The following is an example of a business resumption policy statement at the corporate and business unit levels, respectively:

> The organization recognizes the importance of business survival. To ensure that all critical business functions continue in the event of a disaster, it has committed to develop the business resumption plan. This plan implemented by its staff documents the policy of business survival for the company.
>
> Business resumption planning is the responsibility of all organization management. Each business unit manager is responsible for ensuring that his or her critical business operations are prepared to resume operations within a predefined period following a major disruptive incident.

Once management has stated that it is the policy of the organization to establish a business continuity program, it must follow through to ensure compliance. If the program is abandoned in the future and an incident occurs resulting in major losses, senior management is liable for the failure to comply with a published policy.

Closing the Deal

After completing the initial presentation to senior management, the planner must restate and confirm in writing the objectives, scope, time frame, impact on organizational resources, and cost of the program. A clear set of objectives, agreed-on scope, funding, organizational impact, and time frame are required for the planner to begin the development process. Not having the above may prove disruptive during the project if members of the senior management team assume something other than the initially stated project parameters, change elements of the project plan, or renege on committed resources.

USEFUL RESOURCES

Bulletin boards, journals, federal agencies, and professional organizations can provide information that will prove valuable to the planner. Appendix I-A provides a selected listing of these key resources.

WORKPAPER I1.01 Sample Risk Assessment Report

RISK ASSESSMENT REPORT

The company's disaster recovery plan should assume a worst-case, total-facility disaster, thus also providing for recovery from less severe circumstances. However, the assessment of threats and the risk associated with vulnerability to such threats provides for identification of hazards in terms of potential for occurrence and severity of impact. Emphasis may then be placed on preparation for those hazards of greatest potential and consequence. The primary objective of this analysis has been to identify the most critical risks that could cause an interruption of the company's information processing for a period greater than 24 hours.

Threats have been generally grouped into three categories:

- Natural.
- Human.
- Technical.

Each threat is then qualified by:

- Probability factor (low = 1, medium = 2, high = 3).
- Threat factor (sum of 1 plus speed of onset, where slow = 0, fast = 1; forewarning, where forewarning = 0, no forewarning = 1; duration, where short = 0, long = 1).
- Impact (low = 1, medium = 2, high = 3).

Weighted results are calculated by this formula:

Probability x Threat Factor x Impact = Relative Weight

The following matrix presents findings for a variety of threats to the organization's business operation A.

Threats to Business Operation A

Threats	Applicability	Probability	Threat Factor	Impact	Weight
Human Error: Operation--Response	Applicable	3	4	3	36
Power Outage--External	Applicable	3	3	3	27
Power Flux	Applicable	3	3	3	27
Fire: Internal--Major	Applicable	2	4	3	24
Toxic Contamination	Applicable	2	4	3	24
Water Leak/Plumbing Failure	Applicable	2	4	3	24
Central Computer Equipment Failure	Applicable	2	4	3	24
Human Error: Maintenance	Applicable	2	4	3	24
Hostage Taking	Applicable	2	4	3	24
Power Outage--Internal	Applicable	2	3	3	18
HVAC Failure/Temperature Inadequacy	Applicable	3	2	3	18
Telecommunications Failure Data	Applicable	2	3	3	18
Ancillary Equipment Failure	Applicable	2	4	2	16
Earthquake (Magnitude 5 or more)	Applicable	1	4	3	12
Upstream Dam/Reservoir Failure	Applicable	2	2	3	12
Seasonal/Local Flooding	Applicable	3	2	2	12
Radioactive Contamination	Applicable	1	4	3	12
Fire: Internal--Catastrophic	Applicable	1	4	3	12
Aircraft Crash	Applicable	1	4	3	12
Accidental Explosion--On Site	Applicable	1	4	3	12
Telecommunications Failure Voice	Applicable	2	3	2	12
Sabotage: External--Physical	Applicable	1	4	3	12
Sabotage: Internal--Physical	Applicable	1	4	3	12
Bombing	Applicable	1	4	3	12
Bomb Threat	Applicable	1	4	3	12
Arson	Applicable	1	4	3	12
Volcanic Activity	Applicable	1	3	3	09
Fire: Internal--Minor	Applicable	3	3	1	09
Loss of Key Staff	Applicable	2	2	2	08
Vandalism	Applicable	1	4	2	08
High Winds (70+ mph)	Applicable	1	3	2	06
Labor Dispute/Strike	Applicable	1	3	2	06
Riot/Civil Disorder	Applicable	1	3	2	06
Thunder/Electrical Storm	Applicable	1	2	2	04
Fire: External	Applicable	1	3	1	03
Accidental Explosion--Off Site	Applicable	1	3	1	03
Ice Storm	Applicable	1	2	1	02
Snowstorm/Blizzard	Applicable	1	1	1	01
Major Landslide/Mudslide	Not Applicable		NA		
Subsidence Faulting	Not Applicable		NA		
Tidal Flooding	Not Applicable		NA		
Tsunami	Not Applicable		NA		
Tornado	Not Applicable		NA		
Hurricane/Typhoon	Not Applicable		NA		
Tropical Storm	Not Applicable		NA		
Sandstorm	Not Applicable		NA		
Epidemic	Not in scope of study		NA		
Medical Emergency	Not in scope of study		NA		
Media Failure	Not in scope of study		NA		
Purchased Software Failure	Not in scope of study		NA		
Human Error: Programmers	Not in scope of study		NA		
Human Error: Users	Not in scope of study		NA		
Misuse of Resources	Not in scope of study		NA		
Theft: Data	Not in scope of study		NA		
Fraud/Embezzlement	Not in scope of study		NA		
Theft: Physical Assets ($2500+)	Not in scope of study		NA		
Sabotage: External--Data and Software	Not in scope of study		NA		
Sabotage: Internal--Data and Software	Not in scope of study		NA		

WORKPAPER I1.02 Business Case Support Document

BUSINESS CASE SUPPORT DOCUMENT

Date: ______________________

Overview: ______________________

Project Title: ______________________

Sponsoring Business Unit: ______________________

Contact Person: ______________________

Phone Number: ______________ Mail Stop: ______________

Business Objective: Recover critical business operations in the event of a disaster.

Business Function or Application

Objective: ______________________

____

____

Description: ______________________

____

____

Financial Estimates

Equipment (software): $______________

____

____

Equipment (hardware): $______________

____

____

Communications: $____________________

____

____

Space: $____________________

____

____

Miscellaneous Operating Expense: $____________________

____

____

IS Department Support and Planning: $____________________

____

____

<u>Risk Assessment</u>

Probable Risk (Without Backup Plan): $____________________

Probable Risk (With Backup Plan): $____________________

<u>Risk Assessment Narrative</u>

Option 1:____________________ $____________________

____

____

Option 2:____________________ $____________________

____

____

Organizing the Project

CHAPTER

I-2

This chapter presents the key steps involved in organizing the resumption planning project. These steps include assembling the project team, developing an action plan for carrying out the project, and allocating tasks and responsibilities for meeting plan objectives.

ASSEMBLE THE TEAM

STEP 1

The recovery team should be composed of both senior managers and functional and technical experts. Participation by senior management is critical, because it establishes the appropriate level of authority necessary to obtain resources and cooperation throughout the enterprise. Functional and technical experts are needed because they possess the detailed knowledge of business operations and of the related systems, which is essential for gathering accurate information to create an effective recovery program. These experts are in the best position to determine how the organization really works.

Management

A project manager must be assigned to coordinate the planning activities of team members. This manager must ensure that project participants complete their assigned tasks on schedule and perform work of high quality. This cannot be accomplished by simply ordering participants to meet objectives. Instead, the project manager must act as a leader capable of motivating team members to perform well, especially under the stress of a disaster. Often, the manager's first opportunity to display leadership skills occurs during the first recovery exercise.

The project manager has both budgetary and administrative responsibilities. These are described in the following paragraphs.

Budgetary Responsibilities. Business resumption planning projects often require investments of tens or hundreds of thousands of dollars, depending on the size of the organization. The responsibility for managing this budget rests with the business resumption project manager. The project manager should have (or obtain) basic financial skills for managing the budget—this is a key area on which the manager's performance will be evaluated.

It is difficult to precisely predict the cost of resources until the business impact analysis is completed. The cost of such purchased services as hot sites is usually not determined until late in the first year of planning. The cost of testing and maintenance may vary depending on such factors as the number of participating employees, the number of test sites, and the cost of equipment required for testing.

Nonetheless, the project manager is ultimately responsible for developing a sound initial budget. He or she must be prepared to justify the budget and should monitor the project to quickly detect any budgetary overruns. (Overruns should be reported to senior management as soon as possible; the planner must be prepared to justify any increases in the initial budget.) The project manager should anticipate financial requirements to change over time. In many cases, project costs tend to escalate during the first few years of development and then stabilize. After the initial planning is concluded, some organizations choose to reallocate costs from the project team to specific business units served by the plan.

Administration. The project manager is responsible for establishing meeting schedules, defining and publishing objectives, assigning tasks, monitoring the completion of tasks, documenting the results of meetings, and preparing and conducting presentations to senior management, employees, and auditors and regulators. An effective project manager must possess project management skills that ensure participants are productive. This can be accomplished by such simple things as providing an agenda and planning objectives at each team meeting; each item on the agenda should be tied to a specific task, its schedule for completion, and the names of meeting attendees responsible for completing the task.

Such administrative work may consume more than 80% of the manager's time for the project. If possible, the project manager should obtain clerical support during project planning. This assistance can help free the planner to focus on more important issues.

Functional and Technical Experts

The project manager must identify the appropriate experts within and outside the organization who are to participate in developing and implementing the business operations resumption plan. The following paragraphs describe the various types of experts who should be considered. The actual assignment of individuals to specific recovery planning tasks is performed only after the project scope and objectives have been defined in Step 2.

Consultants. Few organizations have all the internal skills necessary to cover all aspects of business resumption planning. The project manager may therefore wish to consider the use of consultants. Consultants may be employees of a key vendor; their services may be included with purchased services or products. Consultants may be used in the risk analysis, business impact analysis, or other specialized areas to supplement the skills and resources within the organization. In general, consultants should be used as a temporary resource. If at all possible, internal skills comparable to those of the consultants should be developed internally to ensure they are available when needed in a crisis.

Systems Experts. The project manager must recruit as part of the project team experts in the various mainframe, midrange, and small operating system environments. This includes experts in data processing operations, storage media management, printing management, and operating systems security.

Communications Specialists. Experts in communications platforms are a critical resource required in the planning process. Restoration of voice services is fundamental to the start-up of business operations. The technical internal and external expertise required to plan for alternative voice resources must be identified early in the project.

Network Experts. The challenge of quickly connecting central information processing services to business recovery locations is the responsibility of network experts. Their planning for the acquisition of network hardware, data communications lines, and external resources directly affects the recovery time frame. (Acquisition and implementation of network resources often require long lead times.)

Financial Experts. Estimates of potential and actual financial loss depend on information that can be provided only by internal financial experts. Financial experts are key participants in the business impact analysis and may also provide assistance in developing the project budget.

Business Function Representatives. Representatives from the organization's operating units provide the expertise needed to describe how the units function, determine what operations to recover, develop recovery strategies and procedures, and identify appropriate team members.

Vital Records Managers. Legal requirements related to the management of vital records may or may not be clearly documented in the organization. Experts in managing vital records can help provide a focused effort and ensure that applicable laws or regulations are complied with. In addition, the vital records expert can help in defining recovery criteria that might be integrated into the vital records program.

Restoration Resources. Few organizations have the internal expertise or resources to effectively restore a damaged facility, building contents, office equipment, data processing equipment, and magnetic and paper records. Therefore, the project manager needs to identify an external company to provide postdisaster services and help identify the restoration services required during the recovery.

Crisis Management Representative. In some organizations, a crisis management team comprising the organization's senior executives and internal and external experts is organized to handle such specialized problems as criminal activity, product contamination, and hazardous waste spills. If the organization has such a team, one or more representatives of that team should take part in the business operations recovery project.

Legal Experts. A legal representative should participate as a project team member to ensure that issues related to potential organizational liabilities are addressed in the plan. Additionally, lawyers may perform contract review for purchased recovery services.

Clerical and Support Staff. Clerical assistance should be allocated to handle the clerical work associated with the project. Individuals who provide ongoing clerical and administrative support will be more familiar with the plan, its objectives, and the responsibilities of each team. This knowledge makes support personnel more effective in the posting, assigning, and management of information received in the emergency operations or recovery centers.

DEVELOP THE ACTION PLAN

STEP 2

The project manager next develops an action plan that specifies the scope of the plan and its objectives. The objectives should be action oriented; that is, they describe the steps that should be taken to complete discrete tasks. After these tasks have been defined, the manager can then determine who is best suited to perform each task. He or she assigns one or more team members to each task and also identifies any other resources that may be needed to successfully execute the step.

Defining the Plan Scope

Management and project team members need to know what the plan does and does not cover. The scope should define both the business locations and the business functions to be addressed by the plan. These might include:

- Building A.
- A campus of buildings.
- Region B.
- Business operations C and D.
- Local area networks E and F.

The following is an example of a scope statement for a manufacturer:

> This plan includes actions and procedures necessary to recover the business operations and information resources located at the Atlanta and Denver headquarters facilities. Included are the previously identified critical business functions as well as their supporting information and communications resources, including LANs, microcomputers and peripherals, laser and impact printers, routers, bridges, and the PBX.
>
> The plan is designed to recover critical business functions and information processing following the loss of either facility but is not intended to address the simultaneous loss of both centers. The scope of the business resumption plan does not include:
>
> - Recovery of any equipment not located within one of the specified locations.
> - Interim user procedures for performing specialized manufacturing operations using specialized process-related information systems.
>
> The plan does not attempt to address dependences between this recovery plan for the headquarters functions and other plans for recovery of data center, manufacturing, and distribution functions.

Identifying Action-Oriented Objectives

Objectives and planning assumptions should be defined early in the project. A good starting point for developing these objectives is the list of qualities of an effective business resumption plan (as described in Chapter I-1).

To be most useful, the objectives should be expressed as a checklist of actions to be performed in the course of creating, testing, and maintaining the resumption plan. At a high level, these actions include:

1. Conducting project team orientation meetings in which the recovery approach, deliverables, required resources, and schedules are presented.
2. Documenting business functions in order to understand the relationships of these functions. For example, in a disaster, it may become necessary to relocate to alternative locations, which could require separating certain business functions into component operations. The consequences of such separation must be clearly understood to avoid operational problems during the recovery.
3. Performing a business impact analysis. This is needed to better understand the risks and priorities for recovery of key business functions. Even if such an analysis has been performed in the past, it may need to be done again if the company has been reorganized or if certain operations have moved to new locations.
4. Identifying resources required by each business function to perform its duties. For example, resource planning identifies what the business units need to reestablish their operations at an alternative location.
5. Establishing a recovery strategy to ensure an effective transition through emergency response, recovery, and restoration following a disaster.

6. Developing detailed response, recovery, and restoration procedures. Not only do such procedures provide valuable assistance to recovery team members during a crisis, they also serve as a vehicle for training team members in their recovery roles. Such detailed procedures also provide a clear definition of each team member's scope of authority in a crisis.
7. Establishing a testing strategy to ensure the planned recovery approach is effective in a disaster.
8. Establishing a maintenance strategy to ensure that recovery plan information is current and that it can be maintained efficiently.
9. Developing a training and orientation program to ensure the readiness of team members and general awareness of employees. The original team members must be trained to ensure they are able to respond effectively in a disaster. And as the composition of the teams change over time, new team members must be trained in their recovery roles.

   Although not all employees belong to recovery teams, everyone in the organization must understand how to respond to a disaster. Therefore, it is important to orient all employees to the recovery plan, even if they are not assigned to recovery teams.

Workpaper I2.01 provides a list of the actions that should be performed to accomplish the objectives of the recovery plan; it can be modified to address the requirements of specific organizations.

IDENTIFY RELATED TASKS AND RESPONSIBILITIES

STEP 3

After the objectives of the project are defined and agreed on, the planner must identify tasks associated with each objective and determine who within or outside the organization should be responsible for completing the tasks. The project manager must have support in the planning. No one individual has the time or the expertise to successfully address all planning tasks.

Workpaper I2.02 provides an example of how business functions might be assigned to specific tasks. A person's name would also be provided as the project participant responsible for completing the specific task; this ensures accountability. The order in which the responsible functions are listed in Workpaper I2.02 indicates the order of responsibility. For example, in the first task, identifying online intensive users, the business units have primary responsibility and the information systems coordinator provides secondary support, as does the business resumption planning project team.

The tasks should be allocated to those organizations and individuals with the greatest knowledge of the particular area. The planner may provide assistance, tools, and clerical support to the respective units but should not have primary responsibility to collect the information or formulate the recovery strategies. That is the responsibility of the business or information processing unit.

FORMALIZE AND DISTRIBUTE DATA COLLECTION TOOLS

STEP 4

The project manager should provide the forms for project participants to use in gathering information. This helps avoid the misinterpretation of requirements, and it provides a structured data gathering process. It also avoids the added effort of reworking information to a common format after it has been collected.

SCHEDULE TASK COMPLETION DATES

STEP 5

Task completion dates must be set and adhered to. The completion dates for assigned tasks should be established in consultation with project team members to ensure that recovery planning tasks do not conflict with their other commitments. After the schedule for completing tasks has been set, the deadlines become the team members' rather than the planner's.

The schedules should be documented and distributed to all interested parties. A summary of the tasks, schedules, and responsible parties should be communicated to senior management. As the project progresses, senior management should be kept apprised of the status of the project.

STEP 6

DEVELOP FORMAL MEETING SCHEDULES

Regular meetings need to be planned to keep the project on schedule. In the initial stages of the project, it is not uncommon for meetings to be held every two weeks to discuss the status of assigned tasks and any issues related to the information being developed. In addition to regular meetings with the working team, the planner should schedule meetings with senior management on at least a quarterly basis.

WORKPAPER I2.01 Resumption Plan Objectives

RESUMPTION PLAN OBJECTIVES

1. Conduct orientation meetings:
   a. Introduce the project team.
   b. Review the business resumption planning process.
   c. Review the recovery approach and expected results.
   d. Review qualifications for project participants.
   e. Present roles of project participants.
   f. Review deliverables:
      -- Business impact analysis.
      -- Recovery assumptions.
      -- Coping strategies.
      -- Command and control strategies.
      -- Data collection process.
      -- Project management meetings and reports
   g. Review required resources:
      -- Support personnel.
      -- Time.
      -- Data.
      -- Level of responsiveness.
   h. Present project schedule and key dates.

2. Perform business impact analysis. Identify critical business functions providing information about:
      -- Potential threats.
      -- Financial losses expected.
      -- Key asset movement.
      -- Interorganizational dependences.
      -- Appropriate recovery priorities.

3. Document business functions at the task level:
   a. Identify key tasks performed for each critical business unit identified by the business impact analysis.
   b. Identify relationships and interdependences among critical business tasks and functions.

4. Determine required resource.

5. Review current plans and establish a recovery strategy:
   a. Compare the emergency preparedness and recovery plan strategies, assumptions, and priorities with identified business priorities.
   b. Develop an integrated recovery strategy.

6. Develop detailed command and control procedures. Develop response, recovery, and restoration procedures for managing a major disruption.

7. Establish a testing strategy.

8. Establish a maintenance strategy:
    a. Modify planning documents on the basis of the business impact and interdependence analysis to ensure plan information is current and maintainable.
    b. Investigate and select a data base software product to store and manage collected information.

9. Develop business resumption planning training and orientation program:
    a. Train response, recovery, and restoration teams on incident management.
    b. Provide training tools for other divisions to use in developing their own plans.
    c. Develop an orientation program for new employees.
    d. Develop an orientation program for new recovery team members.

WORKPAPER I2.02 Assignment of Tasks and Responsibilities

Tasks	Responsibility
Identify online intensive users.	BU, IS, BRP
Identify PC-intensive users.	BU
Identify midrange intensive users.	BU, BRP, IS
Develop notification list of key personnel.	BRP, BU
Identify applications--mainframe, midrange, PC.	All
Document applications requirements.	IS, BU
Identify impact of loss of applications.	BRP, BU
Document business impact, additional expense, revenue loss, embarrassment.	BRP, BU, IS
Management review and approval of impact results.	BRP, Senior Management
Identify data backup requirements.	BRP, IS, BU
Document off-site data storage.	BRP, IS
Identify dependence and relationship with internal functions.	BRP, BU
Document dependence and relationship with internal functions.	BRP, BU
Identify impact of loss of key internal functions.	All
Document business impact, additional expense, revenue loss, embarrassment.	BRP
Management review and approval of impact results.	BRP
Identify computer and office equipment.	BU
Document equipment requirements.	BRP, BU
Identify paper records, historical documentation.	BU
Document paper record requirements.	BRP, BU
Identify key vendors--services, equipment, supplies.	BU, IS
Document key vendors and contacts.	BU, IS, BRP
Develop notification list of key vendors.	BU, IS, BRP
Identify key customers and contacts.	BU
Document relationship or dependence.	BU, BRP
Develop notification list of key customers.	BU, BRP
Identify critical procedures, manuals, and reports.	All
Identify backup and off-site storage locations.	BRP, IS
Document off-site storage locations.	BRP
Develop interim operating strategies.	BRP, BU
Management review and approval of interim operating strategies.	BRP
Train unit personnel.	BRP
Develop test objectives and criteria.	BU, BRP, IS
Test planning assumptions.	All
Critique test results.	BRP
Modify plan.	BU, BRP, IS

Key

BRP: Business Resumption Planning Group
BU: Business Unit Recovery Coordinator
IS: Information Systems Recovery Coordinator

Conducting the Business Impact Analysis

CHAPTER

I-3

The business impact analysis (BIA) is designed to ensure a thorough understanding of the vital business functions and systems within the organization. The impact of loss on each of these functions is identified, evaluated, and categorized according to the required time frames for recovery of the function. The recovery priorities are set on the basis of this analysis.

The purpose of the BIA is to identify the consequences of the interruption in terms of financial loss, additional expense, embarrassment to the organization, and the maximum period of interruption that the organization can tolerate. The BIA does not take into consideration what type of incident causes a disruption to operations; the cause of the disruption does not matter.

Avoiding financial loss is the primary objective of developing a business resumption plan. Financial losses occur from an interruption or loss of revenue caused by the inability to continue business after a disruptive incident.

The longer a business fails to provide services or products, the more severe the financial losses. Some losses are unavoidable no matter how effective the plan and recovery effort. The objective is to determine what level of financial loss is acceptable to management for the organization as a whole and for specific business functions. Each business unit's financial contribution is determined during the BIA.

Acceptable levels of interruption are defined by the organization's management on the basis of estimates of both financial and nonfinancial losses. Management may be willing to self-insure or cover the potential loss with commercial insurance for a short period. After that, the loss may become permanent and the damage long-term.

As most planners know, the shorter the recovery time frame, the more expensive the recovery capability that must be put in place. Management depends on information from the BIA to make an informed decision on how much financial risk it is willing to assume and how much it should invest in the recovery plan.

After the BIA is complete, it should be reviewed and verified by management and all participants. Management is then ready to establish recovery priorities for critical applications, systems, and business functions. System and application recovery time frames are driven by the business recovery priorities. For example, the priority for recovering networks connecting users to information systems must be consistent with the recovery time frames for the most critical business units. If critical business units plan to recover in five days, the IS function must plan to recover network services at least one day before the recovery of the business unit.

DEFINITION OF BUSINESS IMPACT ANALYSIS

Business impact analysis refers to the process of identifying an organization's exposures to specific threat events and analyzing the potential disruptive impact of those exposures on critical business operations. The BIA can also be used to:

- Assess the impact of a disruption in any functional area of the business on the operations of the enterprise as a whole.
- Determine the extent to which key functional and operational dependences exist within the organization (e.g., the extent of reliance on information processing).
- Establish the priorities and sequences in which critical data processing applications and key business functions should be restored.

There are two generally accepted methods of performing any type of analysis: qualitative and quantitative. Qualitative analysis might be performed by interviewing a knowledgeable person about the relative characteristics, value, or risk associated with a given function. Quantitative analysis attempts to measure value or risk by, for example, assigning numerical values to a scale. The BIA employs both qualitative and quantitative analysis.

PERFORMING A BUSINESS IMPACT ANALYSIS

The process of conducting a business impact analysis can be broken into four steps:

1. Determining the scope of the analysis.
2. Gathering the initial information about business unit functions, support systems, and applications through the use of questionnaires.
3. Conducting interviews to verify the completeness and accuracy of information gathered in the previous step.
4. Analyzing the information to determine priorities for recovery of business operations, systems, and applications, and presenting these results to senior management.

These steps are described in the following sections of this chapter. The chapter concludes with a discussion of insurance options for mitigating financial losses.

STEP 1

DETERMINE THE SCOPE OF THE ANALYSIS

The planner must determine the degree of detailed analysis that the BIA is to provide. A comprehensive BIA requires a significant commitment of resources and time. If the planner needs to establish a recovery capability within a short time frame, a comprehensive BIA may not be appropriate.

In that case, an abbreviated BIA should be considered. The abbreviated BIA relies on information obtained from a group of experts within the organization. Technical systems experts are asked to identify high-volume system users. They do so by using information obtained from performance measurement and billing applications. For example, IS departments usually bill back system use to the business units; individual users and user groups can be identified by their user IDs. These systems experts can therefore determine the volume of application use by employee and identify those critical applications on which the business units depend most heavily. High-volume users can be targeted for follow-up interviews as needed. This process avoids having to question all users about the applications they use, focusing instead on high-use applications and high-volume users.

The second set of organizational experts resides in the financial group. This group can provide the financial contribution of each business unit and assist in determining the per-day loss potential for each business operation.

The third group of organizational experts are the business unit managers. They can assist in identifying any additional expenses associated with the interruption—for example, the cost of additional personnel, legal penalties, and additional purchased resources.

Following this approach, the planner can identify the most critical functions, systems, and applications. Even though this analysis is not comprehensive, it should be sufficient to enable the planner to establish the initial recovery priorities, teams, and resources within a reasonable time frame. After the basic plan and recovery organization is in place, the planner can initiate a more complete BIA to validate the initial information and address new business functions, applications, and systems.

The remaining steps describe how to perform a comprehensive analysis.

GATHER INFORMATION

STEP 2

The planner must gather information from each business unit to determine the cumulative effect on the organization of the loss of the business function, support system, or application. This can be done using a structured set of questionnaires to obtain information from business unit managers and key staff. Workpaper I3.01 provides a complete set of questionnaires along with instructions for their use.

The questions used in the questionnaires and in subsequent interviews should be appropriate to the intended audience and relevant to the purpose of the analysis. In some cases the planner may choose to focus the analysis solely on the recovery of systems and applications; alternatively, the planner may choose to address the recovery of business operations, which includes but is not limited to the recovery of support systems and applications. In either case, the questions presented to managers and users must be within their scope of understanding.

For example, if the initial analysis focuses on systems applications, the names of the applications should be presented in terms the users can understand. The planner should use the popular rather than technical name of the application. The planner should not ask users questions related to the operating systems supporting the applications; most users have no knowledge of the operating system. Similarly, the planner should not question users about issues requiring an understanding of how applications interact. The planner should also assume that such equipment as computer terminals is required; it is not necessary to ask users if they need the equipment.

If the focus of the BIA is on the recovery of business operations, the questions should first attempt to identify the basic systems infrastructure supporting the business operation (e.g., communications, mail services, and general information systems). (Specific applications and systems can then be addressed in a separate impact analysis focusing on recovery of applications.)

The loss of key internal and external business functions can be as crippling as the loss of information systems. The business operations–related BIA attempts to determine the organization's tolerance for disruption of key business functions.

Workpaper I3.01 presents a complete set of questionnaires that address the recovery of business operations, including support systems, applications, and equipment. In general, the questionnaires and the subsequent interviews (described under Step 3) attempt to determine the impact of:

- Interruption of business function or application.
- Loss of revenue.
- Additional expenses.
- Intangible losses.

Business Interruption

The impact of loss of use of a business function, application, or service should be determined. This can be expressed in terms of the number of days the user could tolerate the application not being available. If a network is necessary to provide access to the application, it is not necessary to ask questions about the impact of losing the network.

Revenue Loss

The planner determines what systems or services are directly involved in activities that generate revenue. For example, systems directly involved in billing or collection activities should be identified.

The planner should attempt to determine whether the inability to process certain applications would interfere with the provision of services to customers and other business operations, and if so, how they would be affected.

The inability to perform identified services may cause customers to seek services or products from competitors; if so, the impact of such losses should be assessed. The revenue analysis also determines whether the inability to provide services would cause other indirect impacts on revenue activities (e.g., lost interest on investments).

Additional Expenses

The planner must determine the types of additional expenses the organization would incur with the delay or loss of services or of the processing of applications. The interviewees should be asked to estimate the minimum length of time the support of the applications could be denied their organization without incurring such additional expenses as overtime.

The planner and interviewees should determine whether a delay in the availability of services or applications results in additional expenditures other than for labor or services (e.g., interest expense on bank loans, capital outlays) and should estimate the amount of business backlog (e.g., number of orders, order entries, inquiries) that would be incurred. They should also determine whether a delay in operation would result in any fines or penalties for failure to provide services or to adhere to deadlines or government regulations. If so, the impact should be determined. In addition, the impact should be assessed if a delay in services would result in legal liability, personal injury, or other public harm.

Intangible Losses

Intangible losses include:

- Loss of customer confidence.
- Loss of investor confidence.
- Loss of competitive edge.
- Damage to the organization's reputation.
- Reduced market share.
- Legal or regulatory violations.

It is difficult to estimate the value of intangible losses; such estimates are inherently subjective. The planner should not spend an extraordinary amount of time trying to quantify this category. The planner should determine the most serious sources of embarrassment to the organization with respect to the delay or loss of ability to provide key services or process applications. Interviewees should be asked if there are potential legal, social, or moral liabilities to the organization if key applications or services are disrupted.

The knowledge and credibility of the source of the subjective opinion is critical to the acceptance of this information by the organization's senior management. An example is the loss of customers. When First Interstate Bank conducted its BIA in

1986, it was determined that approximately 2% of the customer base would be lost if an extended outage occurred. Although it does not seem like a large number, this 2% represented the customers generating the most income for the bank. The customers were large, high-volume users who would not tolerate an extended loss of services.

The source of this estimate were the customer account managers servicing these customers on a daily basis. These managers understood the customers' expectations of service and knew how the customers reacted to past minor interruptions of service. They were in the best position to provide an opinion—that is, without directly asking the customer.

In the beginning stages of the BIA, the planner should be cautious in directly approaching customers for input. They may already assume that the organization has a plan in place and may react negatively on finding that it is not the case.

VERIFY THE INFORMATION

STEP 3

After the business units return the questionnaires and the planner completes an initial analysis, interviews should be conducted to verify the completeness and accuracy of the information. In specific, these interviews are intended to identify any discrepancies in the collected information.

All business impact analyses require face-to-face interviews. In addition to interviewing the project participants, the planner should also meet with other independent experts from the contributing business units. The results should also be provided to managers of the contributing business units and reviewed with their next higher level of management. It is important that the key employees and managers of the business units find the collected information credible and be willing to defend the results if required.

The planner should plan to spend at least one to two hours with each interviewee. Group interviews of personnel with related positions can expedite the interview process and may provide a less threatening environment than one-on-one interviews. Issues raised by one team member may jog the memory of another interviewee, thereby uncovering a critical issue that would have been otherwise overlooked.

The interviews should follow the same format as described in Step 2. The planner should attempt to verify the impact of:

- Interruption of business function or application.
- Loss of revenue.
- Additional expenses.
- Intangible losses.

ANALYZE AND PRESENT THE RESULTS

STEP 4

The planner can use automated risk assessment software to help manage and analyze the information collected during the BIA and to summarize the findings. Such software tools include Strohl Systems' B-I-A Professional and Business Resumption Planners' Analysis 2000.

These tools provide algorithms that help the planner to establish a numerical value for each resource being assessed that represents a composite of the potential impact factors. The financial loss potential and additional expenses are presented in monetary values. Numerical values are also assigned to embarrassment and other intangible factors. The tolerance for delays in services are identified and each resource is assigned a numerical rating. Analyzed resources are assigned numerical weightings so that each resource can be compared with other resources. Based on a combination of factors, a total weighting is assigned to each resource or business unit. That composite value identifies the relative severity of the combined impact factors and the priority for recovery of the application or business unit.

The automated tools can also be used to graph the results of the analysis. This makes it easier for team members and management to understand the results.

The management presentation should focus on the highest-priority applications and business functions. The results of the analysis should be presented in a tabular or graphical format. The methodology used, sources of the information, and textual explanations of the results should be presented in a concise format.

After the results are presented, the planner should state the priorities assigned to business units and applications as well as the maximum tolerable disruption time frames. At the conclusion of the management presentation, the planner should explain how the analysis results will be used to establish recovery time frames, strategies, and recovery resources.

REASSESSING BUSINESS IMPACT

The frequency of reassessing the business impact depends on the frequency of change within the organization. If the organization is relatively stable, the reassessment can be less frequent. In most organizations, however, frequent acquisitions of new business activities and technologies constantly change the operations of the organization. With each introduction of a new business operation, application, information system, or network, an assessment should be made to determine where the new function fits among the recovery priorities.

Most organizations should conduct a corporatewide BIA at least every two years. The factors that determine the impact of the loss of a particular function in the organization can be expected to change in that time. For example, the volume of business transactions may increase.

EVALUATING INSURANCE OPTIONS

To offset potential losses, the organization can purchase insurance coverage for identified perils. This coverage is referred to as business interruption or additional expense insurance. Exposures not addressed by insurance must be taken into account in the recovery plan.

The planner should be aware that all disasters are not covered automatically. The exposures need to be identified through a risk analysis, and the policy needs to be tailored to address these exposures.

There are two basic types of insurance: property coverage and time-element coverage. Property coverage covers buildings, personal property, and equipment and machinery. Time-element coverage covers such items as business income, extra expenses, leasehold interest, and rental value. Time-element coverage must generally be purchased separately.

Exhibit I-3-A provides an example of perils covered by insurance and extensions to general coverage that expand the coverage to specific types of losses. Many of the disasters and listed perils will or should be discovered during the initial risk analysis.

Property Coverage

The value of the insured asset may be established based on any of the following:

- Actual cash value.
- Replacement cost value.

EXHIBIT I-3-A INSURANCE OPTIONS

Covered Perils

- Explosion
- Fire or lightning
- Leakage
- Mine subsidence
- Riot or civil commotion
- Sinkhole or collapse
- Smoke
- Vandalism
- Volcanic action
- Wind or hail

Extensions to Normal Coverage

- Electrical arcing
- Falling objects
- Glass breakage
- Mechanical breakdown
- Steam explosion
- Water damage
- Weight of ice, snow, or sleet

EXHIBIT I-3-B VALUATION CONSIDERATIONS

Insured Asset	Consideration
Machinery and Equipment	Original cost of equipment.
	Depreciation of the equipment.
	The current functional costs of using the equipment.
Stock	Cost of stock used by work in progress.
	Cost of raw materials on site.
	Value of finished goods in inventory.
	Value of goods held for sale.
Building	Replacement costs of damaged facilities.
	Rebuilding costs of upgrades required by new building codes.
	Demolition costs for damaged facilities.
	Increased costs of construction compared to when building was built.
Valuable Papers and Records	Costs of restoring damaged records.
	Replacement of blanks.

- Functional replacement value.
- Book value (generally not used for insurance purposes).

Exhibit I-3-B shows valuation considerations for various insured assets.

Time-Element Coverage

The BIA establishes the potential additional expenses incurred during the recovery of critical functions. That information can provide a solid basis for the risk management group to establish time-related coverage for the organization. The following paragraphs describe each of the four types of time-element coverage.

Business Income. For a manufacturing company, business income coverage pays for financial loss because the company cannot manufacture its product. For a mercantile company, business income coverage pays for loss suffered because it cannot sell its products. For a service company, business income coverage pays for loss suffered because it cannot provide a service.

Business income coverage does not pay for damage causing the interruption. (This is covered under hazard-related insurance.) Business income coverage pays for the net profit (or loss) before taxes plus continuing normal operating expenses.

Business income covers the length of time operations are interrupted. The loss is determined on the basis of length of time of the interruption. The deductible may be established in hourly or daily increments.

Extra Expense. This coverage pays for those expenses beyond the normal operating expenses required to continue operations when premises are damaged during an interruption. The damage must be caused by an insured peril. Extra expenses might include:

- Disaster declaration fees.
- Hot-site use fees.
- Rent for alternative office site.
- Rent for fixtures, machinery, and equipment.
- Light, heat, and power at temporary locations.
- Insurance at temporary locations.
- Moving and hauling.
- Installation of operations at temporary location.
- Employee expenses.
- Administrative expenses.
- Emergency command post expenses.
- Operating expenses.

The insured and insurance company establishes a payout pattern in which the insurance company pays 40%, 80%, or 100% up front.

Leasehold Interest. This coverage pays for loss of lease interest when the lease is canceled because of damage to the property. Leasehold interest might include:

- Tenant's lease interest.
- Bonus payments.
- Improvements and betterment.
- Prepaid rent.

Rental Value. This coverage pays for the landlord's loss of rental income when leased property is damaged and rendered untenantable as a result of a covered peril.

SUMMARY GUIDELINES

The following guidelines should help ensure the success of this phase of the planning project.

Set Time Limits. Time limits should be established for completing the business impact analysis. If the process takes too long, the information may become obsolete by the time the analysis is completed.

Use Data Gathering Tools. Such data gathering tools as prepared worksheets and questionnaires can help speed data collection.

Investigate Dependences Among Business Functions. The impact of the loss of one business function on other functions should be evaluated.

Identify Potential Losses. Even with a recovery plan, some losses should be expected. Therefore, the plan should differentiate between losses incurred without the plan and losses incurred with the plan. Losses should be evaluated assuming a worst-case disaster scenario.

Identify Financial Losses. In addition to the direct financial losses due to lost sales revenue, other indirect losses may also accrue. For example, a client may demand compensation if a certain critical function fails to operate. Regulations may require that reimbursements can be made only if certain reporting tasks are performed. Costs may be incurred for reconstructing vital records. Expected revenue from new business projects may be lost or forestalled.

Identify Nonfinancial Losses. Such nonfinancial impacts as loss of customer confidence and disruption of customer service should be included in the analysis.

Evaluate Insurance Coverage. Insurance may compensate for certain losses. Coverage may vary depending on whether the organization has implemented a business resumption plan.

WORKPAPER I3.01 Business Impact Analysis Questionnaires

BUSINESS IMPACT ANALYSIS QUESTIONNAIRES

INTRODUCTION TO QUESTIONNAIRES

A business impact analysis is a methodology used to determine the effect of an interruption of services on each business unit and the organization as a whole. The analysis can provide information on the short- and long-term effects of a disaster on such factors as profit, market share, and goodwill.

The organization's senior executives and general managers have determined the ranges for acceptable and unacceptable losses in several categories. Those ranges are used to set priorities for business functions.

The questions have been developed to elicit such information as the financial impact, time frame for recovery, and resource requirements. The responses will be compiled and analyzed to provide the information required to develop a corporatewide business recovery strategy.

The objective of gathering this information is to:

- Determine the priority for restoring the functions of the organization.
- Determine recovery time-frame requirements for business units.
- Identify critical resources required to support business unit recovery.

This information is required to develop an effective corporatewide business recovery strategy. Using a consistent methodology based on management's criteria for determining the criticality of business functions will enable us to implement a prudent and cost-effective plan.

INSTRUCTIONS

Complete the following questionnaires in the order in which they are presented. To answer certain questions, you will need to gather such statistics as:

- Daily average transaction volume.
- Daily average dollar volume.
- Peak average transaction volume.
- Peak average dollar volume.
- Fixed costs.
- Overhead.
- Contribution or margin.

QUESTIONNAIRE 1: OVERVIEW OF THE BUSINESS UNIT

1. Describe the unit location: ______________________

2. Briefly describe the unit's functions: ______________________
____
____
____
____

3. Which description best fits the unit?

   [ ] Production unit or unit with direct client contact.
   [ ] Unit that directly provides production support.
   [ ] Unit responsible for sales.
   [ ] Provides order taking or order entry.
   [ ] Administrative.
   [ ] Other: ______________________.

4. What time is the unit's start of the business day?
____

5. What time is the unit's end of the business day?
____

6. What is the average daily dollar volume processed by the unit? ______________________

7. What is the average daily item or transaction volume processed by the unit? ______________________
____

8. Does the unit have any peak volume or otherwise critical times? If the unit does, please list the times as well as the average dollar and item or transaction volumes processed at those times: ______________________
____
____

QUESTIONNAIRE 2: WORK FLOW INTERDEPENDENCES

This section is intended to document the flow of work to and from your unit. It also is intended to determine how the work gets to your unit and how your unit sends it out once it has been completed.

WORK RECEIVED

1. Please list the units, in-house central computer systems, data processing service bureaus, or other organizations from which your unit receives work: ______________________
____
____

2. Of the total amount of incoming work your unit receives, what percentage comes through the following routes?

[ ] US mail.
[ ] Telephone or fax.
[ ] Interoffice mail.
[ ] Courier.
[ ] Online information from the central computer systems.
[ ] Reports or fiche generated from the central computer systems.
[ ] Online information from external data processing services.
[ ] Reports or fiche generated by external data processing services.

WORK SENT

3. Please list the units, in-house central computer systems, data processing service bureaus, or other organizations to which your unit sends completed work or information:

____
____
____

4. Of the total amount of outgoing work your unit produces, what percentage is sent through the following routes?

[ ] US mail.
[ ] Telephone or fax.
[ ] Interoffice mail.
[ ] Courier.
[ ] Online information from the central computer systems.
[ ] Reports or fiche generated from the central computer systems.
[ ] Online information from external data processing services.
[ ] Reports or fiche generated by external data processing services.

QUESTIONNAIRE 3: LAN OR PC MICROCOMPUTER RESOURCES

1. Which microcomputer equipment does your unit use?

[ ] Standalone microcomputers.
[ ] Microcomputers connected to a local area network (LAN).

2. How are the microcomputers or LAN used?

[ ] General administrative or office functions (e.g., memos).
[ ] Gateway to the organization's centralized computer systems.
[ ] Other: ______________________________.

3. Are the automation features of the microcomputers or the LAN used by the unit critical to the timing and efficiency of the services the unit provides? Please describe:

____
____
____

4. Do those microcomputers or the LAN directly support or provide information required to control your unit's operations? Please describe: ______________________

____
____
____

5. If the LAN or microcomputers were unavailable for one business day, would there be a data entry or transaction backlog?

[ ] Yes [ ] No (If no, skip questions 6 and 7.)

6. Estimate the amount of backlog in number of entries or transactions:

- On a normal business day: ________________.
- At the unit's most critical peak time: ________________.

7. Estimate the hours it would take your current staff to eliminate the backlog. Please include the average hourly pay rate for the staff:

- Hours at current staffing on a normal business day: ___________________.
- Hours at current staffing at your unit's most critical peak time: ___________________.
- Average pay rate per hour for current staff: ___________________.

QUESTIONNAIRE 4: IN-HOUSE CENTRAL COMPUTER SYSTEMS

System or application: ______________________________

1. Does the system or application allow clients to access the system directly by dialing in?
[ ] Yes [ ] No

2. If the system or application were unavailable to your unit for one business day, would there be a data entry or transaction backlog?
[ ] Yes [ ] No

If you answered yes, estimate the amount of backlog in number of entries or transactions:

- On a normal business day: ____________________.
- At the unit's most critical peak time: ____________________.

Estimate the hours it would take your current staff to eliminate the backlog. Please include the average hourly pay rate for the staff.

- Hours at current staffing on a normal business day: _______________.
- Hours at current staffing at your unit's most critical peak time: _______________.
- Average pay rate per hour for current staff: _______________.

3. Would a one-day business day delay in processing this system or application result in any fines or penalties due to missed deadlines or other reasons?
   [ ] Yes   [ ] No

   If you answered yes, please describe the reason for the penalty, the issuer of the penalty, and an average for such penalties:
   ____
   ____
   ____

4. Would an outage of this system or application affect other revenue activities (e.g., investments, interest on funds, cash management) or balancing? ______________________________
   ____
   ____
   ____

5. After a disaster, within which time frame do you need to have access to this function for the above system/application?

   [ ] 1 - 6 hours
   [ ] 6 - 12 hours
   [ ] 12 - 24 hours
   [ ] 2 days - 1 week
   [ ] Other: ____________________.

6. Are there any peak periods associated with this system or application? Check those time which apply and include a brief explanation of the reason for the peak time for each.

   [ ] Daily
   [ ] Quarterly
   [ ] Monthly

[ ] Month end
[ ] Quarter end
[ ] Year end
[ ] Other (please specify): ____________________.

QUESTIONNAIRE 5: OUTSOURCED DATA PROCESSING

If the organization uses an external provider of information services, an assessment of the impact of the loss of applications must be made. Please answer the following questions. (The questions provided in the in-house computer systems questionnaire can also be used for outside services.)

1. Does the service provider have a disaster recovery plan?
____

2. Has the plan been tested? ____________________
____

3. When was the plan last tested, what were the test objectives, and what was the result of the test? ___________
____

4. What percentage of total applications were tested? _________
____

5. What is the recovery time frame for the service provider's systems? ______________________________

6. Where in the recovery priorities is your organization in relationship to other service provider customers? __________
____

7. Was the network connecting your organization and the service provider tested? ______________________
____

8. Is there a network recovery plan for the service provider?
____

9. Where in the network recovery priorities is your organization? ______________________________
____

QUESTIONNAIRE 6: REGULATORY AND LEGAL ISSUES

<u>Regulatory Issues</u>

1. Are there any reporting requirements or deadlines that would be affected by a delay in or loss of the services your unit provides?

2. Would a delay in or loss of service result in any fines or penalties?

   a. List the regulations.
   b. Describe the conflict.
   c. Describe possible consequences (e.g., penalties).

<u>Legal Issues</u>

1. Will a delay in or loss of the services your unit provides result in possible legal liability, damages, or other public harm?

   a. List the legal issue.
   b. Describe the conflict.
   c. Describe possible consequences.

QUESTIONNAIRE 7: TRANSACTION VOLUME LOSS--NORMAL BUSINESS DAY

Consider that your unit is unable to perform its functions as a result of a disaster on a normal business day. By how much would the transaction volume decrease? If the disaster extended through each period of time listed below, how much transaction volume might the company lose during each period? Fill in the appropriate dollar range (e.g., $0 - 50,000; $50,000 - 100,000) for each time period listed below.

First half hour: ____________________
Hour 1: ____________________
Hour 3: ____________________
Hours 4 - 12: ____________________
Hours 13 - 24: ____________________
Day 3: ____________________
Days 4 - 7: ____________________
Days 8 - 14: ____________________
Days 15 - 30: ____________________
Day 30 and beyond: ____________________

QUESTIONNAIRE 8: TRANSACTION VOLUME LOSS--PEAK BUSINESS DAY

Consider that your unit is unable to perform its functions as a result of a disaster on a peak business day. By how much would the transaction volume decrease? If the disaster extended through each period of time listed below, how much transaction volume might the company lose during each period? Fill in the appropriate dollar range (e.g., $0 - 50,000; $50,000 - 100,000) for each time period listed below.

First half hour: ____________________
Hour 1: ____________________
Hour 3: ____________________
Hours 4 - 12: ____________________

Hours 13 - 24: ____________________
Day 3: ____________________
Days 4 - 7: ____________________
Days 8 - 14: ____________________
Days 15 - 30: ____________________
Day 30 and beyond: ____________________

QUESTIONNAIRE 9: REVENUE LOSS

1. Is this system directly involved in activities that generate revenue? If so, describe. ____________________

2. Is this system directly involved in billing or collection activities? If so, describe. ____________________

3. Would inability to process this application affect business operations so as to interfere with the provision of services to customers? If so, how? ____________________

4. Would inability to process this application cause customers to seek services or products from competitors? If so, please assess this impact. ____________________

5. Would inability to process this application cause other, indirect impacts on revenue activities (e.g., interest lost on funds, investments)? ____________________

6. Summarize other revenue losses associated with impacts related to the inability to process this application.
____

QUESTIONNAIRE 10: ADDITIONAL EXPENSES

1. What are the types of additional expenses your organization would incur with the delay or loss of processing of this application? ____________________

2. Estimate the minimum length of time the support of this application could be denied your organization without incurring additional expense (e.g., overtime, extra services). ____________________

3. Would a delay in the availability of this application result

in additional expenditures other than for labor or services (e.g., interest expense on bank loans, capital outlays)?

____

____

4. Estimate the amount of business backlog (e.g., number of orders, order entries, inquiries) incurred if this application were unavailable. ______________________

____

5. Would a delay in processing this application result in any fines or penalties for failure to provide services or to adhere to deadlines or government regulations? If so, describe. ______________________________

____

6. Would a delay in processing this application result in legal liability, personal damage, or other public harm? If so, describe. ______________________________

____

7. Please describe any other impacts related to the delay or loss of this application that could result in additional expense to your organization. ______________________

____

QUESTIONNAIRE 11: EMBARRASSMENT OR CONFIDENCE LOSS

1. In your estimation, what are the most serious sources of embarrassment to your organization in regard to the delay in or complete loss of ability to process this application or provide this service? ______________________

____

2. Are there potential legal, social, or moral liabilities to your organization in regard to the delay in or complete loss of ability to process this application or provide this service? If so, please describe them. ______________

____

3. What is the potential liability of exposure to these problems and impact on the general public in terms of embarrassment to the organization? ________________

____

4. What are the potential impacts, in terms of loss of public confidence and other measures, from the loss of capability to process this application or provide this service?

____

____

QUESTIONNAIRE 12: CLIENT LOSS

1. Would a delay in the processing of this application or provision of services cause clients to seek competitor services? ____
____

2. If yes, what percentage of corporate income do these clients represent? ____
____

3. How long do you think the client would tolerate an interruption of company services? ___________________________
____

4. Would these clients return when services are resumed? If yes, would there be additional expenses associated with reestablishing the relationship? Please describe: __________
____

Identifying and Documenting Critical Business Processes

CHAPTER I-4

The business impact analysis identifies the critical business functions at the level of business units and their major supporting systems and applications. This next stage of developing the business operations resumption plan builds on that analysis. For each of the identified critical business units, the planner must now identify the critical processes performed by the business unit. An inventory of these processes is developed, and each process is broken down into its component tasks. (For example, order entry is a process; each activity performed to enter an order is a task.) The individual applications that support each of these processes must also be identified. Having established an inventory of processes and related tasks, the processes can be evaluated to identify those that are most critical and that should therefore receive a high priority for recovery.

This chapter describes two structured methods that can be used to obtain the necessary inventories of critical processes and tasks. The first method discussed in this chapter uses a questionnaire to collect data; the second involves interviews of key employees. These data collection methods are independent of each other, and either may be used. The advantages and disadvantages of each method are discussed later in this chapter.

IDENTIFYING CRITICAL PROCESSES BY QUESTIONNAIRE

Workpaper I4.01 provides a questionnaire that can be used to identify recovery priorities for all business processes and related tasks for each of the critical business units identified in the business impact analysis. This questionnaire is divided into 11 sections. The instructions for completing most of these sections (included in this workpaper) are straightforward and do not require additional explanation in text. Other key sections are described in the following paragraphs. Exhibit I-4-A provides a completed sample of this workpaper.

Section 1: Business Process Overview. In this section, the respondent lists the key business processes performed by his or her business unit. The planner should instruct the respondent to limit this description to a paragraph that is no more than one-half page in length. This forces the respondent to focus on identifying the processes and tasks that are central to the business unit's mission (rather than providing a list of everything the department does).

The process of identifying key business processes provides the added benefit of educating recovery team members about how the business unit really works; this is an essential factor in developing an effective recovery program. An organization does not recover discrete processes, nor do recovery managers and team members have discrete decision-making responsibilities. In the event of a business interruption, recovery team members must be able to make decisions about processes that are not

EXHIBIT I-4-A SAMPLE OPERATING STRATEGY QUESTIONNAIRE

Business Resumption Plan

Date: 3-28-94

Division: Finance

Business Unit: Credit

Contact Name: John Smith

Contact Phone: 555-1234

LEGEND

Tier I = Recovery within 24 hours.
Tier II = Recovery within 72 hours.
Tier III = Recovery within 2 weeks.
Tier IV = Recovery within 2 months.
* = Certain tasks within this business process can be delayed or postponed during recovery processing.

1. **Business Process Overview.** What are the business processes performed by your department? Include in your response the business processes and a high-level definition of each process and related task.

Credit provides an assessment service of customer credit worthiness and adjusts the data base to release goods shipments to customer.

Credit review runs Dunn + Bradstreet reports; reviews credit history of existing or potential clients; adds new customers.

Credit hold/release releases shipments based on credit review approval.

Collection contacts customers on past due accounts; adjusts account hold profile.

2. **Business Resumption Processing.** Based on your response to question 1, what business processes and tasks are critical to the recovery of your department? Prioritize the processes and tasks using the legend on page 1 of this questionnaire.

Process	*Priority*	*Task*	*Priority*
Credit Hold	II	Release holds	II
Credit Review	II	Add customers	II
		Run D+B	III
Collection	III	Adjust hold profile	III
		Contact customers	III

3. **Functional Reductions.** What business processes and tasks are less critical to the recovery of your department and can be delayed or postponed? Include why and the potential processing impact of each delay to your area, and impact to other areas (if known).

Process	*Priority*	*Task*	*Priority*
Admin Support	III	Clerical	III

Comments

Recovery focus will be on shipment release and data base maintenance. Clerical support will be resumed within 2 weeks.

4. Business Recovery Strategy Overview. Provide an overview statement explaining the recovery strategy of your department. Include in your response your preferred recovery location, priority of business processes and tasks, and high-level application and system dependences.

Credit will recover critical operations over a two-week period. The hot site recovery facility will be used for recovery of initial critical functions: credit review and credit hold/release.

Credit collection will be recovered at the Grand hotel in two weeks. All functions will be consolidated at hotel site within three weeks.

Approximately 35 persons will be required in Tier II recovery; 10 persons for Tier III.

Credit hold/release will be recovered first. They must be available to release holds on product shipments to new and existing customers.

Credit review will be recovered second. They must be available to establish new customers.

Collection will be recovered as soon as possible. Two weeks is acceptable.

Credit requires these applications:
- Accounts receivable
- Shipping data base
- D+B
- Customer history

5. Recovery Assumptions. List the key assumptions that have been identified in establishing the recovery strategies of your department.

1. Access to the company mainframe system.
2. Access to the business recovery site.
3. A majority of Credit personnel available to respond.

Business Areas Diagram

6. **Business Interfaces.** List the internal and external business interfaces performed by the business processes of your department. Responses should include categories such as type of external companies, agencies, vendors, banks, customers, and internal departments. Prioritize the interfaces using the legend on page 1 of this questionnaire.

Internal Interface	*Priority*	*External Interface*	*Priority*
Finance	II	D+B	II
Distribution	II	Customers	II
Sales	III		

7. **Business Inputs.** List the input/information needed by your department's business processes to perform key tasks. Responses should include the types of reports, telephone calls, transmission feeds, and paper entries and the media type received (i.e., paper, magnetic media, microfiche, electronic, etc.). Prioritize the inputs using the legend on page 1 of this questionnaire.

Input	*Source*	*Media Type*	*Priority*
A/R 1000	IS	Paper report	II
Mail	Company mail	Varies	II
Fax	Customers	Electronic	II
Fax	Internal	Electronic	III
Telephone	Customers	Voice	II
Shipping advices	Distribution	Electronic	III

8. **Business Outputs.** List the output/products produced by your department's business processes. Responses should include the types of reports, telephone calls, transmission feeds, and paper entries and the media type produced for customers and internal areas (i.e., paper, magnetic media, microfiche, electronic, etc.). Prioritize the outputs using the legend on page 1 of this questionnaire.

Output	*Source*	*Media Type*	*Priority*
Credit hold/release	Sales	Electronic	II
Collection stats	Sales/mgmt	Electronic/rpt	III

9. Critical Applications. Name the mainframe applications that are required to support the business processes of your department. Include in your response the names of the applications and whether online access is required. Prioritize the applications using the legend on page 1 of this questionnaire.

Process	*Application*	*Priority*	*Online Access (Y/N)*
Credit Hold	Accts receivable	II	Y
	Shipping database	II	Y
	Customer history	III	Y

10. Critical Applications. Name the midrange, LAN, and personal computer applications and/or software that are required to support the business processes of your department. Include in your response the names of the applications and/or software and whether online access is required. Prioritize the applications using the legend on page 1 of this questionnaire.

Process	*Application*	*Software*	*Priority*	*Online Access (Y/N)*
Credit Review	Imaging	AS/400 Imaging	IV	Y
	D&B	IBM 486/DB2	II	Dial-up
	E-mail	Novell/Server 1	IV	Y

11. Special Needs. List any special needs required by the critical business processes of your unit/department.

Dial-up modem facilities at recovery site.

usually in their area of responsibility or expertise. By participating in the identification of the business unit's core processes and tasks, team members broaden their understanding of the organization and become better prepared to handle a companywide disaster.

Section 2: Business Resumption Processing. In a recovery, the business units will not be able to perform all of the tasks they normally perform; the delivery of certain products and services must be curtailed. Each business unit is therefore asked to identify the most important services that it provides on the basis of their contribution to the primary mission of the business unit and the organization. These critical services become the focus of the recovery effort.

In this section, the respondent lists the mission-critical business processes (a subset of the processes identified in Section 1) and assigns a recovery priority to each process. The respondent is also asked to identify the critical tasks that must be completed for each critical process and to assign a recovery priority to each of these tasks.

Section 3: Functional Reductions. Each process identified by the business unit requires a certain level of resources to recover it. In a disaster, however, resources are limited. Therefore, a decision must be made by the business unit on how to allocate recovery resources; this decision is based on the value of the process to the mission of the company.

This section asks the respondent to identify less-critical business processes that can be reasonably postponed. The impact of such delay must be evaluated and documented here.

Completing the Remainder of the Questionnaire

After the planner and the respondents to the questionnaire have identified and set recovery priorities for key business processes, they must identify how the relationships and dependences among business units and processes influence recovery priorities. A business unit cannot function independently; it both depends on input from other business groups and provides products and services to other areas of the organization. In order to recover the most critical components of a complete business operation, the planner must understand the dependences among these business units and processes.

The remaining sections of the questionnaire focus on documenting the relationships among the business units and processes in several areas:

- In Section 4, the dependences among high-level systems and applications (as identified in the business impact analysis).
- In Section 6, the interfaces among internal and external business groups and the priority for recovery of these interfaces.
- In Section 7, the source and type of inputs to the business unit that it needs in order to function and the priority for their recovery.
- In Section 8, the source and type of outputs produced by the business unit processes and the priority for their recovery.
- In Sections 9 and 10, the critical applications that support each of the critical business processes and the priority for their recovery.

IDENTIFYING CRITICAL PROCESSES BY INTERVIEW

In many cases, the business units are not able to easily identify their most critical processes. Most employees have not given much thought to the relative criticality of

EXHIBIT I-4-B KEY BUSINESS PROCESSES

Business Processes Performed
Order processing
Enter house account orders
Process faxed shipping orders
Issue invoices
Review invoices
Mail invoices
Perform allocation maintenance
Perform product pricing maintenance
Invoice management

the tasks they perform; this is particularly true of clerical and other nonexempt personnel who have responsibility for only a small piece of an operation. On the other hand, although managers may have a sufficiently broad view of overall business operations, they may lack an understanding of processing details that are important to recovery planning.

It is for this reason that many resumption planners find it more effective to obtain this information by conducting interviews of business unit managers and key line staff rather than by using questionnaires. In an interview, the planner can coach the interviewees through the process and help them to achieve a consensus as to those processes that are truly critical to the organization.

Interviews can be conducted as described in the following paragraphs.

STEP 1

Identify Business Processes. The planner asks the interviewees to identify the key business processes they perform. These processes can be described at a relatively high level—for example, processing of customer orders, issuing of purchase orders, and approving invoices. The output of this step is a list of processes, usually in the order in which they are performed.

STEP 2

Identify Critical Business Processes. The planner asks the interviewees to identify the 10 most important functions that, if not completed, would have a significant impact on the organization. An example is provided as Exhibit I-4-B.

STEP 3

Set Recovery Priorities. This is perhaps the most difficult step. The planner asks the interviewees to identify the most critical process (i.e., the process that would cause the greatest impact to the organization if it were not completed). The process of answering this first question helps to clarify the relative priorities of the remaining processes. The first question is repeated until the priorities of the remaining processes have been sorted out. As shown in Exhibit I-4-C, priority levels are established in terms of recovery time frames (e.g., Level 1 might be within one hour or one day, Level 2 within 12 hours or two days). Although it is not required, the list of processes is usually maintained in the order in which they are performed rather than in the order of priority.

EXHIBIT I-4-C RECOVERY PRIORITIES

Legend

Recovery Time Frames:
Level 1 (**L1**) = 1 day
Level 2 (**L2**) = 2 days
Level 3 (**L3**) = 3–4 days
Level 4 (**L4**) = 5–8 days
Level 5 (**L5**) = 2 weeks
Level 6 (**L6**) = 1 month
Level 7 (**L7**) = 2 months

Business Processes Performed

Order processing—**L1**
Enter house account orders—**L1**
Process faxed shipping orders—**L1**
Issue invoices—**L2**
Review invoices—**L2**
Mail invoices—**L2**
Perform allocation maintenance—**L3**
Perform product pricing maintenance—**L2**
Invoice management—**L4**

STEP 4

Identify Key Interfaces and Support Systems. At this step, the planner asks the interviewees to identify the primary business units with which their own business unit must interact; these groups are listed as shown in Exhibit I-4-D. In addition, the planner and interviewees must identify the key information systems and applications that support the critical operations already identified; recovery priorities must also be set for these systems and applications as shown in Exhibit I-4-D.

STEP 5

Identify Interdependences. The planner requests that interviewees identify the sources of work received from other internal and external business units and how this work is received (e.g., telephone, fax). After identifying the incoming work, the planner and interviewees must identify the items of output generated by the business unit and determine the business entities to which this work is sent and how it is sent. Exhibit I-4-E illustrates how the results of this step are documented.

With respect to Steps 4 and 5, the planner should take account of such frequently overlooked support services as mail, PBX communications, and facilities management. These constitute the organization's services infrastructure. The business units may assume that these services will be available and therefore fail to consider them in the analysis of functional dependences. Planning for their loss is especially complex because these functions must recover themselves as well as assist in the recovery of other business units that depend on them. Typically, the recovery resources available to this services infrastructure are spread extremely thin during a recovery.

STEP 6

Set Priorities for Input and Output. The last step is to establish priorities for the recovery of key incoming and outgoing work, as shown in Exhibit I-4-F. This completed view of critical business processes provides a clear picture of how the business unit is expected to function in an actual recovery.

This information should be shared with the other internal and external business entities with which the subject business unit interacts. (It should also be provided to the service provider [e.g., IS department or communications facility] that is responsible for transferring the input and output.) This is necessary to ensure that recovery priorities are coordinated among dependent business units. For example, if the priority

EXHIBIT I-4-D KEY INTERFACES AND SYSTEMS

Primary Business Interfaces

IS
Accounting
Sales
Shipping
Logistics

Business Processes Performed

Order processing—**L1**
Enter house account orders—**L1**
Process faxed shipping orders—**L1**
Issue invoices—**L2**
Review invoices—**L2**
Mail invoices—**L2**
Perform allocation maintenance—**L3**
Perform product pricing maintenance—**L2**
Invoice management—**L4**

Legend

Recovery Time Frames:
Level 1 (**L1**) = 1 day
Level 2 (**L2**) = 2 days
Level 3 (**L3**) = 3–4 days
Level 4 (**L4**) = 5–8 days
Level 5 (**L5**) = 2 weeks
Level 6 (**L6**) = 1 month
Level 7 (**L7**) = 2 months

Information Systems Used

Order entry—**L1**
Accounts receivable—**L2**
Marketing—**L2**
Credit—**L3**
Teleprocessing—**L1**
EDI—**L1**

assigned to an output is higher or lower than that required by the receiving unit, the sending and receiving business units must resolve the discrepancy.

DOCUMENTING THE RESULTS

In preparing to document the results of this analysis, two issues need to be addressed:

- The level of detail to be documented.
- The presentation format.

Level of Detail

Historically, most recovery plan documentation has been developed to address disasters affecting information systems. Because of the inherently structured, procedural nature of information processing activities, they are relatively easy to document at a highly detailed level. Business operations, on the other hand, are not as precisely structured as information processing activities. Business decisions and related tasks

EXHIBIT I-4-E INTERDEPENDENCES

Primary Business Interfaces

IS
Accounting
Sales
Shipping
Logistics

Work Received From	How Received?
Marketing	Telephone and fax
IS	Order-entry system
Sales department	EDI, telephone, and bulletins
Credit department	Online: credit system
Office services	Mail and courier
Regional sales	EDI, telephone, and fax
Shipping/logistics	Telephone and fax
Accounts receivable	Status reports

Business Processes Performed

Order processing—**L1**
Enter house account orders—**L1**
Process faxed shipping orders—**L1**
Issue invoices—**L2**
Review invoices—**L2**
Mail invoices—**L2**
Perform allocation maintenance—**L3**
Perform product pricing maintenance—**L2**
Invoice management—**L4**

Work Sent To	How Sent?
Sales/marketing	Telephone, fax, and reports
MIS operations	Order-entry system
Materials planning	Reports and logistics
Accounts receivable	Reports
Office services	Interoffice mail
Regional sales	Telephone and fax
Shipping	Reports

Legend

Recovery Time Frames:
Level 1 (**L1**) = 1 day
Level 2 (**L2**) = 2 days
Level 3 (**L3**) = 3–4 days
Level 4 (**L4**) = 5–8 days
Level 5 (**L5**) = 2 weeks
Level 6 (**L6**) = 1 month
Level 7 (**L7**) = 2 months

Information Systems Used

Order entry—**L1**
Accounts receivable—**L2**
Marketing—**L2**
Credit—**L3**
Teleprocessing—**L1**
EDI—**L1**

are frequently based on the intuitive skills of business managers and highly trained staff. Most critical business decisions are made by experts without following routine procedures. Such decision-makers operate on the basis of their general knowledge of the organization, its products, its customers, industry standards, and other complex factors that are difficult to document.

Therefore, with the exception of such repetitive operations as order entry, most business operations should be documented at a relatively high level, and such documentation should, of course, focus primarily on critical processes and tasks. Because there will not be comprehensive procedural documentation for most business operations, the recovery planner cannot rely on the use of temporary labor in the recovery effort for anything other than the most routine functions. The planner must therefore assume that key decision-makers (managers, supervisors, and key staff) will be available during the recovery.

Operating under this key assumption, the organization must then determine the appropriate level of documentation for the recovery of nonroutine business operations. It is recommended that recovery scripts be prepared for supervisors of key employees, so that these supervisors are able to perform the most critical operations until the primary employee or his or her alternate becomes available.

Presentation Format

Most developers of resumption plans tend to rely on textual explanations of business processes, supplementing these with organizational charts to clarify relationships

EXHIBIT I-4-F COMPLETED RECOVERY OPERATIONS

Primary Business Interfaces

IS
Accounting
Sales
Shipping
Logistics

Work Received From	How Received?
Marketing—**L2**	Telephone and fax
IS—**L1**	Order-entry system
Sales department—**L1**	EDI, telephone, and bulletins
Credit department—**L3**	Online: credit system
Office services—**L1**	Mail and courier
Regional sales—**L4**	EDI, telephone, and fax
Shipping/logistics—**L3**	Telephone and fax
Accounts receivable—**L3**	Status reports

Business Processes Performed

Order processing—**L1**
Enter house account orders—**L1**
Process faxed shipping orders—**L1**
Issue invoices—**L2**
Review invoices—**L2**
Mail invoices—**L2**
Perform allocation maintenance—**L3**
Perform product pricing maintenance—**L2**
Invoice management—**L4**

Work Sent To	How Sent?
Sales/marketing—**L3**	Telephone, fax, and reports
MIS operations—**L1**	Order-entry system
Materials planning—**L1**	Reports and logistics
Accounts receivable—**L4**	Reports
Office services—**L1**	Interoffice mail
Regional sales—**L3**	Telephone and fax
Shipping—**L3**	Reports

Legend

Recovery Time Frames:
Level 1 (**L1**) = 1 day
Level 2 (**L2**) = 2 days
Level 3 (**L3**) = 3–4 days
Level 4 (**L4**) = 5–8 days
Level 5 (**L5**) = 2 weeks
Level 6 (**L6**) = 1 month
Level 7 (**L7**) = 2 months

Information Systems Used

Order entry—**L1**
Accounts receivable—**L2**
Marketing—**L2**
Credit—**L3**
Teleprocessing—**L1**
EDI—**L1**

among business units. Although such written documentation may contain all of the information needed for recovery planning, it often requires a significant commitment of time and effort both for developers to prepare and for recovery team members to learn.

Graphical representations of work flows, dependences, and recovery priorities, such as those shown in Exhibits I-4-B through I-4-F, are often more useful in guiding recovery teams in a disaster. For example, a comparable textual description of Exhibit I-4-F would be quite lengthy and difficult to refer to quickly, especially under the stress of a recovery operation.

Graphics can also be useful in analyzing business processes and tasks and developing the recovery plan. For example, as the planner walks interviewees through the recovery process for a business unit, he or she can graphically represent the relationships among critical business processes as they are being identified.

Documentation Tools

Various software tools can be used for documenting and presenting the information gathered during the analysis. Many basic word processing and graphics software packages provide the required capabilities for depicting business processes, relationships, and dependences. Most graphics packages cost less than $300.

In selecting a documentation tool, the planner should ensure that the text and graphics can be easily maintained. Most organizations are subject to frequent change, which can require frequent updating of the recovery documentation to ensure it continues to provide an accurate view of business operations.

Sources of Information

The planner should make it a rule to never document anything that is already available elsewhere. For example, in most organizations, documentation of systems maintenance procedures is maintained as a matter of course; this documentation provides the most up-to-date source of information for this activity. Such publications are more likely to remain current than would a recovery plan that incorporates material from these independent sources.

The business operations resumption plan should therefore identify any existing business unit procedures and reference manuals that document processes vital to the recovery effort. The planner must ensure that these documents are available if the primary facility becomes inaccessible. Current copies of critical support documentation should be stored at alternative locations; the recovery plan should provide an inventory of the documents at each of these alternative locations.

WORKPAPER I4.01 Operating Strategy Questionnaire

BUSINESS RESUMPTION PLAN

Date: ____________________

Division: ________________

Business Unit: ________________

Contact Name: ________________

Contact Phone: ________________

Legend

Tier I = Recovery within 24 hours.
Tier II = Recovery within 72 hours.
Tier III = Recovery within 2 weeks.
Tier IV = Recovery within 2 months.

* = Certain tasks within this business process can be delayed or postponed during recovery processing.

---

1. Business Process Overview. What are the business processes performed by your department? Include in your response the business processes and a high-level definition of each process and related task.

2. <u>Business Resumption Processing</u>. Based on your response to question 1, what business processes and tasks are critical to the recovery of your department? Prioritize the processes and tasks using the legend on page 1 of this questionnaire.

Process	Priority	Task	Priority

3. <u>Functional Reductions</u>. What business processes and tasks are less critical to the recovery of your department and can be delayed or postponed? Include why and the potential processing impact of each delay to your area, and impact to other areas (if known).

Process	Priority	Task	Priority

Comments

____

____

____

____

____

____

____

____

____

4. <u>Business Recovery Strategy Overview</u>. Provide an overview statement explaining the recovery strategy of your department. Include in your response your preferred recovery location, priority of business processes and tasks, and high-level application and system dependences.

5. <u>Recovery Assumptions</u>. List the key assumptions that have been identified in establishing the recovery strategies of your department.

Business Areas Diagram

6. Business Interfaces. List the internal and external business interfaces performed by the business processes of your department. Responses should include categories such as type of external companies, agencies, vendors, banks, customers, and internal departments. Prioritize the interfaces using the legend on page 1 of this questionnaire.

Internal Interface	Priority	External Interface	Priority

7. Business Input. List input/information needed by your department's business processes to perform key tasks. Responses should include the types of reports, telephone calls, transmission feeds, paper entries, and the media type received (e.g., paper, magnetic media, microfiche, electronic). Prioritize the inputs using the legend on page 1 of this questionnaire.

Input	Source	Media Type	Priority

8. Business Output. List the output/products produced by your department's business processes. Responses should include the types of reports, telephone calls, transmission feeds, paper entries, and the media type produced for customers and internal areas (e.g., paper, magnetic media, microfiche, electronic). Prioritize the outputs using the legend on page 1 of this questionnaire.

Output	Source	Media Type	Priority

9. Critical Applications. Name the mainframe applications that are required to support the business processes of your department. Include in your response the names of the applications and whether online access is required. Prioritize the applications using the legend on page 1 of this questionnaire.

Process	Application	Priority	Online Access (Y/N)

10. Critical Applications. Name the midrange, LAN, and personal computer applications and/or software that are required to support the business processes of your department. Include in your response the names of the applications and/or software and whether online access is required. Prioritize the applications using the legend on page 1 of this questionnaire.

Process	Application	Software	Priority	Online Access (Y/N)

11. Special Needs. List any special needs required by the critical business processes of your unit/department.

Identifying and Documenting Resource Requirements

CHAPTER

I-5

The business operations recovery planner must identify the resources needed to provide the critical products and services identified in the analysis of business processes described in Chapter I-4. For each process performed by the business unit, a set of resources or tools is necessary to complete the process. Resource planning identifies the resources that business units need to reestablish their operations at an alternate location.

Identifying critical resources involves various stages of analysis. First, the number of personnel needed for the recovery is determined. This information allows the planner to determine such other resource requirements as recovery facilities and equipment because these depend, at least in part, on the number of people that need to be supported during the recovery effort. For example, the number of employees involved in the recovery helps determine the size of the recovery facility and the number of desks, phones, computers, and supplies. Planning for recovery of facilities and such basic resources as voice and data communications requires determining the expected volume and use of these resources. For example, the expected volume of transactions created by the recovery team determines the bandwidth needed to provide sufficient communications support.

Other types of dependences must also be taken into consideration. For example, the power requirements of specific items of equipment must be assessed to determine overall power requirements for the recovery facility. The desired ambient temperature for people and equipment determines the heating, ventilation, and air-conditioning requirements.

Resource planning should also identify who is responsible for installing and configuring equipment. The results of this analysis must be shared with all participants in the planning process so that the parties responsible for providing the necessary resources understand what is expected of them. Depending on the availability of internal resources, the planner and service providers may have to go outside the organization for assistance.

EVALUATING BUSINESS UNIT RESOURCE REQUIREMENTS

The resources used by business units on a daily basis under normal operating conditions provide a starting point for conducting the resource analysis. Although the volume of resources needed during a recovery of critical operations is often significantly less than that needed to support regular operations, the same general set of resources must be provided.

It cannot be assumed that critical resources can be obtained on the fly. Under normal circumstances, vendors do not always have these resources on hand. The planner should ask the purchasing organization how often equipment and supplies are on back order and the lead times for specific resources. Sophisticated equipment often has a significant lead time because it is built only after the order is received. Even such simple tools as custom forms may have a long lead time for typesetting and printing. For any piece of equipment, service, or supply, the planner should determine how long it will take to acquire the resource.

In some cases, it may be acceptable to replace a tool used at the primary business site with one that is less efficient or effective. For example, a telephone might be replaced by courier service during part of the recovery operation; an E-mail system might be replaced by fax machines. But in general, this practice is not recommended. In most recoveries, fewer personnel are asked to handle more work. They should therefore be provided with the most efficient systems available to handle the expected volume of work. It is the planner's responsibility to ensure that recovery team members are not frustrated by having to use older and slower systems.

During a recovery, an organization that currently uses older technology may be required to switch to newer systems provided by the vendors supporting the recovery. Although this satisfies the objectives noted above, it can also create problems. For example, after a major office fire at the First Interstate Bank in 1988, the bank replaced its microcomputers, which used 5¼-inch diskettes, with new machines using 3½-inch diskettes. The data backups were stored on 5¼-inch diskettes. To complete its recovery, the bank was forced to convert 9,000 diskettes from the old to the new disk format. This caused an unexpected delay in the recovery and consumed a significant amount of staff time.

To gather the necessary information, the recovery planner should interview business units managers to determine how many people will be needed during each phase of the recovery. Each business function should identify the minimum number of personnel required during the recovery as well as the maximum expected staffing. Even a recovery planner who has chosen to provide additional resources only as more personnel are put in place during the recovery must plan for sufficient facilities and resources to support the maximum staffing levels. This helps reduce the potential for unnecessary moves during the recovery to accommodate unplanned increases in staffing levels. Moves in the middle of a recovery are disruptive. Most insurance companies pay only for the move to the secondary site and the return to the primary site; any interim moves are usually not reimbursed.

The planner should make use of the following workpapers to gather information needed for identifying resource requirements for supporting business unit functions. Workpaper I5.01 can be used to document personnel requirements of each business unit. Workpaper I5.02 provides a form that can be used to identify relationships and dependences among business units that may influence resource requirements. Workpaper I5.03 is used to identify requirements for proximity of business units to each other.

STEP 1

Identify Computer System Resource Requirements

The mainframe, midrange, and microcomputer resources used by the business functions were identified in the business impact analysis. The recovery planner must determine the demands that will be placed on these resources during a recovery operation.

Many organizations use analytical software to measure application and system use—for example, to bill users for system resources they use. This resource use information provides an accurate profile of what systems are used and how often they are used.

Underestimating processing requirements can result in delays, additional expense, and frustration. Hot-site service providers frequently find that their subscribers have underestimated their requirements for main and secondary storage. This can create serious problems when a disaster occurs that requires use of the hot site. Hot-site vendors now provide a written policy that describes how they will respond when this type of situation is encountered.

Acquisition of computer resources can be a major issue in the recovery process. The lead time to acquire, configure, and install a system determines whether it must be acquired before an incident. If the lead time exceeds the acceptable delay established by the business impact analysis, the equipment must be acquired in advance. In some cases, the organization may attempt to arrange a guaranteed delivery within an acceptable time frame. However, the vendor generally guarantees only to make a best effort to provide the equipment.

The planning for mainframe systems is a complex task requiring the contribution of many technical experts within the organization. The sizing of the mainframe systems depends on the granularity of the existing applications. If the recovering business units need only a subset of the current production applications, the recovery planner must determine the processing requirements of the smaller machines. If the design and dependences of the applications do not permit a modular restoration, the planning becomes much more simple; the recovery requirements almost match the normal production requirements.

In planning capacity requirements, the recovery planner should not forget that as the restoration proceeds, business units will quickly push to run more and more applications. The sizing of the computers should be adequate to support the business units for the entire period that the organization is operating at the recovery center or hot site. Changing mainframe systems during the recovery period is not feasible unless the organization is using a purchased recovery service.

The maximum time frame for occupancy of the hot site by the recovery organization at commercial service providers is six weeks. Although they may permit an extension of that time frame, they cannot guarantee use of the site if another subscriber declares a disaster after the six-week period. Most organizations plan to move to a cold site as soon as possible and start planning immediately after critical operations are stabilized.

Obtaining a replacement mainframe system is not as simple as calling the manufacturer and ordering one. Most systems are built only after they are ordered. Unless the buyer of an existing machine is willing to give it up, the company will have to wait. Resellers and other secondary markets may be able to provide the needed system. However, they are also faced with a constantly changing inventory and cannot guarantee that a specific system will be available when the need arises. If the planner is set on obtaining equipment after an incident, he or she should plan on from 10 to 21 days to acquire, configure, install, test, and load the operating system, applications, and peripherals, assuming a preconfigured cold site is available.

Midrange systems are generally easier to obtain and install. For example, the delay caused by the preparation of the facility does not occur, because most midrange systems can operate in a general office environment. The planner should identify the volume of use and capacity requirements for these systems, including memory, processing, and secondary storage requirements. The planner should also identify multiple sources for the required machines.

The restoration of the same amount of data may take longer on midrange systems than on a mainframe. The planner should determine how long the restoration of data will take to ensure it is consistent with user requirements.

Microcomputers are generally easier to acquire than most types of systems, although such specialized systems as engineering workstations are not as easy to obtain as personal computers. As with most midrange systems, microcomputers work in any office environment and do not require special facility preparation.

The planner does have to determine required specifications, including the processing speed, disk capacity, and memory requirements. It is not sufficient to accept the typical response of business units that they need a certain number of microcomputers without determining the exact specifications.

The planner can take each user's requirement and provide a customized machine for each user, or he or she can provide a standard configuration and let the business units be responsible for the exceptions to the standard. It is usually impractical and seldom justified to provide different systems for each user; use of a standard configuration is the most effective strategy. Workpaper I5.04 provides data collection forms for different types of computer equipment and peripherals commonly found in offices.

STEP 2

Identify Network Resource Requirements

Acquisition of communications and network services generally have long lead times. For example, a T1 service may take weeks to acquire. The recovery planner should review the location of the recovery site to determine whether the required services are available.

The transaction volume of system users determines the type of network resources needed to recover critical operations. The operating hours of the business and recovery teams determine whether it is possible to spread transactions over multiple work shifts. For example, if the organization can split the staffing into three shifts with 100 personnel per shift, each shift would require less bandwidth than one shift with 300 personnel. The reduction in bandwidth may make it more feasible to use readily available equipment and network services.

The recovery planner must address requirements for three layers of network services. The innermost layer consists of internal services, services that exist within the confines of the company premises. Included in this layer are peripheral devices such as terminals, printers, and personal computers that may be connected directly to a server or other type of computer, typically over short distances. Local area networks (LANs) may be used to provide shared access to data bases, to optimize the efficiency of connected devices, facilitate interoffice communications, or provide a gateway to midrange or mainframe systems. The internal layer may also include the voice and data communications network, consisting of a private branch exchange (PBX) and such communications devices as telephones, modems, data communications terminals, and facsimile machines.

The second layer of networks are those of local and regional telephone and communications companies. Local communications vendors control communications traffic that originates and terminates within the local vicinity by means of central offices. Central offices are outfitted with traffic switching equipment and provide a gateway to the third and outermost layer of wide area and long-distance networks. Wide area networks handle data and voice communications both domestically and internationally.

The service providers include public access networks, value-added networks, packet-switched networks, and satellite communications networks. In some cases, organizations circumvent the second layer and connect directly with the third layer for some network services.

The planner must assess the impact of a loss of service to the company and the consequential impact on each business operation. The business impact analysis and the evaluation of critical business processes identifies the dependence of business units and processes on communications networks, criticality of network services, and acceptable disruption time frames (see Chapters I-3 and I-4).

The business operations recovery planner is responsible for planning the recovery of the innermost layer of network services, including LANs. The recovery planner should obtain documentation of the LAN configuration and work with the network administrator to develop a clear understanding of LAN features. This includes LAN topologies and protocols, characteristics of transmission media between network nodes, and traffic patterns, loads, and transmission rates. It is well within the power of the organization to control the time frame for recovery of these internal resources, for example, by stocking replacement equipment. Recovery planning for LANs and microcomputers is covered in Chapter I-7.

Planning for recovery of the intermediate and outer layers of communications services should be handled by the communications recovery team, led by the communications manager. This manager works with the various providers of local and long-distance telephone service and wide area data networks to minimize the potential for interruption due to a communications failure. Communications recovery planning is discussed in Part III of this book.

Certain issues in planning for local voice communications service should be coordinated among the various business units and the communications department (e.g., PBX capacity requirements and call distribution requirements). The following section addresses these concerns.

Voice Communications Requirements. Few business units can function without voice communications. During the initial hours following a disaster, business units must be able to notify key contacts and customers where they have relocated to and what the new telephone numbers are. Reestablishing that link is critical to proving to customers that the business is recovering. Access to computer-based information is secondary at this point.

The volume and distribution of calls and the type of instruments are important elements in voice communications planning. The volume of calls determines the capacity of the required PBX. If the strategy is to move business personnel into an existing facility owned and occupied by the organization, the capability of the PBX to absorb the additional demand should be verified.

The distribution of telephone calls within the recovered group should also be evaluated. Whether an automated call distribution system is required depends on the current environment and whether the alternate site can handle such a function. Telephone operators and a switchboard are a temporary though less effective alternative to an automated call distribution system.

Many organizations depend on voice mail as a primary communications tool for both internal and external contacts. The planner should analyze the voice mail requirements and again determine whether use of operators taking messages is an acceptable short-term alternative. Having someone in the business unit perform this message-taking and distribution function normally is not a good use of resources.

The types of equipment used by the business functions in the production environment should be carefully analyzed. In the emergency operations center, simplicity of equipment is mandatory. The use of sophisticated multiline instruments is not feasible. The high volume of incoming calls would overwhelm recovery personnel. A maximum of two lines should be assigned to each emergency recovery station.

Workpaper I5.05 provides a form that can be used to collect information about telephone equipment requirements and call volume and distribution for each business unit. The business operations recovery planner should work closely with the communications recovery planner to develop a coordinated plan for the entire organization.

STEP 3

Identify Required Facilities

Facilities requirements must be determined on the basis of the number of personnel, placement of personnel, voice and data communications requirements, and power and heating, ventilation, and air-conditioning requirements. Occupying an existing facility may require performing major renovations. For example, many facilities do not have sufficient cabling for data processing and communications equipment. Most commercial facilities do not supply power greater than 220 volts, as is required by some specialized equipment. The time required to bring sufficient power and communications into the facility may be unacceptable and cause delays in recovery.

The amount of space required for the recovering functions is generally less than that used during normal operations. During a recovery, personnel can work in smaller accommodations for an extended period of time. The amount of space is determined by the functions performed by the business unit and the length of time the temporary facilities will be used. Generally, each employee needs at least a 12- to 15-square-foot work surface. Telemarketing functions operating with just a telephone may make do with less space, whereas office personnel working with significant amounts of paper may need as much as 20 square feet. Personnel can tolerate cramped quarters for three or four days, but after that they often become extremely irritated and their work suffers.

If possible, the recovery planner and facilities personnel should establish recovery space standards to be used for evaluating facility options. The standards should apply to all personnel in the recovery effort and, unlike for a normal space allocation, an employee's title within the organization should not matter. All employees should initially receive the same size work surface.

One of the most critical components that is frequently overlooked in recovery planning is the chairs that the employees will be using at temporary facilities. The use of hotel conference chairs is fine for the first 24 hours of the recovery, but after that, more ergonomically designed chairs should be provided. Employees are working longer hours and are under stress. Back problems that are caused by stress will materialize quickly if proper chairs are not acquired quickly after the initial setup.

STEP 4

Identify Power and Climate Control Requirements

Although many data processing facilities plan for emergency power, business operations typically do not. Even if the data center is housed with business functions, the uninterruptible power supply (UPS) and emergency generator are usually dedicated to the data processing facilities. And if these emergency power supplies are shared, the coverage is usually not adequate for any extended business operations. It is ludicrous to have a functional data processing system connected to user terminals disabled by a lack of power. Planning for power requirements should include not only the data processing systems, but also a set of the critical functions that must continue business.

Portable, high-quality power plants have been developed within the past five years. These new units, unlike their less reliable predecessors, provide high-quality power with both redundancy and stability (within half a volt) and excellent noise suppression.

Portable, containerized heating, ventilating, and air-conditioning systems have been developed that provide efficient cooling and heating even under the most adverse conditions. As with the emergency power, these units can be transported and set up within 24 hours of notification.

Identify Equipment and Supply Requirements

STEP 5

The planner should establish three profiles for equipment and supply requirements: short-term, medium-term, and long-term requirements. During the initial stages of planning, the focus must be on short- and medium-term requirements.

Short-term supplies are the least difficult for the planner to determine. Employees participating in the recovery will need a basic set of supplies as soon as they have access to a desk. It is recommended that supply kits be gathered and stored at the off-site facility. Supplies for each employee can be kept in clear plastic bags and stored in labeled boxes. This storage method makes it easy to identify and distribute the initial desk setup during a recovery or recovery exercise.

A basic desk set should include:

- Lined paper pad.
- Adhesive note pad.
- At least two ball-point pens.
- At least two mechanical pencils.
- Small compact stapler.
- Staples.
- Staple remover.
- Highlighter.
- Problem reporting forms.

Additional short-term supplies might include:

- Copies of incident command procedures, the business resumption plan, and workpapers.
- Telephone message pads and telephone books.
- Fax and copier paper.
- Mailing materials.
- Check stock for writing manual checks.

Short-term equipment is immediately required for either start-up of the recovery operation or support of business functions with little or no tolerance for disruption. Such equipment might include:

- Telephones used by public relations, the recovery command center, and essential business functions.
- Fax machines.
- Special-purpose terminals (e.g., for trading operations or engineering).
- Microcomputers used by the incident management group and essential business functions.
- Small copy machines.

In most cases, this equipment is already installed or is warehoused and immediately available if the need arises.

Medium-term supplies and equipment are not immediately needed; they can usually be provided within two days of the incident. They may include additional personal computers, software, fax machines, telephones, printers, and large, fast copy machines. Supplies are delivered in bulk and distributed as required. Usually, a centralized supply function is set up and business recovery team members responsible for acquiring team supplies obtain supplies from that area.

Long-term equipment and supplies are those that are required to bring business operations as close as possible to production volumes while in the temporary recovery facilities. This may include more sophisticated communications equipment, additional copying services, and expanded mail operations.

EVALUATING RESOURCE USE

The recovery planner must determine how resources are used by the business functions. The volume and frequency of use provides key information as to what is important in the performance of the processes and helps to determine the minimum requirements for recovery resources.

If multiple business functions are being recovered in the same location, it may not be feasible to share equipment. For example, a fax machine might be capable of generating the 500 faxes per day required by one business unit. But in an actual recovery, the increased volume of incoming faxes may limit the transmission of outgoing faxes, especially if the fax machine must now be shared.

The ability of personnel to work in shifts and share resources must also be evaluated. Persons working in shifts may or may not be able to share such resources as desks, telephones, and microcomputers. If access to a mainframe is required, the number of shifts may be constrained by the availability of the mainframe system to provide round-the-clock service. (The mainframe must have some downtime to perform maintenance and batch functions.)

The recovery planner must also determine whether multiple personnel can perform the same or similar functions. Because the long hours can create a great deal of stress, relief for all personnel should be planned for. This is especially important for those people directing the recovery effort. Extreme care and vigilance is required in this area of resource planning.

To assist in evaluating resource use, the planner should identify key resource users, key resources that support business operations, and the volume of use. (Precise volume or frequency is not necessary.) The frequency and volume of use of each resource should be graphed in relationship to time.

The planner should identify cycles in which resource use is greater in one period than another. This helps the planner to identify periods of peak resource use. The capacity of the recovery environment should be designed to meet the peak requirements. This includes system processing capacity, communications capacity, and personnel.

ESTABLISHING THE MINIMUM ACCEPTABLE CONFIGURATION

The planner must determine the minimum acceptable equipment, software, and network configuration required to successfully initiate business operations at an alternate site. To accomplish this, the planner must identify the critical application needed by each business unit during the recovery. An inventory of all applications by work unit should first be established. These applications are then assessed for criticality, as part of the business impact analysis. If an application by its own value is not critical and yet provides necessary support to a critical application, it is considered critical. (For further information, see Chapter I-3.)

The planner must also evaluate the portability and interoperability of the systems and applications required by the business units. The planner must identify what types of operating systems the applications will run on. The compatibility of applications to operating systems and operating systems to hardware must be reviewed. Compatibility among different versions of applications software should be investigated.

The minimum configuration will be driven by the number and type of critical applications that must be processed, the compatibility of hardware and software, the number of personnel to be supported, the expected volume of work, and operating hour constraints. The minimum configuration may employ higher-capacity systems than those used in normal operations. A model of the configuration should be documented and shared with all members of the team.

ASSESSING VITAL RECORDS REQUIREMENTS

Records are an organization's memory. Without records, the organization may have great difficulty reconstructing itself and resuming normal activities. To protect against natural and other disasters, many organizations have developed a vital records program. These vital records can be used to reestablish the basic relationship of the organization with its customers and employees.

The vital records program is one element of a total records management system for controlling records from their creation to final preservation or destruction. A general understanding of records management can be of great use to the recovery planner in determining requirements for the preservation and recovery of vital records.

Records and recovery management share similar interests and expertise that can benefit both. For example, the records manager may be able to suggest more effective ways to manage storage and retrieval of records. In fact, the recovery planner may want to assign a member of records management to supervise the off-site records storage program. It is also recommended that the recovery planner include a representative from records management on the recovery team.

The records management program may, in turn, benefit from the recovery planner's expertise. The recovery planner may help identify appropriate locations for the vital records storage facility and may include questions relevant to the vital records program in recovery planning interviews of business units. Working together clearly benefits both groups.

Records Management Program

This section describes the key components of the records management program.

Retention Scheduling. Retention schedules show how long records should remain in the office or in an inactive records area and when they should be discarded. The planner should be aware of the schedule and provide input in the decision making as to where the records should reside while being retained. As records on the schedule and in the plan are discarded, the business resumption plan should be adjusted accordingly.

Microphotography. Microphotography involves microfilming documents and developing and duplicating film. If the retained records are available only in microfilm format, the recovery planner must have this specialized equipment available at the alternate site. In many cases, organizations make microfiche readers available as a backup for loss of online access. A sufficient number of readers should be provided to avoid production slowdowns.

Filing Equipment and Systems. Within the past decade, optical storage has developed into a widely used records creation, maintenance, storage, and retrieval method, offering storage capacities far surpassing any other current media. If the use of optical storage systems is a primary tool for managing the organization's records, the recovery planner should identify both optical and nonoptical alternatives. The acquisition of replacement equipment potentially could cause a delay in the availability of critical business records. In addition, the optical disks and backup of the magnetic indexes used to tie together optical-based records must also be available at the alternate location.

Records Centers. Records centers are centralized areas for housing and servicing inactive records and records whose reference rate does not warrant retention in regular office areas. The records center may be part of the facility destroyed by the disaster. The recovery planner must identify records within this center that would be used to rebuild current files lost in the incident. If there are a substantial number of potentially critical records maintained in this facility, the planner should urge that an alternate storage site be considered. Although the records may be inactive, the potential future impact could be considerable.

Forms Control. Forms control involves the systematic control of business forms creation, production, and use. Planning for the availability of forms is key to determining off-site storage requirements as well as requirements for production of forms if the primary source of forms is destroyed. If the organization has the printer maintain forms at its site, the planner can avoid having to acquire storage facilities. The planner must know the volume of forms used per month by the company to determine how much stock the vendor should maintain at its location. The printer knows the lead time to re-create the number of forms needed by the organization. If the templates used to print the forms are maintained by the organization, a backup copy should be created and stored at an alternate site.

Reports Management. This ensures that the organization's management receives adequate and timely information. A reports management program requires controls on all types of records to ensure that the best possible report is issued at the least possible expense. It eliminates duplicate, redundant, or otherwise unnecessary reports. This aspect of records management is critical to the planner. When print resources are critical, the organization needs to print only that information that cannot be obtained from any other source. If the users can obtain the information from online systems rather than printed reports, they should.

Archives Management. Archives management provides for the retention of documents and records of company history.

Vital Records. Vital records management provides for the protection of records essential to business operations. Vital records are the primary focus of the recovery planner and the organization in the development of recovery plans.

An effective vital records program has three objectives:

- To resume operations following a disaster.
- To re-create the organization's legal and financial position.
- To fulfill obligations to the stockholders, employees, and outside interests.

A well-planned vital records program must assess:

- What information is vital.
- Which records reflect this information.
- How these records can best be protected.
- Who is responsible for the program.
- Where the records are to be housed.
- How records will be reconstructed.

The records required by the business recovery units may or may not be a vital record in the sense used in traditional vital records programs. If the record is required by statute or policy to be maintained for a set period of time and is mandated to be destroyed at the end of that time, it is a vital record. However, this record may not be needed by the business unit to recover its critical operations. In the context of business recovery, it is not vital. On the other hand, business records that have a short life in the business process may not be mandated by statute or policy to be retained but may be extremely vital to the effective recovery of business operations. Ultimately, the recovery planner must identify what records are needed during the recovery. For example, these may include operating and recovery procedures previously documented (see Chapter I-4).

Immediate access to archived records may be needed to rebuild reports or documents destroyed in a disaster. The planner must ensure that an event that would destroy the primary records could not also destroy the archiving facility. Special attention should be given to fire suppression, construction of the facility, and dependence of the archiving facility's vital records operations on data processing (e.g., for records retrieval). A vital records data collection form is provided as Workpaper I5.06.

Critical forms must also be available when needed during the recovery. For each critical form, the planner should obtain from the business unit the form name and number, the source or printer of the form, the lead time for reprinting, the current quantity on hand at the primary facility, the quantity required off site, the location of the off-site facility, and the anticipated volume of use per week. This information can be gathered using the critical forms data collection instrument shown in Workpaper I5.07.

WORKPAPER I5.01 Personnel Requirements--Data Collection Instrument

PERSONNEL REQUIREMENTS--DATA COLLECTION INSTRUMENT

Business unit name: ______________________________
____

Primary charter of business function: ______________________
____
____
____
____.

Locations: ______________________________________
____
____
____

Normal full-time employee requirements (includes modified part-time): ______________________________
____
____
____
____
____
____
____
____.

Exempt: ____
____
____.

Nonexempt: _____________________________________
____
____.

Cyclical increase or decrease in personnel:

	Jan	Feb	Mar	Apr	May	Jun	Jul	Aug	Sep	Oct	Nov	Dec
% Exempt:	___	___	___	___	___	___	___	___	___	___	___	___
% Nonexempt:	___	___	___	___	___	___	___	___	___	___	___	___

Emergency full-time employee requirements:

	Day 1	Day 2	Day 3	Day 4	Day 5	Day 6	Day 7
Exempt	_____	_____	_____	_____	_____	_____	_____
Nonexempt	_____	_____	_____	_____	_____	_____	_____

	Week 1	Week 2	Week 3	Week 4
Exempt	______	______	______	______
Nonexempt	______	______	______	______

Please explain increase in personnel over normal full-time employees: ____
____
____
____
____
____
____
____
____.

Business unit name: ______________________________

Location: ______________________________

Position title: ______________________________

Short description of responsibilities: ______________________________
____
____.

Primary area of expertise: ______________________________
____.

Years in this company: ______________________________.

Other experience: ______________________________.

Secondary area of expertise: ______________________________
____.

Years in this company: ______________________________.

Other experience: ______________________________.

Special skills required (e.g., personal computer company, merchandise marketing): ______________________________
____
____
______________________________.

Other skill areas (e.g., radio, emergency medical technician, police, security, firefighter): ______________________________
____
____
______________________________.

Alternate replacement:

Name: ______________________________

Location: ______________________________

Years of experience: ______________________________

Operations experience: ______________________________

Source of replacement if neither primary nor alternate are available:

Local: ______________________________

Outside 50-mile radius: ______________________________

WORKPAPER I5.02 Interface Analysis--Data Collection Instrument

INTERFACE ANALYSIS--DATA COLLECTION INSTRUMENT

This analysis will determine with what other business units or outside entities you have critical or frequent contact. It will document the department, vendor, and customer with which you interact, the reason for the relationship, the method of interface, and so on.

Business unit name: ______________________________

Location: ______________________________

Contact name: ______________________________

____

Address [street]: ______________________________

Address [city, state, zip code]: ______________________________

Telephone: ______________________________

Summarize the relationship: ______________________________

____

____

____

____

____

____

______________________________.

Method/frequency of interface:

Telephone: ______________ Frequency: ______________

Comments: ______________________________.

Fax: ______________ Frequency: ______________

Comments: ______________________________.

Electronic data interchange: ______________________________

Frequency: ______________________________

Comments: ______________________________.

Mail: ______________________________ Frequency: ______________________

Comments: ____.

Courier: ___________________________ Frequency: ______________________

Comments: ____.

Face-to-face: _____________________ Frequency: ______________________

Comments: ____.

WORKPAPER I5.03 Adjacency Requirements--Data Collection Instrument

ADJACENCY REQUIREMENTS--DATA COLLECTION INSTRUMENT

This analysis is to determine what business units your unit needs to be close to. In an emergency that requires relocation, the planning group needs to know which other business units you need to be near.

Business unit name: ______________________________

Location: ______________________________

Description of unit responsibility: ______________________________
____
____
______________________________.

Proximity requirements: ______________________________
____
____
______________________________.

Critical to be near:

Unit name: ______________________________

Reason: ______________________________
____
____
______________________________.

Maximum distance if separation required: ______________________________

Important to be near:

Unit name: ______________________________

Reason: ______________________________
____
____
______________________________.

Maximum distance: ______________________________

WORKPAPER I5.04 Office Equipment--Data Collection Instrument

OFFICE EQUIPMENT--DATA COLLECTION INSTRUMENT

Business unit name: ______________________

Location: ______________________

Address [street]: ______________________

Address [city, state, zip code]: ______________________

Floor: ______________________

Quadrant of floor: ______________________

Description of primary and secondary use: ______________________
____
____
____
____
____
____
____
______________________.

Microcomputer:

Make: ______________________

Model: ______________________

Size: ______________________

Serial number: ______________________

Peripheral equipment:

Monitor: ______________________

Make: ______________________

Model: ______________________

Serial number: ______________________

Printer:

Make: ______________________________

Model: ______________________________

Serial number: ______________________________

External hard drive:

Make: ______________________________

Model: ______________________________

Serial number: ______________________________

Special-purpose equipment:

Scanner: ______________________________

Optical storage: ______________________________

Other: ______________________________

Standalone or attached systems: ______________________________
____

Local area network:

Make: ______________________________

Model: ______________________________

Operating system/version: ______________________________

Applications: ______________________________
____
____
____
______________________________.

Mainframe attached:

Applications: ______________________________
____
____
____
____
______________________________.

Software: ______________________________

Software configuration: ______________________________

Software/version/license number: ______________________________

Type of media used:

[ ] 5 1/4

[ ] 3 1/2

[ ] Other: ______________________________

Backup: ______________________________

List backup: ______________________________

Files: ______________________________
____
____
____
______________________________.

Programs: ______________________________
____
____
____
______________________________.

Frequency of backup: [ ] Daily [ ] Weekly [ ] Monthly

Storage of backup: ______________________________

Location: ______________________________

Type of storage: ______________________________

Facility: ______________________________

Business unit name: ______________________________

Location: ______________________________

Facsimile:

Make: ______________________________

Model: ______________________________

Telephone number: ______________________________

Purpose (describe primary use): ______________________________
____
____
____
______________________________.

Volume:

Outgoing: ________________ per day

Incoming: ________________ per day

Primary sources of transmissions: ______________________________
____
____
____
____
____
______________________________.

Copiers:

Make: ______________________________

Model: ______________________________

Special functions: ______________________________
____
____
______________________________.

Volume: Daily ________________ Weekly ________________

Primary users: ______________________________
____
____
____
____
____
____
____
____
______________________________.

WORKPAPER I5.05 Voice Communications--Data Collection Instrument

OFFICE EQUIPMENT: VOICE COMMUNICATIONS--DATA COLLECTION INSTRUMENT

Business unit name: ______________________________

Location: ______________________________

Telephones:

Make: ______________________________

Model: ______________________________

Number of instruments: ______________________________

Number of lines: ______________________________

Primary use of instruments (e.g., customer contact, internal calls, ordering, customer service, vendor contact): ____________
____
____
____
____
____
____
____
______________________________.

Volume of calls:

Daily: Incoming: ____________ Outgoing: ____________

Weekly: Incoming: ____________ Outgoing: ____________

Monthly: Incoming: ____________ Outgoing: ____________

Time of volume:

Morning_____ Midday_____ Afternoon_____ Evening_____ Night_____

Cyclical increase or decrease in volume:

	Jan	Feb	Mar	Apr	May	Jun	Jul	Aug	Sep	Oct	Nov	Dec
%	___	___	___	___	___	___	___	___	___	___	___	___

Business unit name: ______________________________

Location: ______________________________

Type of system: ______________________________
______________________________.

Location of system: ______________________________
______________________________.

System capacity: ______________________________
______________________________.

Capacity as configured: ______________________________.

Date: ______________________________

Growth assumptions: ______________________________.

Annual: ______________________________

System topology: Describe dependences on proprietary system, how remote locations are serviced, whether they are tied to a proprietary system, and if so, where and how the nodes are linked. ______________________________
____
____
____
____
____
____
______________________________.

WORKPAPER I5.06 Vital Records--Data Collection Instrument

VITAL RECORDS--DATA COLLECTION INSTRUMENT

This analysis determines the critical vital records on which your unit depends. It determines what needs to be duplicated and stored off site, what has already been stored off site, and what archival records are critical to your operations on a daily, weekly, or monthly basis.

Business unit name: ______________________________

Location: ______________________________

Record name: ______________________________
____

Media (e.g., paper, microfilm): ______________________________
____
______________________________.

Frequency of use: ______________________________
____
______________________________.

Legal retention required? [ ] Yes [ ] No

Length of time: ______________________________
____
______________________________.

WORKPAPER I5.07 Critical Forms--Data Collection Instrument

CRITICAL FORMS--DATA COLLECTION INSTRUMENT

This analysis is to determine what forms are critical to your operation.

Business unit name: ________________________________

Location: ________________________________

Form name: ________________________________

Number of forms: ________________________________

Source of the forms: ________________________________

____

____.

Lead-time for reprints: ________________________________

Quantity on hand: ________________________________

Quantity off-site: ________________________________

Location of off-site: ________________________________

Volume of use: ________________________________

Organizing the Business Operations Recovery Teams

CHAPTER I-6

The business operations recovery teams are responsible for responding to and managing any condition that has caused or has the potential to cause a serious interruption of business operations. Exhibit I-6-A lists the types of disasters that might be handled by the recovery teams.

Some organizations choose to create separate programs and teams for handling specific types of threat events. A disaster recovery team might handle any immediately apparent disaster (e.g., an explosion, fire, or earthquake) that interrupts business operations. A crisis management team might be organized to handle such threats as criminal activity, workplace violence, product contamination, and accidents involving hazardous materials that pose a danger to the organization but do not interrupt operations. An emergency preparedness team might be assigned responsibility for the safety of employees, customers, or the public in a crisis or disaster.

Other organizations choose to manage all types of crises and disasters using primarily two types of teams—one that is chiefly responsible for coordinating the companywide recovery effort and the other for managing recovery of specific business units at the alternate sites designated in the recovery plan. This is the approach presented in this chapter. It should be observed that most of the objectives, principles, and methods of organizing recovery teams presented in this chapter are common to any type of team organized to handle crisis situations.

PRINCIPLES OF RECOVERY MANAGEMENT

The purpose of recovery management (and crisis management) is to minimize damage to the organization and its employees. The first priority is to protect human life, whether of employees or consumers of a company's products or services, while terminating and recovering from the incident as quickly as possible. The recovery teams must act prudently to ensure that a relatively minor incident does not become a major disaster.

The recovery teams must also attempt to protect the organization's assets. These include financial and commercial assets as well as such intangible assets as the company's goodwill and reputation. Any losses should be recovered as rapidly and effectively as possible.

In responding to a disaster, the organization must seek to maintain the confidence of its customers and shareholders. It must also maintain good relations with law enforcement, regulatory, and other governmental agencies and comply with all applicable laws and regulations. A key objective is to minimize the risk of legal liabilities to the organization.

In order to achieve these objectives, the recovery teams should follow these principles, which are common to the management of any type of crisis or disaster. They include:

EXHIBIT I-6-A TYPES OF CRISES AND DISASTERS

- Major Crimes
- Extortion
- Kidnapping
- Crimes Against the Organization—Internal
- Crimes Against the Organization—External
- Crimes by Members of the Organization
- Loss of Key Personnel
- Product Contamination
- Hazardous Materials Releases and Other Environmental Disasters
- Natural Disasters
- Human-made Disasters
- Computer System Failures (Accidental and Intentional)
- Utility Disruptions

- Formal preparation whenever possible.
- Planning for the worst-case scenario.
- Carefully assessing the potential impact on the organization.
- Minimizing the number of people involved in the response.
- Allocating decision making to appropriate levels of authority.
- Communicating in an accurate, efficient, and secure manner.
- Responding consistently to public and legal expectations.
- Documenting the response activities properly.

These common principles are discussed in the following paragraphs.

Preparation. The business operations recovery planner must establish responsibilities, procedures, and standards that the recovery teams are to follow in responding to a disaster. This includes establishing responsibilities for the recovery at the corporate and divisional levels and by facilities where appropriate. Notification lists should be prepared to ensure an orderly process of alerting team members. Such lists should be organized by priority of response, designate who is to issue the alert, and include alternative phone numbers. The notification lists must be easily accessible in a disaster and should be kept current and secure.

Consistent response procedures must be established throughout the organization. These should include checklists of the immediate actions to be taken upon notification of a disaster. Efficient and dependable procedures for activating teams must be established for both regular and nonworking hours. Backups of critical equipment and procedures should be maintained to ensure the organization's ability to respond quickly.

All members of the recovery teams must be trained and rehearsed in their respective roles. Senior management must be informed of the conditions under which the recovery teams will be activated.

Planning for the Worst-Case Scenario. Response preparations should be made assuming the worst-case scenario. (Even if the immediate disaster is not the worst, the recovery teams must be prepared to respond if the situation deteriorates.) Management should avoid communicating an overly optimistic view of the recovery effort until the organization has regained complete control.

Assessing the Potential Impact. The disaster should be carefully analyzed to determine the exact risk to the organization and its employees. The immediate scope of the problem, the most probable scenario, and the worst-case scenario should each be established before agreement on a response strategy is sought.

The assessment of the threat to the organization should be reviewed and updated, as appropriate, throughout the course of the recovery operation. The recovery teams should adhere to preestablished priorities for response and recovery; however, when alternative courses of action are possible, the likely consequences of each should be assessed before any decision is made.

Minimizing the Number of People Involved. Designated recovery management team members and their alternates have the primary responsibility for managing the disaster response. In some cases, experts may be called on to assist a team. All other parties not directly involved in responding to the disaster should be kept away from the disaster site; a method for informing them of the status of the response should be established.

Allocating Decision-Making Authority. Levels of decision-making authority should be assigned to each recovery team member and documented in the recovery plan. Senior management should not preempt lower levels of authority unnecessarily. Team members should be trained and rehearsed in performing their duties according to their assigned level of responsibility.

Communicating Accurately, Efficiently, and Securely. Communications must be accurate and appropriate to the various interested parties. Recovery team management should be trained in how to communicate information during a disaster accurately and efficiently. Information should not be embellished or changed as it is reported through the chain of command.

All sensitive information should be secured. For example, in developing response strategies, the team may be presented with certain options to establish limits of appropriate behavior in alternative disaster scenarios (e.g., restricting physical access to the disaster site or prohibiting use of cellular phones by nonauthorized personnel); team members should be able to present such options without fear of disclosure beyond the management team. Information related to security and alleged criminal activity must be treated with utmost security and should be distributed only on a need-to-know basis. Procedures should be established for confidentially reporting any threatening or suspicious communications directed at the organization or its employees to the security department.

Team members should maintain appropriate channels of communication to external parties to keep them informed of the status of the recovery. A 24-hour emergency phone number should be established and communicated to all employees so that they can obtain information and assistance in the event of a disaster.

The command center should be outfitted in advance with appropriate equipment to support communications and documentation.

Responding to Public and Legal Expectations. The organization's recovery effort will be judged by external observers, who will expect that the organization exhibit an adequate standard of commitment and concern for protection of its employees, customers, and vendors. These expectations may reflect social conventions of behavior

[redacted]

as well as legal requirements. Failure to meet these expectations can damage the company's reputation.

Documenting Response Activities. The actions taken by team members and decision makers during the response and recovery operation should be documented. This can be useful in later assessing the quality of the response and may also serve in the event of litigation.

ORGANIZING THE RECOVERY TEAMS

As noted, organizations vary in the way in which they establish the business operations recovery program. Some organizations establish a centralized management group consisting of senior management of various operational and administrative departments. This type of centralized group would have the responsibility for making recovery decisions about incidents that have a broad impact on the enterprise. Other organizations choose to establish teams to manage different types of crises and disasters (e.g., a crisis management team and an emergency preparedness team).

Most organizations use a hybrid approach in which the overall response and recovery is coordinated by one team at a centralized location while recovery operations are managed locally for each affected business unit. This is the approach presented in this chapter.

Two types of teams are involved: the emergency operations team and the business recovery teams. The emergency operations team assumes primary responsibility for directing and coordinating the recovery. The business recovery teams handle recovery operations for their respective business units at the alternate recovery locations.

Emergency Operations Team

The emergency operations team exists to respond to the needs resulting directly from the business interruption caused by the disaster. Its objectives are to resolve issues related to the disaster and provide the necessary support to the incident manager, emergency operations manager, and the business recovery teams.

The emergency operations team is responsible for the day-to-day direction of the recovery effort. Essentially, because of the disruption of operations, the emergency operations team assumes full control of all operations within the affected facilities. There is a temporary cessation of the normal management reporting structure, and the emergency operations team in effect takes over management of the organization. (Most line managers have no organization to manage until the recovery is completed. If they have responsibilities outside the areas affected by the disaster, they should continue to provide direction to those areas.)

The incident manager and the emergency operations team manager are the primary decision makers during the recovery effort. They have the authority to execute the plan, make decisions related to unplanned requirements, reassess and establish priorities, and authorize the purchase of equipment, services, and other resources as needed. The emergency operations team is led by the incident manager, who is responsible for managing the overall recovery effort. The incident manager is also the primary interface between senior management and the emergency operations team.

The emergency operations team manager is responsible for the daily operation of the recovery effort and for coordinating the activities of the emergency operations team leaders. The team leaders represent various disciplines within the organization. Each of them is an expert in a particular functional area and is responsible for providing assistance to the business units in their recovery efforts. These team leaders are primarily drawn from functional departments throughout the organization. The following sections describe the responsibilities of each member of the emergency operations recovery team.

Emergency Operations Team Manager. This person is responsible for managing the emergency operations recovery team as well as the day-to-day operations of the command center from which all recovery operations are directed. This command center is referred to as the emergency operations center (EOC). Exhibit I-6-B illustrates the layout of the center.

Because it would be impossible for the emergency operations manager to handle all issues directly, recovery coordinators may be designated to assist the manager in responding to the business units. The responsibilities of these coordinators are described in detail in Workpaper I6.01 under the heading "Recovery Coordinators."

Emergency Operations Team Leaders. The following team leaders are responsible for providing dedicated support for specific recovery purposes:

- *IS recovery team leader.* This team leader is responsible for recovery planning as well as postdisaster recovery of information systems. He or she acts as the primary interface between the data center recovery team, the applications support teams, and the emergency operations manager.
- *Communications recovery team leader.* This team leader is responsible for recovery planning and postdisaster recovery of voice and data communications. (Communications recovery is discussed in Part III of this book.)
- *Administrative services recovery team leader.* This team leader has primary responsibility for planning and postincident acquisition and preparation of facilities for relocating business units.
- *Purchasing and transportation recovery team leaders.* These team leaders are responsible for ensuring the expeditious acquisition and delivery of equipment, services, and supplies during the recovery operation.
- *Security recovery team leader.* This team leader is responsible for ensuring the safety and preservation of corporate assets and for ensuring employee safety during recovery operations. He or she coordinates with the incident manager and the emergency operations manager and provides status reports on safety- and security-related issues. This team leader is also responsible for ensuring that only authorized personnel are permitted to access the primary and alternate sites.
- *Risk management recovery team leader.* This team leader is responsible for coordinating all salvage and insurance issues in support of recovery operations.
- *Human resources recovery team leader.* This team leader provides support for personnel and staffing requirements during the recovery operation.
- *Legal recovery team leader.* This team leader provides legal counsel in all matters related to the recovery.
- *Public relations recovery team leader.* This team leader acts as the sole source for disseminating information to the public during the recovery. He or she must coordinate with senior management and the incident manager.
- *Accounting recovery team leader.* This team leader manages financial aspects of recovery operations.
- *Travel and lodging recovery team leader.* This team leader arranges all travel and lodging requirements to support recovery operations.
- *Office services team leader.* This team leader is responsible for providing supplies, copy, and mail services during the recovery.

EXHIBIT I-6-B EMERGENCY OPERATIONS CENTER CONFIGURATION

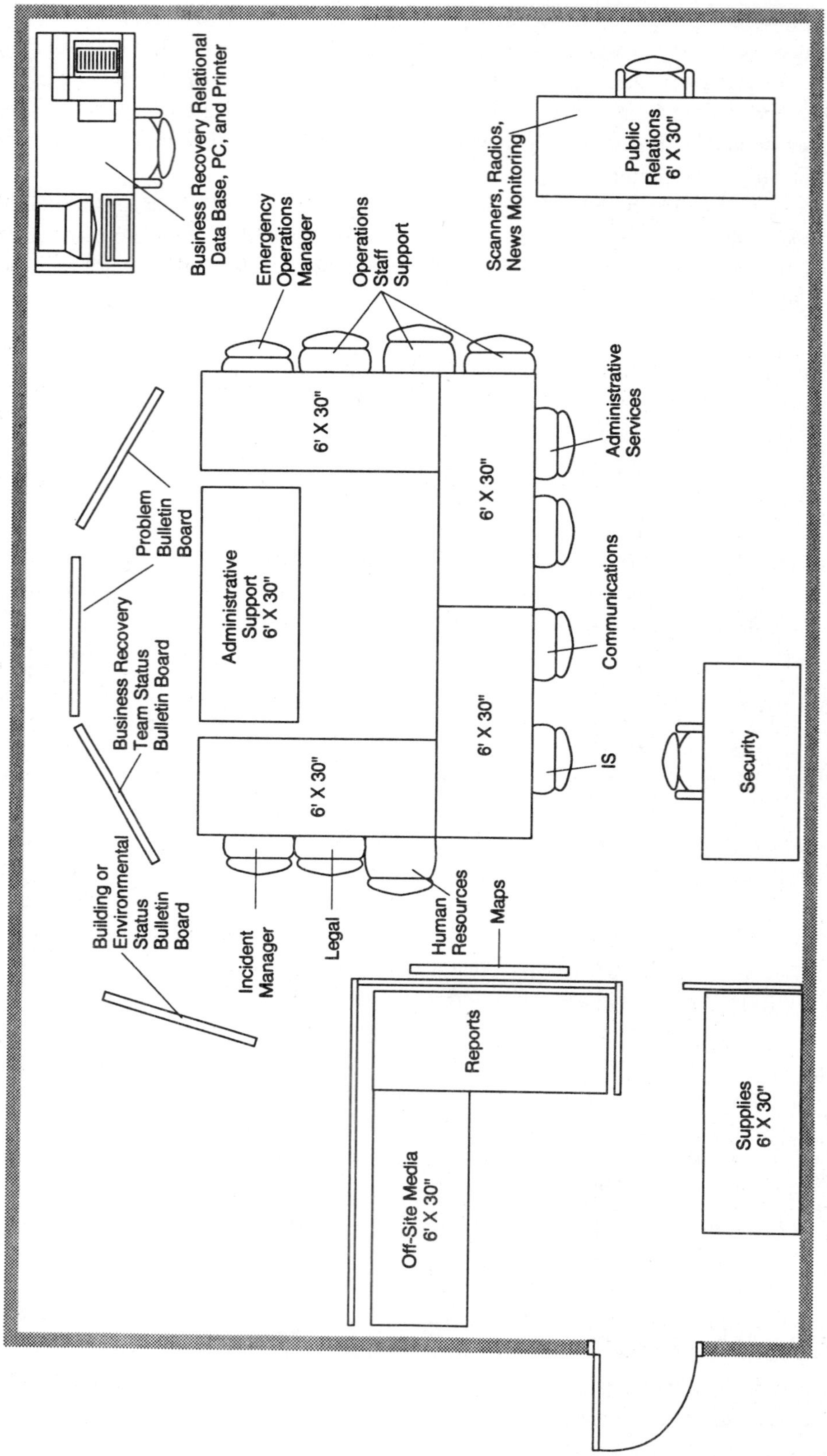

An alternate team leader should be designated for each primary team leader. The composition of the teams may vary depending on the type of incident and availability of personnel. Detailed descriptions of the responsibilities of these team leaders are provided in Workpaper I6.01 under the heading "Emergency Operations Team."

In addition to these functional team leaders, two team leaders are assigned to provide specialized services during the initial response to the disaster:

- *Emergency response team leader.* This team leader is responsible for conducting the initial assessment of the damage to facilities and for providing support to employees forced to evacuate the building.
- *Site evaluation and restoration team leader.* This team leader is responsible for providing a detailed damage assessment report (after the initial report by members of the emergency response team) and for coordinating restoration activities.

Business Recovery Teams

The business recovery teams are responsible for conducting the recovery of business operations at the alternate processing sites. A business recovery team coordinator is responsible for coordinating the activities of these teams. The coordinator is located at the EOC and reports directly to the emergency operations manager. The recovery teams should follow the procedures defined for their business units in the business resumption plan.

SELECTING TEAM MEMBERS

The business operations recovery teams typically include many of the team members who were involved in creating the recovery plan. The process for selecting team members is similar to the process for selecting people to develop the plan (see Chapter I-2). Team leaders may be employees of the organization, or they may come from outside the organization. Team leaders typically include the functional line managers who led the recovery planning effort for their business units; in some cases, team leaders may be key vendors responsible for a technical part of the recovery effort. Team members include staff-level employees as well as vendor representatives and consultants.

In general, external resources are used if the company does not have expertise in a particular area. If external resources are to be recruited for the recovery team, they should also take part in the planning effort and in training exercises.

The recovery planner should recognize that many business units will be asked to provide team leaders and members for both the emergency operations team and the business recovery teams. (Such business units include IS, communications, legal, and human resources.) In essence, they have a twofold responsibility: to provide assistance to the command center in managing issues related to the disaster at the primary site, and to assist in recovery of their business functions at the alternate site. In planning the allocation of personnel, the recovery planner should take care not to assign one person to serve both functions.

MANAGING THE DISASTER

A sample emergency operations center guidebook is provided as Workpaper I6.01. The EOC guidebook provides guidelines on how to set up the emergency operations center and manage the disaster. The guidebook describes the chain of command, areas of responsibility for managing the recovery, and certain basic operational procedures.

It is not possible to document how specific recovery decisions should be made. Such decisions will differ depending on the type of disaster and expected length of the outage, the nature of the affected organization, its organizational structure, and the mix of experts available at the emergency operations center. However, it is possible to outline a basic framework for response and recovery activities.

A Framework for Response and Recovery

The emergency operations team must know under what circumstances it is to respond to a disaster or crisis. In most cases, the response procedures should be based on the expected length of the outage rather than the type of incident. The organization might choose to designate response or escalation levels representing the expected length of the interruption of business operations and the appropriate response for that level. For example, the following levels might be defined:

- *Level 1.* An interruption of less than two days.
- *Level 2.* An interruption of from three to five days.
- *Level 3.* An interruption of more than five days.

In a level 1 incident, the response procedures might simply be to:

1. Initiate notification of the emergency operations team.
2. Meet at the emergency operations center.
3. Assess the damage and determine potential length of the interruption.
4. Make the necessary repairs.

In a level 1 incident, the emergency operations team might wish to consider limited use of a recovery facility for critical online applications and communications. In that event, the procedure would be expanded to include steps for moving the appropriate business units to the recovery facility.

A level 2 incident would include the four steps described for a level 1 incident but would add more specific procedures for notification and use of a recovery center (e.g., hot site). It would also include a step for formally activating the emergency operations team.

A level 3 incident would include all of the steps noted for a level 2 incident but might specify additional steps on the search for and use of temporary facilities for expanded business operations in the local area.

For ease of communication and use, it is recommended that one set of response procedures be developed and communicated to all parties involved in managing the incident. This process incorporates the three-level response and notification criteria described in the preceding paragraphs but incorporates them in a single uniform set of procedures. A sample set of procedures should include these steps:

1. *Disaster occurs.*
2. *Notification.* Members of the emergency response team make an initial report on damage to the facility and communicate their findings to the incident manager and the emergency operations team manager. If a level 2 or level 3 incident is indicated, the predesignated recovery facility or hot site should be notified; executive management and the business recovery teams should also be notified.
3. *Damage assessment.* The site evaluation and restoration team estimates how long the building will be unavailable. If it is not possible to complete such an evaluation within 12 hours, the worst-case assumption should be made. In that event, the business resumption plan is fully activated.
4. *Activation of the emergency operations center.* A decision is made to activate

the emergency operations center on the basis of an analysis of the type of disaster, the condition of the building (e.g., unable to be occupied), and the condition of employees (e.g., employees injured or present in the damaged facility). At different stages of the recovery effort, the emergency operations center may need to be relocated. When first activated, the center should be located at a facility near the damaged site.

A decision to fully activate the emergency response teams is made using the same decision criteria. (In addition to performing the initial assessment, the emergency response team is responsible for managing the evacuation of employees and ensuring their safety.)

5. *Notification of more senior management.* After the initial notification process is completed, more senior levels of management that were not immediately notified should now be advised as to the status of the disaster and the actions they are to take.
6. *Activation of business recovery organization.* After safety issues have been addressed by the response teams, recovery operations can begin. The business recovery teams are activated.
7. *Relocation of the emergency operations center.* If warranted by the type of disaster and length of interruption, it may be decided to move the emergency operations center to the hot site (or other recovery facility) at which recovery operations are being conducted.
8. *Deactivation of the original emergency operations center.* After the operations center has been activated at the hot site, the original operations center should be deactivated. At this point, both command and recovery operations are consolidated at the hot site.
9. *Preparation for deactivation of the hot site.* Most hot-site contracts stipulate that the hot site may be used for six weeks. Planning for relocation to other temporary facilities should begin immediately after the center is fully functional and after critical business operations have been restored.
10. *Restoration of facilities.* The site evaluation and restoration team coordinates the restoration of the damaged facilities or the construction of interim facilities to permit complete restoration of business operations.
11. *Transition to restored facilities or interim facilities.* After the restoration team completes its work, personnel can return to either the restored facilities or interim facilities designed to support full operations.
12. *Closing of the emergency operations center.* The emergency operations center located at the hot site or other temporary facility can be closed.

Communications

The most critical element of managing any disaster is communications. Effective communications procedures help ensure that the emergency management team obtains the information it needs to evaluate the situation and make accurate decisions on how best to respond. They also provide senior management with the necessary information for its review and action.

Information is provided to the emergency operations team members by various means, including couriers, telephones, fax machines, two-way radios, Internet connections, and written documentation. No matter the method of communication, the incoming information should be logged on receipt. The documentation procedure should be as simple and efficient as possible. Logging the information is important to help reduce the possibility that a critical request or item of information is misplaced and therefore not addressed.

The documentation process must be able to handle the incoming volume of information without slowing down the recovery. Often the simplest and most effective solution is to use a logbook to initially capture the information or to immediately log the information on a bulletin board; it can then be entered into a more sophisticated computer-based system after the item has been addressed. Tracking and reconciling requests and responses for action is best accomplished with automated systems.

Posting information on boards is a standard practice in most recovery operations. Boards may vary from a flip chart to sophisticated electronic boards projected by large-screen television systems. The purpose is to make sure that the information is visible to team members who need it to make decisions during the course of the recovery.

The communications and documentation procedures should be thoroughly tested and exercised to ensure they work properly in an actual disaster.

WORKPAPER I6.01 Emergency Operations Center Guidebook

EMERGENCY OPERATIONS CENTER GUIDEBOOK

OVERVIEW OF THE BUSINESS RESUMPTION PLAN

Objectives

Your business resumption plan establishes the organization, actions, and procedures necessary to recover critical headquarters business functions in the event of a disaster. This plan is designed to minimize the operational and financial impacts of such a disaster.

Scope

This resumption plan includes actions and procedures to recover all critical activities at your company's headquarters.

Organization and actions for headquarters personnel safety and survival issues are detailed in the emergency response plan of your company's headquarters for safety and life-sustaining functions and are not included in this plan.

Policy

The business resumption plan is designed to cover all contingencies that may require use of an alternative site. The plan will be maintained and updated on a continuing basis, reflecting all organizational and procedural changes that may occur within the operations of the headquarters.

Although this plan provides guidance for disaster recovery efforts, it is not a substitute for sound judgment nor is it a rigid set of rules to be followed at any cost.

Assumptions

This plan has been developed and is to be maintained on the basis of the following assumptions:

A complete interruption of facilities has occurred, and there is no access to its equipment or its data. Recovery from anything less than complete interruption will be achieved by using appropriate portions of this plan.

Normally available staff members may become unavailable as a result of the disaster. However, sufficient staff with adequate knowledge will be available to implement recovery.

This plan covers interruption for only the first 60 days following the disaster. If it is determined that the interruption will exceed 60 days, all functions at the initial alternate site will develop additional plans to regain full function and use all employees as soon as practical.

Two general classifications of interruption are:

- Local. Basically affects only your company headquarters. Support can be expected from suppliers and local agencies. A local alternative site will be available.

- Regional. Affects the entire area and no local support can be expected. An alternative site out of the area will be available.

All vital records, data, and files required to implement recovery of critical functions are backed up off-site on a regular basis. These items stored off-site are considered to be the only such resources available for executing the recovery.

Recovery Strategy

In the event of a disaster, this plan is designed to recover critical business functions by establishing a business recovery organization that will, upon notification, operate at preselected alternative sites. The site used will be located in or outside the immediate area, depending on whether the interruption is classified as local or regional. This site will accommodate the needs of disaster management and critical business function operations. Required space and equipment will be available on a prearranged basis.

Disaster management will be conducted at the alternative site in the disaster recovery emergency operations centers, staffed by your company senior management and the emergency operations team leaders. All decisions and communications will emanate from these centers.

Business functions will operate at the alternative sites on a minimum, critical-need basis. When functions can perform critical operations through the implementation of prearranged off-site procedures, or out of homes, or through existing alternative facilities for their function, they will do so. These preparations and procedures are included in the business recovery team plans.

Operation of critical business functions at the alternative site will be accomplished in phases over the 60-day interruption period. According to a previously conducted business impact analysis, business functions will begin operating out of the alternative site with minimum personnel meeting critical needs on a prearranged schedule over the 60-day period. In the event of an extended interruption beyond 60 days, the business recovery team plans provide for additional personnel to be brought into the original alternative site to do the planning within the first 60 days that will regain full function for all employees at additional alternative sites as soon as possible.

The final phase of the business resumption plan is the migration to restored or replaced facilities. The conclusion of this phase would end the recovery effort and deactivate the contingency conditions.

AUTHORITY

Key to the recovery management process are the teams assigned to manage the incident. These teams will be executing decisions made during the planning process as well as responding to demands that could not have been anticipated or planned for. The incident manager, emergency operations center manager, and the emergency operations center team are the primary decision makers during the recovery effort. Your company management has given them the authority to execute the plan, make decisions related to unplanned requirements, reassess or establish priorities, and authorize the purchase or acquisition of required equipment, services, space, travel, or whatever other resources are necessary to assure the timely resumption of business operations. During the recovery, your company management will be frequently briefed by the incident manager or alternate on the status of the recovery process, issues originated by the incident, deployment of resources, or assistance required from senior management.

ALTERNATIVE LOCATIONS

The company has identified alternative sites to relocate your company business operations following a disruptive event that renders the facilities not occupiable for three business days or longer.

The primary business recovery site is located at [address].

At this location, your company has contracted for [number] workstations, equipped with a personal computer, telephone, and connection to a LAN. The number of stations will be increased, if space is available, in the event of an actual emergency.

Note: If declaration constraints exist, such as first-call, first-served or other conditions, the planner should document them here.

Identify the personnel who have the authority to declare:

Name	Home Telephone	Office Telephone
Primary:		
______________________	________________	________________
______________________		
______________________		
Alternative 1:		
______________________	________________	________________
______________________		
______________________		
Alternative 2:		
______________________	________________	________________
______________________		
______________________		

The secondary business recovery site is [alternative site]. This facility is configured to resume operations for approximately [number of employees] in [location].

[Alternative site] is located at: ______________________________.

Alternative site phone number: _______________

Emergency operations center phone number: _______________

TEAM ORGANIZATION

Emergency Operations Team

This group is responsible for the day-to-day direction and coordination of the recovery effort. It is managed by the incident manager, who is also a member of senior management. The incident manager is assisted in recovery functions by the emergency operations manager and team leaders of the emergency operations team. During the disaster-caused interruption, the emergency operations team will receive reports of recovery progress and problems. They will maintain an up-to-date status of recovery efforts and will recommend appropriate recovery actions, as needed.

The emergency operations team has primary responsibility for managing the recovery of your company's business units following a major disruptive incident. The emergency operations team makes all operational decisions related to the recovery of business units and coordinates all teams affected by the incident. Its responsibilities include:

- Emergency operations center setup.
- Logging, task assignments, reconciliation of issues.
- Management of priorities:
  - Data processing.
  - Facilities.
  - Services.
  - Other resources.
- Assigning priorities of unplanned requirements.
- Problem resolution.

The emergency operations team is directly managed by the emergency operations manager. The emergency operations team consists of individuals representing various disciplines within the organization. Each team member is a resident expert who provides direction and assistance to the emergency operations manager and business recovery units in their recovery effort.

The emergency operations team includes the leaders of these teams:

- IS recovery team.
- Communications recovery team.
- Administrative services recovery team.
- Purchasing and transportation recovery team.
- Security recovery team.
- Risk management recovery team.
- Human resources recovery team.
- Legal recovery team.
- Public relations recovery team.
- Accounting recovery team.
- Travel and lodging recovery team.
- Office services team.
- Emergency response team.
- Site evaluation and restoration team.

The following sections describe the responsibilities of each of these teams.

IS Recovery Team. This team is responsible for recovery planning as well as postdisaster recovery of information systems. The IS recovery team leader coordinates the support activities of the applications support teams who are responsible for resolving errors and other issues related to the recovered applications. He or she acts as the primary interface between the data center recovery team, the applications support teams, and the emergency operations manager.

Communications Recovery Team. The communications recovery team is responsible for developing and documenting voice and data communication configurations necessary for the business recovery and is to ensure that all components necessary for recovery are available.

When notified, the team is to activate voice and data communications at the recovery sites, with the command center first and then the business recovery areas.

The voice and data recovery teams are coordinated by the communications recovery team leader at the emergency operations center.

Administrative Services Recovery Team. The administrative services recovery team is to plan for and, when notified, activate an effective working environment for the recovery effort at the alternative sites and is to provide the plans for the working environment at the restored or replaced facility.

Following the declaration of a disaster, the team will set up the emergency operations center, which will serve as the business recovery location for the first critical business functions and as the information center for the recovery organization.

The administrative services team will also set up the alternative sites for operation of critical business functions, using planned layouts and equipment requirements. The focus immediately following the setup of the hot-site business recovery facility will be on configuring the alternative site for occupancy by the remaining critical business functions.

The administrative services recovery team will coordinate with the site evaluation and restoration team in planning the working environment of the restored or relocated facilities.

The administrative services recovery team is coordinated by the administrative services team leader, who reports to the emergency operations manager.

Purchasing and Transportation Recovery Team. This team is responsible for planning and postdisaster recovery efforts involving purchasing and transportation services. The team processes requests from the EOC and is responsible for ensuring the expeditious acquisition and delivery of equipment, services, and supplies.

Security Recovery Team. The security recovery team is to ensure the preservation of corporate and employee assets, employee and customer information, and employee safety during recovery operations.

Continuing the emergency response plan responsibilities, the team is to provide security and access control to the damaged facility, and, as required, to the alternative site.

The security recovery team is to coordinate with local agencies to prevent exacerbation of the damage.

Risk Management Recovery Team. The risk management recovery team is to coordinate all salvage and insurance issues in support of the disaster recovery operations.

The team is to notify insurance carriers and request appropriate claims representatives to assemble at the damaged facilities. The team will also maintain close liaison with insurance representatives in processing claims and will obtain authorization from appropriate insurance carrier officials for the disbursement of emergency funds as required throughout the recovery cycle.

With insurance company approval, the team will coordinate the cleanup and restoration of damaged equipment and supplies. They will prepare and maintain records of all salvageable equipment and its disbursement. The team will coordinate with vendors, suppliers, and restoration professional in the restoring and replacing of equipment and supplies.

The risk management recovery team will coordinate the authorization and removal of needed or usable items from the damaged facility without affecting claim settlements. The team will coordinate with the site evaluation and restoration team in the preparation of the insured property damage assessment.

The risk management recovery team is coordinated by the risk management team leader at the emergency operations center.

Human Resources Recovery Team. The human resources recovery team is to provide support of those personnel related issues that are critical to controlling the recovery effort and is to meet the needs of employees and management during the recovery.

The team is to develop a personnel schedule to track recovery staffing at all times. It is to coordinate with other recovery teams regarding staffing requirements and provide personnel as needed.

The human resources recovery team is to provide needed assistance to families of employees, particularly those who are injured or displaced by the disaster. The team is to minimize the emotional aftershock from the disaster and provide counseling for employees affected by the excessive scope of the disaster.

The human resources team is coordinated by the human resources team leader at the emergency operations center.

Legal Recovery Team. The legal recovery team is to ensure the availability of legal counsel, as required, in all matters related to disaster recovery operations. The team will also monitor laws and regulatory issues related to business and industry liabilities for the applicability and possible impact on disaster recovery planning.

The legal recovery team is coordinated by the legal recovery team leader at the emergency operations center.

Public Relations Recovery Team. The public relations recovery team will serve as the sole source for dissemination of information related to the disaster to the public, including news media. The team will continue to manage the employee-family communication program initiated under the emergency response plan.

The public relations recovery team is to ensure the availability of current and correct information announcing the occurrence of a disaster and any follow-up information deemed necessary. The team will monitor all media reporting of the disaster and, with approval of management, will respond as required.

The public relations recovery team is coordinated by the public relations recovery team leader at the emergency operations center.

Accounting Recovery Team. The accounting recovery team will effectively aid in managing all monetary details associated with the recovery operations.

The team will coordinate with all recovery teams to ensure the recording of expenses associated with the recovery and will coordinate with the cashier function to establish an emergency fund systems to support the recovery operation.

Travel and Lodging Recovery Team. The travel and lodging recovery team is to arrange all travel and lodging requirements in support of the disaster recovery operations. The team also coordinates any catering requirements for recovery personnel during the recovery process.

Office Services Team. The office services team reports to administrative services and is responsible for providing supplies, copy services and mail services at the alternative site.

Emergency Response Team. This team is responsible for conducting the initial assessment of the damage to facilities and for providing support to employees forced to evacuate the building.

Site Evaluation and Restoration Team. The site evaluation and restoration team is to assess the results of the disaster and ensure the availability of information necessary to the restoration or relocation of the damaged facilities.

Following the initial damage assessment by the emergency response team, the site evaluation and restoration team is to provide a detailed report on the extent of damages, access restrictions, and an estimate of the length of interruption, using the opinions of civil agencies, utility companies, and other professionals, as needed.

The site evaluation and restoration team is to coordinate with the corporate public relations team for release of information regarding extent of damage, origin of interruption, injuries sustained, and course of action. The team will also coordinate with the risk management team in preparing information required for processing insurance claims.

Upon selection of a restoration alternative, the site evaluation and restoration team is to establish a reconstruction project plan with estimated costs and time frames to reactivate or relocate the facilities. The site evaluation and restoration team reports to the site evaluation and restoration team leader and is coordinated by the emergency operations manager.

Recovery Coordinators

Three special positions exist within the emergency operations center. These positions provide focal points for a number of recovering business units. Each coordinator position is responsible for multiple groups. It would be impossible for the emergency operations manager to handle all recovering business units on a one-on-one basis. The three positions are the business recovery team operations coordinator, business recovery team staff coordinator, and business recovery team support coordinator.

Business Recovery Team Operations Coordinator

The business recovery team operations coordinator reports to the emergency operations manager and operates from the emergency operations center. The business recovery operations coordinator is responsible for acting as the focal point within the command center for the following company business recovery teams.

[The planner should list the line operation teams here.]

Coordinator Tasks. The business recovery team leaders are responsible for providing the following information to the business recovery team operations coordinator as they complete each major recovery step:

- The team leader or alternate arrives at emergency operations center. The business recovery team leader is responsible for initial notification calls. Any critical employees not able to be reached should be identified and the list given to the business recovery team operations coordinator on a problem form.

- Telephones and terminals have been checked, and any problems have been identified on the problem form.

- Supplies have been picked up, and any missing or additional supplies have been identified on the problem form.

- Reports have been picked up, and any missing reports have been identified on the problem form.

- Magnetic media have been picked up, and any missing media have been identified on the problem form.

If the business recovery team leader fails to provide this information within a reasonable time frame, the coordinator is responsible for contacting the business recovery team leader and obtaining the status of the respective task.

It is important that the incident manager, emergency operations manager, and crisis management team are kept current on the status of the recovery effort. Periodic status meetings should be conducted every one or two hours to provide them with the necessary information.

In the event that the business recovery team operations coordinator is the first to arrive at the emergency operations center, he or she is responsible for the setup of the emergency operations center.

Staffing. The business recovery team operations coordinator is responsible for ensuring that an alternate is designated to act in his or her place in the event that the coordinator is not available to respond to the emergency operations center.

The alternate must be trained in the responsibilities of the position, and it is preferable that the individual has participated in at least one recovery exercise.

The business recovery team operations coordinator is dedicated to this position and should not be assigned any functions that require the individual to leave the emergency operations site. If the coordinator is required to leave the site, the alternate must take the coordinator's place.

Business Recovery Team Staff Coordinator

The business recovery team staff coordinator reports to the emergency operations manager and operates from the emergency operations center. The business recovery staff coordinator is responsible for acting as the focal point within the command center for the following company business recovery teams:

[The planner should list the company staff teams here.]

Coordinator Tasks. Business recovery team leaders are responsible for providing the following information to the business recovery team staff coordinator as they complete each major recovery step:

- The team leader or alternate arrives at emergency operations center. The business recovery team leader is responsible for initial notification calls. Any critical employees not able to be reached should be identified and the list given to the business recovery team operations coordinator on a problem form.
- Telephones and terminals have been checked, and any problems have been identified on the problem form.
- Supplies have been picked up, and any missing or additional supplies have been identified on the problem form.
- Reports have been picked up, and any missing reports have been identified on the problem form.
- Magnetic media have been picked up, and any missing media have been identified on the problem form.

If the business recovery team leader fails to provide this information within a reasonable time frame, the coordinator is responsible for contacting the business recovery team leader and obtaining the status of the respective task.

It is important that the incident manager, emergency operations manager, and crisis management team are kept current on the status of the recovery effort. Periodic status meetings should be conducted every one to two hours to provide them with the necessary information.

In the event that the business recovery team staff coordinator is the first to arrive at the emergency operations center, he or she is responsible for the setup of the emergency operations center.

Staffing. The business recovery team staff coordinator is responsible for ensuring that an alternate is designated to act in his or her place in the event that the coordinator is not available to respond to the emergency operations center.

The alternate must be trained in the responsibilities of the position, and it is preferable that the individual has participated in at least one recovery exercise.

The business recovery staff coordinator is dedicated to this position and should not be assigned any functions that require the individual to leave the emergency operations center site. If the coordinator is required to leave the site, the alternate must take the coordinator's place.

Business Recovery Team Support Coordinator

The business recovery team support coordinator reports to the emergency support manager and operates from the emergency operations center. The business recovery operations coordinator is responsible for acting as the focal point within the command center for the following company business recovery teams.

[<u>Planner should list the support teams (e.g., data center, order entry, communications, office services) here.</u>]

Coordinator Tasks. Business recovery team leaders are responsible for providing the following information to the business recovery team support coordinator as they complete each major recovery step:

- The team leader or alternate arrives at emergency operations center. The business recovery team leader is responsible for initial notification calls. Any critical employees not able to be reached should be identified and the list given to the business recovery team operations coordinator on a problem form.

- Telephones and terminals have been checked, and any problems have been identified on the problem form.

- Supplies have been picked up, and any missing or additional supplies have been identified on the problem form.

- Reports have been picked up, and any missing reports have been identified on the problem form.

- Magnetic media have been picked up, and any missing media have been identified on the problem form.

If the business recovery team leader fails to provide this information within a reasonable time frame, the coordinator is responsible for contacting the business recovery team leader and obtaining the status of the respective task.

It is important that the incident manager, emergency operations manager, and crisis management team are kept current on the status of the recovery effort. Periodic status meetings should be conducted every one to two hours to provide them with the necessary information.

In the event that the business recovery team support coordinator is the first to arrive at the emergency operations center, he or she is responsible for the setup of the emergency operations center.

Staffing. The business recovery team support coordinator is responsible for ensuring that an alternate is designated to act in his or her place in the event that the coodinator is not available to respond to the emergency operations center.

The alternate must be trained in the responsibilities of the position, and it is preferable that the individual has participated in at least one recovery exercise.

The business recovery team support coordinator is dedicated to this position and should not be assigned any functions that require the individual to leave the emergency operations center site. If the coordinator is required to leave the site, the alternate must take the coordinator's place.

TASK EXAMPLES

[The planner includes recovery scripts to be used by the emergency operations team members in this section.]

NOTIFICATION AND ESCALATION

The notification plan is designed to be used for mobilization of the complete business recovery organization. If partial mobilization is called for, the appropriate portion of the plan can be executed as needed. When primary members in the recovery organization cannot be reached for their part in the notification plan, their alternates will be contacted.

Initial Notification

Initial notification of an interruption will follow the procedures outlined in the emergency response plan. An event will usually be reported to security, who will notify senior management, the incident manager, and, if appropriate, damage assessment personnel. With the exception of a major earthquake, the crisis management chairperson, or his alternate, or the most senior company manager on-site will determine whether or not to declare a disaster according to the criteria outlined in the disaster declaration section and an estimate of the duration of the interruption. On declaration of a disaster, the incident manager will be notified to mobilize all or part of the business recovery organization.

Command Center Notification

The incident manager will notify senior executives and the emergency operations manager that the business recovery organization is to be mobilized and that the emergency operations centers are to be activated.

The emergency operations manager will notify the emergency operations team leaders as indicated in the preceding section. Emergency operations team leaders will use their team rosters and call lists to notify their team members of the situation and appropriate action to take.

Business Recovery Team Notification

Senior executives will notify their business unit recovery team leaders that the business recovery organization has been mobilized and that they should report to an alternative site as directed in the individual team plans.

Business unit recovery team leaders will notify their business function team leaders. Team leaders will use their team rosters and call lists to notify their team members of the situation and appropriate actions to take.

Notification Process

[<u>Planners should enter the notification process to be used by their company here.</u>]

RECOVERY CENTERS AND FACILITIES

Emergency Operations Center

The emergency operations center is the command center for managing major incidents that may affect your company's operations. The emergency operations center might be located in a variety of locations depending on the type of incident and conditions of the headquarters building.

The emergency operations center may be used by the emergency response team to manage the postevacuation support of company employees forced to evacuate the building. In this case, the planning assumption is that the building is not safe to occupy and the emergency operations center will be located in a safe place close to the headquarters.

The emergency operations center will be used by the business recovery organization and will be located sufficient distance for the headquarters to prevent a regional disaster from affecting both the headquarters and the emergency operations center.

In the event that company headquarters is not occupiable, all locally established emergency operations centers will move to the off-site emergency operations center as soon as the immediate safety issues are stabilized and employees have been returned to their homes.

Hot-Site Vendor Business Recovery Facility

The initial emergency operations center for business recovery will be located at the hot-site vendor business recovery facility in [town name]. This emergency operations center will be used to coordinate the recovery of the critical business operations during the first week following the event. A majority of the critical business operations will be recovered at the [alternative site] business recovery facility from the end of the first week through week three of the recovery effort. Equipment and supplies necessary to support the emergency operations center will be stored at or close to the hot-site location and hotel.

The emergency operations center will be set up in a room configured to provide sufficient telecommunications services to handle the volume of telephone traffic. [Number] telephones will use one phone number, so that incoming calls to roll to the next telephone if one station is busy.

The emergency operations center will contain dedicated incoming and outgoing fax machines.

Status Monitoring

The operating period of the hot-site business recovery facility will most likely overlap the operation of the alternative site emergency operations center, and it will be necessary to have some duplicate information available at both centers. In addition, the contingency of not having the hot site available to initiate recovery operations has been addressed by providing two emergency operations centers and business recovery areas.

At the hot site and the alternative site, status boards have been designed to post and monitor incoming information related to:

- Headquarters building status--Personnel, damage, other issues.
- Environmental status--Roadways, airports, utilities, other infrastructure.
- Business recovery team status--Team availability, equipment, reports.
- Problem and resolution status--Missing resources, absent personnel, communication problems, and equipment problems.

HOT-SITE BUSINESS RECOVERY

Assuming that the declaration of a disaster has been made and the company has access to the hot-site business recovery facility, the following should take place:

1. Hot-site business recovery facility personnel go to the off-site storage facility and retrieve the equipment necessary to configure the emergency operations center.
2. The first person arriving at the hot-site facility signs into the facility and inventories the equipment.
3. Hot-site personnel will assist with the physical configuration if they have sufficient staff available. Their primary responsibility is to establish telecommunications connectivity between the business recovery facility and the company's data center and to set up the required PBX configuration.
4. The emergency operations team table and telephones are set up in the emergency operations center.
5. The telephone operators and the message center person take their stations.

6. If possible, outside subsidiaries or emergency 800 telephone emergency centers are contacted and advised of the telephone number at the emergency operations center.

7. The storage boxes for the emergency operations center are separated from the supplies boxes for the business recovery units.

8. The status boards are set up as identified in the emergency operations center.

9. The partitions separating the emergency operations center area from the supply, off-site data, and reports tables are set up.

10. The emergency operations center supply boxes, containing the following are opened:

    - Emergency operations center supply kit.
    - Emergency operations team name cards.
    - Emergency operations team start up instructions.

11. The emergency operations team positions are established according to the emergency operations center configuration.

12. Two-way radios are set up.

13. Scanners are set up.

14. Map boards for areas potentially affected by the incident are put in place.

15. The business recovery start-up plan is obtained and distributed.

16. The status of arriving emergency operations team and business recovery team members and any problems requiring assignment or resolution are logged.

17. The command of the emergency operations center is turned over to the incident manager, emergency operations manager or their alternates when they arrive at the command center.

RECOVERY PRIORITIES

The following represents the priorities and time frames established for your company's headquarters operations. The chart represents the organization to be recovered, the location at which the recovery will take place, the initial number of staff to be recovered, and the time frame for recovery. The priorities are based on the need to first establish a recovery infrastructure to support the business recovery teams when they begin their recovery and second to continue to service customers. The time frames assume that in a regional incident such as a major earthquake or flood at least three days may pass before most company personnel are able to respond to the recovery. The exception to this constraint are the teams with the responsibility for putting in place the recovery infrastructure. These teams are required to respond as quickly possible given safety restraints.

It is assumed that the data processing resources required by the emergency operations centers and business recovery teams will be in place with the business recovery time frames and that connectivity between the recovery sites and the data center has been established.

EMERGENCY OPERATIONS CENTER EQUIPMENT INVENTORY

Specify number of each item:

- Status boards:
  - -- Problem status boards.
  - -- Magnetic team status board.
  - -- Environmental status board.
  - -- Building status board.
  - -- Easels.
  - -- Flip charts.
  - -- Magnetic status markers.
  - -- Magnetic markers with team names.
  - -- Magnetic markers with task names.
- Two-way radios with spare batteries and three chargers.
- Multichannel emergency-band scanner.
- Supplies:
  - -- Maps of the city, county, and surrounding counties.
  - -- Desk supply kits.
  - -- Erasable board markers.
  - -- Magic markers for flip charts.
  - -- Pads of problem resolution forms.
  - -- Pads of problem forms.
  - -- Company telephone directories.
  - -- First-aid kit.
  - -- Rolls of masking tape.

- Equipment:
  - -- Computers.
  - -- Laser printers.
  - -- Fax machines.
  - -- Copiers or immediate access to copier.
  - -- Bolt cutters for removing padlocks on off-site storage boxes.

The business recovery team status board should contain the following information:

Task	Emergency Operations Team	Telecommunications Team	Data Communications Team	IS Team	Order Entry Team	Finance Team
Team Notified						
Team Arrived						
Phones Checked						
Terminals Checked						
Supplies						
Reports						
Microcomputers						
Data						
Vital Records						
Vendors Notified						
Customers Notified						
Employees Notified						
Location--Hot Site						
Location--Other						

The environmental status board should contain the following information:

Area Damaged	Type of Damage	Comments

The building status board should contain the following information:

Floor	Problem	Status	Comments

CHAPTER I-7

Recovery Planning for Microcomputers and LANs

Many organizations are moving from centralized processing systems to distributed systems that support shared use of data and computing resources and real-time access to information. These distributed systems include standalone microcomputers and local area networks (LANs).

Many applications that previously resided on mainframe systems are being moved to LANs; this includes an increasingly large number of mission-critical applications. The local area networks may in turn be connected to other internal and external networks as well as to mainframes. Even if a system appears to serve a single business application, its applications and data may reside on multiple computers, although the connections may never be apparent to users. In addition to networked systems, standalone microcomputers are now sufficiently powerful to support important, mission-critical applications.

Whereas most companies have comprehensive programs in place for data center recovery, far fewer address recovery of microcomputers and LANs. A recent study by David Michaelson & Associates with ICR Survey Research Group measured the extent to which major US companies are vulnerable to a disaster. It was found that although the data centers of these organizations take significant precautions in the event of an interruption of computer services, LANs are extremely vulnerable to a disaster. This disparity in vulnerability between data centers and LANs results from failure to include LANs in business resumption planning. Whereas almost all of the surveyed plans addressed recovery of mainframes, less than half included recovery plans for LANs. And only 20% of companies with disaster recovery plans included plans for recovery of standalone microcomputers. The results of this survey are summarized in Exhibit I-7-A.

RECOVERY ISSUES

Certain problems common to LAN and microcomputer recovery do not exist in the mainframe environment; other problems are common to all processing environments. In a mainframe environment, for example, the selection and implementation of systems is well controlled, and controls for managing development and maintenance of software are also well established. In a distributed environment, diverse platforms may be located throughout the organization. There are often few controls for managing development and maintenance of software (e.g., change controls) and for ensuring data integrity. Physical and logical access controls are often lacking in distributed systems.

Unlike midrange and mainframe systems, microcomputer-based systems are more closely integrated into the business environment. In many cases they are located on the same floor as the business units they serve. These small systems are often implemented

EXHIBIT I-7-A SURVEY OF BUSINESS UNITS WITH LAN RECOVERY PLANS

	Financial Services	Manufacturing	Services	Wholesale/Retail Trade	Public Administration
Designation of alternate site in event of disruption	46%	16%	20%	21%	26%
Testing and evaluation program for recovery plan	50%	10%	21%	7%	29%
Recovery of critical information	65%	44%	48%	21%	39%
Identifying critical information	54%	34%	43%	21%	36%

without the knowledge or assistance of the IS department, let alone of business resumption planners. Even if the resumption plan attempts to include microcomputers and LANs, it may be difficult to develop a complete inventory of such systems.

Many business units implement local systems to improve operating efficiencies. For example, use of LANs tied to imaging systems can increase the speed of transaction processing while reducing dependence on paper records. However, the loss of paper-based records also eliminates an important source of backup information that can be useful in a disaster that disables computer systems.

With mainframe systems, ownership and responsibility for the system is clear-cut. But this is not always the case with small systems. For example, a LAN server located in one department may provide shared applications to multiple business units. The department in which the server is located may not have critical data on the server and therefore may not consider it a critical priority for recovery. But other units may store critical data on the server. Therefore, planning for system use and recovery requires a coordinated effort by all business units that depend on the server, and not just the one where the server is located.

Network connections are also an important consideration in planning for recovery of LANs. Without the ability to restore the necessary routers and bridges, an otherwise functional LAN may be unable to provide critical services to its remote users. This can also be an issue in recovering centralized business operations. During the recovery, centralized operations are often forced to relocate to multiple facilities; these facilities must be connected to provide temporary services. Rebuilding a large-scale network without a resumption plan is difficult and likely to suffer substantial delays.

In addition to these issues that are unique to the recovery of small systems, there is also a set of recovery issues common to both large and small system recovery. These include:

- Establishment of priorities for recovery of applications.
- Data and application backup procedures and procedures for off-site storage.
- Data and application restoration procedures.
- Planning to ensure equipment availability.
- Planning for use of recovery services.
- Testing of the recovery plans and systems.

The following sections present an approach for recovery of microcomputers and LANs. Some of these procedures are adapted from procedures already used commonly in data center recovery programs; others have been created to address the specific requirements for recovery of small systems.

ESTABLISH RECOVERY PRIORITIES

STEP 1

Classifying data and applications into categories according to their priority for recovery is a common practice in mainframe environments. These categories identify the time frames in which the data and applications should be recovered, as well as recovery strategies for each class. In most organizations, data and applications for microcomputer and LAN systems have not been classified. This must be done to ensure effective and timely recovery of small systems.

To classify this information, the recovery planner must attempt to anticipate the impact of the loss of each application and type of data on critical business operations. Such applications as order processing and fulfillment may be required immediately because they are revenue-generating functions, whereas certain administrative applications may not need to be restored until much later.

To provide consistency within the organization, small systems data and applications should be classified using the same terminology as used in the mainframe recovery program. Data and applications are commonly classified as:

- *Critical.* The business unit cannot recover without this data or application; it must be recovered immediately.
- *Essential.* It would be difficult to recover without this data or application; it must be recovered in the early phases of the recovery effort.
- *Nonessential.* It would be possible to recover all critical business functions without this data or application; it is needed only to reestablish normal business operations.

The results of classification help to determine what data and applications should be backed up and moved to an off-site storage location.

ESTABLISH BACKUP PROCEDURES

STEP 2

Recovery without LAN and microcomputer backup data may be impossible to achieve in the time frame required for recovery. The planner must ensure that the critical data and applications can be restored to business operations at an alternate site when they are needed.

Such planning can be complicated by certain common practices among users of LAN systems. Users who encounter relatively frequent problems on a LAN often choose to maintain their data on the local workstation rather than on the server. They do so to ensure immediate access to their data in the event of a network failure. If they create backups at all, they also usually store the backup on site, for the same reason. These practices create an obvious exposure if the workstation and its surrounding area is the target of a disaster. Most LAN recovery programs involve backing up data and applications from the server. But if critical files are not stored on the server, the backup program will be incomplete.

The recovery planner should establish a small systems recovery program based on a disaster scenario that assumes that all microcomputers and LANs (and their resident data) are lost in a disaster. Therefore, a procedure should be established for the routine backing up of data stored on microcomputers and LANs and their storage in an off-site storage location. To be effective, all users must be required to update and maintain critical files in a server-based repository from which the backups will be made.

Procedures for backup and off-site storage can be manual or automated. Manual backup procedures can be difficult to enforce among end users, especially if users are expected to use individual diskettes to back up large quantities of information stored on a hard drive. Fortunately, an alternative to this inefficient and time-consuming process has been developed. Both LAN and microcomputer data can be easily backed up using high-density digital tape backup systems. Compact digital tape systems are inexpensive and efficient; the user can initiate a backup, go to lunch, and be assured that the backup will be completed upon return.

These compact tape systems provide sufficient capacity for handling the typical volume of backup data generated by microcomputers and LANs. A large number of these small tapes can be readily stored at the off-site facility.

An automated system that does not require user intervention is the most efficient and reliable backup method for LANs. Some systems can automatically move data from the LAN server to a mainframe on a scheduled basis, typically during nonpeak hours. The data is then moved to the off-site storage location when the mainframe is backed up according to its normal cycle. Other systems provide centralized tape storage facilities as remote backup to the distributed systems. These backup systems, which can be attached either directly to the mainframe or indirectly to the LAN, use robotics for tape retrieval and loading. Should the network be destroyed, the backup data could be used to configure a local computer and provide dial-up access to it; alternatively, it could transmit the data to a remote location accessible to the business unit. Centralized tape storage services are provided by such vendors as IBM, Storage Technology Corp, and Memorex.

Automated backup of microcomputers is rarely used, although some organizations have established systems to move data from a networked microcomputer to a central repository with backup and off-site storage facilities. Typically, software running on a LAN is programmed to periodically extract data from the microcomputer and move it to the repository. Systems are being developed that make use of mainframe communications protocols to facilitate the transfer to a host. For example, one application using Novell's NetWare allows LAN users to communicate between NetWare and the IBM SNA environment.

Schedules for backing up data and applications and their rotation to the off-site storage facility need to be established. The frequency of backups and rotation depends on the business impact analysis for the loss of this data. For example, the analysis might indicate that the organization can tolerate only loss of three days' worth of its LAN-based data, whereas it can tolerate a seven-day loss of microcomputer data. Therefore, the recovery planner would establish a weekly schedule for backing up microcomputer-based data and rotating it off site; LAN-based data might be backed up daily and rotated off site every three days. In general, if a thorough loss analysis is not available (which is common, given that most organizations do not have a backup and off-site storage program for small systems), a weekly backup and rotation schedule is a reasonable starting point.

The frequency with which backups are taken may also depend on the organization's experience of network problems. For example, if the organization has experienced disk drive failures that have caused loss of data, it may decide to take more frequent backups. Companies with little tolerance for downtime may also choose to implement duplex disk drives on their servers and maintain a spare drive as a backup. Of course, this would not provide any assurance of recovery if the disaster destroyed the business facility. Off-site storage of critical data and applications is the only method of ensuring the organization's ability to recover from a major disaster affecting business facilities. The off-site storage facilities should be identified early in the planning process.

DETERMINE RESTORATION PROCEDURES

STEP 3

The recovery planner has at least two options for restoring backup data. For restoring a LAN, the first option is to restore the data from a server; this is the most common method. However, this approach requires that a sufficiently large number of servers be available to hold the data; it also requires that connections be established between the servers and the recovering business units.

Connections may be established in several ways. Ethernet or token-ring adapters can be used to attach microcomputers to the servers; if this option is used, the recovery planner should ensure that these adapters are included with the replacement microcomputers. Alternatively, wireless technology might be used; although wireless connections are faster to set up, they are significantly more expensive than hard-wired connections.

A second, less frequently used option is to restore data from a LAN backup tape to an intermediary microcomputer configured to accept the tape and with sufficient storage capacity to hold the contents of a tape. The recovering business user's file directory is established on this interim computer, and the data is then transferred to the end-user's computer using microcomputer-to-microcomputer data transfer cables and software. This process of restoration is slow and it must be repeated for each machine; however, it is an option if a server is not available.

The business resumption plan should specify how LAN directories should be established to segregate categories of critical, essential, and nonessential data and similar categories of servers. During a recovery, the set of systems available for recovery is limited; therefore, only a relatively small percentage of total data and applications can be restored. Establishing appropriately classified directories in advance can help ensure that all critical data and applications can be restored quickly.

ENSURE EQUIPMENT AVAILABILITY

STEP 4

The recovery planner must identify the number of systems required by the recovering business groups. This equipment must be able to handle the quantities of backup data for the business units in the required recovery time frames. Sources of replacement equipment must also be identified.

Plans should be made to acquire the necessary equipment from multiple companies with production and shipping facilities outside of the immediate area. Use of multiple companies ensures that the organization can obtain all items of required equipment. In a regional disaster, a vendor may have committed equipment to many clients and may not have the required amount of inventory on hand to supply all of them. Use of vendors outside the local area helps ensure that the organization will be able to obtain the needed equipment in the event of a regional disaster that affects local suppliers.

It is easiest to obtain off-the-shelf equipment with standard configurations and features. Such specialized equipment as high-performance workstations and large monitors with split-screen capabilities are more difficult to obtain during a disaster, especially if a large number is needed quickly. To ensure that business units can obtain such specialized equipment, multiple sources should be identified and the average product inventory of each vendor determined in advance.

Equipment and Software Configuration. It is most efficient for the recovery planner to establish a standard profile for the equipment and applications to be provided during the recovery. With the exception of specialized equipment, users will be provided with equipment and software that meets the standard configuration.

The standard configuration should provide sufficient memory to operate efficiently and sufficient storage capacity to hold the necessary amount of backup data. For example, if multiple sessions are to be run in a windowed environment, 16M bytes of RAM may be required. Efficiency of memory and storage is especially important, given that business operations are typically restored with fewer people handling more work than they would under normal conditions.

The recovery planner should provide the vendors with a master copy of the standard configuration for equipment and applications. Whenever this configuration changes (not an infrequent event in most companies), the master should be updated and provided to suppliers. The planner should consider having the supplier provide the equipment fully configured when delivered.

After the standard configuration has been selected, the business units can identify and plan for any exceptions to the standard. The business unit should be responsible for backup and restoration of any of its nonstandard applications.

STEP 5

PLAN FOR RECOVERY SERVICES

Most major hot-site vendors provide at least some LAN recovery services for their subscribers. In some cases, the LAN recovery is offered as part of general business recovery services. The business recovery facilities provided by the hot-site provider also support microcomputer recovery. In some cases, the microcomputers provided by the recovery service may not meet the requirements of the business user, in which case an upgrade is required.

STEP 6

TEST RECOVERY PLANS

The recovery plan for microcomputers and LANs should be tested in phases. First, tests should be conducted of equipment and applications acquisition, setup, and recovery. Tests should focus on restoring applications, data, equipment, and connections among network components. If the LAN is connected to a wide area network, the connections should be tested. Any problems identified in this preliminary phase of testing should be resolved by the IS department before it moves on to the second phase of testing.

In the second phase, testing of microcomputer and LAN recovery is conducted as part of testing the recovery plan for the business units. In this phase of testing, the focus is on the recovery of business operations. Actual production systems are used to test recovery of data, applications, and LAN connections. The use of production data is necessary to verify the effectiveness of the recovery plan as well as to sustain the support of management. (Chapter I-8 discusses testing of the business operations recovery plan.)

MICROCOMPUTER AND LAN RECOVERY PLANS

Microcomputer and LAN recovery plans should be part of the corporatewide business resumption plan.

Microcomputer Recovery Plans

The recovery plans for microcomputers should be a part of the business recovery plan for each business unit. The business unit that owns the microcomputer is responsible for including it in the recovery plan. The business unit should identify the microcomputer-based applications and data that have the highest priority for recovery. Location of off-site storage of data and applications should be identified, and the time frame for acquisition and restoration of equipment and data should be documented. If the business unit depends on the IS department to provide assistance in restoring its microcomputer systems, that requirement should also be documented in the plan.

It is preferred that standardized backup software and tape backup systems be used by the business units. If a business unit does not choose to do so, the exceptions should be identified in its plan. The business unit should also identify the planned source of the nonstandard equipment or software. To ensure that the application software is available at the alternate site, copies should be made and stored with the data at the off-site storage facility.

As with LAN recovery plans, microcomputer recovery documentation should be sufficiently comprehensive to enable any recovery team member to restore the system without reliance on the primary user of the system. Any security mechanisms installed on microcomputers should have an override feature so that authorized recovery personnel can access the system and data. If data is encrypted, the master key for decrypting the restored data should be available to authorized recovery team members.

LAN Recovery Plans

Workpaper I7.01 provides an example of the areas to be covered in a LAN recovery plan. In most organizations, the LAN administration group is responsible for planning for the disaster response and recovery of LAN systems. The recovery process should be consistent with the recovery strategies, priorities, and processes of the business units that depend on the LAN as well as that of the organization as a whole.

As shown in Workpaper I7.01, the first section of the LAN recovery plan addresses the immediate steps to be taken following a disaster. These include procedures for notifying the incident manager and the business recovery team coordinator as well as the LAN recovery team leader and team members. This section also describes the procedure for alerting recovery service providers of the disaster.

The next section of the plan describes the operational and environmental restoration procedures at the recovery site. These include procedures for moving tapes to the recovery site, team logistics at the site, verification of the condition of equipment at the recovery site, activation of the LAN operating system, the loading of application software, activation of workstations, and establishing LAN management systems.

The third section of the LAN recovery plan addresses functional recovery procedures, including procedures for restoring data from backups, testing voice communications, establishing connections from the LAN to the host, testing and execution of server applications, and establishing wide area network connections. The fourth section addresses the resumption of business functions, and includes procedures for notifying LAN users of the location of the recovery site and the schedule for restoring the system. At this point, users are able to conduct the necessary business functions using services provided by the recovery center.

The last section addresses procedures for managing the return to the home site. As with the configuration of the recovery site, this section provides information related to installing new equipment (if necessary), loading the network operating system, loading applications, restoring data from the alternate sites, cleaning and restoring equipment at the disaster site, and reestablishing LAN and WAN connections at the home site.

WORKPAPER I7.01 LAN Recovery Plan

LAN RECOVERY PLAN

1. Immediate Response Steps:

   a. Contact LAN recovery team leader.

   b. Contact incident manager and the business recovery team coordinator.

   c. Contact LAN recovery team members following notification procedures.

   d. Declare disaster with alternative site vendor following declaration procedures.

2. Operational and Environmental Restoration:

   a. Notify off-site storage to move tapes to site. Bring parent and grandparent tapes to alternate site.

   b. Team arrives at site.

   c. Verify equipment at site. If equipment is inaccessible, order new equipment. Move printers, tape backup unit, and cabinets.

   d. Activate [operating system], as follows: [Enter detailed procedures here.]

   e. Load application software.

   f. Activate workstations, as follows: [Enter detailed procedures here.]

   g. Configure voice system.

   h. Establish network management systems.

3. Functional Restoration:

   a. Install software backups, restore data.

   b. Test voice communications.

   c. Establish connectivity to host.

   d. Restore workstations to full function.

   e. Log-on, test, and execute server applications.

   f. Establish WAN connections.

4. Resumption of Business Functions:

   a. Notify users of schedule and site.

5. Return to Home Site:

   a. Install new equipment, if necessary.

   b. Load network operating system.

   c. Load applications.

   d. Restore all data from alternative site.

   e. Ensure that vendor removes all data.

   f. Reestablish WAN connections.

   g. Reestablish host connections.

Business Operations Recovery Plan Testing, Maintenance, and Training

CHAPTER

I-8

The business operations resumption plan must change in response to changes in the organization. The plan must be maintained in a timely manner so that it reflects the most recent changes in operations, systems, and management structure. It must be periodically tested to ensure it is workable.

Recovery team members must be trained so that they understand how to perform their duties in a recovery operation. They must also be tested in the documented recovery procedures to ensure they are capable of carrying out the plan in a crisis.

BUSINESS OPERATIONS RECOVERY TESTING

The primary goal of testing is to ensure that the procedures for recovering business operations are feasible in practice. This involves testing the readiness of the organization to recover business operations as well as testing recovery of specific systems and applications. Testing also helps to:

- Determine the compatibility of backup systems and facilities.
- Identify deficiencies in existing procedures.
- Demonstrate the ability of the organization to recover.
- Ensure that recovery teams are capable of working together in a recovery operation.

Whatever the objective of the test, however, a test plan must first be developed.

PLAN THE TEST

STEP 1

As with any aspect of the recovery program, a plan for conducting the tests must be developed and documented. This documentation should clearly outline the objectives of the test, identify test participants, specify test frequency, identify the dates and locations of each test, and specify evaluation criteria. The test plan should be documented far in advance of the actual test, and it should be communicated to test participants for their review and preparation.

The test objectives should be established in concert with test participants. Participants should also be involved in preparing the test plan for their area. Publishing the test objectives in advance can help motivate participants to become involved in test planning. If they are aware that they are to be evaluated on the basis of the test information they provide, they will usually make sure that this information is current and complete.

The evaluation criteria should clearly describe what outcome would indicate that the objective was met. This includes specifying test measurements. For example, success might be measured by the ability to enter 100 transactions in eight hours or to record a certain volume of command center problems with a 95% rate of accuracy.

The planner should also select the business units to be tested and the number of participants from each business unit. The business unit manager should identify the recovery team leader; the team leader in turn selects team members.

Vendors should also be invited to participate in recovery plan testing. Vendors can be a critical part of the recovery program, providing technical resources not available within the organization. Vendor team members can initiate recovery procedures at remote recovery locations, thereby establishing an initial base of operations on which the organization's team members can expand when they arrive at the recovery site. (Hot-site vendors often contract with subscribers to set up the emergency operations center and business recovery facilities.) Vendors typically work under the direction of one of the organization's recovery team leaders.

The names of all test participants should be provided to the recovery planner one month before the test is to be held. If a hot site is to be used, the recovery planner should provide the names of recovery team members to the hot site so that access to the hot-site facility can be arranged. The planner should anticipate potential changes in personnel and arrange for the organization's security representative to be present to identify and sign in personnel not on the original list.

In some business recovery tests, the participants' telephones and fax machines may be forwarded from the original site to the backup site. If this is the case, responsibility for switching telephone or fax numbers must be assigned. A check of the participant roster should be made on the day of the exercise to ensure that telephone and fax numbers match those of participants. Any cancellations, additions, or changes should be communicated to the original site as soon as possible to prevent missed calls or faxes.

Test participants should be briefed before each exercise on test objectives, time of the test, equipment to be provided, work to be taken to the test site, and other relevant issues.

Because of the frequency with which most organizations experience changes in management, operations, and systems, testing of recovery procedures and teams should be conducted at least annually. Introduction of new procedures, systems, and personnel may warrant testing as major changes occur to critical systems and teams.

The recovery planner should be sensitive to the fact that a recovery test requires a significant commitment of time and resources. For example, a two-day test involving 100 recovery and support personnel translates to a loss of 200 person-days from normal business operations. To obtain the necessary commitment, the recovery planner must work closely with senior management, soliciting it for input in defining test objectives and identifying ways to minimize lost productivity during testing.

The recovery plan should also specify the types of tests that are to be conducted. These include tests of recovery procedures and resources, systems and applications recovery, and execution of the recovery plan. Some types of tests can provide an effective evaluation without requiring a major commitment of resources, whereas others may entail significant time and expense. The various types of tests are described in the following sections of this chapter.

STEP 2

TEST THE RECOVERY PLAN

As noted, recovery plan testing can be separated into test categories on the basis of the objective of the test. Some tests focus on testing the adequacy of documented procedures for recovery of business operations; others test recovery of supporting computer systems and applications. Systems testing includes testing the ability to recover microcomputer and network systems upon which the business unit depends. (Testing of mainframe systems is covered by the data center recovery plan, as described in Part II of this book.)

Testing Methods

The organization can perform a number of tests of the plan, including:

- Checklist testing.
- Simulation testing.
- Parallel testing.
- Full interruption testing.

These tests are described in the following paragraphs.

Checklist Testing. A checklist test determines whether adequate supplies are stored at the recovery site, critical records and storage media are stored off site, telephone numbers are current, quantities of forms are adequate, critical procedures and operational manuals are available off site, and copies of the plan are available. With this testing approach, the recovery team reviews the plan and identifies key components that should be current and available. The checklist test ensures that the business units are in compliance with the requirements of the plan.

Simulation Testing. This test simulates a disaster. A simulation test involves these steps:

1. Define test objectives.
2. Establish the scope of the test and how to determine success.
3. Define the scenario.
4. Develop the ground rules and scripts for the test.
5. Create the problems to be solved by the participants.
6. Arrange for the logistics and locations to be involved.
7. Conduct the test.
8. Evaluate the test.
9. Summarize the findings and make recommendations for improvement based on documented results.

Test objectives include:

- Developing an awareness of the business recovery process.
- Validating recovery checklists and scripts.
- Familiarizing recovery teams with recovery locations.
- Familiarizing recovery teams with emergency communications systems.
- Mobilizing recovery teams and validating membership.
- Testing the emergency operations center as the clearinghouse of information and decision making.

The scenario chosen for the exercise should be realistic. It may be a good idea to use a worst-case scenario such as a major flood, hurricane, or regional earthquake, because this also establishes the knowledge needed to recover from less serious events.

Exercise problems must also be solvable by the consensus of participants. To knowingly build failures into the exercise is not wise. Failure only demoralizes participants and hurts the credibility of the planning group. Participants should enjoy the exercise, not dread it.

The test should be self-documenting. As participants are working to solve the problems, they should use the actual problem and resolution forms; these serve as a record of the decisions made during the exercise. The problem and status boards also act as part of the documentation process. Information should either be transcribed from the boards or photographed to provide a permanent record.

The scope of the test should specify the recovery teams to be mobilized and the business functions to be tested. The scope statement should specify if command centers and recovery sites are to be activated at locations designated in the plan. Large-scale simulations are extremely complex and can take as long as three to six months to plan for. A company should not attempt a large-scale simulation until it has conducted more focused exercises of individual business units.

A sample scenario for use in California might involve an 8.3 magnitude earthquake whose epicenter is located 30 miles northeast of Los Angeles. Damage in Los Angeles, Riverside, and San Bernardino counties is widespread and the casualties are heavy. Utility failures are widespread and service is predicted to be unavailable or unstable for six or more days.

The objective of this simulation test might be to document the impact of the quake on employees and its effects on major buildings and operations of the organization. The test scripts and ground rules should specify the time of the day (e.g., six hours after the earthquake; 24 hours later). The time frame for the exercise should be defined, as should be the time units (e.g., whether the test time will be conducted in real time or whether one hour of test time will be equivalent to 24 hours of recovery time). The plan should also specify:

- The rules governing the use of phones and other communications systems.
- Who is participating in the exercise and in what capacity.
- The forms to be used and how will they be used.
- The flow of the exercise.
- Use of facilitators, monitors, transcribers, and evaluators.

Staff involved in the development of exercise problems could serve as group facilitators in their respective areas.

Parallel Testing. A parallel test can be performed in conjunction with the checklist test or simulation test. In this scenario, for example, yesterday's transactions are processed against the previous day's backup files at the organization's recovery site. All reports produced at the alternate site for the current business date should agree with those reports produced at the alternate processing site. Although this type of test is more frequently used in mainframe recovery, it can also be used to test smaller systems supporting business operations.

Full Interruption Testing. A full interruption test activates the total disaster recovery plan. This test is costly and could disrupt normal operations and therefore should be approached with great caution. Actual costs of the exercise should be determined, risks identified, and the potential impact presented to senior management before such a test is considered.

Adequate time must be scheduled for the testing. Initially, the test should not be scheduled at critical points in the normal processing or business cycle. (The end of the month, quarter, or year would not be a prudent time to schedule an exercise.) It may be best to exercise the plan related to small business systems and supporting networks after normal business hours or on weekends to minimize disruptions. Business recovery teams should be exercised during normal business hours and access to production systems provided. The duration of the test should provide adequate response time and avoid commitment conflicts.

Test scenarios should identify the type of disaster, the extent of damage, recovery capability, backup resource availability, and duration of the test. The test plan should also identify the persons responsible and the time they need to perform each activity. Before an attempt of a full test is made, each part of the plan should be tested to verify it functions as planned.

Unannounced Tests. Unannounced tests may be used to test the notification process and exercise recovery teams. Unannounced tests for business recovery teams should be limited to the notification process only. Moving business units to alternate sites would be too disruptive to normal business operations.

Systems Recovery Testing

The computer systems and applications used by the business units should be tested. Small systems generally will be tested as a whole rather than in segmented tests as is done in mainframe testing. Ideally, recovery of both mainframe and small systems should be tested simultaneously. This comprehensive exercise will more closely approximate a worst-case disaster in which both the information systems and business operations are affected by the incident.

Where appropriate, the recovery planner should test logical groups of applications in the logical sequence of production. In most cases, recovery of related business units should be tested along with the logical sets of applications used by the business units.

The following steps should be followed for application testing of small systems:

1. Provide specific information for testing each application. The midrange systems development group should position the test in the work queue.
2. Establish the test plan and discuss tasks.
3. Establish the application testing objectives and criteria.
4. Provide details on dates, tasks, duration, and personnel.
5. Outline actual test steps to be performed.
6. Verify test steps and familiarize personnel with the test.
7. Test the application.
8. Evaluate and document all issues pertaining to the test.
9. Sign off on test results.

Testing the Recovery Teams

For the sake of consistency, the word *test* is used in this chapter to describe both tests of the plan and of the recovery teams. In practice, however, it is recommended that the recovery planner use the word *exercise* to describe testing that relates to human performance. (The word test is better used to refer to testing of inanimate objects such as systems.) The reason for maintaining this distinction is that many people fear being tested and may resist participating if they think they are to be judged and graded.

The objective of recovery team testing is to discover whether the recovery plan assumptions and procedures developed in theory satisfy the organization's recovery needs in practice. Even dedicated recovery team members may not be able to identify all requirements until they actually participate in an exercise. For example, the process of going to an alternate location and using predefined resources may lead team members to discover resources that were overlooked in the planning process. This testing also verifies the readiness of the recovery teams to carry out the procedures documented in the plan.

It is most effective to test recovery teams that have a close working relationship or are interdependent. Choosing three or four business units that represent parts of a product or service life cycle chain more closely approximates the actual recovery mix. During the test, these organizations can experiment with new means of sharing information that may improve their effectiveness.

Grouping interdependent organizations together at the recovery site expedites the internal communications process. The physical proximity may compensate for the lack of E-mail or other facilities normally used by the business units for interorganizational communications.

Command Center Personnel. Testing command center personnel trains them on how to effectively manage an incident and helps them to establish the best process for a particular recovery operation. Command and control exercises enable the command team to handle the type of problems it will face in a major disaster. The communication and decision-making process can be refined over multiple tests.

Recovery Roles. Team leaders and members need to be able to perform multiple roles. In an actual disaster, the primary team leaders or members may not be able to respond following the disaster. Alternate team leaders or members may have to carry the responsibility for ensuring that the critical business processes are restored. Primary and alternate business unit personnel should be rotated as team leaders and members over multiple tests.

Command center personnel typically have specific areas of expertise that they provide to the decision-making and recovery effort. Reality again demands that all emergency operations center team members be able to respond and perform basic tasks for command and control. Command center and business unit recovery status logging and notification of critical personnel are responsibilities that are initiated by the first emergency operations center team member reporting to the command facility.

The roles of team leaders and command center team members should be shared by as many members of the organization as possible. Training multiple organization managers on the function of the command center and ensuring that a broad audience understands the recovery strategies, command process, and general recovery priorities increases the potential for a well-managed response.

STEP 3

DOCUMENT TEST RESULTS

As much of the test should be self-documenting as possible. The information from the various status boards in the command center should be transcribed by someone specifically assigned to the emergency center for that task. The checklists or task lists provided to the business recovery team leaders should indicate the successful completion of their tasks. Test observers should document the flow of information and the problem management process.

Problem and resolution forms filled out by test participants should document such problems as system and software incompatibility, backup data problems, and missing or incomplete reports.

A summary document of the test results should be created and presented to the organization's senior management for its review and comment. The document should present the most significant positive and negative points of the exercise and any planned corrections or additions to the plan.

REVIEW TEST RESULTS

STEP 4

The recovery planner should determine whether the results of the test met, failed to meet, or exceeded the stated objectives. Objectives that were only partially met should also be noted. Review criteria are generally based on both business recovery objectives and technical objectives. Workpaper I8.01 provides a checklist of criteria for evaluation.

The review of test results should be scheduled immediately following the exercise. When all evaluations have been processed and the planning group has conducted an overall evaluation of the exercise, the planner should call a meeting for key participants to discuss lessons learned. The planner should also publish a document summarizing findings and lessons learned, as well as detailing recommendations for improvement. An example of an abbreviated assessment form is provided as Workpaper I8.02.

In addition to publishing the test results summary, the recommendations should be integrated into the resumption plan with specific individuals identified to complete the revisions or additions. Dates for testing the revised plan should be established as soon as possible after the revisions are completed.

A time frame for resolving issues discovered during the test should be established. Each issue should be assigned to recovery personnel with the required corrective action clearly defined. If the time frame for action is greater than 30 days, a report providing the status of the actions should be published monthly and senior management copied on the status report. Monthly meetings should be held to discuss the status of the corrective actions and objectives for the next exercise. After the corrections are completed, copies of the changes should be sent to team leaders and command staff responsible for the part of the plan adjusted.

MAINTAINING THE RESUMPTION PLAN

The primary cause of failure for many plans is lack of proper maintenance. An inaccurate plan can be misleading and cause management to make incorrect decisions or delay the recovery. For example, if key vendor contact information is not valid, the delays in contacting and obtaining a response may extend the interruption.

The users of the plan should provide the information and have primary responsibility to ensure that their specific part of the plan is kept current. The best source of accurate information about operational requirements is from the individuals who use that information and work in that area.

To encourage active participation and maintenance by the recovery plans, ease of plan use and maintenance are key. Plans can be maintained in either a word-processed or data base format.

There are positives and negatives related to both approaches. Word-processed plans are inexpensive to create. Most organizations already have word processing systems and would not need to purchase additional software. However, these plans are difficult to maintain. Overhead related to maintenance of a word-processed plan can be significant, depending on the size of the organization and the frequency of updates. Small organizations with little data and few personnel, however, may find a word-processed plan sufficient. Large organizations with substantial amounts of planning data and a frequently changing organization require automation to help keep the plan current. Use of a relational data base makes it easier to maintain the plan and provides greater flexibility for accessing critical information for reporting.

The planner should compare the cost of maintaining a centralized, word-processed plan against the cost of decentralizing plan maintenance using a data base product. (Relational data base products can cost from $3,000 to $80,000, depending on the type of software and conditions of the license agreement.) Ideally, each individual business unit should be able to access and maintain its section of the recovery plan. Although central administration of the plan provides some control, there may be delays in entering data to change the plan as well as potential for inaccuracy in communication with the centralized data entry function. Decentralized maintenance and data entry, combined with central review to ensure compliance and quality, is the most effective maintenance strategy.

A maintenance policy should describe trigger events that signal the need to modify the plan. Such trigger events might include:

- Changes in personnel, vendor, and customer information.
- Additions or deletions of business operations.
- Additions, deletions, or changes in teams.
- Changes in critical equipment.
- Changes in system software.
- Changes in recovery or incident management locations.
- Changes in recovery time frames.

TRAINING RECOVERY STAFF

Every recovery team member requires training. Without sufficient training before a disaster, the recovery personnel would be unprepared to respond. Training provides an opportunity for team members to address problems that would almost never occur under normal business conditions and to do so in a more relaxed atmosphere.

Tests provide the best training for the recovery teams. Tests simulate problems and provide an opportunity for team members to use systems in an unfamiliar environment, accomplish critical tasks with minimal resources, and develop the team attitude and processes required for successful recovery.

Periodic training compels participants to prepare. Even if the business functions have been delinquent in maintaining the information in their plan, they will most certainly scramble to update the information before having to perform in public. The more frequently they are required to perform, the more current their data will be and the more confident and successful they will be in an actual recovery.

The incident management and emergency operations center team members have the most complicated training requirement because they have the most difficult and complex recovery task. Whereas the business units have a very focused recovery scope, the incident management team must be prepared to handle the full range of recovery activities. Because of the complexity and difficulty of managing an incident, extensive training is needed to prepare the command team for an actual disaster.

If the organization elects to use a relational data base product to maintain its plan, selected team members should be trained on its use. Although the best relational products are fairly easy to use, the planner must ensure that users are comfortable with the new product and can demonstrate their competence with the software. In addition, certain constraints on what data the business units can or cannot change may be imposed by the planner to ensure data integrity. The recovery team members should be advised of these constraints during training.

Users should be trained only on those parts of the product that they need in the near term. Users must also be provided direction on the type and quality of information needed for planning. Training is the key to both the effective planning and performance of the business operations recovery effort.

WORKPAPER I8.01 Test Evaluation Criteria

EVALUATION CRITERIA

General Criteria:

1. Was the notification process successful? [ ] Yes [ ] No

2. Were the key team members contacted? [ ] Yes [ ] No

3. Were the directions to recovery site clear? [ ] Yes [ ] No

4. Were the team members able to find the recovery center? [ ] Yes [ ] No

5. Were the telephones functional? [ ] Yes [ ] No

6. If the telephone system was different from the company's system, was the user documentation adequate? [ ] Yes [ ] No

7. Was the search routine for the recovery groups effective? [ ] Yes [ ] No

8. Were the terminals or personal computers functional? [ ] Yes [ ] No

9. Were modem connections functional and adequate? [ ] Yes [ ] No

10. Did the data provided from off-site backup meet user requirements? [ ] Yes [ ] No

11. Did the users have any problems with restoration? [ ] Yes [ ] No

12. Were needed applications available? [ ] Yes [ ] No

13. Did applications function adequately? [ ] Yes [ ] No

14. Was system response adequate? [ ] Yes [ ] No

15. Were specified reports available? [ ] Yes [ ] No

16. Were any reports required but not specified? [ ] Yes [ ] No

17. Were telephone calls forwarded to team members within a reasonable time frame? [ ] Yes [ ] No

18. Was the recovery environment conducive to effective work performance? [ ] Yes [ ] No

19. Were recovery scripts complete and usable? [ ] Yes [ ] No

Command Center Team Criteria:

1. Were notification procedures effective? [ ] Yes [ ] No

2. Were directions to recovery site clear and easy to follow? [ ] Yes [ ] No

3. Were emergency operations center setup instructions available and clear? [ ] Yes [ ] No

4. Was the emergency operations center equipment available and adequate? [ ] Yes [ ] No

5. Were there adequate personnel available in the emergency operations center to initiate incident management? [ ] Yes [ ] No

6. Were the emergency communications systems easy to use? [ ] Yes [ ] No

7. Were you able to communicate with critical areas? [ ] Yes [ ] No

8. Are there areas of the organization that did not participate that you feel should have? [ ] Yes [ ] No

9. Was the scenario detailed enough? [ ] Yes [ ] No

10. Were recovery checklists validated? [ ] Yes [ ] No

11. Was your awareness of business recovery issues strengthened? [ ] Yes [ ] No

12. How did you find the functioning of the emergency operations center or command center? [ ] Yes [ ] No

13. Do you have any general comments about the exercise?
____
____
____
____
____

WORKPAPER I8.02 Test Assessment Form

TESTING ASSESSMENT FORM

Participant name: ______________________________

Position: ______________________________

Location: How easy was it for you to use the maps and find the location? ______________________________

____

Suggestion for changes: ______________________________

____

____

Supplies: Were the supplies sufficient? If not, what would you need? ______________________________

____

____

____

____

____

Equipment: Was the equipment provided sufficient? If not, what would you need? ______________________________

____

____

____

____

____

Data: Was the data available and sufficient? If not, what would you need? ______________________________

____

____

____

____

Reports: Were the right reports available? If not, which ones do you need? ______________________________

____

____

____

____

Telephone numbers: Were all needed phone numbers available? If not, which ones do you need? ______________________________

____

____

____

____

____

Execution script: Were the execution scripts and the outlined tasks adequate for you to know what to do after reporting to the facility? Were they adequate in assisting you to execute your job? ____

____
____
____
____

Other observations and suggestions: ____________________

____
____
____
____
____
____
____
____
____
____

Disaster Mitigation Controls for Microcomputer Systems

CHAPTER

I-9

An old adage says, "An ounce of prevention is worth a pound of cure." As much as possible, the business resumption planner must ensure that controls are established to protect both microcomputer systems and the information that they contain from abuse, misuse, and theft. As noted in Chapter I–7, the users of microcomputer equipment may not be as sensitive to the fragile nature of the equipment, data, and media as users or personnel responsible for large systems. Increasing the level of awareness and generating a heightened sensitivity is required for successful recovery programs for microcomputers.

In contrast to microcomputer recovery, successful LAN recovery typically takes place in an environment in which knowledgeable LAN administrators support users whose level of expertise may be similar to or lower than that of the users of standalone microcomputers. The business resumption planner should remember that in the past, users of dumb terminals had little or no idea how the terminals were connected or how the applications on the large systems worked, and they really did not care. Although users of small systems are developing greater expertise, the general population still lacks complete knowledge of how to protect information and microcomputer systems effectively.

The responsibility for ensuring application and data integrity rests with both business unit management and microcomputer users. Business unit management has the responsibility for promoting effective controls and ensuring that microcomputer users are provided the tools necessary to protect both the information and the systems. To help ensure that users are aware of their responsibilities, business unit management should publish policies, guidelines, and procedures describing which controls are mandatory within the organization. The policies should be published and an assessment program established to evaluate the effectivenss of the program. By preventing disruption of system operation or loss of system data, an effective control-based program may reduce the possibility that the planner will have to activate the microcomputer recovery procedures.

Workpapers I9.01–I9.08 are checklists covering the tasks that must be completed by the groups that share responsibility for ensuring the effective control of microcomputer resources. The following sections contain suggested policies and recommendations for implementing the required controls. Guidelines are also provided to business unit management for selecting and implementing specific microcomputer controls. The following issues are discussed:

- Complying with legal and ethical standards.
- Ensuring information and application recoverability.

- Preventing unauthorized access to microcomputer hardware, software, and data.
- Protecting against unauthorized access to networks.
- Ensuring information and application integrity.
- Reducing the risk of damage from virus infection.
- Preventing theft of microcomputer resources.
- Protecting against environmental hazards.

COMPLYING WITH LEGAL AND ETHICAL STANDARDS

Corporate management should communicate legal requirements and ethical standards for information handling and microcomputer resource use to both business unit management and employees. Business unit management should educate employees about laws, company policies, and ethical standards governing such issues as:

- Copying of licensed software.
- Handling of internal, confidential, and highly sensitive information.
- Protecting software written by employees or contractors with a copyright notice.
- Using all other corporate computer resources.

Employees must comply with all legal requirements, company policies, and ethical standards. The organization should cooperate fully with law enforcement officials in the investigation and prosecution of criminal activities involving the use of corporate computer resources.

Suggested Policy

All use of corporate microcomputer resources should be in full compliance with legal requirements and ethical standards. Only authorized copies of licensed software should be used. Software written by employees in the performance of their jobs should be protected with a copyright notice, as necessary.

Copying of Licensed Software

Only authorized copies of licensed software should be used. Microcomputer software is typically licensed for use on standalone microcomputers. Each such software package comes with a set of installation diskettes and a user manual. A copy should be considered authorized only if the following conditions are met:

- The user's department has both the installation diskettes and the accompanying manual.
- The software is installed on only one machine.
- The installation diskettes are copied only for backup purposes.

In most companies, users retain the installation diskettes and the accompanying manuals only for the software that they use. There should be a one-for-one correspondence between copies of the software, installation diskettes, and manuals.

If software is to be used by more than one user on a LAN, a special network version of the software may be available, and a fee may be paid to the vendor to allow more than one person to use the software at a time. In these cases, only one set of installation diskettes comes with the package, and the licensing agreement indicates the number of authorized simultaneous users. This type of licensing agreement usually specifies that the number of users of the software at any given time cannot exceed the number of manuals. Depending on the agreement, however, different restrictions may apply. The IS or EUC (end-user computing) department should know the specific provisions of the licensing agreements for LAN software used by an organization.

In a very few cases, copy restrictions differ from those described in the preceding paragraph. Under licensing arrangements with some software vendors, multiple copies are permitted if the license maintains records of the number of copies and compensates the software vendor accordingly.

Licensing agreements usually specify the number of backup copies permitted. Backup copies may be made for recovery purposes only. No other copies should be made. To help prevent the unauthorized copying of software, business unit management should provide enough copies of licensed software to meet employees' legitimate business needs.

It should be a violation of company policy, and it may be illegal to copy licensed software for any of the following purposes:

- Using the software at home, even if it is to be used for company business while the office copy is not in use.
- Allowing a co-worker to use the software on a trial basis.
- Installing the software on another microcomputer when an employee's job responsibilities change, unless the software is first deleted from the original computer.
- Using the software on a temporary basis while waiting for a purchase order to be filled.

Although a vendor may, in rare cases, authorize this type of emergency copying, many companies do not allow it even with vendor approval. In an emergency, the IS or the EUC department may be able to arrange for shipment of licensed software within one or two days at an additional freight charge.

It may be illegal to allow simultaneous use of LAN-based software by more users than are authorized by the vendor. Strict compliance with licensing requirements can prevent an embarrassing and expensive confrontation between the licensing company and the user's organization.

Storage of Licensed Software

Business unit management should be responsible for documenting the inventory of licensed software. Because microcomputer software and hardware manuals may be needed as proof of purchase, they should be secured when they are not in use.

Handling of Internal, Confidential, and Highly Sensitive Information

To help microcomputer users comply with legal, contractual, and ethical standards, information and application owners should communicate information classification and handling requirements. Microcomputer users share responsibility with information owners for ensuring that they are aware of classification and handling requirements for the information with which they work.

Written procedures should be developed governing the release of information to nonemployees. These procedures for obtaining proper authorization should be followed when releasing applications and information to nonemployees.

Protecting Software with a Copyright Notice

Federal registration of a copyrightable work is recommended for works that are going to be widely distributed or for works that have market potential. For assistance in the application process, the business resumption planner should contact the company's legal division.

Certain software (i.e., programs and applications) written by employees or contractors in the performance of their job requires a copyright notice if the intent is to protect the software. Determining which products require a copyright notice involves consideration of several factors. If uncertain, however, it is safest to put the copyright notice on the work.

When determining whether a work should include a copyright notice, the following factors should be considered:

- *Creativity*—The greater the creativity involved in the development of the work, or the more unique the work, the greater the need for including a copyright notice.
- *Complexity*—Copyright protection is more important for complex works than for works that were very simple to develop.
- *Classification (i.e., sensitivity) of the information*—Works that contain general or internal information should be reviewed on a case-by-case basis to determine whether a copyright notice is needed. Works that contain confidential or highly sensitive information should include a copyright notice.
- *Circulation*—If the work is to be circulated to nonemployees or to a large number of employees, a copyright notice should be included on the work.
- *Marketability*—A work with strong market potential should be copyrighted, even though the company may have no immediate plans to market the work.
- *Time, energy, and money*—The more time, energy, or money expended in developing the work, the greater the need for copyright protection.

The copyright notice should be in the following format:

© Copyright. 19xx Your Company. All Rights Reserved.

The copyright notice should be clearly visible at the bottom of the initial application screen and on the first page of any documentation associated with the software. Additional copyright notices are necessary if a user can selectively print screens and if the work includes internal information being disseminated to nonemployees, confidential information, or highly sensitive information. In such cases, following the initial copyright notice, a copyright notice should be placed at the bottom of each screen, using the following abbreviated format:

© 19xx Your Company.

Questions concerning the inclusion of a copyright notice in a program or an application should be directed to the company's legal division.

ENSURING INFORMATION AND APPLICATION RECOVERABILITY

Backup is the process of copying data files and storing the copies in a safe place. The duplicate files are then available if the originals are damaged or lost.

Because microcomputer-based information and applications are extremely vulnerable to damage, destruction, or loss, proper backup procedures are essential to continued, efficient operations. Each department or business function should be required to establish and implement a plan for recovering its critical applications in the event of loss. This plan should provide for regular, periodic backup of the data and software needed to run critical applications. Although backup frequency will vary with the needs of the department, backup should be frequent enough that business will not be impaired by the loss of microcomputer-based data.

Suggested Policy

Each headquarters department or office should develop and implement a backup plan for microcomputer-based applications. The plan should ensure that critical microcomputer applications can be recovered quickly enough after a loss to allow the department or office to continue conducting its business in an effective manner. Information and application owners are responsible for determining backup requirements based on criticality and frequency of change.

Determining Criticality

Owners of information and applications should identify their applications as either critical or noncritical. An application should be designated as critical if the time required to recreate it without backup would impair the department's or an individual's ability to conduct business. An application is noncritical if the department's or the individual's ability to conduct business would not be impaired within the time it would take to recreate the application without backup.

In determining whether an application is critical, the owner should consider the following factors:

- The importance of the application to the business of the department or the company.
- The time required to recreate the application's data and software without backup.
- Whether the application's processing has deadlines.
- Whether the application is needed to comply with federal, state, or local requirements.
- Whether any other critical business processes depend on the application.
- Any other factors that may affect the application's criticality.

Business unit management should establish and implement procedures for periodic review of critical application designation and of the backup schedule for each critical application.

Developing a Backup Plan

Business unit management is responsible for developing, implementing, and monitoring compliance with a backup plan, based on requirements established by the owner. The backup plan should include procedures for:

- Backing up licensed software (if licensing agreements permit).
- Backing up critical application software and data.
- Transferring backup copies of critical applications and data to off-site or valued storage.
- Providing the resources for backing up critical application data and software.
- Testing backup and recovery capabilities periodically.

Business unit management, with the application owner, should establish a schedule for backing up noncritical applications. This may be done with the same frequency as backups for critical applications. For critical applications, backup copies must be stored off site or in a vault. Backup copies of noncritical application software and data may, but need not, be stored off site or in a vault.

Information and application owners and business unit management share responsibility for communicating backup requirements to microcomputer users. Microcomputer users are responsible for complying with the backup procedures established by business unit management to meet the application owner's backup requirements.

Recommendations

The following discussion explains the control objectives of the preceding policy and suggest ways in which it may be implemented. Management should review these recommendations, and select and implement controls appropriate to the business area.

To ensure the effectiveness of the backup procedures for microcomputer-based information and applications, management and the business resumption planner should perform the following:

- Create written procedures for users of the backup system.
- Establish and document a plan for recovering backup copies in the event of a disaster.
- Develop and implement procedures for periodic review and updating of stored documentation.
- Develop and implement procedures for periodic testing of backup capabilities.

Three steps may assist management and the business resumption planner in developing a recovery plan for critical applications:

- **Step 1**—Assigning responsibility for the overall administration of the backup program. Some departments and offices may find it more convenient to assign a specific person with responsibility for making all backups after business hours. Others may elect to make users responsible for their own backups, requiring only that all backups must be completed as scheduled.
- **Step 2**—Determining which information and applications should be backed up if not backing up everything on a hard disk.
- **Step 3**—Determining whether to use a diskette backup system or a tape backup system.

With a diskette backup system, backup copies of data files are stored on diskettes. Although this method is simple, a diskette backup of a high-capacity hard disk can take dozens of diskettes and hours to complete. Therefore, this method is recommended only for low-volume backups. As an alternative, a tape cartridge unit can be used to copy data files from the hard disk onto a magnetic tape. This approach requires purchasing a tape cartridge backup unit, which may be internally or externally installed. For large-volume backups, the tape cartridge method is recommended because a tape cartridge can hold large amounts of data. Because most backup products use data compression to provide increased data storage, an entire hard disk can often be copied onto a single tape cartridge. This method is also relatively fast, usually requiring less than half an hour.

Establish a Backup Schedule. Business unit management should establish a schedule that provides for the timely backup of data files with a minimal disruption of work. The frequency of backup will depend on several factors:

- Whether the application is critical.
- The frequency of changes to the backed up data or software.
- The volume of changes to the backed up data or software.
- The ease of rekeying changes.
- The urgency of recovery in case of loss.

Determine the Number of Backup Generations. Business unit management should determine how many generations of backups will be stored for each application.

Implement the Backup Process. Business unit managers should ensure that their organizations have acquired the diskettes, or the tape cartridges and associated hardware, needed for backup. Standards should be developed and implemented for labeling backup diskettes and tapes to ensure that their contents can be quickly identified. A logging system should be developed and implemented, with a master list maintained of all backup materials stored off site or in the vault. (Setting up this master log on a microcomputer is ideal, because the log file itself is backed up and stored off site during regularly scheduled backups.)

Document the Backup Process. Procedures should be established for filing, maintaining, and recovering documentation on all critical microcomputer applications in the department or office.

Off-Site Storage. A suitable location must be selected for storing the backups. Backups must be stored in a location separate from the originals. For noncritical applications, this may be a separate location in the same building. For critical applications, backup copies must be stored off site or in a vault. Procedures must be established for transferring backups to and from off-site storage or to a central pick-up location.

While the data files are being transported and stored, their physical security must be ensured. Access should be permitted to only authorized individuals.

PREVENTING UNAUTHORIZED ACCESS TO MICROCOMPUTER RESOURCES

Controlling access to microcomputer resources is necessary for protecting corporate information from unauthorized alteration, destruction, disclosure, or loss, whether accidental or intentional. The degree of control necessary for protecting microcomputer resources from unauthorized access is determined by the classification of the information residing on or processed by the resources. Classifications typically used by businesses include:

- General.
- Internal.
- Confidential.
- Highly sensitive.

The microcomputer data and the software that it uses reside on the hard disk within the microcomputer, on diskettes, or both. Controls must therefore limit access to both the microcomputer and the diskettes, as well to as any printed copies of the information produced by the microcomputer application.

Classification is a measure of the sensitivity of information to disclosure or misuse. It is a tool to help determine how much control is needed over users' ability to view or copy the information. Control is not a measure of importance or of the need to ensure integrity. Some critical information may not be particularly sensitive, and some sensitive information may not be critical. Labeling information as to its sensitivity tells the user how much care to use in handling it and whether it resides on a mainframe, a hard disk, a diskette, paper, or any other medium.

Data files on company mainframe (i.e., host) computers may have already been classified. A file downloaded from a mainframe to a microcomputer should have the same classification as it does on the mainframe. The owner of a mainframe data file can identify the classification of that file.

Classifying Information and Applications

Not all information and applications require the same level of protection. To help determine and document the level of protection needed, all microcomputer information and applications should be classified by their owners according to the degree of loss, liability, or other damage to which the company would be exposed by their disclosure. All microcomputer information and applications should be assigned one of the following classifications:

- *General*—The information or application may be made available to any employee or nonemployee, because its disclosure to nonemployees poses no risk to the company (e.g., a table of state abbreviations).
- *Internal*—The information or application may be made available to any company employee, but not to anyone else without specific authorization by the data owner, because its disclosure to nonemployees could expose the organization to some risk. Examples of internal data include customer files, client lists, and internal telephone directories.
- *Confidential*—The information or application may be made available only to those specifically authorized by the owner, because its disclosure to unauthorized individuals could expose the company to some risk. Examples of confidential data include budget information, pre-release product information, and human resources files.
- *Highly sensitive*—The information or application may be made available only to a very limited number of employees because disclosure to unauthorized individuals could expose the company to significant risk. Highly sensitive data includes financial results before they are made public, business planning data, and government affairs data.

When classifying information and applications, the owner should ask the following questions:

- Is the handling of such information and applications governed by federal, state, or local law?
- Is the handling of such information and applications covered by specific company policy dictates?
- What is the time sensitivity of the information and applications?
- What is the potential financial, legal, competitive, or emotional effect from the disclosure or misuse of the information and applications?
- What is the potential damage to the reputation of the company or its employees, customers, or shareholders by the disclosure or misuse of the information and applications?
- What is the potential for fraud or other illegal action resulting from the disclosure or misuse of the information and applications?
- Are there any other factors that may affect the sensitivity of the information and applications?

The owner should classify information and applications according to the most sensitive information that they contain. All copies of information and applications should have the same classification as the originals.

Management in the department or office in which a microcomputer application resides should be responsible for establishing procedures to:

- Obtain classification information from the information owner.
- Ensure that all users of the information and applications are aware of the classification.
- Include the classification in all documentation about the application.
- Design and implement controls, based on data classification, in compliance with company microcomputer control policies and with control requirements established by information and application owners.

Business unit management and information owners should be responsible for reviewing the classification of microcomputer information and applications annually. They should also be responsible for re-evaluating the controls, based on the classifications, to ensure that the information and applications are adequately protected.

Information downloaded from the mainframe to a microcomputer should be classified and protected to prevent unauthorized access. Unclassified information and applications should be treated as internal.

Protecting Information on Diskettes and Hard Disks

Business unit management is responsible for ensuring that the information residing on microcomputer diskettes and hard disks is protected based on its classification and criticality. Business unit management is responsible for:

- Evaluating the specific access control needs of the information and applications within the department or field office, based on control requirements established by the owners of the information and applications.
- Providing appropriate hardware and software controls.
- Developing specific controls to meet control requirements established by information and application owners.
- Ensuring that proper controls are implemented through the policies established by business unit management and the owners of the information and applications.

Classifying Information and Applications

Each business area should develop its own procedures for classifying data on its microcomputers and network servers and for providing protection based on classification. The answers to the following questions can help determine how the information should be protected:

- Does the microcomputer process or store sensitive (i.e., confidential or highly sensitive) information?
- Are all users of the microcomputer authorized to view the sensitive information?
- Does the microcomputer have encryption or access control software that allows protection at the file, subdirectory, drive, or folder level?

Classifying by Filename. One way to classify data is by including a classification code within each filename. Files containing confidential or highly sensitive information should be protected with encryption or with access control software if individuals who are not authorized to view the information have access to the microcomputer on which that information is stored.

Classifying by Subdirectory or Folder. Rather than classifying individual data files, it may be simpler to separate files into subdirectories or folders based on classification and include a classification code in subdirectory or folder names. Subdirectories containing confidential or highly sensitive information should be protected with encryption or with access control software if individuals who are not authorized to view the information have access to the microcomputer on which that information is stored. If the microcomputer does not have encryption or access control software, sensitive data should be stored on a diskette rather than the hard disk. Diskettes containing confidential or highly sensitive information should be labeled with the classification of the information and placed in locked cabinets when they are not in use.

Classifying by Drive (Networks). Confidential and highly sensitive information may be placed on separately defined drives on a LAN. If not all users of the LAN are authorized to view the sensitive data, the LAN administrator should implement controls that limit access to only authorized users.

Protecting Information on Hard Disks

Hard disks should be protected by hardware and software access controls. For each microcomputer that processes confidential or highly sensitive information, one or more of the following hardware access controls should be implemented:

- *Door lock*—If the microcomputer is located within a dedicated or enclosed room, the door to the room should be locked except during business hours and, if practical, whenever the microcomputer is not in use.
- *Cabinet cover lock*—A cabinet cover lock encloses part or all of the microcomputer. It should be locked whenever the microcomputer is not in use.
- *Keyboard cover lock*—The cover encloses the keyboard and prevents access to the microcomputer through the keyboard. It should be locked when the microcomputer is not in use.
- *On/off switch lock*—An on/off switch lock prevents unauthorized persons from turning on the microcomputer. Some microcomputers have built-in switch locks. For other microcomputers, switch locks can be purchased and installed.

Microcomputers that process confidential or highly sensitive information should also be secured with passwords or keyboard cover locks when not attended by an authorized individual. Whenever any type of lock is used, a duplicate key should be available to authorized persons.

In addition to the hardware access controls, one or more software access controls should be implemented on each microcomputer that processes highly sensitive or confidential information. Some microcomputers have password capabilities that can provide security at the machine level (e.g., power-on passwords and keyboard passwords). If a microcomputer has these capabilities, they should be used. The need for these features should be evaluated before purchasing equipment.

An increasing number of licensed software packages include security features, the most common of which are passwords. Some programs require passwords for access to the software, but most provide password protection at the file level. These passwords are applied when creating or saving a file. The security features in licensed software should be used whenever access to data files must be restricted.

If application-level passwords are applied, it is important to ensure that whenever they are changed, all users of the file are informed of the new passwords. Before any licensed software is obtained, its security features should be evaluated. Special security software can also be purchased and installed to provide varying levels of security.

Log-on IDs and passwords provide multiple levels of security that limit the user's ability to use the microcomputer or the software on the microcomputer. Microcomputer users should avoid choosing passwords that can be easily guessed (e.g., the user's name, the name of a family member, the name of a hobby). Individual log-on passwords must be kept confidential.

Lockout features restrict users to specific programs or subdirectories. To implement these features, access levels must be defined for each user of the microcomputer.

Data encryption is a coding method that uses an encryption key (password) to encode data into a form that cannot be read or understood. The data is translated back into its original form only when the encryption key is supplied. Data encryption software is typically applied at the file level. Data encryption can also be handled by special encryption boards, which combine hardware and software features to provide encryption of all software and data on a microcomputer. Data encryption provides a high degree of access protection. Data encryption, through security software or encryption boards, is highly recommended for each microcomputer that processes highly sensitive information.

It is important to remember that erasing a data file only removes its name from the directory on a hard disk. The data remains on the hard disk and can be viewed through the use of special utility programs. Therefore, any confidential or highly sensitive data files must be encrypted or deleted from the hard disk if individuals who are not authorized to view them have access to the microcomputer.

It is also important to remember that when a hard disk malfunctions, the information on it may still be accessible. Precautions (e.g., not exposing the disk to a strong magnetic field) should be taken to prevent disclosure of the information to unauthorized individuals when replacing the disk.

PREVENTING UNAUTHORIZED ACCESS ON NETWORKS

Microcomputers can be connected to other computers in several ways: through local area networks (LANs), through dedicated lines and communications software, and through modems connected to other computer systems (e.g., microcomputers, mainframes, and LANs).

A LAN is a network of microcomputers and other peripheral equipment such as printers, plotters, and modems. By permitting data exchange and equipment sharing among microcomputer users, LANs offer such benefits as reduced equipment costs and increased efficiencies.

Businesses typically use one of two LAN configurations: LANs with dedicated file servers, in which the microcomputers and peripheral equipment are connected to a central microcomputer (i.e., a file server) dedicated to administering the network; and LANs without dedicated file servers, in which microcomputers are linked with one another, and any microcomputer can act as a file server.

A file server controls the network and is capable of storing common data and software. The file server is also commonly used as a central point for sharing peripheral equipment.

Users of microcomputers connected to local area networks or communicating with other computer systems should implement security measures to protect against unauthorized access to information and applications.

Local Area Networks

Business unit management and information owners should be responsible for implementing and monitoring LAN controls to prevent unauthorized access to data, software, microcomputers, and mainframe computers. Each LAN should have a LAN administrator, who is responsible for providing support to the LAN users and for the secure, efficient operation of the LAN. An IS function responsible for communicating LAN practices, procedures, upgrades, and other LAN information to LAN administrators should be identified. To ensure secure, efficient LAN operation, technical training should be provided for LAN administrators and users.

Connecting to Other Computer Systems

Controls should be implemented to protect against unauthorized access to corporate information through microcomputers connected to mainframes or to outside networks or services. Microcomputer users who download information from mainframes should be responsible for protecting the information from access by unauthorized individuals. Specifically, microcomputer users have the following responsibilities:

- Logging off mainframe sessions before leaving a microcomputer unattended.
- Refraining from hard-coding passwords into automatic log-on procedures.
- Complying with corporate controls for accessing the mainframe via modems.

Recommendations

The following recommendations explain the control objectives of the suggested policy and propose ways in which it may be implemented. Business unit management should review these recommendations, and select and implement controls appropriate to the business area. These recommendations apply to the transfer of information (by voice or any electronic means) using facilities such as telephone lines and satellites.

Information owners should be made aware that individuals granted read-only access to information stored on mainframes can download the information to microcomputers, where access controls may not be in effect to protect the information. Individuals given authorized access to confidential or highly sensitive information should not pass the information to any other user without authorization from its owner. To further guard against unauthorized access, microcomputer users should log off a mainframe (i.e., host) session before leaving their computers unattended in their office or in any other location (e.g., at home, in a hotel room, or in a conference room).

It should be a violation of company policy to program passwords into automated log-on procedures (i.e., procedures that provide quick log-on to a mainframe). Programming passwords into command procedures jeopardizes security because these passwords can be discovered by browsing command lists. These automated procedures might also enable an unauthorized user to access the mainframe under another user's log-on ID.

Microcomputer users who engage the services of outside networks or data bases should ensure that the vendors provide controls to prevent unauthorized access to the company's computer resources and information. To prevent unauthorized access to the outside services, users should also secure log-on IDs, passwords, and billing numbers.

All microcomputer controls described in this section also apply to LAN resources. The following section describes additional controls that should be implemented to prevent unauthorized access to information on a LAN.

Local Area Networks. The following controls pertain to all LANs, with or without dedicated file servers:

- Each area using a LAN should assign a LAN administrator with responsibility for properly controlling and securing the network.
- The LAN administrator should establish such security measures as password protection to restrict access on the network.
- LAN users should implement the password and lockout features of the LAN software to prevent unauthorized access to information on the LAN. (This is especially important on LANs that have no dedicated file server.)

For LANs with dedicated file servers, controls should also be implemented to meet these two objectives:

- Providing physical security for the LAN server (e.g., by restricting access to the server or by placing the server in a secured location).

- Controlling access to LAN resources through the LAN server.

The LAN administrator should restrict access to the network file server by implementing password protection. The file server password permits the user to activate the file server and therefore activate the network. Without the file server, other network workstations cannot access the file server's data.

The LAN administrator should establish controls on hard disk directories to prevent unauthorized access to information on the LAN. Through operating software on a LAN with a file server, users can be restricted to selected hard disk directories, based on a hierarchy that is defined by the LAN administrator. The LAN administrator can assign different levels of access to the various users of the network. For example, some users may be permitted to use only certain hard disks, while other users might have unrestricted access to all hard disks on the LAN.

Connecting to Other Computer Systems. Company procedures should address the security issues involved in using modems and other communications devices to access mainframe computers. With a dial-in security system, a user calls the security system and enters an access code. The system instructs the user to hang up and verifies the access code using information in a table. The system locates the user's telephone number in the table, calls the user back, and connects the user to the mainframe.

With a token security system, the user calls the security system and enters a number corresponding to the number provided by the token. A password is usually also required before the user is connected to the mainframe or the LAN.

Users accessing other computers should be required to use the password capabilities of the communications software. Passwords should be required of microcomputer users who perform remote job entry (RJE) to gain access to data files. Users of microcomputers connected to mainframes through a protocol coverter should be required to comply with mainframe security measures.

ENSURING INFORMATION AND APPLICATION INTEGRITY

To ensure the integrity and reliability of microcomputer-based information, controls should be implemented governing the development, testing, documentation, and modification of microcomputer applications. Controls should also monitor output from microcomputer applications.

Corporate management is responsible for ensuring that each business unit has procedures in place for the following tasks:

- Developing and modifying microcomputer applications.
- Testing microcomputer applications.
- Documenting microcomputer applications.
- Monitoring output from critical microcomputer applications.

Corporate management is also responsible for ensuring that these procedures comply with all the policies detailed in this chapter.

An IS unit should be responsible for providing consultation to business unit management for developing and maintaining these procedures. Corporate management, business unit management, and information owners share responsibility for ensuring the integrity of critical microcomputer applications.

Recommendations

The following sections explain the control objectives of the suggested policy and propose ways in which it may be implemented. Management should review these recommendations and select and implement controls appropriate to each business area.

Developing and Modifying Microcomputer Applications. Microcomputer applications used by either more than one business area or for production processing should be developed and maintained following formal systems development procedures. These procedures should be designed to ensure that the following objectives are met:

- The application is appropriate for development on a microcomputer.
- The application satisfies the business requirements of its users.
- The integrity of the information is maintained.
- Security requirements for the information are met.
- Changes to the system are documented and thoroughly tested to preserve the integrity of the information.
- The application is well documented for auditability and ease of maintenance.

An application may be considered used for production if it is processed regularly and if it meets one of the following criteria:

- It is complex or uses a large number of files.
- It creates data for other business systems or reports used by other business areas.
- It creates or modifies data for management or other financial data.
- Its accuracy is critical to the company.
- It is used in making critical business decisions.

Testing Microcomputer Applications. Each microcomputer application used by either more than one business area or for production processing should be tested to ensure the integrity and the reliability of the application. It should also be approved by the application owner to verify that it has been tested. For complex processing, final test results for each newly developed or modified application should be reviewed by an individual other than the developer.

Documenting Microcomputer Applications. The purposes of microcomputer documentation are to provide auditability, to aid individuals other than the developer in using an application, and to facilitate maintenance of the application. Documentation should include the following information:

- Application name.
- Department name.
- Author's name.
- Date on which development of the application was completed.
- List of input and output files and documents.
- Purpose of the application.
- Instructions for running the application.
- Copies of the programs.
- List of changes to the application.
- Test plan and procedures.
- Business recovery priority designation.
- Other appropriate information.

Documentation procedures should be tailored to meet the needs of the department.

Monitoring Output from Critical Microcomputer Applications. Business unit management should ensure that microcomputer output used in making business decisions is accurate and complete. Business unit management and information owners should monitor output from critical applications and ensure that corrections are made to applications producing erroneous or incomplete results.

The following techniques or procedures may be used for monitoring output to ensure the quality and integrity of the information:

- *Balancing and reconciliation*—Comparing the control totals with an outside source.
- *Analytical review*—Using such statistical measures as trends, ratios, or percentages to identify departures from expected or normal values.
- *Transaction calculation*—Verifying the accuracy of the output by calculating the information independently.

REDUCING THE RISK OF DAMAGE FROM COMPUTER VIRUSES

Computer viruses are programs that continually replicate by attaching themselves to other programs. They are spread from computer to computer through networks and by the sharing of data and disks or by the installating of new software. They may replicate on system files or any application program, including word processors, spreadsheets, drawing programs, and data base systems. A virus may destroy and damage data within a computer system. However, it may simply consume a computer's resources in such a way as to impair the computer's efficiency.

Viruses are most prevalent on microcomputers; however, mainframes are also susceptible to infection. A virus can enter a computer through several paths. Most viruses have entered computer systems through software obtained from such outside sources as bulletin board services, microcomputer user groups, and pirated software. The infection most frequently occurs through the use of an infected floppy disk.

Management and microcomputer users should take reasonable and prudent precautions to reduce the risk of losses from computer viruses.

Guidelines for Implementing the Suggested Policy

Management should be responsible for ensuring that microcomputer users understand the precautions that they should take to avoid or minimize the damage from virus infection. If a virus is suspected, microcomputer users should be responsible for:

- Leaving the microcomputer on and stopping processing immediately.
- Notifying the IS help desk or the EUC function.
- Notifying their management of the suspected problem.

The IS help desk or EUC should notify the Data Security and Business Recovery Planning departments that a virus infection is suspected. Viral infections can cause extensive and prolonged disruption of business operations.

Protecting Microcomputers from Viruses

Microcomputer users should be aware that viruses can damage data and system files critical to the company's capability to conduct business. To reduce the risk of infection and to minimize damage if infection occurs, the user should take the following precautions:

- Do not download information or programs from any bulletin board service.
- Whenever possible, purchase software through the company's purchasing agents. When it is impossible to order through the company's purchasing agents, purchase only factory-sealed software from a reputable vendor.
- As suggested by many software companies, before loading a new program, back up the microcomputer's hard disk, and write-protect the original master

diskette before inserting it into a drive. Do not run the application using the original master diskette. The original master diskette should be stored in a locked drawer or cabinet, away from the microcomputer location.

- Never accept illegal copies of software. To do so is a violation of US copyright laws and company policy.
- To restrict access and prevent installation of unauthorized or suspicious software on a microcomputer, take advantage of microcomputer locking devices and security software.
- Understand and abide by the company's policy on the ethical use of computer resources.

PREVENTING THEFT OF MICROCOMPUTER RESOURCES

Asset Identification with Property Tags

Property tags are helpful for identifying corporate microcomputer assets. Management should identify the department responsible for supplying property tags to be attached to all microcomputer hardware. To ensure that records are in agreement and that no equipment has been lost, stolen, or exchanged, the IS department should be responsible for verifying identification numbers periodically with business unit management. This process should be validated during an annual audit.

Building and Work Area Security

Corporate management should be responsible for providing a level of building security that minimizes the risk of theft of microcomputer resources.

Workstation Security

Business unit management should be responsible for evaluating the adequacy of controls provided by building and work area security. Business unit management should also be responsible for implementing additional controls, as needed. Microcomputer users are responsible for storing diskettes and manuals in locked drawers or cabinets. This control provides some protection against loss of data. Only off-site backup of microcomputer disks provides full protection from permanent loss of data if a microcomputer is stolen.

Protection of Portable Microcomputers

Business unit management should be responsible for establishing controls over the removal of corporate microcomputer resources from the department. Because of their size and portability, microcomputer resources are particularly vulnerable to theft. Several levels of control are necessary to protect these resources. These controls are described in the following sections.

Property Tags. Typically, property tags are attached to microcomputers by the company function responsible for managing fixed assets. In some companies, the EUC department has the responsibility for ensuring that the tags are attached. However, the tags are not always available before the equipment is sent to the department that will use the microcomputer resources. In such cases, the tags should be mailed to the department or office that ordered the equipment, and that department or office should be responsible for attaching them.

Building and Work Area Security. In some organizations, security guards are responsible for checking the identification of everyone who enters the building. In such locations, the security guards should be responsible for:

- Preventing unauthorized persons from entering the building or work area.
- Checking the authorization of anyone removing equipment from the building or work area.
- Verifying that removed equipment is accompanied by a property removal pass if removed from the facility by a nonemployee.

In buildings without security guards, an employee may be assigned responsibility for documenting removal of equipment from the building or work area. Whenever practical, doors to work areas where microcomputer resources are kept should be locked except during regular business hours.

Workstation Security. If building or work area security is inadequate to prevent theft or if heavy traffic through the area makes theft more likely, one of the following controls is recommended:

- An anchor, bolt, or locking device to secure the microcomputer hardware to the workstation.
- A locking cabinet to enclose the microcomputer hardware.
- A backplate or cover screw lock to prevent theft of boards.

Perhaps the most important workstation security control is a clean desk. Diskettes and paper containing internal, confidential, or highly sensitive information; critical information; or critical applications should be locked away when not in use.

Microcomputers small enough to be transported or easily concealed (e.g., a laptop computer in a briefcase) should be stored in locked cabinets, drawers, or other secured areas when not in use, or secured to the desk with cables and locks.

PROTECTING AGAINST ENVIRONMENTAL HAZARDS

Microcomputer resources should be protected from environmental hazards. Specifically, measures should be taken to protect microcomputer resouces from damage by water, excessive heat and humidity, power surges and static electricity, magnetic fields and X-rays, and contaminants such as dust, smoke, hair, food particles, and liquids.

Corporate management is responsible for providing environmental conditions that ensure against damage to microcomputer resources. Business unit management is responsible for the following tasks:

- Monitoring environmental conditions.
- Implementing environmental controls if necessary.
- Notifying corporate management of unacceptable conditions.
- Providing for general preventive maintenance of microcomputer hardware.
- Providing additional protection as needed.

Microcomputer users are responsible for:

- Executing environmental controls provided by management.
- Taking precautions to protect microcomputer resources from damage from food, liquids, smoke, and other contaminants.
- Protecting microcomputer resources that they remove from the office from damaging environmental conditions.

Protecting Against Water Damage

Although it is difficult to guard against water damage (e.g., from flooding or leaking pipes), the risk of loss from water damage can be minimized by regularly backing up data. If a microcomputer sustains water damage, it should not be turned on. If a microcomputer is damaged by water, the user should contact the IS help function or an automation coordinator. A company with experience in cleaning and certifying microcomputer equipment should be called to clean the equipment. Such companies should be identified during the business resumption planning process and documented in the business resumption plan.

Protecting Against Extremes in Temperature and Humidity

Office conditions are generally adequate for the safe operation of microcomputer equipment. Equipment taken out of the office should be protected from extremes in temperature and humidity. Specific protection measures may be detailed in the manuals accompanying the equipment.

Protecting Against Damage from Static Electricity

Static electricity can damage microcomputer resources. Static electricity problems in an office may result if humidity is too low. In such cases, a room humidifier may provide the proper humidity level. Most other commonly used methods, such as anti-static mats, strips, and sprays, have minimal effect against static electricity.

Protecting Against Power Surges

Surges in electrical current can damage microcomputer components and destroy data. Surges of electricity can be caused by inadequate wiring facilities, electrical storms, turning off high-energy-use appliances such as air conditioners and coffee pots, and various other factors that may cause electrical current to fluctuate.

The following devices may provide some protection against power surges and loss of power:

- *Surge suppressers*—A high quality surge suppresser will protect the microcomputer from power surges. Many manufacturers provide guarantees and compensation for any damage caused by the failure of a surge suppresser.
- *Line conditioners*—A line conditioner protects a microcomputer from "dirty" power (i.e., power spikes and surges). Line conditioners are relatively expensive (costing approximately $250), but offer some protection to a microcomputer.
- *Uninterruptible power supplies (UPSs)*—An uninterruptible power supply is an auxiliary power source connected to a microcomputer; it is activated in the event of a power loss. An UPS is recommended for any microcomputer that requires uninterrupted processing for critical information and applications as well as for applications in which power loss would create serious problems with processing completion or accuracy of the information. UPS can range in cost from hundreds to several thousands of dollars, depending on its capabilities.

Protecting Against Damage from Magnetic Fields and X-Rays

The magnetic nature of the disks on which software and data are stored makes them vulnerable to damage by contact with magnetic fields and by high dose X-rays. Magnetic fields can be created by magnets of any size, magnetized tools (e.g., magnetic paper holders, screwdrivers, magnetized paper clips), fluorescent lights, and motor-driven and electrical devices.

To reduce the risk of damage to microcomputer resources from magnetic fields and X-rays, microcomputer users can take the following steps:

- Keep all magnets and magnetized tools away from microcomputers and diskettes.
- Keep microcomputers and diskettes as far away from fluorescent lights as possible (diskettes should never be placed on top of a fluorescent light).
- Keep all motor-driven and electrical devices (including coffee pots and personal fans) at least two feet away from microcomputers and diskettes.
- Avoid sending microcomputers and diskettes through airport X-ray machines outside of the United States. US-based X-ray machines pose minimal risk to microcomputer data.

Protecting Against Damage from Contaminants

Microcomputers and diskettes are susceptible to damage or destruction from air impurities such as dust and smoke, hair, food particles, and spilled beverages. To reduce the risk of such damage, microcomputer users should take the following precautions:

- Avoid eating or drinking near a microcomputer keyboard. Keep all food and beverages far enough away from the microcomputer and diskettes that an accidental spill would not touch them. Spilling liquid on a diskette can destroy the diskette.
- Avoid smoking while using the microcomputer. Both smoke and ashes can damage microcomputer components.
- Cover the microcomputer when it is not in use if it is located in an area where dust or other air contaminants are a problem.

Preventive Maintenance

Microcomputer users should follow a regular program of preventive maintenance, including dusting and wiping equipment and cleaning the exterior of keyboards with a damp cloth.

WORKPAPER I9.01 Policies and Program Management

____ A steering committee from executive management has been established.

____ A working committee of business unit management has been established.

____ Policies related to the protection of information have been created.

____ Policies related to the protection of information have been published.

____ Sources of policies, guidelines, procedures, and technical procedures have been identified.

____ Sources of policies, guidelines, procedures, and technical procedures have been published.

WORKPAPER I9.02 Business Impact Analysis

____ The effect of loss of support of key internal functions dependent on microcomputers has been identified.

____ The business impact, additional expense, revenue loss, and embarrassment caused by the loss of the business functions have been identified and documented.

____ Business unit management has reviewed and approved the results of the business impact analysis.

____ Executive management has reviewed and approved the results of the business impact analysis.

____ Priorities have been established based on the business impact analysis, and the priorities have been approved by business unit management and executive management.

____ The business impact, additional expense, revenue loss, and embarrassment caused by the loss of applications have been identified and documented.

____ Management has reviewed and approved the results of the application impact analysis.

WORKPAPER I9.03 Training

____ A formal training program for information security and recovery of microcomputers has been developed.

____ Training of microcomputer users has been completed.

____ Terms used in information security and recovery are published.

____ User training on the use of backup software has been conducted.

____ Microcomputer services (i.e., internal or external support) personnel have been briefed or trained on the recovery process.

WORKPAPER I9.04 Information Backup Program and Facilities

____ Backup strategies for critical data have been defined and published.

____ Facilities for the storage of backup media have been established.

____ Data backup requirements have been identified.

____ Off-site data storage and retrieval procedures have been developed and published.

____ Backup facilities have been reviewed to determine their adequacy for protecting information.

____ Each backup facility has its own plan and resources to ensure that the stored data will be available if both the storage facility and the user organization are affected by the same incident.

____ Backup facilities and off-site storage locations for critical documentation and manuals have been identified.

____ Off-site storage locations and access procedures have been published.

WORKPAPER I9.05 Prevention

____ Antiviral programs are established in the company.

____ Business units having critical microcomputer data participate in the antiviral program.

Microcomputer programs and publications include:

____ Legal and ethical compliance standards.

____ Backup and recovery procedures.

____ Access protection.

____ Information and application integrity.

____ Virus infection protection.

____ Theft prevention.

____ Environmental hazards protection.

WORKPAPER I9.06 Recovery Planning

____ Users with online access have been identified.

____ Users without online access or LAN access (i.e., users of standalone microcomputers) have been identified.

____ Users dependent on dial-up or dial-out services have been identified.

____ Software and modem requirements of users connecting to outside services or facilities have been identified.

____ Microcomputer software and modems have been tested in the business recovery exercises.

____ Notification lists of key microcomputer recovery personnel have been developed.

____ Notification lists of key microcomputer recovery personnel have been published.

____ Mainframe, midrange, and LAN applications using microcomputers for access have been identified.

____ Applications requirements have been documented.

____ Dependencies and relationships with internal functions have been determined.

____ Dependencies and relationships with internal functions have been documented and reviewed by related business units.

____ Alternative sources to replace or augment key internal functions have been identified.

____ Alternative sources for key internal functions have been published, including contact names and telephone numbers.

____ All equipment has been identified, including microcomputers, printers, scanners, optical storage devices, and specialized monitors.

____ Equipment requirements have been documented.

____ Paper records (e.g., invoices, historical documentation) required by microcomputer users have been identified.

____ Paper record requirements have been documented.

____ Key vendors of services, equipment, and supplies have been identified.

____ Contact names and telephone numbers for key vendors have been documented.

____ Notification lists of key vendors have been published.

____ Vendor contracts have been established with specific performance requirements and vendor guarantees.

____ Key customers, contact names, and contact telephone numbers have been identified.

____ Each customer relationship and dependency has been identified and documented.

____ Notification lists of key customers, contact names, and contact telephone numbers have been published.

____ Critical procedures, manuals, and reports have been identified.

____ Critical procedures, manuals, and reports have been documented.

____ Interim operating strategies have been developed for continuing critical business functions without microcomputers.

____ Management has reviewed and approved the interim operating strategies.

WORKPAPER I9.07 Testing

____ Vendor performance is included in the testing of microcomputer recovery plans.

____ Test objectives and criteria have been developed to test microcomputer recovery.

____ Test objectives have been published.

____ Test planning assumptions have been developed and published.

____ Test results are formally critiqued and the results published.

____ Recovery exercises have involved the accessing and use of stored data.

____ The restoration of off-site data has been tested.

WORKPAPER I9.08 Business Resumption Plan Maintenance

____ Formal procedures exist to maintain the plan.

____ Formal update procedures exist to ensure required changes identified during tests are made to the microcomputer recovery plans.

II DATA CENTER RECOVERY

II DATA CENTER RECOVERY

DATA CENTER RECOVERY

PART

II

Part II of this book describes the planning efforts involved in developing the data center recovery plan (DCRP). This part of the book is indispensable for anyone who is responsible for developing a DCRP. It describes in detail the steps that need to be followed to develop the plan, and it provides the key questionnaires, forms, and checklists that can help ensure the plan is well-organized and thorough.

This material should also be useful for data center recovery planners who have taken over the responsibility for an existing DCRP. It can assist them in understanding why many of the recovery responsibilities, procedures, and checklists are contained in their DCRP. It can also be useful in evaluating an existing data center recovery plan to ensure that it is sufficiently comprehensive and employs the procedures and controls recommended here. Last, all business resumption planners should be familiar with the concepts and principles discussed in this section of the book in order to ensure the DCRP conforms with other components of the organization's overall business resumption plan.

The following sections provide a brief overview of each of the chapters of Part II.

INTRODUCTION TO DATA CENTER RECOVERY PLANNING

Chapter II-1 introduces the primary objectives and reasons for developing a data center recovery plan. It provides a brief history of data center recovery planning and reviews the organizational model and other key assumptions for recovery planning used in Part II. In short, this chapter sets the stage for introducing the phases for developing a data center recovery plan. These developmental steps are covered in Chapters II-2 through II-11.

DEVELOPING THE DATA CENTER RECOVERY PLAN

Chapter II-2 describes how to:

- Select the members of the development committee—this is the group that is primarily responsible for developing and documenting the DCRP.
- Establish the scope, the objectives, the premise, the level of detail, and the format to be used in documenting the plan.
- Determine the recovery logistics.

When establishing the scope of the plan, the development committee should clearly identify the areas to be covered in the plan as well as any areas that will not be covered.

In establishing the objectives of the DCRP, the development committee needs to address the different perspectives of data center management, end users of data center services, and the executive management committee of the company. Each has a different perspective on what the objectives should be. The development committee must also define the premise of the plan, meaning the assumptions regarding the readiness of the DCRP as well as the disaster scenario for which the plan has been developed. For example, assumptions may include availability of a computer backup site and thorough training and testing of recovery personnel. The disaster scenario might be a single isolated disaster or a regional disaster.

In considering the level of detail to be used in documenting the plan, the development committee should decide how detailed the DCRP manual needs to be. Some organizations prefer that it be kept simple and identify only what must be accomplished following a disaster and who is responsible for executing the recovery. Others prefer the plan to be more detailed, including specific procedures for performing recovery responsibilities.

The format or organization of the recovery plan documentation must also be decided to ensure the plan covers all necessary topics. The development committee must also resolve certain logistical issues related to basic recovery activities. These include damage assessment, notification, equipment replacement, procurement of recovery material and facilities, recovery of data, and transportation of personnel and material to the backup sites after a disaster.

ORGANIZING THE DCRP DEVELOPMENT PROJECT

Chapter II-3 presents an organizational framework for developing the DCRP. The development committee conducts a series of meetings with the designated recovery teams—individually at first and later in groups—to develop recovery procedures, identify responsibilities, and gather information essential to completing the plan. The development committee determines the information that needs to be collected and assigns to team members the task of gathering this information. Various data gathering forms are used to collect this information—samples are provided as workpapers. Recovery team members later review this information to ensure it is accurate and complete. At the conclusion of the planning project, a turnover meeting is held in which the DCRP is formally presented. Maintenance and training exercises are also planned and scheduled to ensure the DCRP remains current and can be executed as planned.

The next three chapters of Part II provide detailed information on the roles and procedures for each of the major recovery teams beginning with the recovery headquarters team, described next.

THE RECOVERY HEADQUARTERS TEAM

The recovery headquarters team is one of the three data center recovery teams, the others being the computer operations recovery team and the disaster site recovery team. The recovery headquarters team is responsible for internal and external notification and communication activities as well as the administrative support activities that will be needed throughout the disaster recovery operation.

THE COMPUTER OPERATIONS RECOVERY TEAM

The computer operations recovery team is responsible for performing the recovery activities that take place at the computer backup site. This team is made up of experts in systems and applications software, tape operations, data bases, and communications. Its responsibilities are to return services to end users on a timely basis. Team members perform such actions as recovery of systems and applications software, recovery of data bases, and retrieval of backup data from the off-premises storage facility. The

DCRP must describe the actions to be followed in notifying team members of a disaster, transporting the team to the backup site, managing and performing all critical recovery operations, and completing the shutdown of the backup site. Each team leader has a unique set of responsibilities which must be clearly defined in the plan.

THE DISASTER SITE RECOVERY TEAM

The disaster site recovery team is responsible for performing recovery activities at the site of the disaster. This team consists of specialists in facility damage assessment and restoration, equipment damage assessment and salvage, and communications recovery. The team's responsibilities include assessment of damage to facilities, equipment, and supplies, repair or relocation of the damaged facility, replacement or repair of equipment and supplies, and preparation for return of data center operations to the original data center site (if applicable). The DCRP should include procedures detailing the steps to be taken to notify the team of the disaster, coordinate the necessary support at the disaster site, manage and perform assessment activities, and communicate with internal and external entities on the progress of the recovery effort. The facility restoration team leader may also need to assist in finding a temporary data center that meets predesignated criteria established in the plan.

DEVELOPING THE INITIAL DISASTER ALERT PROCEDURE

As described in Chapter II-7, the initial disaster alert procedure addresses the decision-making process from the time data center representatives are notified until the decision is made to activate (or not activate) the DCRP. This procedure establishes who notifies the IS recovery management team of a disaster, who on the team is to be notified, how to verify that the disaster requires activation of the DCRP, and who has authority to activate the recovery plan. The initial disaster alert is important for companies that have determined they would suffer a serious loss if their computers were not quickly operational following a disaster and that have contracts with commercial hot-site vendors or have established their own in-house backup sites.

PERFORMING AN APPLICATIONS IMPACT ANALYSIS

The applications impact analysis is a process used to identify the impact on the organization of not being able to process a computer application as scheduled. It is performed in order to identify which applications are critical to the company and which are less critical. The impact analysis provides information that can be useful in developing the computer backup site strategy. For example, if the results of the impact analysis indicate that an application cannot be delayed long beyond its scheduled processing point without causing a significant negative impact, use of a hot site may be justified. Chapter II-8 describes how to perform the applications impact analysis and provides a sample questionnaire to be used in the analysis.

SELECTING A COMPUTER PROCESSING RECOVERY STRATEGY

An organization can select from a number of strategies for resuming computer processing following a disaster or business interruption affecting the data center. The options include use of a commercial hot site, company-owned backup site, reciprocal agreement, and cold site. Companies that need immediate processing may choose a computer hot site. Companies that do not have an immediate processing need may choose a reciprocal agreement or a cold site. Chapter II-9 assesses the strengths and weaknesses of each of these options.

PROTECTING AND RECOVERING COMPUTER DATA

Chapter II-10 discusses the protection and recovery of data. This is the most important element in the DCRP, because without the data, the recovery operation will fail. The chapter discusses the rotation of backups to the off-premises storage location and the reconstruction steps needed to bring the backup data to a satisfactory point for the user of the application.

TESTING THE DATA CENTER RECOVERY PLAN

Chapter II-11 describes how to test, exercise, and maintain the DCRP. After the DCRP is documented and tested to ensure it works, the plan then moves to a maintenance and exercise phase. The DCRP coordinator needs to establish a policy for plan maintenance; this usually involves reviews and updates on at least a quarterly basis.

The plan should also be flexible enough to allow recovery teams to update their section of the plan whenever a significant change has occurred. For example, changes in routine computer operations may occur frequently during the quarter, and some of these changes may affect the DCRP. These changes should be reflected in the DCRP as soon as possible after they occur.

Introduction to Data Center Recovery Planning

CHAPTER

II-1

Chapter II-1 introduces data center recovery planning concepts and sets the stage for the development project, which is covered in Chapters II-2 through II-11. Chapter II-1 introduces:

- The definition of data center recovery planning and how it differs from business resumption planning.
- The history of data center recovery planning.
- Reasons for developing the DCRP.
- Development assumptions.

DEFINITION OF A DATA CENTER RECOVERY PLAN

The data center recovery plan (DCRP) consists of documented plans and procedures that will be employed by key information systems personnel following a disaster for the express purpose of resuming data center operations in an organized and timely manner. The DCRP lists the documented recovery responsibilities the data processing personnel should carry out. It also documents the resources needed to carry out these responsibilities. These resources include recovery plan procedures, checklists, and forms.

Disaster. Although a disaster is defined in the dictionary as a sudden, calamitous event bringing great damage, loss, or destruction, a disaster will be defined in the DCRP as any extended interruption to data center operations. The interruption can be from physical damage to the building or the data center contents, but it does not have to be. The term *disaster* will be used to indicate any situation in which computer services have suffered an interruption that may extend beyond an acceptable time frame. The following are examples of disasters:

- A hardware failure that causes data center operations to be interrupted over an extended period of time.
- A power company suffers a disaster on its premises, causing an interruption of its services and resulting in a data center outage, similar to the Consolidated Edison substation fire in New York City on August 13, 1990.
- A telephone company suffers a disaster on its premises, causing an interruption of services and resulting in a data center outage, similar to the Illinois Bell Telephone Company fire in Hinsdale IL on May 8, 1988.

Acceptable Time Frame. The definition of an "acceptable time frame" varies among companies. To one company, the acceptable time frame may be one day; to another, it may be five days. Each recovery planner must identify the acceptable time frame for the specific company.

The DCRP contains the recovery responsibilities for data center personnel primarily, but it also includes information as to the support role of both the executive management committee and the staff departments.

Executive Management Committee. The executive management committee is the group of senior executives that deal with all of the major crises that face the company. Although they are not directly involved in the data center recovery operation, they need to be kept informed of its progress throughout. The committee intervenes only when the situation warrants it.

Staff Departments. The staff departments include corporate security, building services/engineering, public relations, human resources, insurance, legal, and purchasing. They are directly involved in assisting the data center during the recovery operation. The DCRP identifies who in each staff department should be notified if there is a disaster and what support they will provide. The DCRP does not document how they will provide the support; that information is included in the companywide business resumption plan.

The Difference Between Data Center Recovery Planning and Business Resumption Planning

The business resumption plan (BRP) consists of documented plans and procedures that will be employed by key company personnel following a disaster for the express purpose of resuming business operations in an organized and timely manner. The BRP contains documented business resumption responsibilities for all departments in the company (i.e., the revenue-generating departments, the staff departments, and the executive management committee). The BRP is covered in detail in Part I of this book. The DCRP is just one component of the overall plan for crisis management. (See Exhibit II-1-A.)

The Data Center Recovery Plan Model

The data center is one of the divisions of the data processing department or the more commonly used term today, the information systems (IS) department. The responsibilities of the IS department include the data center, as well as communications, personal computers, and local area networks. Communications recovery planning issues are covered in Part III of this book; the personal computer and local area network issues are covered in Part I. This part of the book addresses the remaining divisions related to data center recovery.

There is no single IS department organization common to all companies. The organization model that is used in Part II assumes that the IS department comprises five divisions:

- Systems programming.
- Data center operations.
- Applications programming.
- Data base.
- Communications.

The vice-president of information systems manages the department; each of the five divisions is managed by a director. (See Exhibit II-1-B.)

The systems programming division consists of a director and the teams responsible for each of the major operating systems; each team is supervised by a manager. The data center operations division consists of a director and various teams, each supervised by a manager. (See Exhibit II-1-C.)

EXHIBIT II-1-A PLAN COMPONENTS FOR CRISIS MANAGEMENT

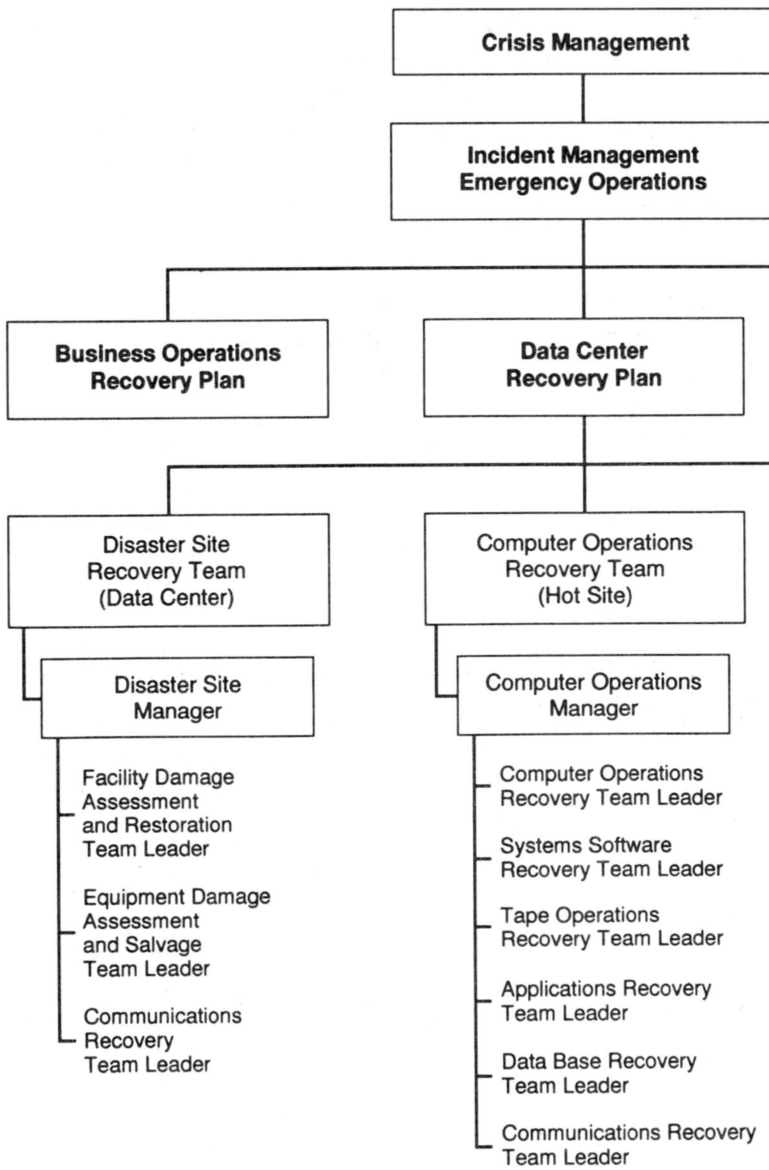

The applications programming division consists of a director and teams for each major application systems (e.g., a financial systems team). The data base division consists of a director and a staff of data base specialists. Last, the communications division consists of a director and two teams—the data communications team and the voice communications team—each of which is supervised by a manager. This model IS department is the subject of the DCRP that is developed in Part II.

HISTORY OF DATA CENTER RECOVERY PLANNING

Data centers throughout the United States started documenting formal recovery plans in 1973. Before 1973, certain segments of the plan were developed, but not complete DCRPs. For example, the data center division of an IS department typically documented

EXHIBIT II-1-B INFORMATION SYSTEMS DEPARTMENT

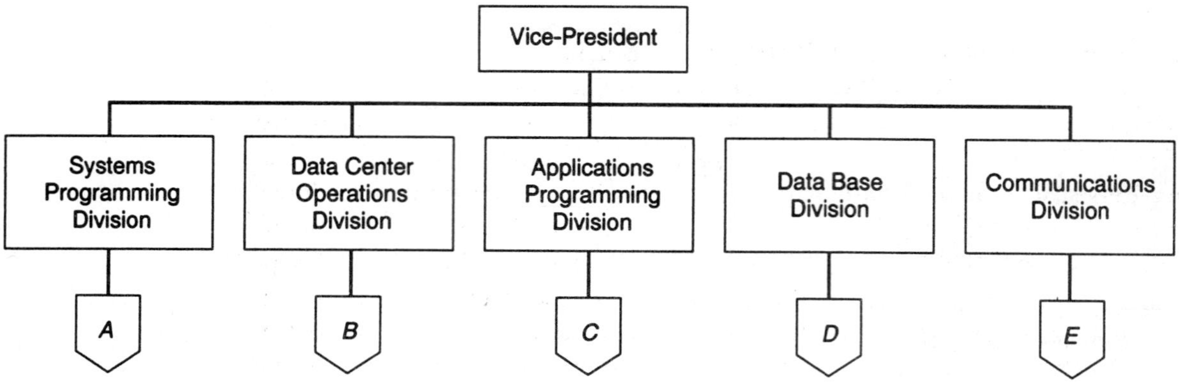

EXHIBIT II-1-C DATA CENTER OPERATIONS DIVISION

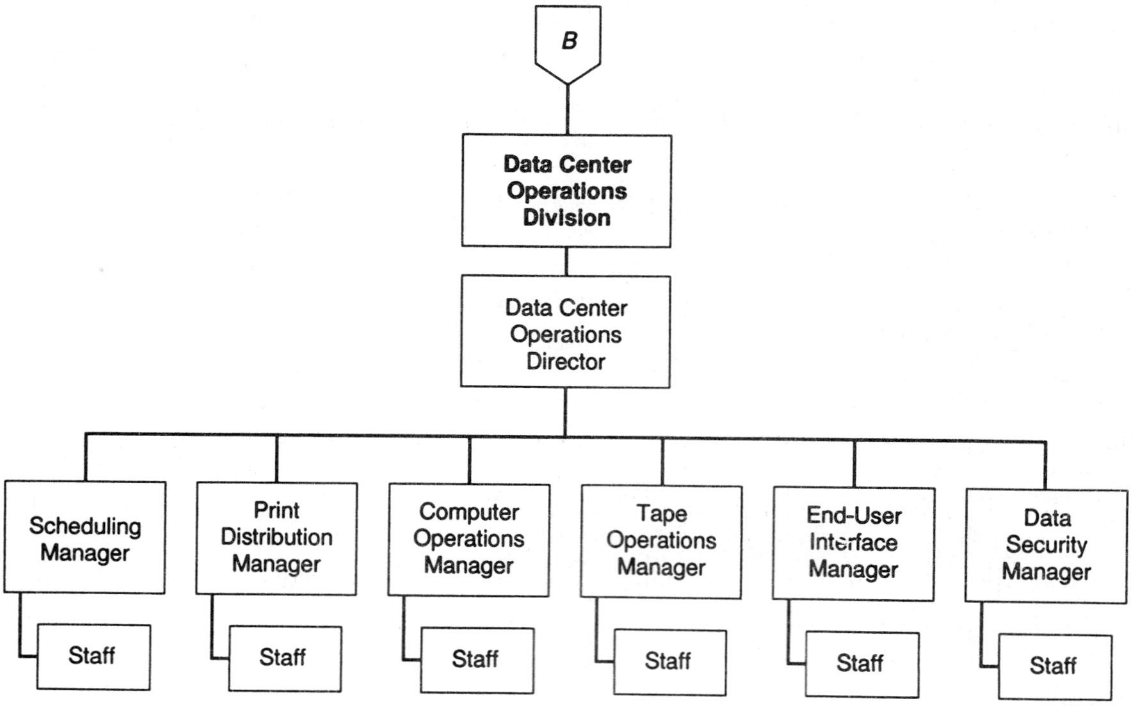

its role in a data center recovery operation, but the systems and the applications programming divisions did not. As these divisions began to prepare recovery plans, they often failed to synchronize them with the other divisions' plans. This situation created the demand for documented, formal plans so that all divisions could establish a uniform set of recovery objectives.

The data center was the focal point for the development of disaster recovery plans during the 1970s, because the revenue-generating departments of most companies needed to provide information to, or obtain information from, the data center in order to accomplish their business objectives. Because the data center was responsible for the processing of this information, it had to developed plans to minimize the length of time the computer would be unable to provide access to this information.

The Evolution of Data Center Recovery Planning: 1970s to 1990s

There are several differences between the DCRPs of the 1970s and the 1990s. First, if a data center was disabled by a disaster in the early 1970s, it would not have prevented the company from performing its essential business functions. Because the computer usually typically acted as an after-the-fact bookkeeper, the business functions would still have been performed; the company could have delivered its product or services, although it would suffer from late billing of customers and the late receipt of receivables. During the 1990s, the disabling of the data center can prevent a company from completing many of its essential business functions. The impact of the interruption could result in a significant loss of revenue, profits, and company credibility.

A second difference is that computer environments of the 1990s are much more complex than they were during the 1970s. During the 1970s, data centers operated in a batch environment. The end users' work was carried into the data entry area, where it was keyed; the keyed input was then sent to the schedulers, who submitted it for processing. After the completion of processing, it was sent to quality control, where it was balanced to the control figures. The output would then be picked up by or delivered to the end user.

If there were a disaster, the end users' work could be taken to another data entry location for keying. (If there were no other data entry locations available, it could be taken to a data entry service bureau or to the computer backup site.) The keyed input would be sent to the schedulers at the computer backup site, where it would be submitted for processing. After processing, it would be sent to quality control, either at the computer backup site or recovery headquarters, where it could be balanced to the controls. The output would then be delivered to the end user.

Data centers of the 1990s operate in an online environment. End users work directly on workstations; the data is sent to the data center electronically. The end user can call up programs remotely to process the input. After processing, the output is sent back to the end user electronically. Such online environments require that complex technical issues be addressed and implemented before a disaster occurs. When a disaster causes an interruption to the data center's processing, the applications must move to a computer backup site. Such an environment requires several technical issues to be addressed, including ensuring:

- The backup site has compatible hardware, processors, disk drives, and tape drives.
- There is sufficient disk space to bring up the operating systems and utilities and run the applications.
- The operating systems and utilities can be loaded.
- Application data files can be loaded onto the disk space provided by the backup site.
- Application data files can be reconstructed from the time of backup of the off-premises tapes to the time of the disaster.
- Data already processed earlier in the day but destroyed before it could be backed up and sent off-premises can be reentered.
- End-user workstation data communications lines can be switched into the backup site.

- The security concerns of critical data in a dial-up network environment are addressed.

The good news is there are now more resources available to help deal with these complex issues. First, there are commercial hot sites. (Hot sites will be discussed in detail in Chapter II-9.) Although such hot sites can meet the needs of most companies today, they cannot meet the disk space and communications requirements of the largest data centers.

Second, testing procedures can help ensure that there is sufficient disk space at the backup hot site for loading of operating systems, utilities, and application data files. During such testing, the reconstruction of application data files can also be verified. (The recovery of data and the problems associated with hot-site testing is covered in Chapter II-9.) Third, electronic vaulting can be used to send current transactions off-premises immediately after they are received by the data center.

The final difference in recovery planning between the 1970s and 1990s is that the recovery plans of the 1970s did not address end users, staff departments, and executive management. Data center personnel felt that if a disaster did strike, they would be the only group in the company prepared to respond. (They often complained that they would be up and running, but they would not have anything to process, because they were the only group in the company that had done any planning.) The DCRPs of the 1990s include planning sessions with end users, the staff departments that will support the recovery operation, and members of the executive management team that will oversee operation. These planning sessions help the rest of the organization in preparing its overall resumption plan.

Importance of the Data Center Today

With increased use of microcomputer-based LANs, the question of the importance of today's data center is often raised. There is no doubt that local area networks have had an impact on the role of the data center in the organization. As local area networks become entwined in wide area networks, however, they often communicate with each other through the data center's mainframe. In many respects, the data center remains the heart of the organization, sending information that allows the company head to make decisions and offices and factories to perform specific functions.

REASONS FOR DEVELOPING THE DCRP

There are four potential catalysts that generate a company's need to develop the DCRP:

- There is a regulatory requirement for the company to have a DCRP.
- The company believes that it could be held liable by its clients or customers for not having one.
- The company is aware of a recent disaster to a company in the same geographic area or industry.
- The company believes that the impact from an extended business outage to the data center is too risky.

Regulatory Requirements. First, companies develop the DCRP to be in compliance with regulations governing their industry. For example, the banking industry has had regulations requiring the documentation of a DCRP since May 1983, when BC-177 was issued by the Comptroller of the Currency, requiring all national banks to have a DCRP. This regulation may have been the result of a fire that extensively damaged the headquarters building of Norwest Bank in Minneapolis MN in November 1982.

The initial version of the BC-177 regulation indicated that the DCRP was needed for any areas of the bank that contained computers. A later version added any areas of the bank that had such electronic equipment as terminals that connect to a mainframe or minicomputer. Currently, this requirement covers any essential business operations of the bank regardless of whether there are any computers.

Liability. Companies have also indicated that a DCRP can help them defend against litigation from customers or clients, even if the plan did not work.

Recent Disaster. Many companies have begun a DCRP project just after a disaster has occurred in their area or to a company in their business. For example, several insurance companies developed or strengthened their DCRPs after the Penn Mutual Insurance Company fire in Philadelphia PA on May 30, 1989. (A contributing factor might have been the public acknowledgment that the fire was caused by an arsonist who was able to gain access to an area restricted by an access control system.)

Impact Analysis. Many companies have analyzed what the business impact would be if the data center were not operational for an extended period of time. This is the most common reason executive management is willing to provide a budget for this process. The results of a comprehensive business impact analysis and a data center application impact analysis often prompt the executive committee to require the development of a data center recovery plan. The business impact analysis analyzes the impact on the company if any of the business functions suffer an extended interruption. The application impact analysis analyzes the impact on the application owner, or any end user, if the data center cannot process a specific computer application for an extended period of time. Typically, other high-profile areas of the company are also required to develop a plan shortly after the data center is.

RECOVERY PLAN DEVELOPMENT ASSUMPTIONS

Because potential recovery issues are related to the size of a company, the size of its data center, the type of disaster, and the level of damage caused by the disaster, the following parameters have been used to structure subsequent chapters:

- The location of the data center is in a separate building from the corporate headquarters.
- The corporate headquarters houses the executives, the staff departments, and the data center end users. The executive personnel are the key officers of the company that have final decision-making authority. The staff department personnel manage departments that are responsible for such functions as corporate security, human resources, public relations, insurance, legal, purchasing, and transportation. These are departments that contribute to the successful operation of the company but do not generate revenue for the company. The data center end users are departments that use the data center mainframe to process information that is used in generating revenue and is essential to their day-to-day operations.
- If the computer center is in the same building as the corporate headquarters, the company must consider the companywide planning elements mentioned in Part I of this book.
- The data center organization that the DCRP is being developed for is as presented in this chapter. It is large enough to staff the different teams that are covered in the various chapters of Part II. For small companies, it may be necessary

to combine the responsibilities of two or more teams into one team. If a suggested team is not needed, it can be eliminated.

- The disaster scenario for the DCRP that is covered in Part II of this book is as follows:
  - —A disaster has occurred causing physical damage to the computer and data communications network equipment, resulting in the inability to use the computer center to support business operations.
  - —The disaster is isolated in the building housing the data center and communications network. (Regional or local disaster logistics are discussed as exceptions.)
  - —The data center is inaccessible following the disaster and may remain inaccessible for an extended period of time.
  - —The data files, supplies, and forms located inside the data center have been damaged or destroyed.
  - —Key data center personnel have not been injured in the disaster and are available to perform the required recovery actions.

This disaster scenario will be discussed in detail in Chapter II-2.

Developing the Data Center Recovery Plan

CHAPTER II-2

Chapter II-1 introduced the concept of the data center recovery plan (DCRP); Chapter II-2 presents the steps to be used in developing the plan. These steps are summarized in Exhibit II-2-A.

Chapter II-2 begins by discussing the process used in selecting members of the development committee and the purpose for establishing the scope, objectives, and premise of the DCRP. This chapter describes how to establish the appropriate level of detail and the format to be used in documenting the DCRP. Chapter II-2 also presents what recovery actions should be included in the plan, who will be assigned the responsibilities, and how the responsibilities will be performed. These are referred to as the recovery logistics.

Chapter II-3 discusses the remaining two steps shown in Exhibit II-2-A. Chapter II-3 describes the procedure to be used in organizing the DCRP development meetings. This chapter concludes with a discussion of common mistakes made during the development cycle that either lengthen the total process or may cause the project to come to an unsuccessful conclusion.

SELECT MEMBERS OF THE DEVELOPMENT COMMITTEE

STEP 1

The first step in developing the DCRP is selecting the development committee. The development committee is composed of the personnel that have been selected to work on the development and documentation of the DCRP.

The selection of who will be on the development committee is important, because this team participates in the development, documentation, implementation, and testing phases of the DCRP project. This group decides on the recovery strategies, the resources, and the procedures that will be used in the recovery program.

The DCRP can be thought of as a chain made up of strong links (the recovery teams) connected to one another. The recovery teams work together to provide a strong resource during a recovery operation, just like the links work together to form a strong chain.

If the person selected to be the representative for a particular division on the development committee is too busy to give the project sufficient time, that team's section of the plan may be a weak link, and a chain is only as strong as its weakest link. Unless all links in the recovery plan are strong, the chain will be likely to break, resulting in a recovery operation that is neither organized nor timely.

The DCRP coordinator initiates the process of selecting the development committee. The DCRP coordinator is the representative of the IS department head who has been given the primary responsibility and authority for carrying out the recovery planning project.

EXHIBIT II-2-A THE DCRP DEVELOPMENT STEPS

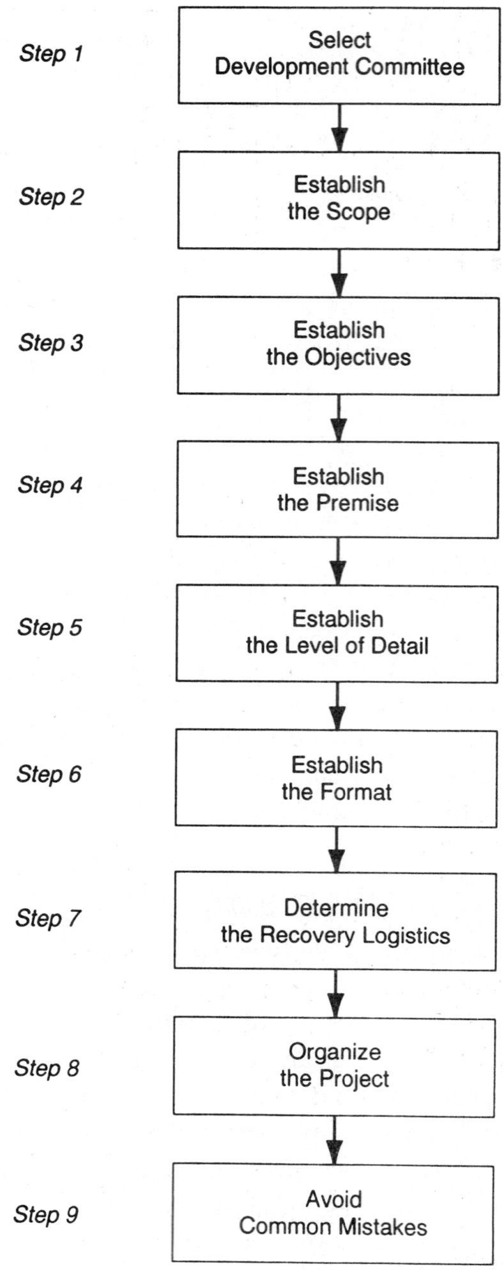

The DCRP coordinator should first obtain an organization chart of the IS department. (See Exhibit II-2-B.) The DCRP coordinator then meets with the head of the IS department and the directors of the divisions to determine who should represent each division on the development committee and what recovery teams will be drawn from each division. As shown in Exhibit II-2-B, the directors are from systems programming, data center operations, applications programming, data base, and communications divisions.

After the directors have designated their choices for the development committee and selected the recovery teams from each division, they should identify which person-

EXHIBIT **II-2-B** INFORMATION SYSTEMS DEPARTMENT

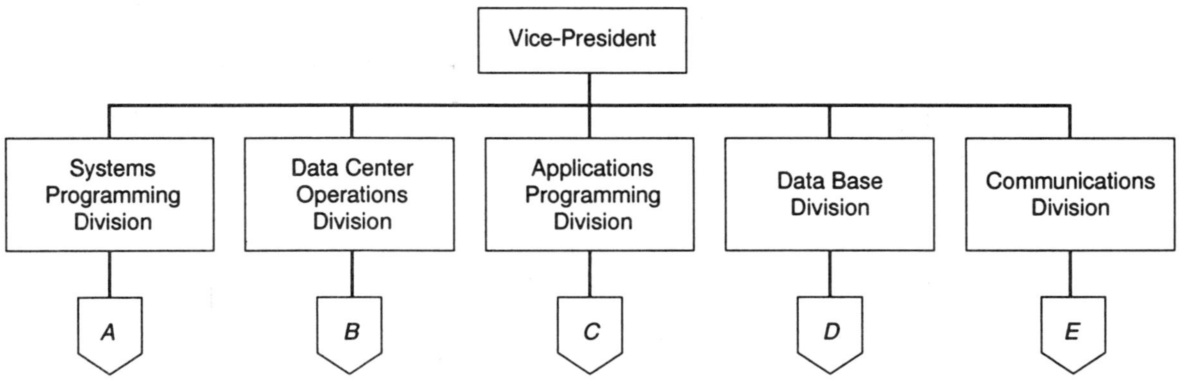

nel will be the recovery team leaders—those with primary recovery team leader responsibilities—and those who will be their alternates or backups. An overview of the major recovery teams is presented in Exhibit II-2-C.

The DCRP coordinator and the development committee will meet with the recovery team leaders and their alternates several times during the development phase of the project—for example, during the formal kickoff meeting, during individual recovery team meetings, and during any multiple team meetings. These meetings are discussed in detail in Chapter II-3. The DCRP coordinator should then meet with the development committee representatives to establish the scope, objectives, premise, level of detail, format, and logistics that will be used in the DCRP.

ESTABLISH THE SCOPE FOR THE DCRP

STEP 2

One of the first steps the development committee takes is to establish the scope of the DCRP. In the DCRP project, the term *scope* refers to establishing the range of operation the DCRP will cover. The DCRP consists of documented plans and procedures that will be employed by key IS personnel following a disaster for the express purpose of resuming data center operations in an organized and timely manner. The critical word is *following,* as opposed to before or during. Those elements that deal with plans and procedures to be employed before and during are parts of other corporate plans. For example, building evacuation procedures may be used during a disaster.

Areas Covered by the DCRP Scope

The scope of the DCRP addresses the responsibilities of data center personnel from the time they are notified of the disaster to the time the data center returns to a normal environment and the DCRP is terminated. These responsibilities are defined by the initial disaster alert procedure, disaster site recovery logistics, backup site operations logistics, and recovery headquarters logistics. The term *logistics* as used in the DCRP means the preplanning for the procurement of recovery resources and material and for the transportation of personnel and resources.

How to Identify the Scope

To identify the elements in the scope, for the DCRP coordinator and the development committee should start with the groups that make up the IS department (as shown

EXHIBIT **II-2-C** MAJOR RECOVERY TEAMS

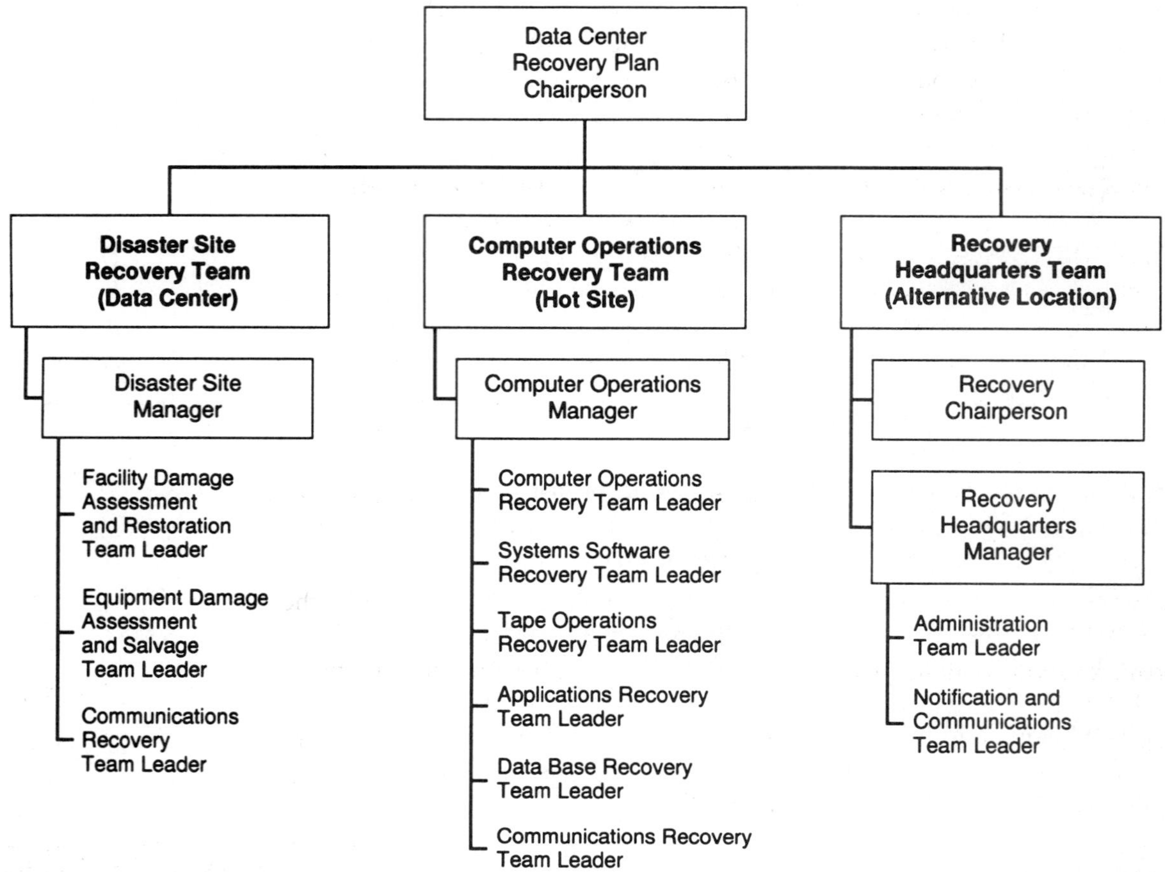

in Exhibit II-2-B). Each of these groups has a role in preparing for the recovery of their area should a disaster strike the department.

For example, the development committee should determine from the data center operations director whether there are any computers housed inside the computer center that are controlled (owned or leased) by other departments. If so, who is responsible for their recovery following a disaster? If they are controlled by the departments that own or lease them, and not by the data center, they should be covered by the business resumption plan (BRP) for that department. If they are controlled by the data center, their repair or replacement is the responsibility of the data center. Another key concern in this type of situation is identifying who is responsible for backing up and protecting the data on these computers: in some cases, it is the department that owns or leases the computer; in others, it is the data center. This should be clarified and clearly documented in the scope.

Areas Not Covered by the DCRP Scope

It is also important for the scope to identify any areas that will not be included in the range of operations covered by the DCRP. The following are some examples of areas not usually addressed within the scope of the DCRP:

- The plans and procedures dealing with situations before a disaster occurs that are intended to minimize the potential for a disaster to occur. That is usually the day-to-day responsibility of the corporate security and corporate buildings services departments. These departments are responsible for minimizing exposures and implementing plans and procedures to accomplish this.

- The policies and procedures that deal with situations during a disaster—for example, attempting to extinguish a fire; evacuating a building; searching for a bomb following a bomb threat; and evacuation to the center of a building during a tornado. These procedures are established as part of emergency response plans. The person responsible for the emergency response plans is either the corporate safety officer or the head of the human resources department. They are the management representatives who have the responsibility to establish the corporate policies on what employees should do during dangerous situations. This includes procedures as to what they should do if they are at work when the disaster occurs and policies on what they should do if they are not at work at the time of an areawide disaster (e.g., earthquake or hurricane).
- Computers installed outside the data center.
- Data centers in other countries.
- The way in which end-user departments react to a disaster that has affected the data center. All end users should have documented how they will temporarily perform their business functions in the BRP.
- The way in which end-user departments resume their business operations if the disaster strikes their department. The end-users procedures to address how the department will continue their business operations is part of the BRP, not the DCRP.

A benefit of clearly documenting the scope is that it clarifies for executive management which areas are covered in the DCRP and which are not. This can eliminate the problem of executive management assuming the DCRP will be used to recover a department other than the data center. An example of the DCRP scope is provided in Workpaper II2.01.

ESTABLISH THE OBJECTIVES FOR THE DCRP

STEP 3

The next step the development committee should take is to establish the objectives of the DCRP. The term *objective* as used in the DCRP project means the goals toward which the DCRP are directed.

There are two types of objectives. The first are the company's objectives. The company's objectives are documented in the DCRP. The second type of objectives are those of participants—for example, objectives of the data center operations director, data center's end users, and executive management. The participants' objectives help determine the strategies and procedures that will be incorporated in the DCRP.

The Company's Objectives

The company's objectives of the DCRP are usually to:

- Limit the magnitude of any loss by minimizing the duration of the interruption of processing to the critical applications.
- Assess damage to the data center facilities and equipment and repair the damage.
- Recover data center information critical to the operation of the company.
- Manage the recovery operation in an organized and timely manner.
- Prepare data center personnel to respond effectively in a recovery situation.

- Prepare the staff departments to provide support during a data center recovery operation.

Limit the Magnitude of Any Loss. In order to limit the magnitude of any loss, the DCRP should have a section that minimizes the duration of the interruption of processing critical applications. This can be accomplished by including a computer backup site strategy in the DCRP that allows the data center to resume the processing of critical applications quickly.

Assess Damage to the Data Center. In order to assess damage to the data center facilities and equipment and repair the damage, the DCRP should have a section that identifies how data center personnel will assess damage to the facilities and equipment and how they will arrange for repairing the damage.

Recover Data Center Information. In order to recover data center information critical to the operation of the company, the DCRP should have a section that identifies how backups of critical information are protected, where they are protected, how they will be retrieved, and how they will be reprocessed and reconstructed.

Manage the Recovery Operation. In order to manage the recovery operation in an organized and timely manner, the DCRP should have a section that identifies what has to be done during the recovery operation, who should do it, and how they should do it.

Prepare Data Center Personnel to Respond. In order to prepare the data center personnel to respond effectively in a recovery, they need to be adequately trained and be given the opportunity to exercise their recovery responsibilities on a periodic basis.

Prepare the Staff Departments. In order to prepare the staff departments to provide support during a data center recovery operation, they should be trained adequately and should participate in periodic exercises.

The Participants' Objectives

When asked what objectives the DCRP should meet, the data center end users have one answer in mind, executive management another, and the data center director yet another. End users typically want the DCRP to provide a means to return the data center to processing end-user applications within hours of the time the interruption occurred. The data center operations director also wants the DCRP to provide a means to return the data center to processing quickly by using the best backup site strategy available—for example, a duplicate computer with the same configuration down to the disk and tape drives. Although this may be the perfect technical solution, it is usually the most costly. The executive management committee also wants the DCRP to provide a means to have the data center return to processing quickly but is concerned with using the most cost-effective backup site strategy.

Reaching Agreement on the Objectives

Despite this seeming impasse, companies are able to resolve these differences through negotiation.

Executive Negotiation. Presenting executives with the results of the applications impact analysis may help them realize that the least expensive solution for a computer backup site may not be in the best interest of the company if it results in the company losing money, credibility, and customers. They are then more open to alternatives. For example, the reciprocal backup site agreement is generally considered the most cost-effective solution; an alternative is the commercial hot site. Although a commercial hot site costs more than the reciprocal agreement, it costs less than a duplicate or near-duplicate in-house site.

Data Center Operations Director Negotiation. Presented with the need to have the most cost-effective backup site strategy (e.g., a reciprocal backup site agreement), the data center director may respond that this solution will not meet the end users' objectives because it does not allow the data center to process many of the end users' applications. But they may then be more willing to consider another alternative (e.g., a commercial hot site) to the more expensive ideal technical solution. The commercial hot site may not have all of the resources the data center director would like, but it is a better solution than the reciprocal agreement.

Once the objectives have been agreed on, the DCRP coordinator and the development committee can determine the resources and options that allow the data center to meet its objectives. This will enable the DCRP coordinator to meet the participants' objective, which is to have a DCRP that will manage any recovery operation in an organized and effective manner. An example of the DCRP objectives is provided in Workpaper II2.02.

ESTABLISH THE DISASTER PREMISE FOR THE DCRP

STEP 4

The next step the development committee should undertake is to establish the premise for the DCRP. The term *premise* as used in the DCRP refers to the assumptions made about the readiness of the DCRP at the time of the disaster. Therefore, the premise contains the assumptions regarding the readiness of the DCRP as well as the disaster scenario on which the DCRP has been developed.

The feasibility of the DCRP depends on the compliance with the premise of the plan. If the items in the premise are not complied with, the DCRP may not be able to meet the objectives for which it was developed.

Assumptions

Some of the key assumptions of the premise are that:

- All personnel with recovery responsibilities have been adequately trained and tested.
- A computer backup site is in place.
- A communications network backup strategy is in place. (This subject is covered fully in Part III of this book.)
- Data protection procedures are in place.
- Systems programming and application data backups are being protected.
- Procedures are in place for reconstructing the application files and data base files.
- Essential documentation and material are available from an off-premises storage location.

Personnel Trained and Tested. This element of the premise assumes either that all recovery personnel have participated in the writing of the responsibilities and the preparation of the procedures or that their role has been thoroughly explained to them. It also assumes that they have taken part in at least one test in which they actually performed the responsibilities and used the procedures.

Computer Backup Site in Place. This element of the premise assumes that a backup site agreement or contract does exist, that the backup site will meet the needs of the DCRP, and that the backup site has been tested to ensure it will work.

Communications Network Backup Strategy in Place. This element is covered in Part III of this book.

Data Protection Procedures in Place. This element of the premise assumes that essential data is being backed up frequently and is being rotated to an off-premises, or off-site, storage location. Off-premises indicates that the essential backup data has been moved outside of the building housing the data center. If a company moves essential backup data out of the computer room or the tape library and stores it in another part of the same building, this does not provide off-premises or off-site protection. For example, if a disaster rendered the building inaccessible for several days, the backup data would be useless because it could not be retrieved.

Systems Programming and Application Data Backups Protected. This element of the premise assumes that all of the necessary data has been identified and is being rotated off-premises. This is not always the case. There are a number of reasons why companies have a partial data recovery capability using their off-premises storage location. These reasons are discussed in detail in Chapter II-3 of this book.

Reconstruction Procedures in Place. This element of the premise assumes that the technical people have analyzed the conditions in which they would be required to recover data center files and information using only the backups stored in the off-premises storage locations. As part of this element, it is assumed that the DCRP contains documented procedures on how to reconstruct the files based on the generation of files that will be retrieved from the off-premises location.

Essential Documentation/Material Available from Off Premises. This element of the premise assumes that all documentation, supplies, and any other resources needed for the recovery of the data center have been identified and are available from an off-premises storage location. An example of the DCRP premise is provided in Workpaper II2.03.

Types of Disasters

The DCRP coordinator should determine the types of disasters that could strike the data center. Generally, disasters can be broken into three categories: acts of nature, accidents, and intentional acts. The acts of nature include earthquakes, hurricanes, tornadoes, and floods. Accidents include explosions and fires, internal flooding, loss of power, and loss of communications. Intentional acts include vandalism, sabotage, terrorism, and arson (see Exhibit II-2-D).

Disaster Scenarios of the Premise

Some of the key elements that relate to the disaster scenario of the premise for which the DCRP has been developed are: the type of disasters that could strike the data

EXHIBIT II-2-D TYPES OF DISASTERS

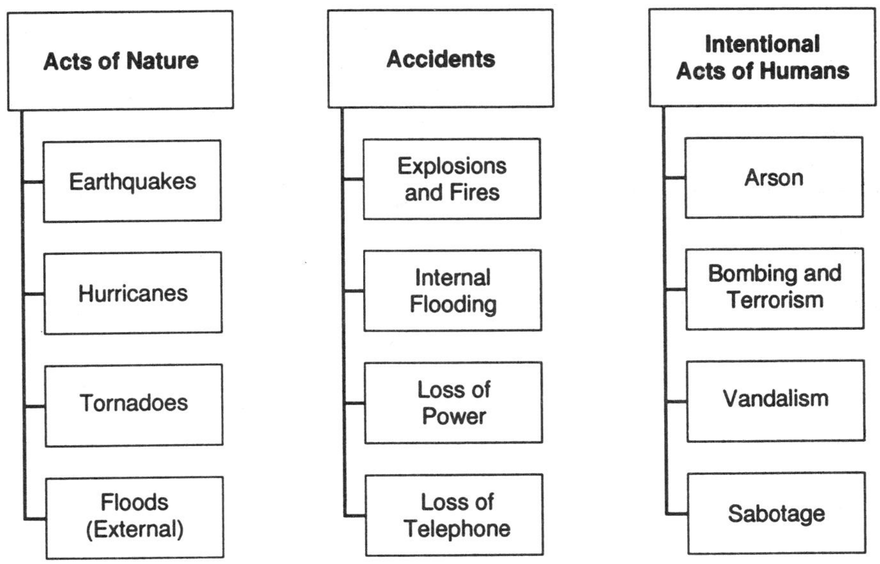

center, the type of damage the disaster could cause, and the areas of the data center that could be affected.

Types of Disaster Scenarios. Two types of disaster scenarios can be addressed: the single, isolated disaster or a wide-area regional disaster. A single, isolated disaster affects only the building housing the data center. There may be other companies in the same building, but only one building is affected by the disaster. A wide-area, regional disaster affects the building housing the data center and additional buildings as well. This happens most often following an earthquake, a flood, or a hurricane.

Levels of Damage. Two levels of damage are evaluated: the best-case situation and the worst-case situation. In the best-case situation, it is assumed that data center personnel will be able to gain access to the site of the disaster quickly and will be able to retrieve all of the resources they would need to move the processing to a computer backup site. It is also assumed that there is a minimum amount of damage to data center equipment and to the building housing the data center, allowing the DCRP personnel to repair the facility rapidly and return the processing from the backup site quickly. An example of a single, isolated, best-case disaster scenario is provided in Workpaper II2.04.

In the worst-case situation, it is assumed that data center personnel will be unable to gain access to the building for at least several days. There will be no retrieval of resources from the building. The data center recovery operation will depend on the resources located outside the buildings (i.e., from the off-premises storage locations or other offices of the company). In the worst case, it is also assumed that equipment and all other contents of the data center are destroyed. Employees will have to resume their operations at temporary locations, where they may need to stay for months before the disaster site can be repaired. An example of a single, isolated, worst-case disaster scenario is provided in Workpaper II2.05.

In a wide-area regional disaster, it is assumed that buildings will be inaccessible for an extended period of time and that the equipment and contents have been destroyed. It is also assumed that vendors will be forced to respond to the problem using a priority-based response plan: for example, support for government locations first, other high-profile industries next, and routine installations last. An example of a wide-area regional disaster scenario is provided in Workpaper II2.06.

Selecting the Scenario. In the initial development phase, the DCRP coordinator and the development committee should use a single, isolated, worst-case disaster scenario. Some members of the development committee may prefer to develop the DCRP using a best-case scenario, because the best-case scenario is much easier to deal with and does not require the same amount of effort and time. However, if this type of scenario is selected, the DCRP will not be usable in the event of a worst-case disaster. On the other hand, a DCRP developed for the worst-case disaster can handle a best-case disaster.

Other development committee members may prefer to develop the DCRP using a wide-area regional disaster scenario. The problem with using the wide-area scenario in the initial stage of the development phase is that it presents a number of logistical issues that require policies to be established or support to be committed above and beyond the needs of a single, isolated disaster scenario. For example, a wide-area scenario might require policies to be set stating that personnel may be expected to travel to the data center to participate on one of the disaster site recovery teams, to the computer backup site, or to the recovery headquarters. A policy on requiring personnel to travel in disaster situations that might be construed to be unsafe is not the responsibility of the DCRP coordinator or the development committee; that authority rests with the corporate safety officer or the human resources department.

The wide-area disaster scenario affects not only the company's facilities but many other companies as well. Recovery service vendors will be forced to respond on the basis of industry classifications, with government and life support given first priority. This would invalidate assumptions of vendor commitment based on a single, isolated disaster.

The wide-area disaster scenario must also address the difficult issues of potential injury or death of employees or family members. The issue of injuries to personnel is brought up often during the development of the DCRP. How would the recovery responsibilities be carried out if both the person assigned the primary role and the alternate were injured in the disaster? Although there have not been many instances in which data center personnel have been injured by a disaster, the development committee does have to consider this in its planning. For example, some companies have assigned a third person the responsibility of carrying out recovery activities if both the primary and the alternate are injured at the same time.

In short, there is no question that the wide-area scenario must be considered, but not until the logistics that deal with the single, isolated, worst-case disaster scenario are finalized.

STEP 5

ESTABLISH THE LEVEL OF DETAIL FOR THE DCRP

The development committee also needs to establish the level of detail that will be used in the DCRP. The level of detail refers to the depth of information documented in the DCRP manual.

Two Levels of Detail

There are two levels of detail that can be used in the DCRP. The first is designed to keep it simple, easy to develop, and easy to maintain. This is referred to as the simple method. The second is designed to include the details on how the recovery teams will perform their recovery responsibilities. This is referred to as the detailed method.

The Simple Method. This method includes the identifying of recovery responsibilities that have to be performed and the recovery teams that will perform those responsibilities. The documentation in this level of detail does not include how the recovery teams will perform their responsibilities.

The strength of this level of detail is in its ease in development and maintenance. If the development committee is under a severe time constraint to complete the DCRP, it may make a decision to use the simple method for the initial version of the plan. More detail can be added as the plan is updated. The weakness in this level of detail is that it requires that knowledgeable technical people familiar with the company's data center be available to perform the responsibilities. If such knowledgeable people are not available, the person who will step in as the alternate may not completely understand how to perform the responsibilities and in fact may know just enough to be dangerous. An example of DCRP level of detail documentation using the simple method is shown in Workpaper II2.07.

The Detailed Method. This method is considerably more complex, because it includes the technical aspects of performing the recovery responsibilities and requires more effort during the development phase and the maintenance phase. The value of the detailed method is that:

- It gives the primary team leader all the information needed to carry out the responsibilities.
- It gives the alternate all of the information needed to carry out the responsibilities. This is important because in most cases the alternate is not as knowledgeable about the data center functions as the primary leader is.
- It gives to other data center employees or vendor representatives the documented procedures and checklists on how to carry out recovery responsibilities in case the persons assigned the primary and alternate responsibilities are unable to perform their assigned responsibilities.

The weakness of this level of detail is that it is somewhat more difficult to develop and maintain. The strength of this level of detail is that it is not people-dependent; it provides how-to information that the alternate leader or another knowledgeable data center person can use to perform the recovery responsibilities. An example of DCRP level of detail documentation using the detailed method is shown in Workpaper II2.08.

ESTABLISH THE FORMAT FOR DOCUMENTING THE DCRP

STEP 6

The development committee should establish the format to be used in documenting the DCRP. The term *format* as used in the DCRP refers to the organization of the documentation for a recovery team. The format consists of the recovery procedure overview, the initial response actions, the recovery actions, and the administrative actions.

Recovery Procedure Overview. This segment explains the general responsibilities of the team leader, the recovery procedures, the recovery checklists in the recovery team's documentation, and the recovery preparedness tasks of the team leader. An example of the recovery procedure overview format is provided in Workpaper II2.09.

Initial Response Actions. This segment explains the actions the team leader should take after the initial notification that a disaster has occurred. It details where to report, whom to meet with, how to plan the staffing of the team, and the importance of reviewing the objectives of the team during the recovery operation. This procedure reminds the team leader that the objectives of the recovery operation will dictate the need for and timing of the responsibilities to be activated. The team leader should read the entire recovery team section before performing any assignments. An example of the initial response actions format is provided in Workpaper II2.10.

Recovery Actions. This segment explains the recovery actions the team could take, depending on the objectives of the recovery operation. It deals with such issues as the need to organize team area at the recovery headquarters, the need to notify vendors that their support is needed, the need to travel to the disaster site or the recovery backup site, and other specific recovery actions documented for the team. An example of the recovery actions format is provided in Workpaper II2.11.

Administrative Actions. This segment explains the administrative actions the team leader is responsible for throughout the recovery operation—for example, maintaining accurate written documentation of changes or modifications, maintaining a record of all personal expenses incurred, and submitting periodic recovery status reports. An example of the administrative actions format is provided in Workpaper II2.12.

STEP 7

DETERMINE THE RECOVERY LOGISTICS

The development committee must also determine the recovery logistics to be used in documenting the DCRP. Broadly speaking, determining the recovery logistics involves identifying what recovery actions should be included in the plan, who should be assigned responsibility for performing these actions, and how the responsibilities should be carried out. These actions include damage assessment, notification, equipment replacement, procurement of recovery material and facilities, recovery of data, and transportation of personnel and equipment to the backup sites after a disaster.

The following sections provide examples of recovery logistics for the disaster site recovery team, computer operations recovery team, and recovery headquarters team. The examples suggest the types of functions that should be performed by each team. (A complete discussion of the actions and responsibilities of each team is provided in Chapters II-4, II-5, and II-6.) The development committee should consult with key team members to modify this basic set of recovery logistics to meet the specific requirements of the organization.

Recovery Logistics for Three Teams

Disaster Site Recovery Team. The disaster site recovery team is responsible for the following logistics:

1. Determining the extent of damage to:
   —Electrical services.
   —Air conditioning and heating systems.
   —Water and plumbing systems.

2. Controlling all building and utility repair activities at the disaster site.
3. Determining the extent of damage to:
   - Equipment.
   - Data.
   - Documentation.
   - Supplies.
   - Work in process.
4. Ordering replacement equipment.
5. Installing and testing repaired or replacement equipment.
6. If a temporary location is required, identifying, selecting, and preparing a location.
7. Controlling the movement of personnel, equipment, and materials to the repaired site and the disaster recovery backup site.

The disaster site recovery team is responsible for all activities related to damage assessment, salvage, repair, and replacement at the site of the disaster. This team consists of the following members:

- The disaster site manager.
- The facility damage assessment and restoration team leader.
- The equipment damage assessment and restoration team leader.
- The communications recovery team leader.

Computer Operations Recovery Team. The computer operations recovery team is responsible for the following logistics:

1. Initiating the backup site disaster alert.
2. Controlling the retrieval of backup data and documentation from the off-premises tape vault.
3. Managing the loading and initiation of operating systems, libraries, and utilities.
4. Loading and restoring disk data.
5. Reloading and recovering data base data and files.
6. Processing systems and jobs according to the approved processing schedule.
7. Enforcing data backup and rotation procedures during the recovery operation.

The computer operations recovery team is responsible for all activities related to restoring the computer services to data center end users. This includes organizing the move to a backup site and the move back to the data center after it is repaired. The computer operations recovery team consists of the following members:

- The computer operations manager.
- The computer operations team leader.
- The systems software team leader.
- The tape operations team leader.
- The applications recovery team leader.
- The data base recovery team leader.
- The communications recovery team leader.

Recovery Headquarters Team. The recovery headquarters team is responsible for the following logistics:

1. Managing the IS department personnel notification activities.
2. Notifying executive and senior management of the disaster situation and recovery plan activation activities.
3. Notifying staff department representatives of the recovery plan activation.
4. Controlling all incoming telephone calls.

5. Providing administrative and clerical support to all recovery personnel throughout the recovery operation.
6. Collecting and processing all expense reports.
7. Collecting, summarizing, and distributing recovery status reports.

The recovery headquarters team is responsible for all activities related to the management of the recovery operation and support of the disaster site recovery team and the computer operations recovery team. The recovery headquarters team consists of the following members:

- Recovery chairperson.
- Recovery headquarters manager.
- Administrative team leader.
- Notification team leader.

For an overview of the three major teams and subteams responsible for DCRP recovery logistics, see Exhibit II-2-C.

WORKPAPER II2.01 Scope Statement

THE DATA CENTER RECOVERY PLAN
SCOPE

The data center recovery plan (DCRP) is designed to respond to a disaster that affects the data center located at [data center address]. The plan documents the data center recovery responsibilities, procedures, checklists, and forms that will be used to manage and control the recovery of essential computer operations following a disaster.

The plans included in the DCRP provide for the recovery of the [company name] critical applications and includes detailed recovery procedures for the following data center areas:

- Systems programming division.
- Data center operations division.
- Applications programming division.
- Data base division.
- Communications division.

The data center recovery plan does not address or provide recovery strategies for:

- Computers installed at any [company name] locations outside the control of the data center, including:
  - -- Midrange computers installed in other departments.
  - -- Personal computers and LANs installed in other departments.
- End-user department operations, including:
  - -- The business operations of end users of data center services. (They are addressed in their departments' plans in the business resumption program.)
- [Company name] data center locations in other countries. (They are addressed in that country's data center recovery plan.)

WORKPAPER II2.02 Objectives Statement

THE DATA CENTER RECOVERY PLAN
OBJECTIVES

The data center group is responsible for responding to any disruption of computer services (short or long term). By activating the data center recovery plan, data center personnel can restore the critical applications in a timely and organized manner consistent with the resources approved by executive management.

The DCRP has been developed to accomplish the DCRP following objectives:

- Limit the magnitude of any loss by minimizing the duration of the interruption to the critical application services.
- Assess damage to the data center facilities and equipment, repair the damage, and activate the repaired computer center.
- Recover data center data and information critical to the operation of the company.
- Manage the recovery operation in an organized and effective manner.
- Prepare the data center personnel to respond effectively in a recovery situation.
- Prepare the staff departments that will provide support during a data center recovery operation.

To accomplish these objectives, the data center team will depend on support from executive management, end users, and staff departments. These support personnel have been identified and included in the DCRP manual.

WORKPAPER II2.03 Premise Statement

THE DATA CENTER RECOVERY PLAN
PREMISE

The feasibility of the data center recovery plan depends on compliance with the premise of the plan.

The premise for the DCRP is:

- All personnel with recovery responsibilities have been adequately trained and tested on their assigned roles.
- A computer backup site strategy has been approved by executive management and is in place. This backup site strategy has been tested and will meet the objectives of the DCRP.
- Data protection procedures (backup and rotation) have been approved by executive management and are in place.
- Essential system and application data has been identified and is being protected.
- The procedures to be used to reconstruct the applications using the backup copies of application data stored in the off-premises location have been documented and tested.
- To ensure proper data is still protected following changes to an application or data base, change control standards and methods are in place. The responsibility for the identification and protection of data has been assigned.
- Essential documentation, materials, and resources are stored off premises.
- The DCRP is reviewed on a regular basis to ensure that it remains current and correct.
- An ongoing DCRP awareness and training program is in place.
- The plan is exercised frequently during the course of the year.

The premise is based on the following disaster scenario:

- A disaster has occurred, causing physical damage to the computer equipment and resulting in the inability to use the data center to support business operations.
- The data center is inaccessible following the disaster and may remain inaccessible for an extended period of time.
- The data, supplies, and forms located inside the data center have been damaged or destroyed.
- Key data center personnel have not been injured in the disaster and are available to perform the required recovery actions (either primary or alternate).

If the items in the premise are not complied with, the feasibility of the DCRP and its ability to meet the objectives for which it was developed are in doubt.

WORKPAPER II2.04 Single, Isolated, Best-Case Disaster Scenario

THE DATA CENTER RECOVERY PLAN

Single, Isolated, Best-Case Disaster Scenario

There has been a disaster in the building housing the data center.

The building is accessible within hours of the disaster:

- The building has not suffered any major structural damage.
- There are no toxic- or hazardous-materials problems.

There is no damage to the data center or its contents:

- The equipment has not suffered any major damage.
- The data on storage media has not been damaged.
- The voice and data communications were interrupted for a few hours but are now working again.

Employees will be able to resume their business operations at their regular locations tomorrow.

WORKPAPER II2.05 Single, Isolated, Worst-Case Disaster Scenario

THE DATA CENTER RECOVERY PLAN

Single, Isolated, Worst-Case Disaster Scenario

There has been a fire in the building housing the data center.

The building will not be accessible for days:

- The building has suffered major structural damage. Local authorities have condemned the building because they deem it unsafe.
- The Environmental Protection Agency has found toxins in the air; it considers the building to have a hazardous-materials problem.

The building has suffered extensive damage and will require a minimum of six months to repair.

Some of the equipment in the data center has been destroyed, and the remaining equipment has been damaged and needs repair.

Much of the information stored on storage media in the data center has been destroyed, and the remaining information has been damaged and needs repair. The voice and data communications are damaged and may not be operational in this location for an extended period of time.

Employees will not be able to resume their business operations at their regular locations.

WORKPAPER II2.06 Wide-Area, Regional Disaster Scenario

THE DATA CENTER RECOVERY PLAN

Wide-Area, Regional Disaster Scenario

A wide-area (regional) disaster has occurred (e.g., earthquake, hurricane, tornado, or flood).

The building housing the data center has been damaged by the disaster. It will not be accessible until local authorities have certified that it is safe to reenter.

There has been some damage to the contents located inside the data center:

- Some computer equipment has been destroyed, and the remaining equipment has been damaged and needs repair.
- Some data and voice communications equipment and lines have been destroyed, and the remaining equipment has been damaged and needs repair.
- Some data and records have been destroyed and needs to be restored.

Employees have suffered personal losses:

- Employees and family members have been injured:
  -- Some while inside the data center.
  -- Some while they were at home.
  -- There have been some fatalities.
- Homes and other personal property have been damaged or destroyed.

The disaster zone has lost a significant amount of its infrastructure:

- Bridges, overpasses, and roads have been damaged.
- Parking areas have been damaged and are not usable.
- Water lines have been damaged or water has been contaminated and is not available.
- Food is not available in the disaster zone.

WORKPAPER II2.07 Level of Detail--Simple Method

THE DATA CENTER RECOVERY PLAN

LEVEL OF DETAIL: SIMPLE METHOD

RECOVERY HEADQUARTERS MANAGER

Primary: ______________________ Alternate: ______________________

1. Manage the recovery headquarters communication efforts:

   - Notification to department personnel.
   - Management of incoming telephone call control functions.

2. Coordinate staff department activities.

3. Direct recovery headquarters activities throughout the recovery operation, to include:

   - 24-hour personnel coverage.
   - Administrative and clerical activities.
   - Recovery status and expense report preparation.

4. Maintain the personnel location control information throughout the recovery operation.

WORKPAPER II2.08 Level of Detail--Detailed Method

THE DATA CENTER RECOVERY PLAN

LEVEL OF DETAIL: DETAILED METHOD

RECOVERY HEADQUARTERS MANAGER

Primary: ______________________ Alternate: ______________________

RECOVERY ACTIONS:

1. Manage the recovery headquarters voice communications efforts. Meet with the data center internal communication team leader:

   a. Authorize that department personnel be notified:

      1. Record the location and telephone number of the recovery headquarters on the personnel notification procedure (Workpaper II4.17). Make copies of this procedure and distribute to all personnel carrying out the department notification. This procedure has been developed to limit the potential of prematurely alarming families of employees who may have been injured by the disaster.
      2. Provide the personnel notification information checklist (Workpaper II4.18).
      3. Review the priority assigned by the recovery management team to identify those individuals who should be called immediately.
      4. Review the instructions for calling personnel believed to have been working during the disaster and potentially injured.
      5. Collect the completed personnel notification status reports and provide information to recovery managers and responsible staff departments.

   b. Manage the incoming telephone call control functions:

      1. Ensure that specific telephone numbers have been assigned to be used for incoming calls.
      2. Ensure that personnel have been assigned to monitor the telephones designated for incoming calls.
      3. Provide copies of the incoming telephone call procedure and form (Workpaper II4.21) to assist in handling all incoming calls correctly.
      4. Inform the company telephone operators to direct all return calls to the assigned extension at the recovery headquarters.

c. Ensure that accurate personnel location control information is being maintained for all recovery personnel.

2. Coordinate staff department support with recovery managers during the recovery operation. Complete a personnel location control form (Workpaper II4.13), identifying who is authorized access to the recovery headquarters, off-premises storage, disaster recovery backup site, and any other location used for recovery.

3. Meet with the security representative to review the need to assign security personnel to secure the disaster site and the recovery operations sites. Depending on the nature of the disaster (e.g., bombing, suspicious fire), tighter-than-usual security may be required:

   a. Arrange for the issuance of appropriate security badges and access cards. Meet with personnel from security administration to assist in the identification of appropriate security clearance levels.

   b. Provide a completed personnel location control form (Workpaper II4.13) to security personnel.

   c. Request that admittance be restricted to only authorized personnel who have proper identification.

4. Meet with the data center end-user interface team leader. (The data center end-user interface team will act as the focal point for all internal end users and all regional office bureaus and customers.) Direct customer interface activities throughout the recovery operation:

   a. Assist with the development of any statements that will be used during initial contacts with internal end users and external customers.

   b. Ensure that user interface team personnel provide end users and customers with continued current status information on the following:

      1. Recovery of critical applications.
      2. Availability of backup network facilities.
      3. Changes in system processing schedules.

   c. Ensure that adequate user interface team personnel are available to support end-user and customer interface activities throughout the recovery operation. Provide personnel staffing on a 24-hour-a-day basis, if required.

5. Identify equipment requirements and arrange for purchasing to provide copy machines and other office equipment and supplies as required.

6. Manage all administrative and clerical support activities throughout the recovery operation. Meet with the administrative and clerical team leader to coordinate:

   a. Travel requirements.
   b. Cash advance and expense requirements.
   c. Recovery status information.
   d. Recovery team meeting arrangements.

7. Schedule recovery headquarters operations so that 24-hour coverage is provided. Around-the-clock coverage of recovery headquarters telephones will be required.

WORKPAPER II2.09 Recovery Procedure Overview

THE DATA CENTER RECOVERY PLAN

RECOVERY PROCEDURE OVERVIEW

NOTIFICATION AND COMMUNICATIONS TEAM

Primary: ______________________ Alternate: ______________________

The responsibilities of the notification and communications team leader during the recovery operation are to:

- Coordinate data processing personnel alert and notification activities.
- Control all incoming telephone calls.
- Maintain the personnel location control information throughout the recovery operation.

The procedures and checklists required to perform these recovery tasks are:

Procedure Checklist	Workpaper
Recovery Procedure	II4.22
Reserved Telephone Numbers List	II4.20

Recovery preparedness tasks include:

- Conducting periodic recovery plan review sessions with personnel who would participate in the recovery operation.
- Maintaining the recovery plan section and checklists in a current up-to-date condition.
- Keeping a copy of the recovery procedures at home.

WORKPAPER II2.10 Initial Response Actions

THE DATA CENTER RECOVERY PLAN

INITIAL RESPONSE ACTIONS

NOTIFICATION AND COMMUNICATIONS TEAM

Primary: ______________________ Alternate: ______________________

Recovery procedures follow. Read the entire section before performing any assignments. The recovery objectives will dictate the need for and timing of all assignments.

1. Report to the recovery headquarters following the initial recovery team alert. Ensure that you bring your off-premises copy of your data center recovery plan, your proximity access card, and your building security badge.

2. Meet with the recovery headquarters manager to review recovery objectives and to receive direction on specific actions to be taken on the basis of the disaster situation.

3. Use the team staffing requirements to assign personnel to the notification and communication team.

4. Complete the personnel location control form (Workpaper II4.13) by identifying the work location and contact phone number of each team member. Retain the completed form for the master recovery file in your area.

WORKPAPER II2.11 Recovery Actions

THE DATA CENTER RECOVERY PLAN

RECOVERY ACTIONS

NOTIFICATION AND COMMUNICATIONS TEAM

Primary: ____________________ Alternate: ____________________

1. Review recovery actions for each phase of the recovery effort.

2. Reserve specific telephone numbers to be used for outgoing and incoming calls. Indicate the phone extension, whether it is an incoming or outgoing line, and who is assigned to monitor the line.

3. Coordinate the department personnel notification activities:

   a. Work with the recovery headquarters manager to assign personnel to perform the department personnel notifications:

      1. Recording the location and telephone number of the recovery headquarters on the personnel notification procedure (Workpaper II4.17). Make copies of this procedure and distribute to all individuals performing the department notifications.
      2. Reviewing the instructions for calling personnel believed to have been working during the disaster and potentially injured. Refer to the personnel notification procedure (Workpaper II4.17). This procedure has been developed to limit the possibility of prematurely alarming families of employees who may have been injured by the disaster.
      3. Reviewing the priority assigned by the recovery management team to identify those individuals who should be called immediately.
      4. Providing the individuals with the personnel notification checklist (Workpaper II4.18).
      5. Obtaining authorization from the recovery headquarters manager to begin department personnel notification activities.

WORKPAPER II2.12 Administrative Actions

THE DATA CENTER RECOVERY PLAN

ADMINISTRATIVE ACTIONS

NOTIFICATION AND COMMUNICATIONS TEAM

Primary: ______________________ Alternate: ______________________

1. Maintain the personnel location control form (Workpaper II4.13). Retain the completed forms for the master recovery file in your area.

2. Maintain accurate written documentation of any changes or modifications to standard operating procedures. Make sure temporary changes or modifications do not carry over to normal operations following the recovery operation shutdown.

3. Maintain a record of all personal expenses incurred during the recovery operation (receipts should be attached).

4. Submit periodic written recovery status reports and expense reports to the recovery headquarters manager.

5. Collect disaster recovery time sheets (Workpaper II4.16) from all team members and submit to the administrative and clerical team leader on a weekly basis.

Organizing the DCRP Development Project

CHAPTER

II-3

In organizing the data center recovery plan (DCRP) project, the development committee should:

1. Conduct the formal kickoff meeting, at which the DCRP coordinator introduces the project to the key players in the data center.
2. Conduct initial individual recovery team meetings for the purpose of developing the first drafts of the team sections of the DCRP manual and for distributing the data gathering forms.
3. Conduct a second round of meetings with the individual recovery teams to review the first draft of their sections of the DCRP and to collect their data gathering forms.
4. Conduct joint recovery team meetings, with two or more teams working together.
5. Conduct the final round of individual recovery team meetings to review the drafts to date and include any input or changes required after the multiple team meetings. This is the step that produces the final documentation that makes up the DCRP manual.
6. Conduct a formal turnover meeting wherein a presentation of the DCRP, in the form of an overview, is made.
7. Establish a maintenance and exercise program that consists of scheduled updates to the information documented in the plan and periodic exercises of the plan to ensure it is both current and correct.

The organizing steps as summarized in Exhibit II-3-A provide a game plan that should help the development committee complete the project in an organized and timely manner. The seven steps are explained in more depth in the following sections of this chapter.

CONDUCT FORMAL KICKOFF MEETING

STEP 1

To officially start the project, the DCRP coordinator should conduct a formal kickoff meeting. The individuals who should be invited are the head of the information systems (IS) department, the IS department representatives that have been selected to be part of the development committee, and all individuals selected to be part of the recovery teams, either in a primary, alternate, or support role.

The value of the kickoff meeting is that it provides an opportunity for the head of the IS department to introduce the project as a priority. This starts the plan development project on the right foot. The head of the IS department wants the project completed, and the DCRP coordinator is his or her assigned representative with the authority to carry out the project. It is also valuable because it allows the DCRP coordinator to set the scene for the development project with all participants, and only have to do it once. The DCRP coordinator can introduce the DCRP scope, the objectives it needs to meet, the premise under which it will be developed, and the level of detail that will be used in developing it. This meeting gives the DCRP coordinator the opportunity

EXHIBIT II-3-A ORGANIZING STEPS FOR THE DEVELOPMENT PROJECT

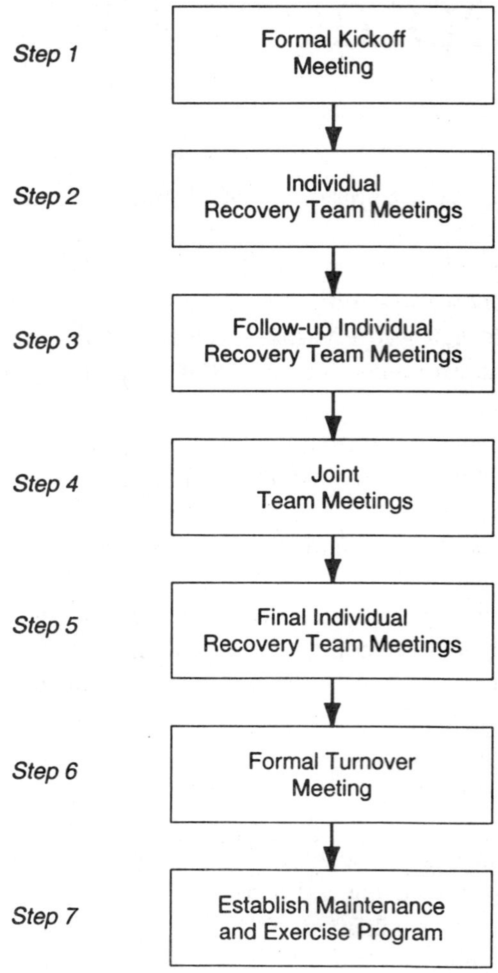

to present actual case studies of disasters that help illustrate the need for, and value of, the DCRP. At the conclusion of the presentation, attendees should be encouraged to ask questions to further clarify the DCRP project.

STEP 2

CONDUCT INITIAL INDIVIDUAL RECOVERY TEAM MEETINGS

After the kickoff meeting, the DCRP coordinator should schedule separate meetings with each of the recovery teams that will be needed for the DCRP. The purpose of this meeting is to discuss the team's recovery logistics, the recovery procedures, and the data that must be gathered to document the DCRP.

During the individual recovery team meeting, the development committee should discuss the recovery logistics that have been assigned to that team. For example, the tape operations recovery team should discuss such issues as how the backups will be identified, how the off-premises storage location will be contacted, and how the backups will be taken from the off-premises location to the computer backup site. For the notification and communications team, there should be a discussion of who will make the outgoing phone calls to data center personnel, why these people must follow the personnel notification procedure, and how to control outgoing and incoming phone calls.

The team should discuss the recovery checklists, which can be used to check off the actions that have been successfully taken or to account for the status of the inventories of equipment, supplies, and forms. The development committee should also discuss the recovery procedures that will be used by the team to perform its recovery responsibilities. Last, this is the time to present the data gathering assignments to the recovery teams. The data to be gathered will be used in creating the recovery checklists and the recovery procedures. The data gathering assignments are described in the following paragraphs.

ISD Personnel Notification Information. This data gathering form is used to create the IS department personnel notification checklist. The checklist is, in turn, used to notify IS department employees of the activation of the DCRP and to advise them of the actions they are to perform.

The information to be gathered includes the:

- Employee name.
- Job title.
- Department name (within the data center).
- Home phone number.
- Car phone number.
- Beeper number.
- Address.

For an example of the personnel notification information data gathering form, see Workpaper II3.01.

DCRP Recovery Headquarters Information. This data gathering form is used to identify the location to be used by the DCRP management team when it meets to assess the level of damage and determine whether any part of the DCRP must be activated. If the DCRP is activated, this location will be used by the recovery headquarters team to manage communication activities and to provide administrative support.

The form provides for information to be gathered about three locations: the primary, an alternate to the primary, and, for contingency reasons, a second alternate. The primary site should be a company-owned property that is close to the data center and would still be accessible at the time of a disaster. An alternate site could be a nearby hotel where rooms could be rented and used as a recovery headquarters. The contingency alternate can be a second hotel location in case the first becomes unavailable.

The information to be gathered for each location includes the:

- Address.
- Contact person to gain access.
- Phone number for contact person.

For an example of the data center recovery headquarters data gathering form, see Workpaper II3.02.

Company Senior Management Notification Information. This data gathering form is used to create the disaster alert procedure for notifying the senior management of the company that the DCRP was activated. The information to be gathered for each senior manager includes the:

- Senior manager name.
- Title.
- Department and location.
- Home phone number.

For an example of the senior manager notification data gathering form, see Workpaper II3.03.

Staff Department Management Notification Information. This data gathering form is used to create the disaster alert checklist for notifying staff department managers that the DCRP was activated. The information to be gathered includes the:

- Staff department manager name.
- Title.
- Department.
- Business phone number.
- Home phone number.

Each staff department should provide information on two people: a primary contact and an alternate contact. For an example of the staff department management notification data gathering form, see Workpaper II3.04.

Computer Equipment Inventory. This data gathering form is used to identify the computer equipment installed in the data center and to create the computer equipment inventory checklist. This checklist is used after the disaster has occurred to determine which pieces of equipment are undamaged, which are damaged but can be repaired, and which are destroyed and must be replaced.

The information to be gathered includes the:

- Vendor name.
- Model.
- Description.
- Serial number.

For an example of the computer equipment inventory data gathering form, see Workpaper II3.05.

Computer Equipment Vendor Notification Information. This data gathering form is used to create the computer equipment vendor notification checklist. This recovery checklist is used to notify vendor representatives after a disaster causes physical damage to computer equipment. The vendor's representatives will assess the damage and determine whether the equipment can be repaired or needs to be replaced.

The information to be gathered includes the:

- Vendor name.
- Vendor address.
- Business phone number.
- Emergency or 24-hour phone number.

For an example of the computer equipment vendor notification data gathering form, see Workpaper II3.06.

Letter Requesting Computer Equipment Vendor's Commitment. As part of the development of the computer equipment inventory checklist and the vendor notification checklist, it is suggested that a letter of commitment be obtained from each vendor indicating the type of support it can provide following a disaster. This letter of commitment is generated in response to a letter of request sent to each vendor.

For an example of a suggested letter that can be used, see Workpaper II3.07. When the vendor responds with its commitment, the DCRP coordinator should review the commitment to ensure that it is satisfactory. If the vendor commitment is not satisfactory, the DCRP coordinator should bring this concern to the attention of the head of the IS department. After receiving a satisfactory response, the letter should be placed in the DCRP manual. (Most companies add an appendix to the manual for letters from vendors.)

Computer Forms Inventory. This data gathering form is used to create the computer forms inventory checklist, which identifies the forms that support data center activities. This checklist is used to determine which forms are undamaged and salvageable and which forms are destroyed and must be replaced.

The information to be gathered includes the:

- Vendor name.
- Form number.
- Description.
- Average monthly use.

For an example of the computer forms inventory data gathering form, see Workpaper II3.08.

Computer Forms Vendor Notification Information. This data gathering form is used to create the computer forms vendor notification checklist. This recovery checklist is used to notify vendor representatives after a disaster causes such physical damage to the computer forms that they must be replaced.

The information to be gathered includes the:

- Vendor name.
- Vendor address.
- Business phone number.
- Emergency or 24-hour phone number.

For an example of the computer forms vendor notification data gathering form, see Workpaper II3.09.

Letter Requesting Computer Forms Vendor's Commitment. As part of the development of the computer forms inventory checklist and the vendor notification checklist, it is suggested that a letter of commitment be obtained from each vendor indicating the type of support it can provide following a disaster. This letter of commitment is generated in response to a letter of request sent to each vendor.

For an example of a suggested letter that can be used, see Workpaper II3.10. When the vendor responds with its commitment, the DCRP coordinator should review the commitment to ensure that it is satisfactory. If the vendor commitment is not satisfactory, the DCRP coordinator should bring this concern to the attention of the head of the IS department. After receiving a satisfactory response, the letter should be placed in the DCRP.

Computer Supplies Inventory. This data gathering form is used to identify the computer supplies used in the data center and to create the computer supplies inventory checklist. This checklist is used after a disaster has occurred to determine which supplies are undamaged and which supplies are destroyed and must be replaced.

The information to be gathered includes the:

- Vendor name.
- Catalog number.
- Description.
- Average monthly use.

For an example of the computer supplies inventory data gathering form, see Workpaper II3.11.

Computer Supplies Vendor Notification Information. This data gathering form is used to create the computer supplies vendor notification checklist. This recovery checklist is used to notify vendor representatives after a disaster causes physical damage to the computer supplies requiring them to be replaced.

The information to be gathered includes the:

- Vendor name.
- Vendor address.
- Business phone number.
- Emergency or 24-hour phone number.

For an example of the computer supplies vendor notification data gathering form, see Workpaper II3.12.

Letter Requesting Computer Supplies Vendor's Commitment. As part of the development of the computer supplies inventory checklist and the vendor notification checklist, a letter of commitment should be obtained from each vendor indicating the type of support it can provide following a disaster. This letter of commitment is generated in response to a letter of request sent to each vendor.

For an example of a suggested letter that can be used, see Workpaper II3.13. When the vendor responds with its commitment, the DCRP coordinator should review the commitment to ensure that it is satisfactory. If the vendor commitment is not satisfactory, the DCRP coordinator should bring this concern to the attention of the head of the IS department. After receiving a satisfactory response, the letter should be placed in the DCRP.

External Support Companies Information. This data gathering form is used to create a notification checklist for external support companies. The external support companies may include such utilities as the power company, the telephone company, and heating, ventilating, and air conditioning companies. It can also include companies that provide electrical, plumbing, access control, and fire suppression services. The external support companies can also include construction, salvage, and cleanup companies.

This recovery checklist is used when a disaster causes physical damage to the facility housing the data center, requiring repairs to be made. This is especially important to IS departments that are autonomous and have the day-to-day responsibility of interacting with these companies. Otherwise, vendor contact information will be maintained by the various support departments (e.g., building services, purchasing).

The information to be gathered includes the:

- Vendor name.
- Vendor address.
- Business phone number.

- Emergency or 24-hour phone number.
- Service provided.

For an example of the external support companies data gathering form, see Workpaper II3.14.

Temporary Location Requirements Information. This data gathering form is used to create the temporary location requirements checklist. This checklist contains information that identifies the minimum requirements needed if the data center has to move to a temporary facility.

The information to be gathered includes the requirements for:

- Floor space.
- Heating, ventilating, and air conditioning.
- Electrical power.
- Access control.
- Fire protection.
- Telephones.

In addition to the information above, the facility considerations can also include the requirements for:

- A motor generator area and the uninterruptible power supply (UPS) system (e.g., batteries and generators).
- The fire suppression system.
- Electrical service area.
- Telephone service room.

For an example of the temporary location requirements data gathering form, see Workpaper II3.15.

Other Data Gathering Assignments

Additional data gathering assignments are discussed later in Part II. These data gathering efforts will result in the following DCRP checklists:

- The critical applications checklist.
- The computer backup site checklist.
- The backup data and tape storage checklist.
- The software vendor notification checklist.

Due Dates

When distributing the data gathering material, the DCRP coordinator must assign due dates for returning the material. If people are not given a time frame in which to return work, they often let this type of assignment slip because they consider other projects more important. The DCRP coordinator must realize that although this is a priority of the head of the IS department, it may be only one of many priorities the managers and supervisors in the data center have received. Because the managers and supervisors receive job performance evaluations on those other projects, they may decide to work on the other projects first. To address this problem, many data centers have begun to include the DCRP as one of the items that employees are evaluated on in their yearly performance review.

Preparing the First Draft

After each recovery team meeting is completed, the DCRP coordinator and the development committee prepare a first draft of the recovery team's section of the DCRP.

Specific information as to how team members should perform their recovery actions will not be prepared until the data gathering forms have been completed and reviewed.

STEP 3

CONDUCT A SECOND ROUND OF INDIVIDUAL TEAM MEETINGS

The follow-up recovery team meetings are conducted for the purpose of reviewing the first draft and for collecting and reviewing the completed data gathering forms distributed in the preceding step.

Reviewing the First Draft

The DCRP coordinator and the development committee review the first draft with the recovery team. This review usually results in steps being added and changes made to the existing documentation. This review, along with a walkthrough exercise (explained further in this step), results in a second draft of the recovery team's DCRP.

Reviewing the Data Gathering Forms

The DCRP coordinator and the development committee should review each completed data gathering assignment with the recovery team. This allows the DCRP coordinator and the development committee to ensure they understand the information provided by the recovery team while it is fresh in everyone's mind. The exhibits in this chapter include several examples of completed data gathering forms:

- Completed computer equipment inventory form, Exhibit II-3-B.
- Completed computer forms inventory, Exhibit II-3-C.
- Completed computer supplies inventory, Exhibit II-3-D.
- Completed temporary location requirements, Exhibit II-3-E.

Later review of data gathering forms is not recommended, because members of the recovery team may be interrupted from more important activities if questions need to be answered.

The Walkthrough Exercise

This step should include a walkthrough exercise to determine if recovery elements or procedures are missing from the first draft. The walkthrough exercise is one in which the recovery team is presented with a disaster scenario prepared by the development committee. The recovery team responds by discussing the actions it would take. This type of exercise is designed to be an informal exercise; it is not a pass/fail test. The concept is to motivate the participants to think about the problems that arise during the exercise and to discuss solutions. After the walkthrough exercise is completed, the solutions can be used to determine what must be added or changed in the DCRP.

After each follow-up recovery team meeting is completed, the DCRP coordinator and the development committee prepare a second draft of the DCRP.

STEP 4

CONDUCT JOINT RECOVERY TEAM MEETINGS

At a point near the conclusion of the development process, the DCRP coordinator and the development committee should conduct meetings in which two or more recovery teams are present. The first reason to have these joint meetings is that it allows the members of the different teams to review the successes of their peers. Second, if any team is having a problem with its recovery strategies, the teams may be able to help solve the problem. Third, such meetings allow the teams to share information on how they plan to respond after a disaster. Teams often find they have

EXHIBIT **II-3-B** COMPUTER EQUIPMENT INVENTORY

This data gathering form is used to identify the computer equipment installed in the data center. This information will be used to document the computer equipment inventory checklist. This checklist will be used after the disaster has occurred to determine which pieces of equipment are undamaged, which are damaged but can be repaired, and which are destroyed and must be replaced.

Fill in the vendor, model, description, and serial number for each piece of computer equipment.

Vendor	*Model*	*Description*	*Serial Number*
IBM	3090-150	CPU	72964
IBM	3092	Process Controller	72795
IBM	3089-3	Power unit	45427
IBM	3180	Console	EV950
IBM	3370	Disk drive	P4400
IBM	3880-003	DASD Controller	22255
IBM	4248-001	Printer	11390
STC	3420-003	Mag Tape [1600 bpi]	48011
STC	3480-A21	Mag Tape Unit	66122
STC	3803-002	Tape Control unit	20309

made incorrect assumptions as to what other teams are going to do. As a result of this meeting, they can eliminate any incorrect assumptions. Fourth, joint meetings allow a more comprehensive walkthrough exercise to take place by sharing information and eliminating incorrect assumptions.

For example, as noted in the preceding chapter, the systems software team has the responsibility to reload systems software and applications software onto the computer at the backup site. In many data centers today, systems and applications software backups are the responsibility of the systems programming division. Systems programming software is usually backed up and rotated on a weekly basis, over a weekend. Often the current backup (from last weekend) is still on-site, in the tape library; the software that is stored off-premises is from the previous weekend. This is not a problem for the systems programmers, because typically they do not make changes to systems software during the week, only on weekends. Therefore, they would be able to recover their software using off-premises backups and have to make only the changes that were made during the last weekend. On the other hand, applications software that is in production may be changed on any day of the week. Applications programmers may assume that their software is backed up nightly and rotated off-premises the next day. Therefore, they may also assume the software recovery team will reload current application software backups onto the backup site computer. In reality, however, the

EXHIBIT II-3-C COMPUTER FORMS INVENTORY

This data gathering form is used to identify the computer forms used in the data center. This information will be used to document the computer forms inventory checklist. This checklist will be used to determine which forms are undamaged and which forms are destroyed and must be replaced.

Fill in the vendor, form number, description, and average monthly usage for each computer form.

Vendor	*Form Number*	*Description*	*Average Monthly Usage*
3M	2424	2x laser labels	3,000
3M	2042	3x laser labels	50,000
Contact Products	64-513	Bin labels	1 box
Williamette	141375	Computer paper	325 boxes
Williamette	9501-74	Continuous paper	4 boxes
Xerox	3R127	Xerox paper (std.)	100 Cases
Xerox	3K727	Legal Xerox paper	5 Cases

application software that will be reloaded at the backup site will be from the previous weekend.

For example, a tape library was damaged by a disaster on a Thursday, and the on-site backups have been destroyed. An application programmer made changes on Tuesday of this week and Wednesday of the prior week, the first change reformatting some data files and the second adding a new report file. If the applications software backups are from two weekends ago (i.e., the most current weekend backup is still on-site in the tape library), the application software will not be able to recognize the reformatted files or the new file. This is a typical example of a logistical problem that needs to be addressed before a disaster occurs. Joint team meetings help to resolve such problems.

Following this step, the DCRP coordinator and the development committee prepare a third draft for review at the final recovery team meetings. The third draft of the recovery team section of the DCRP manual should be nearly complete, requiring only a little fine-tuning at the final meetings.

STEP 5

CONDUCT FINAL INDIVIDUAL RECOVERY TEAM MEETINGS

These meetings are conducted to finalize the third draft of the DCRP. This draft should be reviewed to ensure it meets the objectives of the DCRP. In most cases, only a few changes are needed to complete the plan.

EXHIBIT II-3-D COMPUTER SUPPLIES INVENTORY

This data gathering form is used to identify the computer supplies used in the data center. This information will be used to document the computer supplies inventory checklist. This checklist will be used to determine which supplies are undamaged and which supplies are destroyed and must be replaced.

Fill in the vendor, catalog number, description, and average monthly usage for each type of computer supplies.

Vendor	*Catalog Number*	*Description*	*Average Monthly Usage*
Business Supply	2000 AD	Mag Tape 2400	300
Business Supply	3480	3480 cartridges	200
Business Supply	4245	Printer ribbons	20
Xerox	6R210	8790 printer ink	60
Xerox	5R97	Developer	12
Xerox	8R79	Fuser oil	10
STC	N/A	Printer supplies	N/A

CONDUCT A FORMAL TURNOVER MEETING

STEP 6

The attendees at this turnover meeting should include all personnel in the company that have a role to play in the DCRP (i.e., data center personnel assigned primary or alternate recovery responsibilities). In addition, the heads of the staff departments should also be invited, because they will be expected to provide support to the data center during the recovery operation. These departments include the security, facilities, medical, human resources, public relations, purchasing, insurance, legal, finance, and transportation areas.

At the conclusion of the meeting, people with recovery responsibilities should be presented with their section of the DCRP manual. They should sign a plan distribution form indicating that they have received their recovery responsibilities and that they understand that they are responsible for keeping their section of the program current and correct. In most cases the sections of the DCRP are distributed to recovery personnel on a need-to-know basis. This means that a recovery team leader receives a copy only of the recovery procedures that pertain to his or her area of responsibility.

EXHIBIT II-3-E TEMPORARY LOCATION REQUIREMENTS INFORMATION

This data gathering form is used to create the temporary location requirements checklist. This checklist contains information that identifies the minimum requirements needed if the data center has to move to a temporary facility.

Fill in the Minimum Needed column only for each item shown on the form.

Data Center Computer Site Temporary Location Requirements	*Minimum Needed*	*Sq. Ft. Available*
I. PROCESSING AREA		
A. Floor Space (Sq. Ft.):		
1. Computer Room	12,000 sq.'	
2. Support Area	1,200 sq'	
3. Office Area	1,000 sq'	
Total Floor Space:	14,200 sq'	
B. Raised Flooring:	12,000 sq'	
C. Air Conditioning (BTU):		
1. Computer Room	600,000	
2. Support Area	40,000	
3. Office Area	30,000	
D. Heat and Humidity Control:		
1. Heat	65°–80° F	______ ° F
2. Humidity	50% ± 5%	______ %
E. Electrical Power:		
1. Computer Room	270KVA 60Hz	______ KVA ______ HZ
2. Air Conditioning	180 KVA 60Hz	______ KVA ______ HZ
3. Support Office Area	50 KVA 60Hz	______ KVA ______ HZ
F. Floor Weight Capacity:	0.48#/sq."	______ # per Sq. Inch
G. Access Control:	Cardkey system	
H. Fire Protection:		
1. Computer Room	Halon with preaction sprinkler backup	
2. Support/Office	Halon with high temp sprinkler backup	
I. Telephone:		
1. Lines	20	
2. Handsets	30	

(continued)

EXHIBIT II-3-E TEMPORARY LOCATION REQUIREMENTS INFORMATION (*CONTINUED*)

Fill in the Minimum Needed column only for each item shown on the form.

Data Center Computer Site Temporary Location Requirements	*Minimum Needed*	*Sq. Ft. Available*
II. FACILITY CONSIDERATIONS		
A. Motor Generator Area (as required)	Static inverters on raised floor area	
B. UPS System (batteries and equipment)	208V switch gear if required	
C. Fire Suppression Gas	200 sq'	
D. Other Trash Storage Area	200 sq'	
Electrical Service Room	400 sq'	
Telephone Service Room	400 sq'	
TOTAL SERVICE AREAS:	1,200 sq'	

ESTABLISH A MAINTENANCE PROGRAM

STEP 7

After the DCRP has been documented and distributed to the appropriate team leaders, the DCRP coordinator needs to establish a policy for maintenance efforts. Most DCRPs have a maintenance policy that requires reviews and updates on a quarterly basis. Most also have a provision that provides the capability to update sections of the DCRP whenever major changes in the operation of the data center take place. If these changes could result in the DCRP not working as planned, recovery teams are given the authority to make the necessary updates.

At some point, major revision of the DCRP becomes necessary. This may be caused by major changes in the day-to-day operation of the data center or major changes in the business objectives or operation of the company. (The maintenance program is discussed in Chapter II-11 of this book.)

AVOIDING COMMON DEVELOPMENT MISTAKES

The most common mistakes made during the development of the DCRP are the failure to involve key individuals, conflicting responsibilities, and the failure to implement and test strategies and procedures.

Failure to Involve Key Individuals

A common problem is not getting key individuals involved in the project. Individuals from within the data center or IS department may not get involved in the project because they are too busy with other projects that they consider to be more important. When required to respond during exercises of the DCRP in which internal auditors or consultants are present, they may attempt to excuse their ignorance of DCRP requirements by stating they were not kept apprised of their responsibilities.

Executives who approve expenditures for the program should be involved, but they may also feel too busy to participate. Generally, however, their participation throughout the project should not require a lot of time; perhaps a half hour several times during the course of the project (e.g., the kickoff meeting). Additional time may be required if the development committee uncovers a high-profile exposure that must be remedied immediately (e.g., major discrepancies in the data backup procedure).

Last, executives who provide their department's support to the data center during the recovery operation should also be involved in the DCRP development project. This group of executives manage the building, security, human resources, public relations, legal, insurance, purchasing, transportation, and finance departments. All too often, they delegate this responsibility to one of their managers and then have no first-hand knowledge of the commitments being made—and, in some cases, the commitments not being made.

Conflicting Responsibilities

The DCRP coordinator and the people assigned to the development committee often have other day-to-day responsibilities. Although these responsibilities, which are part of their annual job performance evaluation, may consume most of their time each week, they are still expected to develop the DCRP during the time remaining. Being responsible for two or more projects at the same time results in conflicting priorities for the DCRP coordinator. When this situation occurs, it is usually the DCRP development project that suffers.

Failure to Implement Strategies and Procedures

Although many recovery procedures are documented in the DCRP manual, their implementation may be delayed. The manual may indicate that a specific recovery strategy be used requiring a specific resource, but that resource may not be available. Yet the feasibility of the whole team's recovery strategy may depend on its ability to implement that strategy.

Examples of strategies that are documented but not ready to be implemented include:

- *Computer backup sites.* The DCRP manual may indicate that a hot site will be used to ensure processing of critical applications, but no contract has been made with a hot-site vendor.
- *Data recovery procedure.* The data recovery procedure may indicate that all the critical files are rotated to the off-premises storage location. As part of the development plan, applications programmers were directed to identify the critical files needed to recover and reconstruct end-users' applications. But the programmers failed to perform this task, which makes timely implementation of this procedure impossible.

Failure to Test Strategies and Procedures

After developing the DCRP, a series of tests should be performed to identify any strategies that do not work according to the documentation in the DCRP manual. Data center personnel can then make the necessary corrections and retest the strategies. During development, however, someone may assume that a particular strategy will work and therefore not test it. When that strategy is needed, it may fail to work as planned.

CONCLUSION

Chapters II-2 and II-3 presented the nine steps to be used in developing the DCRP (see Exhibit II-2-A). Chapter II-2 discussed the selecting of the development committee, the establishing of the scope, objectives, premise, level of detail, and format to be used in documenting the plan, and it reviewed the recovery logistics. Chapter II-3 presented the steps involved in organizing the development project (see Exhibit II-3-A), and it concluded with a discussion of common mistakes made in developing the DCRP.

The next three chapters present the teams that will be located at the three recovery locations: the disaster site (the disaster site recovery team); the computer backup site (the computer operations recovery team); and the recovery headquarters (the recovery headquarters team).

WORKPAPER II3.01 IS Personnel Notification Information

IS DEPARTMENT PERSONNEL NOTIFICATION INFORMATION

This data gathering form is used to create the IS department personnel notification checklist. This DCRP checklist will be used to notify employees of the activation of the DCRP and to advise them as to what they are supposed to do.

Fill out the information for each team leader, alternate team leader, required team member, or alternate member.

Employee Name: ____________________

Job Title: ____________________

Department Name: ____________________

Home Phone: ____________________

Car Phone: ____________________

Beeper: ____________________

Address [street]: ____________________

Address [city, state, zip code]: ____________________

____

Employee Name: ____________________

Job Title: ____________________

Department Name: ____________________

Home Phone: ____________________

Car Phone: ____________________

Beeper: ____________________

Address [street]: ____________________

Address [city, state, zip code]: ____________________

WORKPAPER II3.02 DCRP Recovery Headquarters Information

DCRP RECOVERY HEADQUARTERS INFORMATION

This data gathering form is used to identify the location that will be used first by the DCRP management team when it gathers to assess the level of damage and determine whether it will need to activate any part of the DCRP. If the DCRP is activated, this location will be used second by the recovery headquarters team to manage the communication activities and to provide administrative support.

Fill out the form with primary and alternate information for the DCRP recovery headquarters.

DCRP Recovery Headquarters (primary): ____________________

Address [street]: ____________________

Address [city, state, zip code]: ____________________

Phone [contact person]: ____________________

Contact Person: ____________________

DCRP Recovery Headquarters (alternate): ____________________

Address [street]: ____________________

Address [city, state, zip code]: ____________________

Phone [contact person]: ____________________

Contact Person: ____________________

WORKPAPER II3.03 Senior Management Notification Information

COMPANY SENIOR MANAGEMENT NOTIFICATION INFORMATION

This data gathering form is used to create the disaster alert procedure that will be used in notifying the senior management of the company that the DCRP was activated.

Fill in the name, title, department, and home phone number for each senior manager of the company.

Name	Title	Department	Home Phone

WORKPAPER II3.04 Staff Department Management Notification

STAFF DEPARTMENT MANAGEMENT NOTIFICATION INFORMATION

This data gathering form is used to create the disaster alert checklist for notifying the staff department managers that the DCRP was activated.

Fill in the name, title, department, and home phone number for each staff department manager.

Name	Title	Department	Home Phone

WORKPAPER II3.05 Computer Equipment Inventory

COMPUTER EQUIPMENT INVENTORY

This data gathering form is used to identify the computer equipment installed in the data center. This information will be used to document the computer equipment inventory checklist. This checklist will be used after a disaster has occurred to determine which pieces of equipment are undamaged, which are damaged but can be repaired, and which are destroyed and must be replaced.

Fill in the vendor, model, description, and serial number for each piece of computer equipment.

Vendor	Model	Description	Serial Number

WORKPAPER II3.06 Computer Equipment Vendor Notification

COMPUTER EQUIPMENT VENDOR NOTIFICATION INFORMATION

This data gathering form is used to create the computer equipment vendor notification checklist. This recovery checklist is used to notify vendor representatives after a disaster causes physical damage to the computer equipment. The vendor's representatives will assess the damage and determine whether the equipment can be repaired or needs to be replaced.

Fill in the vendor name, address, business phone number, and emergency phone number for each computer equipment vendor.

Vendor Name: ____________________ Business Number: ____________

Address [street]: ________________ Emergency Number: ____________

Address [city, state, zip code]: ______________________________

Vendor Name: ____________________ Business Number: ____________

Address [street]: ________________ Emergency Number: ____________

Address [city, state, zip code]: ______________________________

Vendor Name: ____________________ Business Number: ____________

Address [street]: ________________ Emergency Number: ____________

Address [city, state, zip code]: ______________________________

Vendor Name: ____________________ Business Number: ____________

Address [street]: ________________ Emergency Number: ____________

Address [city, state, zip code]: ______________________________

WORKPAPER II3.07 Request Letter to Equipment Vendor

LETTER REQUESTING COMPUTER EQUIPMENT VENDOR'S COMMITMENT

In addition to obtaining the computer equipment inventory checklist and the vendor notification checklist, it is suggested that a letter of commitment be obtained from each vendor indicating the type of support it can provide following a disaster. This letter of commitment is generated in response to a letter sent to each vendor.

[date]

[address]

Dear [hardware vendor]:

[Company name] is implementing a disaster recovery program for the [department name]. As you know, there are many critical concerns during the development and implementation of a disaster recovery program. In the event the equipment that we have leased or purchased from you is damaged or destroyed, we would need to have your support on an emergency basis.

To solidify our planning, we need you to identify your company's position in responding specifically to a disaster in [company name] [department name].

1. Do you provide backup processing capability? Please explain your position.

2. Do you provide support personnel to assist with damage assessment and salvage activities during the recovery operation?

3. What is your company's policy on the emergency replacement of current equipment?
   a. How long will it take to replace the equipment?
   b. Will you be able to determine the specifications of our equipment (e.g., all special features) at the time of the occurrence? If not, what must we have documented and stored off site to satisfy this requirement?
   c. How long will it take to ship replacement equipment?
   d. How long will it take to install and test replacement equipment?

4. How quickly can you replace the documentation associated with the equipment you supply?

5. Please provide us with the phone number we should use to notify you in the event that a disaster damages equipment we acquired from you. The following phone number is the 24-hours-a-day, 7-days-a-week, 365-days-a-year number where

someone from your company will respond to our emergency: [phone number].

The progress of our project depends on your response. Therefore, would you please respond in writing by [date]? Should you have any questions or require additional information, please call me at [phone number].

We appreciate your assistance.

Cordially,
[name, title]

WORKPAPER II3.08 Computer Forms Inventory

COMPUTER FORMS INVENTORY

This data gathering form is used to identify the computer forms used in the data center. This information will be used to document the computer forms inventory checklist. This checklist will be used to determine which forms are undamaged and which forms are destroyed and must be replaced.

Fill in the vendor, form number, description, and average monthly use for each computer form.

Vendor	Form Number	Description	Average Monthly Use

WORKPAPER II3.09 Computer Forms Vendor Notification

COMPUTER FORMS VENDOR NOTIFICATION INFORMATION

This data gathering form is used to create the computer forms vendor notification checklist. This recovery checklist will be used to notify vendor representatives after a disaster causes physical damage to the computer forms, requiring them to be replaced.

Fill in the vendor name, address, business phone number, and emergency phone number for each computer forms vendor.

Vendor Name: ____________________ Business Number: ____________

Address [street]: _______________ Emergency Number: ___________

Address [city, state, zip code]: ______________________________

Vendor Name: ____________________ Business Number: ____________

Address [street]: _______________ Emergency Number: ___________

Address [city, state, zip code]: ______________________________

Vendor Name: ____________________ Business Number: ____________

Address [street]: _______________ Emergency Number: ___________

Address [city, state, zip code]: ______________________________

Vendor Name: ____________________ Business Number: ____________

Address [street]: _______________ Emergency Number: ___________

Address [city, state, zip code]: ______________________________

WORKPAPER II3.10 Request Letter to Forms Vendor

LETTER REQUESTING COMPUTER FORMS VENDOR'S COMMITMENT

In addition to obtaining the computer forms inventory checklist and the vendor notification checklist, it is suggested that you obtain a letter of commitment from each vendor indicating the type of support it can provide following a disaster. This letter of commitment is generated in response to a letter that you send to each vendor.

[date]

[address]

Dear [forms vendor]:

[Company name] is implementing a disaster recovery program for the [department name]. As you know, there are many critical concerns during the development and implementation of a disaster recovery program. In the event the forms that we purchase from you are damaged or destroyed, we would need to have your support on an emergency basis.

To solidify our planning, we need you to identify your company's position in responding specifically to a disaster in [company name] [department name].

Using the attached list of forms that we currently purchase from you, please provide the estimated time required to ship emergency replacements.

Do you have a disaster recovery program in the event your location suffers a disaster? How soon will you be able to supply [company name]'s needs?

Please provide us with the phone number we should use to notify you in the event that a disaster damages or destroys the forms we purchased from you. The following phone number is the 24-hours-a-day, 7-days-a-week, 365-days-a-year number where someone from your company will respond to our emergency: [phone number].

The progress of our project depends on your response. Therefore, would you please respond in writing by [date]? Should you have any questions or require additional information, please call met at [phone number].

We appreciate your assistance.

Cordially,
[name, title]

WORKPAPER II3.11 Computer Supplies Inventory

COMPUTER SUPPLIES INVENTORY

This data gathering form is used to identify the computer supplies used in the data center. This information will be used to document the computer supplies inventory checklist. This checklist will be used to determine which supplies are undamaged and which supplies are destroyed and must be replaced.

Fill in the vendor, catalog number, description, and average monthly use for each type of computer supplies.

Vendor	Catalog Number	Description	Average Monthly Use

WORKPAPER II3.12 Computer Supplies Vendor Notification

COMPUTER SUPPLIES VENDOR NOTIFICATION INFORMATION

This data gathering form is used to create the computer supplies vendor notification checklist. This recovery checklist will be used to notify vendor representatives after a disaster causes physical damage to the computer supplies requiring them to be replaced.

Fill in the vendor name, address, business phone number, and emergency phone number for each vendor of computer supplies.

Vendor Name: ____________________ Business Number: ____________

Address [street]: ______________ Emergency Number: ___________

Address [city, state, zip code]: ________________________________

Vendor Name: ____________________ Business Number: ____________

Address [street]: ______________ Emergency Number: ___________

Address [city, state, zip code]: ________________________________

Vendor Name: ____________________ Business Number: ____________

Address [street]: ______________ Emergency Number: ___________

Address [city, state, zip code]: ________________________________

Vendor Name: ____________________ Business Number: ____________

Address [street]: ______________ Emergency Number: ___________

Address [city, state, zip code]: ________________________________

WORKPAPER II3.13 Request Letter to Supplies Vendor

LETTER REQUESTING COMPUTER SUPPLIES VENDOR'S COMMITMENT

In addition to obtaining the computer supplies inventory checklist and the vendor notification checklist, it is suggested that you obtain a letter of commitment from each vendor indicating the type of support it can provide following a disaster. This letter of commitment is generated in response to a letter that you send to each vendor.

[date]

[address]

Dear [supplies vendor]:

[Company name] is implementing a disaster recovery program for the [department name]. As you know, there are many critical concerns during the development and implementation of a disaster recovery program. In the event the supplies that we purchase from you are damaged or destroyed, we would need to have your support on an emergency basis.

To solidify our planning, we need you to identify your company's position in responding specifically to a disaster in [company name] [department name].

Using the attached list of supplies that we currently purchase from you, please provide the estimated time required to ship emergency replacements.

Do you have a disaster recovery program in the event your location suffers a disaster? How soon will you be able to supply [company name]'s needs?

Please provide us with the phone number we should use to notify you in the event that a disaster damages or destroys the supplies we purchased from you. The following phone number is the 24-hours-a-day, 7-days-a-week, 365-days-a-year number where someone from your company will respond to our emergency: [phone number].

The progress of our project depends on your response. Therefore, would you please respond in writing by [date]. Should you have any questions or require additional information, please call me at [phone number].

We appreciate your assistance.

Cordially,
[name, title]

WORKPAPER II3.14 External Support Companies Notification

EXTERNAL SUPPORT COMPANIES NOTIFICATION INFORMATION

This data gathering form is used to create an external support companies notification checklist. The external support companies can include such utilities as the power company, telephone company, and heating, ventilation, and air-conditioning companies. It can also include companies that provide electrical, plumbing, access control, and fire suppression services. The external support companies can also include construction, salvage, and cleanup companies. This recovery checklist will be used when a disaster causes physical damage to the facility housing the data center requiring repairs to be made.

Fill in the vendor name, address, business and emergency phone numbers, and the service provided by each external support company.

Vendor Name: ______________________ Business Number: ______________

Address [street]: ________________ Emergency Number: _____________

Address [city, state, zip code]: ____________________________________

Service Provided: ____

____

Vendor Name: ______________________ Business Number: ______________

Address [street]: ________________ Emergency Number: _____________

Address [city, state, zip code]: ____________________________________

Service Provided: ____

____

Vendor Name: ______________________ Business Number: ______________

Address [street]: ________________ Emergency Number: _____________

Address [city, state, zip code]: ____________________________________

Service Provided: ____

WORKPAPER II3.15 Temporary Location Requirements

TEMPORARY LOCATION REQUIREMENTS INFORMATION

This data gathering form is used to create the temporary location requirements checklist. This checklist contains information that identifies the minimum requirements needed if the data center has to move to a temporary facility.

	Minimum Needed	Available
Processing Area		
• Floor Space (in sq. ft.):		
-- Computer Room	________	________
-- Support Area	________	________
-- Office Area	________	________
Total Floor Space (in sq. ft.):	________	________
• Raised Flooring (in sq. ft.):	________	________
• Air Conditioning (in BTUs):		
-- Computer Room	________	________
-- Support Area	________	________
-- Office Area	________	________
• Heat and Humidity Control:		
-- Heat	65° - 80° F	________
-- Humidity	50% ± 5%	________%
• Electrical Power:		
-- Computer Room	________	____kVA ____Hz
-- Air Conditioning	________	____kVA ____Hz
-- Support Office Area	________	____kVA ____Hz

- Floor Weight Capacity (lbs. per sq. in.): ______ ______
- Access Control (type): ______ ______
- Fire Protection (type):
  - -- Computer Room ______ ______
  - -- Support Office ______ ______
- Telephone:
  - -- Lines ______ ______
  - -- Handsets ______ ______

<u>Facility Considerations</u>

- Motor Generator Area (as required): ______ ______
- UPS System (batteries and equipment): ______ ______
- Fire Suppression Gas: ______ ______
- Trash Storage Area: ______ ______
- Electrical Service Room: ______ ______
- Telephone Service Room: ______ ______

Total Service Areas: ______ ______

CHAPTER

II-4

The Recovery Headquarters Team Section of the DCRP

Chapter II-4 presents the actions that the recovery headquarters team takes following the activation of the data center recovery plan (DCRP). The recovery headquarters team is one of the three data center recovery plan teams; the others being the computer operations recovery team and the disaster site recovery team. Each of the DCRP teams receives its name from the location at which it operates—for example, the recovery headquarters team operates at the recovery headquarters, the disaster site recovery team operates at the affected data center, and the computer operations recovery team operates at the computer backup site. The computer operations recovery team is discussed in Chapter II-5, and the disaster site recovery team is covered in Chapter II-6.

THE RECOVERY HEADQUARTERS TEAM

The recovery headquarters team (see Exhibit II-4-A) comprises the:

- Recovery headquarters team manager.
- Notification and communications team leader.
- Administration team leader.

The recovery chairperson will also be located at the recovery headquarters. Although not officially a member of this team, the recovery chairperson's activities are described in this chapter.

The Activation of the Recovery Headquarters Team

The recovery headquarters team is activated after the decision to activate the DCRP has taken place. This occurs after a sequence of events known as the initial disaster alert takes place. (The initial disaster alert is covered in Chapter II-7.) Briefly, that sequence begins when an incident at the data center is first discovered and a member of the IS recovery management team is notified of the incident. (The IS recovery management team comprises the recovery headquarters team manager, the computer operations recovery team manager, the disaster site recovery team manager, and the recovery chairperson, who is typically the head of the IS department.) This IS recovery management team member travels to the data center and assesses the situation. If the situation might require the activation of the DCRP, he or she notifies the other members of the IS recovery management team to report to the recovery headquarters.

The IS recovery management team reviews the results of the damage assessment activities and makes its recommendations on whether to activate the DCRP or terminate any further recovery activities. The recovery chairperson is responsible for the final decision on whether to activate the DCRP.

After the DCRP is activated, the recovery headquarters team manager notifies the team leaders (or their alternates) for the administration team and the notification and

EXHIBIT **II-4-A** RECOVERY HEADQUARTERS TEAM

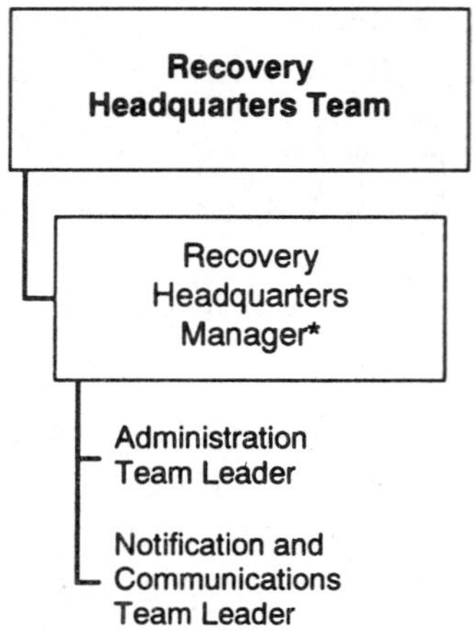

Note:
*Member of the IS recovery management team

communications team to report to the recovery headquarters. The recovery headquarters team manager then attends the chairperson's activation meeting along with the managers of the computer operations recovery team and the disaster site recovery team. At the conclusion of the chairperson's activation meeting, the recovery headquarters team manager conducts an activation meeting for his or her team with the administration team leader and the notification and communications team leader. (See Exhibit II-4-B.)

Responsibilities of the Recovery Headquarters Team

The recovery headquarters team is responsible for the following recovery activities:

- Providing administrative and clerical support to all recovery teams throughout the recovery operation.
- Distributing, collecting, and processing the forms that will be used by all recovery teams during the recovery operation.
- Notifying all IS personnel.
- Managing the incoming telephone calls to the recovery headquarters.
- Maintaining a current copy of the authorized personnel location control form.

THE RECOVERY CHAIRPERSON

After the decision is made to activate the DCRP, the recovery chairperson:

1. Notifies executive management of the situation.
2. Notifies the staff department representatives of the situation.
3. Conducts the chairperson's activation meeting.
4. Conducts a staff department support meeting.
5. Reviews the recovery headquarters team activities.
6. Reviews the computer operations recovery team activities.
7. Authorizes the activation of the computer backup site, if appropriate.

EXHIBIT **II-4-B** DCRP ACTIVATION

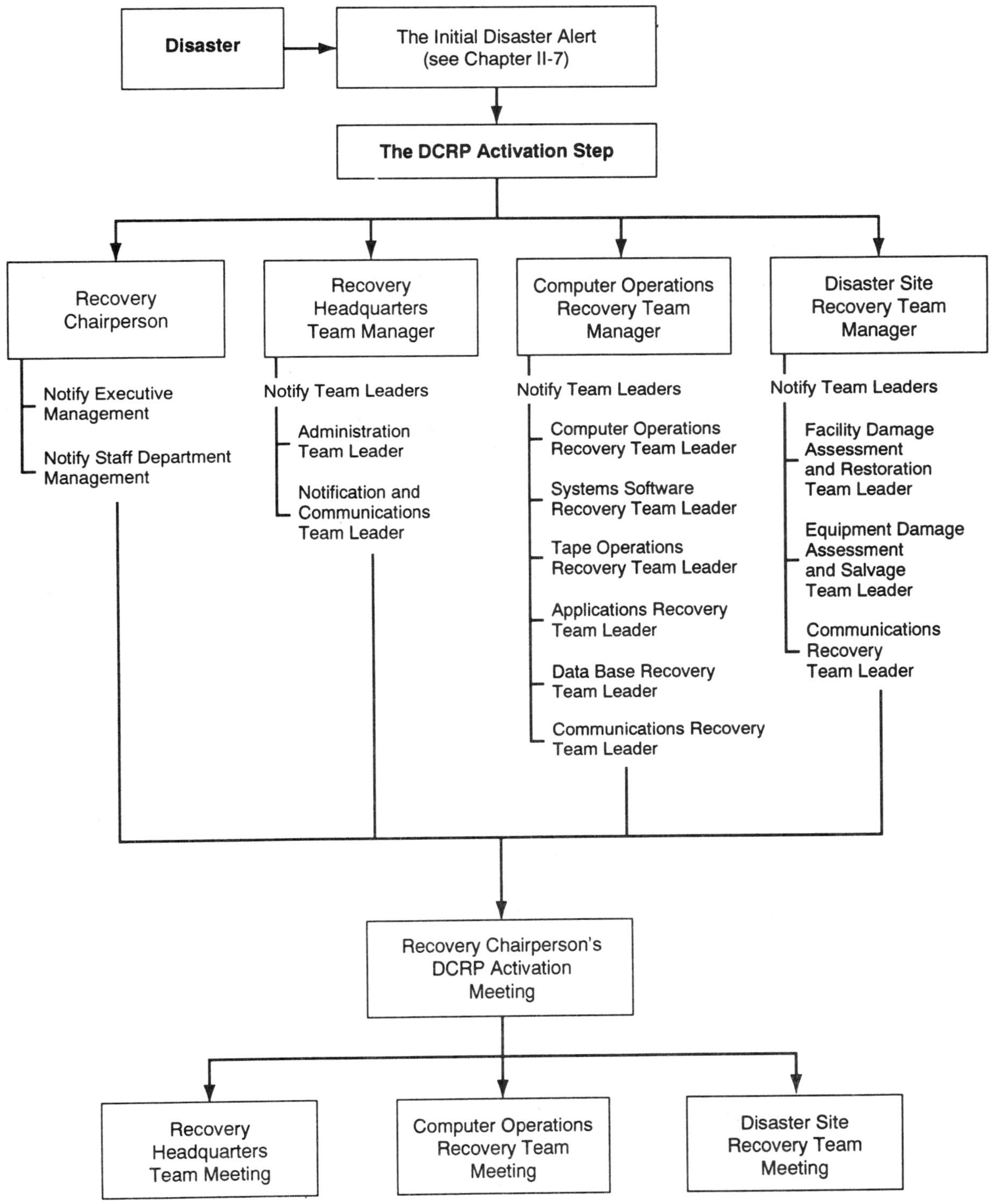

8. Reviews the disaster site recovery team activities.
9. Approves the move to a temporary or permanent data center, if appropriate.
10. Meets with executive management.

These steps are described in the following paragraphs.

STEP 1

Notify Executive Management

After the DCRP has been activated, the recovery chairperson should inform executive management of the situation. During this discussion, the recovery chairperson should provide executive management with an estimate of when services will be available. Executive managers whose business functions will be affected by the data center interruption should alert their personnel of the situation. The recovery chairperson should provide the location and phone number of the recovery headquarters, and assure executive management that it will be notified of any changes to the situation.

STEP 2

Notify the Staff Departments' Management

After notifying executive management, the recovery chairperson should notify the staff departments' management of the situation and request that a support representative report to the recovery headquarters. During the development of the DCRP, the staff departments should have been interviewed to determine the support they would provide to the IS department during a data center recovery operation. Following the interview, a staff department support checklist should have been documented. This checklist should have then been sent to the representative interviewed to allow any additions or changes to be made. This checklist identifies:

- The person to be called and phone number.
- An alternate person who would be called if the primary person was unavailable.
- The specific support activities the department would respond with during a data center recovery operation.

The checklist does not identify how the department performs the support activities. (See sample staff department support checklists, Workpapers II4.01 through II4.10.)

STEP 3

Conduct the Chairperson's Activation Meeting

After the DCRP is activated, the recovery chairperson initiates the actions to be taken during the recovery operation by conducting a meeting with the three DCRP team managers. The chairperson establishes the scope of the recovery operation (e.g., which divisions of the IS department are affected). The chairperson also establishes the objectives (e.g., move computer processing to a backup site). He or she reviews the procedures to be activated (e.g., the recovery headquarters team's procedures and the computer operations recovery team's procedures).

During this meeting, the chairperson asks the recovery headquarters manager to review the notification and communications support and the administrative and clerical support that is to be provided by the recovery headquarters team. The recovery headquarters manager also distributes forms that will be used throughout the recovery operation (e.g., the personnel location control form, the recovery status report form, the travel and expense report form, and the disaster recovery time record form). The purpose and use of these forms is explained in the next section of this chapter, entitled "The Recovery Headquarters Team Manager."

The chairperson asks each of the three recovery team managers to identify the categories of IS personnel to be alerted. When identifying who should be alerted, the recovery team managers should consider who should be involved in the first stages of the recovery operation and who should back them up when the first group gets tired. Several well-respected recovery planners involved in such major disasters as the Loma Prieta earthquake in 1989 and Hurricane Andrew in 1992 have noted the importance of having properly rested personnel available in the later stages of a recovery operation.

The managers should consider the group that will work the first eight-hour shift, the second eight-hour shift, and the third eight-hour shift; they should consider at what point they will replace the personnel on all three shifts. This could be after two or three days, depending on a company's philosophy and travel policy. For example, companies that use a computer backup site located a distance from their present data center often send the computer backup site contingent out of town for approximately one week before replacing them.

The Personnel Notification Checklist. Before any phone calls are placed to the homes of IS employees, the IS recovery management team members should attempt to identify the IS personnel who might have been working at the time of the disaster. Calls made to the homes of employees who were believed to be working in the data center must be made very carefully so as not to alarm any family member who answers the phone. The members of the notification and communications team should follow the personnel notification procedure when calling. (This procedure and form is explained in the section of this chapter entitled "The Notification and Communications Team Leader.")

DCRP Public Relations Policy. The chairperson should direct the recovery team managers to remind all personnel that they should not make any statements to the news media, if it can be avoided. Media representatives should be told to speak with the public relations representative or the recovery chairperson, who is the temporary spokesperson. If IS personnel must speak with the news media, they should use a prepared statement that was developed by public relations and approved by company executive management. (See Workpaper II4.11 for a sample of an initial news media statement.)

Conduct a Staff Department Support Meeting

STEP 4

The recovery chairperson conducts a meeting with staff department support representatives. At this meeting, the chairperson provides any information that is known about the incident (e.g., what happened, when it happened, how it happened, if there were any injuries or deaths, or if the cause is known). The chairperson should request the support identified in the staff department support checklists (Workpapers II4.01–II4.10). Examples of some of the support commitments follow.

Building Services Department. This department assesses the damage to the building and estimates the time required for repairs; manages building repairs; manages residue disposal; activates the temporary location to be used as the recovery headquarters; and obtains a temporary data center location if the current site cannot be repaired quickly. (See the Building Services Department Checklist, Workpaper II4.01, for a more complete list of commitments.)

Finance Department. This department provides travel advances; provides general ledger account numbers to track recovery operations expenses; and provides information to the tax agencies on the situation. (See the Finance Department Checklist, Workpaper II4.02, for a more complete list of commitments.)

Human Resources Department. This department contacts hospitals to determine whether injured personnel have been admitted; notifies families of injured or deceased personnel; assists with the preparation and filing of any benefit insurance program claims (e.g., workers compensation); and hires temporary personnel. (See the Human Resources Department Checklist, Workpaper II4.03.)

Insurance Department. This department notifies the insurance carrier; provides salvage guidance; obtains any special insurance coverage; and provides guidance as to the type of loss or claim records that are required. (See the Insurance Department Checklist, Workpaper II4.04.)

Internal Audit Department. This department provides financial and IS auditing personnel at the computer backup site; reviews the schedules and controls in use for running applications at the computer backup site; reviews controls for processing financial applications in an out-of-balance condition; and reviews any temporary controls established to facilitate the recovery operation. (See the Internal Audit Department Checklist, Workpaper II4.05, for a more complete list of commitments.)

Legal Department. This department provides contract advice on existing equipment and software contracts; provides contract advice on new equipment and software contracts; advises the recovery chairperson regarding legal or regulatory requirements; and advises regulatory agencies of the situation. (See the Legal Department Checklist, Workpaper II4.06.)

Public Relations Department. This department manages the news media press conferences; sets up a news media location in or near the recovery headquarters; provides a formal statement to be used by IS personnel, if approached by the news media; and provides recovery information to the employees. (See the Public Relations Department Checklist, Workpaper II4.07.)

Purchasing Department. This department provides a purchasing department point of contact throughout the recovery operation; coordinates vendor support during the recovery operation; obtains replacements of equipment, forms, and computer supplies; and obtains repair services for furniture. (See the Purchasing Department Checklist, Workpaper II4.08.)

Security Department. This department secures the disaster site immediately; investigates the cause; if its origin is suspicious, provides security protection at the recovery headquarters, the computer backup site, and the off-premises records storage areas; and verifies that personnel are authorized to access recovery locations. (See the Building Services Department Checklist, Workpaper II4.09.)

Transportation Department. This department provides vehicles and drivers to transport computer documents, supplies, and personnel; establishes courier services for the moving of material and supplies to and from the computer backup site; controls the receipt and storage of material and supplies; and provides secured space for the storage of new equipment. (See the Transportation Department Checklist, Workpaper II4.10.)

Review the Recovery Headquarters Team Activities

STEP 5

The recovery chairperson reviews the results of the personnel notification process with the recovery headquarters team manager. They identify which of the personnel assigned as primary team leaders were available, which were not available, and which personnel assigned as alternates have replaced the unavailable primaries.

Review the Computer Operations Recovery Team Activities

STEP 6

The recovery chairperson reviews the status of the systems and applications software vendor notifications and the estimates of the time required to resume the processing of applications with the computer operations recovery team manager. This estimate is the total of the time to: travel to the computer backup site; bring up and test the systems software and libraries; bring up and test the applications software; load the production backups, the data base backups, and the application data file backups; and reconstruct the application data files to an acceptable point in time. It should also include the time to rerun the work-in-process transactions that were destroyed by the disaster.

Authorize the Activation of the Computer Backup Site

STEP 7

If the data center is damaged to the point that it will not be able to process applications in time to meet the critical schedule, the recovery chairperson authorizes the activation of the computer backup site agreement. This decision is usually made by the recovery chairperson because, if the company is using a commercial hot site for the backup site, this decision will result in a significant expenditure.

Review the Disaster Site Recovery Team Activities

STEP 8

The recovery chairperson reviews the damage assessment estimates with the disaster site recovery team manager. The disaster site recovery team manager will present estimates of: the time required to restore the data center; the damage to the equipment, supplies, and forms; and the damage to the computer data on the disks and tapes. The manager also makes recommendations for the protection of undamaged equipment, for the repair of damaged equipment, and for the replacement of destroyed equipment.

The recovery chairperson should review the plans to replace damaged and destroyed equipment with the in-house insurance department representative before authorizing the ordering of replacements. This is important, because a company cannot make a unilateral decision to abandon insured equipment that is believed to be destroyed. The insurance company may find an equipment repair company that can recondition the equipment. If a company replaces equipment that can be salvaged, it could end up owning two identical pieces of equipment after the insurance company delivers the repaired equipment.

Approve Selection of the Temporary or Permanent Data Center

STEP 9

If a temporary or permanent data center facility is needed and a computer cold site is not available, the recovery chairperson will review the information provided by the disaster site recovery manager on potential sites and approve the selection.

Meet with Executive Management

STEP 10

The recovery chairperson meets with executive management to explain the nature of the disaster, when it happened, how it happened, and the cause, if it is known. The recovery chairperson will then explain the anticipated effect on the IS department and the potential impact on the company. The recovery chairperson should provide information on IS personnel injuries; the status of notification to the families; and the extent of damage to the building, the computer equipment, communications facilities, and essential records located in the data center.

The recovery chairperson will explain the recovery operation strategy being used to resume data center operations. The chairperson and executive managers will mutually agree to a time for the next briefing. An example of the recovery chairperson's recovery responsibilities is provided as Workpaper II4.12.

THE RECOVERY HEADQUARTERS TEAM MANAGER

The recovery headquarters team manager is responsible for providing all of the communications and administrative support activities throughout the recovery operation. After the DCRP has been activated, the recovery headquarters team manager will be responsible for:

1. Distributing the forms that will be used throughout the recovery operation.
2. Conducting a recovery headquarters meeting.
3. Providing notification and communications team support—for example, selecting the IS personnel call sequence (categories), authorizing IS personnel notification, and managing incoming phone calls.
4. Providing administration team support—for example, organizing recovery headquarters, providing equipment and supplies, organizing recovery operations team meetings, and providing other administrative support.

The following paragraphs describe each of these actions.

STEP 1

Distribute Recovery Forms

During the chairperson's meeting, the recovery headquarters team manager distributes the forms to be used during the recovery operation. These forms include those described in the following paragraphs.

Personnel Location Control Form. This form is used to identify where IS personnel are located during the recovery operation. For example, employees could be working at the backup site or asleep in the hotel at which backup site personnel are staying. The personnel location control form can be used to locate and contact an employee who may have had a personal emergency during the recovery operation. On the other hand, if an individual is asleep after a 12-hour shift and a call is not an emergency, the recovery headquarters team can take a message or let the caller know when to contact the employee. (See Workpaper II4.13.)

Recovery Status Report Form. This form is used to accumulate all of the facts and figures involved in the recovery operation by the recovery teams. The significant recovery activities should be logged on this form. (See Workpaper II4.14.)

Travel and Expense Report Form. This form is used to reimburse IS employees for the out-of-pocket expenses they incur during the recovery operation. It is also used to account for insurance recovery expenses. (See Workpaper II4.15.)

Disaster Recovery Time Record Form. This form is used by each IS person involved in the recovery operation. It is not intended to be used for payroll purposes. Its major purpose is to account for those employees who put in an extraordinary effort during the recovery operation. The completed forms can help IS management determine who will be considered for any extraordinary compensation provided by the human resources department (e.g., compensatory time off from work). (See Workpaper II4.16.)

Conduct a Recovery Headquarters Meeting

STEP 2

After the chairperson's meeting is over, the recovery headquarters team manager should conduct a meeting for the recovery headquarters team leaders (e.g., the notification and communications team leader and the administration team leader). During this meeting, the recovery headquarters team manager should explain the goals and objectives that were identified during the recovery chairperson's activation meeting. The recovery headquarters team manager should then review the tasks that will be performed by the two recovery teams. The recovery headquarters team manager should distribute copies of forms that will be used during the recovery operation and provide instructions on how and when the forms are to be completed. He or she should also distribute and review copies of the prepared public statement.

Provide Notification and Communications Team Support

STEP 3

The recovery headquarters team manager should assist the other two recovery team managers in determining the order in which remaining IS personnel are to be notified. IS personnel can be classified into five categories:

1. Category 1 refers to those IS personnel who should report to the recovery headquarters immediately. They may be needed at the recovery headquarters for the notification and communications team phone alerts or they may be needed at the headquarters to support one of the other teams.
2. Category 2 refers to those IS personnel who should prepare to travel to—and, if necessary, stay in the area of—the computer backup site. This group should review its copy of its DCRP responsibilities to make sure it takes everything it needs to resume processing at the backup site and to stay at a local hotel if necessary.
3. Category 3 refers to those IS personnel who should report to the disaster site because they will be working on the salvage and repair activities of the disaster site recovery team.
4. Category 4 refers to those IS personnel who should stay home and wait for further notice. Many of these employees are assigned to serve as alternates for the initial team members. They will replace the employees on one of the three teams after a few days.
5. Category 5 may be used to represent any other specific employees a company may need to include.

Authorizing the IS Personnel Notification. The recovery headquarters team manager should authorize the notification and communications team leader to perform a full IS personnel notification process. Before the notification is authorized, the notification and communications team leader records the recovery headquarters location and telephone information on the personnel notification procedure (see Workpaper II4.17) and makes copies for everyone participating in the notification process. The recovery headquarters team manager provides the list of IS personnel to be notified using the personnel notification information checklist (see Workpaper II4.18).

After the members of the notification and communications team complete a first attempt at notifying everyone on the list, they should make a copy of the results and send the copy to the recovery headquarters team manager. A second attempt should be made to notify personnel who were not reached during the first attempt.

Managing the Incoming Telephone Calls. The recovery headquarters team manager should work with the notification and communications team leader to implement a procedure for managing incoming telephone calls. A detailed explanation of the procedure and a form are provided in the next section of this chapter, entitled "The Notification and Communications Team Leader."

STEP 4

Provide Administration Team Support

The recovery headquarters team manager should identify areas in the headquarters in which the recovery chairperson, the notification and communications team, the administration team, the computer operations recovery team, the disaster site recovery team, and the staff department representatives will be located. Twenty-four-hour staffing at the recovery headquarters should be scheduled to ensure support is available for the individual recovery teams.

Providing Equipment and Supplies. The recovery headquarters team manager should establish a supply area and establish procedures for recovery teams to obtain supplies. To facilitate the status reporting process, the manager should obtain battery-operated tape-recording machines for each team, ensure that extra batteries and cassettes are available, and ensure that a copy machine is available at the recovery headquarters.

Organizing Recovery Operations Team Meetings. When the recovery chairperson or any of the three recovery team managers need to conduct meetings, this team supplies the administrative support. This team alerts the recovery team managers or the recovery team leaders who will be attending, organizes the meeting place, and records the minutes of the meeting. Shortly after the meeting is over, the minutes of the meeting should be documented and distributed to the attendees.

Providing Other Administrative Support. Such support might include:

- Ensuring there are adequate cash advances to cover travel, hotel, and other out-of-pocket expenses and collecting and processing all travel and expense reports.
- Controlling all purchases, leases, and rental requisition requests.
- Obtaining the special general ledger account number that will be used throughout the recovery operation to charge recovery expenditures and applying the general ledger number to all expense accounts or recovery invoices.
- Collecting and processing all completed recovery status reports.
- Collecting and processing all daily time record reports.

The recovery headquarters team manager's recovery responsibilities are provided in Workpaper II4.19.

THE NOTIFICATION AND COMMUNICATIONS TEAM LEADER

After the recovery headquarters team activation meeting has been conducted, the notification and communications team leader assumes responsibility for providing the notification and communications support throughout the recovery operation. The notification and communications team acts as a communications control point for all communications made during the recovery operation. The actions it performs include:

1. Managing the notification of IS personnel.
2. Identifying specific telephone numbers to be used for outgoing and incoming calls.
3. Managing all incoming phone calls to the recovery headquarters.

4. Acting as a control point for vendor notifications.
5. Accumulating the personnel location control forms from the recovery team managers and leaders.

The steps described in the following paragraphs may be performed in a different sequence than that suggested here.

Manage the Notification of IS Personnel

STEP 1

The notification and communications team leader is responsible for ensuring that all IS personnel have been notified that the DCRP has been activated and have been given a recovery assignment. The team leader reports the results of the notification calls to the recovery headquarters team manager.

In order to accomplish this, the team leader should assign personnel to notify IS department personnel using the personnel notification information checklist (see Workpaper II4.18). This checklist contains the name, address, and phone number for each employee in the IS department. The information used in the checklist is obtained from the completed data gathering form (as discussed in Chapter II-3).

The team leader reviews the personnel notification procedure (see Workpaper II4.17). This procedure is intended to minimize the possibility of prematurely alarming families of employees who have been injured by the disaster. (If there have been injuries, the company should follow the procedure in the DCRP for notifying families.)

Identify Outgoing and Incoming Telephone Numbers

STEP 2

The team leader is responsible for identifying specific telephone numbers that will be used for outgoing and incoming calls at the recovery headquarters using the reserved telephone numbers list form (see Workpaper II4.20).

The reason for identifying which phones are used for outgoing calls and which for incoming calls is to ensure that people who are trying to return calls have a line that is open. For example, in the early stages of a recovery operation, there is a greater need for outgoing phone calls than for incoming calls. If there were 10 phones available, eight could be used for outgoing calls and two could be reserved for incoming calls. As time goes on, there will be fewer outgoing phone calls and more people calling back to headquarters. Some of the phones used for outgoing calls can then be switched and used for incoming calls.

Manage Incoming Phone Calls

STEP 3

The notification and communications team leader should implement a plan to manage all incoming phone calls to the recovery headquarters. Because recovery personnel will be busy, it is important to ensure they are not interrupted by telephone calls. The incoming telephone call procedure and form can be used to manage these calls (see Workpaper II4.21).

Act as a Control Point for Vendor Notifications

STEP 4

Even though the notification and communications team is not responsible for making phone alerts to the various IS department vendors, the team members do collect the completed vendor notification checklists from the recovery headquarters team members who made the calls. They will assume the responsibility for continuing to try to reach vendors that have not yet been contacted, using the information on the vendor notification checklists.

STEP 5

Accumulate the Personnel Location Control Forms

The notification and communications team should accumulate the completed personnel location control forms from the recovery team managers and leaders. This team should also maintain a master list of all recovery team personnel assignments and work locations. Anyone who needs to contact an IS employee can find the employee through the notification and communications team. A summary of the notification and communications team leader's recovery responsibilities is provided as Workpaper II4.22.

THE ADMINISTRATION TEAM LEADER

After the recovery headquarters team activation meeting has been conducted, the administration team leader assumes responsibility for providing administrative and clerical support throughout the recovery operation. This includes:

- Obtaining equipment and supplies.
- Organizing recovery meetings.
- Providing travel support.
- Accumulating and processing recovery status reports.
- Accumulating and processing travel and expense reports.
- Accumulating and processing daily time record reports.

These actions are not assigned steps because they are performed as needed.

Obtaining Equipment and Supplies

The administration team should obtain battery-operated tape recorders and supplies for use by the recovery teams. If they have to be purchased from outside vendors, arrangements should be made through the purchasing department representative. To obtain this representative's name, the team should contact the recovery headquarters team manager. The members of the team should identify equipment and other supplies that will be needed immediately (e.g., copy machines, personal computers, microfilm/fiche readers).

Organizing Recovery Meetings

The administration team can organize any recovery meetings requested by the recovery chairperson or the recovery team managers. The team notifies the personnel that should attend, organizes the meeting room, and records the minutes of the meeting. It then provides typed minutes, obtains approval, and distributes the minutes to the attendees.

Providing Travel Support

The administration team should provide travel support for the recovery teams. The team leader should obtain travel requirements and cash advance requirements from the recovery team leaders. The team should assist the recovery team leaders in obtaining company vehicles when available. If company vehicles are not available, the team should lease cars, vans, or small trucks. It should coordinate all travel requirements with the transportation department support representative. If air transportation is required, the administration team member should work with the transportation department or the company's travel agency. If the company's transportation department authorizes the recovery headquarters team to make the travel arrangements for the recovery team, the administration team should prepare a travel itinerary form (see Workpaper II4.23) for each person for whom travel arrangements have been made.

Accumulating and Processing Recovery Status Reports

The administration team should accumulate recovery status report forms from the team leaders on a daily basis. If any part of the status reports has been taped, the team member should transcribe the tape. The team member should make a copy of the report, which is sent to the recovery headquarters manager, with the original going to a master recovery status report file managed by the administration team and stored in its area of the recovery headquarters. A control procedure should be established to ensure the receipt of status reports from the team leaders each day.

Accumulating and Processing Travel and Expense Reports

The administration team should accumulate travel and expense report forms from the team leaders on a weekly basis. It should record the general ledger account number that will be used to account for all of the recovery operations expenses. Two copies of each travel and expense report should be made: the first copy is used to process the form for reimbursement through the finance department support representative; the second copy is used to organize one complete set of forms for the insurance department support representative dealing with the insurance carrier. The original of each travel and expense report form should be filed in a master travel and expense report file managed by the administration team and stored in its area of the recovery headquarters. A control procedure should be established to ensure the receipt of travel and expense reports from the team leaders on a weekly basis.

Accumulating and Processing Daily Time Record Reports

The administration team should accumulate the daily time record forms from team leaders on a weekly basis. A control procedure should be set up to ensure the receipt of these forms from the team leaders each week. A summary of the administration team leader's recovery responsibilities is provided in Workpaper II4.24.

WORKPAPER II4.01 Building Services Support Checklist

Company Name____________ Issued________ Section________ Page________
Data Center____________________
Data Center Recovery Plan________________ Supersedes________________

<u>BUILDING SERVICES SUPPORT CHECKLIST</u>

Department	Name	Home Phone	Contact Status
Building Services			
(primary)	____________________	____________	__________
(alternate)	____________________	____________	__________

Support Activities:

1. Provide an interface with local authorities to determine when it is safe to enter the building (e.g., considering structural damage, hazardous materials).

2. Manage all building damage assessment and repair activities, keeping recovery management informed of building and computer facility status.

3. Manage the activities of all building and utility vendors (e.g., contractors, engineers, electric, water, gas).

4. In the event another company location will be used by the data center recovery teams (e.g., recovery headquarters), make all necessary arrangements to provide access to and use of the facilities. Ensure that 24-hour access is available until the location is no longer needed for the recovery operation.

5. In the event a temporary computer center must be acquired, review the minimum facilities requirements, locate potential sites, and review the sites with the disaster site recovery team manager to obtain guidance on which site will be used. Acquire and prepare the site for use.

6. In the event a new computer center must be acquired, review the current facilities requirements with the disaster site recovery team manager. Locate potential sites and review with the disaster site recovery team manager and the head of IS. When a final selection is made, acquire the site and prepare it for use.

WORKPAPER II4.02 Finance Support Checklist

Company Name___________ Issued________ Section_______ Page_______
Data Center__________________
Data Center Recovery Plan_______________ Supersedes______________

FINANCE STAFF DEPARTMENT SUPPORT CHECKLIST

Department	Name	Home Phone	Contact Status
Finance			
(primary)	______________	__________	________
(alternate)	______________	__________	________

Support Activities:

1. Provide the recovery team personnel with expense monies and petty cash during the recovery operation.

2. Make arrangements to notify financial institutions and regulatory authorities of the disaster situation.

3. Provide an account number within the general ledger accounting system to be used to maintain a record of all disaster-related expenses.

4. Verify the status of accounting applications that have been reconstructed during the recovery operation.

5. Coordinate the investigation and resolution of any out-of-balance conditions with accounting applications.

6. Approve any modifications to financial controls requested to facilitate backup site processing.

7. Issue stop-payment notices for destroyed or missing checks.

WORKPAPER II4.03 Human Resources Support Checklist

Company Name____________ Issued_________ Section________ Page________
Data Center____________________
Data Center Recovery Plan_________________ Supersedes________________

HUMAN RESOURCES SUPPORT CHECKLIST

Department	Name	Home Phone	Contact Status
Human Resources			
(primary)	____________________	____________	__________
(alternate)	____________________	____________	__________

Support Activities:

1. Contact local hospitals to determine which personnel have been admitted with injuries sustained during the disaster. Provide this information to IS management at the recovery headquarters.

2. Notify and assist families of injured or deceased personnel. Work with IS management.

3. Advise the recovery headquarters team manager of the status of family notifications.

4. Assist with the preparation and filing of any required benefit insurance plans (e.g., workers' compensation claims).

5. Obtain replacement or temporary personnel to meet recovery operation needs.

6. Consider implementing an extraordinary-compensation program to reward employees who extend special efforts. Work with IS management.

7. Monitor stress situations and provide employee counseling sessions. Assist in monitoring personnel for symptoms of posttraumatic stress disorder. Provide or obtain psychological support for personnel suffering from such symptoms. Work with medical department.

WORKPAPER II4.04 Insurance Support Checklist

Company Name___________ Issued________ Section_______ Page_______
Data Center__________________
Data Center Recovery Plan_______________ Supersedes______________

INSURANCE SUPPORT CHECKLIST

Department	Name	Home Phone	Contact Status
Insurance			
(primary)	_______________________	_____________	__________
(alternate)	_______________________	_____________	__________

Support Activities:

1. Notify all insurance carriers.
2. Provide guidance on what action may be taken to salvage items without affecting insurance coverage.
3. Provide guidance as to the type of loss or claim records required.
4. Act as an interface with the insurance company's adjuster.
5. Prepare and file all insurance claims.
6. Provide any required additional or special insurance coverage.

WORKPAPER II4.05 Internal Audit Support Checklist

Company Name____________ Issued_________ Section________ Page________
Data Center____________________
Data Center Recovery Plan_________________ Supersedes________________

INTERNAL AUDIT SUPPORT CHECKLIST

Department	Name	Home Phone	Contact Status
Internal Audit			
(primary)	__________	__________	________
(alternate)	__________	__________	________

Support Activities:

1. Provide financial and IS auditing personnel at the computer backup site, if required.
2. Review the schedules and controls in use for running applications at the computer backup site.
3. Review the controls in use for processing financial applications in an out-of-balance condition.
4. Review any temporary controls established to facilitate the recovery operation.
5. Notify the external auditors of the situation, if necessary.
6. Monitor the control and use of financial items (e.g., checks, petty cash).
7. Assist security in the investigation of the cause of the disaster.

WORKPAPER II4.06 Legal Support Checklist

Company Name___________ Issued________ Section_______ Page_______
Data Center_________________
Data Center Recovery Plan_______________ Supersedes_______________

LEGAL SUPPORT CHECKLIST

Department	Name	Home Phone	Contact Status
Legal			
(primary)	______________________	____________	__________
(alternate)	______________________	____________	__________

Support Activities:

1. Advise the recovery teams on existing contract terms and conditions:

   a. Computer equipment contracts.
   b. Computer software contracts.

2. Assist the recovery teams with the review and approval of new contracts:

   a. Computer equipment contracts.
   b. Computer software contracts.
   c. Property or real estate contracts.

3. Advise the recovery chairperson on legal or regulatory requirements that may affect recovery processing schedules or priorities.

4. Assist the recovery teams in the preparation of any required notifications (verbal or written) to vendors concerning the activation of the recovery plan.

WORKPAPER II4.07 Public Relations Support Checklist

Company Name____________ Issued_________ Section________ Page_______
Data Center____________________
Data Center Recovery Plan________________ Supersedes________________

PUBLIC RELATIONS SUPPORT CHECKLIST

Department	Name	Home Phone	Contact Status
Public Relations			
(primary)	____________________	____________	__________
(alternate)	____________________	____________	__________

Support Activities:

1. If telephone communications are disrupted, make emergency announcements over radio or TV to communicate with employees.

2. Manage all communications with news media at the disaster site.

3. Set up a news media area in or near the recovery headquarters to conduct and manage all press conferences.

4. Provide a formal statement to be used by IS personnel if approached by the news media. The statement is intended to minimize adverse publicity.

5. Provide employees with information on the recovery progress. Consider using the company's newspaper or magazine.

6. If an external photographer is hired to take pictures of the damage, assist in the contracting process. Ensure the company is purchasing both the pictures and the negatives from the photographer to provide complete control of the future use of the pictures.

WORKPAPER II4.08 Purchasing Support Checklist

Company Name___________ Issued________ Section_______ Page_______
Data Center__________________
Data Center Recovery Plan_______________ Supersedes______________

PURCHASING SUPPORT CHECKLIST

Department	Name	Home Phone	Contact Status
Purchasing			
(primary)	______________________	_____________	__________
(alternate)	______________________	_____________	__________

Support Activities:

1. Provide the recovery headquarters manager with a purchasing department single point of contact throughout the recovery operation.

2. Coordinate vendor support during the damage assessment, salvage and restoration phases of the recovery operation.

3. Obtain replacements of equipment, forms, and computer supplies on an emergency basis during the recovery operation.

   - Use DCRP inventory and vendor checklists.

4. Obtain repair services or replacements for damaged furniture or fixtures.

   - Use DCRP inventory and vendor checklists.

WORKPAPER II4.09 Security Support Checklist

Company Name___________ Issued________ Section_______ Page_______
Data Center__________________
Data Center Recovery Plan_______________ Supersedes______________

SECURITY SUPPORT CHECKLIST

Department	Name	Home Phone	Contact Status
Security			
(primary)	_______________________	_____________	__________
(alternate)	_______________________	_____________	__________

Support Activities:

1. Secure the affected area immediately. Provide 24-hour security.

2. Coordinate and play an active role in any investigations (e.g., into arson, bombing) conducted by local or company authorities.

3. Provide security guards, as required, during the recovery operation. Guards may be required during the transportation of data, reports, and materials between recovery operation locations.

4. Instruct all security personnel to verify that individuals entering the recovery operations sites are authorized by checking the appropriate authorized access list and the company identification of the individual.

WORKPAPER II4.10 Transportation Support Checklist

Company Name___________ Issued________ Section_______ Page_______
Data Center__________________
Data Center Recovery Plan_______________ Supersedes______________

TRANSPORTATION SUPPORT CHECKLIST

Department	Name	Home Phone	Contact Status
Transportation			
(primary)	______________________	_____________	__________
(alternate)	______________________	_____________	__________

Support Activities:

1. Provide vehicles and drivers to transport computer documents and supplies to and from the recovery sites.

2. Provide vehicles or travel services to transport personnel to and from recovery operation work locations, if necessary.

3. Establish courier services for the movement of input, output, material, and supplies to and from the computer backup site.

4. Provide secure space for the storage of new, repaired, and salvaged computer and communications equipment pending repair of the disaster site.

5. Control the receipt and storage of computer and communications equipment. Ensure that proper receiving and security practices are followed.

6. Control the receipt, storage, and distribution of items, materials, and supplies required to support the recovery operation.

7. Provide shipping and transportation support for the movement of equipment, materials, and supplies to the recovery operation locations.

WORKPAPER II4.11 Initial News Media Statement

Company Name___________ Issued________ Section_______ Page_______
Data Center__________________
Data Center Recovery Plan_______________ Supersedes______________

INITIAL DISASTER ALERT PROCEDURE

INITIAL NEWS MEDIA STATEMENT

The emergency is being handled in accordance with the company's emergency procedures. Our management team is meeting with the local authorities right now to obtain official information related to the incident. We want you to publicize the facts regarding the situation. Therefore, we have made arrangements at [location] for your use. Management will be presenting a company statement very shortly. You will be invited.

WORKPAPER II4.12 Recovery Chairperson--Procedure

Company Name___________ Issued________ Section_______ Page_______
Data Center__________________
Data Center Recovery Plan_______________ Supersedes______________

<u>RECOVERY CHAIRPERSON--PROCEDURE</u>

Recovery Actions

1. After activating the data center recovery plan, notify executive management (listed below) that the DCRP has been activated and provide:

    a. A brief description of the disaster situation.
    b. An estimate of when computer services will be available.
    c. A request that it alert all personnel in each business group that will be affected by the data center interruption.
    d. The location and telephone number of the recovery headquarters.
    e. Assurance that it will be notified in the event of any change in recovery status.

Name	Title	Home Phone	Result of Alert

Note: All area codes are [<u>area code</u>] unless otherwise noted.

2. Notify appropriate staff department management of the disaster situation. Request that staff department support representatives report to the recovery headquarters immediately. Provide the location and phone number of the recovery headquarters. Use the staff department support checklists (Workpapers II4.01 - II4.11).

3. Conduct the recovery operation activation meeting with the three recovery team managers:

    a. Establish the recovery operation scope and objectives.
    b. Review the recovery procedures to be activated to support the recovery objectives:
        - If appropriate, approve the notification of the computer backup site by the computer operations recovery team manager.

c. Have each recovery team manager:
   - Attempt to account for all personnel who may have been working at the time of the disaster. During IS personnel notifications, do not unnecessarily alarm families.
   - Identify the category in which the IS personnel should be alerted. Consider:
     -- Additional personnel needed at the recovery headquarters.
     -- Personnel who should stay home and remain on standby (they will be needed when the initial group needs rest).

d. Have the recovery headquarters manager review the services that will be provided through recovery headquarters according to the procedures activated.

e. Have the recovery headquarters manager distribute copies of the following recovery forms, as appropriate:
   - Personnel location control form.
   - Recovery status report form.
   - Travel and expense report form.
   - Disaster recovery time record form.

f. Remind all personnel not to make public statements. If news media representatives inquire into the situation, the recovery chairperson will be the temporary corporate spokesperson until the public relations representatives arrive. Refer to the statement in the initial disaster alert section.

4. Conduct a meeting with staff department support representatives:

   a. The chairperson will provide any information that is known about the incident. For example:
      - What happened?
      - When did it happen?
      - How did it happen?
      - Were there any injuries or death?
      - Is the cause known?

   b. Review the recovery goals.

   c. The chairperson will request support identified in the staff department support checklists (Workpapers II4.01 - II4.11).

   d. Establish a schedule for continued status reporting.

5. Meet with the recovery headquarters team manager to:

   a. Review the results of the IS employee notifications.

   b. Determine which recovery team personnel are available. If primaries are not available, assign alternates.

6. Meet with the disaster site recovery team manager to:

   a. Review the estimates of the time required to restore the affected area.

b. In the event a temporary facility must be obtained, approve a suitable facility and the design layout.
c. Review all computer and network equipment, data, forms, supplies, and documentation damage assessment and salvage reports.
d. Authorize the ordering of replacements for nonsalvageable items (ensure that undesirable equipment is not reordered). When required, meet with vendor senior management to expedite deliveries.
e. Establish a schedule for the reporting of status on:
   - Facility repair.
   - Computer and network equipment repair or replacement.

7. Meet with the computer operations recovery team manager to:

a. Review the status of software vendor notifications.
b. Review the plans for the use of the computer backup site for the processing of critical applications.
c. Review the estimates of the time required to bring up and test system software and libraries.
d. Review the plans for the load and reconstruction of data bases and applications data.
e. Review and approve the initial processing schedule.
f. Establish a schedule for the reporting of status on:
   - The completion of system restoration.
   - The completion of data base restoration and reconstruction.
   - When the computer backup site will be ready for processing.
   - The production processing schedule.

8. Meet with the networking recovery team manager to:

a. Review the status of communications vendor notifications.
b. Review the plans for the activation and use of alternative data communications and network facilities at the computer backup site.
c. Establish a schedule for the reporting of status on the activation of alternative network facilities.

9. Meet with executive management group. Explain the anticipated effect on the IS department and the potential impact on the company. Provide the following information:

a. Personnel injuries and status of notification to families.
b. Damage to assets:
   - Building.
   - Computer equipment.
   - Communications facilities.
   - Essential records.

c. Recovery strategy:
   - Phased approach to recovery.

d. Processing delays:
   - Estimated downtime.
   - Jobs to be processed when computer resources become available.
   - Jobs to be delayed temporarily.

e. Establish a schedule for continued status reporting.

WORKPAPER II4.13 Personnel Location Control Form

PERSONNEL LOCATION CONTROL FORM

COMPLETE AFTER PLAN ACTIVATION

Date: ____________________
Issued by: ____________________
Team: ____________________

After the data center recovery plan has been activated, complete this checklist indicating work location of recovery personnel. Continue to update the information throughout each day during the recovery operation. As updates are made, send a new copy to the notification and communications team for its use in maintaining the recovery operation personnel location control forms.

Name	Recovery Location	Phone Number	Work Schedule From	To

WORKPAPER II4.14 Recovery Status Report Form

RECOVERY STATUS REPORT FORM

Recovery teams can use this form to log significant recovery activities.

After the data center recovery plan has been activated, you are required to submit written recovery status reports daily. Submit completed status reports to the administration team. This status report may be submitted handwritten as long as it is legible.

Date: ______________________ Name: ______________________

Time: ______________________ Team: ______________________

Comments: ____

____

____

____

____

____

____

Conclusions: ____

____

____

____

WORKPAPER II4.15 Travel and Expense Report Form*

WEEKLY EXPENSE REPORT
(ATTACH RECEIPTS)

TO ______________________________ FROM ______________________________

FOR WEEK ENDING ______________

TIME RECORD:
START: HOUR _____ DATE __________

RETURN: HOUR _____ DATE __________

		SUN	MON	TUES	WED	THUR	FRI	SAT	TOTALS FOR WEEK
		CITY / ARRIVE / DEPART	CITY / ARRIVE / DEPART	CITY / ARRIVE / DEPART	CITY / ARRIVE / DEPART	CITY / ARRIVE / DEPART	CITY / ARRIVE / DEPART	CITY / ARRIVE / DEPART	
1	HOTEL–MOTEL								
2	BREAKFAST								
3	LUNCH								
4	DINNER								
5	PLANE–RAIL–BUS FARE								
6	LOCAL TAXIS–BUS FARE								
7	AUTO EXPENSE: REPAIR–TIRES–SUPPLIES								
8	GAS–OIL								
9	LUBRICATION–WASH								
10	GARAGE–PARKING								
11	TOLLS								
12	PHONE–TELEGRAMS								
13	TIPS								
14	ENTERTAINMENT								
	TOTALS								
	NUMBER OF CALLS MADE (LIST CUSTOMER ON REVERSE SIDE)								
	NUMBER OF HOURS WORKED								

STATE BUSINESS PURPOSE—PEOPLE ENTERTAINED—PLACE OF ENTERTAINMENT AND TIME—(LIST GIFTS ON REVERSE SIDE)

I HEREBY CERTIFY THAT THE ABOVE EXPENDITURES REPRESENT CASH SPENT FOR LEGITIMATE COMPANY BUSINESS ONLY AND INCLUDES NO ITEMS OF A PERSONAL NATURE.

Signed ______________________________

DATE	REPAYMENT RECAP	AMOUNT	
	ADVANCE RECEIVED		
	REIMBURSED		
	TOTAL		
	EXPENSE FOR WEEK		
	OVER OR SHORT		

MILEAGE RECORD	
END OF TRIP	
LESS START	
MILES PER TRIP	

APPROVAL

CASHIERS MEMO	
CHECK NO.	
DATE	AMOUNT

*Not available on disk.

WORKPAPER II4.16 Disaster Recovery Time Record Form*

DISASTER RECOVERY TIME RECORDS

Employee Name ____
Last Name *First Name* *Middle Initial*

Social Security Number: ___ ___ ___–___ ___–___ ___ ___ ___

Exempt ______________ Nonexempt ______________

Time	Monday __/__/__	Tuesday __/__/__	Wednesday __/__/__	Thursday __/__/__	Friday __/__/__	Saturday __/__/__	Sunday __/__/__
12:00 am							
1:00 am							
2:00 am							
3:00 am							
4:00 am							
5:00 am							
6:00 am							
7:00 am							
8:00 am							
9:00 am							
10:00 am							
11:00 am							
12:00 pm							
1:00 pm							
2:00 pm							
3:00 pm							
4:00 pm							
5:00 pm							
6:00 pm							
7:00 pm							
8:00 pm							
9:00 pm							
10:00 pm							
11:00 pm							
Total							

Total Hours for the Week	

Date Submitted ________/________/________

Employee Signature ______________________________

FOR DISASTER RECOVERY ADMINISTRATION ONLY

Disaster Recovery Cost Center ______________________________

Reviewed by ______________________________

*Not available on disk.

WORKPAPER II4.17 Personnel Notification Procedure

Company Name____________ Issued_________ Section________ Page________
Data Center____________________
Data Center Recovery Plan_________________ Supersedes________________

PERSONNEL NOTIFICATION PROCEDURE

After the data center recovery plan has been officially activated, use this procedure to alert IS personnel.

IMPORTANT NOTICE: BY USING THE FOLLOWING INSTRUCTIONS, YOU WILL NOT UNNECESSARILY ALARM MEMBERS OF THE FAMILY OF AN EMPLOYEE WHO WAS WORKING IN THE DATA CENTER AT THE TIME OF THE DISASTER.

Place telephone call and say, "May I speak with [individual]?"

1. If available, provide the following information:

   a. Brief description of the problem.
   b. Location of the recovery headquarters:
      ____
   c. Telephone number at the recovery headquarters:
      ____
   d. Any immediate action requirements as noted on the list.
   e. Remind personnel to make no public statements regarding the situation.
   f. Remind personnel not to call co-workers and to advise their family not to call other employees. (This will avoid premature notification to families of personnel working at the time of the disaster.)

2. If not available, say, "Where may I reach [individual]?"

   a. If at any location other than the data center, get the telephone number. Call the other location and provide the above information.
   b. If individual is working in the data center, indicate that you will reach the individual at the data center. (Do not discuss the disaster with the person answering the phone.)
   c. Immediately notify the recovery headquarters manager that the individual was working in the data center at the time of the disaster.
   d. Record the information in the contact status column.

3. If contact is made with an answering machine: make no statement regarding the situation; provide the telephone number at recovery headquarters designated for incoming calls; ask that employee make contact with [your name] at this number as soon as possible.

4. If no answer:

   a. Record the time attempted contacts were made.
   b. Periodically call again, until contact is made.

5. If no answer and the individual has an assigned beeper number:

   a. Place a call to that number.
   b. Insert the telephone number of one of the incoming phone numbers to the recovery headquarters.
   c. Alert the operator at the incoming phone line that you have called the individual and ask the operator to transfer the call to you when it comes in.

6. If contact information is invalid (e.g., wrong number, person moved):

   a. If person has moved, try to get new telephone number and contact the individual.
   b. Notify management of incorrect contact information.

WORKPAPER II4.18 Personnel Notification Information Checklist

Company Name___________ Issued________ Section_______ Page_______
Data Center__________________
Data Center Recovery Plan_______________ Supersedes______________

PERSONNEL NOTIFICATION INFORMATION CHECKLIST

Complete after plan activation:

Computer Operations:

Name	Address	Phone Number	Priority Number	Contact Status

Complete after plan activation:

Applications Programming:

Name	Address	Phone Number	Priority Number	Contact Status

WORKPAPER II4.19 Recovery Headquarters Team Manager's Recovery Procedures

Company Name___________ Issued________ Section_______ Page_______
Data Center__________________
Data Center Recovery Plan_______________ Supersedes_______________

RECOVERY HEADQUARTERS MANAGER RECOVERY PROCEDURE

Recovery procedures follow. Read the entire section before performing any assignments. The recovery objectives will dictate the need for and timing of all assignments.

RECOVERY ACTIONS:

1. During the recovery chairperson's meeting, perform the following:

   a. Distribute copies and explain the proper use for the following recovery forms to be used throughout the recovery operation.

      - Personnel location control form (Workpaper II4.13). All recovery team managers and team leaders are responsible to complete this form if any recovery personnel are assigned to locations other than recovery headquarters. After the recovery operation has been organized or any changes made to personnel assignments of locations, the completed form is to be submitted to the notification and communication team. The notification and communication team will maintain a list of current personnel assignments and work locations.

      - Recovery status report form (Workpaper II4.14). All recovery managers and team leaders are required to submit status reports. Recovery teams can use this form to log significant recovery activities. The status report is to be submitted to the administration team daily. Recovery status reports will be required less frequently as recovery progresses; however, the completed status reports should be maintained until the recovery is officially concluded.

      - Travel and expense report form (Workpaper II4.15). All recovery expenses are to be recorded and charged to the disaster recovery cost center number. Each team leader will ensure that expense reports are prepared by all recovery personnel in accordance with normal company expense policies. The team leader will collect expense reports on a timely basis, obtain approval from their recovery manager, and submit to the administration team for proper processing and reimbursement.

- Disaster recovery time record form (Workpaper II4.16). These forms are provided for all personnel to maintain a log of hours worked during the recovery operation. The forms are to be submitted weekly to the recovery headquarters manager, who is responsible for ensuring that individuals are not overworked. Periodic rests should be taken to ensure the health and effectiveness of all personnel.

b. Assist the recovery team managers to determine the category in which the remaining department personnel will be notified using the following category explanation. Record the category information on the personnel notification checklist (Workpaper II4.18).

Category Number	Explanation
1	Report to the recovery headquarters immediately
2	Prepare to travel to computer backup site
3	Report to the disaster site to work on the salvage efforts
4	Stay home until further notice

c. Determine what type of recovery headquarters facilities will be required by each recovery team, staff department, and vendor representative.

2. Activate the required recovery teams to support the recovery operations:

   a. Administration recovery team.
   b. Notification and communication recovery team.

3. Complete the personnel location control form by identifying the work location and contact phone number for yourself and anyone working directly with you. (See Workpaper II4.13.)

4. Manage the recovery headquarters notification and communications efforts. Meet with the notification and communication team leader:

   a. Authorize that IS personnel notifications be performed:
      - Complete the location and telephone number of the recovery headquarters on the personnel notification procedure. (See Workpaper II4.17.) Make copies of this procedure and distribute to all personnel carrying out the department notification. This procedure has been developed

to limit the potential of prematurely alarming families of employees who may have been injured by the disaster.
- Provide the personnel notification information checklist. (See Workpaper II4.18.)
- Review the category assigned by the IS recovery management team to identify those individuals who should be called immediately.
- Review the instructions for calling personnel believed to have been working during the disaster and potentially injured.
- Authorize the notification and communications team leader to perform the IS personnel notification.
- Collect the completed IS personnel notification information checklists and provide information to recovery managers.

b. Manage the incoming telephone call control functions:
- Ensure that specific telephone numbers have been assigned to be used for incoming calls. Refer to the reserved telephone numbers list. (See Workpaper II4.20.)
- Ensure that personnel have been assigned to monitor the telephones designated for incoming calls.
- Provide copies of the incoming telephone call procedure and form to assist in handling all incoming calls correctly. (See Workpaper II4.21.)
- Inform the company telephone operators to direct all return calls to the assigned extensions at the recovery headquarters.

c. Ensure that accurate personnel location control information is being maintained for all recovery personnel.

5. Coordinate staff department support with recovery managers during the operation. Have them complete a personnel location control form identifying who is authorized access to the recovery headquarters, off-premises storage, disaster recovery backup site, and any other location used for recovery.

6. Identify equipment requirements and arrange for purchasing to provide copy machines, microfilm/microfiche reader/printers, other specific office equipment as required, and miscellaneous paper, pencils, and pens.

7. Manage all administrative and clerical support activities throughout the recovery operation. Meet with the administration team leader to coordinate:

   a. Travel requirements.
   b. Cash advance and expense requirements.
   c. Recovery status information.
   d. Recovery team meeting arrangements.

WORKPAPER II4.20 Reserved Telephone Numbers List Form

RESERVED TELEPHONE NUMBERS LIST

Log the telephone numbers to be assigned for incoming and outgoing calls. Assign monitors to each number.

Phone Extension	(I) Incoming (O) Outgoing	Monitored By

WORKPAPER II4.21 Incoming Telephone Call Procedure and Form

INCOMING TELEPHONE CALL PROCEDURE AND FORM

After the disaster recovery plan has been activated, this form will be used to control incoming telephone calls. Since recovery personnel will be busy, it is important to ensure they are not being interrupted by phone calls.

Follow the procedure as written. Ask whether the incoming call is a return call. If it is, put it through to the appropriate person. If it is not a return call, complete the message sheet. Make a copy and file it in the master file of incoming call forms. Send the original to the person being called.

Is this a return call?

[ ] Yes. Transfer phone call to the appropriate extension.

[ ] No. Take a message following the procedure below:

Message Taken by: ____

Message for: ______________________ Date: ________ Time: ______

Message from: _____________________ Company: ___________________

Area Code/Telephone: ___/________ Purpose of Call: _____________

____

____

____

____

How long will caller be at the noted telephone number? __________

WORKPAPER II4.22 Notification and Communications Team Leader Responsibilities

Company Name___________ Issued________ Section_______ Page_______
Data Center__________________
Data Center Recovery Plan_______________ Supersedes______________

NOTIFICATION AND COMMUNICATIONS TEAM LEADER RECOVERY PROCEDURE

Recovery procedures follow. Read the entire section before performing any assignments. The recovery objectives will dictate the need for and timing of all assignments.

RECOVERY ACTIONS:

1. Identify specific telephone numbers to be used for outgoing and incoming calls. Document the information on the reserved telephone numbers list (Workpaper II4.20). Indicate the phone extension, whether it is an incoming or outgoing line, and who is assigned to monitor the line.

2. Coordinate the IS personnel notification activities:

   a. Complete the location and telephone number of the recovery headquarters on the personnel notification procedure (Workpaper II4.17). Make copies of this procedure and distribute to all individuals carrying out the department notifications. This procedure has been developed to limit the potential of premature notification to families of personnel working at the time of the disaster.

   b. Working with the recovery headquarters manager, assign personnel to perform the department personnel notifications:
      - Review the instructions for calling personnel believed to have been working during the disaster who may be injured. Refer to the personnel notification procedure.
      - Review the priority assigned by the recovery management team to identify those individuals who should be called immediately.
      - Provide individuals with the IS personnel notification information checklist (Workpaper II4.18).
      - Have assigned personnel perform the IS personnel notification.
      - Collect the completed IS personnel notification information checklists and provide the information to the recovery headquarters manager.

3. Coordinate the incoming telephone call control functions:

   a. Assign specific telephone numbers to be used for incoming calls.
   b. Assign personnel to monitor the telephones designated for incoming calls.
   c. Provide copies of the incoming telephone call procedure and form (Workpaper II4.21) to assist individuals with the handling of all incoming calls correctly.
   d. Inform the company telephone operator to direct all return calls to the assigned extension at recovery headquarters.

4. Accumulate the personnel location control forms (Workpaper II4.13) from the recovery managers and leaders. Maintain a master list of current personnel assignments and work locations at the recovery headquarters. Anyone who needs to contact a member of the recovery team should obtain the contact information from the recovery headquarters.

WORKPAPER II4.23 Travel Itinerary Form

TRAVEL ITINERARY FORM

Itinerary for: ______________________________

Airline Reservations:

Date	Airline/ Flight	Depart (city)	Time	Arrive (city)	Time	Remarks

Hotel		Car Rental
Name: ____________	*	Rental Company: ____________
Address: ____________	*	Vehicle Type: ____________
____________	*	Pick-up Location: ____________
Telephone: ____________	*	Date: ____________
Arrival: ____________	*	Confirmed by: ____________
Departure: ____________	*	Confirmation Date: ____________
Accommodation/Rate: ______	*	

Travel Advance: [ ] Yes [ ] No Amount: $__________

Provide once copy to the individual; keep one copy for the recovery headquarters manager's file.

WORKPAPER II4.24 Administration Team Leader Responsibilities

Company Name___________ Issued________ Section_______ Page_______
Data Center__________________
Data Center Recovery Plan_______________ Supersedes______________

ADMINISTRATION TEAM LEADER RECOVERY PROCEDURE

Recovery procedures follow. Read the entire section before performing any assignments. The recovery objectives will dictate the need for and timing of all assignments.

RECOVERY ACTIONS:

1. Work with the recovery headquarters manager to establish the plan to provide administrative and clerical support:

   a. Schedule personnel to provide 24-hour coverage, if required.
   b. Obtain battery-operated tape recorders and supplies (batteries and cassettes) for use by the recovery teams. If they have to be purchased, contact the purchasing representative.
   c. Identify immediate equipment and supply requirements and make arrangements through the purchasing representative to obtain the following, as required:
      - Heavy-duty copy machines.
      - Microcomputers.
      - Microfilm/microfiche reader/printers.
      - Miscellaneous paper, pencils, and pens.
      - Miscellaneous office equipment specified after the disaster.
   d. Organize recovery meetings as requested by the recovery chairperson or the recovery managers.
      - Notify required personnel.
      - Organize a meeting place.
      - Record minutes of the meetings.
      - Type minutes, obtain approval, and distribute.

2. Obtain travel requirements and cash advance requirements from all recovery teams:

   a. Transportation arrangements to the disaster recovery backup site may be required. Assist the team leaders in obtaining company vehicles or issued cars for use during the recovery operation. If required, receive specific directions from the team leaders regarding which personnel may travel in the same vehicles (essential personnel should travel separately in the event of a traffic problem or accident).

b. If air transportation is required, call the travel department or the company's travel agent, [agent's name and phone number]. The travel agent can make reservations, produce and deliver airline tickets, and charge to the corporate account. Prepare a travel itinerary form (Workpaper II4.23) for each IS person traveling by air.

c. Obtain cash advance requirements from the team leaders.
   - Submit cash advance requirements to the finance department representative.
   - Distribute cash advances to recovery personnel.

3. Accumulate recovery status report forms (See Workpaper II4.14) from the team leaders. These should be submitted daily in the early stages, and less frequently as the recovery progresses.

   a. Set up a control checklist to ensure the receipt of status reports from each team leader.
   b. Transcribe any tape-recorded status reports.
   c. Make two copies of all reports and submit the copies to the recovery headquarters manager.
   d. Organize the original reports into a master recovery status report file.

4. Maintain a daily log, for the recovery headquarters manager, of all significant actions, decisions, and events relating to the recovery activities.

5. Accumulate travel and expense report forms (Workpaper II4.15) from all recovery personnel throughout the recovery operation:

   a. Put the general ledger number assigned to the recovery operation (obtain from the finance department representative) on all expense reports.
   b. Make two copies of each expense report.
   c. Review and process one copy for reimbursement through the finance department representative.
   d. Organize one complete set of expense reports for the corporate insurance representative.
   e. Maintain the original reports and organize into a master recovery expense report file.

6. Accumulate daily time records on a weekly basis and submit to the recovery headquarters manager. Ensure that all recovery managers and team leaders submit completed daily time records (Workpaper II4.16) each week.

The Computer Operations Recovery Team Section of the DCRP

CHAPTER

II-5

Chapter II-5 presents the actions that the computer operations recovery team takes following the activation of the data center recovery plan (DCRP). The computer operations recovery team is one of the three major teams in the data center recovery plan, the others being the recovery headquarters team and the disaster site recovery team. The DCRP teams are named for the recovery locations at which they will be operating; for example, the computer operations recovery team operates at the backup operations site; the recovery headquarters team operates at the recovery headquarters; and the disaster site recovery team operates at the data center damaged in the disaster. The recovery headquarters team is discussed in Chapter II-4, and the disaster site recovery team is covered in Chapter II-6.

THE COMPUTER OPERATIONS RECOVERY TEAM

As shown in Exhibit II-5-A, the computer operations recovery team comprises the:

- *Computer operations recovery team manager.* The computer operations recovery team manager is responsible for the recovery activities that take place at the computer backup site. The team leaders report the status of their teams' activities to the computer operations recovery team manager, who in turn reports the teams' status to the recovery chairperson.
- *Computer operations recovery team leader.* This team leader is responsible for the computer processing at the backup site.
- *Systems software recovery team leader.* This team leader is responsible for the recovery of the systems software and, in this book, the applications software.
- *Tape operations recovery team leader.* This team leader is responsible for the retrieval of the backup tapes from the off-premises storage location.
- *Applications recovery team leader.* This team leader is responsible to the data center end users for the recovery of their applications.
- *Data base recovery team leader.* This team leader is responsible for the recovery of the data bases.
- *Communications recovery team leader.* This team leader is responsible for the communications network recovery activities at the computer backup site. (Communications recovery is covered in Part III of this book.)

The Activation of the Computer Operations Recovery Team

The computer operations recovery team is activated after the decision to activate the DCRP has taken place. This occurs after a sequence of events known as the initial disaster alert (see Chapter II-7). That sequence begins when an incident at the data

EXHIBIT II-5-A COMPUTER OPERATIONS RECOVERY TEAM

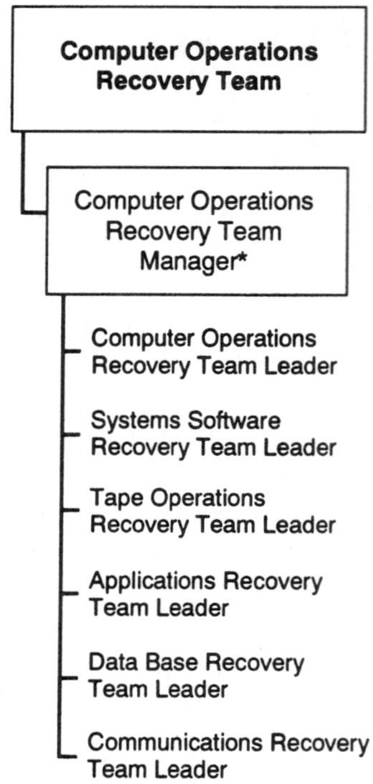

Note:
*Member of the IS recovery management team

center is first discovered and a member of the IS recovery management team is notified of the incident. This IS recovery management team member travels to the data center and assesses the situation. If the situation could require activation of the DCRP, this team member notifies the other members of the IS recovery management team to report to recovery headquarters.

The IS recovery management team reviews the results of the damage assessment activities and makes its recommendation on whether to activate the DCRP or terminate any further recovery operation activities. The recovery chairperson is responsible for deciding whether to activate the DCRP or terminate any further actions.

After the DCRP is activated, the computer operations recovery team manager (who is one of the three members of the IS recovery management team) notifies all of his or her team leaders, or their alternates, to report to recovery headquarters. After attending the chairperson's activation meeting (along with the managers of the recovery headquarters team and the disaster site recovery team), the computer operations recovery team manager conducts an activation meeting for all operations recovery team leaders. (This process is illustrated in Exhibit II-4-B.)

Responsibilities of the Computer Operations Recovery Team

The computer operations recovery team is responsible for the following recovery activities:

- Moving the processing of applications to the computer backup site.
- Retrieving backup tapes from the off-premises storage location.
- Recovering and reloading the systems and applications software at the backup site.

- Reloading and reconstructing the application data files and data bases.
- Providing an orderly shutdown of operations at the computer backup site.

THE COMPUTER OPERATIONS RECOVERY TEAM MANAGER

After the DCRP has been activated, the computer operations recovery team manager:

1. Notifies the computer backup site.
2. Conducts the computer operations recovery team meeting.
3. Meets with the computer operations recovery team leader.
4. Meets with the systems software recovery team leader.
5. Meets with the tape operations recovery team leader.
6. Meets with the applications recovery team leader.
7. Meets with the data base recovery team leader.
8. Meets with the communications recovery team leader.

These steps are described in the following paragraphs. Workpaper II5.01 provides a sample script that the team manager can follow in performing these recovery actions.

Notify the Computer Backup Site

STEP 1

After the recovery chairperson authorizes the activation of the computer backup site, the computer operations recovery team manager should notify the computer backup site using the backup site notification checklist (see Workpaper II5.02), which provides the backup site's phone number and contact name. He or she should verify the backup site's ability to support processing. The computer operations recovery team manager should provide the computer backup site with a list of team personnel who are authorized to enter the computer backup site and request that the backup site refuse entry to anyone not on the list.

In a wide-area disaster, this step may need to occur earlier in the recovery process. In such disasters, a number of data centers may be damaged at the same time, and the commercial hot sites may have to support multiple customers. Each commercial hot site has its own way of dealing with multiple disaster activations (see Chapter II-9). If the commercial hot site cannot support processing in the site the client is contracted to, most commercial hot-site vendors will move the customer to one of their other sites. (Most commercial hot-site vendors have more than one location.) This solution may require the customer to travel to a facility hundreds of miles away from the contracted hot site. The logistics for such contingencies should be covered in the DCRP.

Conduct the Team Meeting

STEP 2

The computer operations recovery team manager conducts a meeting of all operations recovery team leaders. At this meeting, the computer operations recovery team manager should explain the recovery objectives that were identified during the recovery chairperson's activation meeting. The team manager should then review the tasks to be performed by operations recovery team personnel. The computer operations recovery team manager distributes copies of forms to be used during the recovery operation and provides instructions on how and when the forms are to be completed. These forms may include the personnel location control form (see Workpaper II4.13), the recovery status report form (see Workpaper II4.14), the travel and expense report form (see Workpaper II4.15), and the disaster recovery time record form (see Workpaper II4.16). The computer operations recovery team manager also distributes and reviews copies of the prepared public statement (see Workpaper II4.11). At the conclusion of the meeting, the manager should remind all team leaders to discuss the use of the recovery forms with the IS personnel working with their recovery teams.

STEP 3

Meet with the Computer Operations Recovery Team Leader

The team manager should meet with the computer operations recovery team leader to establish the initial processing schedule. The team manager should use the critical application checklist, a sample of which is provided in Workpaper II5.03. The critical application checklist identifies the criticality of the application, the application name, and the frequency with which the application should be processed. The criticality classification identifies when the application should process (e.g., a class 1 application should process within 24 hours after activation of the DCRP; a class 2 application should process within 48 hours). (These classification categories can be changed to meet the needs of specific organizations.) The computer operations recovery team manager should review and approve the processing schedule submitted daily throughout the recovery operation by the computer operations recovery team leader.

STEP 4

Meet with the Systems Software Recovery Team Leader

The team manager meets with the systems software recovery team leader to ensure that the operating systems and libraries can be loaded at the computer backup site. This team leader provides the status of the systems software vendor alert and of the backups that have been retrieved to restore the systems software. The team manager and the systems software recovery team leader meet during the recovery operation to discuss the processing at the backup site and the plan for migrating back to the repaired data center.

STEP 5

Meet with the Tape Operations Recovery Team Leader

The team manager should meet with the tape operations recovery team leader to determine the status of salvageable data that was retrieved from the damaged data center. This team leader next describes the recovery of backups from the off-premises storage location and provides a report of the status of retrieved tapes. He or she should also report on any missing tapes and the potential impact of their loss. The team leader and manager discuss the plan for organizing a tape library at the computer backup site. The team leader also reports on the plan for ensuring the backups taken at the computer backup site are rotated to an off-premises storage location.

STEP 6

Meet with the Applications Recovery Team Leader

The team manager should meet with the applications recovery team leader to discuss the plan for recovering applications. The team leader and manager discuss the problems in recovering any of the applications and identify solutions. They discuss the recovery of the applications backup tapes and any problems uncovered. The team leader should report on the status of the applications software vendor alert and on the status of applications that need to be modified.

STEP 7

Meet with the Data Base Recovery Team Leader

The team manager should meet with the data base recovery team leader to discuss the plan for recovering the data bases. The team leader should provide the status of the data base software vendor alert and explain the most current generation available and the plans to reconstruct it. The team leader also provides the status of the backups that have been retrieved to restore the data bases and reports on the status of applications that have to be modified.

STEP 8

Meet with the Communications Recovery Team Leader

The computer operations recovery team manager must work with the communications recovery team to restore the necessary communications networks. Communications recovery is discussed in Part III of this book.

THE COMPUTER OPERATIONS RECOVERY TEAM LEADER

After the computer operations recovery team manager's meeting, the computer operations recovery team leader should meet with the IS personnel who will assist the computer operations recovery team and explain the forms to be used during the recovery operation. The team leader should complete the personnel location control form (see Workpaper II4.13), identifying who will be working on the computer operations recovery team, their work locations, and the telephone numbers for those locations. After the form is completed, the team leader should make a copy for his or her own records and send the original to the notification and communications team at the recovery headquarters.

The computer operations recovery team leader is responsible for:

1. Organizing an end-user help desk.
2. Obtaining the assessment of damage to the on-site data.
3. Preparing the team for travel to the computer backup site.
4. Supervising the computer processing at the computer backup site.
5. Processing applications based on the approved processing schedule.
6. Performing computer backup site shutdown procedures.

A detailed script of these recovery actions is provided in Workpaper II5.04.

STEP 1

Organize an End-User Help Desk

The computer operations recovery team leader should establish an end-user help desk. The initial purpose is to notify end users of the disaster and of the activation of the DCRP; contact is made using the end-user contact list (see Workpaper II5.05). Users should be informed of the expected delays in processing their applications. At first, the help desk will be set up in the recovery headquarters. After processing has begun at the computer backup site, the end-user help desk should be moved to the backup site. During the recovery operation, the end-user help desk should notify the computer operations recovery team leader of any information obtained from end users that may affect the criticality of an application or cause legal concern. Help-desk personnel should log all calls and record information from end users throughout the recovery operation using the end-user log book (see Workpaper II5.06).

STEP 2

Obtain the Damage Assessment

The computer operations recovery team leader should obtain a damage assessment of all on-site data from the disaster site recovery team manager. If the on-site data is not damaged and can be used at the computer backup site immediately, the team leader along with the tape operations recovery team leader should assign personnel to assist the tape operations recovery team in retrieving the data. This backup data could include systems software, applications software, data base software, network software, and applications data files. The team leader should ensure that no contaminated tapes are shipped to the computer backup site. All tapes and magnetic media should be cleaned and certified before shipment.

If the on-site data is damaged, the team leader should assist the tape operations team in identifying the specific backup data needed to be retrieved from the off-premises storage location using the application recovery checklist (see Workpaper II5.07). This backup data is used for the restoration of the production packs.

If the on-site work in process is damaged, the team leader should contact the end users who entered the input and request that they resubmit the work for reprocessing. If production documentation is damaged, the team leader should provide for the backup documentation to be retrieved from the off-premises storage location and taken to the computer backup site.

STEP 3

Prepare the Team for Travel to the Computer Backup Site

Before traveling to the computer backup site, the team leader should verify that the computer operations recovery team manager has contacted the computer backup site and made the necessary arrangements for the use of the facility. The team leader should then organize the team personnel and the materials that will be traveling to the backup site. The computer operations recovery team leader can prepare the team for travel to the backup site by following the guidelines in Workpaper II5.08.

STEP 4

Supervise Processing at the Backup Site

After arriving at the computer backup site, the computer operations recovery team leader should first call the recovery headquarters and provide the telephone number where the computer operations recovery team can be reached. The team leader should inventory all backup tapes and other materials needed for the resumption of processing. An area should be designated for receiving input from and distributing output to end users. The team leader should determine the need to order tapes, forms, and other computer supplies for processing at the computer backup site. For accounting control purposes, orders should be placed through the recovery headquarters team manager.

The computer operations recovery team leader should meet with the systems software recovery team leader to coordinate the activities needed for loading the systems software and the applications software at the computer backup site. The computer operations recovery team leader should also meet with the applications recovery team leader to discuss the recovery and restart procedures for the applications scheduled for processing at the computer backup site. Last, the computer operations recovery team leader should meet with the data base recovery team leader to identify the status of the data base backups, identifying how long ago they were created and what jobs have to be run to create a more current version.

After the computer backup site has been turned over for applications processing, the computer operations recovery team should restore all applications using the most current backup status. The team should reconstruct the applications by applying recent transaction backups. After applying the recent transactions, team members should determine whether the applications are in balance. If they are in balance, the team leader can have the end users submit the transactions that have occurred since the transaction backups. If they are not in balance, the team leader should have the end users determine which data are missing and have them reenter the data. (They may need to be assisted by the internal auditors.)

STEP 5

Process Applications Based on the Approved Schedule

The computer operations recovery team leader should meet with the computer operations recovery team manager to establish the initial processing schedule using the critical application checklist (see Workpaper II5.03). He or she should develop and submit the processing schedule to the computer operations recovery team manager for approval on a daily basis throughout the recovery operation. The team leader should maintain a record of applications processed at the computer backup site and develop a schedule to catch up on all processing that has been delayed.

The computer operations recovery team leader should set up processing of applications using the critical processing schedule. The team leader should assign personnel to set up jobs in accordance with the recovery processing schedule, review the production control documentation, arrange documentation by application to be processed, and set up procedures to handle report outputs. The team personnel assigned should give special attention to printer output, special forms, and remote output. The personnel should log information on the input, prepare output for distribution, and maintain a log of job abends.

The computer operations recovery team leader may need to reorganize the team periodically during the recovery operation. The team leader should watch personnel for signs of fatigue. Many employees will want to work as long as they can; this is commendable, but it can also lead to errors of omission and commission. The team leader should require team personnel to rest after their shift.

Perform Shutdown Procedures

STEP 6

When the recovery operation is going to shut down, the computer operations recovery team leader should prepare the timing plan to move back into the repaired data center or the new permanent data center. The team leader should ensure that a complete backup of all data is taken and that a library report is processed. He or she should ensure that the computer data, software, applications data, and data bases are backed up before leaving the processing site.

The team leader should take proper steps to overwrite all company data on the disks at the computer backup site. He or she should ensure that no company data or information is left on the backup site's tapes by erasing or overwriting the data.

The team leader should ensure that all backup tapes are packaged for shipment back to the repaired data center. Each tape should have a label identifying its destination. All paper, reports, forms, and data belonging to the company should be removed from the computer backup site for proper distribution or destruction.

THE SYSTEMS SOFTWARE RECOVERY TEAM LEADER

After the computer operations recovery team manager's meeting, the systems software recovery team leader should meet with the IS personnel who will assist the systems software recovery team and explain the forms to be used during the recovery operation. The team leader should complete the personnel location control form (see Workpaper II4.13), identifying who will be working on the systems software recovery team, their work locations, and the telephone numbers for those locations. After the form is completed, the team leader should make a copy for his or her own records and send the original to the notification and communications team at the recovery headquarters.

The systems software recovery team leader is responsible for:

1. Contacting systems software vendors.
2. Identifying backup data that needs to be retrieved from the off-premises storage location.
3. Preparing the team for travel to the computer backup site.
4. Managing the loading of the operating systems, libraries, and utilities at the computer backup site.

Workpaper II5.09 provides a script detailing these recovery actions.

STEP 1

Contact Systems Software Vendors

The systems software recovery team leader should contact the systems software vendors and advise them that their software will be run at the computer backup site. The systems software vendor notification checklist (see Workpaper II5.10) and the systems software inventory checklist (see Workpaper II5.11) should be used for this purpose. The systems software vendor notification checklist identifies the name of the software company, the address, the phone number during regular business hours, and an emergency phone number that can be used 24 hours a day. The results of the phone call should be noted on the form. If the software vendor cannot be contacted during the initial call, follow-up calls will be made by IS personnel in the recovery headquarters. (Recovery headquarters personnel call vendors only if the result of the initial call indicates they have not been reached.) The systems software inventory checklist identifies the product, the vendor, the installed release, and whether it is needed at the computer backup site.

While talking to the software vendors, the team leader should verify that the software will successfully run at the computer backup site. If changes to the software are required, technical support should be requested from the vendor. The team leader should issue a written confirmation to all software vendors that the relocation of the software was due to disaster. Copies of the confirmation letters should be kept in the vendor contract files.

STEP 2

Identify Backup Data That Needs to Be Retrieved

The systems software recovery team leader should identify the software backups needed to provide an operating system and communications environment at the computer backup site using the operating system recovery procedure provided in Workpaper II5.12. This procedure identifies the retrieval requirements for the operating system backup files and the documentation and recovery procedures to be used when the operating system is loaded at the computer backup site.

STEP 3

Prepare the Team for Travel to the Computer Backup Site

The systems software recovery team leader should prepare the team for travel to the computer backup site by following the guidelines in Workpaper II5.08.

STEP 4

Manage the Loading of the Operating Systems

The systems software recovery team should travel to the computer backup site to manage the loading of the operating systems. After arriving, the team leader should call the recovery headquarters with the telephone number where personnel can be reached and then meet with the computer operations recovery team leader to coordinate activities for the loading of the operating systems.

The systems software recovery team leader should identify the status of the operating systems backups to be used at the computer backup site and should determine whether a more current generation of the operating system is needed. If so, the team leader should identify the jobs that will have to be executed to create a more current version of the operating system using the operating system recovery procedure.

Other Responsibilities

When all of the above activities are completed, the systems software recovery team leader should advise the computer operations recovery team leader that the system is available to load production data. The team leader should assist the computer operations recovery team leader with the loading of the production backups onto the systems at the computer backup site. He or she should also assist applications personnel with the allocation of disk resources and the loading of applications data onto the available disks. Finally, the team leader should manage the loading and initiation of the online and communications software and the activation of the networks at the computer backup site.

THE TAPE OPERATIONS RECOVERY TEAM LEADER

After the computer operations recovery team manager's meeting has concluded, the tape operations recovery team leader should meet with the IS personnel who will assist the tape operations recovery team and explain the forms to be used during the recovery operation. The team leader should complete the personnel location control form (see Workpaper II4.13), identifying who will be working on the tape operations recovery team, their work locations, and the telephone numbers for those locations. After the form is completed, the team leader should make a copy for his or her own records and send the original to the notification and communications team at the recovery headquarters.

The tape operations recovery team leader is responsible for:

1. Assisting in retrieving on-site data that was not damaged by the disaster.
2. Coordinating the retrieval of backup data and documentation from the off-premises storage location.
3. Establishing security at the off-premises storage location.
4. Confirming the status of retrieved material and reporting missing items.
5. Preparing tapes for shipping to the computer backup site.
6. Preparing the team for travel to the computer backup site.
7. Organizing the tape library at the computer backup site.
8. Ensuring that the rotation of backup tapes and cartridges is continued while processing is performed at the computer backup site.

Workpaper II5.13 provides a script that the team leader can follow in performing these recovery actions.

Assist in Retrieving Undamaged On-Site Data

STEP 1

The tape operations recovery team leader should obtain the damage assessment status of the on-site data from the disaster site recovery team manager. If the on-site data is not damaged and can be used at the computer backup site immediately, the team leader and the computer operations recovery team leader should assign personnel to assist the disaster site recovery team manager in retrieving the on-site data. This data could include systems software, applications software, data base software, network software, and the applications data files.

Coordinate the Retrieval of Backup Data

STEP 2

If the data located in the computer area has been destroyed by the disaster or if it has been damaged and will not be usable until it can be repaired, the team leader should arrange for the retrieval of backups from the off-premises storage location. In order to do this, the team leader contacts the storage location and advises the facility of the need to retrieve the backup tapes.

The systems software recovery team leader, the applications recovery team leader, and the data base recovery team leader must tell the tape operations recovery team leader which backups are needed. Each of these team leaders uses DCRP checklists from his or her section of the plan to identify the data to be retrieved and how it should be recovered.

Company-Owned Storage Location. If the storage facility is owned by the company rather than a vendor, the team leader should contact the security personnel located at the storage facility. The IS personnel can then travel to the storage facility and retrieve the tapes needed for processing at the backup site.

Commercial Storage Location. If storage is contracted from an outside vendor, the call should be made using the off-premises storage location notification checklist (see Workpaper II5.14). The off-premises storage location notification checklist contains the name of the vendor, the address of the storage facility, the vendor contact's name and phone number, directions to the storage site, and the access procedures used by the vendor. Many vendors encourage their clients to use confidential codes to verify that the IS person making the call is authorized to request the retrieval. Tapes can be retrieved from the off-premises storage vendor by having the IS personnel travel to the vendor's location and select which backup tapes will be retrieved or by having the vendor send the backup tapes to the location designated by the authorized IS person.

STEP 3

Establish Security at the Off-Premises Storage Location

The tape operations recovery team leader should provide to off-premises storage management the names of all personnel who are authorized to access the storage area. The team leader should explain that such authorized personnel must present some form of company identification when they arrive at the off-premises location. The team leader should request that no other personnel be permitted to enter and that the off-premises storage management notify either the tape operations recovery team leader or the computer operations recovery team manager of any unauthorized attempts at access.

STEP 4

Confirm the Status of Retrieved Material

The tape operations recovery team leader should request that the systems software recovery team leader, the applications recovery team leader, and the data base recovery team leader verify that the retrieved tapes are correct. If the verification identifies errors, the team can return to the off-premises storage location and retrieve the missing or correct tapes. If tapes cannot be located, this should be reported by the tape operations recovery team leader to the computer operations recovery team manager.

STEP 5

Prepare Tapes for Shipping to the Computer Backup Site

The tape operations recovery team leader should ensure that tapes are placed in protective containers. The containers should each be labeled with the destination address, return address, and contents.

STEP 6

Prepare the Team for Travel to the Computer Backup Site

The tape operations recovery team leader should prepare the team for travel to the computer backup site by following the guidelines in Workpaper II5.08.

STEP 7

Organize the Tape Library at the Computer Backup Site

After arriving at the computer backup site, the tape operations recovery team leader should first call the recovery headquarters manager and provide the location and telephone number where he or she can be reached. The team leader should next organize the tape library. The backup site tape library contains the tapes retrieved from the off-premises location and new, blank tapes that will be used during the recovery operation. The team leader should initialize the new tapes as well as manage the backup site tape library.

Ensure the Rotation of Backup Tapes

STEP 8

The tape operations recovery team leader should ensure that the backups are being rotated to an off-premises storage location. If the computer backup site is reasonably close to the regular off-premises storage location, the regular off-premises location can be used to house the rotated tapes. If the computer backup site is located at a distance from the off-premises location, a temporary off-premises storage location should be used.

THE APPLICATIONS RECOVERY TEAM LEADER

After the computer operations recovery team manager's meeting, the applications recovery team leader should meet with the IS personnel who will assist the applications recovery team and explain the forms to be used during the recovery operation. The team leader should complete the personnel location control form (see Workpaper II4.13), identifying who will be working on the applications recovery team, their work locations, and the telephone numbers for those locations. After the form is completed, the team leader should make a copy for his or her own records and send the original to the notification and communications team at the recovery headquarters.

The applications recovery team leader is responsible for:

1. Contacting the applications software vendors.
2. Preparing the team for travel to the computer backup site.
3. Providing the means to reconstruct the application's data files to an acceptable point in time. This requires identifying the backup tapes that need to be retrieved from the off-premises storage location.
4. Recovering any work in process that was destroyed during the disaster.
5. Making programming changes needed to process at the computer backup site.

Workpaper II5.15 provides a script that the applications recovery team leader can refer to in performing these actions.

Contact Applications Software Vendors

STEP 1

The applications recovery team leader should assist the systems software recovery team leader in contacting the applications software vendors and advising them that their software will be run at the computer backup site. The applications software vendor notification checklist (see Workpaper II5.16) and the applications software inventory checklist (see Workpaper II5.17) should be used for this purpose. The applications software vendor notification checklist identifies the name of the software company, the address, the phone number during regular business hours, and an emergency phone number that can be used 24 hours a day. The results of the phone call should be noted on the form. If the software vendor cannot be contacted during the initial call, follow-up calls will be made by IS personnel in the recovery headquarters. The applications software inventory checklist identifies the product, the vendor, the release installed, and whether it is needed for processing at the computer backup site.

While talking to the software vendors, the team leader should verify that the software will successfully run at the computer backup site and request any technical support needed to modify it for successful operation. The team leader should issue a written confirmation to all software vendors that the relocation of the software was due to the disaster situation and maintain copies of these letters.

STEP 2

Prepare the Team for Travel to the Computer Backup Site

The applications recovery team leader should prepare the team for travel to the computer backup site by following the guidelines in Workpaper II5.08.

STEP 3

Prepare to Reconstruct the Application's Data Files

The applications recovery team leader should travel to the computer backup site to help reconstruct the application's data files to an acceptable point in time and to make any necessary program changes. The team leader assigns applications recovery team personnel to identify specific retrieval requirements using the application recovery checklist (see Workpaper II5.07). The team leader should contact the computer operations recovery team leader to determine the status of the applications backups retrieved from the off-premises storage location.

If the backups retrieved from the data center are salvageable, the end users should reenter the transactions that had been processed after the backups were taken. The computer operations recovery team reprocesses those transactions, and the end users can then begin entering new input.

If the backups are from the off-premises storage location, the team leader should identify the reconstruction procedure needed to bring the backups to the most current possible status. After the reconstruction is accomplished, the end users reenter the transactions that had been processed after the backup. The computer operations recovery team reprocesses the day's input and balances to the controls, and the end users can then begin entering new input.

STEP 4

Recover Work in Process

The applications recovery team leader should identify the destroyed or missing data from work in process and have end users resubmit the input. End users must be made aware that it is their responsibility to reenter the input for a day. For example, if a disaster struck the data center at 11:00 AM, the backups from the prior day should have already been rotated off premises. (This example is based on the daily rotation of backup tapes to an off-premises storage location, not on the use of electronic vaulting. For more information on electronic vaulting, see Chapter II-10.) If input started at 6:00 AM, users would have to reenter everything they entered from 6:00 AM to 11:00 AM. If the disaster struck at 11:00 PM, the end user would have to reenter everything from 6:00 AM to 11:00 PM, because the backups would not yet have been rotated to the off-premises storage location.

STEP 5

Make Necessary Programming Changes

The applications recovery team leader should ensure the proper functioning of the programs being processed at the computer backup site. If the programs do not function properly, the team leader should make the necessary program changes. The applications recovery team personnel should maintain written documentation of all programming changes made on each application and on all problems encountered. After the changes have been made, the applications data backup tapes should be protected to ensure they cannot be scratched accidently. They will be used again when the processing is returned to the repaired data center.

THE DATA BASE RECOVERY TEAM LEADER

After the computer operations recovery team manager's meeting, the data base recovery team leader should meet with the IS personnel who will assist the data base recovery team and explain the forms to be used during the recovery operation. The team leader should complete the personnel location control form (see Workpaper II4.13), identifying who will be working on the data base recovery team, their work locations, and the telephone numbers for those locations. After the form is completed, the team leader should make a copy for his or her own records and send the original to the notification and communications team at the recovery headquarters.

The data base recovery team leader is responsible for:

1. Contacting the data base software vendors.
2. Preparing the team for travel to the computer backup site.
3. Reloading and recovering the data base data and files.
4. Making any programming changes required to process the data bases at the computer backup site.

Workpaper II5.18 provides a script detailing these recovery actions.

Contact Data Base Software Vendors

STEP 1

The data base recovery team leader should contact the data base software vendors and advise them that their software will be run at the computer backup site. The team leader should use the data base software vendor notification checklist (see Workpaper II5.19) and the data base software inventory checklist (see Workpaper II5.20) for this purpose. The data base software vendor notification checklist identifies the name of the software company, the address, the phone number during regular business hours, and an emergency phone number that can be used 24 hours a day. The results of the phone call should be noted on this form. If the software vendor cannot be contacted during the initial call, follow-up calls will be made by IS personnel in the recovery headquarters. The data base software inventory checklist identifies the product, the vendor, the release installed, and whether it is needed for processing at the computer backup site.

While talking to the software vendors, the team leader should verify that the software will successfully run at the computer backup site and request any technical support required to modify it so that it can be run successfully. The team leader should issue a written confirmation to all software vendors that the relocation of the software was due to the disaster situation and maintain copies of these letters.

Prepare the Team for Travel to the Computer Backup Site

STEP 2

The data base recovery team leader should prepare the team for travel to the computer backup site by following the guidelines in Workpaper II5.08.

Reload and Recover the Data Base Data and Files

STEP 3

The data base recovery team leader should assist the computer operations recovery team leader with restoring the data bases. The data base recovery team leader should determine the status of the data bases after the restores are complete. If the tapes located in the damaged data center are salvageable, the data bases should be restored using the most current backup. If the tapes located in the damaged data center are destroyed, the data bases should be recovered from backups at the off-premises storage location. The team leader should identify the cause of any problems during the restores and correct them.

Make Required Programming Changes

STEP 4

The data base recovery team leader should ensure the proper functioning of the data base programs being processed at the computer backup site. If there are any problems, the team leader should make the necessary program changes required to process the data bases at the backup site. The data base recovery team personnel should maintain written documentation of the programming changes that were made and on all problems encountered. After the changes have been made, the data base backup tapes should be protected to ensure they are not scratched accidently. They will be used again when processing resumes at the repaired data center.

WORKPAPER II5.01 Computer Operations Team Manager's Recovery Procedures

Company Name___________ Issued________ Section_______ Page_______
Data Center__________________
Data Center Recovery Plan_______________ Supersedes_______________

COMPUTER OPERATIONS RECOVERY TEAM MANAGER RECOVERY PROCEDURE

Recovery procedures follow. Read the entire section before performing any assignments. The recovery objectives will dictate the need for and timing of all assignments.

RECOVERY ACTIONS:

1. Activate the required recovery team leaders needed to support the recovery operation:

   a. The computer operations recovery team leader.
   b. The systems software recovery team leader.
   c. The tape operations recovery team leader.
   d. The applications recovery team leader.
   e. The database recovery team leader.

2. Conduct a computer operations recovery team meeting:

   a. Explain the goals and objectives identified during the recovery chairperson's activation meeting.
   b. Review the tasks that will be performed by the team leaders and their assigned personnel.
   c. Distribute copies of the forms that will be used throughout the recovery operation and explain how and when they are to be completed.
   d. Distribute a copy of the news media statement that has been prepared for employees to respond to any news media questions.
   e. Establish meeting schedules for each team leader.

3. Obtain the names of the staff department representatives who will support the computer operations recovery activities from the recovery chairperson. Coordinate the support of the staff department representatives with the computer operations recovery team leaders.

Staff Support Department	Representative's Name
Insurance	____________________
Security	____________________
Transportation	____________________
Legal	____________________
Human resources	____________________

4. Alert computer backup site personnel that they will be needed for processing during the recovery operation. Use the backup site notification checklist (Workpaper II5.02).

5. Complete the personnel location control form (Workpaper II4.13), including staff personnel, by identifying the work location and contact phone number for yourself and anyone working directly with you.

6. Manage all computer operations recovery efforts throughout the recovery operation. Meet with the computer operations recovery team leader to review:

   a. The damage assessment report on the site data.
   b. The initial processing schedule at the backup site.
   c. The on-going status of processing at the backup site.

7. Manage all software recovery efforts throughout the recovery operation. Meet with the systems software recovery team leader to review:

   a. The results of the software vendor notification activities:

      - Verify that the software will run at the backup site.
      - Determine whether software changes will have to be made in order to run for any length of time.
      - Verify that a written confirmation of the disaster situation was tendered to the software vendors.

   b. The results of the loading and testing of the operating system.

8. Manage all data recovery and protection efforts throughout the recovery operation. Meet with the tape operations recovery team leader to review:

   a. The status of the retrieval operation from the off-premises storage location.
   b. The recovery procedure being used to recover any data that is needed for the recovery operation but that was not found in the off-premises storage location.
   c. The status of which tapes have been moved to the computer backup site and which still remain in the off-premises storage location to act as a contingency.
   d. The procedure being used to ensure the backups being created during the processing at the computer backup site are being rotated to an off-premises storage area.

9. Manage all application recovery activities throughout the recovery operation. Meet with the applications recovery team leader to review:

   a. The status of the recovery of all critical applications data files.
   b. The status of the recovery of all less critical applications data files.
   c. The program changes that must be made to successfully process on the computer backup site.
   d. The plan being used to capture and save all transactions being created by those applications that are processing and will be used for input into applications not scheduled for processing until later in the recovery operation.

10. Manage all data base recovery activities throughout the recovery operation. Meet with the data base recovery team leader to review:

    a. The results of the data base vendor notification activities.
    b. The results of the data base restoration activities.

11. When the damaged data center is repaired or has been relocated, meet with the team leaders to review their plans for an orderly shutdown of the computer backup site.

WORKPAPER II5.02 Backup Site Notification Checklist

Company Name___________ Issued________ Section_______ Page_______
Data Center__________________
Data Center Recovery Plan_______________ Supersedes______________

BACKUP SITE NOTIFICATION CHECKLIST

After the recovery chairperson has authorized the activation of the backup site, this checklist will be used to notify the site of the need to move computer operations to the backup site location.

Backup site:

Company name: ____

Address: ____

City, state, zip code: ____

Contacts:

Name (primary): ____

Name (alternate): ____

Contact Status

Business number: _______________ _______________________________

Emergency number: ______________ _______________________________

Computer configuration: ____
____

Availability: ____
____

Authorized personnel: ____
____

Directions: ____
____

WORKPAPER II5.03 Critical Application Checklist

Company Name ____________ Issued ________ Section _______ Page _______
Data Center __________________
Data Center Recovery Plan __________________ Supersedes ________________

CRITICAL APPLICATION CHECKLIST

After the DCRP has been activated, this checklist will be used to assist during the computer backup site processing schedule determination.

			Run Schedule**							
Acronym	Application/ System Name	Priority Number*	d	w	m	q	sa	a	or	bw
_______	Billing	__	___	___	___	___	___	___	___	___
_______	Automated Lease Accounting	__	___	___	___	___	___	___	___	___
_______	Corporate Benefits	__	___	___	___	___	___	___	___	___
_______	Accounts Payable	__	___	___	___	___	___	___	___	___
_______	Stock Status	__	___	___	___	___	___	___	___	___
_______	Plant Payroll	__	___	___	___	___	___	___	___	___
_______	Staff Payroll	__	___	___	___	___	___	___	___	___
_______	Pensioners Payroll	__	___	___	___	___	___	___	___	___
_______	General Ledger	__	___	___	___	___	___	___	___	___
_______	Accounting	__	___	___	___	___	___	___	___	___
_______	Fixed Assets	__	___	___	___	___	___	___	___	___
_______	Shipment Book	__	___	___	___	___	___	___	___	___
_______	Sales	__	___	___	___	___	___	___	___	___
_______	Plant Inventory	__	___	___	___	___	___	___	___	___
_______	Manufacturing Cost	__	___	___	___	___	___	___	___	___
_______	Accounts Receivable	__	___	___	___	___	___	___	___	___
_______	Customer Listing	__	___	___	___	___	___	___	___	___
_______	Quality Control	__	___	___	___	___	___	___	___	___

Notes:

*Priority Number:
- 1 = Must be processed within 24 hours after DCRP activation.
- 2 = Must be processed within 48 hours after DCRP activation.
- 3 = Must be processed within 3 to 5 hours after DCRP activation.
- 4 = Can be processed after the 1s, 2s, and 3s are processed.

**Run Schedule:
- d = daily
- w = weekly
- m = monthly
- q = quarterly
- sa = semiannually
- a = annually
- or = on request
- bw = biweekly

WORKPAPER II5.04 Computer Operations Team Leader's Recovery Procedures

Company Name___________ Issued________ Section_______ Page_______
Data Center__________________
Data Center Recovery Plan_______________ Supersedes_______________

COMPUTER OPERATIONS RECOVERY TEAM LEADER RECOVERY PROCEDURE

Recovery procedures follow. Read the entire section before performing any assignments. The recovery objectives will dictate the need for and timing of all assignments.

RECOVERY ACTIONS:

1. Confirm that the computer operations recovery team manager has notified the computer backup site and made the necessary arrangements for the use of the facility.

2. Obtain the status of all on-site data from the disaster site recovery team manager:

   a. Identify any salvageable data that could be used for recovery.
   b. Provide instructions to the disaster site recovery team manager regarding critical data.

3. If requested, assign someone to assist the tape operations recovery team with the retrieval of backup data and documentation to be used at the computer backup site.

4. Authorize the activation of the help-desk team, which will use the end-user contact checklist to notify the end users of the situation (see Workpaper II5.05). The help desk should notify the computer operations recovery team leader of any information obtained from the end user that may affect the criticality of an application. Help-desk personnel should log all calls and record the information on the end-user log book form (Workpaper II5.06).

5. Assign personnel to support the systems software recovery team. Instruct the computer operations personnel to:

   a. Report to the disaster recovery backup site.
   b. Assist with the installation of the operating system in preparation for critical application processing.

6. Travel to the computer backup site with the required operations personnel.

7. After arriving at the computer backup site, perform the following:

   a. Call the recovery headquarters and provide the telephone number where the personnel can be reached.
   b. Meet with the systems software recovery team leader to coordinate activities for the recovery operation.
   c. Organize documentation, files, and materials for the resumption of processing.
   d. Use any standby time to organize personnel, develop control mechanisms required for recovery processing, and resolve problems.
   e. Be prepared to receive salvaged data. Verify that the disaster site recovery team has properly cleaned and certified all salvaged magnetic media (disk and tape) to prevent contamination of the backup site.
   f. Work with the recovery headquarters manager to establish a security function to ensure unauthorized personnel do not enter the backup site.

8. Assign the computer operations recovery team personnel to support the data base recovery team with the reloading and activation of the data bases.

9. After the computer has been turned over for recovery operations processing:

   a. Verify that all operating systems are loaded and tested.
   b. Process systems and jobs based on the approved processing schedule. Obtain a copy of the critical application checklist (Workpaper II5.03) from the computer operations recovery team manager.

10. Develop and submit for approval the daily processing schedule to the computer operations team manager throughout the recovery operation.

11. Direct all help-desk activities in the backup site for the duration of the backup site processing.

12. Ensure that backups are made for processing at the backup site in accordance with standard procedures.

13. Keep the computer operations recovery team manager advised of pertinent information provided by the end user that may either affect priority processing or raise legal concerns.

14. Be prepared to process on-request jobs to satisfy the immediate report needs of end-user departments affected by the disaster situation.

15. Provide computer operations support at the computer backup site throughout the recovery operation:

    a. Ensure that support is available at the computer backup site on a 24-hours-a-day basis.
    b. Provide the recovery headquarters manager with the names of the operations personnel.
    c. Provide appropriate instructions to the assigned personnel.

16. Reorganize the computer operations recovery team throughout the recovery operation, as required:

    a. Watch personnel for signs of fatigue.
    b. Return personnel to home site at least every two weeks.
    c. Require operations personnel to rest.

17. When backup site processing is no longer required, activate shutdown procedures:

    a. Ensure that all computer data has been backed up before leaving the disaster recovery backup site, as appropriate.
    b. Maintain confidentiality of all data:

        -- Assist the systems software recovery team leader to overwrite all data on disk packs and noncompany tapes that will be left at the disaster recovery backup site.
        -- Ensure that all paper, reports, forms, and data belonging to the company are removed from the backup site for proper distribution or destruction.

    c. Make arrangements for the return of computer operations personnel, documentation, and supplies.

WORKPAPER II5.05 End-User Contact Checklist

Company Name__________ Issued_______ Section______ Page______
Data Center________________
Data Center Recovery Plan______________ Supersedes____________

END-USER CONTACT CHECKLIST

Department	Contact/Alternate	Business Extension

WORKPAPER II5.06 End-User Log Book Form

Company Name____________ Issued_________ Section________ Page________
Data Center____________________
Data Center Recovery Plan_________________ Supersedes________________

END-USER LOG BOOK FORM

Complete after plan activation:

Date	Time	From (Location)	Caller	Question/Problem/Information

WORKPAPER II5.07 Application Recovery Checklist

Company Name___________ Issued________ Section_______ Page_______
Data Center__________________
Data Center Recovery Plan_______________ Supersedes_______________

APPLICATION RECOVERY CHECKLIST

Application name: ______________________________

End user: ______________________________

Introduction: ______________________________

This section contains information relevant to this application.

Application jobs and processing schedule:

Job Number	Job Name	Control Card

File restore jobs:

Job Number	Job Name	Control Card

Program libraries:

Complete after plan activation:

Data Set Name	Tape Number	Date of Work

Application data files:

	Complete after plan activation:	
Data Set Name	Tape Number	Date of Work

Custom forms:

		Complete after plan activation:	
Form Description	Form Number	Required	Date Received

Documentation:

	Complete after plan activation:	
Manual Title	Required	Date Received

Other requirements:

Complete after plan activation:

Printer Forms	Requirement Communicated to Whom and Date	Availability Status or Resolution

Control Cards		

Applications reconstruction procedure:

This section describes the technical procedure for reconstructing the application.

WORKPAPER II5.08 Computer Backup Site Travel Guidelines

Company Name__________ Issued________ Section_______ Page_______
Data Center__________________
Data Center Recovery Plan_______________ Supersedes_______________

GUIDELINES FOR TRAVEL TO A COMPUTER BACKUP SITE

1. The team leader should divide the available personnel into two groups: those who will go to the computer backup site first and those who will be sent as replacements after a few days. The team leader should not overcommit resources during the first few days.

2. The team leader should provide directions to the team members that will be traveling to the computer backup site. In the event that personnel cannot drive to the computer backup site and will need air transportation, hotel accommodations, and advance expense money, the team leader should arrange the details through the administration team leader.

3. The team leader will provide the administration team leader with the names of the individuals, their destination, hotel requirements, an estimate of any travel money needed, and instructions relating to specific personnel who should not travel together on the same airplane (many companies have travel policies that forbid key individuals to fly on the same airplane in case of an accident).

4. The administration team leader will make the travel arrangements (usually with the assistance of the transportation support department) and will provide personnel with itineraries, tickets, and advance travel money.

WORKPAPER II5.09 Systems Software Recovery Team Leader Recovery Procedures

Company Name___________ Issued________ Section_______ Page_______
Data Center__________________
Data Center Recovery Plan_______________ Supersedes______________

SYSTEMS SOFTWARE RECOVERY TEAM LEADER RECOVERY PROCEDURE

Recovery procedures follow. Read the entire section before performing any assignments. The recovery objectives will dictate the need for and timing of all assignments.

RECOVERY ACTIONS:

1. Notify the software vendors that their software packages will be run on a different computer because of a disaster in the data center. Use the systems software vendor notification checklist (Workpaper II5.10) and the systems software inventory checklist (Workpaper II5.11):

   a. Verify that the software package will successfully run on a different computer system.
   b. Request technical support for any changes required to run software on the other computer.
   c. Inform all software vendors in writing of the disaster and the relocation of the software. Copies of these confirmations should be retained for safekeeping in the contract files.

2. Identify the data and items needed to provide an operating system and communications environment at the computer backup site using the operating system recovery procedure (Workpaper II5.12):

   a. Provide retrieval requirements to the tape operations recovery team leader and request retrieval.
   b. Verify that the data and items retrieved are correct.

3. Arrange to have required documentation copied, and return one set to the off-premises storage facility.

4. Assist the computer operations recovery team leader and the data base recovery team leader with the identification of backup data required to restore the data bases onto the backup site disk configuration. Refer to the data base recovery team leader recovery procedures (Workpaper II5.18).

5. Travel to the disaster recovery backup site as directed by the backup site recovery team manager.

6. After arriving at the computer backup site, perform the following:

   a. Call the recovery headquarters and provide the telephone number where personnel can be reached.
   b. Meet with the computer operations recovery team manager to coordinate activities for the recovery operation.

7. Identify which operating system is available at the computer backup site.

   a. Determine whether a more current operating system is necessary.
   b. Identify what jobs, using which volumes, will be executed to create a more current version of the operating system. Use the operating system recovery procedure (Workpaper II5.12).

8. Advise the computer operations recovery team manager when the system is available to load production critical application data.

9. Assist the computer operations recovery team leader in allocating DASD resources to support the recovery operation.

10. Assist the computer operations recovery team with the loading of all required disk data using disk backups and standard disk volume reloading procedures.

    a. If all computer room production data is available for the recovery operation, restore data using the most recent backup.
    b. If some or all computer room data is unsalvageable and will be recovered using backups stored off-premises, restore using off-premises storage data.

11. Load, bring up, and test the network systems. (Note: This is covered in detail in Part III of this book.)

12. Advise the computer operations recovery team manager when the online and communications systems are available for production operations.

13. If the disaster situation has affected any online terminal facilities, assist the network recovery team with the restoration of terminal operations capabilities.

14. Assign personnel to support the computer backup site throughout the recovery operation.

    a. Ensure that support is available to the computer backup site on a 24-hours-a-day basis.
    b. Provide appropriate instructions to the assigned personnel.

15. After the recovery operation is officially concluded, restore the operating system at the repaired or relocated facility.

WORKPAPER II5.10 Systems Software Vendor Notification Checklist

Company Name___________ Issued________ Section_______ Page_______
Data Center__________________
Data Center Recovery Plan_______________ Supersedes______________

SYSTEMS SOFTWARE VENDOR NOTIFICATION CHECKLIST

After the data center recovery plan has been activated, use this checklist in conjunction with the systems software inventory checklist (Workpaper II5.11) to notify vendors of the situation and request their support. In the event they have to report to the site, request that representatives report to the recovery headquarters to obtain temporary security passes.

Vendor Name: ____________________ Business Number: _____________

Address [street]: ________________ Emergency Number: ____________

Address [city, state, zip code]: ________________________________

Result of alert: ____
____

Vendor Name: ____________________ Business Number: _____________

Address [street]: ________________ Emergency Number: ____________

Address [city, state, zip code]: ________________________________

Result of alert: ____
____

Vendor Name: ____________________ Business Number: _____________

Address [street]: ________________ Emergency Number: ____________

Address [city, state, zip code]: ________________________________

Result of alert: ____
____

Vendor Name: ____________________ Business Number: _____________

Address [street]: ________________ Emergency Number: ____________

Address [city, state, zip code]: ________________________________

Result of alert: ____
____

WORKPAPER II5.11 Systems Software Inventory Checklist

Company Name___________ Issued________ Section_______ Page_______
Data Center__________________
Data Center Recovery Plan_______________ Supersedes______________

SYSTEMS SOFTWARE INVENTORY NOTIFICATION CHECKLIST

After the data center recovery plan has been officially activated, use this checklist in conjunction with the systems software vendor notification checklist (Workpaper II5.10) to notify the vendors of the situation.

Product	Vendor	Installed Release	Needed at Backup Site? (yes/no)

WORKPAPER II5.12 Operating System Recovery Procedure

Company Name___________ Issued________ Section_______ Page_______
Data Center__________________
Data Center Recovery Plan_______________ Supersedes_______________

OPERATING SYSTEM RECOVERY PROCEDURE

1. Retrieval requirements:

   a. Operating system backup files:

		Complete after plan activation:	
File Name	Contents	Tape Number	Date of Work
____.__.____			
____.__.____			
____.__.____			
____.__.____			
____.__.____			
____.__.____			
____.__.____			
____.__.____			

   b. Operating system documentation:

   - A complete set of [operating system vendor] software manuals are available at the computer backup site.
   - A complete set of third-party software manuals are available at the computer backup site.

2. Recovery procedures:

   a. Bring up the one-volume minimum system.

   b. Working from the one-volume minimum system:

   - Restore volumes needed to access the catalogs in which the volume backups are catalogued.
   - Restore operating systems volumes.
   - Restore all remaining volumes.

   c. Bring up the production systems.

WORKPAPER II5.13 Tape Operations Team Leader Recovery Procedures

Company Name___________ Issued________ Section_______ Page_______
Data Center__________________
Data Center Recovery Plan_______________ Supersedes_______________

TAPE OPERATIONS RECOVERY TEAM LEADER RECOVERY PROCEDURE

Recovery procedures follow. Read the entire section before performing any assignments. The recovery objectives will dictate the need for and timing of all assignments.

RECOVERY ACTIONS:

1. If requested, assist the disaster site recovery team manager in performing damage assessment and salvage tasks for tapes stored in the computer center tape library. The disaster site recovery team manager may need a complete copy of the tape management system reports when performing the damage assessment. It may be salvaged from the tape library. If it cannot be, arrange for new reports to be printed when the backup site is operational.

2. After receiving authorization from the computer operations recovery team manager, notify the off-premises storage facility that backup data will be retrieved. Use the off-premises storage location notification checklist for contact information (Workpaper II5.14).

3. Establish security procedures for backup data. Request that off-premises storage management restrict access to the off-premises storage facility to all [company name] personnel except those identified by the computer operations recovery team manager.

4. Obtain a copy of the backup data required for restoration of the systems and applications software from the systems software recovery team leader, the applications master files from the applications recovery team leader, and the data base files from the data base recovery team leader.

5. Obtain the following tape library reports from either the on-site or off-premises storage facility:

   a. Complete tape library report--on-site.
   b. Off-premises vault inventories for the off-premises vendor.

6. Identify the correct volume serial numbers for the required backup data. Record the volume serial number in the appropriate column on the list provided from the recovery teams. Refer to step 4. Also record the date of work in the appropriate column.

7. If required, travel to the off-premises storage facility:

   a. Refer to the off-premises storage location notification checklist for access procedures and directions.
   b. Show proper identification and follow the security regulations established by off-premises storage facility management.
   c. Team leader will proceed to the off-premises storage location and obtain the tape management system listing. Tape operations recovery team personnel will also report to the facility and assist in pulling the required tapes.
   d. Retrieve the tapes, supplies, and documentation required for restoration of the applications. Retrieve only one generation of backups requested. Leave other generations in the off-premises storage area for both security and contingency reasons.
   e. Ensure the tapes are placed in protective containers.
   f. Label the containers with destination address, return address and contents.

8. After retrieval, transport the tapes, supplies, and manuals to the location designated, which is either the:

   a. The computer backup site location.
   b. Recovery headquarters location.

9. Request that each recovery team leader verify that the retrieved tapes are correct.

10. If the verification identifies retrieval errors, return to the off-premises location and retrieve the correct tapes. If the required tapes cannot be located, report the missing tapes to the computer operations recovery team manager.

11. Report to the computer backup site:

    a. Organize the tape library, which will contain those available backup tapes retrieved from off premises as well as new blank tapes.
    b. Produce a scratch listing from the tape management system.
    c. Initialize new tapes.

d. Ensure that proper rotation of backups is continued at the computer backup site. If two copies of all backups are made during computer backup site processing:

- One copy should be available on site for normal recovery.
- One copy should be stored off premises for disaster recovery.

e. Review the existing tape scratching policies and procedures with the computer operations recovery team manager to determine whether any changes are required. (Management may decide that it is prudent not to scratch any production data sets during the initial stages of the recovery operation, particularly if the normal production job stream has been altered to accommodate processing at the computer backup site.)

12. Coordinate with the computer operations recovery team leader the printing of microfiche reports. Generate reports on tape reels or cartridges and send them out to be printed or fiched.

13. When the computer backup site operations are no longer required, perform library shutdown activities:

a. Run a library report.
b. Ensure that computer data has been backed up before leaving the computer backup site.
c. Remove all [company name] tapes from the computer backup site tape library and computer room. Package them for shipment to the home site.

WORKPAPER II5.14 Storage Location Notification Checklist

Company Name___________ Issued________ Section_______ Page_______
Data Center__________________
Data Center Recovery Plan_______________ Supersedes______________

OFF-PREMISES STORAGE LOCATION NOTIFICATION CHECKLIST

Off-premises storage location:

Name: ____
Address [street]: ________________________________
Address [city, state, zip code]: _________________

Contacts:

Contact Name	Business Number	Home Number	Beeper Number
________________ Name (primary)	______________	______________	______________
________________ Name (alternate)	______________	______________	______________

Directions to site: ________________________________
____
____
____.

Access procedure: A phone call will be made to the off-premises location requesting that certain tapes be pulled and sent to the computer backup site as soon as possible. The person calling will identify him- or herself and indicate the confidential code. A callback will not be necessary.

Access limitations, off-premises location: Access is limited to authorized personnel from the company who have been assigned a confidential code.

WORKPAPER II5.15 Applications Recovery Team Leader Recovery Procedures

Company Name___________ Issued________ Section_______ Page_______
Data Center__________________
Data Center Recovery Plan_______________ Supersedes______________

APPLICATIONS RECOVERY TEAM LEADER RECOVERY PROCEDURE

Recovery procedures follow. Read the entire section before performing any assignments. The recovery objectives will dictate the need for and timing of all assignments.

RECOVERY ACTIONS:

1. Notify the software vendors that their software packages will run on a different computer because of a disaster in the data center. Use the applications software vendor notification checklist (Workpaper II5.16) and the applications software inventory checklist (Workpaper II5.17):
   a. Verify that the software package will run successfully on a different computer system.
   b. Request technical support for any changes required to run software on the other computer.
   c. Inform all software vendors in writing of the disaster and the relocation of the software. Copies of these confirmations should be retained for safekeeping in the contract files.

2. Direct personnel to investigate the status of all programs, program libraries, and program documentation to identify any required reconstruction activities.

3. If required, assign personnel to travel to the computer backup site. Direct them to:
   a. Assist with the reloading and activation of program libraries.
   b. Meet with the computer operations recovery team manager to review the recovery processing schedule. Review all critical production systems and identify noncritical jobs or programs that can be bypassed. Change the jobs as required.
   c. Identify, develop, and install any required programming or job changes at the backup site.
   d. Provide ongoing support to the computer operations recovery team throughout the recovery operation.
   e. Maintain written documentation of all changes made to production systems, jobs, or programs.

f. Maintain written documentation of all problems encountered.

4. Work with the recovery headquarters team to coordinate end-user communication and support activities.

5. Assist end users with the implementation and maintenance of manual procedures to continue essential business operations during a data processing outage.

6. Assign personnel to use the application recovery checklist (Workpaper II5.07) to identify the specific retrieval requirements. Instruct personnel to review the application restart procedures. If modifications are required, they should prepare recovery instructions based on data in the application recovery checklist.

7. Provide test and verification support to determine the integrity of data:

   a. Assist with reloading and reconstruction of applications.
   b. With end users, review output from restoration and reconstruction activities and assist in identifying destroyed or missing data.
   c. Identify catch-up processing activities.

8. Review all development work in process. Determine whether any development work must continue during the recovery operation. If development work must continue, notify the applications recovery team leader and the computer operations recovery team manager, providing exact details of what development work must be processed.

9. Review all systems and jobs that will not be processed and take whatever actions are necessary to ensure that:

   a. Daily transactions are collected.
   b. Input data is not deleted or scratched.

10. Direct applications development activities for the duration of the recovery operation.

11. Return to normal development and maintenance procedures when processing capacity is available either at the computer backup site or at the restored facility.

    a. Restore programs and jobs to original production status, if changes were made during the recovery operation.
    b. Test all programs changed to ensure that jobs are returned to original status.

WORKPAPER II5.16 Applications Software Vendor Notification Checklist

Company Name___________ Issued________ Section_______ Page_______
Data Center__________________
Data Center Recovery Plan_______________ Supersedes______________

APPLICATIONS SOFTWARE VENDOR NOTIFICATION CHECKLIST

After the data center recovery plan has been activated, use this checklist to notify vendors of the situation and request their support. In the event that they have to report to the site, request that representatives report to the recovery headquarters to obtain temporary security passes.

Vendor Name: ____________________ Business Number: _____________

Address [street]: _______________ Emergency Number: ____________

Address [city, state, zip code]: ________________________________

Result of alert: ____

____

Vendor Name: ____________________ Business Number: _____________

Address [street]: _______________ Emergency Number: ____________

Address [city, state, zip code]: ________________________________

Result of alert: ____

____

Vendor Name: ____________________ Business Number: _____________

Address [street]: _______________ Emergency Number: ____________

Address [city, state, zip code]: ________________________________

Result of alert: ____

____

Vendor Name: ____________________ Business Number: _____________

Address [street]: _______________ Emergency Number: ____________

Address [city, state, zip code]: ________________________________

Result of alert: ____

____

WORKPAPER II5.17 Applications Software Inventory Checklist

Company Name___________ Issued________ Section_______ Page_______
Data Center__________________
Data Center Recovery Plan_______________ Supersedes______________

APPLICATIONS SOFTWARE INVENTORY NOTIFICATION CHECKLIST

After the data center recovery plan has been officially activated, use this checklist in conjunction with the applications software vendor notification checklist (Workpaper II5.16) to notify the vendors of the situation.

Product	Vendor	Installed Release	Needed at Backup Site?

WORKPAPER II5.18 Data Base Recovery Team Leader Recovery Procedures

Company Name___________ Issued________ Section_______ Page_______
Data Center__________________
Data Center Recovery Plan_______________ Supersedes______________

DATA BASE RECOVERY TEAM LEADER RECOVERY PROCEDURE

Recovery procedures follow. Read the entire section before performing any assignments. The recovery objectives will dictate the need for and timing of all assignments.

RECOVERY ACTIONS:

1. Notify the vendors that their software packages will run on a different computer because of a disaster in the data center. Use the data base software vendor notification checklist (Workpaper II5.19) and the data base software inventory checklist (Workpaper II5.20).

   a. Verify that the software package will successfully run on a different computer system.
   b. Request technical support for any changes required to run software on the other computer.
   c. Inform all software vendors in writing of the disaster and the relocation of the software. Copies of these confirmations should be retained in the contract files.

2. Assist the computer operations recovery team leader with the investigation of the exact status of data base backups and the establishment of plans for any reconstruction activities.

3. If required, assign personnel to travel to the computer backup site. Direct them to:

   a. Restore all production data bases using the following procedure:
      [company's data base recovery procedure]
   b. Restore test data bases.
   c. Format the data sets for production data bases. The disk volumes where these data sets reside need to be clipped with the correct volume servers before formatting.
   d. Determine status of data bases after restores are complete.
   e. Provide ongoing support to computer operations recovery team throughout the recovery operation.
   f. Maintain written documentation of all changes made to the production data base system.

4. Direct data base recovery activities for the duration of the recovery operation.

5. Return to normal data base development and maintenance activities when processing capacity is available either at the computer backup site or at the restored facility.

WORKPAPER II5.19 Data Base Software Vendor Notification Checklist

Company Name___________ Issued________ Section_______ Page_______
Data Center__________________
Data Center Recovery Plan_______________ Supersedes_____________

DATA BASE SOFTWARE VENDOR NOTIFICATION CHECKLIST

After the data center recovery plan has been activated, use this checklist to notify vendors of the situation and request their support. In the event they have to report to the site, request that representatives report to the recovery headquarters to obtain temporary security passes.

Vendor Name: ____________________ Business Number: _____________

Address [street]: _______________ Emergency Number: ____________

Address [city, state, zip code]: ________________________________

Result of alert: ____

____

Vendor Name: ____________________ Business Number: _____________

Address [street]: _______________ Emergency Number: ____________

Address [city, state, zip code]: ________________________________

Result of alert: ____

____

Vendor Name: ____________________ Business Number: _____________

Address [street]: _______________ Emergency Number: ____________

Address [city, state, zip code]: ________________________________

Result of alert: ____

____

Vendor Name: ____________________ Business Number: _____________

Address [street]: _______________ Emergency Number: ____________

Address [city, state, zip code]: ________________________________

Result of alert: ____

____

WORKPAPER II5.20 Data Base Software Inventory Checklist

Company Name____________ Issued________ Section_______ Page_______
Data Center____________________
Data Center Recovery Plan________________ Supersedes_______________

DATA BASE SOFTWARE INVENTORY NOTIFICATION CHECKLIST

After the data center recovery plan has been officially activated, use this checklist in conjunction with the data base software vendor notification checklist (Workpaper II5.19) to notify the vendors of the situation.

Product	Vendor	Installed Release	Needed at Backup Site?

The Disaster Site Recovery Team Section of the DCRP

CHAPTER II-6

Chapter II-6 presents the actions that the disaster site recovery team takes following the activation of the data center recovery plan (DCRP). The disaster site recovery team is one of the three major teams in the data center recovery plan, the others being the computer operations recovery team and the recovery headquarters team. The DCRP teams are named for the different recovery locations at which they will be operating; the disaster site recovery team operates at the data center that is the site of the disaster. The computer operations recovery team is discussed in Chapter II-5, and the recovery headquarters team is covered in Chapter II-4.

THE DISASTER SITE RECOVERY TEAM

As shown in Exhibit II-6-A, the disaster site recovery team comprises the:

- *Disaster site recovery team manager.* The disaster site recovery team manager is responsible for the recovery activities that take place at the disaster site. The team leaders report the status of their teams' activities to the disaster site recovery team manager, who in turn reports the teams' status to the recovery chairperson.
- *Facility damage assessment and restoration team leader.* This team leader is responsible for the repair or relocation of the data center facility.
- *Equipment damage assessment and salvage team leader.* This team leader is responsible for the protection, repair, or replacement of computer equipment, supplies, and forms.
- *Communications recovery team leader.* This team leader is responsible for the recovery of the communications network supporting the data center. (Communications recovery is discussed in Part III of this book.)

The Activation of the Disaster Site Recovery Team

The disaster site recovery team is activated after it has been decided to activate the DCRP. This occurs after a sequence of events known as the initial disaster alert (see Chapter II-7). That sequence begins when an incident at the data center is first discovered and a member of the IS recovery management team is notified of the incident. This IS recovery management team member travels to the data center and assesses the situation. If the situation might require the activation of the data center recovery plan, he or she notifies the other members of the IS recovery management team to report to recovery headquarters.

The IS recovery management team reviews the results of the damage assessment activities and makes its recommendation on whether to activate the DCRP or terminate any further recovery operation activities. The recovery chairperson is responsible for deciding whether to activate the DCRP or terminate any further actions.

EXHIBIT II-6-A DISASTER SITE RECOVERY TEAM

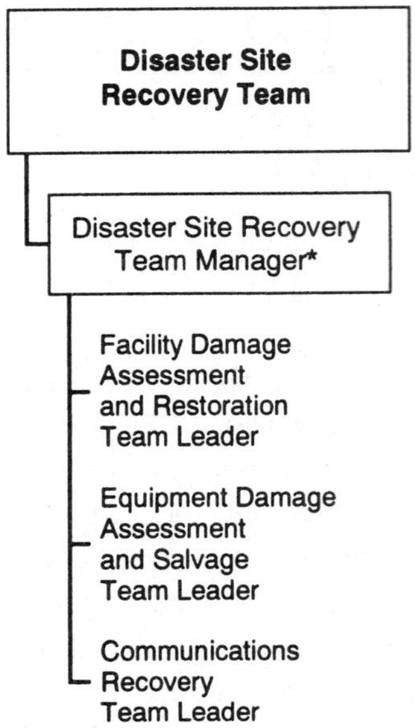

Note:
*Member of the IS recovery management team

After the DCRP is activated, the disaster site recovery team manager notifies his or her team leaders, or their alternates, to report to recovery headquarters. After attending the chairperson's activation meeting (along with the managers of the computer operations recovery team and the recovery headquarters team), the disaster site recovery team manager conducts an activation meeting for all disaster site recovery team leaders. (This process is summarized in Exhibit II-4-B.)

Responsibilities of the Disaster Site Recovery Team

The disaster site recovery team is responsible for the following recovery activities:

- Assessing the damage to the computer equipment; to the computer supplies, forms, and data; and to the communications network.
- Salvaging and protecting computer equipment, supplies, forms, and data against any further damage.
- Making arrangements for the repair and/or replacement of damaged equipment, supplies, forms, and data.
- Acting as a liaison with vendors that will be supporting the recovery operation.
- Providing a coordinated effort during the building damage assessment and repair efforts.
- If the building cannot be repaired on a timely basis, providing assistance in finding an adequate alternative site.

The disaster site recovery team may need to rely on the expertise of the staff support teams. The staff support teams come from departments within the company that have special expertise in areas that support the operations of the data center; these departments include the security department, the building services department, the public relations department, the human resources department, the insurance department, the transportation department, the legal department, and the audit department.

The DCRP contains the support commitments of each of these staff departments. The DCRP does not describe how the staff departments are to provide this support; that is covered in each of the staff department's business resumption sections of the companywide business resumption plan.

THE DISASTER SITE RECOVERY TEAM MANAGER

After the DCRP has been activated, the disaster site recovery team manager:

1. Conducts the disaster site recovery team meeting.
2. Identifies and coordinates support from staff departments.
3. Notifies vendors.
4. Obtains clearance to enter the building housing the data center.
5. Manages the efforts involved in assessing the damage to the data center and the building housing the data center. This may also involve selecting and preparing a temporary location if the damaged data center cannot be repaired on a timely basis.
6. Manages the efforts involved in assessing the damage to the computer equipment, forms, supplies, and data and in repairing or replacing computer equipment, supplies, and forms.
7. Manages efforts in assessing damage to the communications network that supports the data center and in salvage activities.

These steps are described in the following paragraphs. Workpaper II6.01 provides a sample script that the team manager can follow in performing these actions.

Conduct the Team Meeting

STEP 1

After the chairperson's meeting is over, the disaster site recovery team manager conducts a meeting for the disaster site recovery team leaders. At this meeting, the disaster site recovery team manager should explain the goals and objectives that were identified during the recovery chairperson's activation meeting. The team manager should then review the tasks to be performed by the disaster site recovery team personnel. The disaster site recovery team manager should also distribute copies of forms to be used during the recovery operation and provide instructions on how and when the forms are to be completed. These forms may include the personnel location control form (see Workpaper II4.13), the recovery status report form (see Workpaper II4.14), the travel and expense report form (see Workpaper II4.15), and the disaster recovery time record form (see Workpaper II4.16). The disaster site recovery team manager also distributes and reviews copies of the prepared public statement (see Workpaper II4.11). At the conclusion of the meeting, the manager should remind all team leaders to discuss the use of the recovery forms with the IS personnel working with their recovery teams.

Identify and Coordinate Support from Staff Department Representatives

STEP 2

The disaster site recovery team manager should obtain from the recovery chairperson the names of the staff department representatives who will be supporting disaster site recovery activities. These staff department representatives provide support throughout the recovery operations.

Building Services Department. Representatives of this department obtain clearance to enter the building from local authorities. They examine the building to ensure there are no safety problems that could result in injury to members of the disaster site recovery team. They also investigate the cause of the disaster to determine whether it was intentional or accidental or could happen again. Last, they make arrangements to have the building repaired.

Security Department. Representatives of this department secure the site and prevent anyone who is not authorized from entering the building. They investigate the cause of the disaster to determine whether it was intentional or accidental. If they determine that it was intentional, they seal off the area for local authorities and provide security personnel at all critical locations in the company to minimize the potential for a physical attack. These locations might include the computer backup site and the off-premises record storage location.

Public Relations Department. These representatives prepare all official company statements. They manage the relations with news media personnel and are present whenever company members and reporters meet.

Human Resources Department. Human resources representatives notify families of injured personnel. They explain the company benefits available to families and establish the payment policy for personnel, especially for those who will not be able to work for a time following the disaster. They also establish a policy to reward personnel who work beyond normal expectations during the recovery operation.

Insurance Department. These representatives notify the insurance carriers of the situation. They advise IS management of the manner in which information should be gathered, file all claims and supporting documentation, and obtain any special insurance coverage that may be needed during the recovery operation.

Purchasing Department. Purchasing department representatives expedite purchase orders for the replacement of computer equipment destroyed by the disaster. They also place purchase orders for computer supplies and forms that were destroyed by the disaster, account for the delivery of replacement items, and record any insurance-covered delivery charges that may be incurred during the recovery operation.

Legal Department. These representatives review copies of existing contracts to ensure the company is being supported by the vendors properly. They also review any new contracts that may have to be entered into as a result of the disaster.

STEP 3

Contact Vendors

The disaster site recovery team manager should alert major vendors to the situation using the vendor notification checklists. Computer equipment vendors are alerted using the computer equipment vendor notification checklist (see Workpaper II6.02), the computer supplies vendors using the computer supplies vendor notification checklist (see Workpaper II6.03), and the computer forms vendors using the computer forms vendor notification checklist (see Workpaper II6.04). These checklists identify the vendor name, the company address, the phone number during business hours, and a 24-hour emergency phone number. The checklist provides space for the caller to document the result of each vendor alert.

The disaster site recovery team manager provides the vendors with the location of the recovery headquarters. The vendors will be requested to send their representatives to the recovery headquarters, where the security department representative will provide any clearance and credentials needed to enter the building.

The disaster site recovery team manager provides the equipment damage assessment and salvage team leader with checklists containing the current inventories of equipment, supplies, and forms used by the IS department. The team leader returns the checklists at the completion of the assessment with appropriate recommendations to either repair or replace damaged items. The disaster site recovery team manager than meets with the recovery chairperson to review this information. Based on the decisions rendered during this meeting, the disaster site recovery team manager will direct the equipment damage assessment and salvage team leader on which resources to repair and which to replace.

When developing the plan, the DCRP coordinator should gather information on local vendors that supply services that might be needed following a disaster. These include general contractors as well as demolition, cleanup and salvage, heating and air-conditioning, electrical, fire protection, security systems, and plumbing contractors. These companies should be recorded on the recovery services company notification checklist (see Workpaper II6.05).

The disaster site recovery team manager should use this checklist to alert the utility service companies of the situation and request their assistance in assessing the damage, if required. (This step is needed only when the data center is operating autonomously and is not supported by a building services department, which would usually handle this activity.) If needed, the disaster site recovery team manager provides the vendor with the location of the recovery headquarters. The companies will be requested to send their representatives to the recovery headquarters, where the security department representative provides any clearance and credentials needed to enter the building.

Obtain Clearance to Enter the Building

STEP 4

The disaster site recovery team manager should obtain clearance before sending any recovery teams into the building to assess the extent of damage. He or she obtains this clearance from the building services department or local authorities.

Access into the building may be delayed for several reasons. First, the local authorities may have determined that the building is unsafe to enter because there is a danger of collapse or because it has been contaminated by toxic chemicals. Second, local authorities may suspect the disaster was caused intentionally; therefore, the area would be considered a crime scene. During that time, unauthorized personnel would not be allowed to gain entry into the area, because they could accidentally remove or destroy evidence that could point to the criminal. Third, if the company does not own the building, the owner may decide to restrict all tenants from entering the building. Because the owner of the building is usually held responsible for any injuries sustained by tenants' employees, most insurance companies advise their clients to secure the building and keep it closed until the building can be inspected and certified as safe.

Manage the Facility Damage Assessment and Restoration Activities

STEP 5

In conjunction with the team leader, the disaster site recovery team manager manages the activities of the facility damage assessment and restoration team throughout the recovery operation. The manager reviews the reports provided by the team leader. In particular, the manager should review the recommendations made by the team leader on whether the repairs can be made on a timely basis or whether a temporary data center should be used. If the temporary data center is to be used, the disaster site recovery team manager should review the recommendations of the team leader on which of the potential temporary data center sites should be selected. The disaster site recovery team manager should also ask the recovery chairperson for his or her opinion. After the decision has been made, the disaster site recovery team manager should direct the team leader to begin preparations for the selected temporary site. (For more information on this team leader's activities, see the section of this chapter entitled "The Facility Damage Assessment and Restoration Team Leader.")

STEP 6

Manage the Equipment Damage Assessment and Salvage Activities

In conjunction with the team leader, the disaster site recovery team manager manages the activities of the equipment damage assessment and salvage team throughout the recovery operation. The manager first should provide the current vendor inventory checklists (i.e., equipment, supplies, and forms vendors) to the team leader for use during the assessment of damages. The manager should review the assessments made by the team leader as to which equipment, supplies, and forms are salvageable and which are destroyed. The disaster site recovery team manager should direct the team leader to order replacements for the destroyed equipment, supplies, and forms; make provisions for cleaning damaged but salvageable equipment and supplies; and make provisions for protecting undamaged equipment, supplies, and forms. (For more information on this team leader's activities, see the section of this chapter entitled "The Equipment Damage Assessment and Salvage Team Leader.")

STEP 7

Manage Communications Recovery Activities

The disaster site recovery team manager should assess the damage to the communications network that serves the data center and assist in its salvage and restoration. This work is performed in cooperation with the communications recovery team, as discussed in Part III of this book.

THE FACILITY DAMAGE ASSESSMENT AND RESTORATION TEAM LEADER

After the disaster site recovery team manager's meeting, the facility damage assessment and restoration team leader should meet with the IS personnel who will assist the facility damage assessment and restoration team and explain the forms to be used during the recovery operation. The team leader should complete the personnel location control form (see Workpaper II4.13), identifying who will be working on the facility damage assessment and restoration team, their work locations, and the telephone numbers for those locations. After the form is completed, the team leader should make a copy for his or her own records and send the original to the notification and communications team at the recovery headquarters.

The facility damage assessment and restoration team leader is responsible for:

1. Obtaining information on the damage to the data center and the building housing the data center and supervising or assisting the building services department during the repairs of the data center and the building housing the data center.
2. When needed, assisting in finding an adequate location for a temporary data center.

A detailed script of these recovery actions is provided in Workpaper II6.06.

STEP 1

Assess Damage and Estimate Time to Repair Facility

The facility damage assessment and restoration team leader should obtain the names of the staff department support representatives and the recovery services company representatives who will assist the team during the damage assessment and restoration activities. The team leader travels to the damaged facility to participate in evaluating the damage. The team leader acts as a liaison with the building services department representative or the recovery services company representatives; these representatives are ultimately responsible for determining the extent of damage to the building. The team leader is responsible for obtaining an initial estimate of damage to the structure and the estimate of the time required for repair.

If the building is not badly damaged, the team leader should notify the disaster site recovery team manager immediately, so that IS can begin the cleanup operations to move back into the damaged site. On the other hand, if the structure is badly damaged, the disaster site recovery team manager should notify the recovery chairperson, because a temporary data center location will probably be needed.

The facility damage assessment and restoration team leader should use the disaster site damage assessment form to record the initial damage assessment (see Workpaper II6.07). This form identifies areas of the building that should be included in the damage assessment. It covers access to the building (e.g., whether access is limited as a result of safety or security concerns); structural damage to walls, floors, and ceilings; damage to the building equipment and utilities; and damage to such building controls as fire protection and security systems. This report should include the initial estimate of the time to repair the facility.

It should be recognized that the initial estimate may change later. A building may appear as though it can be repaired in weeks, but after a more detailed investigation is performed, it may require many months to repair. For example, after a fire at the C&P Telephone Company information systems facilities in Silver Spring MD, it was originally estimated that it would take only six weeks to repair. Later, asbestos problems were uncovered and the asbestos abatement project took nearly a year to complete.

Damage to Power and Climate-Control Systems. Backup generators can provide a substitute for power equipment that cannot be replaced quickly. For example, in 1982 the Singer Corporation's Kearfott Division in Wayne NJ lost use of its power equipment because of fire. The transformer was destroyed and had to be replaced. It took nine days to acquire and install a similar transformer. During this period of time, Singer used a backup diesel generator to provide power to the IS area and keep the mainframes operating.

If the company does not have backup generators, the disaster site recovery team manager may want to consider obtaining a mobile generator from a commercial vendor. For example, in 1988 Nordstrom Inc.'s data center lost power as a result of an underground fire in the power company's facility in Seattle WA. The head of the IS department was able to obtain a power-on-wheels generator, thereby limiting the computer outage to less than one day. He pointed out that if it had not been a holiday weekend, the company might not have been allowed to operate the generator in the downtown area because of the noise it created.

Data center facilities must maintain a temperature of 72° F, plus or minus three degrees. If it is too hot or too cold, it is not safe to operate the computer.

Mobile climate-control systems can be used to maintain proper temperature and humidity. For example, after a fire at a State Farm Insurance Company service center in 1981, State Farm contracted for four mobile air-conditioning trucks. Even though it was the beginning of August, when temperatures and humidity are very high, the trucks were able to produce enough cool air to service the whole building for several weeks until the necessary repairs to air-conditioning equipment could be made.

Problems in Completing Repairs. Problems that can delay the repair of the building include the need to meet the current fire code and to clean up an area contaminated by toxins or other residues. Meeting current fire codes can be costly and may result in a delayed decision on whether to repair the building or to tear it down. The building may have a toxic contamination problem that restricts entry to those individuals who have been certified for this type of cleanup operation and who are wearing the appropriate protective clothing.

STEP 2

Assist in Finding a Temporary Data Center

If the disaster has damaged the building to a point that it cannot be repaired within a reasonable period of time, the team leader should evaluate the available space in other facilities using the temporary location facilities requirements information checklist (see Workpaper II6.08). (This step assumes that the organization has not already contracted for a hot site or cold site.) This checklist contains information pertaining to the space required for the processing area, the support area, and the office. It identifies the amount of raised flooring, the air conditioning, the heat and humidity control, and the electrical power required. It also provides such information as access control and fire protection requirements.

The facility damage assessment and restoration team leader fills out the temporary computer site facilities review form when analyzing each of the potential temporary locations (see Workpaper II6.09). The form provides the questions the team leader should ask about potential exposures to be avoided (e.g., power and telephone service, location of water lines over the data center room, and presence of external windows). The new site should not be too close to an earthquake fault, flood area, airport, or hazardous areas or businesses. Known earthquake fault lines are identified on maps that can be obtained from local authorities. (Unfortunately, many recent earthquakes have occurred on unknown faults [e.g., the Whittiers Narrow in 1987 and the Northridge in 1994].) Flood areas are also identified on maps that can be obtained from local authorities.

Although an airport is not a safe location for businesses or data centers, industrial parks have been built in areas near airports for the past 20 years. The team leader should ensure that the temporary data center is not too close to an airport. Facilities near a chemical company, oil company, or pipeline should also be avoided.

Personnel Considerations. The proximity of the data center to public transportation should be evaluated. Lack of public transportation access may result in the loss of key employees or in an employee filing an unfair work claim. A move from city to suburb could present a problem in commuting for some employees.

Coordinating the Move into the New Facility. If the data center is to move to a new site, the facility damage assessment and restoration team leader is responsible for preparing the equipment layout for the new facility. In a normal move of a data center to a new location, it is not uncommon for the participants to plan the move for 12 months. In a disaster, they may have six weeks. Little planning can be done, because the company does not know where the data center is going to move. But some information is available that can assist in the coordinating effort. Copies of the present floor plan can be useful. The DCRP includes information from computer equipment vendors and the computer operations manager about required resources.

Use of Commercial Cold Sites. Many customers of commercial hot sites also sign a contract to use a commercial cold site as the temporary location for their data center in the event they cannot repair the damaged data center within the six weeks they contracted for the hot site. This was the case with the Penn Mutual Insurance Company. Following a fire in 1989 in the building that housed the corporate data center, the data center processing activities were moved to the commercial hot site. When it became known that the company would be unable to move back into the damaged facility for at least six months, it activated the commercial cold-site contract and installed computer equipment at the cold site. The company processed at the cold site for more than a year before finally moving into a new, permanent data center.

(For more information on commercial hot sites and cold sites, see Chapter II-9 of this book.)

THE EQUIPMENT DAMAGE ASSESSMENT AND SALVAGE TEAM LEADER

After the disaster site recovery team manager's meeting, the equipment damage assessment and salvage team leader should meet with the IS personnel who will assist the equipment damage assessment and salvage team and explain the forms to be used during the recovery operation. The team leader should complete the personnel location control form (see Workpaper II4.13), identifying who will be working on the equipment damage assessment and salvage team, their work locations, and the telephone numbers for those locations. After the form is completed, the team leader should make a copy for his or her own records and send the original to the notification and communications team at the recovery headquarters.

The equipment damage assessment and salvage team leader is responsible for:

1. Assessing the extent of damage to computer equipment. This requires acting as liaison with the hardware vendor representatives during the assessment of damage. The team leader also arranges to have damaged equipment repaired and destroyed equipment replaced.
2. Assessing damage to supplies and ordering replacements for those that were destroyed.
3. Assessing damage to forms and ordering replacements for those that were destroyed.
4. Assessing the extent of damage to the computer data residing on the disks and tapes in the damaged data center. The team leader ensures that precautions are taken to protect undamaged data from being damaged by the effects of the disaster and makes provisions to have damaged data cleaned and destroyed data reconstructed.

A detailed script of these recovery actions is provided in Workpaper II6.10.

Assess Damage to Computer Equipment

STEP 1

The equipment damage assessment and salvage team leader should obtain the names of the staff department support representatives, the vendor representatives, and the recovery services vendor representatives who will assist the team during the damage assessment activities. When directed by the disaster site recovery team manager, the team leader travels to the damaged facility to evaluate the extent of damage to the computer equipment.

The team leader is not expected to make the decisions on whether computer equipment is repairable. Acting as a liaison with the computer equipment vendor representatives and the insurance company adjuster, the team leader obtains the estimate of damage for the equipment and passes that information on to the disaster site recovery team manager. While examining the equipment, the team leader should record the results on the computer equipment inventory checklist (see Workpaper II6.11). The computer equipment inventory checklist contains a current list of all equipment installed in the data center; it includes the vendor name, the model number, a description, and the serial number for each piece of equipment. A space is provided to record the condition of the equipment. Using the checklist, the team leader or his or her representative identifies and records equipment that is not damaged, equipment that is damaged but repairable, and equipment that has been destroyed. The team leader should also make recommendations on how to protect undamaged equipment from being damaged during the salvage and cleanup operation. A copy of the completed inventory checklist and the recommendations are then forwarded to the disaster site recovery team manager.

Undamaged Equipment. This equipment should be protected from any potential new damage. For example, it can be covered with plastic to prevent exposure to water, smoke, soot, or dust. It is not suggested that the equipment be tightly wrapped in the plastic or waterproof covers, because it might trap moisture inside the chassis; the covers should be laid on top of the equipment. If any significant salvage or reconstruction work is to take place near the equipment, it might be necessary to temporarily move the equipment to a safe storage area.

Damaged but Repairable Equipment. This equipment should be cleaned and repaired by the vendor or a professional equipment-cleaning company. The procedure used by the vendor depends on the type of damage sustained. In most cases, the vendor checks the equipment for contaminant damage, washes the parts with demineralized water, and dries them with fans.

Professional equipment-cleaning companies and vendors usually move the equipment into an air-conditioned and humidity-controlled environment as soon as possible; in some cases they seal off the equipment area from outside elements that could further contaminate the equipment. Some professional equipment cleaners spray the connectors and circuit boards with fluorocarbon-based aerosol contact cleaners, which will leave a thin coating to prevent oxygen from activating chlorides.

The drying process should be started as soon as possible. The longer the equipment stays wet, the more chance there is for oxidation. Professional equipment cleaners usually open the cabinet doors, remove side panels and covers, and pull out chassis drawers to allow water to run out of the equipment. They often set up fans to move air through the equipment to dry it and sometimes use compressed air to blow out trapped water. Hand-held hair dryers may also be used to further dry the equipment.

Destroyed Equipment. The team leader should make recommendations on which equipment should be replaced. The purchasing department should provide support in ordering replacement equipment.

If there is a dispute over whether a piece of equipment is repairable or destroyed, the team leader should let the internal insurance representative negotiate with the insurance company and report on this to the disaster site recovery team manager.

In some cases, the company may need to continue to assess performance of repaired equipment, especially if there has been disagreement about whether the item should have been replaced. For example, in one case several years ago, an online service bureau suffered a fire in the computer center. The computer equipment vendor determined that three of the five mainframes could not be salvaged, but the insurance adjuster determined that two of the three computers identified as unsalvageable could be repaired. The service bureau was forced to have them repaired. After these two computers were installed, the service bureau kept strict records of the repaired computers' downtime. During a period of 90 days, the computers were down more than 50% of the time. Extensive claims were submitted to the same insurance company that held the business interruption coverage; it finally agreed to replace the two computers. What could have been a $2 million settlement right after the fire became a $7.5 million settlement a few months later.

Assess Damage to Computer Supplies

STEP 2

The team leader should direct the computer supplies damage assessment and salvage activities. While examining the supplies, the team leader should record the results on the computer supplies inventory checklist (see Workpaper II6.12). The computer supplies inventory checklist contains a current list of all supplies used in the data center. It identifies the vendor's name and address and includes the catalog number, a description, and the average monthly use. Space is provided to record the condition of the supplies. Using the completed checklist, the team leader or his or her representative should develop a report listing supplies that are not damaged, supplies that can be salvaged, and supplies that have been destroyed. The team leader should copy the completed inventory checklist and make recommendations on how to protect supplies that have not been damaged from further damage. The team leader should also make recommendations on which supplies should be replaced. A copy of the completed inventory checklist and the recommendations should then be forwarded to the disaster site recovery team manager.

Assess Damage to Computer Forms

STEP 3

The team leader should direct the computer forms damage assessment and salvage activities. The team leader records the results of the assessment on the computer forms inventory checklist (see Workpaper II6.13). The computer forms inventory checklist contains a current list of all forms used in the data center. It identifies the vendor's name and address and includes the form number, a description, and the average monthly use. Space is provided to record the condition of the forms. Using the completed checklist, the team leader or his or her representative should develop a report listing forms that are not damaged and forms that have been destroyed. The team leader should copy the completed inventory checklist and make recommendations on how to protect intact forms from damage. The team leader should also make recommendations on which forms should be replaced. A copy of the completed inventory checklist and the recommendations should then be forwarded to the disaster site recovery team manager. The team leader should also salvage any documentation that is not destroyed by the disaster.

Assess Damage to Data

STEP 4

The team leader should assess the damage to the tapes and disks located in the damaged site. If any of them can be salvaged, it could save the company hours of application and data base reconstruction time.

The team leader should consult with representatives from the IS operations area (e.g., in assessing the tape library), the recovery services companies, and the purchasing department. To identify the status of the tapes, the team leader should use a copy of the most current tape library report (from the prior night). If the on-site copy was destroyed, the most current copy should be retrieved from the off-premises storage area. (For more information on the data recovery procedures, see Chapter II-10.)

WORKPAPER II6.01 Disaster Site Recovery Team Manager Recovery Procedures

Company Name___________ Issued________ Section_______ Page_______
Data Center__________________
Data Center Recovery Plan_______________ Supersedes_______________

DISASTER SITE RECOVERY TEAM MANAGER RECOVERY PROCEDURE

Recovery procedures follow. Read the entire section before performing any assignments. The recovery objectives will dictate the need for and timing of all assignments.

RECOVERY ACTIONS:

1. Obtain the names of the staff department representatives who will support the data center restoration activities from the recovery chairperson.

Staff Support Department	Representative's Name
____________________________	____________________________
____________________________	____________________________
____________________________	____________________________
____________________________	____________________________
____________________________	____________________________

2. Provide this information to the facility damage assessment and restoration team leader and the equipment damage assessment and salvage team leader. Based on the extent of damage caused by the disaster, determine the damage assessment, salvage, and restoration activities required. For example:

    a. If the facility is undamaged and the equipment and contents have sustained minor damage, initiate:

        - Equipment and contents salvage activities.
        - Site cleanup activities, if needed.

    b. If the facility has minor damage and the equipment and contents have sustained major damage, initiate:

        - Data, equipment, and contents salvage activities.
        - Equipment cleanup and repair activities.
        - Replacement activities for destroyed items.
        - Site repair and cleanup activities.

    c. If the facility has major damage and the equipment and contents have sustained major damage, initiate:

        - In-depth data salvage activities.
        - In-depth damage assessment and salvage activities.
        - Site reconstruction activities.

- Site-equipping activities.

3. Alert the major vendors to the situation and request their assistance. Provide the location of the recovery headquarters and ask them to have their representative report to that location to obtain security clearance passes. Use the following checklists:

a.	Computer equipment vendor notification	(Workpaper II6.02)
b.	Communications vendor notification	(See Part III of this book)
c.	Forms and supplies vendor notification	(Workpapers II6.03 and II6.04)
d.	Recovery services companies notification	(Workpaper II6.05)

4. Notify recovery service companies to assist in the recovery operation using the recovery services companies notification checklist (Workpaper II6.05).

5. Complete the personnel location control form (Workpaper II4.13), including staff and vendor personnel, and give a copy to the notification and communications team. Obtain temporary access passes from the recovery headquarters manager for any personnel who will be working in a secured area.

6. Obtain clearance to send personnel into the damaged site from authorized individuals (e.g., building services, security, or local authorities).

7. Provide the facility damage assessment and restoration team and the equipment damage assessment and salvage team with the names of representatives from the staff departments and vendors that will be assisting during the recovery activities.

8. Distribute copies of the required checklists to the appropriate team leader for damage assessment and salvage activities:

a.	Computer equipment inventory	(Workpaper II6.11)
b.	Communications inventory	(See Part III of this book)
c.	Computer supplies inventory	(Workpaper II6.12)
d.	Computer forms inventory	(Workpaper II6.13)

9. Direct the facility, equipment, and network damage assessment and restoration teams to travel to the disaster site and initiate damage assessment and salvage activities.

10. After completion, obtain the salvageable data report from the equipment damage assessment and salvage team leader:

    a. Notify the computer operations recovery team leader on the status of data located at the disaster site.
    b. Keep the team leader informed on the status of the recovery of data.

11. Obtain the assessment reports from the facility damage assessment and restoration team leader:

    a. Review the reports, giving special attention to estimate of time to repair the facility.
    b. If the building services department representative feels the building can be repaired quickly, prepare to move back into the damaged site as soon as the cleanup is complete.
    c. If the building services department representative feels the building will not be repaired for months, consider the need to move the data center to a temporary location.
    d. Present this recommendation to the recovery chairperson. If the recovery chairperson approves the move to a temporary or permanent location, direct the facility damage assessment and restoration team leader to locate potential sites.
    e. Obtain a report of findings on the potential temporary sites and a copy of the completed disaster site damage assessment form (Workpaper II6.07).
    f. Review and approve all restoration recommendations and actions. After a decision has been made regarding the reconstruction of the damaged facility and the obtaining of a temporary or new facility, work with the facility damage assessment and restoration team to:

        - Design a layout of the new or repaired site to accommodate equipment and personnel.
        - Color-code a new floor plan to indicate where boxes, furniture, and equipment is to be placed.
        - Post color-coded floor plans to facilitate use by personnel and movers.

12. Obtain the damage assessment reports from the equipment damage assessment and salvage team leader.

    a. Equipment:

        - Review the reports, giving special attention to equipment that is reported as being beyond repair.
        - Meet with the equipment damage assessment and salvage team leader, the insurance representative, and the vendor representatives to review recommended courses of action.
        - Obtain estimated delivery dates from the equipment

damage assessment and salvage team leader for replacement of computer equipment. When required, meet with vendor senior management to expedite shipments of equipment.

- Meet with the recovery chairperson to provide information on the extent of computer equipment damage:

  -- Present recommendations on the replacement or repair of equipment.
  -- Provide estimates of when equipment can be repaired or replaced.
  -- Obtain authorization to proceed with repair and replacement actions.

- Obtain appropriate approvals and coordinate the ordering of any replacement equipment, materials, supplies, and forms:

  -- Maintain lists of ordered equipment, materials, supplies, and forms.
  -- Designate space for delivery, acceptance, and temporary storage.
  -- Establish procedures to control the delivery, receipt, and storage of all items.
  -- Maintain accurate records of materials ordered and received.
  -- Maintain a record of any extraordinary charges resulting from material delivery and storage.
  -- Provide copies of all invoices to the recovery headquarters manager.

- Place orders with vendors requesting emergency response.
- Review and approve all equipment installation activities.

b. Supplies:

- Obtain a copy of the supplies damage report from the equipment damage assessment and salvage team leader.
- Review the report and provide the authorization to order replacements for destroyed items.

c. Forms:

- Obtain a copy of the forms damage report from the equipment damage assessment and salvage team leader.
- Review the report and provide the authorization to order replacements for destroyed items.

WORKPAPER II6.02 Computer Equipment Vendor Notification Checklist

Company Name___________ Issued________ Section_______ Page_______
Data Center__________________
Data Center Recovery Plan_______________ Supersedes______________

COMPUTER EQUIPMENT VENDOR NOTIFICATION CHECKLIST

Vendor Name: ____________________ Business Number: _____________

Address [street]: _______________ Emergency Number: ____________

Address [city, state, zip code]: ________________________________

Result of alert: ____

Vendor Name: ____________________ Business Number: _____________

Address [street]: _______________ Emergency Number: ____________

Address [city, state, zip code]: ________________________________

Result of alert: ____

Vendor Name: ____________________ Business Number: _____________

Address [street]: _______________ Emergency Number: ____________

Address [city, state, zip code]: ________________________________

Result of alert: ____

Vendor Name: ____________________ Business Number: _____________

Address [street]: _______________ Emergency Number: ____________

Address [city, state, zip code]: ________________________________

Result of alert: ____

WORKPAPER II6.03 Computer Supplies Vendor Notification Checklist

Company Name____________ Issued_________ Section________ Page________
Data Center____________________
Data Center Recovery Plan_________________ Supersedes_______________

COMPUTER SUPPLIES VENDOR NOTIFICATION CHECKLIST

Vendor Name: ______________________ Business Number: ______________

Address [street]: ________________ Emergency Number: _____________

Address [city, state, zip code]: ____________________________________

Result of alert: ____

____

Vendor Name: ______________________ Business Number: ______________

Address [street]: ________________ Emergency Number: _____________

Address [city, state, zip code]: ____________________________________

Result of alert: ____

____

Vendor Name: ______________________ Business Number: ______________

Address [street]: ________________ Emergency Number: _____________

Address [city, state, zip code]: ____________________________________

Result of alert: ____

____

Vendor Name: ______________________ Business Number: ______________

Address [street]: ________________ Emergency Number: _____________

Address [city, state, zip code]: ____________________________________

Result of alert: ____

____

WORKPAPER II6.04 Computer Forms Vendor Notification Checklist

Company Name____________ Issued_________ Section________ Page_______
Data Center____________________
Data Center Recovery Plan_________________ Supersedes________________

COMPUTER FORMS VENDOR NOTIFICATION CHECKLIST

Vendor Name: ______________________ Business Number: ______________

Address [street]: ________________ Emergency Number: _____________

Address [city, state, zip code]: ____________________________________

Result of alert: ____
____

Vendor Name: ______________________ Business Number: ______________

Address [street]: ________________ Emergency Number: _____________

Address [city, state, zip code]: ____________________________________

Result of alert: ____
____

Vendor Name: ______________________ Business Number: ______________

Address [street]: ________________ Emergency Number: _____________

Address [city, state, zip code]: ____________________________________

Result of alert: ____
____

Vendor Name: ______________________ Business Number: ______________

Address [street]: ________________ Emergency Number: _____________

Address [city, state, zip code]: ____________________________________

Result of alert: ____
____

WORKPAPER II6.05 Recovery Services Companies Notification Checklist

Company Name__________ Issued________ Section_______ Page_______
Data Center_________________
Data Center Recovery Plan______________ Supersedes______________

RECOVERY SERVICES COMPANIES NOTIFICATION CHECKLIST

Vendor Name: ____________________ Business Number: _____________

Address [street]: _______________ Emergency Number: ____________

Address [city, state, zip code]: ________________________________

Service provided: ____

Result of alert: ____

Vendor Name: ____________________ Business Number: _____________

Address [street]: _______________ Emergency Number: ____________

Address [city, state, zip code]: ________________________________

Service provided: ____

Result of alert: ____

Vendor Name: ____________________ Business Number: _____________

Address [street]: _______________ Emergency Number: ____________

Address [city, state, zip code]: ________________________________

Service provided: ____

Result of alert: ____

Vendor Name: ____________________ Business Number: _____________

Address [street]: _______________ Emergency Number: ____________

Address [city, state, zip code]: ________________________________

Service provided: ____

Result of alert: ____

WORKPAPER II6.06 Facility Damage Assessment and Restoration Team Leader Recovery Procedures

Company Name____________ Issued_________ Section________ Page________
Data Center____________________
Data Center Recovery Plan________________ Supersedes________________

<u>FACILITY DAMAGE ASSESSMENT AND RESTORATION TEAM LEADER RECOVERY PROCEDURE</u>

Recovery procedures follow. Read the entire section before performing any assignments. The recovery objectives will dictate the need for and timing of all assignments.

RECOVERY ACTIONS:

1. Obtain from the disaster site recovery team manager the names of individuals who will assist during the facility damage assessment and salvage activities:

   a.

Staff Support Department	Representative's Name
______________________	______________________
______________________	______________________
______________________	______________________
______________________	______________________
______________________	______________________

   b.

Recovery Services Company	Representative's Name
______________________	______________________
______________________	______________________
______________________	______________________
______________________	______________________
______________________	______________________

2. Travel to the damaged facility to participate in evaluating the extent of damage. Use the disaster site damage assessment form (Workpaper II6.07).

3. Obtain a damage assessment report from the buildings department support team representative:

   a. Damage to the building structure (external and internal).
   b. Damage to the floor housing the data center.
   c. Damage to the utilities.
   d. Access to different areas within the building.
   e. Capability for securing the building.

4. Obtain an estimate of time needed to repair the facility from the buildings department support team representative:

   a. Days: ______________________________.
   b. Weeks: ______________________________.
   c. Months: ______________________________.
   d. Years: ______________________________.

5. If the data center can be repaired, coordinate the cleanup of the area.

6. If the estimate of time needed to repair the facility is months or years, consider a temporary data center site until the damaged site can be repaired or a new permanent data center site. Develop a recommendation on acquiring either temporary space or a new location.

7. In the event that temporary operating sites must be used:

   a. Find suitable space. Use the temporary location facilities requirements information checklist (Workpaper II6.08).
   b. Travel to each potential temporary or permanent site. Evaluate the site for exposures that will lessen the desirability of the site. Use the temporary computer site facilities review form (Workpaper II6.09).

8. After selecting the temporary or permanent location:

   a. Design a proposed layout that will accommodate the equipment and IS personnel.
   b. Color-code the floor plan to indicate where equipment, furniture, and boxes are to be placed. Post color-coded floor plans for employees or movers.

WORKPAPER II6.07 Disaster Site Damage Assessment Form

Company Name____________ Issued_________ Section________ Page________
Data Center____________________
Data Center Recovery Plan________________ Supersedes________________

DISASTER SITE DAMAGE ASSESSMENT FORM

To be completed after plan activation:

1. Access to the building:

- [ ] Open access.
  [ ] Limited access (explain): ____________________________
  ____
  ____.

- [ ] No safety concerns.
  [ ] Safety concerns (explain): ___________________________
  ____
  ____.

- [ ] No security concerns.
  [ ] Security concerns (explain): _________________________
  ____
  ____.

- [ ] Other (explain): _____________________________________
  ____
  ____.

2. Structure:

- Walls:

  [ ] No visible damage.
  [ ] Visible damage (explain): ____________________________
  ____
  ____.

- Floors:

  [ ] No visible damage.
  [ ] Visible damage (explain): ____________________________
  ____
  ____.

- Ceilings:

  [ ] No visible damage.
  [ ] Visible damage (explain): ____________________________
  ____
  ____.

3. Equipment:

- [ ] Moved during disaster: ____.
- [ ] Receiving water from overhead leaks: ____.
- [ ] Contaminated by smoke or soot: ____.
- [ ] Showing signs of electrical problems: ____.
- [ ] Other (explain): ____.

4. Mechanicals/utilities:

- Lighting:

  [ ] Primary working.
  [ ] Not working (explain): ____.

  [ ] Backup working.
  [ ] Not working (explain): ____.

- Heating:

  [ ] Emergency working.
  [ ] Not working (explain): ____.

- Cooling:

  [ ] Working.
  [ ] Not working (explain): ____.

- Ventilation:

  [ ] Working.
  [ ] Not working (explain): ______________________________
  ____
  ____.

- Plumbing:

  [ ] Intact.
  [ ] Ruptures, leaking (explain): ________________________
  ____
  ____.

- [ ] Other (explain): ___________________________________
  ____
  ____.

5. Services:

- Access control:

  [ ] Working.
  [ ] Not working (explain): ______________________________
  ____
  ____.

- Fire protection:

  -- Sprinklers:
  [ ] Not activated.
  [ ] Activated (explain): ____________________________
  ____
  ____.

  -- Halon:
  [ ] Not activated.
  [ ] Activated (explain): ____________________________
  ____
  ____.

  -- Carbon dioxide:
  [ ] Not activated.
  [ ] Activated (explain): ____________________________
  ____
  ____.

- Power:

  [ ] Working.
  [ ] Not working (explain): ______________________________
  ____
  ____.

- Uninterruptible power supply system:

  -- Batteries:
  [ ] Working.
  [ ] Not working (explain): ______________________
  ____
  ____.

  -- Generator:
  [ ] Working.
  [ ] Not working (explain): ______________________
  ____
  ____.

- Other power considerations:

  -- Power regulation:
  [ ] Not damaged.
  [ ] Damaged (explain): __________________________
  ____
  ____.

  -- Power distribution:
  [ ] Not damaged.
  [ ] Damaged (explain): __________________________
  ____
  ____.

  -- Motor generators:
  [ ] Not damaged.
  [ ] Damaged (explain): __________________________
  ____
  ____.

  -- Circuit breakers and power cables:
  [ ] Not damaged.
  [ ] Damaged (explain): __________________________
  ____
  ____.

  -- [ ] Other (explain): ____________________________
  ____
  ____.

Name of report preparer: ______________________________
Date of report: ______________________ Time of report: __________

Damage assessment information provided by:

1) Name: ___________________ Title/Position: ___________________
2) Name: ___________________ Title/Position: ___________________
3) Name: ___________________ Title/Position: ___________________

WORKPAPER II6.08 Temporary Location Facilities Requirements Checklist

Company Name___________ Issued________ Section_______ Page_______
Data Center__________________
Data Center Recovery Plan_______________ Supersedes______________

TEMPORARY LOCATION FACILITIES REQUIREMENTS INFORMATION CHECKLIST

Complete after plan activation:

Data Center Computer Site	Minimum Needed	Available
Processing Area		
• Floor Space (in sq. ft.):		
-- Computer Room	__________	__________
-- Support Area	__________	__________
-- Office Area	__________	__________
Total Floor Space (in sq. ft.):	__________	__________
• Raised Flooring (in sq. ft.):	__________	__________
• Air Conditioning (in BTUs):		
-- Computer Room	__________	__________
-- Support Area	__________	__________
-- Office Area	__________	__________
• Heat and Humidity Control:		
-- Heat	__________ ° F	__________ ° F
-- Humidity	__________%	__________%

- Electrical Power:

  -- Computer Room ______kVA ______Hz ________kVA ________Hz

  -- Air Conditioning ______kVA ______Hz ________kVA ________Hz

  -- Support Office Area ______kVA ______Hz ________kVA ________Hz

- Floor Weight Capacity (lbs. per sq. in.): ____________________ ____________________

- Access Control (type): ____________________ ____________________

- Fire Protection (type):

  -- Computer Room ____________________ ____________________

  -- Support Office ____________________ ____________________

- Telephone:

  -- Lines ____________________ ____________________

  -- Handsets ____________________ ____________________

Facility Considerations

- Motor Generator Area (as required): ____________________ ____________________

- UPS System (batteries and equipment): ____________________ ____________________

- Fire Suppression Gas: ____________________ ____________________

- Trash Storage Area: ____________________ ____________________

- Electrical Service Room: ____________________ ____________________

- Telephone Service Room: ____________________ ____________________

Total Service Areas: ____________________ ____________________

WORKPAPER II6.09 Temporary Computer Site Facilities Review Form

Company Name___________ Issued________ Section_______ Page_______
Data Center__________________
Data Center Recovery Plan_______________ Supersedes______________

TEMPORARY COMPUTER SITE FACILITIES REVIEW FORM

To be completed after plan activation:

1. General information:

   a. Address: ____

   b. City: ____

   c. [ ] Existing building [ ] New building

   d. [ ] Owned [ ] Leased

2. Temporary computer site location:

	Comments:
a. How many floors in the building?	____________________
b. Which floors will the IS department be using?	____________________
c. What type of occupancy is on the floor above?	____________________
d. What type of occupancy is on the floor below?	____________________
e. Are there any companies occupying the building that are a known hazard (e.g., storing chemicals or gases on-site, high-profile organization)?	____________________
f. Hazards:	
Proximity to airport:	____________________
Proximity to earthquake fault:	____________________
Proximity to flood plain:	____________________
Proximity to hazardous industry:	____________________

g. Is multiple-grid commercial power service available? ______

h. Is there proximity to a telephone company office capable of supporting the required teleprocessing load? ______

i. Are parking spaces adequate for the number of employees? ______

j. Is public transportation available? ______

k. Is there proximity to an adequate labor market to staff the site? ______

l. Will this occupancy create any EEOC or union ramifications? ______

3. <u>Building considerations</u>:

Comments:

a. Loading dock truck-bed height: ______

b. Are hallways between loading dock and computer room or forms storage areas wide enough to permit skids of supplies to negotiate corners? ______

c. Will elevators, ramps, doors, and other passageways accommodate large, heavy equipment? ______

d. Is the computer room airtight if a gas fire-extinguishing agent needs to be used? ______

e. Are there water lines above the room? ______

f. Are the walls and ceiling watertight to prevent damage from water entering from above? ______

g. Are there water lines under the floor? ______

h. Is there positive drainage of the area under the raised floor? ______

i. Is there positive check valve to prevent sewer or other drain backup? __________

j. Are there external windows in the computer center? __________

k. Do the external windows have glare-retardant materials to reduce effect of solar heating? __________

l. Are the external windows covered with shatter-resistant material? __________

m. If location is above or below the entrance or lobby, does the building have freight elevators? __________

- Is the door opening width a minimum of 48"? __________
- Is the door opening height a minimum of 90"? __________
- Can weight capacity handle the heaviest unit? __________

n. Power company background:

- Outages:
  - -- Duration (time): __________
  - -- Frequency: __________
- Brownout/low voltage: __________
- Lightning:
  - -- Lightning rods: __________
  - -- Lightning arresters: __________
- Check electrical utility's performance data (interruptions): __________

WORKPAPER II6.10 Equipment Damage Assessment and Salvage Team Leader Recovery Procedures

Company Name___________ Issued________ Section_______ Page_______
Data Center__________________
Data Center Recovery Plan_______________ Supersedes______________

EQUIPMENT DAMAGE ASSESSMENT AND SALVAGE TEAM LEADER RECOVERY PROCEDURE

Recovery procedures follow. Read the entire section before performing any assignments. The recovery objectives will dictate the need for and timing of all assignments.

RECOVERY ACTIONS:

1. Obtain from the disaster site recovery team manager the names of individuals who will assist during the equipment damage assessment and salvage activities:

   a. Staff Support Department / Representative's Name

Staff Support Department	Representative's Name

   b. Vendor / Person's Name

Vendor	Person's Name

   c. Recovery Services Vendor / Person's Name

Recovery Services Vendor	Person's Name

2. Travel with your team to the damaged facility to evaluate the extent of damage to the equipment, supplies, and forms. Use the following checklists:

a.	Equipment inventory checklist	Workpaper II6.11
b.	Supplies inventory checklist	Workpaper II6.12
c.	Forms inventory checklist	Workpaper II6.13

3. Direct the computer equipment salvage activities:

   a. With the assistance of the vendor and insurance representatives, take an inventory of all equipment. Use the computer equipment inventory checklist (Workpaper II6.11).
   b. Develop a list of all salvageable equipment.
   c. Document a list of equipment that is damaged but salvageable.
   d. Document a list of equipment that is damaged and not salvageable.
   e. Develop an equipment damage status report and include a copy of the completed inventory list salvage evaluations and recommendations. Give the completed report to the disaster site recovery team manager.
   f. Stand by for management direction on equipment replacement activities.

4. Direct the computer supplies salvage activities:

   a. Take inventory of all supplies. Use the computer supplies inventory checklist (Workpaper II6.12).
   b. Document a list of supplies that are salvageable.
   c. Document a list of supplies that are damaged but salvageable.
   d. Document a list of supplies that are damaged and not salvageable.
   e. Develop a supplies salvage status report, which should include a copy of the completed inventory lists, salvage evaluations, and recommendations. Give the completed report to the disaster site recovery team manager.
   f. Stand by for management direction on replacement activities.

5. Direct the forms supplies salvage activities:

   a. Take inventory of all forms. Use the computer forms inventory checklist (Workpaper II6.13).
   b. Document a list of forms that are salvageable.
   c. Document a list of forms that are damaged but salvageable.
   d. Document a list of forms that are damaged and not salvageable.
   e. Develop a forms salvage status report, which should include copies of the completed inventory lists,

salvage evaluations, and recommendations. Give the completed report to the disaster site recovery team manager.

f. Stand by for management direction on replacement activities.

6. Direct the documentation salvage activities:

   a. Take an inventory of all documentation.
   b. Provide protection for all salvageable documentation.
   c. Arrange to have all salvageable documentation moved to a safe environment.
   d. Develop a documentation salvage status report and give it to the disaster site recovery team manager.

7. Conduct the following data salvage activities:

   a. Retrieve a copy of the tape library inventory report (in volume serial order) from the off-premises storage location.
   b. Use the tape library inventory report to record the condition of all magnetic media by tape reel number.
   c. Provide temporary storage and protection for all salvageable data.
   d. Develop a salvage report for the data located in the disaster area. Provide the report to the disaster site recovery team manager.
   e. Make arrangements to have all magnetic media checked for contamination:

      Vendor Name: ______________________________
      Contact Name: ______________________________
      Phone: ______________________________

   f. Once magnetic media are certified as clean, arrange for proper storage or prepare for shipment to the computer operations recovery team. Instruct all personnel to avoid sending contaminated items to the computer operations recovery location.

8. Do not initiate any salvage activities until the insurance department representative is on-site. Review planned salvage activities with the insurance department representative to verify that activities do not negatively affect insurance coverage.

9. Ensure that security is provided for all salvageable items:

   a. Clear all plans with security and insurance representatives.
   b. In the event salvageable items are to be moved, provide proper coordination between vendor representatives and the insurance representatives.

c. Designate space for salvageable materials to be relocated and protected.
d. Maintain records of emergency expenses related to the move of equipment and materials.

10. Determine a method to remove the nonsalvageable items to prepare for the facilities cleanup:

    a. Obtain authorization from the insurance representative before removing anything.

11. After the disaster site recovery team manager has ordered replacements, obtain estimated delivery dates from the vendors for computer equipment, supplies, and forms.

12. After delivery, manage and control the installation of all equipment with assistance from the appropriate recovery teams:

    a. Review results of any vendor diagnostic tests to ensure that equipment design specifications are met.
    b. Load and test the operating environment.
    c. Exercise the equipment with sample job streams.
    d. Initiate a controlled production test to ensure that the newly installed equipment will function properly.

WORKPAPER II6.11 Computer Equipment Inventory Checklist

Company Name___________ Issued________ Section_______ Page_______
Data Center__________________
Data Center Recovery Plan_______________ Supersedes_______________

COMPUTER EQUIPMENT INVENTORY CHECKLIST

Vendor	Model	Description	Serial Number	Condition

WORKPAPER II6.12 Computer Supplies Inventory Checklist

Company Name____________ Issued_________ Section________ Page________
Data Center____________________
Data Center Recovery Plan_________________ Supersedes________________

COMPUTER SUPPLIES INVENTORY CHECKLIST

Vendor	Catalog Number	Description	Average Monthly Use	Condition

WORKPAPER II6.13 Computer Forms Inventory Checklist

Company Name____________ Issued_________ Section________ Page________
Data Center____________________
Data Center Recovery Plan_________________ Supersedes________________

COMPUTER FORMS INVENTORY CHECKLIST

Vendor	Form Number	Description	Average Monthly Use	Condition

Developing the Initial Disaster Alert Procedure

CHAPTER

II-7

Chapter II-7 presents the initial disaster alert procedure. This procedure is used to inform a member of the IS recovery management team that the data center may have been affected by a problem at the building. (As noted in earlier chapters of Part II, the IS recovery management team comprises the recovery chairperson, recovery headquarters team manager, the computer operations recovery team manager, and the disaster site recovery team manager.) The IS recovery management team member will evaluate the situation to determine whether there is potential for a computer interruption and whether the situation could escalate into a crisis requiring the activation of the data center recovery plan (DCRP). The initial disaster alert procedure consists of the actions that will be taken from the time the problem at the building is identified to the time the decision is made to either activate or terminate DCRP activities.

The initial disaster alert procedure answers the following questions:

- Who in the IS department will be notified of the situation?
- Who notifies the IS recovery management team member if there is a problem in the building housing the data center?
- What should the IS recovery management team member do after being notified?
- Who activates the DCRP operation when it becomes necessary?

The initial disaster alert procedure consists of four steps:

1. *First alert.* At this step, a member of the IS recovery management team is notified that a computer interruption has occurred.
2. *Disaster verification.* This step is designed to provide a designated IS recovery management team member information on the appropriate actions for verifying that a disaster requiring the activation of the DCRP has occurred.
3. *IS recovery management team contact.* This step provides the IS recovery management team contact person with the actions to take in notifying the remaining IS recovery management team members to assemble at the recovery headquarters.
4. *DCRP activation.* This step provides the IS recovery management team with a procedure to follow to either activate the DCRP or terminate further DCRP activities.

The initial disaster alert procedure must be carefully thought out, because it is vital to ensuring the timely resumption of processing. The procedure needs to be documented and tested, and it should be exercised at least annually to ensure that it continues to meet DCRP objectives.

For an overview of the initial disaster alert, see Exhibit II-7-A. In this exhibit, the initial disaster alert is depicted as a series of logical steps used to determine the need to activate the DCRP or to terminate recovery activities.

EXHIBIT **II-7-A** DISASTER ALERT OVERVIEW

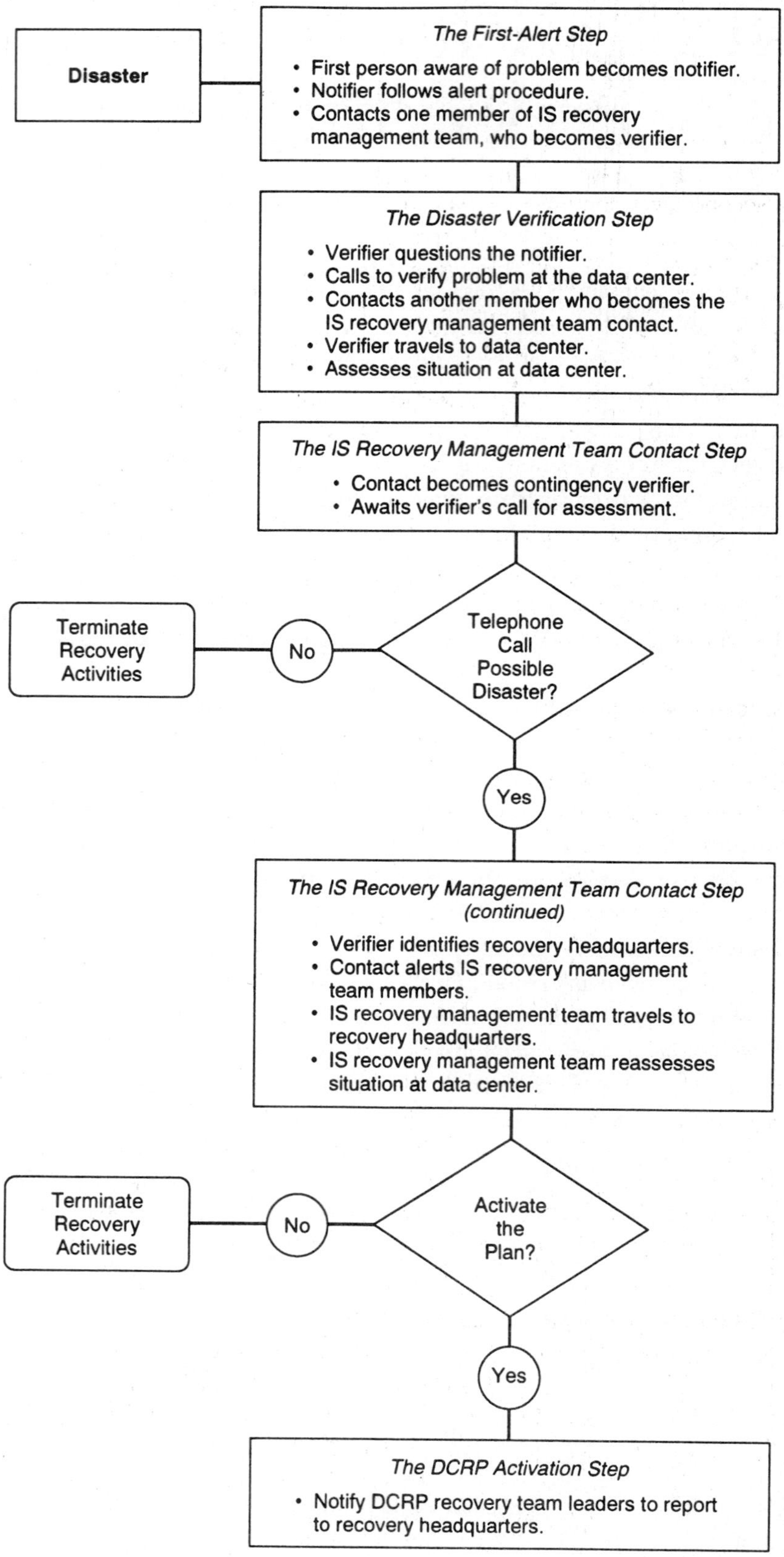

ACTIVATING THE DCRP

The time frame in which the data center has to resume the processing of critical applications determines how quickly the DCRP has to be activated. The shorter the time frame, the faster the department has to make the decision. Some companies have DCRPs with objectives to resume processing within 24 hours, while others have objectives to resume processing within seven days. As an example of a short time frame for recovery, regulations were issued by the New York Clearing House Administration requiring member banks that send a daily average of $20 billion in wire transfers to have a second-level contingency plan that would ensure the institution would be operational within six hours of the declared disaster.

If the data center has to respond by resuming processing within 24 hours, it needs to ensure that the initial disaster alert is not delayed and that the IS recovery management team receives word of a problem at the building housing the data center quickly. If, on the other hand, the computer center can wait to resume processing for seven days, the activation step does not have to be rushed.

When Does the Recovery Clock Start?

In the early days of DCRP planning, the heads of IS departments and the DCRP coordinators often assumed the DCRP clock did not start running until after the computer center declared a disaster and activated the DCRP. Perhaps they believed that the effects of the interruption to computer processing did not begin until they made the decision to activate the DCRP, even if that decision occurred 24 hours after the actual interruption began. Unfortunately, business units in the company would begin to feel the impact several hours after the interruption.

In fact, most were concerned about making a premature decision. There were many instances in which computer center interruptions were caused by hardware problems. In that case, the hardware vendor's representative, not the IS managers were in control of the situation. It was quite common for IS management to be told by the hardware vendor's representative that the hardware would be up and running in an hour. (They might be told this same message for hours before the computer eventually became operational.) IS management was hesitant to activate the DCRP, because the activation could be expensive and would not be justified if the computer actually became operational in an hour. A sizable amount of money might be spent unnecessarily on such tasks as arranging for computer backup site time, moving data center personnel to the computer backup sites, and moving computer forms and data tapes or disks to the backup sites.

As the DCRP process matured, the IS management became aware that it was required to respond to the interruption at the point where the processing of end users' information was stopped. The executive management and the business units of the company started the recovery clock at the point where the computer stopped processing.

Who Notifies the IS Recovery Management Team?

The person responsible for notifying one of the IS recovery management team members that an incident is taking place is the IS staff person working in the data center at the time of the incident. Most data centers today operate on a seven-day-a-week, 365-day-a-year basis. If a disaster strikes a data center, it is both reasonable and likely for an IS person in the data center to contact one of the IS recovery management team members.

If an IS staff member from the data center is not available, the security guard is the next person responsible for notifying the IS recovery management team. The security guard is typically responsible for notifying a number of different groups during a disaster, including the IS department. The guard should first notify an IS recovery management team member of the problem and then notify the remaining groups.

If the security guard is not available, the alarm company that monitors the fire alarms and sprinkler system should be next in line to inform the team. Notification should occur as soon as the company detects that the fire alarms or sprinklers have been activated.

When Should the Initial Disaster Alert Procedure Be Used?

The initial disaster alert procedure is to be used when managers in the IS department are not at work: after normal working hours, on weekends, or on holidays. If an incident occurs during normal working hours, this procedure will not have to be used because presumably managers will already be in the building. In this case, the managers are notified through regular work phone numbers.

STEP 1

THE FIRST ALERT

This step is designed to inform a member of the IS recovery management team that the data center may have been affected by a problem at the building. The purpose of the first alert is to prepare this IS recovery management team member to evaluate the situation to determine whether the computer interruption might possibly escalate into a crisis requiring the activation of the DCRP. If this step is not performed in a timely manner, the resumption of processing will be delayed.

For the purposes of this chapter, the person performing the notification is referred to as the "notifier." The IS recovery management team member being informed of the situation is referred to as the "verifier."

The first-alert step comprises a list of the IS recovery management team members to be notified in the event of a data center problem and a procedure for the notifier to follow.

IS Recovery Management Team List

The first-alert list identifies the IS recovery management team members that are authorized to make decisions on whether a condition exists that might require the DCRP to be activated. The members of this team are selected by the head of the IS department. The IS recovery management team comprises the recovery chairperson, recovery headquarters team manager, the computer operations recovery team manager, and the disaster site recovery team manager. Exhibit II-7-B provides a chart that identifies the individual recovery teams and their relationships. It should be noted that the team leaders for the individual DCRP recovery teams report to their respective managers, each of whom is a member of the IS recovery management team.

During DCRP development, the DCRP coordinator and the development committee document the specific information to be included on the first-alert procedure. The list includes the IS recovery management team members' titles, names, and home phone numbers. (Some companies include beeper numbers as well.) Space is provided at the end of each line to record the results of the phone notification. The notifier should record the result of the phone notification, which is especially important if an IS recovery management team member cannot be reached. This information should be passed on to the verifier by the notifier. This is one of the many control points used throughout the DCRP.

EXHIBIT II-7-B DATA CENTER RECOVERY PLAN TEAMS

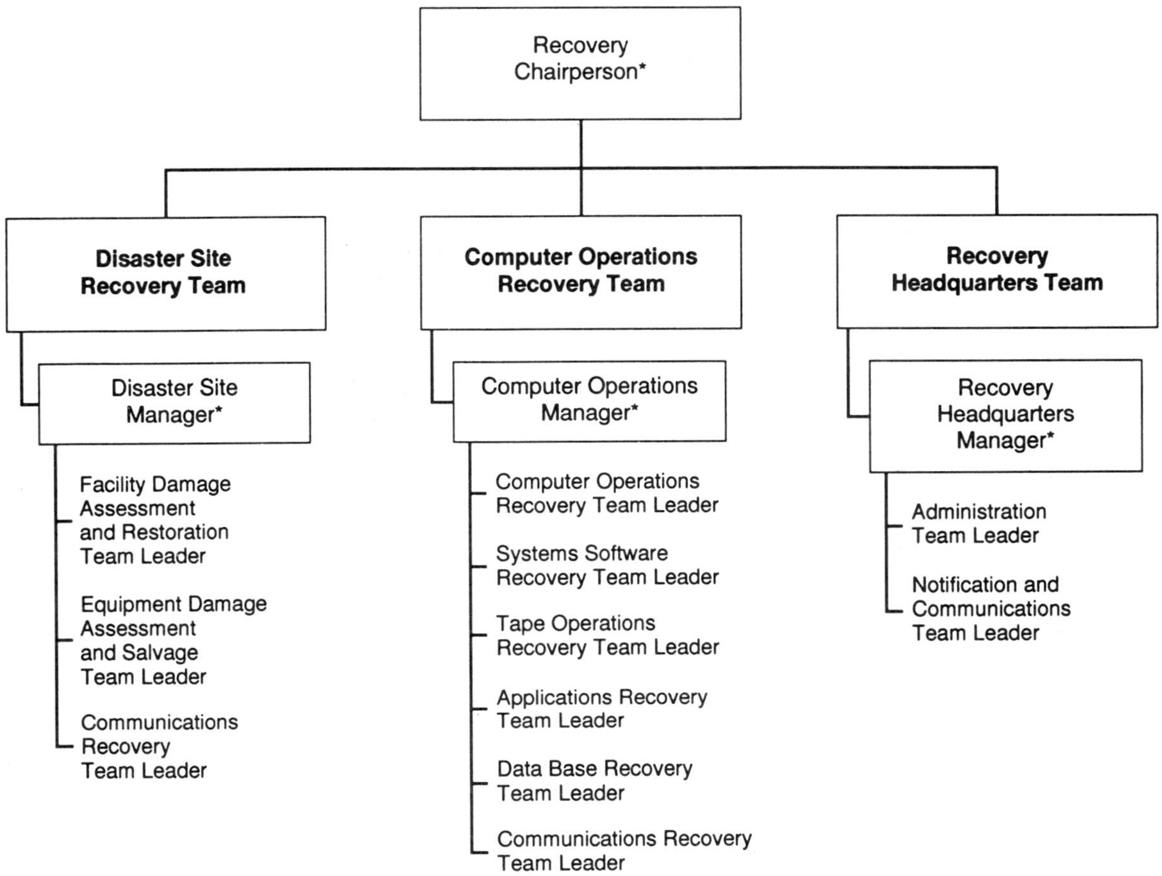

Note:
*Members of the IS recovery management team

At the completion of the recovery operation, management will require a full report on the incident. Information such as that recorded here makes it easier to complete any subsequent incident reports or management presentations. A sample form for use in the first-alert step is provided as Workpaper II7.01.

The Alert Procedure

The first-alert procedure instructs the person assigned to notify one of the IS recovery management team members on how to perform the alert. If the primary IS recovery management team member cannot be contacted, the notifier should call the second person on the list. This procedure should be followed until the notifier reaches one of the listed IS recovery management team members. After this is accomplished, the notifier does not have to make any further telephone calls to any other team members.

The procedure identifies the information the notifier should provide to the verifier. This information includes the notifier's name, the phone number at which the notifier can be reached, a description of the disaster situation, and any early report of damages (including any injuries to IS personnel). If the notifier was unable to contact another member of the IS recovery management team, he or she should inform the verifier of this fact.

History of the First-Alert Step

The first-alert step was added to the DCRP during the mid-1970s after a divisional manager from the IS department of a manufacturing company in Georgia reported on a serious failure in its alert method. The original plan was to have either the on-site operations person or the security guard notify the data center manager in the event of a disaster. This plan failed when a tornado struck the building on a Saturday evening around 6:00 PM, causing the roof to collapse and injuring the two computer operations employees who were working in the data center. Both had to be taken to the hospital and were in no condition to notify the data center manager. Four of the five security guards working at the time were also injured and had to be taken to the hospital; the fifth security guard was so upset that he failed to notify anyone.

The data center manager was notified of the situation by a neighbor who happened to drive by the building and noticed the collapsed roof. The data center manager was finally notified by the neighbor at 10:30 PM, more than four hours after the incident.

STEP 2

THE DISASTER VERIFICATION

The disaster verification step specifies information about how the IS recovery management team member notified of the interruption should verify that a disaster has occurred and determine whether it requires activation of the DCRP. The IS recovery management team member who has been notified of the data center problem is responsible for carrying out the actions of the verifier.

Questions for the Notifier

While on the phone with the notifier, the verifier should determine who is making the alert, the phone number where the notifier can be reached, the nature of the problem, a preliminary report of damages, and the health condition of IS personnel (including any injuries or deaths). The verifier should ask the notifier if the building is accessible or if there are restrictions that might delay access to the building.

The verifier should then ask if the notifier has tried to reach any other IS recovery management team members. If he or she has tried and was unable, the verifier should obtain the names of those persons; this helps eliminate calling people who are not available.

The verifier should also obtain information as to where the notifier can be located when the verifier arrives at the site. After arriving at the site, the verifier must first meet with the notifier to check on any changes in the safety of the building before trying to enter it to make an on-site assessment of damage. This is especially important if the status of the accessibility of the building has changed since the first-alert phone call. For example, the building may have been accessible at the time of the first alert but has been declared inaccessible after the phone call. There have been a number of cases in the past few years in which floors of buildings have collapsed after a fire or earthquake.

The verifier should next estimate and inform the notifier of the time when he or she will arrive at the site. In estimating the expected time of arrival, the verifier should consider the amount of time it takes to drive to the data center as well as any additional time needed to complete the verification step.

Finally, the verifier should advise the notifier that he or she will make all further IS recovery management team contacts, thereby freeing the notifier to handle other pressing issues. Workpaper II7.02 provides a checklist of the questions that the verifier should ask the notifier as part of the disaster verification step.

Verifying with the Data Center

A second verification step consists of phoning the data center to obtain a status report on the condition of the data center from computer operations personnel. The verifier should use the data center phone number listed on the disaster verification procedure (see Workpaper II7.02). If the verifier cannot reach the computer operations personnel, he or she should telephone either the main lobby, the security department, or the alarm company for the building. If none of these locations answer the phone, the verifier should assume that a disaster has either affected the phones or forced personnel to evacuate the building. The outcome of each call should be recorded on the disaster verification procedure form, as shown in Workpaper II7.02.

The verifier should next notify another member of the IS recovery management team. This person is referred to as the IS recovery management team contact. Upon notifying the IS recovery management team contact, the verifier should provide the preliminary assessment information obtained over the phone, the status of all contacts, the name and phone number of the notifier, the estimated time of the verifier's arrival at the data center site, and an estimated time when a follow-up call will be made to the contact. (This IS recovery management team contact step is covered in detail under Step 3 of the initial disaster alert procedure.)

The verifier should next take a copy of the DCRP and travel to the data center location. It may also be necessary to bring a building security ID badge, access control card, beeper, and a cellular phone, if one is available. Upon arrival, the verifier should meet with the notifier and any buildings and security representatives to obtain the following information (see Workpaper II7.02):

- Can the facility be entered?
- If not, when will access be allowed?
- What is the estimated damage to the building?
- What is the estimated damage to the data center floor and contents (other than computers)?
- What is the estimated damage to data center computer equipment?

If the building housing the data center can be entered, the verifier should tour the data center area to evaluate the extent of damage. If the data center facility, equipment, and data are not affected and the problem can be resolved easily by data center personnel with assistance of the equipment vendors' representatives, the verifier should notify the IS recovery management team contact person to terminate any further data center recovery activities. If the data center and its equipment and data have been damaged and a disaster condition apparently exists, the verifier should select which recovery headquarters location will be used to assemble the IS recovery management team.

The selection of the recovery headquarters is made using the different options identified during the data gathering process discussed in Chapter II-3 of this book. Each recovery headquarters location (primary and alternates) should be identified in the disaster verification procedure. As shown in Workpaper II7.02, the information for each should consist of:

- Building name.
- Address.
- Phone number.
- Access requirements.

If the primary location is not usable, one of the alternates will be selected by the verifier. After the recovery headquarters location has been selected, the verifier should call the IS recovery management team contact person and request that he or she notify the remaining members of the IS recovery management team to assemble at the recovery headquarters. The verifier can then make the arrangements with buildings and security representatives to have access to the recovery headquarters. They will report to the headquarters and make arrangements for the arrival of the IS recovery management team.

The verifier must also temporarily act as the news media representative. If approached by any people from the news media, the verifier should use the statement formulated by the public relations department to respond to any questions, as shown in Workpaper II7.02.

STEP 3

THE IS RECOVERY MANAGEMENT TEAM CONTACT

The IS recovery management team contact step provides a method for notifying the remaining IS recovery management team members of the need to report to the recovery headquarters. If, after traveling to the data center and assessing the situation, the verifier decides that a disaster situation exists, he or she should let the IS recovery management team contact person know of the situation. The verifier identifies the location of the recovery headquarters where the IS recovery management team is to assemble.

Because the verifier has a number of actions to handle with regard to setting up the recovery headquarters, the contact person is charged with alerting the remaining IS recovery management team members using the procedure shown in Workpaper II7.03.

Reason for the Contact Role

If anything had happened to the verifier in transit to the data center and a contact person had not been informed of the disaster in advance, no one on the IS recovery management team would be aware of the disaster. (The verifier had told the notifier that he or she would make all further IS recovery management team contacts. This course of action was chosen to allow the notifier to handle other responsibilities following the disaster.) The need for a contact person was identified in response to postrecovery analysis of a data center fire at a company in Pennsylvania in 1977. The assistant IS director received a telephone call at 11:10 PM, alerting him to a fire in the data center. The assistant director traveled to the data center and entered the building 15 minutes later, even though the drive normally took more than a half hour. On being interviewed the next day, the assistant director could not remember whether he had stopped at traffic lights or stop signs. It was determined that he had suffered temporary amnesia caused by stress.

The company was concerned that the assistant director could have had an accident driving to the data center and realized the need to provide a contingency plan for continuing the assessment and recovery activation should anyone get into an accident. Therefore, this company added a step in its DCRP requiring that a telephone call be made to another member of the IS management team—the contact person.

STEP 4

THE DCRP ACTIVATION

The DCRP activation step provides a procedure for assisting the recovery chairperson (or alternate) in deciding whether it is necessary to active the DCRP. A sample procedure is provided as Workpaper II7.04.

After the remaining members of the IS recovery management team have been notified, they should travel to and assemble at the recovery headquarters. If the data center is accessible at that time, all team members should tour the affected area and perform another on-site assessment. If access is restricted, they should obtain an estimate from the local authorities of when the site will become accessible. They should review any reports containing information on the facility and contents damage assessment to determine whether any of the individual DCRP recovery teams should be activated.

If the data center's facilities and contents are not seriously affected and the problem can be handled by IS or vendor personnel, the interruption should be declared a "temporary interruption." No recovery teams will be activated, and DCRP activity will be terminated.

If the data center's facilities and contents are damaged and there will be an outage lasting more than 72 hours, the interruption should be classified as a disaster. The DCRP will be activated, as will some or all of the recovery teams.

If it is recommended that the DCRP be activated, the recovery chairperson should activate the DCRP. If the recovery chairperson is not available, his or her alternate has the authority to activate the DCRP. The alternate for the recovery chairperson is usually not delegated to a lower level of the IS department; rather, it is delegated to the chairperson's manager (e.g., the chief information officer or the chief financial officer). (This came about because it was felt to be unfair to ask lower-level managers to make such a critical decision for which they could be blamed if the DCRP were activated and the data center were then able to resume processing more quickly than estimated.) The name and phone number of one of these officers is included on the first-alert list.

When the DCRP is activated, the DCRP recovery team leaders should be called to report to the recovery headquarters. These are the team leaders for each of the teams participating in the recovery operation (see Exhibit II-7-B). Each of the three team managers is responsible for notifying their particular team leaders using the DCRP recovery team alert checklist, as shown in Workpaper II7.05.

The personnel notification procedure has been developed to minimize the potential of prematurely notifying a family member of a data center employee who was in the data center at the time of the disaster. (A sample of this procedure is provided as Workpaper II4.17.) If a data center employee is injured in a disaster, the family is notified according to the plan adopted by the company management.

IMPORTANCE OF TIMELY DCRP ACTIVATION

One of the key objectives of the DCRP is to limit the magnitude of any loss by minimizing the duration of the interruption to critical applications. The IS department builds its recovery strategies and procedures to meet this objective. That is what makes the activation step so important.

An organization may determine that its data center must resume processing of critical applications within 24 hours to meet end users' needs. But when does the clock for the 24 hours start running?

For example, a disaster occurs at a company's data center at 1:00 AM. The initial disaster alert is made by the security guard at 1:15 AM. The verifier gets dressed and travels to the data center, arriving at 2:15 AM.

During the next hour, the verifier contacts various people from the company and local authorities to get an estimate of the damage to the data center. The verifier decides the situation could escalate into a crisis requiring activation of the DCRP and at 3:15 AM notifies the IS recovery management team contact person to alert the remaining members of the situation. After being alerted, the remaining IS recovery management team members travel to the recovery headquarters, arriving around 4:30 AM.

The members of the IS recovery management team visit the computer location to perform another disaster assessment; this step adds another hour to the process, ending at approximately 5:30 AM. During the next hour, the IS recovery management team members analyze the information to determine which, if any, of the individual DCRP recovery teams will have to be activated. They officially activate the DCRP at 6:30 AM.

According to this scenario, when does the 24-hour recovery clock start running? The IS recovery management team starts the DCRP recovery clock at 6:30 AM and may believe it still has 24 hours to get the critical end users up and running. But end users have started the clock at 1:00 AM, and they expect to have access to the computer by 1:00 AM the next day. Can data center personnel perform all of their DCRP responsibilities and begin processing in 18½ hours?

This hypothetical case reflects a relatively smooth response to the disaster and does not take into account problems that commonly occur in activating the plan. For example, the person making the initial disaster alert may find it difficult to reach any of the members listed on the initial disaster alert checklist; the "notifier" is injured in the disaster and is unable to make the calls; or the verifier cannot get to the data center in the hour provided because the disaster has created travel problems.

Clearly, there are many scenarios that can cause the alert procedure to take longer than expected, further delaying the resumption of processing. To meet the objectives of the DCRP, the end users, and the company, it is critical that IS respond in a timely manner. This requires that the IS recovery management team be notified shortly after the problem is discovered, complete the assessment, and decide on the need to activate or terminate in a reasonable time frame.

CONCLUSION

The initial disaster alert procedure has been left as the last DCRP logistic to be discussed, not because it is unimportant, but because it would not have seemed as important if presented earlier. Much of the focus in prior chapters has dealt with DCRP planning issues relating to time: selection of critical applications that need to be processed quickly after the interruption; selection of a computer backup site strategy to enable quick resumption of processing; analysis of the data protection and recovery processes to ensure a fast recovery. The DCRP is built to respond quickly, because the longer the computer center remains out of operation, the more damage the company will sustain.

WORKPAPER II7.01 First-Alert Step

Company Name___________ Issued________ Section_______ Page_______
Data Center__________________
Data Center Recovery Plan_______________ Supersedes______________

INITIAL DISASTER ALERT PROCEDURE

THE FIRST-ALERT STEP

If you are the first person to become aware of a problem at the building housing the data center, assume the role of the notifier:

1. After completing the other alerts and notifications required by the [company name] emergency procedures, determine whether the problem could have affected the IS data center.

2. If the IS data center could have been affected, notify one of the IS recovery management team members listed.

Title	Name	Home Phone	Record Outcome of Call
Recovery Chairperson	__________	__________	__________________
Recovery Headquarters Team Manager	__________	__________	__________________
Computer Operations Recovery Team Manager	__________	__________	__________________
Disaster Site Recovery Team Manager	__________	__________	__________________
Recovery Chairperson Alternate*	__________	__________	__________________

3. Furnish the following information to the first IS recovery management team member contacted:
   a. Your name.
   b. Phone number where you can be reached.
   c. Description of the disaster occurrence.
   d. Preliminary report of damages and injuries.

* The chief information officer or the chief financial officer will be called as an alternate if the recovery chairperson is not available.

WORKPAPER II7.02 Disaster Verification Step

Company Name____________ Issued_________ Section________ Page________
Data Center____________________
Data Center Recovery Plan________________ Supersedes________________

INITIAL DISASTER ALERT PROCEDURE

THE DISASTER VERIFICATION STEP

1. The first IS recovery management team member contacted and notified of the problem will assume the responsibility of the verifier and perform the following responsibilities.

2. While on the telephone with the notifier, obtain answers to questions a through f and provide the information identified in g through i:

   a. Who is making the alert?

      Name:__________________ Time:_____ Date:_____ Day:________

      Contact Phone:__________ Location:_________________________

   b. What is the nature of the problem? _______________________

      ____

   c. What is the preliminary assessment (e.g., damages and injuries)? ____

      ____

   d. Can access to the building be gained? _________________

   e. Are there any immediate dangers or restrictions? _______

      ____

   f. Have any attempts been made to reach other members of the IS recovery management team? If so, list below.

Name	Results	Time

   g. Provide information as to when you will arrive and where you will meet the notifier.

h. Advise the notifier that you will make all further IS contacts.

i. Remind the notifier not to make any public statements regarding the situation.

3. Verify that a disaster situation exists by calling one of the following:

	Phone Number	Record Outcome of Call
Data Center Area	______________	____________________________
Main Lobby	______________	____________________________
Security Department	______________	____________________________
Alarm Company	______________	____________________________

Note: If telephone contact cannot be established, assume disaster situation and proceed with the verifier responsibilities.

4. Notify one other member of the IS recovery management team that a problem situation exists at the building housing the data center. The person who is being informed of the situation will be referred to as the IS recovery management team contact. Provide the following information:

a. Preliminary assessment information.
b. Status of contacts with any IS recovery management team members.
c. Name and contact phone number of the notifier.
d. Estimated time of arrival at the disaster site.
e. Estimated time elapsed for a second call with activation or termination instructions.

5. Take your copy of the data center recovery plan, travel to the disaster site, and contact the following individuals upon your arrival:

a. The notifier.
b. On-site company building management personnel.
c. On-site company security personnel.
d. Fire and police authorities.

6. Obtain the following information:

a. Can the facility be entered? ____________________________

If not, when will access be allowed? ____________________

b. Estimate of damage to the building: ____________________

____

c. Estimate of damage to the contents: ____________________

____

d. Estimate of damage to the computer equipment: __________

____

7. If the facility can be entered, tour the area and evaluate the extent of damage.

8. Evaluate all information obtained, and decide whether there is the potential for a computer interruption and whether the situation could escalate into a crisis requiring the activation of the data center recovery plan. If all facilities, equipment, and data are unaffected and the problem can be easily solved by operations personnel and vendor systems engineers, notify the IS recovery management team contact to terminate all further DCRP activities.

9. If a disaster situation does exist:

a. Select the location for the recovery headquarters.

Suggested recovery headquarters sites:

1. The affected facility (if accessible).

2. Place ____________________
Street ____________________
City, State ____________________
Phone ____________

3. Place ____________________
Street ____________________
City, State ____________________
Phone ____________

4. Place ____________________
Street ____________________
City, State ____________________
Phone ____________

b. Notify the IS recovery management team contact to proceed with the IS recovery management team alert.

10. Report to the recovery headquarters and make arrangements for the arrival of the remaining IS recovery management team members.

11. Establish an area to house the news media outside of the recovery headquarters.

a. Escort news media to the assigned area.

b. Provide news media with the following initial statement:

Initial News Media Statement

The emergency is being handled in accordance with the company's emergency procedures. Our management team is meeting with the local authorities right now to obtain official information related to the incident. We want you to publicize the facts regarding the situation. Therefore, we have made arrangements at [location] for your use. Management will be presenting a company statement very shortly. You will be invited.

c. Consider ordering refreshments.

WORKPAPER II7.03 IS Recovery Team Contact Step

Company Name___________ Issued________ Section_______ Page_______
Data Center__________________
Data Center Recovery Plan_______________ Supersedes______________

INITIAL DISASTER ALERT PROCEDURE

THE IS RECOVERY MANAGEMENT TEAM CONTACT STEP

The alert of the IS recovery management team members will be completed when authorized by the verifier at the disaster site.

1. The verifier will call after assessing the situation at the data center, with instructions either to notify all members of the IS recovery management team or to cancel any further actions.

   If the verifier does not call within an hour after the estimated time of arrival, the IS recovery management team contact should contact another member of the IS recovery management team. He or she should explain the situation regarding the data center problem and the initial telephone call from [verifier's name]. The original IS recovery management team contact should assume the verifier's role and have the other team member handle the IS recovery management team contact's responsibilities.

2. When instructed by the verifier, the contact person should alert all remaining IS recovery management team members that a disaster situation exists and direct them to report to the recovery headquarters. Provide the following directions and information:

   a. Location and telephone number of the recovery headquarters.

   b. Name of the IS recovery management team member at the disaster site.

   c. Brief description of the disaster situation.

   d. Reminder to:

      1. Make no public statements about the disaster situation.

      2. Bring their copy of the data center recovery plan.

Title	Name	Home Phone	Record Outcome of Call
Recovery Chairperson	____________	____________	____________
Recovery Head-quarters Team Manager	____________	____________	____________
Computer Oper-ations Recovery Team Manager	____________	____________	____________
Disaster Site Recovery Team Manager	____________	____________	____________

WORKPAPER II7.04 DCRP Activation Step

Company Name____________ Issued________ Section_______ Page________
Data Center___________________
Data Center Recovery Plan________________ Supersedes________________

INITIAL DISASTER ALERT PROCEDURE

THE DCRP ACTIVATION STEP

When the IS recovery management team members assemble at the recovery headquarters, the recovery chairperson or alternate will direct the following activities:

1. Dispatch several IS recovery management team members to the affected site to reassess the extent of damage to the facility and its contents. Instruct the individuals to:

   a. Tour the affected area (if access is allowed).

   b. Obtain updated damage reports on the building and its contents.

   c. Obtain injury reports.

   d. If access is restricted, obtain an estimate on when access will be allowed.

   e. Formulate a DCRP activation or termination recommendation.

2. Reassemble the IS recovery management team at the recovery headquarters:

   a. Review the findings of the reassessment activities.

   b. Review the recommendation to activate or terminate activities.

3. If no further recovery activities are required, terminate all recovery activities.

4. If recovery operations are required:

   a. Identify the recovery goals and objectives.

   b. Identify any additional individuals required at the recovery headquarters and authorize the alerting of those persons.

   c. Authorize activation of the data center recovery plan.

5. Alert the DCRP recovery team leaders and instruct them to report to the recovery headquarters. Use the DCRP recovery team alert checklist. (See Workpaper II7.05.)

WORKPAPER II7.05 DCRP Recovery Team Alert Checklist

Company Name____________ Issued_________ Section________ Page________
Data Center____________________
Data Center Recovery Plan_________________ Supersedes________________

DCRP RECOVERY TEAM ALERT CHECKLIST

The IS recovery management team will use this checklist to alert the team leaders and to make any appropriate alternate assignments.

Recovery Responsibility	Primary/Alternate	Home Phone	Contact Status
Administration Team Leader	Primary__________	__________	__________
	Alternate__________	__________	__________
Notification and Communications Team Leader	Primary__________	__________	__________
	Alternate__________	__________	__________
Computer Operations Team Leader	Primary__________	__________	__________
	Alternate__________	__________	__________
Systems Software Team Leader	Primary__________	__________	__________
	Alternate__________	__________	__________
Tape Operations Team Leader	Primary__________	__________	__________
	Alternate__________	__________	__________
Applications Recovery Team Leader	Primary__________	__________	__________
	Alternate__________	__________	__________
Data Base Recovery Team Leader	Primary__________	__________	__________
	Alternate__________	__________	__________
Network Recovery Team Leader	Primary__________	__________	__________
	Alternate__________	__________	__________
Facility Damage Assessment and Restoration	Primary__________	__________	__________
	Alternate__________	__________	__________
Equipment Damage Assessment and Restoration	Primary__________	__________	__________
	Alternate__________	__________	__________
Network Damage Assessment and Restoration	Primary__________	__________	__________
	Alternate__________	__________	__________

Performing an Applications Impact Analysis

CHAPTER II-8

Chapter II-8 describes how to perform the applications impact analysis (AIA) for the data center recovery plan (DCRP). The AIA is a process in which the computer applications that are processed in the data center are analyzed to determine the negative impact on the company if they could not be processed as scheduled.

The issues discussed in this chapter are:

- The value in identifying critical applications.
- The classification of criticality of applications.
- The methodology used to perform the AIA.

The objectives of the AIA are twofold. The first objective is to determine when the impact would begin (e.g., in hours, days, or weeks) if there were a delay in processing any of the applications scheduled at the data center. The second objective is to determine what the impact would be. The types of impacts are discussed later in this chapter.

Performing an AIA is important for two reasons. First, it identifies the need to develop the DCRP. Second, it provides information that can be helpful in determining the computer backup site strategy. The final result of the AIA is the classification of data center applications as either critical or less critical.

VALUE IN IDENTIFYING CRITICAL APPLICATIONS

This section discusses the benefits of performing the AIA. The AIA helps in identifying:

- Potential direct costs.
- Potential indirect losses.
- The need for a computer backup site.
- Antecedent applications—that is, applications that must process before the critical applications can be processed.
- The minimum acceptable configuration for a backup site.
- Network requirements.
- The procedures to be used in recovering computer data.

Potential Direct Costs. The AIA process helps to identify some of the potential direct costs the company could expect to incur as a result of an interruption to the processing of critical applications—for example, the cost to operate temporarily in leased space, the cost to lease equipment temporarily, the cost of employee overtime, and the cost of hiring temporary personnel to supplement the IS department employees during the recovery operation. The direct costs are discussed in detail later in this chapter under the heading "Classification of Criticality of Applications."

Potential Indirect Losses. The AIA process helps to identify some of the indirect losses the company could expect to incur as a result of an interruption in the processing of critical applications—for example, the loss of current business, the loss of future business, and the loss of employees who leave the company as a result of the disaster. The indirect costs are discussed in detail later in this chapter under the heading "Classification of Criticality of Applications."

The Need for a Computer Backup Site. One of the more important benefits of performing the AIA is that it provides information on the need for a computer backup site. If the results of an AIA indicate that an application cannot be delayed long beyond its scheduled processing point without causing a significant negative impact on the company, a computer backup site strategy for quick resumption of processing can be cost-justified. (This type of backup site is referred to as a hot site.) Conversely, if the results of the AIA indicate that the application can be delayed for a week or more without causing any significant impact to the company, a more cost-effective computer backup site strategy can be pursued (e.g., a cold site or transportable shell).

The term *hot site* as used in the DCRP means a fully operational computer center with enough equipment installed to process the critical applications for a period of time. During that time, the DCRP team will either repair and reequip the damaged site or move the data center into a temporary or new facility. The temporary or new facility will be equipped with the same computer configuration housed in the data center before the disaster.

The term *cold site* as used in the DCRP means a nonequipped facility that has been preconditioned to serve as a data center—for example, the facility has a raised floor, the power and air-conditioning requirements needed for a computer, and installed (but not necessarily activated) communications lines. At the activation of the DCRP, the cold site is equipped.

A transportable shell is a temporary cold site. It can be a cold site on wheels that is driven to the site of the disaster and then equipped or one that is assembled at the site of the disaster and then equipped. The cold site and other computer backup strategies are discussed in more detail in Chapter II-9 of this book.

Antecedent Applications. The term *antecedent applications* as used in the DCRP refers to the less-critical computer applications that support the processing of critical applications during normal system processing. Each system is made up of a number of applications. For example, system 1 may have five major applications, A through E. These applications are usually processed in a specific sequence. Applications A and B process first; the output of both applications is used as input for application C. Then application C is processed, followed by applications D and E. Some of the input to applications D and E is the result of processing application C.

As part of the AIA, the end user reported that four of the applications could be delayed for 10 workdays without affecting the department or the company. Those four were classified as less critical. One application, C, had to resume processing in two days or less. Application C was classified as critical, and it will therefore be processed at the computer backup site.

The DCRP would list application C as critical and applications A, B, D, and E as less critical. However, when the IS personnel scheduled application C for processing at the backup site, they determined that 50% of the input comes directly from the end users' workstations and the other 50% comes from the output of applications A and B. The IS department would not want to run a critical application with only 50% of the daily input, so it scheduled applications A and B to run at the backup site as well.

EXHIBIT **II-8-A** IDENTIFYING ANTECEDENT APPLICATIONS

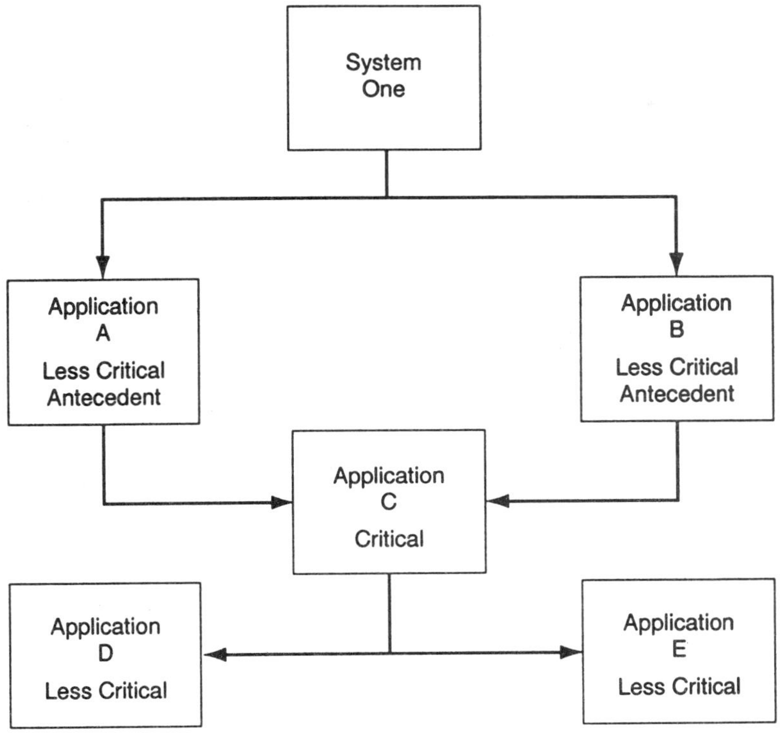

If the less-critical applications A and B were not processed during the time critical application C was processed at the computer backup site, the processing of application C would be incomplete, which would give an inaccurate picture of the business area supported by it. Therefore, the two less-critical applications, A and B, will be processed at the computer backup site before application C, because application C depends on input from applications A and B (see Exhibit II-8-A).

In most cases, the criticality of applications is determined by the end user. In the case where it has been identified as less critical by the end user, it can be changed to critical by the IS department. (For the recovery planning "purist" who believes that only the end user should determine criticality, an antecedent application can be looked at as a separate category of application. It is an application that must be scheduled to process when the critical application is processed but is not itself classified as critical. When the list of critical applications and less-critical applications is developed, a third category, antecedent applications, can be listed if desired.)

As a result of the identification process, the computer backup site minimum acceptable configuration can now be accurately sized to support the total CPU and disk space requirements.

The Minimum Acceptable Configuration. The term *minimum acceptable configuration* refers to the computer configuration needed to support the processing of the critical applications and their antecedents. If the AIA identifies the need for a hot-site backup strategy, the size of the hot site must be determined. In most cases, the critical applications and their antecedents represent only a portion of the normal computer configuration installed in the current data center and therefore the hot-site computer configuration can be sized to meet their needs.

Data center personnel should analyze the resources needed to process the critical applications and their antecedents to determine the minimum resources needed at the hot site. This includes such parameters as the computer size, the amount of disk space, the number of tape drives, and the number of printers. The IS department project personnel can then use these minimum requirements to qualify or eliminate commercial hot-site vendors that are interested in providing this service. The minimum acceptable configuration can also be used to determine the proper configuration for a company-owned backup site.

Network Requirements. The results of the AIA also help to clarify network and communications resource requirements. Applications that will be moved to the backup site must be analyzed to determine the minimum acceptable configuration of the data communications network. (Communications network planning issues are covered in more detail in Part III of this book.)

Procedures to Be Used in Recovering Computer Data. Once the decision has been made to use a computer hot site to resume the processing of critical applications, the length of time before the processing of new input into the critical applications can begin must be determined. To make that determination, data center personnel must analyze several situations. For example, they may need to determine how long it will take to:

- Identify the backups to be sent to the hot site.
- Retrieve and deliver the backups to the hot site.
- Reload the backups onto the hot-site computers.
- Reconstruct the application data files to an acceptable point in time.
- Process the input from the day of the disaster (i.e., the input destroyed before it could be backed up and sent to an off-premises location).

The AIA provides data center personnel with information on which applications will be processed at the hot site. They can then identify the data files that have to be retrieved and reloaded at the hot site in order to process the critical applications.

After the data files have been identified, data center personnel must first analyze the steps involved in reloading the computer software and applications data at the hot site. They will then have to address the time it will take to reconstruct the applications data files to an acceptable point in time. This acceptable point in time has to be agreed on by the end user, the applications programming manager, and the responsible data center personnel.

The amount of time involved in the recovery and reconstruction procedure must be identified by data center personnel for them to determine when the hot site can begin processing new information. The two data recovery situations that the DCRP coordinator and the development committee have to consider in planning are discussed in the following paragraphs.

Situation 1. If the disaster has not caused either the building to become inaccessible or the data at the disaster site to be damaged, data center personnel can retrieve the current backups from the tape library and transport them to the hot site. They will be able to load the most current backup information onto hot-site computers. End users can then reenter any data processed earlier but destroyed before it could be backed up and sent to the off-premises location. At this point, the computer operations recovery team can begin processing the critical applications and their antecedents.

Situation 2. If the disaster has caused the building to become inaccessible or has damaged the data of the disaster site, data center personnel will have to recover using the backups stored in the off-premises storage location. After identifying which of the backups should be retrieved, the backups will be sent to the hot site. When the backups arrive at the hot site, they can be loaded onto the computer. Unfortunately, in most data centers, the backups that will be retrieved from the off-premises storage location are not the most current backups but an older version. After they are loaded onto the hot-site computers, they must be reconstructed to reach the acceptable point in time (agreed on between the end user, the applications programming manager, and the responsible data center staff member). End users can then reenter any data that was processed earlier but destroyed before it could be backed up and sent to the off-premises locations. At the conclusion of this computer processing, the applications should be balanced to the control figures. If there are any out-of-balance conditions, they should be rectified before new input can be processed. At this point, the computer operations recovery team can begin processing the critical applications and their antecedents.

On the basis of analysis of these procedures, IS department personnel can now determine the amount of time between the identification of the backups and beginning the processing of new input. Exhibit II-8-B summarizes the general procedure used to recover data. An estimated time should be assigned to each step in Exhibit II-8-B and the times for each step added to estimate when end users can expect to process new input.

If the estimated time for processing new input is not acceptable to the end user or to executive management, a change to the current data backup and rotation procedure can be made. End users and the executive management must realize, however, that such changes can increase costs.

CLASSIFICATION OF CRITICALITY OF APPLICATIONS

This section defines a critical application and discusses the reasons for classifying an application as critical or less critical. The term *critical* in relation to computer applications is used in the DCRP to mean a condition of being indispensable to avoid negative impacts. A critical application is a computer application that supports an essential business function.

The term *essential business function* refers to the business operations performed in a company that enable the company to meet its business objectives. If a delay in performing the business function results in a significant negative impact on the company and its business operations, the business function would be considered an essential business function. (The identification of the essential business functions is a function of the business impact analysis, which is covered in detail in Part I of this book.)

Classifying Critical Applications

For a computer application to be determined as critical, it must meet the following criteria. First, the essential business function it supports would cause a significant negative impact to the company if it cannot be performed on a timely basis. Second, the length of time it will be delayed is a key to classifying the critical and less-critical applications. If the business function cannot be delayed for a certain period of time, the computer application cannot be delayed for a certain period of time. In this case the application would be classified as critical. Third, the business function must depend totally on the computer—there is no alternate means of performing it.

EXHIBIT **II-8-B** PROCEDURE USED IN RECOVERING DATA

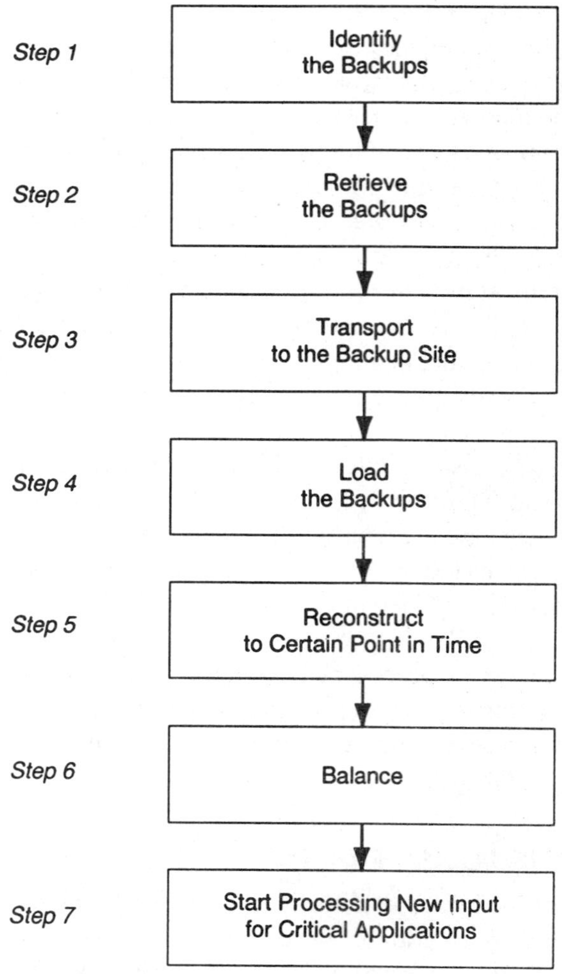

There are five reasons why a company classifies some applications as critical and others as less critical. Specifically, they are that a delay in processing could result in:

- A sizable loss of current business.
- A sizable loss of future business.
- A sizable loss of money.
- Regulatory agency problems.
- A lawsuit against the company.

These are discussed in the following sections.

Sizable Loss of Current Business. An application might be considered critical if the delay in processing would limit the availability of a company's products or services, which could cause a current customer to buy from a competitor. The loss of one customer is a small concern. The real issue is how many customers might do the same thing. During AIA interviews of end users, the DCRP coordinator should attempt to have the end user estimate the percentage of the customers that might be lost.

When working on identifying the loss of current business, the end user should use actual data to estimate loss amounts (e.g., estimate daily loss using figures from annualized sales of a year ago). The key to finding this information is in asking the right questions. Sample interview and questionnaire forms are provided as Workpaper II8.02.

Sizable Loss of Future Business. An application might be considered critical if the delay in processing would result in the company suffering a sizable loss of future business. It is often difficult to estimate the amount of future business that could be lost. The DCRP coordinator needs the opinions of the managers in the end-user departments who are responsible for the product or services. If their answers can be based on prior experience, they should be reported in the AIA report.

To emphasize how important it is to retain market share, some companies, when faced with a delay in producing their product, have purchased, repackaged, and resold a competitor's product to satisfy their customers. Although this is not profitable, it is more important to retain the customer. Most companies are willing to operate at a loss for a short period of time rather than lose some of their share of the market.

In one case, for example, a candy manufacturing company suffered a fire that destroyed its manufacturing facility in July 1988. The company had enough inventory to supply its retail outlets for a couple of months. During that time, the company located a temporary manufacturing site and began producing its products, though at a reduced rate (about half the rate before the fire). Because of this, the company bought raw materials in smaller quantities, which raised the costs per unit. When asked if this was a profitable way of operating, the head of the company responded, "This is not a profitable operation. We're just trying to keep our brand name on the shelf. Loss of shelf space would be critical."

It is not essential to identify estimated losses of future business—in fact, executives often disagree with such estimates and as a consequence may reject the total report. Executives might be requested to estimate the amounts themselves—they sometimes estimate potential losses at a larger number than would their managers. In any case, management should be provided with estimated losses of future business only if those estimates are based on prior experience.

Sizable Loss of Money. An application might also be considered critical if the delay would result in a sizable loss of money. This could be caused by a delay in billing, cash flow problems, or additional interest payments. Other losses that can escalate rapidly are the cost of employees working overtime; calling back retirees to help staff the company during the recovery operation; hiring temporary personnel; renting office space, manufacturing space, or warehouse space; and renting temporary equipment. If the company has business interruption insurance, some of these costs may be recovered.

Regulatory Agency Problems. An application could be considered critical if the delay in processing would result in a regulatory agency investigation of the incident. Disaster recovery compliance requirements for regulatory agencies began in the financial services industry, particularly in banks and savings institutions, as long ago as 1983. On May 26 of that year, the Comptroller of the Currency, the administrator of national banks in the US, issued a new policy, BC-177, which stated that "a number of lines of banking business are critically dependent on EDP support. Some of those lines of business such as demand deposits accounts (e.g., checking accounts) and wire transfer can be so vital to the safety and soundness of a bank's operation that their termination for even a relatively short time (one or two business days) could cause the bank to incur serious financial damage, as well as harm public confidence." The regulation further stated that "the board of directors of your bank must annually review and approve management's assessment of how a loss of EDP support would [affect] your bank's operations and the methods management has employed to reduce or eliminate such risk or impact. This annual review and approval must be noted in the minutes of the board of directors and should be verified at each examination of your institution." The key to the regulation is the statement that "this annual review and approval must be noted in the minutes and will be reviewed." This means that any action regarding the methods management has employed must be documented so that it can be examined, audited, and tested.

The Potential for a Lawsuit. An application might also be considered critical if the delay in processing the application could result in a lawsuit. Lawsuits could be filed by customers that feel that the company has been negligent in failing to provide its products or services.

For example, Consolidated Edison, New York's largest electric utility, was sued by an estimated 350 companies for being "grossly negligent" during the 1977 blackout in New York City and surrounding areas. They sought an estimated $200 million in damages. On November 19, 1981, Consolidated Edison was found grossly negligent by the Court of Appeals, New York's highest court. It upheld a jury award of $40,000 to a New York grocery chain, Food Pageant Inc., which had sued Con Edison for food spoiled and business lost in the wake of the blackout. This decision was overturned by the Supreme Court in 1984, when it ruled negligence, not "gross" negligence, was the cause. (The major difference between gross negligence and plain negligence is that the insurance company is responsible for negligence settlements.) If the finding had not been overruled by the Supreme Court, the directors and officers of Con Edison would have been held personally responsible for the settlements.

Potential damages are not the only consideration; there is also the negative publicity that is associated with a lawsuit. Such negative publicity could cause people to have second thoughts about purchasing the company's products or services in the future.

Industry-Related Considerations. There are also industry-related reasons that may cause an application to be considered critical. For example, a health-care application involved with a patient life support function would obviously be considered critical.

Two companies within the same industry may differ, one company feeling an application is critical and another company in the same industry feeling the same application is less critical. One company cannot take the AIA results of a second company and use them for its own operations. The two companies may have different business objectives, a different business environment, or a different business philosophy. For example, several years ago, two banks from the same state merged into one entity but functioned as two separate and distinct operations for a few years after the merger. During the time they functioned as two operations, an AIA project was performed. During the AIA, the controller from the northern part of the state indicated that the accounts payable application would be classified as less critical. Later the controller from the southern part of the state indicated that the accounts payable application would be classified as critical. The reason for the difference in perspective between the two controllers was that the southern bank had just come out of Chapter 11 bankruptcy. During the time they were in Chapter 11, they did everything they could to instill confidence in their bank with their vendors. The last thing that controller wanted was to be late on paying vendors and starting bankruptcy rumors again.

Classifying Less-Critical Applications

An application could be classified as less critical for one of the following reasons:

- It can be delayed for a reasonable period of time without causing a significant negative impact on the company.
- It supports an essential business function that has an alternative, manual means of performing the function.
- The application supports a less-essential business function.

These are discussed in the following sections.

No Significant Impact. A general ledger application can be an example of an application that may have no significant impact. The general ledger system is an essential business function in a company. It summarizes all of the debits and credits, receives its input from books of original entry, and creates reports used by financial regulatory agencies. The integrity of its information must remain unquestioned. This does not imply, however, that the general ledger application must be processed at the end of every month. Many chief financial officers, treasurers, and controllers have expressed the opinion that processing could be postponed a month without creating significant problems—they could estimate the information accurately for management reports. They had no problems with the general ledger business function being classified as an essential function and the general ledger application being classified as a less-critical application.

In the banking industry, however, the general ledger system provides the chief financial officer with a number of figures that must be submitted to regulatory agencies in daily reports. Therefore, bank management generally wants the general ledger application classified as critical.

Alternative Means. Some essential business functions that currently use the computer as a resource may be able to use an alternative means to accomplish the same goal. An example of this is the payroll function, which most companies agree is an essential business function. The payroll function is supported by the payroll application, which is processed on the computer. If the payroll application could not be processed as scheduled, this does not mean a company could not pay its employees. Such alternative means as cash payments could be used. As a result, the payroll application would not be considered critical during the first days of a disaster recovery operation. This is a common example of an essential business function being supported by a less-critical application.

This is not to say that all companies have an alternative means to pay their employees. A small percentage of companies may find that they have no other means of paying their employees except by processing it on the computer. Therefore, they may consider the payroll application to be a critical application.

Supports a Less-Essential Business Function. Many computer applications provide processing support to business functions that do not have to be performed on schedule in the event of an interruption in the company. For example, the general ledger system can be delayed without causing a significant negative impact on the company. The computer applications that support this type of business function would be classified as less critical.

Classifying Noncritical Applications

The recovery planner must be careful with the terms used to classify noncritical applications. At one time, applications that would not cause a significant problem if they were not processed on a timely basis were referred to as noncritical applications. The term *noncritical,* however, when used in the AIA interview process, causes end users to become very defensive, because they infer that they are performing a noncritical (i.e., unimportant) business function. The end users' concern is that this message might be passed on to executive management through the results of the AIA. This attitude caused a number of AIAs in early DCRP projects to be useless, because end users answered that most, if not all, of their computer applications were critical and should be processed within days of the interruption. It is generally better to use the phrase "a computer application that can be delayed for a certain period of time" rather than the term *noncritical.*

This having been said, some applications processed by the data center can be considered noncritical. For example, mathematical or statistical applications in technical companies often do not have to process on a specific time schedule. Many of these applications are scheduled to be performed over a number of years. If a task had to be delayed for an extended period of time, it would not cause the company a significant loss. Although the processing can be delayed, in a disaster recovery operation the end user of this application needs to ensure the ability to recover the application software following a disaster. The end user may not have to worry about restoring the application data on the computer at the time of the disaster if the application uses different data each time it is processed.

THE AIA METHODOLOGY

The steps involved in an applications impact analysis (AIA) project are to:

1. Obtain a list of applications processed in the data center.
2. Identify which business functions the applications support.
3. Develop the questionnaire that will be used for interviews.
4. Test the questionnaire.
5. Perform the interviews.
6. Analyze the results.
7. Document the list of critical applications.
8. Prepare the AIA report.
9. Use the findings to determine the computer backup site strategy.

These steps are summarized in Exhibit II-8-C.

Data center personnel cannot determine which applications are critical and which are less critical by themselves. Input must come from the end users of the computer applications—the people who are responsible for the essential business functions. Although the answers must come from the end user, the questions should come from the DCRP coordinator and the development committee. The end user is called on to explain the impact on the company. The DCRP coordinator uses this information to determine the priority in scheduling applications identified as critical, the backup site strategy, the network support strategy, and the data recovery strategy.

STEP 1

Obtain a List of Applications. The DCRP coordinator should obtain the list of applications processed in the data center from any of the following sources: the data center operations scheduler, the chargeback system, the security administrator, or the standards manual. Workpaper II8.01 can be used to document this information.

STEP 2

Identify Which Business Functions the Applications Support. After obtaining the list of applications, the DCRP coordinator identifies which business functions use which applications. The DCRP coordinator should prepare a list that identifies which

EXHIBIT **II-8-C** STEPS FOR PERFORMING THE AIA

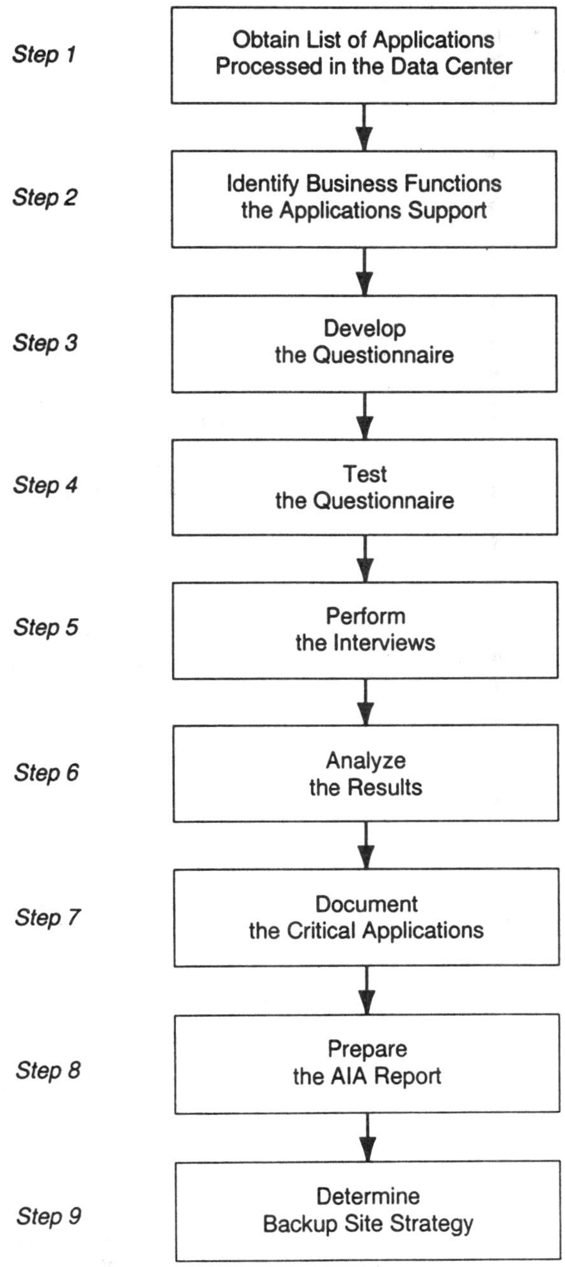

computer applications are supporting the business functions performed in each of the departments in the company. Workpaper II8.01 can be used to document this information.

STEP 3

Develop the Questionnaire. A well-constructed questionnaire is a key element in the success of the DCRP project. Although end users generally cannot answer technical questions about the computer application, they can answer such questions as how they use the information obtained from the application; what the impact on the company is if the application cannot be processed on time; and whether they could perform the business function without the application. An example of an AIA questionnaire is provided as Workpaper II8.02.

STEP 4

Test the Questionnaire. After developing the questionnaire, it is important to test it. Test appointments should be set up with two end users who can be expected to contribute positively to such a test (i.e., offering constructive criticism rather than just criticism). The DCRP coordinator should explain the purpose for the proposed interview and send the end users a copy of the questionnaire so that they can become familiar with it; they should not fill it out. The DCRP coordinator can then meet with the two end users to review the questionnaire and solicit their recommendations. After the interview is completed, the questionnaire should be modified to ensure it is concise, easy to understand, and covers all the important questions.

STEP 5

Perform the Interviews. The DCRP coordinator and development committee members should schedule interviews with data center production systems end users. The objective during the interview is to complete the questionnaire and determine whether there will be a significant impact on the company if the application is delayed and at what point in time this impact will occur (i.e., in hours, days, or weeks). The interview should also establish whether the end user has an alternative means of performing the business function without the computer.

When meeting with end users, the DCRP coordinator or the development committee member should ask only those questions that apply during the interview. There may be some questions listed on the questionnaire that are unnecessary and therefore should be skipped.

An alternative to conducting personal interviews is to mail the questionnaire to end users. Many DCRP coordinators choose this option because multiple end users can complete the questionnaire at the same time, thereby minimizing the total time required to complete this step. The time saved, however, may not be worth the problems that can result from this approach. If end users do not understand a question in the mailed questionnaire, they should contact the DCRP coordinator or the development committee member for an explanation. Often, however, they fail to do so and instead guess as to the meaning of the question. Sometimes they guess right, and sometimes they guess wrong. If they guess wrong, the DCRP strategy selected on the basis of this information may also be wrong.

Not only do end users not phone to discuss the unclear questions, they often do not send back their completed questionnaire at all. The failure to complete and return the questionnaires is one of the most common complaints made by DCRP coordinators.

To ensure that complete and accurate information is collected, it is recommended that the DCRP coordinator or the development committee member set up interviews, scheduling them into the end users' day. The end user will then commit to and participate in the scheduled personal interview and charge the time to the DCRP project in the job accounting system.

Although the personal interview is more time consuming than sending the questionnaire through the mail, it provides a number of benefits. The first benefit is that the interview allows the end user to ask for any question to be rephrased if it is not understood. A second benefit is that it allows the DCRP coordinator to probe beyond the questions on the questionnaire. For example, if end users think that they can perform a function without the support of the computer application, the DCRP coordinator can ask them how they expect to do it. In attempting to respond, they may realize that the approach will not really work, which will force them to come up with a better solution. Use of a personal interview also allows the DCRP coordinator to keep the end user focused on the impact on the company rather than on the department. End users tend to classify applications as critical if their loss would have a negative impact on the department (e.g., department personnel would be idle) even though there would be no financial, regulatory, or legal effects on the company. That may be of concern to a company, but it is not part of the criteria used to determine the criticality of an application.

STEP 6

Analyze the Results. After the AIA interview process is complete, the DCRP coordinator and the development committee should analyze the answers provided by the end users. This analysis may result in changes to the original classifications. For example, it may be found that the estimated loss the end user expects the company to experience is not really significant. In this case, the application may be changed from critical to less critical.

STEP 7

Document the List of Critical Applications. After analyzing the results of the interview process and making any changes in the classification of applications, the DCRP coordinator and the development committee should document the list of critical applications and send the list to the end users for their commitment. An end user who does not agree with any of the classifications should contact the DCRP coordinator for another meeting. During this meeting, the end user and the DCRP coordinator can review the answers from the first interview and identify any necessary changes before the report is prepared and presented to executive management.

Applications can be classified in many ways. The most common classification scheme follows this format:

- *Critical 1.* This application must be processed within 12 hours after the DCRP has been activated.
- *Critical 2.* This application must be processed within one day after the DCRP has been activated.
- *Critical 3.* This application must be processed within three days after the DCRP has been activated.
- *Critical 4.* This application must be processed within one week after the DCRP has been activated.

The number of hours or days assigned to each level of criticality must be determined by each company independently. For one company, critical could be 12 hours; for another, it could be two days. It depends on the company's objectives, its philosophy toward its customers, and the industry in which it operates. For example, a small number of New York banks must resume some applications within eight hours of an interruption; this is not a requirement for other types of banks in New York.

Most companies use either three or four levels of criticality. The criticality designation of the application appears in the DCRP on the critical processing checklist (see Chapter II-6).

STEP 8

Prepare the AIA Report. The written report should consist of four sections:

- Background and scope of the project.
- Executive management summary.
- Detail summaries of the application interviews.
- Exhibits.

The background and scope sections of the report should briefly explain why the project was undertaken and what areas of the company were included in the study. In some cases, companies have also stipulated in the scope those areas that were not included and why they were not included.

The executive management summary section of the report should be a summary of the findings and recommendations from the project. This section of the report should be brief and to the point. This is the one section that each member of the executive committee is sure to read. If it is too long, or if it is not well focused, they will not pay attention.

The detail summaries section of the report should contain the findings of the project for each end user or application covered in the project. Each of the summaries should have been approved by the end user who provided the information before they are presented in the report.

The exhibits section should contain any charts, graphs, and tables that were developed to present the findings of the project.

In presenting the report, the DCRP coordinator should address the losses that the company will experience if an interruption occurs to the data center and it does not have a DCRP to ensure quick recovery of services. Executive management should respond positively if the report focuses on the impact on business functions rather than the impact on the IS department alone.

The presentation of the project findings should be limited to 75% of the time allotted for the total presentation to management; the rest should be reserved for questions and answers. The DCRP coordinator should try to anticipate the questions that executives will ask. Experience has shown that executives do not always agree with the time estimates for recovery of applications processing or with assessments of the total dependence of certain business functions on the computer.

STEP 9

Determine the Computer Backup Site Strategy. On the basis of the findings of the AIA, the DCRP coordinator and the development committee can make a case as to which computer backup strategy best meets the needs of the company. The selection of a computer backup strategy is discussed in detail in the next chapter of this book.

CONCLUSION

Chapter II-8 described how to perform the AIA. It discussed the value in identifying which applications are classified as critical, the process of classifying the criticality of applications, and the methodology used in performing the AIA. The next chapter addresses the process involved in selecting the computer backup site strategy to be used in the DCRP.

WORKPAPER II8.01 Applications and Business Functions Data Gathering Form

Company Name____________ Issued_________ Section________ Page________
Data Center____________________
Data Center Recovery Plan________________ Supersedes________________

APPLICATIONS AND BUSINESS FUNCTIONS DATA GATHERING FORM

Prepare a list of all applications processed in the data center. Beside each application identify the business function that is supported by that application.

Application	Acronym	Business Function

WORKPAPER II8.02 Application Impact Analysis Interview and Questionnaire

Company Name____________ Issued_________ Section________ Page________
Data Center____________________
Data Center Recovery Plan________________ Supersedes________________

APPLICATION IMPACT ANALYSIS INTERVIEW INFORMATION

Department: ____

Department Representative 1: ____

Department Representative 2: ____

Department Representative 3: ____

Department Representative 4: ____

Interview Date: __________________ Interview Time: ____________

Interviewer: ____

Computer applications supporting this department. (This information should be gathered by the DCRP coordinator before any interviews take place with end users.)

____

____

____

____

____

____

____

____

____

____

____

____

____

APPLICATION IMPACT ANALYSIS QUESTIONNAIRE

Complete one questionnaire for each application supporting this department.

1. If the computer processing of [application name] were interrupted, which business functions (e.g., payroll, accounts payable, accounts receivable) would be affected?

   Application Name: ______________________________

   Business Function: ______________________________

2. Do you have an alternative method for performing the business functions other than through the support of [application name]?

   [ ] Yes [ ] No

   If yes, explain the alternative method.

   ____

   ____

   ____

   ____

   ____

   How long can you operate under these conditions?

   ____

   Can you operate under these conditions with your current staff or will you need more personnel?

   ____

3. Have you ever performed this business function using the alternative method?

   [ ] Yes [ ] No

   If yes, complete the following:

   a. When did you do this? (Describe the incident, not the date.)

   ____

   ____

b. How did the alternative method work?

____

____

c. How long did the business operate in that fashion?

____

____

d. What problems occurred? How did you resolve them?

____

____

____

____

4. Identify the type of impact a computer interruption would have on the business function and at what point in time it would have a significant impact on the company.

Type of impact (check all types that apply):

a. [ ] A loss of business (current).

b. [ ] A loss of business (future).

c. [ ] A loss of dollars.

d. [ ] Problems with regulatory agencies.

e. [ ] A lawsuit filed against the company.

f. [ ] Other impacts (explain): ____________________

____

Impact:

a. Twenty-four hours; describe the significant impact.

____

____

____

b. Two to three workdays; describe the significant impact.

c. Four to five workdays; describe the significant impact.

d. Six to ten workdays; describe the significant impact.

e. Ten or more workdays; describe the significant impact.

Selecting a Computer Processing Recovery Strategy

CHAPTER II-9

Chapter II-9 discusses the strategies that can be used to resume computer processing following a disaster or business interruption in the data center. The interruption can be caused by any number of incidents, from an earthquake or tornado to a loss of power company service. The type of incident is not an issue here; the fact that there is an interruption to computer processing is. The term *disaster* as used in this chapter simply means an extended interruption to computer processing.

RECOVERY STRATEGIES

When developing the data center recovery plan (DCRP), the company can choose among three basic strategies for resuming data center computer processing. The strategies include transferring computer processing to a computer backup site; populating a cold site; or delaying computer processing until the damaged site can be repaired.

The first strategy involves transferring computer processing to a computer backup site. A computer backup site is a fully equipped data center to which the IS department can move temporarily and resume computer processing. Three options for the computer backup site strategy are discussed in this chapter:

- *Reciprocal agreements.* The reciprocal agreement is a backup site plan in which each of two companies commit to providing a level of data center support to the other should one company lose its processing capability as a result of disaster.
- *Company-owned backup site (internal hot site).* A company-owned data center backup site is a backup site plan in which a fully operational second data center will be used for the processing of critical applications during a disaster recovery operation.
- *Commercial hot site.* A commercial hot site is a backup site plan in which a fully operational data center has been contracted for to be used for the processing of critical applications during a disaster recovery operation.

The second strategy that a company can choose is to populate a cold site, which is a nonequipped raised-floor facility that has been prepared environmentally to house a computer center. This strategy requires a company to order and install equipment and resume processing as soon as it can get all of the equipment operating. The delay to computer processing is generally 10 to 14 days.

The third strategy is for the company to wait until it can repair and reequip the damaged site. This could result in a significant delay before the processing of critical applications can be resumed. Exhibit II-9-A provides an overview of these strategies and options.

EXHIBIT II-9-A COMPUTER PROCESSING RECOVERY STRATEGIES

1. Transfer processing to a computer backup site. Under this recovery strategy, there are three options:
   — Reciprocal agreement.
   — Company-owned backup site (internal hot site).
   — Commercial hot site.
2. Transfer processing to a cold site (shell facility).
3. Repair and reequip damaged site.

Selecting a Strategy

The question of which strategy a company should select depends on the degree to which the business functions of the company must rely on its computer systems.

This business function dependence on the computer is determined by performing an applications impact analysis. As described in Chapter II-8, the applications impact analysis is a process in which applications are analyzed to determine the impact on the company if the applications could not be processed as scheduled. After completion of this analysis, the company is ready to select which computer processing recovery strategy best fits its needs. For example, if the results from the impact analysis indicate that some applications cannot be delayed without causing a significant impact on a company, the company should probably choose to transfer its critical applications processing to a computer backup site while repairing the damaged site or relocating to another site. If, on the other hand, the analysis indicates that all applications could be delayed for a certain period of time without causing a significant impact, the company might elect to use a cold site or wait until it can repair the damaged site.

Choosing Multiple Strategies

More than one recovery strategy may be appropriate. Companies have sometimes opted to have two or more strategies included in their DCRP. If some computer applications have been identified as critical, a hot site may be the solution for those applications. Because the building housing the data center could require months to repair, and there would be a gap in time between the use of the hot site for critical applications and the return to the original data center, a cold site could be used in the interim. If there were an essential business function that required checks to be printed but not processed, a reciprocal agreement could be used for that application.

Chapter II-9 discusses the various computer processing recovery strategies and options that are available and their strengths and weaknesses. Discussed in this chapter are the reciprocal agreement, the internal backup site, the commercial backup site, and the cold site (also referred to as a shell).

THE RECIPROCAL AGREEMENT OPTION

The reciprocal agreement is a computer backup site option in which two companies pledge a level of data center support to the other company should one company lose its processing capability as a result of a disaster. Many companies have eliminated using reciprocal agreements as a feasible computer backup site option because the complexity in processing the critical applications usually exceeds the capabilities of the reciprocal agreement site. (These drawbacks are discussed in more detail later in this chapter.) However, in certain limited circumstances reciprocal agreements may be useful. The following sections describe how such agreements have been traditionally established and managed and discuss when their use is appropriate.

Establishing the Agreement

Traditionally, when an agreement is reached between two data center managers to provide backup support, a commitment letter is sent by each manager identifying the terms of the reciprocal agreement. These terms include the proposed level of commitment, the configuration of the computer to be used for backup processing, the manner in which the processing support would be given, and any reimbursement that would be required between the two companies. The letter is then included in the DCRP manual.

Types of Reciprocal Agreements

There are three common types of reciprocal agreements: those made between companies located in the same locale; those made between companies in the same industry; and those made between companies in the same corporation.

Same-locale agreements have the advantage of proximity, which can make the recovery easier to carry out. Same-industry agreements provide the ability to support or to gain support from other companies that have the same hardware and software needs. Same-corporation agreements provide an increased level of assurance that the other company in the agreement will do its best to assist during the recovery operation.

Of these three types, the one most commonly used is the same-industry reciprocal agreement. For example, this agreement has been used by companies in the newspaper industry, because they share either unique equipment or unique software requirements.

Drawbacks of Reciprocal Agreements

As noted, many companies have eliminated use of reciprocal agreements because the complexity of processing the critical applications exceeds the capabilities of the reciprocal agreement site. Other reasons companies do not include them as a feasible option are the difficulty in maintaining hardware compatibility, supporting online systems, and testing. Another problem is that such agreements are usually not executed as legal contracts.

Hardware Compatibility. Even though the two companies may be hardware compatible today, there is a good possibility that they will not be compatible in the future. Maintaining hardware compatibility has always been a problem. For example, it could require that a company install new hardware sooner than planned in order to remain compatible with the reciprocal party.

Inclusion of Online Systems. Most computer operations depend heavily on data communications networks. Except for provision of dial-up recovery capabilities, standard reciprocal agreements do not provide recovery support for such data networks.

Testing. For the most part it is difficult to test the reciprocal agreement's data center. In order for the reciprocal agreement data center manager to provide test time, the other site would need to delay processing its own work, something few data center managers would be willing to do.

Contractual Issues. The reciprocal agreement is only a legal contract if it is signed by one of the corporate officers. Most in-house lawyers will not authorize the signing of a reciprocal agreement, because such agreements present more potential exposures than benefits to the company.

In the past, there have also been problems with reciprocal agreements because the company failed to obtain a firm commitment with the other party. With a firm commitment, a company can expect that the agreement will be honored (unless the second company is also experiencing a computer outage at the same time). A key indicator of a firm agreement is testing at the reciprocal data center. With a firm agreement, each company tests its capability to process on the other company's computer. Loose agreements did not provide for testing and generally were made solely to satisfy auditors and executive management.

Use of Reciprocal Agreements

Not all applications that are scheduled for the hot site may need to be processed there. For example, printing applications could be moved to a reciprocal agreement location that can provide a printing capability. This can be a valuable resource during the first few days of the recovery operation. The reciprocal location could be used to print reports for end users to use temporarily until they can start to access their data at their workstations.

A second example where printing support could be used is in a payroll application that needs to be processed during the recovery operation. Instead of processing the computerized payroll application itself, checks could be printed and used as an advance against the employees' payroll; exceptions would be handled manually by the payroll department directly. When the computer resources again became available, the advance payments can be processed during that period's payroll. This payroll strategy is being employed by many companies today, even those using a computer hot site. This strategy allows all of the resources at the hot site to be used to support revenue-generating and customer service functions, while still meeting the company's obligation to pay its employees on a timely basis.

THE COMPANY-OWNED BACKUP SITE OPTION

With a company-owned computer backup site, a second, fully operational data center is used for the processing of critical applications during a disaster recovery operation. This company-owned backup site is not just sitting idly waiting for a disaster to occur. It is an operational data center, with a processing workload capable of accommodating critical applications if necessary. The existing workload that could be preempted to handle such critical applications consists of applications that can be removed from the normal processing schedule—for example, applications being developed or tested. This replaceable work would be off-loaded during a disaster recovery operation, freeing the necessary resources to support processing of critical applications.

Advantages of the Company-Owned Hot Site

A company-owned backup site option is considered the best technical option, but it is also the most costly. Among its advantages, the company-owned hot site can eliminate the problem of hardware and software incompatibility. Network problems can be resolved more readily, and some of the logistical problems with personnel that occur during a recovery operation can be minimized. Last, tests of the backup site can be performed more cost effectively.

Hardware Compatibility. The company-owned backup site option eliminates the problem of hardware incompatibility. It can ensure that any equipment installed in the main data center is duplicated in the backup site. In fact, this option has been used by large corporations with multiple data centers throughout the country to ensure that the unique equipment installed in any of its data centers is also installed in the company-owned backup site. When new and unique equipment is purchased, a second can be installed at the company-owned backup site as well.

Software Compatibility. The company-owned backup site option eliminates the problem of software incompatibility. The concern about getting all of the software loaded and operational at the backup site is eliminated because the software already resides at the backup site. Therefore, the backup site is software compatible at all times.

Network Issues. Network problems can be more readily resolved with this option. For example, a network switching strategy could be designed by in-house network specialists to meet the needs of the company.

Personnel Logistics. The company-owned backup site option minimizes some of the logistical problems with personnel that can occur during a recovery operation. In particular, because the company-owned hot site is already staffed, the need to make travel, hotel, and financial arrangements for a large number of personnel is minimized.

Testing. Tests and exercises of the backup site can be performed in a cost-effective manner with this option. Because the company already has operations personnel working at the backup site, it does not need to send people on the road to test the backup site's capabilities. In addition, the number of test exercises can be increased. Instead of companies testing every six months, they can test more frequently. Finally, companies can schedule unannounced test exercises in which computer center employees are not warned in advance that an exercise is going to take place.

In summary, the company-owned backup site option is an ideal solution to the technical problems associated with commercial hot sites. Despite its advantages, however, fewer companies are choosing this option because of pressures to reduce expenditures and because of the increased use of personal computers and LANs.

THE COMMERCIAL HOT-SITE OPTION

A commercial hot site is a computer backup site in which a fully operational data center has been contracted for processing of critical applications during a disaster recovery operation. The contract must be in effect prior to the disaster; hot-site vendors will not negotiate a contract to use a hot site after the disaster has occurred. The first commercial hot-site option was established by Sungard Inc. during the late 1970s. Currently, there are a large number of commercial hot-site vendors; a list of vendors is provided as Exhibit II-9-B.

Advantages of the Commercial Hot Site

The three major advantages of the commercial hot site are that it is a dedicated facility; it can be used to test and exercise the computer backup site team's recovery responsibilities; and it is cost-effective.

Dedicated Facility. The hot-site facility is a dedicated facility used only as a backup site and not in any other capacity (e.g., as a service bureau). It is to be used primarily to support companies that are in a recovery operation and secondarily as a location

EXHIBIT II-9-B COMMERCIAL HOT-SITE VENDORS

Arel Technologies Inc.
7111 West Broadway
Minneapolis MN 55428
(612) 560-0203
fax: (612) 560-2506

AT&T/NCR Business Recovery Group
1700 S. Patterson Boulevard, SDC-4
Dayton OH 45479
(513) 445-2787
fax: (513) 449-2599

Backup Recovery Services Inc.
1620 NW Gage Boulevard
Topeka KS 66818
(913) 232-0368
fax: (913) 233-6862

Bank Up, Business Recovery Services
2694 Bisahop Drive, Suite 115
San Ramon CA 94583
(510) 275-9474
fax: (510) 275-9515

Bekins Disaster Recovery Services
1601 Leavenworth Street
Omaha NE 68102
(402) 341-2700
fax: (402) 341-5603

Chubb Contingency Trading Facility
100 Williams Street
New York NY 10038
(212) 612-4175
fax: (212) 612-4672

Comdisco Disaster Recovery Services
6111 N. River Road
Rosemont IL 60018
(708) 698-3000
fax: (708) 518-5340

Computer Solutions Inc.
397 Park Avenue
Orange NJ 07050
(201) 672-6000
fax: (201) 672-8069

CRI Disaster Recovery Center
7268 S. Tuscon Way
Englewood CO 80112
(303) 790-4700
fax: (303) 790-4736

CSC Compusource Inc.
118 MacKenan Drive, Suite 500
Cary NC 27511
(800) 671-2948
fax: (919) 380-5562

Data Assurance Corp.
12503 E. Euclid Drive, Suite 250
Englewood CO 80111
(800) 654-1689
fax: (303) 792-5544

Dataguard Recovery Services Inc.
P.O. Box 37144
Louisville KY 40233-7144
(800) 325-3977
fax: (502) 426-3028

Data Processing Security Inc.
200 East Loop 820
Fort Worth TX 76112
(817) 457-9400
fax: (817) 457-9400

Delaney Recovery Services Inc.
888 First Avenue
King of Prussia PA 19406
(215) 992-1081
fax: (215) 992-1084

Digital Equipment Corp.
3555 Salt Creek Lane
Arlington Heights IL 60005-1092
1-800-HOT-SITE
fax: (708) 818-0790

Exchange Resources Inc.
5700 Green Circle Drive
Minneapolis MN 55343
(800) 424-3171 and (612) 933-6340
fax: (612) 933-3834

First Bancorporation of Ohio Disaster Recovery Hotsite
6625 W. Snowville Road
Brecksville OH 44141-3209
(216) 838-4044
fax: (216) 838-4037

First Recovery Inc.
1046 Albemarle Road, P.O. Box 552
Troy NC 27371
(919) 576-0901
fax: (919) 576-1070

Hewlett-Packard
15815 SE 37th Street
Bellvue WA 98006
(206) 644-3362
fax: (206) 643-8748

IBM Business Recovery Services
400 Parson's Pond Drive
Franklin Lakes NJ 07417
(201) 848-3734
fax: (201) 848-3376

Newtrend Disaster Recovery Services
2600 Technology Drive
Orlando FL 32804
(407) 880-9050
fax: (407) 880-2917

Recovery Resources
P.O. Box 2646
Orlando FL 32802-2646
(407) 851-7657
fax: (407) 850-9537

Sun Data Inc.
1300 Oakbrook Drive
Norcross GA 30093
(800) 241-9882
fax: (404) 242-3510

Sungard Recovery Services
1285 Drummers Lane
Wayne PA 19087
(800) 247-7832
fax: (215) 341-8739

Technical Restoration Services Inc.
5600 NW 12th Avenue, #306
Ft. Lauderdale FL 33309
(305) 351-0301
fax: (305) 351-0288

Upsite Disaster Recovery Center
3381 Successful Way
Dayton OH 45414-4317
(513) 237-3400
fax: (513) 236-2503

Wang Laboratories Inc.
One Industrial Avenue
Lowell MA 01851
(508) 967-8701 and 967-3101
fax: (508) 937-7507

Weyerhaeuser Recovery Services
PC2-15
Tacoma WA 98477
(800) 654-9347
fax: (206) 824-4688

XL/Datacomp Inc.
908 N. Elm
Hinsdale IL 60521
(708) 323-1200
fax: (708) 323-2104

where clients can test and exercise their DCRP. Although hot sites usually have enough computer equipment and network resources to satisfy most clients, they will install additional hardware for a client for a fee.

Testing. The commercial hot sites also include in the client's contract a specific number of free hours to test and exercise the DCRP. This a valuable resource for the DCRP coordinator, because it allows the coordinator to verify that the company can process at the backup site and can successfully switch the network to the backup site. It also allows the coordinator to exercise the IS department personnel who have been assigned DCRP recovery responsibilities and to train new employees.

Cost. The commercial hot-site option costs generally include:

- A monthly cost that allows the customer access to the site should it suffer a disaster.
- Communications equipment and line costs to ensure that the network can be switched properly at the time of the disaster.
- A declaration fee associated with activating the agreement.
- Daily use fees during the recovery operation.

Despite these expenses, commercial hot sites can often be justified on a cost basis. First, the cost of the hot site must be compared with the expected losses the company will sustain if it does not have a hot site to move into after a business interruption or disaster. (The expected losses are identified during the applications impact analysis [see Chapter II-8].)

Second, the commercial hot-site option is usually only one-fourth the cost of the company-owned hot site. This is because the costs for the facility and the equipment in a commercial hot site are split among multiple customers of the hot site. (Other costs of the commercial hot site, such as the network lines, are not shared by the other customers of the hot site.)

Third, the commercial hot site is only a fraction of the cost of other functions in most companies. For example, it is typically only about 1% of the annual IS department budget. It is also only a fraction of the cost of premiums paid for employees' medical insurance and wage continuation insurance. If medical and wage continuation insurance are considered a reasonable insurance cost, the commercial hot site, which acts as an insurance policy for the data center, could also be considered a reasonable insurance premium.

Factors in Selecting a Hot-Site Vendor

There are a number of factors that companies consider when selecting a commercial hot-site vendor. These factors include the available configuration; right of access; reliability; cost; and value-added services offered by the vendor.

Available Configuration. The first step in selecting a hot site is to identify the hardware configuration needed to process the critical applications. This is referred to as the minimum acceptable configuration. The minimum acceptable configuration is identified by analyzing all of the applications that will be processed at a backup site during the initial stages of the recovery operation and determining the type of configuration required to support them. Having determined the minimum configuration, the next step is to determine which commercial hot-site vendors provide a configuration that satisfies the minimum requirement. This research can be performed by reviewing the vendors' marketing material; all hot-site vendors identify their system configurations clearly in their marketing material. (However, it should be remembered that these configurations are subject to change.)

Right of Access. This refers to access during a time when the site is being used or when a wide-area disaster has affected two or more hot-site clients. The major concern of hot-site clients is how they can be assured of computer use at the hot site to process critical applications during a wide-area or regional disaster. They need to know whether this is a guaranteed commitment from the hot-site vendor or a first-come, first-served commitment.

Some hot-site vendors have multiple computer locations. If a wide-area or regional disaster strikes, they may first place clients in the backup site in which they have a contract. If more hot-site customers need the contracted site than the site can handle, the vendor moves the overflow to alternative locations.

Hot-site vendors have experience in providing support to multiple clients in various types of disasters, including the Chicago River flood in April 1992, Hurricane Andrew in August 1992, the New York World Trade Center bombing in February 1993, and the Los Angeles earthquake in January 1994.

The prospective client should also evaluate how the vendor will respond if a wide-area disaster affects more clients than the contracted site and the alternative sites can handle. This is a valid question to ask each of the vendors that are responding to a request for proposal. Even though the hot-site vendors have supported all of their customers to date, they should be able to explain how they will support a larger number of disaster activations than it appears they can handle.

Reliability. This refers to the vendors' history of supporting clients during disasters. Have they been able to provide access to the hot site quickly? Have they been supportive of client personnel during this stressful time? Following earthquakes and floods or during the tracking of hurricanes, did the vendors proactively contact their clients in the affected areas to see how they could help? During such specific events as the Los Angeles riots and the Chicago River flood, did they proactively contact their clients do see whether they could help?

Some hot-site vendors go out of their way to assist clients in need, even acting beyond the contract requirements. For example, following Hurricane Hugo, one hot-site vendor was notified by two clients that wanted to activate their backup site contracts because they had lost power to the data center. (These data centers provided computer support to end users located in areas outside the damage zone.) Rather than having these clients incur the cost and effort of activating the hot site, the vendor made arrangements to send auxiliary power generators to them—a much more cost-effective solution.

Cost. The proposal should contain a number of cost items for consideration. These include:

- The monthly cost to have the right to use the facility during a disaster.
- The cost of the declaration fee. (This is a cost the company assumes when it activates the contract.)
- The daily cost for using the facility during a recovery operation.
- The cost of any special equipment that has to be installed to meet the configuration requirements.

The computer backup site options matrix shown in Workpaper II9.01 can be used to determine the estimated costs for different hot-site vendor services. The matrix allows cost information to be compared among three commercial hot-site vendors as well as a company-owned hot site.

The matrix is divided into four sections. The first section addresses availability issues, including the estimated time before the recovery can start; the estimated time before critical processing can begin; and the duration in time that the client can remain in the hot site.

The second section of the matrix identifies the computer equipment that will be provided in the contract, including the CPUs; the number and types of disks; the number and types of tapes; and the number and types of printers.

The third section identifies the teleprocessing resources, including the number and types of communications controllers; the number and types of modems; and the number and types of circuits and lines.

The fourth section of the matrix provides the costs for the site and the computer equipment, the teleprocessing resources, and an estimate of the ongoing costs for maintenance and exercising the plan. The site costs are broken into five categories:

- The one-time costs to establish the site.
- The ongoing costs or monthly contractual costs.
- The declaration costs.
- The use costs (per day).
- The daily use costs for use of a cold site.

The equipment costs and teleprocessing costs are each broken into two categories: one-time costs and ongoing costs. The next set of costs included in the matrix are for maintenance and testing. The maintenance costs are based on an estimate of the salary, plus benefits, of the person responsible to keep the DCRP and the backup site in a current and usable condition. The testing costs are estimates based on the number of IS department personnel that will participate in the tests and the out-of-pocket expenses the company will have to reimburse. Another cost factor to be considered is the estimated annual increase in contract fees charged by the vendor. The increase percentage is usually negotiated when the contract is signed.

Value-Added Services. Additional disaster recovery services beyond the hot site can be an important criterion. Some commercial hot-site vendors have internal consultants to support a customer's DCRP planning needs. The consultants can help in data recovery and network analysis and in performing the various test exercises of the DCRP.

Summary

After determining which vendors can meet the minimum acceptable configuration, the prospective client asks the remaining vendors to submit proposals of how they will provide service to the client. The contract issues that should be covered in their proposals include:

- The cost of meeting the minimum configuration.
- The capacity to expand that configuration, if needed.
- The vendors' length of time in the business and whether this is their primary business.
- Their policy on access to the facility (in a localized disaster, a wide-area disaster, and in any situation in which multiple clients need access at the same time).
- Whether they have any exclusive contracts with clients that would supersede other contracts.
- The number of sites available and the location of these sites.
- Any additional services that the vendor can provide.

THE COLD-SITE STRATEGY

A cold site is a nonequipped backup facility that has been prepared environmentally to house a computer center. This facility does not have a computer installed, but it is set up for a computer and its peripherals to be installed; for example, the facility has a raised floor, the power and air conditioning needed for a computer, and the communications lines installed (but not necessarily activated).

This computer processing recovery strategy is not designed to support the quick resumption of processing critical applications. The problem with a cold site is the length of time it would take to become operational. Most companies estimate that 10 to 14 days is the best that can be expected for the cold site to become operational. In most data centers today, the equipment comes from a minimum of two hardware vendors. Before the cold site could be ready for processing, the vendors would have to deliver, install, and test their equipment. A company could experience additional delays if everything did not work according to the best-case scenario (e.g., hardware or network not up and running as quickly as planned). For these reasons, the cold site is not considered an appropriate solution for processing critical applications in a short period of time.

The primary value of the cold site is that it can be used if the building housing the data center suffers major damage that would require months to repair. In this situation, the company will have an environmentally prepared facility available in which to install equipment.

Many commercial hot sites include space for a cold site in the same building that houses their hot site. If for any reason the damaged data center cannot be repaired within the contracted processing period at the hot site, the customer can install equipment in the cold site. Processing can then be moved to the cold site, where it will continue until the client can move back to either the repaired disaster site or a new, permanent facility.

This was the process that the Penn Mutual Insurance Company followed after a fire in May 1989, which damaged the building housing its corporate computer center in Philadelphia. While the fire itself did not cause significant damage, the side effects of the fire did. Boxes containing old records stored in the room where the fire started were treated with a chemical to protect them. Following combustion, this chemical turned into a toxic gas, which contaminated the rest of the building and caused the building to be unusable for more than a year. During the six weeks the company processed at the commercial hot site, it equipped a cold site, to which it moved and operated for approximately one year. During that time, the company built a new data center in the suburbs of Philadelphia.

CONCLUSION

This chapter has discussed the different recovery strategies that companies can choose on the basis of their dependence on the computer. Selecting the computer processing recovery strategy can often be a frustrating process to go through. DCRP coordinators often identify the criticality of applications, present the information to the executive committee, receive proposals from commercial hot-site vendors, and select the appropriate strategy, only to find out that the executive committee will not authorize expenditures for a backup site.

The DCRP only identifies the critical applications that will need to be processed at a computer backup site. It is not ready to be implemented until the computer backup site has been tested to verify that it is workable. Unless that step is completed, the DCRP will probably fail if activated in a disaster.

WORKPAPER II9.01 Recovery Processing Strategy Matrix*

DATA CENTER RECOVERY PLAN

[COMPANY NAME]

RECOVERY PROCESSING STRATEGY OPTION MATRIX

Evaluation Areas	In-House Company Owned Hot Site	Commercial Vendor Hot Site Vendor No. ____		Vendor No. ____		Vendor No. ____	
		Full Backup with Network	Full Backup with Dial-Up	Full Backup with Network	Full Backup with Dial-Up	Full Backup with Network	Full Backup with Dial-Up
Availability							
A. For Recovery Startup							
B. For Business Unit Use							
C. For What Duration							
Computer Equipment Available							
A. CPU							
B. Disk							
C. Tape							
D. Printer							
Teleprocessing Resources Available							
A. Communications Controller							
B. Modems							
C. Circuits/Lines							

*Not available on disk.

Page 1

Evaluation Areas	In-House Company Owned Hot Site	Commercial Vendor Hot Site					
		Vendor No. ____		Vendor No. ____		Vendor No. ____	
		Full Backup with Network	Full Backup with Dial-Up	Full Backup with Network	Full Backup with Dial-Up	Full Backup with Network	Full Backup with Dial-Up
Costs							
A. Site							
1. One Time							
2. Ongoing							
3. Declaration							
4. Use/Daily							
5. Cold Site							
B. Computer Equipment							
1. One Time							
2. Ongoing							
C. Teleprocessing							
1. One Time							
2. Ongoing							
D. Other Ongoing							
1. Maintenance							
2. Testing							

Page 2

Evaluation Areas	In-House Company Owned Hot Site	Commercial Vendor Hot Site Vendor No. ____		Vendor No. ____		Vendor No. ____	
		Full Backup with Network	Full Backup with Dial-Up	Full Backup with Network	Full Backup with Dial-Up	Full Backup with Network	Full Backup with Dial-Up
Costs (Continued)							
E. Total Facility Cost							
1. One Time							
2. Ongoing (Annual)							
3. Declaration							
4. Use (6 Weeks)							
5. Annual Percentage Increase							

Page 3

Protecting and Recovering Computer Data

CHAPTER

II-10

The recovery of critical data is the most important element in the data center recovery plan (DCRP). If a company suffers a disaster that destroys data in the computer center, it must rely on the data that has been rotated off premises. If the data stored off premises is incomplete or insufficient for recovering applications, the company has a serious problem.

Chapter II-10 therefore discusses the recovery of computer data following a disaster in which the on-site data is either damaged or destroyed. This chapter also presents the methods for protecting critical data. These include backing up the data and rotating the backups to an off-premises storage location so that the company can retrieve the backups and reconstruct the data quickly during the recovery operation.

The strategies discussed in this chapter assume the following disaster scenario. A disaster has damaged the data center, its equipment, and data. The disk drives in the data center and the tapes in the tape library have been destroyed. Backup tapes, which were stored in the basement of the building, are inaccessible, and it is believed they have been damaged. The backup data that is stored in the off-premises storage location is intact and accessible. The recovery operation depends entirely on the ability to restore data from the backups stored off site.

OBJECTIVES OF THE DATA RECOVERY PROGRAM

The objectives of most data recovery programs are to back up critical data, rotate the backups to an off-premises storage location, and retrieve the backups quickly during a recovery operation. Data is backed up and rotated to an off-premises storage location to ensure that there will be no loss of critical information caused by a disaster to the data center. This critical data must be able to be retrieved on a timely basis to meet the recovery commitments that have been made to the end users and executive management. For example, if the computer backup site must be operational in 72 hours, the data backups must be able to be retrieved, reloaded at the backup site, and reconstructed to an acceptable point for the end users within the same 72 hours.

BACKING UP DATA

The types of data usually backed up in data centers include systems software and utilities, applications software, data bases, production data on disk packs, and transaction logs or journal files. In addition to these standard backups, special requests may be made to back up such data as data files stored on tapes only, test packs for applications in development, and private disk drives used by end users or local area network (LAN) administrators for their LAN backups.

Responsibility for Identifying the Data to Back Up

Systems software and utilities backups are usually the responsibility of the systems software manager. The manager identifies which files should be backed up and at what frequency. Applications software is usually the responsibility of the systems software manager as well, because this manager is usually responsible for the system that houses the application libraries. (In some cases, the applications programming manager is responsible.)

Data bases are usually the responsibility of the data base administrator. Production data on disk packs and transaction files are usually the responsibility of the data center operations manager.

Responsibility for backing up data files stored only on tapes may vary. In some cases, the end user of the application is responsible; in others, it is the application project manager who requests the backup. Backups of test packs containing the programs for applications in development are usually the responsibility of the applications programming manager or project leader. Backups of private disk packs are usually the responsibility of the owner (e.g., end user); backups of LAN disk packs are usually the responsibility of the LAN manager. Because there are always exceptions to the usual cases, the DCRP coordinator should verify who the responsible person or group is in his or her organization.

The responsible person identifies which files are to be backed up and at what frequency. This person should also identify which generation of data should be rotated and how long it should be stored before being retrieved and scratched. The data files should be identified when an application is being developed or, if it is already developed and in production, when the DCRP is being developed. The data files can be verified when the DCRP is tested.

Identifying the specific data files that must be available if the on-site data has been destroyed can be difficult. Many methods have been used to identify the data that should be backed up. In the early days of data center recovery planning, application flowcharts were used to identify the critical files that needed to be backed up and rotated off premises. This allowed the DCRP coordinator to identify all incoming data files at a glance. After flowcharts were phased out of the application development process, recovery planners had to resort to using printouts of JCL procedures to identify the applications files that were being used in processing the application. Because the JCL procedures identify input and output files and because these files are repeated throughout the JCL printout, the process of identifying the files was laborious and boring. Even after identifying the data files, the recovery planner still had to meet with the applications project leader to review the list of data files to ensure it was complete. In some cases, input files identified by the JCL were not critical to the running of the application and did not have to be recovered.

Recently, software has been introduced that greatly assists the recovery planner in identifying the files that need to be protected. The software reads internal system management files and selects all incoming files that are used in processing the application. Some of the software can run in a batch environment. Other software runs in an online environment, where it both identifies the files needed and manages the backing up of the files.

Backup Strategies for Disk Drives

A number of methods can be used to back up disk drives. These include full-volume backup, incremental backup, data base backup, data set backup, and journal backup.

The backup strategy is selected on the basis of the needs of the owner of the data. Companies usually use a combination of these backup strategies.

Full-Volume Backup. This strategy copies the entire disk volume. It requires more processing time than some other methods, but it is easy to manage and is less likely to introduce errors. It is normally used for the weekend backup routine, when there is enough time available.

Incremental Backup. This strategy copies only those files that have changed since the last backup. This strategy requires less processing time than the full-volume backup strategy; it is generally used in conjunction with the full-volume backup. The recovery procedure involves reloading the full-volume backups from the weekend prior to the disaster and applying the incremental backups to recover data files that have been updated since the weekend.

Data Base Backup. This strategy copies the data base files in a similar fashion to the full-volume backup. The difference is that the data base files are located on more than one disk drive. The data base to be backed up is taken offline and then all of the elements of the data base are copied at the same time to ensure they are synchronized. The recovery procedure involves restoring the data base backups and reapplying transactions by using data base journals (i.e., logs). A different backup strategy is required for data bases that cannot be taken offline, because they are accessed 24 hours a day.

Data Set Backup. This strategy is used to back up applications and inactive files. This strategy backs up specific data sets that have been identified by the applications programmer and requested to be rotated off premises. Rather than having inactive files occupy disk space, the files are backed up to tape and then sent off site. The tapes are then used to reload the files when they are needed.

Journal Backup. This strategy copies records of transactions that have been processed against a data base.

Backup Strategies for Data on Tapes

The data that is stored only on tapes is often overlooked when backups are rotated off premises. If the data is considered critical, when the tape is created, either the tape should be copied and the copy sent off premises or the next-oldest generation of the tape should be sent off premises.

ROTATING DATA OFF SITE

Critical data should be rotated off premises as soon as possible after it is created. The old data protection procedure of rotating backups off premises on a weekly basis is no longer satisfactory to most companies. The efforts involved in recovering application data files and data bases using backups that are a week old will result in frustration and, more important, lost business opportunities for most companies. Critical data from applications that are processed daily should be rotated no later than the day after it is created.

In the past, critical data was identified for critical applications only, and quite frequently that was the only application data that was stored off premises. But in some cases, less-critical application data may be just as important. Applications are considered less critical if their processing can be delayed for a time. But this does not mean the data used in the applications is less important than that used in critical applications. For example, processing of the general ledger system can often be delayed for a time; therefore, this application is classified as less critical. But the data is not less critical—revenues and expenses must still be accounted for during the recovery of the data.

RETRIEVING DATA

Storing only one copy of the critical backup data files off premises is not recommended. The object of recovery planning is to avoid a single point of failure. The most devastating single point of failure is the loss of the application data files and data bases. Companies should have two or more sets of backups off premises for several reasons. The backups could be destroyed during transport to the backup site. Even if the backup tapes arrived without incident, they may not load on the backup site computer because of tape drive alignment problems or because the tapes are damaged in another manner. If successfully loaded on the backup computer, a software error could still erase the data files.

If there is only one generation of backup tapes stored off premises, the tape operations recovery team should take them to a nearby computer and copy them. One copy should then be left at the off-site storage location.

If there is more than one generation stored off premises, the tape operations recovery team should retrieve only the most current generation. The next-older generation should remain in the off-premises storage location as a backup. If something happens to the tapes that are being taken to the computer backup site, the company still has this full set of backups in the off-premises storage location for recovery purposes.

Archival, regulatory, or legal backups probably should not be retrieved during a data center recovery operation. They should be retrieved only if needed for processing or if they should be scratched. Because most DCRP processing strategies concentrate on production applications, the archival, regulatory, or legal backup files should not be needed.

If the archival, regulatory, or legal tapes are destroyed by a disaster and the only copy in existence is located in the off-premises storage location, it is prudent to make provisions to have another copy made. Although these files are not used often, they are very important. For example, some major corporations guarantee the IRS that these files will be available for audit purposes for at least seven years. If the files are not available, the company may be assessed a large fine and its executives can be prosecuted. Companies in this situation always store two copies of their end-of-year data. One copy is located in the off-premises storage location, and the second copy is located in a different building, usually the data center. If anything happens to the files stored in either facility, the remaining copy should be taken to a computer center to be copied. After being copied, the files are then stored in two separate locations again.

RECONSTRUCTING DATA FILES

The amount of time needed to reconstruct the application data files to a point in time acceptable to the end user depends on the backup version available at the off-site

EXHIBIT II-10-A TERMINOLOGY FOR GENERATIONS OF BACKUPS

When Created	Number	Family	Today Is Friday
Last night	0	Child	Thursday
The prior night	−1	Parent	Wednesday
Two nights prior	−2	Grandparent	Tuesday
Three nights prior	−3	Great-grandparent	Monday

storage location. (Exhibit II-10-A shows the terminology used in referring to generations of backups. The exhibit also shows which day the backup would refer to if today were Friday. A 0 or child generation would have been created on Thursday, and so on.)

If the backup is a 0 (i.e., child) generation, the recovery time will be short and the recovery procedure similar to the operations restart procedure (i.e., the procedure for restarting an application at various program steps, rather than starting at the first step). The 0 generation operations restart procedure requires loading the backups created the previous night and having the end users reenter all current activity. If the backups are a −2 (i.e., grandparent) generation, the recovery process is much more involved and the recovery time is longer. This requires a reconstruction procedure, in which data center personnel load backups from earlier backup generations and then reprocess all of the activity that has taken place since the earlier backups were created.

If the reconstruction procedure is too time-consuming to meet the business objectives of the company, the company may want to consider electronic vaulting. Electronic vaulting is designed to reduce the time required to reconstruct data files.

Electronic Vaulting

There are three types of electronic vaulting: online tape vaulting, remote transaction journaling, and data base shadowing. All three types of electronic vaulting lessen the time required to reconstruct applications at the computer backup site by reducing the exposure of data and applications to the disaster. Even though electronic vaulting would help the DCRP meet the business objectives of resuming the processing of critical applications within a specific time frame, it is often rejected as being too expensive.

Online Tape Vaulting. In this system, backup data is electronically transmitted, or vaulted, to a recovery or storage location. The data center executes the tape backups, but instead of writing to a local tape drive, the tape channel is extended over communications lines to a recovery or storage location, where it is attached to a tape drive. This eliminates the need to ship tapes to an off-premises storage location.

Online tape vaulting requires high bandwidth. To move large amounts of data in a short amount of time may require a T3 circuit. For redundancy purposes, the data center may choose to have two T3 circuits. Although the cost of these lines is coming down, the high cost is still a stumbling block for most companies considering this backup approach.

Remote Transaction Journaling. This system uses the same logging procedure as that for a data base management system. (For example, the data base administrator can recover by restoring the last backup and then reprocessing the data base management system logs or journals.) Remote transaction journaling, in addition to creating the on-site journal, creates a second journal electronically at an off-premises location. This allows the off-premises location to recover the files to the point of interruption, reducing the time required to reconstruct the files and limiting the amount of information destroyed by a disaster.

Data Base Shadowing. This system creates an update to the production data base, journals it, and transfers it to the remote computer. At the production site, the journal record is applied to a copy of the production data base.

A Caution on Reconstructing Data

The DCRP may call for the reconstruction of critical applications first and less-critical applications later. This strategy can create problems because the journal log backups with the transactions needed for the reconstruction of the less-critical applications may not be available when needed later. This occurs when journal or log tapes with transactions for both critical and less-critical applications have been used to reconstruct the critical applications. After they are used, the tape library system may identify them as available scratch tapes and write over them. If they are written over, the end users of the less-critical applications must reenter the missing data, which can be a major undertaking. If the reconstruction of the less-critical applications has been delayed for several days, it will be difficult to identify and reenter the missing input. If the reconstruction of the less-critical applications has been delayed for several weeks, it may be next to impossible to find the missing data.

ESTABLISHING EFFECTIVE DATA RECOVERY POLICIES AND PROCEDURES

The DCRP coordinator should ensure that the organization has established effective policies and procedures that support recovery objectives. This section presents several recommendations of sound procedures governing the backup, rotation, and retrieval of data from an off-site storage location. The risks of not establishing such procedures are also illustrated.

Availability of Access to the Off-Premises Location

The off-premises storage location must be open and available 24 hours a day, seven days a week. It should not be locked with a time lock or be closed on weekends. Commercial off-premises storage companies provide this type of service. Companies that use their own locations for storage of backups are not always so lucky.

A few years back, a bank rotated its backup files to a vault in the basement of a bank-owned building about 10 miles from its data center. When the vault door was closed each evening, it was locked with a time lock that would automatically open at 8:00 AM the next morning. This procedure worked for years without a problem. Then early one morning, the data center needed to retrieve backup tapes to restart its operations and found that it was not possible to enter the vault because of the time lock. The data center manager had to get the assistance of a representative from the lock company. The solution was to have a dual combination lock installed, which would allow two people with the combination to open the vault door.

Security of the Off-Premises Location

The off-premises storage location must be a secure, environmentally controlled facility. It must protect against unauthorized access to the information, which could result in its theft or destruction. In one case, a commercial off-premises vendor stored backup tapes for a number of companies in a vault in its facility; the tapes were stored on racks, out in the open. This company failed to establish any procedures to protect against theft of these tapes. For example, people would have to sign into the vault, but their attaché cases were not inspected on either their entry or exit. This lack of security could have easily resulted in the unauthorized removal of critical files.

Rotation of Backups Off Site

Backups should be rotated to the off-site facility as soon as possible after they have been created. For recovery purposes, rotating the information electronically as it is being created is the best procedure.

The standard procedure for rotating backup files to the off-premises storage location is by using a vehicle to transport tapes. This technique is more time-consuming than the electronic vaulting method mentioned earlier, but it is also less costly. This method backs up the critical data after all batch processing is completed (e.g., midnight), which gives the tape librarian an hour or so after arriving in the morning to select the tapes, box them, and have them ready for the off-premises representative to collect (e.g., 10:00 AM). If a disaster occurs before the off-premises representative collects the backups, however, all of the backups for the previous night as well as yesterday's journals and logs could be destroyed. The application reconstruction procedure would then require that the full-volume backups be reloaded, incrementals up through the day before yesterday be reloaded, and all transaction activity for yesterday be reentered and reprocessed.

On weekends, it is not uncommon to have the weekend full-volume backups completed by Saturday afternoon or early evening. But most companies do not want to pay a premium to have backup tapes picked up on a weekend, so they leave them on site until Monday morning. Clearly then, the worst time to have a disaster is Monday morning before 10:00 AM, because the weekend backups have not yet been rotated off premises.

Sometimes, not all of the backups that are supposed to be rotated are actually rotated. For example, an applications project leader may instruct the tape librarian to keep the backups for an application on site, because he or she is going to use them for testing programming changes. In this case, even though the tape library system indicates that the tapes are being rotated, the tape librarian keeps them on site. This is a data center operational problem as much as it is a data center recovery plan problem. Applications programmers should not be using off-premises backups for testing their applications.

A related problem can result if the tape librarian assumes the applications project leader wants to continue holding the backups on site and waits to be told when to begin rotating them again. This happened at a large manufacturing company a few years ago. The manager of computer programming requested that applications backup files not be rotated to the off-premises storage location and did not instruct the tape librarian to resume rotating the backups. The failure to rotate the critical files was identified 77 days after the original instruction had been given. Although there were a number of generations located on site, there were no backups in the off-premises storage location. Had a disaster occurred at this company during that time and the on-site data destroyed, the company would have suffered a significant loss.

To address these problems, the DCRP coordinator should check the tape library report to verify that the backups identified as needed for recovery are actually scheduled to be rotated to the off-premises location. The DCRP coordinator should also perform desk check validations periodically to verify that the backups listed on the vault report are actually residing in the off-premises location. (See Chapter II-11 for an explanation of desk check validations.)

The backups in the off-premises storage location should be synchronized with each other. The DCRP coordinator should review the DCRP application recovery procedure checklist and the vault report to ensure that the create dates of the backups are synchronized.

The DCRP coordinator should also analyze how many of the tapes in the off-premises storage location can actually be used for recovery purposes. This involves identifying when the backup tapes were created, whether they were created for annual, quarterly, or monthly archiving, and the generations available.

Testing the Data Center Recovery Plan

CHAPTER

II-11

Chapter II-11 presents information on the testing and exercising of the data center recovery plan (DCRP). This chapter discusses the benefits of testing and exercising the plan, when to test, types of tests, and the planning and implementation of tests and exercises.

Recovery planners commonly distinguish between testing and exercising the plan. Testing refers to the process of verifying that a recovery strategy or procedure works correctly. Such tests are intended to isolate errors and omissions in the plan itself rather than in the execution of the plan. The term *exercising* refers to the process of rehearsing recovery teams to both reinforce training and verify their ability to execute the recovery plan. In short, an exercise focuses on performance. It also is used to verify that the recovery plan documents are being kept current and that documented recovery procedures are being routinely observed.

It is recommended that the recovery planner use the word exercise to describe testing that relates to human performance. This helps mitigate fears of being tested, which might cause some team members to resist participating in planned exercises.

In most organizations, the DCRP coordinator is responsible for scheduling the tests and exercises and reporting the test results to management. Other companies may select a member of the EDP audit or internal control departments; this person is referred to as the exercise coordinator. (The responsibilities of the exercise coordinator are described later in this chapter.)

THE BENEFITS OF TESTING

Testing and exercising the DCRP helps to verify that recovery procedures work as planned and that the supporting documentation (e.g., forms and checklists) are accurate and current. Testing also provides an opportunity to identify any omissions in recovery procedures or documentation and to determine whether personnel are adequately prepared to perform their assigned duties.

Verifying That Procedures Work. A test verifies that recovery procedures will work as documented in the DCRP. For example, the ability to process on a computer backup site is verified by loading the system, applications, and files and successfully processing transactions to update files. A test can also identify any omissions in procedures (e.g., a missing step that causes the procedure to terminate before the recovery is completed).

Exercises focus on verifying that recovery information is current. For example, an exercise might be conducted in which all team members on the current notification phone listing are called in order to verify that phone numbers remain up to date. Exercises may also identify strategies that no longer satisfy business objectives. Business objectives often change after the recovery plan is first developed; new products are introduced and new revenue goals are established. An exercise can be used to verify that the recovery plan is still able to meet current business objectives. For example, an exercise might find that the computer operations recovery team is not able to resume processing in sufficient time to avoid an unacceptable loss of market share.

Verifying Effectiveness of Procedures. Tests can also be conducted to verify that a planned strategy or procedure is, in practice, the most effective way of achieving its objective. If not, the recovery team may decide to rewrite the procedure or reassign team member responsibilities for performing particular steps.

Verifying That Personnel Are Prepared. A recovery procedure is tested to show it is complete and accurate. But the procedure will be effective in an actual disaster only if recovery team members are capable of executing the procedure. Exercises are conducted to verify that team members understand how to perform their assigned duties.

Training. An exercise can be used to train alternates to perform the recovery responsibilities. The person assigned primary responsibility can be used to monitor the performance of the alternate during the exercise. Such cross-training is very important, because the primary team member or leader may not be available in an actual disaster recovery operation. For example, recent case studies have found that sometimes primary team members are unavailable because they are traveling at the time of the disaster or have experienced family or personal problems caused by a regional disaster.

Maintaining the DCRP. Policies that require the DCRP to be maintained are often not followed, because other commitments take a higher priority or because of difficulty obtaining the necessary support. Fortunately, the exercise coordinator can use periodic exercises to maintain the plan. The exercise should follow the documented recovery procedures and checklists. After the exercise is over, a written report of the findings should be prepared. The recovery team members should review the areas that worked well and those that did not. Team members should be asked to identify solutions to the problem areas and to revise their section of the DCRP accordingly by a specific date. This date should be shortly before the next recovery team exercise.

WHEN TO PERFORM TESTS AND EXERCISES

The ideal time to perform tests is shortly after the recovery procedure or accompanying documentation has been developed—in other words, during the DCRP development process. As each team develops its team plan, it should test the recovery procedure to ensure it works. For example, after developing a computer equipment inventory checklist, the team should test it to verify that it contains all the computer equipment.

Tests are conducted before exercises. Tests are planned well in advance to ensure that all necessary resources for conducting the test are available; if the test fails, it should be because of an error or omission in the recovery procedure itself and not because of an unplanned environmental factor or performance error. (This is also done to maximize use of the limited free test time provided by the recovery [i.e., hot-site] vendors.) The following example should help clarify how tests are conducted and why they are performed before exercising the plan.

DCRP exercise coordinators usually begin planning for a commercial hot-site test weeks before the test actually takes place. As part of the planning, the exercise coordinator has the application data files to be used during the test retrieved from the off-premises storage location. To ensure that all of the backup tapes needed for processing are actually located in the off-premises storage location, the exercise coordinator arranges to have the data from the applications processed, backed up, and sent to the off-premises storage location weeks before the test. When the test is performed, the tape operations recovery team retrieves backup tapes and transports them to the backup site, where they are loaded onto the computer.

This type of test is limited to verifying that, given use of the correct backup tapes, the preselected applications are able to run on the backup site's computer. Whether the IS department is able to process those same applications following a disaster has not yet been verified, because the exercise coordinator has not determined that the correct backup tapes and cartridges actually reside in the off-premises storage location.

The exercise coordinator cannot know whether the backups being rotated daily to the off-premises storage location are adequate for the recovery of the applications without further evaluation, which now focuses on performance and environmental factors. Therefore, at this stage the coordinator conducts exercises to verify these backup and recovery procedures under more realistic operating conditions.

TYPES OF TESTS AND EXERCISES

Three types of tests and exercises are discussed in this chapter: the walkthrough, the simulation, and the desk check. The walkthrough and the simulation can be used to test elements of the DCRP as they are being developed as well as exercise the plan.

The Walkthrough. In this exercise, participants describe what they will do and how they will do it to the exercise coordinator and any other members of the IS department who may be involved in the exercise. The exercise coordinator provides the participants with a scenario of the disaster that they are to respond to. The participants should be given time to read their section of the DCRP, converse among themselves, plan their recovery activities, and then present how they will respond.

The Simulation. In this exercise, the participants perform recovery actions using the procedures, checklists, and forms. The team travels to the recovery location to execute its responsibilities (i.e., the recovery headquarters team reports to the recovery headquarters location, the computer operations recovery team reports to the backup site, and the disaster site recovery team reports to the data center). During simulation exercises, recovery team members are usually not permitted to return to their offices to retrieve copies of their recovery plan or their recovery resources. They are instructed to meet in a designated room, where they are presented with the scenario of the disaster to which they are to respond. They are then required to report to their recovery location, where they will do their planning and perform their recovery responsibilities. This is the most effective of all the exercises because it verifies that the recovery team personnel can perform their assigned responsibilities. When two recovery teams are being exercised together, the exercise also provides experience with interacting.

The Desk Check. The exercise coordinator can perform this exercise with little or no participation on the part of recovery team managers or team leaders. The exercise coordinator selects one or more checklists and confirms that they are still current and accurate. For example, the exercise coordinator might validate the personnel notification checklist by phoning each person to verify their nonbusiness phone number. The coordinator might validate the computer equipment inventory checklist by performing a physical inventory of all equipment listed on the checklist.

Announced Versus Unannounced Exercises. Exercises are usually announced. However, on occasion, companies authorize the exercise coordinator to perform an unannounced walkthrough or simulation exercise. In this case, participants receive no prior notice of the exercise but are simply told that the recovery plan has been activated. For example, the computer operations recovery team members might be told to report to the recovery headquarters location, where they would be presented with a disaster scenario requiring them to activate the computer backup site, retrieve backup tapes from the off-premises storage location, and resume the processing of critical applications within the time frame identified in the objectives of the DCRP. This is the final culmination of all of the exercises given, because it truly verifies that the participants can perform their recovery activities and that the DCRP works when needed. The desk check exercise is not performed unannounced because it typically requires little or no participation on the part of the recovery teams.

PLANNING FOR AN EXERCISE

If the exercise coordinator runs an exercise that does not work well, participants may feel it was a waste of time. The next time the exercise coordinator wants to exercise that team, the team may not be cooperative.

To minimize the possibility of a poor exercise, planning is essential. Five steps should be followed:

1. Obtaining the required approvals.
2. Identifying measurable objectives.
3. Preparing a strong scenario for the exercise.
4. Scheduling the exercise.
5. Obtaining additional personnel to assist in evaluating the exercise, when needed.

STEP 1

Obtain Required Approvals

Before scheduling an exercise, the exercise coordinator should obtain approval to perform the exercise from the head of the IS department. This is necessary to ensure that the exercise does not conflict with another project. The exercise coordinator should also obtain the authority to perform the exercise from the manager of the area being exercised. (The manager cannot necessarily refuse to allow the exercise to be performed. This step is intended to ensure the exercise does not conflict with another activity already scheduled by the manager.)

STEP 2

Identify Measurable Objectives

After selecting the recovery team and recovery procedures to be exercised, the exercise coordinator should establish the objectives for the exercise. The objectives should focus on evaluating the DCRP documentation, the personnel's understanding of the recovery procedures, and the recovery strategies and procedures.

The first objective is to evaluate whether the documented DCRP procedures are current and correct and to determine whether the recovery team members use the DCRP when performing the recovery and from where the DCRP documentation was obtained. The second objective is to evaluate the personnel's awareness of the recovery procedures and their ability to perform the required actions. The final objective is to evaluate the recovery plan strategies and procedures. This analysis can be complex, as illustrated by this example involving verification of notification procedures. The exercise coordinator obtains the completed notification checklists. A complete analysis must address the following issues:

- How many IS personnel are listed on the checklist.
- How many IS personnel were reached.
- How many were not reached.
  - —How many were recovery team managers.
  - —Whether their alternates were reached.
  - —How many were recovery team leaders.
  - —Whether their alternates were reached.
- How many phone calls were made to incorrect phone numbers.
- How many ex–IS personnel are still listed on the checklist.
- How many new IS personnel are not on the checklist.

Prepare a Strong Disaster Scenario

STEP 3

Developing an effective disaster scenario may be the most important part of the exercise coordinator's planning activities. If the disaster scenario is weak, incomplete, or not specific, the recovery team may be confused and misinterpret elements of the exercise. The disaster scenario should identify the type of disaster, describe the incident, and provide an estimate of damage.

Identifying the Type of Disaster. The first element in developing the scenario is to identify the type of disaster (e.g., fire, flood, or earthquake). The type of disaster should be believable. A disaster that is not believable often leads to a loss of credibility in the scenario and in the exercise. An example of a weak and arguable scenario would be to use an earthquake as a scenario in an area in which earthquakes are not only rare but relatively mild and people do not expect buildings to be seriously damaged or the transportation system to be severely affected.

Describing the Incident. The coordinator can use actual examples of disasters to provide details of the disaster scenario (e.g., the bombing of the World Trade Center in New York or the Midwest floods of 1993; the Los Angeles riots in 1992; and the loss of telephone service following the fire at the Hinsdale IL central office in 1988). The exercise coordinator may want to show slides of a disaster similar to the one used in the scenario. The pictures can be used to demonstrate the type of damage sustained.

In describing the incident, the exercise coordinator should identify when the incident happened—the day of the week, date, and time of day. Identifying when the incident happened could affect the manner in which certain teams perform their recovery responsibilities. For example, if the incident happened on a Monday, the tape operations recovery team would probably only have to retrieve the weekend backups from the off-premises storage location. The computer operations recovery team would only have to reload the weekend backups and reenter any work for Monday to resume new processing. If, on the other hand, the incident occurred on a Friday, the tape operations recovery team would probably have to retrieve the previous weekend's backups and all of the incremental or daily transaction backups that were taken from Monday through Thursday. The computer operations recovery team would reload last weekend's backups and then reprocess the backups that were taken on Monday, Tuesday, Wednesday, and Thursday evenings before resuming new processing.

The date of the incident may be a concern if it coincides with the critical applications processing schedule (e.g., month-end or year-end closing). This affects the criticality of applications that would have to be processed at the computer backup site. The time of day is also a concern for the recovery of data (e.g., if the incident occurred before the backups were rotated to the off-premises location).

Providing an Estimate of Damage. The exercise coordinator presents the estimated damage that has been sustained (e.g., two or more floors in the building damaged or destroyed). If the scenario used is a fire, the exercise coordinator can add to the damage estimate fire-fighting water damage sustained on floors lower than the fire and smoke and soot contamination on floors above the fire. The exercise coordinator can also provide an estimate of time to put the building back into operation.

STEP 4

Schedule the Exercise

When planning the exercise, the coordinator must consider the time of the week and year. Every company has a different opinion as to when exercises should be performed. Some companies schedule exercises on the basis of their production work load. For example, if the work load is heavy in the beginning of the week, they would prefer the exercise be performed at the end of the week. Some companies feel the beginning of the week is a good time to schedule an exercise because most IS personnel are relaxed and may therefore perform better. Sometimes companies prefer that the exercise be performed on a weekend or a holiday so as not to conflict with production activity.

The following examples illustrate differences in planning based on the time of week and time of year.

Case 1. The objective for this exercise is to have the computer operations recovery team process applications at the computer backup site. The critical application recovery procedure has been documented in the application recovery checklist. The applications recovery team leader uses the full production backup created over the weekend and the incremental backups created at the conclusion of processing each day, indicating that if the exercise is performed in the beginning of the week, the recovery team must reload the production backup files from the weekend and then apply any incremental backups since the weekend to recover to the night before the exercise. Any transactions processed during the day of the exercise must be reentered and reprocessed. If, on the other hand, the exercise is performed at the end of the week, the reprocessing of all incremental backups made since the weekend would be much more involved, with more chances for problems in recovering the data.

Case 2. The objective for this exercise is to have the notification and communications team leader contact the recovery team managers and team leaders, or their alternates, using the personnel notification information checklist. The length of time it takes to notify the IS personnel may vary depending on the day of the week. It might be very informative to see how long it would take to contact the recovery team managers, team leaders, and technical personnel on a Tuesday evening, a Thursday evening, or a Saturday evening. This step in the DCRP may not be as important to data centers with a recovery objective to begin processing critical applications at the backup site within three to five days, but it is important to those data centers with a recovery objective to begin processing within 24 to 48 hours. The inability to reach recovery team managers and team leaders and their alternates could result in a significant delay in the recovery. (It should be noted that many tests of notifying key people are performed after participants have been warned they would be called. An unannounced notification exercise can produce markedly different results.)

Case 3. In this exercise, IS recovery personnel are notified of a disaster in different seasons. The time of the year does influence the availability of key personnel. People take vacations during different seasons of the year. (Anytime someone is scheduled for vacation, an alternate should be assigned to handle the vacationers' activities. The assigning of alternates can be verified by repeating the exercise in each season.) Some companies have work loads that are seasonal. Exercises do not have to be avoided during these times, but they should be authorized and carefully planned to avoid causing conflicts with other business priorities.

Obtain Additional Personnel

STEP 5

The exercise coordinator acts as the referee of the exercise as long as the exercise is being performed in one location. If the exercise takes place at more than one site (e.g., at the recovery headquarters and at the computer backup site), the coordinator may have to obtain assistance. This can be accomplished by obtaining support from team leaders who are not being exercised or from the EDP audit department.

IMPLEMENTING AN EXERCISE PROGRAM

In order to implement a program for testing and exercising the DCRP, the exercise coordinator should:

1. Establish a schedule for the exercises to be performed and a record of exercises performed.
2. Prepare the guidelines for each exercise performed.
3. Prepare the teams being exercised.
4. Act as a referee during the exercise.
5. Evaluate the exercise.
6. Prepare a report of findings, including recommendations for improvements.

Establish a Schedule of Exercises

STEP 1

The exercise coordinator is responsible for scheduling, monitoring, and evaluating the exercises performed throughout the year. To assist in scheduling the exercises, the exercise coordinator can use the exercise performance schedule form shown in Workpaper II11.01. This form contains seven columns. The first column is used to identify the section number of the DCRP teams, procedures, checklists, or forms to be exercised. (The number refers to the section of the DCRP in which they appear.) The second column contains the name of the item to be exercised—a team manager or leader, procedure, or form, for example. The third column is used to identify the number of exercises planned for each year. The fourth column is used to record the date the first exercise for the year is scheduled, while the fifth column is used to record the actual date it was performed. The sixth column is used to record the date the second exercise for the year is scheduled, while the seventh column is used to record the actual data it was performed. (Additional columns can be added as needed for more frequent exercises.)

Exhibit II-11-A illustrates a completed exercise performance schedule form. Column 1 begins with the section number for the initial disaster alert (section number 200). Column 3 indicates that two annual exercises are planned. The first was scheduled and performed on January 13; the second is scheduled for July. (The specific day has not been listed because it is too soon to set the day.)

Another form that is very helpful to the exercise coordinator is the exercise performance history form shown in Workpaper II11.02. This form indicates the history of exercises that have been performed since the DCRP was documented and distributed.

EXHIBIT II-11-A COMPLETED EXERCISE PERFORMANCE SCHEDULE

DATA CENTER RECOVERY PLAN

[COMPANY NAME]

EXERCISE PERFORMANCE SCHEDULE FORM

Section Number	Personnel/Team Responsibilities, Procedures, Checklists, Forms	Annual Exercises Scheduled	Exercise 1: Scheduled Date	Date Performed	Exercise 2: Scheduled Date	Date Performed
200	Initial Disaster Alert	2	01/13/9X	01/13/9X	07/ /9X	
300	Recovery Chairperson	1	01/26/9X	01/26/9X	NA	
300.10	Staff Department Support Checklists	1	01/26/9X	01/26/9X	NA	
310	Recovery Headquarters Team Manager	2	02/09/9X	02/09/9X	09/ /9X	
310.10	Personnel Location Control Form	2	02/09/9X	02/09/9X	90/ /9X	
310.20	Recovery Status Report Form	2	02/09/9X	02/09/9X	09/ /9X	
310.30	Travel and Expense Report Form	2	02/09/9X	02/09/9X	09/ /9X	
310.40	Disaster Recovery Time Record Form	2	02/09/9X	02/09/9X	09/ /9X	
320	Notification and Communications Team Leader	2	03/08/9X	03/08/9X	10/ /9X	
320.10	Personnel Notification Procedure	2	03/08/9X	03/08/9X	10/ /9X	
320.20	Personnel Notification Information Checklist	1	03/08/9X	03/08/9X	NA	
320.30	Reserved Telephone Numbers List	1	03/08/9X	03/08/9X	NA	
320.40	Incoming Telephone Call Procedure and Form	2	03/08/9X	03/08/9X	10/ /9X	
330	Administration Team Leader	2	04/19/9X	04/21/9X	10/ /9X	
330.10	Travel Itinerary Form	2	04/19/9X	04/21/9X	10/ /9X	
400	Computer Operations Recovery Team Manager	2	05/16/9X		11/ /9X	
400.10	Backup Site Notification Checklist	2	05/26/9X		11/ /9X	

The first column identifies the section number, and the second column the name of the team, procedure, checklist, or form in the DCRP. The successive columns identify the dates on which the various exercises were performed. This form shows clearly the number of times each item has been exercised. It can help the exercise coordinator quickly recognize areas of the DCRP that require further testing.

STEP 2

Prepare the Exercise Procedure Guidelines

The exercise coordinator first selects the elements in the DCRP to be exercised. Second, he or she determines the type of exercise to be used—a walkthrough, simulation, or desk-check exercise. Third, the coordinator determines the day and hour to perform the exercise and establishes the time limit that will be allowed for the exercise. (All exercises should have a definite time limit established.)

At this point, the exercise procedures can be written. The exercise coordinator should write the exercise procedures using the DCRP exercise planning form shown in Workpaper II11.03. This form should be used whenever an exercise is to be performed, even if it is a desk-check validation performed by the exercise coordinator alone. The form provides areas for identifying the type of exercise, the purpose of the exercise, the sections of the DCRP to be exercised, the scenario of the exercise, the measurement criteria to be used to evaluate the exercise, and the results of the exercise.

STEP 3

Prepare the Teams Being Exercised

To eliminate questions and confusion during an exercise, the exercise coordinator should start each exercise by meeting with the participants and explaining the scope, the objectives, the disaster scenario, and how the exercise will be evaluated. The following example explains this process. The exercise involves the notification and communications team informing the IS personnel that the DCRP has been activated. This exercise tests the use of the IS notification information checklist and the IS notification procedure.

The Scope. The notification and communications team leader is given the scope of the specific exercise being performed at this time. (The scope of the same exercise may differ each time it is performed.) The scope includes the time allotted to the exercise and the extent to which the team will attempt to reach the IS personnel (e.g., if someone is not home, but the family member knows where the IS person is, whether they should call the second place rather than just record this information).

The Objectives. The objective is to determine how many IS personnel can be reached within the given time frame and how many can not be reached. As part of the objective, it may be important to note which recovery team managers and team leaders were reached and which were not reached.

The Scenario. The scenario includes the type of incident that happened, the day and time of the incident, and the information known about the type of damage suffered. After the scenario has been described, the exercise coordinator should answer any questions the members of the team have about the disaster scenario to ensure there is no confusion. The exercise coordinator should also monitor the exercise to make sure that the notification and communications team members do not change the scenario during their phone calls (e.g., adding details not in the scenario).

The Evaluation. The team members should understand how the exercise will be evaluated for two reasons: to carry out their responsibilities properly, and to obtain the right information for the exercise coordinator.

STEP 4

Act as a Referee

The exercise coordinator acts as a referee during the exercise in the event something happens in the course of the exercise that might delay or stop it. For example, if the computer operations recovery team discovered that a backup tape needed for loading the operating system at the commercial hot site was missing, the exercise coordinator might decide to allow another copy from the on-site tape library to be sent to the hot site to continue the exercise so as not to lose the test time arranged at the hot site. (Obviously, this is not an ideal solution, since after an actual disaster the on-site tape library might be destroyed or made inaccessible and such tapes would not be available.)

STEP 5

Evaluate the Exercise

The exercise coordinator reviews the use of the recovery procedures, checklists, and forms and the performance of the recovery teams during the exercise. He or she should note what worked properly according to the DCRP documentation and what did not. The exercise coordinator should evaluate problems to determine whether they were caused by errors involving people, strategy, or documentation. After determining the cause of the problems, the exercise coordinator should prepare a report of findings.

STEP 6

Prepare a Report of Findings

The exercise coordinator should prepare a documented report each time an exercise is performed. After completing the report, the exercise coordinator should review the report with the management of the area that was exercised. During this meeting, the positive points should be presented first and then the problem areas and recommendations. It is as important to present the areas in the DCRP that functioned as planned as it is to identify problem areas. In the areas where problems were encountered, the report should indicate the type of problem and offer recommendations for improvement.

WORKPAPER II11.01 Data Center Recovery Plan—Performance Schedule*

DATA CENTER RECOVERY PLAN

[COMPANY NAME]

EXERCISE PERFORMANCE SCHEDULE FORM

Section Number	Personnel/Team Responsibilities, Procedures, Checklists, Forms	Annual Exercises Scheduled	Exercise 1: Scheduled Date	Date Performed	Exercise 2: Scheduled Date	Date Performed

*Not available on disk.

WORKPAPER II11.02 Data Center Recovery Plan—Performance History*

DATA CENTER RECOVERY PLAN

[COMPANY NAME]

EXERCISE PERFORMANCE HISTORY FORM

Section Number	Personnel/Team Responsibilities, Procedures, Checklists, Forms	Date Exercise 1 Performed	Date Exercise 2 Performed	Date Exercise 3 Performed	Date Exercise 4 Performed	Date Exercise 5 Performed

*Not available on disk.

WORKPAPER II11.03 Data Center Recovery Plan Exercise Planning Form

Company Name___________ Issued________ Section_______ Page_______
Data Center__________________
Data Center Recovery Plan_______________ Supersedes_______________

DATA CENTER RECOVERY PLAN EXERCISE PLANNING FORM

Type of exercise:

[ ] Walkthrough exercise
[ ] Simulation-type exercise
[ ] Desk-check validation exercise

Objectives of exercise: [Identify the purpose for the exercise.]

____
____
____
____
____
____
____.

Scope of exercise:

____
____
____
____
____
____.

Sections to be exercised: [Identify the sections of the data center recovery plan that will be exercised (e.g., the recovery team managers or team leaders, the recovery checklists or forms).]

____
____
____
____
____
____
____
____
____
____
____
____.

Scenario of exercise: [Describe the type of incident that has occurred. Provide initial assessment information.]

____.

Measurement criteria: [Identify the measurement criteria that will be used to evaluate the exercise results.]

____.

Results of exercise: [Document the results of the exercise.]

____.

Preventive Controls

CHAPTER

II-12

Preventive controls can be used by the management of the Information Systems (IS) department to protect the data center from damage caused by a disaster. As detailed in this chapter, the following steps can be employed for identifying which preventive controls could be used to limit the damage a disaster can cause and, in some cases, to minimize the potential for a disaster to occur:

- Identifying threats to data centers.
- Determining the probability that a threat might become a reality (i.e., a disaster).
- Establishing preventive controls that can limit the damage a disaster can cause.

Preventive controls are defined as defense mechanisms implemented to minimize the damage that a disaster could cause. The preventive controls discussed in this chapter include:

- The selection of the site at which the data center will be located.
- The means used to limit or prevent access to the data center.
- The controls implemented to minimize the damage from a disaster.

In some cases, preventive controls may result in preventing a disaster. For example, access control systems and procedures can prevent a person from planting a bomb or starting a fire from gaining access to the building. However, even excellent access control systems cannot guarantee that such destruction will not occur. Absolute security is impossible.

Some of the preventive controls discussed in this chapter involve issues outside the auspices of the IS department, including:

- Building management.
- Security management.
- Emergency response management.

Although the data center resumption planning manager does not have the authority to make decisions for these management planning areas, if the DCRP project manager believes that the company should implement certain controls and procedures that are not currently being used by the company, a meeting should be held with the management responsible for that area. During this meeting, the data center resumption planning manager should discuss the potential threats and the controls that could be implemented to minimize those threats. That meeting should disclose whether the company has considered these controls and determine the status of those controls. Perhaps the controls have not been installed because the cost is prohibitive.

This chapter does not discuss preventive controls for hardware failures, software failures, or day-to-day operational errors, because they are usually addressed by data centers as part of their problem escalation procedure. In addition, the strategies and procedures required for the resumption of data center operations after the disaster is over are not covered, because those procedures are covered in the overall data center business resumption plan.

IDENTIFY THREATS TO DATA CENTERS

STEP 1

As mentioned in Chapter I-1, many different types of threats, if they became a reality, could interrupt processing at a data center (see Exhibit II-12-A). However, many of

EXHIBIT II-12-A THREATS TO DATA CENTERS

- Accidental explosion—off site
- Accidental explosion—on site
- Aircraft crash
- Ancillary equipment failure
- Arson
- Bomb threat
- Bombing
- Central computer equipment failure
- Data theft: physical assets ($2,500+)
- Earthquake (magnitude 5+)
- Epidemic
- Fire: external
- Fire: internal—catastrophic
- Fire: internal—major
- Fire: internal—minor
- Fraud/embezzlement
- High winds (70+ mph)
- Hostage taking
- Human error: maintenance
- Human error: operation
- Human error: programmers
- Human error: users
- Hurricane/typhoon
- HVAC failure/temperature inadequacy
- Ice storm
- Labor dispute
- Loss of key staff
- Major landslide/mudslide
- Media failure
- Medical emergency
- Misuse of resources
- Power flux
- Power outage—external
- Power outage—internal
- Purchased software failure
- Radioactive contamination
- Riot/civil disorder
- Sabotage: external—data and software
- Sabotage: external—physical
- Sabotage: internal—data and software
- Sabotage: internal—physical
- Sandstorm
- Seasonal/local flooding
- Snowstorm/blizzard
- Strike
- Subsidence faulting
- Telecommunications failure—data
- Telecommunications failure—voice
- Theft
- Thunder/electrical storm
- Tidal flooding
- Tornado
- Toxic contamination
- Tropical storm
- Tsunami
- Upstream dam/reservoir failure
- Vandalism
- Volcanic activity
- Water leak/plumbing failure

these threats should not be classified as a disaster. As defined at the beginning of Chapter II-1, a disaster is any extended interruption to data center operations. Emphasis should be placed on the word, *extended*. Many of the threats mentioned in Exhibit II-12-A will not usually result in an extended interruption. The data center resumption plan would probably not be activated in these cases, because IS would be able to resume its normal processing at the data center before it could initiate processing at the plan's back-up data center.

As also mentioned in Chapter II-2, disasters can be broken into three categories: acts of nature, accidents, and intentional acts. Acts of nature include earthquakes, hurricanes, tornadoes, and floods. Accidents include explosions and fires, internal flooding, loss of power, and loss of communications. Intentional acts include vandalism, sabotage, terrorism, and arson (see Exhibit II-12-B). This chapter addresses preventive controls for all three categories of disasters.

STEP 2

DETERMINE THE PROBABILITY THAT A THREAT WILL BECOME A REALITY

The most effective way to determine whether a threat will become a reality is to perform a threat analysis or risk analysis. The risk analysis process is discussed in

EXHIBIT **II-12-B** CATEGORIES OF DISASTERS

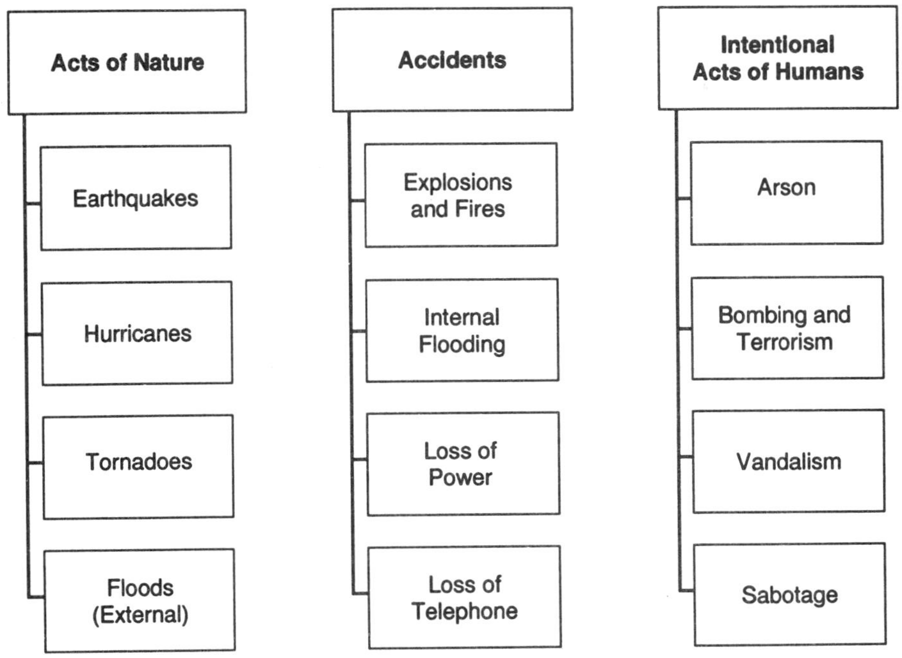

Chapter I-1. A threat or risk analysis uses various sources of information to determine the probability of whether a company's building is subject to a disaster. The predictability of a threat and the frequency of a threat help to determine the probability of its occurrence. The risk analysis process also involves examining the disaster prevention controls or measures the company uses to minimize the probability that a disaster will occur.

When examining the predictability of a threat, the risk analysis project leader should identify the history of the threat. The project leader may ask the following questions:

- Does this area tend to experience a particular type of disaster, such as earthquakes, hurricanes, tornadoes, or floods?
- What is the predictable history for this type industry? For example, is this an oil or chemical company, with a history of fires and explosions? Is it a high-profile international company that has experienced acts of terrorism, bombings, sabotage, or arson?

When examining the frequency of the threat, the risk analysis project leader should identify the number of times this type of threat actually occurred. The following questions should be asked:

- How often has the threat affected companies in the same region of the country as this company is located?
- How often has the threat occurred to companies in the same type of industry as this company?
- Does the threat occur once a week, once a month, once a year, once every 10 years, or once every 100 years?

The risk analysis project leader should also use statistics that have been reported in newspapers, periodicals, or other printed literature. However, such statistics can be misleading, because they might not be based on facts. They might be the result

EXHIBIT II-12-C ENVIRONMENTAL RISKS FOR METROPOLITAN CONCENTRATIONS OF DATA CENTERS

City	Annual Snowfall	Storm Days	Annual Rainfall	Earthquake Risk	Hurricane Risk	Tornado Risk	Nuclear Power Exposure
Atlanta	2 in.	30	48 in.	Moderate	Moderate	High	Low
Boston	42 in.	19	48 in.	Moderate	Extreme	Low	High
Chicago	40 in.	40	34 in.	Low	None	High	Extreme
Cleveland	52 in.	36	35 in.	Moderate	None	Moderate	Moderate
Dallas	3 in.	46	32 in.	Low	Low	Extreme	None
Denver	60 in.	41	16 in.	Moderate	None	None	Moderate
Detroit	39 in.	33	32 in.	Low	None	High	Low
Houston	0 in.	69	48 in.	Low	Extreme	Extreme	Moderate
Indianapolis	21 in.	45	39 in.	Low	None	High	None
Los Angeles	0 in.	3	12 in.	Extreme	Low	None	Low
Miami	0 in.	75	60 in.	Low	Extreme	Extreme	Extreme
Minneapolis	46 in.	36	26 in.	Low	None	Low	High
Montreal	95 in.	43	38 in.	Moderate	None	High	Low
New York	29 in.	20	40 in.	Low	Extreme	Low	Extreme
Ottawa	110 in.	42	40 in.	Moderate	None	High	Low
Pittsburgh	45 in.	36	35 in.	Low	None	Moderate	High
St. Louis	18 in.	45	36 in.	Moderate	None	Extreme	None
San Francisco	0 in.	2	21 in.	Extreme	Low	None	Low
Seattle	15 in.	7	39 in.	Moderate	None	None	Low
Toronto	80 in.	28	35 in.	Moderate	None	High	High
Washington, DC	16 in.	29	39 in.	Low	Moderate	Moderate	Extreme

SOURCE: *Data compiled from* World Weather Guide *by E.A. Pearce and Gordon Smith, published by Contingency Planning Research, Jericho, N.Y.*

of marketing tactics used by a vendor, who either misquoted a fact or made up a statistic. It is important to verify the statistics before presenting them to corporate management. Corporate management might question the statistics and ask to have them validated.

Sources of Information

Each threat has a history that the risk analysis project leader can use to determine the potential that a threat might become a reality. The project leader can use different sources to obtain information on the history associated with each type of threat, including the public library, the company's risk or insurance manager, insurance carriers, the National Fire Protection Association (NFPA), and government agencies. A recent survey by Contingency Planning Research, Inc. provides information on incidents from the most common disasters (see Exhibit II-12-C).

Public Library. The most cost-effective information source is the public library, which contains books and periodicals that report data on disasters. Information on all of the threats to be researched is available from the public library at little cost. The largest investment in using the public library is the amount of time necessary for conducting the research.

Risk or Insurance Manager. An alternative to the public library is the individual in charge of the company's risk management or insurance function. Part of this individual's day-to-day responsibility is evaluating the different threats to each company's location and determining the probability that a threat will become a reality. This information is used to justify recommendations for security or insurance expenditures. Even if data about a specific threat has not already been gathered and evaluated, the risk or insurance manager will probably be able to help the risk analysis project leader find the information.

Insurance Carrier. Statistics and other disaster information may also be obtained from the company's insurance carrier. Insurance carriers often communicate this type of information through literature that they send to their clients.

National Fire Protection Association. An excellent source of information on fires is the National Fire Protection Association (NFPA). This organization maintains an extensive data base on fire occurrences, and it publishes a bimonthly magazine. For a fee, the NFPA will provide case study reports on major fires. The NFPA also maintains statistics on which fires were believed to be incendiary or suspicious. NFPA is located at 1 Batterymarch Park, Quincy MA 02269-9101.

Government Agencies. Various federal government agencies provide information on disasters. Among these agencies are: the National Weather Service, US Army Corps of Engineers, US Geological Survey, and the Federal Insurance Administration.

Natural Disasters

Earthquakes. In the United States, earthquakes are generally thought to occur primarily in California. People are familiar with the names of earthquake faults, such as the San Andreas, Heyward, the Imperial fault, and Garlock. The San Andreas is the longest and most publicized fault in California. The Heyward, actually a branch of the San Andreas, has been the site of some of the more publicized San Francisco quakes. The Imperial, also a branch of the San Andreas, was the site of the 1979 Imperial Valley quake that severely damaged the earthquake-resistant, seven-story Imperial County Building to the point that it could not be salvaged. Although the Garlock is the second largest fault in California, a great earthquake has not yet been blamed on this fault. Sizable earthquakes have occurred in areas of the country other than California, such as Puget Sound, near Olympia, Washington; the Utah-Idaho border; New Madrid, Missouri; Charleston, South Carolina; Giles County, Virginia; Sharpsburg, Kentucky; Grand Banks, Maine; and, probably the most powerful of them all, the Prince William Sound quake, near Anchorage, Alaska.

Typical Damage from Earthquakes. Earthquakes result in a number of problems. Buildings can be damaged to the point that they are condemned and must be destroyed. In some cases, people can go back into the building for a short time to salvage whatever they can. In other cases, the building must be demolished without ever allowing time for salvage efforts. In some earthquakes, the violent shaking has caused equipment to move across the data center floor or fall off walls. Windows have been knocked out, and pipes in buildings have ruptured, causing water damage to data center equipment, as well as to other areas of the building.

Data Centers Affected by Earthquakes. The October 1, 1987 Whittiers Narrows earthquake measured 5.9 on the Richter scale. Numerous data centers were affected by this quake. The data center for one savings and loan (S&L) used its backup sites to resume critical application operations because the building housing the S&L's data center suffered significant damage. Data center management notified the data center resumption planning alternate sites that the S&L would be using those facilities to process critical applications. Although operations were moved to backup sites, the damaged data center was repaired and resumed processing on the second day after the quake.

Numerous data centers were damaged by the October 17, 1989 Loma Prieta quake (7.1 on the Richter scale), and they had to move their processing to alternate sites. For example, a department store, a chemical manufacturing company, two banks, a bank card processing company, a stock trading company, and a transportation company moved their data center processing to Comdisco. Similarly, a number of companies moved their data center operations to back-up sites following the January 17, 1994 Northridge quake (7.1 on the Richter scale). IBM and Comdisco supported numerous companies with their commercial hot sites.

Damage from Hurricanes, Tornadoes, and Floods. The occurrence of hurricanes in the United States is generally thought to be concentrated in Florida. However, hurricanes are not just a problem in Florida. They can strike anywhere along the Gulf coast and the east coast. Tornadoes occur most often along tornado alley—the continental plains of North America. However, tornadoes can occur in all 50 states, and no season of the year is free of them.

High winds, especially during hurricanes or tornadoes, can damage the roof and the exterior of a building. If a roof is damaged, the contents of the building are exposed to the rains that usually accompany these storms. Roof coverings, skylights, roof-mounted equipment, flashing, and insulation can also be damaged by strong winds. Walls, or parts of walls, can be blown inward. The strong winds can also take down trees, causing power outages. Without an emergency backup power source, the data center equipment will lose power.

Flooding from heavy rain can also soak the contents of the building, which might be subject to further damage from the force of the water's flow. After a flood, heavy deposits of silt and debris may be left behind, making cleanup and salvage a slow, expensive operation. Data centers have been shut down by flooding. In some cases, equipment on the lower floors of a building should be moved to a safer location.

To determine whether a building is at risk from a flood, information can be obtained from reports by the US Army Corps of Engineers, and flood maps can be obtained from the Federal Insurance Administration or the US Geological Survey. These reports will indicate the locations of known flood plains and the potential flood severity within each area. A flood plain is a low-lying area adjacent to a body of water that either has flooded or could flood. Flood severity is expressed by its recurrence interval (i.e., 10-year, 50-year, 100-year, and 500-year floods). The greater the time interval, the greater the severity of the flood. These ratings are based on yearly average estimates of the longest obtainable record of storms or stream flows.

Data Centers Affected by Hurricanes, Tornadoes, and Floods. Hugo (1989) affected data centers in South Carolina and North Carolina. One data center in South Carolina suffered a collapsed roof, flood damage, a power outage, and a damaged telephone switch (PBX). The data center processing was moved to its disaster recovery backup site, CSC Compusource's commercial backup site in Niles, OH. The Atlanta-based Sun Data commercial vendor had a Charleston company relocate to its Philadelphia site, and a bank temporarily set up shop in the Atlanta facility.

Bob (1991) affected data centers in New England. A bank in Hempstead, NY switched to generator power before power was lost. Andrew (1992) affected data centers in Florida and Louisiana. Commercial hot sites, such as IBM and Comdisco, provided a great deal of assistance to their clients during recovery operations.

A computer services company in Atlanta experienced tornado conditions when a large tree brought down power lines running to the data center. Damage to the data center's roof allowed rain to pour down on computer equipment. An insurance company in Minnesota experienced severe damage to its roof, affecting data center equipment. In Connecticut, a tornado caused severe damage to the roof of a bank, affecting data center equipment.

The Great Flood of the Mississippi and Missouri Rivers (1993) caused several banks, an insurance company, and a manufacturing company to relocate their data centers to back-up sites. The Chicago River Flood (1992) affected power to 226 buildings in the center of Chicago. The computer hot-site vendors worked around the clock to help data centers in those buildings resume operations.

Damage from and Data Centers Affected by Internal Flooding. Internal flooding can cause damage to computer equipment and data. Internal flooding is typically caused by leaking pipes. Most leaks in pipes occur as a building ages or as aging pipes corrode. However, internal floods have also been caused by leaking pipes in new buildings, which are usually the result of improper installation of poorly manufactured pipes. Leaks have also been the result of renovations to a data center or the building housing the data center. Pipes have been damaged when workers pulled cables through the ceiling above the data center. Leaks have also occurred because pipes ruptured during extremely cold winter weather.

In 1992, a data center in Connecticut experienced flooding from a pipe leak, which required shutdown of the electric supply. The data center operations were moved to a backup site. In 1991, a bank in Minnesota moved to its backup site in Virginia after a pipe that carried water for the air conditioning system burst above the computer room. In 1987, mainframes and computer tapes in a stockbroker's data center in New York were soaked when a pipe burst, shutting down the systems for two workdays.

Damage from Explosions and Fires. To determine whether a building's location exposes the data center to explosions, an evaluation should be made of the functions that are being performed in the building. This evaluation should investigate whether the company, or any other company inhabiting the building, uses explosive materials, chemicals, or gases. The evaluation should determine whether the building has any history of explosions, and what corrective action was taken to eliminate the possibility of recurrences.

Fires continue to be a significant threat to office buildings. Out of the 1,964,000 fires in the United States in 1992, 637,000 occurred in structures. Exhibit II-12-D lists the NFPA's estimates of 1992 US structure fires and property loss by property use.

Fires in offices and data centers can have various causes. In any investigation of office fires, the usual cause is the electrical system. In fact, various defects in electrical wiring or the improper and careless use of electrical equipment were the probable cause of 30% of the office fires that occurred over a four-year period according to a study by Factory Mutual Engineering and Research.

EXHIBIT II-12-D ESTIMATES OF 1992 US STRUCTURE FIRES AND PROPERTY LOSS BY PROPERTY USE

	Structure Fires		Property Loss[1]	
Property Use	**Estimate**	**Percent Change from 1991**	**Estimate**	**Percent Change from 1991**
Public assembly	17,000	+3.0	$ 361,000,000	−0.3
Educational	9,500	+5.6	68,000,000	+17.2
Institutional	12,000	0	35,000,000	+25.0
Residential (total)	472,000	−1.3	3,880,000,000	−30.1**[4]
One- and two-family dwellings[2]	358,000	−1.4	3,178,000,000	−5.3
Apartments	101,000	−0.5	597,000,000	−2.0
Hotels and motels	6,000	−7.7	56,000,000	+7.7
Others	7,000	0	49,000,000	+32.4
Stores and offices	33,000	+1.5	1,105,000,000[5]	+18.7**
Industry, utility, defense[3]	19,500	0	597,000,000	−1.3
Storage in structures	42,000	−4.5	734,000,000	+23.6**
Special structures	32,500	+12.1	177,000,000	−6.8
Total	637,500	−0.5	$6,957,000,000	−16.4**

Notes: The estimates are based on data reported to the NFPA by fire departments that responded to the 1992 National Fire Experience Survey.

[1] This includes overall direct property loss to contents, structures, vehicles, machinery, vegetation, or anything else involved in a fire. It does not include indirect losses such as business interruption or temporary shelter costs. No adjustment was made for inflation in the year-to-year comparison.

[2] This includes manufactured homes.

[3] Incidents handled only by private fire brigades or fixed suppression systems are not included in the figures shown here.

[4] This decrease reflects the Oakland Hills Fire in 1991 that caused an estimated $1.5 billion in property damage.

[5] This figure reflects fire losses that occurred during the Los Angeles Civil Disturbance of April 1992. An estimated 862 structures containing 1,037 occupancies had fire damage resulting in an estimated loss of $567,371,476.

** Change was statistically significant at the .01 level.

SOURCE: *September/October 1993 NFPA Journal, adapted.*

Data Centers Affected by Fires. In 1993, the data center equipment at a credit union in California suffered considerable water damage when a fire occurred on a floor above the data center. The data center backup site was used to resume critical processing. In 1990, the data center equipment at a bank in California suffered significant damage from a fire. Again, the data center backup site was used to resume critical processing. In 1989, an arson fire that started one floor above the data center at an insurance company in Pennsylvania created considerable water damage to the data center equipment. The data center backup site was used to resume critical processing.

Loss of Power or Communications. Loss of power can be the result of a transformer problem for the building; it can also result from a problem with the power company's service. Power failures have been caused by fires at electrical substations (Consolidated Edison, New York, NY, August 13, 1990) or in the electrical company's underground cables (City Light, Seattle, WA, September 1, 1988).

The loss of communications might occur because of an incident in the communications room. It might also be caused by contractors accidentally cutting the communications lines outside the building or by a problem with the communications company's service.

Data Centers Affected by Loss of Power or Communications. In 1993, a defective cable knocked out power to the computer center for a bank in West Virginia. An estimated 300 data centers in 1990 were affected by a power disruption in Manhattan caused by a fire in an electrical substation. More than 40 data centers were without power for up to six days. IBM supported three hot-site clients and Comdisco supported 12.

In 1988, the power company serving Seattle had six main cables destroyed by an underground fire. As a result, a department store's data center moved its processing to a Comdisco backup site.

Vandalism, Sabotage, Arson, Bombing, and Terrorism. The potential for damage to the data center from sabotage, arson, bombing, or terrorism is high. Most incidents of this type are never publicized. Companies recognize that it is not in their best interest to advertise that they have experienced one of these incidents. The most effective way for the data center recovery project manager to obtain statistics about such threats is to ask their practitioners for information about off-the-record cases.

Based on the case studies that have been published, the number of incidents of vandalism, sabotage, arson, bombing, and terrorism seem to be increasing. Recent newspaper articles suggest that the increase in vandalism, sabotage, and arson may be related to more frequent corporate downsizing.

Statistics on these problems may be obtained from managers of the company's facilities and security departments. They should have current and historical data on such occurrences. Although the local police department is another information source, particularly for statistics on the numbers of recent incidents, this information is not always made public. Other possible sources of information are the ASIS organization and numerous security industry periodicals. Exhibit II-12-E shows data from the NFPA on estimates of 1992 losses from incendiary and suspicious structure fires.

IDENTIFY PREVENTIVE CONTROLS THAT CAN MINIMIZE THE POTENTIAL FOR A DISASTER TO OCCUR OR LIMIT THE DAMAGE IT CAN CAUSE

STEP 3

Step 3 deals with the preventive controls (i.e., defense mechanisms) that can be implemented to minimize the damage caused by a disaster. This step identifies suggestions on how to limit damage from the various threats discussed in the preceding section.

A risk analysis must be performed to determine which preventive controls a company should implement to protect its data center. This analysis includes evaluating the existing physical security controls, such as the access control system and the fire protection system. It should also evaluate the following plans:

- Contingency plans that the company has established.
- Plans that deal with the site location and the type of construction used for the building.
- Alternate plans in the event of the loss of electrical power or telephone service to the building.

Preventive Controls for Data Centers Located in Areas Subject to Natural Disasters

If the building housing the data center is located in an earthquake zone, the building should be of earthquake-resistant construction. If a new building will be located in

EXHIBIT **II-12-E** ESTIMATES OF 1992 US LOSSES IN INCENDIARY AND SUSPICIOUS STRUCTURE FIRES

	Number of Fires		Number of Civilian Deaths		Direct Property Loss[1]	
Type of Fire	**Estimate**	**Percent Change from 1991**	**Estimate**	**Percent Change from 1991**	**Estimate**	**Percent Change from 1991**
Structure fires of incendiary origin	58,000	−6.5	465	+27.4	$1,493,000,000[2]	+39.3**
Structure fires of suspicious origin	36,000	0	140	+12.0	506,000,000	+10.2
Total structure fires of incendiary or suspicious origin	94,000	−4.1	605	+23.5	1,999,000,000	+30.6**

Notes: The estimates are based on data reported to the NFPA by fire departments that responded to the 1992 National Fire Experience Survey.

[1] This includes overall direct property loss to contents, structures, vehicles, machinery, vegetation, or anything else involved in a fire. It does not include indirect losses, such as business interruption or temporary shelter costs. No adjustment was made for inflation in the year-to-year comparison.

[2] This figure reflects fire losses that occurred during the Los Angeles Civil Disturbance of April 29, 1992, resulting in an estimated loss of $567,371,246.

** Change was statistically significant at the .01 level.

SOURCE: *September/October 1993 NFPA Journal, adapted.*

a flood plain, the company may want to locate the site on the highest available ground. The building should also have protection that will force flood waters away from the building. The data center should be located on floors that are above ground level, not on or below ground level. The mechanicals that support the operation of the data center should also be located on floors that are above ground level.

If the building is located in an area subject to tornadoes, the building should be constructed to handle the strong, swirling winds. In these areas, data centers are often located in low-rise buildings, specifically designed to avoid damage from the force of the winds.

If the building is located in an area subject to hurricanes, the location and the construction should incorporate the flood and tornado planning previously mentioned. The building must be able to cope with both flooding and high winds.

How to Limit Damage from Earthquakes

Because earthquakes cannot be prevented, the first step in limiting damage from an earthquake involves site selection for the building housing the data center. The building should not be located near a known fault line. However, some earthquakes have occurred in areas where the faults were unknown, such as the Whittiers Narrow fault line. Numerous companies had buildings close to the epicenter, because the fault line was unknown prior to the earthquake.

The building should be built to withstand the effects of a strong earthquake. Most new buildings in earthquake zones must conform to seismic building codes and standards. Many existing buildings are being reinforced to meet those same seismic standards.

A real concern for data center managers on the east coast is whether the buildings will stand up to the shaking caused by an earthquake. The buildings on the east coast are not built to meet seismic building codes.

How to Limit Damage from Storms

The high winds of hurricanes, tornadoes, and blizzards can result in damage to a data center's roof. The weight of the snow from a blizzard can also cause a roof to collapse. For example, following the Blizzard of 1993, the roof on a building housing a data center in Clifton, NJ collapsed due to the weight of the snow. The data center had to be moved out of the damaged building into a new permanent facility, which was accomplished in 12 days.

Water damage can result if rain enters a building through a damaged roof and drips on materials and equipment. This type of water damage often accounts for much of the dollar loss from a storm. Water can also spread along the floor and damage goods stored on the floor.

Based on a study performed after Hurricane Andrew, representatives of the Factory Mutual System found that damage to roofs was the most widespread type of building damage. They found deficiencies in the design and installation of many of the damaged roofing systems. These deficiencies involved flashing, roof covering, insulation, and even the deck itself. They also had the following findings:

- Buildings located adjacent to open terrain are more likely to be damaged by high winds.
- Glass wall construction and large glass windows are vulnerable to breakage by wind-blown debris and direct wind forces.
- Inadequately fastened base sheets on lightweight, insulating concrete roofs can result in roof covers being torn off, followed by additional damage to the insulating concrete.

(These findings were reported in the July/August 1993 issue of the **Record,** published by the Factory Mutual System.)

If the operations and the contents of a building are particularly susceptible to water damage, a company should place extra emphasis on securing the roof. The company should also avoid storing products or materials directly on the floor. In the event that the company receives a warning of an impending threat, anything that can be moved, should be moved off the floor to minimize the potential for its loss.

How to Limit Damage from Fires

The steps that data center managers can take to limit damage from fires include removing combustibles from the room, installing fire detectors and fire alarms, and installing an automatic fire suppression system.

Remove Combustibles. The primary fire hazards in data centers are combustibles, such as computer paper that are in storage. A fire protection strategy is to move the reserve computer paper out of the data center and into a separate room. A fire detection and suppression system should also be installed in the room used for storaging combustibles.

Install Fire Detectors. Early detection of a fire in the data center is essential. The sooner the fire is discovered, the sooner the fire suppression system can be activated

EXHIBIT II-12-F FIRE DEPARTMENT RESPONSE TIME MODEL

IGNITION
The event that causes the fire.

DETECTION
A person or an automatic system discovers the fire or its products of combustion.

NOTIFICATION
The fire department is notified by some means that a fire has occurred.

DISPATCH
The time it takes to decide the location of the fire, which units shall respond, and the transmission of the alarm.

TOTAL RESPONSE TIME
The time it takes from dispatch to the arrival of men and equipment at the fire scene.

SETUP TIME
The time it takes to locate a hydrant, lay supply lines, position the apparatus, and stretch sufficient offensive hose lines to a position that will ensure an effective fire attack.

APPLICATION OF AGENT
Water is finally applied to the fire.

CONTROL
The fire is confined and extinguished.

and the fire department can be called. The fire department needs time to react to the initial call before the fire can be controlled and extinguished (see Exhibit II-12-F).

The three types of fire detectors commonly used throughout buildings are: smoke detectors, ionization detectors, and heat detectors. A smoke detector is effective when a fire reaches a smoldering or smoke stage; no flame or high heat needs to be present. An ionization detector is effective before heat or smoke are present; that is, at the earliest stage of a fire. A heat detector is effective when heat is rising from the site of the fire. For data centers, it is usually recommended to have both smoke detectors and ionization detectors installed. The detectors should be installed throughout the data center room, as well as under the raised floor and in the air conditioning ducts.

Install Fire Alarms. A fire alarm signals that a fire has been detected. The alarm can sound in the data center, in the building security station, in a security station in another building, at the fire department, or it can be sent to an external alarm monitoring company. The alarm can also be sent to any combination of these alternatives.

If the alarm sounds only in the data center, the company must ensure that employees are working in the data center 24 hours a day, seven days a week, and 365 days a year. If the alarm sounds and no one is within hearing distance, the fire can burn out of control, causing a great amount of damage.

Companies that have a fire alarm signal sent to a guard station in another building should ensure that the employees in the other building follow the prescribed procedures when an alarm is activated. For example, a midwest telephone company had alarms sounding in its monitoring room signaling a fire in a building 200 miles away. The employee receiving the alarm assumed that severe storms in that area were causing electrical shorts in the system, thus activating the alarms. The employee did not notify the fire department until nearly one hour after the first alarm was sent to the monitoring station. This delay contributed to the damage caused by the fire.

A fire alarm usually sounds in the data center and at the building security station. Many companies choose to have an alarm activated at an external alarm monitoring company. Because some fire departments in the United States fine commercial customers for false alarms, some companies choose not to send alarms to the fire department.

Install Fire Suppression Systems. Automatic fire suppression systems should be installed in the data center. The automatic suppression can use water (i.e., sprinklers) or a gas (i.e., Halon 1301 replacement or carbon dioxide) to control the fire.

Sprinklers use water, the most effective extinguishing agent known. Water arrests heat and cools adjacent areas. A sprinkler system will not turn on unless heat from the fire causes the individual sprinkler heads to activate. Sprinkler systems are designed to apply water in the proper amount at the earliest practical moment. Sprinklers are considered safe, because they do not release any toxic materials when activated, such as carbon dioxide gas.

According to fire prevention specialists, properly installed and well-maintained automatic sprinkler systems and other basic protection equipment can virtually eliminate the chance of significant fires in the office.

Halon gas is a fire suppressant that was used to provide effective, safe protection of sensitive equipment, such as computers, for more than 40 years. However, because it has been determined to be harmful to the earth's ozone layer, it is no longer being produced.

A project sponsored by the US armed forces and the Federal Aviation Administration has brought together 40 researchers from the National Institute of Standards and Technology (NIST), universities, and manufacturers of aircraft, equipment, and chemicals to find alternatives to Halon 1301. Out of 12 possible replacements, NIST has recommended three chemicals: HCFC-124, HFC-125, and FC-218. The Air Force has announced its plans to begin installing new fire-fighting agents in its fleet in early 1996.

Carbon dioxide gas is another effective fire suppressant. It operates by removing some of the oxygen from the air. A fire needs oxygen to remain active. The problem with carbon dioxide gas is that it removes too much oxygen for human safety. If employees remain in the room after carbon dioxide has been activated, they will become unconscious and eventually die.

In the past, many data centers had both a Halon 1301 system and a dry-charged sprinkler system. Such a combination is recommended for new data centers, except a replacement is needed for Halon.

How to Limit Damage from Internal Flooding

Water detectors should be installed in the data center. If two or more sensors activate, the data center equipment can automatically power down. In addition, plastic covers or sheeting should be stored near the data center equipment. If water starts to enter the room or fall from the ceiling, the equipment should be powered down, and the plastic covers or sheeting should be placed over the equipment.

How to Limit the Length of Interruption from a Loss of Power

Power outages can occur at a data center for a number of reasons. Most data centers that are processing critical applications have installed backup generators to supply a continuous stream of power, even after the power company's source has been cut. Although expensive, this is justifiable if the applications being processed are considered critical.

How to Limit the Length of Interruption from a Loss of Communications

Most large data centers have a voice and data communication contingency plan to minimize the effect of the loss of service from the primary vendor. This contingency plan provides for two or more communications companies to provide service to the company's building. Most communications department managers have planned for the lines to enter their building at two different points, minimizing the number of single points of failure. The data center recovery project manager should review the contingency plan in detail with the responsible communications department manager.

How to Limit the Damage from Sabotage, Vandalism, Terrorism, Bombing, and Arson

Concern has grown about the possibility of a data cener being bombed. For instance, although explosives were not planted near a computer center in the World Trade Center (New York City) bombing of 1993, many computer centers in the complex were unable to function for an extended period of time. Some companies moved their data center operations to their data center backup sites.

The most effective means for limiting the damage from an intentionally malicious act is to limit access to the data center and its periphery; that is, the floors above and below the data center and the adjacent areas. Restricted access can be accomplished by installing an access control system and implementing effective access control procedures. The benefits of a properly installed access control system and properly implemented procedures are that they help to secure the building and reduce risk to the data center environment.

Install Access Control Systems. Access control systems can include the use of magnetic card entry systems, security guards, a closed circuit television (CCTV) system, or a combination of these devices. Card access systems can use either magnetic stripes or proximity cards. The magnetic stripe system uses cards similar to a bank credit card. The card is inserted into a slot on a card reader where a tape-recorder-like head reads information off the stripe. The proximity card does not have to be inserted into the card reader. It is simply held a few inches from the card-reading sensor, which compares the information on the card with its access criteria information and grants or denies access accordingly.

Closed circuit television systems use cameras to show who, if anyone, is present in high-profile areas. The cameras also may be able to record the action on a video tape.

Security guards can be employees either of the company or of a professional guard service. The hiring of a guard as a full-time employee allows a company to perform a background check. (In numerous cases, companies have discovered that guards working for an external, professional guard company were ex-employees of the company, who may have been terminated for cause.)

Develop a Bomb Threat Emergency Response Plan. All companies cannot and should not respond to bomb threats in the same way. A company's response might be based on policies established by executive management or on the capacity of the security staff. Despite these differences, all companies should develop bomb threat response plans.

Advance planning for responding to bomb threats might include the following steps:

- Establishing bomb search teams.
- Identifying where and how to look for bombs.
- Specifying what to do if a suspicious item is found.
- Identifying and obtaining required equipment.
- Determining when to evacuate the building.
- Specifying where employees should go if evacuation is necessary.

The plan can also establish the sequence of notifications to be executed if the bomb threat is believed to be real, such as first local law enforcement personnel (bomb squad), then army explosives center and fire department, followed by executive management, the FBI, local hospitals, and the public relations department.

Train Personnel on How to Respond to Bomb Threats. Telephone switchboard operators should be trained to know what they should do if a bomb threat is received. If recording equipment has been installed to record threats, the operator should activate the device. If an emergency notification device has been installed to notify the security director of an emergency condition, the operator should activate the device. If such a device is not installed, the operator should notify the company's security director and facilities manager of the threat, without losing contact with the bomb threat caller. The person receiving the threat should attempt to engage the caller in an extended conversation to draw out any details that might help establish the authenticity of the threat. The person receiving the threat should fill out a bomb threat form (see Exhibit II-12-G).

Security managers should evaluate the seriousness of the threat. Generally, the more specific the detail provided by the caller, the more seriously the warning should be taken. If the threat is believed to be real, a law enforcement agency should be notified. This notification should include an evaluation of the threat, and the law enforcement agency should be informed that security will begin a facility search immediately.

Security managers should then initiate the search. They should also assign someone to meet the local authorities when they arrive. After a bomb threat is over, the steps taken during the threat should be reviewed to determine whether vulnerabilities were uncovered. If so, they should be eliminated or corrected. The cause or purpose of the threat should also be determined, whether it was real or a hoax. For example, was the threat from an outside dissident, a disgruntled employee, or a former employee?

What Type of Support Should be Expected from the Fire Department?

According to the June 1991 issue of *Fire Engineering,* "In many cities, firefighters receive some training in explosives, incendiaries, and chemicals, and the ways they are used to construct improvised devices" (i.e., bombs). However, unless firefighters

EXHIBIT II-12-G BOMB THREAT FORM

FBI BOMB DATA CENTER

PLACE THIS CARD UNDER YOUR TELEPHONE

QUESTIONS TO ASK:

1. When is bomb going to explode?
2. Where is it right now?
3. What does it look like?
4. What kind of bomb is it?
5. What will cause it to explode?
6. Did you place the bomb?
7. Why?
8. What is your address?
9. What is your name?

EXACT WORDING OF THE THREAT:

____
____
____
____
____
____
____
____
____

Sex of caller: ________ Race: ________

Age: ________ Length of call: ________

Number at which call is received:

____

Time:____________ Date: ___/___/___

CALLER'S VOICE:

___ Calm	___ Nasal
___ Angry	___ Stutter
___ Excited	___ Lisp
___ Slow	___ Raspy
___ Rapid	___ Deep
___ Soft	___ Ragged
___ Loud	___ Clearing throat
___ Laughter	___ Deep breathing
___ Crying	___ Cracking voice
___ Normal	___ Disguised
___ Distinct	___ Accent
___ Slurred	___ Familiar
___ Whispered	

If voice is familiar, who did it sound like?

____
____

BACKGROUND SOUNDS:

___ Street noises	___ Factory machinery
___ Crockery	___ Animal noises
___ Voices	___ Clear
___ PA System	___ Static
___ Music	___ Local
___ House noises	___ Long distance
	___ Booth
___ Motor	Other __________
___ Office machinery	________________

THREAT LANGUAGE:

___ Well spoken (educated)	___ Incoherent
	___ Taped
___ Foul	___ Message read by threat maker
___ Irrational	

REMARKS: ______________________________

____
____
____

Report call immediately to:

____

Phone number________________________

....

Date ___/___/___

Name ____________________________

Position __________________________

Phone number ______________________

are specifically authorized by law with the ultimate responsibility for dealing with all aspects of these devices, they usually perform only limited functions and receive minimal training.

SUMMARY

Preventive controls are needed to minimize the damage caused by a disaster that could not be prevented. Numerous preventive controls have been suggested, but data center recovery project managers should not limit themselves to the ones discussed in this chapter. New, sophisticated controls are continually being introduced. The data center recovery project manager should constantly research and look for controls to determine whether they will enhance the company's security at an acceptable price.

CHAPTER II-13

Life Safety/Emergency Response Actions for Natural Disasters

This chapter has been added to *Business Resumption Planning* because companies are merging their Protection Plan and their Response Plans together with their Business Resumption Plan (BRP) to form their company's overall Business Continuity Plan (BCP). The Business Continuity Plan includes the controls, the procedures, and the policies designed to:

- Prevent a disaster from occurring (prevention).
- Respond to a disaster during and immediately after it has occurred (response).
- Resume time-sensitive business operations quickly after a disaster has occurred (resumption).
- Recover all other business operations that have been delayed (recovery).
- Restore the damaged site or find another operating location (restoration).

The Business Continuity Planning concept of prevention, response, resumption, recovery and restoration is also referred to as the PR^4 principle as shown in Exhibit II-13-A.)

The resumption and recovery sections of the BRP are discussed in Chapter II-5, and the restoration section is discussed in Chapter II-6. Preventing a disaster from occurring (prevention) is discussed in Chapter II-12. Chapters II-13 and II-14 cover the Response Phase of the PR^4 methodology. Chapter II-13 discusses LS/ERP actions that employees should take to respond to a natural disaster, such as an earthquake, a hurricane, a tornado, or a flood. Each of these disasters requires a different strategy to be used for life safety. Chapter II-14 discusses LS/ERP actions that employees should take to respond to a fire or bombing.

THE LIFE SAFETY/EMERGENCY RESPONSE PLAN

The Life Safety/Emergency Response Plan (LS/ERP) is part of the response section of the BCP. The response section, as shown in Exhibits II-13-B, and C includes four areas:

- The life safety/emergency response actions.
- The emergency operations center actions.
- The recovery headquarters damage assessment actions.
- The crisis management actions.

This chapter covers only the life safety/emergency response actions.

The LS/ERP identifies those actions that the company expects the employees to take to minimize the potential for injuries, as well as to minimize the damage to the assets of the company when a disaster occurs. LS/ERP actions should be developed by the manager in Information Systems (IS) responsible to ensure that the IS personnel know what to do before (in the case of hurricanes and floods), during, and immediately after a disaster. As noted in Chapter II-2, three types of disasters are: acts of

EXHIBIT II-13-A REPRESENTATION OF A BUSINESS CONTINUITY PLAN

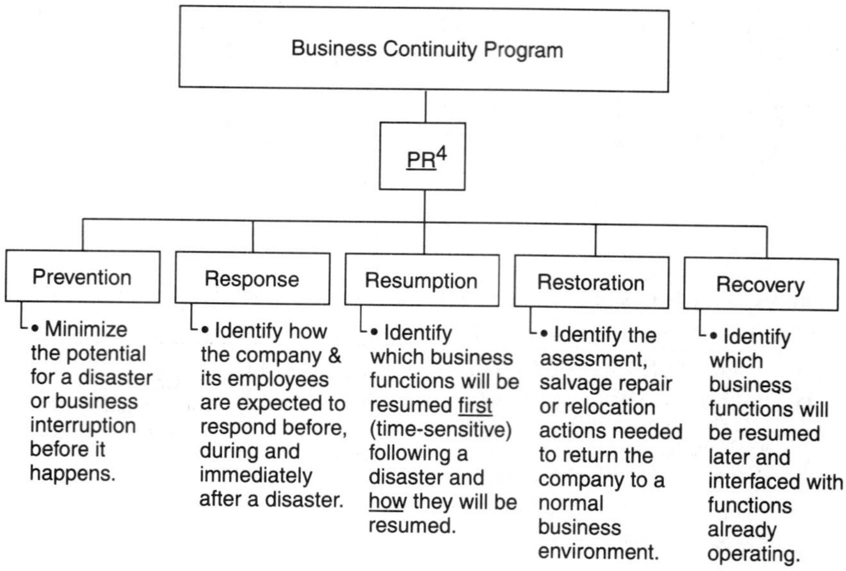

EXHIBIT II-13-B SUMMARY OF BCP RESPONSE ACTIONS

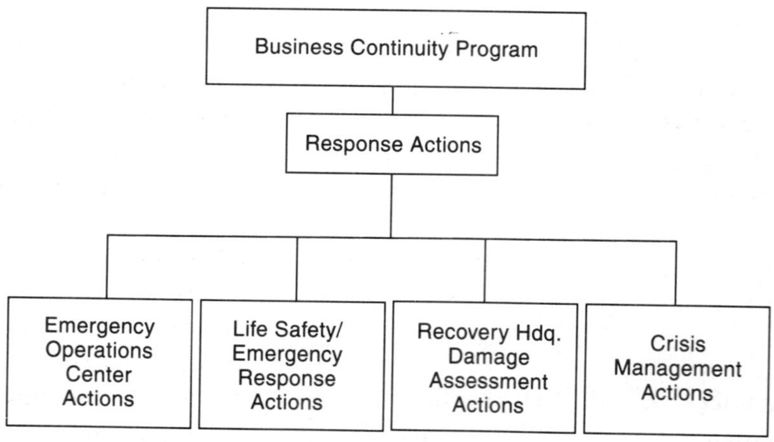

nature, accidental disasters, and intentional acts. The LS/ERP actions that employees should take in response to an arson or explosion would be the same as those covered for a fire or bombing. No LS/ERP actions are discussed for loss of power or telephone, because these situations do not involve life safety concerns. Internal flooding may not require an evacuation or be concerned with life safety issues, but if the circumstances are such that life safety is involved, external and internal flooding could have the same LS/ERP actions. For vandalism and sabotage, they could result in one of the other disasters. For example, vandals could set fire to the data center for revenge. In that case, the LS/ERP actions for fire are followed.

The Data Center Recovery Plan (DCRP) is written from the point of view of the worst case scenario. (See Chapter II-2.) This scenario does not concern the specific type of disaster that caused the problem, but rather the type of damage, extent of

EXHIBIT II-13-C SUMMARY OF LS/ERAs

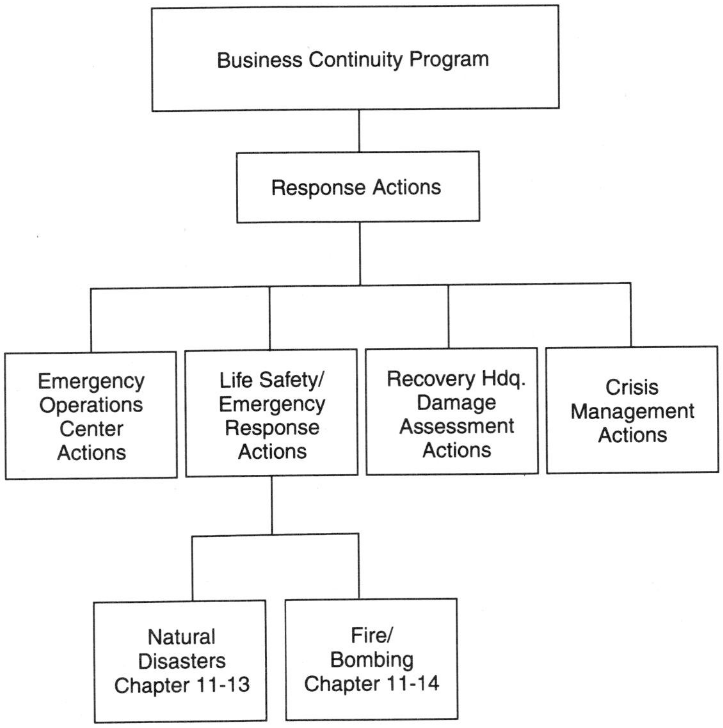

damage, and how to recover. In this way, employees are able to respond properly and efficiently to the actual situation. During most actual recovery operations, only portions of the DCRP have had to be activated. However, the companies that had to recover indicated that they felt in complete control, because their plan covered the situation more than adequately. On the other hand, the Life Safety/Emergency Response Plan is written for the specific type of disaster, because the type of disaster dictates the type of response actions to be used by the employees. The Life Safety/ Emergency Response Plans contain some unique actions for each specific type of disaster. For example, during an earthquake, employees are instructed not to leave the building. During most fires, employees are instructed to evacuate the building. In another example, the procedure for evacuating a building during or after a fire or bombing is quite different than after an earthquake or a tornado. For these specific disasters, employees should follow these evacuation procedures:

- After an earthquake, if evacuation is advisable, employees should check stairways to ensure that they have not collapsed.
- After a tornado, if evacuation is advisable, employees, exiting the stairwell, should be aware of fallen wires (i.e., live electrical wires) that have been downed by the violent winds of a tornado.
- During a fire, employees should check stairwell doors to determine if they are hot before they attempt to evacuate using that stairwell.

Most companies already have an LS/ERP that documents the specific information that employees should know to respond to a specific disaster:

- When and how to evacuate the building.
- Where to assemble following the evacuation.

- How to protect the critical assets of the company without endangering themselves.
- What is expected of them if they are not at work at the time an earthquake or tornado strikes (i.e., whether they should report to work immediately after an earthquake or a tornado).

During a disaster, a company's concern should be the health and safety of their employees, as well as the property and assets of the company. The safety of personnel is always a company's first concern and more important than the property of the company. The actions taken by employees at the time of a disaster, if they are the correct actions, can avoid injuries; and, in some cases, save their lives. If the actions taken by employees are incorrect, they can lead to injuries, and, in some cases, death. There are many examples in which employees have followed the procedures identified in the life safety section of their company's emergency response plan (ERP) and have successfully minimized or eliminated injuries. Most employees at work when the 1989 earthquake struck northern California followed their ERP procedures. Although there were injuries and some fatalities, most of these could not have been prevented by following the ERP actions. During August of 1990, a cluster of tornadoes raked a 12-mile path of destruction through several northern Illinois towns. At a Plainfield, Illinois School District Building, 25 people took refuge in a records vault in the center of the building. The building they were in suffered damage from the tornado, but their ERP actions may have saved their lives.

However, even in companies with a life safety section in their ERP, there have been some examples of employees either not knowing what to do or not following its instructions. For example, during the 1987 Whittier Narrows earthquake near Los Angeles, CA, many employees ran out of their company's building and into the streets or parking lots. One woman was killed when she fled her building and was crushed by a slab of falling concrete.

Most company executives believe that their employees know what to do before, during, and immediately after a disaster because the company has a documented ERP. However, simply having an ERP is not enough. Companies must have the plan documented and continually updated. It is also extremely important for companies to allocate time to exercise and evaluate the effectiveness of the emergency response actions in the plan. In addition, companies should require all employees to read the emergency response actions and verify that they have read and understand the various ERP procedures and policies. Time may be required to train or re-train employees. By doing these things, companies will ensure that their ERPs will be effective when they are needed; and, in so doing, protect their employees, their property, and their assets to the best of their ability.

This chapter provides information on particular acts of nature, such as earthquakes, tornadoes, hurricanes, or floods. It provides general information about the type of disaster, the typical damage caused by the disaster, and the suggested life safety/ emergency response actions that readers may want to consider for their companys' LS/ERP sections of their BCPs. These suggested actions are actions that employees should be prepared to take while they are working in the company's facility, as well as suggested actions companies have recommended that their employees take for their safety at home.

EARTHQUAKES

An earthquake is the sudden and traumatic displacement of the earth's crust caused by the faulting of rocks. Earthquakes occur most often in areas where weak rocks

EXHIBIT II-13-D EARTHQUAKE MAGNITUDE RICHTER SCALE

Magnitude	Damage
2	Normally felt by humans.
3.5	Can cause slight damage.
4	Can cause moderate damage.
5	Can cause considerable damage.
6	Can cause severe damage.
7	Major earthquake, capable of widespread, heavy damage.
8	A "great" earthquake, capable of severe damage.
8.9	Highest ever recorded.

Note: The highest recorded number, estimated years after the scale was developed, was 8.9, for an earthquake off the coast of Ecuador in 1906 and one off Japan in 1933.

are located and volcanic activity takes place and where high mountains and deep oceans are close together. About 80% of all earthquakes occur around the edge of the Pacific Ocean. Earthquakes generate waves or vibrations that can cause damage to rigid structures on the surface. The source of the earthquake waves can be either near the surface or be hundreds of miles below the surface. When identifying the quake's location, it is usually referred to as the epicenter. The epicenter is the part of the earth's surface directly above the origin of the earthquake, whether the origin is on the earth's surface or hundreds of miles below the surface.

Aftershocks and Foreshocks

Sometimes the earthquake occurs as one large movement along a fault, followed by a number of smaller tremors or aftershocks. Major earthquakes are usually followed by several aftershocks. Sometimes there is a small earthquake that precedes a larger earthquake. This is called a foreshock. It originates at or near the focus of the larger earthquake. For example, the magnitude 5.9 earthquake that shook Fairbanks, Alaska, on June 21, 1967, was preceded by a magnitude 5.6 foreshock, followed by a magnitude 5.5 aftershock, and over the next 24 hours, by more than 2,000 smaller aftershocks.

Magnitude and Intensity

The study of earthquakes is called seismology. Earthquake strength is commonly measured based on two concepts: magnitude and intensity.

Magnitude or total energy of an earthquake attempts to compare the energy of various earthquakes. The Richter Magnitude Scale measures the magnitude based on a mathematical scale derived from seismographical records. It is based on the one developed in 1935 by Charles F. Richter of the California Institute of Technology. (See Exhibit II-13-D.) It is more objective than the Mercalli Scale and provides a better determination of the energy released in an earthquake. The mathematical nature of the magnitude scale means that each whole number increase represents a tenfold increase in size of the waves. Each whole number increase also corresponds to the release of approximately 31 times more energy. The seismograph is the instrument that is used to measure the movements of the earth's crust during an earthquake. It combines a seismometer, which senses earth motion with recording equipment, which provides a permanent continuous record of the motion, which is called a seismogram. Adjustments are made in the magnitude formula to allow for the distance between the various seismographs that are measuring the movements and the focus of the quake. Theoretically, calculations of magnitude from various seismic stations should give the same value for the same earthquake. The duration of the earthquake's waves is not accounted for in the magnitude concept.

While an earthquake's damage is related to its magnitude, the distance from the quake and the nature of the soil determine how much damage is actually done. For example, a 6.5 magnitude quake under a city will do more damage than an 8.5 magnitude quake in a remote area.

On the average, one earthquake of 8.0 occurs somewhere in the world each year. Although the Richter Scale has no upper limit, the largest known shocks have had the magnitudes in the 8.8 to 8.9 range. These highest numbers, estimated years after the Richter scale was developed, occurred off the coast of Ecuador in 1906 and off the coast of Japan in 1933. The 1906 Good Friday earthquake in San Francisco and the 1964 Good Friday earthquake near Anchorage Alaska had magnitudes of 8.0 or higher.

Intensity classifies the degree of shaking or the effect of the earthquake on the earth's surface. The severity of the earthquake can be evaluated by individual's observations of the damage and other effects of an earthquake without any technical equipment or knowledge. This damage is usually the greatest closest to the epicenter. Although numerous intensity scales have been developed over the last several hundred years to evaluate the effects of earthquakes, the one currently used in the United States is the Modified Mercalli Intensity Scale. It was developed in 1931 by the American seismologists Harry Wood and Frank Neumann. The scale, composed of 12 increasing levels of intensity that range from imperceptible shaking to catastrophic destruction, is designated by Roman numerals. It does not have a mathematical basis. Instead, it is an arbitrary ranking based on subjective observations and feelings. As shown in Exhibit II-13-E, information about a particular earthquake is gathered from replies to questionnaires and from specialists' reports of the damage that is seen in an area.

Typical Damage

Earthquakes cause numerous problems:

- Buildings have been severely damaged and some have collapsed.
- Streets, highways, and bridges have been severely damaged and some have collapsed.
- Electric wiring short circuits.
- Gas pipelines and storage tanks rupture.
- Water lines burst.

Structures. Quakes have damaged buildings in cities throughout the world with millions of lives lost. Earthquakes move a building's foundation back and forth, while any load borne by the foundation works diligently at staying put. Short buildings are, as a rule, more vulnerable to earthquake damage than tall buildings, because they vibrate at higher frequencies.

The failure of buildings, bridges, or dams to withstand the shock waves and movements of an earthquake have resulted in the loss of many lives. However, structures can be designed to resist quakes. The buildings that collapsed in San Francisco during the Loma Prieta quake in October of 1989 were old ones, many of them made of stucco or unreinforced brick and built on soft, unstable soil. Following the 1933 Long Beach earthquake, California banned the building of new buildings with unreinforced masonry. However, the state still has over 50,000 such buildings from the days before the ban. Some of these have been reinforced to withstand

EXHIBIT II-13-E EARTHQUAKE INTENSITY MODIFIED MERCALLI INTENSITY SCALE

Number	Effects
I	Not felt except by a very few under especially favorable conditions.
II	Felt by only a few persons at rest, especially on upper floors of buildings. Delicately suspended objects may swing.
III	Felt quite noticeably by persons indoors, especially on upper floors of buildings. Many people do not recognize it as an earthquake. Standing motor cars may rock slightly. Vibration similar to the passing of a truck.
IV	Felt indoors by many, outdoors by few during the day. At night, some awakened. Dishes, windows, doors disturbed; walls make cracking sound. Sensation like heavy truck striking building. Standing motor cars rocked noticeably.
V	Felt by nearly everyone; many awakened. Some dishes, windows broken. Unstable objects overturned.
VI	Felt by all, many frightened. Some heavy furniture moved; a few instances of fallen plaster. Damage slight.
VII	Damage negligible in buildings of good design and construction; slight to moderate in well-built ordinary structures; considerable damage in poorly built or badly designed structures; some chimneys broken.
VIII	Damage slight in specially designed structures; considerable damage in ordinary substantial buildings with partial collapse. Damage great in poorly built structures. Falling of chimneys, factory stacks, columns, monuments, walls. Heavy furniture overturned.
IX	Damage considerable in specially designed structures; well-designed frame structures thrown out of plumb. Damage great in substantial buildings, with partial collapse. Buildings shifted off foundations.
X	Some well-built wooden structures destroyed; most masonry and frame structures destroyed with foundations. Rails bent.
XI	Few, if any (masonry) structures remain standing. Briges destroyed. Rails bent greatly.
XII	Damage total. Lines of sight and level are distorted. Objects thrown into the air.

Source: US Dept. of the Interior, Geological Survey.

earthquake vibrations, but reinforcing can be costly. Many owners choose not to pay the price.

Liquefaction. Buildings that are built on soft, unstable soil can have a process known as liquefaction occur during a quake. Liquefaction occurs when sandy soil and a high water table shake so violently that the solid particles separate from the liquid and a gooey lake of mud forms. Buildings are often thrown off their foundations. Some can even sink partially into the muck. When this happens, a structure sinks or tilts a couple of feet or as much as an entire floor. Coastal communities are especially vulnerable to liquefaction because they are built on landfills, former marshes or old stream beds. The soil is sandy, and the underground water table is near the surface. Liquefaction occurred in parts of Long Beach and Compton when a 6.3 quake struck Long Beach in 1933.

Earthquake-Resistant Building Design. Today, buildings are being designed to withstand the forces of an earthquake. Engineers are using metal straps, braces, or other strengthening parts called reinforcing on buildings for vibration resistance.

Some taller buildings have ductile frames, called moving frames, that move with the earth, absorbing much of the destructive energy of the earthquake. Engineers can also use a technique where there is the installation of shear walls, reinforced concrete walls positioned perpendicular to each other, which absorb the force that would otherwise crack the building. The state-of-the-art building construction in earthquake-prone areas is to employ bearings, called isolation bearings, that separate the ground from the building, so that if the ground shakes, the building does not. The bearings are composed of alternate layers of steel and rubber, which act like shock absorbers between a building and the shaking ground. The technique is not well suited to tall, flexible buildings, which require a firm anchor to avoid tipping over when they sway, but it can eliminate the need for extensive reinforcement within short, rigid structures. These earthquake-resistant building techniques can help companies to eliminate or minimize the loss of life and property in the earthquake-prone areas. As new buildings are purchased or built by companies, these engineering designs can be incorporated into the plans of the building, and they become part of the prevention aspect of the BCP.

Tsunami. An infrequent side effect of an earthquake is the tsunami. The tsunami, or seismic sea waves, are waves in the ocean caused by a submarine volcanic explosion or a major earthquake. The Japanese word "tsunami" is more appropriate to use than the common term, "tidal wave," because these waves have nothing to do with "the tide." When these waves are formed, the tsunami is not noticeable. The water rises very little initially, but when the wave nears shore, it begins piling up and can rush onshore as a wall of water. Tsunamis move incredibly fast with the speed depending on the depth of the water. In water that is 30,000 feet deep, a tsunami moves at 670 miles per hour. In 3,000 feet of water, it will slow down to 212 miles per hour, and in 60 feet of water to 30 miles per hour. Almost all tsunamis occur in the Pacific Ocean.

The tsunami that wrecked Hilo, Hawaii, on April 1, 1946, originated in the Aleutian Islands and generated waves 30 to 55 feet high. It was so forceful that it bent parking meters in half. Following this 1946 tsunami, a warning system was set up at the Honolulu Observatory for the entire Pacific Ocean. Whenever a large earthquake occurs, its details are immediately reported to Honolulu from earthquake observatories around the world. This information, combined with measurements of water levels made by tide gauges in the region of the earthquake, provides the basis for whether a tsunami warning will be issued or not. Once a tsunami starts, it cannot be stopped. This warning system has been set up to minimize injuries or deaths and to warn citizens of the impending danger so they can evacuate from the danger area. Despite the loss of life, the system is believed to be very effective, because most people do evacuate from low-lying areas. The loss of life appears to be adventurers and curiosity seekers who want to experience these rare, life-threatening events.

Earthquake Emergency Response Actions

The Life Safety/Emergency Response Plan for earthquakes should clarify for employees what actions the company wants them to take during and immediately after an earthquake strikes the area. The plan should stress to all employees to remain calm and not panic during the quake. Many people, who have experienced an earthquake, indicate that they have heard sounds a split second before they felt the actual earthquake. Personnel should use this time to protect themselves. Although the earth's movement may be violent, and frightening, it usually does not injure them.

If the Employee is Inside a Building They Should Stay in the Building. They should take cover under a desk, a table, or some other substantial furniture that can absorb any falling debris from the ceiling. If there is no substantial furniture to crawl under, the person should brace themselves in a doorway, in an inside corner of the room, or a hallway. These locations provide protection from falling objects such as ceiling tiles, light fixtures, and pictures. They should stay away from windows, glass doors, and mirrors because they often shatter during the violent motion. In addition, they should stay away from tall book cases, shelves, and cabinets that could fall or slide into them. These items have been known to travel great distances across the room during a violent quake. Employees should shield their heads and faces against falling or flying debris by using their arms, coats, sweaters, or anything that is nearby.

The employee should never rush outside of the building. The greatest danger is from falling debris from a building. Numerous people have been injured, and some killed, by falling debris from the building they were exiting. For example, during the Loma Prieta earthquake in October, 1989, five employees from the offices of Major Legal Services were killed in their cars on the street when the walls of the building collapsed. During the Whittier Narrows earthquake in 1987, a student was crushed to death by a concrete block that had fallen from the college's parking facility. During Loma Prieta and again during the Northridge earthquake in 1994, a number of office buildings and parking facilities had partial collapses.

If the Employee is Required to Evacuate the Building for Safety Reasons. Use stairwells. Before rushing into the stairwell, employees should check the stairways to ensure they have not collapsed. For example, two buildings housing computer centers in Mexico City experienced emergency stairwell collapses after the 1985 earthquake. In one case, two IS employees fell down an empty shaft that held the flight of steps that had collapsed, and they were severely injured. In the second case, the IS employees noticed the collapsed steps before entering the stairwell. They contacted emergency personnel, who brought them out of the building using ladders.

If the Employee is Inside an Elevator They Should Stop at the Nearest Floor and Get Out of the Elevator. Elevators are frequently inoperable following an earthquake, or they may become inoperable during an aftershock, so that employees should attempt to get out of them as soon as possible. After leaving any elevator, they should take cover by using the same procedures as those previously if the person is inside a building. If employees are trapped inside elevators, they should use the elevator emergency notification controls, which will inform the building management personnel that someone is trapped in the elevator, and they can begin the process of extracting the trapped personnel. According to a Coopers and Lybrand study, during the Loma Prieta earthquake in San Francisco in October, 1989, 87% of the buildings surveyed had lost elevator service and on the average for 35 hours.

If the Employee is Outside of a Building or on the Street When the Quake Takes Place, They Should Move Away to an Open Area from Walls and Sides of Buildings, Power Lines, or Trees. Employees should watch for falling debris, while quickly moving to an open area. If the shaking starts again while they are in the clear area, they should lie down to avoid falling.

If the Employee is in a Moving Car When the Quake Takes Place, He or She Should Stop the Car as Quickly as Safety Permits. Employees should avoid

EXHIBIT II-13-F EARTHQUAKE SUPPLY CHECKLIST

Survival

- Sturdy footlocker or plastic boxes to store earthquake supplies.
- Water—one gallon per person per day.
- Food for three days (canned, packaged, and dried).
- Blankets or sleeping bags.
- Portable radio, flashlight, and lots of spare batteries.
- Money, essential medication, and eyeglasses.
- Fire extinguisher: A-B-C type.
- Food and water for pets.
- Whistle to call for help.

Sanitation

- Large plastic trash bags and cans.
- Resealable plastic bags.
- Bar soap and liquid detergent.
- Pre-moistened towelettes.
- Personal toiletries and toilet paper.
- Household bleach.
- Newspapers to wrap garbage and waste.

Safety and Comfort

- Sturdy shoes and gloves.
- Tent, knife, candles, and matches.
- Change of clothing, including a hat.
- Garden hose for siphoning and fire fighting.

Cooking

- Barbecue, camp stove, fuel for cooking, and chafing dish.
- Disposable plates, cups, and utensils.
- Manual can opener and paper towels.

Tools and Supplies

- Ax, shovel, broom, and crowbar.
- Crescent wrench for turning off gas and water.
- Screwdriver, pliers, and hammer.
- Coil of half-inch rope.
- Plastic tape and sheeting.
- Toys for children.

Car Mini Survival Kit

- Bottled water.
- First Aid kit, book, and medications.
- Fire extinguisher and tools.
- Battery-operated or reflectorized warning device (safer than flares).
- Extra clothes and sturdy walking shoes.
- Blankets or sleeping bags.
- Flashlight, including extra batteries and bulbs, street maps, and money.
- Nonperishable food.
- Resealable plastic bags and tissue.
- Pre-moistened towelettes.

For Disinfecting Water

- Before attempting disinfection, first strain water through a clean cloth or handkerchief to remove any sediment, floating matter, or glass.

(*continued*)

EXHIBIT II-13-F EARTHQUAKE SUPPLY CHECKLIST (*CONTINUED*)

- Water may be disinfected with eight drops per gallon of sodium hypochlorite solution (i.e., household chlorine bleach). Do not use solution in which there are active ingredients other than hypochlorite.
- Mix water and bleach thoroughly by stirring or shaking in the container. Let it stand for 30 minutes before using. A slight chlorine odor should be detectable in the water. If not, repeat the dosage and let it stand for additional 15 minutes before using.
- Water may be purified by bringing it to a rapid boil.

Source: The ACP Communicator: Second Quarter 1994.

overpasses and underpasses if possible. If necessary, employees should use the emergency survival kit they should be required to carry in their trunks. For example, most Californians carry survival kits in their cars as well as storing them in their homes. This survival kit should contain water, food, a first aid kit, flashlight, and blankets. For an earthquake supply checklist, see Exhibit II-13-F.

Actions to Take After the Earthquake is Over. Employees should check for injuries. If they are not injured, they should check around them to determine if other personnel have been injured. The general rule is that first aid should only be administered by adequately trained personnel. Seriously injured personnel should not be moved, because the movement may result in more injury, unless the seriously injured person was in immediate danger of further injury. Employees should listen to the radio or television (battery operated) to obtain emergency bulletins. The telephone should be used for emergency purposes only, and employees should not go sightseeing.

Companies that have suffered damage will want to get their employees and repair personnel to their location. Some areas will have local authorities limiting access so that they can rescue injured and trapped people and respond to any fires. For their employees to gain access to their building locations, many companies review their emergency response plans with the local authorities before an incident takes place. As a result of this review, the company is able to make arrangements to obtain passes for key personnel to enter limited access controlled areas because they will be needed at the company's site. Eventually, the access controls will be relaxed by local authorities, and employees will not have a problem getting to any location.

Specific employees should be assigned to assess damage after the quake is over. Although this task is usually the responsibility of the facilities department personnel, IS departments should also assign key, knowledgeable personnel with this responsibility.

If the Employee is Responsible to Assess the Damage to the Building After the Quake is Over. This employee should check the building for fire hazards, especially gas leaks and damaged electrical wiring. If the employee determines that the structure of the building may not stand up to an aftershock, he or she should evacuate the building immediately by following the same procedures for evacuating the building as detailed previously. Because earth movement may have ruptured gas lines, the employee should avoid striking a match, using a lighter, or even turning on a light switch, because the spark could cause an explosion. If not enough light is available, the employee should use a flashlight. If the employee smells gas, he or she should open windows; shut off the main valve, if its location is known; leave the building; report the gas leakage to authorities; and he or she not re-enter until a utility official indicates that it is safe. If water mains are ruptured, the employee should shut off the supply at the main valve. If electrical wiring is shorting out, the employee should shut the electricity off at the main box. The employee should be cautious when moving around the building, and remember that there may be aftershocks. Any items damaged or loosened by the initial quake may fall during the aftershock.

Other Questions to be Answered for Emergency Response Planning for Earthquakes

The following questions should be answered and included in the emergency response action plan for earthquakes:

- Will the repair personnel need access passes as well as other employees?
- Will the repair personnel and employees need transportation?
- If employees or repair personnel use their personal cars to get to their companys' location, will they have a place to park?
- If the area suffers a power outage, how will employees or repair personnel obtain gasoline for their personal cars?
- Can public transportation be used to get to any companys' location? Even if available, it may not be functioning. Trains may have their tracks damaged, and buses may have to contend with road closures due to damaged bridges and overpasses.
- How will employees and repair personnel obtain food and water? Based on recent quake damage, there have been few food establishments operating during the first few days following an earthquake.

Employees should be instructed to incorporate in their family emergency response plans many of their employers' earthquake response suggestions. A sample family earthquake response plan is presented in Exhibit II-13-G.

HURRICANES

The general term for all atmospheric disturbances originating over tropical waters is tropical cyclone. Cyclones are large, circular atmospheric systems in which barometric pressure steadily diminishes to a minimum at the center. The winds spiral inward, turning clockwise in the southern hemisphere and counterclockwise in the northern hemisphere. The atmospheric system is accompanied by stormy weather with heavy rains. Normal systems usually spread over a circular or elliptical width of between 100 to 200 miles, but on occasion, they have spread over widths of 1,000 miles. Cyclones originating over the tropical waters of the Atlantic Ocean are known as hurricanes. Those originating over the Pacific Ocean are known as typhoons. Those originating over the Indian Ocean and around Australia are known as tropical cyclones. For a general understanding of the various terms associated with hurricanes see Exhibit II-13-H.

Hurricanes, typhoons, and tropical cyclones originate only in specific areas of the west Atlantic, east Pacific, south Pacific, western north Pacific, and south and north Indian Oceans. Curiously, none have ever developed in the south Atlantic Ocean. They seldom move closer to the equator than latitude four to five degrees north or south, and they never cross the equator. They are more common at certain times of the year, which vary from ocean to ocean. In the Atlantic, the high season is August and September, but hurricanes can also occur as early as June or as late as November. Hurricanes usually last from five to 10 days, but due to their unpredictable behavior they have lasted for several weeks. Their unpredictability also explains the erratic

EXHIBIT II–13–G PERSONAL FAMILY EARTHQUAKE RESPONSE PLAN

Before

- Decide on a reunion or message point if family members are separated.
- Be aware of children's school emergency plans.
- Make provisions for elderly or disabled family members.
- In each room, know the safest "duck and cover" spots (i.e., under desks and sturdy tables or against hallway walls).
- In each room, know the most dangerous spots: near windows, mirrors, hanging objects, fireplaces, and tall, unsecured furniture.
- Learn first aid and CPR.
- Keep a list of emergency phone numbers handy.
- Learn how to shut off gas, water, and electricity in case the lines are damaged.
- Secure water heater and other appliances that could move and rupture utility lines.
- Secure heavy, tall furniture that can topple such as bookcases, china cabinets, and wall units.
- Secure hanging plants and heavy picture frames or mirrors (especially over beds).
- Move heavy and precious objects to bottom shelves.
- Put latches on cabinet doors to keep them closed during shaking.
- Keep flammable liquids such as paints, pest sprays, or cleaning products in cabinets or secured on lower shelves.
- Know all possible exits from the house.
- Maintain emergency food, water, and other supplies, including a flashlight, a portable battery operated radio with extra batteries, medicines, first aid kit, and clothing in a place that is readily accessible even if the house is damaged.

During

- If indors, stay there. Get under a desk or table or stand in a corner. Stay away from windows and objects that may fall.
- If outdoors, go to an open area away from trees, buildings, walls, and power lines.
- If in a high-rise, stay away from windows and outside walls. Do not use the elevators.
- If driving, pull over to the side of the road and stop. Avoid over-passes and power lines. Stay inside until the shaking is over.
- If in a crowded public place, do not rush for the doors. Move away from display shelves containing objects that could fall.

After

- Hunt for damage and hazards
- Be prepared for aftershocks.
- Check for gas and water leaks, broken electrical wiring, or ruptured sewage lines. If there is damage, turn the utility off at the source.
- Check food and water supplies. Emergency water can be obtained from water heaters, melted ice cubes, toilet tanks, and canned vegetables.
- Turn on a portable radio for information, instructions, news, and damage reports.
- Cooperate fully with public safety officials.
- Do not use vehicles unless there is an emergency. Keep the streets clear for emergency vehicles.
- Do not use the telephone except to report medical emergencies, fire, or violent crimes.
- Stay calm and lend a hand to others.
- If there is a need to evacuate, post a message inside the house telling family members where the assembly point is located.

Source: The ACP Communicator. Second Quarter 1994.

EXHIBIT II–13–H TROPICAL STORM AND HURRICANE GLOSSARY

Tropical Disturbance:	A storm, but with no strong winds.
Tropical Depression:	An area of low atmospheric pressure originating over tropical waters with winds blowing counter-clockwise around the center at speeds of 38 miles per hour or less.
Tropical Storm:	A storm of tropical origin with winds near its center greater than 38 miles per hour, but less than 74 miles per hour.
Hurricane Advisory:	Message concerning tropical storms and hurricanes giving warning information along with details on where the storm is located, how intense the storm is, where it is moving, and what precautions should be taken.
Hurricane Watch:	An announcement to the public whenever a tropical storm or hurricane becomes a threat to coastal areas. This announcement is not a warning; it indicates the hurricane is near enough. Everyone in the area covered by the watch should listen for subsequent advisories and be prepared to take precautionary action in case hurricane warnings are issued.
Hurricane Warning:	An announcement indicating that hurricane winds of 74 miles per hour or higher are expected in a specified coastal area. It may also describe coastal areas where dangerously high water or waves are forecast. When a hurricane warning is announced, hurricane conditions are imminent and may begin within 24 hours. Precautionary actions should be started immediately.
Bulletin:	A release presented between advisories giving the latest details of the storm.
Storm Surge:	The rise in sea level caused by a storm. It is caused by a combination of low atmospheric pressure in the storm's center and by water pushed by wind. The height depends on the strength of the storm and the nature of the ocean floor offshore. When the surge pushes into bays or rivers, it can pile up water higher than on open beaches. Over the years, storm surge has been a bigger killer than wind.
Eye:	The center of a tropical cyclone where winds are nearly calm. As a storm grows, the eye becomes better developed. Often, on satellite photos, the eye is seen as a clear area in the middle of the storm.
Eye Wall:	The wall of clouds, usually extending 40,000 feet or higher around the hurricane's eye that contains the fastest winds.
Spiral Band:	A line of thunderstorms that spirals into a hurricane's wall.

paths that hurricanes will take. They may stay over the warm waters, from which they derive their strength, or move inland and eventually weaken and die. A hurricane may move back and forth between land and water several times before dying. Moreover, a hurricane generates more energy in one hour than all the electric power generated in the United States in one year.

Hurricanes begin as tropical depressions. A tropical depression is a low pressure area that contains winds blowing around its center at 38 miles per hour or less. When the winds of a tropical depression increase to more than 38 miles per hour at the center, but less than 74 miles per hour, a tropical storm has developed. If those winds increase above 74 miles per hour, the tropical depression is called a hurricane. As the winds, water vapor, and clouds of a hurricane increase in strength, an "eye," is formed. An "eye" of a hurricane is a calm and clear area. Many people over the years have mistaken the calm, clear eye for the end of the hurricane. When they have left their shelters, they have been hit again by the hurricane's fury from the opposite direction. An eye can vary in size from as small as three miles wide to as large as 50 miles wide, depending on the size of the hurricane.

Hurricanes frequently spawn tornadoes, such as in: Hurricanes Camille (1969), Allen (1980), and Gilbert (1988). The tornadoes that are spawned by hurricanes usually are small and short-lived and do not pose as great a danger as those occurring following heavy rain or thunderstorms.

The National Weather Service

The National Weather Service is a major element of the US Commerce Department's National Oceanic and Atmospheric Administration (NOAA). It is the mission of the NOAA to help mitigate the threat to life and property from natural hazards. It provides weather reports and predictions and issues hurricane, tornado, and flood warnings. The National Weather Service office in Coral Gables, Florida, is known as the National Hurricane Center. Interestingly, in 1992, the Center was in a direct path of Hurricane Andrew. Andrew cut off power and water supplies to the Center, and blew the Center's radar unit off the roof. The Center has the responsibility for forecasting tropical storms and hurricanes in the Atlantic Ocean, Caribbean Sea, Gulf of Mexico, and the Pacific Ocean east of the International Date Line. Since the 1970s, the National Hurricane Center has classified hurricanes on the Saffir/Simpson Hurricane Damage Potential Scale (see Exhibit II-13-I) to give public safety officials an assessment of potential wind velocity, potential damage, and potential storm surge height for the hurricane in progress. The National Weather Service, in conjunction with the National Hurricane Center, makes periodic reports over the radio and television stations on storm activity during the hurricane season, from June 1 through November 30. Exhibit II-13-J shows the frequency of hurricanes by month. By listening to the bulletins issued by the National Weather Service concerning tropical storms or hurricanes, employees can be alerted in time to respond in a timely and efficient manner to protect their lives and the company's property.

Typical Damage

Hurricanes destroy property and kill people and in four principal ways: heavy rains, winds, the tornadoes they sometimes spawn, and storm surges. A typical hurricane brings six to 12 inches of rainfall in a short period of time, which causes floods throughout the area. Winds above 75 miles an hour will damage many buildings, stripping them of their roofs and shattering windows. Because hurricanes spawn tornadoes, there is related damage from these as well. Finally, the storm surge is the most lethal, damaging element of a hurricane.

The heavy rainfall that accompanies a hurricane can cause severe flooding. Data centers can be affected when the flood waters inundate basement levels of office buildings where the power and generator systems are located. Without the necessary electricity, heating, or cooling equipment, and water supply, a data center will cease to function properly. Another side effect of heavy rainfall is the collapse of roofs or that weakened roofs will collapse with the combined weight of both water and air-conditioners on them. This occurred during Hurricane Hugo in 1989 to a manufacturing company in Charleston, SC, where the heavy rain and high winds caused the ceiling to collapse onto the CPU along with the ultimate flooding of the data center with all of its equipment and records.

EXHIBIT II–13–I HURRICANE DAMAGE POTENTIAL SCALE SAFFIR/SIMPSON SCALE

This scale is used by the National Hurricane Center to give public safety officials an assessment of potential wind velocity, potential damage, and potential storm surge height for the hurricane in progress.

Category	Wind Speed	Storm Surge	Damage
1	74–95 mph	4–5 feet	Minimal damage. Primarily to shrubbery, trees, foliage, and unanchored mobile homes. Low lying coastal roads inundated, and minor damage to piers and small craft in exposed anchorage.
2	96–110 mph	6–8 feet	Moderate damage. Trees blown down, major damage to mobile homes and signs. Damage to piers and small craft; marinas flooded. Evacuation of some shoreline residences and low-lying island areas required.
3	111–130 mph	9–12 feet	Extensive damage. Large trees blown down and mobile homes destroyed. Some structural damage to small buildings. Serious flooding to coast. Small buildings destroyed, large buildings damaged by waves and floating debris. Evacuation within several blocks of shoreline required.
4	131–155 mph	13–18 feet	Extensive damage. Destruction of roofs, windows and doors, complete failure of roofs on small residences. Complete destruction of mobile homes. Major damage to lower floors of structures near the shoreline due to flooding. Evacuation within 500 feet of shoreline required. Evacuation of single-story residences on low ground within 2 miles of shore.
5	156 mph and up	18+ feet	Catastrophic damage. Small buildings overturned or blown away and extensive damage to roofs, windows and doors. Complete failure of roofs on industrial buildings and some complete building failures. Extensive shattering of glass. Complete destruction of mobile homes. Major damage to lower floors of all structures less than 15 feet above sea level within 500 yards of the shoreline. Massive evacuation of residential areas on low ground within 5–10 miles of shoreline possibly required. Escape routes cut off 3–5 hours before the hurricane center arrives.

EXHIBIT II-13-J THE HURRICANE SEASON

The total number of tropical storms and hurricanes in the Atlantic Ocean, Caribbean Sea, and Gulf of Mexico by month from 1886 through 1993.

Month Formed	Tropical Storms	Hurricanes
January through April	4	1
May	14	3
June	57	23
July	68	35
August	221	152
September	311	196
October	188	96
November	42	22
December	6	3

The gusting winds of a hurricane may cause tall structures to oscillate until the structure fails. Although hurricane winds are not as strong as those in a large tornado, a hurricane more than makes up for this factor with its size and duration. A mile-wide tornado is huge, but a 100-mile-wide hurricane is small. Few tornadoes last an hour, but hurricanes can last a week or more. Even the biggest tornado will devastate only part of an area or community, but a large hurricane can devastate entire communities, as was the case in Hurricane Andrew in August 1992. In tornado-hit communities those, who are not affected by the tornado, can rally to help the tornado victims. However, when an entire community is affected, the victims must depend on the help and services from other parts of their state or the country. Although wind is the least destructive of the hurricane's elements, wind-driven barrages of debris can be dangerous. Pieces of roofs, parts of houses, trees, outdoor structures and furniture, and even trash containers can hurdle through the air like projectiles damaging anything in their path. Electricity and communication lines can be easily affected, which in turn affect the voice and data communications in a data center. Here are three examples:

- Following Hurricane Iniki in 1992, the entire power system had to be rebuilt on the Island of Kauai.
- During Hurricane Hugo in 1989, wind and debris shattered windows in high-rise office buildings in Charlotte, SC. Computers were damaged, and company records were damaged, destroyed, or missing.
- During Hurricane Andrew in 1992, a food services company's headquarters building, and its information services data center in Miami was damaged so severely by the hurricane's winds that it was unable to provide services for a number of days. Voice and data lines were either out completely or unreliable for days. The electricity to the building was also either out completely or unreliable for weeks. In addition, the homes of many of the company's employees were destroyed or severely damaged.

A storm surge occurs when the high winds combine with low pressure in the eye of a hurricane to suck up the sea; the effect is a wall of water that strikes the land as the hurricane makes landfall. These walls of water have been known to exceed 50 feet. A storm surge lessens as the hurricane smashes its way inland. The mean water level may increase by 15 feet or more, which is important because much of the Atlantic and Gulf Coast lies at less than 10 feet above mean sea level. Water weighs 1700 lbs./cubic yd. Any extended pounding by giant waves can demolish any structure not specifically designed to withstand such forces. Hurricane waves can erode 30–50 feet of beach within an hour, or wash away 15 feet high and 100 feet wide dunes in six hours. One half day of battering by hurricane waves is the equivalent of a century's normal wave action. It accounts for over 90% of hurricane destruction and deaths.

Tropical storms, the weaker sisters of hurricanes, although not usually as destructive as hurricanes, can sometimes create the same type of destruction as a hurricane. For example, Tropical Storm Alberto's flood waters (August 1994) destroyed hundreds of bridges and roads in Georgia and Florida. Businesses were damaged or destroyed by the extremely high flood waters, and several water treatment plants were damaged.

Hurricane Emergency Response Actions

Although hurricanes are dangerous and destructive, they are relatively slow forming, slow moving, and fairly predictable as to when and where they will strike land. Because of these characteristics of hurricanes, companies have time to prepare and respond to them. The Life Safety/Emergency Response Plan should clarify for employees what the company wants them to do before, during, and immediately after a hurricane strikes the area.

When an area is covered by a Hurricane Watch, employees should continue normal activities, but they should stay tuned to radio or television for any further National Weather Service advisories. The company should have a National Weather Service radio in their Emergency Operations Center, which they can use to monitor all advisories. They should make all employees aware of any changes to the situation.

When the National Weather Service issues a hurricane watch advisory, company personnel should ensure that emergency supplies that may be needed are on-hand:

- Rolls of water resistant sheeting.
- Rolls of nylon tape.
- Rolls of masking tape.
- Flashlights and extra batteries and bulbs.
- Signs indicating the office may be closed temporarily, but will open as soon as conditions permit.

When a Hurricane Warning is placed (approximately 12 to 24 hours before the actual storm is expected to make landfall), the company should:

- Decide on which locations will close during the storm.
- Designate the location of the emergency headquarters, set it up before the storm hits, and have the emergency response committee meet there after the storm.
- Ensure that the company's assets are secure.
- Notify any tenants in the building that upon notification of a hurricane warning advisory, the company will be closing the building. In that case, their employees will be required to leave.
- Be prepared to have personnel leave the building if the company does not own the building, and if the owner feels that it is a safety problem for them to stay.
- Make arrangements for:
  - —Sump pumps.
  - —Wet vacs.
  - —Dehumidification units.
  - —Blankets and pillows.
  - —Bottled drinking water.

—Cooler.
—Hot water dispensers.
—Battery operated radios and flashlights with extra batteries and flashlight bulbs.
—Emergency generators and extra fuel for at least three days.
—Disinfectants and first aid equipment.
—Soap, paper towels, and toilet paper.
—Portable toilets if possible.

- Excuse personnel as soon as reasonably possible, advising them to listen to the designated radio or TV stations for instructions regarding their return to work. The public announcement messages should either be prepared or be reviewed before sending them to the appropriate radio or television stations.

Company personnel should also ensure that these actions are completed:

- All emergency generating equipment should be test started.
- All company vehicles should have full gas tanks. Gasoline stations are often shut down after the hurricane is over, because the stations have lost the electrical power needed to pump the gasoline. The gas tanks should be kept as full as possible until the threat is over.
- Upon instructions to close the building, all assets and vital records should be secured in appropriate files, safes, or vaults.
- Where possible, all electrical and electronic equipment should be unplugged and moved to a centralized location that affords the best protection against water damage. This will also protect the equipment against power surges.
- Electrical cords should be raised off the floor.
- Equipment should be covered with water resistant sheeting. Where possible all items should be moved away from windows to the most secure area.
- Before the last person leaves the building, he or she should ensure that:
  —No one is left in the building.
  —All electrical outlets have been turned off.
  —The building is secure.

There is a possibility that after a Hurricane Warning is placed, building services management may want to talk with their regular contractors to discuss the potential for what emergency supplies may be needed after the hurricane is over.

During the Hurricane. Employees should stay in a sheltered area, either at home, or in an evacuation center. Employees should listen to the radio or television for tornado warnings. Tornadoes spawned by hurricanes are among the storms' worst killers. A tornado watch means that tornadoes are expected to develop. A tornado warning means that a tornado has actually been sighted. When an area receives a tornado warning, employees should seek inside shelter immediately, preferably below ground.

After the Hurricane is Over. All employees should remain at home or in a shelter area until advised that it is safe to travel or be outdoors. Each employee should contact his or her department manager as soon as possible to report their availability based on damage sustained to his or her living quarters, personal property, or injuries to his or her family. If anyone has been injured, he or she should seek medical care at a hospital or Red Cross location. Employees should stay out of disaster areas, unless they are qualified to help. The employees presence might hamper first-aid and rescue work.

After the Hurricane is Over and it is Safe to Travel. All personnel that are members of the response team should assemble at the previously designated emergency headquarters. Members should drive carefully along the debris-filled streets when travelling to the emergency headquarters. Roads may be undermined and collapse under the weight of the car. Loose or downed wires should be avoided and reported to the power company as soon as possible. Any broken sewer or water mains should be reported to the water department as soon as possible. Emergency communications can be made by using the telephone, by using previously designated radio stations, or by mobile radio or by cellular telephone units. Those members of the response team responsible to make damage assessments, should return to the emergency headquarters to report their findings. The complete response team should then evaluate the reports of damage sustained and initiate pre-planned procedures.

To protect the assets of the company, employees may be required to perform emergency functions that are not in their documented job description. They may even be required to report to work at a different location than their normal work location because of the hurricane. If members of the response team are required to travel to another location by auto, remember that transportation can be a nightmare. For example, after Hurricane Andrew, street signs had been blown away by the hurricane's winds, and the only people that could find their way to alternate locations were those that were familiar with the area ahead of time.

It is important for companies to minimize the potential damage from a hurricane or to be able to resume operations quickly following a hurricane. In 1972, Hurricane Agnes killed 134 persons, destroyed 128,000 homes and businesses, and caused more than $60 billion worth of damage. One unexpected casualty of Agnes was the Erie-Lackawanna Railroad. Already in deep financial trouble, the Lackawanna filed for bankruptcy on June 26, 1972, citing the damage caused by the storm as one of the main factors prompting this move.

If the IS department has to operate in an off-line mode until data lines can be restored, pre-planned operating procedures should be used by the business units. For example, banks have pre-planned limits for cash withdrawals and certain check cashing limitations at the branches. If critical paper documents or records have been subjected to flooding, arrange for refrigeration units, or freeze-drying chambers. Exhibit II-13-K lists a number of companies that can provide these services.

Employees should be instructed to incorporate in their family emergency response plans many of their employers' hurricane response suggestions. A sample family hurricane response plan is presented in Exhibit II-13-L.

TORNADOES

A tornado is defined as a violently rotating column of air in contact with the ground. When a tornado touches the ground, there is usually a swirl of dust and debris even when the visible cloud portion fails to reach all the way to the ground. When the column of air is aloft, the visible portion is called a funnel cloud. A funnel cloud that is in contact with water, rather than land, is called a waterspout.

Tornadoes occur worldwide. They are common in Europe, and even more so in the British Isles, but rarely in Africa and India. However, the United States holds the world record for tornadoes. Approximately 1% of all thunderstorms in the US produce a tornado. Annually, there are between 700 and 1200 tornadoes, and those numbers are rising. About one-third of US tornadoes occur only in three states: Texas, Oklahoma, and Kansas. The warm, moist air of the Gulf of Mexico flows north and meets the cool, dry air from Canada that flows down along the eastern Rockies. This

EXHIBIT II–13–K RESTORATION OF PAPER DOCUMENTS OR RECORDS

Advanced Restoration
Specialists, Inc.
16324 South Main Street
Gardenia, CA 90248
(310) 329-2755
FAX (310) 769-6633

BMS Catastrophe (BMS CAT)
303 Arthur St.
Ft. Worth, TX 76107
(800) 433-2940
FAX (817) 332-6728

CATCO—Catastrophe Cleaning and
Restoration Co.
3318 Choteau St.
St. Louis, MO 63103
(314) 772-9010
FAX (314) 772-3348

Disaster Recovery Services Inc.
414 Blue Smoke Court W.
Ft. Worth, TX 76105
(800) 856-3333
FAX (817) 536-1167

Moisture Removal Technologies
54 Eleventh St.
Atlanta, GA 30309
(404) 892-8455

The Restoration Company
3120 Medlock Bridge Rd., Bldg. J
Norcross, GA 30071
(404) 448-7250
FAX (404) 448-6196

Servpro of Western Lake County, OH
811 Lafayette Rd.
Medina, OH 44256
(216) 975-9585
(800) 933-7179

turbulent region, which is 460 miles in length and 400 miles in width, is known as Tornado Alley. In 1991, of the 1125 tornadoes in the US, 378 hit this area of the midwest. Texas records a greater number of tornadoes each year than any other state.

Tornadoes vary greatly in size, intensity, and appearance. As seen in Exhibit II-13-M, the intensity or severity of tornadoes is charted on the Fujita-Pearson or "F" scale. Tornadoes can produce winds greater than 200 miles per hour. Scientists are still trying to determine just how fast the winds in a tornado can blow. They are sure that 200 mile per hour winds occur, and there is a chance that higher speeds are possible. The strongest tornadoes can rip apart even well-built houses, but these tornadoes are rare. Weaker tornadoes, which are more common, are dangerous to mobile homes, cars, and people caught outside. Most of the tornadoes that occur each year fall into the weak category. Wind speeds are in the range of 100 miles per hour or less. About one out of every three tornadoes is classified as strong, with winds speeds that reach 200 miles per hour.

Eight General Characteristics of Tornadoes

Eight general characteristics of tornadoes are:

1. *Time of day*. Mid-afternoon, generally between 3:00 and 7:00 PM, is the most likely time, but they have occurred at all times of the day.
2. *Direction of movement*. It usually moves from southwest to northeast. Their direction of travel can be erratic and change suddenly. Tornadoes that occur with hurricanes can move from an easterly direction.
3. *Length of path*. The path is approximately four miles long, but can be 300 miles. On May 26, 1917, a tornado traveled 293 miles across Illinois and Indiana.
4. *Width of path*. They are approximately 300 to 400 yards in width, but some have been a mile or more in width.

EXHIBIT II–13–L PERSONAL FAMILY HURRICANE RESPONSE PLAN

Plan before the storm arrives:

- Leave low lying or coastal areas, as well as mobile homes, for more substantial shelter and relocate outside of the threatened area. The storm surge, the most dangerous part of the hurricane, is a dome of water that comes across the coast as the hurricane makes landfall. Tides are five to 25 feet above normal, and superimposed on these high tides are large wind-driven waves. Nine out of ten deaths caused by hurricanes occur in the surge.
- If the dwelling is sturdy and on high ground and staying is an option, then;
  - —Board up the windows, or protect with storm shutters, boards or tape.
  - —Secure outside objects or store them inside: trash cans, furniture, signs, garden tools, and toys.
  - —Store drinking water (enough to last for a couple days): jugs, bottles, cooking utensils, and bathtub.
  - —Fill up the car's gas tank.
  - —Bring pets indoors.

Listen carefully to local officials before the storm hits and evacuate the area if told to do so.

During the hurricane:

- Stay indoors.
- Stay away from the windows on the downwind side of the house.
- Beware of the eye of the hurricane. This calm storm center can be deceptive by its clear sky and light winds. The hurricane's eye is bordered by winds and rains of maximum force that blow from the opposite direction to the winds and rains in the beginning half of the storm.

Suggested supplies to keep on-hand:

- Boards or tape for windows.
- Battery operated radio (and clock) and extra batteries.
- Flashlight, extra batteries, and extra flashlight bulbs.
- Emergency cooking facilities, propane or butane stove, and fuel.
- Nonperishable canned foods and milk and hand can opener.
- Bottled drinking water.
- Bleach.
- Cooler.
- Lantern and propane or butane.
- Fuel.
- Candles, matches, and lighter.
- First-aid kit with family prescriptions and extra medicine.
- Insect repellant.
- Snake bite kit.
- Toiletries.
- Fire extinguisher.
- Warm clothing.
- Blankets.
- Tool box.
- Plastic garbage bags.
- Toilet paper.
- Important family documents.

Check to be certain that all emergency equipment is in good working order and that supplies are adequate to last several days if necessary.

If expected to evacuate, make contingency plans in advance, where to stay, and how to get there.

EXHIBIT II–13–M TORNADO INTENSITY FUJITA-PEARSON SCALE

The severity of tornadoes is charted on the Fujita-Pearson or "F" scale.

Rating	Wind Speed	Damage
F-0	Up to 72 mph	Broken tree branches.
F-1	73–112 mph	Moving cars pushed off the road and mobile homes overturned.
F-2	113–157 mph	Mobile homes demolished and roofs torn off frame houses.
F-3	158–206 mph	Cars lifted off ground and trains overturned.
F-4	207–260 mph	Houses demolished and cars tossed and destroyed.
F-5	261–318 mph	Cars and houses carried hundreds of feet.

5. *Speed of travel.* It travels approximately 25 to 40 miles per hour, but some have ranged from stationary to 68 miles per hour.
6. *Type of cloud.* The cloud of a tornado is a dark, heavy cumulonimbus (i.e., thunderstorm cloud). The air column or funnel extends from this cloud.
7. *Type of precipitation.* Rain, often with hail, usually precedes the tornado. A heavy downpour usually occurs immediately to the left of the tornado's path.
8. *Type of sound.* The sound of a tornado has been described as a roaring noise, similar to a train speeding through a tunnel or the engines of many planes.

Other Characteristics of Tornadoes

Tornadoes are extremely complex. Often they have more than one vortex and, at times, these mini-vortices turn in the opposite direction of the main vortex. A vortex can be defined as a whirlpool drawing into its center all that surrounds it. A tornado's direction of movement can change quite suddenly, and its exact path can not be predicted. Tornado damage can be devastating in one street, and absolutely nothing on an adjacent street. The most promising technology for tornado detection is Doppler radar. During the 1990s, a Doppler radar network is to be installed across the US as part of a series of experiments and studies to observe storm systems across the nation.

Tornadoes can be spawned by tropical storms and hurricanes, such as Hurricanes Camille (1969), Allen (1980), and Gilbert (1988). The tornadoes that are spawned by hurricanes usually are small and short-lived and do not pose as great a danger as those occurring following heavy rain or thunderstorms. The hurricane-type tornado has a thin, rope shape, and the rain or thunderstorm-type tornado has a funnel shape. The main differences between the hurricane type and the tornadoes formed after rain or thunderstorms are their diameter, wind speed, and pressure. A rope tornado has very little pressure drop in the vortex, and in a funnel type tornado there is a tremendous pressure drop that acts as a vacuum.

Typical Damage

Tornado winds can cause extraordinary destruction. These incredible winds have also caused numerous roofs to collapse and even entire buildings to collapse. Powerful winds have been known to rip building's HVAC systems off their stands on roofs and send them hurtling through space as units of destruction toward other buildings.

Some examples of tornado damage are:

- On April 26, 1991 the worst tornado disaster of that year started southeast of

Clearwater, Kansas and traveled 69 miles to Andover, Kansas, where it destroyed 84 houses and 14 businesses.

- Physicians Hospital in Wylie, Texas, closed after extensive damage to the building in May of 1993 following a tornado.
- The Enron Corporation Office Tower in Houston, Texas, experienced smashed tower windows, office damage, and injured employees following a tornado in November 1993.
- The Dow Chemical plant in Midland, Michigan in June 1994 had a significant leak caused in the building due to lightning from the rainstorm associated with a tornado.

Tornado Emergency Response Actions

The National Weather Service provides the first line of defense against the tornado through its tornado and severe thunderstorm watches and warnings. A tornado watch means tornadoes are expected to develop. A tornado warning means a tornado has actually been sighted or indicated by weather radar. These watches and warnings give people and businesses the time needed to respond properly when a tornado approaches their area. The emergency response plan should clarify for employees, what the company wants them to do during and immediately after a tornado strikes the area.

After a tornado watch has been issued, employees should keep a battery operated radio or television nearby and listen for weather advisories. A tornado watch means tornadoes are expected to develop.

After a tornado warning has been issued, employees should seek shelter inside and stay away from the windows. A tornado warning means a tornado has actually been sighted or indicated by weather radar.

Employees should have the following responses given a particular circumstance:

- If the approaching tornado is heard or seen, employees should go to the basement and curl up so that their heads and eyes are protected.
- If a tornado has been sighted and employees are in a high-rise office building, they should go to the lower floors or basement; or take shelter in interior rooms, such as, closets, utility rooms, rest rooms, or interior corridors. Once there, employees should protect their heads from flying and falling debris.
- If a tornado is sighted and employees are in a factory, they should move to areas of the plant that are below ground level. If there is no below ground level, employees should take shelter in interior corridors or in small interior rooms, such as rest rooms, closets and storage rooms, on the east or north side of the building. Employees should avoid the southwest corner of the plant, as well as large rooms or work areas with long freespan roofs, and they should stay away from all windows.
- If a tornado is sighted and an employee is in a moving car, he or she should stop as quickly as safety permits. He or she should leave the car and take shelter in a building or in a storm cellar if one is available. Employees should stay away from areas where there is a large amount of glass. If no building is available, he or she should take shelter in a ditch or ravine upwind from his or her car, or, if an overpass or concrete viaduct is available, he or she should take shelter behind it. It is very dangerous to attempt to flee to safety in an automobile. Over half of the deaths in the Wichita Falls, Texas tornado in 1979 were attributed to people trying to escape in motor vehicles.

EXHIBIT II–13–N PERSONAL FAMILY TORNADO RESPONSE PLAN

If at home:

- Take shelter in the basement. Move under sturdy items in the basement, such as concrete laundry tubs, heavy duty work benches or tables, pool tables, or a staircase.
- If there is no basement, take cover either under heavily stuffed furniture in the center of the house, in a bathroom, or in an interior closet.
- Avoid bathrooms with an outside wall on the south or west side of the home. Do not get locked in a closet because there is no inside latch or door handle.

Many people used to suggest that some windows should be opened on at least two sides of the house, preferably those on the east and west side. Now, experts are saying that the tornadoes atmospheric pressure drop plays, at most, a minor role in the damage process. Most structures have sufficient venting to allow for the sudden drop in atmospheric pressure. Opening a window to minimize damage by allowing inside and outside atmospheric pressure to equalize is not recommended. If the tornado gets close enough to a structure for the pressure drop to be experienced, the strong tornado winds probably already will have caused most of the significant damage.

Although most tornado damage is caused by violent winds, most tornado injuries and deaths are caused by flying debris. Small rooms, such as closets or bathrooms, in the center of the home offer the greatest protection from flying objects. Such rooms are less likely to experience roof collapse. Always stay away from windows or exterior doors.

Suggested supplies to keep on-hand:

- Battery operated radio and extra batteries.
- Flashlight, extra batteries, and extra flashlight bulbs.
- Emergency cooking facilities.
- Lantern.
- Fuel.
- Candles.
- Matches.
- First Aid kit.
- Canned foods and milk.
- Bleach.
- Extra medicine.
- Toiletries.
- Boards or tape for windows.
- Fire extinguisher.

Employees should be instructed to incorporate in their family emergency response plans many of their employers' tornado response suggestions. A sample family tornado response plan is presented in Exhibit II-13-N.

FLOODS

A flood is any overflow from a body of water that spreads out over adjacent land areas, usually resulting in the harmful inundation of property and lands used by man and often with the loss of life. Flooding occurs because the soil, vegetation, or atmosphere is unable to absorb excess water. Flooding often accompanies and contributes to the destructiveness of earthquakes, volcanic eruptions, hurricanes, and storms. However, floods, particularly those of the world's large rivers, can by themselves be dangerous. Few regions of the earth are secure from floods, except for the Gobi Desert, the central Sahara, and the Atacoma Desert of northern Chile.

By studying the patterns of rivers over centuries, certain general statements can be made. A river overflows its banks and floods nearby low places once every two years on the average. About once every five to 10 years a truly large flood occurs, causing significant damage and possible loss of life. Even greater floods can be expected once every 25 to 50 years. Moreover, once a century, a truly spectacular flood of catastrophic proportions can be expected.

Floods are difficult to classify. Any attempt to classify floods by the amount of the water involved would rank relatively minor Mississippi River floods above important floods on smaller rivers. Estimates of the economic losses are unreliable, especially those of many years ago. However, floods can be classified as either accidental or recurrent. Both are considered natural phenomena. Recurrent floods are those that are a yearly occurrence, regardless of any other conditions. The Mississippi River in the United States, the Nile River in Egypt, and the Yellow River in China are examples of rivers that have recurrent flooding. The accidental flood is considered a natural disaster when it is caused by such phenomena as landslides or excessive rainfall. These floods occur unpredictably and abruptly after intense rain that lasts anywhere from one-half hour to several days. Sometimes called flash floods, they are a natural phenomena that occur all over the world. It was the excessive rainfall that caused the severe flooding in the midwest in June and July of 1993.

Typical Damage

Flood damage can be both destructive and varied. The overloading pressure and abrasive action of floods washes away parts of buildings. The rushing water creates transportation havoc by flooding roads and destroying bridges; creates problems with communications by knocking down telephone poles and damaging telephone lines; and contaminates water and food supplies.

Some examples of typical flood damage during the Great Flood in 1993 are:

- The Midwest authorities had to cut power and phone service to many companies because of the high flood waters. This circumstance resulted in many companies' data centers having to move to their computer backup sites to continue to provide computer processing and access to vital information. Some examples of data centers that had to move to their backup sites included a chemical company in St. Louis, a manufacturing company in Des Moines, and a major bank in Des Moines.
- There was a danger of electrocution and of dams collapsing. Bridges and roads were flooded out. Because the water treatment plants were damaged, there was the danger of bacteria invading the water supply. It was recommended that all contaminated wells be professionally cleaned, and that any food that could have been tainted by the floodwaters or by lost electricity be thrown away.
- In Des Moines, 250,000 people went without tap water for 12 days. The entire public water system of Des Moines was shut down. After the water was returned to service, residents could use it for bathing and flushing toilets, but not for drinking for two more days.
- Drinking water was not the only problem for businesses. Sprinkler systems were inoperative, creating a fire hazard in the commercial buildings serviced by the water treatment plants. The buildings were required to shut down operations until they could eliminate the fire hazard.

Numerous companies were also affected by the flooding in the Chicago Loop area in May 1992. River water poured through an aging tunnel system beneath a 12-square block area of Chicago's Loop, paralyzing the downtown area. Power was cut off to the area after as much as 30 feet of water flowed into the high-rise office building's basements. According to the *Chicago Resource Magazine,* 229 buildings were affected by the flood. An estimated 7,500 business tenants in those 229 buildings were out of business temporarily. The flood caused numerous company's data centers to move their processing to their computer backup sites. The flood produced a power glitch in one of the law firms located in one of the buildings affected and a few seconds of fluctuating electricity corrupted key data on a data base that took more than 400 work hours to restore.

During a severe storm in New Jersey in October 1991, the flooding knocked out the transformer carrying electricity from two power grids to a vendor's backup site data center. One building used a generator for power; the second had electronic vaulting service knocked out for 24 hours.

Flood Emergency Response Actions

The emergency response plan should clarify for employees, what the company wants them to do during and immediately after a flood strikes the area.

If a flood threatens a company's location, company personnel should:

- Assist in moving company assets onto the top of desks, tables and file cabinets.
- Assist in moving equipment from the lower floors to either the upper floors or out of the building.
- Keep their automobile's gas tank filled (if electric power is cut off, gas stations may not be able to operate pumps).
- Listen to their radio or TV station for information.

Company personnel must be moved to safety. To do this, employees must act with time to spare, and they should know the best evacuation routes. The loss of life from flooding can be substantially reduced by basic precautionary measures. Whenever there is any danger of flooding, low-lying areas should be evacuated. Those who must remain in a flood-prone area should have bottled water, canned food, and other necessary supplies.

During the Flood. Company personnel must be aware of one flood-related hazard; that is, electrocution from current traveling through water. This will happen if water has come into contact with electric appliances or with a power source. This hazard can be eliminated in buildings by turning off the electricity at its main source before flooding occurs. People should not enter a flooded basement or structure of any type in which water is in contact with a source of electricity.

After a Flood has Taken Place. Company personnel should:

- Not visit the disaster area. Local authorities will be attempting to limit access to only emergency and rescue personnel.
- Not handle live electrical equipment in wet areas. It should be dried and checked before use.
- Exercise caution in using lanterns, torches, or matches to examine buildings, because flammables may be inside.
- Report all broken utility lines that they discover to appropriate authorities.
- Test drinking water for potability. Wells should be pumped out before using.
- When eating food, they should not use fresh food that has come in contact with flood waters.

When Employees are Travelling to Perform Response Actions. Employees should not attempt to drive over a flooded road or attempt to walk through a rapidly flowing stream, especially when the water is above their knees. As waters rise, the velocity of the water increases. Although the water in a stream may have a velocity of one mile per hour normally, during a flood, this can increase to 10 miles per hour. In rivers with a normal velocity of six to seven miles per hour, flooding has produced a velocity of 20 miles per hour. This increased velocity can carry a car or truck downstream, resulting in the deaths of the occupants. According to a recent statistic in the *US News and World Report,* about 165 people are swept away in flash floods following storms each year.

When Employees are Performing Response Actions. Employees should proceed immediately to check the sub-floor for water accumulation. They should:

- Have the building engineer disconnect or cut all power to the area.
- Ensure that water is not affecting any of the wiring in the sub-flooring.
- Have the building engineer cut power to any electrical equipment within the area where water is accumulating.
- Protect all electronic equipment with plastic material. The plastic should be placed in a way to ensure that water does not run or drip onto or into the equipment. They should also ensure that air will be able to circulate around the equipment.
- Request the building engineer to pump all of the water out of the building.

When Employees are Performing Response Actions. If employees find that the source of the water is not controllable, they should:

- Instruct all personnel to put their documents and working materials in plastic bags and secure them with a twister.
- Ensure that each bag is identified with the company's name and address, department name, and the type materials that are in the bag.
- Store the bags in highest area of the building.
- Cover all electronic equipment with plastic material and ensure that the material is secured so they do not float or blow away.

Other Less-Common Examples of Flood Dangers. These include snakes in the water and open manholes in the streets. Several examples are:

- Police warned of poisonous water moccasins swimming in the flood waters on April 14, 1980 in the floods in New Orleans, Louisiana.
- Officials said highly venomous cottonmouth snakes, which normally live in riverside brush, were being flushed into flood waters along the Pearl River during the May 25, 1983 floods in Jackson, Mississippi.
- Officials warned that the force of the flood waters in Great Bend, Kansas on June 17, 1981 had blown off manhole covers, providing potential death traps to waders.

Supplies to Keep On-hand for Floods. All employees should be instructed to gather these supplies:

- First aid supplies.
- Food that requires no refrigeration and little cooking.
- Drinking water.
- Portable radio.
- Emergency cooking equipment.
- Emergency lights and flashlights.

EXHIBIT II–13–O PERSONAL FAMILY FLOOD RESPONSE PLAN

Prepare before floods arrive:

- Keep your car's gas tank filled. Floods can cut off electrical power, making gas pumps inoperable for days.
- Store drinking water. Often regular water service is cut or water reservoirs and treatment plants become contaminated during floods.
- Stock up on food that needs little cooking and no refrigeration.
- Keep first aid supplies and any necessary medications on hand.
- Keep weather radio, a battery-powered portable radio or television, emergency cooking equipment, and flashlights in working order.
- When evacuation orders are given by local authorities, all persons should evacuate. Staying behind to try to save a home, business, or car can be deadly.
- When driving a car, do not drive into water covering a road, especially if the water is moving. The water can hide a washed-out roadway and only a little water is needed to wash a car away.
- If driving through flood water and the car stalls, leave it immediately and wade to safety. The water could rise rapidly and wash the vehicle away. Escaping from a worse danger is the only reason to wade in flood water.

- Spare batteries and bulbs.
- Sandbags.
- Plastic sheeting.

Employees should be instructed to incorporate in their family emergency response plans many of their employers' flooding response suggestions. A sample family flood plan is presented in Exhibit II-13-O. Exhibit II-13-P shows how employees can evaluate and correct damage to their homes after a flood.

BLIZZARDS AND WINTER STORMS

During the winters from 1993 to 1996, the East Coast experienced a series of blizzards and ice storms that have also wrecked havoc on companies that are located in that area.

A blizzard can be defined as a snowstorm that is accompanied by three hours of sustained 35 mile-per-hour winds and quarter-mile visibility. Precipitation that falls through the air in liquid form and freezes on coming in contact with the ground is known as freezing rain and occurs during the winter months when temperatures are below freezing. This differs from snow in that snow is precipitation that falls through the air in crystal form. Examples of damage from blizzards and winter storms are:

- In March 1993, Electronic Data Systems Corporation in New Jersey had its roof collapse as a result of a blizzard and the weight of the snow on the roof. There was no service to ATMs for several days.
- During that same storm, Leggett's Department Store in Maryland experienced a roof collapse.
- The winter of 1993–94 produced a number of winter storms. Severe ice and water damage caused major roof damage to businesses in the Middle Atlantic states. Snow backed up in the eves and rain gutters, which eventually formed ice. As warmer rains and thawing came, water flowed down the inside of walls and resulted in flooding that caused high moisture levels in various buildings. At the Morris Township Public Library in New Jersey, this unusual occurrence threatened a mold and mildew attack on rare books and historic documents.

EXHIBIT II–13–P EVALUATING DAMAGE AFTER A FLOOD

Problem	Effect	Type of Cleanup
Wiring, appliances	Wiring, electrical panel often corrode.	Furnace, water heater, air conditioning, other appliances must be cleaned and checked. Some may have to be replaced.
Furnishings	Carpeting, upholstered furniture, other belongings become mildewy and ruined.	Must be ripped out and sent to the dump. If salvageable, disinfectants can be applied to stop bacteria, mold, and mildew.
Insulation	Wet insulation in walls.	Needs to be replaced. Plastic foam insulation can be washed off.
Interior walls	Drywall soaks up water like a sponge and dries to a crumbly texture	Needs to be removed and replaced.
Exterior walls	Water pressure can crack and buckle walls.	Needs to be dried and exterior material replaced.
Supports and joists	Water can buckle floors and weaken support beams, wall studs, and floor joists.	Support beams, wall studs and floor joists tested should be replaced if weakened.
Basement leaks	Water seeps through cracks, weakens walls, and fills basements.	Remove standing water with pumps; giant dehumidifiers can remove water; huge fans can help dry out walls, floors, and even furniture.

Generally, getting the house dry is the first order of business. Salvageable walls, floors, and cupboards can be cleaned with a detergent or disinfectant mix. Deodorant can be applied to mask flood odors.

This flow of water and moisture could certainly cause similar problems in a company's data center.

- The extraordinary Blizzard of 1996 caused numerous roofs to collapse with the weight of the huge amount of snow and then flooding when the thaw and rain arrived. The normal roof is not constructed to work under the weight of heavy snow and a repeated pattern of freezing and thawing. Roofs were lost at AFL Printing Co. in New Jersey, a Borders Bookstore in Delaware, and the Potomac Mills Mall in Maryland.

The emergency response actions for these unusual natural disasters are similar to those that have already been suggested in the previous section on floods.

CONCLUSION

The Life Safety/Emergency Response Plan (LS/ERP) is part of the Response Section of the Business Continuity Plan. The LS/ERP identifies those actions that the company expects its employees to take to protect their health and safety, as well as to protect the assets of the company when a disaster occurs. The LS/ERP actions should be developed by the manager in Information Systems responsible to ensure that IS personnel know what to do before, during, and immediately after a natural disaster, such as an earthquake, a hurricane, a tornado, a flood, or blizzard. The LS/ERP is written for the specific type of disaster, because each type of disaster dictates the type of response actions to be used by the employees. The LS/ERPs contain some separate actions for each specific type of disaster.

Most companies already have an LS/ERP, but simply having an ERP is not enough. If companies are serious about their emergency response plans, they must:

- Ensure that the emergency response section of the business continuity plan is documented.
- Ensure that all employees have read those portions of the ERP that explain what the company expects them to do before, during, and after an emergency.
- Verify that this is being accomplished by having all employees sign-off as having read their applicable section of the ERP.
- Ensure that all employees review the ERP actions annually to evaluate the effectiveness, validity, and completeness of those actions.
- Ensure that exercises are performed to train or re-train the employees.

Life Safety/Emergency Response Actions for Fires and Bombs

CHAPTER II-14

Most companies already have a Life Safety/Emergency Response Plan (LS/ERP) that documents the specific information that employees must know when a fire occurs in the building. This includes such information as:

- Who to notify if an employee discovers a fire.
- The proper use of fire extinguishers.
- When and how to evacuate the building.
- The proper use of elevators during a fire.
- Where to assemble following the evacuation.
- What is expected of employees following a fire.

Most companies already have an LS/ERP that documents the specific information employees must know when a bomb threat or bombing occurs in the building. This includes such information as:

- What actions the employee who receives the bomb threat should take.
- How to conduct a search for the bomb.
- If a bomb is found, what to do and what not to do.
- When and how to evacuate the building.
- Where to assemble following the evacuation.
- What is expected of employees following the threat.

During a disaster, a company's concern should be the health and safety of their employees, as well as the property and assets of the company. The safety of personnel should always be a company's first concern and more important than its property. The actions taken by employees at the time of a disaster, if they are the correct actions, can avoid injuries; and, in some cases, save their lives. If the actions taken by employees are incorrect, they can lead to injuries, and, in some cases, death. There have been many examples where employees have followed the procedures identified in the life safety section of their company's ERP and have successfully minimized or eliminated injuries. In 1992, there was an explosion and resulting fire on the first floor of a four-story office building. As the fire spread, workers on the upper floors followed the procedures identified in the life safety section of their company's ERP and used the stairwells properly to escape the flames and smoke and reach safety outside.

However, even in companies with a life safety section in their ERP, there have been some examples of employees either not knowing what to do or not following the instructions in the LS/ERP. For example, notifying the fire department on a timely basis when a fire is discovered is part of the LS/ERP actions that employees should know. The following two examples demonstrate the importance of the prompt notification of the fire department.

In 1988, a fire started in the generator room of a supermarket in Massachusetts. When employees tried to phone the fire department, the phones were inoperative.

Immediately one employee went to the nearby police station to notify the fire department. The sprinklers in the corridor outside the generator room fused and confined the fire until the firefighters arrived. The prompt notification and arrival of the firefighters shortly after the sprinklers activated lessened the damage to the store.

Fire erupted in a water heater on the 33rd floor of the Rainier Bank Tower in Washington in 1981. The fire itself did little damage and was quickly extinguished by the sprinkler system. However, because the fire department was not notified promptly by any of the employees, the sprinklers continued to drench the area and the floors below for an hour and 40 minutes. Employees were safe because the fire was out quickly. However, consider the water damage to the computers, their accompanying equipment and supplies, paper records, and the resulting costs involved in the cleanup.

Most company executives believe that their employees know what to do before, during, and immediately after a disaster, because the company has a documented Emergency Response Plan. However, simply having an ERP is not adequate. Companies must have their plans documented and continually updated. It is also extremely important for companies to allocate time to exercise and evaluate the effectiveness of the emergency response actions in the plan. In addition, companies should require all employees to read the emergency response actions and verify that they have read and understand the ERP procedures and policies. Time may be needed to train or re-train employees. By taking these actions, companies will ensure that their ERPs will be effective when they are needed. As a result, companies can more effectively protect their employees, their property, and their assets.

An example of an effective industry emergency response program, is in the chemical and oil industry. Most of the companies in this industry have developed company-wide emergency response programs. Because of the risks associated with their industry, these companies spend a great deal of time and put forth much effort to protect their employees, as well as their visitors. This author has participated in safety preparedness sessions at numerous companies in this industry, in which they identify exactly what employees are supposed to do in emergency situations. At the conclusion of the sessions, each employee signed a paper indicating that he or she went through the safety briefing and understood what to do.

If a company is serious about its emergency response plan, it should perform an unannounced exercise. However, it is the opinion of many people that it is more likely that an employee will be injured during an unannounced exercise than during an actual emergency evacuation. This author also believes that a large number of employees intentionally avoid taking part in evacuation exercises that have been pre-announced. They think that they will know how to evacuate when an actual disaster occurs. However, these employees are the same ones who are out-of-control during the emergency, because they have not participated in the controlled exercises.

Here is an example of such a situation occuring in a company in Milwaukee, Wisconsin. The fire alarms began activating in the middle of the morning. The evacuation procedure for the high-rise tower was for the employees to assemble at the stairwells, then to wait for word as to whether they would need to evacuate, and to be told which stairwell should not be used. In any case of fire, one stairwell is used by the fire department personnel, who would be coming up the stairwell with 65 to 100 pounds of gear. The firefighters would also have the door on the fire floor open, allowing smoke into the stairwell. As the employees waited at the doors to the stairwells, several employees began to get concerned. The public address system was not working. The floor wardens were using radios to communicate. There was definitely a fire of some sort in the lower areas of the building. It was not long until the concerned employees began to lose control, telling the floor warden that they were going to leave the building. They began to argue with the floor warden when he would not let them enter the stairwell to leave. Fortunately, the all clear was announced; there was no need to evacuate the building because the fire was declared under control. In reviewing the situation, the floor wardens reported that the individuals that began to panic missed all of the fire drill exercises in prior years because they were too busy to participate. These employees used to brag about the fact that they used to schedule themselves to be out of the building when the fire drill was to take place.

This chapter provides general information on fires and bombings and the typical damage that results from each. It also provides suggested actions for the Life Safety/Emergency Response Plan section of the Business Continuity Plan. These suggested actions are actions that employees should be prepared to take while they are working in the company's facility.

FIRES

Fire has several definitions. First, it is a chemical reaction, combining oxygen, fuel, and heat. Second, it is an oxidation reaction that emits heat and light. Third, it is called an exothermic reaction, because it creates a substance, char and ash, that contains less energy than the original burned combustible material. (An endothermic reaction creates a substance with more energy.) Fourth, fire can be called combustion, and it produces four deadly products—heat, flame, smoke, and gases—that kill and injure people.

There are generally four classifications of fires based on the type of combustible that the fire consumes:

- *Class A.* These fires are those involving ordinary, solid combustibles such as paper, wood, cloth, rubber, and plastics. This type of fire is best extinguished by a cooling agent such as water.
- *Class B.* These fires are those involving flammable liquids, such as gasoline, acetone, greases, oils, and flammable gases, such as methane or hydrogen. This type of fire is best extinguished by a surface-acting agent such as dry chemicals.
- *Class C.* These fires are those involving energized electrical equipment, appliances, and wiring. This type of fire is best extinguished by a nonconductive agent.
- *Class D.* These fires are those involving combustible metals, such as magnesium, lithium, and potassium.

Most fires are accidental, some are intentional and are usually referred to as incendiary or suspicious. An incendiary fire is one in which the physical evidence indicates that the fire was set deliberately. A suspicious fire is one in which circumstances indicate the possibility that the fire may have been set deliberately, such as when multiple ignitions are found, when there are suspicious circumstances, and no accidental or natural ignition factors can be found. A BLEVE (Boiling Liquid Expanding Vapor Explosions) is a fire in which boiling liquid generates an explosion.

Fire Safety Regulations

Companies can attain the best degree of fire safety for their employees, their property, and their assets by emphasizing fire prevention and detection. Fire safety regulations or fire prevention codes have been important in society and business for many years.

Today's codes require exit stairs to have heavy self-closing doors of metal. Fire retardant paints and fabrics have been developed to delay the spread of fires. Numerous types of fire detection devices are used in buildings today, such as smoke detectors and heat sensitive detectors. The development of many of today's fire safety regulations and fire prevention systems are a direct result of "lessons learned" from prior major fires.

These are some examples of major historical and present-day fires:

- It was the fire in the Triangle Shirtwaist Company in New York City in 1911 that marked the beginning of fire safety regulations in the workplace. One-hundred and forty-five workers died as a result of inadequate exits, locked doors, and doors that only opened inward. This tragedy not only resulted in New York fire safety laws, but those laws were the basis for fire protection laws in workplaces throughout the United States.
- The Coconut Grove fire in Boston on November 28, 1942 prompted major efforts in the field of fire prevention and control for nightclubs and other types of places of assembly.
- The Beverly Hills Supper Club fire in South Gate, Kentucky on May 28, 1977 spurred new demands for improved fire safety measures, including inspection improvements. Many of the patrons in the club at the time of the fire were from other jurisdictions that strongly enforced codes for public assembly occupancies. National political leaders raised the question of the propriety of citizens of one jurisdiction being exposed to fire danger when visiting an area where code enforcement is not as stringent.
- The Imperial Foods Processing Plant fire in Hamlet, North Carolina on September 3, 1991 caused the death of 25 workers and another 45 were injured. It is alleged that workers were unable to escape from the unsprinklered building due to locked fire doors and blocked exits. In addition, there were no adequate exits from the building and no emergency evacuation plan was in place. The plant did not have a safety inspection since it began operation 10 years ago. Following this tragedy, OSHA urged employers and employees throughout the country to conduct an immediate review of the adequacy of fire safety measures in their workplaces. State and local public authorities were urged to examine all aspects of their building and fire code enforcement process. Amendments were adopted by the North Carolina Building Code Council to the state's fire prevention code, which mandates all cities and counties to maintain a periodic inspection schedule to identify those activities and conditions that present a fire safety threat to employees.
- On May 8, 1988 a fire occurring at the Hinsdale switching station of Illinois Bell caused the melting and fusion of 118,000 long distance fiber-optic phone lines, 36,000 data lines were dead for more than two weeks, and local service over 35,000 voice lines was completely out. Normal service was not restored even three weeks later. This fire, which disrupted phone service to thousands of business and residential customers for weeks, prompted the state of Illinois to pass legislation that requires a state-approved emergency telephone service plan for telephone companies operating in the state. It also calls for the Illinois Commerce Commission, the State Fire Marshal, and the state's Emergency Services and Disaster Agency to coordinate efforts to establish the fire and alarm standards for the telephone companies. It mandates that telephone companies can be fined up to $10,000 for each violation of these future standards and up to $1,000 for each day that a violation continues. As a result, telephone companies

and users across the nation began to rethink the design of their emergency plans and network requirements.

Generally, the fire department enforces those fire safety regulations that relate to fire protection equipment, fire safety inspections, fire code enforcement, maintenance and use of buildings, and hazardous materials and machinery in buildings. The building department of a building enforces fire safety regulations in relation to the construction, location, and use of the building. It is recommended that fire departments and building departments work together concerning the fire safety regulations in the prevention effort. All of these recommendations should be part of the prevention section of a company's Business Continuity Plan. In fact, when fire departments and building departments enforce the fire safety regulations, it enables employees to carry out their LS actions promptly, effectively, and efficiently if a fire does erupt. These LS actions include maintaining a building's emergency systems, instituting an evacuation plan, and enforcing the guidelines contained in the Americans With Disabilities Act.

Building Emergency Systems. Companies that own buildings install emergency systems designed to protect the employees and the physical assets of the company. Examples of these emergency systems are:

- A backup electrical system.
- The backup emergency lights for stairwells to be used during an evacuation.
- Emergency lights throughout the building.

The emergency electrical system and backup electrical system provide emergency power to any area of the building that has lost commercial power. This is used to power the emergency elevators that allow firefighters faster access to the building's floors, or to provide power for the ventilating system so that it can be reversed to force most of the smoke out of the building. The emergency lights and backup lights have two major uses: during a temporary loss of power, not associated with a fire, they allow employees to see to continue their business operations, and during a loss of power associated with a fire, they allow employees in the building to see their way to the evacuation exits. The emergency lights in the stairwells assist employees to evacuate the building safely.

Smoke management can be accomplished through air-handling systems and smoke barriers that dispose of fire products and limit their spread. The design goals for such systems are to provide clear air in evacuation routes for occupants and to make it easier for firefighters to approach the blaze. For small fires, air-handling systems and smoke barriers together can remove smoke from the fire area by using negative air pressure, and preventing its spread by using positive air pressure in areas adjacent to the fire. However, a hostile fire burning freely will grow to the point at which the volume of smoke and gases produced and the rate of energy released will overwhelm the mechanical systems.

Companies that lease space in buildings must also be sure that emergency systems have been installed that will protect their employees and the physical assets of their company. Large companies that lease space in buildings usually have their building engineering management personnel review the building to ensure that it meets the safety and security policies of the company. If the building does not meet the company's policies, it has three choices: require the building's owners to install the missing emergency systems; install the emergency systems at their own expense; or not lease the space. Some small companies that lease space in buildings usually do not have building engineering management personnel as employees. They usually assume that the owner of the building has installed all of the emergency equipment that is available to protect their company's employees and assets. Other small companies do not give emergency response planning a thought, until after an emergency has occurred. At that point, they begin to realize that they have a responsibility for the safety of their employees, as well as their assets. Unfortunately, at that point, it is sometimes too late.

The Evacuation Plan. The evacuation plan is inherently tied in with the emergency systems. The emergency systems (i.e., alarms) announce the need to evacuate to all people in a building and how and where evacuations (i.e., through public address systems) will take place. This section of the LS/ERP should be distributed to all employees. An important question is: has this procedure been explained and distributed to all employees, including part-time employees, vendors, and contractors?

Most companies have developed and documented an evacuation plan as a section in the Life Safety/Emergency Response Plan, which explains to employees how they will be notified that an evacuation is necessary, how to evacuate the building (i.e., which stairwell to use), and where to assemble after exiting the building. If the building has elevators, the plan will stress that employees should not use the elevators for evacuation.

Part of the evacuation plan strategy is determined by the type of building and the use of the building. If the building is a high-rise office tower, the initial evacuation procedure for a fire is for the affected floor and the two nearest floors to evacuate first. Most high-rise buildings are constructed to minimize the spread of a fire to other floors quickly, so that the remainder of the employees are usually instructed to stay on their floors until notified otherwise. This provides for an orderly and controlled evacuation, which will minimize panic. If the building is a manufacturing facility, the decision to evacuate all employees quickly may be necessary. This decision will depend on the type of manufacturing the company does. For example, does it use flammable or combustible chemicals in the process? It is common to see the evacuation section of the emergency response plan for chemical plants to have one set of policies and procedures, and the evacuation section of the emergency response plan for the corporate headquarters building to have a different set of policies and procedures.

Because the executives of the company have approved large expenditures to install the emergency systems and a great deal of time to test or exercise the procedures in the ERP, they assume that they will work 100% of the time. Unfortunately, emergency systems only work 97.4% of the time. Mechanical systems are bound to fail. These failures of emergency systems have been the cause of employees not knowing what to do during the emergency. Two examples of emergency systems failing are:

Example One. When a fire occurred in a 38-story high-rise office building in Philadelphia in February 1991, many of the emergency systems failed. Specifically, the emergency electrical system, the backup emergency electrical system, the emergency lights, the backup emergency lights, the internal fire pumps and the water pressure failed.

The electrical system failure caused the emergency elevators to fail. Because the firefighters could not use the elevators to move their gear to the command center on the 20th floor, they had to climb the stairwells. After climbing 20 floors, with an estimated 65 to 100 pounds of gear on their back, they were in no condition to fight the fire until they took a short rest.

The electrical system failure caused the HVAC system to fail. If the electric system functioned properly, the HVAC system would have switched into reverse and removed most of the smoke from the building. It was a combination of the dense smoke and the lack of emergency lighting, that led to the loss of three firefighter's lives. The three firefighters ran out of air in their air packs while searching the building for people who may have been trapped on the upper floors. When they requested assistance from the command center, they mistakenly identified themselves as being on the 30th floor. Because of the dense smoke and the lack of adequate lighting, they could not tell that they were on the 28th floor. The firefighter's rescue team searched for them on the wrong floor. By the time the rescue team found the trapped firefighters, it was too late.

The failure of the internal fire pump system probably was the single most contributing factor that permitted the fire to spread, according to a fire marshal's report. The settings on the standpipe systems were too low, preventing firefighters from getting enough water onto the fire.

Example Two. When a fire occurred in a 60-story high-rise office building in Boston in August 1992, many of the emergency systems failed. Specifically, two of the three service elevators, the primary power system, the emergency power system, the emergency lighting, and the public address system all failed. The systems failure occurred because the fire was located on the 7th floor where all of the emergency systems were located.

As a result of the building's emergency system failure, the employees and tenants were unaware of what to do when the building was being evacuated. They had to evacuate without receiving any of the instructions they had expected to receive over the public address system. They had to walk down dark stairwells when they expected to have the emergency lights working. People were angry because they did not know what they should do or what they should not do. A major tenant said the skyscraper's safety system was "a complete failure."

According to the statements made by the Boston Fire Department after the fire was under control, this opinion about no contingency plan was totally inaccurate. The fire department felt the reason that there were few injuries, was because the company that owned the building had an excellent fire prevention and emergency response plan. The company's emergency response plan is usually exercised twice a year. They, in fact, had conducted a very extensive and successful exercise in October 1991 that involved the Boston fire department, the Boston police department, and the Boston emergency medical services people. In preparation for this exercise, the company held a series of joint meetings with the outside emergency forces to discuss the roles and responsibilities of the participating organizations, as well as issues concerning safety, communications, elevator use, site security, and property preservation.

Despite having a plan, exercising it twice a year, incorporating all of the local emergency response organizations in an extensive exercise, this company's experience is another example that any plan cannot absolutely ensure that employees will know how to respond correctly when a disaster occurs and unusual circumstances prevail.

Americans With Disabilities Act. The Americans With Disabilities Act (ADA) was signed into law on July 26, 1990. The Act defines a disability as a physical or mental impairment that substantially limits one or more of the major life activities of an individual. The Department of Justice issued the final guidelines on July 26, 1991, which were then published in the Federal Register, and are known as the Americans

With Disabilities Act Accessibility Guidelines (ADAAG). All new building construction started after January 26, 1992 has to comply with the ADAAG and all corrective actions were to be completed for existing public buildings by January 26, 1995. The ADAAG has several sections that directly affect the LS/ERP. These include:

- *Means of egress*. Previously, it was necessary for only the main entrance to be made accessible. Under the ADAAG at least 50% of all entrances and 100% of all building and fire safety code exits must be fully accessible.
- *Areas of rescue assistance*. The ADAAG requires "areas of rescue assistance" in all buildings that are not protected throughout by an approved, supervised automatic sprinkler system. These "areas of rescue assistance" can be a portion of a stairway landing within a smokeproof enclosure that complies with the local code requirements or a portion of a one-hour fire resistive corridor that complies with the local code requirements and is located immediately adjacent to an exit enclosure.
- *Fire alarm systems*. Under the ADAAG, fire alarm systems must have a minimum audible signal of at least 15dbA over the normal ambient and no more than 120 dbA. Visual alarms for the hearing impaired must be located in all corridors, restrooms, and general usage areas such as meeting rooms and lobbies.
- *Elevators*. The ADAAG requires that in new construction at least one passenger elevator be installed to serve each level for all three-story or higher buildings and this includes shopping centers and malls and professional office buildings with health care providers.
- *Public reporting systems*. The ADAAG also affects public reporting systems. Telephone emergency services, including 911 services, must provide direct access to individuals with speech or hearing impairments. This requires installing telecommunications devices for deaf persons.
- *Protruding objects and controls*. Objects protruding from the walls, such as fire extinguishers with their leading edges between 27 inches and 80 inches above the floor, cannot protrude more than four inches. This is also true of standpipe outlets in hallways and stairwells. Controls must be mounted so that the operating mechanism is not more than 48 inches above the floor. Controls and operating mechanisms must be operable with one hand and not require tight grasping, pinching, or twisting of the wrist. The force required should not be more than five pounds.

Typical Damage

Fires can cause major property damage, which includes all forms of direct loss to contents, structure, and machinery. Fire damage can also include loss of paper records and supplies, microfilm, discs, and tapes. Fires also cause indirect losses, such as losses due to the interruption of a company's business or losses for the necessary costs involved for a company to set up temporary operating locations following a fire. These losses can be the result of the fire or the fire-fighting water or chemicals used to extinguish the fire.

Fire Life Safety/Emergency Response Actions

The Life Safety/Emergency Response Plan should clarify for employees what the company wants them to do during and immediately after a fire strikes the building. The following sections contain recommendations that the IS manager, who is responsible for the LS/ERP, may want to include in his or her plan.

EXHIBIT II-14-A BASIC FIRE EXTINGUISHER OPERATION

The all-class fire extinguisher, which may be used on Class A, B, or C fires has simplified procedures for using it. The basic fire extinguisher operation can be remembered by the simple acronym PASS.

- P—PULL the safety pin (twist-pull action).
- A—AIM the nozzle at the base of the fire.
- S—SQUEEZE the trigger handle.
- S—SWEEP slowly from side to side.

If the Employee is the First Person to Discover a Fire. The employee should:

- Not attempt to extinguish the fire until they first call the fire department. He or she should provide the fire department with his or her location, the location, and the description of the fire.
- Then call the person identified by the company in the LS/ERP (e.g., a fire safety director) and tell them the location of the fire.
- Then pull the nearest fire alarm and alert other personnel in the fire area. This is a generally recommended procedure. Not all companies use it; some prefer for the employee to notify his or her manager, who will then notify the Building Manager, who will then assess the situation before calling the fire department. The problem with this procedure is that the delay in notifying the fire department can result in unnecessary damage being sustained by the company. The reason that companies select this procedure is because the local fire departments have begun charging companies fees anytime they are called out for false alarms.

Should the Employee Fight the Fire Using a Hand-Held Fire Extinguisher? If the situation arises, employees should respond appropriately:

- Make a decision as to whether they think they can quickly and safely extinguish the fire.
- If they feel that the fire is small and if they know how to use a hand-held extinguisher, they can use the closest fire extinguisher to extinguish or control the fire. They should follow the basic fire extinguisher operation procedure as presented in Exhibit II-14-A.
- If they are successful in controlling the fire, it is recommended that a Class A fire be doused with water to ensure extinguishment of all deep-seated smoldering. Otherwise, it may recur a few hours later.
- If they have already used one fire extinguisher and have been unable to get the fire under control, they should evacuate the building. In December 1985, a small fire occurred in a manufacturing company in Rhode Island. The plant manager stayed in the building attempting to contain the fire with a hand-held fire extinguisher until the firefighters arrived. The fire department personnel arrived about five minutes after receiving the alarm, but by this time the plant manager had succumbed to smoke and carbon monoxide inhalation.

When the Employee is Evacuating the Building. Should the situation arise, employees:

- Should close all doors as they leave. This will prevent the fire from travelling.
- Should only use the stairways when exiting the building and never use the elevators. A cardinal rule of fire protection is to never use an elevator for evacuation during a fire.

- When using a stairway for evacuation, check the door first:
  - —If the door is hot, do not open the door. Follow the procedures identified if conditions prevent safe evacuation.
  - —If the door is not hot, open the door cautiously. If conditions provide for a safe evacuation, they should walk down the stairs to the ground level. They should not run and remove shoes or clothing that could cause them to trip or fall. They should leave the building and continue to the assembly area, and not re-enter the building until notified that it is safe.

If the Employee Must Go Through Smoke During the Evacuation. Should the situation arise, employees should:

- Remember that smoke rises, so they should keep their face close to the floor where the air will be cleaner and cooler.
- Crawl on their hands and knees to the emergency exit.
- Breathe in a shallow manner through their nose to minimize the amount of smoke that they inhale. They should also hold a cloth, dampened with water if possible, over their nose and mouth.

Evacuate to the Roof Only if Told to do so. Persons designated in the ERP or the fire department will instruct employees to proceed to the roof where they should move away from the exit so others may follow them.

If it is Decided to Evacuate by Helicopter. If the situation arises employees should not climb to the helicopter pad until the helicopter has landed. They should face away from the approaching craft, cover their eyes to protect them from flying dust and debris, and wait for directions. They should always approach a helicopter from the front.

If Conditions Prevent a Safe Building Evacuation. In this situation, employees should:

- Follow the same procedures as if the door is hot.
- Not panic. The calmer they stay, the less air they will breathe, and the longer they can survive in foul air.
- Stuff any cloth they can find (e.g., clothing, drapes, or rags) into the air ducts and the cracks around doors. Because wet cloth will block out smoke better than dry cloth, cloth should be soaked in any available water—from drinking fountains, in restrooms, in flower vases, even coffee or tea.
- Retreat from the area. They should close as many doors as possible between them and the fire.
- Find a room with an outside window. If it opens, they should open it only slightly at both the top and bottom. They should then signal from the window to attract attention to their location. They should not break a window unless it absolutely necessary, because once it is broken, it can no longer keep the outside smoke from entering. If they must break a window to remain conscious, they should first check to ensure that no people are below the window, then they should break the window with a heavy object.
- If they are on the third floor or above, they *should not jump*. They will probably not survive the fall. They will have a better chance if they stay where they are.
- Call the fire department again. They should tell them their exact location and

the location of the fire. They should then follow fire department instructions and wait for assistance.

If employees hear a fire alarm sounding in their area of the building, they should evacuate immediately. They should walk quickly and quietly to the nearest stairway door and proceed down the stairs to the ground level. If employees hear a fire alarm sounding in the building but it is not in their area, they do not have to evacuate unless they are instructed to by the fire safety director or fire warden. They should not go up the stairs unless directed by the fire department or emergency personnel. Upon leaving the building, they should report to the designated assembly area.

Related Information for Fire LS/ERP Actions

The following sections describe other safety precautions and LS/ERP actions to be carried out during a fire.

Notification of the Fire Department. According to the fire experts, the most important step taken following the discovery of a fire is the notification of the fire department. This step has been instrumental in the saving of lives. On the other hand, many times the loss of lives can be attributed to the delay in notification of the fire to the fire department. There have been cases in which individuals have failed to notify the fire department immediately after discovering a fire. Instead, they attempted to extinguish it. If they are unsuccessful, the fire will cause a great more damage than it would have caused if the department had been notified immediately. The LS/ERP should explain how the employee should call the fire department, using 911, or the direct telephone number. As a means to notify employees of the fire department's phone number, many companies have applied stickers to all telephones throughout the company.

During a fire in the late 1980s at a bank in California, the fire alarm was silenced at least three times, and a building maintenance helper was sent to check conditions on the floor from which the alarms were being received. He made the fatal mistake of taking the elevator directly to the floor from which the alarms were being received.

Management of any organization cannot, and must not, justify endangering its employees for any reason, no matter how noble. Nor must management ever encourage, by commission or omission, employees taking any initiative without regard for their own safety.

In other cases, employees who have smelled smoke assume that it is not in their area and do not react. This happened recently at the Philadelphia Zoo on December 24, 1995. Although this is not in a commercial building and that the deaths were animals, not humans, an analogy still holds. The security guards on duty that night smelled smoke hours before they became aware that it was coming from the primate's building. They explained that they thought it was burning wood on the railroad tracks across the street from the zoo, so they disregarded it. Twenty-three primates died of smoke asphyxiation. They Philadelphia Fire Department said that if the security guards would have followed the documented procedures, the primates could have survived.

The Proper Use of Fire Extinguishers. A major weakness in the LS/ERP is the assumption that employees know how to use a fire extinguisher. Employees must know how to operate the fire extinguisher before attempting to extinguish the fire. They must also be trained on how to make the decision that the fire is small enough to extinguish. How else will they know if they can safely contain the fire? The company must provide the training on how and when to use the hand-held fire extinguishers. Companies all over the United States make arrangements for the local fire departments to visit companies annually and provide hands-on training on how to use the fire extinguishers.

A need exists for more education in the proper use of portable fire extinguishers, particularly in recognizing their limitations. Although there are thousands of instances in which fire extinguishers have successfully controlled fires, there have also been many fires involving large losses where extinguishers have been used improperly. The main limitation is that the extinguisher is a portion of a total system, which is dependent on the proper behavior of a human being. The behavior must be predetermined by having the individual educated on the operation of the extinguisher. Fire extinguishers are sometimes complex and may be somewhat intimidating to an individual who has never used one before. An important fact to remember is to never re-hang an extinguisher once it has been discharged, even if it is only used for a few seconds. Employees should notify the appropriate person to have the extinguisher recharged.

The Proper Use of Elevators During an Evacuation. Another weakness in the LS/ERP is ensuring that employees do not use elevators to evacuate the building. Companies must educate their employees on the dangers involved in using an elevator during a fire. There have been numerous cases in which individuals have attempted to use an elevator during a fire, only to have it fail:

- On November 23, 1980, the MGM Grand Hotel in Las Vegas, Nevada suffered a fire in which 21 victims were found in corridors and elevator lobbies between the 19th and 24th floors, five victims were found in elevators, and nine were found in stair enclosures.
- On June 23, 1980, the New York City Fire Chief handling a high-rise office building fire had a bad experience with the elevators. He used a service elevator to get to the 18th floor to set up a command station. Later, when he attempted to return to the lobby in the elevator, the elevator began rising toward the fire floor. It stopped somewhere between the 18th and 20th floors. The fire chief knew that if the elevator stopped at the fire floor, when the door opened, the fire might rush in and kill him. He also knew that if the elevator never moved, he could die from lack of oxygen. Fortunately, when he pushed the lobby button again, the elevator went down to the lobby.
- On April 15, 1985, a New York City Fire Chief and several firemen working a fire on the 28th and 29th floors of a 41-story high rise on Seventh Avenue were trapped briefly on the 20th floor in an elevator that had stalled when its electrical system was short circuited by water. The Fire Chief and the other firefighters forced the door open and left the elevator for the stairwells.

The Use of Helicopters for Evacuation. Helicopters have a great use at high-rise fires, but evacuation is not one of them—at least not until used as a last resort. Helicopters should be used to deliver operational personnel to the roof level and for reconnaissance. They should look at the building, fly away for at least one block, and then wait for instructions. On the other hand, for example, they were used to rescue people in the MGM Grand Hotel fire in Las Vegas.

Fire Drills. To promote fire safety awareness, fire drills should be conducted by companies regularly, at least once a year. During fire drills, orderly evacuation is far more effective than a speedy, but disorganized exit. Personnel should be aware of the procedures to follow at all times. The company should ensure that all personnel know who the fire wardens and the fire safety director are, so that they will be prepared to follow their instructions during a real fire.

The most prepared people to respond to a fire in the United States are school children. Fire response education in the schools is outstanding. The students are trained what to do, and they practice what to do. They respect the people that are giving them instructions. As part of learning self-control, they have learned to control their emotions. The National Fire Protection Association (NFPA) sponsors a "Learn Not To Burn" program. This school program has been designed for children from kindergarten through eighth grade. It has been credited with saving many children's lives when fires have occurred in schools. For high school students, the NFPA sponsors a "Fire Safety for the Rest of Your Life" program.

Personnel should treat every alarm as though their lives depended on it. If the alarm is caused by a real fire, the person has a head start in the evacuation. If the alarm is a drill, the person will have lost only a few minutes of work, but will have gained valuable experience in dealing with the real thing. In addition, all companies should schedule an evacuation exercise at least once a year, in which all employees are expected to participate. In many cases, the company notifies the employees several weeks in advance as to the date the drill will be taking place.

Human Reactions. A complicating factor, which can lead to unnecessary deaths and injuries, that occurs during any disaster is that of human reactions. A company's LS/ERP must be designed to prepare the employees to respond to a fire to protect their lives. Individuals taken by surprise in a stressful situation may panic. The greatest loss of life in hotel, department store, and theater fires is primarily because of the panic that is caused by unfamiliarity with the layout of the facility and the location of the exits. For example, after the fire at a hotel in Harrison, NY, six bodies were found in a closet, which victims had apparently mistaken for an exit route. Three bodies were found next to an exit that had been bolted shut to protect an artificial Christmas tree that stood on the other side. An electronics company located in Greenwich, CT lost 13 of their executives in the fire, including their president and the executive vice-president. Eleven food company executives were also killed in the fire.

If employees are able to evacuate the building in an orderly fashion without delay, they can usually escape the dangers created by the fire. On the other hand, panic is easily triggered in a crowd. A sudden movement toward the exit could lead to panic, which could lead to injuries or death. The following are some of the measures that can be included in the LS/ERP to minimize panic:

- Emergency lighting, throughout the building, as well as in the stairwells that will be used for evacuations, has been found to be helpful in preventing panic.
- A public address system, used in concert with the fire bell or fire horn, has been found to be helpful in preventing panic. Often the emergency messages that will be used on the public address system have been pre-recorded to avoid showing any stress by the person using the system at the time of the emergency.
- Advance notice of emergency actions can help prepare people for responding without panic if the situation arises. For example, at conferences, seminars, and symposiums, the organizers should explain emergency response actions at the

start of the session. These actions should explain how they will be notified of an emergency and where the exit doors are.

Companies can help employees to control these human reactions by developing complete response actions, training their employees on these actions, practicing them, and evaluating the actions on a timely basis. An integral part of Life Safety/ Emergency Response Planning is education to instill in the employees what they are supposed to do during and immediately after a fire, a bomb threat, or a bombing. By doing these things, a company will maintain the confidence of their employees when a disaster occurs. In that way, they will be able to act assuredly and effectively at the time of a fire or bombing, and not panic.

BOMBS AND BOMBING

A bomb is a receptacle of any size or shape that contains an explosive. The explosives are detonated in various ways by terrorists, criminals, or deranged people to kill or destroy. The detonation or explosion can be achieved by means of impact, proximity to an object, a timing mechanism, an electronic device, or some other predetermined means.

The three kinds of explosives used in bombs are:

- High explosives such as dynamite, TNT, nitroglycerine, and nitro starch.
- Low explosives such as black powder and smokeless powder.
- Blasting agents such as blasting caps.

The explosive power of all types of explosives is basically the same. The difference is in the amount of heat or shock it will take to detonate each one. A blasting agent can be just as powerful as dynamite when it is detonated.

Five types of bombs are used today:

- A pipe bomb is a bomb that is made from a section of pipe that is capped at both ends. It may have a fuse extending from one of the ends. The flying metal pieces that result after it explodes will kill and injure.
- A bottle bomb is a bomb that is made by filling a bottle with gasoline and sulfuric acid. It is then wrapped in a sock and coated with potassium chlorate and sugar. When the bottle is thrown and broken, the sulfuric acid and potassium chlorate combine to produce an explosion and fire.
- A car bomb is a bomb that is placed inside the motor of a car. It is a sealed canister, which will have a spark plug attached through the lid. The wire of spark plug 1 of the car's engine is attached to the spark plug on the bomb or canister. When the car is started, the bomb explodes.
- A bag bomb is a bomb that is placed in a shoulder type bag. Some dynamite and one or two small liquid propane cylinders can cause the explosion and fire when detonated.
- A mail bomb is a bomb that is placed inside a package or letter and sent through the mail. Sometimes a mail bomb can be identified before it harms anyone. The mail bomb often kills or injures the wrong person. For example, when a relative or co-worker opens it instead of the addressee. The following is a list of the most obvious indications of a mail bomb:
  - —Letters or packages that are very heavy, firm, or bulky.
  - —Wrappings with oily stains.
  - —Packages with excess postage.
  - —No return name and address.
  - —Addressed using cut-out or poster letters instead of being handwritten or typed.

— Packages with strange odors.
— Packages with visible string or wire.
— Packages or letters that are difficult to open.
— Packages with soft spots, bulges, or previous traces of glue or tape.
— Packages with irregular shapes.

Typical Damage

A bomb is a weapon of destruction that can cause great loss of life and massive damage. Buildings and all of their contents can be severely damaged or destroyed completely. Entire buildings can be rendered unusable following a bombing. One of the greatest causes of death and injury in connection with a bombing is the flying glass. Jagged and sharp fragments are blasted through the air.

Damage from a bomb is largely caused by the pressure of the shock wave set off by the blast, measured in pounds per square inch (psi). One psi is roughly equivalent to having a small car dropped on an individual from about 10 feet. For example, during the bombing at the Murrah Federal Building in Oklahoma City on April 19, 1995:

- *At 30 feet.* The blast hits the front door of the Federal Building with 160 psi.
- *At 250 feet.* The blast loses energy in the parking lot before hitting the Journal Record Building across the street with 20 psi.
- *At 517 feet.* The blast reaches the 8th floor of the Bell Building one block away with 9 psi.

Because of the size of this bomb there was, in a sense, double destruction that resulted upon detonation. High-pressure gas at about 5,000 degrees exploded out of the truck carrying the deadly bomb at 3,500 yards a second, more than 7,000 miles per hour. The expanding gas pushed normal air out of the way and smashed everything in its path. This gas evaporated about a half-second after the blast, creating a vacuum. Air and debris forced outward during the initial phase came rushing back, causing a second blast and more damage to already weakened structures.

The police department is in charge of a bombing incident, and they are the first on the scene during a bomb threat. At times, the police department will ask the fire department to assist them on the scene with evacuation, forcible entry, use of ladders, first aid, bomb search, collapse search and rescue, and putting out any fire that erupts. However, the fire department will arrive first: if the bomb has already exploded, fire has started, and collapse has occurred.

Bombing is most definitely on the increase. According to a five-year study done by the Bureau of Alcohol, Tobacco, and Firearms between 1989 and 1993, annual bombings have nearly doubled in the United States. In 1992, there were 2,989 reported bomb incidents, which includes threats, attempts, actual attacks, and recovered explosives. These incidents killed 26 people, injured 375 and caused $12.5 million in damage. The most common reasons that have been determined for bombing incidents are in descending order: vandalism, revenge, protest, extortion, homicide or suicide, labor-related, and insurance fraud.

Data centers have been the favorite targets of terrorists throughout the world. Terrorists regard the computer as the symbol of capitalism and its politics. Companies or data centers that are the most likely to be bomb targets are: computer companies, national and local government agencies, defense contractors, chemical companies, pharmaceutical companies, banking facilities, nuclear power plants, universities, and the military.

Bomb Life Safety/Emergency Response Actions

The Life Safety/Emergency Response Plan should clarify for employees what the company wants them to do during and immediately after a bombing or a bomb threat at their building. The following information contains recommendations that IS managers, who are responsible for the LS/ERPs, may want to include in their plan.

Evacuating a building due to a bombing or a bomb threat is slightly different from a fire evacuation. The first thing employees have to know is that if they find a bomb or questionable object, they should never attempt to move, disarm, or tamper with it. Most companies instruct their employees to call security.

When evacuating during a bomb threat, employees should take all belongings with them, so that there are fewer items to look through for the bomb. They should also leave offices, desks, and lockers unlocked to aid in the search and to prevent unnecessary damage during the search. There should be a specific, announced stairway that employees will use to evacuate. Before employees use that exit, police will have searched for the bomb along the access to the stair, the stairway itself, and the area where the stair leads out. The evacuation route should be away from glass windows and doors if possible. Elevators should not be used in case the bomb does explode. The evacuation area should be at least 300 to 500 feet away from the building to prevent injuries from the resulting toxic vapors that occur following the explosion. This distance may be increased because of the type or size of the bomb, hazardous materials present, or large quantities of glass that are part of the building.

Related Information for Fire LS/ERP Actions

When the World Trade Center bombing occurred in February 1993, the heart of the Port Authority Police Department was badly damaged. This is the area that controlled the building's elevators, alarms, and public address system. The loss of that room resulted in the failure of the elevators, the alarm bells, and the loss of the public address system that would provide instructions for the building's tenants and their employees.

Tenants were unaware of what action to take. There had been no alarm bells and no instructions from the building's intercom or emergency workers. Some people in the building used cellular phones to call television stations where they received information on the status of the incident. When people did decide to evacuate, they were faced with a walk down dark stairwells because the emergency lights were not working. It was so dark in the stairwells, people had to feel their way down each step, causing the trip from the upper floors to take over an hour. The whole time, the people were breathing in smoke that had gotten into the stairwells from the open stairwell doors and elevator shafts that had been damaged by the explosion. Although it was pandemonium, to the credit of the people from the building, it was controlled, civilized pandemonium. There were no stampedes. People cursed the darkness or the building management, but not each other.

The World Trade Center buildings have Emergency Response Plans. These plans are tested twice a year. However, as a result of the loss of the Port Authority Police Department control room and the emergency equipment throughout the building, tenants did not know what to do. The message received from the World Trade Center bombing is that people must know what to do during an emergency, especially when the building's emergency systems are unable to function. When these controls fail, employees have to be aware of the company's or building's contingency plans that they should use instead. If the Emergency Response Plan does not include contingencies, the company will probably experience employee injuries, potential lawsuits, negative publicity, and the loss of some credibility in the community. Building owners have the responsibility to ensure that employees, tenants, and visitors know when and how to evacuate the building.

World Trade Center Improvements

The World Trade Center has made a number of improvements in emergency response systems, controls, and procedures after the experience from the bombing. Companies and managers who are responsible for developing their company's LS/ERP actions should look at these improvements to see if they would be worthwhile including in their buildings.

The improvements in the emergency response systems, controls, and procedures after the experience from the bombing in the World Trade Center include the following:

- Emergency battery-powered lights have been installed in exit stairwells, elevator lobbies, and all elevators. The total for the World Trade Center was 1,600.
- Phosphorescent signs have been installed to guide the way to floor entry doors in floor stairwells.
- Phosphorescent tape-paint has been applied to stair threads, handrails, and to the perimeters of doorways in the fire stairwells.
- A battery backup system has been installed to the elevator car position indicator, which will enable passengers to see which floor they are on if the elevator gets stuck in an express shaft.
- The elevator emergency call button will be tied into a battery power supply on top of the elevator car. In the event of a power loss, World Trade Center personnel can communicate with trapped elevator passengers. In 1993, there were a number of people trapped in elevators for hours.
- Fire safety directors will be linked to central communications office stationed at the 44th and 78th floor skylobbies.
- Improved fire alarm and communications systems have been installed.

CONCLUSION

The Life Safety/Emergency Response Plan (LS/ERP) is part of the response section of the Business Continuity Plan. The LS/ERP identifies those actions that the company expects the employees to take to protect their health and safety, as well as to protect the assets of the company when a disaster occurs. The LS/ERP actions should be developed by the manager in the IS department responsible to ensure that all IS personnel know what to do if a fire or bombing occurs. The LS/ERP is written for the specific type of disaster, because the type of disaster dictates the type of response actions to be used by the employees. LS/ERPs contain some actions for each specific type of disaster.

Most companies already have an LS/ERP, but simply having an ERP is not adequate preparation. If companies are serious about their ERPs, they will:

- Ensure that the emergency response section of the Business Continuity Plan is documented.
- Ensure that all employees have read those portions of the ERP that explain what the company expects the employee to do before, during, and after an emergency.
- Verify that this is being accomplished by having the employees sign-off after having read their section of the ERP.
- Ensure that all employees review these actions annually to evaluate the effectiveness, validity, and completeness of the ERP actions.
- Ensure that exercises are performed to train or re-train the employees.

Evaluating the Recovery Headquarters Team Following an Actual Recovery Operation

CHAPTER

II-15

INTRODUCTION

Chapter II-15 presents a series of workpapers that can be used to evaluate the effectiveness of the data center's recovery plan (DCRP) recovery teams' responsibilities and their procedures, checklists, and strategies following an actual recovery operation. The recovery procedures and checklists explain "how" the IS personnel will perform their responsibilities. The recovery strategies explain the resources that will be used by IS personnel to perform their responsibilities.

IS personnel should have already determined the strengths and weaknesses of the DCRP when they had the individual recovery teams exercise their section of the plan at various times throughout the year. As a result of these exercises, IS should have adjusted its plan to minimize any weaknesses. However, the evaluation of the results of an actual recovery operation, gives a different perspective of the components within the DCRP. When the DCRP is merely exercised, the disaster scenarios cannot anticipate all of the different situations that will be faced during an actual recovery operation. Many exercise scenarios have been structured by the participants to include assumptions. They assume this will happen, that this resource will be there, that this vendor will be able to respond immediately, that no one in the same vicinity is affected by the same disaster, and so on. However, during an actual disaster, some, if not all, of those assumptions become useless. During the actual disaster, recovery teams will run into many unforeseen roadblocks. Even though the unforeseen was not addressed in the plan, the DCRP teams will have to find ways to work around those situations. How can they navigate around the roadblocks? That question cannot be answered as yet, but that is the value in performing the evaluation. The purpose of the evaluation is to identify how the plan and its strategies really performed in an actual recovery operation.

This evaluation is best performed after the company fully recovers from the disaster, and IS operations have returned to normal. An evaluation before this time could lead to inaccurate conclusions. On the other hand, IS should not wait too long after the company returns to normal operations, because the personnel involved could easily forget how the recovery actually took place.

Myth: The Recovery Manual is Unnecessary

There are many people who believe that after the DCRP has been developed, the teams do not need to refer to the manual to recover following an actual disaster. They feel that the knowledge gained during the developing, implementing, and exercising of the DCRP, will provide the IS personnel with the knowledge necessary to carry off the DCRP recovery actions. Although there is a great deal of value in participating in this process, the DCRP manual provides a wealth of information for people faced with a crisis. During a crisis, people will operate on adrenalin. The adrenalin provides the stamina, not the knowledge. The knowledge of what to do is found in the written plan, the manual. The plan is a resource. It provides the leaders and members of the recovery teams with responsibilities, resources, and strategies to use, depending on the disaster scenario.

Moreover, a different organization exists today than the one that existed when DCRPs were first developed. Companies have gone through downsizing, many of the IS staff who were involved in the development process may no longer be with the company. Some of the IS personnel that will be required to perform recovery responsibilities may be performing them for the first time. They will depend on the documented plan to know what they are supposed to do and how they are supposed to accomplish it.

Chapter II-15 provides workpapers that can be used to evaluate the effectiveness of the recovery headquarters team. The recovery headquarters team's responsibilities are in Chapter II-4.

EVALUATING THE RECOVERY HEADQUARTERS TEAM

Chapter II-4 defined the recovery headquarters team's responsibilities as: providing administrative and clerical support to all recovery teams; distributing, collecting, and processing the forms that were to be used during the recovery operation; notifying all IS personnel of the situation; managing incoming phone calls to the recovery headquarters; and maintaining copies of the authorized personnel location control forms. Chapter II-4 identified the recovery headquarters team as being comprised of: the recovery headquarters team manager; the notification and communications team leader; the administration team leader; and the IS recovery chairperson. Workpapers II-15.01 through 11-15.04 are provided for each team leader to assist him or her in determining which areas of the DCRP were used during the recovery operation and how effective those areas were during the actual recovery.

The DCRP coordinator can evaluate the completed workpapers to determine which areas of the plan worked as planned and which areas did not work as planned. After performing this analysis, the coordinator can then make the necessary changes to the data center recovery plan to ensure that all areas of the plan will work when needed the next time.

CONCLUSION

This chapter provides workpapers that can be used to evaluate the effectiveness of one of the major teams in the IS DCRP, the recovery headquarters team. The workpapers show how to evaluate each of the four teams that comprise the recovery headquarters team.

Workpaper II15.01 Used in the Evaluation of the IS DCRP Recovery Chairperson Activities

During the recovery operation, did the IS DCRP recovery chairperson:

1. Notify the executive management group of the situation.

   Yes ___ No ___

   - Which executives were notified?

     ____

     ____

   - Which executives were not able to be reached?

     ____

     ____

2. Conduct a staff department meeting to request their "support."

   Yes ___ No ___

   - Which staff department representatives were notified?

     ____

     ____

   - Which staff department representatives were not able to be reached?

     ____

     ____

   - Which staff department alternates had to be notified?

     ____

     ____

- Which staff departments were needed to supply "support"?

  ____

  ____

- At this staff department meeting, did the chairperson provide information known about the incident; e.g.,
  - What happened? Yes ___ No ___
  - When it happened? Yes ___ No ___
  - How it happened? Yes ___ No ___
  - If there were any injuries or deaths? Yes ___ No ___
  - What the cause is believed to be, if known. Yes ___ No ___

3. Conduct an activation meeting for the IS recovery team. Yes ___ No ___

- Was there a review of the recovery team procedures that were activated, e.g., the computer operations recovery team's procedures? Yes ___ No ___
- Was there a review of the support that was provided by the recovery headquarters team? Yes ___ No ___
- Were personnel reminded that they should not make any statements to the news media? Yes ___ No ___
- Did any IS personnel speak with the news media? Yes___ No___

- Did they use the pre-prepared statement from the Public Relations representative?

  Yes___ No___

4. Review the activities that would be taking place in the recovery headquarters throughout the operation.

   Yes ___ No ___

   - Which recovery headquarters team activities were activated?

     ____

     ____

   - Were the results of the IS personnel notification procedure reviewed? Yes ___ No ___
   - Did the members of the notification and communications team follow the personnel notification procedure when calling? Yes ___ No ___
   - How many IS personnel were reached?

     ____

     ____

   - How many were not reached?

     ____

     ____

   - How did they find out about the situation?

     ____

     ____

- How many IS personnel were not available to participate in the recovery operation immediately?

  ____

  ____

5) Determine if there were any IS personnel injured in the disaster.

   ____

   ____

6) Review the backup site recovery team activities throughout the operation. Yes___ No ___

   - Which backup site recovery team activities were activated?

     ____

     ____

   - Was the activation of the computer backup site authorized? Yes ___ No ___
   - Was the status of the systems and applications software vendor notifications reviewed? Yes ___ No ___
   - If there were any problems, how were they resolved?

     ____

     ____

   - Were the estimates of the time required to resume the processing of applications reviewed with the backup site recovery team manager? Yes ___ No ___

- Were the estimates met?

  ____

  ____

7) Review the disaster site recovery team activities throughout the operation. Yes ___ No ___

- Which disaster site recovery team activities were activated?

  ____

  ____

- Were the damage assessment estimates reviewed?

  Yes ___ No ___

- Were estimates of the time required to restore the data center obtained? Yes ___ No ___

- Were estimates of the damage to the equipment, the supplies, the forms, and the computer data residing on the disks and tapes obtained?

  Yes ___ No ___

- Were the plans to replace damaged and destroyed equipment reviewed?

  Yes ___ No ___

- Was the information from the team manager on potential sites, temporary or permanent, reviewed and the selection approved? Yes ___ No ___

- If a temporary or permanent site was used during the

recovery operation, where was it obtained?

____

____

8) Meet with executive group to provide information on:

- The IS personnel injuries. Yes ___ No ___
- How the families of injured IS personnel were notified.

  ____

  ____

- The status of notification to the families.

  Yes ___ No ___
- The damage to assets, the building, the computer equipment, communications facilities, and essential records located in the data center.

  Yes ___ No ___
- The damage to the building housing the computer center.

  ____

  ____

- The damage to the computer equipment.

  ____

  ____

- The damage to the communications facilities.

  ____

  ____

- The damage to the essential records.

  ____

  ____

- The recovery operation strategy being used to resume data center operations. Yes ___ No ___

- The strategy that was used.

  ____

  ____

- How the strategy worked.

  ____

  ____

  ____

  ____

During the recovery operation, were all of the procedures, checklists, and strategies satisfactory? Explain what should be changed or improved and why.

____

____

____

____

____

____

____

Workpaper II15.02 Used in the Evaluation of the Recovery Headquarters Manager

During the recovery operation, did the recovery headquarters manager:

1. Distribute the recovery forms.
   - The personnel location control form used to identify where the IS personnel are located anytime during the recovery operation. Yes ___ No ___
   - The recovery status report form used to accumulate all of the facts and figures involved in the recovery operation by the recovery teams. Yes ___ No ___
   - The travel and expense report form used to reimburse the IS employees for the out-of-pocket expenses that they incur during the recovery operation. Yes ___ No ___
   - The disaster recovery time record form used to account for those employees who put in an extraordinary effort during the recovery operation. Yes ___ No ___
2. Conduct a recovery headquarters meeting. Yes ___ No ___
   - Were the tasks that were performed reviewed? Yes ___ No ___
3. Assist the recovery team managers to determine the order in which the remaining IS personnel will be notified. Yes ___ No ___

4. Authorize the IS personnel notification. Yes ___ No ___

5. Manage the incoming telephone calls. Yes ___ No ___

6. Schedule 24-hour staffing at the recovery headquarters to ensure support is available for the recovery teams.

   Yes ___ No ___

7. Provide equipment and supplies. Yes ___ No ___

8. Organize recovery operation team meetings.

   Yes ___ No ___

   - Were the minutes of the meetings documented and distributed to the attendees? Yes ___ No ___

9. Ensure that there are adequate cash advances to cover travel, hotel, and other out-of-pocket expenses; collect and process all travel and expense reports. Yes ___ No ___

10. Control all purchases, leases, or rental requisition requests. Yes ___ No ___

11. Obtain the special general ledger account number that will be used throughout the recovery operation to charge recovery expenditures; apply the general ledger number to all expense accounts or recovery invoices. Yes ___ No ___

12. Collect and process all completed recovery status reports.

    Yes ___ No ___

13. Collect and process all daily time record reports.

    Yes ___ No ___

During the recovery operation, were all of the procedures, checklists, and strategies satisfactory? Explain what should be changed or improved, and why.

Workpaper II15.03 Used in the Evaluation of the Notification and Communications Team

During the recovery operation, did the notification and communications team leader:

1. Reserve telephone numbers for "outgoing" and "incoming" calls at the recovery headquarters. Yes ___ No ___
2. Did the people who were trying to return calls have any difficulty in reaching their party? Yes ___ No ___
   - If yes, what difficulty did they experience?

     ____

     ____
3. Instruct personnel to use the personnel notification information checklist. Yes ___ No ___
   - Was the information on this checklist accurate? Yes ___ No ___
   - Which employees' names were incorrect?

     ____

     ____
   - Which employees' phone numbers were incorrect?

     ____

     ____
   - Which employees' addresses were incorrect?

     ____

     ____

4. Ensure the use of the personnel notification procedure.

Yes ___ No ___

- Did it help to avoid notifying the families of IS personnel who were working at the data center at the time of the disaster?

  ____

  ____

5. Implement a plan that managed all in-coming phone calls to the recovery headquarters. Yes ___ No ___

- How did it work?

  ____

  ____

6. Continue trying to reach those vendors that had not been contacted during the first attempt. Yes ___ No ___

- Was the vendor notification checklists used?

  Yes ___ No ___

- When were they all reached?

  ____

  ____

7. Accumulate the completed personnel location control forms from the recovery team managers and leaders.

Yes ___ No ___

- Were the forms ever needed to contact an IS employee during the recovery operation? Yes ___ No ___

- How well did the procedure work?

  ____

  ____

During the recovery operation, were all of the procedures, checklists, and strategies satisfactory? Explain what should be changed or improved, and why.

____

____

____

____

____

____

____

____

Workpaper II15.04 Used in the Evaluation of the Administrative Team

During the recovery operation, did the administrative team leader:

1. Obtain battery-operated tape recording machines and supplies for use by the recovery teams. Yes ___ No ___
   - Copy machines. Yes ___ No ___
   - Personal computers. Yes ___ No ___
   - Microfilm or fiche readers. Yes ___ No ___
2. Organize recovery meetings.
   - Notify the personnel. Yes ___ No ___
   - Organize the meeting room. Yes ___ No ___
   - Record the minutes of the meeting. Yes ___ No ___
   - Distribute the minutes of the meeting. Yes ___ No ___
3. Provide travel support for the recovery teams. Yes ___ No ___
   - Obtain travel requirements. Yes ___ No ___
   - Obtain cash advances. Yes ___ No ___
   - Obtain company vehicles when available. Yes ___ No ___
   - Obtain leased cars, vans, or trucks. Yes ___ No ___
4. Coordinate travel requirements with the transportation department support representative. Yes ___ No ___

5. Accumulate recovery status report forms. Yes ___ No ___
   - On a daily basis. Yes ___ No ___
   - Other basis. ______________________

6. Accumulate travel and expense report forms from the team leaders. Yes ___ No ___
   - On a weekly basis. Yes ___ No ___
   - Other basis. ______________________

7. Accumulate the daily time record forms from the team leaders. Yes ___ No ___
   - On a weekly basis. Yes ___ No ___
   - Other basis. ______________________

8. Attempt to identify any IS personnel who were believed to have been working at the time of the disaster.

   Yes ___ No ___

   - How were the calls made to the homes of employees who were believed to be working in the data center?

     ____

     ____

   - Were any of the family members prematurely notified of the event going on?

     Yes___ No___

   - Did the members of the notification and communications Team follow the personnel notification procedure when calling? Yes___ No___

During the recovery operation, were all of the procedures, checklists, and strategies satisfactory? Explain what should be changed or improved, and why.

Evaluating the Computer Operations Recovery Team Following an Actual Recovery Operation

CHAPTER II-16

INTRODUCTION

Chapter II-16 presents a series of workpapers that can be used to evaluate the effectiveness of the data center's recovery plan (DCRP) recovery team's responsibilities, their procedures, checklists, and strategies following an actual recovery operation. The recovery procedures and checklists explain how IS personnel will perform their responsibilities. The recovery strategies explain the resources that will be used by IS personnel to perform their responsibilities.

Chapter II-16 provides Workpapers II-16.01 through II-16.06 that can be used to evaluate the effectiveness of the computer operations recovery team. The computer operations recovery team's responsibilities can be found in Chapter II-5 of this book. The DCRP coordinator can evaluate the completed workpapers to determine which areas of the plan worked as planned and which areas did not work as planned. After performing this analysis, the coordinator can then make the necessary changes to the Data Center Recovery Plan to ensure that all areas of the plan will work when needed.

CONCLUSION

This chapter provides workpapers that can be used to evaluate the effectiveness of one of the major teams in the IS DCRP, the computer operations recovery team. The workpapers show how each of the six teams that make up the computer operations recovery team can be evaluated.

Workpaper II16.01 Used in the Evaluation of the Computer Operations Recovery Team Manager

During the recovery operation, did the computer operations recovery team manager:

1. Notify the computer backup site. Yes ___ No ___
   - Use the backup site notification checklist to notify the computer backup site. Yes ___ No ___
   - Was the backup site's phone number and contact name accurate and current? Yes ___ No ___
   - Was the backup site able to provide the computer processing resources needed? Yes ___ No ___
2. Provide the computer backup site with a list of IS personnel who were authorized to enter the site. Yes ___ No ___
3. Use the critical application checklist to identify which applications would be scheduled at the backup site.

   Yes ___ No ___

During the recovery operation, were all of the procedures, checklists, and strategies satisfactory? Explain what should be changed or improved, and why.

____

____

____

____

____

Workpaper II16.02 Used in the Evaluation of the Computer Operations Recovery Team Leader

During the recovery operation, did the computer operations recovery team leader:

1. Establish the help desk. Yes ___ No ___

   - Where?

     ____

     ____

   - Did any information obtained from the end user by the help desk result in a change in the "criticality" of an application? Yes ___ No ___

   - If yes, what was the reason?

     ____

     ____

   - How valuable was the recording of information in the end user log book?

     ____

     ____

2. Obtain the damage estimate to the on-site data.

   Yes ___ No ___

   - Was there any on-site data that was not damaged and was used at the computer backup site immediately?

     Yes ___ No ___

- If the on-site data was damaged, were the damaged tapes, and other magnetic media cleaned and certified before shipment? Yes ___ No ___
- If work-in-process was damaged, did the team leader need to contact the end user to request that they resubmit the work? Yes ___ No ___

3. Notify the recovery headquarters after arriving at the computer backup site. Yes ___ No ___
4. Organize an area to be used for the receiving of any input from the end users or for the distribution of any of the output to the end users. Yes ___ No ___
5. Order tapes, forms, and other computer supplies for processing at the computer backup site. Yes ___ No ___
6. Meet with the systems software recovery team leader to coordinate the loading of the systems and applications software. Yes ___ No ___
7. Meet with the applications recovery team leader and discuss the recovery and restart procedures for the applications scheduled for processing. Yes ___ No ___
8. Meet with the data base recovery team leader and identify the status of the database backups that were available, how long ago were they created, and if jobs had to be run to create a more current version. Yes ___ No ___

9. Restore all applications data using the most current backup status. Yes ___ No ___

10. Reconstruct the applications by applying recent transaction backups. Yes ___ No ___

- Were the applications in balance? Yes ___ No ___
- If not, who determined which data was missing? Yes ___ No ___
- Who re-entered the missing data? Yes ___ No ___
- Did the internal auditors assist? Yes ___ No ___

11. Establish with the computer operations recovery team manager the initial processing schedule using the critical application checklist. Yes ___ No ___

12. Maintain a record of applications processed. Yes ___ No ___

13. Develop a processing schedule to catch up on applications delayed. Yes ___ No ___

14. Reorganize the team periodically. Yes ___ No ___

15. Prepare the shutdown plan to move back into the repaired data center. Yes ___ No ___

16. Ensure that the computer data, software, applications data and databases were backed up before leaving the processing site. Yes ___ No ___

17. Ensure that a library report was processed. Yes ___ No ___

18. Take proper steps to ensure that all company data residing on the disks at the computer backup site could not be read or accessed. Yes ___ No ___

19. Ensure that all paper, reports, forms, and data belonging to the company were removed from the computer backup site for proper distribution or destruction. Yes ___ No ___

During the recovery operation, were all of the procedures, checklists, and strategies satisfactory? Explain what should be changed or improved, and why.

____

____

____

____

____

____

____

____

Workpaper II16.03 Used in the Evaluation of the Systems Software Team

During the recovery operation, did the systems software recovery team leader:

1. Contact the software vendors and advise them that their software will be run at the computer backup site.

   Yes ___ No ___

   - Use the systems vendor notification checklist.

     Yes ___ No ___

   - Use the systems software inventory checklist.

     Yes ___ No ___

   - Verify that the software would successfully run at the computer backup site. Yes ___ No ___

   - Issue a written confirmation to all of the software vendors that required notification in writing.

     Yes ___ No ___

   - Request technical support from the vendor.

     Yes ___ No ___

2. Load the systems software onto the backup site computer.

   Yes ___ No ___

   - Were there any problems encountered in loading the operating system and libraries at the computer backup site? ______________________________

     ____

3. Assist the applications personnel with the allocation of disk resources and the loading of application data onto the available disks. Yes ___ No ___

4. Manage the loading and initiation of the on-line and communications software and the activation of the networks at the computer backup site. Yes ___ No ___

During the recovery operation, were all of the procedures, checklists, and strategies satisfactory? Explain what should be changed or improved, and why.

____

____

____

____

____

____

____

____

Workpaper II16.04 Used in the Evaluation of the Tape Operations Recovery Team

During the recovery operation, did the tape operations team leader:

1. Obtain the damage assessment status of the on-site data from the disaster site recovery team manager. Yes ___ No ___
   - If data was accessible, assign personnel to retrieve the on-site data. Yes ___ No ___
2. Arrange for the retrieval of backups from the off-premises storage location. Yes ___ No ___
   - Contact the storage location using the off-premises storage location notification checklist. Yes ___ No ___
   - Was the information on the checklist accurate? Yes ___ No ___
   - If IS personnel went to the off-premises storage location to retrieve the backups, what procedure was used by the vendor to identify that the IS person making the call was authorized to request the retrieval?

     ____

     ____
   - Provide the names of the IS personnel authorized to access to the storage area. Yes ___ No ___

- Did the authorized personnel have company identification with them when they arrived at the off-premises location? Yes ___ No ___
- Document any problems encountered in identifying or retrieving the backups tapes or cartridges from the off-premises storage location. Yes___ No ___
- What were some of the problems?

___

___

3. Obtain information from the systems software recovery team leader, the applications recovery team leader, and the data base recovery team leader. Supply the tape operations recovery team leader as to which backups they needed.

   Yes ___ No ___

   - Did these team leaders use DCRP application recovery checklists from their section of the plan?

     Yes ___ No ___
   - Did the team leaders verify that the retrieved tapes were correct? Yes ___ No ___
4. Ensure that tapes were placed in protective containers.

   Yes ___ No ___

   - Ensure that each container was labeled with the destination address, return address, and contents.

     Yes ___ No ___

5. Organize the tape library at the backup site.

Yes ___ No ___

- Have any difficulties organizing a tape library at the computer backup site? Yes ___ No ___
- If yes, what were they?

____

____

6. Initialize any new tapes and manage the backup site tape library activity.

Yes ___ No ___

7. Ensure that the backups created during the recovery processing were being rotated to an off-premises storage location. Yes ___ No ___

8. Encounter any missing tapes or cartridges. Yes ___ No ___

- How was this resolved?

____

____

During the recovery operation, were all of the procedures, checklists, and strategies satisfactory? Explain what should be changed or improved, and why.

____

____

____

____

Workpaper II16.05 Used in the Evaluation of the Applications Recovery Team

During the recovery operation, did the applications recovery team leader:

1. Contact the applications software vendors and advise them that their software will be run at the computer backup site due to the recovery operation in progress.

   Yes ___ No ___

   - Use the applications software vendor notification checklist and the applications software inventory checklist. Yes ___ No ___
   - Verify that the software would run successfully at the computer backup site. Yes ___ No ___
   - Request any technical support changes be provided to run the software at the computer backup site.

     Yes ___ No ___
   - Issue a written confirmation to all of the software vendors that the relocation of the software was due to the disaster situation. Yes ___ No ___
   - Were any problems encountered with the procedure or checklists?

     ____

     ____

2. Assign applications recovery team personnel to identify the specific retrieval requirements using the application recovery checklist. Yes ___ No ___

3. Arrange for end users to re-enter any transactions entered into the system after the backups were taken.

   Yes ___ No ___

   - If yes, how did this work?

     ____

     ____

4. Identify the reconstruction procedure that brought the backups to reflect the current status, e.g., the conclusion of processing the prior day.

   ____

   ____

5. Identify the destroyed or missing data from the work in process and have the end user resubmit input.

   Yes ___ No ___

6. Document problems encountered during the reconstructing of files to a current status when using the most current generation available from the off-premises storage location.

   Yes ___ No ___

   - What problems were encountered?

     ____

     ____

- How were they resolved?

  ____

  ____

7. Ensure the proper functioning of the programs being processed at the computer backup site or make the necessary program changes that enabled the application to process at the computer backup site. Yes ___ No ___

   - Maintain good written documentation of all of the programming changes that were made on each application and also on all problems encountered. Yes ___ No ___
   - Who monitored the modifying of the software?

     ____

     ____

8. Protect the applications data backup tapes and ensure that they could not be scratched accidently. Yes ___ No ___

   - How was this done?

     ____

     ____

During the recovery operation, were all of the procedures, checklists, and strategies satisfactory? Explain what should be changed or improved, and why.

____

____

____

Workpaper II16.06 Used in the Evaluation of the Database Recovery Team Leader

During the recovery operation, did the database recovery team leader:

1. Contact the database software vendors and advise them that their software will be run at the computer backup site due to the recovery operation in progress. Yes ___ No ___
2. Issue a written confirmation to all of the software vendors that the relocation of the software was due to the disaster situation. Yes ___ No ___
   - Was the database software vendor notification checklist accurate? Yes ___ No ___
   - Were there any problems encountered in reaching the vendors on a timely basis? Yes ___ No ___
   - Was the database software inventory checklist accurate? Yes ___ No ___
   - Were the checklists actually used to record information during the recovery operation? Yes ___ No ___
3. Request any technical support changes be provided to run the software at the computer backup site. Yes ___ No ___
4. Have any problems reconstructing the files to a current status when using the most current generation available from the off-premises storage location? Yes ___ No ___

During the recovery operation, were all of the procedures, checklists, and strategies satisfactory? Explain what should be changed or improved, and why.

Evaluating the Disaster Site Recovery Team Following an Actual Recovery Operation

CHAPTER

II-17

INTRODUCTION

Chapter II-17 presents a series of workpapers that can be used to evaluate the effectiveness of the data center's recovery plan (DCRP) recovery teams' responsibilities, their procedures, checklists, and strategies following an actual recovery operation. The recovery procedures and checklists explain how IS personnel will perform their responsibilities. The recovery strategies explain the resources that will be used by IS personnel to perform their responsibilities.

Chapter II-17 provides Workpapers II-17.01 through 11-17.03 that can be used to evaluate the effectiveness of the disaster site recovery team. The disaster site recovery team's responsibilities can be found in Chapter II-6 of this book. The DCRP coordinator can evaluate the completed workpapers to determine which areas of the plan worked as planned and which areas did not work as planned. After performing this analysis, the coordinator can then make the necessary changes to the Data Center Recovery Plan to ensure that all areas of the plan will work when needed.

CONCLUSION

This chapter has provided workpapers that can be used to evaluate the effectiveness of one of the major teams in the IS DCRP, the disaster site recovery team. The workpapers show how each of the four teams that make up the disaster site recovery team can be evaluated.

Workpaper II17.01 Used in the Evaluation of the Disaster Site Recovery Team Manager

During the recovery operation, did the disaster site recovery team manager:

1. Obtain the names of the staff department representatives who were supporting the disaster site recovery activities.

   Yes ___ No ___

2. Alert the major vendors to the situation using the vendor notification checklists. Yes ___ No ___

   - The computer equipment vendors. Yes ___ No ___
   - The computer supplies vendors. Yes ___ No ___
   - The computer forms vendors. Yes ___ No ___
   - Document the result of the alert for each vendor.

     Yes ___ No ___

3. Provide the vendors with the location of the recovery headquarters. Yes ___ No ___

4. Provide the equipment damage assessment and salvage team leader with checklists containing the current inventories of equipment, supplies, and forms used by the IS department.

   Yes ___ No ___

   - Were the checklists returned completed with appropriate recommendations to either repair or replace that which had been damaged? Yes ___ No ___

5. Alert the utility service companies of the situation and request their assistance in assessing the damage.

Yes ___ No ___

- Was the recovery services companies notification checklist used? Yes ___ No ___

6. Obtain clearance before sending any recovery teams into the building to assess the extent of damage. Yes ___ No ___

7. Review the recommendations made by the team leader on whether the repairs could be made on a timely basis, or whether a temporary data center should be used.

Yes ___ No ___

8. Review the recommendations of the facilities damage assessment and restoration team leader on which of the potential temporary data center sites should be selected.

Yes ___ No ___

9. Review the recommendations made by the team leader as to which equipment, supplies, and forms were salvageable, and which were destroyed. Yes ___ No ___

10. Direct team leaders to order replacements for the destroyed equipment, supplies, and forms. Yes ___ No ___

11. Direct team leaders to make provisions for cleaning damaged, but salvageable equipment and supplies. Yes ___ No ___

12. Direct team leaders to make provisions for protecting undamaged equipment, supplies, and forms. Yes ___ No ___

The evaluation of the disaster site recovery team manager's role with the communications damage assessment and salvage team is covered in Part III of this book.

During the recovery operation, were all of the procedures, checklists and strategies satisfactory? Explain what should be changed or improved, and why.

Workpaper II17.02 Used in the Evaluation of the Facility Damage Assessment and Restoration Team Leader

During the recovery operation, did the facility damage assessment and restoration team leader:

1. Obtain the names of the staff department support representatives and the recovery services company representatives that would be assisting the team during the damage assessment and restoration activities.

   Yes ___ No ___

2. Participate in the evaluation of the extent of damage.

   Yes ___ No ___

3. Obtain information on the extent of damage.

   Yes ___ No ___

4. Obtain the initial estimate of damage to the structure and the estimate of the time required to repair it.

   Yes ___ No ___

   - Record the information they obtained on the disaster site damage assessment form. Yes ___ No ___

5. Notify the disaster site recovery team manager if IS could begin the cleanup operations to move back into the damaged site, or would need to obtain a temporary data center location. Yes ___ No ___

6. Use the disaster site damage assessment form to record the initial damage assessment. Yes ___ No ___

7. Contract with, or recommend contracting with, general contractors, demolition contractors, cleanup and salvage contractors, heating and air conditioning contractors, electrical contractors, fire protection contractors, security systems contractors, and plumbing contractors?

Yes ___ No ___

8. Evaluate the available space in other facilities if the building could not be repaired in a reasonable period of time. Yes ___ No ___

- Use the temporary location facilities requirements information checklist. Yes ___ No ___
- Use the temporary computer site facilities review form when each of the potential temporary locations were analyzed. Yes ___ No ___

During the recovery operation, were all of the procedures, checklists, and strategies satisfactory? Explain what should be changed or improved, and why.

____

____

____

____

____

____

____

Workpaper II17.03 Used in the Evaluation of the Equipment Damage Assessment Team

During the recovery operation, did the equipment damage assessment and salvage team leader:

1. Obtain the names of the staff department support representatives, the vendor representatives, and the recovery services vendor representatives that would assist the team during the damage assessment activities.

   Yes ___ No ___

2. Evaluate the extent of damage to the computer equipment, supplies, and forms. Yes ___ No ___

3. Obtain the estimate of damage for the equipment.

   Yes ___ No ___

   - Record the results on the computer equipment inventory checklists. Yes ___ No ___
   - Develop a report that lists equipment that was not damaged, the equipment that was damaged but repairable, and the equipment that had been destroyed.

     Yes ___ No ___

   - Arrange to protect damaged equipment from any potential new damage.

     Yes ___ No ___

4. Obtain the estimate of damage for the computer supplies.

   Yes ___ No ___

- Record the results on the computer supplies inventory checklists. Yes ___ No ___

5. Obtain the estimate of damage for the computer forms. Yes ___ No ___

   - Record the results on the computer forms inventory checklists. Yes ___ No ___

6. Assess the damage to the tapes, cartridges, and disks located in the damaged site. Yes ___ No ___

During the recovery operation, were all of the procedures, checklists, and strategies satisfactory? Explain what should be changed or improved, and why.

____

____

____

____

____

____

____

____

III VOICE AND DATA COMMUNICATIONS RECOVERY

III VOICE AND DATA COMMUNICATIONS RECOVERY

VOICE AND DATA COMMUNICATIONS RECOVERY

PART

III

Today's communications-dependent applications have become an integral part of conducting business. Government entities conduct lotteries, dispense entitlements, and track criminals using computers and sophisticated communications systems virtually unheard of a decade ago. Communications systems are used to activate gasoline pumps, verify credit cards, make automated teller machine transfers, order products and services, trade stock, and facilitate thousands of other applications.

It is difficult to think of an application that is not communications-dependent, even in companies far removed from what are historically considered to be information services. For example, manufacturing operations were thought to be immune from disasters in communications and other automated systems; production lines would not stop because of a communications failure. But times have changed. Today, automated systems control production lines, and systems for processing inbound manufacturing orders are connected by communications links to other parts of the company, including product design, engineering, production, and postsales support. These systems allow constant tracking and quality control of every stage of the process. They are key to such modern production methods as just-in-time inventory management and affect everything from production cycle time to overall customer satisfaction.

A COMMUNICATIONS REVOLUTION

The following example helps put increases in network use in perspective. In 1968, the size of the AT&T network, at that time the only telephone network in the US, was roughly the size of the MCI network in 1993. MCI currently holds about 10% of US market share. The rest represents growth, most of which has been in the past decade alone.

Due to increased competition, first in long distance and now in local telephone service, communications has become a bargain. And as with most other commodities, reductions in cost have spurred increases in use. It was not so long ago that long-distance calls were in the 50-cent-per-minute range. Even as late as 1985, the average per-minute rate for many US corporations—after factoring in volume discounts, dedicated access lines, WATS line optimization, and other advantages—was about 35 cents per minute. Today, even the smallest company can get a 20-cent-per-minute rate without much trouble at all. The largest companies command rates as low as five cents a minute. It has also become common for a call anywhere in the continental US to be rated at the same price, regardless of distance. The implications have been profound. Such telephone order services as 1-800 FLOWERS would not have been profitable when long-distance service cost 50 cents a minute, but it is at eight cents a minute.

The change in pricing in data communications has been even more pronounced. For example, in 1984, a 56K-byte circuit from Dallas to Houston cost about $3,500 per month. Today, an organization can lease a full T1 circuit—24 times the capacity—for about $900 per month. That is 24 times the capacity at 25% of the price.

This is only the beginning. It is estimated that only about 1% of the theoretical maximum capacity of US fiber-optic lines is in use at any one time; the rest sits idle. A single fiber-optic strand the thickness of a human hair can simultaneously handle more than 250,000 calls. With new transmission technologies, potentially millions of calls could be handled over a single fiber-optic line.

In a world of access to fiber optics, capacity on demand will be the rule. This in turn will create a host of new services. PC-based data will be automatically backed up by uploading to a central repository over a high-speed network. Engineers working on a joint project at remote locations will be able to view and manipulate full-color, three-dimensional objects on a screen while conversing with each other. Brain scans will be sent to specialists hundreds of miles away. Customers will be able to request that product information be sent to a multimedia mailbox; the reply, delivered in minutes, might be in the form of written literature, a voice message, or a technical diagram.

In the bold new world we are entering, the only certainty is that our dependence on the network will increase. For this reason, it is important that we gain an understanding of the vulnerabilities of these systems and how to protect and recover critical communications resources. Part III of this book is designed to help achieve that goal.

METHODOLOGY FOR DEVELOPING A COMMUNICATIONS RECOVERY PLAN

The process of developing a communications recovery plan can be broken into distinct phases, each with its own action items, objectives, and deliverables. Breaking the project into phases makes it easier to establish and monitor progress against objectives. Although there are several alternatives, a six-phase development methodology is suggested. These phases are covered in the following six chapters of Part III, beginning with Chapter III-2 (Chapter III-1 providing an introduction to communications recovery planning focusing on the causes of communications disasters):

- *Chapter III-2.* Performing a preliminary risk analysis and presenting the results to senior management in order to obtain its commitment to the planning project.
- *Chapter III-3.* Identifying the internal and external resources needed to complete the communications recovery plan.
- *Chapter III-4.* Evaluating the communications environment against a set of operating standards to ensure the organization's ability to recover as well as to prevent disasters from occurring in the first place.
- *Chapter III-5.* Documenting global recovery procedures that affect the organization as a whole. These procedures are common to any type of recovery operation, including communications recovery. These procedures should be documented before the recovery planner attempts to identify and document communications-specific recovery procedures.
- *Chapter III-6.* Documenting communications-specific recovery procedures. These include procedures for recovery of communications following a companywide disaster as well as procedures for recovering from the failure of specific network components.

- *Chapter III-7.* Planning for the testing, maintenance, and training needed to ensure the communications recovery plan can be executed successfully.

It typically takes an organization at least 18 months to complete all six phases; larger and more complex projects might take as long as 30 months to complete. One of the reasons for this relatively long time frame is that the recovery strategies must adapt to the technical environment. In most cases, changes in system configuration required by the plan must evolve slowly; it is not reasonable or cost-effective to simply scrap the existing network because it does not conform to the ultimate recovery objectives.

The following paragraphs provide a brief overview of each of the chapters of Part III.

UNDERSTANDING THE CAUSES OF COMMUNICATIONS DISASTERS

To develop an effective voice and data communications recovery plan, the planner must thoroughly understand the causes of communications disasters. Disaster types can be divided into four categories: natural causes, human error, intentional causes, and equipment failure. Most communications failures are caused by human behavior, despite the fact that many of these failures could be prevented by implementing appropriate security standards and safeguards.

OBTAINING MANAGEMENT COMMITMENT

Management commitment is essential for ensuring the success of the recovery planning effort. Management must be informed as to what communications resources need to be protected and why they need protection. To accomplish this, senior managers must be interviewed to determine the financial damage to the company of the interruption of communications to a critical business function or system. Various checklists and questionnaires can be used in these interviews, as provided in the workpapers. The results of this survey are reported to the executive committee to obtain its permission to initiate the project and to obtain sufficient funding and resources.

IDENTIFYING RESOURCES FOR THE PLANNING PROJECT

The best persons to write the communications recovery plan are the people who built and who run the network—typically, operations personnel. Unfortunately, these people are often extremely busy handling their routine duties and may lack incentives to participate in the planning project. The recovery planner must overcome these hurdles by identifying and recruiting internal resources and integrating these resources, drawn from multiple departments, into effective teams. A wealth of external resources is also available. For example, local and long-distance carriers offer a variety of useful products and services that can form key components of the recovery plan.

EVALUATING THE COMMUNICATIONS ENVIRONMENT USING STANDARDS

Standards and procedures for the operation and security of communications systems are essential components of the communications recovery plan. They affect every aspect of how the organization provides, uses, and recovers communications services. These include standards governing equipment installation, fire protection, housekeeping, access control, and network operations as well as standards for assigning responsibility and obtaining technical support. These standards can be used to evaluate existing communications facilities to identify operations that do not comply with recommendations. The results of this evaluation can be used to implement the necessary controls of routine operations to both prevent disasters and ensure that the plan, once activated, executes smoothly.

DOCUMENTING GLOBAL RECOVERY PROCEDURES

The primary reason for documenting recovery plan procedures is to ensure that critical systems can be recovered even if the persons usually responsible for those systems are unavailable because of the disaster. Certain global recovery procedures are common to any type of recovery operation, including communications recovery. These include procedures for the initial disaster alert, damage assessment, recovery team activation, and certain general recovery operations. These global recovery procedures should be documented before communications-specific recovery procedures are.

DOCUMENTING COMMUNICATIONS-SPECIFIC RECOVERY PROCEDURES

Communications-specific recovery procedures need to address two types of disaster scenarios: companywide disasters such as those caused by an earthquake or hurricane; and failure of specific network components such as PBX hardware and software, communications cables, or a long-distance service. Recovery procedures might cover command routing of an incoming 800 service, redirection of T1 lines, reestablishing dial-in data ports, and restoration of communications bridges and gateways. Workpapers provide detailed examples of these procedures.

COMMUNICATIONS RECOVERY PLAN TESTING, MAINTENANCE, AND TRAINING

The success of the recovery plan depends not only on how well it has been developed but on its testing and maintenance and on the training of recovery team members. Routine testing can help ensure that the procedures actually work as planned. Maintenance activities must be documented and enforced to keep the plan up to date with changes in the business environment. A program of regular training must be implemented to ensure recovery team members understand their responsibilities and can execute them quickly and efficiently. It is also necessary to educate new employees about correct recovery procedures.

Understanding the Causes of Communications Disasters

CHAPTER

III-1

The recovery planner must thoroughly understand the causes of communications disasters in order to develop recovery plans that effectively address them. This introductory chapter presents a comprehensive review of the threat environment confronting communications-dependent organizations. The chapter discusses the causes of communications disasters—both general causes and those that are specific to communications systems. Several case studies of actual disasters are also presented.

GENERAL CAUSES OF COMMUNICATIONS DISASTERS

With dramatic growth in communications technology has come an increase in vulnerability to disruptions in the network. Ten years ago, communications interruptions were inconveniences; today they are disasters. For example, on October 17, 1987, the day the Dow Jones Industrial Average dropped more than 500 points, telephone and trading systems were overwhelmed. Some people lost 25% of their stock market equity that day because they could not reach their brokers. The volatility of the financial markets graphically illustrates the dependence on communications and the vulnerability of organizations when systems do not work. Businesses with high dependence on communications systems are summarized in Exhibit III-1-A.

There are many causes of communications disruptions and disasters. Some, such as fire, water, intrusion, and sabotage, are familiar to traditional contingency planners accustomed to disaster planning for the data center. Others, however, are completely communications-specific.

Telephone fiber-optic and cable cuts are the most common cause of network disruptions. Although cable cuts occur frequently, they are disastrous only in extreme circumstances. Nonetheless, they cost businesses billions of dollars in lost revenue per year. Telephone cable and optical fiber cuts due to weather, construction, or excavation can last from a few hours to several days. A breakdown of the causes of fiber-optic cable damage excerpted from a June 1993 FCC technical report is provided in Exhibit III-1-B.

Disaster types can be divided into four categories: natural causes, human error, intentional causes, and catastrophic equipment failure. As shown in Exhibit III-1-C, most communications disasters are caused by human behavior. This is particularly ironic, because it is the one area in which it is possible to protect against disasters by implementing security standards and safeguards.

Natural Causes

Natural causes of communications disasters include fires, floods, hurricanes, tornadoes, earthquakes, and severe temperatures.

EXHIBIT III-1-A COMMUNICATIONS-DEPENDENT ORGANIZATIONS

- Airlines
- Online reservations systems
- Hotel chains
- Car rental services
- Bank card companies
- Banks
- Brokerages
- Telemarketers
- Retailers (especially mail order)
- Service bureaus
- Many manufacturing companies
- Government
- 911 and emergency services

EXHIBIT III-1-B CAUSES OF FIBER-OPTIC CABLE DAMAGE

(Total of 160 Outages)

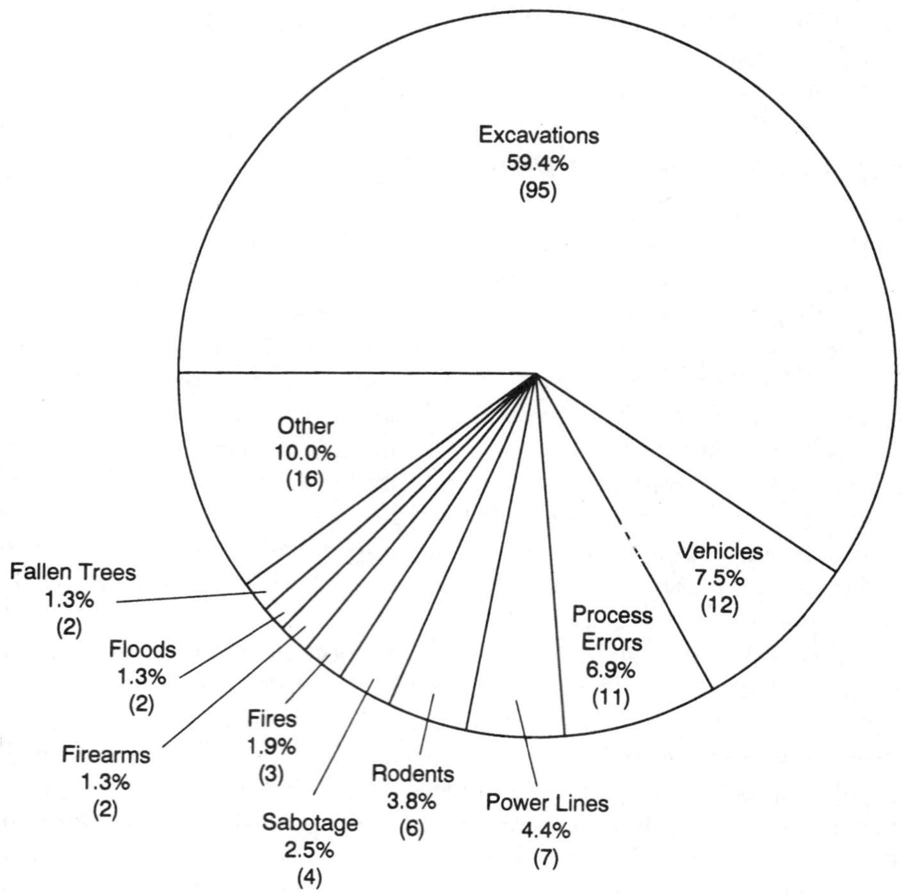

Fires. Probably one of the most noteworthy fires involving automated systems was the 1988 First Interstate Bank fire in Los Angeles. The bank experienced a major fire on a Saturday evening but opened for business the next Monday morning. The recovery plan worked, and the business was spared. The most infamous disaster involving communications was the May 8, 1988 fire in the Hinsdale central office in suburban Chicago, which affected half a million users for up to six weeks.

EXHIBIT **III-1-C** CAUSES OF DISASTERS TO NETWORK INSTALLATIONS

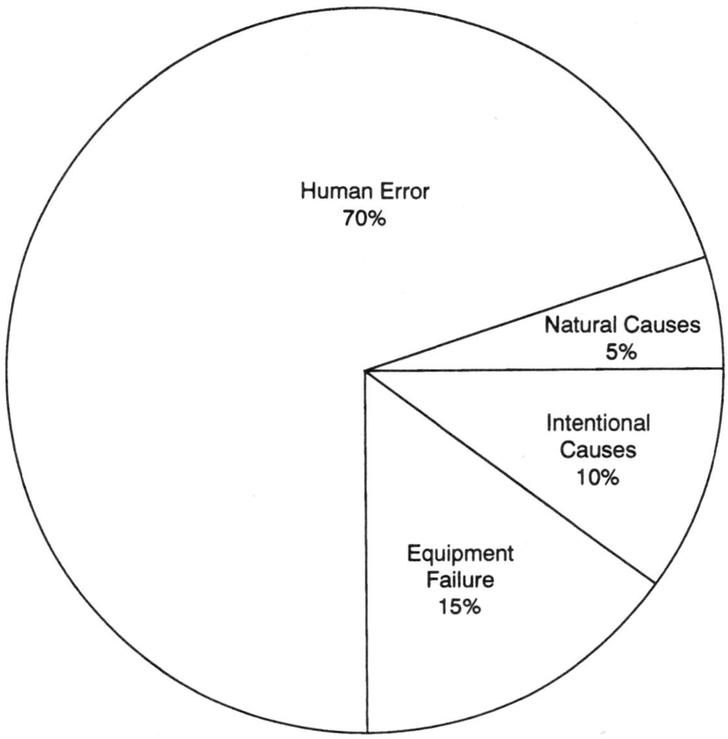

Floods. There have been many incidents involving flooding over the past few years. For example, in 1992, a break in a wall between the river and a tunnel system beneath Chicago resulted in massive damage, isolation of communications facilities and carriers, and multiple disaster recovery center activations. Even disaster recovery centers themselves have not been spared. A major recovery company in New Jersey experienced flooding in its recovery facility during a series of severe storms on the East Coast in 1991. In the American Midwest, 1993 was a banner year for flooding as unprecedented rainfalls swelled rivers.

Flooding of communications facilities need not be so dramatic, however. A burst pipe in an equipment room or a flooded utility hole can be equally catastrophic.

Hurricanes. In 1992, Hurricane Andrew slammed south Florida, becoming the costliest disaster in US history in terms of property damage and destroying thousands of homes and businesses. Hurricane Iniki pounded the Hawaiian island of Kauai only months later. In fact, the cellular telephone system on Kauai became the largest mobile phone company in the country for several months following the hurricane, basically because it was the only phone system that survived.

Tornadoes. There have been numerous documented cases of central offices and data center facilities sustaining damage due to tornadoes. There have been several documented cases of tornadoes destroying telephone central offices. With wind speeds to 600 miles per hour, even the sturdiest communications facilities can be completely incapacitated with little or no warning. The central and south central US are prime breeding grounds for tornadoes.

Thunderstorms and hail are also problems. During the first two years of 1990, insurance companies in Texas paid out more in claims for hail damage than any other cause. There has been at least one documented case over the past few years of a central office being destroyed by baseball-size hail when a roof collapsed.

Earthquakes. The 1989 earthquake that rocked the San Francisco area forced 360 Pacific Bell and GTE central offices to go on backup power. Remarkably, the system held up with little interruption of telephone service. (This was in marked contrast to the 1986 quake in Los Angeles, when service was severely disrupted.)

Often when a major earthquake strikes, the primary long-distance carriers change the mix of incoming and outgoing trunk lines to the affected area. They increase the amount of outgoing lines and decrease the amount of incoming lines. The presumption is that people in the affected area may need help and will need to dial out more than people need to dial in to check on their status. This should be kept in mind when an organization is developing a response plan in an earthquake-prone area. The plan should call for the facility in the earthquake area (e.g., California) to call a facility outside the area (e.g., Georgia). Persons in other areas of the country would then call Georgia for status reports about the California facility. This arrangement helps conserve trunks for other users who may be involved in relief efforts.

Temperature Changes. A failure in a major air-conditioning system could have dire consequences by subjecting equipment to heat-related stresses. This could be due to a power failure or even a failure in the water system if outside water is used for cooling. But temperature changes also mean sensitivity to cold. Flooding due to frozen and broken pipes is a major cause of disasters.

Human Errors

More than two-thirds of all communications disasters are ultimately attributed to human error. In one case, for example, a major long-distance company sustained a one-and-a-half-day outage of its automated systems because a technician pressed an emergency system shutdown button thinking it was the shutoff switch for a fire alarm. The result was the loss of all administrative systems from Minneapolis to Mexico for 36 hours. Other causes of people-related disasters are described in the following paragraphs.

Software Programming Errors. Many people do not realize that software errors occur in communications systems as well as data systems. In 1990, for example, a Dallas telephone company introduced a new extended metro service prefix designed to give callers a wider local calling area. On the day of the cutover, thousands of users received access to hundreds of new telephone prefixes in the Dallas area—but not to any of the original prefixes. This problem illustrates the frailty of today's communications systems. As they rely more on computers, they also demand the same kinds of protection. For example, PBX software and class-of-service indicators must be backed up and stored off-site.

Lack of Training. Untrained or undertrained persons have a much higher probability of causing damage to automated systems. This could involve technical service persons with direct responsibility for equipment. For example, in one case a testboard technician sent a loop-back tone down the line of a multipoint data circuit and in the process knocked out an entire airline network for two hours. Standardization of testing practices can help reduce these kinds of outages.

Carelessness or Inattention. Major disruptions can also be caused when overworked and stressful persons make irrational decisions. Similarly, when tasks become too ingrained, mistakes can be made on even the most routine activities. For example, seasoned telephone company technicians know not to smoke in cable vaults because cable vaults can produce hydrogen gas, which is flammable. In one case, a pipe-smoking technician followed the correct procedure by putting out his pipe before entering the vault. But after exiting the vault and relighting his pipe, he suddenly recalled that he had left something behind. This time he forgot about the pipe; the resulting explosion badly damaged the vault.

Cable Cuts. Telephone cable cuts are the most common cause of communications disruptions. There are hundreds of examples of accidental cable cuts. In 1992, a technician accidentally cut a major cable in a utility hole in New Jersey. Unfortunately, this cable was a 1.7-gigabyte fiber-optic cable that carried the equivalent of 250,000 simultaneous telephone calls. It isolated 60% of New York City's AT&T long-distance traffic for most of a business day.

Telephone, electric, fiber-optic, and television cable, gas and waterlines, and other facilities are most often installed in the same public rights-of-way, mainly along streets and thoroughfares. In many cities, particularly older ones on the eastern seaboard, these rights-of-way date back many years. Consequently, a contractor digging to repair or install facilities is often not sure what the backhoe will find on the way down. Even with warning signs and other precautions, buried cables remain vulnerable.

Record-keeping can also be a problem when rights-of-way have been in continuous use for decades or more. Being off even a few inches with a backhoe can have devastating consequences to buried utilities of all types.

During recent years, some companies have begun laying fiber in abandoned steam tunnels, subway tunnels, and other public rights-of-way. Although this eliminates one problem by making the facility more accessible, it could be creating another by making the facility visible and susceptible to other disruptions (e.g., tampering by unauthorized personnel). There is also the question of what happens to the cable every time it must cross highway, road, or river. Cables run under bridges, sometimes in conduit, sometimes not. There have been several documented cases of persons under bridges building fires to stay warm and in the process burning the cable. One such incident disrupted communications to several towns.

A number of precautions can be taken to prevent accidental disruption to cables. But in general a good first step is to arrange a meeting with the local telephone company account representative to assess the company's exposure in this area. Alternative or diverse routing may be available in the company's service area for little or no cost. (These lines should not be brought into the building through the same conduit, however; this creates a single point of failure that can undermine the use of diverse routing.)

Intentional Causes

Communications hubs are increasingly becoming deliberate targets of attack. The deliberate causes of disasters in communications systems are discussed in the following sections.

Sabotage and Terrorism. Communications centers are often located in physically well-protected buildings designed to protect the facility against natural disasters and unauthorized intrusion. But even the most secure facility can be vulnerable to sabotage by disgruntled employees. Intentional destruction by such employees can cause major damage, because these people know where damage will have the greatest effect. For example, it is common for fiber-optic cables to be cut intentionally by striking employees.

Major communications hubs can also become targets for terrorism. The 1992 World Trade Center bombing badly damaged the facilities of a major access provider for the New York area. If the bomb had been placed across the street near a major New York Telephone office, the damage would have been far greater, possibly isolating major stock exchanges.

Measures to protect against sabotage and terrorism include monitoring of employee behavior to detect any marked changes that might suggest personal or financial problems; this is especially important for employees in high-pressure positions. Physical access controls should also be implemented to limit entry to communications facilities to authorized personnel only.

Vandalism. There are many forms of vandalism. In one example, an electric utility company with its own microwave network had a constant problem with people shooting at its microwave dish, rendering it unusable every few months. The communications manager finally took matters into his own hands. He had a bull's-eye painted on an unused dish and then put it back on the tower. Afterward, he reported no more problems with new dishes being shot.

Theft. Communications equipment is often stolen. One major problem involves people stealing copper, often by cutting live lines off poles. Several local telephone companies have begun marking cable for easy identification when it turns up in scrap yards. There is also an active secondary market for used PBX cards. Certain types of microcomputers also enjoy a high resale value, which is worrisome for communications managers who increasingly rely on such equipment.

Catastrophic Equipment Failure

An unbreakable system has never been built. Sometimes this breakage can be traced to failure of a specific component, a power surge, or lightning strike. Other times the cause is less clear.

Power Impairment. Whether through power spikes, surges, brownouts, blackouts, or noise, power impairments can damage solid-state equipment. After human-caused damage such as cable cuts and water damage, power problems are the next leading cause of communications disasters.

There are steps one can take to mitigate threats due to power impairment. (These are discussed in greater detail later in this part of the book.) Because power-rectifying equipment is also known to fail, installing redundant power supplies should be mandatory for mission-critical functions.

Lightning. Although this is technically a natural cause of disaster, it is included here because it can cause such major damage to communications equipment. Nothing can protect a building or equipment from a direct lightning hit. Lightning has destroyed telephone central offices, despite how well these facilities are grounded. Lightning can interrupt power and destroy the uninterruptible power supply (UPS) at the same time, resulting in a lengthy outage.

The old proverb that lightning does not strike twice is false. A major midwestern long-distance company sustained two lightning strikes on its digital cross-connect system one year apart, sustaining a day-long outage each time. It should be noted that certain areas are especially prone to lightning—for example, Florida experiences the most lightning of any state in the US.

Rodent Damage. Rodents cause considerable damage every year by gnawing through cables. Standard controls include baited traps and rat poison. Telephone companies have had success with the use of yellow or orange jackets on cables, which rats tend to avoid. (Most fiber-optic cable is yellow or orange.)

Summary

These represent some of the more general categories of disasters. The next section of this chapter reviews several communications-specific disasters and discusses how to avoid catastrophic interruptions of service.

COMMUNICATIONS-SPECIFIC CAUSES OF FAILURE

Communications disasters often differ drastically from those disasters on which most computer center recovery plans are based. A disaster with a key communications supplier can cause hundreds of companies to lose service. Often, no priorities for recovery have been established (other than for recovery of police, 911, and other essential services), so most business users must simply wait for restoration of service. In short, in a major disaster the company is at the mercy of the vendor for its recovery and ultimately its survival. This is why proactive recovery planning is so important.

Central Office Failure

Loss of a telephone central office probably represents the worst-case scenario for the communications contingency planner. A central office serves an area that averages 18 square miles, representing a potentially large number of lines out of service (see Exhibit III-1-D). The typical telephone central office is designed to serve an area averaging 18,000 feet from the central office; this area is smaller in central cities and can be significantly larger in outlying areas.

The loss of a telephone central office differs dramatically from the loss of a computer center. When a computer center burns, dozens of equipment vendors and suppliers join in to help the affected customer. Even so, recovery is extraordinarily taxing and difficult. When the telephone company has a fire, the exact opposite is true. Hundreds of users are out of service, and only one company, the telephone company, is coordinating its own recovery. Historically, telephone central offices have taken from 10 days to six weeks to restore, although intermittent problems may continue within the affected central office for years afterward.

Modern communications equipment becomes more automated every year. Seasoned IS professionals would not install a major computer node in a 75-year-old building with no sprinklers, no Halon, and no fire alarms, nor would they fail to make backups or store software off-site. But this is exactly the state of affairs that exists in thousands of central offices nationwide.

Failure of a Long-Distance Carrier

What does a user do when a long-distance carrier fails? There are numerous examples of long-distance failure involving AT&T, MCI, Sprint, and other companies. In this area, users have alternatives. In fact, currently the United States is the only country

EXHIBIT III-1-D CENTRAL OFFICE SERVING AREAS

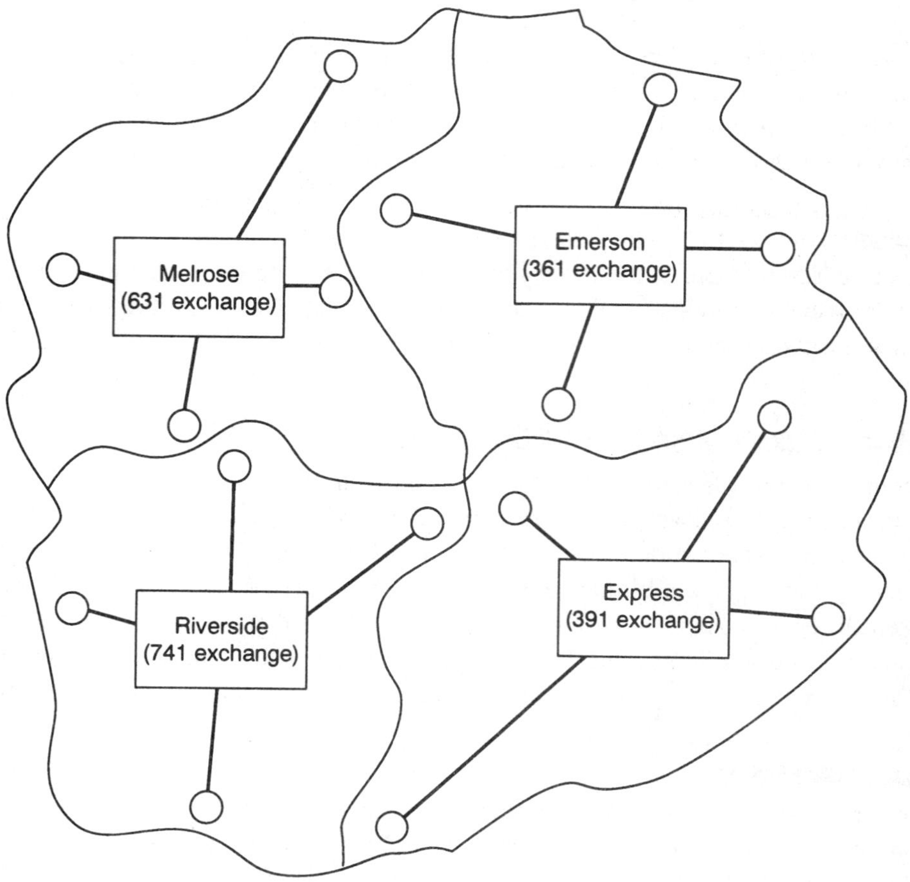

EXHIBIT III-1-E SELECTED LONG-DISTANCE ACCESS CODES

AT&T	10288
MCI	10222
Sprint	10333
LDDS/Metromedia	10084
ATC	10987

in the world in which customers can dial around a long-distance failure using a system designed for equal access through all carriers.

This has a direct bearing on disaster recovery. Equal access was originally intended as a means for all long-distance companies to enjoy the same connections to the local telephone network as AT&T. Even though a customer selects a primary carrier, other carriers can be reached by dialing a five-digit override code. By knowing which codes to dial, users can easily protect against long-distance failures.

Equal access codes for the major carriers include those listed in Exhibit III-1-E. These numbers should be kept on hand. It should be remembered, however, that

EXHIBIT III-1-F SAMPLE EMERGENCY CARRIER OVERRIDE PROCEDURES FOR USE IN A LONG-DISTANCE COMPANY FAILURE

1. In the event that users complain of not being able to complete long-distance calls, attempt to call our primary carrier, MCI (10222), at the following number:

   (800) 555-1212

2. If the problem is going to take a long time to repair or in the event MCI cannot be contacted because of a busy telephone number or other cause, program the PBX to insert the following override code before all 1+ calls. Detailed instructions for doing this can be found in the operating instructions for PBX model SL-100.

Backup Carrier	**Access Code**
AT&T	*10288*

   If customers experience an all-circuits-busy recording, try the next carrier:

Sprint	*10333*

   If customers experience an all-circuits-busy recording, try the next carrier:

ATC	*10987*

   If customers experience an all-circuits-busy recording, consult the metropolitan-area white pages telephone directory for other codes.

3. Call MCI every 30 minutes for status reports until the outage has been resolved, then return to the primary long-distance carrier.

because different carriers typically occupy the same right-of-way or cable, more than one carrier may be affected by the same accident. And other carriers not directly affected by a disaster may nonetheless become overwhelmed as users defect from affected carriers. It may therefore be necessary to dial several codes to get a call through.

Exhibit III-1-F presents emergency carrier override procedures for use in the event of a long-distance company failure. Exhibit III-1-G illustrates equal access using override codes.

Failure of Incoming 800 Service

By now everyone has seen commercials about what happens to a business when 800 service fails. There are many steps that can be taken with the major carriers to reroute 800 numbers. Because of advanced command-routing features available from all major carriers, 800 calls can be answered at virtually any 10-digit telephone number. The switch can be made in as little as 10 minutes by the carriers. Even small companies can enjoy these benefits. Critical 800 numbers can even be answered at home when a major disruption makes this necessary. They can also be easily redirected to computer disaster recovery centers.

Exhibit III-1-H presents emergency recovery procedures for use in a failure of an inbound call center. Exhibit III-1-I illustrates the routing in such a failure.

Internal Building Communications Disasters

It is also useful to evaluate the equipment within the building to protect against communications disasters. (Checklists for evaluating equipment are provided as work-papers in Chapter III-4.)

EXHIBIT III-1-G USE OF ACCESS CODES IN A LONG-DISTANCE COMPANY FAILURE

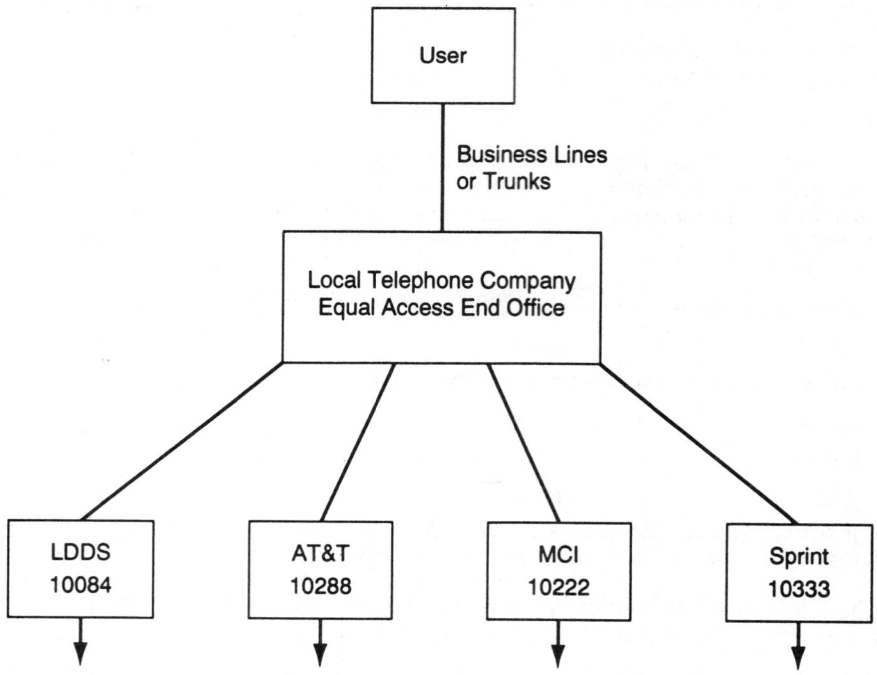

EXHIBIT III-1-H SAMPLE EMERGENCY RECOVERY PROCEDURES FOR USE IN AN INBOUND CALL CENTER FAILURE

CONFIDENTIAL

1. In the event that our primary inbound 800 service center is incapacitated and unable to answer calls, the following three 800 numbers have top recovery priority:

   Inbound Sales and Customer Service: *(800) 555-5555*

   Investor Hot Line: *(800) 555-2211*

   Field Service Support: *(800) 555-3322*

2. The corporation has determined that it can operate without its other 800 numbers for as long as 48 hours. If the disaster is expected to last beyond 48 hours, you will be instructed to consult your disaster recovery plan. Because of the criticality of these numbers on corporate operations, recovery must take place within 60 minutes.

3. The three numbers listed will be redirected to the following alternative location by order of availability:

   Alternative Emergency Call Center Location:

   National Engineering Headquarters (100-line hunt group): *(214) 555-2000*

4. The National Engineering Headquarters will suspend normal operations for the duration of the emergency. For further information, consult your corporate disaster recovery plan document.

EXHIBIT **III-1-1** USE OF 800 SERVICE COMMAND ROUTING IN A TELEMARKETING CENTER FAILURE

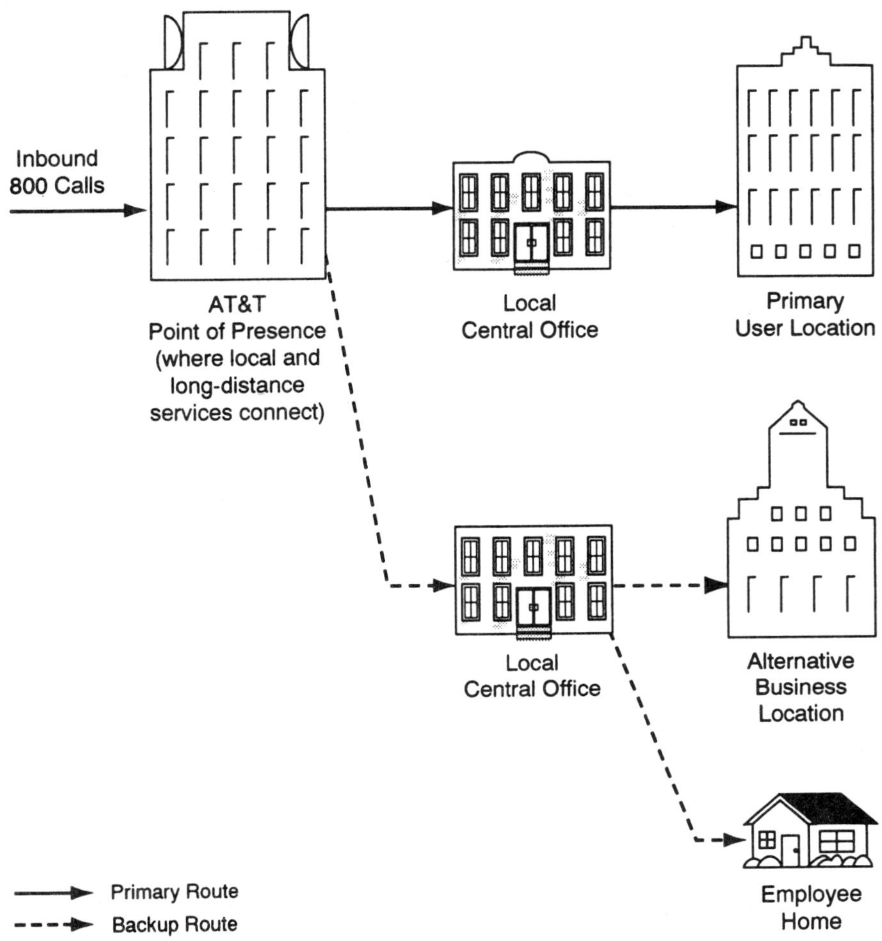

Infrared scanning can be used to identify electrical faults and shorts before they cause fires. It is highly recommended for companies residing in old buildings with antiquated wiring as well as in new buildings that may have not been wired to code. AT&T and other companies provide infrared scanning (also referred to as thermographics service). After the Hinsdale fire, many local and long-distance telephone companies adopted schedules for infrared scanning of their facilities.

Summary

Disasters must be interpreted in a different context when they involve communications. Hundreds of users with limited recovery resources may be affected. It is therefore in the best interest of all communications users to take steps to protect against these disruptions.

CASE STUDY: CENTRAL OFFICE DISASTER

Actual disasters in communications are common. The following paragraphs describe a case involving the destruction of a telephone central office—generally believed to be the worst-case scenario in a communications disaster. Although this is but one

EXHIBIT III-1-J CENTRAL OFFICE STANDARDS ADOPTED AS A RESULT OF HINSDALE FIRE

- Smoke removal systems in large central offices.
- Regular testing with infrared scanners.
- Compartmentalization of central office floor space.
- Direct circuits to the fire department.
- Joint training with fire department.
- New procedures to review power supply protection.
- Alarm reporting procedures reviewed.
- Better management of combustibles in central offices.
- Better management of subcontractors.
- Increased 24-hour human monitoring.
- Improved metropolitan area network routing plans.
- Improved fire detection systems.

well-known example, it should be remembered that in the past 10 years there have been no fewer than 40 telephone central offices destroyed in the US and Canada.

Hinsdale Central Office

This central office fire in suburban Chicago was the first such disaster to occur in a populated area after the AT&T divestiture was complete. By this time, end offices were providing a much broader array of services than just dial tone. For example, carriers derived access lines from Hinsdale; paging companies bought connections into the public network through Hinsdale; and cellular companies connected through Hinsdale. As a Class 4 central office, tens of thousands of calls switched daily between various areas of Chicago through this central office. The fire, which struck on Mother's Day (the busiest calling day of the year) in 1988, affected more than half a million people.

The cause of the fire was found to be a damaged electrical cable, run in a distribution frame along with telephone cables. (It is generally considered a safety hazard to run electrical and telephone cables in the same troughs. A technician expecting to encounter only 48-volt telephone cables could be quite surprised to find 208-volt electrical cables in the same area.) The cable was damaged in a cable mining operation (to recover old copper cable) several months before the fire.

On this particular afternoon, there was a series of thunderstorms moving through the Chicago area, creating electrical disruptions. On weekends, telephone central offices are monitored remotely from a central point, a typical way to save on labor costs. Unstaffed central offices are monitored on the weekends and after hours for such events as fire and intrusion. On this particular afternoon, the central monitoring point was experiencing a number of false alarms because of the thunderstorms. In response, the technician on duty reset the alarms to see whether the condition repeated itself. Therefore, when a valid fire alarm was received, it was initially ignored; the technician simply reset it.

After a second alarm came in 10 minutes later, the technician called the duty supervisor at home, who ordered another technician to survey the central office.

At the scene, the technician immediately detected fire and smoke and attempted to call for help. But by this time, telephone service to the surrounding area was no

EXHIBIT III-1-K OVERVIEW OF SS7 NETWORK CONFIGURATION

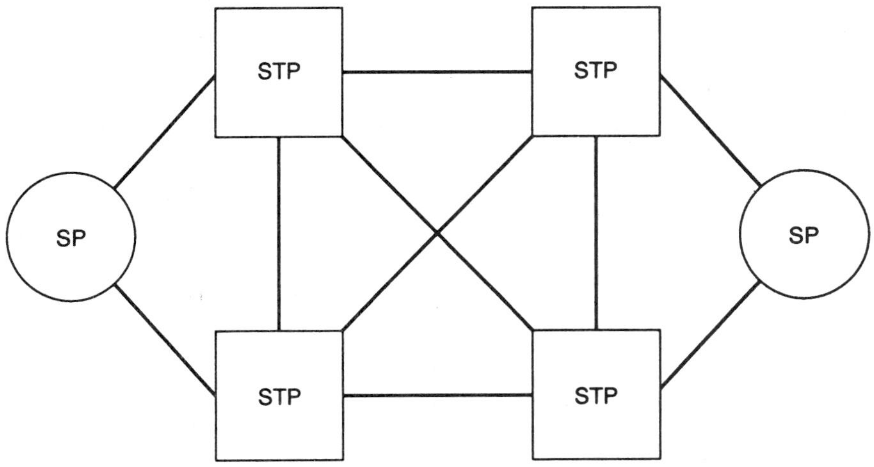

Notes:
STP Signaling transfer point
SP Signaling point

longer available. The technician had to flag down a motorist and drive to the nearest fire department.

When the fire department arrived, the first thing it did was take charge of the building. In effect, the Hinsdale central office no longer belonged to Illinois Bell, and accordingly, all technical personnel were asked to leave.

The fire department next attempted to cut power. After the first attempt to shut down power, a backup generator kicked in. When this was shut down, battery backup went online and, despite the best efforts of the fire fighters, the air conditioning continued to run.

The fire department next set out to control the fire—in this case, with water. The fire was centered in an overhead cable rack filled with burning PVC-coated cable. The water put the fire out, but burning PVC created sulfides, which, when mixed with water, create sulfuric acid. In addition to equipment getting wet, it also became contaminated with sulfuric acid. Because the air conditioning was still running, droplets of sulfuric acid were dispensed into other areas of the building. After a few hours, the fire was declared out, and control was returned to Illinois Bell.

The building suffered a destroyed switch, damaged ancillary equipment, and a burned-out wire center. It would take nearly six weeks to recover.

The Hinsdale fire is a classic example of a major central office disaster. It will be referred to in later chapters of this book to illustrate how to avoid similar occurrences. As shown in Exhibit III-1-J, various central office safety standards were adopted as a result of the Hinsdale fire.

CASE STUDY: SOFTWARE-INDUCED NETWORK FAILURE

In addition to destroyed central offices, catastrophic software failures have also played a large role in communications disasters. The following is one example.

EXHIBIT **III-1-L** BELLCORE RECOMMENDATIONS FOR SS7*

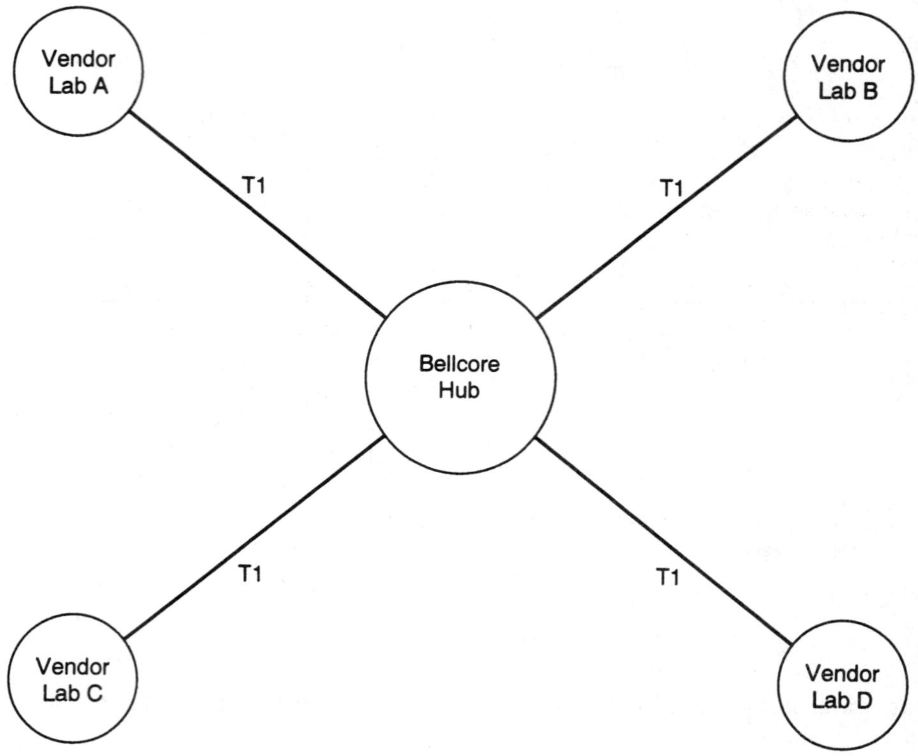

Recommendations to prevent SS7 network outages include:

- Reduce SS7 link oscillation (in and out of service).
- Improve congestion control procedures.
- Avoid compounding congestion problems through increased testing and notification.
- Improve network restoration procedures.

Note:
*Bellcore, the research arm for the local Bell operating companies, provides multicompany test capabilities between numerous equipment vendors.

AT&T Network Failure (1990)

In January 1990, a software upgrade designed to provide greater network robustness caused one of the most widespread communications disasters in US history. An error in the operating code for the AT&T Signaling System 7 (SS7) network caused cascading failures throughout all of AT&T's signaling transfer points—the processors that control the setup and teardown of calls.

In lay terms, the SS7 network is a data network that overlays the public switched telephone network. The SS7 network is composed chiefly of signaling transfer points, signaling points (such as tandems or end offices), and a diversely routed network of links between processors (see Exhibit III-1-K). SS7 networks are engineered for less than 10 minutes of outage per year, or 1 in every 10 million messages. Constant monitoring and performance analysis are required to achieve this goal.

The SS7 network provides for fast call setup and such enhanced features as "look ahead" to determine the availability of a phone in a distant city before setting up a call. (If that phone is busy, the network never bothers setting up a trunk to the distant

EXHIBIT III-1-M SAMPLE EMERGENCY CIRCUIT RECOVERY PRIORITY

Emergency Circuit Recovery
(Priority to Be Used in Declaration of Disaster)

CONFIDENTIAL

The following circuits, in the order shown, shall be redirected to the company's disaster recovery facility at 100 Forest Oaks Drive, Anytown MA, in the event of a formal disaster declaration by the company. For further information, refer to your disaster recovery plan.

Priority	Circuit Number	Speed	Function
1	DDEZ121212 *Vendor:* AT&T	1.544M-bps	Inbound voice service to NCC and customer support (required for coordination, command, and control)
2	DDEZ124455 *Vendor:* AT&T	1.544M-bps	Router link; customer support/sales
3	DDEZ124456 *Vendor:* AT&T	1.544M-bps	Remote Chicago 3725 processor; serves northern US operations
4	DSEC123456 *Vendor:* AT&T	64K-bps	Router link; Midwest sales support
5	DSEC123457 *Vendor:* AT&T	64K-bps	Corporate finance
6	DDEZ124457 *Vendor:* AT&T	1.544M-bps	Los Angeles IDNX node; western US operations
7	All remaining digital private line circuits. *Vendor:* AT&T/MCI		
8	All remaining analog private line circuits. *Vendor:* AT&T/MCI		
9	Voice telephone numbers identified in recovery plan. *Vendor:* New England Telephone		
10	Other services, as instructed.		

city; instead, it simply directs a busy signal at the calling party.) SS7 also provides for much better use of facilities and the ability to identify and move 800 numbers between carriers.

In 1990, an outage was caused by a software coding error that was present in all network processors and that responded to the same conditions; 50 million calls were blocked during one day. By restoring to a version of the code made before the error and stored in a routine backup, it was possible to stabilize the network. (The conditions were then replicated in a laboratory to verify the cause of the failure.) Exhibit III-1-L lists recommendations for preventing SS7 network outages.

MEASUREMENT OF COMMUNICATIONS OUTAGES

In June 1991, a series of major failures hit the public switched telephone networks of Pacific Telephone and Bell Atlantic as a result of equipment compatibility problems and problems with managing data congestion on the SS7 network. A new term was developed to describe the effect of these outages: user lost erlangs (ULE).

Telephone companies employ Erlang theory to determine the number of interoffice trunks, dial tone senders, and other components to provide a given level of service and to determine the rate of calls that will be blocked because trunks are busy. For example, a PO5 level of service indicates that 5 out of 100 callers will experience a busy signal. User lost erlangs refers to a measurement of the level of degraded service and resulting lost calls. For example, an outage with a ULE of 6.0 equates to one million customers out of service for one hour. The Hinsdale fire measured 6.0; the 1990 AT&T network failure described measured 6.3.

PRIORITY IN DISASTER RECOVERY

The following list represents the order in which most communications managers would prefer communications services to be recovered:

1. T3 service.
2. T1 service.
3. Digital data service.
4. Analog data service.
5. Business telephone service.
6. Residential telephone service.
7. Pay telephones.

Experience shows, however, that the order of recovery is actually reversed. Telephone companies start with recovery of pay telephones, the idea being to provide some limited service to a wide area for 911 and emergency services. After the Hinsdale fire, for example, it took up to six weeks to restore T3, T1, and other types of private lines—they were the last type of service to be restored.

There have been some minor modifications made to this order by some local operating companies. (The restoration priority is usually a closely guarded policy and it is not possible to mention which ones.) Some do take into account such uses as banking or telephone-dependent retail operations in their priority scheme. This has been a relatively new change, occurring over the past three or four years. Nonetheless, as a rule of thumb, it is still best to keep a roll of quarters on hand—pay phones will generally work first. It is recommended that the organization document its own internal priority scheme for circuit restoration, similar to the one shown in Exhibit III-1-M.

Obtaining Management Commitment

CHAPTER

III-2

This phase of recovery planning attempts to answer the questions of what communications resources need to be protected and why they need protection. Answering these questions requires identification of critical business systems. To accomplish this, senior managers in the major business units are interviewed to estimate the financial damage to the company of the interruption of communications to a critical system (e.g., a telemarketing or telephone order center) for a given period of time. This chapter provides a variety of checklists and questionnaires that can be used in interviewing senior management (see Workpapers III2.01 through III2.09).

The results from individual interviews are next cross-checked with results from other departments and with corporate financial managers to provide a comprehensive estimate of financial loss. A presentation of these findings is then made to the executive committee, in which the focus is on the relevant business issues and not on technical matters related to recovery strategies and procedures. The objective of this collaboration is to obtain management support, both in terms of money and resources, to pursue the recovery project.

In summary, the following actions are performed:

1. Interview senior management to identify critical business areas and systems and to obtain estimates used in the preliminary loss analysis.
2. Quantify potential losses using the information obtained in Step 1.
3. Present the results to senior management.

DEFINING CRITICAL SYSTEMS

As with all business resumption plans, plans for the recovery of communications services focus primarily on mission-critical systems. The definition of mission critical depends on a number of factors, including how critical the system is to the conduct of business as well as the organization's tolerance for disruption. For the purposes of this discussion, mission-critical systems are those that, when unavailable, may result in severe financial loss to the organization.

There are two basic ways to gauge mission criticality in communications: size of the installation and function. Often, the only method used in many departments is size of the installation. For example, common sense dictates that a 1,000-line PBX is more critical than a 12-line key system. What is often overlooked, however, is the function that the equipment is intended to serve. For example, a company might have certain customers who routinely place large orders. In appreciation, these customers get their own telephone numbers to place orders and do not wait in queue with other customers. The company naturally does not tell its other customers that this "inner circle" is assigned special numbers. These are very important incoming numbers for the company, ones it would want answered at all times. For this reason, a recovery plan should be in place to ensure these calls are always answered.

In summary, size alone should not be the measure of whether a system is mission critical. It is also important to consider the business function being served. This requires effective communication with management and internal users, centering on the needs of their revenue-producing customers.

STEP 1

INTERVIEW SENIOR MANAGEMENT

In general, managers at the level of senior vice-president or director are interviewed to provide quantifiable input regarding the loss to the company in the event of a disaster. It can be difficult to obtain cooperation in arranging interviews about disaster recovery. Soliciting the direct support of the CEO or CIO can help add a sense of urgency to the effort. There are a number of specific actions that can also be taken to increase awareness within the organization. (These are discussed in more detail in Chapter III-3.)

The interview should concentrate on issues that are meaningful to management. These include such broad-based topics as effects of disasters on sales, market share, customer and investor confidence, corporate cash flow and financial stability, and corporate image. Any one or all of these could become the "hot button" that works to sell the plan.

However, it is first necessary to quantify loss information, which necessitates face-to-face interviews with corporate policymakers, division chiefs, and other senior management. In conducting such interviews, the recovery planner should:

- Maintain a competent and professional bearing. It is important to have a firm, concise agenda before going in.
- Use questions like those provided in the workpapers but avoid reading the questions if possible.
- Encourage the executive to talk about related issues if he or she chooses but be careful to keep on track.
- Limit the initial meeting to 30 minutes or less. If there are other issues to address, another meeting should be scheduled.
- As the interview draws to a close, be the first to wrap it up; the executive should not end the meeting before the recovery planner is ready. This reinforces the image that the planner is competent and in control.
- Wrap up the meeting with a promise that a concise synopsis of the responses of other managers will be provided for the review of the executive (and follow through on this commitment). The executive should be invited to comment on the statements of other peers (presented anonymously if needed) and encouraged to stay active in the planning process.

Sample Interview Questions

Workpapers III2.01 through III2.08 provide a representative sample of questions for determining how dependent specific business operations are on communications services. It is important to obtain the input from these sources to broaden the planner's perspective in the planning effort and ensure that the information is believable to executive management. Some of these questions are repeated; this is intentional, because asking the same questions of different departments makes it possible to cross-check figures to ensure they are accurate.

Sales Department. Aside from the corporate controller, there is no better source for determining the source of incoming cash to the company than the sales department. Because sales executives are generally compensated on the basis of performance, it is usually possible to gain very accurate figures.

After obtaining this information, the interviewer must then consider the effect of each technical support system used in generating sales. For example, a PBX that supports a major sales group can be easily quantified in terms of value. Once again, the interviewer should concentrate not on the size of the group but on the function it performs. Workpaper III2.01 provides sample interview questions for executive management of a sales department.

Marketing Department. Much like the interview performed with the sales department, this interview addresses issues related to market share, market development, customer profile, cash flow, revenue requirements, and other broad factors of the company's operation. The questions are very similar. This is to allow cross-checking between departments to ensure the figures are valid and meaningful. Workpaper III2.02 provides sample interview questions for executive management of a marketing department.

Operations Department. These questions are geared more toward the actual operation of the company. Most of this interview should be directed toward understanding the operation of the core business of the enterprise. This makes it easier to gauge the effect on key business operations of the failure of supporting communications systems and to determine the priority for their recovery. Workpaper III2.03 provides sample questions for interviewing executive management of an operations department.

Facilities Department. This interview is important to clearly identify who is really responsible for the physical structure of the facilities. (There are often conflicts among departments over control of business facilities.) It is also important to identify work already completed in disaster recovery to avoid unnecessary work. For example, the facilities department may have already developed a company policy on the appropriate response by employees to a fire. Existing policies and procedures governing such issues may be effectively incorporated in the plan. Workpaper III2.04 provides sample questions for interviewing the facilities manager.

General Counsel. The legal department should be familiar with the requirements for disaster recovery for its particular industry and can provide useful information to justify the recovery plan to senior management. Also, in most companies the corporate general counsel can provide direct access to the chairperson's office, should this be required. Obtaining the support of the legal department can be important in securing long-term executive support. Workpaper III2.05 provides sample questions for interviewing the general counsel.

Information Systems Department. Senior management in IS and other technical service departments should be interviewed to garner information on such items as equipment replacement times and existing disaster recovery plans (e.g., mainframe recovery plan, software packages used in the plan). It is also useful to establish a relationship with the IS department; a significant number of recovery team members will be recruited from IS because of their technical experience in recovery planning. Workpaper III2.06 provides sample questions for interviewing executive management of an IS department.

Communications Department. Interviews with senior management in communications should address such issues as equipment replacement times, expected vendor response, and communications auditing procedures. Workpaper III2.07 provides sample questions for interviewing executives of a communications department.

Finance Department. This should be the last interview. The controller should be able to validate most of the financial data received from other department heads. In addition, senior management holds this person in confidence, making his or her acceptance of the plan critical to a successful outcome. Workpaper III2.08 provides sample questions for interviewing executive management of a finance department.

Benefits of Interviews

In addition to the valuable information that can be gained by interviewing division heads, the interview process also provides a number of ancillary benefits. The relationships developed during this planning phase can help in recruitment of recovery team members. Also, by involving other departments at this stage, it becomes easier to obtain support of critical managers later in the recovery project.

Using Questionnaires

It may be impossible to conduct formal interviews with everyone in the company. A well-written questionnaire can do much to augment the information collected from the executive interview process, as well as to help quantify and substantiate the results. In some cases, more accurate information can be gleaned by use of questionnaires, because it allows the user to remain anonymous. (The decision regarding anonymity of respondents must be made when the questionnaire is developed.) Also, some people are better at committing their sentiments to paper rather than face to face.

The risk with questionnaires is that they will be ignored. But if sufficiently well written and presented, the questionnaire can be an effective tool. In short, although interviews are the primary tool in this phase of planning, questionnaires can also play an important role in information gathering. A sample questionnaire is provided as Workpaper III2.09.

Types of Questionnaires. Essentially there are two kinds of questionnaires. One, commonly known as the multiple-choice questionnaire, has several advantages. It is less complex than other alternatives and thus faster to fill out. And because it looks less imposing, it tends to get a higher response rate than more complex questionnaires.

There are some disadvantages to multiple-choice formats. Because they are more highly structured, they tend to limit the answers from users. If the objective is to gain a perspective of the user environment that is unknown to the technical services area, it is self-defeating to have technical services personnel decide the content of the questions.

For these reasons, a less structured and more open-ended questionnaire may be more appropriate. Although the quality of information may be better with open-ended questionnaires, they are much harder to tabulate and compile than their more structured counterpart. Workpaper III2.09 is a hybrid that uses parts of each type.

Response Rate. The response rate for a typical questionnaire in a corporate environment can be initially very low. In fact, a response rate of 10% is considered quite good. It may be necessary to try several times before getting an adequate response.

Departments Receiving Questionnaires. The selection of departments to receive questionnaires depends largely on the results of the executive interviews. Because the primary purpose of the questionnaire is to augment or verify information from these interviews, it is reasonable to include the same seven or eight departments approached in the interview process.

A strong cover letter can help obtain a high response rate, especially if it is written by someone with authority to ensure the questionnaire is returned promptly (e.g., a senior-level manager). The letter should include a date by which the questionnaire is to be returned.

QUANTIFY POTENTIAL LOSSES

STEP 2

There are many ways of measuring the cost of communications disasters. The most logical measure for most companies is financial. How much will the company lose in revenues and profits if a critical support system is lost? Financial metrics, however, are not the only way to quantify network disasters. For example, hospitals may measure loss in terms of lost lives; government agencies might evaluate loss in terms of entitlement checks delayed or lost or felons whose activities cannot be adequately monitored. For most commercial purposes, however, a financial quantification is appropriate.

This section presents an analysis of projected losses given a specific disaster scenario at a hypothetical company that offers photocopier supplies and maintenance services to a broad base of users. Although the number of suppliers is relatively few, the services of this company can be replaced with relative ease through the use of wholesale office supply outlets and other sources. This case helps demonstrate how quickly business can erode as a result of a communications disaster.

Sample Loss Analysis

The ABC Photocopy Company serves northern Texas and offers most brands of photocopier supplies. It has a customer service center of 15 full-time employees that handles an average of 750 calls per day. Ninety percent of its business is conducted by telephone, including:

- Requests for routine maintenance.
- Service calls from customers with maintenance contracts.
- Calls from customers interested in purchasing supplies.
- Calls from customers interested in purchasing maintenance contracts.

The company has two major competitors, of similar size, serving the same area.

Last year, the company had revenues of $11 million. Revenue was derived from the following sources:

- Maintenance contracts: 33%.
- Service calls: 25%.
- Copier supplies: 40%.
- Other: 2%.

Disaster Scenario

The disaster scenario assumes a loss of telephone service as a result of a fire in the serving phone company's central office. It is assumed that the company has no recovery plan that would provide for an alternative site to conduct business. It is estimated that it would take seven days to establish an alternative site, install telephone lines, procure office supplies, and connect (i.e., call forward) phone lines.

EXHIBIT III-2-A LOSS OF SERVICE CALL REVENUE

1. Compute revenue by time period:

Yearly revenue:	$11,000,000
Weekly revenue:	211,538
Daily revenue:	30,220

2. Compute daily revenue from service calls (25% of business):
   $30,220 × 0.25 = $7,555
3. Apply weighting formula $(\frac{1}{3}, \frac{1}{3}, \frac{1}{3})$:

Day 1:	$7,555 × 0.33 =	$ 2,518
Day 2:	7,555 × 0.67 =	5,037
Days 3–7:	7,555 × 5.00 =	37,775

4. Total for estimated loss in this business segment: $45,330

Loss Estimates

The following paragraphs provide estimates of losses for each revenue-generating business segment.

Loss of Maintenance Contract Revenue. The fairly large portion (33%) of this company's revenue coming from maintenance contracts would presumably continue. The assumption is that the automated systems that generate invoices and statements are still intact and that the mail is still running. These are reasonable assumptions. Therefore, the estimated loss of maintenance contract revenue is zero.

Loss of Service Call Revenue. Twenty-five percent of the company's revenue comes from service calls. Because many businesses have only one copier, it can be assumed that their ability to wait will be at a minimum. Therefore, the first assumption is that no user requiring service will wait more than three days. It is assumed that one-third will defect to a competitor on day 1, one-third on day 2, and the remainder on day 3, regardless of whether or not they have a service contract. The projected loss of revenue due to loss of service call capability is calculated as shown in Exhibit III-2-A. The projected loss in this revenue area is $45,330.

Loss of Copier Supply Sales. Forty percent of the company's revenue comes from sales of supplies, many to existing customers with maintenance contracts. Virtually 100% of these sales are accomplished by means of voice telephone contact or fax. Because copier supply items are important to users, they would probably not wait before defecting to ABC's two competitors. The exception would be those under service contracts. Because routine supplies are often included in the cost of the monthly maintenance contract, some users might be inclined to wait. This example weights users three ways. For purposes of clarity and simplicity, the same weighting formula is used here as was used in the previous example for loss of service call revenue. The weighting factors vary in practice depending on the organization's loss assumptions. Losses are calculated as shown in Exhibit III-2-B. The estimated loss of copier supply sales is $72,528.

After review of these figures by responsible management, an estimate of the total loss to the company from such an event is determined to be $117,858. This provides a basis for evaluating how much the company should spend to minimize the effects

EXHIBIT III-2-B LOSS OF COPIER SUPPLY SALES

1. Compute revenue by time period:

Yearly revenue:	$11,000,000
Weekly revenue:	211,538
Daily revenue:	30,220

2. Compute daily revenue from copier supply sales (40% of business):
   $30,220 × 0.40 = $12,088
3. Apply weighting formula ($\frac{1}{3}$, $\frac{1}{3}$, $\frac{1}{3}$):

Day 1:	$12,088 × 0.33 = $ 4,029
Day 2:	12,088 × 0.67 = 8,059
Days 3–7:	12,088 × 5.00 = 60,440

4. Total for estimated loss
   in this business segment: $72,528

EXHIBIT III-2-C SUMMARY OF TOTAL LOSSES FOR KEY BUSINESS OPERATIONS

- $11 million/year in revenue.
- 90% of business by telephone.
- Revenue sources:[a]
  - Maintenance contracts (33%)
  - Service calls (25%)
  - Copier supply sales (40%)
  - Other (2%)
- Assumptions:[b]
  - Maintenance contract revenue stays stable.
  - 100% loss of service call revenue after three days.
  - 100% loss of copier supply sales after three days.
- Total loss by business segment:

Maintenance contracts:	$ 0
Service calls:	45,330
Copier supply sales:	72,528

- Total possible loss due
  to seven-day disruption: $117,858[c]

[a] According to VP sales, VP marketing, and corporate controller.
[b] According to VP sales and VP operations.
[c] Plus lost market share, lost customer confidence, and lost employee productivity (not quantified here).

of an interruption. Exhibit III-2-C provides an example of how the loss information for this case might be summarized for management.

OBTAIN PERMISSION TO PLAN

STEP 3

The final step in this phase is selling the plan to executive management—that is, obtaining approval to proceed with the recovery planning project. It is important to

EXHIBIT III-2-D FUNDING REQUEST FORM (COMPLETED)

Event	Probability of Occurrence (%)	Cost with Plan	Cost without Plan	Lost Operation (days)	Cost to Protect	Improvement
Electrical Cable Cut	10	0	$50,000	1	$5,000	Run redundant circuit
Telephone Cable Cut	20	0	$25,000	1/2	$25,000	Microwave to MCI
Switch Room Fire	5	$3,000	$750,000	14	$30,000	Halon System
"					"	
"					"	
"					"	
"					"	
"					"	
"					"	
"					"	
"					"	
Total					$130,000	

present the problem in terms management can comprehend and in sufficient detail to secure firm commitment. This means using business terms, not technical terms.

There are two principal reasons for this approach. First, if management is asked to make a major decision based solely on complex technical arguments, the project will likely be delayed by endless requests for clarification. In short, the contingency planner can expect to walk out of each meeting with a longer list of questions than he or she went in with. This is why recovery plans often take years to complete.

The second major reason for presenting in business terms is that if the arguments are understandable to a nontechnical manager, they will be understandable to third parties as well. This can be important in the event of litigation after a disaster. If the plan was presented in terms understandable only to other technicians, it will be difficult to convince a court that sufficient warning of the exposure was given to management. An effective warning must be understood by its intended audience.

Building an Effective Business Case

The need for a disaster recovery plan often originates at the highest levels of the company. Some of the typical reasons companies begin disaster recovery plans include:

- *Threat of shareholder suits.* In the US, if there is any wrongdoing at a corporation, the president and board of directors are held responsible. This is why these persons generally carry insurance (on themselves) and why they are interested in disaster recovery.
- *Government mandates.* Certain government agencies mandate demonstrable disaster recovery plans. For example, several banking circulars issued by the US Comptroller of the Currency require disaster recovery plans; some make direct reference to communications (e.g., bank wire transfers). Other directives deal with hazardous materials and other concerns.
- *High-profile exposure.* Such organizations as hospitals and poison-control centers depend highly on public perception of their ability to recover from communications interruptions. If a poison-control line, for example, is out of service and someone dies as a consequence, media reports could be ruinous. If a small subcontractor fails to provide necessary components and shuts down a company's assembly line, the press reports can seriously damage its reputation among clients.

It can be difficult to sell expenditures on disaster recovery planning. Basically, an executive need know only the following to approve the disaster recovery plan:

1. What can happen?
2. What is the probability that it will happen?
3. What does it cost when it happens, in terms of:
   —Lost sales?
   —Lost market share?
   —Lost productivity?
   —Lost customer confidence?
   —Legal liability?
4. What will it cost to make this problem go away?

Presenting these points convincingly should help get the necessary funding and support. Workpaper III2.10 presents a form that can be used to present funding requests to management. A partially completed sample is provided as Exhibit III-2-D.

WORKPAPER III2.01 Sales Interview Questions

INTERVIEW QUESTIONS FOR A VICE-PRESIDENT OR DIRECTOR OF SALES

1. What is the total of gross monthly sales generated by this company? $____________

2. What percentage of the total is generated through the direct use of your:

   Telephone system: ______%

   Automated call distribution unit: ______%

   LAN platform: ______%

   Telemarketing or sales center: ______%

   Other critical system: ______%

3. In your opinion, how long could your department survive a total loss of communications? ______________________________

4. What are the characteristics of the customer base? How long would the typical user of our services wait for us in the event of problems, before giving up and ordering from our competitor? Days? Weeks? Hours? __________________________

   ____

5. What kinds of customers do we have? Are they under exclusive arrangements, or would they order from competitors immediately? ____

   ____

6. What other specific needs or requirements in your department depend on communications that we have not mentioned here?

   ____

   ____

7. Do any of our customers have special requirements such as just-in-time assembly operations or other special considerations? ____

   ____

WORKPAPER III2.02 Marketing Interview Questions

INTERVIEW QUESTIONS FOR A VICE-PRESIDENT OR DIRECTOR OF MARKETING

1. What is the total of gross monthly sales generated by this company? $____________

2. What percentage of the total is generated through the direct use of your:

   Telephone system: ______%

   Automated call distribution unit: ______%

   LAN platform: ______%

   Telemarketing or sales center: ______%

   Other critical system: ______%

3. In your opinion, how long could your department survive a total loss of communications? ______________________________

4. What are the characteristics of the customer base? How long would the typical user of our services wait for us in the event of problems, before giving up and ordering from our competitor? Days? Weeks? Hours? ______________________________

   ____

5. What kinds of customers do we have? Are they under exclusive arrangements, or would they order from competitors immediately? ______________________________

   ____

6. How much did this company spend on its last marketing campaign? How much market share did we pick up as a result?

   ____

   ____

7. Is this company capable of picking up double-digit increases in market share from customers of other companies if those companies were unable to quickly recover after a disaster? (Market share losses of 30% to 50% are not uncommon in competitive industries that have major disruptions.)

   ____

   ____

8. What other specific needs or requirements in your department depend on communications that we have not mentioned here?

____

____

9. What effect does customer confidence have on our operation? If the users begin to think we are an unreliable service provider, in your opinion, how would this affect our market share? ____

____

WORKPAPER III2.03 Operations Interview Questions

INTERVIEW QUESTIONS FOR A VICE-PRESIDENT OR DIRECTOR OF OPERATIONS

1. What is the total of gross monthly sales generated by this division? $____________

2. What percentage of the total is generated through the direct use of your:

   Automated call distribution unit: ______%

   LAN platform: ______%

   Telephone system: ______%

   Telemarketing or sales center: ______%

   Other critical system: ______%

3. How long could your department survive a total loss of communications? ______________________________

4. What are the characteristics of the customer base? How long would the typical user of our services wait for us in the event of problems, before giving up and ordering from our competitor? Days? Weeks? Hours? ______________________________

   ____

5. What kinds of customers do we have? Are they under exclusive arrangements, or would they order from competitors immediately? ______________________________

   ____

6. What other specific needs or requirements in your department depend on communications that we have not mentioned here?

   ____

   ____

7. Are some customers more important than others? For example, do some callers or customers order millions of dollars in product, command large investment portfolios, or have other urgent needs that require priority? ______________________________

   ____

8. Do important customers require priority in disaster recovery? ______________________________

WORKPAPER III2.04 Facilities Interview Questions

INTERVIEW QUESTIONS FOR A FACILITIES MANAGER

1. Does a disaster recovery plan for this physical building exist?

   [ ] Yes [ ] No

2. Who is responsible for coordinating cleanup operations after a disaster? ______

3. Who in your organization is responsible for coordinating security after a disaster? ______

4. What is the procedure for notifying police, fire, and emergency medical support within this company? ______

   ______

5. Are all emergency calls routed through facilities or the security department, or do employees call 911 or other emergency numbers directly? ______

   ______

6. What is the policy on containing small fires? Should an employee ever, under any circumstances, attempt to put out a fire? ______

   ______

7. Have you ever handled a bomb threat? What is the procedure for handling these? ______

   ______

8. Has business ever been suspended due to:

   [ ] Heavy snow?

   [ ] Building contamination?

   [ ] Major storm?

   [ ] Building facility failure?

   [ ] Water flooding?

   [ ] Other? If so, when and what? ______

9. Who gives the order to evacuate the building or activate a backup operations center? ______

WORKPAPER III2.05 General Counsel Interview Questions

INTERVIEW QUESTIONS FOR GENERAL COUNSEL

1. Is our company held to any additional regulations that are not common practice in business in general? (Look closely at this if company is involved in banking, brokerage, service bureau, hazardous-materials handling, nuclear power, or other business line with special federal requirements.)

   ____

   ____

2. Is the company contractually liable to provide a given service level to its customers or to any particular customer that you know of? (This could be commitments to a just-in-time delivery schedule in cases of manufacturing, guaranteed system availability in cases of banking or service bureaus, or other commitments.) ______________________________

   ____

3. Are there any other contractual requirements, guarantees to creditors, or any other obligation we should be aware of in terms of providing our service? ______________________

   ____

WORKPAPER III2.06 Information Systems Interview Questions

INTERVIEW QUESTIONS FOR VICE-PRESIDENT OR DIRECTOR OF INFORMATION SYSTEMS

1. What are the estimated equipment replacement times for the following critical network and mainframe components?

   Mainframe configuration: __________.

   Distributed LAN networks: __________.

   Front-end processors: __________.

   Channel extension equipment: __________.

   Terminals, attendant positions: __________.

   Building wiring systems: __________.

2. Who activates a disaster recovery center?

   [ ] Executive management team/CEO.

   [ ] The IS VP/manager.

   [ ] The facilities VP/manager.

   [ ] Operations VP/manager.

   [ ] Disaster recovery manager.

   [ ] Other: ____________________________.

3. What kinds of physical protective systems exist in major equipment installations (e.g., Halon, sprinklers, access controls)? ____

   ____

4. Do mainframelike security standards apply to local area networks? ____

   ____

5. What is the status of mission-critical applications migrating from mainframe to distributed platforms?

   ____

6. Does a formal set of operating and security standards exist for the computer room? ____________________________

7. Has your department ever been the subject of a security audit? What were the results? ______________________________

____

WORKPAPER III2.07 Communications Interview Questions

INTERVIEW QUESTIONS FOR VICE-PRESIDENT OR DIRECTOR OF COMMUNICATIONS

1. What are the estimated equipment replacement times for the following critical network and mainframe components?

   A major network hub: __________.

   A critical LAN bridge, router or gateway: __________.

   Front-end processors: __________.

   PBXs: __________.

   T1/T3 multiplexers: __________.

   Automated call distribution unit: __________.

   Terminals, telephone sets, attendant positions: __________.

   Building wiring systems: __________.

2. Who activates a disaster recovery center?

   [ ] Executive management team/CEO.

   [ ] The IS VP/manager.

   [ ] The facilities VP/manager.

   [ ] Operations VP/manager.

   [ ] Disaster recovery manager.

3. What kinds of physical protective systems exist in major network installations (e.g., Halon, sprinklers, access controls)? ______________________________

   ____

4. Do mainframelike security standards apply to the communications network and network installations with regard to:

   [ ] Physical security?

   [ ] Change control?

   [ ] Formal maintenance logs?

5. Does a formal set of operating and security standards exist for:

   [ ] Major communications installations?

   [ ] Major local area network installations?

6. Has your department ever been the subject of an audit? What were the results? ______________________________

   ____

   ____

WORKPAPER III2.08 Finance Interview Questions

INTERVIEW QUESTIONS FOR VICE-PRESIDENT OR CONTROLLER OF FINANCE

1. What is the total of gross monthly sales generated by this company in terms of:

   Direct on-site or walk-in sales: $__________.

   Telephone sales: $__________.

   Other types of sales: $__________.

2. How much of the company's sales come from:

   Customers with formal vendor relationships: _____%

   Independent customers who can order elsewhere: _____%

   Specialized product customers who must order from us: _____%

   Sales of products not available elsewhere: _____%

3. How long could the company survive a total loss of communications? __________

4. What are the characteristics of the customer base? How long would the typical user of our services wait for us in the event of problems, before giving up and ordering from our competitor? Days? Weeks? Hours? __________

   ____

5. What kinds of customers do we have? Are they under exclusive arrangements, or would they order from competitors immediately? __________

   ____

6. What other specific needs or requirements in this company depend on communications that we have not mentioned here?

   ____

   ____

7. We have been given a figure of $__________ in gross monthly sales, generated by the critical systems we have identified. Is this figure correct? (If not, explain.)

   ____

8. Are there any extenuating financial circumstances regarding the company's debt structure, contractual obligations to creditors, or other areas that we should be aware of when developing the recovery plan? ______________________________

____

WORKPAPER III2.09 Communications Standards and Practices Questionnaire

SAMPLE COMMUNICATIONS STANDARDS AND PRACTICES QUESTIONNAIRE

INSTRUCTIONS: This multiple-choice survey should require only a minimum amount of time to complete. Your candid answers to the following carefully selected questions will greatly aid us in providing improved quality services in your organization. The survey is divided into five areas of interest:

I. Major uses of communications in your organization.

II. Technical issues.

III. Communications support issues.

IV. Communications security procedures.

V. Future plans.

We appreciate your taking time out to assist us, as this information will be of great use to other communications network service users.

Respondent Information

Name: ______________________ Title: ________________

Organization: ______________________________________

Address: ____

City: ______________ State: __________ Zip Code: ______

Telephone: ___________

I. Major Uses of Communications in Your Organization

1. What is the primary business function performed in your organization? In cases in which there is a multiple purpose, select the top three.

[ ] Accounting [ ] Administration [ ] Inventory

[ ] Sales Support [ ] Manufacturing [ ] Engineering

[ ] E-Mail [ ] Customer Support [ ] Order Entry

[ ] Financial [ ] Other: ____________________

2. In terms of mission criticality, what are the three most important functions for the telephone in your organization?

   a. ______________________________

   b. ______________________________

   c. ______________________________

3. How many employees are at your location?

   [ ] 2 - 10.

   [ ] 11 - 24.

   [ ] 25 - 100.

   [ ] 100+.

4. What type of communications facilities are primarily used in your location? (Indicate all that apply.)

   [ ] Voice.

   [ ] Data.

   [ ] Fax.

   [ ] Image/Video.

   [ ] Other: ______________________________.

5. How much is your monthly telephone bill for both local and long-distance service?

   [ ] Less than $500.

   [ ] More than $500 but less than $1,500.

   [ ] More than $1,500 but less than $5,000.

   [ ] More than $5,000 but less than $10,000.

   [ ] More than $10,000.

   [ ] Do not know.

II. Technical Issues

1. What is the current transmission medium used to the individual workstation?

   [ ] Shielded twisted-pair wire.

   [ ] Unshielded twisted-pair wire.

   [ ] Fiber-optics cable.

   [ ] Other: ______________________________.

III. Communications Support Issues

1. What is the primary job responsibility of the person who supports the technical functions associated with the PBX? (This includes new service, moves, additions, changes, system backups, and troubleshooting.)

   [ ] Communications technician.

   [ ] System administrator/LAN manager.

   [ ] Office manager/site manager.

   [ ] Other administrative function.

   [ ] Other technical function.

   [ ] Other: ______________________________.

2. Are daily system data backups performed?

   [ ] Yes [ ] No [ ] Yes, but not daily

3. How is training handled?

   [ ] On the job.

   [ ] Vendor-sponsored classes.

   [ ] On-site vendor instruction.

   [ ] Online tutorials.

   [ ] No formal training programs.

   [ ] Other: ______________________________.

4. Have you ever had to deal with a problem associated with a given communications system that was beyond the scope of expertise of your on-site staff?

   [ ] Yes [ ] No

5. Did this problem cause an extensive period of downtime?

   [ ] Yes [ ] No

6. If you answered yes to Question 5, how long were you down?

   [ ] Less than half a day.

   [ ] More than half but less than one day.

   [ ] More than one day but less than two days.

   [ ] More than two days but less than three days.

   [ ] More than three days.

7. Who handles major changes, such as upgrades of switch software?

   [ ] Person identified in Question 1, this section.

   [ ] Vendor.

   [ ] Other internal person (title): ____________________.

IV. <u>Communications Security Procedures</u>

1. Is there a designated person responsible for communications security?

   [ ] Person identified in Question 1, Section III.

   [ ] Vendor.

   [ ] Other internal person (title): ____________________.

2. Where is the PBX physically located?

   [ ] Office environment, equipment closet.

   [ ] Office environment, common closet.

   [ ] Manufacturing environment, equipment closet.

   [ ] Manufacturing environment, on the floor.

   [ ] Other location: ______________________________.

3. How long would it take to replace the PBX in the event of fire, water damage, or a major failure?

   [ ] Immediate (within the day).

   [ ] Two to four days.

   [ ] More than four days but less than seven days.

   [ ] More than seven days.

   [ ] Do not know.

4. Are backups of software and class-of-service designators stored off-site?

   [ ] Yes [ ] No

5. Does a formal disaster recovery plan for the PBX exist?

   [ ] Yes [ ] No

6. Does your PBX, voice mail system, or other communications equipment permit dial-in access to maintenance functions?

   [ ] Yes [ ] No

7. If dial-in communications is employed by the equipment above, what kinds of precautions are taken to safeguard access? (Check all that apply.)

   [ ] Password protection.

   [ ] Unpublished numbers.

   [ ] Limited access.

   [ ] Dial-back modems.

   [ ] Password protected modems.

   [ ] Termination after [<u>n</u>] unsuccessful attempts.

   [ ] Other: ____.

   [ ] None of the above.

V. Future Plans

Please briefly describe your future communications plans with regard to your organization. Concentrate on the adaptations in technology that will be required to serve your organization over the next 24 months and on the support you will require to accomplish these goals. ______________________________

____

____

____

____

____

WORKPAPER III2.10 Management Funding Request Form

MANAGEMENT FUNDING REQUESTS

Event	Probability of Occurrence (%)	Cost with Plan	Cost without Plan	Lost Operation (days)	Cost to Protect	Improvement

Identifying Resources for the Planning Project

CHAPTER

III-3

Most network operations managers and voice and data communications managers are capable of performing the steps needed to recover communications following a disaster. However, they often do not understand the need for documenting the plan. The lack of a plan can create a problem if, in the event of a disaster, the key technical people are not available to implement the plan. It is not unthinkable that a key technical person might be injured in a disaster or might simply be on vacation halfway around the world. The point is that a properly designed recovery plan is written for someone else to execute, the assumption being that key personnel may not be available after a disaster. The plan must be documented to assure continuity in the event key personnel are incapacitated or unavailable.

Clearly, the best persons to write the communications recovery plan are the people who built the network in the first place—typically, IS and operations staff. Unfortunately, these persons are often extremely busy handling their routine duties. Even if the planner is able to find people willing to cooperate, they may not have sufficient time to spare. Another problem is that these people typically do not report directly to the person responsible for completing the plan. Because the planner has no input in the team member's performance evaluation—nor is he or she even in a position to provide a bonus or any other kind of substantial recognition for a job well done—motivation becomes a serious issue. In short, recruitment and motivation of the planning teams pose a serious challenge to the recovery planner.

This chapter examines the potential sources of expertise for completing the communications recovery plan. Integrating the internal resources of multiple departments is necessary to provide strength and depth to the plan. Therefore, the chapter first describes how to identify internal resources. It next describes how external resources can be used to provide additional expertise. This chapter also presents a number of motivational techniques for helping to secure scarce resources in an organization.

IDENTIFY INTERNAL RESOURCES

STEP 1

Using internal company personnel is usually considered to be the most cost-effective way to complete the plan. It is estimated that each team member will need to devote 25% of the workday to the planning effort. As noted earlier, given the heavy existing work loads of technical personnel, this time commitment can be difficult to achieve. The following sections discuss methods of persuading senior departmental managers of the need to provide the necessary time commitment; techniques to improve the efficiency of internal resources are also discussed.

Recruiting the Teams

In the first phase of the planning project (described in Chapter III-2), the recovery planner conducted interviews with senior management in each of the key departments.

By now, these department heads should understand that this project is a priority of the company.

In this phase, the planner returns to department management, this time to recruit staff for the various recovery teams. (The specific teams are discussed later in this chapter.) The planner should schedule a 30-minute meeting with each of the key department heads. He or she should remind the manager of the CEO's commitment to the success of this project and of the deadlines that must be met. Department managers should be assured that the planner will take charge of organizing and training the teams and that time commitments of team members will be limited only to those actions absolutely required to complete the plan on time. The planner should offer to provide periodic status reports to the departmental managers.

The next step is to identify and recruit personnel from each of the key departments. It is strongly recommended that the planner reserve the right of refusal in assigning individuals to the teams. A person may be unacceptable for a number of reasons, including:

- The candidate is involved in a major project that already requires overtime.
- The candidate lacks the technical expertise.
- The candidate is a poor performer.

Obtaining a blanket right of refusal at the outset of the project helps avoid the problem of having to make negative judgments explicit.

Each candidate should be interviewed and selected based on such qualifications as technical expertise, availability and commitment, and an ability to work well in a team environment. The recovery planner lacks the typical incentives available to direct managers, and a team member's performance on the planning project may have no bearing on the employee's performance review or pay raise. In fact, in most organizations, the team member does not even report to the recovery planner. The only way to ensure that the project goes well is to find talented and dedicated people and to inspire them as a leader.

Coordinating Plans

In most organizations, numerous entities claim ownership of the building and its equipment. The facilities manager may feel that he or she is in charge of the physical property, while the IS manager assumes that he or she owns the data center and other computer-related installations. Such conflicting assumptions can create havoc when it comes to responding to a disaster. For example, if the fire department vacates the building after putting out a fire but the building is now exposed to unauthorized intruders, the IS manager might decide to call in an independent security firm to secure the building. The facilities manager and the security manager, however, may also assume that this is their responsibility and independently call additional security. The result may be 30 security guards converging on an already confused and potentially dangerous situation.

To avoid such problems, it is important that the planning project represent an integrated, interdepartmental approach to recovery that clearly defines who is responsible for specific recovery actions. For example, to ensure coordination among departments, the plan should specify who is responsible for:

- Air conditioning in equipment rooms.
- Power in computer rooms.
- Network and telephone communications wiring.
- Physical security.

- The initial damage assessment (i.e., who goes into the building first following a disaster).
- Disbursement of cash and travel advances.

Departments from Which to Recruit

It is not necessary that every member of every team be a technical expert. It is important to recruit from a broad cross-section of the organization, including both technical and nontechnical areas. The specific departments from which to recruit should mirror those whose management was interviewed in the first planning phase. These include sales, marketing, operations, communications, facilities, finance, legal, and public relations.

The need for a broad skills set can be illustrated by this example. Following a disaster, the planning team may need money for equipment purchases, travel expenses, and other requirements. An operations technician might have considerable trouble negotiating the complexities of the finance department (especially if that department has been seriously affected by the disaster) to learn about backup accounting systems and temporary bank accounts. Someone from the finance department would be much better suited to handling responsibility for this task.

IS Department. The IS department is often, by default, the focal point of the recovery planning effort. This makes sense for a number of reasons. IS departments have a long history of recovery planning. A mainframe recovery plan may already be in place, with a recovery or security manager assigned responsibility for the plan. IS personnel are experienced in technical standards for equipment installations and understand the requirements for such precautionary systems as uninterruptible power supplies (UPSs) and fire prevention systems. Many of these mainframe-oriented precautionary systems may directly apply to recovery of communications systems.

Internal Auditors. Internal auditors often possess vast knowledge of the protective controls for mainframe systems. Auditors can also be useful because of their established credibility with the organization's senior management. However, auditors often lack knowledge of communications systems and must therefore be carefully directed in communications recovery planning.

LAN Management. LAN systems have become an important component of the overall processing environment. Therefore, management responsible for corporate LANs should be involved in the communications recovery project. For example, LAN managers should coordinate with the communications department to ensure that critical router links are moved to the recovery center when necessary (assuming a recovery center is used). (It should be noted that LAN recovery itself is considered an element of business operations recovery and is covered in detail in Part I of this book.)

Operations Department. The operations (or engineering) staff includes the people responsible for building the communications network. These people are often thought to be in the best position to take a lead in writing the plan. From a technical standpoint, they know the communications environment better than anyone in the organization, including equipment location and configuration. In too many organizations, however, this attitude results in assigning operations full responsibility for completing the plan. This is not an effective solution, for several reasons.

First, technical staff in this area are often the least able to take the necessary time for training in communications recovery planning. Often, writing of the plan must be accomplished after regular work hours, which can jeopardize the completion schedule.

Second, these technical specialists often lack sufficient understanding of the business operations of other departments to make judgments about how critical an area is to the profitability of the business. For example, a technician cannot know with any certainty the revenue generated by a department that uses a support system. An automated call distribution unit might support a busy telemarketing center, leading him or her to the assumption that the center is critical to generating revenue. But the technician is not in a position to specify the amount of revenue generated or, more specifically, such issues as how long users could function without the support system.

The best approach is to use operations personnel to assist in the planning project, but only under the careful guidance of the recovery planner and with assistance and input from other departments.

STEP 2

IDENTIFY EXTERNAL RESOURCES

Given limitations of knowledge and availability of internal staff, many organizations also look to external sources of assistance. These may include:

- Consultants.
- Computer hot-site providers.
- Long-distance carriers.
- Local telephone companies.

The following sections discuss each of these options.

Consultants

The Big 6 accounting firms as well as smaller consulting firms can provide significant expertise to the communications recovery planning project. An organization might consider using consultants if additional staffing is necessary to meet project deadlines or if specific expertise is needed to address individual components of the plan. The major accounting firms have been involved in disaster recovery planning for many years. In addition to their hands-on experience in recovery planning, they also possess the financial background that can be useful in quantifying the projected losses due to a communications outage.

Senior management may also be more receptive to the findings of external consultants. Consultants are experienced in dealing with executive management and may be in a better position to champion the project in the initial executive committee meetings. The projected loss figures provided by major accounting firms may also be more believable to management because of their reputation as financial experts.

Despite these advantages, however, it must be recognized that use of consultants can be costly, with total charges for a recovery planning project in the hundreds of thousands of dollars. And although such firms are usually very thorough, their plans are often very lengthy and complex. In the worst case, the plan may be too difficult to follow in an emergency because of this complexity or its length may discourage users from reading and understanding it as they should.

Another concern in the use of consultants is ownership of the plan. If the consultant fails to adequately engage all key departments within the organization, these departments may not commit to the final plan or may reject it outright.

A further consideration involves updates to the plan. A communications recovery plan must be updated at least quarterly, and critical components should be verified

EXHIBIT III-3-A SELECTED LISTING OF RECOVERY COMPANIES

Agway Data Services Inc.
IBM
Syracuse NY
(315) 477-6510

Backup Recovery Services Inc.
IBM/Unisys
Topeka KS
(913) 232-0368

Bekeen Computer Corporation
IBM
Missisaga, Ontario
(416) 826-7780

Cadre Inc.
Unisys
Avon CT
(203) 515-6566

Comdisco
IBM, Unisys
Rosemont IL
(312) 698-3000

Corporate Contingency Services
IBM
New Hudson MI
(313) 486-2110

DCI (Sungard)
Unisys
Warminster PA
(215) 355-7800

Disaster Recovery Services
IBM/Unisys
Calgary, Alberta
(403) 234-9533

Elongane Corp. (Sungard)
IBM
St. Paul MN
(612) 644-0882

Hotsite
IBM
Cary NC
(919) 460-1234

LDI
IBM/Unisys
Solon OH
(216) 248-0991

NCR Disaster Recovery
NCR
Dayton OH
(513) 445-3150

Recovery Resources Inc.
Unisys
Orlando FL
(407) 422-5991

Sungard
IBM, DEC, Tandem
Philadelphia PA
(215) 341-8700

Wang Emergency Backup Services
Wang
Burlington MA
(617) 270-8519

Weyerhauser Recovery Services
IBM, HP, Honeywell, DEC
Tacoma WA
(206) 924-3479

Reprinted with permission from "Writing Disaster Recovery Plans for Telecommunications Networks and LANs" by Leo Wrobel, © 1993 Artech House Books, Norwood MA.

even more frequently. This could prove to be expensive if the consultant must be brought in for each update. It is generally much less expensive to have the consultant train internal staff members on how to maintain the plan so that these costly reengagements can be avoided.

Regardless of the decision to use a consultant, it must be remembered that the project will still require some level of time and commitment by internal operations and IS staff. A network operations manager, for example, might be designated as project manager responsible for directing the activities of the consultants.

Hot-Site Providers

Another option is to use a hot-site provider. Exhibit III-3-A provides a selected listing of companies specializing in disaster recovery and backup services. Hot-site providers have extensive experience in communications recovery. Many have formed alliances with major long-distance communications providers, in some cases even locating their

EXHIBIT III-3-B LONG-DISTANCE COMPANY PRODUCTS AND SERVICES

- Switched 56K-bps, 64K-bps, 1.536M-bps, and 45M-bps services.
- Diverse long-haul circuit routing.
- 800 service command routing/service guarantees.
- Access to a second toll office.
- Foreign exchange service.
- T1 access service bundling.
- Long-distance fraud control.
- Central office multiplexing and fan-out features.
- Customer-controlled reconfiguration.
- Central office colocation of customer-owned equipment.

Reprinted with permission from "Implementing a Successful Telecommunications Disaster Recovery Program" by Leo A. Wrobel, © 1993 IS Management Group, Carlsbad CA.

recovery centers on major fiber-optic routes to allow fast connectivity. Others have leased T1 and T3 networks that operate full time. These firms can provide seasoned technical personnel adept at configuring emergency networks and plans.

In many cases, management has already signed a contract with one of these firms for data center recovery, which can make it easier to sell management on establishing a relationship to address communications recovery.

Hot-site providers also share some of the drawbacks cited for consultants. Issues of ownership, updates, and complexity and length of plans may need to be clarified and resolved. Because their primary expertise is in data center (i.e., mainframe) recovery, it is also necessary to carefully screen the capabilities of individual hot-site providers to determine their capabilities in communications network recovery.

Long-Distance Carriers

Long-distance telephone companies have considerable experience in creating communications recovery plans for customers. Long-distance company products and services useful in communications recovery are listed in Exhibit III-3-B. Several key products and services are also discussed in detail in the following paragraphs of this section.

Long-distance carriers have made great strides in disaster recovery services since the 1988 Hinsdale fire (described in Chapter III-1). They have invested heavily to make their own systems more reliable and capable of recovery. Capital-intensive requirements of a recovery plan may have already been implemented by the carriers themselves, which can save the company considerable expense in implementing its plan.

Because of fierce competition, long-distance carriers are also often quite amenable to exploring options for providing these services, especially if providing these services may tie the client more closely to their basic long-distance business. For this reason, carriers can offer much assistance in developing a recovery plan, often for little or no cost.

The carrier's account representative may not be familiar with contingency planning but should be able to identify the appropriate persons and arrange a meeting. At a minimum, such meetings can provide an excellent springboard for generating ideas. If the appropriate personnel are involved, the carrier may be able to help devise solutions for all or at least part of the recovery plan.

EXHIBIT III-3-C USE OF SWITCHED 56K-BPS SERVICE TO RESTORE REMOTE LAN FROM RECOVERY CENTER

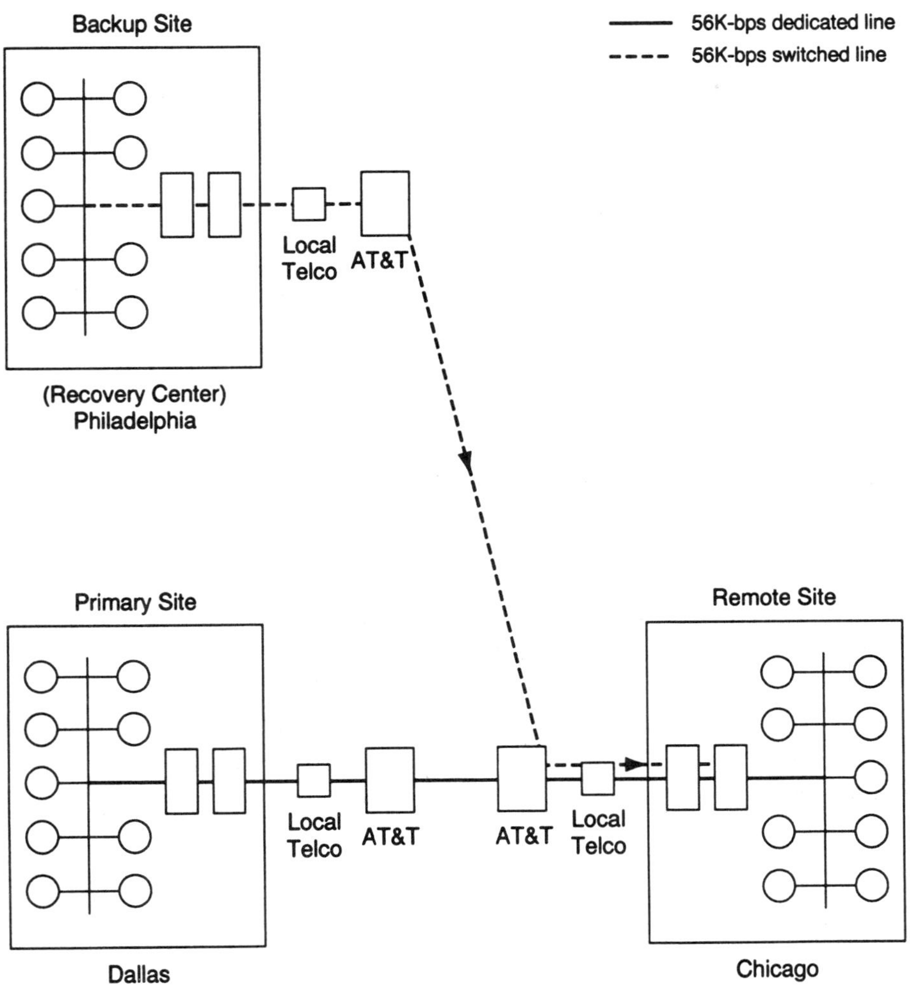

Carriers may have different strengths and weaknesses in their recovery capabilities. It is important to evaluate several carriers in order to make the best selection.

The following sections describe key products and services provided by long-distance carriers that can be useful in recovery operations.

Switched 56K- and 64K-bps Digital Service. Switched 56K- and 64K-bps service has found a place over the past few years as one of the most useful disaster recovery services available for restoration of critical data links. Switched 56K-bps service is not new. Technically speaking, most public switched telephone networks in urban areas have been 56K-bps since the 1960s. Interexchange telephone calls today are transmitted over switched 56K-bps lines.

In terms of data service, a single switched 56K-bps service link can support up to 300 terminals in an IBM synchronous data link central (SDLC) environment. Switched 56K- and 64K-bps service is a very cost-effective way to back up remote routers, front-end processors, and other equipment. For high-capacity users, the cost can be as little as that for a common voice call, but each link can back up hundreds of remote users.

EXHIBIT **III-3-D** DIVERSE LONG-DISTANCE CIRCUIT ROUTING

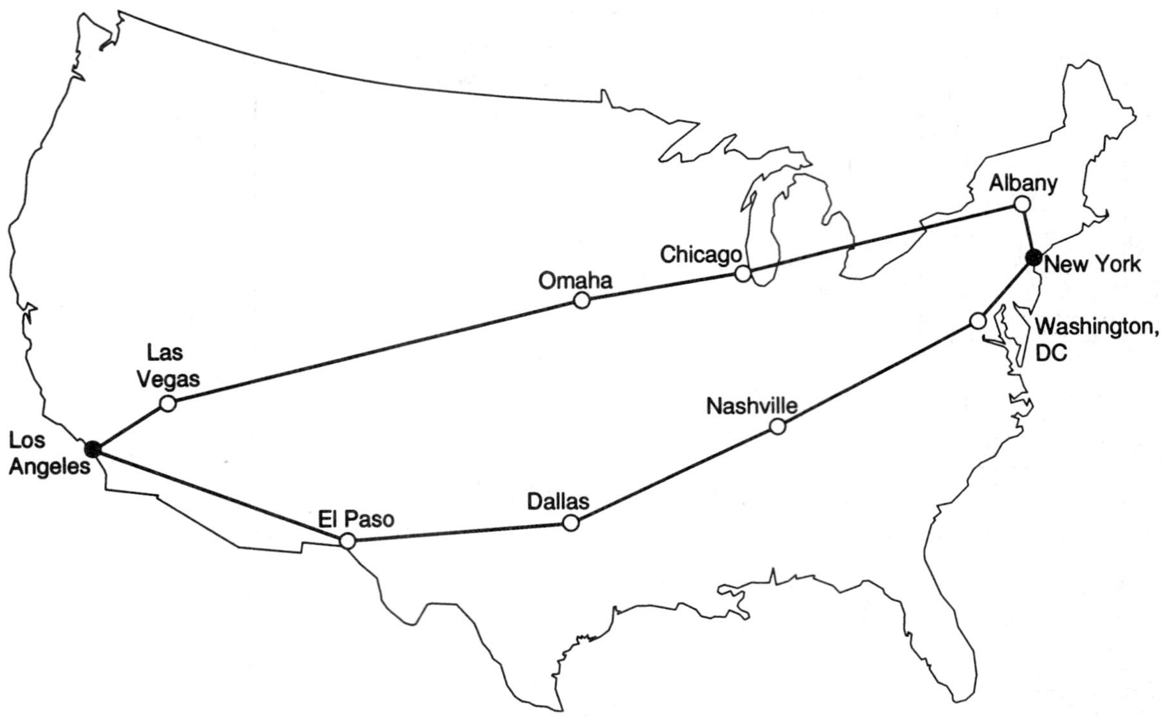

Exhibit III-3-C illustrates the use of switched 56K-bps service to restore a remote LAN from a recovery center.

Diverse Long-Haul Circuit Routing. Companies today take great pains to ensure they have diverse long-haul circuit routing, and the interexchange telephone companies can be very helpful in this regard. This ensures that a single incident will not sever both of a company's critical T1s, for example. To ensure route diversity, telephone companies must provide detailed routing diagrams, which many are reluctant to do. For years these diagrams were proprietary. In this era of communications competition, however, if one company will not provide routing information, another will. Out of competitive necessity, most long-haul carriers will now release this material on a customer-by-customer basis, albeit reluctantly. Some carriers also provide services to secure network integrity (e.g., AT&T's FASTAR).

Diversity on long-haul circuits should be carefully considered, particularly on fiber-optic routes, because a single mishap can disrupt multiple carriers. Microwave can make an effective complement to these points of failure, as can fiber-optic loops. Exhibit III-3-D provides an example of diverse long-haul routing.

800 Command Routing and Service Guarantees. Most long-distance companies recognize the importance of incoming 800 service to the conduct of business and offer comprehensive service guarantees. Again, because an 800 number can be easily directed to any number in the North American numbering plan, there is no excuse for not exploring these options with the long-distance carrier.

EXHIBIT III-3-E ACCESS TO A SECOND TOLL OFFICE

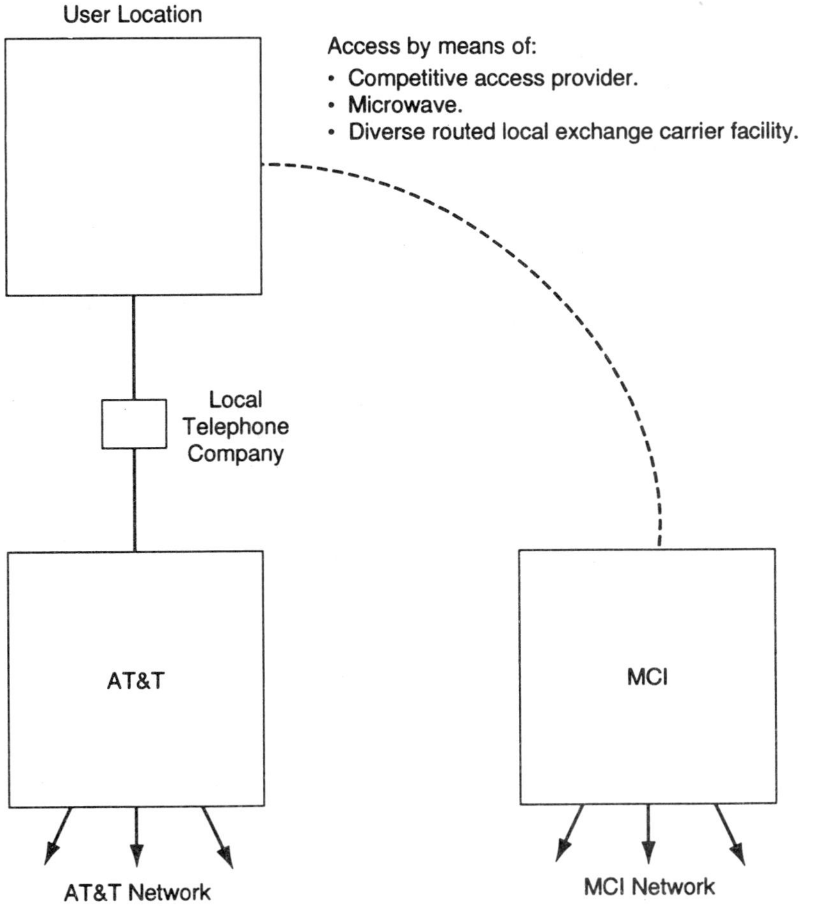

Access to a Second Toll Office. A disaster affecting any long-distance carrier automatically affects its customers. Companies can now protect against loss of a major long-distance point of presence through the use of a second toll office, provided either by the primary or secondary interexchange carrier. As this service becomes more available and affordable, access to a second toll office, either with the same or a different carrier, should become a standard of good practice. Exhibit III-3-E provides an example of access to a second toll office.

Foreign Exchange Service. One way of insulating against switching failures is through the use of foreign exchange (FX) or foreign central office (FCO) service. Although designed mainly for providing dial tone from distant telephone exchanges (reducing toll charges), these services can be readily used to provide network integrity. As shown in Exhibit III-3-F, FX lines pass through the serving central office but actually derive their dial tone from another location, often in another city. In this fashion, a company can still function in the event of a catastrophic failure in its local switch by using its FX lines. By publishing the numbers of the FX lines in the company directory, incoming calls can also be received after a failure, without end users having to learn new numbers. Even in cases where central offices have burned, FX lines have often continued functioning, as long as the physical wire path was still in place. FX service

EXHIBIT **III-3-F** USE OF FOREIGN EXCHANGE SERVICE

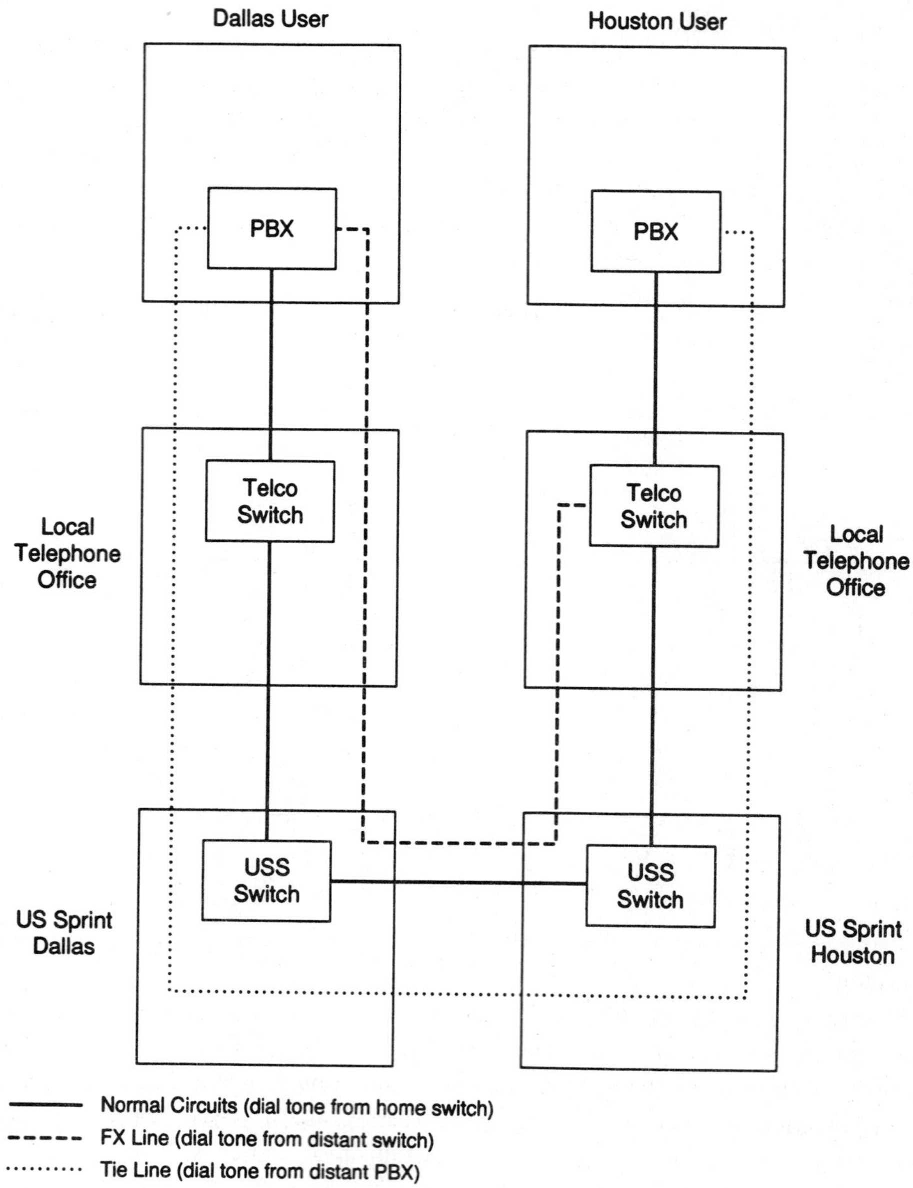

is available from virtually every serving office in the US as a tariffed service. In optimal situations, by placing FX lines to areas often called by the company, it is often possible to reduce overall long-distance charges enough to pay for the lines and in the process fund the additional protection they provide.

T1 Access Service Bundling. The most cost-effective restoration of private line circuits can be accomplished by using high-capacity digital access facilities such as T1. A T1 circuit consists of 24 individual circuits. By multiplexing these circuits into a single T1, recovery is greatly simplified. Only a single four-wire circuit (the T1) need be redirected to restore 24 circuits to a recovery facility. Coupled with services such as switched 1.536M-bps service (switched-on-demand T1), this service bundling

EXHIBIT **III-3-G** T1 ACCESS SERVICE BUNDLING

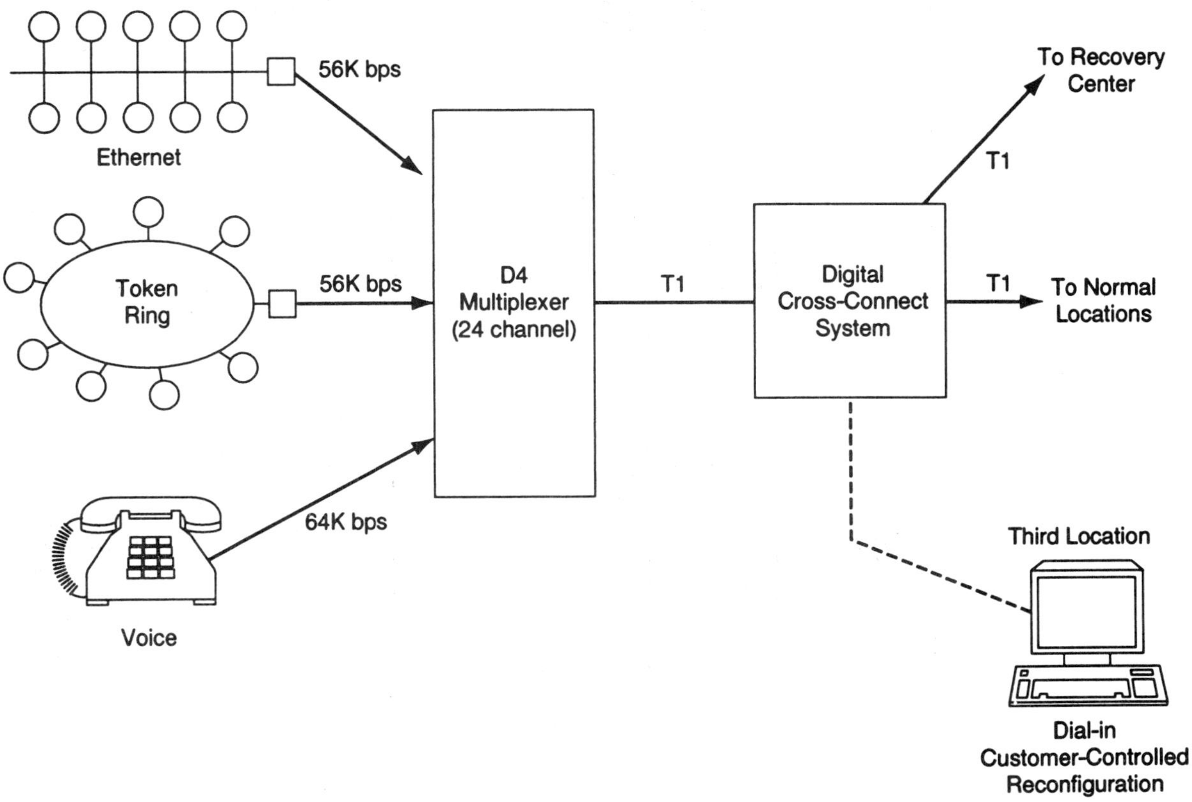

becomes a powerful option. Exhibit III-3-G provides an example of T1 access service bundling.

One of the most commonly used methods of delivering large quantities of private line circuits to a computer disaster recovery center is through the use of switched 1.536M-bps service or related services, such as AT&T's Accunet Reserve 1.5. Exhibit III-3-H illustrates the use of switched 1.536M-bps service to support a recovery center.

Long-Distance Fraud Control. Companies have lost billions of dollars because of long-distance fraud involving automated systems. Long-distance companies can offer suggestions on how to avoid this exposure as well as various fee-based plans to ensure against this contingency. Absent such steps, the user may be responsible for any bill, even if it is fraudulent. Various steps for avoiding such abuse are described later in Part III of this book.

Central Office Multiplexing and Fan-Out Features. Numerous central office features are accessible through high-capacity services. These access links are currently T1- and T3-based, but many companies have begun to introduce SONET OC-3 and OC-12 access links. (Optical carrier [OC], the new SONET standard, starts at OC-3 for access links, which is roughly three times the capacity of a DS-3, currently the largest pipe available in a communications network.) As these services proliferate, access to

EXHIBIT **III-3-H** USE OF SWITCHED 1.536M-BPS SERVICE TO SUPPORT A RECOVERY CENTER

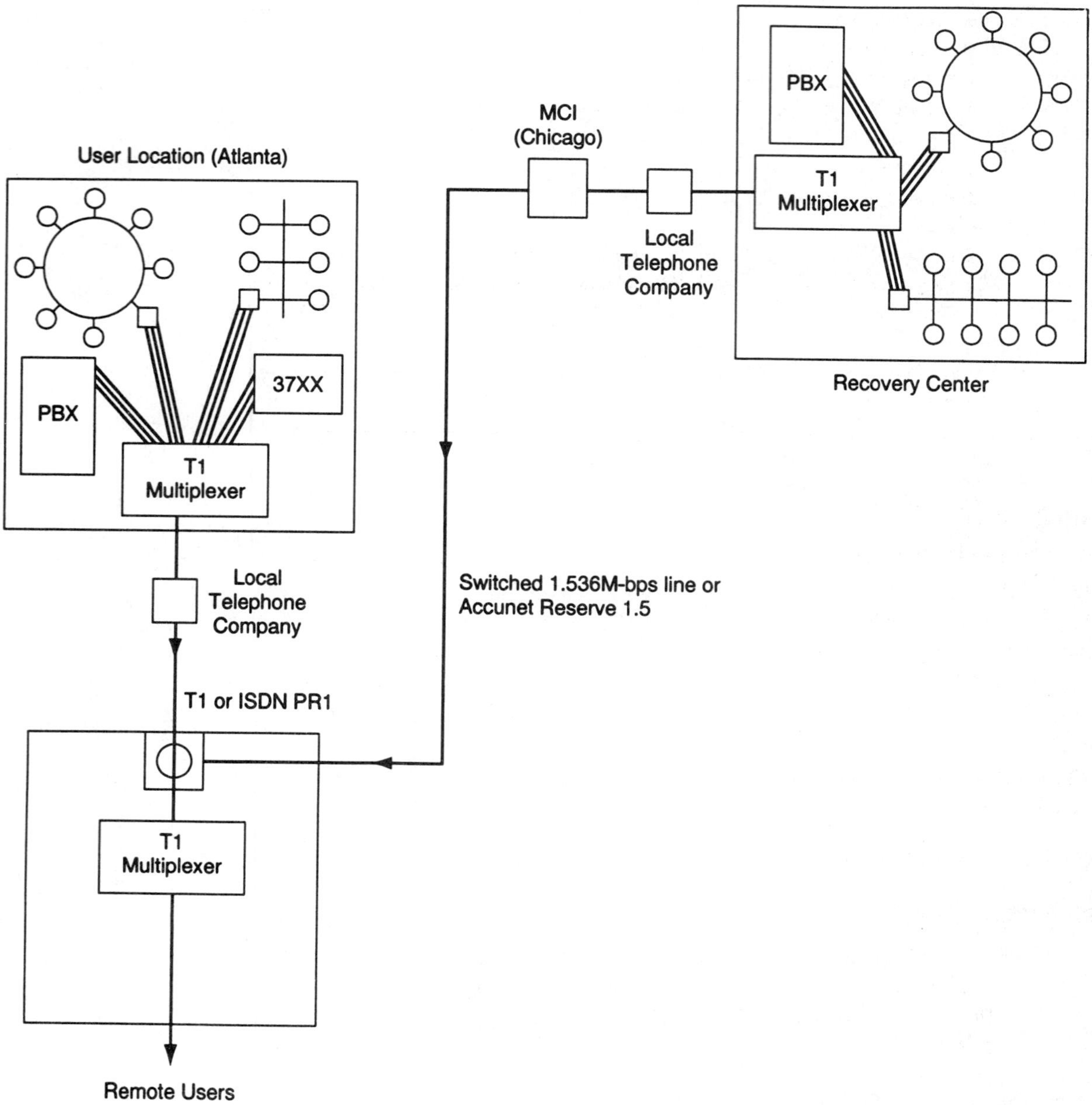

other central office resident features such as asynchronous transfer mode (ATM) hubs should also increase.

Customer-Controlled Reconfiguration. Digital cross-connect systems (DCSs) provide a fast and efficient means for telephone companies to connect and disconnect private line circuits. This has a great bearing on disaster response, where time is of the essence. Customer-controlled reconfiguration can add to this efficiency by allowing the customer to connect and disconnect its own private lines. This is particularly helpful in a disaster because it keeps the customer in control and avoids delays.

EXHIBIT III-3-I LOCAL TELEPHONE COMPANY PRODUCTS AND SERVICES

- Alternative or diverse cable routing.
- T1 access service bundling.
- Foreign exchange or foreign central office service.
- Optinet recovery service.
- Central office colocation of customer-owned equipment.
- Centrex (useful for backing up a PBX).
- Access to a second local serving office.
- Remote call forwarding.
- Local switched 56K-bps and 64K-bps services.
- Central office multiplexing and fan-out features.
- Fiber-optic building entrance facilities.

Central Office Colocation. Many large communications users have actually become communications providers themselves. Recent FCC rulings have also made colocation (with telephone companies) a reality for competing local exchange companies. Colocation is the ability to locate customer-owned equipment inside public telephone offices. It has been in existence in one form or another since the early 1980s in the long-distance company arena and is now spreading to local telephone companies. Workpaper III3.01 provides a checklist of issues that should be considered when an organization is colocating equipment.

(Telephone companies and high-volume users have begun to establish partnerships in which they locate equipment with one another in order to provide service. This is referred to as reverse colocation.)

Local Telephone Companies

Local telephone companies have introduced many services that can be of help in communications recovery. These products and services are listed in Exhibit III-3-I. Several key products and services are also discussed in detail in the following sections.

One major advantage of using local telephone companies for assistance in recovery planning is that they freely recommend solutions that encompass more than one long-distance carrier. (Long-distance carriers, on the other hand, try to keep as much business as they can and discourage the use of other carriers.)

Even relatively simple recommendations by local phone companies can have a significant impact on recovery. For example, it might be recommended that every supervisor in the organization have a Centrex line and every staff person a PBX line to ensure that a major PBX failure does not completely isolate the company. Local carriers also offer various options for fast circuit restoration (e.g., digital cross-connect systems). The local carrier's account representative should be able to recommend an expert on disaster recovery planning.

It can also be useful to take a tour of the central office at the local telephone office. This can help in evaluating potential exposures within the local carrier's operations, as well as provide valuable contacts at the phone company that may be helpful in the event the disaster plan is activated.

EXHIBIT III-3-J ALTERNATIVE VERSUS DIVERSE CABLE ROUTING

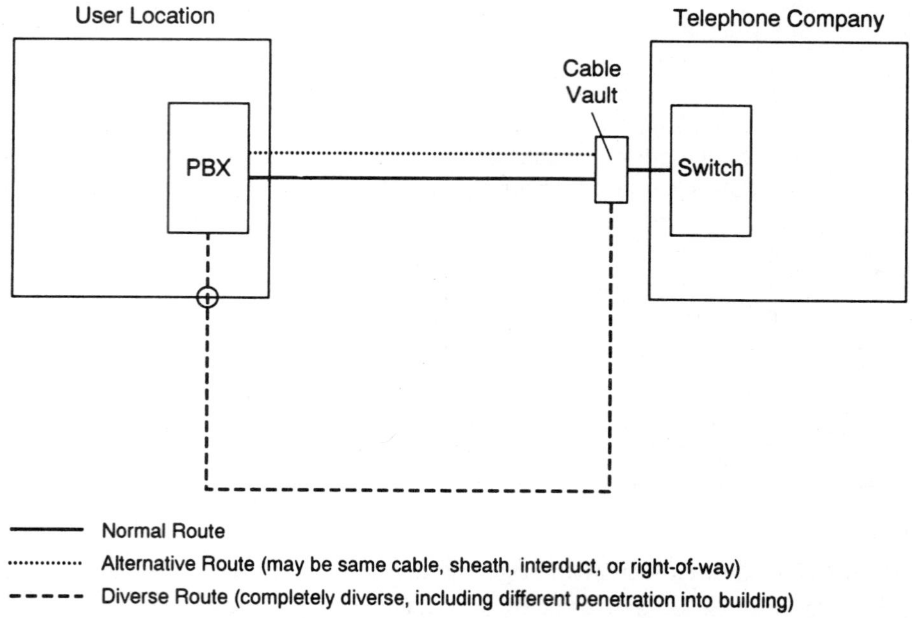

Alternative or Diverse Cable Routing. It is a common mistake to use the terms *alternative routing* and *diverse routing* interchangeably. Alternative routing refers to any communications route other than the one the company's circuits usually ride over; the same cable, sheath, or right-of-way may be used. Diverse routing implies no common rights-of-way or equipment (except when protected by redundant power, common logic, and back planes, for example) and no other common components or facilities. The recovery planner should understand this difference before attempting to talk with the local carrier about routing options.

Routing diagrams should be used when the planner is evaluating diverse and alternative routing from the telephone company. Exhibit III-3-J provides an example of each routing type.

T1 Access Service Bundling. The same rules apply with regard to bundling services for access to central offices as was discussed for long-distance carriers. Bundling greatly simplifies the recovery process, especially when dealing with private line circuits by allowing them to be switched in multiple capacities if required. For example, with such services as switched 45M-bps service, even fiber-optic entrance facilities can be easily accommodated to recovery centers, restoring 672 circuits or more in the process. Exhibit III-3-K illustrates this.

Foreign Exchange or Foreign Central Office Service. Foreign exchange (FX) service can provide a cost-effective means of protecting against central office hardware and software failures for many businesses. And because FX lines draw their dial tone from a remote (as opposed to the home) serving office, there is automatic protection against software failures in the home serving office. In addition, there have been documented cases of FX lines that continued to work even after a major fire in the home serving facility.

EXHIBIT **III-3-K** FIBER-OPTIC BUILDING ENTRANCE FACILITIES

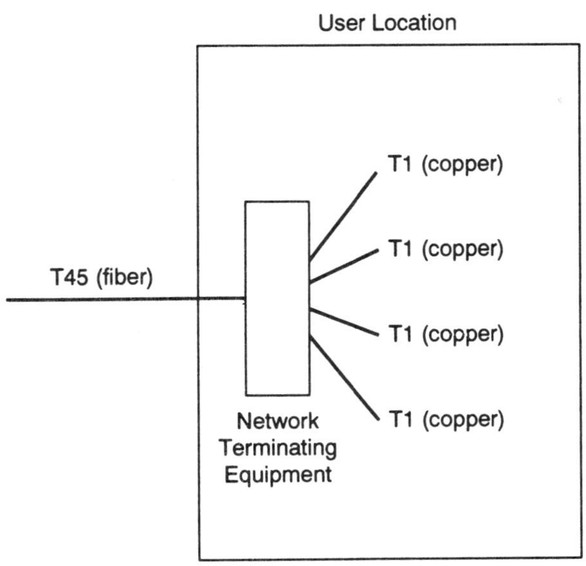

This was the case in the Hinsdale disaster for some users. Even though the switch was destroyed by the fire, many FX lines still were wired in. When power was restored, these lines worked because they drew dial tone from a distant switch that was unaffected by the fire. Similar cases were noted after the main telephone office in Baghdad was bombed during the Persian Gulf War.

Digital Cross-Connect System Reconfiguration Services. Ameritech's Advanced Optinet Restoral Service (AORS) and Southwestern Bell's Network Recovery Service (NRS) are two examples of local exchange company digital cross-connect system reconfiguration services, similar to those described in the long-distance section. Again, from the standpoint of simplifying the recovery of private lines, these services are invaluable. Exhibit III-3-L provides an example of the configuration of these services.

Central Office Colocation. It is possible to locate customer-owned equipment inside Bell, GTE, and other local serving central offices on a case-by-case basis. Such competitive access providers as Teleport and MFS can also locate equipment and couple it with diverse (privately provided) fiber-optic links to ensure network integrity.

Centrex. Even a service as seemingly mundane as central office residence telephone systems (Centrex) can have a positive impact on the overall recovery plan. If every worker gets a PBX line and every supervisor gets a Centrex line, the company is not isolated if there is a failure of a major PBX. Centrex is a feasible, cost-effective system for backing up the PBX. By combining this with the diverse facilities techniques described earlier, a strong voice recovery plan can be established and tested on a daily basis through live use. Exhibit III-3-M depicts the use of Centrex as a backup facility.

Access to a Second Local Serving Office. The local serving office is increasingly being recognized as a primary choke point because virtually all network traffic channels

EXHIBIT III-3-L OPTINET RESTORAL SERVICE OR NETWORK RECOVERY SERVICE

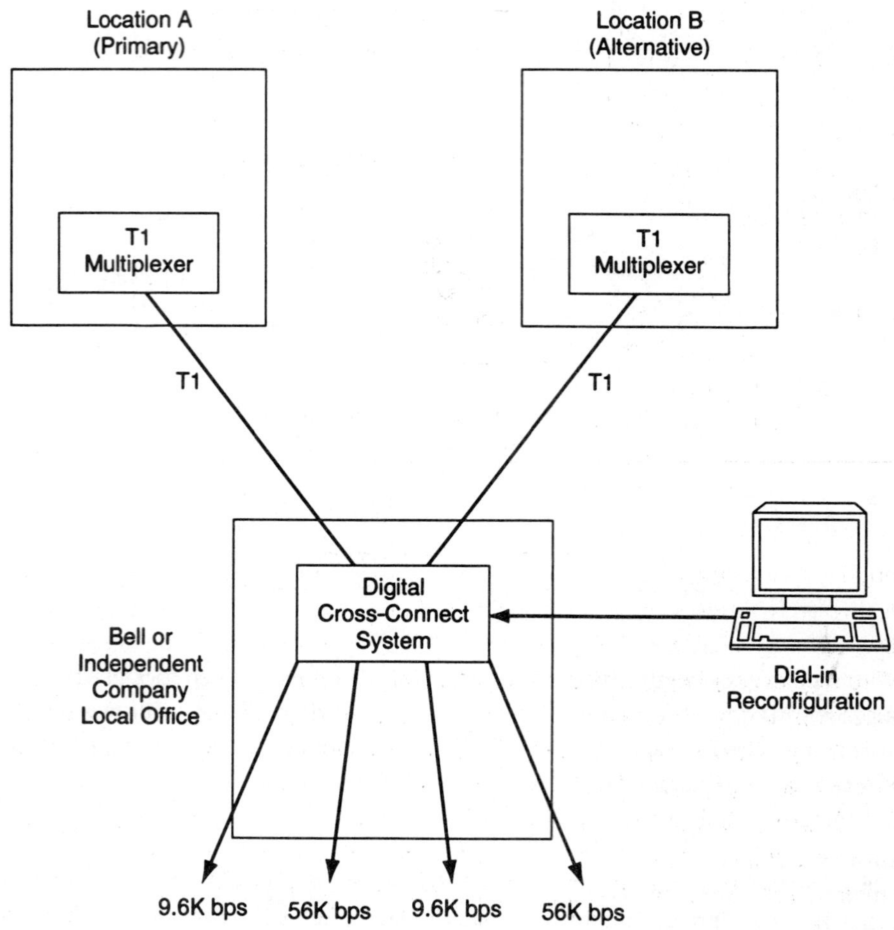

EXHIBIT III-3-M CENTREX USED AS BACKUP FOR PBX

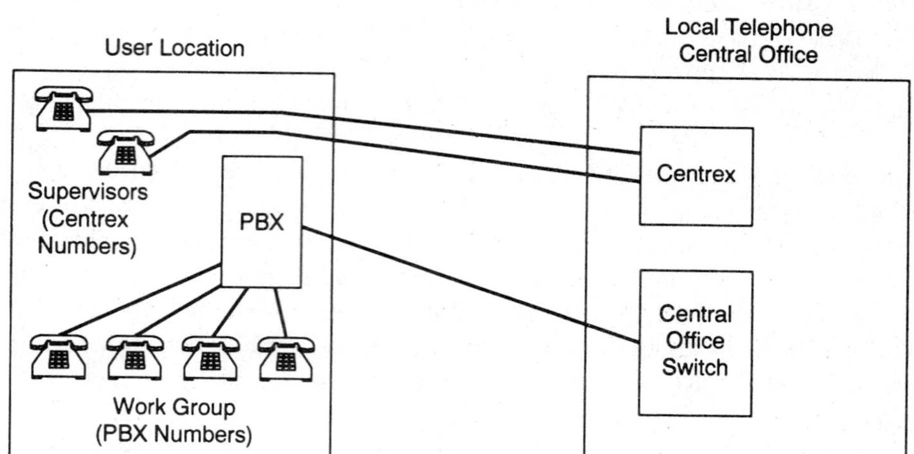

EXHIBIT III-3-N REMOTE CALL FORWARDING

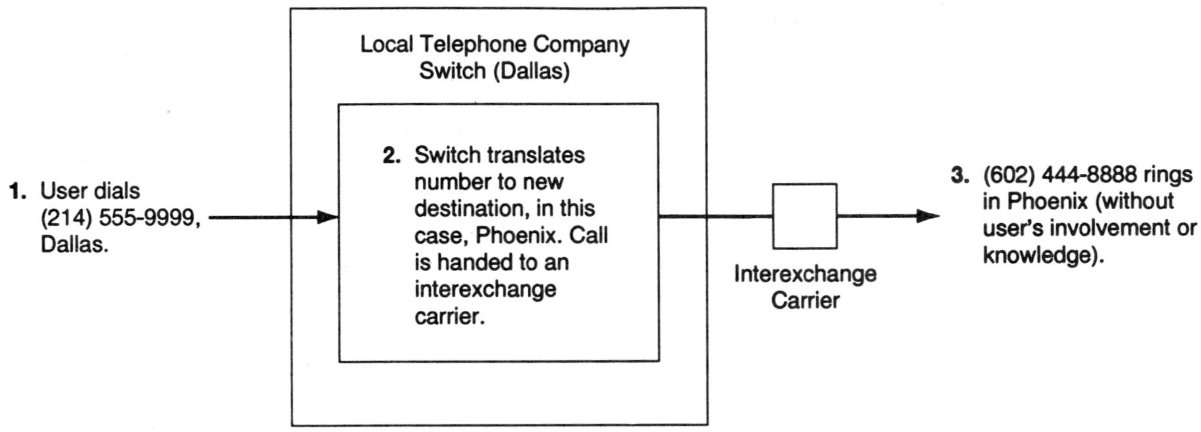

through it. As a result, users are demanding access to two separate local serving offices over diverse facilities. This can be accomplished through the local telephone company or by means of microwave facilities or the services of competitive access providers.

With the advent of high-capacity fiber optics, dual access is becoming more feasible economically. For example, Southwestern Bell Telephone offers Secure-Net Service for this purpose. Although limited in availability, it is competitively priced and provides diverse paths and central offices where available.

Remote Call Forwarding. Remote call forwarding can ensure command and control are maintained after a disaster. Circuits can be call-forwarded from the testboard, for example, in case the building cannot be entered immediately following the disaster. Users do not have to learn new numbers for the recovery facility. Exhibit III-3-N shows how this works.

Local Switched 56K-bps Service. Many of the local telephone companies now offer switched 56K-bps service in local metropolitan areas. For example, Southwestern Bell offers this service at a Feature Group A access rate (about nine cents per minute). This service is use based; users do not pay until they use it. A user with a nine-cents-per-minute Southwestern Bell charge, a 15-cents-per-minute charge from AT&T for the long-distance portion, and a nine-cents-per-minute charge from New York Telephone could set up an 1,800-mile switched 56K-bps access link for 33 cents per minute, or about what a long-distance voice call of the same distance cost a few years ago—only now that circuit is capable of restoring more than 300 devices if properly engineered.

Central Office Multiplexing and Fan-Out Features. The same fan-out features available from the long-distance companies are in most cases available from the local carriers. The same advantages apply. In the future, high-capacity fiber links will access myriad service offerings in the local servicing offices, from DCSs to ATM hubs. The local operating companies can also be expected to develop an interest in reserve colocation systems, in which they install equipment on the user's site. Either can substantially benefit the network recovery plan.

Using PC-Based Software Packages

PC- or LAN-based software planning tools are available from a variety of sources. The more expensive packages generally include a few days to a few weeks of on-site consulting and training in use of the package. These software planning tools provide the user with a template of a recovery plan, often in a convenient fill-in-the-blank format. This helps the planning process to get moving quickly and makes it relatively easy to keep them up to date. Because communications environments change so quickly, updates should be undertaken at least quarterly.

STEP 3

ORGANIZE THE TEAMS

Communication between departments fosters strength and continuity in the recovery plan. One method of fostering communication among organizations is through a standards committee. Standards committees are involved not only in disaster recovery planning but in other key areas of the business. The communications standards committee should attempt to answer these questions:

- What types of hardware and software platforms are supported by a help desk?
- How does an end user get a new network device approved? What is the process for introducing a new device to the product acceptance and quality control program conducted by the communications department? How does the user secure approval from the communications department for installation and maintenance support?
- Are remote users required to carry maintenance contracts to avoid placing an undue burden on the communications department?
- What precautions are end users and the communications department itself required to take to secure equipment in large and small network installations?
- What equipment is considered mission critical?
- Are remote users expected to document network recovery plans?
- Can a remote user sign up for a long-distance carrier that is different from the primary long-distance carrier used by the corporate communications department? If so, how?
- Can the communications department disconnect any LAN user who refuses to take adequate precautions against virus contamination?
- What kinds of safeguards should an end user employ if using dial-up access?

Forming the Emergency Management Team

The company should have an emergency management team that coordinates the overall recovery. When this team is formed, it is also necessary to address the policy decisions surrounding when and how the team is activated in an emergency and what constitutes a true disaster. The emergency management team may comprise various policy makers but at a minimum should include the CEO or CIO, the directors of the major technical service divisions (e.g., IS and communications), one or two administrative persons for support, and a corporate communications person to serve as a media representative.

The emergency management team is activated in the event of a disaster. But what constitutes a disaster? The following events all interrupt processing:

- A major fire guts the data center and cripples companywide information processing.
- The file server that previously served the human resources department is found to be missing and is suspected of having been stolen by the cleaning crew.
- The PBX for a major corporate location is rendered inoperable as a result of a broken water pipe over the equipment room during a long holiday weekend.

There is little debate that the first event would activate the emergency management team; the disaster is companywide in scope and requires the coordination of numerous unrelated departments.

Although the second event is serious, a response would probably be coordinated by the manager in charge of network processing and corporate security. The emergency management team would not be activated; instead, the directors coordinating the recovery would simply report progress to any concerned executives through normal channels.

The third event is a gray area. The decision to activate the emergency management team would depend on the size, cost, function, and business purpose of the flooded PBX. The recovery might be coordinated by the director of communications, but if severe enough, the emergency management team would be activated.

These examples illustrate the need to resolve and clearly document the appropriate response to different levels of possible business interruption.

Forming the Communications Recovery Team

The communications recovery team is subordinate to the emergency management team. The communications recovery team is formed only after the policy issues involved in forming the emergency management team have been resolved. In general, the communications recovery team is responsible for:

- Activating the network disaster recovery plan.
- Testing the network disaster recovery plan.
- Updating the network disaster recovery plan.
- Restoration activities including specification of members responsible for:
  - Entering the building after a disaster.
  - Filing the initial emergency management team report about damage.
  - Coordinating equipment suppliers.
  - Coordinating circuit vendors.
  - Coordinating delivery of administrative supplies.
  - Preparing the emergency recovery center.

Staff Size. The size of the communications recovery team varies with the size of the organization. The initial response team may consist of as few as six persons. Given the task list, it should be clear that many of them might have to wear several hats.

It is not prudent to have a entire staff report after a disaster; this might only add to the confusion. When the plan is activated, a smaller number of persons should be expected to report to work immediately, and the majority put on standby. These alternates may be called on to provide additional help if needed or to fill in for members of the primary team who are called but do not show up. (In widespread disasters, employees will often first go home; this fact should be taken into account in the recovery plan.)

In summary, a six-person team for the initial response should be more than adequate, provided the remainder of the staff is standing by. If there are six recovery teams in the corporate plan and each has six members, a total of 36 would respond initially, which should be adequate in most cases.

Team Member Duties and Responsibilities. In general, communications recovery team members are responsible for a variety of actions. The team leader is responsible for:

- Notifying and assembling the communications recovery team members.

- Conducting a preliminary damage evaluation in conjunction with on-site vendors and local authorities as appropriate.
- Summarizing in writing all actions and events that took place during the recovery operation or test.
- Meeting with the overall recovery management team for a debriefing and critique.

Team members are responsible for:

- Ordering and expediting the delivery of replacement equipment for the damaged site as directed by the team leader.
- Coordinating the installation of replacement equipment.
- Establishing online communications (e.g., dial-up, multiplexer scripts, switched digital links).
- Testing newly established backup circuits.
- Establishing voice communications (e.g., 800 command routing, remote call forwarding) and coordinating installation of the necessary complement of business lines at the recovery location.
- Monitoring the backup network for performance during the recovery operation or test.

Workpaper III3.02 provides a sample form listing specific team member responsibilities for a hypothetical project.

Motivating Team Members

There are a number of methods for motivating team members, from bringing in a dozen doughnuts for team meetings to providing rewards for good performance. One consultant gave team members a windup doll, which cost about a dollar. The effect was surprising. The fact that he thought enough to say "thank you" in an innovative way motivated team members to put forth an extra effort. It also helped make the project fun.

While it is important to attempt to establish team spirit, team leaders must also instill a sense of dedication and responsibility for meeting deadlines. If the team gets behind, it should be notified in a positive manner. Regular management reviews can be used as checkpoints to indicate the status of the project to management and the team. Time lines and PERT charts are useful tools for keeping the project on track.

PROJECT DURATION

A realistic time frame should be set for completion of the effort—generally, a period of 18 to 30 months. There are many reasons for this. First, it takes time to obtain management commitment and schedule executive interviews. Second, there is the task of verification. For example, something as simple as obtaining a list of current employees can be difficult. Finding a current list is one thing; keeping it up to date is another thing altogether. A large amount of time in the planning process is spent simply finding and documenting data bases of personnel, equipment inventories, contracts, software inventories, vendor lists, and other components of the plan. The integrity of these sources must be verified; it is difficult to take shortcuts without sacrificing quality.

INCREASING AWARENESS

Even when the best motivational skills are used, it can be difficult to inspire employees of a large organization. For this reason, it is often necessary to spread the message that a disaster recovery planning effort is under way and that it is a priority. Increasing awareness is important to keep the effort from being perceived as just another project among many. Without such awareness throughout the organization, a recovery project will likely fail no matter how capable and motivated recovery team members are.

One way of increasing awareness is to have the CEO or CIO write a corporatewide memorandum introducing the recovery planning team and stating that recovery planning for the network is a priority. Another method is to publish an article in the company newsletter on a disaster recovery theme. People have a natural curiosity about disasters that happen to other people. Stories which might affect the reader are even more attention-getting. For example, a story entitled, "What Would You Do Without Telephones for Three Weeks?" would likely get attention. Many people have never thought of the possibility of losing telephone service. In the story, the recovery planning team should be introduced and the CEO quoted about the importance of the project.

In one unorthodox approach, a disaster recovery planner cut out articles about disaster recovery and sent them to division managers in an interoffice envelope—with no return address. After a few weeks, he would call one of the managers, presumably to inquire about the nature of these "phantom" articles he had been receiving. The technique proved to be a good door opener, and his calls did in fact get returned.

USING PROFESSIONAL ORGANIZATIONS

It is also possible to get a substantial amount of support for the recovery planning project at no cost from professional organizations. In addition to such traditional organizations as the American Red Cross, many other societies and organizations exist to help systems and communications professionals with recovery planning. These include the Association of Contingency Planners and the Delaware Valley Disaster Recovery Information Exchange Group (DVDRIEG). Memberships in these organizations can provide the opportunity to meet with disaster recovery experts in an informal forum. Such organizations as DVDRIEG sponsor yearly conferences (typically heavily subsidized by disaster recovery vendors) that provide much useful information on all facets of resumption planning. Appendix I-A provides a listing of professional organizations and services with contact information.

WORKPAPER III3.01 Equipment Colocation Checklist

CENTRAL OFFICE COLOCATION OF EQUIPMENT CHECKLIST

[ ] Access to colocated equipment is monitored on a 24-hour basis.

[ ] The carrier provides test assists, such as rebooting colocated equipment.

[ ] The location provides adequate security.

[ ] The location provides adequate power.

[ ] The location provides adequate ventilation and air conditioning.

What does the carrier expect in return for allowing your organization to colocate? ____________________________________

____

____

WORKPAPER III3.02 Communications Recovery Team Member Recovery Procedures

SAMPLE FORM: TEAM MEMBER RECOVERY PROCEDURES

1. The team leader notifies and assembles the communications team members, through the use of one of the following (in order of preference):

    a. Dial home telephone number.
    b. Sky pager.
    c. Messenger.

2. Team member 1 serves as coordinator, providing damage reports to the team leader for submission to the emergency management team, and coordinates other recovery resources, vendors and serves as focal point of contact for the communications recovery team. Team member 1 also serves as the backup help desk in case the primary one is incapacitated; however, the member will handle only emergency calls and those associated with the recovery operation.

2. Team member 2 notifies appropriate vendors and requests an on-site representative to be dispatched immediately. The vendors identified in the plan as primary suppliers will be summoned immediately.

3. Team leader assists in conducting a preliminary damage evaluation in conjunction with on-site vendors and local authorities as appropriate.

4. Team member 3 orders and expedites new replacement equipment for the damaged site as directed by the team leader.

5. Team member 4 coordinates the installation of replacement equipment at the recovery center and will take the first outbound flight to the center.

6. Team members 5 and 6 establish online communications while coordinating with circuit vendors and the company representative at the recovery center.

7. Team members 4, 5, and 6 test newly established backup circuits.

8. Team members 4 and 5 establish voice communications and coordinate installation of the necessary complement of business lines at the recovery location.

9. Team members 5 and 6 monitor backup network for performance during the length of the recovery operation or test.

10. Team leader summarizes in writing all actions and events that took place during the recovery operation or test.

11. Team leader meets with the overall recovery management team for debriefing and critique.

Evaluating the Communications Environment Using Standards

CHAPTER

III-4

Standards and procedures for the operation and security of communications systems are essential components of the communications recovery plan. This chapter presents a basic set of operational standards that should be in place to both prevent disasters and ensure the organization's ability to recover.

Operating and security standards affect every aspect of how the organization provides, uses, and recovers communications services. These include standards governing equipment installation, fire protection, housekeeping, software change control, access control, and network operations. They include procedures for the routine backup and recovery of information as well as for preventing theft of long-distance services and for securing dial-in terminals. They may address such mundane matters as the correct procedure for changing passwords and such basic questions as who is authorized to call for help in the event of a disaster.

Standards also address general issues of technical support, identifying support vendors and service providers that are critical resources in both day-to-day and recovery operations. They also define the authority and levels of responsibility for communications resources throughout the organization, not just within the communications department itself.

At their highest level, standards reflect the core policies of the organization. For example, an organization may establish as an overriding principle that the preservation of human life is the first objective in any response to a disaster. It may further define specific procedures to be followed, as well as employees' responsibilities in a disaster. Such policies and procedures obviously have profound implications on how the recovery plan is written and carried out.

Some organizations go so far as to incorporate security and operational standards in the communications recovery plan. It is suggested, however, that these standards documents be maintained separately from the recovery plan, for two reasons. First, the standards are resources that govern day-to-day operations of the communications department; they are not solely for use in emergencies. Second, the resumption plan should be kept as lean as possible so that it is quick and easy to refer to in a disaster.

This chapter focuses on those operational and security standards that have the greatest impact on disaster prevention and recovery. As shown in Workpapers III4.01 through III4.08, the recommended standards are presented in the form of checklists that can be used to evaluate existing communications facilities to identify operations that do not comply with the recommended standards. The results of this evaluation can be used to implement the necessary controls of day-to-day operations to both prevent disasters and ensure that the plan, once activated, executes smoothly.

These results can also be used to identify weaknesses in the organization's existing set of standards. Because it may be necessary to revise or create new standards as a result of the evaluations, this chapter begins with a brief set of guidelines on their development.

DEVELOPING STANDARDS

Standards documents for the communications department should be written only with the support and participation of other related departments. An organization can establish a communications standards committee to develop new standards and revise existing standards as business requirements change. For example, the standards committee might be called on to decide such broad companywide issues as which hardware and software services the communications department will support for end-user departments. This type of standard should include a list of supported services and vendors; otherwise, end users might independently acquire products and services that communications personnel are not able to support. (It is not just difficult to routinely maintain such diverse systems; the need to restore multiple systems can create a significant burden in a recovery operation in which recovery resources are spread thin.) The communications standards committee also provides a forum for qualified experts to evaluate new technologies in terms of cost, operational benefits, and recovery requirements.

Standards should not be so rigid as to reduce employee productivity. Most users require some level of flexibility in performing their functions.

To be workable, communications standards should be organized in tiers based on the size and complexity of the targeted communications environment and the criticality of the services it provides. It would be ridiculous, for example, to require a location with a six-line telephone system to provide HALON backup and other precautions more suited to a large installation. In short, two tiers should be established:

- *Tier I.* Standards for communications networks, regardless of size.
- *Tier II.* Standards for large communications networks.

The organization must decide what constitutes an appropriate division between types of installations.

EVALUATING SMALL INSTALLATIONS

The discussion of evaluating the communications environment using operational standards begins with the evaluation of a Tier I installation. Physical standards for small, noncritical installations include access to the equipment room, housekeeping of the equipment room, power supply, and the general physical condition of support services such as heating and plumbing. These basic standards would apply to communications facilities of any size. A checklist for this evaluation is provided as Workpaper III4.01.

The standards used in this evaluation may seem obvious but are often overlooked. For example, a surprising number of organizations have placed communications equipment for small installations in janitor's closets, which exposes the equipment to access by unauthorized persons or persons who might not understand how such equipment can be damaged. When possible, it is recommended that communications equipment be installed in a secured room.

Housekeeping also has an impact on both disaster prevention and recovery. For example, to prevent fire- and smoke-related damage, a no-smoking policy for equipment rooms should be enforced. Fire extinguishers of the appropriate type should be installed along with instructions for their use. The room temperature should be adequately controlled to prevent damage to equipment.

To prevent interruption of service, electrical power service should meet equipment manufacturer's specifications with respect to control of power sags and surges. Backup power should be provided to ensure recovery. Maintenance contracts should be current.

EVALUATING LARGE INSTALLATIONS

Large, mission-critical installations present an entirely different set of problems and should be much more intensively controlled than small networks. The following sections of this chapter describe key areas to be evaluated against operational and security standards, including those governing:

- Access to equipment areas.
- Housekeeping.
- Power supply.
- Change control for critical software resources.
- Protection of direct inward system access (DISA), voice mail, and remote access services.
- Local area networks.
- Fire and water protection systems.

Access to Equipment Areas

The communications standards document should bar any unauthorized individuals from equipment rooms unless they have a documented reason to be there. This includes other employees and visitors of all types. The room should employ additional protection, such as locks on the door and cipher locks. Any large glass areas in the building should be reinforced to prevent damage from outside sources of intrusion.

The physical review of the facility should include all cable entrance points into and out of the building. For example, diverse cable access should not be through the same entry point; this creates a potential single point of failure. All cabling should be assessed for single points of failure, including cable that goes between floors. A checklist for evaluating equipment area access controls is provided as Workpaper III4.02.

Equipment Room Housekeeping

In terms of housekeeping in a large network installation, a number of items should be mandatory. This includes a ban on eating, drinking, and smoking within the communications equipment room. Workpaper III4.03 provides a checklist for evaluating housekeeping.

Electrical Power Supply

Power to large network installations must be thoroughly tested. In areas where mission-critical applications are supported by communications systems, the use of such precautions as uninterruptible power supplies should be seriously considered.

In many buildings, particularly those housing a computer center, controls to prevent power fluctuations and outages are already in place. In a new building, however, power should be tested by a qualified electrician or electrical contractor before a communications node is installed. Not only should controls be able to prevent or mitigate power outages, they should also be able to handle power spikes, surges, brownouts, blackouts, and other conditions.

If the organization already has a data center in the building, an uninterruptible power supply (UPS) has probably been installed. The communications manager should rely on the IS manager for information on installing a UPS; it may also be possible to connect to the existing UPS.

Electrical cable should not be run in the same conduit with telephone cable. As noted in the previous discussion of the Hinsdale disaster, fire can be caused by electrical cable run in the same cable trough as telephone cable.

This also presents a safety hazard to technicians working on telephone cables. Workpaper III4.04 provides a checklist for evaluating power to the equipment room.

Software Change Control

Communications equipment is every bit as vulnerable to software-induced disasters as is the computer center. As noted earlier in Part III, two of the largest communications disasters in US history—the AT&T network disaster in 1990 and the SS7 disaster in 1991—were attributed to software failures.

Firm change control procedures should be in place to control software changes to critical communications systems. Such systems may include PBXs, digital cross-connect systems, multiplex and voice-mail services, and communications-related LAN servers. A key component of change controls is the audit trail.

Audit trails record information about each change to a major system, including the nature and purpose of the change and the person making the change. Without such a record, in the event of a software failure, it would be impossible to retrace the software development steps that led to the introduction of the software error, which may be necessary to identify and correct the error. It would also be impossible to identify an uncorrupted previous version of the software that might be needed for a quick recovery.

Such control records allow the communications manager to identify who made the changes, when, and for what purpose. This is especially important in large departments in which numerous people may have access to critical programs and data bases. The point is not to assign blame, but to control the number of people who are authorized to make changes and to ensure that these people are sufficiently trained. This is an essential control for preventing software-induced disasters.

Change controls should provide for a formal sign-off procedure for authorizing changes to critical production systems. They should include a listing of persons authorized to make changes to software, as well as procedures for password protection of software maintenance functions, particularly those that are remotely accessed. These controls should also dictate that a complete backup of software be made before any updates to the software to allow restoration from the previous version in the event of a disaster. Workpaper III4.05 provides a checklist for evaluating communications software change controls.

Remote Access

Controls for safeguarding remote access to long-distance services should also be evaluated. Such controls include access control of direct inward system access (DISA) lines, password protection, monitoring of reports for suspicious call activity, class-of-service restrictions for lobby phones, which could be used to make unauthorized long-distance calls, and an operator transfer policy. These controls are designed to protect against unauthorized access to communications services. Although this is primarily a security issue, it has implications for both the prevention of and recovery from disasters. Hackers who are able to gain remote access to long-distance services may not be interested only in theft; they may take advantage of such access to disable a communications system. For this reason, the resumption planner should ensure that effective controls for remote access are in place. Workpaper III4.06 provides a checklist for evaluating remote access to communications equipment.

Various standards of good practice should be evaluated. A policy should be established to limit operator-initiated transfers to outside phone lines, for example. Operator transfers are a common source of abuse. This can occur when a person calls an employee of an organization and is connected to his or her voice mail. Typically, voice mail gives the caller the opportunity to connect to the operator. The caller can then request that the operator give him or her an outside line in order to reach the absent employee or another party. Because it is the employee's phone number that appears on the operator's console, a busy operator is not likely to challenge the caller. Once an outside line is established, the caller is free to call anywhere in the world. To prevent this type of abuse, a standard should restrict transfers to outside lines for emergency (i.e., 911) calls only.

Standards for management of telephone credit cards should also be evaluated. For example, it is important to ensure that these cards are deactivated immediately after an employee leaves the company. Absent this precaution, a vindictive employee could easily post the company's credit card number, resulting in significant fraud.

Other security concerns include dial-up terminal access to both maintenance functions and online services. As an absolute minimum, these services should be password protected, and the passwords changed on a regular basis. It is imperative that anything that contains an access code or other confidential information be shredded, just as it would be in the computer room, to avoid it being intercepted.

One of the most common forms of telephone fraud takes place on DISA lines. DISA lines are primarily used by executives and salespeople who travel. They can dial an 800 number, receive a dial tone, enter an access code, and make calls through the company's PBX.

Hackers have another name for DISA—dial in–steal away. Hackers can download a program from a computer bulletin board that dials random 7- or 10-digit telephone numbers and creates a list of every number that answered with a dial tone (or a carrier tone for a modem). Once they have this list, they execute a second program that hits each of these access codes with random three-, four-, five-, and six-digit access numbers, until they crack one. At this point, the hacker is free to call long distance, leaving the unsuspecting company to pick up the tab for the call.

Innovative hackers can dial through a number of PBXs in succession to thwart being caught. (This is also often done to mask the automatic number identifier of the hacker.) As shown in Exhibit III-4-A, a hacker dials first into a PBX in New York, then goes out, either on a 950 or 1-800 number, to a PBX in Chicago. At this point, the process is repeated, and the hacker dials out to a PBX in Dallas, and finally, repeating the same procedure, dials into a PBX in Atlanta. At this point, the hacker uses the PBX in Atlanta to make overseas phone calls. If the hacker is discovered by the communications manager in Atlanta, he or she can simply fall back one step to Dallas and repeat the process there. It is very difficult to track a hacker using this methodology. However, there are a few steps that an organization can take to ensure that it is not a victim.

In the initial phases, even though the user in Atlanta is paying for the call, there

EXHIBIT **III-4-A** HACKER ATTACK ON DISA LINES

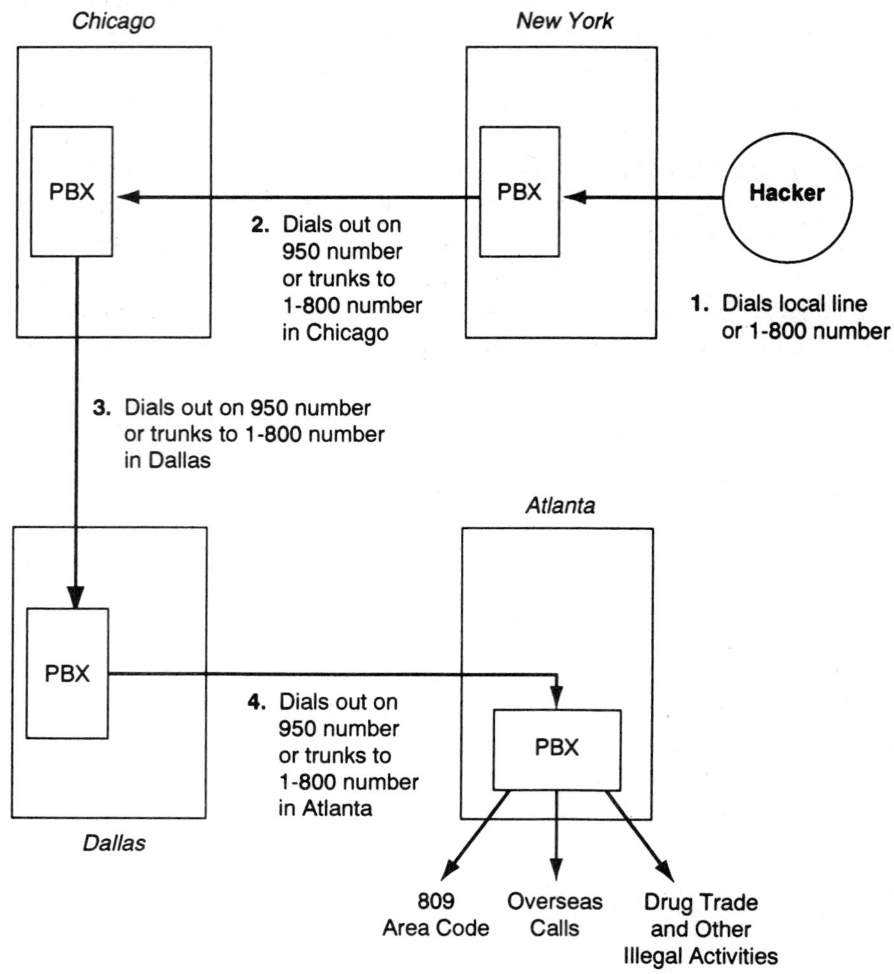

are warning signs within the PBXs in Dallas and Chicago. Use of the 800 service, for example, may be increasing. Also, various types of outbound service may be going up. If the communications managers in Dallas and Chicago are monitoring the traffic, they can contact different departments within the company to determine whether this increase is legitimate.

The communications manager in Atlanta could also take certain precautions to ensure the organization is not victimized. The first involves blocking overseas access on DISA lines. If the company has no overseas offices, blocking the 0-1-1 access code should be required. Second, blocking the 809 area code to the Caribbean addresses many types of fraud, because much of this activity involves calls by immigrants to relatives in the Caribbean. Third, reports can be generated within the PBX to identify suspicious calling patterns (e.g., calls that exceed a certain duration, go to unusual locations, or take place during nonstandard business hours).

LAN Connectivity Standards

The operation and security of departmental LANs should also be evaluated to identify weaknesses that could result in compromise or disruption of critical functions. Although issues related to the recovery of LANs are covered in Part I of this book as part of business operations recovery, connections among LANs should be evaluated as part of the communications recovery program.

The communications manager must monitor various exposures to multiple connected LANs. For example, a finance department running mission-critical applications may have implemented strong controls to prevent unauthorized access and virus infection. Such controls might include automatic scanning of files to detect viruses. The sales department, on the other hand, may be relatively uncontrolled, with sales staff downloading public domain software from bulletin boards and using borrowed diskettes, thereby running the risk of virus contamination. If the sales department LAN is connected to the finance department LAN, the strict antivirus controls in finance could be jeopardized. It is the communications manager's responsibility to monitor such connections and determine whether to isolate a particular LAN in the interest of the overall security of the organization. Appropriate standards for connecting LANs should be documented and evaluated, as shown in Workpaper III4.07.

Fire and Water Protection Systems

A number of precautions should be taken to protect against both fire and water damage. This section begins with a review of the fire suppression mechanisms that may need to be evaluated. There are primarily three means of fire suppression used in large commercial buildings: carbon dioxide, sprinkler systems, and HALON. The following paragraphs describe each of these methods. Workpaper III4.08 provides a checklist for evaluating fire and water protection systems.

Carbon Dioxide. Carbon dioxide is very effective in fighting fires. It works by removing oxygen from the air, thereby stopping combustion. However, there are two problems with the use of carbon dioxide. First, because carbon dioxide removes the oxygen from the air, people and other living things cannot be in the room in which it has been released. Second is the problem of thermal shock. Carbon dioxide quickly freezes objects with which it comes into contact. For these reasons, carbon dioxide is restricted to unstaffed areas.

Sprinkler Systems. Sprinkler systems are very effective at fire suppression. Their use is increasingly required in commercial buildings, regardless of the types of communications and computer systems installed there. (For example, sprinkler systems may be required by providers of business resumption insurance as well as by city and state fire codes.) However, such water-based systems can also create problems in the recovery of electronic equipment. The recovery planner needs to understand these potential problems in order to determine appropriate recovery measures.

In general, after a fire in which water is released into a communications or computer equipment room, specialists in the recovery of water-damaged equipment can be brought in. Typically, they remove circuit boards and other components, dip them in special solutions, dry the equipment using blow dryers, and reassemble and test the equipment. Although it is much cheaper to revitalize water-damaged equipment than to replace it (some industry experts estimate the cost of repair to be as little as 30% of the replacement cost), the restored equipment often remains prone to failure in the future. This is because of the nature of the damage to electronic components caused by water.

Equipment is often both electrically and physically hot when water is released during a fire. If equipment is electrically active, components may short-circuit. The water that is released is not distilled; it typically contains such minerals as iron, which act as conductors of electrical current. Therefore, the release of such mineralized water can damage electronic equipment, especially if it is still electrically charged. If equipment is physically hot, sudden contact with cold water can cause rapid contraction of circuit boards, which can be especially damaging to multilayered circuit boards.

Even the process of restoring the equipment can cause damage. For example, circuit boards must be protected against static charges, but the blow dryers used to dry the inside of equipment can generate significant static.

Although sprinklers are installed according to exacting specifications, they can cause damage, even without being activated by fire. For example, in equipment rooms where there is a 10-foot clearance for sprinklers, someone may transport an 11-foot crate and break off a sprinkler head. Or technicians crawling through a suspended ceiling area to service cable may step on a sprinkler pipe, causing a leak.

One way of avoiding these types of problems is to use a dry-pipe, preaction, or precharged sprinkler system. A dry-pipe sprinkler system does not store the water overhead in the equipment room. The dry pipe, as the name implies, keeps the water out of the equipment room until such time as the fire alarm is tripped. An electromechanical device and a valve located outside the equipment room keep the water outside the room until it is needed. When the first alarm system trips, the valve opens, allowing the water into the pipe inside the equipment room. When the filament for the sprinkler system melts, the water is released. In a false alarm, however, the valve will open, and the water will enter the pipe in the equipment room. After a false alarm, it is usually necessary to evacuate the water from the pipe. Preaction and precharged sprinkler systems work on a similar basis, some using an inert gas inside the sprinkler system to hold the water back and others using a valve.

In summary, although there are a number of competent companies that specialize in emergency restorations, restoration of mission-critical communications equipment should be carefully weighed. If the operation of the equipment is questionable, the components should be replaced to avoid continuing problems after the recovery.

HALON Systems. Another option for fire suppression is a HALON system. HALON works in somewhat the same fashion as carbon dioxide, with one major exception. HALON can be used in rooms with humans, and it is not harmful to breathe or be exposed to. Rather than depleting the oxygen, the HALON molecule interrupts the combustion cycle required to sustain a fire. It only takes a small amount of the oxygen out of the air; therefore, it is possible for people to remain in the room and breathe during a HALON discharge.

This is not to say that a HALON dump is pleasant. The force of the gas as it is discharged into the room can knock ceiling tiles loose and blow items off desks.

To be effective, HALON must be released in a confined area. For example, if the door to the communications equipment room were open at the time the HALON discharged, or if the force of the discharge was sufficient to open that door, HALON would escape and oxygen would enter the room, allowing the fire to burn. The integrity of the room itself may be compromised by people putting holes through sheet metal walls to run cable or water pipes. This is especially a concern above dropped ceilings and below raised floors.

HALON is not effective against deep-rooted electrical fires, which require very little oxygen to burn. Should a fire start in cabling under the floor, HALON is not likely to put it out. (That is why fire detectors or particle detectors should be installed under the floor to ensure a quick alert.)

Problems can also occur in installing HALON systems. For example, in one case, the building manager ordered that a large fan be installed for the floor serving a communications equipment room. In the event of a fire, the fan would exhaust any smoke within the building in order to save lives. Of course, with a HALON system, the fan would immediately compromise the integrity of the HALON. To resolve this conflict, it was decided to keep the fan in place and put it on a manual switch. In the event of a fire, the alarm would go off and the HALON would discharge; the fire department would arrive on the scene, assess the situation, and after ascertaining that the fire was out, turn on the fan and exhaust the smoke. The key to solving these conflicts is to work with fire inspection and building management to reach a compromise.

It should be noted that because HALON is damaging to the ozone layer of the atmosphere, many governments have mandated that its use be phased out. Although a complete ban on HALON is unlikely, it is going to become prohibitively expensive to use because of its limited availability and production. Already, there are laws in place for systems to recover HALON and other types of chlorofluorocarbons so that they are not vented into the atmosphere. In short, it will be very expensive to replace HALON after it is released. Currently, there is no cost-effective, long-term replacement for HALON. This should be taken into account in planning.

Fire-Retardant Cable. The preponderance of the cable within the communications facility is polyvinyl chloride, which burns and creates nauseous fumes as well as hydrochloric and sulfuric acid compounds when wet. It is therefore recommended that fire-retardant communications cable be specified when possible. Traditionally, this has been Teflon cable; however, other materials are beginning to be used for fireproof cable as well, including Halar, Stolsis, and Kevlar.

Other Fire Prevention Controls. Smoke and particle detectors should be mounted above the ceiling (i.e., at the highest point within the room), on the ceiling, and below the raised floor. Similarly, moisture detectors should be installed below the raised floor, where they can detect water before it becomes a disaster. Last, a no-smoking policy is absolutely essential within equipment areas for obvious safety reasons but also to prevent what could be a very expensive HALON discharge should a detector be set off accidentally.

Fire extinguishers within the work area should be labeled as to their contents or for the type of fire they are designed to fight. Using the wrong type of fire extinguisher on a fire, particularly one involving complex communications equipment, could be an expensive mistake, complicating cleanup efforts considerably. There are also safety considerations involved in using the wrong type of fire extinguisher against live electrical fires.

An infrared scan can be used to detect heat sources, identifying possible locations of fires before they begin. Infrared scanning equipment is used to scan the walls, ceilings, and floors in buildings. In one case, a scanning device found a great deal of heat coming from a breaker box. After the circuit breakers had been repeatedly tripped, they eventually fused and were running dead shorts. The infrared scan saved the company from a potentially damaging fire. It is recommended that the communications equipment room undergo a complete infrared scan on an annual basis at least.

Infrared scanning is available from a variety of sources. Many of the local Bell operating companies and long-distance carriers perform infrared scans as part of their normal maintenance services.

Water Damage

There are probably more disasters due to water in equipment areas than due to fire and other causes. There are many sources of water within a commercial building, including leaky roofs, plumbing, and air conditioning.

Drains themselves can become sources of water damage if they become clogged with debris. Sewers can create water disasters as well. Any type of drainage out of the building must have an approved back-flow device.

If a water problem occurs in the building, the water ultimately goes to the basement, which is where PBX equipment is often installed. When possible, the PBX should be kept out of the basement.

Several steps can be taken to avert the possibility of a water-related disaster. First, pipes should be labeled. In a disaster, it can be difficult to distinguish whether a pipe carries water or sewage or is an electrical conduit. By labeling these, it becomes very easy to find the correct shutoff quickly.

Second, moisture detectors should be installed under the floor, particularly in areas that are especially prone to water problems. These might be immediately under or adjacent to air-conditioning units, along major routes of water pipes running under the floor, in low-lying areas, or adjacent to drains.

Third, water pipes should be protected against freezing. This, ironically, is more of a problem in areas like Atlanta, Dallas, and Memphis than in such areas as Minneapolis and New York, where people prepare for cold weather. In more temperate areas, a sudden cold wave can freeze and break water pipes.

Last, loss of water service to a building could cause problems if outside water is used in cooling systems, either for technical systems or air conditioners. There have been a number of reported outages because of a water shutoff.

Lightning Exposure

There should be adequate lightning protection on incoming circuits and proper grounding. One lightning strike can have devastating consequences on electronic equipment.

Although little can be done about direct lightning strikes, there are many things that can be done about indirect lightning strikes. One of the prime candidates for an indirect lightning strike are the telephone lines coming into the building. Adequate lightning protection should be installed on these outside lines to help protect communications equipment.

VENDOR ASSISTANCE

Vendors can help ensure the recoverability of the network on site. They can assist in developing an inventory of all communications equipment installed on site, including the date of installation, the serial number of the equipment, the revision numbers of any software or hardware associated with the equipment, the existence of a maintenance contract for the equipment, and any replacement guarantees provided by the vendor. The planner should document any contractual obligations the vendor may have made in writing to support the system in a disaster. Procedures to be followed in the event of a disaster, including escalation lists for emergency response personnel (both within the company and at the vendor), should be documented. (An escalation list provides contact information on personnel who can be called in the event the primary contact is not available).

The vendor may also be able to provide general assistance in disaster recovery planning. Many equipment vendors offer elaborate disaster recovery liaison programs that can be invaluable in developing a plan.

USING STATE PUBLIC UTILITY COMMISSIONS

A wealth of information about the telephone companies can be obtained at little or no cost from state public utility commissions. Much of the information filed with these commissions is in the public domain. (The address and phone number of the state public utility commission are normally provided in the front section of the telephone directory under the section on consumer rights.)

The state commissions can provide information about central office areas that can be useful in evaluating whether to build diverse facilities to a separate serving office. The commission can also provide exact definitions of exchange boundaries and calling areas, which can be useful in estimating communications costs, and they can also provide information on proposed new central offices.

Information on distances to other central offices can be obtained, which may be of interest if the company is considering diverse access to other central offices. There is also information on central office upgrades and central office capacity. Although it is rare, central offices may get close to saturation, making it difficult to install large blocks of dial tone, because of either lack of facilities or available numbers. If a large company is looking to move into a rural area, information can be obtained about the capacity of the central office for that area to ensure it can handle the anticipated traffic.

Some companies have sought to obtain access to more than one local telephone company. Service from two central offices can provide improved flexibility as well as protection in the event of a disaster at one of the central offices.

Diverting facilities to another local operating company's territory, however, may affect the rate base. The state public utility commission may become involved in approving such dual certification, ensuring there is no negative effect on the rate base or on public telephone service due to this change in service.

WORKPAPER III4.01 Checklist for Evaluating Tier 1 Installations

EVALUATING TIER 1 INSTALLATIONS

1. Tier 1--Equipment room access:

   a. Are equipment rooms locked and accessible to authorized persons only? (Location of janitorial and other functions in the equipment area is strongly discouraged to discourage both tampering and theft of equipment.)

      [ ] Yes [ ] No

2. Tier 1--Equipment room housekeeping:

   a. Are paper and other combustibles stored in an equipment room kept in metal or fireproof cabinets? (Large quantities of these materials must be stored in areas other than the equipment room.)

      [ ] Yes [ ] No

   b. Are trash and other unnecessary items regularly removed from the equipment room?

      [ ] Yes [ ] No

   c. Are waste containers of a fire-resistant type, with lids capable of suffocating small fires?

      [ ] Yes [ ] No

   d. Is there a policy to discourage eating and drinking in the equipment room?

      [ ] Yes [ ] No

   e. Is smoking in the equipment room prohibited?

      [ ] Yes [ ] No

3. Tier 1--Equipment room electrical power:

   a. Is backup power installed in the equipment room?

      [ ] Yes [ ] No

   b. Are backup generators installed in the equipment room?

      [ ] Yes [ ] No

c. When backup generators are installed for emergency power generation, are they periodically tested through actual use?

[ ] Yes [ ] No

d. Is emergency lighting available for use during a power failure?

[ ] Yes [ ] No

e. Are circuit breakers clearly marked and easily accessible? (Where practical, communications equipment should be installed on a separate circuit and breaker from other circuits.)

[ ] Yes [ ] No

f. Does the installation conform with manufacturers electrical specifications and local building codes with respect to cable size, individual electrical circuits, and twist lock electrical outlets?

[ ] Yes [ ] No [ ] Yes, except for: ____________

g. Is all communications equipment properly grounded in accordance with vendor specifications?

[ ] Yes [ ] No [ ] Yes, except for: ____________

4. Tier 1--Equipment room general building facilities/condition:

a. Is all nonelectrical piping in the equipment room identified and labeled to allow for easy shut-off in the event of a problem?

[ ] Yes [ ] No

b. Are air conditioning, heating, and humidity levels of the equipment room controlled by building maintenance personnel? (Every effort should be made to ensure that the temperature and humidity levels are maintained within the range specified for the equipment installed as specified by the manufacturer, and building maintenance should be aware of this fact.)

[ ] Yes [ ] No

5. Tier 1--Equipment room, miscellaneous items:

a. Are emergency instructions maintained in a conspicuous location within the equipment room? These should ideally include:

- Police and fire department numbers.
- Emergency and trouble reporting numbers for the corporate communications department in sites where owned equipment resides.
- Fire exit maps as required by local code.
- Procedures for an emergency shutdown of equipment, as well as for electrical, gas, and water.

[ ] Yes [ ] No

b. Is a portable fire extinguisher located in the equipment room, with an adjacent sign clearly indicating the type of fire for which it is intended?

[ ] Yes [ ] No

WORKPAPER III4.02 Checklist for Evaluating Equipment Area Access

EVALUATING EQUIPMENT AREA ACCESS

1. Tier 2--Equipment room access:

   a. Are equipment rooms locked at all times, and accessible to authorized persons only? (Only persons with a definite need to be in the area to perform their assigned duties shall be authorized to enter on a regular basis. Location of janitorial and other functions in the equipment area is prohibited.)

      [ ] Yes [ ] No

   b. Is a card key or cipher lock entry system installed?

      [ ] Yes [ ] No

2. Tier 2--Equipment room access to visitors:

   a. Are visitors limited and controlled through proper authorization and access controls? (Visitors other than customer engineer, telephone company, equipment maintenance and service personnel should be accompanied by communications personnel at all times while in the equipment room. A log for visitor signatures should be maintained for all people entering a computer facility who are not regular communications employees of the company.)

      [ ] Yes [ ] No

3. Tier 2--Equipment room additional physical protection:

   a. Is there a single general entrance to the equipment room that is controlled by a locking mechanism, receptionist, or other similar restriction? Other entry points such as windows, emergency exits, duct work, service panels, conduit paths must also be modified to prevent access.

      [ ] Yes [ ] No

   b. Is the room windowless?

      [ ] Yes [ ] No

   c. If not, do alternative window protections such as steel bars, unbreakable glass, or secondary walls exist?

      [ ] Yes [ ] No

d. Does exterior building protection include adequate lighting at night, guard surveillance, intrusion detection systems, and physical barriers at doors, windows, and ramps?

[ ] Yes [ ] No

WORKPAPER III4.03 Checklist for Evaluating Equipment Room Housekeeping

EVALUATING EQUIPMENT ROOM HOUSEKEEPING

1. Equipment room housekeeping: Are paper and other combustible materials stored in the equipment room in minimum amounts and in metal cabinets? (Large amounts of these materials must be stored in areas other than the equipment room.)

   [ ] Yes [ ] No

2. Are solvents or flammable liquids stored in closed fire-retardant containers away from paper, forms, and other combustible materials?

   [ ] Yes [ ] No

3. Are trash and other unnecessary items prevented from accumulating in the equipment room?

   [ ] Yes [ ] No

4. Are waste containers of a fire-resistant type with lids to suffocate small fires?

   [ ] Yes [ ] No

5. Are eating and drinking in the equipment room prohibited, except in specially designated areas?

   [ ] Yes [ ] No

6. Is smoking in the equipment room prohibited and are signs visibly posted?

   [ ] Yes [ ] No

WORKPAPER III4.04 Checklist for Evaluating Equipment Room Electrical Power

EVALUATING EQUIPMENT ROOM ELECTRICAL POWER

1. Are there at least eight hours of backup power (mandatory for large Tier 2 network installations) for the equipment room?

   [ ] Yes [ ] No

2. Are backup generators installed?

   [ ] Yes [ ] No

3. Where generators are installed for emergency power generation, are they periodically tested through actual use?

   [ ] Yes [ ] No

4. Is emergency lighting available for use during a power failure in all large installations?

   [ ] Yes [ ] No

5. Is one main breaker provided for all equipment and secondary breakers for each major piece of equipment?

   [ ] Yes [ ] No

6. Are breakers clearly marked and easily accessible? (Critical communications equipment should be on a separate power circuit and breaker.)

   [ ] Yes [ ] No

7. Are manufacturers' electrical specifications and local building codes followed with respect to cable size, individual electrical circuits, and twist lock electrical outlets?

   [ ] Yes [ ] No [ ] Yes, except for: ______________

8. Is all communications equipment properly grounded in accordance with vendor specifications?

   [ ] Yes [ ] No

9. Has commercial power been tested (before installing any major network component) for spikes, surges, brownouts, noise, and other impairments that may affect the equipment?

   [ ] Yes [ ] No

10. Power conditioning equipment:

    [ ] Installed.

    [ ] Under consideration.

    [ ] Not under consideration.

WORKPAPER III4.05 Checklist for Evaluating Network Software Security and Change Control Management

EVALUATING NETWORK SOFTWARE SECURITY AND CHANGE CONTROL MANAGEMENT

1. Are major software changes to network components approved in advance by the communications manager and documented (in the event follow-up action is required)?

   [ ] Yes   [ ] No

2. Are only specifically authorized individuals permitted to make major software changes? (Major is defined as any change that affects multiple users such as with a T1 multiplexer or major PBX system change.)

   [ ] Yes   [ ] No

3. Is all access to maintenance systems associated with these changes password protected, with passwords changed at least monthly and on a regular basis?

   [ ] Yes   [ ] No

4. Are backups of critical software, routing tables, and other critical information routinely made before any major network software change (in the event a fallback to the old information is required)?

   [ ] Yes   [ ] No

WORKPAPER III4.06 Checklist for Evaluating Remote System Access to Equipment Rooms

EVALUATING REMOTE SYSTEM ACCESS TO EQUIPMENT ROOMS

1. Is dial-in access to remote systems (designed for maintenance) restricted to employees having a need for such access to perform their specific job responsibilities?

   [ ] Yes [ ] No

2. Are requests for passwords made in writing to the communications department and approved by same?

   [ ] Yes [ ] No

3. Do controls for remote access include:

   [ ] Passwords to prevent unauthorized access to a maintenance function?

   [ ] A procedure for changing the access password on at least a monthly basis?

   [ ] A procedure for immediately reporting the termination of an individual possessing a password to prevent a terminated employee from accessing a maintenance function?

   [ ] When possible, passwords hidden on screens during sign-on?

   [ ] The ability to detect suspicious activity or failed log-on attempts to maintenance functions?

   [ ] Are printed materials containing password information or log-on information disposed of as proprietary information by shredding, incinerating, or other accepted practice?

4. Is all direct inward system access (DISA) disabled when possible to prevent unauthorized use?

   [ ] Yes [ ] No

5. When DISA must be used, is it assigned in accordance with written policies and procedures strictly on an individual, as-required basis?

   [ ] Yes [ ] No

6. Are other precaution for safeguarding DISA used, including:

   [ ] Eight-digit access codes?

   [ ] Answering of the DISA line with silence rather than dial tone?

   [ ] Stepped-up monitoring of reports detailing activity on DISA lines?

   [ ] Shutting down [<u>number</u>] area code?

   [ ] Automatic number identification?

   [ ] Caller ID?

7. Are lobby phones and other high-abuse areas restricted from completing long-distance calls?

   [ ] Yes [ ] No

8. Are all autoattendant and voice mail systems certified as incapable of transferring a call to an outside line, regardless of whether the caller has an access code?

   [ ] Yes [ ] No

9. Does a policy exist stating that operators shall not be permitted to transfer a caller to an outside line or location under any circumstances, with the exception of police, fire, and emergency services?

   [ ] Yes [ ] No

10. Are passwords assigned to control dial-in access by unauthorized persons to all maintenance and operations systems?

   [ ] Yes [ ] No

11. Does a corporate policy on privacy of phone conversations and data transfers exist?

   [ ] Yes [ ] No

WORKPAPER III4.07 Checklist for Evaluating LAN Connectivity Standards

EVALUATING LAN CONNECTIVITY STANDARDS

1. LAN standards set or enforced by corporate communications may include the following (check each instance where the policy is in place):

   [ ] Users may be expected to conform to specific standards that allow for simplified recovery of the private-line network. These usually include connection to the corporate T1 backbone network when possible to aid in a major recovery.

   [ ] LAN users are expected to take reasonable precautions when using public domain or non-factory-sealed copies of software because of the threat of virus contamination. If a local area network threatens other networks because of such contamination, the communications department may disconnect such a user to protect the integrity of the remainder of the network.

   [ ] LAN users interconnecting over the corporate backbone network are expected to conform to a prespecified list of supported vendors and services to expedite recovery in a disaster.

   [ ] Remote users are expected to keep all installed communications equipment associated with their LAN or PBX in good working order.

   [ ] Maintenance contracts are required of all end users covering the period from the time the initial warranty expires until a period five years from that date or until the equipment is retired, whichever is less. Exceptions are as follows:

      a. Trained technical personnel on-site who perform the maintenance function in lieu of a service contract.

      b. The site manager who signs a document stating that the site will absorb all preventive and demand-maintenance charges incurred in keeping the equipment in working order.

      c. In either of these two cases, the end user who relinquishes support from the communications staff to avoid creating an undue burden on limited resources.

[ ] All new PBX- or LAN-connection equipment contacts bid by communications department shall include a five-year maintenance in the request for proposal.

WORKPAPER III4.08 Checklist for Evaluating Fire and Water Protection Systems

EVALUATING FIRE AND WATER PROTECTION

1. Fire exposure standards should be based on the National Fire Protection Association (NFPA) standard. All new construction of major network nodes or installations must follow NFPA standards, local building codes, and applicable insurance standards. Are you familiar with these standards?

   [ ] Yes [ ] No

2. Is the building or equipment (e.g., walls, floors, suspended ceilings, and internal partitions) constructed of fire-resistant material?

   [ ] Yes [ ] No

3. Is the equipment area located to minimize exposure from environmental risks, away from areas where hazardous process are conducted (e.g., factory floors)?

   [ ] Yes [ ] No

4. Do interior walls extend from the slab to the structural ceiling, even below and above dropped ceilings and raised floors?

   [ ] Yes [ ] No

5. Do the surrounding walls have at least a two-hour fire rating?

   [ ] Yes [ ] No

6. Are air-conditioning ducts through interior walls equipped with fire dampers?

   [ ] Yes [ ] No

7. Are shut-off valves for overhead sprinkler systems installed and marked to prevent accidental discharge?

   [ ] Yes [ ] No

8. Are fresh-air intakes covered with protective screening and located to prevent the intake of pollutants and debris from outside?

   [ ] Yes [ ] No

9. Are approved smoke and heat detectors installed:

   [ ] Throughout the equipment room?

   [ ] In associated storage areas?

   [ ] In cable vaults?

   [ ] Above the ceiling?

   [ ] Under raised ceilings?

10. Are floor panels, ceiling tiles, or air registers that hide smoke detectors marked?

    [ ] Yes   [ ] No

11. Is Halon 1301 in use?

    [ ] Yes   [ ] No

12. Do alarms for fire, intrusion, and Halon discharge forward to a guard station or other area occupied 24 hours a day located away from the equipment room?

    [ ] Yes   [ ] No

13. Do automatic sprinkler systems exist? If so, what type?

    [ ] Normal sprinklers

    [ ] Dry pipe

    [ ] Preaction

    [ ] Precharged

    [ ] No sprinklers

    In an equipment room equipped with a sprinkler system, the risk of water damage is high due to accidental release or false alarm. Delayed quenching precautions as explained in the fire precaution section of this document provides protection against accidental release.

14. Do procedures and shut-off devices allow for emergency manual power-down before a water release in sprinkler-protected equipment rooms?

    [ ] Yes   [ ] No

15. Do Halon systems that are automatically activated smoke detectors have manual overrides to release or stop discharge?

[ ] Yes [ ] No

16. Does an alarm exist to warn employees of pending Halon discharge?

[ ] Yes [ ] No

17. Does the air-conditioning system (which could exhaust the Halon agent) automatically shut off when the Halon system is activated?

[ ] Yes [ ] No

18. Are all doors in equipment rooms equipped with Halon modified to open inward, toward the equipment area? (A sudden release of Halon will most probably force the door closed if it is inadvertently left open by an employee exiting the area.)

[ ] Yes [ ] No

19. Does drainage exist below raised floors, with proper traps and back-flow devices where practical?

[ ] Yes [ ] No

20. Is all nonelectrical piping inside the equipment room labeled and associated shut-off valves located? (Floor or ceiling panels hiding such piping should also be labeled where practical.)

[ ] Yes [ ] No

21. Are moisture detectors installed under the raised-floor areas in places where water could be a concern such as under air handling units or adjacent to drains?

[ ] Yes [ ] No

22. Does a policy exist with regard to equipment accidentally doused with water, specifying that the equipment be turned off immediately and remain off until manufacturers representatives have inspected the equipment and approved reuse?

[ ] Yes [ ] No

Documenting Global Recovery Procedures

CHAPTER

III-5

This phase of communications resumption planning involves documenting the scope of the plan and specific recovery procedures. Certain global recovery procedures affect the organization as a whole; these procedures are addressed in Chapter III-5. Other recovery procedures are specific to the communications function; these are documented separately, as described in Chapter III-6.

The primary reason for documenting recovery plan procedures is to ensure that critical systems can be recovered even if the persons usually responsible for these systems are unavailable because of the disaster. Workpaper III5.01 provides a sample table of contents of the key global procedures that should be documented in the recovery plan.

It should be noted that the sample global plan shown in Workpaper III5.01 has been compiled from several actual plans of real organizations. As such, it reflects the general requirements of most organizations. Of course, in developing its recovery plan, a company may need to add specific recovery procedures to this generic plan. For example, is not unusual for businesses in earthquake-prone regions of California to include provisions for storage of food on site.

Before documenting the plan, the recovery planner should also decide on the appropriate level of detail for the plan. Highly detailed plans may be fine if the recovery is being conducted by employees who are familiar with company procedures and related equipment configurations. However, people involved in the recovery who are not employees and hence are not familiar with the organization and its related procedures and equipment may find such highly detailed plans difficult to understand and follow. In addition, providing too much detail may discourage people from using the plan in a disaster, because it appears too complicated and imposing.

WRITE THE POLICY STATEMENT

STEP 1

The policy statement should be the first section of the recovery plan. It should include a high-level statement of the reasons for developing the recovery plan and the objectives of the plan. Because of its broad-based character, the policy statement should be written by a senior manager (e.g., a chief information officer or chief executive officer) who reports directly to the board of directors. The completed policy statement should not exceed two pages. Workpaper III5.01 provides a checklist of items that organizations often choose to include in the policy statement.

Most policy statements include the objective of protecting human life, if not for ethical then for financial reasons. There are, however, exceptions to this practice. For example, a pharmaceutical company rationalized that recovery of the process for developing certain life-saving drugs should take precedence over the protection of human life in a recovery operation, because losing the ability to produce these drugs would have a far more damaging impact on human life. Absent such extreme considerations, however, most organizations would choose protection of human life as the foremost priority in a recovery.

The policy statement should also include the objective of minimizing risk to the organization. For example, if an automated call distribution system is implemented to permit continued operation of the business, it should not expose the company to undue increased risk. The consequence of such a policy might be that such systems must provide a baseline set of access controls to prevent intrusions during the recovery period.

Certainly a key objective of the plan is the recovery of critical operations that ensure the company remains profitable. As noted earlier, this has an impact on developing the communications-specific recovery plan in that it determines the priority for recovery of communications systems.

The policy statement should also address the avoidance of litigation in the form of shareholder suits or government-initiated action because of failure to take prudent precautions against disasters. Lawsuits might be brought because such a failure results in substantial loss in the value of shareholder assets or in an inability to generate government-mandated services.

The preservation of the organization's competitive position and customer confidence and goodwill are related. Failure to provide products and services may result in loss of customers, as competitors step in to fill the void. The lost market share may be very difficult to recover. It can be effective to emphasize the impact of such a loss on profits by adding a statement to the policy detailing the expected financial loss per day of a communications failure.

The company's inability to recover operations in a timely manner may also erode the customer's confidence in the business, which also has an impact on competitive position. Loss of goodwill may be especially severe if it becomes known that the company did not adequately prepare for the disaster.

The policy statement should conclude with a synopsis of the recovery strategy—for example, "Mission-critical automated communications systems will be restored within eight hours."

ESTABLISHING RECOVERY PROCEDURES

Recovery procedures can be divided into two categories:

- Procedures for reacting to a disaster and activating the recovery plan.
- Procedures for performing recovery activities.

Section II of Workpaper III5.01 presents a listing of the key activities to be performed. Subsections II.A through II.D relate to the preparatory steps involved in activating the plan; subsection II.E focuses on recovery activities.

As noted earlier, this chapter describes recovery procedures that involve a companywide response, including, for example, notification of police and fire departments, filing of damage assessment reports, and activation of disaster recovery teams. These activities are typically covered in the corporatewide plan for recovery of business operations and automated systems; as such, they need only be referenced in the communications recovery plan. For example, it makes no sense for the communications recovery planner to document the procedure for notifying the police of a disaster if that procedure has already been developed in the business operations or data center recovery plan. For this procedure, the communications plan might simply provide the phone number for the police department, with a reference to the corporatewide plan if more detailed information is needed.

STEP 2

DOCUMENT ALERT AND ACTIVATION PROCEDURES

As shown in section II of Workpaper III5.01, the following procedures must either be established or identified and referenced from existing recovery documents:

- *Subsection II.A.* Initial reaction and alert procedures.
- *Subsection II.B.* Damage assessment procedures.
- *Subsection II.C.* Activation procedures.
- *Subsection II.D.* Related procedures.

The following paragraphs describe how to document each of these sets of procedures.

Initial Reaction and Alert Procedures

In the minutes and hours following a disaster, a number of actions must be performed in rapid succession. Protection of human life is of primary importance. Therefore, immediate steps should be taken to protect employees, including evacuating the building and disconnecting power. The initial disaster may be reported to any one of several organizations within the company. For example, a communications disaster due to water damage to a PBX may first be reported to the facilities department or to the security department. Because the damage may affect not only the PBX but also multiplexer equipment, and LAN servers, it may not be immediately apparent who to notify of the disaster.

Nonetheless, it is possible to codify basic procedures for use in these situations, which should apply to any type of technical service department. Police, fire, and emergency medical professionals should be notified immediately if required, without a formal activation of the recovery plan. A procedure should also be in place to notify management. Because building-related disasters are often discovered first by the facilities or security departments, there should be a procedure in place in these departments' recovery plans to alert responsible management throughout the organization. Notification might flow from a building security guard to a building security manager, to a director of technical services, to the disaster response team, and to the appropriate departmental managers. The response team is responsible for notifying the emergency management team of the situation and for then determining the cause of the disaster, evaluating the extent of the damage, and filing an initial damage report to the emergency management team.

Damage Assessment Procedures

Within the departments designated to respond to the scene of a disaster, an individual should be assigned responsibility for notifying the emergency management team of the disaster, assessing the extent of the damage, preparing the initial damage report, and communicating the report to the management team, all of which must usually be done within 90 minutes. Procedures should describe how and when the emergency management team is to be provided this assessment and the required format of the damage reports. In most cases, the damage report should be written; however, oral reports may suffice under extraordinary circumstances. The decision to activate the recovery plan is made on the basis of the initial damage report.

The corporate recovery plan should identify the persons responsible for notifying cleanup companies that specialize in handling recovery of technical equipment, hazardous spills, or other specific requirements. This plan should also identify persons responsible for contacting such local authorities as police and fire departments. The communications recovery plan would include the names and phone numbers of the responsible contact people, with a cross-reference to the corporate plan for more detailed information on contact procedures and responsibilities.

Workpaper III5.02 provides a script of the actions to be performed in assessing damage to company facilities.

The Emergency Management Team. An emergency management team is called together only for the most severe disasters, which are corporatewide. The emergency management team consists of a core group of executives responsible for coordinating disaster response for the company as a whole. Typically comprising a half dozen individuals, this group may include a chief information officer, president of the company, the IS director, the director of distributed processing, the director of communications, and the director of facilities. The emergency management team should also include one or two individuals to handle phones and routine administrative tasks, as well as coordinate supplies, materials, and other support required by the emergency management team.

The emergency management team should have a designated meeting place a safe distance from the main place of business. This meeting place could be an alternate company location, an employee's home, or even a hotel. The location must be accessible at any hour and be known to the emergency management team and recovery planners well in advance. It should also be a place where communications could be quickly established after a disaster. A fax machine should also be available in the alternate facility. Telephone numbers to the emergency management team should be arranged with the telephone company in advance and reserved so that calls can be forwarded in a disaster. This allows the numbers to be published in advance in company telephone directories and in the recovery plan.

Activation Procedures

The decision to activate the recovery plan is made by the emergency management team on the basis of the initial damage report. If the damage warrants such action, the first step is to activate the full emergency management team at its designated command center. The emergency management team in turn activates the individual disaster recovery teams and the necessary backup plans. It is important that the corporatewide plan clearly define how the communications department is involved in the overall recovery effort. Obviously, if the disaster involves communications facilities and services, the communications recovery plan and recovery team are activated.

The decision to formally declare a disaster is made by the emergency management team after the damage reports have been received. The emergency management team also decides whether to relocate operations to a backup recovery center or processing facility.

Coordination with local authorities is important in the initial hours following a disaster. For example, in the event of a fire, the local fire department assumes control of the building. Employees may not be allowed to enter the building, even after the fire is contained, for their own safety. (The recovery plan should assume that, in such an event, documents and magnetic media will be unavailable and ensure that the necessary backups are stored off site.) The recovery plan should take into account any restrictions on the organization's recovery efforts that might be imposed by local authorities immediately following the disaster. The recovery team should cooperate with local authorities in pursuit of their duties, which ultimately benefits the overall recovery effort.

Disasters frequently draw the attention of the news media. The emergency management team should coordinate press releases and other forms of contact with the media through a well-organized communications effort. The objective is to project an image of an organization that is in control of the situation. Adverse publicity can seriously damage the company's reputation with customers and investors.

To this end, the recovery plan should establish a media liaison between the emergency management team and the public. This liaison can issue periodic statements on the progress of the recovery, either in written form or by means of a recorded message available by calling a toll-free number. Recorded messages can be used to provide information not only to the news media but also to concerned employees and family members not directly involved in the recovery.

Workpaper III5.03 provides sample procedures for activating a recovery plan in response to a companywide disaster affecting communications.

Related Procedures

The recovery plan should also define procedures for assisting the emergency management team prepare its statements, handling emergency equipment purchases and cash disbursements, and ensuring the security of the damaged site and the recovery center.

Critical Events Log. Persons involved in the recovery effort make many critical decisions in rapid succession. It is important to document these decisions in a critical events log. This may require no more than a loose-leaf notebook; an audiotape recorder might also be used.

Every major command decision or equipment purchase should be noted in the critical events log. This record is helpful later on in analyzing the organization's response to the disaster, in dealing with litigation that may arise from the disaster, and for honoring employees who make exceptional contributions during the recovery.

Equipment Purchases and Cash Disbursements. After a disaster, midlevel managers may be called on to replace expensive equipment very quickly. Procedures should be established in the recovery plan to modify signing authority, allowing midlevel management, under certain extraordinary conditions, to have high levels of statutory spending authority to accomplish replacement of equipment. Other procedures should be in place to account for these expenditures, particularly when they are made in emergency situations and in very rapid succession. This requires close coordination with the finance department of the company and the midlevel managers making these purchases.

The recovery plan should also set procedures for cash disbursements to employees. For example, technical employees may require funds to travel to disaster recovery centers or other locations. One solution is for the company to sign an agreement with its primary bank that requires the bank to have a mobile branch on site within a certain number of hours of the disaster. This mobile bank should be responsible not only for the dissemination of cash after a disaster, but also for the accounting systems, recording who the cash was given to and in what amounts. If the company does a large amount of business with a bank, the bank will usually agree to this type of stipulation.

Transportation. In many disasters, nontechnical as well as technical employees must move rapidly to recovery centers to do their jobs. Procedures for such matters as air travel reservations and car rentals should be identified in the recovery plan. A travel agency should be designated in advance and have emergency instructions for the company on file. Employees could call the travel agency on a toll-free number and be given a predetermined itinerary.

Maintaining Security. Security must be maintained at the damage site. Many employees have no business being on the site in the initial phases of a disaster, because they are not directly involved in the recovery effort. Their presence can complicate recovery efforts. For example, their use of mobile phones to report on the disaster to friends could tie up critical mobile phone frequencies needed for command center communications. For this reason, the recovery plan should bar these employees from visiting the company during a disaster. It should also forbid employees from using mobile phones in the vicinity of the company immediately following a disaster.

To identify authorized personnel, one company issued its authorized employees a hard hat, an orange vest, and an identity badge—the hard hat, for safety reasons, the orange vest, for visibility and to immediately identify the person as an authorized on-site employee, and an employee badge for more precise identification.

Other security-related concerns include potential looting. If recovery is taking place at the damaged site, equipment will be moving in and out quickly; it will be very easy for theft to occur. The recovery plan should identify the persons responsible for security on site.

Security is also a concern at the recovery center, particularly in areas where equipment is being transported. Security should also be established at the mobile funds-disbursement center; one or two security guards should be sufficient.

DOCUMENT RESTORATION PROCEDURES

STEP 3

After the recovery teams have been notified and activated, recovery activities begin. The majority of the recovery plan is devoted to procedures for restoring business, systems, and communications functions.

Subsection II.E of Workpaper III5.01 lists the types of recovery activities involved in a corporatewide recovery effort. Unlike the recovery of mainframe or communications systems, which are handled by their respective departments, the recovery activities described here address the recovery of systems owned and shared by several departments. As such, the recovery effort must be coordinated among these departments.

For example, certain distributed software applications may be shared by the payroll, accounting, and finance departments; their restoration may require a coordinated effort by all groups. Restoration of power services is perhaps the most common example. Data center managers may have special power requirements for the mainframe (e.g., 400 Hz rather than standard 60 Hz), whereas communications managers may require elaborate, 48-volt battery systems. And, of course, regular electrical power is shared among all departments. The corporate recovery plan should identify one department that will take the lead in restoring power (e.g., the facilities department), coordinating with the various technical departments that may have special power requirements. The facilities department may also be called on to coordinate restoration of other types of common systems, including fire suppression systems (e.g., building sprinkler systems).

The following sections describe several of these restoration activities.

Rewiring. Modern business facilities include a large variety of types of wiring, all of which will need to be restored following a disaster. The recovery plan should include a wiring schematics, detailing the various levels of cable required to support LANs and communications services; the diagrams should illustrate the physical pathways in which the cable is run. Rewiring is a joint effort, because it is impractical during restoration to have separate contractors for the communications and IS departments, for example, vying for space in crowded crawl spaces and conduit throughways. A single contractor should coordinate the rewiring with all concerned departments.

Testing New Hardware and Software. New hardware and software installed after a disaster must be tested. Otherwise, the organization runs the risk of back-to-back disasters. Procedures should be established for testing the hardware and software to ensure they function correctly.

Training. Operations personnel may have to be trained on the newly installed software and hardware if different software versions and hardware models have been installed. End users may also have to be retrained, for the same reasons. It is not unusual for an organization to upgrade its equipment following a disaster. For example, an organization that employed 286-class microcomputers for low-level functions would most likely replace these with more up-to-date equipment. New hardware often entails new software. It could be major stumbling block to the recovery if data entry clerks were unable to perform their duties because they were unfamiliar with changes in the user interface or function keys for entering transactions.

Returning to the Damaged Site. Scheduling and coordinating the migration back to the original site (assuming a recovery center was used) can be a daunting task. Most recovery center contracts are established for a relatively short period (e.g., six weeks). At the end of this period, many organizations are faced with the decision to incur the considerable expense of remaining at the recovery center or attempt an early return to the damaged site. Moving back too quickly runs the risk of creating another disaster if new but untested systems are hurriedly put in place.

Some companies choose to run in parallel (e.g., two network nodes) until the conversion to the original site is complete. This arrangement may buy added security, but it also can be difficult to operate with the existing staff spread between two sites. The recovery plan should address the issue of the migration approach, recognizing the trade-offs of the financial costs and risks to the organization of each approach.

Other Recovery Issues. Subsection II.E provides a generic set of companywide recovery activities. Individual companies may have unique concerns that should be addressed in the recovery plan. For example, organizations on the West Coast might include procedures for responding to an earthquake; companies in the Midwest would more likely include procedures for conducting tornado drills.

Organizations might also want to include a procedure for responding to evidence of potential sabotage or vandalism (detected during an initial damage assessment, for example). Most companies have documented procedures for responding to bomb threats. These procedures are often included in the corporate recovery plan.

WORKPAPER III5.01 Sample Organizationwide Recovery Procedures

RECOVERY PROCEDURES

I. Policy Statement

A. Objectives of the Project:

1. Protect human life.
2. Minimize risk to company.
3. Prepare to recover critical operations.
4. Safeguard against lawsuits.
5. Protect competitive position.
6. Preserve customer confidence and goodwill.

B. Overview of Preliminary Business Impact Analysis.

C. Synopsis of Recovery Strategy.

II. Overview of Recovery Procedures

A. Initial Reaction and Alert Procedures:

1. Protection of human life.
2. Notification of police, fire, and medical emergency services.
3. Notification of management.
4. Initial determination of cause.

B. Damage Assessment Procedures:

1. Coordinating with the emergency management team:
   - Responsibilities of the emergency management team.
   - When to notify emergency management team.
2. Notification of emergency management team:
   - How to notify emergency management team.
   - Support services required by the emergency management team.
3. Damage assessment reports to emergency management team:
   - Format of reports.
   - Frequency of reports.
   - Format and procedure for initial reports.

4. Notification of cleanup companies:

   - Responsibilities.

5. Interfacing with local authorities:

   - Responsibilities.

C. Activation Procedures:

1. Activation of emergency management team.
2. Activation of disaster teams.
3. Activation of network backup plans.
4. Decision to activate recovery center.
5. Relocation to recovery center.

D. Related Procedures:

1. Assisting emergency management team in preparation of statements.
2. Opening a critical events log for audit purposes.
3. Modified signing authority for equipment purchases.
4. Providing cash disbursements.
5. Transportation.
6. Maintaining physical security.
7. Security at the damaged site.
8. Security at the recovery center.
9. Security at emergency funds disbursement centers.

E. Restoration of Critical Business Functions:

1. Coordination of restoration of the original site.
2. Restoration of hardware systems.
3. Restoration of software systems.
4. Restoration of power.
5. Replacement of fire-suppression systems.
6. Addition of security.
7. Rewiring of the facility.
8. Restoration of the LAN.
9. Restoration of the WAN.
10. Testing new hardware and software.
11. Training operations personnel.
12. Training employees.
13. Scheduling migration back to original site.
14. Coordinating return to original site.

WORKPAPER III5.02 Damage Assessment Procedures for a Companywide Disaster

DAMAGE ASSESSMENT PROCEDURES

Date: ________________ Company Name: ________________________

---

1. Begin preliminary damage assessment. Companywide objectives for damage assessment are as follows:

   - Within 60 minutes of an outage, provide the emergency management team a verbal damage report and an estimated time to repair. You will also recommend whether or not to declare a disaster and move into a recovery facility on the basis of this assessment.
   - Within 90 minutes of the outage, assess damage to the communications facility and deliver a written report to the emergency management team outlining the estimated time to repair. This will also include a recommendation whether or not to declare a disaster based on the situation.
   - Resume normal operations within 24 hours of the outage.
   - Prevent premature activation of backup facilities.

   The responsible team members should perform these actions:

   a. Report to the damage assessment team leader as defined in the corporate disaster recovery plan. The damage assessment team leader is [name].

   b. Receive damage assessment reports from subordinates and make recommendations regarding implementation of backup and recovery operations.

   c. Fill out a damage assessment maintenance form.

   d. Direct supervision of damage assessment activities related to the network or network facilities.

   e. Determine the status of any personnel who may have been on duty in the area during the disaster.

   f. Aid with maintaining security in the affected area.

   g. Check other responsibilities regarding vendor coordination shown in the next section.

   Responsible Team Member: ________________________________

2. Notify vendors, request an on-site representative.

   Responsible Team Member: ______________________________

3. Coordinate with vendors at the affected site. In cases that involve on-site equipment, the individuals responsible for damage assessment will contact the vendors involved and request an on-site representative immediately to aid in damage assessment and facilitate fast restoral of the equipment. (Refer to the equipment inventories and vendor escalation lists contained in the resumption plan.) Before calling vendors, check for possible roll-in replacement guarantees for equipment for which [company name] may have been contracted.

   Responsible Team Member: ______________________________

4. Coordinate with carriers. In cases where equipment involves outside vendors (e.g., telephone companies), the network operations center or alternate network operations center will coordinate these activities. (Refer to the carrier escalation lists documented in the resumption plan; first verify the carrier's contractual obligations.)

   Responsible Team Member: ______________________________

5. Coordinate with other recovery teams. The on-site damage assessment personnel associated with the communications department will be subordinate to the facilities recovery team designated in the overall corporate recovery plan. Follow this team's instructions carefully and lend all possible support. The team leader for the facilities recovery team is [name]. For further information, contact the communications team leader.

   Responsible Team Member: ______________________________

WORKPAPER III5.03 Activation Procedures for a Companywide Disaster

ACTIVATION PROCEDURES

Date: ____________________ Company Name: ____________________

____

1. Activate the emergency management team:

   a. The leader of the on-site disaster response team [name] or, if this person is not available, the communications department manager [name] should contact a member of the emergency management team to provide an initial damage report:

      Primary Contact: ______________________________
      (The primary contact is usually the company president.)

      Alternate Contact: ______________________________

   b. The contacted emergency management team member should evaluate the initial damage report and consult with the other members of the emergency management team to decide whether to declare a disaster and activate the recovery plan. The emergency management team members should be contacted, as follows:

Team Member	Phone Number

   c. If a disaster is declared, the primary or alternate activates the full emergency management team at the emergency operations center (also referred to as the command center).

   d. Direct inquiries to the emergency operations center at one of the following telephone numbers: ____________
      ____
      ____

   e. Status of all major facility outages is provided by [department name, usually the corporate communications department] at [phone number]. This is a confidential number, which is not to be released outside the company.

2. Activate the disaster recovery teams. The company president should activate the disaster recovery teams denoted in the corporatewide recovery plan. In the event the telecommunications team is activated, the president will contact each team leader or his or her alternate to implement one of the preplanned network disaster recovery plans contained in this document, place his or her resources on alert, or take other appropriate action.

   Operations/Recovery Management Team:

   Primary: ______________________________
   Alternate: ______________________________

   Engineering/Network Reconfiguration Team:

   Primary: ______________________________
   Alternate: ______________________________

   Field Services/Facility Restoral Team:

   Primary: ______________________________
   Alternate: ______________________________

   Distributed Systems Recovery Team:

   Primary: ______________________________
   Alternate: ______________________________

3. Establish an emergency operations center. To effectively maintain command and control of the recovery process, a meeting place must be designated from which to coordinate recovery activities. The activation of the plan will not, however, depend on this center, since personnel at the corporate headquarters building may not be immediately available to staff it, or coordinate recovery activities. The command post is the staging area from which to reestablish command and control for the recovery of corporate headquarters.

   Two locations have been designated as staging areas for recovery activities:

   Primary Command Center:

   Address [street]: ______________________________
   Address [city, state, zip code]: ______________________________
   Phone: ________________

   Alternate Command Center:

   Address [street]: ______________________________
   Address [city, state, zip code]: ______________________________
   Phone: ________________

A complement of PBX and Centrex phones has been installed at this location.

4. Activate network backup plans. The following teams and team members will have the primary responsibilities shown in implementation of the network disaster recovery plan for corporate headquarters.

Team Name: Network operations recovery management team

Primary Team Leader: ______________________

Alternate Team Leader: ______________________

a. Provide, if required, personnel to staff an emergency network operations center and recovery base to coordinate further recovery operations, unless this center is rendered unusable by the disaster. If such center is unusable, the command center will locate at the company's alternate emergency network operations center at [address] or at a site specified by the emergency operations center at the time of the disaster.

b. Coordinate recovery activities, including equipment installations, notification of vendors, and testing with on-site personnel at the disaster recovery center from a primary or alternate network control center.

c. Perform tasks as requested by the emergency management team.

d. Contact [carriers] and other vendors regarding implementation of emergency call-forwarding arrangements.

e. Make timely damage assessment reports to the emergency management team at the emergency operations center.

Team Name: Network engineering reconfiguration team

Primary Team Leader: ______________________

Alternate Team Leader: ______________________

a. Provide personnel to activate an emergency command center and recovery base to coordinate further recovery operations, unless this center is rendered unusable by the disaster.

b. Provide high-level engineering support to the company network control center or alternate network control center (in case the primary is damaged) in the implementation of the alternate network configuration for support of systems previously located at corporate headquarters.

[Enter the equipment to be recovered in order of priority, according to the following classes of service]:

- Priority A--Mission critical (e.g., high-speed channel connections; ACD voice lines for customer support).
- Priority B--High-visibility but not mission critical (e.g., non-priority A T3 circuits).
- Priority C--All other (e.g., low-speed data circuits).

c. Provide at least one high-level telecommunications analyst on site at the recovery center or the specified recovery center if requested to aid in T1 circuit activations.

d. Perform tasks as requested by the emergency management team or [company name] team leader.

e. Submit timely status reports to the emergency operations center during the course of the disaster.

f. Install a predetermined complement of emergency router links for all distributed platforms (e.g., LANs) located at corporate headquarters in cooperation with the distributed systems recovery team to support the selected recovery site.

Team Name: Field services restoral team
Primary Team Leader: ______________________
Alternate Team Leader: ______________________

a. Initiate on-site damage assessment of affected communications facilities, act as liaison to emergency management team, and submit initial damage reports within 60 minutes to the emergency management team.

b. Coordinate new equipment installations, deliveries, and vendor coordination, both at the damaged facility at corporate headquarters and at the selected recovery center.

c. Coordinate with [company name] security with regard to building security issues.

d. Work with [vendor] at [vendor phone number] for damage evaluation and cleanup.

e. Submit timely status reports to the emergency operations center during the course of the disaster.

f. Aid in the emergency restoration of hardware and software systems associated with all distributed platforms (e.g., LANs) located at corporate headquarters, in cooperation with the distributed systems recovery team, at the selected recovery site, and at corporate headquarters.

Team: Distributed systems recovery team
Primary Team Leader: ______________________
Alternate Team Leader: ______________________

a. Coordinate emergency equipment replacement with vendors of LAN platforms in use at corporate headquarters and its installation at the selected recovery site.

b. Provide equipment configuration and connectivity requirements to the engineering network reconfiguration team so that emergency router links can be established.

c. Provide equipment configuration diagrams to the field services or facility restoral team so that installation can take place concurrently with other building wiring and equipment installations.

d. Submit timely status reports to the emergency operations center during the course of the disaster.

In the event the recovery plan calls for relocation of operations to the designated recovery center, the network engineering team will provide one data communications person on site at the center to coordinate activation of T1 circuits, equipment installation (if required), and overall coordination of the move. This activity will be assumed by recovery center personnel as soon as the situation becomes stable, and the [company name] person will return to home base.

5. Redirect network facilities. Network facilities will be redirected according to the detailed plans listed in the recovery plan or as directed by a team leader, the emergency management team, or the president, [company name]. All network reconfigurations will be performed by or under the supervision of principal analysts unless otherwise directed.

Responsible Individuals:

- Principal Data Communications Analyst: ______________________
- Alternate: ______________________

Documenting Communications-Specific Recovery Procedures

CHAPTER

III-6

As discussed in Chapter III-5, the recovery planner must document global recovery procedures that affect the organization as a whole. These include procedures for the initial disaster alert, damage assessment, recovery team activation and related procedures, and general restoration procedures. As noted in Chapter III-5, these procedures are common to any type of recovery operation, including (but not limited to) a communications recovery effort. That is, any communications recovery effort requires a core set of procedures that address the initial alert, damage assessment, and activation of the recovery team. However, additional procedures must be documented to address such communications-specific issues as command routing of an incoming 800 service, redirection of T1 lines, reestablishment of dial-in data ports, and recovery from failure of communications-specific equipment such as PBXs and communications bridges and gateways.

Chapter III-6 addresses the documentation of these communications-specific recovery procedures. Workpaper III6.01 provides a sample table of contents of the major communications-specific procedures that should be documented in the recovery plan. Subsequent workpapers provide detailed examples of these procedures. Note that these procedures have been compiled from the actual plans of organizations and therefore reflect the general requirements of most companies. Specific types of organizations may need to tailor these procedures to meet special requirements.

As shown in Workpaper III6.01, communications-specific recovery procedures can be divided into two categories:

- Procedures for recovery of communications services following a company-wide disaster caused by an earthquake or tornado for example.
- Procedures for recovery of communications services caused by the failure of specific network components such as PBX hardware and software, communications cables, or long-distance service. In addition, procedures may be needed to address communications failures on the basis of the cause of damage—for example, power surges or theft of equipment.

Much of the information needed to develop these procedures should already be available to the recovery planner. The recovery planner should have identified the internal and external resources needed for developing the recovery plan (see Chapter III-3). For example, as noted in Chapter III-3, long-distance carriers and local telephone companies provide a variety of services that are useful in recovering from the loss of long-distance service and the loss of a central office. Therefore, in documenting communications-specific recovery procedures, the recovery planner should be able to select from those previously identified options and document procedures that incorporate the services that best satisfy the organization's recovery needs.

Similarly, as discussed in Chapter III-4, the recovery planner should have evaluated the organization's requirements for protection and recovery of such key resources as the power supply, software, remote access services, and fire and water protection systems. The information gathered in that phase of recovery planning can also be used to develop and document communications-specific procedures. For example, the identified requirements for protecting the power supply to communications equipment help determine the procedure for handling a power surge.

STEP 1

DOCUMENT PROCEDURES FOR A COMPANYWIDE DISASTER

Section III.A of Workpaper III6.01 provides an overview of the procedures required to restore specific types of companywide communications services that have been lost as a result of a companywide disaster. In this context, a companywide disaster refers to a disaster in which loss of communications is caused by an event other than failure of an isolated communications system or component. Companywide disasters may result from a variety of causes, including:

- Natural disasters such as flood, earthquakes, tornadoes, or extreme weather conditions (e.g., heavy snow and extreme cold).
- Sabotage or vandalism.
- Security breach.

In a companywide disaster, it is assumed that several departments or facilities have suffered damage and must therefore be involved in the recovery effort. Close coordination among departments is essential for avoiding unnecessary duplication of effort and ensuring that the organization meets its recovery objectives in an efficient manner.

As shown in Section III.A of Workpaper III6.01, the first five procedures address the initial reporting of the disaster, notification of recovery teams, damage assessment, protection of human life, and activation of recovery services. These procedures are common to any type of disaster. They are described in Chapter III-5 on documenting global recovery procedures. The remaining procedures in Section III.A address recovery actions that must be taken to restore specific types of companywide communications services, including incoming 800 services, remote call forwarding, T1 communications lines, local area network router links, wide-area network services, and dial-in data ports.

The following sections describe the procedures for recovery of companywide communications services. The first section begins with a brief review of the requirements for the initial disaster alert, notification of the emergency management and recovery teams, damage assessment, plan activation, and establishment of command and control.

Alert and Notification Procedures

During the initial reaction phase, the communications manager or other responsible person receives an initial report of a communications systems failure. The communications manager should record this in the critical events log by documenting the time of the report and the action taken. Depending on the nature of the report, the communications manager may decide to notify the emergency management team and begin the procedure for notifying the response teams and any supporting vendors.

The notification process can be accomplished in several ways. The first choice is to phone the response team members by using the phone numbers documented in the recovery plan. However, in a communications-related disaster, telephone service may not be available in the local area; therefore, alternative methods of contact should also be identified in the plan, including, by order of preference:

1. Public telephone network.
2. Cellular phone or pager.
3. High-frequency radio (useful in the event of a regional disaster).

The process of notification can be complicated, even if communications systems are not seriously damaged in the disaster. Disruptions in the public telephone network can result simply because demand on the network exceeds its capacity. For example, after the 1994 California earthquake, many people experienced difficulty in reaching family and friends. As the earthquake subsided, hundreds of thousands of people attempted to make calls; the networks were unable to handle that level of demand.

Shared Access and Blocked Calls. The capacity of the public phone systems is engineered to provide service for the average expected amount of traffic at a given day and time. Shared use is assumed; it is simply too expensive to guarantee an open line for every subscriber.

Erlang theory is used to estimate the number of phone lines needed to handle a given level of calls, based on estimates of the number of attempted calls and the duration of these calls at different times of day. During workdays, public phone use tends to peak at around 10:30 A.M., taper off during the lunch hour, and then peak again around mid-afternoon. Demand decreases dramatically after 5:00 P.M., when most businesses close.

Network providers use this information to decide on the most cost-effective number of lines to install to support these varying levels of demand. At peak hours, a certain level of blocked calls is considered acceptable (e.g., 10%).

In a disaster, the problem is that both the number of calls and the duration of calls skyrocket. As more and more people attempt to make calls, it becomes more likely that these calls will be blocked on the first try. Most people, after receiving the taped message that "all circuits are busy, please try your call again later," immediately try again until the call is successfully completed, which of course adds to the load on the network. Once a call does go through, people are reluctant to be brief, because they fear that they may be unable to get through the next time. Therefore, the call duration increases as well. In a disaster, as many as 75% of calls may be blocked on the first attempt, depending on the day of the week and the time when the disruption takes place.

Getting Through. In an emergency, users often assume the phone line is dead because they do not receive an immediate dial tone on lifting the receiver. This is not always true. If there is power to the keypad used for touch dialing and some line "noise" heard through the receiver, the phone is not dead. In such a case, the user should hold on; the dial tone usually comes on in 30 to 60 seconds.

The recovery team manager can also take advantage of differences in peak call demand between the switched public phone companies and cellular phone companies. The call distribution pattern for switched phone services is the opposite of that for cellular services. For example, whereas the demand for switched phone lines peaks during workday mornings at around 10:00 A.M., the demand for cellular access peaks between 7:00 A.M. and 8:00 A.M., because people are on their way to work. Other peak periods for cellular phone service include the lunch hour, when people are running errands, and between 5:00 P.M. and 8:00 P.M., as people are returning home from work. As noted, these are the least active periods for switched public telephone networks. Therefore, if a disruption occurs during the peak period for switched public networks, the recovery team managers and staff would be well advised to shift to cellular service. Cellular networks are also indispensable if the outage is caused by failure of a switched network component (e.g., a cable cut or central office fire).

Although cellular technology provides an excellent alternative for maintaining command in a recovery effort, it has certain limitations. First, a cellular system is a finite medium; a limited number of send and receive frequencies are available for a given area. Second, cellular has a transmission speed limit of typically 2,400 to 4,800 bps. (Most faxes transmit at 9,600 bps, for example.)

A user expecting to back up a telemarketing center of 200 people using transportable cellular phones is probably in for a rude shock. However, this problem can be mitigated through the use of microcell technology. A microcell is a piece of equipment not unlike the cell sites that dot the landscape throughout the metropolitan area. In this case, however, the particular cell site is a small, low-power version dedicated to a single user or to users within a given building. Two types are available. With the first, a direct microwave connection is established from the user's location to a mobile telephone switching office. This microwave system is then terminated in a microcell, the output of which provides two wire ground-start trunks. In the event of a major cable cut, for example, the PBX equipment is smart enough to sense the loss of the trunk and begin routing the traffic over the microcell. The traffic goes out over the cellular network without the user even being aware that it is happening.

This works very well except in cases in which the PBX is disrupted in the disaster. In these cases, a second technique is used in which an antenna (commonly called a leaky coax) is strung between floors in the building. Users can then use regular hand-held cellular phones to bypass the crippled PBX, completing calls over the microcell to the mobile telephone switching office.

Damage Assessment and Plan Activation Procedures

After the response team members have been notified, the next order of business is to conduct the initial on-site damage assessment. The damage assessment includes an initial determination of the nature of the disaster, its extent, the equipment affected, and, if possible, the cause of the disaster. This assessment may be led by the communications department manager, who acts as team leader. If the communications manager is a member of the emergency management team, he may choose to designate another person to lead the on-site assessment.

The initial damage report should be provided to the emergency management team within a predesignated period (e.g., 90 minutes after notification of the disaster). At that time, the emergency management team decides whether to activate the company-wide disaster recovery plan or, if the disaster primarily affects communications facilities, to allow instead the communications recovery team to respond. If the second course is taken, the communications recovery team should provide periodic reports of progress to the emergency management team.

Establishment of Command and Control

In addition to assessing damage, the team leader is responsible for ensuring the safety of human life at the scene of the disaster and for securing the damaged facility as well as possible. The communications recovery team leader coordinates with the team leaders for other technical service departments as well as with such local authorities as fire and police.

The team leader should request that a vendor representative for each major system affected by the disaster be called to the disaster site. The end users of the affected systems should also be advised as to what systems have been damaged and the expected length of time that they will not be available. In general, it is more efficient to provide periodic reports to end users than to have to handle multiple calls from dissatisfied users.

If the recovery plan provides for guaranteed replacement of damaged equipment, the team leader (or his representative) should contact the vendors as soon as possible to begin this process. Calls should also be made to companies that provide disaster-related services called for in the plan—for example, insurance providers and cleaning companies.

While the communications recovery team leader is on site assessing the damage and establishing control, other recovery team members may be assigned to handle other matters. For example, a team member at an alternate location might contact the local phone company and equipment vendors to provide the phone numbers for contacting recovery personnel.

Team members should also be assigned to recover specific communications services, including restoring the network control help desk and rerouting incoming 800 numbers and call-forwarding local phone service to key command and control numbers. Team members may also need to contact long-distance carriers to redirect lines. These communications-related recovery procedures, which are listed under Section III.A on Workpaper III6.01, are described in the following paragraphs.

Restoring Help Desk and Network Control Numbers

Command and control is of paramount importance, especially in the first hours of a disaster. For this reason, help numbers and network control numbers must receive special consideration. After a disaster, end users may no longer be able to access an application over a wide-area network. Instinctively, they dial the help desk or network control. If there is no planning to ensure that these numbers work in a disaster, users may ring into a dead line or, if they do connect, receive no recordings or other indicators informing them of what has happened. Installing new numbers after the fact is not practical, given the logistics of distributing a new telephone number to perhaps hundreds of end users in an already chaotic situation.

The most effective solution is to arrange for remote call forwarding. A procedure should direct the telephone company to forward the most critical incoming numbers to an alternate location. If there are too many of them, and it proves impractical, all supervisor lines should be redirected instead. (Users typically call the supervisor number if the primary number is unanswered.) Even if only one line in 10 is restored, a persistent user will eventually get through, receiving emergency instructions and a status report on the recovery. Workpaper III6.02 provides a procedure and form for redirecting key phone numbers.

Command Routing of 800 Numbers

Similar to the remote call-forwarding features provided by local telephone companies, long-distance companies offer command routing of 800 numbers. In an emergency, 800 numbers can be forwarded easily to any working 10-digit telephone number. These may be located at:

- An alternate company location.
- The company's computer recovery facility.
- A nontraditional recovery facility, such as an employee residence.
- A telephone company redirect recording.

The last of these options has come into widespread use, both for disasters as well as for routine events. Customers might receive a message such as this:

> Thank you for calling ABC company. Because of the earthquake, many customers are experiencing trouble calling our San Francisco processing center. Rest assured, we are open for business in all operations. We hope you will excuse this temporary condition while we help free the telephone company's phone lines for those most in need after this disaster. If you can delay your call until Monday, we will have extra agents on hand to process your business with minimal delay. If your call is an emergency, please call (415) 555-1234. Thank you for your understanding.

It would also be possible to provide such recordings using a line at the company's recovery center. Whatever method is selected, the image to the customer is that everything is under control, which is exactly what should be communicated. Workpaper III6.03 provides a sample procedure for redirecting critical inbound 800 phone numbers.

Redirection of Backbone T1 Network

With planning, T1 circuits can also be moved quickly. Because most T1 lines are hard-wired and specially engineered, they provide unique challenges for recovery. The easiest way to move T1 and other private lines is to have the telephone company direct them through a digital cross-connect system. A digital cross-connect system is a piece of equipment in the telephone central office that makes the cross connections between circuit facilities—for example, from local cable to a company location to a long-distance intercity facility. These are software controlled from a terminal, which allows a telephone company technician to make fast connections. In a disaster, this same feature may help by allowing the telephone company to insert quickly a new facility assignment to move a private line circuit to a recovery center. Some digital cross-connect systems even allow for emergency configurations to be stored in advance. This permits the user to call the telephone company or long-distance carrier and activate the plan with a single command. Other schemes even allow dial-in access by end users to the telephone company's digital cross-connect system to make these connections for themselves. Workpaper III6.04 presents a procedure for reconfiguring communications equipment and redirecting T1 circuits.

Redirection of Dial-In Maintenance and Production Ports

The same remote call-forwarding and command-routing approaches described here can be applied to the redirection of dial-in ports of all types. For example, it is much easier for a credit-card verification company to command route or remote call-forward incoming verification numbers than to reprogram thousands of remote terminals. Similarly, dial-in facilities to maintenance functions allow for fast trouble resolution. A dial-in port at the recovery center, for example, could allow personnel engaged at the disaster site to dial in and help with activities at the recovery center as well. Workpaper III6.05 provides a procedure for redirecting dial-in ports. Workpaper III6.06 is a form that can be used to record priorities for recovery of circuits in the event of a disaster. A completed sample of this form is provided as Exhibit III-1-M.

STEP 2

DOCUMENT PROCEDURES FOR COMPONENT-SPECIFIC DISASTERS

Section III.B of Workpaper III6.01 provides an overview of the procedures required to restore communications that have been lost because of the failure of specific network components—for example, failure of PBX hardware or software. In general, the alert and notification procedures are the same as those described in Step 1 and do not need to be discussed further. Step 2 focuses on the recovery activities as they pertain to the type of component-related failure that caused the disaster. These can be summarized as:

- Software failures.
- Hardware and equipment component failures.
- Cable cuts.
- T1 service failures.
- Loss of the central office.
- Loss of the long-distance carrier.
- Equipment room and building disasters.

It should also be noted that some organizations choose to document recovery procedures according to the cause of failure. Workpaper III6.01 lists examples of three: power surges, lightning, and equipment theft.

Because of the tremendous diversity of packaged and custom computer and communications systems, it is impossible to provide detailed procedures for recovery of specific hardware and software components—there would be literally thousands of possible procedures depending on the type of product and application. The technical specialists responsible for installing and maintaining these components must be recruited to draft the recovery procedures. The workpapers presented in this section of Chapter III-6 provide a general framework for constructing recovery procedures for such system components.

Procedures for Recovery from Software Failure

Disasters to PBXs, voice mail systems, and other major communications components are not always the result of such common threats as fire and water damage; they may be due to a catastrophic software failure. In such cases, the actions taken to recover the affected equipment may differ significantly from the actions for responding to physical damage. Although the same procedures for the initial disaster alert and notification of the emergency management team are used, the procedures for determining the cause of the disaster are different. The causes of software-induced failures can be difficult to pinpoint; they might result from a software coding error or from a hacker attack or virus infection. Specially trained IS personnel are needed to identify such causes of failure.

The communications recovery plan should identify the appropriate recovery procedures. The most common approach is to recover by using a backup copy of the affected software. The procedure for this method of recovery should include instructions on where to obtain this backup copy—it should be stored off site—and how to reload it.

An outage caused by a hacker attack requires a different set of recovery procedures. If the attack was made through a remote maintenance port, for example, the recovery team should be directed immediately to shut down this port and contact law enforcement authorities. In the case of a virus infection, a procedure should specify the appropriate virus detection and eradication software to use, where to obtain this software, and how to use it.

If necessary, the software vendors should be notified of the disaster and a vendor representative called in to consult at the disaster site. As with any recovery operation, periodic reports should be provided to the emergency management team on the progress of the recovery. This is especially important because, if the software-induced disaster is severe, it may require activation of the companywide recovery plan.

A software-related disaster may not necessarily require activation of the entire communications recovery team. However, all team members should be notified and kept on alert in case they are needed. Workpaper III6.07 presents a framework for developing a procedure for recovery from a software-induced disaster.

Hardware and Equipment Component Failures

A communications outage may result because of the failure of a hardware component in any number of systems. These might include failure of a PBX, a front-end processor, or a communications bridge, router, or gateway connection.

The recovery plan should specify who is responsible for recovery of specific communications components. For example, a front-end processor used for certain communications functions may belong to the IS department; therefore, the recovery may be led by the IS recovery team and not by the communications recovery team. The communications team might be called to provide support, including recabling and redirecting circuits.

Similarly, recovery of a critical bridge or router circuit may fall under the jurisdiction of the LAN manager rather than the communications department. Again, the communications recovery team may be called on to provide support. It is essential that the recovery plan clearly spell out who is responsible for leading the recovery effort for specific types of hardware components. Workpaper III6.08 presents a framework for developing a procedure for recovery from failure of equipment.

Cable Cuts

The communication recovery plan should also include procedures for dealing with a major cable or fiber-optic cut. The plan should not necessarily include procedures for dealing with minor cable cuts, because these are basically everyday occurrences. However, major cable cuts, particularly of fiber-optic links between cities or different portions of cities, can be disastrous.

In one case, a group of homeless people in Missouri built a fire under a bridge during the winter to keep warm. A major fiber-optic link also passed under that bridge and was destroyed by the fire. The result was an outage that lasted several days and isolated several cities.

Human errors by technical personnel performing routine maintenance are also major contributors to cable cuts. For instance, an AT&T technician in New Jersey cut a 1.2G-bps fiber-optic cable, isolating New York City for most of the day.

All of these would be classified as major cable cuts. The communications recovery plan should include procedures to address their occurrences. These procedures would include contacting the cable vendor or phone company and determining the location of the cable cut, the extent of damage, and the cause of the disaster. The cable vendor or utility should be contacted immediately, because cable cuts invariably take a long time to repair.

If the cable cut affects mission-critical systems for the company, the communications recovery manager, team leaders, and critical users should be notified. Normal procedures for reporting on site and providing a damage assessment report to the emergency management team will apply, because if the cable cut is severe enough, it may necessitate activating the companywide plan. The team manager should determine whether to implement procedures for activating backup communication links or for load-sharing critical traffic over the remaining open links.

Companies can take many precautions to protect against cable cuts. These include diverse routing and self-healing networks, microwave transmission, and using competitive access providers. However, these items must be documented in the plan and implemented before the disaster event. For companies that have not taken precautions against cable cuts, the only recourse is to wait until the telephone company, interexchange carrier, or cable vendor has repaired it.

Failure of T1 Service

The recovery plan should address the failure of a major T1 node. Because most major companies use T1 lines for transmission of both voice and data services, the T1 multiplexer creates another single point of failure. Often, advanced T1 multiplexers employ vendor-proprietary technologies. Because of their custom configuration, these multiplexers can be very difficult to recover during a disaster. If a vendor-specific multiplexer is used as part of the communications network, a similarly configured multiplexer should also be installed at the disaster recovery center in order to multiplex the same network traffic, particularly private line circuits.

Advanced multiplexers are also increasingly software driven, which opens new doors to vulnerability in terms of software errors and hacker attacks through maintenance ports. T1 circuits may also be partitioned into nonstandard sizes. Although 128K-bps, 512K-bps, and 1,024K-bps circuits are part of the domain of the data communications manager who employs proprietary T1 solutions, these are completely foreign to telephone companies. Therefore, in the event of a disaster to the T1 facility itself, the communications manager is on his own in recovering the T1 node.

Participation of the primary T1 multiplex vendor is critical in this regard, and a vendor representative, as in any major failure, should be requested on site immediately. T1s carry a variety of traffic, including voice communications, data communications, and video; anyone with service running on the affected T1 line should also be advised of the disaster. This would include LAN managers, because critical router links usually traverse the T1 as well.

A mirror image of the software and all of the circuit designators defined in the software for the T1 multiplexer should be copied to tape and safely stored off site. In the event of a disaster, it is then possible to recover using the backup copy of the software.

As noted, a similarly configured T1 multiplexer should be stored at the recovery center at all times, because replacement of this equipment can be difficult to accomplish in a timely fashion after a disaster. If this equipment is connected using reserve or on-demand T1s, they can be activated quickly after a disaster, and they have the capability to learn the configuration of other multiplexers in the network, in a dynamic on-line fashion. This greatly simplifies the recovery process.

Although using vendor proprietary equipment creates a new area of exposure for communications managers, it also allows for elegant recovery solutions. Some vendor proprietary systems can restore literally hundreds of circuits to a recovery center over a single 1.536M-bps T1 circuit.

The procedures for recovery of a major T1 node should also include the procedures for recovery of technical systems already noted, including determining the cause, extent, and nature of the disaster; securing the installation from theft; and notifying team members and the emergency management team. Workpaper III6.04, previously introduced, presents a procedure for redirecting T1 circuits.

Failure of a Local Central Office

Failure of a local operating company central office falls under the auspices of the communications recovery team. A telephone company's central office typically serves up to 35 square miles of a metropolitan area; hundreds of thousands of subscribers could be out of business as a result of a failure of a central office.

Central office failures are often the worst of all communications disasters. A central office disaster requires the telephone company to coordinate the disaster response while its subscribers wait for service. Companies that have not planned for central office disasters must simply wait until the central office is restored. This can take as long as six weeks to accomplish, even with the best of support.

It is important that the communications recovery team verify the cause and extent of the disaster. It is sometimes determined that the outage is not due to a central office failure. For example, a cable cut may affect a large area and initially be misidentified as a central office failure.

A company can use several approaches to avoid becoming the victim of a central office failure. These include diverse routing, access to a second toll office, and use of a foreign exchange service.

Diverse Routing. Diverse routing can help ensure that a single incident does not isolate the company. Diverse cable routing can be provided by the local telephone companies as well as by long-distance carriers. (Diverse routing is discussed in Chapter III-3. Exhibits III-3-D and III-3-J provide examples of diverse routing.)

Access to a Second Toll Office. A disaster affecting any long-distance carrier automatically affects its customers. Companies can protect against loss of a major long-distance point of presence through use of a second toll office, provided by either the primary or secondary interexchange carrier. (Exhibit III-3-E provides an example of access to a second toll office.)

Foreign Exchange Service. One way of insulating against switching failures is through the use of foreign exchange (FX) or foreign central office (FCO) service. Although designed mainly for providing dial tone from distant telephone exchanges (thereby reducing toll charges), these services can be readily used to provide network integrity. FX lines pass through the serving central office but actually derive their dial tone from another location, often in another city. In this fashion, a company can still function in the event of a catastrophic failure in its local switch by using its FX lines. By publishing the numbers of the FX lines in the company directory, incoming calls can also be received after a failure, without end users having to learn new numbers. Even when central offices have burned, FX lines have often continued functioning, as long as the physical wire path was still in place. FX service is available from virtually every serving office in the United States as a tariffed service. In optimal situations, by placing FX lines to areas often called by the company, it is possible to reduce overall long-distance charges enough to pay for the lines and, in the process, fund the additional protection they provide. (Exhibit III-3-F illustrates the configuration of FX service.)

Failure of a Long-Distance Carrier

As noted in Chapter III-1, the United States is the only country in which customers can dial around a long-distance failure using a system designed for equal access through all carriers. This has a direct bearing on disaster recovery. Equal access was originally intended as a means for all long-distance companies to enjoy the same connections to the local telephone network as AT&T. Even though a customer selects a primary carrier, other carriers can be reached by dialing a five-digit override code. By knowing which codes to dial, users can easily protect against long-distance failures.

Equal access codes for the major carriers are listed in Exhibit III-1-E. These numbers should be kept on hand. It should be remembered, however, that because different carriers typically occupy the same right-of-way or cable, more than one carrier may be affected by the same accident. In addition, other carriers not directly affected by a disaster may nonetheless become overwhelmed as users switch from affected carriers. It may therefore be necessary to dial several codes to get a call through. Workpaper III6.09 presents emergency carrier override procedures to use in the event of a long-distance company failure.

Equipment Room and Building Disasters

Although the communications recovery plan should address recovery from equipment room and building disasters, in the event of such disasters, the communications recovery team may not be the primary response team. For example, if a major piece of communications equipment fails, the communications team will presumably be responsible for its restoration. However, if the entire building is destroyed, the emergency management team will be in charge and will direct all of the other response teams.

In cases of major equipment loss, the communications recovery team must be notified immediately. It is equally important to determine quickly the type of disaster and the necessary scope of the response.

Exhibit III-6-A illustrates the process of determining the primary response team during an equipment room or building disaster. The first step in the process is notification, which may not come from anyone in the communications recovery team's chain of command. More likely, the notification will come from someone such as a security guard, the facilities manager, or even the fire department.

During this early notification phase, careful consideration of how information flows is important. For example, if a security guard is making rounds late at night and discovers that the air conditioning in a major equipment room has failed, will the guard know to notify the communications team directly, or will the problem be treated strictly as a facilities failure? Needless to say, loss of air conditioning is a serious matter in a room full of expensive (and heat-producing) equipment.

Most building security organizations have a book or written procedure specifying who to call if something unusual happens after hours. The communications recovery team members should be sure that they are listed as part of this procedure and that they are called at the first hint of trouble.

After the response teams have been notified of a serious event, a quick assessment must be made of whether the damage affects the entire building and thus involves multiple departments, or whether the damage is confined to the communications equipment. The results of this assessment are reported by using the damage reports shown as Workpapers III6.10 and III6.11.

The procedures that are implemented will be based on this initial assessment. For example, failure of a PBX or a multiplexer power supply certainly affects the company as a whole, but if the damage is confined to communications equipment, the response is coordinated principally by the communications recovery team. In such cases, the communications recovery team will report to the emergency management team or other corporate entity about the status of the recovery, but it will be basically acting on its own. The communications recovery team will also be expected to coordinate with other teams as necessary (e.g., the facilities recovery team in situations involving

EXHIBIT III-6-A EQUIPMENT ROOM AND BUILDING DISASTERS—DETERMINING THE PRINCIPAL RESPONSE TEAM

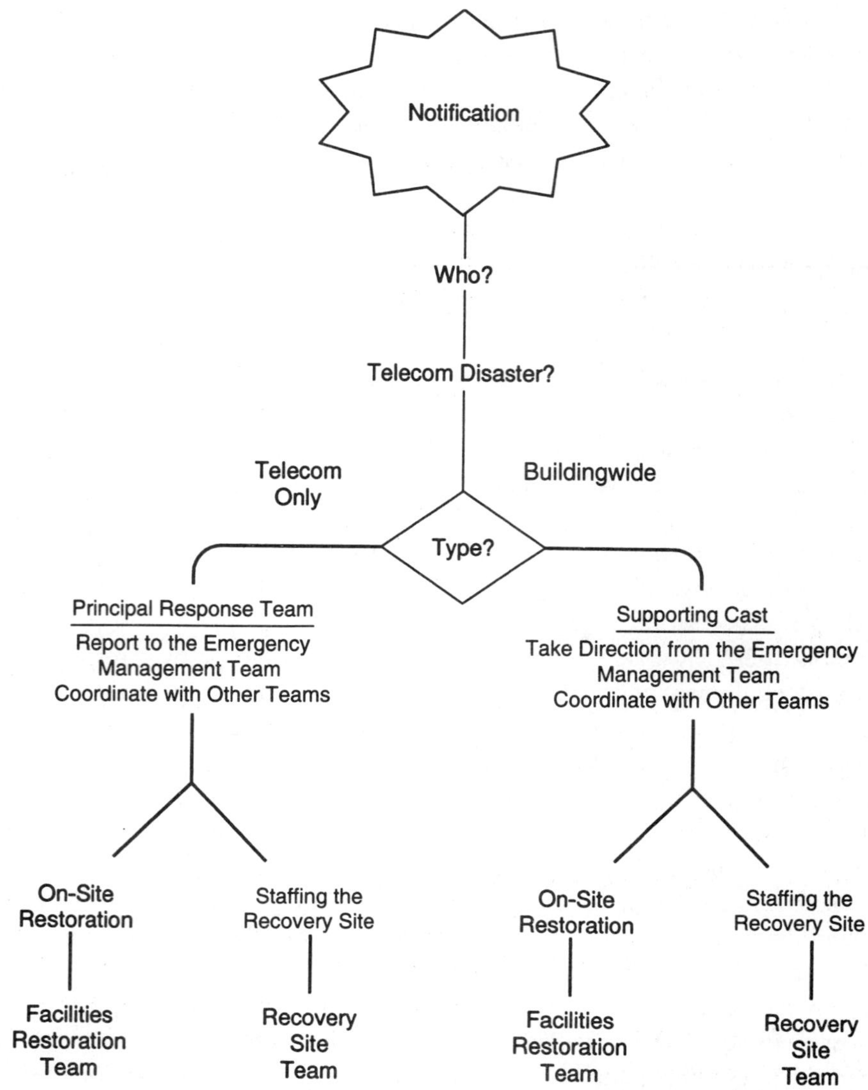

power failure or common facilities). Workpapers III6.12 through III6.23 outline the support activities that may be provided by other departments during a recovery operation.

If the disaster is more global in nature, such as fire or water damage affecting the entire building, the communications recovery team will act in a supporting role and will take direction from the emergency management team. In this capacity, the communications recovery team may be called on to perform tasks that are outside the auspices of communications. This typically occurs in a companywide disaster, because communications are not the only concern.

Whether the disaster is confined to communications or affects the entire building, the communications recovery team may be split into at least two subgroups to control various aspects of the disaster. If the company is using a backup and recovery center, one subgroup will be responsible for staffing and configuring that location. The other

EXHIBIT III-6-B RESPONSIBILITIES OF COMMUNICATIONS SOFTWARE RESTORATION TEAM

1. Provide a representative at recovery headquarters.
2. Specify filenames of media to be picked up by MIS at the off-site storage facility.
3. Make duplicate copies of software upon delivery, return original to storage.
4. Verify software and hardware configurations.
5. Notify vendor to assure software releases are compatible with new equipment installation.
6. Request software patches, if available, if software hardware incompatibilities are possible.
7. Request an on-site vendor representative if required.
8. Make all remote loads of PBX and multiplexer software.
9. Review software installation for correctness.
10. Test final configuration.
11. Place new configuration in service.

subgroup will be expected to remain on site to oversee restoration activities so that the business can return to its original location as soon as possible. Although the names of these subgroups vary, for purposes of this discussion, the team that remains on site is referred to as the communications facilities restoration team. The team that travels to the backup facility is referred to as the communications recovery site team.

Various specialty teams can also be created. For example, creation of a communications software reconfiguration team is typically prudent, because a lot of equipment for the network is software driven (e.g., multiplexers and PBXs). Exhibit III-6-B lists the responsibilities of the communications software reconfiguration team.

Once responsibilities are delegated, personnel are trained, and everyone is comfortable with the game plan, it is time to move to the next phase of the effort—testing the plan. This is discussed in Chapter III-7.

APPENDIXES TO THE RECOVERY PLAN

Section III.C of Workpaper III6.01 contains appendixes to the communications-specific recovery plan. These contain primary information essential to the conduct of the recovery effort and include call lists for notifying the recovery team, vendor contact lists, maintenance and report forms, team member responsibilities, network and equipment room diagrams, contracts and maintenance agreements, and hardware and software inventories. The following paragraphs describe the contents of these appendixes.

Emergency Call Lists

Emergency call lists of management and recovery teams should be obtained from sources that are known to stay accurate and are subject to periodic updates. These sources might include human resources and the company telephone directory. These directories should include home and business telephone numbers, pager numbers, and an alternative means of contacting these personnel should communication services not be available (e.g., home addresses). Because confidentiality is a concern, it might be prudent to use pointers in this appendix to another data base that is kept confidential.

Vendor Escalation Lists

Vendor escalation lists should already exist within the organization, because most local and long-distance telephone companies offer well-defined escalation procedures. Escalation procedures involve the identification of alternative contacts in the event that the primary contact is not available in an emergency. These usually stem from the primary contact, who may be a mid-level manager, up to a division manager or vice-president. The vendor should be able to provide an accurate escalation list if one is not already available within the company. Whatever the source of the original list, the vendor should provide updates on a monthly basis or when such information changes. The recovery team should test it periodically during monthly and quarterly checks to ensure that it is up-to-date. The vendor should be happy to help keep these lists current, because this confirms that the company will continue to use their services.

Recovery Forms

The various forms used in the recovery process should be stored with the disaster recovery plan. These include forms for notification of recovery team members (primary and alternates) as well as forms for changes in equipment, software configurations, and software revisions. The notification forms are usually administered by the human resources department responsible for recording employees' changing jobs.

Recovery Team Member Duties and Responsibilities

This appendix includes key recovery team member duties and responsibilities. The team leader is responsible for establishing the duties and responsibilities of team members in a disaster; these should be approved by senior management. For example, members of the off-site storage team might be responsible for picking up magnetic and printed media from off-site storage locations; logistical team members for providing administrative support for persons in a disaster; and voice communications recovery team members for routing 800 service, remote call-forwarding, and providing command and control at the disaster site, coordinating with the emergency management team. Specifically, this appendix should identify persons responsible for voice and data communications, restoring critical communications links, T1 service, and other types of services. It may also identify people responsible for damage assessments.

Network Schematic Diagrams

The communications recovery plan should be compiled so that any technically competent person could pick it up and ascertain what the installation once looked like and how it should look in its emergency configuration. This is done in case persons directly responsible for recovery are unavailable during the disaster. To accomplish this objective, the recovery plan should include schematics illustrating the network configuration. Supporting text should be provided as required. Graphics software programs can be used to generate the necessary drawings.

Equipment Room Diagrams

Diagrams of the equipment room floor grid are useful to ensure that proper clearances and air flow are maintained between equipment as it is restored. This also provides a picture of the equipment installation to aid persons who are not familiar with the layout.

Contracts and Maintenance Agreements

This appendix should contain contracts and maintenance agreements, including agreements for replacement of equipment and major components, hot-site contracts, and service contracts. Absent this information, the company may not realize that a roll-in replacement for a critical piece of equipment already exists and may purchase a maintenance contract again.

Cellular Telephone Agreements

An inventory of cellular telephones and the service company agreements should be included in this appendix. This is very important, because cellular telephones play a major role in command and control in most communications disasters. Every management employee within the company, with a role in the recovery process, should be identified, along with his or her cellular telephone number and equipment. It should also be noted whether the equipment is a car-mounted unit or a portable unit that could be brought into the building.

This appendix should also include a policy for employees, stating which employees are not authorized to use cellular phones in the vicinity of the company when a disaster has been declared. Because there are only a limited number of transmission frequencies per cell site, it is important to conserve these frequencies for critical recovery applications.

Hardware and Software Inventories

This appendix includes an itemized list of hardware serial numbers to aid in rapid replacement of the equipment in a disaster. Helpful data to include here includes the date that the equipment was purchased, original cost of the equipment, critical rating and power requirements, the name, address, and telephone number of both the manufacturer and the distributor of the equipment, and an amortization schedule for the equipment.

For example, if the equipment is depreciated over a five-year life and is four years old, the decision may be simply to replace rather than repair the equipment, because much of its useful life has already been booked. This is important information to have at a time when many command decisions regarding replacement of the equipment will have to be made rapidly.

A separate inventory should be maintained of all equipment residing at the disaster recovery center. This inventory might also specify whether the equipment is on a rolling rack, which could be moved off of the floor quickly, or whether it requires dollies. It might also indicate what types of power plug the equipment uses.

A separate appendix should include software lists and license numbers, as well as names and contact numbers for the software vendors, to assist in identifying and restoring critical software.

DEVELOPING INVENTORIES

The most effective method for keeping track of the hardware, software, and personnel necessary for the recovery process is through a process called importing data. This process involves finding accurate sources of information within the organization that can be reasonably expected to stay up-to-date and importing from these sources whenever possible. Importing can be accomplished by simply assigning responsibility to a key person to go to the source department on a regular basis, copy the appropriate file, and update the recovery plan. If this option is chosen, it is important to ensure that it is enforced. For example, if the employee responsible for copying the equipment inventory file for the recovery plan fails to do so, that employee's salary increase may be affected. Absent such measures, it becomes too easy for employees to fail to update the plan.

The optimal method of importing data is to update the plan automatically whenever the source data is changed. This can be done in a networked environment in a number of ways.

Object linking Microsoft Word files, for example, is one way of accomplishing this task. By linking to a specific file in the accounting department, a technical service manager can ensure that every time that the department updates an equipment repository file, the file in the recovery plan is also updated.

Identifying an accurate source of information can be difficult. For example, there are many places within the organization to find home telephone numbers for key employees; these include human resources and company telephone directories. At some companies, human resources may be the best place to get this information. However, at others, the information in human resources is often out of date.

The telephone numbers for key equipment vendors and suppliers can be found in the network control center, help desk, or other operational environment with day-to-day vendor contact. When telephone numbers for key vendors and suppliers change, operations personnel are informed first.

A circuit inventory can come from a number of sources, including a circuit analysis department, a communications analyst who is responsible for ordering these circuits, the network control center, and even from circuit call records contained in intelligent multiplexers. Such intelligent multiplexers as the IDNX series multiplexer (Network Equipment Technologies) provide for data dumps of all circuit calls established within the multiplexer. This provides for quick and easy reestablishment of these circuits by means of a taped copy or a manual process from a printed record, either of which can be safely stored off site. The important point is to back up regularly this data contained within the multiplexer and have it included in the regular pickup schedule for magnetic media for the data center. This backup should take place at least weekly, and daily in intensive operations that change rapidly.

Other items that may be useful in an equipment inventory include the location of third-party or secondary market equipment suppliers. These suppliers can be instrumental in locating equipment, particularly equipment that is a few years old.

Maintaining a current equipment inventory helps to ensure that the company takes advantage of any equipment replacement and maintenance guarantees. For example, a PBX vendor may have agreed to supply another PBX of similar capabilities and capacity within 24 hours of a disaster—this is referred to as a roll-in replacement guarantee. If this information is not imported into the recovery plan, it may be forgotten during a disaster, resulting in an unnecessary expenditure.

An inventory should also be developed to identify software required for recovery. This inventory should include the acquisition date of the software, the original cost of the software, the license number, and the version number. Particular attention should be paid to software versions. Using software that is significantly outdated is an open invitation to problems in a disaster, because the version of the software may no longer be available. Using out-of-date software can cause significant delays in the recovery process. Software should also be backed up regularly and stored off site.

Samples of hardware and software inventory forms are provided as Workpapers III6.24 and III6.25, respectively.

WORKPAPER III6.01 Communications-Specific Recovery Procedures

COMMUNICATIONS-SPECIFIC RECOVERY PROCEDURES

III. Communications-Specific Recovery Procedures*

A. Communications Emergency Procedures--Companywide Disaster:

1. Receive initial report.
2. Notify emergency management and response teams.
3. Initial damage assessment.
4. Safeguard human life.
5. Activation of recovery services.
6. Restoral of help desk and network control numbers.
7. Command routing of 800 numbers.
8. Redirection of backbone T1 network.
9. Reestablishment of production dial-in ports.
10. Reestablishment of maintenance dial-in ports.

B. Communications Emergency Procedures--Component-Specific Disaster:

1. PBX, automated call distribution unit, or voice mail system software failure.
2. PBX, automated call distribution unit, or voice mail system hardware failure.
3. Failure of major front-end processor.
4. Loss of critical bridges, routers, or gateways.
5. Major cable cut.
6. Failure of major T1 node.
7. Loss of central office.
8. Loss of long-distance carrier.
9. Power surge.
10. Lightning strike.
11. Theft of equipment.

C. Appendixes to the Communications-Specific Recovery Plan:

Emergency call lists of management and recovery teams.
Vendor escalation lists.
Team member duties and responsibilities.
Network schematic diagrams.
Equipment room diagrams.
Contract and maintenance agreements.
Cellular telephone inventory and agreements.
Hardware lists and serial numbers.
Software lists and license numbers.

*Part III completes the overall communications recovery plan. Parts I and II appear in Workpaper III5.01, Sample Organizationwide Recovery Procedures.

WORKPAPER III6.02 Redirection of Phone Numbers

CRITICAL INTERNAL NUMBER REDIRECTION CHECKLIST

Call [company name]'s centralized trouble reporting number and request that the main telephone number for network control be forwarded to the emergency network operations center to provide transparency to end users and maintain command and control. After this has been accomplished, the following numbers should be forwarded within one hour:

Normal Number	Function	Emergency Number

Test all numbers by dialing the old number to verify that they forward to the new numbers.

Responsible Team Members: ____________________

WORKPAPER III6.03 Redirection of Inbound 800 Numbers

INBOUND CALL CENTER FAILURE EMERGENCY RECOVERY PROCEDURES

CONFIDENTIAL

1. In the event that our primary inbound 800 service center is incapacitated and unable to answer calls, the following three 800 numbers have top recovery priority.

   Phone number: ________________
   Function: ____

   Phone number: ________________
   Function: ____

   Phone number: ________________
   Function: ____

2. The corporation has determined that it could operate without its other 800 numbers for up to 48 hours. If the disaster is expected to last beyond 48 hours, you will be instructed to consult your disaster recovery plan. Because of the criticality of these numbers on corporate operations, recovery must take place within 60 minutes.

3. The three numbers listed above will be redirected to the following alternate location by order of availability:

   [alternate emergency call center location]
   Phone number: ________________

4. For further information, consult your corporate disaster recovery plan document.

WORKPAPER III6.04 Reconfiguration of Equipment and Redirection of T1 Circuits

INSTALLATION OF EMERGENCY EQUIPMENT CONFIGURATION

On activation of the plan, the communications recovery team will dispatch at least one principal analyst to the recovery center by regular scheduled airline service or other available means. The following is intended to be used as a checklist for the analyst's activities on arrival:

[ ] Open a critical events log to chronicle recovery operations for future review.

[ ] Conduct an initial meeting with internal recovery center personnel and review the plan.

[ ] Review installation of all equipment set up before your arrival for correctness and conformance with desired specifications.

[ ] Provide an initial verbal status report to the emergency management team as to the recovery center's progress, and estimated time the equipment configuration will be usable.

[ ] Ensure proper configuration and operation of the T1 local loops. If these have been in use by other subscribers, it is possible that options and configurations could have changed.

[ ] Test with carriers and the local telephone company. Ensure that the network operations can run a loopback test to the channel service unit on all T1 circuits.

[ ] Make a final check of all equipment cabling, power connectors, and configurations. Power up equipment and run self tests to ensure proper operation.

[ ] Make one final equipment check of all T1 circuits, cabling, and matrix switch patches.

[ ] Call network operations by a three-way conference call. Begin configuration of the multiplexers.

[ ] After equipment is configured, have emergency network operations run a loopback test to verify connectivity between the network and the newly established node.

[ ] Await direction from network operations as to when to bring the network up.

[ ] Work as required to resolve any outstanding issues. Remain at the recovery center unless specifically requested to return by the emergency management team.

Responsible Team Members: ______________________________

WORKPAPER III6.05 Redirection of Dial-In Ports

REDIRECTION OF DIAL-IN PORTS

These instructions for redirecting dial-in ports should be invoked as soon as possible after a disaster.

[ ] Call [carrier name] and establish circuits according to the configuration shown in the normal and emergency circuit configuration. [Carrier name] number can be found in the vendor escalation list.

[ ] Escalate to [carrier name] management at your discretion using the same appendix if progress seems slow.

[ ] Conduct acceptance tests with [carrier name] and on-site [company name] personnel at the recovery center to ensure end-to-end connectivity of the newly established circuits.

Dial-in modem banks will be call forwarded to the recovery center by the telephone company test board serving the damaged area, unless access to the area permits [company name] to conduct this operation itself.

[ ] Provide the number of the appropriate recovery center group to which these numbers will be forwarded and to the emergency network control center and ensure its proper operation.

The emergency network control center will be responsible for directing long-distance company 800 numbers for the data communications department.

[ ] Provide the number of the appropriate recovery center group to which these numbers will be forwarded and to the emergency network control center and ensure its proper operation.

Dial-in equipment maintenance ports will be call forwarded to the recovery center by the telephone company test board serving the damaged area, unless access to the area permits [company name] to conduct this operation themselves.

[ ] Provide the number of the appropriate recovery center business lines to which these in-dial ports will be forwarded and to the emergency network control center and ensure their proper operation.

Responsible Team Member: ______________________________

WORKPAPER III6.06 Emergency Circuit Recovery Priorities

EMERGENCY CIRCUIT RECOVERY PRIORITIES

CONFIDENTIAL

The following circuits, in the order shown, shall be redirected to the company's disaster recovery facility at [street, city, state] in the event of a formal disaster declaration by the company. For further information, refer to your disaster recovery plan.

Priority	Circuit Number	Speed	Function

WORKPAPER III6.07 Recovery From Software-Induced Disaster

PBX, AUTOMATED CALL DISTRIBUTION, OR VOICE MAIL SOFTWARE DISASTER

1. Determine the nature of the disaster:

   [ ] Software error.

   [ ] Critical file corrupted.

   [ ] Virus.

   [ ] Other [explain]: ____
   ____.

2. Determine the extent of the disaster: ______________________
   ____
   ____.

3. Request on-site software vendor.

   Software vendor telephone: ________________.

4. If virus, run virus-cleanup software.

   Location of software: ______________________________.

5. Alert emergency management team representative.

   Emergency management team representative telephone:
   ________________.

6. Make report to emergency management team representative.

   If directed, implement recovery plan beginning on page ____.

WORKPAPER III6.08 Recovery From Equipment Failure

PBX, AUTOMATED CALL DISTRIBUTION, OR VOICE MAIL SYSTEM HARDWARE DISASTER

1. Determine the nature of the disaster: ________________________.

2. Protect human life. If it is a water-related disaster, disconnect all power.

   Location of power shut-off switch: ___________________________
   ____.

3. Notify facilities department.

   Corporate facilities telephone: ________________.

4. Call equipment vendor, request on-site representative.

   Equipment vendor telephone: ________________.

5. Secure the installation from theft.

   Corporate security telephone: ________________.

6. Alert emergency management team representative.

   Emergency management team representative telephone: ________________.

6. Make report to emergency management team representative.

   If directed, implement recovery plan beginning on page ____.

WORKPAPER III6.09 Carrier Override Procedures

EMERGENCY CARRIER OVERRIDE PROCEDURES
FOR LONG-DISTANCE COMPANY FAILURE

1. In the event that users complain of not being able to complete long-distance calls, attempt to call our primary carrier.

   Primary carrier: ______________________________
   Phone number: ____________

2. If the problem is going to take a long time to repair or if the carrier cannot be contacted, program the PBX to insert the following override code before all 1+ calls. Detailed instructions for doing this can be found in the operating instructions for the [PBX system name].

   If customers experience an all-circuits-busy recording, try the next listed carrier:

Backup Carrier	Access Code
________________	____________
________________	____________
________________	____________
________________	____________
________________	____________
________________	____________

   Consult the white-pages telephone directory for other codes.

3. Call primary carrier every 30 minutes for status reports until the outage has been resolved, then return to the primary long-distance carrier.

WORKPAPER III6.10 Telecommunications Recovery Plan (Initial EMT Damage Report)

*Fax this form to ABC Company EMT at (214) XXX-XXXX within 90 minutes of your arrival on site.

LOCATION ______________________________

TIME OF DISRUPTION ______________________________

NATURE OF DISRUPTION ______________________________

____

____

EXTENT OF DAMAGE ______________________________

____

____

____

____

INJURIES ______________________________

PRESENT STATUS ______________________________

____

____

____

____

TIME OF NEXT REPORT ______________________________

____

WORKPAPER III6.11 Equipment Damage Report

*Fax this form, along with your initial notification to BMS catastrophe (site clean-up company) at (817) XXX-XXXX.

NATURE OF DAMAGE:

[ ] FIRE

[ ] SMOKE

[ ] WATER

[ ] CONTAMINATION

[ ] SABOTAGE

[ ] SOFTWARE

[ ] POWER SURGE

[ ] LIGHTNING

[ ] OTHER: ____________________

TYPE OF RESTORATION REQUIRED:

[ ] MAGNETIC MEDIA

[ ] DOCUMENT

[ ] EQUIPMENT--PBX

[ ] EQUIPMENT--MULTIPLEXER

[ ] EQUIPMENT--ACD

[ ] EQUIPMENT--POWER

[ ] EQUIPMENT--OTHER: ____________________

[ ] EQUIPMENT--OTHER: ____________________

[ ] EQUIPMENT--OTHER: ____________________

WORKPAPER III6.12 Support Activities Provided by the Communications Departments

Department	Primary/Alt	Home Phone	Result of Alert
Telecommunications	______	______	______
	______	______	______
Communications (Voice Data)	______	______	______
	______	______	______

SUPPORT ACTIVITIES:

- Provide a representative at the EMT Headquarters.
- Provide immediate notification to all communications carriers.
- Coordinate telephone company's input to the damage assessment status reports.
- Coordinate equipment installation at the recovery sites.
- Coordinate repair or replacement of any damaged communication facilities.
- Coordinate the establishment of voice communications with the telephone company (Command and Control).

WORKPAPER III6.13 Support Activities Provided by the Human Resources Department

Department	Primary/Alt	Home Phone	Result of Alert
Human Resources	____________	____________	____________
	____________	____________	____________

SUPPORT ACTIVITIES:

- Provide a representative at the EMT Headquarters.
- Notify families of injured personnel; explain benefits program.
- Obtain temporary personnel during the recovery operation.
- Provide special considerations for employees who were required to work during recovery versus those who were required to stay home.
- Provide guidance on pay and compensation for employees.
- Be prepared to provide list of employee home addresses if needed during the recovery operation.

WORKPAPER III6.14 Support Activities Provided by the Facilities Department

Department	Primary/Alt	Home Phone	Result of Alert
Facilities	______________	______________	________________
	______________	______________	________________

SUPPORT ACTIVITIES:

- Provide a representative at the EMT Headquarters.
- Provide guidance to local authorities while accessing the facility as related to the existence of unique preventative measures (e.g., lexon windows, automatic locking doors, raised floors)
- Provide assessment of investigation of the cause.
- Assist in the assessment of building damage, including:
  - -- Architectural.
  - -- Electrical.
  - -- Utilities.
  - -- Environment (HVAC).
- Manage building repairs and reconstruction activities.
- Manage disposal of damage residue.
- Obtain temporary recovery headquarters location.
- Obtain temporary work locations.

WORKPAPER III6.15 Support Activities Provided by the Finance Department

Department	Primary/Alt	Home Phone	Result of Alert
Finance	__________	__________	__________
	__________	__________	__________

SUPPORT ACTIVITIES:

- Provide a representative at the EMT Headquarters.
- Alert appropriate corporate and company financial departments.
- Provide immediate emergency credit arrangements, petty cash, and travel advances.
- Provide communications with Tax Regulatory Agencies (Federal, State, and Local)
- Assist in the investigation to account for any "lost" or destroyed negotiable items.

WORKPAPER III6.16 Support Activities Provided by the Risk Management Department

Department	Primary/Alt	Home Phone	Result of Alert
Risk Management	______	______	______
	______	______	______

SUPPORT ACTIVITIES:

- Provide a representative at the EMT Headquarters.
- Notify the appropriate insurance companies.
- Obtain written releases.
- Obtain Proof of Loss documentation instructions (photographs).
- Obtain claims filing instructions.
- Provide guidance regarding actions to be taken during the salvage operations.
- Process all insurance claims.
- Advise Recovery personnel as to the type of records and information to be retained for insurance purposes.
- Collect and record all recovery-related costs.

WORKPAPER III6.17 Support Activities Provided by the Internal Audit Department

Department	Primary/Alt	Home Phone	Result of Alert
Internal Audit	________	________	________
	________	________	________

SUPPORT ACTIVITIES:

- Provide a representative at the EMT Headquarters.
- Assist SECURITY as required to coordinate investigations during the recovery.
- Verify that controls are in place for applications modified to meet limited resources available at the computer back-up site.
- Review recovery procedures to ensure assets control.
- Notify external auditors, if necessary.

WORKPAPER III6.18 Support Activities Provided by the Legal Department

Department	Primary/Alt	Home Phone	Result of Alert
Legal	________	________	________
	________	________	________

SUPPORT ACTIVITIES:

- Provide a representative at the EMT Headquarters.
- Handle legal issues with "next of kin".
- Advise Recovery personnel on contractual obligations.
- Provide copies of contracts destroyed by the disaster.

WORKPAPER III6.19 Support Activities Provided by the Medical Department

Department	Primary/Alt	Home Phone	Result of Alert
Medical	______________	______________	______________
	______________	______________	______________

SUPPORT ACTIVITIES:

- Provide a representative at the EMT Headquarters.
- Handle minor medical requests.
- Coordinate with local hospitals for additional medical requirements.
- Identify and locate injured personnel already moved to the hospital.
- Assist in obtaining proper nourishment for recovery personnel during initial sates of the recovery operation.
- To avoid exhaustion, ensure recovery team members work reasonable hours.

WORKPAPER III6.20 Support Activities Provided by the Office Services Department

Department	Primary/Alt	Home Phone	Result of Alert
Office Services	______________	______________	______________
	______________	______________	______________

SUPPORT ACTIVITIES:

- Provide a representative at the EMT Headquarters.
- Alert Post Office to advise of the situation.
- Establish a Mail Services area within the Recovery Headquarters to handle mail for recovery personnel.
- Coordinate with the Corporate Security Officer.
- Provide security at the affected site.
- Provide security at all recovery operation locations.
- Coordinate with the RISK MANAGEMENT representative to get approval for the removal of any material from the damaged site.
- Establish area to accept deliveries 24 hours a day.

WORKPAPER III6.21 Support Activities Provided by the Public Affairs Department

Department	Primary/Alt	Home Phone	Result of Alert
Public Affairs	__________	__________	__________
	__________	__________	__________

SUPPORT ACTIVITIES:

- Provide a representative at the EMT Headquarters.
- Coordinate radio and TV announcements to notify employees as to where they will report.
- Prepare official company statement to minimize adverse publicity.
- Direct and coordinate all press conferences.
- Provide, monitor, and control photographers.
- Develop recovery progress notifications for publication.

WORKPAPER III6.22 Support Activities Provided by the Purchasing Department

Department	Primary/Alt	Home Phone	Result of Alert
Purchasing	__________	__________	__________
	__________	__________	__________

SUPPORT ACTIVITIES:

- Provide a representative at the EMT Headquarters.
- Obtain office equipment, furniture, forms, and supplies, as needed.
- Issue purchase orders for all recovery requisitions.

WORKPAPER III6.23 Support Activities Provided by the Transporation Department

Department	Primary/Alt	Home Phone	Result of Alert
Transportation	__________	__________	__________
	__________	__________	__________

SUPPORT ACTIVITIES:

- Provide a representative at the EMT Headquarters.
- Provide ground transportation.
- Provide courier coordination and scheduling.
- Provide air transportation.
- Obtain hotel accommodations.

WORKPAPER III6.24 Sample Communications Equipment Inventory Form

COMMUNICATIONS EQUIPMENT INVENTORY FORM

Equipment:

Manufacturer:

Serial number:

Purpose:

Criticality rating (1,2,3,4):

Date of purchase:

Remarks:

WORKPAPER III6.25 Sample Communications Software Inventory Form

COMMUNICATIONS SOFTWARE INVENTORY FORM

Software Package:

Vendor:

License number:

Software version:

Purpose:

Criticality rating (1,2,3,4):

Date of purchase:

Remarks:

CHAPTER

III-7

Communications Recovery Plan Testing, Maintenance, and Training

The success of the organization's recovery planning program depends not only on the development of the plan but on testing, maintenance, and training activities designed to ensure the plan can be carried out successfully.

A thorough program of regular tests is intended to ensure that the complex procedures for responding to and recovering from a disaster function properly; this is especially important in companywide disasters in which different recovery plans (e.g., business operations, data center, and communications) must be coordinated. To this end, department managers should develop tests based on simulated disasters within their own departments. Wide-scale tests of multiple departments' recovery capabilities should also be conducted, though less frequently than the more isolated tests. Test procedures for both types of simulated disasters are discussed in this chapter.

Maintenance activities must also be documented and enforced to ensure the plan stays up to date with the changing business environment. Chapter III-6 discussed the concept of importing data from repositories of information that can be assured of being current. If this is done manually, strict procedures should be written and specific individuals assigned responsibility—and held accountable—for carrying out these maintenance procedures. The most reliable and costly method of importing is by means of automated updating of the plan, as was also discussed in Chapter III-6.

Employees must also be trained to respond appropriately to a disaster. Training varies, depending on the level of involvement of the employee in the recovery plan. Nonessential employees may simply be trained to stay away from the recovery site until notified to return to work. Recovery team members and managers must be trained in the recovery procedures for which they are responsible, as documented in the recovery plan. Training must be ongoing to both refresh the memory of current employees and to educate new hires about correct recovery procedures.

Workpaper III7.01 provides a checklist of the issues that should be addressed in developing effective testing, maintenance, and training procedures.

RECOVERY PLAN TESTING

Testing procedures should be documented both for recovery from isolated disasters involving communications equipment and facilities and for recovery from disasters affecting companywide communications.

Establishing a Testing Schedule

Tests should be conducted periodically throughout the year. The type of test depends on the frequency with which it is given. Tests may be given monthly, quarterly, semiannually, or annually; it can also be effective to stage unannounced tests as well.

Monthly Tests. These are usually paper-based trials for the purpose of verifying plan information that was previously identified to ensure it remains accurate. Information that might be reviewed includes:

- Recovery team member rosters and emergency numbers.
- Dates of last backups of PBX class of service indicators.
- Dates of last backups of multiplexer call assignments.
- Equipment configuration data.
- Vendor call-out and escalation lists.
- Equipment inventories (to ensure they include any new equipment installed that month).
- Software inventories (to ensure they include any new systems or applications installed that month).

These tests are usually conducted by the communications director or his or her designee. These reviews should have no effect on operations in the communications or other departments.

Quarterly Tests. Quarterly tests should be conducted to verify information, as done in the monthly tests, as well as to test command and control procedures. This might involve calling numbers on the team member roster to ensure they are correct and activating remote call-forwarding numbers to the emergency management team site to verify they work as planned. Procedures that should be tested include:

- Call forwarding of key command and control numbers.
- Calling vendors using contact numbers for both regular business hours and after hours.
- Calling vendors to verify current equipment replacement times.

These tests are usually conducted by the communications director or his or her designee.

Semiannual Tests. These tests include most areas of the recovery plan, including the dispatch of personnel to recovery centers, activation of emergency switches and communications links, and command routing of critical control systems.

These tests usually involve all technical service departments (e.g., communications, LAN management, and data center management), but they do not affect current operations. Testing should be orchestrated by the directors of the technical service units involved.

Because these tests involve more than one department, they can be quite complex. Flowcharts can help clarify the logical sequence of steps. They can also be helpful for recovery procedures that must be performed by more than one person or unit. Exhibit III-7-A provides an example of the use of flowcharts to describe activation and recovery steps.

Annual Tests. These are intensive tests involving the entire company. In these tests, such major corporate departments as manufacturing operations, facilities, and finance take the lead; the technical service departments operate in a supporting role as directed by the emergency management team. Annual tests do not affect current operations, but they are intended to completely exercise the recovery plan, especially elements involving cooperation among departments. These tests are conducted by the company president, CEO, or other senior member of the emergency management team.

Unannounced Tests. Unannounced tests can be the most effective for determining how well the organization is prepared to cope with a disaster. Such tests may be

EXHIBIT **III-7-A** ACTIVATION AND RECOVERY FLOWCHARTS

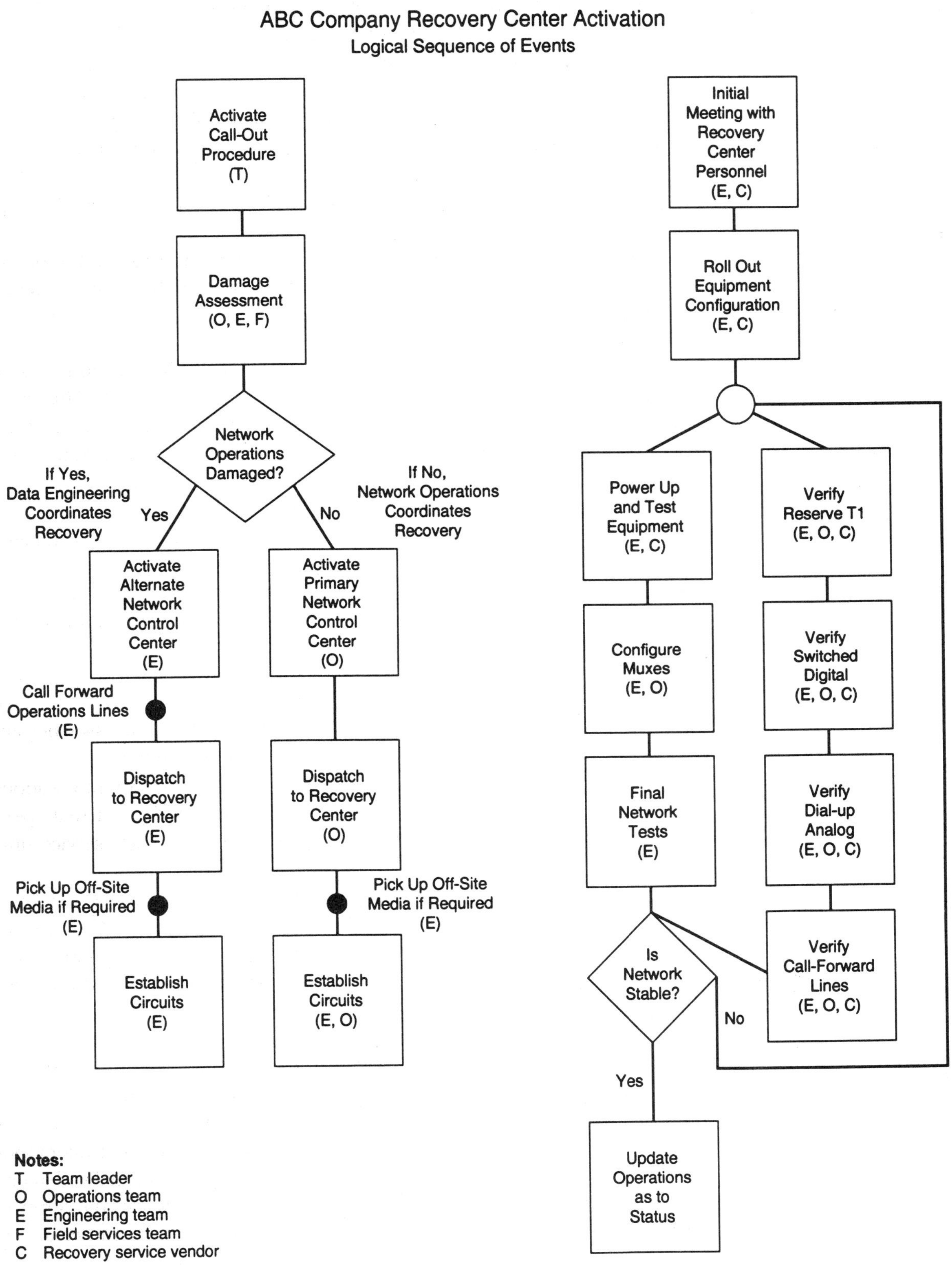

designed to test services in operation; if so, they should be conducted with caution because a failure of the test could result in a costly disruption of service.

The content of these unannounced tests may vary. For example, they may be used to verify adherence to the plan, which is similar in kind to the monthly tests designed to verify information. At a routine weekly staff meeting, for example, the communications manager might declare that a disaster has occurred and escort the staff out of the building with the announcement that they should begin the recovery process. It will quickly become apparent whether recovery team members have stored their recovery plan off site as required and whether they have been kept up to date. More rigorous tests involving multiple systems and departments can be difficult to coordinate without advance warning.

Procedures for Conducting Tests

The type of test to be given determines the departments that will be mobilized. In monthly and quarterly tests, each technical service department tests its own internal systems only; other departments are neither involved nor affected by these tests. Semiannual and annual tests involve coordination among several departments. In annual tests, the technical service departments carry out their own internal tests, while providing recovery support to other departments (e.g., communications recovery support for field sales).

It is difficult to justify disrupting critical communications during a business day for recovery testing. For this reason, few companies perform invasive tests on the production network. Nonetheless, there are tests that can be performed without interrupting production. These might include activating emergency T1 nodes or router links at a recovery center in a manner that isolates them from the production network. Test equipment of various types can simulate live data and serve as a measure of the effectiveness of the emergency links. Much of this kind of testing can also take place after hours.

If a test might affect the production environment, the communications department may need to take certain steps in advance of the test to protect ongoing services from disruption. For example, if the planned test requires software changes to switching equipment and multiplexers, these changes should be coordinated in advance. Some corporate policies require that such changes be made during nonwork hours; this typically means that the communications department would need at least 24 hours' notice of a test.

As the testing program evolves and staff members become accustomed to these tests, they may become complacent. To counteract this tendency, it is recommended that additional levels of complexity be added to test scenarios. For example, in a real disaster, it is likely that at least some recovery team members will not be available. It can be useful to test how the recovery team handles the recovery without one or more key members. This would require that other staff members who are not as familiar with the plan take over the functions of these missing employees. This can provide an especially good test of the adequacy of the documented recovery procedures.

Evaluating Results

The results of each test should be evaluated with respect to both the performance of staff members and the adequacy of documented procedures. Procedures may need to be modified so that they can be executed more efficiently. The object is to identify improved methods of conducting the recovery operation that can minimize expenses, conserve resources, and improve efficiency. The person responsible for evaluating test results—typically the test administrator—should be on the lookout for such improvements as:

- Replacing manual procedures for updating contact information with automated procedures that import data from selected data bases. It may be possible to identify new data bases that already capture the necessary information and that can be used as a source for automatic updates to the recovery plan.
- Shortcuts for performing such processes as installing new equipment at a recovery center or loading critical software to tape for storage.
- Improvements in automated methods for moving data to a recovery center (e.g., remote software loading) so that human resources can be freed to perform other more critical duties. It may also be possible to make better use of existing recovery center personnel so that there is less need to transport people to the recovery center.
- Improved procedures for notification of employees and vendors. These might include network conferencing, recorded announcements, and voice mail messages.

RECOVERY PLAN MAINTENANCE

The communications recovery plan can quickly become useless if it is not properly maintained. Changes in personnel and in systems configurations must be reflected in the recovery plan. To ensure this is done, the recovery planner must clearly identify the parties responsible for updates, the frequency of updates, and the procedures for updates reflecting replacement and modification of equipment and software. In addition, changes in information regarding external contacts must be included in the plan. These might result from contract renewals and changes in contact information for emergency services.

Assigning Responsibility for Updates

Many departments have direct responsibility for maintaining various sections of the recovery plan. Exhibit III-7-B provides a sample flowchart that illustrates how three departments might be assigned responsibility for maintaining such information as multiplexer call assignments, vendor contact lists, and hardware inventories.

These departments may need to create specialized procedures for capturing information on resource changes and updating the recovery plan. For example, human resources may need to develop a form to track changes in membership of recovery teams. (A sample form is provided as Workpaper III7.02.)

Identifying Frequency of Updates

The frequency of updates to the recovery plan should reflect the pace of change within the organization. In general, many organizations are in a constant state of change, in part because of corporate downsizing and technological advances.

Frequent changes to network components require a similar frequency of change to the recovery plan. For example, class of service indicators for PBX equipment may need to be updated daily. Call assignments in intelligent multiplexers might require updating every 30 days. Critical telephone numbers and data base assignments may need to be updated at least monthly. As noted previously, the best and most accurate method of performing these updates is to automatically import this information from repositories of critical data; whenever the repository is updated, the change will be automatically imported to the recovery plan without the need for human intervention.

EXHIBIT **III-7-B** RESPONSIBILITY FOR RECOVERY MAINTENANCE

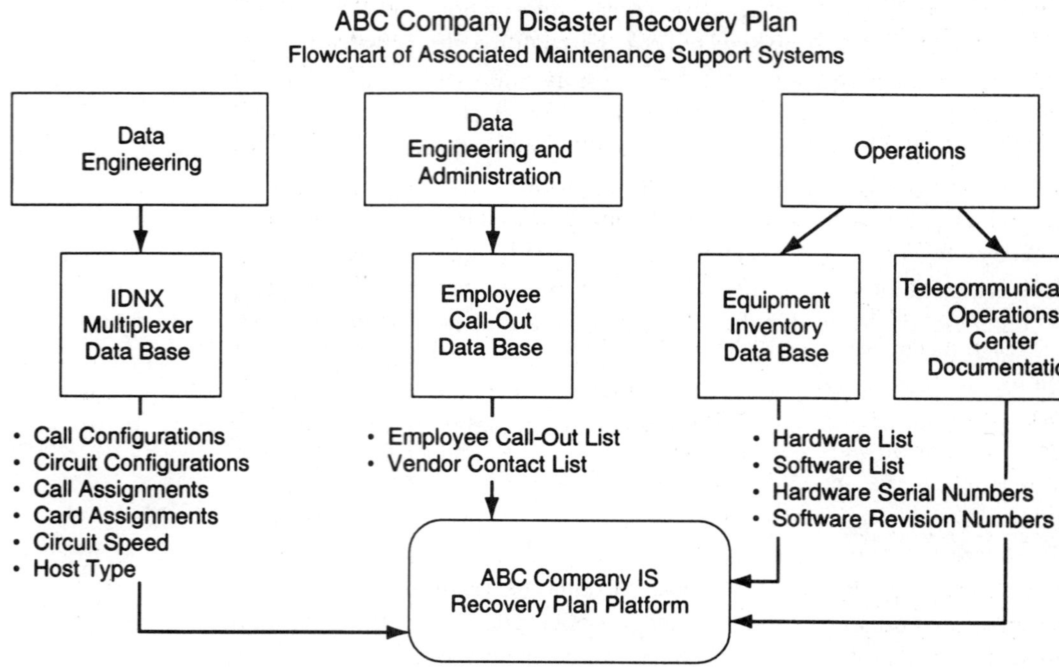

Types of Resource Changes

Procedures should be in place to record changes involving major hardware and software system components. These might be due to a system reconfiguration, as well as upgrades of equipment and software. Installation of new equipment may also require updating vendor-related information, including emergency contacts and such contracted services as equipment replacements and the time frames for such replacements. A newly negotiated contract with a major communications equipment vendor might, for example, specify the lead time the vendor requires for restoring a major asynchronous-transfer-mode switch.

The recovery planner should also keep track of the renewal dates of all contracts which have a bearing on recovery capabilities. Items that should be reflected in the recovery plan include termination dates of contracts with hot-site providers, expiration dates of maintenance contracts on mission-critical equipment, and scheduled replacement dates for such equipment. The recovery planner may want to take the opportunity to negotiate with vendors for improved disaster recovery support—for example, for a roll-in replacement guarantee. Contract renewal is the best time to negotiate such additional commitments from the vendor, because the vendor is usually eager to do what is necessary to retain the client.

It is also critical to maintain current contact information for emergency assistance. These might include telephone numbers for police and fire departments—especially important if the organization is in an area without 911 service—and for emergency services such as toxic cleanup companies.

RECOVERY TRAINING

Ongoing training of employees is critical to the successful implementation of the communications recovery plan. Procedures should be established not only to train technical staff in recovery procedures but also to build awareness of recovery objectives among end users.

The first step is to identify the most cost-effective method of training personnel. Various methods of training are available; these include periodic issuance of memos, videotape presentations, and seminars. The audience for each training method should also be identified. For example, reminder memos and posters might be useful for building awareness among end users, whereas seminars may be more appropriate for managers and key technical staff who are more directly involved in managing the recovery effort.

Identifying Scope of Training

Most departments require some level of training. At a minimum, nonessential personnel might receive training about what to do in the event of a natural disaster such as a tornado or earthquake. Technical service departments should be provided more in-depth training.

Members of recovery teams should receive training to ensure competence in their primary area of responsibility. However, it is recommended that they also be exposed to recovery requirements and procedures in other critical areas. For example, a communications recovery team might also be taught procedures for recovering a LAN. Such cross-training can be invaluable in a disaster in which key personnel are unavailable and must be replaced.

Recovery operations often require close cooperation, not only among members of the same recovery team, but among different recovery teams as well. For this reason, joint training sessions should be held among recovery teams that focus on areas of cooperation and mutual support. For example, the communications recovery team may need to work closely with the data center recovery team to ensure correct restoration of support software.

Assigning Responsibility for Training

Technical department managers should assume responsibility for training technical employees in recovery procedures. Training of end users is usually conducted by the operations or corporate training department.

WORKPAPER III7.01 Communications Plan Testing and Maintenance

COMMUNICATIONS PLAN TESTING AND MAINTENANCE

IV. Testing and Maintenance of the Communications Plan

A. Testing Procedures

Identify:

1. Affected departments.
2. Responsibilities.
3. Reference documents.
4. Frequency of testing.
5. Pretest coordination.
6. Scheduled tests.
7. Unscheduled tests.
8. Introduction of complications.
9. Evaluation of results.

B. Maintenance Procedures

Identify:

1. Affected departments.
2. Responsible personnel.
3. Frequency.
4. Hardware change procedures.
5. Software change procedures.
6. Staff or team member changes.
7. Vendor list updates.
8. New technologies or equipment.
9. Contract renewals.
10. Emergency assistance changes.

C. Training Procedures

Identify:

1. Scope of training.
2. Affected departments.
3. Responsibilities.
4. Reference documents.
5. Frequency of training.
6. Required versus optional training.
7. Media to be used.
8. Specialty team training.
9. General new hire training.

WORKPAPER III7.02 Personnel Change Notification Form*

PERSONNEL CHANGE NOTIFICATION

DELETIONS

To ______________________________

From ______________________________

The following individuals' names should be deleted from the Disaster Recovery notification checksheets from the positions noted below. These changes should be made immediately.

	Name	Department	Position on Team	LIST	Telephone Numbers			Reason for Change
					Home	Office	Pager	
1.								
2.								
3.								
4.								
5.								

Signature ______________________________ Date ______________

FOLD HERE

Note: For each deletion on the list above, an addition must be created below.

PERSONNEL CHANGE NOTIFICATION

ADDITIONS

To ______________________________

From ______________________________

The following individuals' names should be added to the Disaster Recovery notification checksheets in the positions noted below. These changes should be made by ______________________.

	Name	Department	Position on Team	LIST	Telephone Numbers			Replaces
					Home	Office	Pager	
1.								
2.								
3.								
4.								
5.								

Signature ______________________________ Date ______________

CONFIDENTIAL

*Not available on disk.

Evaluating the Results of a Plan Activation

CHAPTER

III-8

The first six chapters in Part III provide guidance for developing a comprehensive disaster recovery plan for voice and data communications. Those chapters provide the foundation for developing an effective, well-documented procedure.

However, developing and documenting a disaster recovery plan is only the beginning. As detailed in Chapter III-7, the plan must be tested and maintained. Regardless of whether the disaster recovery plan has been activated for testing purposes or in response to a real disaster, the results of the plan activation must be evaluated and the plan adjusted accordingly. To accomplish this, measurement criteria must be in place for evaluating the plan's effectiveness. By reviewing these measurement criteria following activation of a recovery plan, and then making the necessary adjustments to the plan, an organization can ensure that its documented procedures provide effective guidance for the recovery of voice and data communications capabilities following a disaster.

EVALUATING THE RESPONSE OF THE EXECUTIVE MANAGEMENT TEAM

As discussed in Chapter III-3, the executive management team is responsible for the overall coordination and management of an organization's response to a highly visible and destructive disaster. For example, the executive management team would be convened if a disaster forced the company to vacate its primary place of business and move to a disaster recovery facility. An executive management team might also be assembled if a disaster posed a difficult public relations problem, such as a hazardous chemical spill. An executive management team might also be activated if a disaster posed a threat to investors, shareholders, or customers dependent on the organization, and a high level of public contact was required to assure the community that the situation was under control.

An executive management team's first requirement is for a place to work. This could be a training facility, a hotel suite, or even one of the executive's homes. The important points are that the place is specified in the disaster recovery plan and that the executives know to report there after a disaster has rendered the primary place of business unusable.

When evaluating a disaster response that requires activation of the executive management team, the key questions that should be considered involve the ease with which members of this team are contacted and assembled. For example:

- Was the executive management team successfully contacted? Although this may seem academic, in a disaster, contacting key executives is often difficult.
- Do these key executives have unlisted telephone numbers, which are not documented in the plan?
- Does each member of the executive management team have a backup device, such as a pager or a cellular telephone, if telephone service is out in the area?
- Did the executive management team take the notification seriously and report promptly to the specified location?

Special care is needed for any telephone calls to employees' homes regarding disasters at a facility. The persons making calls to employees' homes must be prepared to deal with concerned, possibly hysterical relatives wondering about the safety of family members who were at work during the disaster. The following questions are helpful for evaluating this aspect of the disaster response:

- Was the calling procedure scripted?
- Did the people making the calls follow the script?
- Did the script work as intended, or were modifications needed?

The most effective method for making the necessary calls to assemble the executive management team is to provide a pre-approved check list, containing not only names and telephone numbers, but a brief procedure to follow when contacting an employee's family.

Other points to consider when evaluating the executive management team's response to a disaster notification include the following questions:

- *Did the correct executive management team members actually assemble at the predetermined location or, at least, know where to go?*
- *Did the members of the executive management team require directions to the command center?* If so, were directions to the command center clear and easy to follow? This issue can be mitigated in large part by establishing the command center at a landmark, such as a hotel or other facility that is easy to find and has ready access to telephone service.
- *Did the required equipment arrive at the command center on time and in a usable configuration?* When members of the executive management team arrive at the command center, they should not have to wait for such items as telephones, fax machines, a small copier, and other necessary equipment that might be overlooked during the planning process (e.g., a place to sit).
- *Did the equipment require installation?* If so, were diagrams available to technical personnel to assist in the set up of equipment? Set up of the command center should be documented in advance; the site chosen should be a room that is not only immediately available, but an acceptable work environment for several very busy executives.
- *Were emergency telephones easy to use?* During an emergency, the members of the executive management team cannot stop to ask how to use the telephone system. A simple, analog touch-tone telephone set will minimize the time spent showing people how to use the telephone, as well as plug in a fax, laptop computer, or modem.
- *Did the executive management team receive critical status reports within the prescribed time?* Once notified of the disaster, teams will fan out citywide, or perhaps nationwide, implementing the company's recovery plan. One team might be dispatched to the disaster recovery center, if one is in use; another team might be dispatched to the affected facility, to aid in restoration; and still more teams might travel to various locations, retrieving stored magnetic media, picking up and delivering equipment, and performing various other functions. Within a designated period of time, these teams typically must provide damage assessments and progress reports to the executive management team.
- *Were there organizational functions that should have been represented on the executive management team, but were not?* As mentioned in Chapter III-3, the executive management team should include the CEO, the directors of the major technical services divisions (e.g., IS and communications), a corporate communications person, and a small administrative staff. However, this is only a

EXHIBIT III-8-A THREE-PHASE METHODOLOGY FOR RECOVERY PLANNING

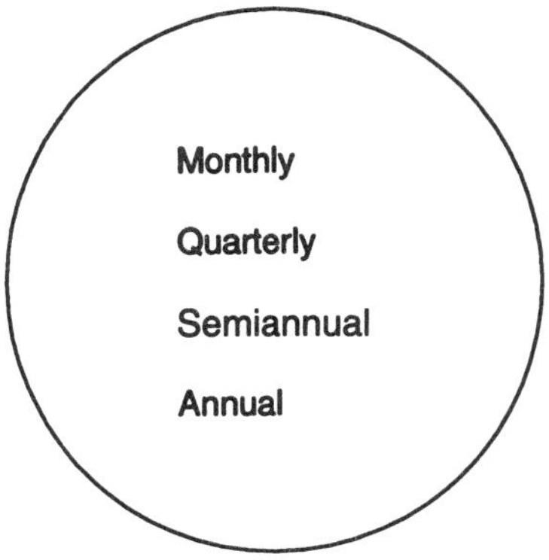

TYPE OF TEST	EXAMPLE OF SCOPE
Monthly	Review telephone numbers and verify accuracy.
Quarterly	Internal joint test with LAN and MIS Departments. (Paper only.)
Semiannual	Joint test with LAN and MIS Departments. Activate back-up circuits, but no live data. Use test patterns to verify continuity.

minimum; other departments could also be involved. Perhaps, the executive management team should include a representative from the company's real estate department or a representative from human resources. The business resumption planner should review the makeup of the executive management team and determine what is needed to make it more effective. During such reviews, members of the executive management team should be asked who else should have been included.

- *What was learned from the exercise?* The business resumption planner should take notes during and after the plan activation so that the recovery plan can be improved, as necessary.
- *What should be changed?* Following activation of a recovery plan, the recovery plan and test procedures should be immediately reviewed.

ENSURING THE EFFECTIVENESS OF COMMUNICATIONS RECOVERY PLAN TESTING, MAINTENANCE, AND TRAINING

Exhibit III-8-A depicts a three-phase methodology for recovery planning. The first phase involves gaining executive commitment to the plan, as well as putting together a preliminary loss analysis. During the second phase, logistical issues are addressed—for example, identifying data bases and selecting data that is to be imported into the disaster recovery plan. The second phase involves selecting an appropriate platform for the plan; this platform should simplify the process of updating the plan. During the third phase, testing, maintenance, and training issues are addressed.

As suggested in this exhibit, the level of effort required for testing, maintenance, and training (i.e., Phase III) is inversely related to the effort expended during Phase II. In other words, if the business resumption planner takes shortcuts during Phase II, particularly in the critical area of identifying data bases, these tasks must be performed manually during Phase III, at great cost in terms of time and effort.

For the purposes of this chapter, it is assumed that the business resumption planner has diligently completed the tasks in Phase II, as they are described in the previous chapters of this book. These tasks having been completed, the task of maintaining the plan becomes simpler, because the required information is gracefully imported from known sources. As a result, the organization can focus its efforts on testing the plan, refining the plan as necessary, and providing the necessary training.

FINDING RECOVERY SPACE

Depending on the nature of a company's business, the company may already subscribe to a commercial recovery facility. However, not all companies subscribe to such services. For firms that choose not to subscribe to a commercial facility, it will be necessary to improve the liaisons between technical services and other divisions within the company—for example, the real estate function, which must be able to quickly locate suitable office space after a disaster.

Finding suitable recovery space is usually not a problem, because most cities have at least a modest surplus of available office space. If possible, however, the recovery space should be documented in the business resumption plan. A commercial recovery center has the advantage of providing a forwarding address in the event of a disaster. Such a site also provides a focal point for recovery planning, thereby simplifying the planning process.

Many companies use off-site disaster recovery facilities from various commercial sources. Although these facilities are well suited to their purpose, they generally cannot single-handedly recover an organization.

The key question to ask when mobilizing technical service personnel involved in staffing and configuring a recovery center is: Were the responsible technical services teams successfully notified? These teams usually include representatives from the mainframe computing operation. Because the mainframe is typically the oldest component in the recovery plan, the entire recovery process may center around recovery of the mainframe. However, a mainframe is only one component of the business and its recovery plan. Unlike the computing environments of a few decades ago, many other components are now connected to the mainframe, including LANs.

It is important to remember that the recovery of a LAN involves more than simply restoring a server. Effective recovery of a LAN-based business function requires a business recovery outlook that ensures that the recovery encompasses the following items:

- An attendant position (i.e., a place to sit).
- The data that resided on the LAN.
- The telecommunications link, which turns the employees who use the LAN into revenue generators for the company.

Without all three of these, recovery of a LAN may be an exercise in futility. Telecommunications will play a prominent role in this effort, for both voice and data communications.

THE BUSINESS RECOVERY CONCEPT

To understand the importance of a business recovery solution, consider the example of a company that has a mainframe disaster recovery center and a long-standing plan aimed at restoring the mainframe. The mainframe supports the company's financial applications (e.g., payroll and accounts payable). LANs support the company's customer support centers, engineering, operations, and production—that is, all of the company's revenue-generating functions.

This company would be better off with no recovery plan at all rather than its current, mainframe-oriented plan. By restoring the mainframe, the company is in a position to restore payroll, accounts payable, and other functions that support the capability to move money out of the company to suppliers, vendors, and employees. If a LAN is down, however, no money is coming in, because the LAN is an integral component of the company's production mechanism. In other words, by focusing recovery efforts on the mainframe instead of the LAN, the company can pay its bills, but it is not making any money.

Although this example is simplistic, it illustrates the importance of focusing on recovery of the core business and the systems that support it. In any recovery operation, the recovery teams will have to make difficult choices. For example, scarce resources should be allocated to functions that make money for the company, even at the expense of something as seemingly important as payroll. Most employees will understand why their paychecks must be a few days late, especially if it means the difference between keeping their jobs or losing them because the company has gone out of business.

DELEGATING RESPONSIBILITY

Chapter III-6 discussed the role of telecommunications recovery teams, and split these into two major categories: teams that remain at the damaged building to aid in restoration activities, and teams that travel to the recovery center to staff the site and restore critical business functions immediately.

If possible, the responsibilities of the various recovery teams should correspond closely with their members' areas of expertise. This is particularly important when they are working under pressure during a disaster. When assigning responsibility for emergency installation of new equipment, it is preferable to select a field service team or other department with employees skilled in installations as part of their regular jobs.

Other teams will also be involved in this effort. For example, field service personnel who normally perform maintenance of microcomputers or terminals probably have the tools and training necessary to serve as emergency installation technicians for the new configurations. Various engineering teams or teams of senior analysts may also be involved to provide high-level troubleshooting and support when complex equipment configurations must be built quickly, literally overnight.

Assuming that one team is dedicated to on-site restoration activities, and the other team is responsible for staffing the recovery site, the following questions are helpful for evaluating how well these teams performed during a disaster or a test:

- *Did the correct team members meet at the recovery center?* This can often be a problem, especially in cases of widespread disasters, because many employees will stop to check on their homes and families before reporting to work. Following a widespread disaster, they could find injured family members, destroyed property, or a neighborhood that seems vulnerable to looting. In such cases, it is not at all unusual to have less than 50% of the team members report for their recovery assignments.
- *Does the recovery plan work in the absence of key personnel?* When testing the recovery plan, it is helpful to evaluate how well the recovery teams compensate

for the absence of a few key personnel. The persons chosen to be absent from the test should be key technologists or those staff members who immediately come to mind as the most pivotal people in the recovery process because of their knowledge of the environment. In addition to rewarding these people with compensatory time while the rest of the team tests the plan, this allows the business resumption planner to evaluate how well the other team members respond without these key individuals, as well as how the team works under stress.

- *Were directions to the recovery center available and easy to follow?* This is particularly important in cases of widespread disaster. If the disaster is an earthquake or a flood, employees will face enough delays in reporting to the center without having to stop for directions. The recovery service vendor should provide maps and written directions, or this information should be documented and included as an integral part of the recovery plan.
- *Was the necessary equipment in a usable configuration?* It is important to remember that the recovery center is also used by other organizations. As a result, the configurations will probably have changed since the last test.
- *Were diagrams available to assist technical personnel in the setup of the equipment?* Previous chapters have emphasized the importance of documenting the recovery plan. Recovery center personnel who are not familiar with a company's day-to-day environment will want to see diagrams showing where equipment goes, and exactly how it should be connected. Although a company's key technical people will know this information, they might not be available during a disaster, and their replacements might not know this information without a detailed guide.
- *Were recovery center personnel available and knowledgeable?* If a company is using (and paying for) the services of a recovery center, it makes sense to evaluate the performance of the recovery center and its personnel during any disaster or test. Although commercial recovery centers provide a useful service, such services are not inexpensive, and it is important to ensure that recovery center personnel are available to provide the necessary guidance for the operation of the recovery center. For example, a commercial recovery center should be staffed with knowledgeable employees who can explain the subtleties of complex matrix switches and other equipment that will be used at the center.
- *Was the telephone system easy to use?* As mentioned previously in this chapter, the preference is for simple touch-tone, analog telephone sets. If these are not available, documentation should be obtained and recovery center staff should receive advance training to avoid unnecessary delays.
- *Were critical status reports dispatched in the prescribed time frame to the executive management team?* To provide effective control of the recovery process, the executive management team must have timely information. Within 90 minutes of disaster notification, the executive management team should receive faxed, written, or verbal reports from each team, both on site and at the recovery center.
- *Were telephone help desk numbers successfully diverted?* When a large amount of technical equipment must be installed in a short period of time, it is helpful to keep the same help desk or network control number. In this way, vendors supporting the recovery process can easily contact the members of the recovery team without unnecessary delays caused by having to learn new telephone numbers.

- *Was dial-in data service successfully established?* Most companies use some type of dial-in data communications service, with the state-of-the-art being 28.8-Kbps v. 34 modems (although many 1,200- and 2,400-bps modems are still in use). Replacement equipment should not be a concern, because modems are fairly standardized and readily available from various sources. The focus should be on the telephone numbers; just as with voice telephone numbers, modem numbers should not change. These numbers can be diverted by either the local telephone operating company or the long-distance carrier to any 10-digit working number in North America. Because commercial recovery companies have hundreds, or perhaps thousands of such numbers, careful planning should permit prompt recovery of this circuit.
- *Were switched digital service and ISDN links successfully established?* As users continue to demand ever-increasing amounts of switched bandwidth, services such as switched 56-KB and ISDN are becoming more widespread. Recovery of these services is somewhat more complex than that of regular dial-up phone lines. ISDN requires special access lines, which may not be available in all areas. Specialized terminal adapter equipment is also required. A careful review of circuit and equipment inventories is helpful for determining how extensively these services are used in an organization. If these have become mission-critical services for the organization, they must be restored. If they are simply conveniences, however, users might be able to fall back to slower speed transmission mediums, such as dial-up phone lines or telephone conferences in lieu of video.
- *Were T1 loops intact, and were these properly optioned?* T1 local loops to recovery centers are typically shared among a broad user community. Because each customer using these links may be using a different line code for the T1, the links may have been re-optioned since the last test or plan activation. If so, they will not work without modification. The recovery plan should detail the procedures for re-optioning channel service unit (CSUs) and other components that may have changed since the last test or plan activation. In all cases, the most effective test is a live test. Even if live production data is not transmitted, a test pattern should be run across these telecommunications facilities to ensure that they work properly and would support the company's data if it ever became necessary.
- *Was data stored off site delivered successfully to the recovery center for mainframe and LAN data?* Most companies have procedures for the off-site storage of mainframe data, with regular pick-up schedules for the tapes. However, procedures for LAN data are sometimes less formal. A LAN administrator might make a backup and simply take the tape home, rather than include it in a formal pick-up schedule. Although this does get the tape off site, problems could arise if the LAN administrator is injured or dies in a disaster. Depending on the type of disaster, access to an off-site storage facility might also be a problem. For example, an earthquake might result in blocked roads or the destruction of bridges. The recovery testing procedure should address this possibility. For example, the script for a test might instruct employees to retrieve off-site storage data as usual, but without using normal routes.
- *Was data stored off site delivered successfully to the recovery center for telecommunications, switches, and multiplexers?* Data should also be stored off-site for telecommunications switches, PBXs, and multiplexers. As mentioned previously, recovery of a 1,000-line telephone switch is a difficult task, and it should not be

further complicated because a list of telephone numbers was not stored off site. Similar problems exist for sophisticated multiplexer equipment, which is also largely software defined.

- *Was data stored off site delivered successfully to the recovery center for the voice mail system?* Voice mail can be indispensable for command and control during a disaster. However, if the voice mail system resides on site, it is likely to be affected in a buildingwide disaster. Fallback procedures could be implemented for using a commercial voice mail vendor, with the normal telephone numbers call-forwarded to allow for transparent use.
- *Was data stored off site delivered successfully to the recovery center for automated call distribution units (ACDs)?* Automated call distribution units (ACDs) are highly customized and heavily software-driven equipment. Therefore, their restoration in a disaster could be slow. Such devices merit careful consideration, both before and during a test, because they are complicated and they generally support a company's core business, such as incoming sales groups.
- *Did technical services have problems with the installation or restoration of any software components?* Subtleties of operating systems, or even minute differences in components such as tape drives, can create lasting and severe problems for employees attempting to uninstall software from one system and reinstall it on another. Through testing, many shortcuts can be identified, which work toward a more graceful reload on the new systems.
- *Was the test equipment available?* If not, what was needed? Like any project, the recovery process requires having the proper tools to finish the job.
- *Did test equipment at the recovery center function properly?* The recovery service vendor probably has test equipment installed at the center for general use. If so, this equipment should be examined in advance to ensure that it is suitable or adaptable for the processes for which it is intended.
- *Were proper small items, such as hand tools, available and adequate?* Personnel at the recovery center should not need to search for a pair of pliers, a note pad, or other seemingly insignificant items.
- *Was response by equipment vendors prompt and adequate?* It is highly recommended that any principle equipment vendors should be asked to provide an on-site representative at the recovery center. Each vendor's responsiveness should be evaluated. If the company has vendor-sponsored disaster recovery programs, or roll-in replacement guarantees, they should be implemented.
- *Were any equipment service or installation manuals required?* Possibly overnight, the people at the recovery center are trying to install a system that originally took years to create. They should have all documentation necessary for this task.
- *Was the overall environment at the recovery center reasonably conducive to performing the necessary work?* In other words, could the recovery team members get their jobs done? Could they do so over time? This is especially important in cases of distributed processing. As mentioned previously, effective backup of distributed processing requires an attendant position, the data that the attendant is supposed to manipulate, and a telecommunications link to turn that attendant into a revenue producer (e.g., in a telemarketing function).
- *Were there other areas of the organization that should have been represented at the recovery center but were not?* In other words, was any function represented at the center that did not need to be there? These questions focus on the issue

of effective utilization of personnel. Someone who may not be needed at the recovery center could be more effectively used at the damaged facility as part of the restoration effort. Personnel will be at a premium in any recovery center test or activation, and they must be used properly and efficiently.

- *What was learned?* Even the most advanced organizations learn something each time the recovery plan is activated or tested. If an organization consistently produces flawless results on its recovery tests, this probably indicates that the standards should be tightened. Management must understand that the plan should be tested until it fails; otherwise, the test is not a true measure of the plan's effectiveness. After each activation or test, the business resumption planner should document the lessons learned as well as any necessary changes.

  A critical events log (i.e., a notebook for logging command decisions) should be opened as soon as a disaster occurs and notification is received. This log is a convenient tool for reviewing performance after a disaster or test. This review should be used to tighten up procedures and to identify possible additions or modifications to the plan. The critical events log can be stored in the jacket of a written disaster recovery plan; it will find immediate use when the plan is activated.

SUMMARY

Management should not expect everything to go perfectly during the first test of a recovery plan. Instead, testing of the recovery plan should be viewed as an iterative process in which employees learn by doing, and the plan is continually refined. When a plan component does fail, procedures can be strengthened to avoid a recurrence of that particular failure. When the activations start to run consistently smoother, the test criteria should be tightened.

By introducing complications during a test (e.g., the absence of a key employee) a company can identify the limits of the plan. By producing failures during the testing procedures, the company can be more secure in the knowledge that the plan will work when it is really needed, under actual disaster conditions.

CHAPTER

III-9

Recovery Procedures for Communications-Intensive Businesses

Recovery planners are encountering new types of enterprise: businesses without storefronts. To understand the subtleties of recovery planning for these types of businesses, it is important to know about the new modes of operation that characterize these enterprises, as well as to know how they can generate revenues and profits without ever having customers come through the front door. This capability depends on the strong integration of telecommunications and IS functions, which is often referred to as a seamless solution.

Although the notion of a seamless solution using relatively low-cost, easy-to-use microcomputers seems like a cost-effective alternative to mainframe-based operations, the cost of migrating from a mainframe environment to a client-server configuration is often much greater than businesses initially realize. The migration to client-server computing involves many costs beyond those for hiring and training staff and installing the microcomputers. The cost of hiring staff and installing equipment can be as little as 10% of the total cost of the migration.

For example, every time a user turns on a workstation and sees an error message such as, "Unable to read drive C," the company incurs additional cost in the form of lost productivity. Other costs related to the migration to a client-server environment arise from the hundreds of pieces of ancillary equipment (e.g., tape drives and modem boards) that are needed, as well as the lack of effective security and control over these devices.

With so many costs involved, it is reasonable to ask why so many organizations are migrating to client-server environments. The answer is that client-server technology, by putting the equivalent of a 1970s-class mainframe on every desktop, can contribute significantly to an organization's profitability. However, this benefit can be realized only if the organization manages the technology correctly. In other words, to enjoy the benefits of client-server computing and seamless solutions, an organization must implement effective security procedures and controls.

The following section explains the concept of the seamless solution and describes the distinctive operating characteristics of communications-intensive businesses. Chapter III-9 also focuses on effective recovery planning and controls for this new type of organization, businesses without storefronts.

BUSINESSES WITHOUT STOREFRONTS

Exhibit III-9-A illustrates the concept of a seamless solution for a hypothetical manufacturing company that is highly dependent on both LAN and telecommunications technology. Starting with the first circle, Customer Service, Exhibit III-9-A traces the path of a typical order through the company, illustrating how fast access to information strengthens the entire process and makes the company more profitable.

EXHIBIT **III-9-A** SEAMLESS SOLUTION

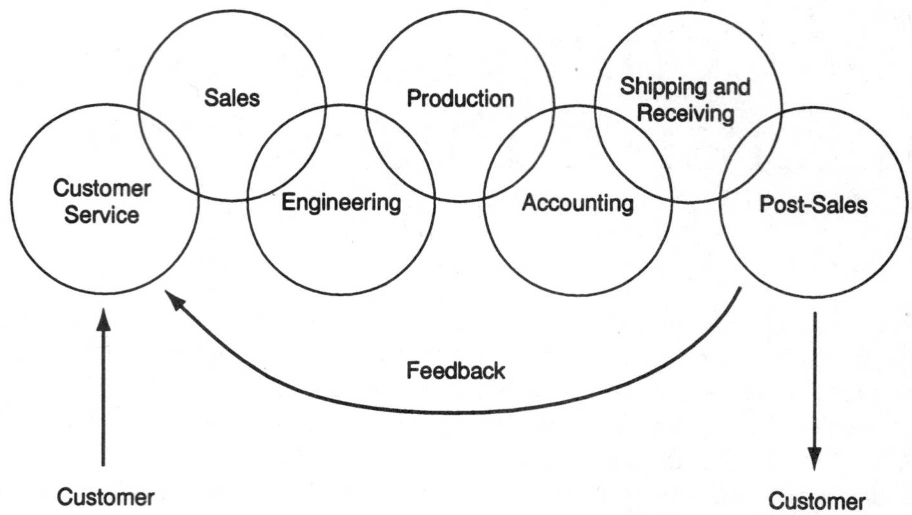

The Flow of Information in a Seamless Solution

The seamless solution depicted in Exhibit III-9-A begins and ends with the customer. The process begins with a customer dialing in, probably on an incoming 800 toll-free number to a customer service center. The customer service center uses many types of technology to handle its workload, including the following:

- Automated call distribution units (ACDs).
- Connections to some type of data processing capability—typically a LAN.
- An attendant position—that is, a place where people can sit and answer calls.
- Telecommunications services, which transform the entire operation into a revenue generator, even though the business has no storefront.

In this example, the customer service center might receive a call from a customer inquiring about a product—for example, a specific type of computer chip—and its suitability for an automotive application. The customer service representative probably would not know whether the product is suited for this application. However, this might represent a new market for the company. Rather than telling the customer, "Leave your name and number, and I'll call back with the answer," the customer service representative can seek a more immediate response by using the company's automated system. For example, customer service can make an on-line inquiry to the sales department, asking whether there have been any recent sales of this product for similar automotive applications. An on-line inquiry to the engineering department would allow customer service and sales to ascertain the feasibility of adapting an existing product for this application. To complete this line of inquiry, customer service, sales, and engineering might contact the production department to find out how long it would take to adapt this product.

Access to this information allows the customer service center to respond quickly, efficiently, and accurately to a customer's inquiry, while the customer is on the telephone and ready to buy. Rather than saying, "I'll call you later," the customer service center can tell the customer, "Yes, we can adapt an existing chip to your application. Engineering says it will take a week to design, and we can produce it within two weeks. How many would you like to order?"

The last circle in Exhibit III-9-A, Post-Sales, represents a function that contacts the customer approximately one week after the sale to request feedback about the company's products and services. The following questions are representative of the type of information collected by this post-sales function:

- Is the product functioning properly?
- Did the product meet the needs of your application?
- Would you like to place another order?
- Are you aware that we offer other products that may be suitable for your application?
- May we send you information about these products?

This feedback allows the customer service center to strengthen its operation in preparation for the next call.

This simple example demonstrates how the entire business process is strengthened because various functions in the company each have access to the others' information. The capability for seamlessly integrating these disparate functions into one synergistic operation is probably the most important reason for migrating to a client-server architecture.

Recovery Planning for a Seamless Solution

From the perspective of disaster recovery and the company's long-term profitability, customer service is probably the most important function in the process shown in Exhibit III-9-A. Because the walk-in market for customized computer chips is small, most of this company's business is conducted via telephone and is, therefore, totally dependent on automated systems.

Effective recovery planning for this organization requires identifying which technical platforms support the customer service center and making these as fault-tolerant and resilient as possible. Part of this process is the selection of equipment for use within the organization with very low failure rates. Just as important, however, is the selection of telecommunications providers with services that are fault-tolerant and resilient. Even the most sophisticated and fault-tolerant network topology is quickly rendered useless if customers are unable to call in.

BRINGING BUSINESS CLOSER TO THE CUSTOMER

Such companies as 1-800-FLOWERS and the Home Shopping Club are representative of the competitive advantage that can be gained simply by making it easier for customers to avail themselves of a company's services. With an easy-to-remember name that is also the company's telephone number, 1-800-FLOWERS makes it easy for customers to use the company's service, i.e., delivery of floral arrangements. At the same time, however, the company is highly dependent on telecommunications.

The second example, Home Shopping Club, depends on very fast turnover of products to be profitable. The products advertised on Home Shopping Club may reside in their warehouse only for a few days. Rapid inventory turnover through selling to consumers generates revenue; storing inventory raises costs. The company's products are advertised on television, and the consumer is given a toll-free number for ordering UPS delivery of the products. Again, the company's success is highly dependent on telecommunications. A single cable cut by a careless contractor, for example, could isolate this company for several days, resulting in a 100% revenue interruption.

THE ROLE OF TELECOMMUNICATIONS IN SEAMLESS SOLUTIONS

All long distance carriers have periodic troubles. For example, a client calling a travel agent was told that the travel agency was not doing any business that day because of a major cable cut on their long-distance carrier's network. The client was able to reach the travel agency only because the client used another long-distance carrier that was unaffected by the outage.

In this example, the travel agency lost nearly a full day of business because of the cable cut. However, the fact that one long-distance company experienced problems while another was unaffected suggests that more effective planning might have avoided this loss of business. For example, if the travel agency had diversified its incoming service among several carriers, the likelihood of being isolated during a major failure would have been reduced.

Many long-distance carriers offer service guarantees for incoming 800 service and private-line service. For example, AT&T guarantees that an interruption in 800 service can be redirected to another working number in less than 10 minutes. Similar guarantees are being developed for private-line service. US Sprint has built its network into a series of fault-tolerant fiber optic loops, which provide a measure of protection. Other carriers diversify by using digital radio to back up fiber optic groups, which may be prone to accidental cuts. All of these measures are indicative of long distance carriers' heightened awareness of the importance of telecommunications in the core business operations of their customers. By mixing both telecommunications carriers and services in an optimal configuration, a high level of network reliability and availability can be achieved.

THE BUSINESS RECOVERY CONCEPT

The focus for disaster recovery planning has shifted over time. During the mid-1960s, companies became increasingly dependent on mainframe computers, which resided in carefully controlled environments. All necessary preventive measures were taken to ensure that a disaster never hit these critical operations. Controls included everything from halon fire protection, to no-smoking policies, and water detectors under the floor.

During the early 1980s, telecommunications began to gain importance, particularly after the price of these services dropped following the AT&T divestiture. By the mid- to late 1980s, client-server computing was becoming more widespread, and both auditors and technologists were faced with the migration of mission-critical applications from secure mainframe platforms to relatively unproven client-server environments.

Client-server technology has evolved to become a reliable platform—in some cases, even rivaling mainframes in terms of availability and support. By successfully applying these technologies to core business applications, as illustrated in Exhibit III-9-A, companies have become much more profitable and efficient.

However, these technologies have created new vulnerabilities, particularly in the area of telecommunications. The recovery solutions for these businesses without storefronts must ensure the rapid restoration of all of the services required to complete a sales transaction, including:

- An attendant position (i.e., a place to put employees).
- Connection to some type of automated data processing facility (LAN, mainframe, or both).
- Telecommunications capability for voice and data.

An effective business recovery solution must address all three of these components. Without any one of these three, a company's core business and revenue-earning capability can grind to an abrupt halt. The following sections focus on restoring the critical telecommunications link that turns the people and the automated platforms of the company into revenue generators.

Restoring Incoming 800 Service

Various carriers have invested considerable amounts of marketing expense advertising service guarantees for 800 service. This is probably money well spent, because all businesses recognize the importance of being able to answer incoming calls. Probably the most compelling commercials are those that show offices full of people doing everything except answering the phones. The implied message is that no business can survive this type of disruption.

With planning, switched telephone services of all types, including 800 service, are among the simplest components to back up. For example, as mentioned previously, service guarantees offered by AT&T promise the redirection of any 800 number to any working 10-digit telephone number in North America, within 10 minutes. This service guarantee would allow an organization to redirect calls to another company location, or perhaps, in extreme cases, to employees' homes. Following a disaster, a company might redirect calls to a hotel suite or meeting room. In addition to available space for putting people back to work, hotels often offer fast availability to telecommunications services, because they have large PBXs.

After identifying the possible locations for redirecting critical 800 lines within the company, the business resumption planner can document this information using the form shown in Workpaper III9.1.

Restoring Incoming Telephone Service

Like 800 service, incoming telephone service can be quickly redirected in many cases. Rather than calling the long distance company, however, the request to redirect service is made to the local telephone company, such as Ameritech or Bell South. In a matter of minutes, critical incoming numbers can be redirected to any working 10-digit number. Moreover, many local operating companies even allow for the redirection of direct inward dial (DID) trunks under a special assembly basis. Workpaper III9.2 shows a form that can be used to document the planned redirection of these critical numbers.

Restoring Private Line Service

Unlike incoming 800 service and incoming telephone service, private line circuits, such as T-1s, digital lines, and dedicated data service, can be difficult and complex to restore. Nonetheless, they provide essential access to data bases and ordering systems. Without such access, the company cannot function. For switched services, such as 800 lines and telephone service, a company could probably muddle through, even without documentation, by depending on the telephone company. Of course, this assumes that the disaster is limited to one company, and the telephone company is not busy elsewhere.

For the recovery of private line services, however, planning and coordination are absolutely essential, because these are customized, hard-wired data services that are not easily moved. At a minimum, the business resumption planner should document the circuit number of each private line circuit, as well as its intended use and priority. Workpaper III9.3 can be used to record this information. This information should be reviewed with local and long-distance telephone companies to identify possible solutions for backing up these services.

DAY-TO-DAY PROTECTION

For a communications-intensive business—for example, the businesses without storefronts discussed previously—significant disruptions can occur even in the absence of a dramatic disaster. A cable cut that isolates a network all day might deprive such a company of $\frac{1}{22}$ of its monthly income. Because telephone cable cuts are such a common occurrence, the following sections provide a brief review of various means for protecting against them.

Fiber Optic Cable Cuts (Long Haul)

An example in a previous section of this chapter described a travel agency that was out of business all day because of a cable cut on a fiber optic cable. When selecting a long-distance carrier, a company should evaluate the type of protection that the carrier provides against such occurrences. Workpaper III9.4 is a checklist that can be used as a guide when making inquiries about a long-distance company concerning their contingency plans for handling a major fiber optic cable cut.

Local Cable Cuts

Local telephone cables, commonly referred to as the "last mile," are a frequent source of disruption. These cables often run through metropolitan areas, where construction is ongoing. Construction crews can easily dig up or core through these cables. Workpaper III9.5 is a checklist that can be used for evaluating the local operating company's capability for avoiding such disasters.

Software and Traffic Management Disruptions

In many cases, disruptions to telecommunications systems—particularly switched telephone service—are due, not to hardware failure, but to software or traffic management failure. For example, during a recent four-hour-long disruption, it was difficult to place any type of telephone call in the Dallas metropolitan exchange. This was not caused by a cable cut, a tornado, or a hurricane. Instead, radio announcers had mentioned the availability of tickets for an upcoming concert, and their listeners overloaded the system with calls to the radio stations and the various ticket outlets.

Software failures may also affect the network. Most modern central office switches have an elaborate series of software codes, blocks, and classes of service, which can be difficult to troubleshoot in the event of software failure. In even the most competent local operating companies, the personnel are still more comfortable with telephone test sets than with data scopes. The checklist is Workpaper III9.6 can be used for evaluating the potential for this type of problem.

SUMMARY

Telecommunications should be part of an overall business recovery solution that encompasses the following elements:

- Attendant positions.
- Connection to the data.
- The telecommunications services that transform these elements into revenue generators.

The business resumption planner should carefully evaluate the business and the core services that it offers, paying particular attention to the technical platforms that support these core businesses and provide revenue to the company. In communications-intensive businesses without storefronts, revenue production is impossible without the automated systems. For these companies, continued success, productivity, and profitability depends on effective measures for protecting mission-critical systems.

WORKPAPER III9.01 Priority and Redirection Form for Incoming 800 Service

Call AT&T at ________________ to implement redirection of these numbers. For further information, see Appendix ______.

Number	Department	Use	Priority	Emergency Number

WORKPAPER III9.02 Priority and Rediretion Form for Incoming Telephone Service

Call Southwestern Bell at ____________ to implement call forwarding of these numbers. For further information, see Appendix ______.

Number	Department	Use	Priority	Emergency Number

WORKPAPER III9.03 Priority and Redirection Form for Private-Line Service

Circuit Number	Dept Use	Original Destination	Emergency Destination	Priority
______	______	______	______	______
______	______	______	______	______
______	______	______	______	______
______	______	______	______	______
______	______	______	______	______
______	______	______	______	______

WORKPAPER III9.04 Checklist for Evaluating Fiber Optic-Based Long-Haul Carriers

The following make good discussion topics for your long distance carrier.

1. Does your company employ fault-tolerant ring topology?
2. Is our company on a ring?
3. Is the ring LIT (electronics installed)?
4. Will your company redirect our service in the event of an accidental fiber cut?
5. If so, will you redirect switched service only, or private line service as well?
6. Will such a transfer be a manual patch or automatic?
7. Will we experience network blockage when this happens?
8. If so, how much (what percentage of normal capacity)?
9. Can you, as a carrier, suggest any improvements that can help us?

WORKPAPER III9.05 Checklist for Evaluating Local Access Carriers

The following makes good discussion topics for your local carrier.

1. Does your company employ fault tolerant ring technology?

2. Is our facility on a fiber ring?

3. If we are not served by fiber, can it be economically provided to us?

4. Where is the next nearest central office? Can we get a second path to it?

5. Exactly where do our present facilities run (.eg., by street or side of street)

6. Is this area prone to frequent digging or construction?

7. Can you, as a carrier, suggest any improvements that can help us?

Note:
Providing fiber where none exists can be expensive. Because it is more convenient for the carrier, however, many carriers have provided it free to companies expecting significant growth. If a company expects significant growth, the carrier should be informed, and the company should request a fault-tolerant ring, if the carrier plans to install fiber.

WORKPAPER III9.06 Software and Traffic Management Disruptions

1. Do users frequently hear "all circuits are busy" recordings on local calls.

2. Do users frequently hear "all circuits are busy" recordings on long-distance calls.

3. Do callers frequently report hearing rapid busy signals?

4. Are problems encountered calling specific prefixes or area codes?

Performing a Business Impact Analysis

CHAPTER III-10

WHAT IS A BUSINESS IMPACT ANALYSIS?

The Business Impact Analysis, or BIA, is probably the most important component of a recovery project. It defines and quantifies all the reasons for going through the trouble of producing a Business Resumption Plan. More importantly, the more factual, understandable, and informative your BIA is, the better the chances are of success. If BIA clearly communicates to executive management the vulnerabilities of the systems, there is a better chance of winning endorsement, support, and funding from higher-ups. The specifics of conducting a hard-hitting BIA meets this objective and allows for a fast-track approach to a successful project completion follow.

CONDUCT A BUSINESS DYNAMICS OVERVIEW

A preliminary business impact analysis of core businesses and processes is helpful in directing efforts to the most meaningful areas. It is "preliminary," since there usually isn't time for a detailed business-process analysis. This first phase should take no more than a month. A detailed business analysis can take six months or more by the most expensive outside consultants in the business. Nonetheless, within one month you should be able to draw some interesting conclusions about a business and its ability to withstand service disruptions. In the process, management will understand the relationship between technical disruptions and lost business vividly enough to earn their support and buy-in. Here's how.

Exhibit III-10-A compares the resistance to disruptions of the parent company with that of its two subsidiaries — a heavy-manufacturing company and a real estate company. It includes a few assumptions:

- The parent company is ABC Polymers, Inc., a specialty films company whose primary business is making bags for snack foods.
- The company also has two other kinds of businesses — a snack-food company (a natural outgrowth of the core business) and a second, more speculative venture, ABC Real Estate Investments, Inc.
- ABC Real Estate Investments Inc. invests money and collects rents for the parent company.

The graph illustrates how quickly the daily revenues of each of the company's business lines declines in the event of a major disruption.

The snack-food supplier loses most of its revenue after the first day because in a commodity market, a customer orders from a competitor almost immediately. It is difficult for this company to recover lost customers, since with a profit margin of next-to-nothing there is little room to discount the product or make other concessions. This company would be in the most serious trouble after a disaster.

The subsidiary involved in real-estate ventures is also in trouble, but not as serious as the snack-food supplier. Most people pay their rent monthly; therefore, unless a disaster occurred on the last day of the month (thus preventing cash

EXHIBIT III-10-A DYNAMICS OF ABC POLYMERS INC.

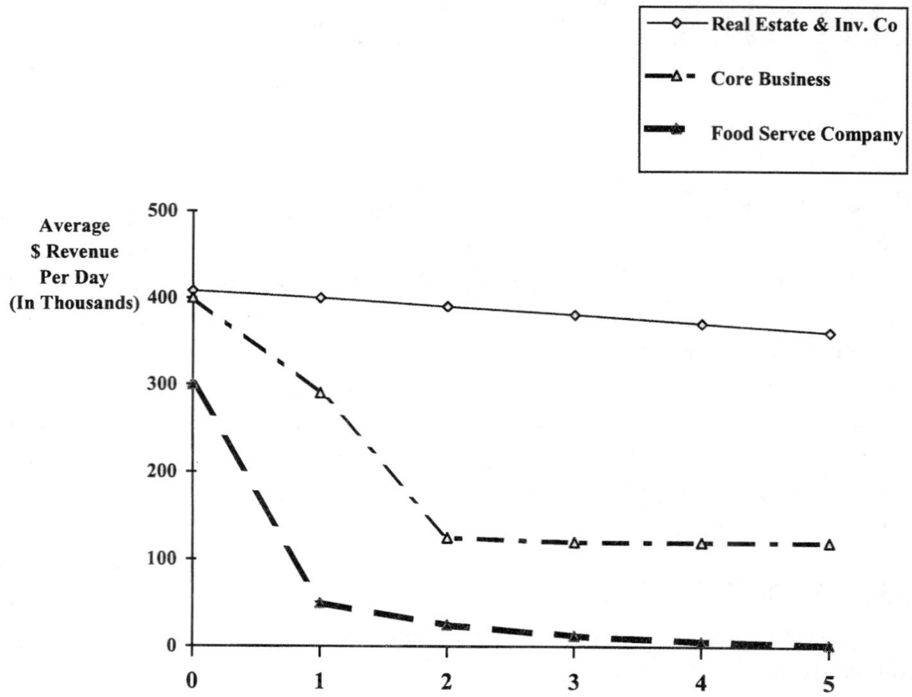

Revenue = $354,706,000 per year
Business Days = 320
Daily Revenue = $1,108,000

Other Issues: Lost Productivity
Lost Market Share
Lost Customer Confidence

Number of Idled Employees in Total Outage: 1000

posting) the effect would be nominal (if the system were back up by posting time). This is not to say that these folks wouldn't scream if their system was down, but they would nontheless survive.

The situation with ABC Polymers, the core manufacturing company, is more complicated. It has several distinct *classes* of customers. One-third of them buy plastic meat wrap, a product easily obtained on day one from other suppliers.

Another third of its customer base are "aligned distributors" who *could* order elsewhere, but would probably wait a few days longer since the company holds them with a lucrative commission or bonus structure. This particular customer mix produced the center line showing a significant, but less immediate revenue loss.

The last third of the customer base orders specialized or customized products that no other company makes. It would be too time consuming for the customer to find a new supplier to transfer complex graphics used for bag labels to a competitor.

They are stuck, and their ultimate success depends on how quickly ABC Polymers gets back in business. These monopoly customers staked their business fortunes on the company and were the ones who were most severely let down. In the words of one executive in a similar business, "They are the hardest to lose, but the hardest to get back if you ever do." This is the scenario of a major disaster with ABC Polymers Inc. core manufacturing:

- Non-exclusive customers (one-third of the business) bail out day one.
- Exclusive customers (another one-third) jump ship day three.
- Monopoly customers (the last one-third) take days to leave, but years to get back.

What kinds of companies have the shallowest graphs? These include companies with a high rate of word-of-mouth referrals, those perceived to offer really good deals, such as discount airlines. Imagine a family getting ready to fly to Disneyland, and the airfare is $850 per person. A reputable air carrier starts a fare war by putting the same seats up for $99 each way. Chances are that if the carrier is perceived to be equal in safety and comfort, the ticket buyer will wait on hold for a long time to make reservations and will even try again tomorrow. Other kinds of businesses, like limited buying service companies, also fall into this category. These companies serve a clientele who have often paid a fee to join or were referred by a friend. Personal referrals are perceived by potential customers as inside tips on a good deal. Users who believe they are getting a good deal are more persistent and more tolerant of waits. Indeed, for many companies in this category, when customers haven't been serviced in a timely fashion because of major call influxes or other reasons, there was no immediate reduction in sales.

So who has the steepest curve on the graph? Since most people are gun-shy with their money, banks are high on the list, brokerage houses maybe even more so. If your broker is out of service and you absolutely must make a trade today, you will call a competitor no matter how good a relationship you have with your present broker. Other companies with steep curves include catalog-sales organizations, television networks, and the like, particularly those geared to impulse sales. Nobody calls back tomorrow to make an impulse purchase.

ASSESS THE EFFECTS OF INTERRUPTION ON CASH FLOW

It's a good idea to present another important topic — to the organization the ability to post cash. Again, a detailed financial analysis will not be possible in a one-month timeframe, but a preliminary examination should reveal major concerns.

As stated earlier, some companies (such as home-shopping clubs) depend on a very rapid turnover of working capital in order to remain viable. Others enjoy longer timeframes because of the nature of their product or service, or because of their financial stability being more simple than that of more leveraged companies. These companies could probably weather interruptions better than most. Consider the effects of losing interest or "float" on money for the duration of an outage.

As illustrated in Exhibit III-10-B, ABC Polymers has little cause for alarm, however, the issue cannot be disregarded.

INTERRUPTION IN THE CUSTOMER SERVICES FUNCTION

Where do customers go for post-sale support? Obviously, to customer service. Again, the level of support required varies widely among companies. Assume that ABC Polymers enjoys a loyal clientele who, in almost all cases, has already paid for

EXHIBIT III-10-B FAILURE WHICH PREVENTS CASH POSTING (EXAMPLE: PARENT COMPANY/CORE BUSINESS)

YEARLY REVENUE	$ 128 Million
BUSINESS DAYS / YEAR	320
AVERAGE CASH POSTED /DAY	approx. $ 4 Million
DAILY "FLOAT" (Get from controller)	$ 3.1 Million
COST IN INTEREST (6%) PER DAY	$ 600.00

CONCLUSION:

"No Big Deal." Only a prolonged outage creates real problems in terms of cash posting.

products. Therefore, the interruption in cash flow from a limited outage is minimal. The important consideration is customer confidence and perception. Jeopardizing ABC Polymer's reputation for reliability is probably much worse than any financial hit. Some of its customers may have been considering implementing a "JIT" or Just-in-Time delivery system. This would be good for ABC, since becoming an integral part of its customers' production system is great for building customer loyalty. It's a good deal for customers too, since its inventory costs would be much lower. The catch for them is that a disaster for ABC Polymers becomes their disaster too, since ABC Polymer is now part of their production process.

DISASTER IN THE ABC POLYMERS FOOD SERVICE DIVISION OR OTHER SUBSIDIARIES

The client bases of the subsidiaries are slightly less loyal, particularly in the foods division, which has significantly more competitive pressure and special considerations associated with managing multiple retail operations. The subsidiaries also have processes and requirements that don't apply to the core business.

For the following reasons, ABC Polymers must make extra contingency plans for its subsidiaries:

- Smirching highly visible disaster in a subsidiary company would smirch the name of its well-regarded parent company.
- In almost all cases, the subsidiaries will have different recovery requirements from the parent company.
- The subsidiary companies, which are often newer or more speculative, may be least able to finance improvements.

Manhours of Outage

Another valuable measurement of loss is manhours of outage. Once again, this varies widely between companies and subsidiaries. Reliable estimates are necessary. Estimates of the costs of certain types of outages can be based on loaded personnel costs (Human Resources has them; see Exhibits III-10-A through C). Manhours of

EXHIBIT III-10-C MANHOURS OF OUTAGE (MHOO) - PARENT COMPANY IN TERMS OF AVERAGE LOADED PERSONNEL COST

(Selected Examples)

COMPONENT	DURATION IN HOURS	USERS AFFECTED	AVG MHOO COST	RPN
MAJOR ROUTER FAILURE	8	650	$26,000	320 - 480
LOCAL ROUTER FAILURE	4	200	$2,600	40 - 480
MAIN PHONE SWITCH FAILURE	8	800	$12,000	60 - 240
LAN RING FAILURE	8	50	$180	24 - 48
MAU FAILURE	8	8	$103	96 - 160
TOTAL BUILDING DISASTER / EVACUATION	40	1000	$80,000	120 - 200

* Assumes Average Loaded Personnel Cost Of $100.00 Per Day (given by Human Resources)

** RPN = Rating Probability Number, derived from FMEA (Failure Mode Effects Analysis) described later.

EXHIBIT III-10-D MANHOURS OF OUTAGE (MHOO) - REAL ESTATE COMPANY IN TERMS OF AVERAGE LOADED PERSONNEL COST

(Selected Examples)

COMPONENT	DURATION IN HOURS	USERS AFFECTED	AVG MHOO COST	RPN
MAJOR ROUTER FAILURE	8	108	$5,189	320 - 480
LOCAL ROUTER FAILURE	4	34	$530	40 - 480
MAIN PHONE SWITCH FAILURE	8	134	$2,412	60 - 240
LAN RING FAILURE	8	9	$40	24 - 48
MAU FAILURE	8	8	$155	96 - 160
TOTAL BUILDING DISASTER / EVACUATION	40	125	$12,000	120 - 200

* Assumes Average Loaded Personnel Cost Of $120.00 Per Day (given by Human Resources)

** RPN = Rating Probability Number, derived from FMEA (Failure Mode Effects Analysis) described later.

outage is intended as a high-level estimate of the lost productivity of network outages based on selected components. The estimate is also very useful as a preliminary stab at the cost of an outage, especially when presented in a group setting.

The bottom line is that due to the nature of its business, ABC Polymers appears more able than most companies to tolerate a protracted network outage. However, considering the business dynamics between divisions, careful scrutiny *by business unit* is advised. The next section is designed to foster such scrutiny in the context of ABC Polymer's diverse core business operations.

EXHIBIT III-10-E MANHOURS OF OUTAGE (MHOO) - SNACK FOOD COMPANY IN TERMS OF AVERAGE LOADED PERSONNEL COST

(Selected Examples)

COMPONENT	DURATION IN HOURS	USERS AFFECTED	AVG MHOO COST	RPN
MAJOR ROUTER FAILURE	8	163	$8,476	320 - 480
LOCAL ROUTER FAILURE	4	50	$520	40 - 480
MAIN PHONE SWITCH FAILURE	8	200	$3,900	60 - 240
LAN RING FAILURE	8	13	$61	24 - 48
MAU FAILURE	8	8	$135	96 - 160
TOTAL BUILDING DISASTER / EVACUATION	40	250	$26,000	120 - 200

* Assumes Average Loaded Personnel Cost Of $130.00 Per Day (given by Human Resources)

* * RPN = Rating Probability Number, derived from FMEA (Failure Mode Effects Analysis) described later.

Evaluating Vulnerability Analysis by Line of Business

How does one present something as complex as a business vulnerability analysis, not only to peers, but to competing interests in the typical large corporation? Exhibit III-10-F illustrates the technical criteria which can be used for the network vulnerability assessment.

The remaining Exhibits in this chapter, deal with specific business dynamics by business division, with ABC Polymers, Inc. and its subsidiaries as an example. Each of the business division is illustrated with diagrams dealing with three issues: focus, dynamics, and cost/benefit.

- The "**Focus**" diagram depicts high-level issues and a business overview
- The "**Dynamics**" diagram, as described earlier, is designed to show how long the business could operate in the event of a disruption of a major automated system.
- A **Cost/Benefit** diagram represents the line of business need compared to its perceived benefit.

Some business divisions have additional diagrams to emphsize additional points, as will be seen in our examples.

Let us begin by looking at the parent company/core business of ABC Polymers Inc. The Focus diagram (Exhibit III-10-G) and the Dynamics diagram (Exhibit III-10-H) are relatively self explanatory.

With the ABC Polymers, Inc. parent company, we have included a diagram depicting the cost of executive complaints (see Exhibit III-10-I), is appropriate here to emphsize that complaints due to a disrupted system can be far-reaching and some of the costs are not easily quantified.

Finally, we want to include the Cost/Benefit diagrams. These diagrams appear in black and white but should be color-coded in your presentation slides to illustrate and emphasize the relative cost based on the associated risks to the components in the environment. An example is provided in Exhibit III-10-J.

Where the risk is high and the costs are very low, the decision to protect against exposures requires little thought. These are indicated by medium shading. However,

EXHIBIT **III-10-F** EVALUATION CRITERIA FOR NETWORK VULNERABILITY

High Risk	Moderate Risk	Low Risk	Low-No Risk
No alternate site or connection available No planned action to fall back on after failure	No alternate site or connection available, but recovery on site is possible	Alternate location is available to recover quickly	No alternate site is needed to recover
Impacts Greater than 75% Total Network	Impact on Total Network is Greater than 50% but less than 75%	Impact on Total Network is between 25-50%	Impact on Total Network is less than 25%
High Probability of Event or Failure (.8-1.0)	Moderate Probability of Failure (.5-.8)	Low Probability of Failure (.25-.5)	Unlikely Probability of Failure (0-.25)
No spares on site or within immediate access recovery takes greater than one hour	Spares within local area and available within 1 hour	Spares on site, technician on site	Spares on hand, hot swappable and total redundancy available
Affects an entire core business function or a whole building (>200 users)	Affects less than 50% of an entire core business function (40-200 users)	Affects only a small portion of a core business function (30-40 users)	Affects a few users (7-10 users)
High Cost of Replacement or protection ($100K +)	Costs are moderate to high ($50-100K)	Costs are minimal ($25-50K)	Costs are considered petty or no costs involved ($0-25K)
High impact on Users. Users cannot access network or host.	Impact on Users is moderate	Impact on users is hardly noticed. Recovery is within minutes (10-15)	Impact is minor, recovery is automatic
Users Screaming, all work has ceased	Users Call to report outage	Users mention it casually	Users never knew it happened
Entire Building is out of service with longer term recovery required	One floor is out of service	Two or more beams are out, but not a whole bay	Less than one beam is affected

where the risk is low and the costs are high to very high, it is unlikely that the business line would want to go through with the action. These areas are indicated by dark shading. The bulk of the areas — those with moderate costs and moderate risks — are the ones worthy of further discussion. These are indicated by light shading.

Data for the Cost/Benefit diagram(s) is based on results of the yet-to-be introduced FMEA, (That's Failure Mode Effects Analysis run chiefly on the equipment) the business impact analysis, face-to-face interviews, and the opinions of the project manager.

For ABC, our parent company, we have opted to include multiple Cost/Benefit diagrams broken down by various systems and other considerations. See Exhibits III-10-K through N.

Moving on to the Food Services subsidiary of ABC Polymers Inc., we generate a Focus diagram and a Dynamics diagram (Exhibits III-10-O and P), two of the three "standards".

By now, these two diagrams will probably look familiar. We then insert two additional diagrams (see Exhibits III-10-Q and R) to emphasize the Food Services company's dependence/relationship with suppliers and strategic partners around the nation.

Depending on the type of company a business is in, the diagrams can be very enlightening. Some companies are extremely dependent on outside suppliers or other strategic partners. Where are those partners located? How reliable are they? What if one of them just "went away"? How would the company be affected?

Next, the Food Services company will have its own set of Cost/Benefit diagrams (see Exhibits III-10-S through V).

EXHIBIT III-10-G FOCUS ON ABC POLYMERS INC. PARENT COMPANY/CORE BUSINESS

- Answers All New Customer Inquiries - 95% of All First Time Inquiries Call In To Call Center in Home Office Complex.
- Well Known In Industry - 70 Year Old Company
- Perceived by Customers as Reliable, and As Good Value
- Number of Sales (1997)
  -- Primary 121,011
  -- Cross Sales 22,005
- Average Sale = $895
- 1997 Incoming Calls (Includes Fax) = 151,684 (95% of Orders)
- 1997 Incoming Mail = 7,983 (5% of Orders)
- Customers Demand Timely Customer Service - 90/10 Rule with 3% Abandon Rate
- Backup System Exists for Short Outages - Paper
- Technology: Centralized Mainframe Now - Going to PC's
- "JIT" (Just In Time) Environment for Select Customers
- Increasingly Astute End User W/Regard to Technology -- Developing Internal Support
- Lines Blurring Between Core Business Operation and Technology

Although these may look identical to the earlier Cost/Benefit diagrams for the parent company, look closer. The shading has changed. That's because each Division's level of need and willingness to pay will be different, based on the Focus and Dynamics of that particular company. Compare these diagrams with thsoe presented previously for the parent company and you will see what we mean.

Finally, let's look at the Real Estate subsidiary. Again, you will see the Focus and Dynamics diagrams. (See Exhibits III-10-W and X). Don't be tempted to skip over these.

Remember, these are the foundation for determining which of the recommendations on you Cost/Benefit diagrams (see Exhibits III-10-Y through BB) should be addressed first. Again, compare the shading on this last set of Cost/Benefits diagrams with the previous two sets to see what we mean.

Once again, please bear in mind that all of these graphics are estimates. In order to keep the project on track, it will not be possible to do a detailed business-impact analysis in most cases. Still, this does not mean the information should be unreliable, just not as detailed as one would like optimally. It is possible to save some time and not sacrifice quality. For example, most of the money figures could come from business-line financial controllers, since they are in a position to know, and generally give straightforward answers. Operational capabilities for the most

EXHIBIT III-10-H DYNAMICS OF ABC POLYMERS INC., PARENT COMPANY/CORE BUSINESS

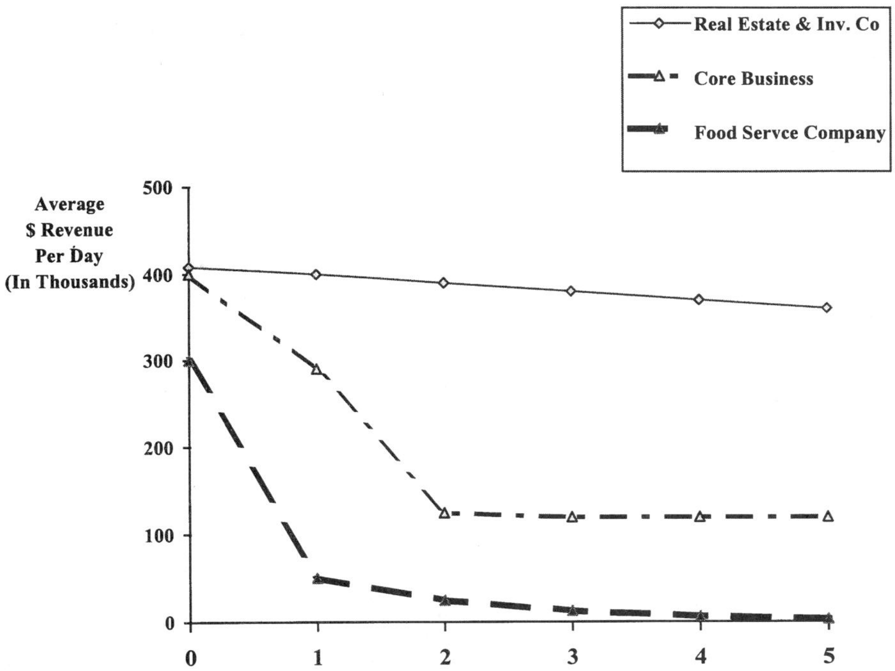

Revenue = 143,016 Sales x $895 = $127,999,320
Business Days = 320
Daily Revenue = $399,997

Other Issues: Lost Productivity
Lost Market Share
Lost Customer Confidence

Number of Idled Employees in Total Outage: 550

part should come from the AVP or VP level, in order to provide both a core business and technical perspective.

The slides that you produce from these diagrams will be the cornerstone of your executive presentations for support and funding as well as the catalyst to discussion and technological planning.

A QUICK REVIEW

As outlined earlier in this section, the diagrams illustrate the example technical recommendations we used for the network vulnerability assessment, according to each line of business, with specific business dynamics considered.

Each business line is illustrated by at least three diagrams (slides):

1. A "Focus" diagram showing high-level issues and a business overview
2. A "Dynamics" diagram showing how long the business could operate in a major network failure

EXHIBIT III-10-I WHAT DO EXECUTIVE COMPLAINTS COST ABC?

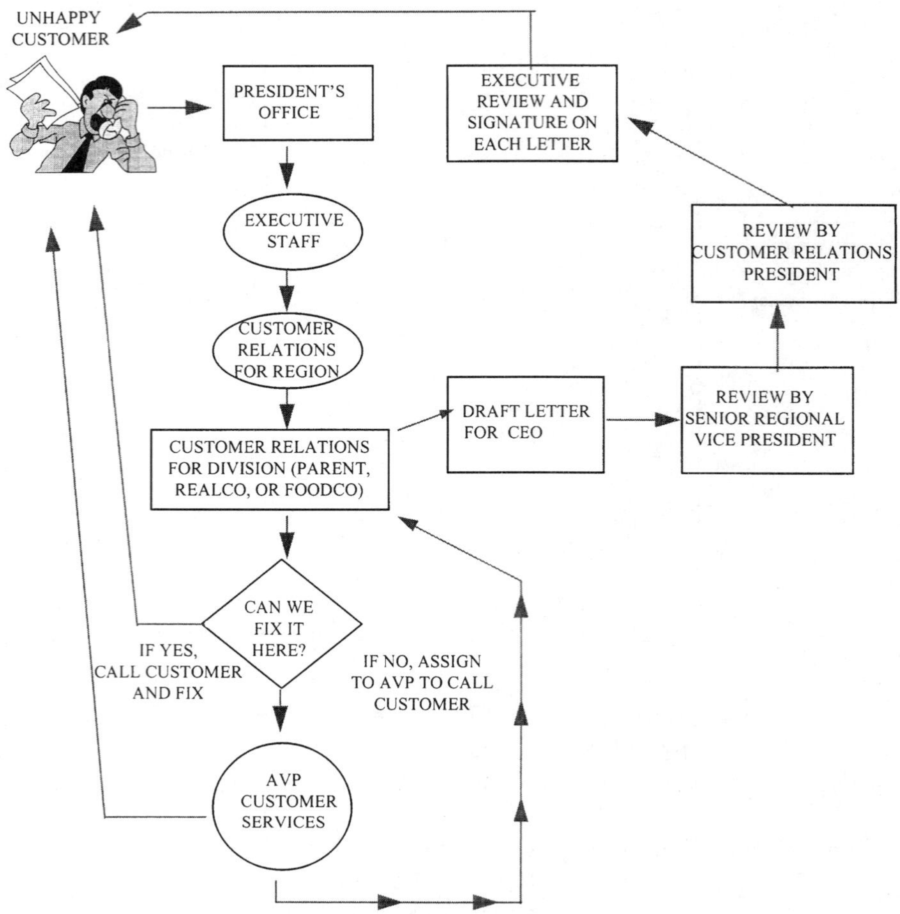

ISSUES:

- ✓ COMPLAINTS ARE COSTLY - $300 to $800 in personnel costs to process each.
- ✓ COMPLAINTS DAMAGE CUSTOMER CONFIDENCE AND TRUST.
- ✓ BESIDES ALL THIS, WE COULD LOSE THE CUSTOMER!
- ✓ Source: Office of the President, senior staffer

3. A Cost'/Benefit diagram designed to represent the line of business need compared to its perceived benefit.

These diagrams are to illustrate the relative cost/benefit by business unit. Data is based on results of the FMEA (described later in this supplement), the business impact analysis, face-to-face interviews, and the opinion of the consultant.

There are additional diagrams for a few business lines; for example, what an executive complaint costs, and how to illustrate alliance partners in order to paint a more complete picture.

The tables at the end of each business-impact section show the relative cost based on the associated risks to the components in the nevironment.

EXHIBIT III-10-J TECHNOLOGY COST VS. NEED, BY BUSINESS DIVISION

COSTS $				
Very High	MEDIUM	SHADING MEANS PROBABLY	UNIT WON'T DO IT	
High				
Moderate		LIGHT SHADING MAY	MEANS UNIT DO IT	
Low				
Very Low / None			DARK SHADING MUST DO IT.	MEANS UNIT
Exposure	Very Low / None	Low	Moderate	High

EXHIBIT III-10-K OVERVIEW OF EXPOSURE IN TERMS OF COST BENEFIT: CORE BUSINESS NETWORK SYSTEMS

COSTS $				
Very High	Want to eliminate all possibility of cable failure? Rewire the whole building and run two cables to each workstation.	Move all servers to a computer room environment.	Arrange for duplicate access facilities from the telephone company.	Duplicate all power supplies and logic cards for all Routers to prevent single point of failure.
High	Keep the same wiring, but run a second wire to all users.	Duplicate only main fiber and cable runs.	Replace or duplicate all MAUs with managed MAUs to prevent beaconing from taking down entire rings	Install new, comprehensive network management system for a "Johnson Space Center" level of command and control.
Moderate	Duplicate wiring to the bay areas only, run single threaded out to workstations.	Install water detectors in cable shafts near restrooms	Duplicate power cards, logic cards and software in company's Internet firewall server.	Duplicate 64Kb circuits to all outlying regional offices.
Low		Install more pay telephones on site in case of a major C.O. failure.	Train users and develop standards.	Change Routers to accommodate dual porting for mission critical applications.
Very Low / None			Keep spare parts on site by all manufacturers for Router cards, switch cards and hub cards	Change and monitor passwords on network routers and issue separate passwords to users. Keep a log of all major changes.
Exposure	Very Low / None	Low	Moderate	High

EXHIBIT III-10-L OVERVIEW OF EXPOSURE IN TERMS OF COST BENEFIT: CORE BUSINESS EQUIPMENT SYSTEMS

COSTS $				
Very High	Install 22 gage cable to overcome distance limitations and allow greater intermixing of service.		Relocate furnace equipment which backs up to interface room.	Rehome all station-side cable which presently is single-threaded through the PBX distribution frame.
High	Upgrade Cisco 4000's to 5000/6000 "Ultra" series to provide redundant power, CPU and logic.	Rehome 50% of incoming "800" service to a second "Class-1" CO outside Dallas.	Install dry-pipe sprinkler system in transmission services room.	Install a Network Management System for the WAN, including SNMP "hooks" to read network (SONET) data from circuit providers.
Moderate	Install a development / test firewall, duplicate firewall WAN connections, and increase manpower.	Install power failure rollover phones for supervisors in all critical work areas.	Eliminate or re-route water pipes in interface rooms.	Install backup AC rectifier power AT&T G3 switches in switch room, etc.
Low	Firm up responsibilities for security between mid-range and firewall groups.	Install a backup circuit to ADVANTIS.		Install -48V battery backup power for DACS and SONET equipment in transmission services.
Very Low / None	Install additional pay telephones. Keep supply of quarters on hand.	Keep extra cellular phone batteries on hand. Add procedures for utilizing two way radio in major system failures.	Install emergency "1FB" lines on copper facilities in strategic equipment and command areas.	Organize and document contingency procedures for dealing with major network and system failures, including rerouting, recordings, response teams, etc. Document and test.
Exposure	Very Low / None	Low	Moderate	High

EXHIBIT III-10-M OVERVIEW OF EXPOSURE IN TERMS OF COST BENEFIT: CORE BUSINESS DOCUMENTATION AND POLICY CONSIDERATIONS

COSTS $				
Very High		Standardize equipment and software inventory lists. Import into formal procedures.	Object link critical databases to formal emergency procedures to aid in updates and changes.	Develop a list of operating and security standards for all network services.
High				Define recovery team leaders and members. Organize groups concerned with recovery, restoration, salvage operations and other players.
Moderate			Implement a new HR policy to notify Network Services of terminations in order to cancel dial-in access.	Document scripted "First-Alert" procedures to get word of system wide disruptions out quickly. Must not be solely dependent on the phone.
Low		Institute policy requiring key vendors to provide monthly escalation lists on magnetic media.	Install a low power AM radio broadcast station and post signs alerting employees of the frequency.	Equip a pre-arranged EXECUTIVE MANAGEMENT TEAM (EMT) location and publish the number in company directory.
Very Low / None		Install a dial-in service to provide emergency info to employees and to aid in command and control.	Assemble listing of all cellular phones. Distinguish users not authorized for cell phone use in a major emergency.	Script and standardize home call-out information. Train personnel. Test procedures including introduction of complications, such as key personnel lost.
Exposure	Very Low / None	Low	Moderate	High

EXHIBIT III-10-N OVERVIEW OF EXPOSURE IN TERMS OF COST BENEFIT: CORE BUSINESS WORKSTATION AND PC CONSIDERATIONS

COMPLEXITY				
Very High		Review and document all Help Desk support and escalation procedures	Move all servers to hardened site for security and control	Form high level LAN Standards Committee
High		Strengthen procedures for physical inventory of equipment	Document a formal process for PC rollout which can be standardized and duplicated	Appoint and document an interdepartmental "Change Control Czar" or Configuration Board to approve all changes
Moderate	Identify and document applications slated for operating system conversion	Strengthen performance/availability management systems	Refine Client/Server System certification and test process	Establish a separate Help Desk number for standardized production (revenue impacting) workers
Low			Document and clarify high level responsibility for PC rollout	Revisit PC rollout schedule for 1997/98 -- Document a sustainable deployment rate
Very Low / None	Establish vendor arrangement for on-site depot or storage of servers and parts	Verify problem tracking systems for informal floor support	Implement a procedure for disposal of transitioned PCs and equipment (proprietary data)	Eliminate PC software acquisitions through informal channels
Exposure	Very Low / None	Low	Moderate	High

The tables at the end of each business-impact section show the relative cost based on the associated risks to the components in the nevironment.

- Where the risk is high and the costs are very low, the decision to protect against exposures requires little thought. These are indicated by the medium shading. For example, "Keep spare parts on site by all manufacturers for router cards, switch cards, and hub cards" and "Change and monitor passwords on network routers and issue separate passwords to users. Keep a log of all major changes."
- However, where the risk is low and the costs are high to very high, it is unlikely that the business line would want to go through with the action. These areas are indicated by the dark shading. These are considerations which will probably never be acted upon unless in combination with another project in order to mitigate the cost. Things like: "Want to eliminate all possibility of cable failure? Rewire the whole building and run two cables to each workstation."
- The bulk of the costs in the moderate range and the moderate risk areas are the ones worthy of further discussion. These are indicated by the medium shading. These are "Let's talk about it" alternatives, like: "Replace or duplicate all MAUs with managed MAUs to prevent beaconing from taking-down entire rings" or "Install water detectors in cable shafts near restrooms."

The recommendations are the same for each diagram. Only the shade of grey changes in order to represent the business line's level of need and willingness to pay.

Once again, please bear in mind that the numbers in the example slides are estimated, but well-scrubbed estimates. Most of the money figures for the examples should come from business line financial controllers, and operational capabilities

EXHIBIT III-10-O FOCUS ON ABC POLYMERS INC., SUBSIDIARY/FOOD SERVICE CO.

- Answers All New Customer Inquiries - 95% of All First Time Inquiries Call In To Call Center in Home Office Complex.
- New, Relative Unknown in Industry - 2 Year Old Company
- Number of Sales (1997)
  -- Primary 217,061
  -- Cross Sales 54,266
- Average Sale = $355
- 1997 Incoming Calls (Includes Fax) = 262,780 (95% of Orders)
- 1997 Incoming Mail = 13,830 (5% of Orders)
- Customers Demand Timely Customer Service - 90/10 Rule with 3% Abandon Rate
- Backup System Exists for Short Outages - Paper
- Technology: Centralized Mainframe Now - Going to PC's
- "JIT" (Just In Time) Environment for Select Customers
- Increasingly Astute End User W/Regard to Technology -- Developing Internal Support
- Lines Blurring Between Core Business Operation and Technology
- Dependent on Core Business For Technology Needs
- Known as "Most Demanding" User by Corporate
- Least Able to Pay for Technology Improvements

have for the most part come from the AVP or VP level, in order to provide both a core business and technical perspective.

We believe that these diagrams will serve as a springboard to fruitful discussion and thoughtful technological planning, and help you more accurately present you case to non-technical executives.

EXHIBIT III-10-P DYNAMICS OF ABC POLYMERS INC., FOOD SERVICES SUBSIDIARY

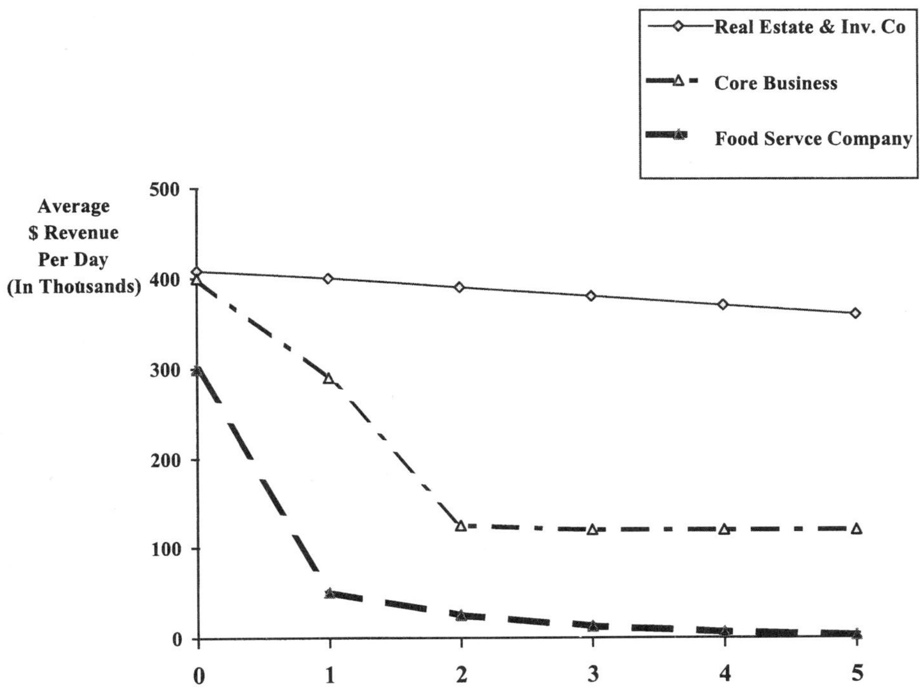

Revenue = 271,327 Sales x $355 = $96,321,085
Business Days = 320
Daily Revenue = $301,003

Other Issues: Lost Productivity
Lost Market Share
Lost Customer Confidence

Number of Idled Employees in Total Outage: 350

EXHIBIT III-10-Q FOOD CO. STRATEGIC VENDOR RELATIONSHIPS

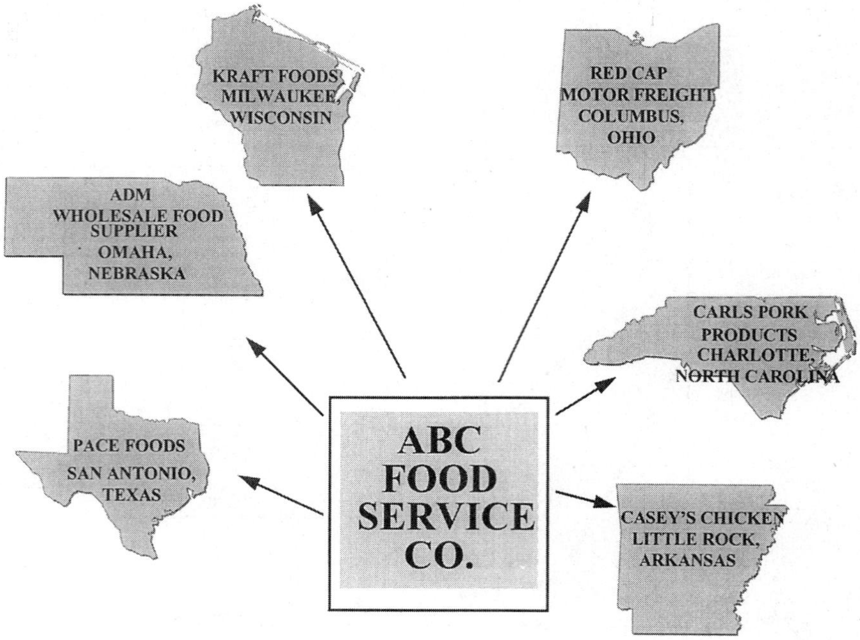

✓ **Dependence on networks (local and wide area) is high.**

EXHIBIT III-10-R ABC POLYMERS CO. CORE BUSINESS (BUSINESS SUPPORT SYSTEMS) ALLIANCE PARTNERS AND DATA SERVICES

Priority	System Name	Use	Delivery	Frequency	Users
Portfolio Management and Trading Activities:					
HIGH	PACE FOODS	Supplier	Satellite	Daily	25
HIGH	ADM	Supplier	Dedicated Telecom	Daily	50
HIGH	KRAFT	Supplier	Dedicated Telecom	Daily	50
MED	RED CAP MOTOR FREIGHT	Transportation Scheduling	Dial-Up Telecom	Daily	25
MED	KARL'S PORK	Specialty Orders	Dial-Up Telecom (ISDN)	Weekly	10
LOW	CASEY's CHICKEN	Holiday Products	Dial-Up Telecom (Analog)	Only at Thanksgiving	20
	"ETC"				

EXHIBIT III-10-S OVERVIEW OF EXPOSURE IN TERMS OF COST BENEFIT: FOOD SERVICE SUBSIDIARY NETWORK SYSTEMS

COSTS $				
Very High	Want to eliminate all possibility of cable failure? Rewire the whole building and run two cables to each workstation.	Move all servers to a computer room environment.	Arrange for duplicate access facilities from the telephone company.	Duplicate all power supplies and logic cards for all Routers to prevent single point of failure.
High	Keep the same wiring, but run a second wire to all users.	Duplicate only main fiber and cable runs.	Replace or duplicate all MAUs with managed MAUs to prevent beaconing from taking down entire rings	Install new, comprehensive network management system for a "Johnson Space Center" level of command and control.
Moderate	Duplicate wiring to the bay areas only, run single threaded out to workstations.	Install water detectors in cable shafts near restrooms	Duplicate power cards, logic cards and software in company's Internet firewall server.	Duplicate 64Kb circuits to all outlying regional offices.
Low		Install more pay telephones on site in case of a major C.O. failure.	Train users and develop standards.	Change Routers to accommodate dual porting for mission critical applications.
Very Low / None			Keep spare parts on site by all manufacturers for Router cards, switch cards and hub cards	Change and monitor passwords on network routers and issue separate passwords to users. Keep a log of all major changes.
Exposure	**Very Low / None**	**Low**	**Moderate**	**High**

EXHIBIT III-10-T OVERVIEW OF EXPOSURE IN TERMS OF COST BENEFIT: FOOD SERVICE SUBSIDIARY EQUIPMENT SYSTEMS

COSTS $				
Very High	Install 22 gauge cable to overcome distance limitations and allow greater intermixing of service.		Relocate furnace equipment which backs up to interface room.	Rehome all station-side cable which presently is single-threaded through the PBX distribution frame.
High	Upgrade Cisco 4000's to 5000/6000 "Ultra" series to provide redundant power, CPU and logic.	Rehome 50% of incoming "800" service to a second "Class-1" CO outside Dallas.	Install dry-pipe sprinkler system in transmission services room.	Install a Network Management System for the WAN, including SNMP "hooks" to read network (SONET) data from circuit providers.
Moderate	Install a development / test firewall, duplicate firewall WAN connections, and increase manpower.	Install power failure rollover phones for supervisors in all critical work areas.	Eliminate or re-route water pipes in interface rooms.	Install backup AC rectifier power AT&T G3 switches in switch room, etc.
Low	Firm up responsibilities for security between mid-range and firewall groups.	Install a backup circuit to ADVANTIS.		Install -48V battery backup power for DACS and SONET equipment in transmission services.
Very Low / None	Install additional pay telephones. Keep supply of quarters on hand.	Keep extra cellular phone batteries on hand. Add procedures for utilizing two way radio in major system failures.	Install emergency "1FB" lines on copper facilities in strategic equipment and command areas.	Organize and document contingency procedures for dealing with major network and system failures, including rerouting, recordings, response teams, etc. Document and test.
Exposure	Very Low / None	Low	Moderate	High

EXHIBIT III-10-U OVERVIEW OF EXPOSURE IN TERMS OF COST BENEFIT: FOOD SERVICE DOCUMENTATION AND POLICY CONSIDERATIONS

COSTS $				
Very High		Standardize equipment and software inventory lists. Import into formal procedures.	Object link critical databases to formal emergency procedures to aid in updates and changes.	Develop a list of operating and security standards for all network services.
High				Define recovery team leaders and members. Organize groups concerned with recovery, restoration, salvage operations and other players.
Moderate			Implement a new HR policy to notify Network Services of terminations in order to cancel dial-in access.	Document scripted "First-Alert" procedures to get word of system wide disruptions out quickly. Must not be solely dependent on the phone.
Low		Institute policy requiring key vendors to provide monthly escalation lists on magnetic media.	Install a low power AM radio broadcast station and post signs alerting employees of the frequency.	Equip a pre-arranged EXECUTIVE MANAGEMENT TEAM (EMT) location and publish the number in company directory.
Very Low / None		Install a dial-in service to provide emergency info to employees and to aid in command and control.	Assemble listing of all cellular phones. Distinguish users not authorized for cell phone use in a major emergency.	Script and standardize home call-out information. Train personnel. Test procedures including introduction of complications, such as key personnel lost.
Exposure	Very Low / None	Low	Moderate	High

EXHIBIT III-10-V OVERVIEW OF EXPOSURE IN TERMS OF COST BENEFIT: FOOD SERVICE SUBSIDIARY WORKSTATION AND PC CONSIDERATIONS

COMPLEXITY				
Very High		Review and document all Help Desk support and escalation procedures	Move all servers to hardened site for security and control	Form high level LAN Standards Committee
High		Strengthen procedures for physical inventory of equipment	Document a formal process for PC rollout which can be standardized and duplicated	Appoint and document an interdepartmental "Change Control Czar" or Configuration Board to approve all changes
Moderate	Identify and document applications slated for operating system conversion	Strengthen performance/availability management systems	Refine Client/Server System certification and test process	Establish a separate Help Desk number for standardized production (revenue impacting) workers
Low			Document and clarify high level responsibility for PC rollout	Revisit PC rollout schedule for 1997/98 -- Document a sustainable deployment rate
Very Low / None	Establish vendor arrangement for on-site depot or storage of servers and parts	Verify problem tracking systems for informal floor support	Implement a procedure for disposal of transitioned PCs and equipment (proprietary data)	Eliminate PC software acquisitions through informal channels
Exposure	**Very Low/ None**	**Low**	**Moderate**	**High**

EXHIBIT III-10-W FOCUS ON ABC POLYMERS INC., SUBSIDIARY/REAL ESTATE CO.

- Answers All New Customer Inquiries - 95% of All First Time Inquiries Call In To Call Center in Home Office Complex.
- Little known outside ABC Co. Primarily handles informal investments for ABC parent
- Number of Sales (1997)
  - -- Primary 1,159
  - -- Cross Sales Not Available
- 1997 Incoming Calls (Includes Fax) = 3300 (25% faxes)
- 1997 Incoming Mail = 640
- Backup System Exists for Short Outages - Paper
- Technology: Already on PC's/Mainframe gone
- Increasingly Astute End User W/Regard to Technology -- Developing Internal Support
- Lines Blurring Between Core Business Operation and Technology
- Lots of non-standard, knowledge-based PC users.
- Often creates headaches for Help desk due to non-standard applications.

EXHIBIT III-10-X DYNAMICS OF ABC POLYMERS INC., REAL ESTATE & INVESTMENT CO.

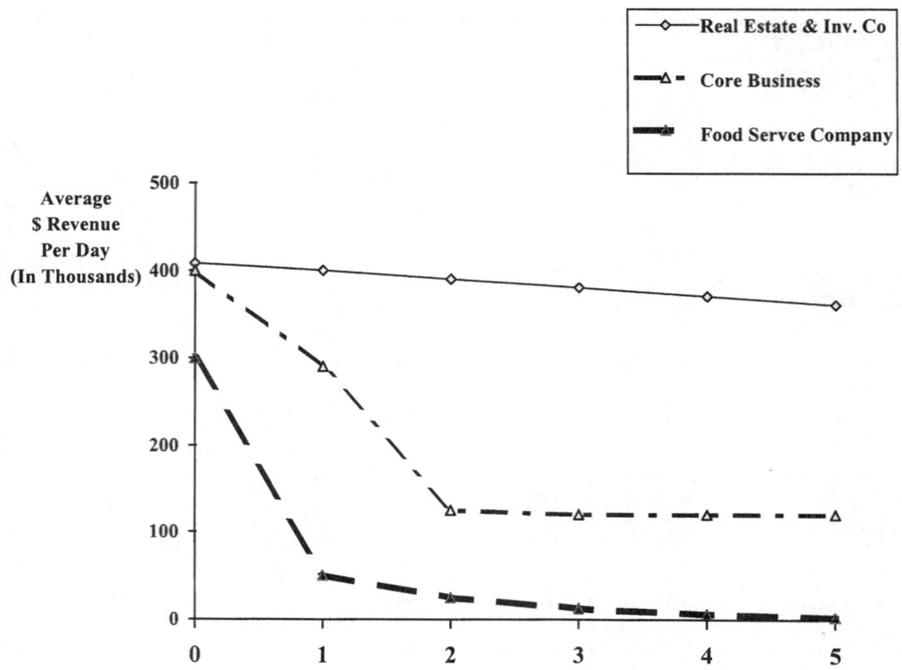

Revenue = 1,159 Sales x $112,894 = $ 130,385,182

Business Days = 320

Daily Revenue = $ 407,453

Other Issues: Lost Productivity
Lost Market Share
Lost Customer Confidence

Number of Idled Employees in Total Outage: 100

EXHIBIT III-10-Y OVERVIEW OF EXPOSURE IN TERMS OF COST BENEFIT: REAL ESTATE & INVESTMENT SUBSIDIARY NETWORK SYSTEMS

COSTS $				
Very High	Want to eliminate all possibility of cable failure? Rewire the whole building and run two cables to each workstation.	Move all servers to a computer room environment.	Arrange for duplicate access facilities from the telephone company.	Duplicate all power supplies and logic cards for all Routers to prevent single point of failure.
High	Keep the same wiring, but run a second wire to all users.	Duplicate only main fiber and cable runs.	Replace or duplicate all MAUs with managed MAUs to prevent beaconing from taking down entire rings	Install new, comprehensive network management system for a "Johnson Space Center" level of command and control.
Moderate	Duplicate wiring to the bay areas only, run single threaded out to workstations.	Install water detectors in cable shafts near restrooms	Duplicate power cards, logic cards and software in company's Internet firewall server.	Duplicate 64Kb circuits to all outlying regional offices.
Low		Install more pay telephones on site in case of a major C.O. failure.	Train users and develop standards.	Change Routers to accommodate dual porting for mission critical applications.
Very Low / None			Keep spare parts on site by all manufacturers for Router cards, switch cards and hub cards	Change and monitor passwords on network routers and issue separate passwords to users. Keep a log of all major changes.
Exposure	Very Low / None	Low	Moderate	High

EXHIBIT III-10-Z OVERVIEW OF EXPOSURE IN TERMS OF COST BENEFIT: REAL ESTATE & INVESTMENT SUBSIDIARY EQUIPMENT SYSTEMS

COSTS $				
Very High	Install 22 gage cable to overcome distance limitations and allow greater intermixing of service.		Relocate furnace equipment which backs up to interface room.	Rehome all station-side cable which presently is single-threaded through the PBX distribution frame.
High	Upgrade Cisco 4000's to 5000/6000 "Ultra" series to provide redundant power, CPU and logic.	Rehome 50% of incoming "800" service to a second "Class-1" CO outside Dallas.	Install dry-pipe sprinkler system in transmission services room.	Install a Network Management System for the WAN, including SNMP "hooks" to read network (SONET) data from circuit providers.
Moderate	Install a development / test firewall, duplicate firewall WAN connections, and increase manpower.	Install power failure rollover phones for supervisors in all critical work areas.	Eliminate or re-route water pipes in interface rooms.	Install backup AC rectifier power AT&T G3 switches in switch room, etc.
Low	Firm up responsibilities for security between mid-range and firewall groups.	Install a backup circuit to ADVANTIS.		Install -48V battery backup power for DACS and SONET equipment in transmission services.
Very Low / None	Install additional pay telephones. Keep supply of quarters on hand.	Keep extra cellular phone batteries on hand. Add procedures for utilizing two way radio in major system failures.	Install emergency "1FB" lines on copper facilities in strategic equipment and command areas.	Organize and document contingency procedures for dealing with major network and system failures, including rerouting, recordings, response teams, etc. Document and test.
Exposure	Very Low / None	Low	Moderate	High

EXHIBIT III-10-AA OVERVIEW OF EXPOSURE IN TERMS OF COST BENEFIT: REAL ESTATE & INVESTMENT SUBSIDIARY DOCUMENTATION AND POLICY CONSIDERATIONS

COSTS $				
Very High		Standardize equipment and software inventory lists. Import into formal procedures.	Object link critical databases to formal emergency procedures to aid in updates and changes.	Develop a list of operating and security standards for all network services.
High				Define recovery team leaders and members. Organize groups concerned with recovery, restoration, salvage operations and other players.
Moderate			Implement a new HR policy to notify Network Services of terminations in order to cancel dial-in access.	Document scripted "First-Alert" procedures to get word of system wide disruptions out quickly. Must not be solely dependent on the phone.
Low		Institute policy requiring key vendors to provide monthly escalation lists on magnetic media.	Install a low power AM radio broadcast station and post signs alerting employees of the frequency.	Equip a pre-arranged EXECUTIVE MANAGEMENT TEAM (EMT) location and publish the number in company directory.
Very Low / None		Install a dial-in service to provide emergency info to employees and to aid in command and control.	Assemble listing of all cellular phones. Distinguish users not authorized for cell phone use in a major emergency.	Script and standardize home call-out information. Train personnel. Test procedures including introduction of complications, such as key personnel lost.
Exposure	Very Low / None	Low	Moderate	High

EXHIBIT III-10-BB OVERVIEW OF EXPOSURE IN TERMS OF COST BENEFIT: REAL ESTATE & INVESTMENT SUBSIDIARY WORKSTATION AND PC CONSIDERATIONS

COMPLEXITY				
Very High		Review and document all Help Desk support and escalation procedures	Move all servers to hardened site for security and control	Form high level LAN Standards Committee
High		Strengthen procedures for physical inventory of equipment	Document a formal process for PC rollout which can be standardized and duplicated	Appoint and document an interdepartmental "Change Control Czar" or Configuration Board to approve all changes
Moderate	Identify and document applications slated for operating system conversion	Strengthen performance/availability management systems	Refine Client/Server System certification and test process	Establish a separate Help Desk number for standardized production (revenue impacting) workers
Low			Document and clarify high level responsibility for PC rollout	Revisit PC rollout schedule for 1997/98 -- Document a sustainable deployment rate
Very Low / None	Establish vendor arrangement for on-site depot or storage of servers and parts	Verify problem tracking systems for informal floor support	Implement a procedure for disposal of transitioned PCs and equipment (proprietary data)	Eliminate PC software acquisitions through informal channels
Exposure	Very Low / None	Low	Moderate	High

WORKPAPER III10.01

FINANCIAL SUMMARY

YEARLY REVENUE	____________
BUSINESS DAYS / YEAR	____________
AVERAGE CASH POSTED PER DAY	____________
DAILY "FLOAT" (Get from controller)	____________
COST IN INTEREST (__%) PER DAY	____________

CONCLUSION: "No Big Deal."

Only a prolonged outage creates real problems in terms of cash posting.

WORKPAPER III10.02 Man Hours of Outage — Mainframe Systems part 1

MAN HOURS OF OUTAGE - MAINFRAME SYSTEMS IN TERMS OF AVERAGE LOADED PERSONNEL COST

COMPONENT	DURATION	USERS AFFECTED	COST	RPN
1. 3745 Processors			$	
2. Channel Extension Equipment			$	
3. Main CPU			$	
4. DASD			$	
list other components below			$	
5.			$	

* Assumes Average Loaded Personnel Cost Of $ ____ Per Hour. (given by Human Resources)

* * RPN = Rating Probability Number, derived from FMEA (Failure Mode Effects Analysis) described later.

WORKPAPER III10.03 Man Hours of Outage — Mainframe Systems part 2

MAN HOURS OF OUTAGE - MAINFRAME SYSTEMS IN TERMS OF AVERAGE LOADED PERSONNEL COST

COMPONENT	DURATION	USERS AFFECTED	COST	RPN
6.			$	
7.			$	
8.			$	
9.			$	
10.			$	
11.			$	

* Assumes Average Loaded Personnel Cost Of $ ____ Per Hour (given by Human Resources)

* * RPN = Rating Probability Number, derived from FMEA (Failure Mode Effects Analysis) described later.

WORKPAPER III10.04 Man Hours of Outage — Mainframe Systems part 3

MAN HOURS OF OUTAGE - MAINFRAME SYSTEMS IN TERMS OF AVERAGE LOADED PERSONNEL COST

COMPONENT	DURATION	USERS AFFECTED	COST	RPN
12.			$	
13.			$	
14.			$	
15.			$	
16.			$	
17.			$	

* Assumes Average Loaded Personnel Cost Of $ ____ Per Hour (given by Human Resources)

* * RPN = Rating Probability Number, derived from FMEA (Failure Mode Effects Analysis) described later.

WORKPAPER III10.05 Man Hours of Outage — Mainframe Systems part 4

MAN HOURS OF OUTAGE - MAINFRAME SYSTEMS IN TERMS OF AVERAGE LOADED PERSONNEL COST

COMPONENT	DURATION	USERS AFFECTED	COST	RPN
18.			$	
19.			$	
20.			$	
21.			$	
22.			$	
23.			$	

* Assumes Average Loaded Personnel Cost Of $ ____ Per Hour (given by Human Resources)

* * RPN = Rating Probability Number, derived from FMEA (Failure Mode Effects Analysis) described later.

WORKPAPER III10.06 Man Hours of Outage — Mainframe Systems part 5

MAN HOURS OF OUTAGE - MAINFRAME SYSTEMS IN TERMS OF AVERAGE LOADED PERSONNEL COST

COMPONENT	DURATION	USERS AFFECTED	COST	RPN
24.			$	
25.			$	
26.			$	
27.			$	
28.			$	
29.			$	

* Assumes Average Loaded Personnel Cost Of $ ____ Per Hour (given by Human Resources)

* * RPN = Rating Probability Number, derived from FMEA (Failure Mode Effects Analysis) described later.

WORKPAPER III10.07 Man Hours of Outage — Telecommunications Systems part 1

MAN HOURS OF OUTAGE - TELECOMMUNICATIONS SYSTEMS IN TERMS OF AVERAGE LOADED PERSONNEL COST

COMPONENT	DURATION	USERS AFFECTED	COST	RPN
1. AT&T POP			$	
2. MCI POP			$	
3. US SPRINT POP			$	
4. Bell Primary CO			$	
5. Bell Local Serving CO			$	
6. MFS CO			$	

* Assumes Average Loaded Personnel Cost Of $ ____ Per Hour, (given by Human Resources)

* * RPN = Rating Probability Number, derived from FMEA (Failure Mode Effects Analysis) described later.

WORKPAPER III10.08 Man Hours of Outage — Telecommunications Systems part 2

MAN HOURS OF OUTAGE - TELECOMMUNICATIONS SYSTEMS IN TERMS OF AVERAGE LOADED PERSONNEL COST

COMPONENT	DURATION	USERS AFFECTED	COST	RPN
7. Teleport CO			$	
8. DACS Equipment			$	
9. SONET / Lightguide Co,			$	
10. Physical Fiber Cable			$	
11. PBX			$	
12. IDNX Multiplexers			$	

* Assumes Average Loaded Personnel Cost Of $ ____ Per Hour (given by Human Resources)

* * RPN = Rating Probability Number, derived from FMEA (Failure Mode Effects Analysis) described later.

WORKPAPER III10.09 Man Hours of Outage — Telecommunications Systems part 3

MAN HOURS OF OUTAGE - TELECOMMUNICATIONS SYSTEMS IN TERMS OF AVERAGE LOADED PERSONNEL COST

COMPONENT	DURATION	USERS AFFECTED	COST	RPN
13. Channel Banks			$	
14. ATM Switches			$	
list other components below			$	
15.			$	
16.			$	
17.			$	

* Assumes Average Loaded Personnel Cost Of $ ____ Per Hour (given by Human Resources)

* * RPN = Rating Probability Number, derived from FMEA (Failure Mode Effects Analysis) described later.

WORKPAPER III10.10 Man Hours of Outage — Telecommunications Systems part 4

MAN HOURS OF OUTAGE - TELECOMMUNICATIONS SYSTEMS IN TERMS OF AVERAGE LOADED PERSONNEL COST

COMPONENT	DURATION	USERS AFFECTED	COST	RPN
18.			$	
19.			$	
20.			$	
21.			$	
22.			$	
23.			$	

* Assumes Average Loaded Personnel Cost Of $ ____ Per Hour (given by Human Resources)

* * RPN = Rating Probability Number, derived from FMEA (Failure Mode Effects Analysis) described later.

WORKPAPER III10.11 Man Hours of Outage — Telecommunications Systems part 5

MAN HOURS OF OUTAGE - TELECOMMUNICATIONS SYSTEMS IN TERMS OF AVERAGE LOADED PERSONNEL COST

COMPONENT	DURATION	USERS AFFECTED	COST	RPN
24.			$	
25.			$	
26.			$	
27.			$	
28.			$	
29.			$	

* Assumes Average Loaded Personnel Cost Of $ ____ Per Hour (given by Human Resources)

* * RPN = Rating Probability Number, derived from FMEA (Failure Mode Effects Analysis) described later.

WORKPAPER III10.12 Man Hours of Outage — LAN Systems part 1

MAN HOURS OF OUTAGE - LOCAL AREA NETWORK SYSTEMS IN TERMS OF AVERAGE LOADED PERSONNEL COST

COMPONENT	DURATION	USERS AFFECTED	COST	RPN
1. Server			$	
2. Backbone Fiber Net			$	
3. Distribution Closets			$	
4. Cable to Desktop			$	
5. NIC Cards			$	
6. Power/Logic - Server			$	

* Assumes Average Loaded Personnel Cost Of $ ____ Per Hour (given by Human Resources)

* * RPN = Rating Probability Number, derived from FMEA (Failure Mode Effects Analysis) described later.

WORKPAPER III10.13 Man Hours of Outage — LAN Systems part 2

MAN HOURS OF OUTAGE - LOCAL AREA NETWORK SYSTEMS IN TERMS OF AVERAGE LOADED PERSONNEL COST

COMPONENT	DURATION	USERS AFFECTED	COST	RPN
7. Power/Logic - Routers			$	
8. Power/Logic - Fiber Mixes			$	
list other components below			$	
9.			$	
10.			$	
11.			$	

* Assumes Average Loaded Personnel Cost Of $ ____ Per Hour (given by Human Resources)

* * RPN = Rating Probability Number, derived from FMEA (Failure Mode Effects Analysis) described later.

WORKPAPER III10.14 Man Hours of Outage — LAN Systems part 3

MAN HOURS OF OUTAGE - LOCAL AREA NETWORK SYSTEMS IN TERMS OF AVERAGE LOADED PERSONNEL COST

COMPONENT	DURATION	USERS AFFECTED	COST	RPN
12.			$	
13.			$	
14.			$	
15.			$	
16.			$	
17.			$	

* Assumes Average Loaded Personnel Cost Of $ ____ Per Hour (given by Human Resources)

* * RPN = Rating Probability Number, derived from FMEA (Failure Mode Effects Analysis) described later.

WORKPAPER III10.15 Man Hours of Outage — LAN Systems part 4

MAN HOURS OF OUTAGE - LOCAL AREA NETWORK SYSTEMS IN TERMS OF AVERAGE LOADED PERSONNEL COST

COMPONENT	DURATION	USERS AFFECTED	COST	RPN
18.			$	
19.			$	
20.			$	
21.			$	
22.			$	
23.			$	

* Assumes Average Loaded Personnel Cost Of $ ____ Per Hour (given by Human Resources)

* * RPN = Rating Probability Number, derived from FMEA (Failure Mode Effects Analysis) described later.

WORKPAPER III10.16 Man Hours of Outage — LAN Systems part 5

MAN HOURS OF OUTAGE - LOCAL AREA NETWORK SYSTEMS IN TERMS OF AVERAGE LOADED PERSONNEL COST

COMPONENT	DURATION	USERS AFFECTED	COST	RPN
24.			$	
25.			$	
26.			$	
27.			$	
28.			$	
29.			$	

* Assumes Average Loaded Personnel Cost Of $ ____ Per Hour (given by Human Resources)

* * RPN = Rating Probability Number, derived from FMEA (Failure Mode Effects Analysis) described later.

WORKPAPER III10.17 Man Hours of Outage — Other Systems part 1

MAN HOURS OF OUTAGE - OTHER SYSTEMS IN TERMS OF AVERAGE LOADED PERSONNEL COST

COMPONENT	DURATION	USERS AFFECTED	COST	RPN
1. UPS			$	
2. Power Distortion Systems			$	
3. Sprinklers			$	
4. Water Detectors			$	
5. Fire/Particle Detectors			$	
6. Cable Risers			$	

* Assumes Average Loaded Personnel Cost Of $ ____ Per Hour (given by Human Resources)

* * RPN = Rating Probability Number, derived from FMEA (Failure Mode Effects Analysis) described later.

WORKPAPER III10.18 Man Hours of Outage — Other Systems part 2

MAN HOURS OF OUTAGE - OTHER SYSTEMS IN TERMS OF AVERAGE LOADED PERSONNEL COST

COMPONENT	DURATION	USERS AFFECTED	COST	RPN
7. Equipment Room - PBX			$	
8. Equipment Room - Server			$	
9. Equipment Room - Mainframe			$	
10. Roof			$	
11. Plumbing/Drainage			$	
12. Access/ Egress			$	

* Assumes Average Loaded Personnel Cost Of $ ____ Per Hour (given by Human Resources)

* * RPN = Rating Probability Number, derived from FMEA (Failure Mode Effects Analysis) described later.

WORKPAPER III10.19 Man Hours of Outage — Other Systems part 3

MAN HOURS OF OUTAGE - OTHER SYSTEMS IN TERMS OF AVERAGE LOADED PERSONNEL COST

COMPONENT	DURATION	USERS AFFECTED	COST	RPN
13. Accessibility to People			$	
list other considerations below			$	
14.			$	
15.			$	
16.			$	
17.			$	

* Assumes Average Loaded Personnel Cost Of $ ____ Per Hour (given by Human Resources)

* * RPN = Rating Probability Number, derived from FMEA (Failure Mode Effects Analysis) described later.

WORKPAPER III10.20 Man Hours of Outage — Other Systems part 4

MAN HOURS OF OUTAGE - OTHER SYSTEMS IN TERMS OF AVERAGE LOADED PERSONNEL COST

COMPONENT	DURATION	USERS AFFECTED	COST	RPN
18.			$	
19.			$	
20.			$	
21.			$	
22.			$	
23.			$	

* Assumes Average Loaded Personnel Cost Of $ ____ Per Hour, (given by Human Resources)

* * RPN = Rating Probability Number, derived from FMEA (Failure Mode Effects Analysis) described later.

WORKPAPER III10.21 Man Hours of Outage — Other Systems part 5

MAN HOURS OF OUTAGE - OTHER SYSTEMS IN TERMS OF AVERAGE LOADED PERSONNEL COST

COMPONENT	DURATION	USERS AFFECTED	COST	RPN
24.			$	
25.			$	
26.			$	
27.			$	
28.			$	
29.			$	

* Assumes Average Loaded Personnel Cost Of $ ____ Per Hour (given by Human Resources)

* * RPN = Rating Probability Number, derived from FMEA (Failure Mode Effects Analysis) described later.

WORKPAPER III10.22 Example: Technology Cost vs. Need

EXAMPLE
Technology Cost vs Need, by Business Division

COSTS $				
Very High	MEDIUM SHADING	MEANS UNIT <u>PROBABLY</u>	<u>WON'T</u> DO IT	
High				
Moderate		LIGHT SHADING	MEANS UNIT <u>MAY</u> DO IT	
Low				
Very Low / None			DARK SHADING	MEANS UNIT <u>MUST</u> DO IT.
Exposure	Very Low / None	Low	Moderate	High

WORKPAPER III10.23 Technology Cost vs. Need: Mainframe

Technology Cost vs Need, by Business Division
MAINFRAME

COSTS $				
Very High				
High				
Moderate				
Low				
Very Low / None				
Exposure	Very Low / None	Low	Moderate	High

WORKPAPER III10.24 Technology Cost vs. Need: Telecommunications

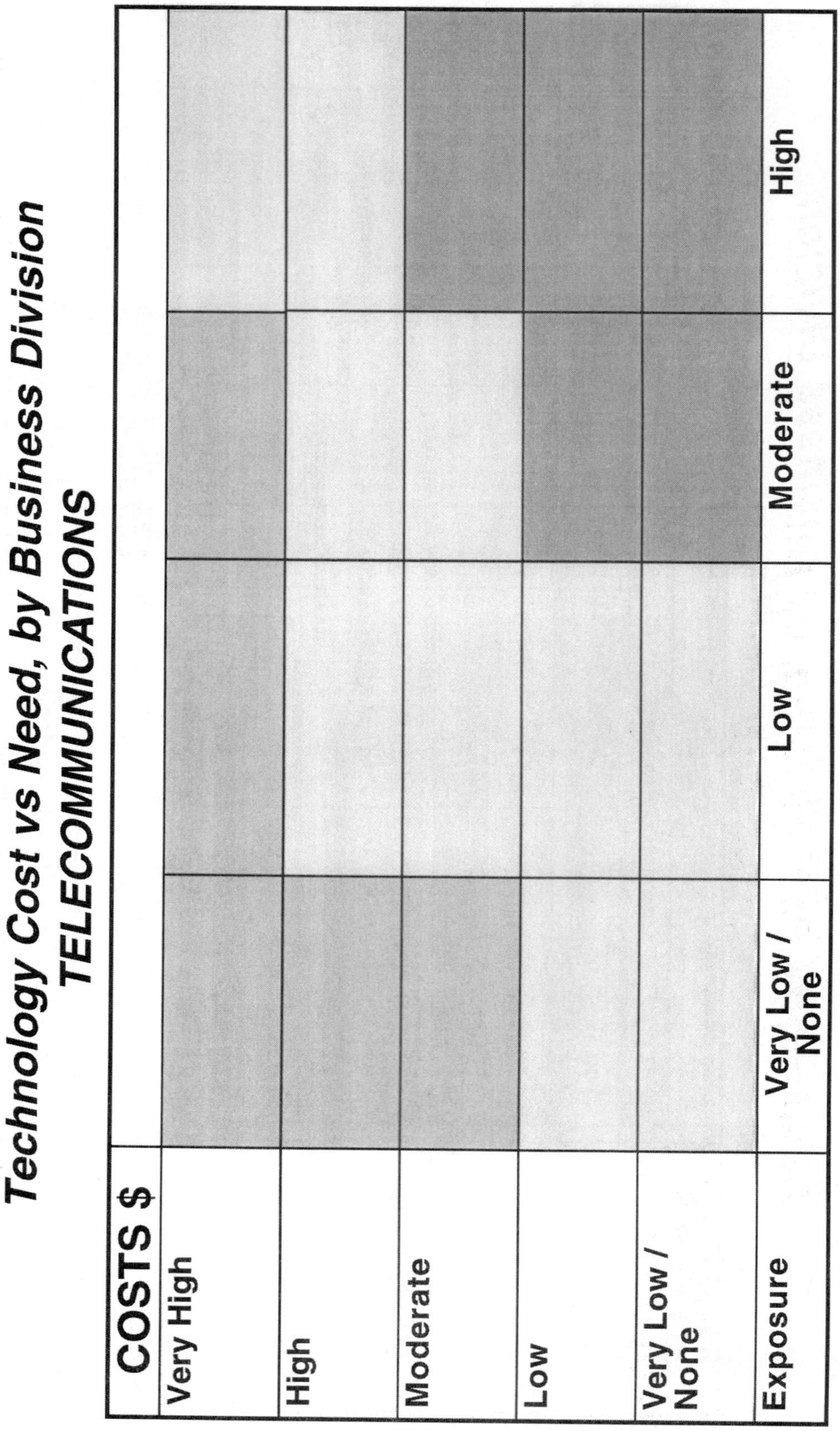

WORKPAPER III10.25 Technology Cost vs. Need: LAN

Technology Cost vs Need, by Business Division
LOCAL AREA NETWORK

COSTS $				
Very High				
High				
Moderate				
Low				
Very Low / None				
Exposure	Very Low / None	Low	Moderate	High

WORKPAPER III10.26 Technology Cost vs. Need: Other

Technology Cost vs Need, by Business Division
OTHER

COSTS $				
Very High				
High				
Moderate				
Low				
Very Low / None				
Exposure	Very Low / None	Low	Moderate	High

WORKPAPER III10.27 Evaluation Criteria for Network Vulnerability: Mainframe

EVALUATION CRITERIA FOR NETWORK VULNERABILITY
MAINFRAME

High Risk	Moderate Risk	Low Risk	Low-No Risk

WORKPAPER III10.28 Evaluation Criteria for Network Vulnerability: Telecommunications

EVALUATION CRITERIA FOR NETWORK VULNERABILITY TELECOMMUNICATIONS

High Risk	Moderate Risk	Low Risk	Low-No Risk

WORKPAPER III10.29 Evaluation Criteria for Network Vulnerability: LAN

EVALUATION CRITERIA FOR NETWORK VULNERABILITY
LOCAL AREA NETWORKS

High Risk	Moderate Risk	Low Risk	Low-No Risk

WORKPAPER III10.30 Evaluation Criteria for Network Vulnerability: Other

EVALUATION CRITERIA FOR NETWORK VULNERABILITY
OTHER

High Risk	Moderate Risk	Low Risk	Low-No Risk

WORKPAPER III10.31 Focus On: (division)

FOCUS ON

____

NOTE: Copy this worksheet and fill out for **each** subordinate company or business division.

- Operations criteria and mission: _____________
- How long in business?
- What kind of reputation with customers?
- Number of Sales
  -- Primary __________
  -- Cross Sales __________
- Average Sale = $_____________
- 1997 Incoming Calls (Includes Fax) = __________ calls (__________% of Orders)
- 1997 Incoming Mail = __________ pieces (__________% of Orders)
- Criteria for operation and call servicing:
- Backup Systems Exist for Core Functions? ______________
- Technology: ____________________________ PC ☐ Mainframe ☐
- "JIT" (Just In Time) Environment for Select Customers? ___Y ___N
- Other considerations:

WORKPAPER III10.32 Dynamics Of (division)

DYNAMICS OF

____

NOTE: Copy this worksheet and fill out for **each** subordinate company or business division.

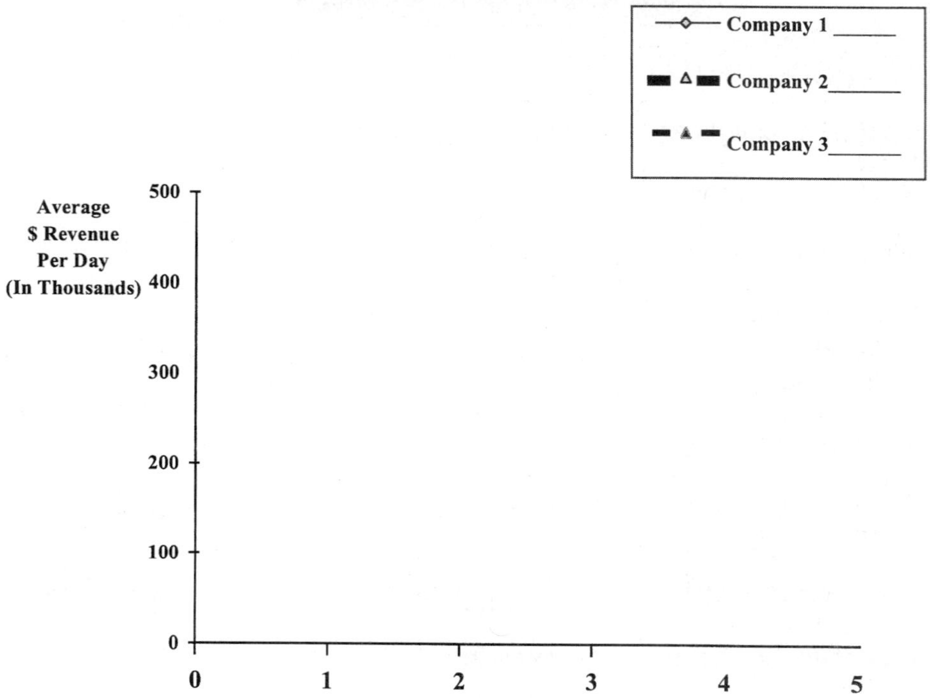

Revenue =

Daily Revenue =

Other Issues:
1. Lost Productivity
2. Lost Market Share
3. Lost Customer Confidence
4.
5.

WORKPAPER III10.33 Cost of Executive Complaints Flow Chart

WHAT DO EXECUTIVE COMPLAINTS COST ________?

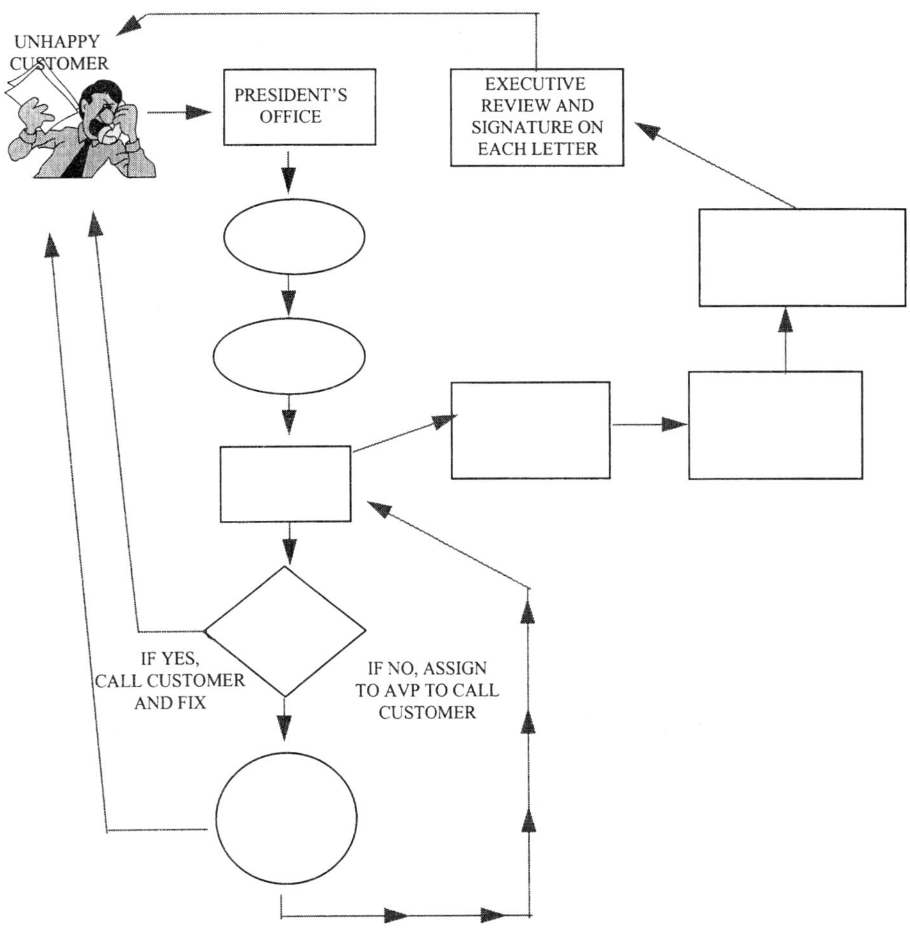

ISSUES:

- ✓ COMPLAINTS ARE COSTLY - ________ in personnel costs to process each.
- ✓ COMPLAINTS DAMAGE CUSTOMER CONFIDENCE AND TRUST.
- ✓ BESIDES ALL THIS, WE COULD LOSE THE CUSTOMER!
- ✓ Source: Office of the President, senior staffer

NOTE: Copy this worksheet and fill out for **each** subordinate company or business division.

Conducting a Technical Vulnerability Analysis of the Physical Environment

CHAPTER III-11

WHAT IS A FAILURE MODE EFFECTS ANALYSIS? (FMEA)

Failure Mode Effects Analysis (FMEA) is a convenient term that originated (or is at least commonly used) in the U.S. military. The CIO of a $25-billion organization, who was also an ex-Air Force general and telecommunications officer, once said with the voice of experience:

> **"When we send up a military satellite, everything has to be perfect. Everything. This is because no one has yet invented a 23,000-mile-long screwdriver to fix it if it is not."**

This is why the military is fond of FMEA. Find everything that can go wrong, evaluate MTBF (Mean Time Between Failure) for each component, then combine them into a single mathematical factor that describes the probability of failure of the whole system. It's not easy, but corporations can adapt a similar methodology for contingency planners. Here's how.

Imagine performing a detailed analysis of the installed backbone network and the related equipment attached to the backbone. The object is to determine single points of failure, critical components that cause failures to multiple users, and an overall assessment of past performance of these devices. This information can be described using the following information outlines.

A Failure Mode Evaluation Analysis (FMEA) is broken down into three components:

1. **Problem Identification.** When designing or evaluating a network, both in hardware and software, the rule of thumb is to ask *"what can possibly go wrong?"* This includes failure of the equipment itself as well as external factors (heat, water, air, people, etc.) that could affect the equipment.
2. **Risk Priority Number (RPN).** Assign a value to each of the probabilities from 1 to 10. The higher the number, the greater the risk except in the case of problem resolution, where the higher the number, the faster the problem is fixed.
3. **Reaction Planning Process.** This is the *"How fast can we fix the problem?"* step. This is best done by modifying your company's operating and security standards to change the environment to make the selected system less vulnerable.

Then assign failure rates from the probability or statistical and historical data accumulated from manufacturers data or other sources. Next, weight the following three factors:

- Severity
- Frequency
- Detection

Severity is assigned a numerical value from 1 to 10 (the higher the number the more severe) based on the probability of an event and how damaging it would be.

Frequency of the occurrences by part type is assigned a value (the higher the number the more often it happens) based on how often it can be expected to happen.

Difficulty of **detection** and repair is weighted the same way, but in this case, the higher number means you can respond and fix it faster.

Multiply the three factors to get the **RPN**. The RPNs help the team assign priorities to address or assess higher priority treatment on specific elements. This is not a qualifier or disqualifier, but a determination of what can and will go wrong. Capital or human resources can be assigned to shore up the risks associated with these areas. The issues with the highest RPNs are the areas where your organization is most vulnerable and needs to spend the most time and resources. Exhibits III-11-A to III-11-D illustrate the procedure:

The final component is the "what are we going to do about it" step, the **Standards Refinement** step. Routine maintenance and repair procedures should be refined, but how do you prevent disasters before they happen? Change control and management control over a system is even more important, and these issues are defined in your network **Standards**. Well-designed systems often become vulnerable over time as the standards governing their maintenance and operation fall victim to changes in budgets or philosophies or undocumented changes in equipment.

Operating and Security Standards are adjusted to cover testing strategies, frequencies of tests and reviews, preparedness training, and documentation. The standards are useful for re-evaluating and reconstructing systems and procedures in order to prevent future repetitions.

PHYSICAL AND ENVIRONMENTAL SECURITY AND CONTROL

Following are a few tips for evaluating the physical environment for the Failure Mode Effects Analysis (FMEA) part of the study.

Basic Physical Standards for All Installations

It is no longer necessary to differentiate between different types of equipment. Telecommunications switches act like — and are — large computers, and they deserve the same protection as mainframes. By and large, mainframes don't require the maintenance they used to (chilled water, 400 Hz power, etc.), so they can be sustained in a well air-conditioned space, although not necessarily an "environment." LANs are taking the place of mainframes, and mission-critical applications are migrating to LANs every day. The standards that applied yesterday's mainframe should apply to LAN servers now. This includes:

Access to Equipment Rooms

Who can get in and out? In many organizations, the telecommunications department makes a change on an important server, and 10 minutes later the LAN department makes a change, and then later in the day the mainframe guys makes another change. Then the system crashes and it's nobody's fault! Consider a sign-in log to track interdepartmental changes.

EXHIBIT III-11-A SEVERITY RATING

Severity rating:

When a component on the network fails, the severity is classified in a ten-point system. IF:

Description	Rating
If one user is affected	1
If a workgroup is affected	2
If an entire bay is affected	4
If a single floor is affected	6
If an entire building is affected	8
If the entire backbone is affected	10

The single point of failure in this scenario is the backbone network, however many components make up this single point of failure. Such things as the building environmental conditions, or the building and closet entrance facilities for the cabling and the power all would have a severity of 10 if they failed even though the building is intact. We have a list of commonly neglected places to look later in this chapter.

EXHIBIT III-11-B OCCURRENCES

Occurrences:

The frequency distribution of an event is a concern, regardless of the severity, if it occurs often enough. IF:

Occurrence Level or Frequency	Rating
If every day	10
Weekly intervals	8
Monthly intervals	6
Quarterly intervals	4
Every 12 months or longer	2

If the occurrences continually happen, or manifest themselves on a daily basis, then the critical rating here is the highest.

Access to Visitors

A true story: A very nice lady — an IS manager — went into her staff office with her five-year-old son to check on a few pressing matters. Her staff repeatedly assured her that everything was under control (and also chided her for not enjoying her day off), she took her eyes off the little boy for a moment. The key for the main UPS, which was about 12 inches off the floor, was irresistible to the child, and ... well, she still works for the company.

EXHIBIT III-11-C DETECTION/REPAIR OF THE FAILURE

Detection / Repair of the Failure:

Detection works in the reverse of the occurrences, whereby the easier it is to detect the problem and begin to corrective measures, the lower the critical rating. The longer it takes then the higher the rating. IF:

Description/ Detection	Rating
Is easy and resolution can be achieved within 1 hour	2
Greater than 1 hour but less than 4 hours	4
Greater than 4 hours but less than 8 hours	6
Greater than 8 but less than 24 hours	8
Greater than 24 hours	10

EXHIBIT III-11-D RISK PRIORITY NUMBERS (RPN)

What finally comes out of these numerical values is an assessment or the

Risk Priority Numbers (RPN)

This is a mathematical computation of:

$$S \times O \times D = RPN$$

$$10 \times 10 \times 10 = 1000$$

The higher the RPN; the higher the risk associated with a specific component and the higher the value that would be placed on solving the problem. If a network was comprised of several critical components that had very high values of RPN, one would have to show where the network can be improved to support the service levels that are expected.

Additional Physical Protection

Many LAN environments are installed where no equipment should be installed such as basements and closets. How is the air flow in that cramped closet? Do the doors lock? Does the janitor go in there? Should a server area or computer room be lined with big, glass windows?

Other Building Improvements

It's a good idea to keep the location of major network nodes a family secret. Sad but true, computer centers and telecommunications hubs are inviting targets for sabotage and terrorism.

Remote System Access

Check controls for remote access. Confidential information could be leave an organization at a moments notice on an unknown $79 fax modem from someone's workstation.

Controls for Remote Access

Who is allowed remote system access, and at what level of security? Everybody? Unlimited? That means trouble!

Housekeeping

Large piles of paper or other combustibles in the server area are a fire hazard. Is smoking banned? Pop a floor tile and look under it. Does it look like a teenager's bedroom?

Electrical Power

Spikes, shorts, brownouts, blackouts, sags. Many buildings were wired long before clean power was a consideration. Take adequate precautions with mission critical equipment. UPS are cheap these days and will save lots of problems.

Fire Protective Systems

Don't try to be the expert — bring one in for a survey. Check for:

- Fire-protection requirements in your area
- General fire-protection standards
- New construction requirements
- Existing facility requirements
- Fire-detection devices
- Water exposure (pipes, roof, drains, and ground water)

ASSESSING CHANGE CONTROL PROCEDURES

People are probably the most common cause of disasters. Control over people is exercised through Standards and Change Management procedures. See Exhibit III-11-E.

Network Software Security and Change Control Management

Every technical system should have a documented **change control** system, defining at least the following:

1. LANs and mainframe chug control and procedures
   - Major software changes
   - Persons authorized to make changes
   - Password protection of maintenance functions
   - Back-up during software changes
2. Telecommunications change control and procedures
   - DISA (dial into PBX, called "Direct Inward System Access")
   - Report monitoring
   - Class of service restrictions
   - Securing of auto-attendants
   - Operator transfer policy

EXHIBIT III-11-E ENTERPRISE - WIDE CHANGE CONTROL

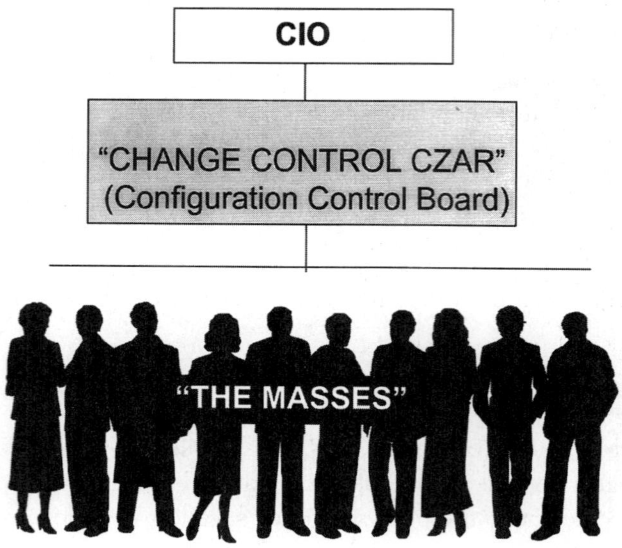

3. Security of remote dial-in devices (for mainframes, LANs, and telecom)
   - Restriction to authorized persons
   - Password protection
   - Responsibility for system and network security
4. Other concerns: sensitive applications and data
   - Disposal of confidential materials
   - Privacy of conversations
   - Availability of scrambling technologies
   - Fax and cellular security
   - Availability of encryption for fax and cellular phones
5. End-user support systems
   - Help desk staffing considerations
   - Listing of supported services and vendors
   - Maintenance contract requirements for end-users

Other Concerns

Hackers. Hackers are unauthorized users, often juveniles, who try to break into a system for kicks. They often use "demon dialers," which dial every number in a prefix to find modem lines (e.g., (210) 498-0000, 498-0001, 498-0002, etc.) Some rudimentary precautions can prevent their entering a system:

- Modems that dial back the user
- Modems that screen the caller's ID
- Modems or equipment that initially answers with silence rather than a modem tone
- Equipment that does not have an initial welcoming screen (e.g., "Welcome to ABC Co."), which can further encourage unauthorized users
- Equipment that logs and tracks unsuccessful log-in attempts
- Equipment that requires a special hardware key for access

While none of these is itself a solution, several or all of them used together can provide a nearly bulletproof defense against unauthorized access.

Saboteurs. The most unsettling types of attacks come from people who know your environment. Disgruntled employees, for example, can cause the most damage, since they know exactly where to hit. Precautions include:

- Eliminating log-in access when an employee leaves the company voluntarily
- Eliminating log-in access when any employee is terminated. Also include the following: protect against "tailgating," an old ploy for accessing a system that goes like this:
  1. A super user or system administrator dials into a remote system;
  2. The hacker dials the number (obtained through a demon dialer) and gets a busy signal;
  3. The hacker dials "0" and asks the operator to verify the line;
  4. The operator interrupts the line, which drops the authorized super user while the hacker is dialing out on another line;
  5. If timed perfectly, the modem sees the interruption as a temporary line hit and re-establishes the session with the hacker's modem instead of the authorized users;
  6. The hacker is online with super-user access.

Other good features include accounting systems, paging systems, and hardware keys.

Each solution presented to management should also provide a record of all call attempts. This gives a paper trail of dial-in access. Strong screening, reporting, and presentation of this information should be a key selection criteria. Some systems or inbound numbers that require high security provide for automatic pager notification. When a user logs in, a system administrator's pager goes off.

Many companies use hardware keys for some applications as well as protection software, which prevents a hard drive from being copied or read, in case a laptop is stolen. They are inexpensive and easy to plug into a parallel port.

BACKUP –48V POWER FOR TELECOMMUNICATIONS EQUIPMENT

One of the worst common threats is the lack of some type of -48 volt backup station power for the DACS (Digital Access Crossconnect Systems), SONET and lightguide transmission equipment, and other telecommunications equipment.

Many companies have crossed the invisible line between being a large corporate user and being a central office server provider and are learning which standards for backup power and procedures apply to prudent operation of a central office. The situation is analogous to trying to save a patient's kidneys after the heart had stopped beating. All other recovery activities pale in comparison.

The SONET lightguide termination equipment is the heart of many communications-intensive businesses. It is the fundamental first layer of raw transport upon which all other systems are built. For example, if this equipment includes a -48 volt battery backup, technical personnel would have an additional eight to sixteen hours of "forgiveness" while they isolated problems on say, the UPS bus, other cause of failure. Don't assume UPS will be enough. They fail too. Phone companies use batteries, and so should you. Even though your switches could be down (but they can be protected with batteries, too), critical private line circuits would be up and running. Alliance partnerships, depending on their connections, need not necessarily be disrupted.

A backup -48 volt power supply for critical transmission equipment, an accepted and common practice in central office locations, is absolutely necessary.

CONSIDER ACQUIRING OR UPDATING A NETWORK MANAGEMENT SYSTEM

Part of reducing network vulnerability, particularly on the wide-area network side, deepens on proactive maintenance and nonintrusive troubleshooting. Most companies can improve appreciably in this regard.

Many large firms are served by SONET access facilities, which are a vast improvement over traditional T3 service. SONET is an intelligent network topology. Much in the way of network diagnostics can be gleaned from the data, which is a function of the network itself. For example, many of the functions of T1 test sets are built into the SONET bit stream.

SONET will replace T1/T3 as the backbone transmission media in the U.S. It will be at least a 30-year technology. With this long planning window, which is quite rare in our business, businesses should use the capabilities of its SONET access facilities. Here's one way to do it.

A well-conceived network management system with the appropriate SNMP "hooks" helps companies read, extrapolate, and act upon data before routine problems turn into emergencies. The system can also be expanded to interpret the automatic fault protection switching overhead built into the SONET frame to provide fast recovery of failed telecommunication links without human intervention. Other capabilities, such as being able to "see behind" major components, greatly simplifies network troubleshooting and repair, since it permits diagnosis of blind spots in the network.

A system should, at the very least, be able to extrapolate useful data from intelligent networks for use in fault tolerance, trend analysis, trouble isolation, automatic protection switching, and seamless integration with comparable systems used by service providers. A goal might be to troubleshoot a "mission-critical" system, such as a bank's fraud line, without interrupting its service. Even better, it might be able to pinpoint and take action on a problem before it affects service through a performance trend analysis program.

Organizations should explore the installation of a "Johnson Space Center" level of network management and control as described above.

INTERNET CONCERNS

In the haste of jumping on this new and exciting communications medium, many organizations overlook what are rudimentary precautions in many other traditional environments, such as:

Responsibility for Internet Security

Many organizations still have some unresolved organizational issues with regard to security responsibilities for the Internet, which may traditionally have been the responsibility of mainframe or midrange computer groups in the IS department. Other departments may have separate groups of technologists responsible for the actual operation of the Internet firewall and other components. They may reside in data security, LAN operations, or other departments.

There have been some minor snafus (i.e., holes or vulnerabilities temporarily left exposed in the system) from unclear policy defining exactly who is responsible for which system and under what circumstances. While ultimate responsibility could gravitate by default to a Mainframe or Midrange computer group, it's best for this function to be closely monitored by a security group, at least until the technology matures.

Companies should also consider a nominal increase in manpower to avoid creating too small a pool of "specialists" and to provide better depth. Once an organization has some experience with Internet access and is confident that any security breeches or holes are closed, it can reconsider organizational changes.

Installation of Test Firewall

Past analyses of physical components comprising corporate firewalls show that there is usually *no* firewall platform earmarked exclusively for testing and backup. For all intents and purposes, the present technology is single threaded in almost every way. This is not a major concern at the outset, but it will be when a company's firewall starts to affect revenue, if it has not already.

Just as with mainframes and LANs, it is important to establish a protocol for not introducing new applications directly into a production environment. Also, a test firewall can also double as a backup in the event of a major equipment failure in the primary. Last, because the Internet is relatively new to most organizations, its staff should be encouraged to dabble. It would not be prudent to experiment on a production platform. See Exhibits III-10-F and III-10-G.

EXHIBIT III-11-F "FOCUS ON FIREWALLS"

✓ **PRIMARY MISSION TODAY:**

GENERALLY LIMITED TO ACCESS BY I.S. PERSONNEL AND MODEM CONTROL / REPLACEMENT

✓ **FUTURE MISSIONS:**

- →**CUSTOMER SUPPORT**
- →**ROVING NOMADIC USERS**
- →**MODEM REPLACEMENT**
- →**USER AFFECTING APPLICATIONS**
- →**REVENUE IMPACTING APPLICATIONS**

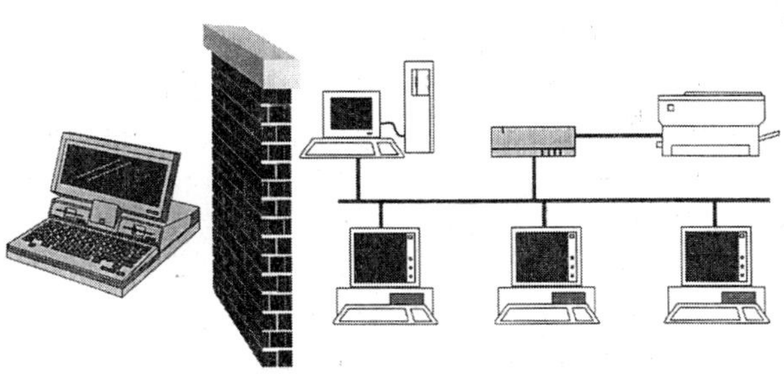

EXHIBIT III-11-G FIREWALL HARDWARE CONCERNS

- ✓NO "TEST" FIREWALL
- ✓MANPOWER CONCERNS
- ✓FAULT TOLERANCE OK FOR NOW, BUT NOT UP TO SPEED FOR REVENUE IMPACTING SYSTEM
- ✓Consider these common problems:
  - →CISCO 4000s HAVE NO REDUNDANCY
  - →USUALLY ONLY SINGLE T1 CONNECTION to the Internet Service Provider (ISP)
  - →NO "ROUND ROBIN DNS"
  - →NO SPARE CSU / DSU, HARD DRIVES, OTHER CRITICAL COMPONENTS
- ✓EVERYTHING IS SINGLE THREADED...NOT A PROBLEM NOW, BUT WILL BE WHEN SYSTEM BECOMES REVENUE IMPACTING

UPGRADE 4000 SERIES TO "ULTRA"

The CISCO 4000 series routers currently in use have no redundancy. The 5000 series in turn has redundant power and a redundant CPU, which will be required later. Network diversity is another concern. Often, there is only one T1 to the ISP (Internet Service Provider), which again creates a single point of vulnerability. A second T1, along with "Round Robin DNS," adds greater resiliency on the wide-area network connectivity to the ISP. Other components, such as CSUs and DSUs, are often single threaded with no redundancy. Check the status of these items if Internet access for your company is revenue impacting.

WORKPAPER III11.01 FMEA Worksheet #1: Severity

FMEA WORKSHEET #1
SEVERITY

Severity rating:

When a component on the network fails, the severity is classified in a ten point system. IF:

Description	Rating
	1
	2
	4
	6
	8
	10

WORKPAPER III11.02 FMEA Worksheet #2: Occurrences

FMEA WORKSHEET #2
OCCURRENCES

Occurrences:

The frequency distribution of an event is a concern, regardless of the severity, if it occurs often enough. IF:

Occurrence Level or Frequency	*Rating*
If every day	
Weekly intervals	
Monthly intervals	
Quarterly intervals	
Every 12 months or longer	

If the occurrences continually happen, or manifest themselves on a daily basis, then the critical rating here is the highest.

WORKPAPER III11.03 FMEA Worksheet #3: Detection/Repair

FMEA WORKSHEET #3
DETECTION / REPAIR

Detection / Repair of the Failure:

Detection works in the reverse of the occurrences, whereby the easier it is to detect the problem and begin to corrective measures, the lower the critical rating. The longer it takes then the higher the rating. IF:

Description/ Detection	*Rating*
Is easy and resolution can be achieved within 1 hour	
Greater than one hour but less than four hours	
Greater than four hours but less than eight hours	
Greater than eight but less than twenty-four hours	
Greater than twenty-four hours	

WORKPAPER III11.04 FMEA Worksheet #4: Computing RPN

FMEA WORKSHEET #4
COMPUTING RPN

Risk Priority Numbers (RPN)

COMPONENT	S x	O x	D =	RPN
1. Example	10 x	10 x	10 =	1000
2.				
3.				
4.				
5.				
6.				
7.				

WORKPAPER III11.05 Focus on Firewalls

"FOCUS ON FIREWALLS"

✓PRIMARY MISSION TODAY:

✓FUTURE MISSIONS:

→ ______________________________

→ ______________________________

→ ______________________________

→ ______________________________

→ ______________________________

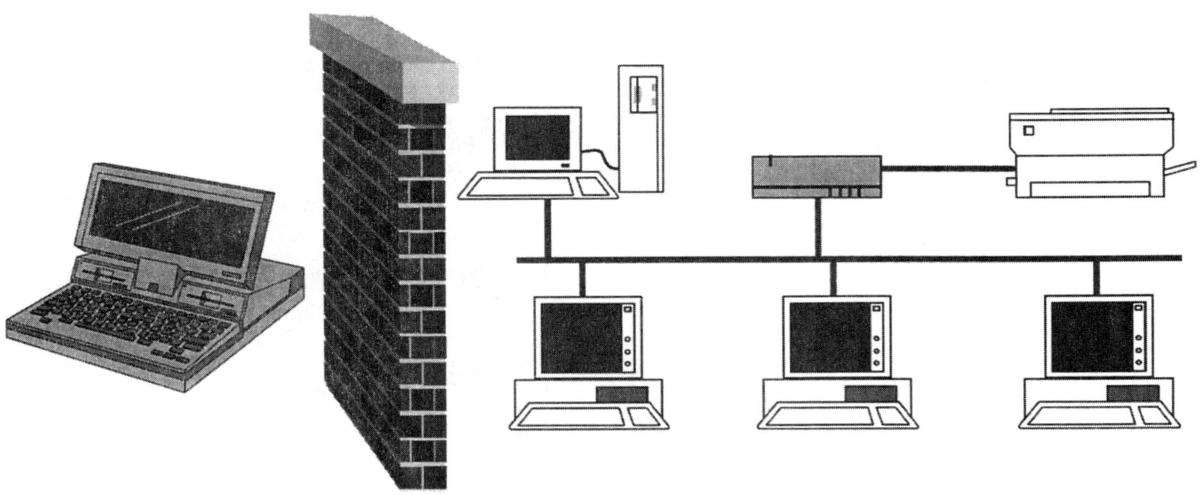

WORKPAPER III11.06 Firewall Hardware Concerns

FIREWALL HARDWARE CONCERNS

___ "TEST" FIREWALL?

___ MANPOWER CONCERNS?

___ FAULT TOLERANCE UP TO SPEED FOR REVENUE IMPACTING SYSTEM?

___ CONSIDER THESE COMMON PROBLEMS:

- ___ CISCO ROUTERS HAVE REDUNDANCY?
- ___ ONLY SINGLE T1 CONNECTION TO THE INTERNET SERVICE PROVIDER (ISP)?
- ___ "ROUND ROBIN DNS"?
- ___ SPARE CSU / DSU, HARD DRIVES, OTHER CRITICAL COMPONENTS?

___ EVERYTHING IS SINGLE THREADED?

Assessing Standards and Controls

CHAPTER III-12

ENTICING USERS INTO ACCEPTING STANDARDS

There are opportunities and threats associated with the need for proper **controls and standards**, which are discussed primarily in the context of protecting the network from disasters. Standards are also used to keep a handle on the operating environment. If properly implemented, standards improve operations in general. Although some of this section is not disaster–recovery oriented, many of the standards required for network fault tolerance can be equally beneficial to the general operating environment. Because of the opportunities addressing disaster recovery — and a lot of other user concerns — through thoughtful planning, standards are addressed in this section.

The following consumer themes emerged from interviews with clients and main users. *The extent to which a company can craft solid networking solutions to each of the following user concerns is the measure of its success in tomorrow's networks.*

- **Expense** — Distributed processing is people-intensive and expensive to maintain. Management skill sets are in serious question. The workforce, trained in distributed processing, is young. The focus is toward the technical platform — such as the building blocks — rather than necessarily on the core business.
- **Reliability** — In many cases, distributed processing is inherently unstable. Ten years ago, in the mainframe environment, network uptime of 98.5% was grounds for burning down the executive suite; today 80% network uptime on the LAN can be the norm. Part of the reason users accept such a low figure today is that they own much of the platform, in contrast to the "glass house," which someone else ran. Even though they own the platform, however, they may not be soliciting help with it.
- **Unproven Track Record** — Business process integrity is a hot button with executives when mission-critical core business applications, currently residing in reliable mainframe computers, move to unproven LAN platforms.
- **Security** — Security is a major concern. Many of the most rudimentary precautions taken in a mainframe environment go by the wayside in the LAN environment. These include development LANs, which keep new applications from being thrown directly into the production environment, and difficulty policing some of the most rudimentary security precautions, such as how often backups are performed, how often passwords are changed, and where the filer server is located.
- ***WHAT* Help Desk?!** — Help desk support can be a nightmare in a LAN environment. In the mainframe environment, it was usually possible to call a help desk telephone number and get real help. This is often impossible now, given the broad cross section of equipment and software options available in a client/server environment.
- **Responsibility:** "It's a TELCO Problem", — Wide-area network support is also an issue. Despite their huge economies of scale, even the largest organizations

EXHIBIT III-12-A PAY NOW OR PAY LATER?

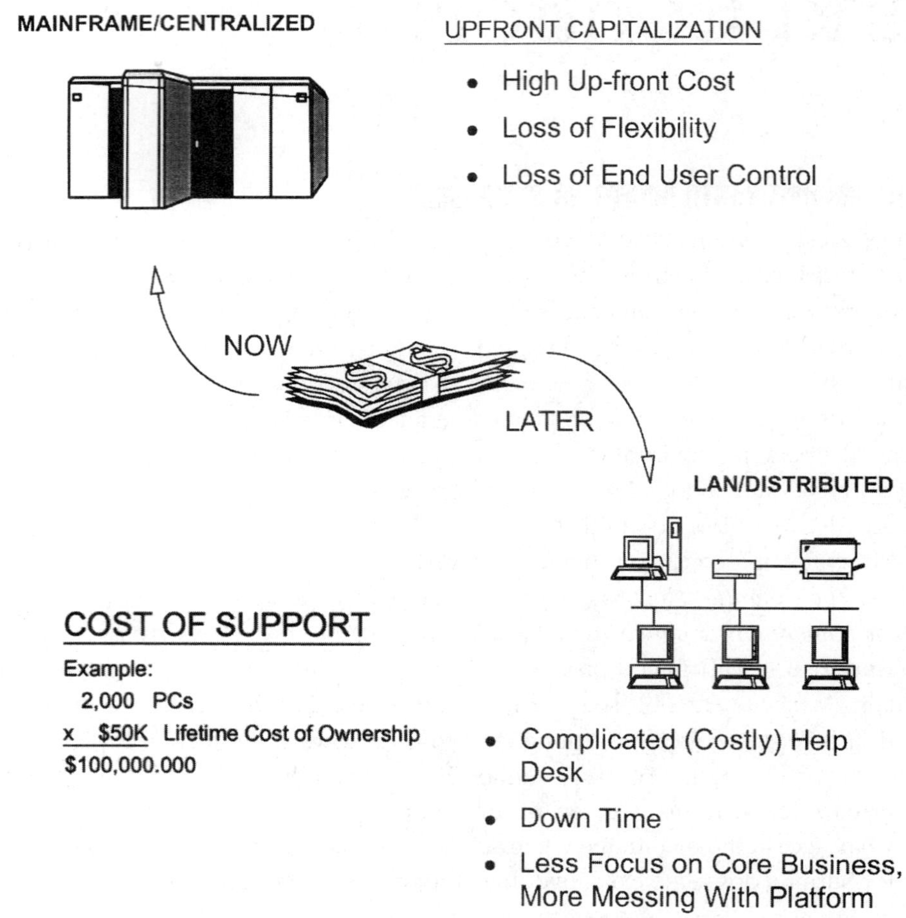

have a rough time coordinating service and reacting to the ever-increasing pressure for bandwidths from users. To believe that individual internal users, who lack these economies of scale, would be any more successful in providing proactive support for a wide-area network is optimistic indeed. These customers, however, do accept that their destinies are in the hands of outside entities, such as AT&T and the Bell operating companies, whose performance criteria does not necessarily match their own.

What follows is a discussion of networking solutions and recommendations that address these themes.

COST OF OWNERSHIP ISSUES

We are going to deploy client/server technology and we are going to save tons of money.

People once made such claims, but not anymore. One thing has become apparent over the last few years of the client/server revolution: it is expensive —

prohibitively expensive — if control of the operating environment is lost, and catastrophic if numbers are alienated in the process. These fears can help attempts to get users to buy-off on standards.

Currently, many companies realize that a client/server migration will not by itself be a money-saving proposition; rather, it would be a productivity-improving proposition. Even so, most firms may underestimate the true cost of an environment consisting of hundreds, or thousands, of PCs.

The lifetime cost of ownership of a personal computer for corporations, according to widely regarded industry sources, could be as high as $50,000 per device over the life of the equipment. This includes not only the original purchase price and installation of the equipment (which constitutes only a fraction of the eventual cost of ownership) but other intangible items, such as productivity loss when the device malfunctions, locks up, or has other problems.

In the world of the mainframe, companies pay now; in the world of client/server, companies pay later. It's almost that simple. A centralized mainframe environment has historically required upfront capitalization but yielded a fairly stable environment later. A client/server environment, on the other hand, requires less upfront cost but much more cost of ownership later on. Loss of control over the environment during roll-out means big trouble. Today, client/server is widely used not only for back-office operations, but for honest-to-god revenue-impacting systems. Proceed with care!

Keeping up With the Environment

Even with the most rigid hardware and software standards, the PC environment can rapidly diversify beyond control. Vendors update PCs about every six months, and the average company can probably expect a major software revision yearly. Even with minimal standardization of equipment, such as three PC configurations and two software loads, the number of hardware/software combinations at the end of 24 months could be as high as $6 \times 6 \times 6 \times 6 = 1{,}296$. Imagine training the help desk for this! This could severely tax support systems for the platforms, to say nothing of equipment incompatibilities and learning curves.

The best way to control cost and complexity in any Client/Server environment is through strong **standards and practices**, careful equipment and vendor selection, meticulous user training, rigorous security, and adequate audit control on the environment. Other actions, such as an active virus-protection program and major organizational changes including formations of quality assurance committees and standards bodies, are required as well.

SEGREGATE USERS

For companies with several different lines of business, it stands to reason that they have several different classes of end user. Segmenting them based on business need helps provide a higher level of day-to-day support and establishing priorities later when considering who recovers first in a disaster. Split user bases two ways:

- Production workers
- Knowledge workers

Production workers are engaged in customer support, sales, or other departments with a direct and immediate impact. Generally, companies do not want to grant a lot of intellectual personal computer freedom to this group. If they lock something up while playing around, they are shut down until the problem is fixed. They have a fairly fixed pallet of software and hardware that is easy to standardize.

Knowledge workers run all kinds of oddball applications and are not easily categorized. They are the finance and HR people, accountants, line managers, and engineers. They usually have something else to do if the PC is down, and they have a better established network of tap-on-the-shoulder support from co-workers when something breaks. However, because of the complexity of their setups, they can tie-up prodigious amounts of a help desk's time if something goes really wrong. Because their applications are unique, they are also the most difficult to recover in a disaster.

Given these dynamics, splitting production workers and knowledge workers into two groups allows management to make some good high-level decisions on such questions as:

1. Should production workers, due to their immediate revenue impact, have a separate help desk number, with personnel trained in their applications?
2. Should production workers be afforded special priority in a disaster because they impact revenue?
3. Should knowledge workers pay a premium or tariff to support the additional costs they impose on the help desk?
4. How far should the company go in limiting acquisition of nonstandard hardware and software for knowledge workers?

These are a few considerations that have a profound impact on both daily operations and your recovery posture after a disaster. Consider them carefully.

Connectivity, standards, and network management are an organization's tools to turn a disorganized gaggle of distributed users into a comprehensive business team. Benefits are profound, not only in business resumption but also in terms of cost, control, and productivity.

STANDARDIZING THE DEVELOPMENT AND BETA TEST PROCESSES

Many organizations lack sufficient coordination between development groups, proving grounds, skunk works, development organizations, and other entities. Coordination of these groups is necessary for backup and recovery and for synergy from the whole organization. These goals are complicated when each group insists on "doing its own thing."

FORMATION OF A LIST OF SUPPORTED SOFTWARE AND HARDWARE

Help desk support could become a nightmare without standards for hardware and software. A mainframe level of support with a distributed level of productivity helps, but it isn't easy for any company today. If a company goes too far to the right, the system gets too complicated to control and most of the productivity gain is lost. If a company goes too far to the left, users are "shoe-horned" into someone else's solution and lose productivity. The solution is to pick a happy median where productivity is enhanced and affords a controlled and manageable environment.

There are financial reasons for appropriate support as well as business resumption reasons. For example, even large increases in help desk personnel won't be enough if standards are not enforced as power moves to the desktop. Companies are urged to use caution as they move in this direction.

EXHIBIT III-12-B PROFILING USERS

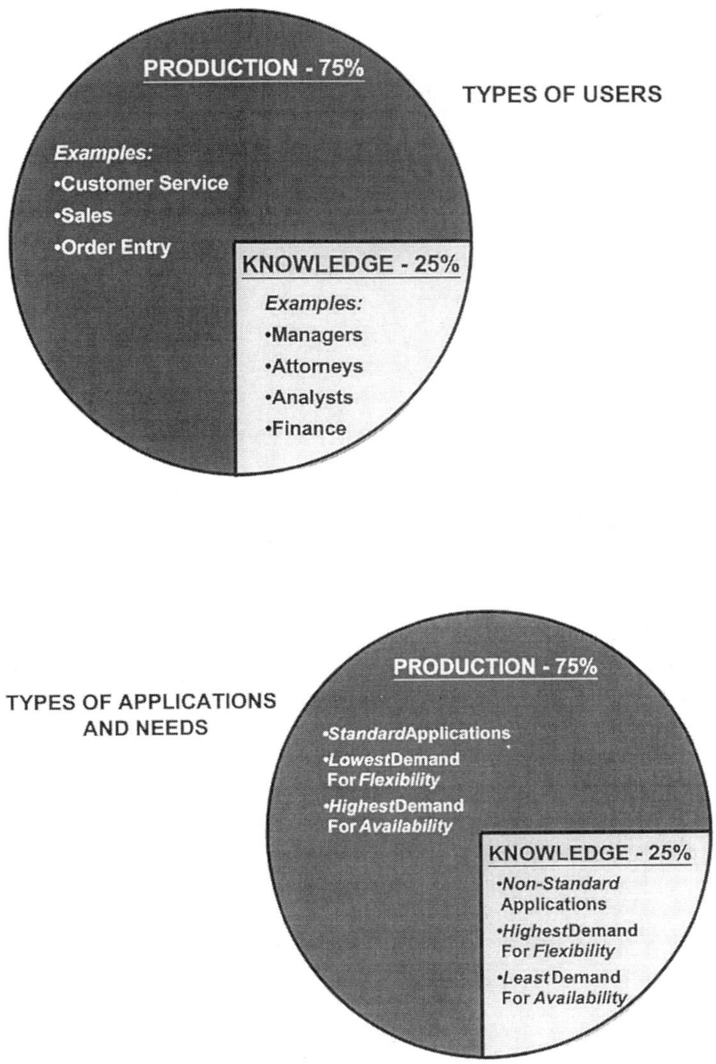

TIGHTENING OPERATIONAL AND SECURITY STANDARDS

Companies should document operating and security standards, particularly for the wide-area network, specifying particular interfaces and equipment that will be used. This will be especially important during the shift to client/server computing, when many business units will define their own technology.

In a diverse client/server environment, standardized interfaces to the wide area network are absolutely necessary. Other components that should be added to the standards document include operating procedures, such as how often passwords should be changed on maintenance ports. The controls defined in the operating securities standards document should also support any future business resumption plan.

EXHIBIT III-12-C PROFILING USERS RELATIONSHIP TO HELP DESK

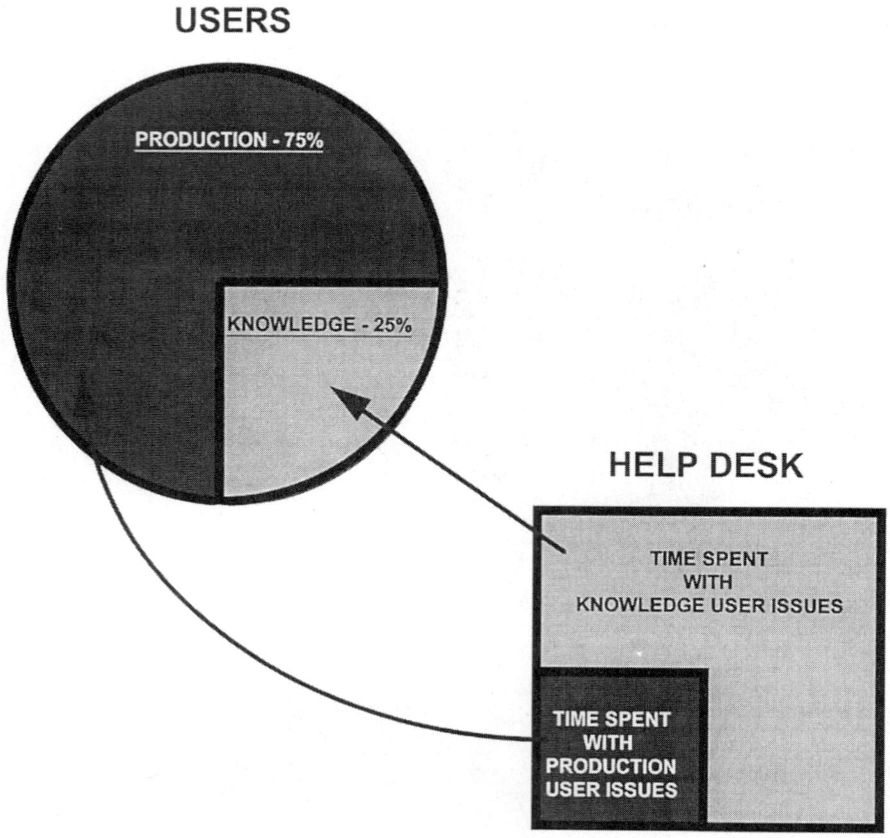

DEFINITION OF RECOVERY TEAMS AND TEAM LEADERS FOR MAJOR FAILURES

It is likely that staffs will be split in three ways in the event of a major systems failure: (1) Employees dedicated to the recovery aspects of the situation, namely finding suitable office space and recreating a usable configuration there in order to support a business unit or work group; (2) employees involved in the restoration phase, namely rebuilding the existing environment so work can get back to normal as quickly as possible. These individuals will also be involved in salvage operations, trying to repair any expensive equipment and getting it recertified for services as quickly as possible; and (3) employees jumping a plane to a disaster recovery center to recreate a configuration there.

Definitions of all of these functions should be organized at the team level with designated recovery team leaders and team members. A diagram of a typical recovery team follows. These are not necessarily cast in stone, but teams and responsibilities should be adjusted to best fit a company. Staffs may run in three different directions, quite a trick for a staff of two!

MAINTAINING CRITICAL DATABASES BY OBJECT LINKING

The standards document should also include the people responsible for updating critical databases. These databases may contain equipment inventories, software

EXHIBIT III-12-D COMMUNICATING BUSINESS VISION

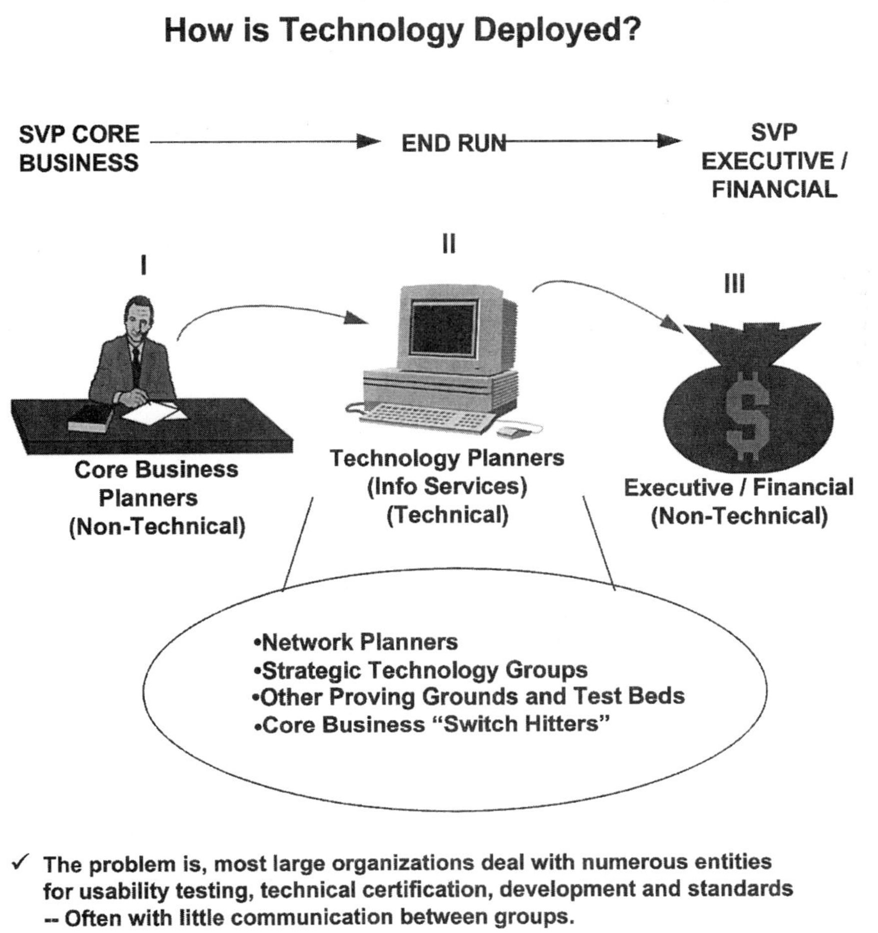

inventories, home telephone numbers, vendor call-out and escalation lists, carrier call-out and escalation lists, cellular telephone lists, and other key components.

Optimally, these databases should be object-linked to the network Business Resumption Plan so that when an operational change is made in a given department, the change is automatically reflected in the business resumption plan through a predetermined "hooked" or linked file in the software. Bear in mind that this is more than a clever convenience. It is an absolute necessity if you ever expect to keep up with the diverse cross section of software, hardware, and ancillary equipment associated with modern client/server environments. To prevent a staff member having to count things manually, take heed. As with many aspects of business resumption planning, the more invested at this initial phase, the less need for manual inventory later. Lucky companies may have a consultant, contractor, or outside resource to help at this juncture. Later, companies are on their own.

STANDARDIZING EQUIPMENT INVENTORY LISTS

To support critical databases, it will be necessary to standardize these databases in some easily importable format to the business resumption planning document. For

EXHIBIT III-12-E ENTICING USERS INTO ACCEPTING STANDARDS

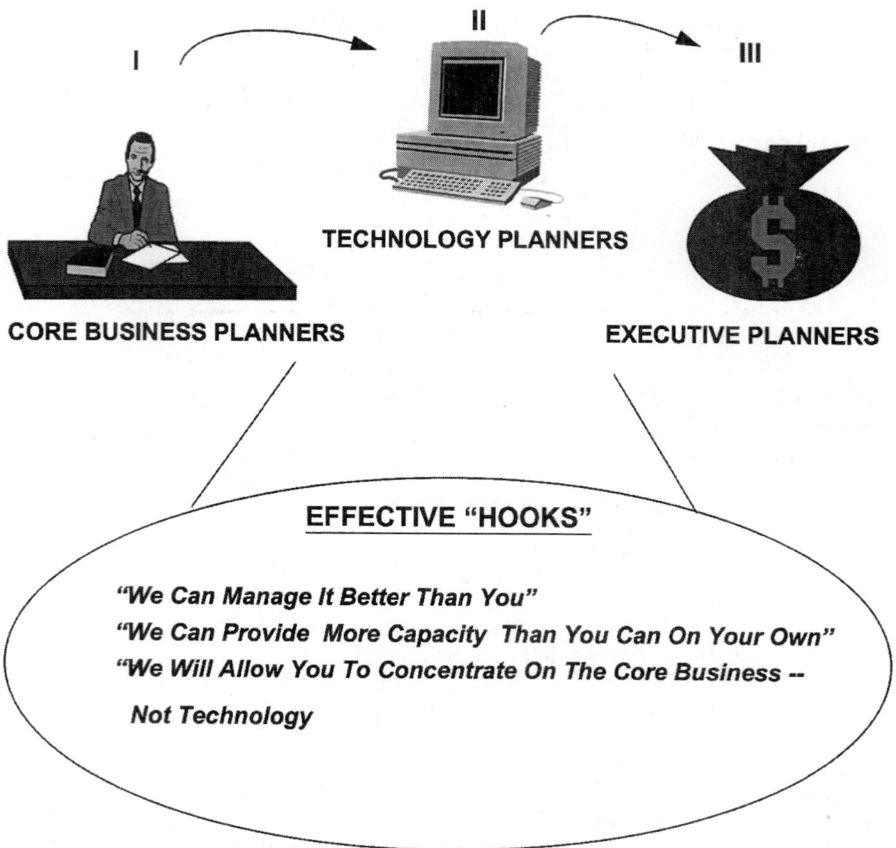

- ✓ **A diverse user base probably can't be forced to accept standards, but can be enticed.**
- ✓ **Advantages: Better support, lower incidence of outage, better backup and recovery, lower cost, greater operational control.**

example, a standardized equipment inventory could be imported automatically to an Excel spreadsheet, which will import into any of the Microsoft Suite of office products.

An equipment inventory of this type should record the type of equipment, the purchase date, the amortization period, the original cost, and other pertinent information. This would allow a technologist operating under emergency conditions to identify damaged equipment and make fast decisions as to whether to dispose, salvage, or buy new equipment. The ultimate complexity and difficulty level in maintenance for the final business resumption planning document would depend largely on how much work goes into these early phases.

DEVELOPING NEW HUMAN RESOURCE DEPARTMENT POLICIES

Another vulnerability is disgruntled ex-employees dialing in on their passwords and sabotaging a critical system. To eliminate this risk, we recommend a procedure with Human Resources to promptly cancel passwords of key employees when they leave the company. The IS or network services group should also be notified of their departure.

EXHIBIT III-12-F CONTROL OF CLIENT/SERVER — WHAT'S THE ISSUE?

Control of Client/Server
WHAT'S THE ISSUE?

"PRODUCTIVITY"

Mainframe Processing	Distributed Processing
• Rigid	• Close-to-Business
• Controlled	• Flexible
• Inflexible	• Productive
• Inhibited	• Unlimited Software Options
• Limited Software Options	• Easily Customized to Core Business
• User Can't Easily Customize to Business	

"SUPPORT"

Mainframe Processing	Distributed Processing
• Well Established	• "What Help Desk?!" Difficult To Train
• Cheap	• Immature Maintenance Tools
• Well Developed Maintenance Tools	• Expensive - Lots of "Quantity 1" Deployments
• Comparatively Easy to Train Help Desk	• Low Device To Support Personnel Ratio
• High Device To Support Personnel Ratio	

✓ The Key Is To Provide A Distributed Processing Level of Productivity With A Mainframe Level of Reliability and Support.
✓ This Is A Constant Balancing Act Industry-Wide.

DOCUMENTATION OF "FIRST-ALERT" PROCEDURES

The first people notified of a catastrophic event affecting an MIS or network system may not be an MIS or network member. In fact, they probably will not be. Detailed "**first-alert**" procedures will ensure that the proper IS and/or network management personnel receive immediate notice of a disruption.

MAINTENANCE AND UPDATES OF ESCALATION LISTS

Many employees probably have memorized contact information for key personnel and vendors. This is commendable but ineffective if these employees were unavailable or incapacitated.

Optimally the vendor or carrier should provide magnetic escalation lists every month that can be imported easily into a business resumption planning or first-alert procedure document.

EXHIBIT III-12-G THE KEYS TO USING THE NETWORK AS THE INTEGRATING FACTOR TO UNITE USERS INTO AN ENTERPRISE-WIDE SOLUTION

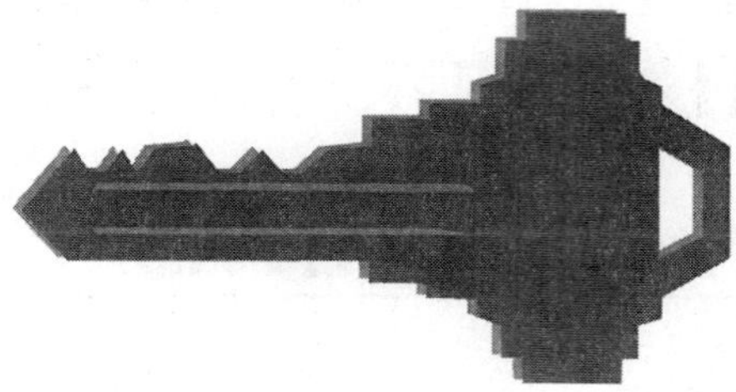

Observation: IF CONNECTIVITY, STANDARDS, AND NETWORK MANAGEMENT ARE THE KEYS....

Mainframe Connectivity *Higher Speed Bandwidth* *Video!*

Detect / Diagnose / Fix / Control *PC Implementations*

Higher Device to Personnel Ratios *Televaulting*

Quality *Proactive vs Reactive* *Systems Integration*

"Native LAN" Connections *Take Over Entire Processes*

Conclusion: THEN ORGANIZATIONS SHOULD USE THE NETWORK AS THE INTEGRATING FACTOR TO UNITE USERS INTO AN ENTERPRISE-WIDE SOLUTION!

EXECUTIVE MANAGEMENT TEAM (EMT) LOCATION

For many companies, an emergency command center or executive management team location is not firmly defined; rather, this function is established on an as-needed basis.

An EMT location needs to be predetermined and equipped with fax machines, direct telephone numbers (which have been preinstalled and published in the company directory), administrative support, copy machines, and other things required to coordinate an emergency response.

After identifying databases that can be reasonably expected to stay up-to-date, systems can be set up to import personnel lists, escalation lists, equipment inventories and components from other plans into a department's disaster recovery document.

EXHIBIT III-12-H TODAY'S QUESTION: WHAT WILL USERS NEED? HOW WILL YOUR INFORMATION SERVICES FOLKS PROVIDE IT? AND AFTERWARDS, HOW WILL YOU PROTECT IT?

"Connectivity, Standards and Network Management Are the Keys"

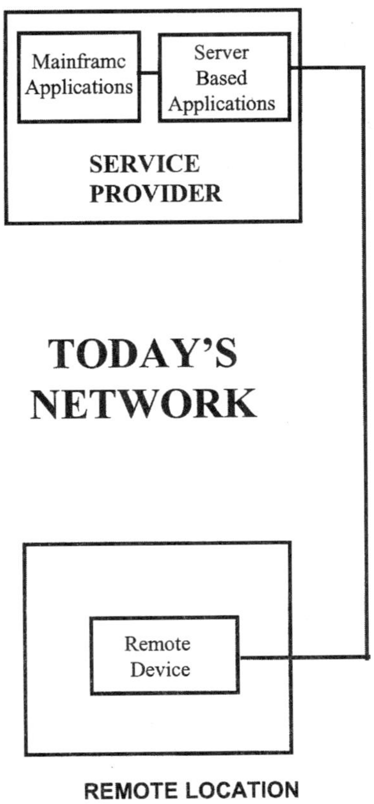

1) INFORMATION SERVICES CAN CONTINUE TO OFFER ITS CUSTOMERS:
   - Quality Hardware
   - Convenient Financing
   - Customer Support (Equipment & Software)
   - Capital Dollars Become Operating Expense
2) INFORMATION SERVICES MUST BE ABLE TO:
   - Provide Customer Intimacy
   - Exhibit Technical Leadership
   - Improve Operational Effectiveness
   - Move Huge Amounts of Information
   - Manage The Network Better Than The Customer Can Himself
3) THEN IT CAN ALSO PROVIDE CUSTOMERS
   - Higher Capacity Than The Customer Can Get On His Own
   - Better Network Management Than the Customer Can Do On His Own
   - Lower Maintenance Costs
4) TO ACHIEVE THESE GOALS, WE NEED TO MODIFY THIS MODEL SOMEWHAT

Reprinted with permission of
NaSpa Technical Support Magazine, Milwaukee, WI

IMPORTING A PLAN INTO OTHERS

Finally, a department's plan will eventually have to be integrated into the company-wide recovery plan. Again, care should be taken to identify the "right" components of the network plan to import into the corporate plan. Importing 200 pages of network procedures and standards, for example, will needlessly clutter the company-wide document. Not importing enough will hamper command and control in a major disaster plan activation. One suggestion is to incorporate a "yellow pages" section into the network recovery plan. Just as a telephone directory has yellow and blue pages to call attention to certain functions, it can be advantageous to print the first and most critical 10 pages on yellow paper. The first 10 pages should contain:

- The mission statement
- A readily understandable flow chart
- The basic game plan, including responsible teams

EXHIBIT III-12-I TOMORROW'S ANSWERS: AVAILABILITY OF ADVANCED CONNECTIVITY WILL CHANGE FUTURE NETWORK DYNAMICS

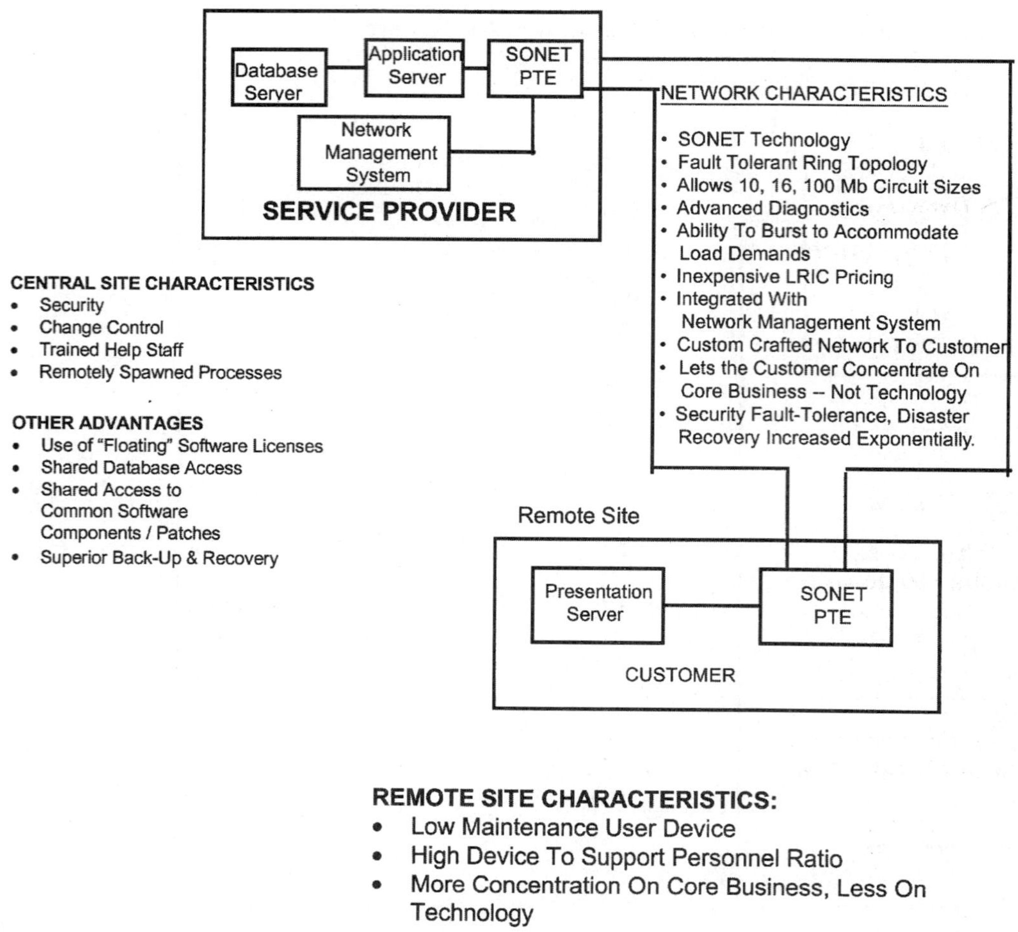

Reprinted with permission of
NaSpa Technical Support Magazine, Milwaukee, WI

This allows the RMT (Recovery Management Team) activating a company-wide plan to know of pertinent activities without overwhelming them with hundreds of pages of details. Many times, the RMT will activate or test a plan and never get beyond page three. As long as the RTM has the flow chart, for example, it can chart the activities of a department without micromanaging.

TELEPHONE INFORMATION LINES

Just getting the word out about major problems can itself be problematic. Any type of dial-in service that gives employees information on emergency situations, from snow storms to major disasters, can be a significant effort for a large work force.

EXHIBIT III-12-J SEAMLESS SOLUTION: AGGRESSIVE USE OF TECHNOLOGY WITH APPROPRIATE STANDARDS FORMS A WORD-CLASS SOLUTION

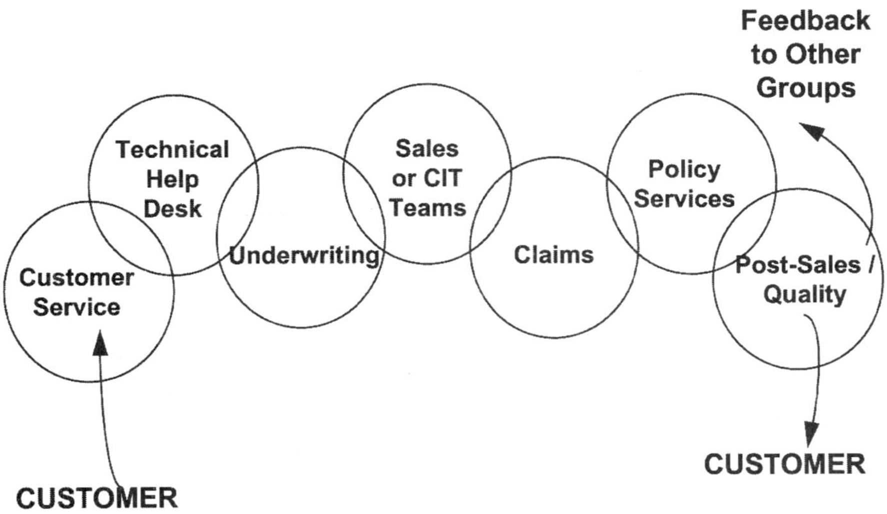

- ✓ **Impossible to do without distributed processing.**
- ✓ **Impossible to manage without standards.**
- ✓ **Requires mainframe level support w/distributed flexibility.**
- ✓ **Provides seamless access to all company resources by people actively on the phone selling.**
- ✓ **Assures the last question to the customer is not "May we call you back?", but "How many would you like to buy now?"**

Reprinted with permission of
NaSpa Technical Support Magazine, Milwaukee, WI

Optimally, the system should reside in an AT&T, Bell, or GTE switch, which would presumably be untouched by a disaster in a company's home office.

LISTING OF CELLULAR PHONES

Maintain a list of cellular telephone numbers for all employees with company-owned cell phones. First, convert it into a format which can be easily transferred into the future business resumption planning document with an Excel spreadsheet or something else that's easily importable.

Second, the company should decide which employees should *not* be authorized to use cellular phones in the work area after a disaster or emergency. Adopt a policy in advance. The largest companies enjoy the luxury of on-site microcells which provide additional capacity, but most companies do not. Therefore, most companies would probably be competing with the surrounding business community for the same cellular frequencies. Anyone who has ever been on a highway at 5:00 PM on a Friday and couldn't make a cellular call because all circuits were busy understands this problem. Since cellular phone is so important to coordinating a

EXHIBIT III-12-K RECOVERY TEAMS

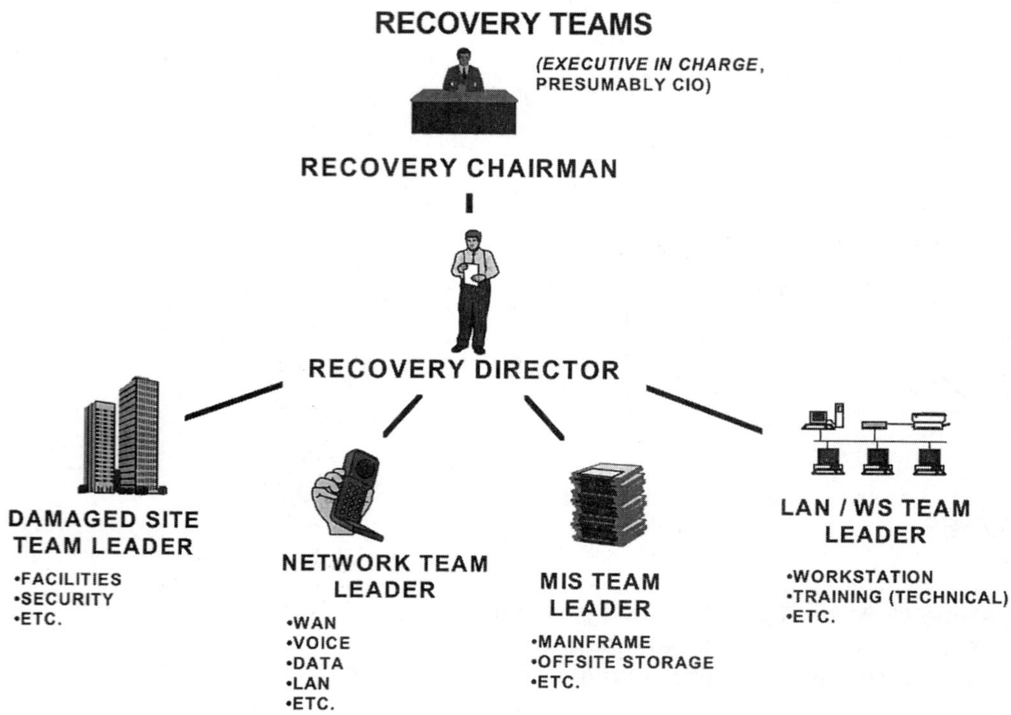

disaster response, don't waste it on employees who do not even belong at the disaster scene and are driving by rubber-necking the disaster and talking to friends. A corporate policy, while not eliminating this problem, will discourage it.

SCRIPTING OF CALL-OUT PROCEDURES

A very convincing story is probably the best way to illustrate why scripting what to say in case of emergencies are needed.

> **A key employee is called into work at 3:00 AM after a gas explosion levels an equipment room and starts a severe fire that results in a total loss of a technical platform. A wife answers. "There's been an explosion. The building is a total loss. I need Bill to come to work immediately." The wife responds, "Bill is at work." Now you have *two* problems: the equipment damage plus an hysterical family member!**

A script for calling people back to work can avoid needlessly alarming the family. Also, make company plans for professional grief counselors to step with Human Resources or other departments if injuries or fatalities are involved. An untrained person in any of these areas could be disastrous for everybody.

EMERGENCY "1FB" LINES FOR COMMAND AND CONTROL

Large companies should install independent "1FB" business lines in critical com-

EXHIBIT III-12-L "IMPORTING" CRITICAL DATA

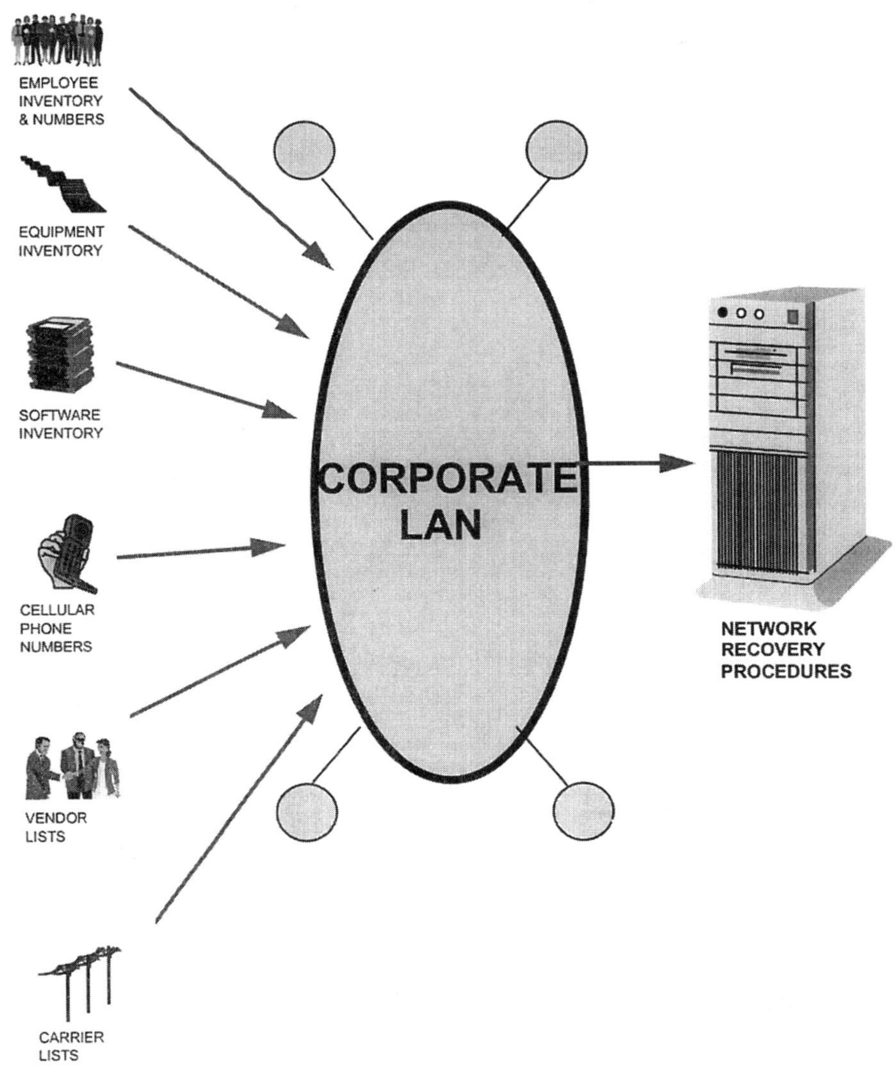

mand locations throughout the building. These should be terminated on copper wire, not fiber optics, in order to use central office station power for extra robustness. Companies using strictly fiber-optic entrance facilities for communications are particularly vulnerable, since these may not operate during power failures. Many organizations moved their telephone service facilities to fiber optics long ago, not realizing that when the telco-provided box in the basement loses power, the optics are out and so are the phones. Besides bringing some service in on copper (which is powered by the telco) companies should also consider adding an 8-hour supply of station battery to all 48-volt powered telephone equipment that they maintain, and coerce the telephone company to the same thing to any on-site equipment that they maintain.

EXHIBIT III-12-M WHERE TO IMPORT DATA: GOOD SOURCES

- ***Personnel Call-Out Lists*** Try using the organization's internal telephone book or any regularly used call-out list for after hours coverage, which can be assumed to be up-to-date. Care should be taken when identifying this database, as home telephone and other contact numbers invariably become stale and out-of-date. It is important to seek out the most accurate repository of this information. Some suggestions might be Payroll, Human Resources, etc.

- ***Software Inventories*** These must be complete with acquisition date, original cost, license number, and version number. Pay particular attention to software VERSIONS.

- ***Equipment Inventories*** The Finance Department, or other formal database, may track equipment after installation. Also, any CAD-like diagrams from one of the many equipment room design packages could be quite useful if up-to-date. Equipment inventories must be complete with acquisition date, original cost, revision number, software complement, and any relevant maintenance agreements. Possible repositories might include, among other places, the Finance Department, or the final resting place of contracts and agreements after equipment is purchased.

- ***Key Vendor Escalation Lists*** Get this from a central support function, if you have one. If any names or numbers have changed, they will know first, since they initiate most of the escalation for routine problems. Nonetheless, verify the list for accuracy, especially with regard to home telephone numbers, which could have changed since the last escalation was performed. All vendor lists should be available, especially if the vendor provides any kind of roll-in replacement guarantees on specific equipment.

- ***Wiring Diagrams*** All wiring layouts, technologies, and topologies must be defined to the point that a person unfamiliar with the organization would be capable of orchestrating reinstallation and recovery.

- ***Floor Grid Diagrams*** These should show all equipment, footprint sizes, clearances, and any special environment specifications, such as required air flow, etc.

- ***Associated Departments*** These can be imported, where required, into your department's disaster recovery plan. What is more probable, however, is that all parts of the network disaster recovery plan will be imported into the CORPORATE disaster recovery plan. For that reason, reasonable access to selected files should be granted to the overseers of the overall company plan, to assure the overall plan stays up-to-date as well.

- ***Components of the Company-Wide Recovery Plan*** These "selected" components may include items like physical security, fire procedures, bomb threat procedures, and other times, which are company-wide, rather than departmental in scope.

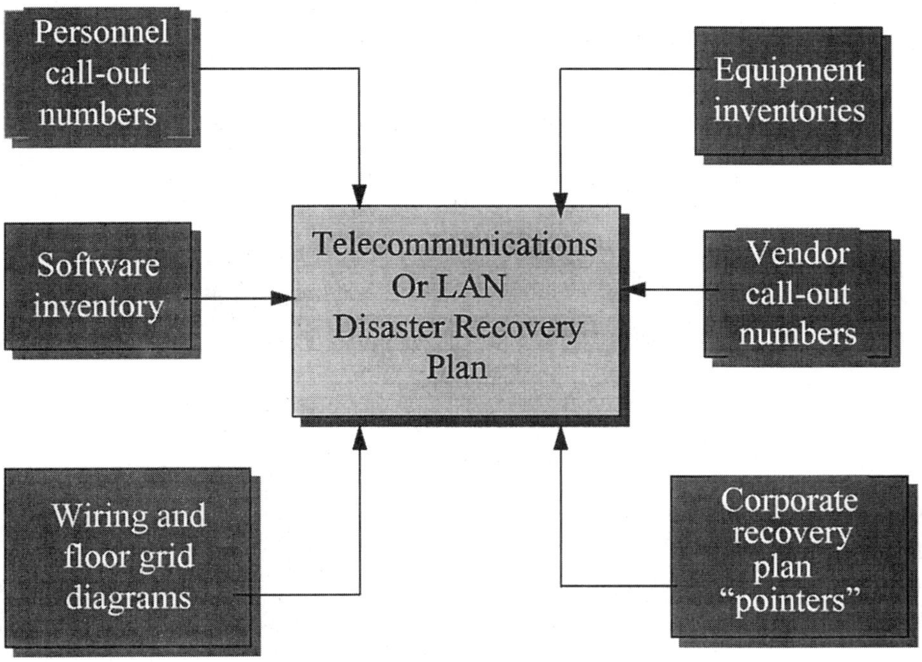

EXHIBIT **III-12-N** IMPORTING RECOVERY PLAN COMPONENTS (TELECOM PLAN)

NETWORK CONTINGENCY PROCEDURES

As we would expect in an organization of size and sophistication, network operations personnel in large, sophisticated companies have good technical skills for responding to major service disruptions. But how would the company fare if these people were unavailable? Documented network services contingency procedures, which would be understandable to outside vendors brought in during major system failures are essential.

As a technical environment gets more complex, organizing formal network contingency procedures into an understandable format is paramount. These would include programming intelligent multiplexers, remote loading, PBXs in regional offices, which recording to put on incoming telephone lines under what circumstances, which regional offices back up which other regional offices (and under which circumstances), initiating new command routing and remote call forwarding tables, establishing Switched 56 Kb service, ISDN BRI Service or Accunet Reserve T1 services to support major data hubs, and a host of other concerns.

MORE PAY PHONES

Since an area-wide telecommunication disaster would also affect the data communication services used for billing and collection on long distance phone calls, it could be expected that only sent paid (i.e., cash) calls would be processed. In cases of widespread service disruptions, telephone companies put special priorities on restoration of pay telephone service. Someone should keep a supply of quarters nearby; since one immediate consequences of an area-wide telecommunication outage is a cash economy.

A LOW-POWER AM BROADCAST STATION

Getting the word out can be a baffling proposition in a large organization. Because of the large number of employees who would require emergency information under adverse conditions, a low-power AM broadcast station might be in order. This equipment is widely used and operates in the standard AM broadcast band from 550 to 1610 kilocycles. The effective range, according to manufacturers, is about 10 miles, with a broadcast power of about 10 watts. Although the solution sounds expensive, this is probably the least expensive way of getting word out to hundreds of employees in a disaster. For about $18,000, the company can acquire a system, complete with digital memory, that is about eight minutes to broadcast emergency messages or messages of general interest to employees.

Signs could be posted at doors and parking lots alerting employees to the frequency. Mount the unit and antenna on a standard telephone pole or other vehicle to get the antenna to a height not to exceed 48 feet by FCC requirements.

Dial the unit to change the recordings using a standard 1FB telephone line. The company's security organization could easily be responsible for maintaining and controlling this function. During non-emergency times, the system could be used to broadcast items of interest. Employees in most metropolitan area would receive the signal, although it degrades the further it is from the broadcast tower.

Since almost everyone has an AM radio, at least in the car, these systems are quickly installed and become a valuable resource. Many cities today are adopting them for municipal information as well as an accompaniment other emergency warning systems, such as sirens.

Author's note: As the Mayor of the city of Ovilla, Texas, I purchased such a system recently for about $15,000, which included installation and frequency coordination. The system has gained widespread acceptance and usage. Combined with other warning systems, such as sirens, the city now enjoys a best-in-class public warning and information system. Surrounding cities have already begun duplicating Ovilla's example.

SUPPORT FOR NOMADIC USERS AND TELECOMMUTERS

Companies shouldn't forget roving work forces in their planning. Many employees work at home, and many roam as part of their jobs. More and more workers rely on dial-in services to upload their work or access critical systems. They include outside utility personnel, insurance claims adjusters, traveling salespeople, and telecommuters, to name a few. Talk to these special users and make sure provisions are made for them.

Besides, it could be convenient. Since these employee's "offices" are wherever they happen to be (home, hotel, airplane, or wherever) where to put them in the main location after a disaster isn't a worry; the principal worry is re-establishing the support systems they rely on. By learning about remote support systems, you may also be able to adapt them to support larger number of users (people who work at home, for example) if they can't get to the traditional office. Some categories of service are listed on the following page.

EXHIBIT III-12-O SUPPORT FOR NOMADIC USERS

Modem Access
Modem Access to Internet
Internet and BBS E-Mail
Voice Mail with Pager Notification
ISDN
Laptops
Home Offices
Executive Suites
Call Forward BNA
Remote Access to Call Forwarding
Caller ID/ANI
800 Service
500 Service
Nationwide Alpha Paging
Residential and Business Calling Plans

WORKPAPER III12.01 Company or Division

COMPANY OR DIVISION - ______________
PCs - APPLICATIONS, NEEDS, AND USERS
(Local Area Networks)

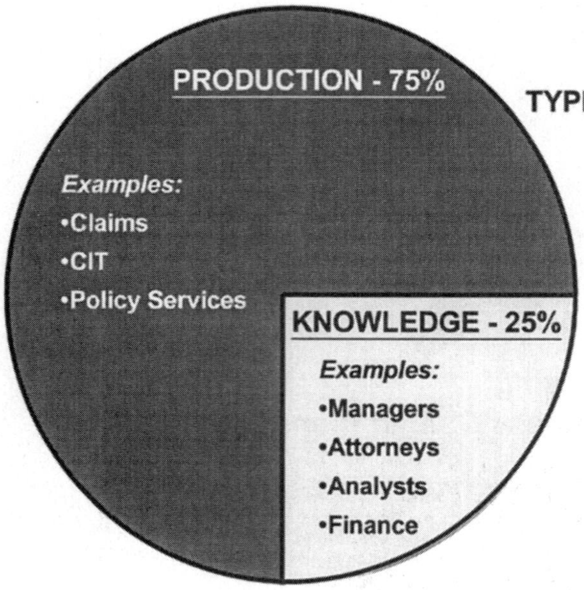

TYPES OF PRODUCTION USERS

1. ______________
2. ______________
3. ______________
4. ______________
5. ______________
6. ______________
7. ______________
8. ______________
9. ______________
10. ______________

TYPES OF KNOWLEDGE USERS

1. ______________
2. ______________
3. ______________
4. ______________
5. ______________
6. ______________
7. ______________
8. ______________
9. ______________
10. ______________

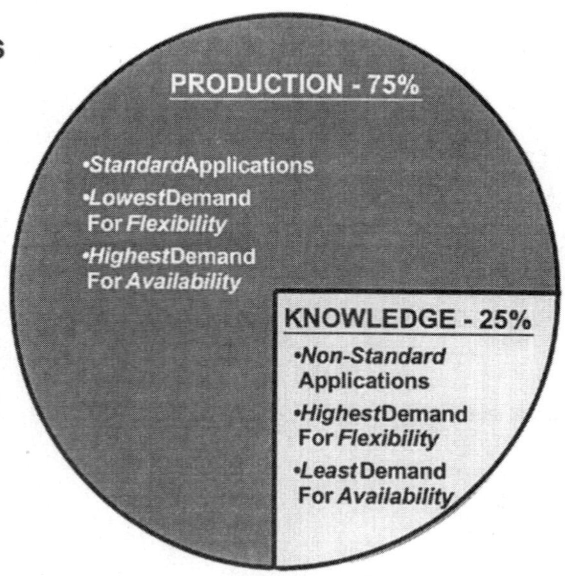

NOTE: Copy this worksheet and fill out for **each** subordinate company or business division. Percentages will vary, of course.

WORKPAPER III12.02 Relationship to Help Desk

RELATIONSHIP TO HELP DESK

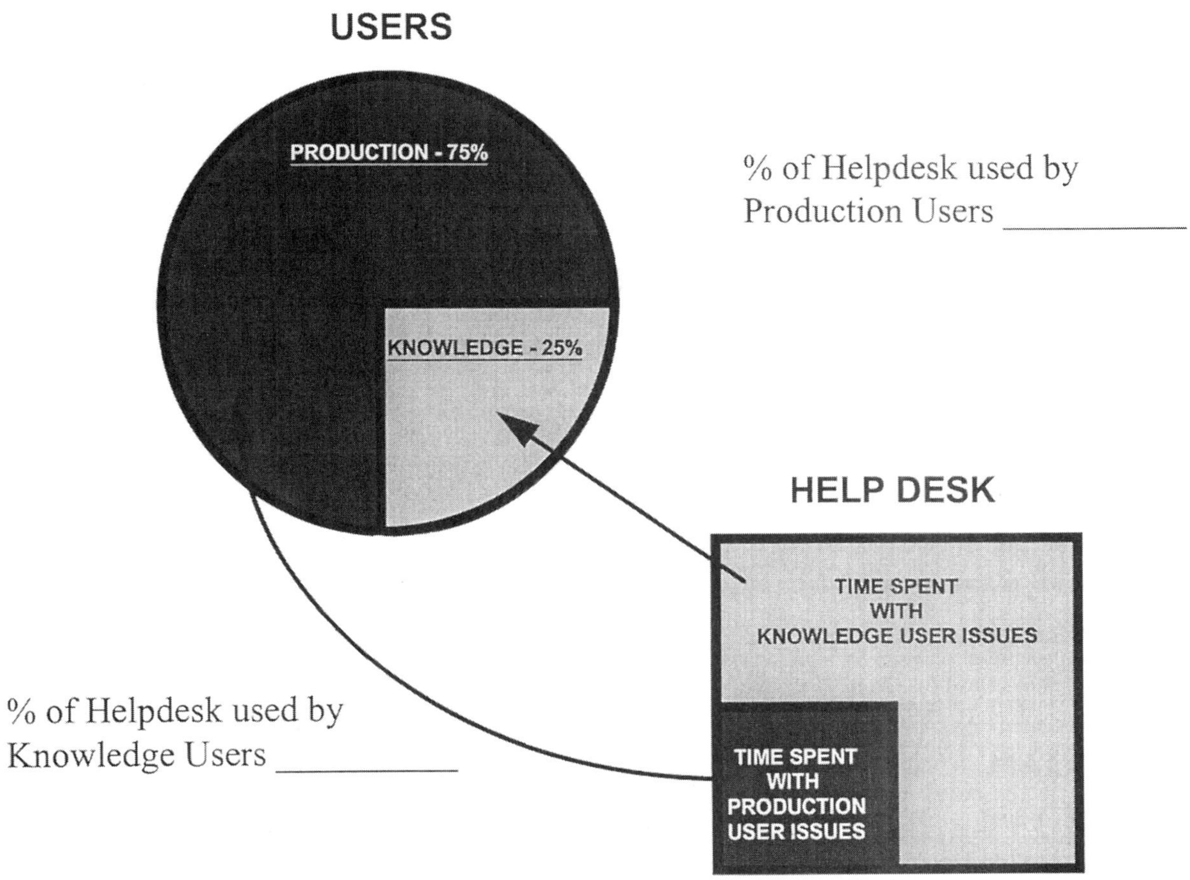

Interview several principal business units managers for an accurate reading of the percentage figure. Managers to include:

NAME:		TITLE:	
NAME:		TITLE:	
NAME:		TITLE:	
NAME:		TITLE:	

WORKPAPER III12.03 Today's Question

Today's Question:

What will users need? How will your Information Services Folks Provide It? And afterwards, how will YOU Protect It?

"Connectivity, Standards and Network Management Are the Keys"

Fill in the company specific ways your organization can make itself irresistible to its end users.

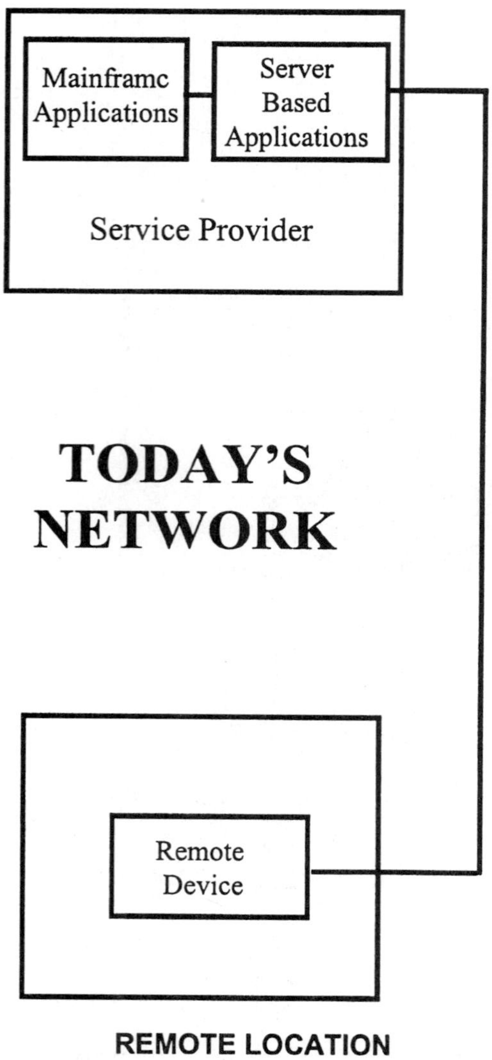

1) INFORMATION SERVICES CAN CONTINUE TO OFFER ITS CUSTOMERS:
- ____________________
- ____________________
- ____________________
- ____________________
- ____________________

2) INFORMATION SERVICES MUST BE ABLE TO:
- ____________________
- ____________________
- ____________________
- ____________________
- ____________________

3) THEN IT CAN ALSO PROVIDE CUSTOMERS
- ____________________
- ____________________
- ____________________

4) TO ACHIEVE THESE GOALS, WE NEED TO MODIFY THIS MODEL SOMEWHAT

WORKPAPER III12.04 Tomorrow's Answers

Tomorrow's Answers:

Availability of Advanced Connectivity will change future Network Dynamics

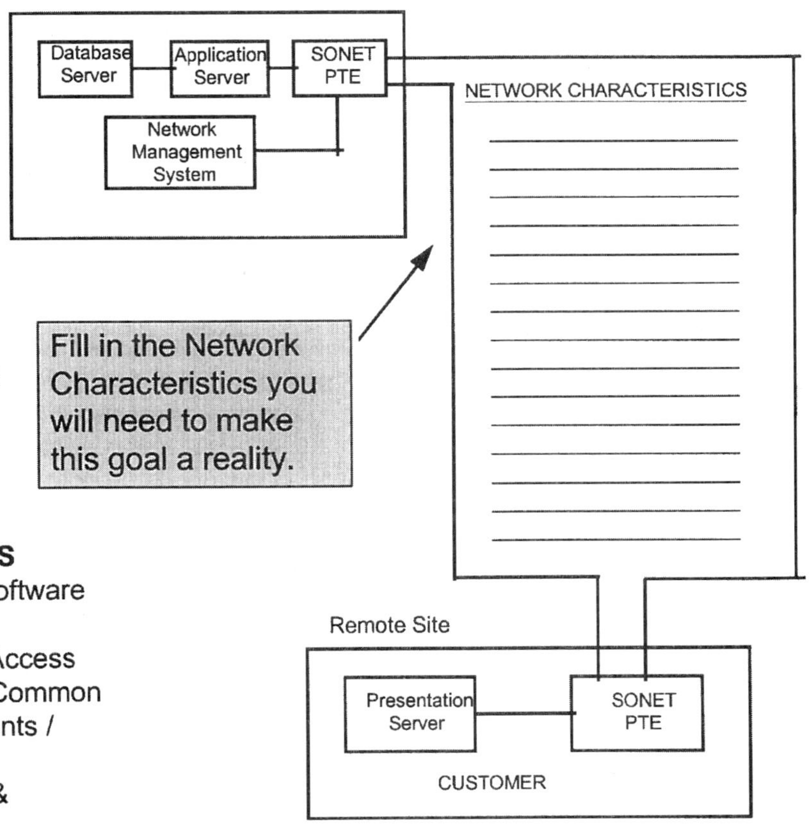

CENTRAL SITE CHARACTERISTICS

- Security
- Change Control
- Trained Help Staff
- Remotely Spawned Processes

OTHER ADVANTAGES

- Use of "Floating" Software Licenses
- Shared Database Access
- Shared Access to Common Software Components / Patches
- Superior Back-Up & Recovery

REMOTE SITE CHARACTERISTICS:

- Low Maintenance User Device
- High Device To Support Personnel Ratio
- More Concentration On Core Business, Less On Technology

WORKPAPER III12.05 Seamless Solution

SEAMLESS SOLUTION

Aggressive Use of Technology With Appropriate Standards Forms a Word-Class Solution

NOTE: Copy this worksheet and fill out for **each** subordinate company or business division.

- ✓ **Impossible to do without distributed processing.**
- ✓ **Impossible to manage without standards.**
- ✓ **Requires mainframe level support w/distributed flexibility.**
- ✓ **Provides seamless access to all company resources by people actively on the phone selling.**
- ✓ **Assures the last question to the customer is no "May we call you back?", but "May we set this up now?"**

Fill in your company specific departments into your own "seamless solution".

WORKPAPER III12.06 Supported Software and Hardware (Workstation)

Supported Software and Hardware (Workstation)

Component	Company "A" (or Division)	Company "B"	Company "C"	Req. Exec. Approval
Processor				
Vendor				
Type				
Video Memory				
Ram (Mbytes)				
Monitor *				
Hard Drive (EIDE)				
CD-ROM				
Enhanced Video Adapter				
Operating System				
Emulator				
Software Dist.				
Office 95				
Token Ring Adapter				
Browser				

*** High End profile requires Executive approval**

Pre-loaded Software:

____

____

____

____

____

WORKPAPER III12.07 Supported Software and Hardware (Notebook)

Supported Software and Hardware (Notebook)

Component	Company "A" (or Division)	Company "B"	Company "C"	Req. Exec. Approval
Vendor				
Processor				
Type				
Screen				
Memory Mbytes (EOD)				
Hard Drive				
CD-ROM				
Floppy Drive				
Modem				
Connectivity				
Browser				
Operating System				
Emulator				
Software Dist.				
Office 95				

*** High End profile requires Executive approval**

Pre-loaded Software:

____

____

____

____

____

WORKPAPER III12.08 Example: The Need for Controls

EXAMPLE - THE NEED FOR CONTROLS

IN JUST 2 YEARS
(EVEN WITH THE MOST RIGID STANDARDS)
UP TO 45 UNIQUE PERMUTATIONS OF HARDWARE / SOFTWARE COMBINATIONS
COULD EXIST AT ABC CO.

Time Line	0 mo.	6 mo.	12 mo.	18 mo.	24 mo.
High End Desktop					
Hardware Possibilities	1	2	3	4	5
Software Possibilities	1	1	2	2	3
Possible HW & SW Combinations	**1**	**2**	**6**	**8**	**15**
Low End Desktop					
Hardware Possibilities	1	2	3	4	5
Software Possibilities	1	1	2	2	3
Possible HW & SW Combinations	**1**	**2**	**6**	**8**	**15**
Laptop					
Hardware Possibilities	1	2	3	4	5
Software Possibilities	1	1	2	2	3
Possible HW & SW Combinations	**1**	**2**	**6**	**8**	**15**
Total Possible HW & SW Combinations for 3 Types of PCs	**3**	**6**	**18**	**24**	**45**

Assumptions: HW updated once every six months.
Major SW revisions once every year.

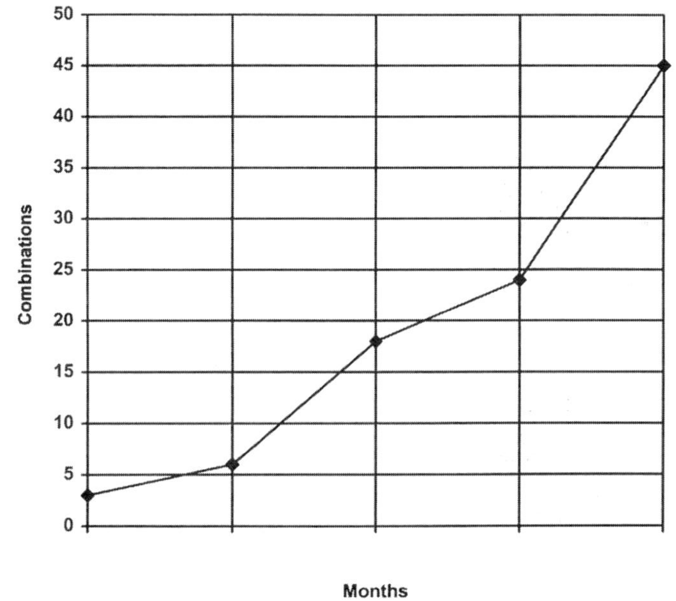

WORKPAPER III12.09 The Need for Controls

THE NEED FOR CONTROLS

IN JUST 2 YEARS
(EVEN WITH THE MOST RIGID STANDARDS)
UP TO ____ UNIQUE PERMUTATIONS OF HARDWARE / SOFTWARE COMBINATIONS
COULD EXIST AT ______________________

Time Line	0 mo.	6 mo.	12 mo.	18 mo.	24 mo.
Total Possible HW & SW Combinations for ____ Types of PCs					

Assumptions: HW updated once every six months.
Major SW revisions once every year.

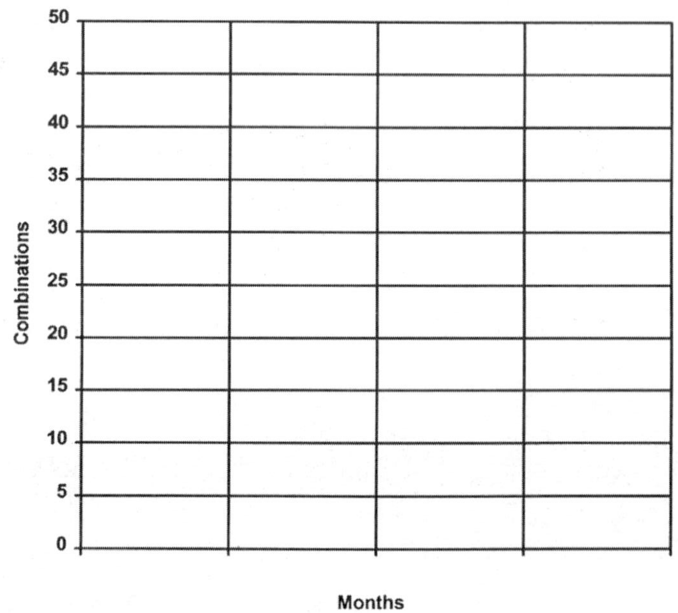

WORKPAPER III12.10 Recovery Teams

RECOVERY TEAMS

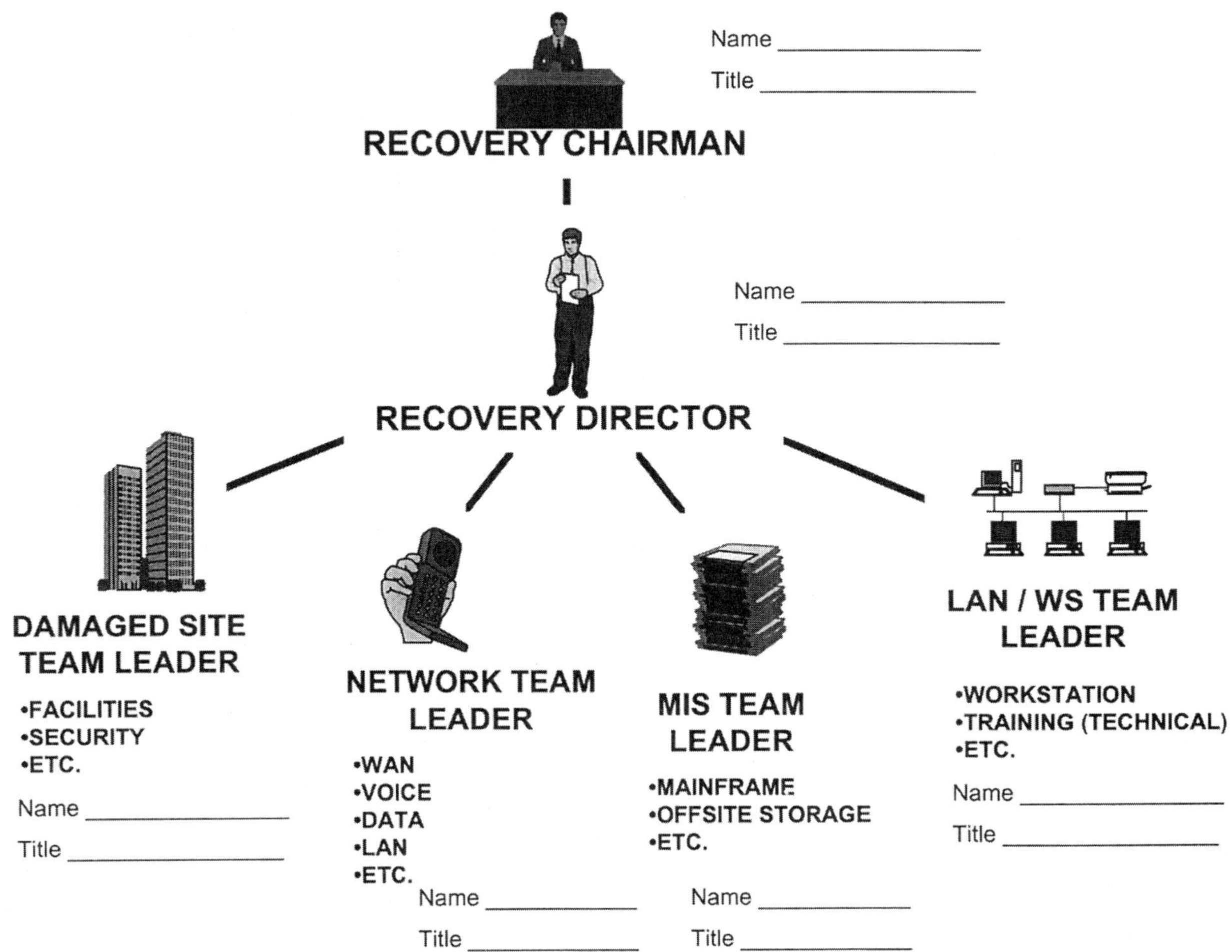

WORKPAPER III12.11 Example: Maintaining Critical Databases by Object Linking

EXAMPLE

Maintaining Critical Databases by Object Linking

DATABASE FILE	PURPOSE	SERVER/ DIRECTORY	FILENAME IN RECOVERY PLAN	RESPONSIBLE INDIVIDUAL
1. *(example)* CALLOUT.DOC	TELEPHONE NUMBERS	F:\DISASTER	APPX11.DOC	JOHN DOE
2. *(example)* INV97.XLS	EQUIPMENT INVENTORY (LAN)	F:\ACCT\INV	APPX13.DOC	JAN SMITH
3.				
4.				
5.				
6.				
7.				

WORKPAPER III12.12 Maintaining Critical Databases by Object Linking

Maintaining Critical Databases by Object Linking

DATABASE FILE	PURPOSE	SERVER/ DIRECTORY	FILENAME IN RECOVERY PLAN	RESPONSIBLE INDIVIDUAL
1.				
2.				
3.				
4.				
5.				
6.				
7.				

WORKPAPER III12.13 Mainframe Equipment Inventory Lists

Mainframe
Equipment Inventory Lists

COMPONENT	USE	ORIGINAL COST	PURCHASE DATE	PRIORITY
1.				
2.				
3.				
4.				
5.				
6.				
7.				

WORKPAPER III12.14 Telecommunications Equipment Inventory Lists

Telecommunications Equipment Inventory Lists

COMPONENT	USE	ORIGINAL COST	PURCHASE DATE	PRIORITY
1.				
2.				
3.				
4.				
5.				
6.				
7.				

WORKPAPER III12.15 LAN Equipment Inventory Lists

Local Area Networks
Equipment Inventory Lists

COMPONENT	USE	ORIGINAL COST	PURCHASE DATE	PRIORITY
1.				
2.				
3.				
4.				
5.				
6.				
7.				

WORKPAPER III12.16 Other Equipment Inventory Lists

Other
Equipment Inventory Lists

COMPONENT	USE	ORIGINAL COST	PURCHASE DATE	PRIORITY
1.				
2.				
3.				
4.				
5.				
6.				
7.				

WORKPAPER III12.17 Documentation of 'First Alert' Procedures

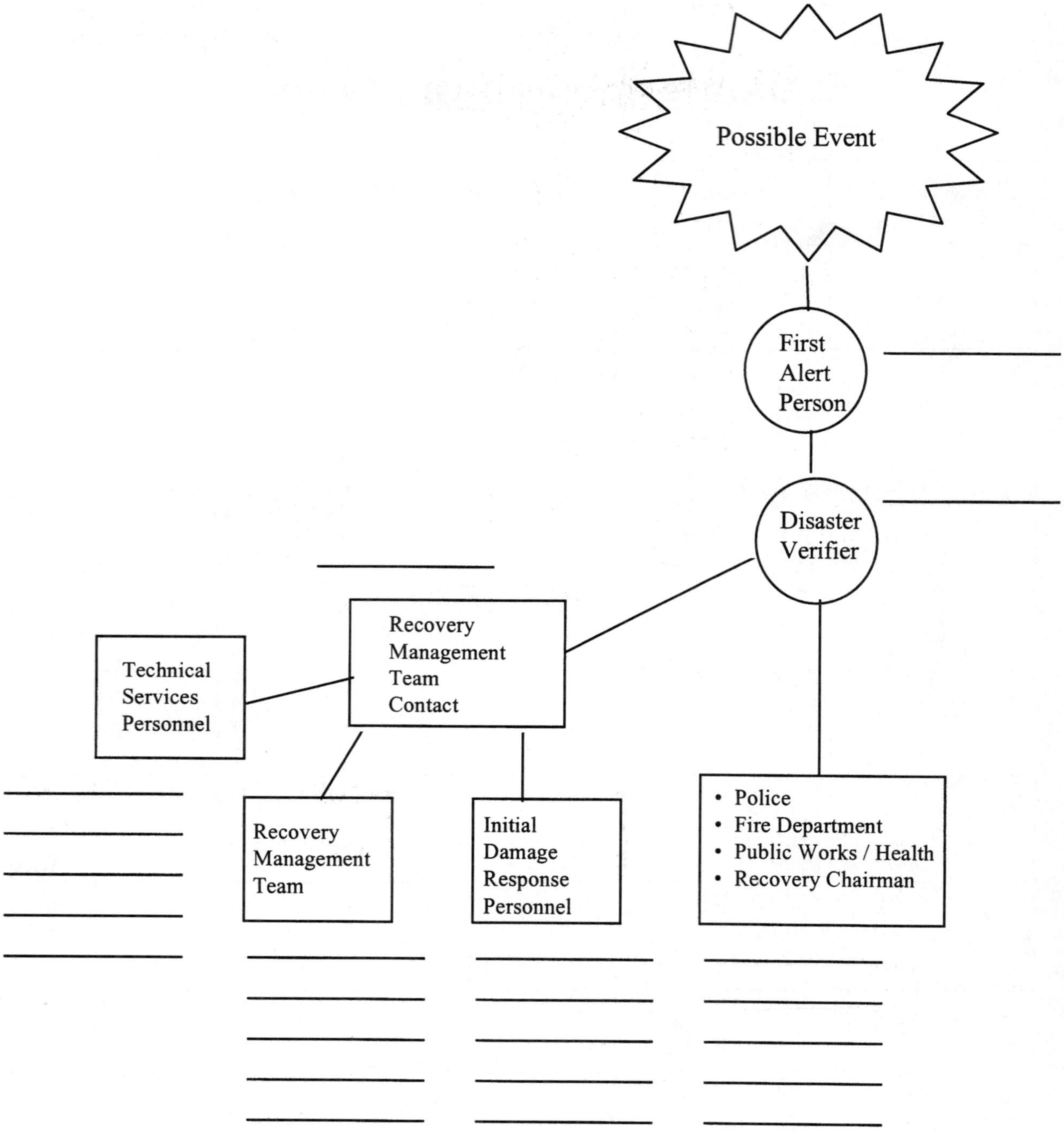

WORKPAPER III12.18 What To Do If You Are The First-Alert Person

WHAT TO DO IF YOU ARE THE FIRST-ALERT PERSON

IF YOU are the first person to become aware of a problem at the building, assume "FIRST-ALERT PERSON" responsibilities.

1. Immediately after completing the alerts and notifications required by existing emergency procedures, determine whether the disaster may affect the operation of company business.
2. If disruption of company business is possible, or if the situation creates a major safety concern, notify one of the INITIAL DISASTER RESPONSE PERSONNEL listed below.

NAME	HOME PHONE #	RECORD OUTCOME OF CALL
	(All area codes are _____ unless otherwise noted)	
______________________	_________________	____________________
______________________	_________________	____________________
______________________	_________________	____________________
______________________	_________________	____________________
______________________	_________________	____________________
______________________	_________________	____________________
______________________	_________________	____________________
______________________	_________________	____________________

WORKPAPER III12.20 Importing Recovery Plan Components: Mainframe

Importing Recovery Plan Components
MAINFRAME
(Relationships Between Plans)

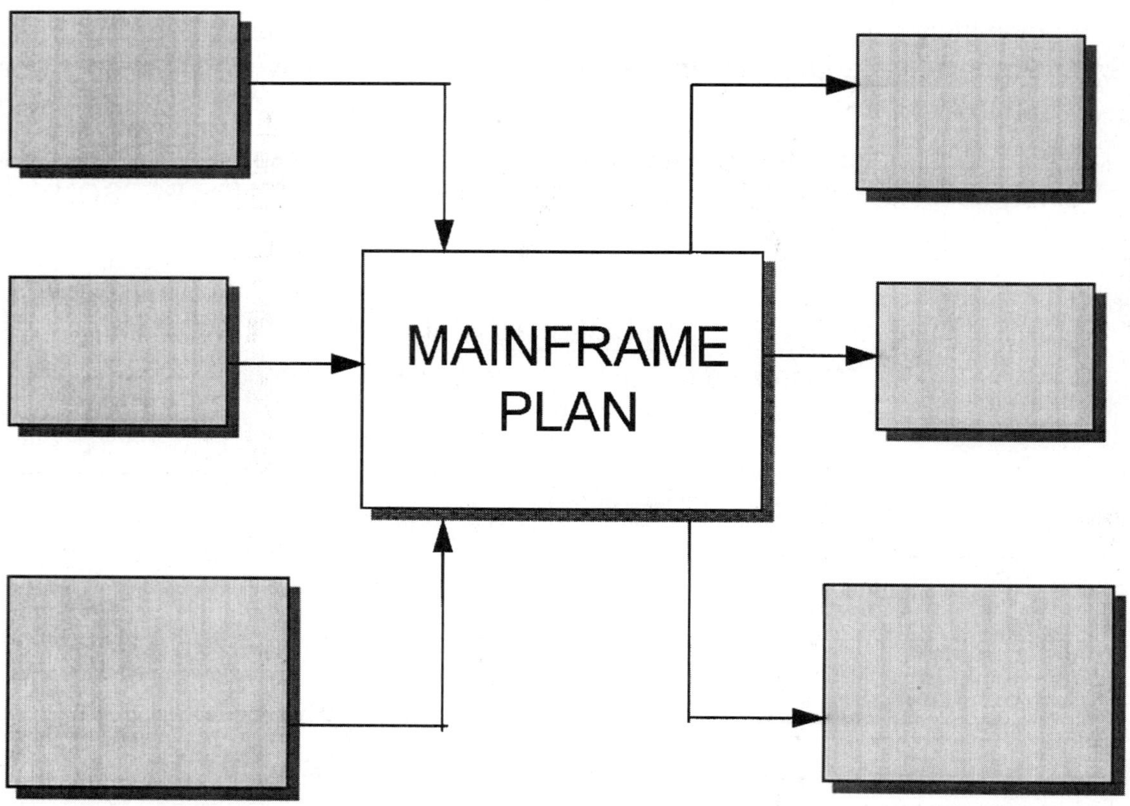

ITEMS WHICH WILL IMPORT (FILL IN)

ITEMS WHICH WILL EXPORT (FILL IN)

WORKPAPER III12.19 'Importing' Critical Data

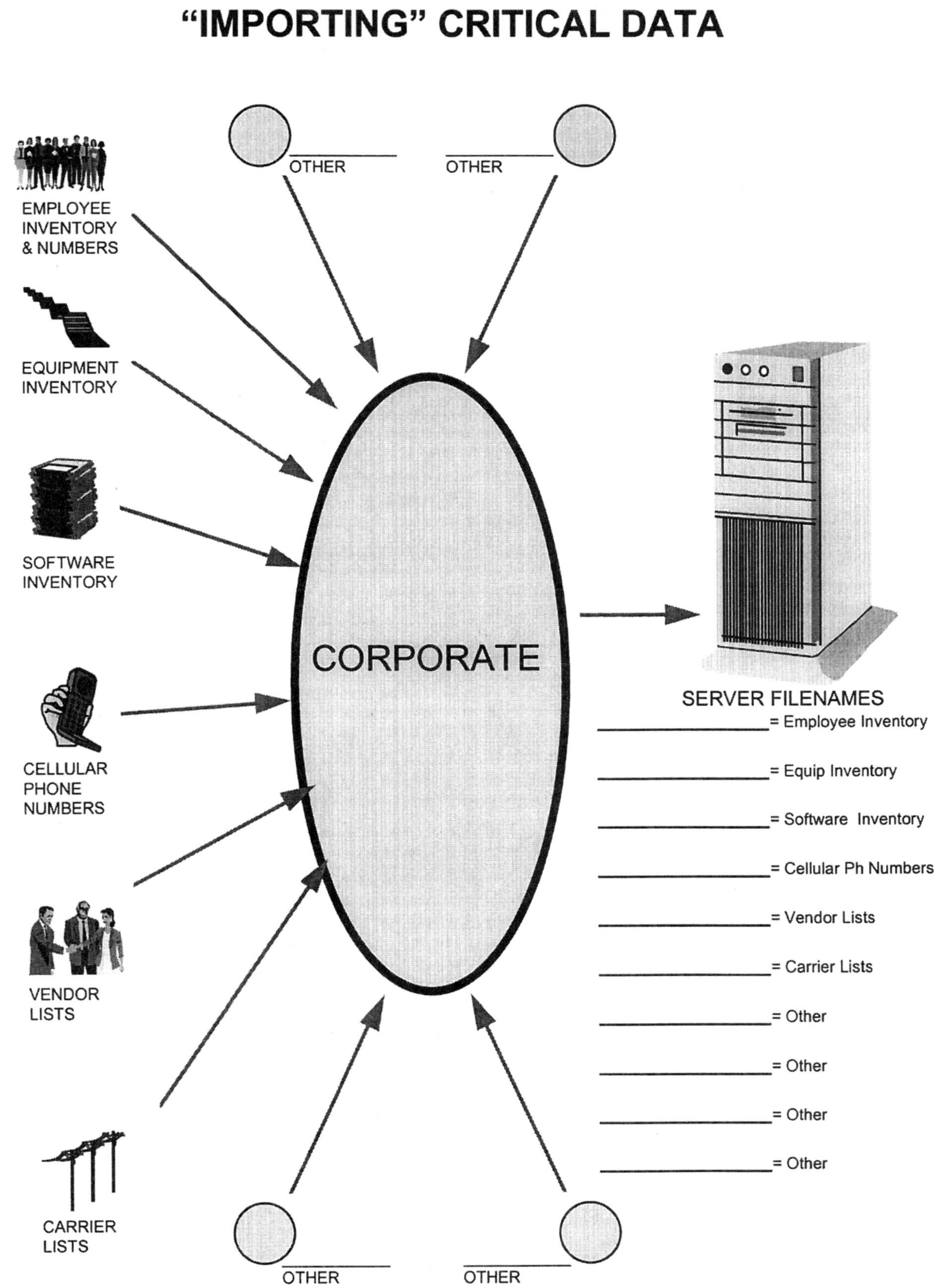

WORKPAPER III12.21 Importing Recovery Plan Components: Telecommunications

Importing Recovery Plan Components
TELECOMMUNICATIONS
(Relationships Between Plans)

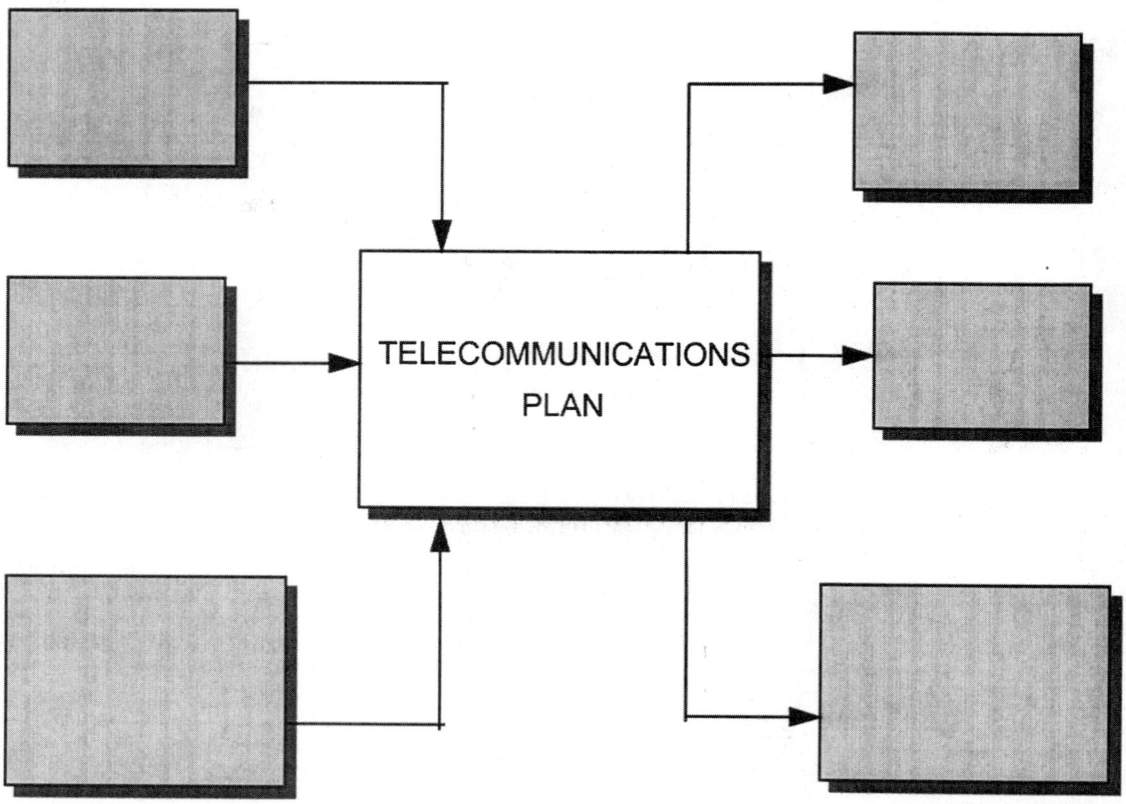

ITEMS WHICH WILL IMPORT (FILL IN)

ITEMS WHICH WILL EXPORT (FILL IN)

WORKPAPER III12.22 Importing Recovery Plan Components: LAN

Importing Recovery Plan Components
LOCAL AREA NETWORKS
(Relationships Between Plans)

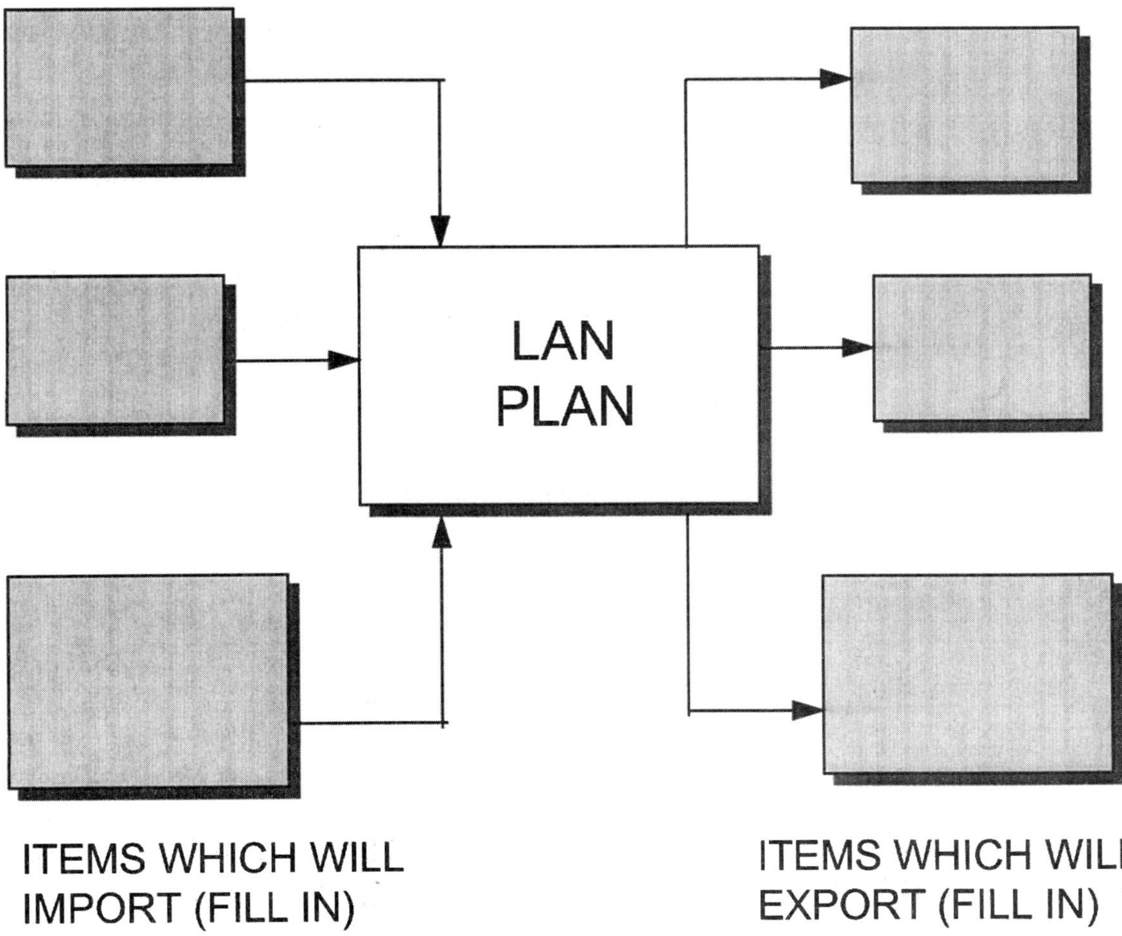

WORKPAPER III12.24 Listing of Cellular Phones

Listing of Cellular Phones

NAME	CELLULAR NUMBER	HOME NUMBER

WORKPAPER III12.23 Importing Recovery Plan Components: Other

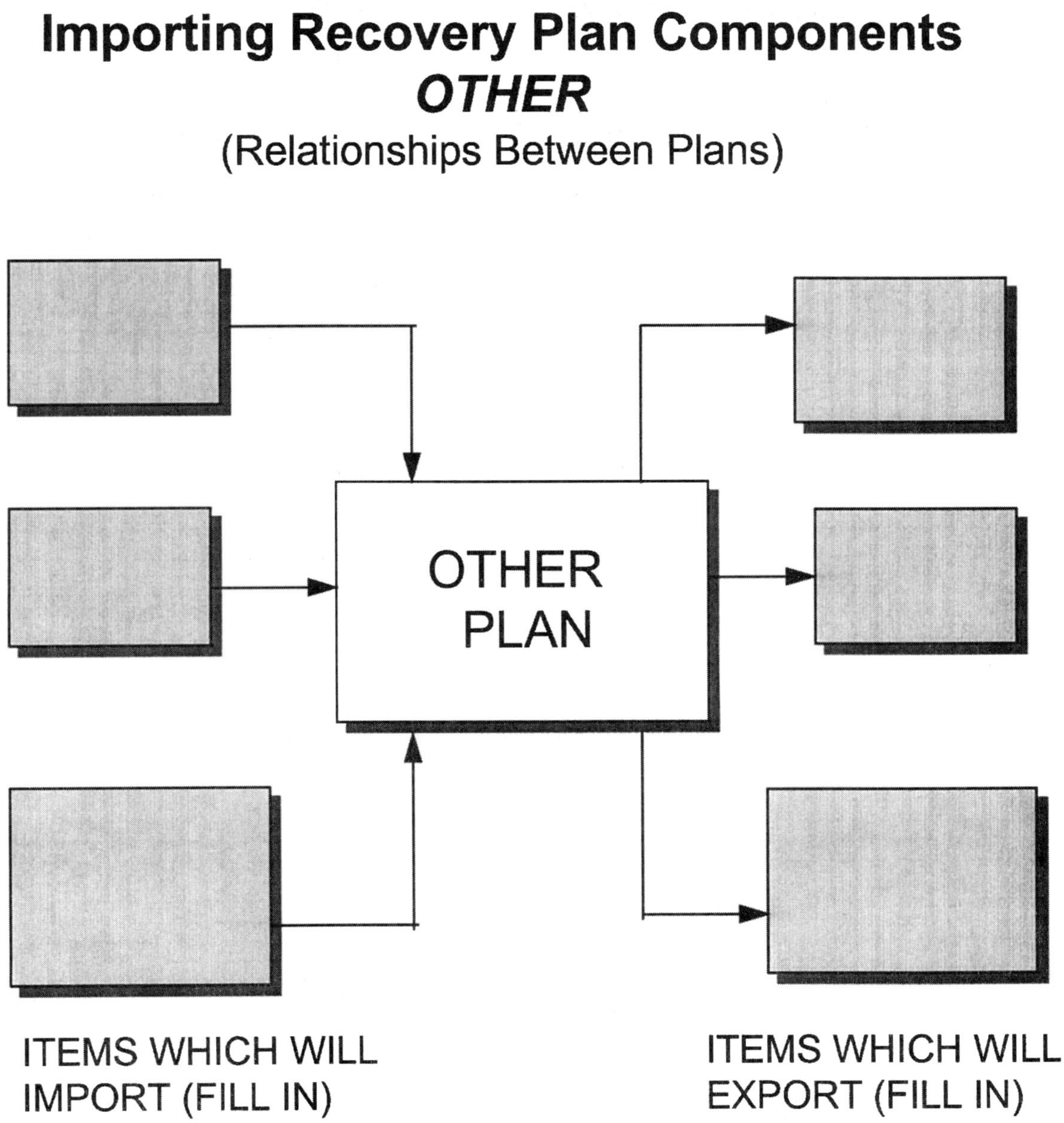

Pulling It Together

CHAPTER

III-13

CHARTING THE PATH

The first bar on the graph on the following page represents Phase I of a three-phase project. The process often breaks itself into three logical phases, each with its own action items and objectives. In this case they are:

- **Phase I Management commitment and preliminary risk analysis**
- **Phase II Education and defining standards**
- **Phase III Documentation of the recovery plan**

MANAGEMENT COMMITMENT AND PRELIMINARY RISK ANALYSIS

PHASE 1

Let's assume this first phase is being performed by a Big-6 accounting firm. The client pays a high rate for this service but for only for a relatively short time. The following action items are undertaken during this phase:

Initial Executive Meeting

For people who are not comfortable giving stand-up presentations in an executive forum, consider a "Big-6" consultant to help. Big-6 firms (external auditors) already have credibility with executive management, helping to break the ice and bridge the credibility gap. These companies also know how to speak to executive management in terms they understand. And management may already know them.

Presenting the Case to Management

It is a well-known fact that the human attention span is about 90 seconds. If a presenter at a meeting doesn't say something meaningful in that time, eyes and thoughts start to wander. This attention span shortens to about 15 seconds with executives, not because they are inhuman, but because they can size up what is said in about 15 seconds. If it doesn't command their immediate attention, they know someone else in the meeting will listen. Another problem in such a forum is that there are three possible answers to requests for permission to plan:

A. YES   B. NO   C. Let's study this some more

Which is the answer given most often? And why do recovery plans take 10 years to complete? It's because technical people are not always good at presenting their needs to management. Sure, technical services people know exactly what they need, but they go about asking for it all wrong. Consider the following presentation opening:

"Good morning. As you can see from the agenda, I am here to alert you to some problems with the telecommunications network. We need a disaster recovery strategy for the company's network resources. For starts, we need a UPS in the switch room, and would also like to upgrade our T1 multiplexers with redundant power and logic and hot stand-by switching. The telco says they will evaluate route diversity but this could be costly, and..."

EXHIBIT III-13-A PULLING IT TOGETHER: THREE PHASES OF THE PLANNING PROCESS

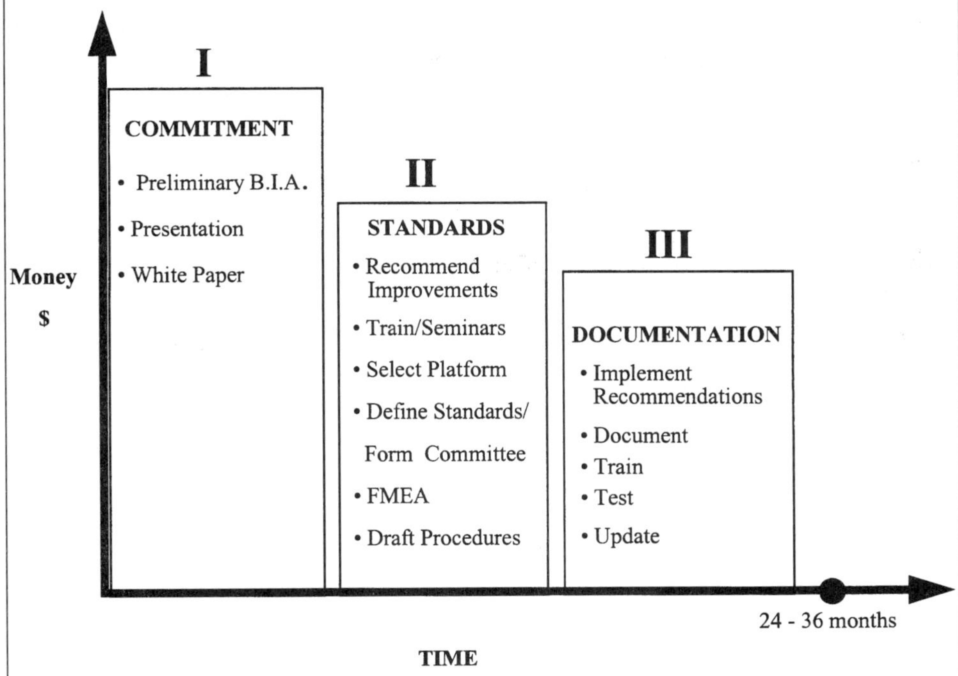

By this time, executives are looking at the ceiling, doodling, or looking at the next agenda item and expecting someone else to listen to the presentation. What is the most likely answer? Not "Yes." Not "No." (Management does not want to go on record as being against whatever is asked for!) So what is left? Why of course, let's study it some more. And why do recovery plans take 10 years? The presenter made a critical mistake by speaking to management in technical terms rather than business terms.

Here's an alternative:

> **"Good morning. Are you aware that we run the risk of a $500,000 per day financial loss to this company from disasters in our inbound call center? We have identified several areas of exposure, and would like you to help us consider preventive measures."**

How's that for an opening? Will that get management's attention? You bet! That's about how long it will take the CEO to look around the table and ask, "Where did that figure come from?" When all shrug their shoulders, the meeting is over. Sure, they will listen, but no action will be taken since the figures are in doubt. What answer can you expect? You guessed it: "Let's study this some more." Why do disaster plans take 10 years?

The key to getting around this problem is to get your figures validated before the meeting, during the Phase I interview process. This way, heads will nod, not shoulders shrug. You will also spend the meeting discussing your plan, not debating the numbers.

The best way to "sell" management is to produce believable loss scenarios and verify your figures with people the manager trusts. These include vice presidents (or equivalent) of sales, marketing, operations, engineering, finance, legal, and other divisions that can truly assess the effect of a disaster on revenue. A competent consulting company or the company's auditors can demonstrate the interview process. The only thing you should expect to walk away with from Phase I with is permission to plan! Once you have this solid commitment, it is time to move on. Once everyone hears the executive announce that this is a priority and who the point person is, things will move more easily.

STAFF EDUCATION AND DEFINING STANDARDS

PHASE II

Phase II is a very busy time. Activities in Phase II should include:

- Training of internal staff in recovery planning methodologies (i.e., hosting seminars)
- Selecting and retaining a consultant for the BIA and other necessary modules
- Developing a document outlining basic telecommunication operating standards and security procedures
- Continued information gathering via interviews and questionnaires
- Identifying critical data bases associated with the planning document
- Making long-term network improvement recommendations
- Recommending a suitable platform for the plan (e.g., LAN based, PC-based, etc.)
- Integrating the telecommunications network recovery plan into the information systems and overall corporate plans

The purpose of this phase is to not only accomplish the above items, but to transfer the *methodology* from the selected consulting firm to the internal staff. When staff members work with the consultant, they learn the methodology of recovery planning to avoid costly re-engagements of the consultant in the future. Staff also learn how to update the plan in Phase II to keep it current. Like the old saying goes: Give a man a fish, and he eats today. Teach a man to fish, and he eats for a lifetime.

Staff Training

What is required to write a disaster recovery plan and to keep it up to date? In most cases, operation personnel need training both in disaster recovery concepts as well as the mechanics of the planning process. One approach is to host some type of on-site training class covering the topic in detail.

The seminars can usually be hosted in a week, with half of an organization's staff attending alternating two-day sessions. The fifth day is reserved for wrap up, questions, and discussion. Each operations staff member is afforded two days of uninterrupted instruction on the fine points and concepts of disaster recovery planning, something very rare in busy operations environments! Other tips to follow before scheduling this time include:

- Host the seminar off-site at a hotel or another location to avoid interruptions
- Leave the beepers and mobile phones at the office
- Do not interrupt the attendees at the seminar unless it is absolutely unavoidable

This may be the only time busy operations personnel ever have the chance to actualize about disaster recovery outside the world of hung terminals, ringing phones, and constant interruptions. When everyone attends the same seminar, the staff knowledge level comes up, a common frame of reference is established, and the latter phases of the plan, when everything is pulled together, is easier.

Gathering Additional Information via Questionnaires

Phase II involves gathering additional information that is impractical to gather by direct interviews due to travel, logistics, time constraints, or other factors. One well-used alternative is a carefully written questionnaire in one of two formats: multiple choice or fill-in-the-blanks. Each has strengths and weaknesses. A competent consulting company or the Internal Audit Department can help you in developing the questionnaire.

PHASE III

DOCUMENTATION

Documenting the Plan

The consultant engaged for Phase II should also help decide on what kind of platform the recovery document will reside. There are many good PC-based telecommunications recovery plans on the market. They range from marginally useful to very useful. Expect to pay from $1,000 to $50,000, depending on the bells and whistles. The higher-end products often include an on-site consultant for a limited engagement of days or weeks to instruct your staff how to use the package.

These packages have resided on personal computers in the past; however, with the advent of Local Area Networks, there are new uses for these packages. The most notable is the ability to important data from interconnected LANS.

Lists that the company keeps up-to-date (which can be very difficult to find!) can be imported into the package as part of the normal business operating procedures. Many systems can be adapted to LAN environments, where importing lists can be done much more easily. A current list of home telephone numbers, for example, might be imported from the LAN serving human resources or payroll, assuring that phone numbers stay current. Personnel call-out rosters, circuit inventories, wiring diagrams, equipment inventories, and other key plan components should also be imported in this fashion.

One of the main deliverables of any well-run recovery project is the accurate definition of databases, which will be critical to the long-term accuracy of the plan. Where possible, standards should be defined to assure that information from these databases is automatically imported into the plan on a regular basis, without human intervention. Where automatic importation is not possible, responsible individuals must be designated to accomplish this by floppy disk transfers or other means.

After identifying databases that can be expected to stay reasonably up-to-date, set up systems to import personnel lists, escalation lists, equipment inventories, and components from other plans (such as LAN disaster recovery plans) into the network disaster recovery document.

To best utilize the import/export features in most PC- and LAN-based recovery tools, take extra care in identifying databases. Accuracy over time should be the primary criteria. If a system is in daily use, chances are it will be more accurate than one which is updated quarterly, semi-annually, or less often. The consultant can help identify these databases and automate the update process so that lists stay up-to-date, often without human intervention.

Integrating the Network Plan Into the Corporate Plan

The network plan will eventually have to be integrated into the corporate recovery plan. Again, take care to identify the "right" components of the network plan to import into the corporate plan. Importing 200 pages of network procedures and standards, for example, will needlessly clutter the corporate document, but not importing enough will hamper command and control in a major disaster plan activation. Incorporating a "blue pages" section into the network recovery plan can help. Just as a telephone directory has yellow and blue pages to identify certain functions, the first 10 pages printed on blue paper will call attention to the most critical parts. These first 10 pages of the plan should contain:

- The policy and mission statement
- A readily understandable flow chart
- The BASIC game plan, including responsible teams.

The idea behind this concept is to allow an EMT (Emergency Management Team), which will activate a corporate-wide plan, to know of your activities without being overwhelmed with hundreds of pages of details. Often an EMT will activate or test a plan and never get beyond page three. As long as the members have the flow chart, for example, they can chart the activities of the network department without micromanagement. The network plan itself, however, has the full complement of pages to allow for successful implementation even if key personnel are lost or unavailable. In short, management has all it needs to conduct a recovery operation in the 10 blue pages and it reduces management's temptation to micromanage the recovery process.

Writing/Updating the Plan

For the inexperienced disaster recovery planner, the most difficult part of the planning process is often simply getting off square one. Disaster recovery planning is a methodical process, and most experienced managers can make judgments about what needs to be done or replaced first after a disaster. Sometimes, however, seeing a process laid out on paper is helpful. The following information was drawn from a number of sources, mostly from actual disaster recovery plans. It allows planners to customize the plan to their own requirements. An understanding of this guide and consultation with other sources, a rudimentary disaster recovery plan outline should be achievable. Good luck!

EXHIBIT III-13-B

Section I Administrative / Mission Statement

A. Objectives of the Project - Overriding Themes

1. Protection of Human Life
2. Minimize Risk to Company
3. Prepare to Recover Critical Operations
4. Safeguard Against Lawsuits
5. Protect Competitive Position
6. Preserve Customer Confidence and Goodwill
7. Overview of Preliminary Business Impact Analysis
8. Synopsis of Recovery Strategy

Section II The Action Plan

A. Detailed Emergency Procedures

1. P.B.X. Hardware Failure
2. P.B.X. Software Failure
3. Failure of Major T1 Node
4. Failure of Major Front End Processor
5. Loss of Data Center
6. Loss of Critical Bridge / Router / Gateway
7. Loss of Bell Operating Company Central Office
8. Loss of AT&T POP (Point of Presence)
9. Loss of MCI POP
10. Loss of a Building
11. Fire
12. Flood
13. Earthquake
14. Tornado
15. Sabotage / Vandalism

EXHIBIT III-13-B (continued)

16. Bomb Threat

17. Power Loss

18.. Security Breach

19. Heavy Snow or Weather Related Disruption

B. Damage Assessment

1. Activation of the Emergency Management Team (EMT)
2. Notification of Emergency Management Team
3. Reports to Emergency Management Team
4. Notification of Clean-Up Companies
5. Interfacing with Local Authorities

C. Initial Reaction Procedures to a Disaster Report

1. Notification of Police, Fire, Medical
2. Notification of Management
3. Determination of Cause
4. Filing of Initial Damage Assessment Reports

D. Business Resumption

1. Activation of Emergency Management Team (EMT)
2. Activation of Disaster Teams
3. Activation of Network Backup Plans
4. Decision to Declare a Disaster
5. Decision to Activate Recovery Center
6. Relocation to Recovery Center
7. Coordination with Local Authorities
8. Notification of Customers, Financial Lenders and Media
9. Activation of the Recovery Center Equipment Platforms

EXHIBIT III-13-B (continued)

E. Rerouting of Network Facilities to the Recovery Center

1. Restoral of Network Control Help Number
2. Restoral of Help Desk Incoming Numbers
3. Command Routing of Incoming 800 Service
4. Remote Call Forwarding of Local Telephone Service
5. Redirection of Backbone T1 Network
6. Redirection of Critical LAN Router Links
7. Redirection of Other Dedicated Wide Area Network Services
8. Re-establishment of Production Dial-In Data Ports
9. Re-establishment of Maintenance Dial-In Ports
10. Verification of Software Configurations

F. Concurrent Recovery Activities

1. Assisting EMT in Preparation of Statements
2. Opening a Critical Events Log for Audit Purposes
3. Modified Signing Authority for Equipment Purchases
4. Where to Get Cash
5. Maintaining Physical Security
   - A. Security at the Damaged Site
   - B. Security at the Recovery Center

G. Restoration of Critical Business Functions

1. Coordination of Restoration of the Original Site
2. Restoration of Hardware Systems
3. Restoration of Software Systems
4. Restoration of Power / UPS
5. Replacement of Fire Detection and Suppression Systems

EXHIBIT III-13-B (continued)

6. Additional Security Concerns
7. Rewiring of the Facility
8. Restoring Original Local Area Network Configuration
9. Restoring Original Wide Area Network Configuration
10. Testing new hardware and software
11. Training Operations Personnel on new equipment
12. Training Employees on new equipment
13. Scheduling migration back to original site
14. Coordinating return to original site

H. Wrap Up Activities

1. Review of Critical Events Log
2. Evaluation of Vendor Performance
3. Recognition of extraordinary achievements
4. Preparing Final Review and Activity Report
5. Aid in Liability Assessments
6. Schedule Compensatory Time Off
7. Schedule the PARTY

Section III Testing and Maintenance of the Plan

A. Testing and Testing Procedures

1. Affected Departments
2. Responsibilities
3. Reference Documents
4. Frequency of Testing
5. Pre-Test Coordination
6. Scheduled Tests

EXHIBIT III-13-B (continued)

7. Unscheduled Tests

8. Introduction of Complications

9 Evaluation of Results

B. Plan Maintenance and Maintenance Procedures

1. Affected Departments

2. Responsible Personnel

3. Frequency

4. Hardware Change Procedures

5. Software Change Procedures

6. Staff or Team Member Changes

7. Vendor List Updates

8. New Technologies or Equipment

9. Contract Renewals

10. Emergency Assistance Changes

Section V Training

A. Training and Training Procedures

1. Scope of Training

2. Affected Departments

3. Responsibilities

4. Reference Documents

5. Frequency of Training

6. Required Vs Optional Training

7. Media to be used

8. Specialty Team Training

9. General New Hire Training

EXHIBIT III-13-B (continued)

Section VI Appendices

Appendix 1	Emergency Call Lists of Management and Recovery Teams
Appendix 2	Team Member Duties and Responsibilities
Appendix 3	Inventory and Report Forms
Appendix 4	Maintenance Forms
Appendix 5	Hardware Lists and Serial Numbers
Appendix 6	Software Lists and License Numbers
Appendix 7	Vendor Call Out and Escalation Lists
Appendix 8	Carrier Call Out and Escalation Lists
Appendix 9	Network Schematic Diagrams
	A. Normal Configuration B. Disaster Configuration
Appendix 10	Equipment Room Floor Grid Diagrams
	A. Normal Configuration B. Disaster Configuration
Appendix 11	Contract and Maintenance Agreements
Appendix 12	Special Operating Instructions for Sensitive Equipment
Appendix 13	Cellular Telephone Inventory and Agreements
Appendix 14	All Other

WORKPAPER III13.01 Rate Your Organization's Disaster Recovery Procedures

The following worksheet is reprinted with permission of NaSpa Technical Support Magazine, Milwaukee, WI

Rate Your Organization's Disaster Recovery Procedures

How does your organization's disaster recovery plan stack up? Are you taking reasonable precautions to prevent disasters? Will your plan work when you need it? Find out the answers to these questions and more by taking this handy quiz!

A successful disaster recovery plan begins with implementing effective *Operating and Security Standards* for all technical platforms. These include items such as LANs, Mainframes, Telecommunications, attendant positions, and other components necessary to the conduct of the core business. Standards are designed essentially for two reasons:

I. To assure that necessary changes are made in the day-to-day operations environment to assure that emergency procedures execute gracefully.

2. To assure that necessary changes are made in the day-to-day operations environment which will prevent disasters from happening in the first place.

For example in the first case, if an organization's emergency procedures dictate that someone will call all essential employees to help with the recovery effort, some kind of policy must be in place to assure that this list of employees and their home telephone numbers is there in the first place! This is handled in the standards document, or more specifically, in the section which deals with *documentation* standards.

In the second case, it might be a good idea to ban smoking and eating in equipment rooms for example. This would also be documented in the standards document, specifically in the section which deals with *housekeeping* standards.

It is probably a safe bet to say that some of the most successful recovery plans start with strong operating and security standards documents.

Does your organization underwrite technical service standards? If so, how well do your organization's standards stack up? Use the following items and explanations to "rate" your organization's present standards. The scores are just for fun, but by taking the quiz you will learn some important lessons about how to protect your valuable technical systems - and your job!

I. Physical Standards

There are many things which should be done pro-actively to protect mission critical LAN and Telecommunications equipment installations in terms of physical protection. Check your organization for the following, and award yourself **five** points for each item you have.

1. Do equipment room doors lock? ______
2. Does a sign-in list exist? ______
3. Are emergency instructions posted in the equipment room? ______
4. Are instructions posted for a “graceful” equipment shut-down in an emergency? ______
5. Is smoking and eating prohibited in the equipment room? ______

6. Does a "parcel pass" system exist for signing in equipment prone to theft, such as laptop computers, modems, etc? ______
7. What kind of fire protection is available in equipment areas?
   A. Sprinklers

      Dry pipe or pre-action *add* five points ______

      Regular Sprinklers *subtract* five points ______
   B. Smoke and Particle Detectors ______
   C. Fire Extinguishers ______
8. Is fire-retardant cable such as Teflon, HALAR, Kevlar or STOLSIS in use? ______
9. Are all cable risers fire-stopped with approved material? ______
10. Does building security have a procedure to call you in case of a problem in the equipment room? ______

Bonus Question!!!

11. Have you ever run an infrared scan on your facility? (Special equipment designed to pick up heat sources often used as a preventative measure to prevent fires before they start. If the answer is yes, award yourself **twenty** points. If the answer is no, contact AT&T and ask about Safety-Net Service Assurance Solutions Thermographics Service (wow, that's a mouthful) or your local fire system contractor. ______

II. Protection Against Water Damage

Do protections exist for possible water damage for equipment? Since damage due to water, whether it be from plumbing, outside flooding, air conditioning chillers, drains, or other causes is a major cause of disasters, you may add **ten** points for each of the following:

1. Are water pipes in equipment rooms labeled for easy shut-off? ______
2. Do moisture detectors exist under raised floors? ______
3. Do you keep plastic sheets or pre-fitted covers in the equipment room to cover equipment in an emergency? ______
4. Are there drains in the equipment room? ______
5. Do drains employ back flow devices? ______
6. Is your PBX or LAN Server in the Basement?

   If YES, subtract ten points ______

   If NO, add ten points ______

7. Do you have a procedure which tells employees what to do if a magnetic tape gets wet? (You store them in the freezer!)

   If yes, add ten points ______

8. Does a procedure exist which tells employees how to dehumidify an equipment room? (Fans, space heaters, etc)

   If yes, add ten points ______

9. Do you know where to find a blow dryer on site? (Great for drying out equipment) If yes, add ten points ______

10. Does your building have a previous history of water damage which has gone uncorrected? If so, subtract ten points (and get it corrected for god's sake!) ______

Bonus Question!!!

11. Does your company have a contingency plan for a possible **cut off** of your commercial water supply? If so, award yourself **fifty** points! ______

III. Operating Standards for LANS and Telecom (Five Points Each)

1. General LAN Protection Standards (Twenty Points Each)
   A. Does a formal change control procedure exist? ______
   B. Are specific persons authorized to make major system changes? ______
   C. Does a policy exist to make a complete system backup before all major system changes? ______
   D. Are all maintenance terminals password protected? ______
   E. Have all factory default passwords been changed, for all equipment? ______

2. LAN Virus Protection (Twenty Points Each)
   A. Virus Software Regularly Run ______
   B. Unauthorized Public Domain Files Deleted ______

C. Access to Computer Bulletin Boards Controlled ______

D. Transportation of Floppies Controlled ______

E. Use of Fax/Modem Boards Controlled ______

3. LAN Documentation Standards (Twenty Points Each)

A. Does your organization have a corporate policy regarding electronic mail privacy? ______

B. Are all applications for the general LAN population documented? ______

C. Is a vendor call-out list maintained up to date at all times? ______

D. Is a key employee call-out list maintained up to date at all times? ______

4. General Telecommunications Protection Standards (Twenty Points Each)

A. PBX Class-of-Service Data Stored Off Site? ______

B. Default Passwords on Voice Mail System Changed? ______

C. Operator Transfer Policy NOT to transfer ANY caller off site, except to 911? ______

D. Is DISA (Direct Inward System Access) in Use? If so, *subtract* five points. ______

E. Are modem pools restricted from unauthorized long distance calls, the same as voice lines? ______

F. Are reports from all systems utilizing dial-in access routinely monitored for unauthorized log in attempts? ______

G. Does a formal change control procedure exist? ______

H. Are specific persons authorized to make major system changes? ______

I. Does a policy exist to make a complete system backup before all major system changes? ______

J. Are all maintenance terminals password protected? ______

K. Have factory default passwords been changed, for all equipment? ______

5. Telecommunications Documentation Standards (Twenty Points Each)

   A. Does your organization have a corporate telecommunications privacy policy? ______

   B. Are all "call assignments" for software driven multiplexers documented in an understandable format? ______

   C. Is a carrier call-out list maintained up to date at all times? ______

   D. Is a key employee call-out list maintained up to date at all times? ______

Bonus Question:

6. Do you maintain a listing of 10XXX override codes for use in case of a long distance company failure? If so, award yourself 100 points. If you have these programmed into your PBX as an "automatic" recovery fall-back feature, double it to 200 points and pat yourself on the back. If not, contact your local telephone company, long distance company or switch vendor for details on how to use these codes to "dial around" long distance company failures. ______

IV. Disaster Recovery Standards (Fifty Points For Each YES)

1. Have you designated a meeting place from which to assemble and coordinate a disaster if your building is inaccessible? ______

2. Have you arranged several methods of contacting key personnel in the event telephone service is disrupted? Award ten points for each of the following which is documented in your plan:

   A. Home Telephone Number ______

   B. Pager Number ______

   C. Cellular Telephone Number ______

   D. Home Address (for personal contact or courier) ______

   E. Two Way Radio ______

   F. Other method not listed ______

3. Do you keep a roll of quarters handy? (ATM's won't work if there is a major communications failure and pay phones come back up first!) ______

4. Do you maintain a current equipment inventory stored off site? ______

5. Do you maintain an employee call-out list stored off site? ______

6. Do you maintain a vendor call-out list stored off site? ______

7. Does your recovery plan make provisions for getting cash? ______

8. Does your recovery plan make provisions for travel? ______

9. Does your recovery plan make provisions for emergency equipment purchases? ______

10. Do you HAVE a documented recovery plan? If not, deduct **450** points, i.e., all the stuff you don't have from the first nine questions! ______

APPENDIXES AND INDEX

APPENDIXES AND INDEX

Research Sources

APPENDIX

I-A

Bulletin Boards

All telephone numbers are modem numbers; 2,400 bps, except for California Office of Emergency Services and Emergency Preparedness Information Exchange, which function better at 1,200 bps.

California Governor's Office of Emergency Services
(916) 424-7204

COM-SEC Online Information Resource
(415) 495-4642; (415) 495-1811

Disaster Research—National Hazards Research and Applications Information Center
(303) 492-2151

Emergency Management Institute
(301) 477-6434, ext. 3283

Emergency Preparedness Information Exchange
(604) 291-4921

Hazmat Information Exchange
(708) 972-3275

Safety Net Forum
CompuServe Information Services
(800) 848-8990

State and Local Emergency Management Data Users Group
(202) 646-2887

Consultant Liaison Programs

Most major vendors offer a consultant liaison program, and many of these include disaster recovery. AT&T has an active program. Most of the switch vendors also offer similar programs, which can give valuable insights into such items as rapid replacement plans for a damaged telephone switch, for example.

Federal Agencies

American Red Cross—National Headquarters
17th and D Streets NW
Washington DC 20006
(202) 737-8300

Federal Emergency Management Agency
500 C Street SW
Washington DC 20472
(800) 525-0321

US Geological Survey
Middlefield Rd.
Menlo Park CA
(415) 853-8300

Professional Journals

Bank Disaster and Contingency Planner
200 West 57th St.
New York NY 10019
(212) 399-1084

BICEPP (Business and Industry Council for Emergency Planning and Preparedness)
PO Box 57905
Los Angeles CA 90057
(213) 386-4524

Disaster Recovery Journal
PO Box 510110
St. Louis MO 63151
(314) 894-0276

Disaster Recovery News
c/o BWT Associates
PO Box 515 Turnpike Station
Shrewsbury ME 10545
(508) 842-0050

Emergency Management Journal
CESA Inc.
1012 Fair Oaks Ave. #368
Pasadena CA 91030-3310

Networks
Bay Area Regional Earthquake Preparedness Project
Metro Center
101 8th St., Suite 152
Oakland CA 94607
(510) 286-0895

Power Quality
PO Box 6209
Lafayette IN 47903-6209
(800) 841-7881

Survive!
c/o The Kingswell Partnership
20 Gael Court, Suite 100
Turnersville NJ 08012
(609) 228-7525

Professional Associations

Association of Business Recovery Planners
c/o Downs Campbell, AmSouth Bank, NA
PO Box 11007
Birmingham AL 35288
(916) 326-5648

Association of Contingency Planners
National Headquarters
PO Box 341
Brigham City UT 84302-0341
(800) 445-4ACP

For information on the following chapters, contact the Association of Contingency Planners National Headquarters:

- Atlanta Chapter
  Norcross GA
- Capital of Texas Chapter
  Austin TX
- Colorado Rocky Mountain Chapter
  Englewood CO
- Los Angeles Chapter
  Woodland Hills CA
- Middle Florida Chapter
  Orlando FL
- Middle Tennessee Chapter
  Nashville TN
- Northeast Florida Chapter
  Jacksonville FL
- North Texas Chapter
  Dallas TX
- Oklahoma Chapter
  Tulsa OK
- Orange County Chapter
  Irvine CA
- San Diego Chapter
  San Diego CA
- St. Louis Chapter
  St. Louis MO
- South Texas Chapter
  Houston TX
- Utah Chapter
  Sandy UT

Business and Industry Council for Emergency Planning and Preparedness
PO Box 57905
Los Angeles CA 90057
(213) 386-4524

Carolinas Contingency Planning Association
Bill Branigan
First Union National Bank
301 South College St.
Charlotte NC 28288
(704) 383-5190

Contingency Planners of Ohio
John Ofcar
May Department Stores
Great Lakes Data Center
219 Sheffield Center
Lorain OH 44055
(216) 233-7162

Hawaii Association of Contingency Planners
Bob Yoder
Bank of Hawaii
PO Box 2900
Honolulu HI 96846
(808) 526-7125

Iowa Contingency Planners
Ed Pearce, CDRP
Communications Data Services Inc.
1901 Bell Ave.
Des Moines IA 50315-1099
(515) 246-6859

Mid-Atlantic Disaster Recovery Association
Mike Slingluff
PO Box 2739
Baltimore MD 21225
(703) 759-8065

Midwest Contingency Planners
Samuel J. Brunnett
EDS/ATD
4700 West 10th St.
MS-H04
Indianapolis IN 46222
(317) 242-5710

Northern New England Disaster Recovery Info Exchange
Bill Bruce
PO Box 3457
Boston MA 02101
(617) 570-3121

Survive! Inc.
Jack Bannan
PO Box 1614
Mt. Laurel NJ 08054
(609) 778-5702

A Case Study in Disaster Recovery

APPENDIX

II-A

INTRODUCTION

This case study is presented not only for the facts of how this company responded to the disaster and the lessons they learned, but it also represents an excellent example of a company's effort to analyze its performance to identify what worked and what did not. The successful recovery from a disaster is not sufficient. Following disaster each company should conduct a post-disaster or post-incident analysis. The company's disaster recovery planner should use the areas that the company focused on as a guide to formatting a post-incident or even post-exercise analysis.

Early July 11, 1993 the Great Flood of 1993 affected The Principal Financial Group in Des Moines, Iowa. This organization lost power and water to its entire corporate center. The disaster affected all of the buildings that they owned in downtown Des Moines, as well as the buildings where they leased space. In addition, the disaster affected their data center located in the US West Building in downtown Des Moines.

The Information Services (IS) team immediately responded to evaluate the effects of the flood on the company's US West data center location, as well as the corporate square data center. The recovery control team leader called the recovery control team members together to evaluate the need to declare a disaster at approximately 9:00 am Sunday, July 11. During this meeting, they decided to declare a disaster and began to implement the corporate business resumption plan. The corporate center operated in a business resumption mode from Sunday, July 11, 1993 through Sunday, July 26, 1993. On Monday, July 27 employees returned to their own desks.

OBJECTIVES FOR POST-DISASTER ANALYSIS

The Principal's overall objectives in conducting the post-disaster analysis were to:

- Verify that the business resumption plans performed effectively and recovered the affected functions.
- Identify areas of the plan to improve.
- Evaluate the flow of communication between different teams.
- Evaluate the effectiveness of the business resumption period.

To accomplish these objectives they:

- Monitored the recovery efforts of the corporate center from July 11th through July 27th.
- Interviewed senior management and business unit representatives.
- Surveyed employees, business resumption team leaders, and field offices.

This case study addresses the following areas of concern identified by the Principal Financial Group:

- Recovery control issues.
- The Information Services department.
- Facility issues.
- Support issues.
- Corporate relation issues.

- Management team issues and general changes to the disaster recovery or, in this case, the corporate business resumption plan.

The company performed the response and recovery evaluation by using the objectives defined in its business recovery plans. In general, the company found that its plan implementation and recovery efforts were effective. However, its evaluation identified many important findings and made many recommendations to enhance its existing plan. The following section presents an overview of key recommendations derived from the company's experience and evaluation.

OVERVIEW OF KEY RECOMMENDATIONS FROM EVALUATION OF THE PLAN, COMMUNICATIONS, AND OVERALL RECOVERY EFFECTIVENESS

Plan Effectiveness

The company evaluated the business resumption plan's effectiveness in recovering the affected functions. As a result of the team's opinion, the key recommendations were:

- Document within each business team plan a list of employees with modem-equipped PCs at their homes.
- Provide these employees with dial-in instructions so that they can continue critical functions from home.
- Develop and test a plan to address recovery of the backbone and LANs.
- Investigate locating a data center outside the Des Moines area to provide mainframe service from a different telephone, electrical, and water company.
- Obtain information from critical vendors about what service the company can expect from the vendors if a disaster affects the company, the vendors, or both.
- To provide more effective notification and communications of a disaster to support teams, develop a management team with the responsibility to coordinate the 22 support teams.

Communications Effectiveness

The company evaluated the flow of communication between teams during the business resumption period. As a result of that evaluation, the key recommendations were:

- Include a task in the recovery control team's plan to have an agenda and minutes provided for each meeting held during a recovery period.
- Document how each business unit would prefer to have telephones handled if a disaster occurs. Research possible ways to meet these preferences and provide alternatives, if necessary.
- Develop and document a program for addressing safety and security issues during a recovery.
- Re-evaluate the company's working relationships with management of leased spaces. Document the facilities management plan to address all space where corporate center employees are located.
- Document in the government relations plan who will be responsible for providing coordination with local officials if a disaster or business interruption occurs.
- Change the employee emergency telephone number to an 800 number instead of a local number. Add wording to all plans to provide employees this number when notifying them of a disaster.
- Develop and document guidelines for handling the media in different disaster situations.

- To allow timely communication to employees, include the human resources staff list for each department in the plan.
- Develop a consistent means of communication from business resumption teams to their staff during a business resumption period.

Overall Recovery Effectiveness

The organization evaluated its overall effectiveness during the business resumption period. The key recommendations related to recovery effectiveness were:

- Include a task in the recovery control team plan to have management services evaluate procedures implemented for a recovery.
- Develop a specific plan for senior management.
- Develop a complete emergency plan that ties together the IS and corporate business resumption plans.
- Research and document realistic options for processing outgoing mail if a disaster affects the mail services equipment.
- When researching data base software for the plan, include criteria requiring the software to provide for easy access to contact information.

RECOVERY CONTROL ISSUES

Customer Calls

Background. The company's ability to answer calls from their customers in a disaster situation is critical. The recovery control team plan did not specifically address incoming calls. The intention was to decide on how to handle incoming calls at the time of a disaster.

Finding. The recovery control team did not preplan and document in the plan a process to address incoming calls. They called in the telecommunications team to set up a bank of telephone staff to handle all incoming calls.

The telecommunications team set up its operation based on normal procedures for the telecommunications department by using a standard telephone log to record telephone messages. Although the team did its best, several departments thought that it was difficult to sort messages. If the log contained more specific information, it would be more useful. Department involvement in the sorting process will help ensure that telephone logs are complete. In addition, some people had long delays in receiving telephone messages, which would have been a perfect situation to have management services evaluate during the recovery effort.

Survey Results. Nine percent of employees and 20% of business resumption team leaders were dissatisfied to very dissatisfied with the handling of telephone messages.

Recommendations. To allow proper handling of customer calls during a recovery effort:

- Include a task in the recovery control team plan to contact telecommunications for telephone support.
- Develop a telephone log that is acceptable to all departments and document the log within the plan.
- Include a task in each management team plan to assign people to work with telecommunications to help sort messages.

- Include a task in the recovery control team plan to use management services to evaluate procedures implemented for the recovery.
- Document in the telecommunications plan a procedure for handling incoming calls and for sorting and distributing telephone logs.

Areas Responsible. The areas responsible for implementing these recommendations are risk control and management and telecommunications.

Staffing the Recovery Control Center

Background. The recovery control center is the location of the recovery control team throughout the recovery effort. Business resumption teams need access to the recovery control team for business resumption related issues. Employees will handle emergency situations by contacting security. The recovery control team plan did not address specific staffing of the recovery control center.

Finding. There was a difference of opinion about how many hours a day to staff the recovery control center. The recovery control team did provide 24-hour staff the first day and night. Beginning with the second day, the security staff took telephone coverage of the recovery control center beginning at 9:00 PM each night. By the first weekend however, the recovery control team began to provide 24-hour staff in the recovery control center. This continued until July 27 when everyone returned to their normal work locations.

Recommendations

- Document the recovery control team plan to staff the recovery control center from 5:00 am to 12:00 midnight throughout a recovery effort.
- Document the plan for security to take any calls between 12:00 midnight and 5:00 AM.

Area Responsible. Risk control and management.

Recovery Control Center Equipment

Background. The recovery control center needs all equipment essential to the recovery control team. Having the necessary equipment will allow the team to be most effective. This plan includes a list of resources they need in the control center.

Finding. The recovery control team had not planned for several items that they actually needed. It was obvious that they needed a television to monitor weather and information from local authorities. In addition, there was a need for a FAX and copy machine. They used two banks of telephones. One for incoming calls and the other for outgoing calls.

Recommendations. Document in the recovery control team plan the additional resources needed by this team.

Area Responsible. Risk control and management.

Status Reports

Background. The recovery control team needs to receive status reports from each department during the recovery effort. These status reports allow the recovery control team to make decisions and changes throughout the recovery effort. Task #20 in the plan calls for a team member to determine a status reporting schedule and to notify the management teams.

Finding. The recovery control team did not request regular status reports from the management teams. They received informal status reports. At times, the team needed information about a department, but did not have it. Using a schedule for status reporting provides the necessary information, which eliminates having to track down department managers between meetings to get the information.

Recommendations. To ensure that proper communication flows between the recovery control and management teams:

- Review the status report form and make any changes necessary to ensure that the recovery control team receives information that they need.
- Remove task #20 from the recovery control team plan.
- Include notification of status report schedule in tasks #16 and #17. These tasks cover initial notification of the disaster to the management teams.

Area Responsible. Risk control and management.

Recovery Control Center Support

Background. The recovery control center must operate in an organized manner, which allows for the recovery control team to manage a recovery effort. The recovery control team plan covers having the control center set up, but not for management of the center.

Finding. The recovery control team did not preplan for someone to manage the telephone bank and other coordination needed for the control center. The first day it was chaotic. Beginning with the second day, the team began to coordinate scheduling people to cover the telephones each day. This coordination was important to the services being available to people contacting the control center.

Recommendations. To provide support, the recovery control team should develop a list of people to coordinate telephone and administrative services for the control center and develop a list of responsibilities for this person. All changes within the plan should be documented.

Area Responsible. Risk control and management.

Recovery Control Meetings

Background. The recovery control team needs a formal meeting with the management teams to keep them updated. Designated employees should receive in writing, information presented and discussed during recovery control team meetings, which ensures effective communication, understanding of responsibilities, and an effective recovery. In addition, agendas for each meeting ensure that everyone knows what to expect from a meeting.

The recovery control team plan calls for them to provide information to and to receive information from different areas of the company. However, it does not specify how or when this communication should happen.

Finding. The recovery control team did begin meetings with the management teams on the second day. The team did not provide agendas or minutes from these meetings, but took notes during each one. However, the team did not formalize them into meeting minutes or distribute them. In the beginning, neither the recovery control or management teams knew what to expect, which caused confusion during the first few days.

During the recovery control team meetings, issues were assigned to different people. They were to report their progress at the next meeting. However, often, they did not give any progress reports because they forgot or did not understand their responsibilities. This lack of understanding caused confusion, and the meetings took longer.

Recommendations. To ensure effective and accurate status meetings during the recovery effort:

- Document within the recovery control team plan a task to determine a formal meeting time each day and a means to notify the management teams of these meetings.
- Include a task in the recovery control team plan to have agenda and minutes provided for each meeting.
- Include a task in the management team plan to receive meeting information from the recovery control team plan.

Area Responsible. Risk control and management.

Control Center Locations

Background. The recovery control team should have several (in different buildings) recovery control center options pre-arranged. These locations must have immediate access to all resources that this team needs. The plan indicates that this team should have the control center established. From this disaster, the team learned ways to plan for a more organized control center.

Finding. The executive conference room on T-2 worked well for this disaster. However, they need to ensure they have similar options in case the Tower is the affected building. The recovery control center was the hub of activity throughout the recovery effort. The control center had heavy traffic throughout the day, and at times it was hectic. Having food in the same room as the control center caused more activity. The food was then moved to a conference room down the hall.

Members of the corporate relations team began using the recovery control center for their headquarters. It was effective to have this team nearby. However, having them in a nearby room would have helped remove some commotion. In addition, senior executives set up headquarters in a conference room down the hall, which was most effective because they were close by when needed.

The recovery control center would have been more effective if they had preplanned and documented resources nearby for the other critical areas. Electricity and telephones are essential to these areas.

Recommendations. To provide necessary space for the recovery control center locate several possible locations for a recovery control center and ensure the availability of electricity, telephones, and wiring for PCs. In addition, document these options in the plan.

Areas Responsible. The areas responsible for implementing these recommendations are risk control and management and various support teams.

Role of Senior Management

Background. Coordination between senior management and the recovery control team is crucial throughout a recovery process and to be effective, the roles of both need to be clear. The recovery control team's task #12 requires them to notify management that a disaster is being declared. Task #21 requires this team to maintain communication with senior management. However, currently this task does not specify the role of senior management with respect to the recovery control team.

Finding. The role of senior management was ambiguous during the recovery. In addition, responsibility roles between senior management and the recovery control team were unclear. Members of senior management actually functioned as a part of recovery control team. They attended all recovery control meetings and gave specific direction. Because senior management's role was not clear, they assumed its normal role, which was effective. However, if senior management plans to have direct involvement, it is necessary for them to understand the plan design.

Recommendations. To clarify the role of senior management:

- Document and train senior management and the recovery control team of senior management's role.
- Change the membership of the recovery control team to include one member of senior management. This person will serve as a liaison between the recovery control team and the senior management team. Train the new team members as to their roles within a recovery effort.
- Develop a specific plan for senior management.

Control Center Locations

Background. The emergency and IS plans should feed into the business resumption plan. To implement the business resumption plan, the recovery control team leader needs notification. The plan indicates in task #1 that Tom will notify the recovery control team leader of a situation for which the recovery control team may need to activate its plan.

Finding. The recovery control team leader did not receive correct or timely notification. The recovery control team leader actually received notification from Tom in IS of the situation in the downtown locations. This notification did not occur until 5:00 am on July 11, 1993. Because the electricity and water went out between midnight and 3:00 am, the notification to the recovery control team leader could have been sooner.

Recommendation. Develop a complete emergency plan that connects both the IS and corporate business resumption plans. This will ensure correct contacts in future disasters.

Areas Responsible. The areas responsible for implementing these recommendations are risk control and management and facilities management.

THE INFORMATION SERVICES DEPARTMENT

Remote Mainframe Access

Background. Access to the mainframe computer by corporate center employees is critical to their ability to perform essential services during a recovery effort. Some employees can work from home if space is an issue. Not all employees have PCs with modems at home. Not all employees with PCs at home know how to use the dial-in option. In addition, the company has only 64 lines that employees can use to dial-in to the mainframe.

Finding. Many employees could not return to work because of the lack of available corporate center space. Better access to the mainframe from homes would allow work to continue outside the corporate center. The company could not provide enough space for all of the departments, and the employees could not work at home without the proper equipment.

Survey Results. Six percent of employees responding used the dial-in method from home. Some comments mentioned that employees could have worked from home if they had mainframe and LAN access.

Recommendation. To allow the most employees access to the mainframe during a recovery effort:

- Document within each functional team plan a list of employees with PCs at home with modems. Provide these employees with dial-in instructions.
- Analyze the lists from the functional teams and determine the correct number of dial-in lines.
- Analyze the need to provide PCs to employees at home.

Areas Responsible. The areas responsible for implementing these recommendations are risk control and management, functional team leaders, and information services.

LAN Access

Background. LAN access is critical for some areas of the company to service customers. They rely on the LAN to perform some applications previously performed by the mainframe. The business resumption plan addresses replacement of departmental equipment. To access the LANs, employees need to use the corporate backbone. Recovery of the backbone is not a part of the business resumption plan.

Finding. LAN access was unavailable initially and was then only available on a limited basis. The recovery control team had IS shut down access to the backbone to keep employees off unsafe floors in the buildings. Some teams moved LANs to temporary space, which caused a timing concern for moving the equipment back to the normal location.

Survey Results. Fifteen percent of employees and 33% of business resumption team leaders responding were dissatisfied to very dissatisfied with LAN access. Many comments mentioned difficulty in obtaining LAN access.

Recommendations. To ensure the necessary LAN access during a recovery effort develop and test a plan to address recovery of the backbone and develop procedures for other likely LAN/backbone recoveries.

Areas Responsible. The areas responsible for implementing these recommendations are risk control and management and information services.

Telephone Options

Background. Telephone service is essential to provide customer service. When policyholders and contract holders need help they must be able to reach company representatives. The plan addresses the recovery of departments' critical telephone numbers. However, this information was not necessary for the solution that the recovery control team implemented.

Findings. The recovery control team decided to intercept incoming telephone calls to ensure the answering of all calls. Quickly implementing a solution eliminated missing customer calls.

The solution used was to forward all telephone numbers to an announcement. This announcement gave customers the status of their situation and an 800 number to use if they needed help. The 800 number was then answered by the telecommunications staff. They took messages and delivered them to the appropriate departments. Some departments preferred to have the flexibility of using Audix, a voice-answering machine system.

Survey Results. Nine percent of employees and 7% of business resumption team leaders responding were dissatisfied to very dissatisfied with the telephone service. Comments were also received about the lack of flexibility.

Recommendations. To provide special handling of telephones during a recovery effort:

- Document how each department would prefer to have telephones handled if a disaster occurs.
- Research possible ways to meet these preferences. If preferences are met, provide the departments with alternatives.
- Document the plan with realistic telephone options.

Area Responsible. The area responsible for implementing these recommendations is risk control and management.

Data Center Locations

Background. Access to the mainframe computer by corporate center and field employees is crucial to their ability to service customers. The company has two data centers. One located in the Square, and the other at 900 Keo. Lack of electricity, water, or telephone service to these data centers could cause employees to lose access to the mainframe system.

Finding. Data centers located close together (i.e., within a few blocks) share service from the same telephone, electrical, and water companies. Disaster affected both data centers. This arrangement does not provide a safe backup to the company's mainframe system.

The Corporate Square data center began running off backup power and its self-contained air conditioner immediately. The 900 Keo data center did have a backup generator to provide electricity, but it needed an outside water supply to run the air conditioning. The mainframe computer cannot operate without air conditioning. The company installed a pool of water to feed the water to the air conditioner on the roof of 900 Keo. However, this did not occur immediately.

The company purchased an agreement with IBM for the use of a computer and data center if necessary. This agreement costs $88,000 per month. It is unclear how long it would take to set up the company's operating system and applications at the IBM site.

Recommendations. To provide critical back-up to the mainframe, investigate locating a data center outside the DSM area to provide service from a different telephone, electrical, and water company. In addition, develop a method to test the IBM site to determine a realistic recovery time-frame if the company decides to keep this option.

Areas Responsible. The areas responsible for implementing these recommendations are risk control and management and information services.

FACILITY ISSUES

Alternate Space

Background. The plan does not document specific alternate site spaces for most teams. Facilities management provides space for teams at the time of a disaster. Depending on the disaster, facilities may not find space for everyone.

Finding. The recovery control team did research available space satellite offices at the time of this disaster. This option did not generate much interest. The Residential Mortgages and Casualty division used space at its West Des Moines field offices. The Princor division used space in Dallas, Texas.

Plan Intent. Use satellite or field office space during a recovery effort if necessary. The company controls this space, and it already has mainframe connections and telephones.

Recommendations. To use alternate space with computer telephone connections document management team plans with alternate sites to consider, and document functional team plans with a list of employees able to travel to a satellite office.

Area Responsible. The area responsible for implementing these recommendations is risk control and management.

Working at Home

Background. A pre-arranged alternate site is space that a team will have access to during a recovery effort. Most corporate center teams do not have pre-arranged alternate sites. If a team does not have one, facilities management will provide them space at the time of a disaster. This can be difficult, especially if the disaster affects more than one of the company's buildings.

Finding. The recovery control team worked with facilities management and move coordination services to locate a small amount of space for each business unit. In this disaster, they were unable to locate large amounts of space for employees because of a lack of water availability. To compensate for the lack of space, some employees worked at home. This option allowed some work to continue.

Survey Results. Many comments indicated that employees could have worked from home with the necessary equipment. Fifteen percent of the employees responding said that they worked from home. Half of the business resumption team leaders said some of their employees worked from home.

Recommendations. To ensure work space during a recovery effort document each management team plan to consider the option of employees working at home, and document each functional team plan with a list of employees who could pre-plan to work at home.

Area Responsible. The area responsible for implementing these recommendations is risk control and management.

Safety and Security

Background. The safety and security of the company's employees during a disaster and recovery is critical. To ensure this, the recovery control team needs safety and security resources available to them immediately. The plan did not call for the recovery control team to address safety or security concerns as a team, and it did not have a safety resource mentioned. The plan called for facilities management to handle security. However, this disaster made them aware that such resources should be directly accessible to the recovery control team.

Finding. The recovery control team did not have contact information easily accessible for safety and security resources. However, they did locate resources for both security and safety during the recovery. The team had many safety and security related issues to address during the recovery period.

Recommendations. To ensure that necessary safety and security needs are met:

- Include security and safety as team advisors in the recovery control team plan.
- Add a task to the recovery control team plan that reminds this team (in addition to facilities management) to address safety and security concerns.
- Develop and document a program for addressing safety and security issues during a recovery in the facilities management plan.

Areas Responsible. The areas responsible for implementing these recommendations are risk control and management and facilities management.

Leased Space

Background. Information about available space is critical during recovery. This includes both space that the company owns and space that it leases. A good working relationship with management of space that is leased allows both the company and the leased space management to understand their responsibilities. It also helps ensure open communication lines during a recovery effort.

Finding. Facilities management concentrated on the buildings that the company owned. It overlooked leased space when giving update reports at the daily meetings. Management of its own buildings attended the daily meetings. However, the management of the leased buildings did not. The leased facilities did not have bathroom facilities or air conditioning as soon as the buildings that the company owned.

Recommendations. To ensure the necessary control of space in which to have employees located:

- Re-evaluate the working relationships with management of leased spaces.
- Establish a division of responsibilities during a recovery between leased space management and the company.
- Document all space where employees are to be located within the facilities management plan.

Areas Responsible. The areas responsible for implementing these recommendations are risk control and management and facilities management.

SUPPORT ISSUES

Mail Distribution

Background. Mail sorting and distribution is critical to some areas of the company. The company must process investment checks, premium payments, and EDP output (e.g., claim checks) from the mainframe. The records' plan was not specific enough to indicate delivery of mail to the different teams located at alternate site locations.

Finding. Records sorted mail on A–1, but did not deliver it. It was each department's responsibility to pick up mail from A–1. After several days, they delivered mail to each building. Each department then picked the mail up from a central location. Mail services processed outgoing mail as usual.

Some areas receive large amounts of mail. They found it difficult to pick up the mail from A–1. Confusion existed about why they had to pick up mail during the recovery effort when normally records delivers it. Mailing EDP Output from the mainframe to customers is important. This continued because the disaster did not affect the mail service's equipment.

Plan Intent. Provide necessary support services for recovering functional teams.

Recommendations. To allow proper distribution of mail within the company and outside the company.

- Document clearly in the records' plan to deliver mail in the normal fashion to alternate site locations. Records should notify the recovery control team if this is not possible.
- Document clearly in the recovery control team's plan to notify records immediately of alternate site locations and to have mail delivery scheduled.
- Research realistic options for the processing of outgoing mail if a disaster affects the mail service's equipment. Document those options in the mail services' plan.

Areas Responsible. The areas responsible for implementing these recommendations are risk control and management, records, and mail services.

Vendor Support

Background. At the time of a disaster, the company must know what it can expect from its vendors. This is critical to the company's ability to recover critical functions.

Team plans call for teams to contact vendors about the service that they can expect from them if a disaster affects the company. Team plans do not address what service they can expect if a disaster affects one of the company's vendors.

Finding. It was unclear or unacceptable what service the company could expect from a vendor if a disaster occurs. One example is the company's use of lock boxes. Lock boxes were a critical issue during this recovery period. They allow the business units to make deposits to bank accounts. Some banks continued service during the recovery without a problem. However, areas of the company use different banks, and some had trouble with lock box service.

Recommendations. To ensure necessary vendor support during recovery effort, get information from critical vendors about the service that the company can expect from them if a disaster affects the company, the vendors, or both. Document this information in the plan.

Areas Responsible. The areas responsible for implementing these recommendations are risk control and management and the affected plan team leaders.

Additional Vendors

Background. Support teams require service from vendors during a recovery effort to help the company resume business. The business resumption plan provides a location for teams to list vendors that they might need support from if a disaster occurs.

Finding. Some support team plans do not include all possible vendors that might be used during a recovery effort. Most include a list of vendors that they work with on a day-to-day basis. However, support teams found that they needed access to different vendors in a recovery effort. These teams spent additional time tracking down vendors that could provide items such as water and portable toilets.

Recommendation. Document in the plan vendors for all possible services that support teams might require during a recovery effort.

Areas Responsible. The areas responsible for implementing this recommendation are risk control and management and all support teams.

Communications with Local Officials

Background. During a disaster, the company needs to coordinate with local officials and service related contacts such as water, electrical, and telephone. This coordination allows for effective communication of information necessary to plan recovery efforts. The plan calls for each team to coordinate communication with vendors.

Finding. The company did not have this type of coordination pre-planned for or documented in its plan. The facilities management team did not have time to coordinate a continuous communication effort with local officials. The first few days they did not have direct contact with local officials or the water utility. It became clear to the recovery team that they would need direct contact. The recovery control team assigned the government relations team to handle coordination with local officials, which made sense because it was its normal area of expertise. In addition, senior management made some contacts to negotiate the special use of water, which appeared to work. However, senior management did not establish a specific reporting structure for the Government relations team to use for communicating with the recovery control team, and this caused confusion at times.

Recommendations. To ensure effective communication with proper local officials:

- Document in the government relations' plan that that team will be responsible for providing coordination with local officials if a disaster or business interruption occurs. Include any resources that they might need to accomplish this coordination. Document a procedure to communicate effectively with the recovery control team.
- Document in the recovery control team plan the requirement to coordinate with the government relations team for contact with local officials.
- Document in both the government relations and recovery control plans to include senior management in negotiations when appropriate.

Areas Responsible. The areas responsible for implementing these recommendations are risk control and management and government relations.

Support Staff

Background. During a recovery effort, the following groups need additional staff to support the corporation: facilities management (security), telecommunications, and the recovery control center. The security, telecommunications, and recovery control team plans did not address the additional staff needed should the recovery control team expand the groups' roles during a recovery effort.

Findings. Security, telecommunications, and the recovery control center did not know what additional staff were available to them. The recovery control team used security to provide floor monitors, security guards, and escorts. The team also used telecommunications to handle all incoming calls for the company. Both security and telecommunications needed more than the normal complement of staff and did not know who was available within the company, which caused confusion because the areas did not know who to ask for additional support staff. The recovery control center also needed additional support staff. The recovery control center tried to coordinate the staffing effort. However, if well organized, it could have been more effective.

Recommendations. To ensure all the staff necessary for an effective recovery effort:

- Develop a list of areas that would be available to help in other areas during a disaster and document this list in the recovery control team's plan.
- Include a task in the recovery control team's plan to coordinate additional staff for the recovery control center and support areas required to perform additional functions during a recovery effort.
- Include a task in the facilities management (i.e., security) telecommunication plans to contact the recovery control team.

Area Responsible. The area responsible for implementing these recommendations is risk control and management.

Employee Emergency Telephone Number

Background. An employee emergency telephone number currently exists within the company (555-1212).

Finding. The recovery control team worked with the corporate relations and communications teams to develop a message for the employee emergency telephone number. The message was intended to provide the status of the situation for employees calling that number. The team found that changing the message was difficult and time-consuming. The telephone system limited the length of the message. Therefore, the teams could not provide all the information that they felt was needed.

In addition, employees did not appear to use this telephone number as much as the recovery control team anticipated. Employees outside the Des Moines area had to dial long distance to use the number. The company felt that a central number is an excellent way to communicate information to employees, and its use in the future will be increased.

Survey Results. The employee survey indicates that 72% of employees responding did not use the employee emergency telephone number. In addition, 51% of the employees responding were less than satisfied with the employee emergency telephone number.

Recommendations. To ensure that employees use the employee emergency telephone number in the event of a disaster:

- Change the emergency number to an 800 number instead of a local number.
- Evaluate options to lengthen the message.
- Evaluate options to shorten the time to change the message.
- Increase employee awareness of this number by including it in the common section of the plan.
- Add wording in all plans to give employees this number when notifying them of a disaster.

Area Responsible. The area responsible for implementing these recommendations is risk control and management.

CORPORATE RELATION ISSUES

Customer Communications

Background. In the recovery control team's plan, a task calls for coordination between corporate relations, management teams, information services, and mail services to develop and distribute status letters to customers and policyholders.

Finding. Coordination did occur between the proper areas to develop and distribute a status letter. The company sent the letter around August 4, 1993 about two and one-half weeks following the beginning of their business resumption efforts. They created and ran a program to prevent customers from receiving multiple copies of the status letter. However, some customers still received multiple copies.

Business units agree they should not send a letter until the immediate crisis is over. However, sending the letter the week of July 27th when they returned to normal work would be more effective.

Recommendations. To ensure impressive communications to customers following a disaster:

- Review the current business resumption customer list kept by IS to ensure that it includes customers of each critical business unit.
- Review the program that generates the customer list to eliminate duplication.
- Document the recovery control and corporate relations plans to show sending the customer letter as soon as business is back to normal.

Areas Responsible. The areas responsible for implementing these recommendations are risk control and management, information services, and media relations.

Media Relations

Background. The corporate relations' plan addresses contact with the media, but not specifically. It does not address how they will handle media relations in an area-wide disaster versus a disaster only affecting the company. The plan also does not document the involvement of senior management in making media related decisions.

Finding. The media portrayed the company incorrectly at times. The company maintained a low profile throughout the recovery period. The media made assumptions and subsequent statements to the public that the company did not agree with or support.

The mayor's proclamation was one example. The media made it appear that the company was not following the proclamation. In addition, the employee's involvement in community efforts were not visible. Although the company made a large donation to the Red Cross and United Way to help in flood relief efforts, this was not very visible.

Recommendations. To position the company to manage public reaction develop and document guidelines for handling the media in different disaster situations. In addition, document senior management's involvement and potential issues with the media in the senior management plan.

Areas Responsible. The areas responsible for implementing these recommendations are risk control and management and corporate relations.

Communication Pieces

Background. Corporate relations' role during business resumption is to handle all media and communications related situations. Its plan covers media contact and internal communications in general.

Plan Intent. Provide necessary communication to employees and the community/ media.

Finding. This team had to create different pieces of communication without the benefit of having pre-planned formats. Some items developed include: daily fact sheets, special update issues, special changes to the internal magazine, and public address announcements. It would have saved time if they had samples of communication pieces included in their plan.

Recommendations. To help provide communications during a recovery effort, document all the types of communication that the corporate relations team will be expected to handle. Include samples of these in the plan as well as on a diskette stored offsite. Although these samples would have to be altered at the time of a disaster, they could provide a framework.

Areas Responsible. The areas responsible for implementing these recommendations are risk control and management and corporate relations.

MANAGEMENT TEAM ISSUES

Contacting Support Teams

Background. Initially, support teams are the most critical because they help the other teams to recover. Therefore, notification of the support teams must happen as soon as the recovery team declares a disaster. The recovery control team plan requires notification of the corporate service support team leaders.

Finding. Some support teams did not receive official notification of the disaster. The coordination of the support teams has caused confusion from the beginning of plan development. During this disaster, it became clear that the recovery control team had a tremendous number of tasks to accomplish. The company felt the need to limit the number of teams that it directly contacted. The company now has seven management teams and about 22 support teams.

Plan Intent. Provide support necessary to recover critical functions of all business units.

Recommendation. To allow proper notification of support teams, develop a management team to coordinate the 22 support teams.

Area Responsible. The area responsible for implementing this recommendation is risk control and management.

Initial Communication

Background. Management teams play a critical role once a disaster is declared. They are the key to getting the plans implemented and employees contacted. If they declare a disaster, the plan initially provides each management team with a conference room in the corporate center for meetings. The teams can make calls from there and begin making plans for their business units recovery.

Finding. The management teams could not get to their pre-assign initial assembly points to begin the implementation process. This was not possible because of a lack of electricity in downtown Des Moines. Because the management teams did not have access to downtown, they each had to come up with a different initial assembly point, which caused confusion. In addition, it caused a problem for communication to flow from the recovery control team to the management teams. Initially, the recovery control team did not know the locations of the different management teams.

Plan Intent. Provide a smooth flow of communication between all teams.

Recommendations. Ensure initial communication between teams by documenting each management team plan with an alternate initial assembly point. This is only used if the team cannot have access to downtown Des Moines. Include wording in the task to notify the recovery control team of a telephone number of the alternate initial assembly point.

Areas Responsible. The areas responsible for implementing these recommendations are risk control and management and each management team.

GENERAL PLAN CHANGES

Contacting Employees

Background. The recovery control team plan indicates to order human resource staff lists from the human resource team. This departmental list includes each employee's address and telephone number. The recovery control team distributes the staff list to the management and functional team leaders.

Finding. The recovery control team did request the staff list from the human resource team. However, the list was not accurate. The recovery control team did not distribute the staff list, but it was available if teams requested it.

Survey Results. The company received several comments about the difficulty in obtaining the staff list.

Plan Intent. Business resumption team leaders must contact their team members and staff to notify them of a disaster.

Recommendations. To provide proper notification of team members and staff include the HR staff list in each functional plan, and remove the recovery team's responsibility to acquire the HR staff lists from the recovery control team plan.

Areas Responsible. The areas responsible for implementing these recommendations are risk control and management, human resources, and all functional teams.

Contact Between Teams

Background. The plan indicates that the recovery control team will notify teams of all other team locations. However, it does not provide any telephone numbers to be used to contact the teams.

Findings. Functional and management teams needed to contact each other during the recovery effort for business and recovery related purposes. In addition, the recovery control team needed to contact support teams and business unit management teams. This was difficult without telephone numbers.

Plan Intent. Teams need to communicate with each other to conduct a recovery.

Recommendations

- Develop a format to develop a telephone directory to use during a recovery effort.
- Assign a team to be responsible for the telephone directory and its distribution.
- Document a telephone directory in the plan.

Area Responsible. The area responsible for implementing these recommendations is risk control and management.

Senior Management

Background. The plan did not specifically define senior management's role during a disaster. The legal department's plan mentions senior management, but senior management had no working knowledge of the plan. Therefore, its role during the recovery was ambiguous.

Finding. Senior management initially used the recovery control center space. By the second day, it needed its own space to work. For example, one senior executive needed to conduct a conference call with London, and board business also had to continue. Senior management set up offices near the recovery control center in two conference rooms.

Plan Intent. Provide for senior management and its support staff to operate critical functions during a recovery.

Recommendations. Develop a plan for senior management to define its role during a recovery and address the following items in the plan:

- Space near the recovery control center.
- Board issues.
- Community involvement issues.
- Creative thinking.

Areas Responsible. The areas responsible for implementing these recommendations are risk control and management and senior management.

Contact Information

Background. The teams' plans refer to the common section topics, but not to specific pages. The plans' common section includes: contact information for teams, a list of how soon functions need to recover, and other information needed for the recovery process.

Finding. Team members thought contact information and telephone numbers for teams were difficult to locate in the common sections.

Plan Intent. Plan implementation occurs by notifying team leaders of the decision to declare a disaster. Team leader contact information is in the plan's common section.

Recommendations. When researching data based software for the plan, include a criteria to find contact information easily and quickly. If new software is not developed, develop additional tabs for the common section to make it easier to locate often used topics.

Area Responsible. The area responsible for implementing these recommendations are risk control and management.

Shift Work

Background. Most disasters place companies in a position of having access to limited space. Working shifts of employees can be critical during a recovery effort. The plan mentions scheduling staff, but not shifts.

Finding. The recovery control team decided at the time of the disaster to recommend shift work because of a lack of space. Management teams coordinated shift work within each critical unit. Shifts were not always consistent from day to day. Some employees did not have enough notice to report to work. In addition, employees were confused about why they had to work hours other than their normal shifts.

Plan Intent. Schedule employees to recover critical functions.

Recommendations. To manage staff scheduling document the recovery control and management team plans to consider shift schedules for employees and document each functional team plan with a probable shift schedule to implement if necessary. In addition, have team leaders educate their staff about this option.

Areas Responsible. The areas responsible for implementing these recommendations are risk control and management and the functional team leaders.

Employees Working

Background. The recovery control team must know how many employees are working for safety purposes. The team also needs this information to provide appropriate support services. The plan does not address having teams report this information to the recovery control team.

Finding. The recovery control teams originally approved the number of employees that each business unit could have in the corporate center. However, afterward, the number of employees working did not get reported.

The fire department visited their facilities during the recovery. They wanted to know how many people were on the premises. To determine this, the recovery control team went floor to floor to count heads. Conducting a count of employees each day would help answer the fire department questions and help the company's food service vendor plan for food and water.

Recommendations. Develop a form to report the number of employees working each day during a recovery, and include this form in the management teams' plans. They will provide this form to the recovery control team at the daily meeting.

Area Responsible. The area responsible for implementing these recommendations is risk control and management.

Employee Communications

Background. Consistent communications to employees is especially important during a recovery effort. Employees must understand exactly what the company expects of them during a recovery effort and whether they work or not.

The company plan clearly addresses communication from the recovery control team to the management and functional teams. However, the plan is not specific on communication to the general employee population.

Finding. Communications from the recovery control team to the management and functional teams was effective. However, functional teams each handled employee communication separately. Some did a good job, and others did not. Some teams updated employees regularly, others did not. Some teams gave employees enough notification of when to report to work, and others did not. Employees were not clear about exactly what "staying on call" meant. The lack of consistent communication caused confusion among employees.

Survey Results. Fourteen percent of employees were dissatisfied to very dissatisfied with communications received. Eighty-five percent of business resumption team leaders were satisfied to very satisfied with communications received. Personnel reported more comments about inconsistencies in communications than any other area.

Plan Intent. Effectively communicate necessary information to all employees.

Recommendations. For effective communication of consistent information:

- Develop specific guidelines for functional teams to use when contacting employees. Include these guidelines in the plans' common section.
- Develop a task for each team's plan addressing the use of these guidelines.
- Develop a task in the recovery control and management team plans to provide information to functional teams outlined in the guidelines.

Areas Responsible. The areas responsible for implementing these recommendations are risk control and management, management teams, and corporate relations.

Workpaper AppII-A.01 Checklist for General Flood Related Issues

1. Are the primary and recovery sites accessible?

2. Are there local or government agency restrictions that will prohibit access to these areas?

3. Are the roadways flooded?

4. Have alternate roadways been identified?

5. Is there a possibility that access could be blocked by collapsed bridges? Is there any history in the area of such an event occurring?

6. Is the off-site storage facility accessible?

7. Are vendors responsive?

8. Are there vendors to move backup media and records?

Workpaper AppII-A.02 Flood Insurance Rate Maps--A Planning Resource

The Federal Emergency Management Agency (FEMA) publishes a collection of maps as part of the National Flood Insurance Program that identifies flood potential within most of the United States. The flood potential is measured on a 100, 300, and 500 per year potential. The maps are relatively inexpensive and provide great detail of areas where flooding may occur. The planner can use these maps to determine the potential for the loss of a facility, vendor's operation, or the best alternate routes to the facility. These maps can be obtained from the FEMA Publication Office in Washington, D.C.

Workpaper AppII-A.03 Contamination and Damage to Equipment

Do plans exist for the restoration of facilities, contents, records, and equipment damaged by flood water? The restoration and cleaning process requires the assistance of a professional organization specifically equipped to restore water damaged assets. It is important that the company identify qualified vendors before the incident. The vendors will be able to provide support for all types of disasters such as fire or chemical contamination. Because most states have restrictions on the types of cleaning chemicals used, it is advised to establish a relationship with such a vendor and to create a profile of the company's restoration requirements. With this information on file, the restoration company will be able to expedite the movement of equipment and supplies to the agreed upon site and still comply with state restrictions. For example, a firm had manual typewriters used for completing multipart forms and these had to be removed from the premises and taken to the company performing the cleaning because the cleaning solvents could not be used in an occupied area.

Workpaper AppII-A.04 Employee Communications

1. Is there an emergency telephone number?
2. Is there an 800 number or are all calls local?
3. Is the location of the PBX or 800 service location susceptible to the same disaster that could affect the company?
4. Does the emergency communications system have emergency power and redundant lines?
5. Are procedures for the emergency communications system documented?
6. Do these procedures cover activation of the system?
7. Where are these procedures published?
8. Who is the keeper of these procedures?
9. Does the emergency communication system provide voice mail or does it require a team of people to support it?
10. Is there a standard form to communicate procedures to the employees, vendors, and customers?

Workpaper AppII-A.05 Vendor Communications

1. Are vendors' telephone numbers documented?

2. Who has access to the numbers?

3. Are the numbers available under emergency conditions?

4. Could a certain type of disaster cause the numbers to be unavailable?

5. Do vendors have access to the company's emergency numbers?

6. If communication with vendors is not available, are there procedures to respond within a certain time frame without notification by the client?

Workpaper AppII-A.06 Command Communications

1. Are there procedures and forms for gathering and documenting information about:
   - Status of the environment.
   - Status of transportation.
   - Status of facilities.
   - Status of equipment.
   - Access issues.
   - Response of teams.
   - Response of vendors.
   - Availability of equipment.
   - Availability of software.
   - Availability of supplies.
   - Availability of vital records.

2. Are there formal, documented emergency telephone procedures?

3. Are there alternate procedures for documenting and publishing new telephone numbers?

4. Are security and safety issues for the damaged sites, recovery sites, and command locations documented in the recovery plans?

Workpaper AppII-A.07 Facilities Issues

1. Is the required space for all critical business, operational, and support functions documented?

2. Have alternate sources of space been identified?

3. Have leased versus owned space been identified?

4. Are the leasing company representatives' telephone numbers documented in the recovery plans?

5. Has the company and the leasing company discussed decision-making authority in the event of a disaster?

6. Have legal contracts for potential sites been reviewed by the legal department to expedite approval and acquisition?

7. Are all employee locations documented in the plan?

8. Are all business functions within each facility documented in the recovery plan?

9. Have ownership versus leased responsibilities been identified and documented?

Workpaper AppII-A.08 Public Relations

1. Are media procedures and guidelines documented?

2. Is the public relations group aware of the leased versus owned relationship at each facility?

Workpaper AppII-A.09 Customer Contact

1. Do customers have the company's emergency telephone numbers?

2. If not, how will the telephone numbers be published?

3. If not published, how will the telephone numbers be communicated to the customers immediately following the incident?

4. Has a time frame for reestablishing customer contact been identified?

5. Are there procedures, information, and tools required to contact key customers proactively?

6. Are messages placed on the original numbers if they are disabled by the disaster?

7. Who is involved in the wording of that message?

8. Are there provisions for the handling of customer complaints during the crisis period?

9. Are there ways to expedite the time from acquiring the calls to getting them to the appropriate business units?

10. Are the calls received centrally or distributed?

11. Are there procedures and tools to document and distribute incoming telephone calls?

12. How are these new telephone numbers communicated to:
    - Employees.
    - Command personnel.
    - Customers.
    - Vendors.
    - Press.

Workpaper AppII-A.10 Command Center Issues

1. Has an appropriate span of control been established to ensure effective management of the incident?

2. Is there a senior management plan covering:
   - Roles.
   - Responsibility.
   - Normal versus critical scope of authority.

3. Have the roles and responsibilities of the command control team versus the roles and responsibilities of senior management been defined?

4. Has senior management made provisions to separate the normal mode of work from the emergency requirements? Are they aware of any differences?

5. If senior management is directly involved in the recovery and command centers, have they been frequently briefed on the plan design and have they participated in any disaster recovery planning exercises?

6. If senior management is not directly involved, is there a member of senior management who has been designated to act as a liaison with the command center team?

Workpaper AppII-A.11 Staffing the Command Center

1. Have procedures addressing the staffing of the command center been developed, published, and exercised?

2. Is there any overlap between shifts to provide for the transition and communications of status, pending issues, and problems?

3. What does the staff need to know?

4. Can security guards take calls?

5. Can specific conditions be identified?

6. Can some team members be on call?

7. Can the on-call member have access to the necessary information?

Workpaper AppII-A.12 Equipping the Command Center

Has the equipment to provide adequate communications been identified?

Voice system:

1. Has the volume of both inbound and outbound calls been determined?

Data:

1. Is the equipment used to connect the command center to critical systems in place of at least identified?
2. Will command center personnel require access to systems such as E-mail or other production systems?

Fax:

1. Has the incoming and outgoing volume of fax traffic been estimated?
2. Are there incoming fax machines and outgoing fax machines?

Miscellaneous Equipment:

1. Scanners--Are they pretuned to the appropriate frequencies?
2. Radios and base station--Is there two-way communication between the command center and other locations? Does this include other floor operations even within the same building?
3. Are television monitors and VCRs available to record public broadcasts?

Workpaper AppII-A.12 Equipping the Command Center (continued)

Office Equipment and Supplies:

1. Are the following items available:

   - Copy machines.
   - Office supplies such as paper, pens, pencils, erasers, envelopes, paper clips, post-its, and so on.
   - Status boards.
   - Markers for the status boards in red, brown, or black only.
   - Flip charts.
   - Diskettes.
   - Power strips.
   - Surge suppressors.
   - Extension cords.
   - Fax paper.
   - Copy paper.
   - Toner for the copy and fax machines.
   - Batteries and battery chargers for portable radios and TVs, cellular phones, and calculators.

Workpaper AppII-A.13 Control Center Support Team

1. Have clerical support teams been planned to assist the decision makers?

2. Are procedures to manage the command center, post information, and the handling of telephone traffic been developed and documented?

Workpaper AppII-A.14 Control Center Locations

1. Have the locations of the control centers been preestablished?

2. Are there multiple locations?

3. Will resources be available at the locations in a timely fashion?

4. Will the utilities at the backup locations have redundancy?

5. Are locations situated far away enough from each other so as not to be affected by the same incident?

6. Are there provisions for communicating to senior management or for providing access for them to the control center?

7. Do all employees know where to go?

Workpaper AppII-A.15 Recovery Team Control Meetings

1. Has the frequency of meetings between the groups making the tactical decisions and the groups executing those decisions been identified?

2. Have the meetings been structured to include:
   - Management briefings.
   - Formal agenda.
   - Minutes.
   - Taping and transcribing.

Workpaper AppII-A.16 Status Reports

1. Have the types of status reports been defined and documented?

2. Have templates been created?

3. Have procedures to use, distribute, and reconcile the documentation been developed and exercised?

APPENDIX

III-A

Certification and Qualification of Business Continuity Professionals

All of us know how smart we are and how qualified we are to do our job, right? For the most part, our real competency is limited to certain planning niches.We excel in specific business continuity planning areas and are generally knowledgable about many other areas. The field is too large for anyone to be considered an expert in all aspects of the field. Professionals understand their limitations and consult experts to augment their own general knowledge. In many cases, the experts needed to assist business continuity planners move within their own organizations. These experts typically do not have the planning expertise or specific knowledge of what the recovery objectives, strategies, and requirements are. Given that business continuity professionals are able to define, articulate, and document them, the experts can define the best practice to meet the goals. The bottom line is that the professional must be able to define the problem before the experts can be effective in helping them.

Recognizing that business continuity professionals must have a broad experience and knowledge to define the planning objectives, strategies, and requirements, members of the Disaster Recovery Institute Certification Board, under the auspices of the Disaster Recovery Institute, started the definition process in 1991. A committee comprised of senior practitioners from various disciplines was established to define what a professional should know and be able to do for their organizations. In other words, the group felt the need for a "common body of knowledge" to use as a measurement for practitioners seeking certification as a Certified Disaster Recovery Planner (CDRP). Most other organizations granting certification in other industries or activities have defined a common body of knowledge used by members of the profession in their work. The common body of knowledge is usually abstract, stable, and technology-free and its language must facilitate communications between members of the profession.

The Institute felt that a common body of knowledge was necessary, but that it was not the sole evidence of professional capabilities. For certification purposes, professionals must demonstrate minimum continuity involvement and experience in addition to passing an exam based on the common body of knowledge. The demonstrated experience must also be related to the content of the common body of knowledge. The board created a document that defined the business continuity profession and the knowledge that must be considered to certify as a CDRP. In addition to being used as the standard to evaluate the competency of professionals, it also gives new professionals guidance as to what areas they must gain knowledge and competency. It also provides criteria for management to better understand the planner's responsibilities, evaluate whether their organization's program includes these basic components, and whether planner's are fulfilling their responsibility to the organization.

The document detailing the common body of knowledge document was divided into nine subject areas. Each provides:

- a description of the area
- the role of the professional
- an outline of the knowledge that the professional should master to perform their role in that subject area

BUSINESS CONTINUITY — COMMON BODY OF KNOWLEDGE

Subject Area **Title and Description**

1. Project Initiation and Management

Establish the need for a Business Continuity Plan that includes management support and the elements needed to organize and manage the project to completion.

2. Risk Evaluation and Control

Determine the events that can adversely affect an organization, the damage that such events can cause and the control needed to prevent or minimize the effects of potential loss.

3. Business Impact Analysis

Identify the effects of disruptions on the organization and how to quantify and qualify such effects.

4. Recovery Strategies

Determine and guide the selection of alternative recovery operating strategies to be used to maintain the critical functions.

5. Emergency Response

Develop and implement procedures to respond to and stabilize an incident or event.

6. Implementation of the Plan

Design, develop and implement business continuity plans.

7. Corporate Awareness Programs and Training

Prepare a program to create corporate awareness and enhance skills required to develop, implement, maintain and execute the Business Continuity Plan.

8. Plan Testing

Pre-plan, coordinate, evaluate, test and exercise the plan, and document the results.

9. Plan Maintenance

Develop processes to maintain the currentness of continuity capabilities and the plan document in accordance with the strategic direction of the organization.

PROJECT INITIATION AND MANAGEMENT

SUBJECT AREA 1

Establish the need for a Business Continuity Plan that includes management support and the elements needed to organize and manage the project to completion.

THE ROLE OF THE PROFESSIONAL IS TO:

1. Lead sponsors in defining objectives and policies including:
   - Scope and objectives
   - Legal and requirements reasons
   - Case histories
2. Coordinate and organize
3. Oversee
4. Present (sell) to management and staff
   - Job description
   - Assimilate
   - Negotiate
   - Compromise
   - Mediate
   - Validate
5. Develop project plan and budget
6. Define and recommend management and project structure
7. Manage the process

THE PROFESSIONAL SHOULD KNOW HOW TO:

1. Define the problem
2. Communicate the need for a continuity plan
   - Awareness
   - Project justification
   - Need for high-level support
   - Commitment
   - Mission statement/charter
   - Benefits of plan
3. Understand executive management's role
4. Understand and communicate management's accountability and liability
5. Establish a planning/steering committee
   - Role of members
   - Type of organization
   - Control and development
   - Membership
6. Develop budget requirements
   - Financial
   - Manpower
7. Identify planning team(s) and responsibilities
8. Develop and coordinate action plans
9. Develop project management and documentation requirements

RISK EVALUATION AND CONTROL

SUBJECT AREA 2

Determine the events that can adversely affect an organization, the damage that such events can cause, and the controls needed to prevent or minimize the effects of a potential loss.

THE ROLE OF THE PROFESSIONAL IS TO:

1. Understand the role of probabilities and risk reduction within the organization
2. Identify potential risks to organization
   - Probability
   - Consequences
3. Identify outside expertise needed
4. Identify vulnerabilities/threats/expenses
5. Identify risk reduction alternatives
6. Identify credible information systems
7. Interface with management to determine acceptable risk levels
8. Document and present findings

THE PROFESSIONAL SHOULD KNOW HOW TO:

1. Understand loss potentials
   - Natural
   - Manmade
   - Accidental
   - Intentional
   - Internal
   - External
2. Determine the organizationís vulnerability to such potential loss
3. Identify controls and safeguards to prevent or minimize the effect of the potential loss
   - Location
   - Physical construction
   - Facilities infrastructure
   - Protection
     - — detection
     - — notification
     - — suppression
   - Security and access controls
   - Personnel procedures
   - Information backup and protection
   - Information security
     - — hardware
     - — software
     - — data
     - — network
   - Preventative maintenance and equipment preplanning
   - Utilities
     - — duplication
     - — redundancy
   - Interact with outside agencies
4. Utilize risk analysis tools
   - Qualitative and quantitative
   - Advantages and disadvantages
   - Reliability/confidence factor
   - Basis of mathematical formulas
5. Utilize information gathering activities
   - Forms and questionnaires
   - Interviews

- Meetings
- Documentation review
- Analysis

6. Determine the probability of events
   - Information sources
   - Credibility
7. Evaluate the effectiveness of controls and safeguards
   - Cost/benefits
   - Implementation procedures and control
   - Testing
   - Audit functions and responsibilities

BUSINESS IMPACT ANALYSIS

SUBJECT AREA 3

Identify the effects of disruptions on the organization and how to quantify and qualify such effects.

THE ROLE OF THE PROFESSIONAL IS TO:

1. Identify organization functions
2. Identify knowledgeable and credible functional area representatives
3. Identify and define criticality criteria
4. Present criteria to management for approval
5. Coordinate analysis
6. Identify interdependencies
7. Define recovery windows
   - Priorities
   - Times
   - Losses
8. Identify information requirements
9. Identify resource requirements
10. Define report format
11. Prepare and present

THE PROFESSIONAL SHOULD KNOW HOW TO:

1. Determine the effect of disruptions
   - Loss of assets
     - —physical
     - —information
     - —intangible
   - Continuity of
     - —service
     - —operations
   - Violation of law/regulation
   - Public perception
2. Understand the impact
   - Financial
   - On customers and suppliers
   - On public relations/credibility
   - Legal

- Regulatory requirements/considerations
- Environmental
- Operational
- On personnel
- On other resources

3. Understand assessment techniques
   - Quantification
   - Qualification
4. Define criticality
5. Determine loss exposure
   - Quantitative
     - — property loss
     - — revenue loss
     - — fines
     - — cash flow
     - — accounts receivable
     - — accounts payable
     - — legal liability
     - — human resources
     - — additional expenses
6. Determine critical functions
   - Business
   - Support
   - Interdependencies
7. Prioritize functions
8. Determine minimum resource requirements
   - Internal
   - External
   - Owned
   - Non-owned
   - Existing
   - Additional
9. Identify resource-recovery time frames

DEVELOPING RECOVERY STRATEGIES

SUBJECT AREA 4 Determine and guide the selection of alternate recovery operating strategies for maintaining critical functions.

THE ROLE OF THE PROFESSIONAL IS TO:

1. Understand available alternatives
   - Advantages
   - Disadvantages
   - Cost ranges
2. Identify viable recovery strategies with business functional areas
3. Consolidate strategies
4. Identify off-site storage requirements and select alternate facilities
5. Develop business unit consensus
6. Present strategies to management to obtain commitment

THE PROFESSIONAL SHOULD KNOW HOW TO::

1. Identify recovery strategy requirements
   - Time frames
   - Type
   - Location
   - Personnel
   - Communications
2. Identify alternate recovery strategies
   - Do nothing
   - Defer action
   - Manual procedures
   - Reciprocal agreements
   - Alternate site or business facility
   - Service bureau
   - Consortium
   - Distributed processing
   - Alternate communications
3. Select alternate site(s) and off-site storage
   - Criteria
   - Communications
   - Agreement considerations
   - Comparison techniques
   - Acquisition
   - Contractual consideration
4. Prepare cost/benefit analysis

SUBJECT AREA 5

EMERGENCY RESPONSE

Develop and implement procedures to respond to and stabilize following an incident or event. This should include establishing and managing an emergency operations center to be used as a command center during emergencies.

THE ROLE OF THE PROFESSIONAL IS TO:

1. Confirm existence of emergency response procedures
2. Recommend the development of emergency procedures if none exist
3. Integrate disaster recovery procedures with emergency response procedures
4. Identify the command and control requirements for emergency managment
5. Recommend command and control procedures that clearly define roles, authority, and communications processes necessary to manage an emergency.

THE PROFESSIONAL SHOULD KNOW HOW TO:

1. Identify emergency response procedures
   - Reporting procedures
     - — internal (escalation procedures)
       - local
       - corporate (decision-making)
     - — external
       - public
       - vendor

- Pre-incident preparation
  - by types of disaster
    - acts of nature
    - accidental
    - intentional
  - management continuity and authority
  - roles of designated personnel
- Emergency actions
  - evacuation
  - medical care
  - hazardous material response
  - fire fighting
  - notification
  - other
- Facility stabilization
- Damage mitigation
- Testing procedures and responsibilities

2. Identify command and control requirements
   - Design of and equipment for an emergency operations center
   - Command and decision authority during an incident
   - Communication vehicles such as radio, messengers and cellular telephones
   - Logging and documentation methods
3. Command and control procedures
   - Opening of the emergency operations center (EOC)
   - Security of the emergency operations center
   - Scheduling of EOC team meetings
   - Management and operations of the EOC
   - Closing of the EOC

SUBJECT AREA 6 — DEVELOP AND IMPLEMENT THE PLAN

Design, develop and implement business continuity plans.

THE ROLE OF THE PROFESSIONAL IS TO IDENTIFY THE COMPONENTS OF THE PLANNING PROCESS

- Planning
- Organization
- Direction of efforts
- Control of the process
- Staffing the process
- Implementation of the plans
- Testing
- Maintenance

THE PROFESSIONAL SHOULD KNOW TO:

1. Determine the plan development requirements
   - Planning aids
   - Use of:
     - job descriptions
     - action plans

    — checklists
    — matrix
    — forms
    — other supporting documentation

2. Define recovery management and control requirements
   - Recovery team concept
     — team description
     — team organization
     — responsibilities
       recovery coordinator
       group coordinators
     — support staff
     — emergency operations center
3. Identify and define the format and structure of major plan components
4. Develop a general introduction of overview
   - General information
     — introduction
     — scope
     — objectives
     — assumptions
     — responsibility overview
     — testing
     — maintenance
   - Plant activation
     — notification
       primary
       secondary
     — disaster declaration procedures
     — mobilization procedures
     — damage assessment concepts
       initial
       detailed
       team members
   - Team organization
     — team description
     — team organization
     — team leader responsibilities
   - Policy statement
   - Emergency operations center
5. Develop an administration section
   - Identify recovery functions for specific support functions
     — personnel/human resources
     — security
     — insurance/risk management
     — equipment/supplies purchasing
     — transportation
     — legal
   - Understand need for public relations/media communications coordinator
     — qualifications
     — responsibilities

- Other specialist coordinator/team responsibilities
  - — government relations
  - — investor relations
  - — other
- Identify components of vital records program
- Action sections
  - — department/individual plans
  - — checklists
  - — technical procedures

6. Develop the business operations plan
   - Operating department plans
     - — essential business functions
     - — information protection and recovery
     - — activation actions
     - — disaster site recovery/restoration actions
     - — end user computing needs
   - Identify components of a vital records program
   - Action sections
     - — recovery team
       - personnel
       - responsibilities
       - resources
   - Action plans
     - — specific department/individual plans
     - — checklists
     - — technical procedures
7. Develop information technology plan
   - Recovery site activities
     - — management
     - — administration/logistics
     - — new equipment
     - — technical services
     - — application support
     - — network communications
     - — network engineering
     - — operations
     - — inter-site logistics and communications
     - — data preparation
     - — production control
     - — end user liaison
   - End user requirements
   - Identify components of vital records program
   - Action sections
     - — recovery teams
       - personnel
       - responsibilities
       - resources
   - Action plans
     - — specific department/individual plans
     - — checklists
     - — technical procedures

8. Develop communications systems plan
9. Develop end-user applications plans
10. Establish plan distribution and control procedures
11. Implement the plan
    - Develop and education program
      —standard guidelines
      —roles and responsibilities
      —procedures
      —training and awareness
      —presentations
    - Complete required tasks
      —acquisition of additional equipment
      —contractual arrangements
      —preparation of backup and off-site storage
    - Develop test plans and schedules and reporting procedures
    - Develop maintenance, updating and reporting procedures

CORPORATE AWARENESS PROGRAMS AND TRAINING

SUBJECT AREA 7

Prepare a program to create corporate awareness and enhance skills required to develop, implement, maintain, and execute the Business Continuity Plan.

THE ROLE OF THE PROFESSIONAL IS TO:

1. Establish objectives and components of training program
2. Identify functional training requirements
3. Develop training methodology
4. Develop an awareness program
5. Acquire or develop training aids
6. Identify external training opportunities
7. Identify vehicles for corporate awareness

THE PROFESSIONAL SHOULD KNOW HOW TO:

1. Define the objectives of training
2. Develop the type of training programs
    - Computer-based
    - Classroom
    - Test-based
3. Develop awareness programs
    - Management
    - Team members
    - New employee orientation
4. Identify other opportunities for education
    - Professional business continuity planning conferences and seminars
    - User groups
    - Publications

PLAN TESTING

SUBJECT AREA 8

Coordinate, evaluate, test, and exercute the plan. Document the results.

THE ROLE OF THE PROFESSIONAL IS TO:

1. Pre-plan the tests
2. Coordinate the tests
3. Evaluate the test plans
4. Execute the test plans
5. Document the results
6. Evaluate the results
7. Update the plan
8. Report results/evaluation to management

THE PROFESSIONAL SHOULD KNOW HOW TO:

1. Establish a test program
2. Determine test requirements
   - Objectives of testing and establishment of levels of success
   - Types of tests (advantages and disadvantages)
     - simulations and walk-through
     - modular
     - functional
     - announced
     - unannounced
   - Establish and document scope of the test
   - Test growth or expansion
   - Test frequency
   - Logistics and pre-planning
3. Develop realistic scenarios
   - Create test scenarios to approximate likely incidents and associated problems
   - Train team members in new roles and decision making outside normal requirements of their permanent positions
   - Exercise the opening, communications, logging, and documentation requirements of the EOC
     - reconstruction
       - damage assessment
       - facility
       - equipment
       - environment
       - salvage/restoration (specialized services)
       - insurance
4. Establish test evaluation criteria
   - Observation
   - Documentation
   - Evaluation
     - expected vs. actual results
     - plan updates

SUBJECT AREA 9

PLAN MAINTAINANCE

Develop procesdures to keep the continuity capabilities current and the plan consistent with the organization's strategic direction.

[redacted]

THE ROLE OF THE PROFESSIONAL IS TO:

1. Understand strategic directions of the business
2. Attend strategic planning meetings
3. Coordinate plan maintenance

THE PROFESSIONAL SHOULD KNOW HOW TO:

1. Establish review criteria
   - Periodic review
   - Key change events
   - Test results
2. Maintain the plan
   - Select tools
   - Monitor activities
   - Establish update process
   - Audit and control
3. Establish status reporting procedures
4. Establish plan distribution and control procedures

DISASTER RECOVERY INSTITUTE CERTIFICATION BOARD MEMBERS	
NAME	**ORGANIZATION**
Melvyn Musson	Johnson & Higgins
Chuck Perkins	Cooper & Lybrand
Cole Emerson	Cole Emerson & Associates
William C. Martin	US Fidelity & Guarantee
Sally Meglathery	New Stock Exchange
Fred Luevano, Jr.	Northrup
William J. Rider	Blue Cross Blue Shield of Maryland
Benny D. Taylor	Texas Instruments
Barney F. Pelant	Barney F. Pelant & Associates
Cris R. Castro	SRI International
Kenneth W. Hargrove	AGT Limited, Canada
James H. McCown	EDS
Raja K. Iyer	University of Texas, Arlington
Edmond D. Jones	Phoenix Consulting
Curt Hartog	Washington University, St. Louis, MO
Tom Doemland	ACP Liaison — Farmers Insurance Group
Curtis A. Edfast	ACP Liaison — Great-West Life Assurance Co.
William Langendoerfer	Director of Education, Disaster Recovery Institute
Jay G. Bender	Executive Director, Disaster Recovery Institute

Index

C

S

T

V

W

BUSINESS RESUMPTION PLANNING

1999 EDITION

EDWARD S. DEVLIN

COLE H. EMERSON

LEO A. WROBEL, JR.

MARK B. DESMAN

AUERBACH

Boca Raton London New York Washington, D.C.

ISBN 0-8493-9945-9
ISBN 0-8493-9975-0

Printed in the United States of America

Auerbach
CRC Press LLC
2000 Corporate Blvd., N.W.
Boca Raton, FL 33431

About the Authors

Edward S. Devlin is often called "The Father of Disaster Recovery Planning." A leading consultant for over 20 years, Mr. Devlin has assisted hundreds of companies in formulating their emergency plans. He is the president of Edward Devlin and Associates, and can be reached at (610) 429-9029.

Cole H. Emerson is president of Cole Emerson & Associates. A recognized leader in the field of business resumption planning, he has assisted companies throughout the world in recovery planning. Emerson has written and spoken at numerous domestic and international conferences. He is a founder of the Information Systems Security Association and a charter member of the Disaster Recovery Institute Certification Board. He can be reached at (916) 729-6055.

Leo A. Wrobel, Jr., president of Premiere Network Services, Inc., has more than two decades of experience in emerging network technology, disaster recovery planning, and technical training. An active author and lecturer, he as published nine books and dozens of trade articles on a wide variety of technical subjects. He can be reached at Premiere's web site (http://www.dallas.net/~premiere) or by calling (972) 515-5000.

Mark B. Desman has been a practitioner in information security and contingency planning for the past 19 years. His background includes being one of the first Information Security managers for American Savings of California as well as CalFed Bank (now NationsBank) and Gibraltar Savings in Southern California. Most recently, he was Manager of Information Security, contingency planning, and the technical Help Desk for a multi-state bank-holding company in New England. Currently, Mr. Desman is Manager of Information Security at Micron Technology, Inc.

Contents

Part III

Voice and Data Communications Recovery

WORKPAPERS

Introduction

Traditionally, resumption planning has focused on the recovery of computer systems. But experience has shown that the ability to recover computer systems does not necessarily guarantee the survival of an organization following a disaster. Quick recovery of a data center is useful only if the business units themselves are able to function–to communicate with customers and vendors, to receive and enter orders, to produce goods and services, and to collect revenue. The only way to ensure that is to plan for the resumption of all of the critical components of the business enterprise–its business operations, including personal computers and LANs, the data center, and voice and data communications services.

Business Resumption Planning is designed to provide a practical, hands-on guide for developing a comprehensive business recovery plan. The book consists of three modules:

- *Part I.* Business operations recovery.
- *Part II.* Data center recovery.
- *Part III.* Voice and data communications recovery.

Each module provides a step-by-step approach for developing the recovery plan; supporting checklists, questionnaires, procedures, and forms used in developing the recovery plan are provided on paper and on the accompanying CD-ROM.

Each of the three modules can be read and used independently of the other two. For example, if your company has already established a data center recovery plan, you may want to establish a plan for communications recovery. In that case, you can turn directly to Part III of this book and begin the process of developing the communications plan; all of the procedures, checklists, and forms you will need are provided in Part III. Of course, if your company has no recovery plan in place, you can begin with any of the three modules. (In practice, however, it makes most sense to proceed in sequential order, beginning with Part I. This is because information gathered in planning for business operations recovery can be useful when planning for data center and communications recovery.)

Business Resumption Planning is not only useful for developing recovery plans; it is also an invaluable source for evaluating the completeness of existing plans. For example, if your organization has already established a data center recovery plan, you might use Part II to ensure that the existing recovery plan is complete and follows the proven techniques described here. Given the step-by-step approach used in this book, its is easy to adapt specific procedures and forms to an existing plan and to the needs of specific organizations.

Now that you have an idea of what this book can do for you, let's look at why you need to plan for disasters.

DEFINING DISASTER

It is impossible to describe all of the events that might be considered disasters, but in the context of this book a disaster is any incident that causes an extended disruption of business functions. The first thought that comes to most minds are such common disasters as fire, hurricane, flood, and earthquake–that is, catastrophic acts of nature. This isn't surprising, given the unprecedented number of disasters the world has suffered in the past decade. The US, for example, has experienced three major earthquakes, several major hurricanes, and a massive flood that covered a large section of the Midwest. Hundreds of people were injured or killed in these natural disasters, tens of thousands lost their homes, and thousands of businesses were disrupted. Business and property losses were in the billions of dollars.

Despite the widespread association of disasters with natural disasters, most recovery specialists have expanded the definition of disaster to include any event that disrupts business operations. Given the variability in causes of disasters, recovery planners should not attempt to focus on specific types of disasters; rather, they should broaden their view to include any type of event that might disrupt business activity.

WHY PLAN?

Business survival is the primary rationale for planning. Avoidance of financial loss and embarrassment as well as ethical and legal obligations to employees, customers, and shareholders all support the need for planning. Without effective planning, the organization is forced to react to a disaster without an understanding of its recovery priorities, the time and resources needed to reestablish business functions, and sources of products and services needed during recovery. The delays caused by such lack of planning may be financially fatal. (For example, such technical resources as hot sites and communications services require long lead times to acquire and configure.) Indeed, history shows that most companies that suffer a disaster causing an extended disruption to information processing do not survive more than two years after the disaster.

The Need for Focus

Even with the most comprehensive plans for all major disruptions, the company can still be surprised. Therefore, it is recommended that organizations plan for the worst-case event rather than for specific types of disasters. The theory, proven many times, is that the company that is ready to respond to the worst disaster will also be able to handle lesser disruptions. If the planning team anticipates, plans for, and documents the recovery requirements and the company is prepared to meet most of those requirements at the time of a disaster, the recovery will succeed.

In addition, the recovery planner must plan within the scope of his or her control. It is always better to have an effective plan for one site than to be in the midst of planning for the world and not survive a single-site disaster. Ensuring that the highest-risk location is ready to respond and recover from an incident is always the more effective approach.

Hidden Benefits

As noted, the primary benefit of a recovery plan is ensuring the organization's survival in the event of a disaster. Yet other, less-obvious benefits are frequently overlooked. For example, in some cases a recovery plan may be a prerequisite for obtaining a business contract; conversely, lack of a plan may disqualify a company from consideration.

An effective recovery plan can also provide a competitive edge. Companies that have been able to quickly recover from regional disasters are often able to increase their share of the market because competitors are unable to conduct business. For example, one company reported that it was able to book $30 million in sales following the Hinsdale central office fire during a period when its competitors were unable to recover.

In developing a comprehensive plan, the recovery planner must learn how the business functions and how information, goods, and services move within and outside the organization. This may create opportunities for identifying potential cost reductions and improved operating efficiencies. The planner may also find opportunities for cost savings in business interruption insurance coverage and in company directors' and officers' insurance. Insurance professionals indicate that companies with resumption plans should save at least 10% on the cost of insurance premiums.

The planning process also forces a review of vital records management. One company was able to eliminate more than 110 tons of paper records, which in turn reduced the potential costs of restoring these records following a disaster.

HOW TO USE THE BOOK AND CD-ROM

Each part of this book is designed to provide a complete step-by-step approach to developing a recovery plan for its respective area; therefore, the chapters within each part should be read in sequential order. Although there are differences in methodology among the three parts, they do share a basic developmental framework:

- Obtaining senior management commitment and sponsorship of the planning project.
- Organizing the project and assembling the teams responsible for planning and recovery.
- Identifying recovery priorities, assumptions, and strategies.
- Gathering information to be included in the recovery plan.
- Developing detailed recovery procedures to be followed by the recovery teams in the event of a disaster.
- Establishing a program for testing and maintaining the recovery plan and for training recovery team members.

Differences among the three planning areas reflect the unique requirements of these areas as well as the practical experience of the authors in developing plans for clients.

In addition to providing step-by-step instructions on how to create the business resumption plan for each area, supporting checklists, questionnaires, procedures, and forms used in developing the recovery plan (collectively referred to as workpapers in this book) are provided on paper and on the accompanying CD-ROM.

On the CD-ROM, each workpaper is provided as a separate Microsoft Word 6.0 file. The file name matches the number of the workpaper referenced in the book.

The electronic files are designed so that users can easily customize the workpapers to meet the recovery planning requirements of his or her organization. Wherever possible, the files are formatted using Microsoft Word default settings; the base font is Courier, 10 characters per inch. Every attempt has been made to ensure that the page layout of the screen version of each workpaper matches the corresponding printed version contained in the book. The owner of this publication is permitted to make either paper or electronic copies of the workpapers without having to obtain permission from the publisher.

Obtaining Senior Management Sponsorship

CHAPTER

I-1

No business resumption project can succeed without the initial and ongoing sponsorship of senior management. Starting the program is difficult; keeping it alive and growing is even more difficult. The object of the planner is to obtain and maintain senior management sponsorship. Without senior management sponsorship, neither the money nor the time will be made available to successfully complete the project.

How then does the planner obtain and keep this commitment? The most effective way to gain and maintain senior management commitment is to first make management aware of the risks of not having a recovery capability and then get them involved in the planning and recovery process. If senior managers do not understand the potential operations are interrupted, they cannot fully support the Process.

The steps involved in obtaining senior management support include:

- Performing a preliminary risk analysis.
- Identifying any relevant laws or regulations.
- Building the business case for the business operations recovery plan.
- Obtaining management approval.

The following sections of this chapter describe these steps.

PERFORM A PRELIMINARY RISK ANALYSIS

STEP 1

The preliminary risk analysis identifies risks, their probability of occurrence, and their potential impact on the organization. The risk analysis differs from a business impact analysis in two important aspects:

- A risk analysis identifies specific threats and severity of impact of a disaster on the organization. It does not attempt to identify financial and logical impacts on specific organizational departments and functions; that is the purpose of the business impact analysis.
- The business impact analysis does not consider what types of accidents cause a disruption to the business operations; it is concerned only with identifying consequences in terms of financial loss, additional expense, embarrassment, and the expected length of the interruption.

A full business impact analysis is conducted only after approval for the recovery planning project has been obtained from senior management. (Chapter 1-3 describes how to perform the business impact analysis.)

In preparing to perform a risk analysis, the planner must accept that all possible risks cannot, and should not, be identified. The planner has neither the time nor money to invest in identifying every possible event that can interrupt business operations. It is a fact that meteors could do serious damage to business operations. But the potential is so remote and occurrence so infrequent that it would be a waste

EXHIBIT I-1-A THREATS LIST

- Accidental explosion—off-site
- Accidental explosion—on-site
- Aircraft crash
- Ancillary equipment failure
- Arson
- Bomb threat
- Bombing
- Central computer equipment failure
- Data theft: physical assets ($2,500+)
- Earthquake (magnitude 5+)
- Epidemic
- Fire: external
- Fire: internal—catastrophic
- Fire: internal—major
- Fire: internal—minor
- Fraud/embezzlement
- High winds (70+ mph)
- Hostage taking
- Human error: maintenance
- Human error: operation
- Human error: programmers
- Human error: users
- Hurricane/typhoon
- HVAC failure/temperature inadequacy
- Ice storm
- Labor dispute
- Loss of key staff
- Major landslide/mudslide
- Media failure
- Medical emergency
- Misuse of resources
- Power flux
- Power outage—external
- Power outage—internal
- Purchased software failure
- Radioactive contamination
- Riot/civil disorder
- Sabotage: external—data and software
- Sabotage: external—physical
- Sabotage: internal—data and software
- Sabotage: internal—physical
- Sandstorm
- Seasonal/local flooding
- Snowstorm/blizzard
- Strike
- Subsidence faulting
- Telecommunications failure—data
- Telecommunications failure—voice
- Theft
- Thunder/electrical storm
- Tidal flooding
- Tornado
- Toxic contamination
- Tropical storm
- Tsunami
- Upstream dam/reservoir failure
- Vandalism
- Volcanic activity
- Water leak/plumbing failure

to include such an event in any risk analysis. What the planner should focus on is the identification of the most probable set of risks that have the greatest impact on the company's business operations.

The objective of the risk analysis at this preliminary stage is to:

- Identify various risks to an organization.
- Identify the requirements of an organization to resume or continue business functions.
- Identify the general impact on the organization, both functionally and financially, of an occurrence of the risks.
- Identify a preliminary estimate of the costs to the organization to establish effective controls to reduce the risks.
- Establish priorities to address identified risks.

Before proceeding, it may be useful to clarify some terminology commonly used in risk analysis — the terms *threat, risk, controls,* and *vulnerabilities*. Threats are the triggers that cause a risk to become a loss. For example, the risk of fire is always present. If a threat called lightning or equipment failure occurs, a fire may happen and property may be damaged. Threats can also be risks. For example, sabotage is both a risk and a threat. A major objective of the planner is to identify the loss exposure due to threats. A comprehensive list of threats that the planner should be concerned with is illustrated in Exhibit I-1-A.

A primary objective of the risk analysis is to identify effective and appropriate controls. Controls are designed to either deter the threat or reduce the loss. Controls cannot do both. Controls may:

- Reduce the occurrence rate of a given threat.
- Reduce the magnitude of the loss.
- Reduce the intensity or severity of the threat, thereby reducing either the occurrence rate or the loss.

Fire sprinkler systems are an example of a control that can reduce loss. Access controls can help deter the threat of intrusion.

Cost effectiveness must be considered for controls. Cost is the initial investment in the control plus the annual maintenance. Because controls have a life expectancy and a return on investment, their benefits can be measured financially; the planner should always spend the most time identifying effective controls for those risks that are most likely to occur.

Some controls are specific in nature; others address more than one threat. A backup site acts as a control applicable to multiple threats including earthquake, tornado, fire, and extended utility failure. An uninterruptible power source (UPS) addresses one threat, power failure.

Vulnerabilities are a weakness in the system of controls. If the control is absent, weak, or inadequate and cannot reduce the threat, the object of the threat is considered to be vulnerable.

Risk Assessment Tools

Explaining how to perform a risk analysis beyond the scope of this book. Fortunately, there are a number of automated risk assessment tools that can be used to assist the business resumption planner at this stage. These include the Bayesian Decision Support System (Ozier, Peterse & Assoc) or RISKWATCH (Expert Systems Software Inc.). These tools can help decrease the amount of time required to complete the risk analysis. However, risk assessment tools are not intuitive and require experienced risk analysis professionals to ensure a valid and useful result. The analyst will need to be trained to use the products; in addition, most users require ongoing assistance from the vendor in resolving problems using the software or interpreting the results.

Risk assessment tools address array of threats, both natural and humanmade, ranging from small fire to nuclear holocaust. The applicability of each threat and its impact on business operations are assessed. In addition, the tools identify the probability of the threat occurring and, by using a mathematical formula, determine the relationship between the threat, the impact on the operations, and the probability of occurrence. A risk priority is established along with financial loss potential.

The classic school of risk analysis uses this information to establish how much should be invested to eliminate the threat or reduce its impact on operations and to set priorities for risk mitigation, Although historical data on such threats as earthquakes is not sufficiently detailed t provide a precise probability weighting, the authors of the tools claim o have a comprehensive set of historical occurrences that establish a credible probability of an occurrence. Nonetheless, there are often major debates within the organization about the validity of the probability algorithms used by these products.

Many risks that planner should concern themselves with are fairly evident and can be assessed without automated tools. For example, in southern California, earthquakes are the most significant risk that could cause catastrophic damage to business operations. Fires, both internal and external, pose major threats to business operations. Even if a fire does not directly affect a facility, it may require that it be evacuated. If the fire destroys employees' homes, the employees may not be available for several days. Power and communications failures also provide frequent challenges to businesses in both southern and northern California. Floods and landslides occur less frequently and with lesser impact. Without too much analysis, most California planners can identify and plan against threats that are most probable and have the most catastrophic effect on business operations.

For the U.S. Southeast and Gulf Coast, hurricane and tornadoes are the major threats. In the Midwest, floods and tornadoes are major threats, with earthquakes being less likely but having a potentially catastrophic impact on the area. The Northeast faces both hurricanes and blizzards, sometimes simultaneously.

Risk assessments should address the threat of disruption of telephone, power, and water utilities. There are also subtler threats that might escape a novice planner — for example, contamination by a toxic spill near a company facility or a minor fire that causes a fluorescent light ballast containing PCBs to burn, thereby discharging carcinogenic agents into the surrounding area. Proximity to industries that use hazardous material in their manufacturing process or actually manufacture the hazardous materials may pose a threat. So too may labor action that shuts down the manufacturing lines of a critical sole-source supplier. Major crimes against employees in the work place seem to be an increasing threat.

In the effort to present a solid business case for senior management, the planner should be ready to present the most likely risks. This preliminary risk analysis should be conducted at a high level; a more comprehensive risk assessment can be conducted after basic recovery capabilities have been established for the organization. The result of this high-level risk analysis may be expresses as a quantified risk value, but not to the degree that would be provided by a comprehensive risk assessment.

Sample Risk Assessment Report

Workpaper I1.01 provides a sample of an actual risk assessment extracted from a final report. This particular risk assessment focused on a data center and was conducted primarily as a qualitative, although numerical weighting was assigned to risk factors. Instead of a complicated, a simplified analysis was used with the objective of establishing priorities to address risks rather than determining the appropriate amount of money to spend to reduce or eliminate the risk.

STEP 2

IDENTIFY LEGAL AND REGULATORY MANDATES

It is only in the past ten years that federal and state regulators have recognized that resumption planning should include business operations and not just data processing. A legal or regulatory requirement to establish a plan does not necessarily mean that the company will comply with the requirement. All regulations are subject to the interpretation; often a company can comply with the regulations without having actually implemented an effective business resumption plan. Nonetheless, management needs to be aware of how the recovery plan will be evaluated in the context of law and regulations.

The key regulations are summarized in the following paragraphs. Much of the regulatory focus is on financial institutions; therefore, the majority of the available regulations apply to a small but important set of business operations. The key legal and regulatory requirement include:

- Executive Order 11490.
- The Foreign Corrupt Practices Act of 1977.
- Comptroller of the Currency banking circulars.
- Federal Home Loan Bank Board regulations and memorandums.

In addition, common law related to negligence may also bear on the corporation's responsibility for recovery plan. Other regulations that may apply include: Office of Management and Budget Circular A-71; IRS Procedure 64-12; IRS Ruling 71-20; Occupational Safety and Health Administration regulations; and Environmental Protection Agency regulations.

Executive Order 11490

Since October 30, 1969, financial institutions have been mandated by Executive Order 14490 to prepare emergency plans that address the following issues:

- Assigning responsibility for emergency operations preparedness to a specific individual.
- Developing and distributing written emergency preparedness procedures.
- Truing personnel periodically in emergency response procedures.
- Developing an effective program for safeguarding and duplicating records.
- Defining plans for succession of senior officers.

The Foreign Corrupt Practices Act

The Foreign Corrupt Practices Act is probably the most misused though frequently mentioned regulation in both the security and disaster recovery fields. In 1977, the Securities and Exchange Act of 1934 was amended by the Foreign Corrupt Practices Act to require all publicly held companies to keep accurate records and maintain internal control systems to safeguard assets. The courts have defined assets as including the computer system and all the data it contains. Critical records and original documents are also assets and should be protected. The company that fails to generate a record is as liable as the company that fails to preserve it. A company without adequate business resumption plans may nit be able to create records for an extended period of time.

Commentators discussing computer recovery generally agree that Section 13(b)(2) of the Securities and Exchange Act (as added by the Foreign Corrupt Practices Act of 1977) may be read to require executives of public companies to take reasonable precautions to preserve computer records from destruction. The act's internal audit and control requirement could conceivably extend into every aspect of corporate operations.

Courts have already indicated that its requirement apply not only to written documents, but to the preservation of accurate computer records as well (SEC. vs World-Wide Coin Investments Ltd.). The courts defined *reasonable* on the basis of economic cost/benefit analysis: implementation of the required procedures was not to create a fail-safe system at all costs; rather, the cost should not exceed expected benefits.

Corporate executives who fail to determine the proper measure of disaster recovery preparation could become subject to certain criminal penalties. The Securities Exchange Commission, in enforcing this statute, may seek an injunction against noncompliance, institute administrative proceedings, or even institute criminal proceedings.

Originally corporate officers were personally responsible even if they were not aware of the deficiency. In 1992, Congress modified the law and significantly changed the responsibility of senior management. With the new amendment, senior management is not responsible unless it "knowingly" fails to put in place appropriate controls.

Comptroller of the Currency

The administrator of national banks is the Comptroller of the Currency. Over the past decade, the Comptroller has issued several requirements related to disaster recovery planning. The following summarizes each publication.

Banking Circular 177. The Comptroller of the Currency originally issued Banking Circular 177 on June 29, 1983. Initially BC 177 emphasized contingency planning for computer systems processing but was revised on April 16, 1987 to include business operations. It states that contingency planning for bank's information systems should extend beyond the data center to the key operational areas of the bank. This is increasingly critical as information expands beyond traditional central operations. A principal objective of any contingency plan should be to ensure the ability of user departments to function effectively in an adverse environment.

Banking Circular 187. The Comptroller of the Currency issued Banking Circular 187 on January 18, 1985 to address the importance of reviewing the financial status of organizations that provide information-processing services. Financial institutions using bureaus should assure themselves of continued, uninterrupted data processing support. BC 187 states that to satisfy its fiduciary responsibilities regarding information processing services, a board of directors or its appointed committee should obtain and analyze the financial condition is deteriorating or unsound, alternative servicing arrangements should be considered to ensure continued information processing support. Prudent banking practices would usually include the documentation of contingency plans.

Banking Circular 226. One of the growing problems within the office environment is the protection of information resident on small distributed systems. The Comptroller of the Currency issued Banking Circular 226 on January 25, 1988. This circular was issued jointly by the Federal Financial Institutions Examination Council. This council includes the following organizations.

- Board of Governors of the Federal Reserve System.
- Federal Deposit Insurance Corporation.
- Federal Home Loan Bank Board.
- Office of the Comptroller of the Currency.

The circular addresses the risks associated with end-user computing activities. End user computing includes information processing activities using microcomputers, minicomputers, small mainframes, or other computers to control and process data at the user level. BC 226 encourages bank management to evaluate the associate risks with its end user computing networks and other forms of distributed computer operations. Control practices and responsibilities to manage these activities should be incorporated into an overall corporate information security policy. Such a policy should address areas such as:

- Management controls.
- Data security.
- Documentation.
- Data and file storage and backup.
- Systems and data integrity.
- Contingency Plans.
- Audit Responsibility.
- Training.

For each operational system, plans should be made to ensure that users adequately recover from damage to hardware, software, and data. For some systems, an inability to process during recovery may mean that work can be held for later processing. For other systems, a manual backup may be appropriate. For some time-critical, highly automated systems, arrangements may have to be made for data reconstruction or for processing on other hardware. At a minimum, for all systems, there should be secure and remote backup storage of data files and programs. Beyond this, the backup and contingency requirements for individual systems may differ and need to be addressed separately.

Banking Circular 87-3. Banking Circular 87-3 was issued by the Comptroller of the Currency on February 12, 1987. It addresses risks associated with contracting long-term IS services. The comptroller recommends several considerations for contracts of information processing services, including establishing a method to develop and test contingency plans.

Federal Home Loan Bank Board

The Federal Home Loan Bank Board has issued several requirements related to disaster recovery planning. Regulation PA-17-1a states that a written contingency plan should be maintained for response to a wide variety of disasters, including potential disruption of the computer room, loss of computer hardware, and loss of data files. Contingency and use of backup hardware should be reviewed periodically and tested where appropriate.

Memorandum R67. The Federal Home Loan Bank Board issued Memorandum R67 on September 4, 1986. This regulation describes guidelines on contingency disaster recovery plans required for insured institutions and service corporations. Memorandum R67 addresses several important concerns, including reciprocal agreements and use service bureaus. With respect to reciprocal agreements, the memorandum states that institutions often obtain a written letter of agreement from another institution, which provides for backup capability to each other, to serve as a contingency disaster plan. However, such agreements are often insufficient because:

- Agreements are not always current.
- The system owned by the institution providing backup may not be capable of supporting the agreement.
- Backup capacity is not tested periodically to ensure compatibility of the systems.
- There is no guarantee that backup equipment will be available when needed.

With respect to service bureau users, the memorandum states that if an institution is using an IS service bureau, the institution must establish policies and responsibilities to ensure that the appropriate contingency disaster plans are developed and maintained. The institution must document a review of the service bureau's contingency plan to ensure that it is compatible with the institution's plan. If an institution uses both its own system and a service bureau, a combined plan must be developed and maintained.

Memorandum R67-1. The Office of Regulatory Policy, Oversight, and Supervision of the federal Home Loan Bank System issued Memorandum R67-1 on March 22, 1988. This regulation is the same as Banking Circular 226, which addresses the risks associated with end-user computing activities.

Common Law Negligence

If a corporation owes a third party a duty and the corporation agent fails to perform that duty, the injured party may recover for the omission. However, recovery has been traditionally rewarded only for physical damages; awards for monetary losses are usually granted only in cases in which the corporation is acting as a fiduciary or trustee.

Under common law, the legal responsibilities of a corporation's directors and officers include a fiduciary duty to the corporation. These executives must therefore exercise due care to safeguard corporate assets.

STEP 3

BUILD THE BUSINESS CASE

Although some organizations are mandated by regulations to establish a recovery plan, most organizations are not. The decision to put in place a resumption plan is a business decision. The investment of time and money must bring some benefits to the company.

As with any business plan, the objective is to identify benefits of having a plan. In most cases, the planner is faced with having a non-profit-generating project that only offsets potential losses. The return on investment is loss avoidance contrasted with the cost of the program. In presenting the case, the planner must identify both the potential financial loss without the plan as well as the potential loss with the plan. The difference between the two provides the basis for justifying the investment.

At this preliminary project phase, the planner must create an informal business case providing a high level analysis for management. Workpaper I1.02 provides a sample format for presenting the business case.

Financial estimates are developed using an interative process, beginning with loss estimates determined in the preliminary risk analysis. The final estimates of potential loss for specific business functions and the cost of equipment, personnel, and services are determined by conducting a business impact analysis (see Chapter 1-3).

The planner should establish a minimum baseline of investment needed to initially recover the most critical business functions. As part of a more comprehensive business plan, the expansion of the program can be addressed. Each expansion of the program should be able to demonstrate a reduction in the loss potential of the organization.

STEP 4

OBTAIN MANAGEMENT APPROVAL

The most effective way for a planner to present a case for the planning project to senior management (as well as project participants) is to use a case study of a type of disaster that would most likely affect the organization. The planner should always use organizations that have been successful responding to and recovering from major incidents. Describing those actions that were most effective — as well as those that were not — can help senior management better understand how the plan should be implemented. Although what worked for one organization will not necessarily guarantee success for another, it is more convincing to use actual incidents.

Conducting the Initial Presentation

The objective of the initial management presentation is to first gain management's interest and second present he intended message. The presentation must always address management's concerns before those of the planners. The level of presentation must remain at a high level, detail should be provided in handouts that can be read before the presentation.

The presentation materials should be provided to senior management a few days before the meeting for its review. The planner should anticipate that most managers will not read the materials. Therefore, the most important information should be presented in a crisp, concise format during the presentation.

The time provided by senior management will be short and the message must be precise and targeted for the audience. An initial meeting of one hour should be planned, though the planner may be given additional time for questions and answers. Any follow up and status meetings should be about 30 minutes long.

The following sections describe the key components of an effective presentation.

Introduction and Meeting Objectives. The presentation starts with a statement of objectives for the meeting. If the planner has a senior management sponsor, the sponsor should state the purpose of the presentation and introduce he planner.

Case Studies. During the initial meeting, the planner should present a brief synopsis of disasters that have occurred at peer companies in the industry. The objective of this summary is to obtain management attention.

Qualities of an Effective Plan. The planner next describes what the plan should do. This can be accomplished by presenting the qualities of an effective business resumption plan. An effective plan should:

- Identify the most likely potential threats.
- Identify critical business and support.
- Estimate impacts because of the disruption of operations; these may include revenue loss, additional expenses, and embarrassment to the organization.
- Document how key assets move within and outside the business. Such assets include information and transactions, goods, and funds.
- Determine relationships interdependencies within the organization (e.g., between order entry and sales) and external to the organization (e.g., between telephone power and utilities and corporate emergency service).
- Determine space and supporting facility requirements, such as percentage of normal requirements for space, and proximity of related business units.
- Develop the prevention, planning, response, recovery, restoration, and resumption teams.

The purpose and objectives of the teams should also be introduced. In general, the objectives are to:

- Establish preventive engineering to eliminate threats or mitigate the consequences of the incident.
- Plan and prepare by identifying critical components, team members, impact of loss, time frame for recovery, proposed course of action, and roles of the participants.
- Respond through effective command and control to maintain the safety of personnel and transition to business and processing recovery.
- Initiate the recovery involving the movement of people, data, equipment, and operations to alternative locations.
- Initiate cleanup of facilities, paper, magnetic media, and equipment and rebuilding of the facilities.
- Transition from the temporary facilities and services to a precise operational status.

Current Planning Status. The planner presents where the company is in the planning process, focusing on the highest-priority items first.

Mission Statement. The planner presents the mission statement of the business resumption planning organization. For example, the mission might be to "provide a cost-effective approach to mitigating the financial impact of a significant business interruption."

Planning Project Objectives. The planner then presents the objectives of the planning project, which should flow from the mission statement. These objectives might include:

- Establishing a business resumption plan for critical headquarters functions.
- Establishing a command structure for effectively managing the response and recovery efforts.
- Training recovery team members in Procedures required to recover critical business operations.
- Testing and exercising the recovery plan to ensure it can effectively respond to an actual disaster.

Defining Corporate Policies

After management's approval is obtained, a policy statement should be issued that clearly states the organization's commitment to ensuring continued business operations. In addition, policies for each business unit within the organization should establish responsibility for plan development, activation, and maintenance at the business unit level. The policy lays the initial foundation for establishing plan ownership at the most appropriate and most effective level within the organization. The following is an example of a business resumption policy statement at the corporate and business unit levels, respectively:

> The organization recognizes the importance of business survival. To ensure that all critical business functions continue in the event of a disaster, it has committed to develop the business resumption plan. This plan implemented by its staff documents the policy of business survival for the company.
>
> Business resumption planning is the responsibility of all organization management. Each business unit manager is responsible for ensuring that his or her critical business operations are prepared to resume operations within a predefined period following a major disruptive incident.

Closing the Deal

After completing the initial presentation to senior management, the planner must restate and confirm in writing the objectives, scope, time frame, impact on organizational resources, and cost of the program. A clear set of objectives, agreed-on scope, funding, organizational impact, and time frame are required for the planner to begin the development process. Not having the above may prove disruptive during the project if members of the senior management team assume something other than the initially stated project parameters, change elements of the project plan, or renege on committed resources.

USEFUL RESOURCES

Bulletin boards, journals, federal agencies, and professional organizations can provide information that will prove valuable to the planner. Appendix 1-A provides a selected listing of these key resources.

WORKPAPER I1.01 Sample Risk Assessment Report

RISK ASSESSMENT REPORT

The company's disaster recovery plan should assume a worst-case, total-facility disaster, thus also providing for recovery from less severe circumstances. However, the assessment of threats and the risk associated with vulnerability to such threats provides for identification of hazards in terms of potential for occurrence and severity of impact. Emphasis may then be placed on preparation for those hazards of greatest potential and consequence. The primary objective of this analysis has been to identify the most critical risks that could cause an interruption of the company's information processing for a period greater than 24 hours.

Threats have been generally grouped into three categories:

- Natural.
- Human.
- Technical.

Each threat is then qualified by:

- Probability factor (low = 1, medium = 2, high = 3).
- Threat factor (sum of 1 plus speed of onset, where slow = 0, fast = 1; forewarning, where forewarning = 0, no forewarning = 1; duration, where short = 0, long = 1).
- Impact (low = 1, medium = 2, high = 3).

Weighted results are calculated by this formula:

$$\text{Probability} \times \text{Threat Factor} \times \text{Impact} = \text{Relative Weight}$$

The matrix on the following presents findings for a variety of threats to the organization's business operation A.

Threats	Applicability	Probability	Threat Factor	Impact	Weight
Human Error: Operation — Response	Applicable	3	4	3	36
Power Outage — External	Applicable	3	3	3	27
Power Flux	Applicable	3	3	3	27
Fire: Internal — Major	Applicable	2	4	3	24
Toxic Contamination	Applicable	2	4	3	24
Water Leak/Plumbing Failure	Applicable	2	4	3	24
Central Computer Equipment Failure	Applicable	2	4	3	24
Human Error: Maintenance	Applicable	2	4	3	24
Hostage Taking	Applicable	2	4	3	24
Power Outage — Internal	Applicable	2	3	3	18
HVAC Failure/Temperature Inadequacy	Applicable	3	2	3	18
Telecommunications Failure Data	Applicable	2	3	3	18
Ancillary Equipment Failure	Applicable	2	4	2	16
Earthquake (Magnitude 5 or more)	Applicable	1	4	3	12
Upstream Dam/Reservoir Failure	Applicable	2	2	3	12
Seasonal/Local Flooding	Applicable	3	2	2	12
Radioactive Contamination	Applicable	1	4	3	12
Fire: Internal — Catastrophic	Applicable	1	4	3	12
Aircraft Crash	Applicable	1	4	3	12
Accidental Explosion — On Site	Applicable	1	4	3	12
Telecommunications Failure Voice	Applicable	2	3	2	12
Sabotage: External — Physical	Applicable	1	4	3	12
Sabotage: Internal — Physical	Applicable	1	4	3	12
Bombing	Applicable	1	4	3	12
Bomb Threat	Applicable	1	4	3	12
Arson	Applicable	1	4	3	12
Volcanic Activity	Applicable	1	3	3	09
Fire: Internal — Minor	Applicable	3	3	1	09
Loss of Key Staff	Applicable	2	2	2	08
Vandalism	Applicable	1	4	2	08
High Winds (70+ mph)	Applicable	1	3	2	06
Labor Dispute/Strike	Applicable	1	3	2	06
Riot/Civil Disorder	Applicable	1	3	2	06
Thunder/Electrical Storm	Applicable	1	2	2	04
Fire: External	Applicable	1	3	1	03
Accidental Explosion — Off Site	Applicable	1	3	1	03
Ice Storm	Applicable	1	2	1	02
Snowstorm/Blizzard	Applicable	1	1	1	01
Major Landslide/Mudslide	Not Applicable		NA		
Subsidence Faulting	Not Applicable		NA		
Tidal Flooding	Not Applicable		NA		
Tsunami	Not Applicable		NA		
Tornado	Not Applicable		NA		
Hurricane/Typhoon	Not Applicable		NA		
Tropical Storm	Not Applicable		NA		
Sandstorm	Not Applicable		NA		
Epidemic	Not in scope of study		NA		
Medical Emergency	Not in scope of study		NA		
Media Failure	Not in scope of study		NA		
Purchased Software Failure	Not in scope of study		NA		
Human Error: Programmers	Not in scope of study		NA		
Human Error: Users	Not in scope of study		NA		
Misuse of Resources	Not in scope of study		NA		
Theft: Data	Not in scope of study		NA		
Fraud/Embezzlement	Not in scope of study		NA		
Theft: Physical Assets ($2500+)	Not in scope of study		NA		
Sabotage: External — Data and Software	Not in scope of study		NA		
Sabotage: Internal — Data and Software	Not in scope of study		NA		

WORKPAPER I1.02 Business Case Support Document

BUSINESS CASE SUPPORT DOCUMENT

Date: ______________________________

Overview: ______________________________

Project Title: ______________________________

Sponsoring Business Unit: ______________________________

Contact Person: ______________________________

Phone Number: ______________________ **Mail Stop:** ______________________

Business Objective: Recover critical business operations in the event of a disaster.

Business Function or Application

Objective: ______________________________

____

____

Description: ______________________________

____

____

Financial Estimates

Equipment (software): $______________________

____

____

Equipment (hardware): $______________________

____

____

Communications: $______________________

____

____

Space: $______________________

____

____

Miscellaneous Operating Expense: $______________________

____

____

IS Department Support and Planning: $______________________

____

____

Risk Assessment

Probable Risk (Without Backup Plan): $______________________

Probable Risk (With Backup Plan): $______________________

Risk Assessment Narrative

Option 1: ______________________ $______________________

____

____

Option 2: ______________________ $______________________

____

____

Conducting the Business Impact Analysis

CHAPTER

I-3

The business impact analysis (BIA) is designed to ensure a thorough understanding of the vital business functions and systems within the organization. The impact of loss on each of these functions is identified, evaluated, and categorized according to the required time frames for recovery of the function. The recovery priorities are set on the basis of this analysis.

The purpose of the BIA is to identify the consequences of the interruption in terms of financial loss, additional expense, embarrassment to the organization, and the maximum period of interruption that organization can tolerate. The BIA does not take into consideration what type of incident causes a disruption to operations; the cause of the disruption does not matter.

Avoiding financial loss is the primary objective of developing a business resumption plan. Financial losses occur from an interruption to or loss of revenue caused by the inability to continue after a disruptive incident.

The longer a business fails to provide services or products, the more severe the financial losses. Some losses are unavoidable no matter how effective the plan and recovery effort. The objective is to determine what level of financial loss is acceptable to management for the organization as a whole and for a specific business function. Each business unit's financial contribution is determined during the BIA.

Acceptable levels of interruption are defined by the organization's management on the basis of estimates of both financial loss and nonfinancial impact. Management may be willing to self-insure or cover the potential loss with commercial insurance for a short period. After that, the loss or impact may become permanent and the damage long term.

As most planners know, the shorter the desired recovery time frame, the more expensive the resources and recovery capabilities that must be put in place. Management depends on information from the BIA to make an informed decision on how much financial risk it is willing to assume and how much it should invest in the mitigation effort and recovery plan.

Once the BIA is complete, it should be reviewed and verified by management and all participants. Management may then be ready to establish or confirm recovery priorities for critical applications, systems, and business recovery priorities. For example, the priority for recovering networks connecting users to information systems must be consistent with the recovery time frames for the most critical business units. If critical business units plan to recover in five days, the IS function must plan to recover network services at least one day before the recovery of the business unit. This timing for provision of the recovery infrastructure applies to all aspects of planning.

DEFINITION OF BUSINESS IMPACT ANALYSIS

Business impact analysis refers to the process of identifying an organization's exposures to specific threat events and analyzing the potential disruptive impact of those exposures on critical business operations. The BIA can also be used to:

- Assess the impact of a disruption in any functional area of the business on the operations of the enterprise as a whole.
- Determine the extent to which key functional and operational dependencies exist within the organization (e.g., the extent of reliance on information processing or other services).
- Establish the priorities and sequence which critical data processing applications and key business functions should be restored.

There are two generally accepted methods of performing this type of analysis: qualitative and quantitative. Qualitative analysis might be performed by interviewing a knowledgeable person about the relative characteristics, value, or risks associated with a given function. Quantitative analysis attempts to measure value or risk by, for example, assigning numerical values to a scale. The BIA employs both qualitative and quantitative analysis.

PERFORMING A BUSINESS IMPACT ANALYSIS

The process of conducting a business impact analysis can be broken into five steps:

1. Determining the scope of the analysis.
2. Gathering the initial information about business unit functions, support systems, applications, and interdependencies through the use of questionnaires.
3. Conducting interviews to verify the completeness and accuracy of information gathered in the previous step.
4. Analyzing the information to determine priorities for recovery of business operations, systems, and applications, and,
5. Present these results to senior management.

These steps are described in the following sections of this chapter. The chapter concludes with a discussion of insurance options for mitigating financial losses.

STEP 1

DETERMINE THE SCOPE OF THE ANALYSIS

The planner must determine the degree of detailed analysis that the BIA is to provide. A comprehensive BIA requires a significant commitment of resources and time. If the planner needs to put in place recovery capabilities within a short time frame, a comprehensive BIA may not be appropriate. In that case, an abbreviated BIA should be considered. The abbreviated BIA relies on information obtained from various experts within the organization. Technical systems experts are asked to identify high-volume system users. They do so by using information obtained from performance measurement and internal billing applications. For example, IS departments usually bill back system use to the business units; individual users and user groups can be identified by their user IDs. These systems experts can therefore determine the volume of application use by employee and identify those critical applications on which the business units depend most heavily. High-volume users can be targeted for follow-up interviews as needed. This process avoids having to question all users about the applications they use, focusing instead on high-use applications and high-volume users.

The second set of organizational experts reside in the financial group. This group can provide the financial contribution of each revenue-generating business unit and assist in determining the per-day loss potential for each business operation. Groups required to support these revenue generators are also identified. Revenue related questions are not asked of support groups.

The third group organizational experts are the business unit managers. They can assist in determining any additional expenses associated with the interruption-for example, the cost of additional personnel, legal penalties, and additional purchased resources.

Following this approach, the planner can identify the most critical functions, systems, and applications. Even though this analysis is not comprehensive, it should be sufficient to enable the planner to establish the initial recovery priorities, teams, and resources within a reasonable time frame. After the basic plan and recovery organization is in place and validated by exercises, the planner can initiate a more complete BIA to validate the initial information and address new business functions, applications, and systems.

The remaining steps to describe how to perform a comprehensive analysis.

GATHER INFORMATION

STEP 2

The planner must gather information from each business unit to determine the cumulative effect on the organization of the loss of the business function, support system, or application. This can be done using a structured set of questionnaires to obtain information from business unit managers and key staff. Workpaper 13.01 provides a complete set of questionnaires along with instructions for their use.

The questions used in the questionnaires and in the subsequent interviews should be appropriate to the intended audience and relevant to the purpose of the analysis. In some cases the planner may choose to focus the analysis solely on the recovery of systems and applications; alternatively, the planner may choose to address the recovery of business operations, which includes but is not limited to the recovery of support systems and applications. In either case, the questions presented to managers and users must be within their scope of understanding and knowledge.

For example, if the initial analysis focuses on system applications, the names of the applications should be presented in terms the respondents can understand. The planner should use the popular rather than technical name of the application. The planner should not ask users questions related to the operating systems supporting the applications; most users have no knowledge of the operating system. Similarly, the planner should not question users about issues requiring an understanding of how applications interact. The planner should also assume that such equipment as computer terminals is required; it is not necessary to ask if they need the equipment.

If the focus on the BIA is not the recovery of business operations, the questions should first attempt to identify the basic systems infrastructure supporting the business operation (e.g., communications, mail services, and general information systems). (Specific applications and systems can be addressed in a separate impact analysis focusing on recovery of applications.)

The loss of key internal and external business functions can be as crippling as the loss of information systems. The business operations-related BIA attempts to determine the organization's tolerance for disruption of key business functions.

Workpaper I3.01 presents a complete set of questionnaires that address the recovery of business operations, including support systems, applications, and equipment. In general, the questionnaires and the subsequent interviews (described under Step 3) attempt to determine the impact of:

- Interruption of business function or application.
- Loss of revenue.
- Additional expenses.
- Intangible losses.

Business Interruption

The impact of loss of a business function, application, or service should be determined. This can be expressed in terms of the number of hours and days the user could tolerate the application not being available. If a network is necessary to provide access to the application, it is not necessary to ask questions about the impact of losing the network.

Revenue Loss and Non-Revenue Loss

The planner determines what systems or services are directly involved in activities that generate revenue. For example, systems directly involved in billing or collection activities should be identified. Order taking and EDI facilities and systems also fall into this category.

The planner should attempt to determine whether the inability to access certain applications would interfere with the provision of services to customers and other business operations, and if so, how they would be affected.

The inability to perform identified services may cause customers to seek services or products from competitors; if so, the potential for and impact of such losses should be assessed. The revenue analysis also determines whether the inability to provide services would cause other indirect impacts on revenue activities (e.g., lost interest on investments).

Non-Revenue Generating Units

Non-revenue generating units are those providing the infrastructure and services upon which the revenue generating units are dependent. The planner should separate these units and customize the questionnaire accordingly. Asking revenue-generating questions of facility engineers is not appropriate and places the respondent in an awkward and potentially embarrassing position. Additional expenses are focused on rather than revenue.

Additional Expenses

The planner must determine the types of additional expenses the organization would incur with the delay or loss of services or the processing of applications. The interviewees should be asked to estimate the minimum length of time access to the applications could be denied their organization without incurring such additional expenses as overtime or hiring temporary personnel to augment existing staff.

The planner and interviewees should determine whether a delay in availability of services or applications results in additional expenditures other than for labor or services (e.g., interest expenses on bank loans, capital outlays) and should estimate the amount of business backlog (e.g., number of orders, order entries, inquiries) that would incurred. They should also determine whether a delay in operation would result in any fines or penalties for failure to provide services or to adhere to deadlines or government regulations. If so, the impact should be assess if a delay in services would result in legal liability, personal injury, or other public harm.

Intangible Losses

Intangible losses include:

- Loss of customer confidence.
- Loss of investor confidence.
- Loss of competitive edge.
- Damage to the organization's reputation.
- Reduced market share.
- Legal or regulatory violations.

It is difficult to estimate the value of intangible losses; such estimates are inherently subjective. The planner should not spend an extraordinary amount of time trying to quantify this category. The planner should determine the most serious sources of embarrassment to the organization with respect to the delay or loss of ability to provide essential services or applications. Interviewees should be asked if there are potential legal, social, or moral liabilities to the organization if key applications or services are disrupted.

The knowledge and credibility of the source of a subjective opinion is critical to the acceptance of this information by the organization's senior management. An example is the loss of customers. When First Interstate Bank conducted its BIA in 1986, it was determined that approximately 2% of the customer base would be lost if an extended outage occurred. Although it does not seem like a large number, this 2% represented the customers generating the most income for the bank. The customers were large, high-volume users who could not and would not tolerate an extended loss of services.

The source of this estimate were the customer account managers servicing these customers on a daily basis. These managers understood the customers' expectations of service and knew how the customers reacted to past minor interruptions of service. They were in the best position to provide an opinion — that is, without directly asking the customer.

In the beginning stages of the BIA, the planner should be cautious about directly approaching customers for input. They may already assume that the organization has a plan in place and may react negatively on finding this not the case.

VERIFY THE INFORMATION

STEP 3

After the business units return the questionnaires and the planner completes an initial analysis, interviews should be conducted to verify the completeness and accuracy of the information. These interviews are specifically intended to identify any discrepancies in the collected information.

Any business impact analysis requires face-to-face interviews. In addition to interviewing the project participants, the planner should also meet with other independent experts from the contributing business units. The results should also be provided to managers of the contributing business units and reviewed with their next higher level of management. It is important that the key employees and managers of the business units find the collected information credible and be willing to defend the results if required.

The planner should plan to spend at least one or two hours with each interviewee. Group interviews of personnel with related positions can expedite the interview process and may provide a less threatening environment than one-on-one interviews. Issues raised by one team member may jog the memory of another interviewee, thereby uncovering a critical issue that may have been otherwise overlooked.

The interviews should follow the same format as described in step 2. The planner should attempt to verify the impact of:

- Interruption of business function or application.
- Loss of revenue.
- Additional expenses.
- Intangible losses.

STEP 4

ANALYZE AND PRESENT THE RESULTS

The planner can use software tools to help collect, manage, analyze, and present the information collected during the BIA and to summarize the findings in a variety of graphical formats. An example of a widely used software tool is Strohl Systems' B-I-A Professional.

These tools provide formulas which assist the planner to establish a numerical value for each resource being assessed which actually represents a composite of the potential impact factors. Financial loss potential and additional expenses are presented in monetary values. Numerical values are also assigned to embarrassment and other intangible factors. The tolerance for delays in service are identified and each resource is assigned a numerical rating. Analyzed resources can be compared with other resources. Based on a combination of factors, a total weighting is assigned to each resource or business unit. That composite value identifies the relative severity of the combined impact factors and the priority for recovery of the application or business process or function.

The automated tools can also be used to graphically present the results of the analysis. This makes it easier for team members and management to understand the results.

The management presentation should focus on the highest-priority applications and business functions. The result of the analysis should be presented in a tabular and/or graphical format. The methodology used, sources of the information, and actual explanations of the results should be presented in a concise format.

After the results are presented, the planner should state the priorities assigned to business units and applications as well as the minimum tolerable disruption time frames. At the conclusion of the management presentation, the planner should explain how the analysis will be used to establish recovery time frames, strategies, and recovery resources.

REASSESSING BUSINESS IMPACT

The frequency of assessing the business impact depends on the frequency of change within the organization. If the organization is relatively stable, the assessment can be less frequent. In most organizations, however, frequent acquisition of new business activities and technologies constantly change the operations of the organization. With each introduction of a new business operation, application, information system, or network, an assessment should be made to determine where the new function fits among the recovery priorities.

EXHIBIT I-3-A INSURANCE OPTIONS

Covered Perils

- Explosion
- Fire or lightning
- Leakage
- Mine subsidence
- Riot or civil commotion
- Sinkhole or collapse
- Smoke
- Vandalism
- Volcanic action
- Wind or hail

Extensions to Normal Coverage

- Electrical arcing
- Falling objects
- Glass breakage
- Mechanical breakdown
- Steam explosion
- Water damage
- Weight of ice, snow, or sleet

Most organizations should conduct a corporate wide BIA at least every two years. The factors that determine the impact of the loss of a particular function in the organization should be expected to change in that time. For example, the volume of business transactions may either increase or decrease.

EVALUATING INSURANCE OPTIONS

To offset potential losses, the organization can purchase coverage for identified perils. This coverage is referred to as business interruption or additional-expense insurance. Exposures and loss potential not nitigated or addressed by insurance must be taken into account in the recovery plan.

The planner should be aware that all disasters are not automatically covered. The exposures need to be identified through a risk analysis, and the policy tailored to address these exposures.

There are two basic types of insurance: property coverage and time-element coverage. Property coverage covers buildings, personal property, and equipment and machinery. Time-element coverage covers such items as business income, extra expenses, leasehold interest, and rental value. Time-element coverage must generally be purchased separately.

Exhibit I-3-A provides an example of perils covered by insurance and extensions to general coverage that expand the coverage to specific types of losses. Many of the disasters and listed perils will or should be discovered during the initial risk analysis.

Property Coverage

The value of the insured asset may be established based on any of the following:

- Actual cash value.
- Replacement cost value.
- Functional replacement value.
- Book value (generally not used for insurance purposes).

Exhibit I-3-B shows valuation consideration for various assets.

EXHIBIT I-3-B VALUATION CONSIDERATIONS

Insured Asset	Consideration
Machinery and Equipment	Original cost of equipment
	Depreciation of the equipment.
	The current functional costs of using the equipmnent.
Stock	Cost of stock used by work in progress.
	Cost of raw materials on site.
	Value of finished goods in inventory.
	Value of goods held for sale.
Building	Replacement costs of damaged facilities.
	Rebuilding costs of upgrades required by new building codes.
	Demolition costs for damaged facilities.
	Increased costs of construction compared to when building was built.
Valuable Papers and Records	Costs of restoring damaged records.
	Replacement of blanks

Time-Element Coverage

The BIA establishes the potential expenses incurred during the recovery of critical functions. That information can provide a solid basis for the risk management group to establish time-related coverage for the organization. The following paragraphs describe each of the four types of time-element coverage.

Business Income. For a manufacturing company, business income coverage pays financial loss because the company cannot manufacture its product. For a mercantile company, business income coverage pays for loss suffered because it cannot sell its products. For a service company, business income coverage pays for loss suffered because it cannot provide a service.

Business income coverage does not pay for damage causing the interruption. (This is covered under hazard-related insurance.) Business income coverage pays for the net profit (or loss) before taxes plus continuing normal operation expenses.

Business income covers the length of time operations are interrupted. The loss is determined on the basis of length of time of the interruption. The deductible may be established in hourly or daily increments.

Extra Expense. This coverage pays for those expenses beyond the normal operating expenses required to continue operations when premises are damaged during an interruption. The damage must be caused by an insured peril. Extra expenses might include:

- Disaster declaration fees.
- Hot-site fees.
- Rent for alternative office site.
- Rent for fixtures, machinery, and equipment.
- Light, heat, and power at temporary locations.
- Insurance at temporary locations.

- Moving and hauling.
- Installation of operation at temporary location.
- Employee expenses.
- Administrative expenses.
- Emergency command post expenses.
- Operating expenses.

The insured and insurance company establishes a payout pattern in which the insurance company pays 40%, 80%, or 100% up front.

Leasehold Interest. This coverage pays for loss-of-lease interest when the lease is canceled because of damage to the property. Leasehold interest might include:

- Tenant's lease interest.
- Bonus payments.
- Improvements and betterment.
- Prepaid rent.

Rental Value. This coverage pays for the landlord's loss of rental income when leased property is damaged and rendered untenantable as a result of a covered peril.

SUMMARY GUIDELINES

The following guidelines should help ensure the success of this phase of the planning project.

Set Time Limits. Time limits should be established for completing the business impact analysis. If the process takes too long, the information may become obsolete by the time the analysis is completed.

Use Data Gathering Tools. Such data gathering tools as prepared worksheets and questionnaires can help speed data collection.

Investigate Dependencies Among Business Functions. The impact of the loss of one business function on other functions should be evaluated.

Identify Potential Losses. Even with a recovery plan, some losses should be expected. Therefore, the plan should differentiate between losses incurred without the plan and losses incurred with the plan. Losses should be evaluated assuming a worst-case disaster scenario.

Identify Financial Losses. In addition to the direct financial losses due to lost sales revenue, other indirect losses may also accrue. For example, a client may demand compensation if a certain critical function fails to operate. Regulations may require that reimbursements can be made only if certain reporting tasks are performed. Costs may be incurred for reconstructing vital records. Expected revenue from new business projects may be lost or forestalled.

Identify Nonfinancial Losses. Such nonfinancial impacts as loss of customer confidence and disruption of customer service should be included in the analysis.

Evaluate Insurance Coverage. Insurance may compensate for certain losses. Coverage may vary depending on whether the organization has implemented a business resumption plan.

WORKPAPER I3.01 Business Impact Analysis Questionnaires

BUSINESS IMPACT ANALYSIS QUESTIONNAIRES

INTRODUCTION TO QUESTIONNAIRES

A business impact analysis is a methodology used to determine the effect of an interruption of services on each business unit and the organization as a whole. The analysis can provide information on the short- and long-term effects of a disaster on such factors as profit, market share, and goodwill.

The organization's senior executives and general managers have determined the ranges for acceptable and unacceptable losses in several categories. Those ranges are used to set priorities for business functions.

The questions have been developed to elicit such information as the financial impact, time frame for recovery, and resource requirements. The responses will be compiled and analyzed to provide the information required to develop a corporatewide business recovery strategy.

The objective of gathering this information is to:

- Determine the priority for restoring the functions of the organization.
- Determine recovery time-frame requirements for business units.
- Identify critical resources required to support business unit recovery.

This information is required to develop an effective corporatewide business recovery strategy. Using a consistent methodology based on management's criteria for determining the criticality of business functions will enable us to implement a prudent and cost-effective plan.

INSTRUCTIONS

Complete the following questionnaires in the order in which they are presented. To answer certain questions, you will need to gather such statistics as:

- Daily average transaction volume.
- Daily average dollar volume.
- Peak average transaction volume.
- Peak average dollar volume.
- Fixed costs.
- Overhead.
- Contribution or margin.

QUESTIONNAIRE 1: OVERVIEW OF THE BUSINESS UNIT

1. Describe the unit location: ____________________

2. Briefly describe the unit's functions: ____________________

____

____

____

____

3. Which description best fits the unit? ____________________

   [ ] Production unit or unit with direct client contact.
   [ ] Unit that directly provides production support.
   [ ] Unit responsible for sales.
   [ ] Provides order taking or order entry.
   [ ] Administrative.
   [ ] Other: ____________________.

4. What time is the unit's start of the business day?

____

5. What time is the unit's end of the business day?

____

6. What is the average daily dollar volume processed by the unit?

____

7. What is the average daily item or transaction volume processed by the unit? ____________________

____

8. Does the unit have any peak volume or otherwise critical times? If the unit does, please list the times as well as the average dollar and item or transaction volumes processed at those times:

____

____

QUESTIONNAIRE 2: WORK FLOW INTERDEPENDENCES

This section is intended to document the flow of work to and from your unit. It also is intended to determine how the work gets to your unit and how your unit sends it out once it has been completed.

<u>WORK RECEIVED</u>

1. Please list the units, in-house central computer systems, data processing service bureaus, or other organizations from which your unit receives work: ____________________

____

____

2. Of the total amount of incoming work your unit receives, what percentage comes through the following routes?

[ ] US mail.
[ ] Telephone or fax.
[ ] Interoffice mail.
[ ] Courier.
[ ] Online information from the central computer systems.
[ ] Reports or fiche generated from the central computer systems.
[ ] Online information from external data processing services.
[ ] Reports or fiche generated by external data processing services.

WORK SENT

3. Please list the units, in-house central computer systems, data processing service bureaus, or other organizations to which your unit sends completed work or information:

____
____
____

4. Of the total amount of outgoing work your unit produces, what percentage is sent through the following routes?

[ ] US mail.
[ ] Telephone or fax.
[ ] Interoffice mail.
[ ] Courier.
[ ] Online information from the central computer systems.
[ ] Reports or fiche generated from the central computer systems.
[ ] Online information from external data processing services.
[ ] Reports or fiche generated by external data processing services.

QUESTIONNAIRE 3: LAN OR PC MICROCOMPUTER RESOURCES

1. Which microcomputer equipment does your unit use?

[ ] Standalone microcomputers.
[ ] Microcomputers connected to a local area network (LAN).

2. How are the microcomputers or LAN used?

[ ] General administrative or office functions (e.g., memos).
[ ] Gateway to the organization's centralized computer systems.
[ ] Other: ______________________________

3. Are the automation features of the microcomputers or the LAN used by the unit critical to the timing and efficiency of the services the unit provides? Please describe:

____

____

____

4. Do those microcomputers or the LAN directly support or provide information required to control your unit's operations? Please describe: ______________________________

____

____

____

5. If the LAN or microcomputers were unavailable for one business day, would there be a data entry or transaction backlog?

   [ ] Yes [ ] No (If no, skip questions 6 and 7.)

6. Estimate the amount of backlog in number of entries or transactions:

   On a normal business day: ____________________

   At the unit's most critical peak time: ____________________

7. Estimate the hours it would take your current staff to eliminate the backlog. Please include the average hourly pay rate for the staff:

   - Hours at current staffing on a normal business day: ____________________
   - Hours at current staffing at your unit's most critical peak time: ____________________
   - Average pay rate per hour for current staff: ____________________

QUESTIONNAIRE 4: IN-HOUSE CENTRAL COMPUTER SYSTEMS

System or application:

1. Does the system or application allow clients to access the system directly by dialing in?

   [ ] Yes [ ] No

2. If the system or application were unavailable to your unit for one business day, would there be a data entry or transaction backlog?

   [ ] Yes [ ] No

If you answered yes, estimate the amount of backlog in number of entries or transactions:

- On a normal business day: ____________________
- At the unit's most critical peak time: ____________________

Estimate the hours it would take your current staff to eliminate the backlog. Please include the average hourly pay rate for the staff.

- Hours at current staffing on a normal business day: ____________________
- Hours at current staffing at your unit's most critical peak time: ____________________
- Average pay rate per hour for current staff: ____________________

3. Would a one-day business day delay in processing this system or application result in any fines or penalties due to missed deadlines or other reasons?

   [ ] Yes [ ] No

   If you answered yes, please describe the reason for the penalty, the issuer of the penalty, and an average for such penalties:

   ____
   ____
   ____

4. Would an outage of this system or application affect other revenue activities (e.g., investments, interest on funds, cash management) or balancing? ____________________

   ____
   ____
   ____

5. After a disaster, within which time frame do you need to have access to this function for the above system/application?

   [ ] 1 – 6 hours
   [ ] 6 – 12 hours
   [ ] 12 – 24 hours
   [ ] 2 days – 1 week
   [ ] Other:

6. Are there any peak periods associated with this system or application? Check those time which apply and include a brief explanation of the reason for the peak time for each.

   [ ] Daily
   [ ] Quarterly
   [ ] Monthly

[ ] Month end
[ ] Quarter end
[ ] Year end
[ ] Other (please specify): ____________________

QUESTIONNAIRE 5: OUTSOURCED DATA PROCESSING

If the organization uses an external provider of information services, an assessment of the impact of the loss of applications must be made. Please answer the following questions. (The questions provided in the in-house computer systems questionnaire can also be used for outside services.)

1. Does the service provider have a disaster recovery plan?
____

2. Has the plan been tested? ____________________
____

3. When was the plan last tested, what were the test objectives, and what was the result of the test? ____________________
____

4. What percentage of total applications were tested?
____

5. What is the recovery time frame for the service provider's systems? ____________________

6. Where in the recovery priorities is your organization in relationship to other service provider customers? ____________________
____

7. Was the network connecting your organization and the service provider tested? ____________________
____

8. Is there a network recovery plan for the service provider?
____

9. Where in the network recovery priorities is your organization?
____

QUESTIONNAIRE 6: REGULATORY AND LEGAL ISSUES

Regulatory Issues

1. Are there any reporting requirements or deadlines that would be affected by a delay in or loss of the services your unit provides?

2. Would a delay in or loss of service result in any fines or penalties?

   a. List the regulations.
   b. Describe the conflict.
   c. Describe possible consequences (e.g., penalties).

<u>Legal Issues</u>

1. Will a delay in or loss of the services your unit provides result in possible legal liability, damages, or other public harm?

   a. List the legal issue.
   b. Describe the conflict.
   c. Describe possible consequences.

QUESTIONNAIRE 7: TRANSACTION VOLUME LOSS — NORMAL BUSINESS DAY

Consider that your unit is unable to perform its functions as a result of a disaster on a normal business day. By how much would the transaction volume decrease? If the disaster extended through each period of time listed below, how much transaction volume might the company lose during each period? Fill in the appropriate dollar range (e.g., $0 — 50,000; $50,000 — 100,000) for each time period listed below.

First half hour: ______________________
Hour 1: ______________________
Hour 3: ______________________
Hours 4 — 12: ______________________
Hours 13 — 24: ______________________
Day 3: ______________________
Days 4 — 7: ______________________
Days 8 — 14: ______________________
Days 15 — 30: ______________________
Day 30 and beyond: ______________________

QUESTIONNAIRE 8: TRANSACTION VOLUME LOSS — PEAK BUSINESS DAY

Consider that your unit is unable to perform its functions as a result of a disaster on a peak business day. By how much would the transaction volume decrease? If the disaster extended through each period of time listed below, how much transaction volume might the company lose during each period? Fill in the appropriate dollar range (e.g., $0 — 50,000; $50,000 — 100,000) for each time period listed below.

First half hour: ______________
Hour 1: ______________
Hour 3: ______________
Hours 4 – 12: ______________
Hours 13 – 24: ______________
Day 3: ______________
Days 4 – 7: ______________
Days 8 – 14: ______________
Days 15 – 30: ______________
Day 30 and beyond: ______________

QUESTIONNAIRE 9: REVENUE LOSS

1. Is this system directly involved in activities that generate revenue? If so, describe. ______________

2. Is this system directly involved in billing or collection activities? If so, describe. ______________

3. Would inability to process this application affect business operations so as to interfere with the provision of services to customers? If so, how? ______________

4. Would inability to process this application cause customers to seek services or products from competitors? If so, please assess this impact. ______________

5. Would inability to process this application cause other, indirect impacts on revenue activities (e.g., interest lost on funds, investments)? ______________

6. Summarize other revenue losses associated with impacts related to the inability to process this application. ______________

QUESTIONNAIRE 10: ADDITIONAL EXPENSES

1. What are the types of additional expenses your organization would incur with the delay or loss of processing of this application? ______________

2. Estimate the minimum length of time the support of this application could be denied your organization without incurring additional expense (e.g., overtime, extra services).
____

3. Would a delay in the availability of this application result in additional expenditures other than for labor or services (e.g., interest expense on bank loans, capital outlays)?
____
____

4. Estimate the amount of business backlog (e.g., number of orders, order entries, inquiries) incurred if this application were unavailable. ______________________________
____

5. Would a delay in processing this application result in any fines or penalties for failure to provide services or to adhere to deadlines or government regulations? If so, describe.
____
____

6. Would a delay in processing this application result in legal liability, personal damage, or other public harm? If so, describe. ______________________________
____

7. Please describe any other impacts related to the delay or loss of this application that could result in additional expense to your organization. ______________________________
____

QUESTIONNAIRE 11: EMBARRASSMENT OR CONFIDENCE LOSS

1. In your estimation, what are the most serious sources of embarrassment to your organization in regard to the delay in or complete loss of ability to process this application or provide this service? ______________________________
____

2. Are there potential legal, social, or moral liabilities to your organization in regard to the delay in or complete loss of ability to process this application or provide this service? If so, please describe them. ______________________________
____

3. What is the potential liability of exposure to these problems and impact on the general public in terms of embarrassment to the organization? ______________________________
____

4. What are the potential impacts, in terms of loss of public confidence and other measures, from the loss of capability to process this application or provide this service?

____

____

QUESTIONNAIRE 12: CLIENT LOSS

1. Would a delay in the processing of this application or provision of services cause clients to seek competitor services?

____

____

2. If yes, what percentage of corporate income do these clients represent? ______________________________

____

3. How long do you think the client would tolerate an interruption of company services? ______________________________

____

4. Would these clients return when services are resumed? If yes, would there be additional expenses associated with reestablishing the relationship? Please describe: ______________________________

____

Planning for Y2K — Staying Focused

CHAPTER I-10

The impending and unmovable requirement to address the infamous Millennium Bug or Y2K problem has caused a major worldwide panic. Is the panic partially justified, I think so. For those companies who have not yet addressed the problem, I offer condolences. For those companies who have already identified, tested and fixed the internal systems within their organization, I salute your foresight because you must have recognized the problem several years ago and actually acted to resolve it. Moreover, for business continuity professionals this is the first major disaster that we know will occur and exactly when it will occur. Never in our lifetime have we had this type of opportunity to know the disaster about to affect our company or organization.

How can I call it an opportunity you ask? First, because it is a "potential" disaster with worldwide recognition to which management has committed tremendous amount of dedicated resources and focus. Second, it is a problem requiring extensive analysis and data collection of the types of information needed to plan for and recover the organization. Rarely would the business continuity planner be able to convince management to go through that level of analysis just to support the business continuity program. Think of their reaction if you suggested that they analyze and inventory every single electronic component they use to conduct their business, provide services or manufacture products. So here is the opportunity to make the best of a bad situation and establish an information base needed to recover the technologies used by your organizations. In most cases, it will be some contracted consulting organization doing the bulk of the work with guidance from internal project managers. Identify what the consultants are using to collect and maintain the data.

Additionally, the other less obvious benefit is to identify the vendor or service provider dependencies within and outside of your organization. While there has been widespread recognition of the need to fix internal systems, there is less focus on the implications of having essential external resources damaged, disabled or handicapped by the Y2K bug.

With the compulsive, short-sighted, but profitable behavior of companies rushing to the just-in-time (JIT) dance, a major disruption threat now exists. The rise in use of JIT inventory practices during the past five years may become the business continuity issue once Y2K passes. There is no argument that the financial benefits are significant when all elements of the system works. Raw materials and finished goods once warehoused at a high capital cost are now moving from the vendor to the production line in record time and volumes. As the supplier's truck with the parts pulls up to your company's loading docks, the apparatus needing those parts is sometimes starting to move down the assembly line. This is extremely efficient and profitable as long as nothing in the chain breaks. When one element of that delivery chain breaks, production ceases. Most of the automobile manufacturers are intimately and painfully familiar with the disruption caused by a strike at one sub-assembly plant causing company wide shutdown of manufacturing operations. This fragile system has interdependencies totally outside of the organization's immediate control. This JIT issue is very typical of the business continuity problems planners must face, question and plan for Y2K. While the consequences of the problem are similar, the solution is very different. Having the striking workers return to work will not fix the problem. Work will resume, but the primary cause and vulnerability remains intact. With current trends and movement of business operations to even more aggressive inventory programs, we have to accept the problem as ongoing and plan accordingly.

Time is not on our side with Y2K. This chapter should have been written two years ago rather than one year before the disaster occurring. I plead guilty and apologize for the delay, but hope this chapter will provide some insight into the problem and options to deal with it. Just how, as planners, can we deal with this oncoming issue?

WHAT IS THE PROBLEM?

Unless you have recently moved to this planet, you know that the basic problem is that when programmers decided to code dates they used two digits such as 00 to save memory. At the time this coding structure was designed memory was at least 1000 times more expensive than it is now. Since current systems cannot differentiate between 00 meaning 1900 or 00 meaning 2000, any program using the date as part of program logic will assume the date is 1900. Because many application decisions are based on date, the systems may do unexpected things, or just stop working. The problem gets even more complex and difficult to correct when the logic is burned into computer chips and then embedded in systems that control everything from traffic lights and elevators to major manufacturing systems. With software or embedded systems, to fix the problem, the occurrence of the date field has to be located in billions of lines of program code. It must then be changed from a two-byte to a four-byte field so that it can handle the complete dates of 1900 and 2000. All associated and interdependent programs have to be changed and tested to ensure they will also function properly.

COST OF THE PROBLEM

The bill for eradicating the Y2K or Millenium bug from the global economy's software has been estimated at $300 billion to $600 billion by the Gartner Group, a computer-industry research firm in Stamford, Conn. Even with this cost, the experts believe complete success is by no means assured. The ultimate costs could be pushed past $1 trillion by hardware replacements and other expenses.

Companies such as GM are investing $400 to $500 million dollars to fix the problem. Estimates are that 180 billions lines of software code will have to be reviewed world-wide at a cost of $1 to $1.50 a line. Gartner Group estimates that the Top 100 FORTUNE companies will spend $50 million, on average to fix the year while smaller companies will invest an estimated $7.5 million.

STATUS OF THE PROBLEM

According to a report released in March 1998 by Forrester Research in Cambridge, MA, says that on average, large corporations are only 34% of the way through the year 2000 job.[1] The surveyed companies, on average, had completed 66% of the task of assessing the dimensions of the problem and the risks, but have made only 40% of the necessary fixes and have tested only 18%.

The problem is even worse in manufacturing according to Bill Thompson, senior analyst at Automation Research Corporation in Dedham, MA. One major problem is that much manufacturing software was custom made for specific applications and most authors are no longer available to de-bug the software. According to articles, only half of manufacturing standard software is written in Cobol. The rest is described as a Tower of Babel, written in hundreds of tongues and added like onion layers to other software.

The experts went on to say that the year 2000 problem has exposed another major area of vulnerability for GM; it's 100,000 suppliers world-wide. Modern manufacturing mastery of just in time parts deliver and business-to-business electronic commerce has "created a beast that can bite." GM stated that "Just-in-Time delivery has streamlined our supply chain to make it highly sensitive to any interruption. Production could literally stop at our plants if supplier's computer systems are not year 200 compliant."

SCOPE OF THE PROBLEM

If your company is not already participating in the Y2K mitigation effort, it may be too late to do anything other than:

- Try to identify the damage potential.
- Mitigate what you can.
- Establish strategies for those areas outside of your control.

There are three planning areas dealing with the problem covered in the following sections.

PLANNING AREAS

The Y2K planner's prayer should be "Grant me the knowledge and strength to change the areas I can; understand and accept the areas I cannot change; and wisdom to know the difference." See Exhibit I-10-A.

The planner must understand that there are three planning domains. The first are areas you have no control over. The second are areas you have limited control over and the last are areas you have total control over. It is critical to understand that the shortage of both time and resources mandates a project strategy. You first focus on those areas you have total control over, then address those areas of limited control and be aware or make contingencies to address areas totally outside of your control. While I am not saying that you should just ignore the last category, there is nothing you can do to change it. Dedicate all organizational time and resources to the first two categories.

Areas You Have No Control Over

If you are one of the U.S. or foreign government agencies trying to resolve this issue in time, I apologize if I include you in this general category. However, U.S. Government Accounting Office (GAO) reports indicate that many critical federal agency systems are not Y2K compliant. Should they not be fully tested by 12/31/99 it is reasonable to assume that there will be system failures causing interruption of other federal systems dependent on their information. Even if the individual agency systems are functional, those agencies feeding the functioning agency may not be

EXHIBIT I-10-A. LEVELS OF CONTROL

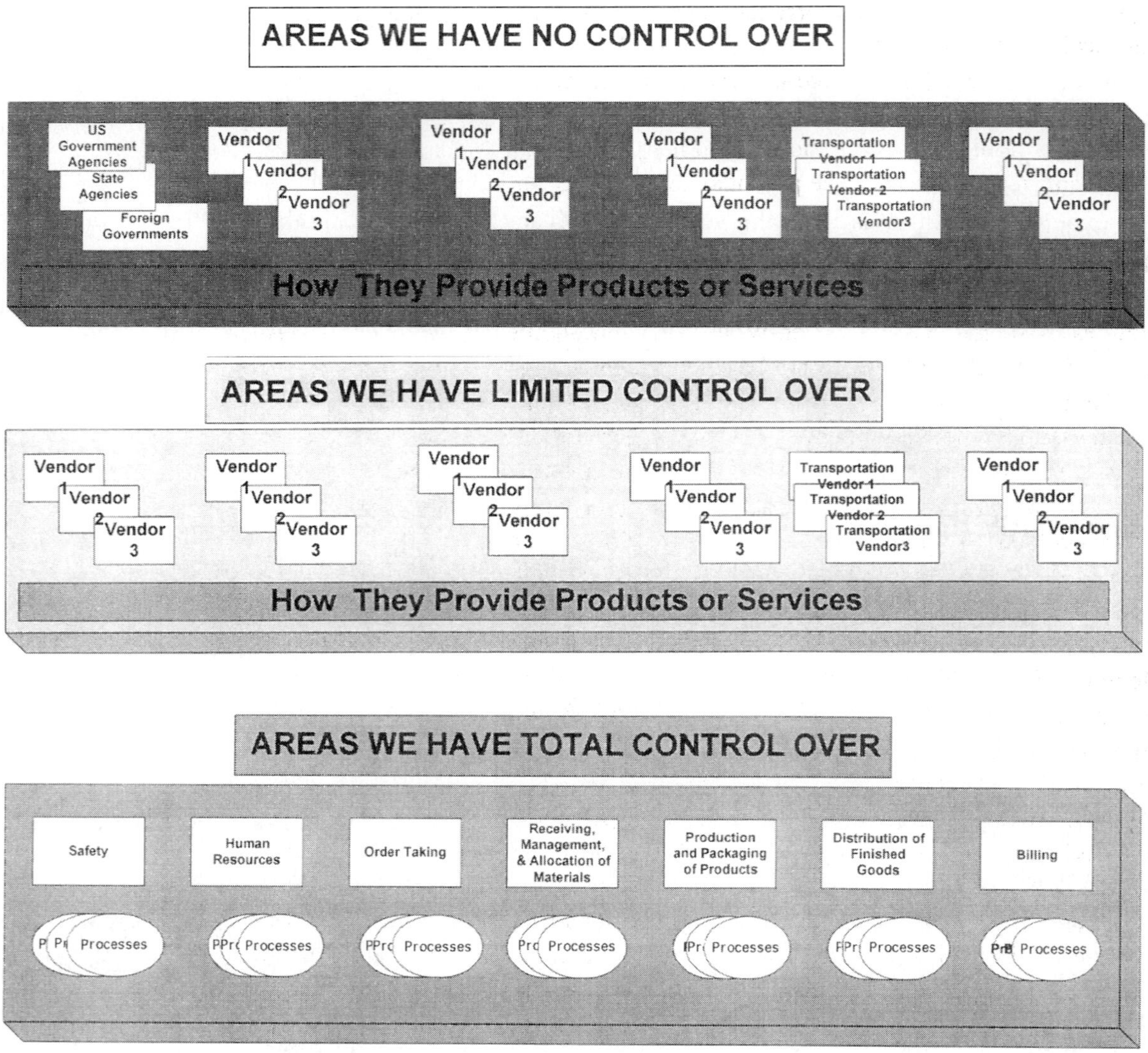

available. The domino effect of that failure is difficult to predict but will have some type of affect on all citizens, organizations, and companies.

Failure of air-traffic-control (ATC) systems either in or outside of the U.S. could cause not only a disruption of passenger transportation but also interrupt thousands of shipments and tons of commercial cargo. As part of the product distribution chain, it can slow the ground cargo carriers while the systems are de-bugged and certified as safe. Recently, GAO has published some more positive information related to the ATC systems in the U.S. indicating that the problem may be resolved in time. However, commercial marine, rail and trucking companies are heavily dependent on computer systems to manage both the carriers and the cargo. Dispatch of trucks, identification of cargo-container contents, loading of container ships, location of containers in yards, movement of trains, ships, warehousing of in-transit products all depend on computers systems. Regulatory and financial agencies such as U.S. Customs, the Coast Guard, issuers of bills of lading, letters of credit, those responsible for tracking of hazardous cargo, or dangerous criminals, all are subject to an interruption of services. All have a heavy dependence on computer systems, networks, and equipment with embedded computer chips. All communicate with other agencies and organizations and much of that information is electronically communicated.

Agencies are struggling to make the date and with perseverance and luck, they will. The planner needs to identify the potential impact on their organization should a failure occur in this domain. Although you may not be able to change the results, you can warn management of the potential consequences and impacts.

Areas You Have Limited Control Over

The dependency on vendors, their products and services are the areas where companies have limited control over. While you cannot force them to mitigate their interruption potential and you cannot be sure of their continuity until 1/1/2000, you may be able to plan around the possibility of an interruption. As with any risk issue, you must identify whether you have a "sole-source issue" or a "single-source issue." The first category "sole source" means that there are no other sources for the material, products or services. The second category may indicate that the organization has decided to limit their relationship to a single provider. Quality, price, relationship, or a number of other reasons may drive that choice. While the company may have other provider options, in many cases, it is not as simple as just changing providers. For many industries, the re-qualification of the supplier, capacity of the provider and other factors may make a transition to an alternate provider difficult and lengthy. In some industries, the qualification of parts or materials takes months of analysis before they are qualified. Assays of new materials and products must be performed by quality organizations. The product using the new part or material must prove that it meets expectations or licensing requirements. Cost typically is not a constraint should the organization unexpectedly lose a single source provider.

There are several positions taken by organizations in dealing with their key service providers and suppliers. Some are taking a legal stance and hard-line approach of threatening loss of business if the provider does not get into compliance. Realistically, no dependent organization has sufficient access to the providers internal systems and processes and regardless of written contracts or statements to know, until it is too late, that critical systems were not compliant. Successful tests of systems and production lines are the only indication that the supplier may have compliant systems. Paper agreements, contracts and vendor compliance statements without accompanying test results are worthless. Legal action after the fact does little to ensure continuity of operations.

With any risk issue, mitigation of loss usually provides a higher level of protection than postdisaster response. Minimizing the number of sole-source providers should be a high priority and area of focus. You must first determine if they are indeed, sole source rather than single source. If they truly are the only suppliers for that material, product or service, then the company must consider a stockpiling strategy to mitigate potential impact. If the vendor is actually a single-source supplier, then locating and qualifying alternate suppliers is a sane mitigation strategy. How much safety stock should the company maintain? That will depend on how long the supplier will not be able to supply the service or product. When do you start the search for alternate suppliers? How many do you identify? That depends on how long it takes to qualify a new supplier and if the supplier has the capacity to service your needs. It really is anyone's guess and warrants a conservative approach to protect your organization's business continuity.

Areas You Have Total Control Over

Since there is a time constraint within which we have to focus the organization limited resources, we must pick our targets carefully. While all systems and processes within the organization are probably essential, there are those that maintain the lifeblood of the organization. The planner usually conducts a business impact analysis to identify the high priority, time-sensitive processes without which the organization will suffer serious financial loss or other significant impacts. This effort is similar, but if the organization has not already completed a recent BIA, I would suggest it may be too late to do anything other than a high-level analysis. Identifying and fixing a majority of the most critical problems is better than completing a comprehensive analysis but run out of time before the systems proved compliant.

The planner's focus must be on the following core elements of the business or organizational processes, the resources supporting those processes, and the supply chain:

- Taking orders.
- Obtaining materials or services.
- Manufacturing products or providing services.
- Maintaining human resources.
- Distributing products or services.
- Billing for services.
- Collection of revenues.

Divide resources (systems, suppliers, other resources) potentially affecting your organization's ability to continue doing business into the three categories. Create a matrix of those dependencies with these resources for which you have no control over, those you have some control over and those you have total control over.

For the last two categories, identify the internal/external organizations and contacts. Identify specifically what they supply that is essential to those processes. Identify systems used to support these functions. Identify communication resources to provide access to the order-entry functions. Determine if each is Y2K compliant.

Core Business Process: The organization must be able to take and process orders.

Are orders taken electronically through EDI? Are orders taken through customer-service functions? Are these internal or external functions? Does your organization place orders electronically with your suppliers? Are there any manual systems to take the place of the electronic systems? Does the organization have the capacity to manually handle the electronic volume? Are the internal and external systems compliant? Have they been tested and if so are the test results available for review?

Core Business Process: The organization must be able to acquire, inventory, and use materials.

Again, for the last two categories, identify the internal/external organizations and contacts. Are suppliers of materials Y2K compliant? Will they be able to acquire, process, and ultimately provide your company with their materials? Remember that they are vulnerable to their suppliers. Once you receive the materials, can your organization manage the inventory of materials? Will the company be able to get the appropriate types and volume of materials to the manufacturing or assembly functions? Identify communication facilities to provide access between logistical and manufacturing operations. Determine if each is Y2K compliant.

Core Business Process: Must be able to manufacture products or provide services.

Can your organization make their products or provide services? Are the systems, process machines, and other equipment required to produce product or provide services Y2K compliant? Are components within complex manufacturing systems compliant? Are the on-site spare parts, used to maintain machines and systems, compliant? Is the spare-parts-management system compliant?

Core Business Process: Must have adequate human resources to build, process, or provide services.

Can you continue to pay employees, provide benefits, and provide access to retirement funds should the need arise? Are the payroll, benefits and IRA systems compliant? Are the contracted service providers systems compliant? Have they tested and can they prove this compliance?

Core Business Process: Must be able to collect the monies required to continue to pay employees, pay vendors, finance produce production, or support provision of services.

Systems used by internal or external functions to pay employees or vendors must be addressed. Accounts receivable systems, lock box functions provided by third party providers, must be reviewed and determined to be compliant. Management of monies is another issue that should be examined. Are the company's cash-management systems compliant? If the company is using third party software, encryption hardware, and communications for treasury operations has this been reviewed and tested for compliance?

While the above areas do not encompass all areas of the organization's systems, it does address the core functions required to survive as a business.

Management Expectations

The first thing management should expect is some failure of internal and external systems. While this expectation is typically not the case, it is the reality of the problem. The complexity makes it nearly impossible for some system(s) not to have problems. The objective of planners' effort is to mitigate the impact in the most essential areas of the business. Meaning that some systems may not be addressed therefore the potential for failure remains for those systems.

Management must be advised that this effort is imperfect at best and only those areas totally under control of the organization and proven compliant have a high probability of working correctly on 1/1/2000. Systems not addressed by lack of time or resources and those outside of the organization may or may not work on that date.

For all other ancillary processes work should be deferred and resources allocated only after the core systems are proven compliant.

NOTE

1. *Fortune Magazine,* April 28, 1998, "Industry Wakes Up To The Year 2000 Menace.

Case Study: Illinois Bell Telephone-Hinsdale Central Office Fire — May 8, 1988

CHAPTER I-11

May of 1988 was a bonus month for disasters. On May 4, 1988 First Interstate Bank suffered the largest high-rise fire in U.S. history and on May 8th of the same year, Illinois Bell suffered the single most devastating central office fire is U.S. history. While the incident is a decade old, it still warrants the planner's attention to the potential for this type of disaster and the consequences of issues discovered during the incident. Some risk elements of the case no longer exist. Many telephone-service providers learned how not to design alarm systems. They learned how not to design emergency power systems and the consequences of failing to properly document the facility's critical shut-off procedures. Much was learned from this major disaster but little has been written about it since. Billions of dollars of business loss resulted from this incident. Major business operations in the Chicago area were severely impacted by this incident. Much of the losses may have been mitigated if the businesses were aware of the potential for such an occurrence and they, the business operations, had informed the telephone service provider of their critical requirements. It is easy to be a Monday morning quarter back ten years after the disaster but risking dragging up old issues, think this case is still relevant to business continuity planning.

INTRODUCTION

The Hinsdale Central Office (HCO) is one of the largest switching stations in the Illinois Bell Telephone (IBT) system, processing an estimated 3.5 million calls every day. The facility provides local telephone service for approximately 38,000 customers with almost 42,000 lines. Because the HCO provides long distance telephone service routing for several local offices, it is considered a "Hub" station; because it also handles long distance routing for other local hub stations, it is call a "Gateway Hub" station.

The fire, which occurred on one of the busiest days of the year — May 8, Mother's Day — lasted 6.5 hours from detection until it was extinguished.

This document summarizes the most critical issues identified during the investigation of the fire and provides a detailed report of the incident.

While this incident affected a telephone switching office, many of the issues that exacerbated the disaster are applicable to many companies. Many large organizations have complex and large-scale communications facilities and may suffer the same level of vulnerability in some areas.

CRITICAL ISSUES

- Inability to shut off power to the burning cables because of inadequate emergency back-up capabilities and poor documentation
- Delay in responding to the alarm caused by a failure to follow established procedures
- Smoke damage and severe corrosion damage due to unconfined corrosive gases carried in the smoke
- Severe impact on community businesses and personal services
- Damage to cables by contractors and mixing of incompatible cables in the same cable run.

Although this event affected a telephone-switching station, these critical issues are applicable to most companies that have large proprietary PBX systems and extensive vertical and horizontal cable runs. The detailed report below presents the most relevant conditions that would apply to most large organizations. It also provides a foundation for considering the possibility of a similar disaster occurring to a planner's provider of service.

THE DETAILED REPORT

Inability to Shut Off Power to the Electrical Equipment; Poor Procedural Documentation

In any electrical fire, one of the most critical actions to be taken is to shut off the power to the burning cables and/or equipment. Most data processing areas protected by fire suppression systems such as Halon 1301 assumed that a manual or automated power interruption facility has been engineered into the fire detection system and would shut down power to the equipment before the fire suppressant is discharged. However, as long as power continues to flow, the cables and equipment will remain energized and continue to burn. As the energized cables are heated by the electrical short, combustible gases are given off that can be re-ignited by fire or sparks. The energized equipment also creates a hazard for the fire suppression personnel due to electrical shock potential.

The Hinsdale fire started at 3:50 P.M.; fire fighters arrived at 5:03 P.M. When the fire officers realized that the power to the building circuits needed to be shut off, a team of three fire fighters was assigned to locate and turn off the emergency power generators. Because the telephone system of the area was interrupted, the fire department could not contact and tell the local utility company to shut off the building power. The equipment continued to be energized by external power.

IBT personnel gave the firemen instructions for shutting down the emergency generators and at approximately 6 P.M., these were disabled. Nevertheless, heavy arcing and spitting of debris continued to occur whenever water was applied to the overhead fire. Power was still feeding the burning circuits.

A second attempt was made to determine the source of the power with assistance from an IBT employee who was familiar with the power system of the building. Dressed in full fire-fighting gear, the IBT employee entered the building and began pulling fuses and disconnecting switches. These efforts did not stop power from reaching the fire areas.

At about 6:15 P.M., the fire fighters, who were still attempting to disconnect the power, manually tripped circuit breakers in the first floor. Despite this action sparks and arcs still erupted when water was applied, and were present at 7 P.M.

Fire fighters again entered the basement and removed all remaining fuses in the electrical panels, finally shutting down the power. The fire had burned more than three hours because of the electrical problem. It was determined that although commercial power and the diesel generators were shut down, the batteries installed to provide emergency power were still energizing the cables until the fuses were pulled.

Power System:

- Two (2) diesel-powered generators.
- 500-gallon tank adjacent to the generators.
- Four (4) hours of operations under full load with the above fuel.
- 10,000-gallon underground tank for extended power loss.
- Two (2) banks of large batteries and rectifiers with sufficient reserve to operate the system **under full load for a minimum of 4 hours** after loss of both utility power and diesel generator power.

Multiple attempts to disable the power were required because of the lack of established documentation and procedures that would enable IBT and fire fighting personnel to quickly interrupt both normal and emergency power. Consequently, the fire and smoke damage continued unabated for more than 2 hours despite all fire fighting efforts.

Failure to Follow Established Procedures — Causing a Delay in Response to the Fire

At 3:50 P.M., the detectors in the Hinsdale Central Offices initiated audible alarms, illuminated a local annunciated panel, shut down the building air handling system, and sent an alarm signal to the Division Alarm Reporting Center (DARC) in Springfield, about 200 miles from Hinsdale. No alarm signals went directly to the local fire department.

The DARC received the signals from the HCO indicating commercial power failure, an air-dryer alarm, a fire alarm, and a battery-discharge alarm. The DARC technician recognized that the fire-alarm trouble alarm and the fire alarm activate whenever there is a break in continuous electrical power at the facility. The technician believed the fire alarm to be an indication of loss of commercial power and not an indication of fire.

At 3:53 P.M., the alarm signal cleared and the reporting center received signals for the HCO that the diesel engines had started and that the backup electric generators were operating properly.

At 3:59 P.M., DARC received indications of diesel power failure, another air-dryer alarm, a fire alarm trouble, and a fire alarm — again coincidental alarms indicating a break in commercial power. The commercial power was restored at 4:00 P.M. and the fire alarm cleared.

At 4:05 P.M., the DARC technician tested the HCO alarm system and the results showed battery discharge and diesel engine failure. The fire and fire alarm trouble alarm had cleared.

At 4:14 P.M., the DARC technician called the duty supervisor and reported the power failures and battery discharge.

At 4:20 P.M., the DARC technician received a fire alarm signal and within minutes began receiving reports of switch and carrier system failures. The DARC technician did not immediately call the Hinsdale Fire Department as required by IBT operating procedures and instead called the duty supervisor.

After receiving the initial DARC calls relating to the power and diesel failures, the duty supervisor referring to her on call roster attempted to call the listed technicians. She received no answer from the first two people on the roster.

At 4:21 P.M., she received the call from the DARC technician regarding the fire alarm.

At 4:24 P.M., the duty supervisor called the Dowens Grove Central Office and directed a technician to investigate the alarm conditions. She continued her attempts to locate on call personnel and finally reached one.

At 4:30 P.M., the duty supervisor attempted to call the Hinsdale Fire Department and received a fast busy signal "no circuit indication." She then attempted to call Downers Grove Fire Department and received the same signal.

At 4:52 P.M., the Downers Grove technician arrived at the scene and saw smoke. He attempted to use the local telephone, which was not working. He then attempted to use his cellular telephone in his car and this failed. He flagged down a motorist and asked him to drive to the fire department and report the fire.

At 4:56 P.M., the DARC stopped receiving signals from Hinsdale.

At 5:03 P.M., the Hinsdale Fire Department arrived at the scene, one hour and thirteen minutes after the first alarm.

The delay allowed the fire and smoke damage to spread.

The response to the fire was delayed by two major factors:

- Failure of the technician to follow procedures. Had he done so, the fire department would have been notified at 4:20 P.M., reducing burning time by 40 minutes. Timely notification would have been by telephone rather than flagging down a motorist.
- The design of the alarm system, which is questionable in that it masked the true fire problem by including multiple conditions in the set of alarm indicators. This engineering problem apparently was not resolved.

Smoke Damage and Severe Corrosive Damage Due to Corrosive Gases Carried in the Fire

In most fires, combustion by-products add to or in some cases are responsible for a majority of the damage to the building contents and equipment. This was true in the case of the HCO fire.

The cables used by IBT included switchboard cable, terminating cable, shielded station wire, fabric-braid covered DC power cable, AC power armored shielded cable, coaxial cable, textile served, plastic-insulated wires loosely twisted together, and cross-linked polyethylene DC power cable.

Tests conducted after the fire indicated that all the sample insulation and jacket materials were based on rubber, polyethylene, or polyvinyl chloride, and were typical formulation used from the mid-1950s through the mid 1970s.

The investigation determined that the cable insulation materials produced large volumes of smoke and corrosive gases. The extent of the damage was primarily due to nonthermal effects. Lack of smoke control features in the HCO allowed for a rapid and total spread of corrosive by products throughout the first floor.

There was no adequate horizontal control for smoke and fire; even if an active smoke control system had been in place, it would have been of no benefit without horizontal compartmentalization.

The insulation of the power cables used in the HCO had undesirable fire-resistant characteristics and contributed to the spread of the fire. The cables themselves did not meet the normal desired burn limits in comparison tests.

Hydrochloric acid was formed when chlorine, released during the pyrolysis and burning of the insulation materials, combined with the natural moisture in the air as well as the water vapor from the fire fighter's spray. This acid immediately began to corrode the equipment that survived the fire, rendering it unreliable for providing telephone service over an extended period.

All equipment was removed from the building and brought to a warehouse for evaluation, and none was reused at Hinsdale. All of the wiring and cables on the first and second floors also were replaced. Estimates of damage to the building and equipment were between $40 million and $60 million.

Although the fire damage was confined to 1200 of the 14,000 square feet of first floor usable space, the extensive smoke damage accounted for a majority of the loss.

Immediately following the fire, an attempt was made to clean the existing equipment and lower the humidity levels in the building to retard corrosion as much as possible. This allowed some customers limited use of their telephones within a few days of the fire, a number that grew as more of the equipment was reconditioned.

SEVERE IMPACT ON COMMUNITY BUSINESS AND PERSONAL SERVICES

As noted above, the Hinsdale Central Office is one of the largest switching stations in the Illinois Bell system. It processes an estimated 3.5 million calls every day, and provides local telephone service for approximately 38,000 customers with almost 42,000 lines. The equipment at the HCO provides dial tone, ringing, busy signals, and connections for local calls.

The HCO also operates 118,000 trunk lines for local and long distance call routing and provides switching for about 13,000 special service lines, such as data transmission lines. In addition to providing services to the communities of Hinsdale, Claredon Hills, Willowbrook, parts of Burr Ridge, Dover, Oak Brook, Westmount, and unincorporated areas in south Du Page County, the HCO provided 800 and WATS service and provides links to AT&T, MCI, and other interexchange carriers as well as cellular phone carriers.

The HCO provides long distance telephone service routing for several local offices, and thus is considered a "hub" station. It also performs long distance routing for other local hubs stations, and thus it is called a "Gateway Hub" station. This configuration contributed greatly to the scope of the disruption; similar configurations, less complex, exist throughout the United States and other countries. The concentration of traffic through such a centralized point is both technically and economically efficient. It does, however, create a single point of failure, as this incident shows so dramatically. Note: Many companies are centralizing multiple communications in a similar hub fashion without providing for alternate routing should the gateway be removed by some type of disaster.

The impact of the fire was immediately felt with disruption of services starting shortly after 4 P.M. on May 8.

The fire department was unable to contact the utility company and have it respond to disconnect power. Similarly, other agencies such as the Environmental Protection Agency (EPA), hospitals, and mutual aid fire departments, could not be reached by telephone.

- The Federal Aviation Agency (FAA) air traffic control facilities at Chicago O'Hare and Midway airports were effected because of the disruption of traffic between them and the FAA air traffic control facility in Aurora, Illinois. Flight delays and cancellations occurred as a result of this 1 day interruption. Partial service was restored in 12 hours and full services resumed in 3 days.
- A nationwide hotel chain whose 800-based reservation system was disrupted, lost 35,000 calls per day until the 800 service was transferred to a main reservation center in North Carolina.

EXHIBIT I-11-A RESTORATION OF HINSDALE SERVICES

Date	Number of Lines with Dial Tone
May 11	12,000
May 13	15,000
May 14	21,000
May 16	27,000
May 17	30,000
May 19	36,000
May 20	All lines serviced

Total Lines Serviced = 41,455

- A major florist delivery service lost its computer connection to 12,500 florists around the nation on Mothers Day.
- Banks in the area lost their ability to effect wire transfers and lost communication with the Federal Reserve Bank.
- Public safety calls to the fire, police, and paramedical services were disrupted.
- Local financial and trading operations were disrupted for up to 5 days.
- Hinsdale Hospital lost both external and internal services. Several other local hospitals were also affected but not as severely.
- Customers served by central offices west and southwest of Hinsdale could call one another and reach emergency services within their area but generally could not make or receive calls from Chicago or long distance points.

In all, approximately 9000 businesses and some 100,000 employees were affected by the outage.

RESTORATION

- Fire, police, and hospital services were given first priority.
- Three (3) special centers with a total of 200 lines were set up to provide interim services to business customers.
- 120 coin telephones at 16 locations throughout the affected area were set up.
- 200 lines in Chicago were made available for business use.
- Restoration of the 13,000 special service circuits, such as data transmission lines, was carried out simultaneously with network restoration; however, this work presented special problems. Restoring these circuits involved locating records containing facility and equipment specifications, reengineering each circuit, and testing for the correct operational characteristics. Most companies had not provided the IBT with this information prior to the incident.
- First inter-office circuits were reestablished by the end of the first week.
- Additional circuits were reestablished day by day and by May 22, 14 days after the fire, normal inter-office trunk circuit capacity was available.

Exhibit I-11-A summarizes the restoration.

Other than for the emergency-service agencies, IBT had very little prior information from the business community to aid in establishing a logical recovery priority. As a result of this lack of information, restoration was prioritized based on IBT's best judgment or ad hoc requests/demands from the community.

Also, a majority of business in this area had no knowledge of what IBT's recovery process or priorities were.

Damage to Cables By Contractors and Mixing of Incompatible Cables in the Same Cable Run

Primary cause of the fire was damaged cables and mixing of incompatible cables in the same cable run.

An armored cable sheath became energized when it contacted a damaged DC power cable. This contact was caused by cable movement. The damage to the DC power cable most likely occurred during "mining operations" some time before the fire. During cable mining operations, wood wedges are used to separate cables in a tray until the cable to be removed is exposed. Once it is exposed, it is cut into small sections and removed.

A subcontractor had performed the most recent mining in the HCO. During the mining operations, damage to the insulation on the dc power cables exposed energized conductors. The exposed conductors coming in contact with the grounded armor cable sheath resulted in shorting, arcing, and overheating. Tests conducted after the fire verified the above deduction by duplicating repeatedly the above condition. One or two power cables would short to a smaller cable causing it to overheat and burn. This fire would then cause the insulation to break down (through heating and melting) of adjacent power cables that would fail and perpetuate the fire growth. Low-voltage multi-conductors and coaxial cable would readily ignite and add to the fire.

RECOMMENDATIONS

ISSUE: Inability to shut off power to the burning cables due to emergency backup capabilities and inadequate procedures for shutting down the system

- The facility power supply equipment should be redesigned to enable a practical, safe disconnection of all interior circuits using as few circuits as practical and installed at a single location.
- A fire department preplanning education program should include a specific procedure for safely disconnecting all electrical power to the facility to which a particular fire department will respond. Facility personnel should be educated in these procedures and the written procedures made available to the emergency response personnel when needed.

ISSUE: Failure to follow established procedures and multiple alarm indicators

- Procedures that require the notification of emergency service personnel in case of an alarm are frequently not followed. This is typical of systems with a frequent false alarm rate, or, as in this case, with multiple alarms masking the true condition. Ironically the same type of problem occurred at First Interstate Bank only four days prior to the Hinsdale fire.
- Procedures that are well thought out should be followed, especially when related to life safety issues such as fire. Procedures that are cumbersome or impractical should be streamlined or eliminated. Systems that provide multiple alarm conditions due to one unrelated event should be reengineered to segregate the most critical alarms from equipment or power failure. Systems that have repeated false alarms should be repaired and if determined to be uncorrectable, replaced.
- Direct connection to the local emergency services should be given serious

consideration. The typical objection is the false alarm problems and the potential charges by the fire department. Again, a system with repeated false alarms should be repaired or replaced.

ISSUE: Smoke damage and severe corrosive damage due to corrosive gases carried in the fire

- For existing installations there may be no practical way to avoid having cables that give off corrosive gases when burned. The existing cabling within most large office buildings would be prohibitively expensive and extremely disruptive to replace. In new installations, the type of cabling may be an option; choosing cables that have resistance to combustion should heavily weigh in the evaluation. Many companies have spools of cabling stored in warehouses, purchased in bulk, that should be examined to assure that it meets current fire resistance standards.
- Knowing the burn characteristics of existing cabling will provide the continuity planners with some insight into the potential damage and skills necessary to mitigate the damage. The skills necessary to address the neutralizing of corrosives on equipment and media are not available in most organizations; the planners should identify organizations qualified to perform this type of restoration.
- Horizontal and vertical compartmentalization is critical in limiting the spread of both the fire and the smoke. Wherever possible, operational areas should be partitioned from floor to ceiling to segregate fire and smoke from the most critical equipment. Air-handling equipment should always be tied into the smoke detection equipment, and should shut down air exchange and circulation within the building immediately after an alarm is detected.

ISSUE: Severe affect on community business and personal services

- In most cases, customers are oblivious to the continuity plans of the telephone service provider. It is imperative that the business resumption planner contact the telephone service provider and find out what level of priority has been assigned to their company. It may not be possible to change that priority, but with some speculative input from the telco, the planner will be able to estimate the length of the outage. If the potential length of the outage is unacceptable, the organization can plan for alternatives to support its critical communication requirements. Unfortunately, many companies assume that the telco's plan is adequate and make no alternate arrangements.
- Hinsdale dramatically illustrates the tremendous dependence on telecommunications services. The total loss for this disaster has not been fully tallied, but the impact is said to be in excess of $9 billion. Many companies declared bankruptcy because of revenue and business losses resulting from the outage.

ISSUE: Damage to cables by contractors and mixing incompatible cables in the same cable run

- Contractors and subcontractors should be bonded, monitored closely by the hiring organization, and before hiring, should undergo a reference check to determine competency. Any damage to company property should be the responsibility of the contractor or subcontractor; the hiring organization should be contractually and financially protected. An incident such as Hinsdale can be a catastrophic loss to an organization that is forced to legally defend its actions and show that it took reasonable and prudent steps to assure continuity of services. The fact that a contractor or subcontractor committed the act does not release the hiring organization from liability.

- One of the most significant findings of the investigation dealt with the mixing of armor shielded ac power cables and unshielded dc power cables in the same cable run. Many organizations, because of limited cable run capacity, have mixed these two types of cables together. If damage occurs to the shielding on the dc power cable, it will short to the metal shielded cables, and the resulting resistance will cause the wiring to heat up and eventually burn the damaged cable or adjacent cables. The mixing of metal shielded cables and "plastic" shielded should not be allowed; where this condition currently exists, the two types of cables should be separated.

Selecting a Computer Processing Recovery Strategy

CHAPTER

II-9

Chapter II-9 discusses the strategies that can be used to resume computer processing following a disaster or a business interruption in the data center. Any number of incidents can cause the interruption, from an earthquake or tornado to a loss of power company service. The type of incident is not an issue here; the fact that there is an interruption to computer processing is. The term disaster as used in this chapter simply means an extended interruption to computer processing.

RECOVERY STRATEGIES

When developing that data center recovery plan (DCRP), the company can choose among three basic strategies for resuming the data center computer processing. The strategies include transferring computer processing to a computer backup site; populating a cold site; or delaying computer processing until the damaged site can be repaired.

The first involves transferring computer processing to a computer backup site. A computer backup site is a fully equipped data center to which the IS department can move temporarily and resume computer processing. Three options for the computer backup site strategy are discussed in this chapter:

- *Reciprocal agreements.* The reciprocal agreement is a backup site plan in which each of two companies commit to providing a level of data center support to the other should one company lose its processing capability as a result of disaster.
- *Company-owned backup site (internal hot site).* A company-owned data center backup site is a backup site plan in which a fully operational second data center will be used for the processing of critical data applications during a disaster recovery operation. *As will be seen later, a client/server environment may be backed up in a company owned facility that is not truly a data center.*
- *Commercial hot site.* A commercial hot site is a backup plan in which a fully operational data center has been contracted to be used for the processing of critical applications during a disaster recovery operation.

The second strategy that a company can choose is to populate a cold site, which is a nonequipped raised-floor facility that has been prepared environmentally to house a computer center. This strategy requires a company to order and install equipment and resume processing as soon as it can get all of the company equipment operating. The delay to computer processing is generally 10 to 14 days.

The third strategy is for the company to wait until it can reequip the damaged site. This could result in a significant delay before the processing of critical applications can be resumed. Exhibit II-9-A provides an Overview of these strategies and options.

EXHIBIT II-9-A COMPUTER PROCESSING RECOVERY STRATEGIES

1. Transfer processing to a computer backup site. Under this recovery strategy, there are three options:
   — Reciprocal agreement.
   — Company-owned backup site (internal hot site).
   — Commercial hot site.
2. Transfer processing to a cold site (shell facility).
3. Repair and reequip damaged site.

SELECTING A STRATEGY

The question of which strategy a company should select depends on the degree to which the business functions of the company must rely on its computer systems.

This business function dependence on the computer is determined by performing an applications impact analysis. As described in Chapter II-8, the applications impact analysis is a process in which applications are analyzed to determine the impact on the company if the applications could not be processed as scheduled. After completion of this analysis, the company is ready to select which computer processing recovery strategy best fits its needs. For example, if the results from the impact analysis indicate that some applications cannot be delayed without causing a significant impact on the company, the company should probably choose to transfer its critical applications processing to a computer backup site while repairing the damaged site or relocating to another site. If, on the other hand, the analysis indicates that all applications could be delayed for a certain period of time without causing a significant impact, the company might elect to use a cold site or wait until it can repair the damaged site.

Choosing Multiple Strategies

More than one recovery strategy may be appropriate. Companies have sometimes opted to have two or more strategies included in their DCRP. If some computer applications have been identified as critical, a hot site may be the solution for those applications. Because the building housing the data center could require months to repair, and there would be a gap in time between the use of the hot site for critical applications and the return to the original data center, a cold site could be used in the interim. If there were an essential business function that required checks to be printed but not processed, a reciprocal agreement could be used for that application.

Chapter II-9 discusses the various computer processing recovery strategies and options that are available and their strengths and weaknesses. Discussed in this chapter are reciprocal agreement, the internal backup site, the commercial backup Site, and the cold site (also referred to as a shell).

THE RECIPROCAL AGREEMENT OPTION

The reciprocal agreement is a computer backup site option in which two companies pledge a level of data center support to the other should one company lose its processing capability as a result of a disaster. Many companies have eliminated using reciprocal agreements as a feasible computer backup site option because the complexity in processing the critical applications usually exceeds the capabilities of the reciprocal agreement site. (These drawbacks are discussed in more detail later in this chapter.) However, in certain limited circumstances reciprocal agreements may be useful. The following sections describe how such agreements have been traditionally established and managed and discussed when their use is appropriate.

Establishing the Agreement

Traditionally, when an agreement is reached between two data center managers to provide backup support, a commitment letter is sent by each manager identifying the terms of the reciprocal agreement. These terms include the proposed level of commitment, the configuration of the computer to be used for backup processing, the manner in which the processing support would be given, and any reimbursement that would be required between the two companies. The letter is then included in the DCRP manual.

Types of Reciprocal Agreements

These are three common types of reciprocal agreements: those made between companies located in the same locale, those made between companies in the same industry, and those made between companies in the same corporation.

Same-locale agreements have the advantage of proximity which can make the recovery easier o carry out. Same-industry agreements can provide the ability to support or gain support from other companies that have the same hardware and software needs. Same-corporation agreements will do its best to assist during the recovery operation.

Of these three types of agreements, the most commonly used is the same-industry reciprocal agreement. For example, this agreement has been used by companies in the newspaper industry, because they share either unique equipment or unique software requirements.

Drawbacks of Reciprocal Agreements

As noted, many companies have eliminated use of reciprocal agreements because of the complexity of processing the critical applications exceeds the capabilities of the reciprocal agreement site. Other reasons companies do not include them as a feasible option are the difficulty in maintaining hardware compatibility, supporting online systems, and testing. Another problem is that such agreements are usually not executed as legal contracts.

Hardware Compatibility. Even though the two companies may be hardware compatible today, there is a good possibility that they will not be compatible in the future. Maintaining hardware compatibility has always been a problem. For example, it could require that a company install hardware sooner than planned in order to remain compatible with the reciprocal party.

Inclusion of Online Systems. Most computer operations depend heavily on data communications networks. Except for provision of dial-up recovery capabilities, standard reciprocal agreements do not provide recovery support for such data networks.

Testing. For the most part, it is difficult to test the reciprocal agreement's data center. In order for the reciprocal agreement data center manager to provide test time, the other site would need to delay processing its own work, something few data center managers would be willing to do.

Contractual Issues. The reciprocal agreement is only a legal contract if it is signed by one of the corporate officers. Most in-house lawyers will not authorize the signing of a reciprocal agreement, because such agreements present more potential exposures than benefits to the company.

In the past, there have always been problems with reciprocal agreements because the company failed to obtain a firm commitment with the other party. With a firm commitment, a company can expect that the agreement will be honored (unless the second company is also experiencing a computer outage at the same time.) a key indicator of a firm agreement is testing at the reciprocal data center. With a firm agreement, each company tests it capability to process on the other company's computer. Loose agreements did not provide for testing and generally were made solely to satisfy auditors and executive management.

It is important not to forget the chances of a regional occurrence (flood, earthquake, tornado, etc.) affecting your reciprocating organization as well as your own. Too often, the probable mutual user is within a short distance of your site. Should this occur, two companies are out of business rather than just one. For that reason, if a reciprocal agreement is thought to be the best option, try to make such an agreement with a more remote site, one less likely to be included in your regional event.

Use of Reciprocal Agreements

Not all applications that are scheduled for the hot site may need to be processed there. For example, printing applications could be moved to a reciprocal agreement location that can provide printing capability. This can be a valuable resource during the first few days of the recovery operation. The reciprocal location could be used to print reports for end users to Use temporarily until they can start to access their data at their workstations.

A second example where printing support could be useful is in a payroll application that needs to be processed during recovery operation. Instead of processing the computerized payroll application itself, checks could be printed and used as an advance against employee's payroll; exceptions would be handled manually by the payroll department directly. When the computer resources again become available, the advance payments can be processed during the period's payroll. This payroll strategy is being employed by many companies today, even those using a computer hot site. This strategy allows all of the resources at the hot site to be used to support revenue generating and customer service functions, while still meeting the company's obligation to pay its employees on a timely basis.

THE COMPANY-OWNED BACKUP SITE OPTION

With a company-owned computer backup site, a second, fully operational data center is used for the processing of critical applications during a disaster recovery operation. This company-owned backup site is not just sitting idly waiting for a disaster to occur. It is an operational data center, with a processing workload capable of accommodating critical applications if necessary. The existing workload that could be preempted to handle such critical applications consists of applications that can be removed from the normal processing schedule — for example, applications being developed or tested. This replaceable work would be off-loaded during a disaster recovery operation freeing the necessary resources to support processing of critical applications.

Advantages of the Company-Owned Hot Site

A company-owned computer backup site option is considered the best technical option, but it is also the most costly. Among its advantages, the company-owned hot site can eliminate the problem of hardware and software incompatibility. Network problems can be resolved more readily, and some of the logistical problems with personnel that occur during a recovery operation can be minimized. Last, tests of the backup site can be performed more effectively.

Hardware Compatibility. The company-owned backup site option eliminates the problem of hardware incompatibility. It can ensure that any equipment installed in the main data center is duplicated in the backup site. In fact, this option has been used by large corporations with multiple data centers throughout the Country to ensure that the Unique equipment installed in any of its data centers is also installed in the company-owned backup site. When new and unique equipment is purchased, a second can be installed at the company-owned backup site as well.

Software Compatibility. The company-owned backup site option eliminates the problem of software incompatibility. The concern about getting all of the software loaded and operational at the backup site is eliminated because the software already resides at the backup site. Therefore, the backup site is software compatible at all times.

Network Issues. Network problems can be more readily resolved with this option. For example, a network switching strategy could be designed by in-house network specialists to meet the needs of the company. *The company owned backup site should be at least a node on the corporate network and have the capability of being a hub, should processing be transferred. Movement of corporate information along the network through this site is neither cost intensive nor inefficient. In fact, shadow backups, or mirroring of data, can be accomplished in this manner (see Chapter II-10).*

Personnel Logistics. The company-owned backup site option minimizes some of the logistics problems with personnel that can occur during a recovery operation. In particular, because the company-owned hot site is already staffed, the need to make travel, hotel, and financial arrangements for a large number of personnel is minimized.

Testing. Tests and exercises of the backup site can be performed in a cost-effective manner with this option. Because the company already has operations personnel working at the backup site, it does not need to send people on the road to test the backup site's capabilities. In addition, the number of test exercises can be increased. Instead of companies testing every six months, they can test more frequently. Finally, companies can schedule unannounced test exercises in which computer center employees are not warned in advance that an exercise is going to take place.

THE COMMERCIAL HOT-SITE OPTION

A commercial hot site is a computer backup site in which a fully operational data center has been contracted for processing of critical applications during a disaster

EXHIBIT II-9-B COMMERCIAL HOT-SITE VENDORS

Arel Technologies Inc.
7111 West Broadway
Minneapolis MN 55428
(612) 560-0203
fax: (612) 560-2506

AT&T/NCR Business Recovery Group
1700 S. Patterson Boulevard, SDC-4
Dayton OH 45479
(513) 445-2787
fax: (513) 449-2599

Backup Recovery Services Inc.
1620 NW Gage Boulevard
Topeka KS 66818
(913) 232-0368
fax: (913) 233-6862

Bank Up, Business Recovery Services
2694 Bisahop Drive, Suite 115
San Ramon CA 94583
(510) 275-9474
fax: (510) 275-9515

Bekins Disaster Recovery Services
1601 Leavenworth Street
Omaha NE 68102
(402) 341-2700
fax: (402) 341-5603

Chubb Contingency Trading Facility
100 Williams Street
New York NY 10038
(212) 612-4175
fax: (212) 612-4672

Comdisco Disaster Recovery Services
6111 N. River Road
Rosemont IL 60018
(708) 698-3000
fax: (708) 518-5340

Computer Solutions Inc.
397 Park Avenue
Orange NJ 07050
(201) 672-6000
fax: (201) 672-8069

CRI Disaster Recovery Center
7268 S. Tuscon Way
Englewood CO 80112
(303) 790-4700
fax: (303) 790-4736

CSC Compusource Inc.
118 MacKenan Drive, Suite 500
Cary NC 27511
(800) 671-2948
fax: (919) 380-5562

Data Assurance Corp.
12503 E. Euclid Drive, Suite 250
Englewood CO 80111
(800) 654-1689
fax: (303) 792-5544

Dataguard Recovery Services Inc.
P.O. Box 37144
Louisville KY 40233-7144
(800) 325-3977
fax: (502) 426-3028

Data Processing Security Inc.
200 East Loop 820
Fort Worth TX 76112
(817) 457-9400
fax: (817) 457-9400

Delaney Recovery Services Inc.
888 First Avenue
King of Prussia PA 19406
(215) 992-1081
fax: (215) 992-1084

Digital Equipment Corp.
3555 Salt Creek Lane
Arlington Heights IL 60005-1092
1-800-HOT-SITE
fax: (708) 818-0790

Exchange Resources Inc.
5700 Green Circle Drive
Minneapolis MN 55343
(800) 424-3171 and (612) 933-6340
fax: (612) 933-3834

First Bancorporation of Ohio Disaster Recovery Hotsite
6625 W. Snowville Road
Brecksville OH 44141-3209
(216) 838-4044
fax: (216) 838-4037

First Recovery Inc.
1046 Albemarle Road, P.O. Box 552
Troy NC 27371
(919) 576-0901
fax: (919) 576-1070

Hewlett-Packard
15815 SE 37th Street
Bellvue WA 98006
(206) 644-3362
fax: (206) 643-8748

IBM Business Recovery Services
400 Parson's Pond Drive
Franklin Lakes NJ 07417
(201) 848-3734
fax: (201) 848-3376

Newtrend Disaster Recovery Services
2600 Technology Drive
Orlando FL 32804
(407) 880-9050
fax: (407) 880-2917

Recovery Resources
P.O. Box 2646
Orlando FL 32802-2646
(407) 851-7657
fax: (407) 850-9537

Sun Data Inc.
1300 Oakbrook Drive
Norcross GA 30093
(800) 241-9882
fax: (404) 242-3510

Sungard Recovery Services
1285 Drummers Lane
Wayne PA 19087
(800) 247-7832
fax: (215) 341-8739

Technical Restoration Services Inc.
5600 NW 12th Avenue, #306
Ft. Lauderdale FL 33309
(305) 351-0301
fax: (305) 351-0288

Upsite Disaster Recovery Center
3381 Successful Way
Dayton OH 45414-4317
(513) 237-3400
fax: (513) 236-2503

Wang Laboratories Inc.
One Industrial Avenue
Lowell MA 01851
(508) 967-8701 and 967-3101
fax: (508) 937-7507

Weyerhaeuser Recovery Services
PC2-15
Tacoma WA 98477
(800) 654-9347
fax: (206) 824-4688

XL/Datacomp Inc.
908 N. Elm
Hinsdale IL 60521
(708) 323-1200
fax: (708) 323-2104

recovery operation. The contract must be in effect prior to the disaster; hot-site vendors will not negotiate a contract to use a hot site after the disaster has occurred. The first commercial hot-site option was established by Sungard Inc. during the late 1970s. Currently, there are a large number of commercial hot-site vendors; a list of vendors is provided as Exhibit II-9-B.

Advantages of the Commercial Hot Site

The three major advantages of the commercial hot site are that it is a dedicated facility; it can be used to test and exercise the computer backup site team's recovery responsibilities; and it is cost-effective.

Dedicated Facility. The hot-site facility is a dedicated facility used only as a backup site and not in any other capacity (e.g., as a service bureau). It is to be used primarily to support companies that are in a recovery operation and secondarily as location where clients can test and exercise their DCRP. Although hot sites usually have enough computer equipment and network resources to satisfy most clients, they will install additional hardware for a client for a fee.

Testing. The commercial hot sites also include in the client's contract a specific number of free hours to test and exercise the DCRP. This is a valuable resource for the DCRP coordinator, because it allows the coordinator to verify that the company can process at the backup site and can successfully switch the network to the backup site. It also allows the coordinator to exercise the IS department personnel who have been assigned DCRP recovery responsibilities and to train new employees.

Cost. The commercial hot-site option generally include:

- A monthly cost that allows the customer accesses to the site should it suffer a disaster.
- Communications equipment and line costs to ensure that the network can be switched properly at the time of the disaster.
- A declaration fee associated with activating the agreement.
- Daily use fees during the recovery operation.

Despite these expenses, commercial hot sites can often be justified on a cost basis. First, the cost of the hot site must be compared with the expected losses the company will sustain if it does not have a hot site to move into after a business interruption or disaster. (The expected losses are identified during the applications impact analysis [see Chapter II-8]).

Second, the commercial hot-site option is usually one-fourth the cost of the company-owned hot site. This is because the costs for the facility and the equipment in a commercial hot site are split among multiple customers of the hot site. (Other costs of the commercial hot site, such as the network lines, are not shared by the other customers of the hot site.)

Third, the commercial hot site is only a fraction of the cost of other functions in most companies. For example, it is typically only about 1% of the annual IS department's budget. It is also only a fraction of the cost of premiums paid for employees' medical insurance and wager continuation insurance. If medical and wage continuation insurance are considered a reasonable insurance cost, the commercial hot site, which acts an insurance policy for the data center, could also be considered a reasonable insurance premium.

Factors in Selecting a Hot-Site Vendor

There are a number of factors that companies consider when selecting a commercial hot site vendor. These factors include the available configuration, right of access, reliability, cost, and value-added services offered by the vendor.

Available Configuration. The first step in selecting a hot site is to identify the hardware configuration needed to process the critical applications. This is referred to as the minimum acceptable configuration. The minimum acceptable configuration is identified by analyzing all of the applications that will be processed at a backup site during the initial stages of the recovery operation and determining the type of configuration requires to support them. Having determined the minimum configuration, the next step is to determine which commercial hot-site vendors provide a configuration that satisfies the minimum requirement. This research can be performed by reviewing the vendors marketing material; all hot-site vendors identify their system configuration early in their marketing material. (However, it should be remembered that those configurations are subject to change.)

Right of Access. This refers to access during a time when the site is being used or when a wide area disaster has affected two or more hot site clients. The major concern of hot-site client's is how they can be assured of computer use at the hot site to process critical applications during a wide-area or regional disaster. They need to know whether this is a guaranteed commitment from the hot-site vendor or a first-come, first-served commitment.

Some hot-site vendors have multiple-computer locations. If a wide-area or regional disaster strikes, they may first place clients in the backup site in which they have a contract. If more hot-site customers need the contractual site than the site can handle, the vendor moves the overflow to alternative locations.

Hot-site vendors have experience in providing support to multiple clients in various types of disasters, including the Chicago River flood in April 1992, Hurricane Andrew in August 1992, the New York World Trade Center bombing in February 1993, and the Los Angeles earthquake in January 1994.

The prospective client should also evaluate how the vendor will respond if a wide-area disaster affects more clients than the contractual site and the alternative sites can handle. This is a valid question to ask each of the vendors that are responding to a request for proposal. Even though the hot-site vendors have supported all of their customers to date, they should be able to explain how they will support a larger number of disaster activation's than it appears they can handle.

Reliability. This refers to the vendor's history of supporting clients during disasters. Have they been able to provide access to the hot site quickly? Have they been supportive of client personnel during this stressful time? Following earthquakes and floods or during the tracking of hurricanes, did the vendors proactively contact their clients in the affected areas to see how they could help? During such specific events as the Los Angeles riots and the Chicago River flood, did they proactively contact their clients to see whether they could help?

Some hot-site vendors go out of their way to assist clients in need, even acting beyond the contract requirements. For example, following Hurricane Hugo, one hot-site vendor was notified by two clients that wanted to activate their backup site contracts because they had lost power to the data center. (These data centers provided computer support to end-users located in areas outside the damage zone.) Rather than having these clients incur the cost and effort of activating the hot site, the vendor made arrangements to send auxiliary power generators to them — a much more cost-effective solution.

Cost. The proposal should contain a number of cost items for consideration. These include:

- The monthly cost to have the right to use the facility during a disaster.
- The cost of the declaration fee. (This is a cost the company assumes when it activates the contract.)
- The daily cost for using the facility during the recovery operation.
- The cost of any special equipment that has to be installed to meet the configuration requirements.

The computer backup site options matrix shown in Workpaper II9.01 can be used to determine the estimated costs for different hot-site vendor services. The matrix allows cost information to be compared among three commercial hot-site vendors as well as a company-owned hot site.

The matrix is divided into four sections. The first section addresses availability issues, including the estimated time before the recovery can start, the estimated time before critical processing can begin, and the duration in time that the client can remain in the hot site.

The second section of the matrix identifies the computer equipment that will be provided in the contract, including the CPUs, the number and types of disks, the number and types of tapes, and the number and types of printers.

The third section identifies the teleprocessing resources, including the number and types of communications controllers, the number and types of modems, and the number and types of circuit and lines.

The fourth section of the matrix provides the costs for the site and the computer equipment, the teleprocessing resources, and an estimate of the ongoing costs for maintenance and exercising the plan. The site costs are broken into five categories:

- The one-time cost to establish the site.
- The ongoing costs or monthly contractual costs.
- The declaration costs.
- The use cost (per day).
- The daily use costs for use of a cold site.

The equipment costs and teleprocessing costs are each broken into two categories: one-time costs and ongoing costs. The next set of costs included in the matrix are for maintenance and testing. The maintenance costs are based on an estimate of the salary, plus benefits, of the person responsible to keep the DCRP and the backup site in a current and usable condition. The testing costs are estimates based on the out-of-pocket expenses the company will have to reimburse. Another cost factor to be considered is the estimated annual increase in contract fees charged by the vendor. The increase percentage is usually negotiated when the contract is signed.

Value-Added Services. Additional disaster recovery services beyond the hot site can be important criterion. Some commercial hot-site vendors have internal consultants to support a customer's DCRP planning needs. The consultants can help in data recovery and network analysis and in performing the various test exercises of the DCRP.

Summary

After determining which vendors can meet the minimum acceptable configuration, the perspective client asks the remanding vendors to submit proposals of how they

[redacted]

will provide service to the client. The contract issues that should be covered in their proposals include:

- The cost of meeting minimum configuration.
- The capacity to expand that configuration, if needed.
- The vendors' length of time in the business and whether this is their primary business.
- Their policy on access to the facility (in a localized disaster, a wide-area disaster, and in any situation in which multiple clients need access at the same time).
- Whether they have any exclusive contracts with clients that would supersede other contracts.
- The number of site available and the location of these sites.
- Any additional service that the vendor can provide.

THE COLD-SITE STRATEGY

A cold site is a nonequipped backup site that has been prepared environmentally to house a computer center. This facility does not have a computer installed, but it is set up for a computer and its peripherals to be installed; for example, the facility has a raised floor, the power and air conditioning needed for a computer, and the communications lines installed (but not necessarily activated).

This computer processing recovery strategy is not designed to support the quick resumption of processing critical applications. The problem with a cold site is the length of time it would take to become operational. Most companies estimate that 10 to 14 days is the best that can be expected for a cold site to become operational. In most data centers today, the equipment comes from a minimum of two hardware vendors. Before the cold site could be ready for processing, the vendors would have to deliver, install, and test their equipment. A company could experience additional delays if everything did not work according to the best-case scenario (e.g., hardware or network not up and running as quickly as planned). For these reasons, the cold site is not considered an appropriate solution for processing critical applications in a short period of time.

The primary value of the cold site is that it can be used if the building housing the data center suffers major damage that would require months to repair. In this situation, the company will have an environmentally prepared facility available in which to install equipment.

Many commercial hot sites include space for a cold site in the same building that houses their hot site. If for any reason the damaged data center cannot be repaired within the contracted processing period at the hot site, the customer can install equipment and use the cold site. Processing can then move back to either the repaired disaster site or a new, permanent facility.

This was the process that the Penn Mutual Insurance Company followed after a fire in May 1989, which damaged the building housing its corporate computer center in Philadelphia. While the fire itself did not cause significant damage, the side effects of the fire did. Boxes containing old records stored in the room where the fire started were treated with a chemical to protect them. Following combustion, this chemical turned into a toxic gas, which contaminated the rest of the building and caused the building to be unusable for more than a year. During the six weeks the company processed at the commercial hot site, it equipped a cold site, to which it moved and operated for approximately one year. During that time, the company built a new data center in the suburbs of Philadelphia.

RE-FURNISHING A SITE

This option differs from that mentioned above in that we are not discussing using the same facility and awaiting delivery of mainframe equipment. It assumes the establishment of a backup site from one contracted for earlier, floor space in the same building or complex — or the original data center — or the use of more informally prepared facilities. We speak here only of building a server and local-client environment that may be housed in a less conditioned site than would be required for a mainframe installation.

This option is premised upon the need to re-establish a client server based processing scheme. While any one of the above noted location options may be executed, the chances for using an owned site (assuming a multi-location organization) are enhanced. Cost factors, can then be controlled to the extent of not having an outlay of consequence unless the plan is activated.

With today's increasing implementation of network-based client/server processing, the equipment and software used are generally more available than are mainframe processors and peripherals, as well as their included complex operating systems and applications. For this reason, it is often easier to locate an alternate site that provides the security, network interfaces, space, and environment needed than it was to locate a full-blown data center or even shell. For this reason, a DCRP should include accurate references to sources of such equipment and software. In most instances, re-sellers are as much a part of this semi-local availability picture as are manufacturers.

To expedite the rapid obtaining and installation of servers and local clients, establish relationships with these organizations and have a clear picture as to what can be expected and under what circumstances. Include contacts and 24-hour telephone numbers where representatives can be reached. Do not forget to evaluate the included and potential communications resources and the vendors that can put them in place. Don't forget to include the vendors of specialized software products.

One of the characteristics of re-sellers in the client/server field is that they generally handle the software necessary to build a mirror image of your lost data center. Even when they do not have all of the software components of your environment, you can contact the software vendors while they are re-implementing your environment.

In those instances where particular software is known to be difficult to obtain in a timely manner, backups should be designed to include it. Remember the capabilities of ADSM as described earlier.

CONCLUSION

This chapter discussed the different recovery strategies that companies can choose on he basis of their dependence on the computer. Selecting the computer processing recovery strategy can often be a frustrating process to go through. DCRP coordinators often identify the criticality of applications, present the information to the executive committee, receive proposals form commercial hot-site vendors, and select the appropriate strategy, only to find out that the executive committee will not authorize expenditures for a backup site.

The movement of corporations toward more network centric and client/server processing creates opportunities as well as problems. Equipment is more available and less expensive and if the design of the network is thoughtfully prepared, the recovery will be for a smaller sub-set of overall processing. In many instances, the need for "computer room" conditioned backup facilities are lessened, if not removed.

Communications, on the other hand, is probably going to be the biggest factor in a successful recovery. Whatever option is chosen for a backup site, the availability of linkup to your network is imperative. Network equipment must be available, as must the ability to connect. The DCRP now needs to pay special attention to having contacts for these resources clearly spelled out.

The DCRP only identifies the critical applications that will need to be processed at a computer backup site. It is not ready to be implemented until the computer backup site has been tested to verify that it is workable. Unless that step is completed the DCRP will probably fail if activated in a disaster.

WORKPAPER II9.01 Recovery Processing Strategy Matrix*

DATA CENTER RECOVERY PLAN

[COMPANY NAME]

RECOVERY PROCESSING STRATEGY OPTION MATRIX

Evaluation Areas	In-House Company Owned Hot Site	Commercial Vendor Hot Site Vendor No. ____		Vendor No. ____		Vendor No. ____	
		Full Backup with Network	Full Backup with Dial-Up	Full Backup with Network	Full Backup with Dial-Up	Full Backup with Network	Full Backup with Dial-Up
Availability							
A. For Recovery Startup							
B. For Business Unit Use							
C. For What Duration							
Computer Equipment Available							
A. CPU							
B. Disk							
C. Tape							
D. Printer							
Teleprocessing Resources Available							
A. Communications Controller							
B. Modems							
C. Circuits/Lines							

*Not available on disk.

Page 1

Evaluation Areas	In-House Company Owned Hot Site	Commercial Vendor Hot Site					
		Vendor No. ____		Vendor No. ____		Vendor No. ____	
		Full Backup with Network	Full Backup with Dial-Up	Full Backup with Network	Full Backup with Dial-Up	Full Backup with Network	Full Backup with Dial-Up
Costs							
A. Site							
1. One Time							
2. Ongoing							
3. Declaration							
4. Use/Daily							
5. Cold Site							
B. Computer Equipment							
1. One Time							
2. Ongoing							
C. Teleprocessing							
1. One Time							
2. Ongoing							
D. Other Ongoing							
1. Maintenance							
2. Testing							

Page 2

Evaluation Areas	In-House Company Owned Hot Site	Commercial Vendor Hot Site Vendor No. ____		Vendor No. ____		Vendor No. ____	
		Full Backup with Network	Full Backup with Dial-Up	Full Backup with Network	Full Backup with Dial-Up	Full Backup with Network	Full Backup with Dial-Up
Costs (Continued)							
E. Total Facility Cost							
1. One Time							
2. Ongoing (Annual)							
3. Declaration							
4. Use (6 Weeks)							
5. Annual Percentage Increase							

Page 3

Protecting and Recovering Computer Data

CHAPTER

II-10

The recovery of critical data is the most important element in the data center recovery plan (DCRP). If a company suffers a disaster that destroys data in the computer center it must rely on the data that has been rotated off premises. If the data stored off premises is incomplete or insufficient for recovering applications, the company has a serious problem.

Chapter II-10 therefore discusses the recovery of computer data following a disaster in which the on-site data is either damaged or destroyed. This chapter also presents the methods for protecting critical data. These include backing up the data and rotating the backups to an off-premises storage location so that the company can retrieve the backups and reconstruct the data quickly during the recovery operation.

The strategies discussed in this chapter assume the following disaster scenario. A disaster has damaged the data center, its equipment, and data. The disk drives in the data center and the tapes in the tape library have been destroyed. Backup tapes, which were stored in the basement of the building, are inaccessible, and it is believed they have been damaged. The backup data that is stored in the off-premise storage location is intact and accessible. The recovery operation depends entirely on the ability to restore data from the backups stored off site.

OBJECTIVES OF THE DATA RECOVERY PROGRAM

The objectives of most data recovery programs are to back up critical data, rotate the backups to an off-site storage location, and retrieve the backups quickly during a recovery operation. Data is backed up and rotated to an off-premises storage location to ensure that there will be no loss of critical information caused by a disaster to the data center. This critical data must be able to be retrieved on a timely basis to meet the recovery commitments that have been made to the end users and executive management. For example, if the computer backup site must be operational in 72 hours, the data backups must be able to be retrieved, reloaded at the backup site, and reconstructed to an acceptable point for the end users within the same 72 hours.

Backing Up Data

The types usually backed up in data centers include systems software and utilities, applications software and utilities, databases, production data on disk packs, and transaction logs or journal files in addition to these standard backups, special requests may be made to back up such data as data files stored on tapes only, test packs for application development, and private disk drives used by end users or local area network (LAN) administrators for their LAN backups.

It is expedient for LAN servers to be backed up in an automated manner — with a backup job kicking off during down hours — on a daily basis. Generally, tape cartridges can be scheduled to complete before the daily rotation for any mainframe application tapes and included in a single shipment.

Along with the potential for using these tapes for recovery from an untoward event, there is the potential for clients on the network to have more individualized problems and, on a daily basis. If company PCs (network attached) are configured to use an "F" (server-based) drive for all application file storage, the onus for backing up sensitive files is removed from them as they will be picked up by the nightly server backup.

Further, the newer storage technology available for contemporary PCs, (JAZ or ZIP drives) allow a tremendous amount of information to be stored quickly and effectively. These devices allow the back up of the newer, gig plus disk drives with a minimum amount of media to handle and store. Although the above described network backup is more formal and therefore, more easily controlled. This technology should not be overlooked for standalone PCs or network attached units where server resources may be limited. Of course, when security concerns preclude the remote backup of working information. These new removable media drives are ideal.

Another technology that has evolved with the advent of complex and multi-platform networks is IBM's Adstar Distributed Storage Manager (ADSM). This tool allows the selective backup of new or changed information (or all information, at the administrator's whim) on both servers and client workstations. The system runs automatically in accordance with a preset schedule against all resources on a network. The flexibility of such a system — crossing platforms, reviewing files or databases for incremental changes since the last backup, etc. — makes it a powerful tool for managing the backup of network attached resources.

Responsibility for Identifying the Data to Back Up

Systems software and utilities backups are usually the responsibility of the systems software manager. The manager identifies which files should be backed up and at what frequency. Applications software is usually the responsibility of the systems software manager as well, because this manager is usually responsible for the systems that houses the application libraries. (In some cases, the application programming manager is responsible.)

Databases are usually the responsibility of the database administrator. Production data on disk packs and transactions files are usually the responsibility of the data center manager.

Responsibility for backing up data files stored only on tapes may vary. In some cases, the end user for the application is responsible; in others it is the applications project manager who requests the backup. Backups of test packs containing the programs for applications in development are usually the responsibility of the applications programming manager or project leader. Backups of private disk packs are usually the responsibility of the owner (e.g., the end user); backups of LAN disk packs are usually the responsibility of the LAN manager. Because there are always exceptions to the usual cases, the DCRP coordinator should verify who the responsible person or group is in his or her organization.

The responsible person identifies which files are to be backed up and at what frequency. This person should also identify which generation of data should be rotated and how long it should be stored before being retrieved and scratched.

The data files should be identified when application is being developed or, if it is already developed and in production, when the DCRP is being developed. The data files can be verified when the DCRP is tested.

Identifying the specific data files that must be available if the on-site data has been destroyed can be difficult. Many methods have been used to identify the data that should be backed up. In the early days of data center recovery planning, application flowcharts were used to identify the critical files that needed to be backed up and rotated off premises. This allowed the DCRP coordinator to identify all incoming data files at a glance. After flowcharts were phased out of the application development process, recovery planners had to resort to using printouts of JCL procedures to identify the application files that were being used in processing the application. Because the JCL procedures identify input and output files because these files are repeated throughout the JCL printout, the process of identifying the files was laborious and boring. Even after identifying the data files, the recovery planner still had to meet with the applications project leader to review the list of data file to ensure that it was complete. In some cases, input files identified by the JCL were not critical to the running of the application and did not have to be recovered.

Recently, software has been introduced that greatly assist the recovery planner in identifying the files that need to be protected. The software reads internal system management files and selects all incoming files that are used in processing the application. Some of the software can run in a batch environment. Other software runs in an online environment, where it both identifies the files needed and manages the backing up of the files.

Backup Strategies for Disk Drives

A number of methods can be used to back up disk drives. These include full-volume backup, incremental backup, database backup, data set backup, and journal backup. The backup strategy is selected on the basis of the needs of the owner of the data. Companies usually use a combination of these backup strategies.

Full-Volume Backup. This strategy copies the entire disk volume. It requires more processing time than some other methods, but it is easy to manage and is less likely to introduce error. It is normally used for weekend backup routine, when there is enough time available.

Incremental Backup. This strategy copies only those file that have changed since the last backup. This strategy requires less processing time than full-volume backup strategy; it is generally used in conjunction with the full-volume backup. The recovery procedure involves reloading the full-volume backups from the weekend prior to the disaster and applying the incremental backups to recover data files that have been updated since the weekend.

Database Backup. This strategy copies the data files in a similar fashion to the full-volume backup. The differences is that the database files are located on more that one disk drives. The database to be backed up is taken offline and then all of the elements of the database are copied at the same time to ensure they are synchronized. The recovery procedure involves restoring the data backups and reapplying transactions by using database journals (e.g., logs). A different backup strategy is required for databases that cannot be taken offline, because they are accesses

24 hours a day. Here again, network-based backup systems such as ADSM can automate the activity while ensuring complete data recovery capability.

Data Set Backup. This strategy is used to back up applications and inactive file. This strategy backs up specific data sets that have been identified by he applications programmer and requested to be rotated off premises. Rather than having inactive files occupy disk space, the files are backed up to tape and then sent off site. The tapes are then used to reload the files when they are needed.

Journal Backup. This strategy copies records of transactions that have been processed against a database.

Backup Strategies for Data on Tapes

The data that is stored on tapes is often overlooked when backups are rotated off premises. If the data is considered critical, when the tape is created, either the tape should be copied and the copy sent off premises or the next-oldest generation of the tape should be sent off premises.

ROTATING DATA OFF SITE

Critical data should be rotated off premises as soon as possible after it is created the old data protection procedure rotating backups off premises on a weekly basis is no longer satisfactory to most companies. The efforts involved in recovering application data files and databases using backups that are a week old will result in frustration and, more important, lost business opportunities for most companies. Critical data from applications that are processed daily should be rotated no later than the day after it is created.

In the past, critical data was identified for critical applications only, and quite frequently that was the only application data that was stored off premises, but in some cases, less-critical application data may be just as important. Applications are considered less critical if their processing can be delayed for a time. But this does not mean the data used in the applications is less important than that used in the critical applications. For example, processing of the general ledger system can often be delayed for a time; therefore, this application is classified as less critical. But the data is not less critical — revenues and expenses must still be accounted for during the recovery of the data.

RETRIEVING DATA

Storing only one copy of the critical backup data files off premises is not recommended. The object of recovery planning is to avoid a single point of failure. The most devastating single point of failure is the loss of the application data files and databases. Companies should have two or more sets of backups off premises for several reasons. The backups could be destroyed during transport to the backup site. Even if the backup tapes arrived without incident, they may load on the backup site compute because of tape drive alignment problems or because the tapes are damaged in another manner. If successfully loaded on the backup computer, a software error could still erase the data files.

If there is only one generation of backup tapes stored off premises, the tape operations recovery team should take them to a nearby computer and copy them. One copy should then be left at the off-site storage location.

EXHIBIT II-10-A TERMINOLOGY FOR GENERATIONS OF BACKUPS

When Created.	Number	Family	Today Is Friday
Last night	0	Child	Thursday
The prior night	−1	Parent	Wednesday
Two nights prior	−2	Grandparent	Tuesday
Three nights prior	−3	Great-grandparent	Monday

If there is more than one generation stored off premises, the tape operations team should retrieve only the most current generation. The next-older generation should remain in the off-premises storage location as a backup. If something happens to the tapes that are being taken to the computer backup site, the company still has this full set of backups in the off-premises storage location for recovery purposes.

Archival, regulatory, or legal backups probably should not be retrieved during a data center recovery operation. They should be retrieved only if needed for processing or if they should be scratched. Because most DCRP processing strategies concentrate on production applications, the archival, regulatory, or legal backup files should not be needed.

If the archival, regulatory, or legal tapes are destroyed by a disaster and the only copy in existence is located in the off premises storage location, it is prudent to make provisions to have another copy made. Foe example, some major corporations guarantee the IRS that these files will be available for audit purposes for at least seven years. If the files are not available, the company may be assessed a large fine and its executives can be prosecuted. Companies in this situation always store two copies of their end-of-year data. One copy is located in the off premises storage location, and the second copy is located in a different building, usually the data center. If anything happens to the files stored in either facility, the remaining copy should be taken to a computer center to be copied. After being copied, the files are then stored in two separate locations again.

RECONSTRUCTING DATA FILES

The amount of time needed to reconstruct the application data files to a point in time acceptable to the end use depends on the backup version available at the off-site storage location. (Exhibit II-10-A shows the terminology used in referring to generations of backups. The exhibit also shows which day the backup would refer to if today were Friday. A 0 or child generation would have been created on Thursday and so on).

If the backup is a 0 (i.e., child) generation, the recovery time will be short and the recovery procedure similar to the operations restart procedure (i.e., the procedure for restarting an application at various program steps, rather than starting at the first step). The 0 generation operations restart procedure requires loading the backups created the previous night and having the end users reenter all current activity. If the backups are a — 2 (i.e., grandparent) generation, the recovery process is much more involved and the recovery time is longer. This requires a reconstruction procedure, in which the data center personnel load backups from earlier backup generations and then process all of the activity that has taken place since the earlier backups were created.

If the reconstruction procedure is too time-consuming to meet the business objectives of the company, the company may want to consider electronic vaulting. Electronic vaulting is designed to reduce the time required to reconstruct data files.

Electronic Vaulting

There are three types of electronic vaulting: online tape vaulting, remote transaction journaling, and database shadowing. All three types of electronic vaulting lessen the time required to reconstruct applications at the computer backup site by reducing the exposure of data and applications to the disaster. Even though electronic vaulting would help the DCRP meet the business objectives of resuming the processing of critical applications within a specific time frame, it is often rejected as being too expensive.

Online Tape Vaulting. In this system, backup data is electronically transmitted, or vaulted, to recovery or storage location. The data center executes the tape backups, but instead of writing to a local tape drive, the tape channel is extended over communication lines to a recovery or storage location, where it is attached to a tape drive. This eliminates the need to ship tapes to an off-premises storage location.

Online tape vaulting requires high bandwidth. To move large amounts of data in a short amount of time may require a T3 circuit. For redundancy purposes, the data center may choose to have two T3 circuits. Although the cost of these lines is coming down, the high cost is still a stumbling block for most companies considering this backup approach.

Remote Transaction Journaling. This system uses the same logging procedure as that for a database management system. (For example, the database administrator can recover by restoring the last backup and then reprocessing the database management systems logs or journals.) Remote transaction journaling, in addition to creating the onsite journal, creates a second electronically at an off-premises location. This allows the off-premises location to recover the files to the point of interruption, reducing the time required to reconstruct the files and limiting the amount of information destroyed by a disaster.

Database Shadowing. This system creates an update to the production database, journals it, and transfers it to the remote computer. At the production site, the journal record is applied to a copy of the production database.

A Caution on Reconstructing Data

The DCRP may call for the reconstruction of critical applications first and less-critical applications later. This strategy can create problems because the journal log backups with the transactions needed for reconstruction of the less critical applications may not be available when needed later. This occurs when journal or log tapes with transactions for both critical and less-critical application have been used to reconstruct the critical applications. After they are used, the tapes library system may identify them as available scratch tapes and write over them. If they are written over, the end users of less critical applications must reenter the missing data, which can be a major undertaking. If the reconstruction of the less critical applications has been delayed for several days, it will be difficult to identify and reenter the missing input. If the reconstruction of the less-critical applications has been delayed for several weeks, it may be next to impossible to find the missing data.

ESTABLISHING EFFECTIVE DATA RECOVERY POLICIES AND PROCEDURE

The DCRP coordinator should ensure that the organization has established effective policies and procedures that support recovery objectives. This section presents several recommendations of sound procedures governing the backup, rotation, and retrieval of data from an off-site storage location. The risks of not establishing such procedures are also illustrated.

Availability of Access to the Off-Premises Location

The off-premises storage location must be open and available 24 hours a day, seven days a week. It should not be locked with a time lock or be closed on weekends. Commercial off-premises storage companies provide this type of service. Companies that use their own locations for storage backups are not always so lucky.

A few years back, a bank rotated it backup files to a vault in the basement of a bank-owned building about 10 miles from its data center. When the vault door was closed each evening, it was locked with a time lock that would automatically open at 8:00 A.M. the next morning. This procedure worked for many years without a problem. Then early one morning, the data center needed to retrieve backup tapes to restart its operations and found that it was not possible to enter the vault because of the time lock. The data center manager had to get the assistance of a representative from the lock company. The solution was to have a dual combination lock installed, which would allow two people with the combination to open the vault door.

Accessibility of Tapes in Off-Premises Location

Quite often, tapes or other storage media are stored in relatively local facilities. As mentioned, this may be another site owned by the company that meets the criteria for safe storage or be operated by a document management or other commercial storage facility.

If a company owned facility is used, it is wise to set up a contract with the security organization that provides guards or other security services for the company to be a party to emergency retrieval of backups. If no such service is used, have a bonded third party involved in tape rotation for purposes of backup and retrieval. In the worst case — where company staff provide transportation for regular rotation — make the staff that performs the task a part of the process.

Assuming the use of a commercial storage facility, make sure that your contract provides for off hours or emergency delivery of backups when needed.

In either case, it is wise to allow those charged with reloading systems, in any location, to do just that and not be involved in the movement of the tapes needed.

Security of the Off-Premises Location

The off-premises storage location must be a secure, environmentally controlled facility. It must protect against unauthorized access to the information, which could result in its theft or destruction. In one case, a commercial off-premises vendor stored backup tapes to a number of companies in a vault in its facility; the tapes were stored on racks, out in the open. This company failed to establish any procedures to protect against theft of these tapes. For example, people would have to sign into the vault, but their attaché cases were not inspected on either their entry or exit. This lack of security could have easily resulted in the unauthorized removal of critical files.

Rotation of Backups Off Site

Backups should be rotated to the off site facility as soon as possible after they have been created. For recovery purposes, rotating the information electronically as it is being created is the best procedure.

The standard for rotating backup files to the off premises storage location is by using a vehicle to transport tapes. This technique is more time-consuming than the electronic vaulting method mentioned earlier but it is also less costly. This method backs up the critical data after all batch processing is completed (e.g., midnight), which the tape librarian an hour or so after arriving in the morning to select the tapes, box them, and have them ready before the off premises representative collects the backups, however, all of the backups for the previous night as well as yesterday's journals and logs could be destroyed. The application reconstruction procedure would then require that the full volume backups be reloaded, incremental up through the day before yesterday be reloaded, and all transaction activity for yesterday be reentered and reprocesses.

On weekends, it is not uncommon to have the weekend full volume backups completed by Saturday afternoon or early evening. But most companies do not want to pay a premium to have tapes picked up on a weekend, so they leave them on site until Monday morning. Clearly, then the worst time to have a disaster is Monday morning before 10:00 A.M., because the weekend backups have not yet been rotated off premises.

Sometimes, not all of the backups that are supposed to rotate are actually rotated. For example, an application project leader may instruct the tape librarian to keep the backups for an application on site, because he or she is going to use them for testing programming changes. In this case, even though the tape library system indicates that the tapes are being rotated, the tape librarian keeps them on site. This is a data center operational problem as much as it is a data center recovery plan problem. Applications programmers should not be using off-premises backups for testing their applications.

A related problem can result if the tape librarian assumes the applications project leader wants to continue holding the backups an site and waits to be told when to begin rotating them again. This happened at a large manufacturing company a few years ago. The manager of computer programming requested that applications backup files not be rotated to the off premises storage location and did not instruct the tape librarian to resume rotating the backups. The failure to rotate the critical files was identified 77 days after the original instruction had been given. Although there were a number of generations located on site, there were no backups in the off premises storage location. Had a disaster occurred at this company during that time and the on-site data destroyed, the company would have suffered a significant loss.

To address these problems, the DCRP coordinator should check the tape library report to verify that the backups identified as needed for recovery are actually scheduled to be rotated to the off premises location. The DCRP coordinator should also perform desk check validations periodically to verify the backups listed on the vault report are actually residing in the off-premises location. (See Chapter II-11 for an explanation of desk check validations.)

The backups in the off-premises storage location should be synchronized with each other. The DCRP coordinator should review the DCRP application recovery procedure checklist and the vault report to ensure that the create date of the backups are synchronized. It might be noted here that a quarterly or semi-annual review of the materials held off site as well as the applicability of the backup scheme may be conducted by internal auditors. This is leveraging an available resource as well as getting a fresh pair of eyes to review procedures and stored media on a regular basis.

The DCRP coordinator should also analyze how many of the tapes in the off-premises storage location can actually be used for recovery purposes. This involves identifying when the backup tapes were created, whether they were created for annual, quarterly, or monthly archiving, and the generations available.

The Human Services Function

CHAPTER II-18

Throughout this section, we have discussed the technical aspects of recovering a business and its associated data center. We detailed the processes through which we would gather the necessary people, media, and equipment and re-establish processing at an alternate or refurbished site. What we did not address is the means by which we can guarantee that a subset of our normal staff or that a contingent of technically competent persons will be available and capable of implementing the provisions of the plan.

Most of us are well aware that the employees of any organization are its most important assets. Unfortunately, we often pay lip service to their importance, stand up and salute at the appropriate moments, but fail to recognize their needs in conditions such as those that would force the activation of the DCRP.

WHERE DOES KEY STAFF FIT INTO THE PICTURE?

When we begin to design a plan, we tend to perform all of the steps necessary to ensure the maintenance of information resources, software inventories and both replacement and potentially re-usable hardware. Dutifully, we prepare lists of backups, vendor contacts, and casually, the telephone numbers and addresses of the persons currently on our staff.

Not once do we consider that, in a regional disaster that disables our facility, the personal lives of the staff might well be impacted as well. And, that impact can easily be added to our corporate burden.

About ten years ago, the concept of the Human Services Team was first introduced. This was a proactive group that took the steps necessary to first, ensure the ready location of staff members, should plan activation occur during off hours and second, ensure that once located, the employees would exhibit the behavior necessary to implement all aspects of the plan. Despite the impact that any regional event might have on their personal lives, the employees felt loyalty to the company, and were comforted to know that their families and/or property would be taken care of in the difficult time.

These things do not happen by accident. As many companies have learned in less stressful conditions, employee loyalty has to be cultivated in good times and in bad. It is no coincidence that the companies adjudged as the best places to work have the lowest turnover rates. Thoughtfulness tends to be repaid in kind.

HUMAN SERVICES FUNCTIONS

Let us examine the duties the Human Services team. As the name implies, the major duty of this team is to see to the needs and comfort of company staff during an untoward event that leads to the activation of the plan. In this instance, however, the responsibility is extended. Rather than just look after employees during working hours, this team will provide the necessities of life for as long as necessary. In addition, that provision of service will extend to the family and property of each individual employee. A worker traveling on behalf of the company will only be able to concentrate on his or her work to the extent that he or she is not occupied with concerns for those left behind. In short, the company will provide the necessities of life for traveling employees families for the duration of the temporary assignment or until such time as their assistance is no longer needed. Services provided might include:

- Arranging for temporary housing in the event that property is rendered uninhabitable by the incident.
- Providing names, and where necessary, contacts with contractors to repair and or rebuild the employee's residence.
- Paying for such repairs pending insurance or reimbursement of funds extended.
- Providing transportation (when the absence of the employee causes hardships in these areas) to schools, medical appointments, or other needed areas.
- Making sure that paychecks arrive on time and that provisions for encashment, if necessary, are in place.
- Arranging and financing medical care when necessary.
- Providing long-distance (as required) service to ensure that family members are kept in contact during the recovery effort.
- Generally ensuring that the quality of life enjoyed in normal times by the family is maintained in the employee's absence.

Some of the functions of the team are based on the needs of the traveling employee as well. This usually takes the form of providing assurances of the services listed above, travel and accommodations arrangements while traveling and such funds and services as are required to allow the employee to work the probably extended hours that conditions will most certainly require.

Admittedly, some of the latter functions begin to sound like the old Human Resources functions that are a part of every plan. To be sure, they are present, but the function of this team is far extended. It is one of the most proactive teams within the planning process, building rapport and confidence in the staff members long before any incident caused activation of the plan.

PRE-EVENT ACTIVITIES

In October of 1989, an event occurred in San Francisco that removed any doubt that employees' first loyalties were with their families. The Loma Prieta earthquake hit at approximately 5:10 in the afternoon. People across the nation, tuned into the World Series saw a stadium rock and the lights go out. What was not visible to the casual observer was that at the time of the quake, first-shift people were ending their work day in the Bay area and second shifters were coming on, or were supposed to.

It is unknown just how many people coming to work were stopped by the inability to use the bridge and mass transit routes into the city and how many simply turned around and headed for home due to concerns for family and property. What is known is that first-shift people manned many a data center on the peninsula that night. When the West wall of your home crumbles with the help of a Richter 6.9 earthquake, you take a personal day — without calling in.

How then, do we prevent this from happening? Certainly, we cannot foresee nor stop an earthquake, but we can have assured the employee that the company would look after his or her interests. As we move forward with this section, the ways to do that will become apparent.

MAKEUP OF THE HUMAN SERVICES TEAM

As with most teams established to deal with emergency responses, this team will be made up of a cross section of responsibilities. It is important to realize that many functions often associated with other functions rightly belong here. Payroll, although an accounting/personnel function, should be handled here. That being the case, the necessary Payroll Department staff should be represented on this team. As the Human Services team will be the primary interface with staff, this is the correct home for the function.

Similarly, health, insurance and other benefits specialists must be represented on this team. In many instances, a relationship with health care providers, pharmacies, and other organizations catering to human well-being (and perhaps veterinarian practitioners, also!) can expedite the care needed for members of employees' families. The close relationship with insurance carriers guarantees that payments can be processed in as short a time as feasible, thereby reducing the stress on those injured in the event.

One of the most important concerns for any individual — beyond potential injury to family — is the condition and return to serviceability of one's home. And, on the assumption of a regional disaster, damage could most certainly occur to an employee's home. The first order of business, then, to the employee is to salvage and repair his or her residence.

By having members of the facilities or building services departments on this team, knowledge of construction, repair, and most important, relationships with contractors and vendors, is readily available. In the instance of a flood, for example, the obtaining of pumps, clean-up services, and other actions needed to repair and return the residence to usability would be best served in the hands of those with business relationships with the contractors and suppliers who can perform such functions. Likewise, these persons can act as a liaison with such contractors and suppliers as repairs continue. The latter is an important issue in that these persons will also most likely be called upon to oversee repairs and rebuilding to the company site. Utilizing their skills and time in this manner must be sold to management as a necessity, given the importance of the staff members whose interests they are serving.

Public relations are a major portion of the recovery effort in any event of this nature. In general, employees need to be told up front not to make statements nor talk to the media without specific clearance from senior management. A single source of information for media consumption must be available (as discussed elsewhere). This person must be a part of this team and have a direct link to the highest management level in the organization. The picture the public sees with regard to the event and the way your company is responding to it will come from the information given to the media. Control over it, then, is of the first order of importance.

Unfortunately, a second function for the public relations/management representative of this team is also present and important. In any disabling event, particularly a regionally involved one, there is often injury and, sometimes, loss of life. The handling of this sensitive issue must be in the hands of senior management as well as the individuals direct supervisor. When serious injury or death occur, much time will be spent with the family, not just hand holding, but provision of assistance in providing medical care and, where necessary, arrangements.

Should an employee be injured and required medical care, it is up to the members of this team to make transportation arrangements, keep track of the movement of the injured party, and directly communicate with his or her family with regards to what happened — where the employee was taken and a brief description as to how the events occurred. This will not be simple reporting, but a sympathetic relating of details.

In the far worse case of death resulting from the event or activities following, notification must be made in person — by a member of senior management and a single representative of the Human Resource department. The information must be passed along in a caring manner and be accompanied by assurances of assistance with whatever arrangements have to be made. It is up to both parties to clearly communicate that the company will cover financial concerns previous to insurance payouts.

It has always been the concern of Human Resources to make certain that traveling employees — those that are manning the bulwarks of remote processing — are housed, fed, compensated, and rotated on a timely and ongoing basis. This puts the function of arranging travel and funding into the hands of this team. If your company is big enough to have a Travel department, it would be logical for them to be represented on this team. If not, someone from HR or Administration must take over this task. Actually, the obtaining of tickets and reservations for hotels and cars is not a long-term undertaking. Absent the Travel department, it is certain that a relationship with a travel agent exists. If one can give a clear and complete description of where staff is going, how many are going, and their exact needs (transportation, hotels, rental cars, etc.) and how long they are likely to be assigned there, most travel agents can take it from there.

We need, then, for the team to be made up of:

- A senior HR manager to oversee all HR-type functions (payroll, insurance, assignment of staff, travel, dependent care, etc.)
- A manager-level Facilities or Building services person to oversee not only the refurbishing or replacement of the facility, but to ensure that traveling staff members' residences are likewise repaired and returned to service as quickly as possible.
- A member of the senior management team to act as a public relations liaison, a channel of communications between the recovery effort and senior management and a recognizable member of management to interact with employees' families.
- A time coordinator, most probably from HR, to coordinate work and rotation schedules, timecard preparation, and retrieval and salary disbursement. Most important, this individual must look for trends on time reports, to guard against anyone trying to do too much.

This is, perhaps, the propitious moment to discuss employee conscientiousness, adrenalin, and the need for rest. An event of the nature that would cause the activation of the plan tends to have all involved parties keyed up. The understanding of the need to re-establish processing can cause someone to address themselves to that end for a great number of hours. Generally, a conscientious employee will not recognize the onset of fatigue nor the need to get a reasonable amount of rest before continuing. It is imperative that the time coordinator or someone on his/her staff keeps close watch on the hours worked by all parties. Recognition of the occurrence of extending hours means that additional steps might have to be taken; add more remote staff, rotate staff in place back to the home site, demand that time off be taken. While this person may or may not have the authority to direct such activities, he or she is duty bound to communicate it those having that authority. Fatigue impairment, more likely to happen under these circumstances than any other, can negatively impact recovery effort. Needless to say, it can also impact the health of the individual involved and for both reasons, the health of the organization.

- An employee-relations person. This individual and his or her support staff will not, strictly speaking, be involved with the employee. Rather, he or she will be involved in the lives of the families of traveling employees, making certain that their needs are met. In short, and beyond the repair and rebuilding of the employee's home, they will act as a replacement for the employee in terms of his or her actions in support of the family. For instance, either with company personnel or by paying for local transportation, this individual will make sure that Junior gets to his orthodontist's appointment and that transportation for shopping, if needed, is provided. The employee need not concern himself for his family's lifestyle or comfort.
- Such other individuals whose work-related duties can provide shortcuts or fast-track resolution of issues relating to the moving and housing of staff, of displaced families (assuming damage from a regional event), of repairs to the homes of said families, or any other aspect of returning to full service in the shortest possible time.

Of course, each of these specialists will require a certain amount of staff support in accomplishing the responsibilities noted. The numbers and types of such staff will vary markedly — dependent upon the size and complexity of the company — but this is one area that cannot be shortchanged. Remember that the public image of your organization will be much enhanced by demonstrating — very publicly — how you take care of your employees. This is another instance where a negative experience can be turned into a positive by the way it is handled and the overall results.

DETAILED FUNCTIONS OF THE HUMAN SERVICES TEAM

We have noted thus far that the Human Services team will be charged with moving employees to and from a remote processing site, handling the repair of their homes, substituting for the missing part of the family, and making sure that the best interests of both the employee and his/her family are effectively taken care of — effectively, but unobtrusively.

The facilities member(s) of the team is charged with building, maintaining, and sharing a list of contractors capable of performing repairs not only to the site but to the homes of traveling employees, if necessary. This will usually be a list of business with which the company does business on a regular basis. However, there are some issues that might be more directed at residential rather than commercial applications. For instance, masonry, drywall, or electrical contractors that normally do commercial work only might wish to provide the names of colleagues that specialize in residential work. Contact should be made with these organizations now, before an incident, to inform them of your intent to utilize their services in an emergency. This action alone could provide the required assistance in putting your needs in front of some of the odd work that will most certainly result from a regional incident.

Also, it is up to the Facilities member to have a list at hand of suppliers and rental companies that can provide needed equipment when necessary. An example is a sump pump, to clear out flooded areas or carpet cleaning equipment needed to remove mud or stains. Again, preliminary contacts can ease the way in an emergency.

The PR member of the team should, as mentioned earlier, be a member of corporate management. The position creates immediate credibility not only with the media, but also in interfacing with employees and their families. The press releases will be issued by someone whose credentials will not be questioned and whose position makes him or her privy to the manner in which information must be released. Make no mistake, effective handling of a difficult situation, when correctly publicized, can be a positive with both staff and customers.

The second aspect of this member's duties is to interface with employee's families. In those instances where injury or death is involved, the need for discretion cannot be overstated. What is important is that contact be made before the information can be received from any other source: in the case of injury, by telephone, in case of death, in person. It is important that the latter item be fully reviewed very quickly (include offers of assistance with arrangements, insurance information, honoraria, etc.) before presentation. Presentation should be done by the key executive, with no more than one accompanying HR representative. (*Note:* In some instances, local authorities might insist on delivering the news. Under no circumstances should they be allowed to precede you by more than minutes. Remember that you cannot control their schedule, so you must make certain that you are ready to accompany them.)

The time coordinator will be dealing with both remote and local staff. It is his or her duty to ensure that timecards are given to traveling staff and that they are returned on time and complete. He or she will then make sure that paychecks are delivered to the location requested by the employee and on time. At the same time, the coordinator must review the cards to note the hours worked by each individual. He or she needs to recognize excessive hours worked and lack of off time and communicate it to management on a timely basis. He or she should be able to recommend rotation for any employee that has supported the remote operation for more than 12 hours per given day, has not taken time off in 2 weeks, or has been remote for more than 3 weeks. Each of these is an indication of burnout potential and must be immediately addressed.

The Human Resource representatives (more than one will probably be assigned) must coordinate travel matters, insurance and benefits issues, and act as a surrogate for the traveling employee with regard his or her family responsibilities. Provisions must be made for transportation and other needs of the family. This could include; appointments, shopping, etc. and staff members can perform these services for the family or a car or taxi service can be retained.

A materialistic aspect to this team is the potential for adding a photographer as an adjunct. Pictures of staff members taking family members shopping or supervising rebuilding of homes can be distributed to the press along with periodic reports. Again, we are attempting to gain positive image from a negative event.

Another area that needs to be touched upon: the emotional impact of a crisis event and its consequential impact on the individual are only now coming into clear focus. During the Whittier Narrows earthquake of 1987 in California, a number of persons in the immediately adjoining area to the epicenter were so badly shaken by the event that they did not wish to return to work. The use of accredited counselors assisted many in getting their lives together again. Later, with the knowledge gained from this experience, many companies in the Bay Area had psychological counseling available immediately after the Loma Prieta earthquake. Make certain that in your lists of contractors and other service providers there is an ample number of psychologists and/or psychiatrists specializing in trauma recovery available. You may well need to request their services by the time the dust has cleared.

BUILDING THE FOUNDATION

As was mentioned, this is one of the most proactive teams within the recovery structure. It is through this team that publication of the plan in general and the functions of this team will become known.

The means of publication may vary, through a company informational newsletter, a separate document dedicated to the planning effort, or by some general information periodical. The most important factor is that employees in general are not only aware of the planning going on, but can identify with what might be expected of them and of their co-workers in the event of activation. While this knowledge will create a degree of comfort, it will, at the same time, raise numerous questions. This is the prime moment to introduce the concept of the Human Services team.

Job security is important to most workers we know. The security of their families and property are as important, but is dependent on the former. The previous being true, the questions that will be raised can be forecast and answered as a part of the publicity campaign.

Foremost in the minds of those workers who find that they are expected to support a recovery at a remote location is their family and/or property. By defining the Human Services team and giving a general overview of its function, many of the basic questions will be answered. But, you ask, what about the focused questions?

This type of interest is the best tool for gaining employee buy-in to the plan provisions. If they are given a place to ask (a telephone number, a mailbox, etc.) they will indeed ask. Upon evaluation of these questions, some trends will certainly be noted. Let us take, for example: "What happens if my home is damaged in an earthquake?" Assuming that you live in an area where this is a possibility, the question will come from a number of directions. Rather than answer these queries individually, make the response to the most-asked general question the subject of your next information release. In this instance, detail the charter and function of the Facilities member of your team. Go over the types of contractors and vendors that are available and how one would go about securiting their services. In fact, if a deal can be worked with a contractor or vendor for employee discounts, both sides will be served. The business will get additional customer flow and the employee will gain a valuable perk for being associated with the company. A byproduct of this relationship is the bond that will be strengthened by the interaction. That bond could be a valuable tool in a recovery scenario. Above all, detail the fact that the company has made these arrangements on their behalf in order to guarantee their peace of mind if they are called away for a recovery effort.

In short, make certain that the rank and file are aware of:

- The planning process underway.
- What is likely to occur in a situation where the facility is disabled.
- Where they fit into the picture.
- Why the company is doing this.
- How the actions of the Human Services team will support them and their families during the employee's absence from the area.

SUMMARY

Recovering from a facility loss is far more than a technical issue. It is an issue of people, and their loyalty and availability are directly proportional to their comfort that their family and property will be taken care of during the period of time that they are traveling on behalf of the recovery effort.

Once you have taken the steps to allay their concerns and actually meet their needs, let them know about it, during downtime, before the crisis takes place. Their first concerns will be for their own well-being, their families, and their possessions. Their second thought will go to the services that you are providing.

Continuing the Program

CHAPTER

II-19

Up to this point we have discussed building a planning program, staffing it, and testing it. We have covered the details of risk assessment and the management of both the planning project and the recovery effort itself. Now, let us go a step further in defining what is needed to make this a living document (or data set) and for it to continue providing protection for the organization.

One of the biggest errors made by planners, or more accurately, those who employ planners, is to complete the project, place a hard copy in a conspicuous place, and abandon any further efforts. In Section I-8, we visited upon the mechanical aspects of plan maintenance. Now let us get into the mind set that will allow the plan to not only stay in place, but guarantee is applicability and currency.

BUILDING A "REAL" PLAN

With the awareness that has been promulgated over the years, many organizations have built, or are in the process of building, contingency plans. Despite the exposure that has been obtained in the business world, the driving force in the planning effort still seems to emanate from the information systems area. A plan for the "data center" is the precedent for other planning throughout the company.

I put the term "data center" in quotes in the previous paragraph for a very good reason. The statement connotes a potential pitfall for the contemporary information systems area. To expand on the point: today's information processing environment is rarely the encapsulated computer room of only a few years ago. Today, networks interconnect company facilities and business partners throughout the world and the technology that drives it is far different that the mainframe centric operation of the past.

The mistake we continue to make is to prepare plans with the assumption that somehow, processing reflects the management hierarchy in place — ultimately, everyone reports to a single entity.

To plan along these same lines is certainly possible, but tends to create a monstrous volume of work, nearly impossible to keep up-to-date. Obviously, we have to adopt a different methodology to make the function workable.

TOTAL BUSINESS CONTINUATION PLANNING

This is the current catch phrase for building plans to cover the entire enterprise. For the sake of this discussion, we shall use the term "modular planning" which more closely describes the end we are trying to attain. That is, to create a number of closely interlocked plans, or segments, that serve the purpose of providing a recovery strategy for each significant business unit. This is not unlike what we have discussed elsewhere in this manual — scope parameters are set and planning ensues. In this instance, parameters are set around a number of functions and the planning is done with a central controlling point in place.

As warned before, we must guard against the monolithic plan that proves a challenge even to pickup, much less test and update. There is simply too much material for efficient handling. This is the manual that gathers dust on the executive vice president's credenza, but never gets looked at except at audit time. This is usually the impetus for rushing around for some rudimentary updating.

Now if the plan being updated were of a limited enough scope that the person responsible for planning had a basic knowledge of all aspects of it, the appropriate persons could be run down for updates quickly and regularly. As you will see, "regularly" is a key term.

Based upon the above description, "Modular Planning" will be defined as: A number of plans, each encompassing an identifiable business unit, with similar structures, maintained by individuals with similar training in planning, using similar tools and being subjected to coordinated communication with regard content and update. In implementing this form of planning, a number of key individuals, each representing a business unit with which they are familiar, will be responsible for building, maintaining, and coordinating testing for their departmental specific plan. They will also take responsibility for communicating each update made to their plan to those responsible for all other plans. A corporate Planning Specialist will be responsible for facilitating the creation of the plans, training the individuals to the extent needed, and creating the communications link that forces the sharing of update material.

Using this mouthful of a definition, the planning process can be:

- Broken down into several manageable segments.
- Utilize a centralized planner training methodology and, where applicable, common planning tools to develop a group of planning coordinators.
- Cause the coordinators of the respective segments to confer regularly, communicating updates to their segments to all of the others.
- Allow for cross-updating, where impact on one or more segments, caused by updates to another, can be addressed and added in the necessary places.
- Allow testing of specific segments on a more regular basis due to the lowered impact on the total organization.
- Produce verifiable evidence of the currency and applicability of each segment of the plan.

The ideal for this situation is to apply one of the many available planning tools to the overall project. By this means, the training curve is shortened as the individuals simply need to familiarize themselves with the provisions of the tool (aided by documentation) rather than the intricacies of contingency planning as an art. The expertise supplied by the corporate Planning Specialist will be used to oversee of each independent effort, as it will in coordinating the information exchange that ensures that updates to each segment are communicated among all coordinators.

Now, a contingency planning team is in place. Each coordinator is charged with gathering the information necessary to create his or her segment of the overall plan in accordance with the template laid out by the Planning Specialist or as required by the selected software planning tool. Despite this individual responsibility, the function is not independent. On a regular basis, throughout the initial planning phase, the coordinators will meet to discuss common issues and to identify and resolve points of interdependency among the various segments. The Specialist will moderate these meetings, guiding the coordinators in their pursuit of information, understanding of components needed, and resolving common or dependent issues.

Throughout the process, a testing of common issues must take place. As an example: If a business unit has been designated to in a move to an alternate location for the recovery effort, that facility will not be available to a second business unit. By the same token — assuming that the division of business unit definition is accurate — one section may be more likely to be forced to move than the other. This could create a priority agreement between the coordinators allowing the most likely user first access to the common desired site with the secondary users locating and securing a second, perhaps less desirable, site.

A second positive result from this method of planning is the understanding by each coordinator of the needs of his/her colleagues. For example, if the accounting department secures a site that will accommodate the entire staff and function in a building remote from the home site, it is important that the network coordinator is aware of the need to get connections to that site. Here again, planning is independent; communication is imperative.

Assuming the successful completion of these modular plans, testing must take place as soon as possible. Due to the limited scope of these plans, testing can often be conducted on one segment even before the completion of other segments. What is learned from these tests will often impact the continued development of the segments not yet completed. Again the cooperative effort impacts the content of other, related plans. Throughout this process, the Specialist must ensure that all parties share the results of their testing with all other coordinators. This is best done in formal meetings, rather than happenstance one-on-one conversations among the coordinators.

Once all plan segments are complete and testing has been conducted and the Specialist is comfortable that the work done is viable, the maintenance cycle begins. This is the point at which the planning function is most likely to break down. The tendency to sit back after plan completion and consider the project "done" is one of the greatest hazards to having a valid plan in place some period of time down the road. It is up to the Specialist to put the tools in place to not only guarantee that this will not happen among the coordinators, but to make certain that management still budgets both the coordinators' time and the necessary funding to keep the activity afloat.

The first task for the Specialist is to set up a common ground meeting schedule for updating. This may or may not be a sit-down meeting, given the ability to use internal e-mail to keep contact. What must be done is to create a routine that:

- Verifies that each coordinator reviews and updates his/her segment on a monthly basis. This may be something as basic as new staff members, a change of address or phone number, or as impacting as the changing of alternative sites.
- Verifies that if no update takes place, the coordinator has reviewed the documentation and states that no update is required.
- Verifies that all other coordinators are made aware of any alterations made to any segment. If this action forces a change in a corresponding segment, that change, too, must be communicated to all other coordinators.
- Communicates and/or distributes changes to planning software tools, company direction or any other alteration in direction that can impact the plans in place.
- Verifies, and advises where necessary, that no deviation from the goal of the multiple plans takes place. This could take the form of discussion of departmental actions that could negatively affect the ability to execute, should conditions demand.
- Coordinates testing, at least annually, for all segments.

As can be seen, having a Planning Specialist on staff is a virtual imperative. While a consultant can get the project underway and see it to completion, someone familiar with company business must be available to see the process through the update and maturation phases.

Contemporary automated calendaring and e-mail services may serve as useful tools in establishing and maintaining an update schedule and the required interaction. By setting monthly deadlines for updates, including reminders when updates or notification of no updates are not received, the Specialist can be assured that review is taking place. Those updates may be forwarded to all other coordinators with the admonition that they must be reviewed for potential impact on the other respective segments. A second variation on this function would be to place these updates into a common database for review. It is a relatively simple task to verify accessing of such databases by the necessary individuals and for the Specialist to remind those that fail to make such accesses in an appropriate time frame.

Another function that falls upon the Planning Specialist is to audit the plans on a rotating basis. This may turn out to be one of the areas where diplomacy can be tested. An audit is essentially a verification that things are being done as prescribed. The unmentioned, yet significant consideration is that suspicion as to performance exists. The easiest way to dodge this bullet is to make the reviews just that — reviews by an expert for the purpose of validating the applicability of the plan. Should evidence be discovered that updates have not been done as needed, it is relatively easy to "suggest" means for modifying the plan to better address company needs, all the while noting any failure to follow through on the assigned task. Obviously, recurrence should be treated more directly. A plan that will not work as a result of the coordinator's failure to keep it current not only puts the company at risk, but reflects poorly on both the coordinator and the Planning Specialist.

The importance of having these plans coordinated at all times cannot be overstated. When they get at cross-purposes, they can defeat, rather than facilitate a recovery effort. The previously mentioned change of recovery site by the Accounting Department, never mentioned to Network, gives an image of a network engineer, cable plug in hand, scratching his head while trying to figure out where to plug it in.

SECTION SUMMARY

The creation of a monolithic plan, whether as a dataset, database, or multi-volume paper document is a short route to guarantee the inability to keep it current. There is simply too much information in one place to be weeded through and updated on a regular basis. Also, the problem of getting the changes into the field is an awe-inspiring issue. Ultimately, the plan is so unwieldy as to quickly become outdated and consequently, of little use.

By breaking the organization down into logical business units and assigning at least one party from each unit to prepare a plan in accordance with detailed instructions and where possible, a common software tool, we have a planner who is knowledgable about the area the plan covers, knows the staff to a greater or lesser extent, and is present for any changes taking place. Multiply this coordinator by the number of business units identified, and an overall corporate planning team has been identified. Now, by having a Planning Specialist in place to lead this group, the planning process will move forward at an unfettered pace.

Assuming that management buyoff is a given and the project has been approved, the first function of the Specialist is to locate the tools to be used. This may include software, manuals, or an internally produced class (hopefully, prepared by that Specialist!). Once these items are available, the team is drawn together to develop a scope for the project and learning the skills necessary to complete it.

There are a number of ways to determine the makeup of the team. Usually, one can start at the operational management level and sort through the obvious fitting parts of the puzzle. Building assignment is one criterion; for instance that might identify a group that can be melded together. Similar functions or those using common equipment might be another identifier. In each organization these break-outs will take shape as one investigates location, responsibilities, tools used and other common ground.

Using the information that has been put forward above, the right persons and the right tools can be brought together to create a series of interlocking plans that will serve the company that caused their creation.

A Word of Caution: The Planning Specialist called for in this type of project must have significant people- and project-management skills as he or she will be directing the efforts of many. And, once the planning process has matured, the facilitation of communications among the coordinators is imperative to ensure that the plans are kept in synch with one another. At any given moment, the Specialist should know the status — with regard completeness and currency — of each modular plan within his/her purview.

As with so many aspects of the technical world, management skills must be developed and implemented along with technical knowledge.

THE GROWING PLAN

The tendency to put a plan in place, introduce it at a board meeting, and subsequently shelve it as a curiosity has been greatly overcome in recent years. Still, without a clear-eyed evaluation of what a final product should look like and how it will be maintained can cause a plan to fall into disuse almost as quickly. Previously in this chapter we demonstrated the means to make sure that your planning project runs smoothly and continues to do so for as long as need be.

However, we cannot always control the environment which we are expected to include in our planning activities. Systems change, areas of responsibility are moved about, new technology and systems are introduced, the business world itself is in constant flux. Have you produced a plan (or series thereof) sufficiently flexible to address change. Let us look at a few ways by which to do exactly that.

We will look first at the potential for re-stacking of buildings or chain-of-command changes crossing the delimiters or your modular plans. This is a task for the Specialist and the coordinators responsible for the modules in question. Upon scrutiny, a few knowns do exist. First: rarely are departments turned over to persons unfamiliar with their function. This would assume that few changes would take place due to management reassignments.

On the other hand, re-stacking of a building can cause dissimilar functions to become neighbors. Handling this means extricating information specific to the functions involved from one plan and inserting them in another. Most of the software tools in the field today are set up to move sections in and out as needed. By keeping the modularity concept in mind while planning, this turns into a cut-and-paste exercise. Phone and vendor lists can be duplicated and edited as needed.

The area most likely to cause major changes to the plan(s) is the addition, deletion, or modification to hardware, software, platforms, or systems. While modifications are readily handled by echoing what occurs in the text, vendor lists, and inventories, the addition of new systems, platforms, or network components is something else entirely. Still, this too can be addressed with a minimum of disruption to business as usual. To be sure, the plans will be modified and a certain investment in time is present. Still, it can be done relatively quickly and in a manner that enhances the utility of the plan rather than diminishing it. It may be accomplished as follows:

Most, if not all organizations of any size have a change control system that evaluates a product for inclusion into production. This may be a new system, a new piece of hardware, or an entire turnkey platform addition. Or, it could be as simple as an upgrade to something already in place. To be placed into production, the project team responsible must demonstrate that the change is compatible with the world as it exists today, that new provisions to accommodate the modification are in place and working, that the user community is satisfied that the change will meet their needs, and that proper testing and results evaluation have taken place. Systems documentation is provided to the change committee including reasons for the implementation, sponsor (who do we blame for this), instruction on how rank-and-file staff are to support the new system/application/modifications/whatever else is involved. A package that allows the change to move smoothly into production is provided. Incomplete? The change doesn't go.

Why not hook the contingency planning effort into this program? It is reasonable to expect any modification to the production environment to be capable of being backed up and restored at whatever facility has been chosen for recovery. Therefore, it is reasonable to expect the project team, working with the respective coordinator(s) and the Planning Specialist, to provide full information on how the system is to be backed up, vendor names, contacts, and telephone numbers, and full instructions for bringing it up in an emergency mode. And, until this information is provided to the planning committee and is signed-off by the Planning Specialist, the change is not implemented.

Not a difficult function to add to the change process. And, it is also not too much to expect for a project team to support their product under recovery circumstances. Once development and procurement functions are aware of the need to provide recovery data for each implementation, it will be simple enough to get them to comply. The hard sell here? Getting management to be willing to hold up implementation until such time as the appropriate plan(s) can be brought up to speed to address the modification to the environment.

It has become apparent — painfully sometimes — that helter-skelter changes to any computer-based environment causes more problems than it solves. We have learned, albeit the hard way, sometimes, that without planning, it is unlikely that an environment can continue to evolve without major problems and major expense. Getting management to accede to including recovery provisions, as a part of the implementation process is not that difficult. It is the responsibility of the Planning Specialist to prepare and present the case for inclusion.

In the current business environment it is not uncommon for on company to take over another company, buy components of another company, or to be bought-out themselves bought. The upshot of this massive change of ownership and style will impact the planning process no matter which end of the stick you are holding. You will have to adapt to someone else's style or they will have to adapt to yours.

Let us take a look at the first scenario; that all or part of another organization is purchased and becomes a part of your responsibility. If the matter is a foregone conclusion before you become involved, you have missed your first best shot.

When a major (or even relatively minor) takeover or business unit purchase is planned, a period of time is set aside for due diligence. Literally, one company makes an in-depth study of the other to verify that the prospective purchase is "as advertised" — all the assets, books, warts, and liabilities are put on the table and evaluated. As a part of that due diligence, the planning already done by the acquired organization should be reviewed for completeness, currency, and validity against the environment into which it will come. Can it be adapted to the modular system you have installed? Can the information they have amassed be inserted into your framework? Is their work valid at all?

These questions need to be asked before the deal is completed and should be a part of the report to senior management. If their planning is not up-to-snuff or is absent completely, there will be added cost to the purchase in putting it in place. Also, there is the additional risk factor in operating a business unit that will be staffed by either unfamiliar or displaced employees at a time when it is most exposed to damage.

If you were not able to get involved during due diligence, make certain that you do a review as soon as possible and raise such flags as necessary. It might have been their problem at one time, but it is yours now.

CONCLUSION

This section has dealt with advanced methods in planning that has as its product a series of compact, easily managed plans that interlock for execution. Through the efforts of the Planning Specialist, the coordinators that have built these modular plans are kept apprised of all of the update work of their colleagues. At the same time, they are prompted to make sure that they at least review their plans for currency on a monthly basis and notify the rest of the planning committee of the lack of need for update.

The Planning Specialist will do little actual planning in this scenario. He or she will choose the tools to be used, select appropriate staff to be planning coordinators, train them in planning process, and monitor their success. He or she will be called upon to coordinate efforts where responsibilities cross business unit lines and ensure that nothing "falls through the cracks" between these modular plans.

Once the process is under way, the Specialist will maintain a project plan and manage the efforts of all coordinators. He or she will be in a direct reporting line with corporate management with regard to this subject.

Once the process is complete, the Specialist will oversee the regular, periodic updating of the individual plans and see that those updates are communicated among the other coordinators. He or she will schedule and oversee testing and will perform regular reviews of the plans, verifying currency, completeness, and responsiveness to need.

Once all plans are complete and are on a regular update cycle, the Specialist will turn his or her eyes toward change management. It is imperative that all modifications to the operational environment go through a change–control process. By agreement with the change committee, a standard must be set up to include the necessary input to the respective modular plan(s) for update, recovery documentation, and a backup schedule a scheme that will cause the least exposure to the company should the system be lost.

In this time of refining technique and fitting the growing environment into the planning process, the Planning Specialist must become a manager as well as a technician. By addressing and improving those skills, you not only enhance your value to the company; you add the skills for your own advancement.

Index

C

D

E

F

N

O

P

Q

R

Here is Your 1999 Supplement to

BUSINESS RESUMPTION PLANNING

Disaster recovery and contingency remains a field where you need to keep your plans up-to-date or risk the success and safety of your organization.

The 1999 Supplement to *Business Resumption Planning* both updates and adds to your contingency plan. There are four new chapters. The first covers contingency planning for Y2K. The second is a case study of the Illinois Bell Telephone Hinsdale Central Office fire of 1988. The case study clearly illustrates the potential for disaster and the consequences of being unprepared. You can use this to help sell the need for continued contingency planning to your management. The third chapter covers the human services function and the importance of maintaining the personnel issues surrounding a business resumption effort. The final new chapter discusses the means and measures you need to take to ensure that your contingency plan, once established, is kept current and correct.

Additionally, there are four chapters updated to reflect changing times and new contingencies. The first two discuss current strategies in obtaining senior management sponsorship and conducting a business impact analysis. The others detail selecting a computer recovery strategy and protecting and recovering computer data.

Planning for business resumption, whether due to natural disasters or man-made causes, is a never ending project. This supplement to *Business Resumption Planning* will help ensure your organization is always ready.

FILING INSTRUCTIONS

REMOVE:

- The old title page, author page, and table of contents
- Chapter I–1
- Chapter I–3
- Chapter II–9
- Chapter II–10
- The old index

ADD:

- The new title page, author page, and table of contents
- Chapter I–1 (updated)
- Chapter I–3 (updated)
- Chapter I–10 (new)
- Chapter I–11 (new)
- Chapter II–9 (updated)
- Chapter II–10 (updated)
- Chapter II–18 (new)
- Chapter II–10 (new)
- The new index